A Treatise
on the
Measure of Damages

A Treatise
on the
Measure of Damages

OR

AN INQUIRY INTO THE PRINCIPLES WHICH GOVERN
THE AMOUNT OF PECUNIARY COMPENSATION
AWARDED BY COURTS OF JUSTICE

BY

THEODORE SEDGWICK

AUTHOR OF "A TREATISE ON STATUTORY AND CONSTITUTIONAL LAW"

CUM PRO EO QUOD INTEREST DUBITATIONES ANTIQUAE IN INFINITUM PRODUCTAE SINT,
MELIUS NOBIS VISUM EST, HUJUSMODI PROLIXITATEM, PROUT POSSIBLE EST, IN ANGUSTUM COARCTARE.
Cod. De sent. quae pro eo quod int. prof. lib. vii, tit. xlvii

NINTH EDITION

REVISED, REARRANGED, AND ENLARGED
BY
ARTHUR G. SEDGWICK
AND
JOSEPH H. BEALE

Volume II

BeardBooks
Washington, D.C.

§ 319.ª Change of judicial opinion in favor of interest.

The great diversity of view in the cases just considered can only be explained by noticing a gradual change of judicial opinion in favor of allowing interest, or damages for delay in the nature of interest and equal to it, in all actions where damages are sought for a pecuniary loss. In the earlier cases the opinion was universal that, damages in actions of tort being by their very nature unliquidated, interest could not be given in any form.[359] The courts then gradually adopted the view that damages in the nature of interest for delay in settling a claim might be added by the jury in their discretion. Finally, courts have come to allow interest as a matter of law in all cases of pecuniary damage, whether the cause of action sounds in tort or in contract. The process is far from complete; and decisions may still be found illustrating all stages of the progress here described. Thus in many States the jury is allowed in its discretion to give damages in the nature of interest in some actions of tort, where formerly interest could not have been added in any case.[360] It is still sometimes

Illinois: Chicago & N. W. Ry. *v.* Shultz, 55 Ill. 421.

Massachusetts: Frazer *v.* Bigelow Carpet Co., 141 Mass. 126, 4 N. E. 620 (*semble*).

New York: Hinds *v.* Barton, 25 N. Y. 544; Wilson *v.* Troy, 135 N. Y. 104, 32 N. E. 44, 18 L. R. A. 449; Home Ins. Co. *v.* Pennsylvania R. R., 11 Hun, 182; Reiss *v.* New York S. Co., 12 N. Y. Supp. 557; Brush *v.* Long Island R. R., 10 App. Div. 535, 42 N. Y. Supp. 103; Jamieson *v.* New York & R. B. Ry., 11 App. Div. 504, 42 N. Y. Supp. 915.

Pennsylvania: Plymouth *v.* Graver, 125 Pa. 24, 17 Atl. 249, 11 Am. St. Rep. 867.

South Dakota: Uhe *v.* Chicago, etc., R. R., 3 S. D. 563, 54 N. W. 601.

In Lucas *v.* Wattles, 49 Mich. 380, it was said to be in the discretion of the jury in such a case to allow interest from the date of the writ; and see Taylor *v.* Bay City S. Ry., 80 Mich. 77, 59 N. W. 447.

ª For § 319 of the eighth edition, see § 313a.

[359] *United States:* Gilpins *v.* Consequa, Pet. C. C. 85.

Virginia: Philips *v.* Williams, 5 Gratt. 259.

[360] *United States:* Brent *v.* Thornton, 45 C. C. A. 214, 106 Fed. 35 (detention of property).

Georgia: Central R. R. *v.* Sears, 66 Ga. 499 (action for death of husband); Gress Lumber Co. *v.* Coody, 104 Ga. 611, 30 S. E. 810 (trespass on land); Snowden *v.* Waterman, 110 Ga. 99, 35 S. E. 309 (breach of warranty of quality of chattels).

Indiana: Chicago, etc., R. R. *v.* Barnes, 2 Ind. App. 213, 28 N. E. 328 (damage by fire).

New York: Walrath *v.* Redfield, 18 N. Y. 457; Duryee *v.* New York, 96 N. Y. 477; Moore *v.* New York El. R. R., 126 N. Y. 671, 27 N. E. 791; Reiss *v.* New York Steam Co., 59 N. Y. Super. Ct. 57, 12 N. Y. Supp. 557;

said that though the jury cannot award interest in ordinary cases of tort *eo nomine*, yet it may consider the lapse of time since the injury in estimating the damages.[361] Even in actions of contract for delay in delivery of property, it has been held that the jury may only adopt an amount equal to interest on the value of the property, as a fair compensation for loss of use of the property.[362]

The cases show a tendency toward the allowance of interest as compensation for delay in settling a claim, except where such delay is paid for in some other way, as by compensation for use: in other words, a rule analogous to that allowing profits in proper cases. Such a rule would clearly bring the law much nearer to completeness of compensation.

§ 320.[a] The rule in Pennsylvania.

In an action for the destruction of property by the defendant's negligence, where interest was claimed on the value of the property, the Supreme Court of Pennsylvania has said: [363]

"Interest as such is recoverable only where there is a failure to pay a liquidated sum due at a fixed day, and the debtor is in absolute default. It cannot, therefore, be recovered in actions of tort, or in actions of any kind where the damages are not in their nature capable of exact computation, both as to time and amount. In such cases the party chargeable cannot pay or make tender until both the time and the amount have been ascertained, and his default is not, therefore, of that absolute nature that necessarily involves interest

Brush *v.* Long Island R. R., 10 App. Div. 535, 42 N. Y. Supp. 103 (damage by fire); Jamieson *v.* New York & R. B. Ry., 11 App. Div. 50, 42 N. Y. Supp. 915.

North Dakota: Ell *v.* Northern Pac. R. R., 1 N. D. 336, 48 N. W. 222, 26 Am. St. Rep. 621, 12 L. R. A. 97 (negligent personal injury).

Ohio: Lawrence R. R. *v.* Cobb, 35 Oh. St. 94 (trespass on real estate); Zipperlein *v.* Pittsburg, C. & S. L. Ry., 8 Ohio S. & C. P. Dec. 587 (personal injury).

Pennsylvania: Bare *v.* Hoffman, 79

Pa. 71 (diverting water); Hollister *v.* Donahoe, 92 N. W. 12 (refusal to perform official duty).

[a] For § 320 of the eighth edition, see § 316.

[361] Clement *v.* Spear, 56 Vt. 401.

[362] *Michigan:* Grosvenor *v.* Ellis, 44 Mich. 452.

Wisconsin: Hinckley *v.* Beckwith, 13 Wis. 31.

And see *Kentucky:* Stark *v.* Price, 5 Dana, 140.

[363] Richards *v.* Citizens' N. Gas. Co., 130 Pa. 37, 39, per Mitchell, J.

for the delay. But there are cases sounding in tort, and cases of unliquidated damages, where not only the principle on which the recovery is to be had is compensation, but where also the compensation can be measured by market value, or other definite standards. Such are cases of the unintentional conversion or destruction of property, etc. Into these cases the element of time may enter as an important factor, and the plaintiff will not be fully compensated unless he receive, not only the value of his property, but receive it, as nearly as may be, as of the date of his loss. Hence it is that the jury may allow additional damages, in the nature of interest, for the lapse of time. It is never interest as such, nor as a matter of right, but compensation for the delay, of which the rate of interest affords the fair legal measure. . . . Interest is recoverable as of right, but *compensation for deferred payment in torts* depends on the circumstances of each case. The plaintiff may have set his damages so inordinately high as to have justified the defendant in refusing to pay, or in other ways the delay may be plaintiff's fault; or, the liability of defendant may have arisen without fault." [364]

§ 321.[a] In Massachusetts.

In Massachusetts interest upon the value of property has always been allowed in actions of trover; but the allowance of such interest in other actions of tort was first discussed by the court in Frazer *v.* Bigelow Carpet Co.,[365] where the trial judge, sitting in place of a jury, had allowed interest. The Supreme Court said:

"It is allowed as of right in trover and other like actions; and although it is suggested that, in such cases, the defend-

---

[a] For § 321 of the eighth edition, see § 319.

[364] This represents the settled doctrine of the court in the case of pecuniary damage: Bare *v.* Hoffmann, 79 Pa. 71, 21 Am. Rep. 42; Plymouth *v.* Graver, 125 Pa. 24, 17 Atl. 249; Richards *v.* Citizens' Natural Gas Co., 130 Pa. 37, 18 Atl. 600; Emerson *v.* Schoonmaker, 135 Pa. 437, 19 Atl. 1025.

If the court in its instruction to the jury uses the word *interest*, this is not reversible error. Mengells *v.* Mohnsville Water Co., 73 Atl. 201, 224 Pa. 120.

No damages for delay can be allowed for mere physical injury. Pittsburgh Southern R. R. *v.* Taylor, 104 Pa. 306, 49 Am. Rep. 580.

[365] 141 Mass. 126, per Holmes, J.

ant may be presumed to have had the use of the goods since the conversion, this is not necessarily the fact, and, if it were, would have no bearing on the indemnity due the plaintiff. . . . *We will assume* that the sum ultimately found by the jury cannot be said to have been wrongfully detained before the finding, in such a sense that interest is due *eo nomine*. But we have heard no reason suggested why, if a plaintiff has been prevented from having his damages ascertained, and, in that sense, has been kept out of the sum that would have made him whole at the time, so long that that sum is no longer an indemnity, the jury in their discretion, and as incident to determining the amount of the original loss, may not consider the delay caused by the defendant. In our opinion they may do so; and, if they do, we do not see how they can do it more justly than by taking interest on the original damage as a measure."

§ 322.[a] In the Supreme Court of the United States.

In the case of Lincoln *v.* Claflin,[366] an action to recover the value of goods obtained by fraud, the appellant contended that interest upon the value had been wrongly allowed. The Supreme Court of the United States held that the question was not properly brought before them, and refused to reverse the judgment below. Field, J., however, said: "Interest is not allowable as a matter of law, except in cases of contract, or the unlawful detention of money. In cases of tort its allowance as damages rests in the discretion of the jury." [367] In Brent *v.* Thornton [368] the trial judge instructed the jury that upon any damages found for plaintiff, three years' interest should be allowed. This was held to be erroneous. "They might have been charged that they could take into consideration the time intervening from the commission of the tort. . . . It was an element of damage they had a right to consider, and it was their province to consider it, and to

---

(a) For § 322 of the eighth edition, see § 320.

[366] 7 Wall. 132, 139, 19 L. ed. 107.

[367] *Acc.*, The Scotland, 118 U. S. 507, 30 L. ed. 153, 6 Sup. Ct. 1174; Mobile & M. Ry. *v.* Jurey, 111 U. S. 584, 4 Sup. Ct. 566, 28 L. ed. 527; Washington & G. R. R. *v.* Harmon, 147 U. S. 571, 37 L. ed. 284, 13 Sup. Ct. 557.

[368] 104 Fed. 839, 44 C. C. A. 213.

pass upon it, and was not the province of the court to decide, as matter of law."

§ 323.[a] Interest in patent suits.

In an action for infringement of a patent, where damages are unliquidated, no interest will be added, in accordance with the general doctrine of the Federal courts;[369] though interest may be allowed as part of the damages in the discretion of the jury.[370] But if the damages are liquidated in any particular case by the agreed amount of a royalty, interest will be allowed from the date of the infringement.[371]

§ 324.[b] Interest in admiralty.

In admiralty proceedings interest is in the discretion of the court.[372] In The Wanata [373] it was held that the libellants could recover interest on the costs and damages, against the stipulators for value, by way of damages for the delay, as the amount should have been paid before the appeal was taken.

C.—RATE OF INTEREST

§ 324a. Rate of interest.

Where interest is recovered as damages, the rate is that established by statute.[374] This was held in an action of re-

---

[a] For § 323 of the eighth edition, see § 321.

[b] For § 324 of the eighth edition, see § 322.

[369] Tilghman v. Proctor, 125 U. S. 136, 160, 8 Sup. Ct. 894, 31 L. ed. 664; Mowry v. Whitney, 14 Wall. 620, 20 L. ed. 860; Littlefield v. Perry, 21 Wall. 205, 22 L. ed. 577. Allowed from master's report in Westinghouse v. New York A. B. Co., 133 Fed. 936.

[370] Bates v. St. Johnsbury, etc., R. R., 32 Fed. 628.

[371] Locomotive Safety Truck Co. v. Pennsylvania R. R., 2 Fed. 677; Creamer v. Bowers, 35 Fed. 206.

[372] The Scotland, 118 U. S. 507, 6 Sup. Ct. 1174, 30 L. ed. 153; Mitchell v. Kelsey, 17 Fed. Cas. No. 9,664; Gammell v. Skinner, 9 Fed. Cas. No. 5,210, 2 Gall. 45; Milburn v. Thirty-

Five Thousand Boxes of Oranges and Lemons, 57 Fed. 236, 6 C. C. A. 317; The Eliza Lines, 132 Fed. 242, 65 C. C. A. 538; Willis v. Commissioners of Appeals, 5 East, 22.

[373] 95 U. S. 600, 24 L. ed. 461.

[374] *Alabama:* Clay v. Drake, Minor, 164; Moore v. Davidson, 18 Ala. 209.

Colorado: Machetts v. Wanless, 2 Colo. 169; Willard v. Mellor, 19 Colo. 534, 36 Pac. 148.

Illinois: Prevo v. Lathrop, 2 Ill. 305; Chumasero v. Gilbert, 24 Ill. 293, 651; Ford v. Hixon, 49 Ill. 142.

Iowa: Vennum v. Gregory, 21 Iowa, 326.

Kentucky: Evans v. Chapel, 13 Bush, 121.

Minnesota: Talcott v. Marston, 3 Minn. 339; Daniels v. Bradley, 4

plevin for a savings-bank book; where the statutory rate of interest was given as damages for detention of the book, though the bank paid a lower rate on deposits.[375] Where no rate is fixed by statute, the customary rate may be recovered.[376] If the statutory rate is changed after the right of action accrues, interest is reckoned at the old rate until the change, then at the new rate.[377] Where a judgment by its terms bore interest, it was held that the rate should not be changed with a change in the statutory rate.[378] And in New Jersey it was held that where the judgment is on a contract to pay money,

Minn. 158; Hollinshead v. Von Glahn, 4 Minn. 190.

Nebraska: Morse v. Rice, 36 Neb. 212, 54 N. W. 308.

Oregon: Duzan v. Meserve, 24 Ore. 523, 34 Pac. 548.

Texas: Houston C. S. Ry. v. Storrie, (Tex. Civ. App.), 44 S. W. 693.

Canada: Archbold v. Building, etc., Assoc., 15 Ont. 237 (affirmed in 16 Ont. App. 1).

[375] Wegner v. Second Ward Savings Bank, 76 Wis. 242.

[376] Davis v. Greely, 1 Cal. 422; Perry v. Taylor, 1 Utah, 63. Where the statute permits any agreed rate, but fixes a rate in the absence of agreement, the parties may by their course of dealing with one another establish a customary rate which will be allowed in their transactions. Sayward v. Dexter, 72 Fed. 758, 19 C. C. A. 176.

[377] *United States:* Saling v. Bolander, 125 Fed. 701, 60 C. C. A. 469.

California: White v. Lyons, 42 Cal. 279.

Connecticut: Hinman v. Goodyear, 56 Conn. 210, 14 Atl. 804.

Illinois: Firemen's Fund Ins. Co. v. Western Refrigerating Co., 162 Ill. 322, 44 N. E. 746 (see Bauer Grocer Co. v. Zelle, 172 Ill. 172, 50 N. E. 238).

New Jersey: Woodward v. Woodward, 28 N. J. Eq. 119; Wilson v. Cobb, 31 N. J. Eq. 91; In re Doremus, 33 N. J. Eq. 234; Jersey City v. O'Cal-

laghan, 41 N. J. L. 349; Gilmore v. Tuttle, 34 N. J. Eq. 45 (but see Wyckoff v. Wyckoff, 44 N. J. Eq. 56, 13 Atl. 662).

New York: Reese v. Rutherford, 90 N. Y. 644; Sanders v. Lake S. & M. S. Ry., 94 N. Y. 641; O'Brien v. Young, 95 N. Y. 428; Ferris v. Hard, 135 N. Y. 354, 32 N. E. 129 (see First Nat. Bank v. Fourth Nat. Bank, 89 N. Y. 412); Hewett v. Chadwick, 8 App. Div. 23, 40 N. Y. Supp. 144.

Oregon: Stark v. Olney, 3 Ore. 88; Graham v. Merchant, 43 Ore. 294, 72 Pac. 1088; Thompson v. Hibbs, 45 Ore. 141, 76 Pac. 778.

Texas: Gulf, C. & S. F. R. R. v. Humphries, 4 Tex. Civ. App. 333, 23 S. W. 556; Rio Grande R. R. v. Cross, 5 Tex. Civ. App. 454, 23 S. W. 529; Worsham v. Vignal, 5 Tex. Civ. App. 471, 24 S. W. 562; Gulf, C. & S. F. R. R. v. Gray (Civ. App.), 24 S. W. 921; Emerson v. Skidmore, 7 Tex. Civ. App. 641, 25 S. W. 671; Watkins v. Junker, 90 Tex. 584, 40 S. W. 11.

Wisconsin: State v. Guenther, 87 Wis. 673, 58 N. W. 1105.

In Washington a change in the legal rate of interest does not affect the interest on debts already due. Union Savings Bank & Trust Co. v. Gelbach, 8 Wash. 497, 24 L. R. A. 359, 36 Pac. 467; State v. Bowen, 11 Wash. 432, 39 Pac. 648.

[378] Prouty v. Lake S. & M. S. Ry. 26 Hun (N. Y.), 546.

41

the legal rate of interest, in the absence of a stipulated rate, became part of the contract; and the rate could not be changed by statute, even after judgment.[379] An annuity was created when interest was at the rate of 5 per cent., which was afterwards changed; it was held that interest on the arrears of the annuity should continue to be allowed at the rate of 5 per cent.[380] But these cases seem in conflict with the current of authorities; and it has been held in other jurisdictions that a change in the statutory rate of interest changes the rate on judgments as well as upon other claims.[381]

§ 325. Interest on overdue paper—Contract and statute rate.

As we have seen, interest is always recoverable on mercantile securities. Where interest is payable by the terms of such a contract, it is recoverable, not as damages for detention of money, but under the contract. After the contract matures, if the amount secured by the contract is unpaid a further question arises, on which there is great conflict of authority. It is claimed on the one side that interest continues to accrue by the terms of the contract, and at the stipulated rate; on the other side it is urged that the contract calls for payment at maturity; if it is broken then, the only right that remains is a claim for damages; and any further interest will be given, not in accordance with, but as damages for breach of the contract, and at the statutory rate.

The decision must rest on the question, whether there is in such cases an implied agreement to pay the contract rate after maturity, or whether interest after maturity is to be given as damages for the delay. In First Ecclesiastical Society v. Loomis,[382] the action was on a note payable three years from date, with interest at $7\frac{3}{10}$ per cent. per annum, the statutory rate being 6 per cent. The court allowed interest after maturity at 6 per cent. only. In Seymour v. Continental Insurance Co.[383]

[379] Cox v. Marlatt, 36 N. J. L. 389, 13 Am. Rep. 454.
[380] Thorntons v. Fitzhugh, 4 Leigh (Va.), 209.
[381] Montana: Stanford v. Coram, 28 Mont. 288, 72 Pac. 655, 98 Am. St. Rep. 566.

Wyoming: Wyoming Nat. Bank v. Brown, 7 Wyo. 494, 53 Pac. 291, 75 Am. St. Rep. 935.
[382] 42 Conn. 570.
[383] 44 Conn. 300.

this last case was referred to and approved. The action was on a demand note, with interest at 8 per cent., payable semi-annually. After referring to Hubbard v. Callahan,[384] where the note had provided for interest at 15 per cent. after maturity, and the court had allowed this rate, and to First Ecclesiastical Society v. Loomis, Carpenter, J., said that the contract must be enforced according to the intention of the parties. That the note was due immediately, but it was manifest from all the circumstances of the transaction that the parties intended to make a loan for a term of years and have the note stand as a continuing security, and hence the stipulated interest should be given. In Eaton v. Boissonnault [385] the action was on a promissory note, payable one year from date, with interest at 8 per cent., payable annually. It was held that after maturity the note only bore 6 per cent., the statutory rate. This case was affirmed in Paine v. Caswell,[386] where the action was on a note for $500, with 10 per cent. interest. No time for payment was fixed. Peters, J., said that it was the intention of the parties to make a continuing security, and interest should therefore run at the contract rate. In the course of his opinion, however, he said: "Where a note is payable on time with interest exceeding six per cent., no more than six per cent. is recoverable after maturity, there being no bargain for interest after that time. In such case interest after the note is due is allowed only by way of damages." The same general rule was followed in Kentucky, in Rilling v. Thompson,[387] where the plaintiff sued on a promissory note payable one year after date, with interest semi-annually at 10 per cent. Cofer, J., said: "If the right to interest depended alone upon the contract, and was not given by law, the appellee would not be entitled to any interest after the maturity of the note, and could only recover, if at all, by way of damages for withholding the money due." So, also, in Minnesota, in Moreland v. Lawrence,[388] where Berry, J., said: "The notes involved in this action drew interest

[384] 42 Conn. 524.
[385] 68 Me. 80.
[386] 67 Me. 540, 24 Am. Rep. 52.
[387] 12 Bush, 310. See also Thomas
v. Bruce, 20 Ky. L. Rep. 818, 50 S. W. 63.
[388] 23 Minn. 84.

from date at 5 per cent. per annum, but contained no stipulation as to interest after maturity. Under such circumstances it was proper to allow interest by way of damages, at the rate of 7 per cent., after the maturity of the notes." The rule is upheld in many jurisdictions.[389]

[389] The following list will show that courts of the highest authority generally allow the statutory rate:

Alabama: Ellis v. Bible, 2 Stew. 63 (see Montgomery Branch Bank v. Harrison, 1 Ala. 9).

Arkansas: Gardner v. Barnett, 36 Ark. 476; Pettigrew v. Summers, 32 Ark. 571; Newton v. Kennerly, 31 Ark. 626; Woodruff v. Webb, 32 Ark. 612; Johnson v. Meyer, 54 Ark. 437, 16 S. W. 121; Johnson v. Downing, 76 Ark. 128, 88 S. W. 825. (See Badgett v. Jordan, 32 Ark. 154.)

California: Kohler v. Smith, 2 Cal. 597; Cummings v. Howard, 63 Cal. 503; Malone v. Roy, 107 Cal. 518, 40 Pac. 1040. The stipulated rate is now allowed by the terms of the statute. Richardson v. Diss, 127 Cal. 58, 59 Pac. 197; Casey v. Gibbons, 136 Cal. 368, 68 Pac. 1032.

Colorado: Clark v. Russell, 1 Colo. 52.

Connecticut: First Ecclesiastical Society v. Loomis, 42 Conn. 570, explaining but practically overruling Adams v. Way, 33 Conn. 419; Beckwith v. Hartford & N. H. R. R., 29 Conn. 268, 76 Am. Dec. 599.

District of Columbia: Sullivan v. Snell, 1 MacArthur, 585.

Florida: Jefferson County v. Lewis, 20 Fla. 980.

Kansas: Robinson v. Kinney, 2 Kan. 184; Searle v. Adams, 3 Kan. 515.

Kentucky: Rilling v. Thompson, 12 Bush, 310; Cunningham v. Carrico, 2 Ky. L. Rep. 310; Posey v. Mayer, 3 Ky. L. Rep. 613; Robertson v. Waltrip, 4 Ky. L. Rep. 627; Snelling's Adm'r v. Atchison, 7 Ky. L. Rep. 752; Joseph v. Lyon, 9 Ky. L. Rep. 324,

(Ky. Super. Ct.); Sanford v. City Nat. Bank, 15 Ky. L. Rep. 607 (and after the death of the payer his representative can be called upon to pay no more than the statute rate: Sinton v. Greer, 11 S. W. 366, 10 Ky. L. Rep. 1011; Fenley v. Kendall, 18 S. W. 637, 13 Ky. L. Rep. 836).

Maine: Duran v. Ayer, 67 Me. 145; Eaton v. Boissonnault, 67 Me. 540, 24 Am. Rep. 52.

Maryland: Brown v. Hardcastle, 63 Md. 484.

Minnesota: Talcott v. Marston, 3 Minn. 339; Daniels v. Ward, 4 Minn. 168; Chapin v. Murphy, 5 Minn. 474; McCutcheon v. Freedom, 15 Minn. 217; Moreland v. Lawrence, 23 Minn. 84; Thorenson v. Minneapolis Harvester Works, 29 Minn. 341, 13 N. W. 156; Holbrook v. Sims, 39 Minn. 122, 39 N. W. 74, 140. (See Brewster v. Wakefield, 1 Minn. 352, 69 Am. Dec. 343.)

Nevada: McLane v. Abrams, 2 Nev. 199.

New Hampshire: Ashuelot R. R. v. Elliott, 57 N. H. 397.

New York: Macomber v. Dunham, 8 Wend. 550; U. S. Bank v. Chapin, 9 Wend. 471; Hamilton v. Van Rensselear, 43 N. Y. 244; Ferris v. Hard, 135 N. Y. 354, 32 N. E. 129; Southern C. R. R. v. Moravia, 61 Barb. 180; but *contra*, Miller v. Burroughs, 4 Johns. Ch. 436; Andrews v. Keeler, 19 Hun, 87; Genet v. Kissam, 53 N. Y. Super. Ct. 43; Respectable A. I. F. R. Association v. Eagleson, 60 How. Pr. 9; Patterson v. Whitlock, 14 Daly, 497, 1 N. Y. Supp. 2; Elmira Iron & Steel Rolling Mill Co. v. Elmira, 5 Misc. 194, 25 N. Y. Supp. 657.

§ 326. Conflict of authority.

But a number of courts insist that there is an implied contract to pay the stipulated rate after maturity.[390] In Cecil v.

In Kelly v. Phœnix Nat. Bank, 31 App. Div. 496, 45 N. Y. Supp. 537, the general rule was stated to be, that the statute rate is due after maturity; but where the obligor of a bond notified the holder that the stipulated rate would be continued after maturity, and in consequence the holder failed to present the bond for payment, the court allowed the stipulated rate until payment.

Ohio: Tuffli v. Ohio L. Ins., etc., Co., 2 Disn. 121.

Pennsylvania: Ludwick v. Huntzinger, 5 W. & S. 51.

Rhode Island: Pearce v. Hennessy, 10 R. I. 223.

South Carolina: Langston v. South C. R. R., 2 S. C. 248; Briggs v. Winsmith, 10 S. C. 133; Maner v. Wilson, 16 S. C. 469; Thatcher v. Massey, 20 S. C. 542; Bell v. Bell, 25 S. C. 149.

Texas: Roberts v. Smith, 64 Tex. 94, 53 Am. Rep. 744 (qualifying Pridgen v. Andrews, 7 Tex. 461; Hopkins v. Crittenden, 10 Tex. 189).

Utah: Perry v. Taylor, 1 Utah, 63; Stevens Implement Co. v. South Ogden Water Co., 20 Utah, 267, 58 Pac. 843.

England: Cook v. Fowler, L. R. 7 H. L. 27; Goodchap v. Roberts, 14 Ch. Div. 49; *contra,* Keene v. Keene, 3 C. B. (N. S.) 144.

Canada: People's Loan, etc., Co. v. Grant, 18 Can. 262; Freehold Loan Co. v. McLean, 8 Manitoba, 116; Hanford v. Howard, 1 N. B. Eq. 241; Powell v. Peck, 12 Ont. 492; Delaney v. Canadian Pac. R. R., 21 Ont. 11. (*Contra,* Howland v. Jennings, 11 Up. Can. C. P. 272; Montgomery v. Bousher, 14 U. C. C. P. 45; Young v. Fluke, 15 U. C. C. P. 360.)

In an action on a note where, after the note was given, the debtor got a

discharge in insolvency, but afterwards promised to pay the debt, it was held, that after such new promise there was a new contract, and the debt would bear interest only at the legal rate. Lambert v. Schmalz, 118 Cal. 33, 50 Pac. 13.

In similar cases where the suit was not on a note but on a simple contract the legal rate was allowed after the time during which the rate was fixed by the contract.

Louisiana: Hepp v. Ducros, 3 Mart. (N. S.) 185.

New York: Lawrence v. Leake Orphan House, 2 Den. 577.

[390] *United States:* H e n d e r s o n v. Desham, Hempst. 231; Farmers' L. & T. Co. v. Northern Pac. R. R., 94 Fed. 454.

Arizona: Greenhaw v. Holmes, 8 Ariz. 94, 68 Pac. 537.

Illinois: Phinney v. Baldwin, 16 Ill. 108; Etnyre v. McDaniel, 28 Ill. 201; People v. Getzendaner, 137 Ill. 234, 34 N. E. 297; Starne v. Barr, 17 Ill. App. 491; Bressler v. Harris, 19 Ill. App. 430. But where the notes were destroyed when security was given, interest was thereafter allowed at the statutory rate only. Conant v. Riseborough, 139 Ill. 383, 28 N. E. 789.

Indiana: Kilgore v. Powers, 5 Blackf. 22; Shaw v. Rigby, 84 Ind. 375; Kimmell v. Burns, 84 Ind. 370; Kerr v. Haverstick, 94 Ind. 178.

Iowa: Hand v. Armstrong, 18 Ia. 324; Thompson v. Pickel, 20 Ia. 490.

Massachusetts: Brannon v. Hursell, 112 Mass. 63, 37 Am. Rep. 305; Union Institution v. Boston, 129 Mass. 82; Forster v. Forster, 129 Mass. 559; Downer v. Whittier, 144 Mass. 448, 11 N. E. 585.

Michigan: Warner v. Juif, 38 Mich. 662.

Hicks [391] the question was considered at some length. This action was on a promissory note payable in six months after date, with interest at 12 per cent. per annum from date. The statute rate was 6 per cent. After citing several decisions of the Virginia courts, that interest is an incident of the debt, due by contract in the absence of an express stipulation to the contrary, Moncure, P., said:

"We think their contract ought to be construed precisely as if the words 'till paid' had been inserted therein after the words 'from date,' and that such was their obvious meaning. They no doubt omitted the words 'till paid' because they considered it only necessary to agree on some legal rate of interest and the date from which it should commence, believing that it would, of course, continue to run until payment. They never could have intended that if default were made by the debtor in the payment of the debt at maturity, he should thereafter pay interest at only one-half of the rate he had agreed to pay for the period during which he had a right under the contract to withhold the principal. . . . At the date of the contract in question, the parties were authorized to agree upon a rate not exceeding 12 per centum per annum. In this case they agreed on that rate; no doubt because the money, at that time and under the circumstances which then existed, was considered to be worth interest at that rate, both to the lender and the borrower; and they stipulated ac-

Mississippi: Meaders v. Gray, 60 Miss. 400.

Missouri: Broadway Sav. Bank v. Forbes, 79 Mo. 226; Borders v. Barber, 81 Mo. 636; Macon Co. v. Rodgers, 84 Mo. 66; Briscoe v. Kinealy, 8 Mo. App. 76.

Nebraska: Kellogg v. Lavender, 15 Neb. 256, 18 N. W. 38, 48 Am. Rep. 339.

Ohio: Monnett v. Sturges, 25 Oh. S. 384; Marietta Iron Works v. Lottimer, 25 Oh. S. 621; Hydraulic Co. v. Chatfield, 38 Oh. S. 575.

Tennessee: Overton v. Bolton, 9 Heisk. 762; Wade v. Pratt, 12 Heisk. 231.

Virginia: Cecil v. Hicks, 29 Gratt. 1; Evans v. Rice, 96 Va. 50, 30 S. E. 463.

West Virginia: Shipman v. Bailey, 20 W. Va. 140; Pickens v. McCoy, 24 W. Va. 344.

Wisconsin: Spencer v. Maxfield, 16 Wis. 178; Pruyn v. Milwaukee, 18 Wis. 367; Thorn v. Smith, 71 Wis. 18, 36 N. W. 407.

In Crockett v. Mitchell, 88 Ga. 166, 14 S. E. 118, a note was extended by a new promise after the running of the statute of limitations. It was held that it would bear interest at the contract rate.

[391] 29 Gratt. 1.

cordingly, agreeing and expecting, no doubt, that at the end of six months the principal and interest would be paid by the borrower to the lender, to be used by the latter as might be most to his interest. . . . There is no evidence of the extent of the loss, on the side of the lender, or gain on the side of the borrower, which has resulted from this default. Is it right to let the borrower, who could not obtain the money for *six months* at a less rate than 12 per cent. per annum, have it for an indefinite period thereafter at half that rate, against the will of the lender?"

The question was considered, and many of the authorities on the subject collected in Overton *v.* Bolton,[392] and the court came to the conclusion that the contract rate should be allowed. The principle was not discussed at length, the court merely saying that they considered that the decisions in favor of the contract rate rested on stronger grounds than those on the other side. In Brannon *v.* Hursell,[393] the Supreme Court of Massachusetts adopted the same rule, Morton, J., without discussing the question, merely saying: "The plaintiff recovers interest, both before and after the note matures, by virtue of the contract, as an incident or part of the debt, and is entitled to the rate fixed by the contract." In support of his decision, he cited four cases. The first, Ayer *v.* Tilden,[394] was an action on a note, made and payable in New York, and which contained no provision about interest. Hoar, J., held that the *contract* must be governed by New York law, but that *interest* was only given as damages, and must therefore be given at the Massachusetts rate. Of the other three cases, two were English decisions, and did not decide the point, and the third was an old New York case which is at variance with the later decisions of that State.

§ 327. Rules in the Supreme Court of the United States.

In the early decisions in this court [395] the statutory rate

[392] 9 Heisk. 762.
[393] 112 Mass. 63, 37 Am. Rep. 305.
[394] 15 Gray, 178.
[395] Brewster *v.* Wakefield, 22 How. 118, 16 L. ed. 301; Burnhisel *v.* Firman,

22 Wall. 170, 21 L. ed. 766; Hunneman *v.* Milwaukee, 12 Fed. Cas. No. 6,878; but see Northwestern Mut. L. Ins. Co. *v.* Perrill, 18 Fed. Cas. No. 10,339.

was adopted as the true rule; but in a later case,[396] which was an action on an Iowa contract, the court held that it was bound by the decisions of the Iowa courts, as on a question of local law. In still later cases [397] the court reaffirms the earlier cases as expressing its own rule of decision, when unembarrassed by any local rule adopted by State courts. Hence the authority of the Supreme Court can only in fairness be cited in favor of the statutory rate.

§ 328. Conflict of decisions in Indiana.

We have cited Indiana as one of the States in which the contract rate is allowed after maturity. This result was reached in that State by a process of reasoning which seems open to criticism. On a note payable on demand, or in one day, it has been decided, as we shall see, in the courts of States upholding the statute rate,[398] that the intention is clearly to make a continuing security on which the contract rate runs till paid. In Indiana after some conflict the rule in favor of the statute rate was established.[399] In a case, however, turning on a note payable one day from date, the court allowed interest at the stipulated rate, but considering it to be necessary in order to reach this conclusion, overruled the decisions just cited, and now the rule of the contract rate is held to be the law of Indiana.[400] The Indiana cases cannot be regarded as giving much substantial support to the authority of the rule of the contract rate.

§ 329. General conclusion.

The arguments on which these opinions are based are open to various criticisms. In the first place, the doctrine that

[396] Cromwell v. County of Sac, 96 U. S. 51, 24 L. ed. 681.

So in a contract governed by the law of *Illinois:* Ohio v. Frank, 103 U. S. 697, 26 L. ed. 531; U. S. Mortgage Co. v. Sperry, 138 U. S. 313, 11 Sup. Ct. 321, 34 L. ed. 969 (affirming 26 Fed. 727); and of *Mississippi:* Burgess v. Southbridge Sav. Bank, 2 Fed. 500.

[397] Holden v. Freeman's Sav. & Tr. Co., 100 U. S. 72, 25 L. ed. 567; Ewell v. Daggs, 108 U. S. 143, 2 Sup. Ct. 408,

27 L. ed. 682; Massachusetts Ben. Assoc. v. Miles, 137 U. S. 689, 11 Sup. Ct. 234, 34 L. ed. 834; Nash v. El Dorado County, 24 Fed. 252; Sherwood v. Moore,. 35 Fed. 109.

[398] See § 330.

[399] Burns v. Anderson, 68 Ind. 202; Richards v. McPherson, 74 Ind. 158.

[400] Shaw v. Rigby, 84 Ind. 375; Kimmell v. Burns, 84 Ind. 370; Kerr v. Haverstick, 94 Ind. .178.

interest is an incident of the debt, due by contract, is an assumption of the very question to be decided. In the next place, the contract which the parties have made, and not that which we think they intended to make, is the one to be enforced. It seems also particularly objectionable to assume an intention to violate the contract. The decision must, of course, in each case depend upon the language used, but variations merely in the rate of interest can make no difference in the decision of the general question. Any valid arguments, therefore, employed to prove that the contract rate governs, will be equally applicable, whether the contract rate is above or below the statute rate. Apply this test to the case of Cecil *v.* Hicks, and it is apparent that the whole argument is founded upon the hardship of compelling the creditor to take 6 per cent. after maturity, when, perhaps, he might have obtained 12 per cent. for his money if the debtor had kept his agreement. To imply a promise to pay the stipulated rate after maturity is, we think, to introduce into the contract a provision which the language does not cover, and to violate both the principles upon which interest is given, and the rules governing the interpretation of written instruments. With great deference to the high authority for the other view, the above review of the case seems to justify the conclusion that the decisions upholding the statutory rate after maturity are based upon a sounder foundation of reasoning.

§ 330. Expressed intention always governs.

In every jurisdiction, however, the clearly expressed intention of the parties governs. Thus where a contract bears interest at a stipulated rate "until paid," interest will be allowed at that rate after maturity.[401] And so in South Caro-

---

[401] *Illinois:* Latham *v.* Darling, 2 Ill. 203.

Kansas: Dudley *v.* Reynolds, 1 Kan. 285; Small *v.* Douthitt, 1 Kan. 335; Young *v.* Thompson, 2 Kan. 83.

Maine: Augusta Nat. Bank *v.* Hewins, 90 Me. 255, 38 Atl. 156.

Massachusetts: Lamprey *v.* Mason, 148 Mass. 231, 19 N. E. 350.

Missouri: Broadway S. B. *v.* Forbes, 79 Mo. 226.

Nebraska: Hager *v.* Blake, 16 Neb. 12.

Nevada: Cox *v.* Smith, 1 Nev. 161, 90 Am. Dec. 476.

New York: Taylor *v.* Wing, 84 N. Y. 471; Wilcox *v.* Van Voorhis, 12 N. Y. Supp. 617.

lina, when interest was to be paid annually at a certain rate "upon the whole amount unpaid," it was held that interest at the stipulated rate should be allowed after maturity, the words practically meaning "till paid." [402] So where on a note payable in one year interest was payable "annually" at a certain rate, that rate was allowed after maturity. [403] So where the intention can be clearly implied to continue the stipulated rate it will be given, as on a note payable in one day ("practically a demand note"), [404] or on demand. [405] But on the other hand, where a contract bears interest at the stipulated rate "till the principal sum shall be payable," the stipulated rate cannot be recovered after maturity. [406] And where the note was indorsed "no interest to be charged on this note," interest at the statute rate was allowed after maturity. [407]

§ 331. Stipulation for a higher rate after maturity.

Where a higher rate of interest is stipulated to be paid after maturity than before, some courts have refused recovery on the ground that interest at the higher rate is a penalty; [408] but it is generally held to be recoverable. [409] The question

Rhode Island: Lanahan v. Ward, 10 R. I. 299.

South Carolina: Mobley v. Davega, 16 S. C. 73.

England: Ex parte Fewings, 25 Ch. Div. 338.

But see St. John v. Rykert, 10 Can. 278; Reg. v. Grand Trunk R. R., 2 Can. Exch. 132.

[402] Miller v. Hall, 18 S. C. 141; Miller v. Edwards, 18 S. C. 600.

[403] Westfield v. Westfield, 19 S. C. 85.

[404] *Arkansas:* Casteel v. Walker, 40 Ark. 117, 48 Am. Rep. 5.

Kentucky: Gray v. Briscoe, 6 Bush, 687.

South Carolina: Sharpe v. Lee, 14 S. C. 341; Piester v. Piester, 22 S. C. 139.

[405] Paine v. Caswell, 68 Me. 80.

[406] *Kentucky:* Rushing v. Sebree, 12 Bush, 198.

Mississippi: Hamer v. Rigby, 65 Miss. 41, 3 So. 137.

Wisconsin: Spaulding v. Lord, 19 Wis. 533.

[407] Harnish v. Miles, 111 Ill. App. 105.

[408] *Indiana:* Brown v. Maulsby, 17 Ind. 10 (but see Wernwag v. Mothershead, 3 Blackf. 401).

Iowa: Gower v. Carter, 3 Iowa, 244, 66 Am. Dec. 71.

Minnesota: Mason v. Callender, 2 Minn. 350; Talcott v. Marston, 3 Minn. 339; Kent v. Bown, 3 Minn. 347; Daniels v. Ward, 4 Minn. 168; Newell v. Houlton, 22 Minn. 19; White v. Iltis, 24 Minn. 43.

Missouri: Watts v. Watts, 11 Mo. 547.

Where the stipulation was to pay the higher rate *from the date of the note* it was held to be a penalty in *Nebraska:* Hallam v. Telleren, 55 Neb. 255, 75 N. W. 560.

[409] *United States:* Scottish-American Mort. Co. v. Wilson, 24 Fed. 310; Vermont Loan & Trust Co. v. Dygert, 89

should, it would seem, be determined upon the principles of liquidated damages, for the higher rate is in the nature of a liquidation of damages for delay in performing the contract to pay money; and if the rate is grossly excessive, payment should not be enforced, and so it was held in an early case in Alabama.[410] The courts, however, have not generally regarded the stipulation for a higher rate of interest after maturity in this light.

D.—INTEREST IN SPECIAL CASES

§ **331a. Property taken by eminent domain.**
Where land is taken by right of eminent domain, the owner recovers interest on the value of the land from the time of taking.[411] In Old Colony Railroad v. Miller [412] the plaintiff brought an action to have his damages assessed for land taken

Fed. 123; Linton v. National L. Ins. Co., 44 C. C. A. 54, 104 Fed. 584.
Arkansas: Miller v. Kempner, 32 Ark. 573; Portis v. Merrill, 33 Ark. 416.
Colorado: Browne v. Steck, 2 Colo. 70; Buckingham v. Orr, 6 Colo. 587.
Illinois: Lawrence v. Cowles, 13 Ill. 577; Smith v. Whitaker, 23 Ill. 367; Gould v. Bishop Hill Colony, 35 Ill. 324; Davis v. Rider, 53 Ill. 416, 85 Am. Dec. 368; Witherow v. Briggs, 67 Ill. 96; Downey v. Beach, 78 Ill. 53; Funk v. Buck, 91 Ill. 575; Reeves v. Stipp, 91 Ill. 609.
Maine: Capen v. Crowell, 66 Me. 282.
Mississippi: Rogers v. Sample, 33 Miss. 310, 69 Am. Dec. 349.
Montana: Davis v. Hendrie, 1 Mont. 499.
Nebraska: Havemeyer v. Paul, 45 Neb. 373, 63 N. W. 932 (overruling Richardson v. Campbell, 34 Neb. 181, 51 N. W. 753, 33 Am. St. Rep. 633); Home F. Ins. Co. v. Fitch, 52 Neb. 88, 71 N. W. 940; Crapo v. Hefner, 53 Neb. 251, 73 N. W. 702; Sanford v. Lichtenberger, 62 Neb. 501, 87 N. W. 305.

Texas: Huddleston v. Kempner, 1 Tex. Civ. App. 211, 21 S. W. 946.
Wisconsin: Fisher v. Otis, 3 Chand. 83.
England: Herbert v. S. & Y. Ry., L. R. 2 Eq. 221.
Canada: Young v. Fluke, 15 U. C. C. P. 360. In Camp v. First Nat. Bank, 44 Fla. 497, 33 So. 241, the increased rate was refused because of defective pleadings.
[410] Henry v. Thompson, Minor (Ala.), 209.
[411] *Illinois:* Chicago v. Palmer, 93 Ill. 125; Phillips v. South Park Com'rs, 119 Ill. 627, 10 N. E. 230.
Iowa: Hartshorn v. Burlington, C. R. & N. R. R., 52 Ia. 613; Hayes v. Chicago, M. & S. P. Ry., 64 Ia. 753, 19 N. W. 245; Guinn v. Iowa & S. L. Ry., 131 Ia. 680, 109 N. W. 209.
Kansas: Cohen v. St. Louis, F. S. & W. R. R., 34 Kan. 158.
Maine: Bangor & P. R. R. v. McComb, 60 Me. 290.
Massachusetts: Reed v. Hanover B. R. R., 105 Mass. 303; Kidder v. Oxford, 116 Mass. 165; Chandler v. Jamaica P. A. Co., 125 Mass. 544; Drury v.

[412] 125 Mass. 1.

by the company. Colt, J., said: "If not agreed on, the damages are assessed by a jury, on the application of either party; but they are assessed as of the time of the location, and the jury may properly allow interest upon the amount ascertained as damages, for the detention of the money from the time of taking." He then quotes the language of Chief-Justice Shaw, in Parks v. Boston,[413] to the effect that taking the land is equivalent to a purchase, and the delay in payment must be compensated by interest. To the same effect is Delaware, Lackawanna & Western Railroad v. Burson,[414] where Thompson, C. J., said:

Midland R. R., 127 Mass. 571; Imbescheid v. Old Colony R. R., 171 Mass. 209, 50 N. E. 609; Dodge v. Rockport, 199 Mass. 274, 85 N. E. 172.

Minnesota: Weide v. St. Paul, 62 Minn. 67, 64 N. W. 65.

Missouri: Plum v. City of Kansas, 101 Mo. 525, 14 S. W. 65; Webster v. Kansas City S. Ry., 116 Mo. 114, 22 S. W. 474.

Nebraska: Sioux C. R. R. v. Brown, 13 Neb. 317.

New Jersey: North H. C. R. R. v. Booraem, 28 N. J. Eq. 450.

Ohio: Atlantic & G. W. Ry. v. Koblentz, 21 Oh. St. 334.

Tennessee: Alloway v. Nashville, 88 Tenn. 510.

Texas: Sabine & E. T. Ry. v. Joachimi, 58 Tex. 456.

Vermont: Bridgeman v. Hardwick, 67 Vt. 653, 32 Atl. 502.

Washington: Bellingham, B. & B. C. Ry. v. Strand, 14 Wash. 144, 44 Pac. 140.

Wisconsin: Sweaney v. U. S., 62 Wis. 396, 22 N. W. 609; Velte v. United States, 76 Wis. 278, 45 N.W. 119.

England: Rhys v. Dare Valley Ry., L. R. 19 Eq. 93, 23 Wkly. Rep. 23.

Canada: Drury v. Reg., 6 Can. Exch. 204.

Contra, California: Himmelman v. Oliver, 34 Cal. 246; Haskell v. Bartlett, 34 Cal. 281 (statutory).

Kentucky: Conner v. Clark, 15 Ky. L. Rep. 126.

And see *District of Columbia:* Hetzel v. Baltimore, etc., R. R., 6 Mackey, 1.

In Ohio and Pennsylvania, interest as such cannot be recovered; but the jury may (and perhaps should) allow damages for delay equal to interest.

Ohio: Lawrence R. R. v. Cobb, 35 Ohio St. 94; Cincinnati v. Whetstone, 47 Ohio St. 196, 24 N. E. 409.

Pennsylvania: Railroad Co. v. Gesner, 20 Pa. 242; Norris v. Philadelphia, 70 Pa. 332; Pennsylvania, etc., R. R. v. Ziemer, 124 Pa. 560, 17 Atl. 187; Reading, etc., R. R. v. Balthaser, 126 Pa. 1, 17 Atl. 518.

In Devlin v. New York, 131 N. Y. 123, 30 N. E. 45, interest was allowed from the award.

[413] 15 Pick. 198.

[414] 61 Pa. 369, 380. But in Klages v. Philadelphia & R. T. R. R., 160 Pa. 386, 28 Atl. 862, it was held that the owner was not entitled to interest from the time of taking possession though the jury might consider the lapse of time in determining the amount of compensation. The decision was based on the ground that interest on unliquidated damages in tort is not allowed in Pennsylvania. See also Reading & P. R. R. v. Bathasar, 126 Pa. 1, 17 Atl. 518; Becker v. Philadelphia & R. T. R. R., 177 Pa. 252, 35 Atl. 617.

"Nor was there error in charging the jury to allow interest. If the plaintiff was entitled to compensation by reason of her property being taken at a particular time, she was certainly entitled to interest as a compensation for its wrongful detention. The company, as well as the plaintiff, could have had the damages assessed as soon as they pleased after locating the road, and it was no reason for withholding compensation that its amount was unknown or unascertained. As the company was the party to pay, it ought to have had the amount ascertained, and paid it; failing to do so, it has no right to complain at having to meet an incident of the delay in the shape of interest."

But interest runs only from the time when possession is taken; and therefore if the award is made before the land is actually taken, interest cannot be included in the award.[415] In some States the owner, after the notice of taking has been filed, has a right to give up his land and demand compensation. Where such a rule prevails, interest may be recovered from the time of the demand.[416] Where the defendant, a corporation, to save an injunction against obstructing the plaintiff's way, paid damages into court *pendente lite* and continued

<hr/>

[415] *Illinois:* Chicago v. Barbian, 80 Ill. 482; South Park Comm'rs v. Dunlevy, 91 Ill. 49.
Louisiana: Hale v. New Orleans, 13 La. Ann. 499.
Maine: Gay v. Gardiner, 54 Me. 477.
Missouri: Hilton v. St. Louis, 99 Mo. 199, 12 S. W. 651.
New Hampshire: Fiske v. Chesterfield, 14 N. H. 240; Concord R. R. v. Greely, 23 N. H. 237.
New Jersey: Metler v. Easton & A. R. R., 37 N. J. L. 223.
New York: Donnelly v. Brooklyn, 121 N. Y. 9, 24 N. E. 17.
Pennsylvania: Stewart v. Philadelphia County, 2 Pa. 340; Second St., Harrisburg, 66 Pa. 132; Wilson v. County, 1 Del. Co. Rep. 422.
Texas: Morris v. Coleman Co. (Tex. Civ. App.), 35 S. W. 29.

Wisconsin: Uniacke v. Chicago, etc., R. R., 67 Wis. 108, 29 N. W. 899 (interest from time of award).
Contra, Missouri: Martin v. St. Louis, 139 Mo. 246, 41 S. W. 231; see Hilton v. St. Louis, 99 Mo. 199; Randolph v. Town Site, 103 Mo. 451, 15 S. W. 437; Doyle v. Lamson, C. & S. Ry., 113 Mo. 280, 20 S. W. 970; Webster v. Kansas C. & S. Ry., 116 Mo. 114, 22 S. W. 474.
When an award had been made but not paid and plaintiff sued to enjoin taking possession, it was held he was entitled to interest on the award, but must account for the mesne profits. Plum v. City of Kansas, 101 Mo. 525, 14 S. W. 65.
[416] *New Hampshire:* Clough v. Unity, 18 N. H. 75.
New York: People v. Canal Comm'rs, 5 Denio, 401.

the obstruction, it was held it must pay interest from the time the damages were paid into court till final decree.[417]   In New Jersey, by statute, interest runs from the date of the assessment.[418]

§ 332. Taxes.

Where a defendant is in default in the payment of taxes, and is sued to recover the amount of them, he is not liable, in the absence of a statutory provision, for interest.[419]   This principle has been held to extend to the case of a county delinquent in paying its quota of taxes to the State.[420]   This principle, however, is confined to taxes in the strict sense; it does not apply to other fees payable to the state, which are given as compensation for special benefits. Thus it has been held that where by statute the expense of improving a street

[417] Carpenter v. Easton & A. R. R., 28 N. J. Eq. 390. And see Baldwin v. San Antonio, 125 S. W. 596 (Tex. Civ. App.).

[418] Beebe v. Newark, 24 N. J. L. 47. The same rule was adopted in Beveridge v. Park Comm'rs, 100 Ill. 75.

[419] *Alabama:* Perry County v. S. M. & M. R. R., 65.Ala. 391.

California: Perry v. Washburn, 20 Cal. 318, 350 (*semble*).

Connecticut: Sargent v. Tuttle, 67 Conn. 162, 32 L. R. A. 822, 34 Atl. 828.

Kentucky: Louisville, & N. R. R. v. Sharp, 91 Ky. 411, 16 S. W. 86, 12 Ky. L. Rep. 973 (see Licking Valley Building Assoc. v. Commonwealth, 26 Ky. L. Rep. 730, 89 S. W. 682).

Massachusetts: Danforth v. Williams, 9 Mass. 324.

Mississippi: Illinois Cent. R. R. v. Adams, 78 Miss. 895, 29 So. 996.

Missouri: Eyerman v. Provenchere, 15 Mo. App. 256.

New Jersey: Camden v. Allen, 26 N. J. L. 398; Brennert v. Farrier, 47 N. J. L. 75.

New York: People v. Gold & Stock Tel. Co., 98 N. Y. 67.

Texas: Heller v. Alvarado, 1 Tex. Civ. App. 409, 20 S. W. 1003.

In *Michigan:* Lake Shore & M. S. R. R. v. People, 46 Mich. 193, 9 N. W. 249, it was held that a railroad company was not chargeable with interest on taxes until an assessment was made and notice given to the company, since it was not in default until that time; for no promise to pay interest can be implied where none is made until the principal falls due.

It was held in *Texas* that where one wrongfully enjoined the collection of taxes from himself he should pay interest on the taxes by way of damages. Rosenberg v. Weekes, 67 Tex. 578.

If the court gives a judgment for taxes, it will draw interest like any other judgment; but a mere order to pay the amount of taxes alleged to be due into court does not bear interest. Louisville Water Co. v. Clark, 29 S. W. 309, 16 Ky. L. Rep. 585.

Statutory interest will run, though after legal proceedings part of the tax is abated, on the portion legally assessed. Western U. T. Co. v. State, 64 N. H. 265, 9 Atl. 547.

[420] State v. Multnomah County, 13 Ore. 287. *Contra,* State v. Van Winkle, 43 N. J. L. 125.

is assessed upon the abuttors, interest may be recovered from a delinquent abuttor; [421] and interest has also been allowed upon unpaid license fees. [422]

§ 333. Fines and penalties.

No interest can be recovered for delay in paying a fine imposed in a criminal case. [423] And similarly where a national bank, for taking usurious interest, is liable to a penalty in favor of the debtor, though it is recovered in a civil action, the debtor cannot have interest upon it before judgment. [424] This principle would prevent the recovery of interest in any *qui tam* action. So where by statute the highest market value of property destroyed between the time of destruction and of trial is allowed, this statute is held to be a penal one, and interest is not allowed. [425] And where double or treble damages are allowed by statute, interest cannot be given on the amount; [426]

[421] *Missouri:* Buchan v. Broadwell, 88 Mo. 31.

Ohio: Gest v. Cincinnati, 26 Oh. St. 275.

Of course, no interest will run until all the conditions making the assessment payable are fulfilled:

New Jersey: Brennert v. Farrier, 47 N. J. L. 75.

Oregon: Mall v. Portland, 35 Ore. 89, 56 Pac. 64.

[422] *Alabama:* Southern Car & F. Co. v. State, 133 Ala. 624, 32 So. 235.

Wisconsin: Travelers' Ins. Co. v. Fricke, 99 Wis. 367, 41 L. R. A. 557, 74 N. W. 372.

[423] State v. Steen, 14 Tex. 396.

So of a fine for usurping a franchise: People v. Sutter St. R. R., 129 Cal. 545, 62 Pac. 104, 79 Am. St. Rep. 137.

Or for failing to make an official return and settlement: Davenport v. McKee, 98 N. C. 500, 4 S. E. 545.

And so of an annual sum ordered to be paid in bastardy proceedings: State v. Sarratt, 14 Rich. (S. C.) 177.

[424] *Kansas:* First Nat. Bank v. Turner, 3 Kan. App. 352, 42 Pac. 936.

Ohio: Highley v. First Nat. Bank, 26 Oh. St. 75.

Pennsylvania: Columbia Nat. Bank v. Bletz, 2 Penny. 169.

So in an action to recover money paid on stock: Baldwin v. Zadik, 104 Cal. 594, 38 Pac. 363, 722; Parker v. Otis, 130 Cal. 322, 21 Pac. 571, 927.

[425] *Georgia:* Central R. R. & B. Co. v. Atlantic & G. R. R., 50 Ga. 444; Ware v. Simmons, 55 Ga. 94.

Wisconsin: Smith v. Morgan, 73 Wis. 375, 41 N. W. 532; Everett v. Gores, 92 Wis. 527, 66 N. W. 616.

[426] *Iowa:* Brentner v. Chicago, M. & S. P. Ry., 68 Ia. 530; Hopper v. Chicago, etc., R. R., 91 Iowa, 639, 650, 60 N. W. 487.

Pennsylvania: McCloskey v. Ryder, 21 Atl. 150.

So where a statute provides for a penalty in case of delay in addition to the principal debt, interest is recoverable on the debt but not on the penalty. Boyd v. Randolph, 91 Ky. 472, 16 S. W. 133.

No interest can be allowed on exemplary damages: Dunshee v. Standard Oil Co. (Ia.), 132 N. W. 371.

but valid liquidation of damages not being a penalty, interest
may be recovered on liquidated damages.[427]

§ 334. Judgments.

The allowance of interest on judgments generally has been
a subject of much discussion. In England, the doubt was solved
by a statute, which declared that every judgment debt shall
carry interest at the rate of four per centum per annum, from
the time of entering up the judgment, or from the time of the
passage of the act in cases of judgment then entered up and not
carrying interest, until the same shall be satisfied; and that
such interest might be levied under a writ of execution on
such judgment.[428]

In New York, it has been decided that interest is recoverable
in an action of debt on a judgment, whether the original demand
carried interest or not.[429] And this is generally followed, either
by statute or by interpretation of the common law.[430] It is,

[427] Ante, § 301.

[428] 1 & 2 Vict., c. 110, § 17. See Fisher v. Dudding, 3 M. & G. 238. See, also, Crafts v. Wilkinson, 4 Q. B. 74.

[429] Arizona: Daggs v. Bolton, 57 Pac. 511.

Illinois: Spooner v. Warner, 2 Ill. App. 240.

Kansas: Thomas v. Edwards, 3 Kan. 804.

Kentucky: Smith v. Todd, 3 J. J. Marsh. 306.

New York: Klock v. Robinson, 22 Wend. 157, where the English cases are reviewed.

[430] Alabama: Crawford v. Simonton, 7 Port. 110.

California: Burke v. Carruthers, 31 Cal. 467.

Georgia: Houston v. Mossman, T. U. P. Charlt. 138. See Wilcher v. Hamilton, 15 Ga. 435.

Illinois: Palmer v. Harris, 100 Ill. 276; Dilworth v. Curts, 139 Ill. 508, 29 N. E. 861; Gage v. Thompson, 161 Ill. 403, 49 N. E. 1062; Rogan v. Illinois Sav. Bank, 93 Ill. App. 39.

Kansas: Grund v. Tucker, 5 Kan. 70;

Lombard Invest. Co. v. Burton, 5 Kan. App. 197, 47 Pac. 154.

Maine: Edwards v. Moody, 60 Me. 255.

Maryland: Gwinn v. Whitaker, 1 H. & J. 754.

Nebraska: Trompen v. Hammond, 61 Neb. 446, 85 N. W. 436; Rawlings v. Anheuser-Busch Brewing Assoc., 94 N. W. 1001, 1 Neb. (Unof.) 555.

New Hampshire: Hodgdon v. Hodgdon, 2 N. H. 169; Mahurin v. Bickford, 6 N. H. 567.

Pennsylvania: Com. v. Vanderslice, 8 Serg. & R. 452.

Tennessee: Edenton v. Dickinson, 2 Tenn. Cas. 324.

Virginia: Mercer v. Beale, 4 Leigh, 189; Beall v. Silver, 2 Rand. 401.

Wisconsin: Booth v. Ableman, 20 Wis. 602.

In several jurisdictions the allowance of interest rests on statute, and in the absence of statute no interest will be allowed on a judgment.

United States: Amis v. Smith, 16 Pet. 303, 10 L. ed. 303; Perkins v. Fourniquet, 14 How. 328, 331, 14 L. ed. 82;

however, generally held that interest cannot be included in a levy on the judgment or in a *scire facias*.[431]

Washington & G. R. R. *v.* Harmon, 147 U. S. 571, 37 L. ed. 284, 13 Sup. Ct. 557; The New York, 108 Fed. 102.

California: Burke *v.* Carruthers, 31 Cal. 467; Dougherty *v.* Miller, 38 Cal. 548; Columbia Sav. Bk. *v.* Los Angeles County, 137 Cal. 467, 70 Pac. 308.

Kentucky: Brigham *v.* Vanbuskirk, 6 B. Mon. 197.

Louisiana: Baudin *v.* Pollock, 2 La. 184; Weaver *v.* Cox, 15 La. Ann. 463; Factors', etc., Ins. Co. *v.* New Harbor Protection Co., 39 La. Ann. 581.

Mississippi: Easton *v.* Vandorn, Walk. 214; Hamer *v.* Kirkwood, 25 Miss. 96.

Missouri: New York, Lake Erie & W. R. R. *v.* Estill, 147 U. S. 591, 622, 13 Sup. Ct. 444, 37 L. ed. 292 (Missouri law); State *v.* Vogel, 14 Mo. App. 187; Coquard *v.* Prendergast, 47 Mo. App. 243.

New York: Todd *v.* Botchford, 86 N. Y. 517.

North Carolina: Moore *v.* Pullen, 116 N. C. 284, 21 S. E. 195.

South Carolina: Glover *v.* Holmes, 1 Brev. 454; Harrington *v.* Glenn, 1 Hill, 79; Trenholm *v.* Bumpfield, 3 Rich. 376; Nelson *v.* Felder, 7 Rich. Eq. 395.

Texas: Coles *v.* Kelsey, 13 Tex. 75; Hagood *v.* Aikin, 57 Tex. 511; Cun-

ningham *v.* San Saba County, 11 Tex. Civ. App. 557, 32 S. W. 928.

Utah: Reece *v.* Knott, 3 Utah, 451.

In Kentucky, in an action of covenant on an agreement to pay for property, judgment was obtained. Suit was brought on that judgment, and the jury were told that *they were bound to give interest on the judgment.* The original agreement contained no stipulation for interest. The Court of Appeals said: "It is true, according to the ancient course of the common law, although the value of the thing covenanted to be performed usually regulated the amount of damages, the jury in an action sounding altogether in damages did in some instances exceed that measure; but they did not so because the law subjected the covenantor to the payment of interest, but in the exercise of a sound discretion with which they were invested, regulated by what, under the peculiar circumstances of the case, they might think just." And for the reason that the charge controlled the discretion of the jury, the judgment was reversed. Guthrie *v.* Wickliffs, 4 Bibb, 541; s. p. Cogwell's Heirs *v.* Lyons, 3 J. J. Marsh. 38.

In a few jurisdictions interest is allowed only in actions sounding in con-

---

[431] *United States:* Perkins *v.* Fourniquet, 14 How. 328, 331, 14 L. ed. 82.

Nevada: Solen *v.* Virginia & T. R. R., 14 Nev. 405.

New Hampshire: Barron *v.* Morrison, 44 N. H. 226.

New Jersey: Walton *v.* Vanderhoof, 2 N. J. L. 73.

New York: Watson *v.* Fuller, 6 Johns. 283.

South Carolina: Mann *v.* Taylor, 1 McC. 171; Williamson *v.* Broughton, 4 McC. 212.

Vermont: Hall *v.* Hall, 8 Vt. 156.

See *Pennsylvania:* Flanagin *v.* Wetherill, 5 Whart. 280.

By statute, however, interest is often included in the execution. So in *New York:* Sayre *v.* Austin, 3 Wend. 496; Co. Civ. Proc., § 1211. On all judgments in civil cases in the United States District or Circuit Courts, interest is allowed wherever, by the law of the State in which such Circuit or District Court is held, interest may be levied under execution on judgments recovered in the State courts. Laws 1842, ch. 188, § 8 (5 U. S. Stat. at Large, 518).

In Vermont it is held that all claim for interest is waived by suing out a *scire facias;* [432] but in New Hampshire it is held that if any part of the principal is unsatisfied, the balance of the principal with all the accrued interest may be recovered by action on the judgment. [433] In some States interest is allowed only on the principal sum due; [434] in others, on the principal and interest. [435] In most States, interest is allowed on the

tract, and is not given where the cause of action on which the judgment was rendered was a tort.

District of Columbia: Washington & G. R. R. *v.* Harmon, 147 U. S. 571, 13 Sup. Ct. 557, 37 L. ed. 284 (but see *contra,* Fifth Baptist Church *v.* Baltimore & O. R. R., 2 Mackey, 458; Hellen *v.* Metropolitan R. R., 4 Mackey, 519; Woodbury *v.* District, 19 D. C. 157).

South Carolina: Daub *v.* Martin, 2 Bay, 193; Crowther *v.* Sawyer, 2 Spear, 573.

In other jurisdictions interest is allowed upon judgments given in actions of tort:

California: Atherton *v.* Fowler, 46 Cal. 320.

Virginia: Fry *v.* Leslie, 87 Va. 269, 12 S. E. 671.

West Virginia: Fowler *v.* Baltimore & O. R. R., 18 W. Va. 579.

So in *Kentucky,* by statute, since 1888: Wagers *v.* Irvine, 103 Ky. 544, 45 S. W. 872 (personal injuries).

Where there were several similar suits pending, and a stipulation was made that all others should abide by the decision of a single test case, interest in the other cases runs from the date of the judgment in each case, and not from the date of judgment in the test case. Schaeffer *v.* Siegel, 9 Mo. App. 594.

In the Federal courts, when the judgment of an inferior court is affirmed, interest is allowed at the rate prescribed in the State or Territory where such judgment was affirmed. Section 966, U. S. R. S. Rules of Court, 11 C. C. A.

cxii. Under the law of Nevada, when the judgment is silent as regards interest, none can be collected; and this practice is followed in the Federal court, although it seems to be considered contrary to principle, and is not in harmony with authority elsewhere. Moran *v.* Hagerman, 69 Fed. 427.

[432] Hall *v.* Hall, 8 Vt. 156.

[433] Hodgdon *v.* Hodgdon, 2 N. H. 169.

[434] *United States:* Downs *v.* Allen, 22 Fed. 805, 23 Blatch. 54.

Alabama: Billingsbley *v.* Billingsbley, 24 Ala. 518.

Louisiana: Hyde *v.* Brown, 5 La. 33.

Maryland: Mobray *v.* Leckie, 42 Md. 474; Boarman *v.* Patterson, 1 Gill, 372.

Mississippi: Stricklin *v.* Cooper, 55 Miss. 624.

Nevada: Hastings *v.* Johnson, 1 Nev. 613.

North Carolina: Reade *v.* Street, 122 N. C. 301, 30 S. E. 124.

South Carolina: Pinckney *v.* Singleton, 2 Hill, 343.

[435] *California:* Emeric *v.* Tams, 6 Cal. 155; Guy *v.* Franklin, 5 Cal. 416; McCann *v.* Lewis, 9 Cal. 246; Mount *v.* Chapman, 9 Cal. 294; Corcoran *v.* Doll, 32 Cal. 82.

Massachusetts: East Tennessee Land Co. *v.* Leeson, 185 Mass. 4, 69 N. E. 351.

Texas: International, etc., R. R. *v.* Dimmit County Pasture Co., 5 Tex. Civ. App. 186, 23 S. W. 754.

West Virginia: Ruffner *v.* Hewitt, 14 W. Va. 737.

In Quivey *v.* Hall, 19 Cal. 97, the

whole amount, principal, interest, and costs.[436]   As the judgment is looked upon as a debt, there is no reason for making any distinction between the different constituents of the debt. In Pennsylvania, interest is allowed on such costs only as have actually been paid, and then from the time of payment. This is founded on the local custom of that State as to costs.[437] It was intimated in an early case in Pennsylvania that where several successive suits were brought on a judgment, interest would be allowed only on the amount of the original judgment; [438] but it was decided, later, that interest would in each case be allowed on the amount of the preceding judgment.[439]

Since interest is given as damages for the detention of the judgment debt, the rate should be that established by statute.[440]

administrator of an estate refused to pay a judgment against the deceased, and suit was therefore brought on the original judgment against the administrator. It was held that interest must not be compounded but must be computed according to the rate fixed in the original judgment since the judgment in this case is nothing more than a recognition of the former judgment as a proper claim against the estate.

[436] *California:* Huellmantel v. Huellmantel, 124 Cal. 583, 57 Pac. 582.

Colorado: Bates v. Wilson, 18 Colo. 287, 32 Pac. 615.

Illinois: Healy v. Protection M. F. I. Co., 107 Ill. App. 639.

Kansas: Sharp v. Barker, 11 Kan. 381.

Ohio: Emmitt v. Brophy, 42 Oh. St. 82.

Texas: Llano I. & F. Co. v. Watkins, 4 Tex. Civ. App. 428, 23 S. W. 612; Lyons v. Iron City Nat. Bank, 24 S. W. 304 (see Ghent v. Boyd, 18 Tex. Civ. App. 88, 43 S. W. 891); Carver v. J. S. Mayfield Lumber Co., 29 Tex. Civ. App. 434, 68 S. W. 711.

Virginia: Laidley v. Merrifield, 7 Leigh, 346.

Washington: Ritchie v. Carpenter, 2 Wash. 512, 28 Pac. 380, 26 Am. St. Rep. 877.

Contra, Kentucky: Cockrill v. Mize, 11 Ky. L. Rep. 637, 12 S. W. 1040.

Even though the judgment is for costs alone, interest may be allowed upon it.

Illinois: Linck v. Litchfield, 31 Ill. App. 104.

Iowa: Hoyt v. Beach, 104 Iowa, 257, 73 N. W. 492, 65 Am. St. Rep. 461.

Michigan: Hayden v. Hefferan, 99 Mich. 262, 58 N. W. 59.

[437] Rogers v. Burns, 27 Pa. 525; Wetherell v. Stillman, 65 Pa. 105; Baum v. Reed, 74 Pa. 322.

This principle is carried so far that a sheriff suing to recover his costs is not allowed interest on them: Galbraith v. Walker, 95 Pa. 481.

[438] Meason's Estate, 4 Watts, 341.

[439] Fries v. Watson, 5 S. & R. 220.

[440] *United States:* Mitchell v. Harmony, 13 How. 115, 14 L. ed. 75; National Steamship Co. v. Tugman, 82 Fed. 246, 27 C. C. A. 116; Evans v. White, 8 Fed. Cas. No. 4,572a, Hempst. 296.

Arkansas: Harbison v. Vaughan, 42 Ark. 538 (see Henry v. Ward, 4 Ark. 150).

California: San Joaquin Land, etc., Co. v. West, 99 Cal. 345, 33 Pac. 928.

Illinois: Mason v. Eakle, 1 Ill. 52; Tindall v. Meeker, 2 Ill. 137; Wayman

Some States, however, provide by statute that a judgment recovered on an interest-bearing obligation shall continue to bear interest at the stipulated rate.[441] A judgment ordinarily bears interest from the time it is entered.[442]

v. Cochrane, 35 Ill. 152; Corgan *v.* Frew, 39 Ill. 31; Hunter *v.* Hatch, 45 Ill. 178.

Kansas: Simmons *v.* Garrett, McCahon, 82.

Massachusetts: West *v.* White, 165 Mass. 258, 43 N. E. 103.

Missouri: Hawkins *v.* Ridenhour, 13 Mo. 125; Ransom *v.* Cobb, 67 Mo. 375 (changed by statute later; see next note).

New Hampshire: Sanborn *v.* Steele, 20 N. H. 34.

New Jersey: Verree *v.* Hughes, 11 N. J. L. 91; Wilson *v.* Marsh, 13 N. J. Eq. 289.

New York: Taylor *v.* Wing, 84 N. Y. 471.

Ohio: Calahan *v.* Babcock, 21 Ohio St. 281, 8 Am. Rep. 63; Neil *v.* Bank, 50 Ohio St. 193, 33 N. E. 720.

Oregon: Brauer *v.* Portland, 35 Ore. 471, 58 Pac. 861, 59 Pac. 378.

Tennessee: Ward *v.* Kenner, 37 S. W. 707.

Texas: Sheldon *v.* Martin (Tex. Civ. App.), 8 S. W. 61; Gunn *v.* Miller (Tex. Civ. App.), 26 S. W. 278 (but see the Texas cases cited in the next note as to judgments on written contracts).

Washington: Roeder *v.* Brown, 1 Wash. Terr. 112.

England: Ex parte Fewings, 25 Ch. Div. 338.

If the statutory rate is changed before payment of the judgment, the new rate prevails from the time of the change.

New York: Wells, Fargo & Co. *v.* Davis, 105 N. Y. 670, 12 N. E. 42.

Washington: Palmer *v.* Laberee, 23 Wash. 409, 63 Pac. 216.

Wyoming: Wyoming Nat. Bank *v.* Brown, 7 Wyo. 494, 53 Pac. 291.

[441] *California:* Corcoran *v.* Doll, 32 Cal. 82.

Georgia: Daniel *v.* Gibson, 72 Ga. 367, 53 Am. Rep. 845; Neal *v.* Brockham, 87 Ga. 130, 13 S. E. 283.

Indiana: Burns *v.* Anderson, 68 Ind. 202, 34 Am. Rep. 250.

Iowa: Burrows *v.* Stryker, 47 Ia. 477; Rand *v.* Barrett, 66 Ia. 631, 24 N. W. 530.

Mississippi: Leaders *v.* Gray, 60 Miss. 400, 45 Am. Rep. 414.

Missouri: Rogers *v.* Lee County, 1 Dill. 529 (Mo.); Crook *v.* Tull, 111 Mo. 283, 20 S. W. 8; Catron *v.* Lafayette County, 125 Mo. 67, 28 S. W. 331; Evans *v.* Fisher, 26 Mo. App. 541.

Nebraska: Bond *v.* Dolby, 17 Neb. 491, 23 N. W. 351; Connecticut Mut. L. Ins. Co. *v.* Westerhoff, 58 Neb. 379, 78 N. W. 724, 76 Am. St. Rep. 101.

Ohio: Hydraulic Co. *v.* Chatfield, 38 Oh. St. 575.

South Carolina: Thomas *v.* Wilson, 3 McCord, 166.

Texas: Jewett *v.* Thompson, 8 Tex. 437; Hagood *v.* Aikin, 57 Tex. 511; Williams *v.* Nat. Park. Bank (Tex. Civ. App.), 26 S. W. 171; Cruger *v.* Sullivan, 11 Tex. Civ. App. 377, 32 S. W. 448.

[442] *California:* Bibend *v.* Liverpool, etc., Ins. Co., 30 Cal. 78.

Colorado: Bates *v.* Wilson, 18 Colo. 287, 32 Pac. 615.

Georgia: Guernsey *v.* Phinizy, 113 Ga. 898, 39 S. E. 402.

Illinois: Healy *v.* Protection M. F. I. Co., 107 Ill. App. 632.

Massachusetts: Payne *v.* McIntier, 1 Mass. 69.

It is not all orders of the court which will bear interest. An order, decree, or judgment by which a party is required to do an act will not bear interest; only judgments or decrees for the payment of money are capable of bearing interest. Mere interlocutory orders,[443] as for the payment of money into court,[444] do not bear interest. But final decrees for the payment of money bear interest like judgments,[445] for instance, decrees of foreclosure, fixing the amount due.[446] Orders in probate proceedings for the payment of money by an administrator bear interest;[447] so does an award of damages included in a decree for restitution in admiralty.[448]

§ 335. Between verdict and judgment.

In some jurisdictions interest is not recoverable between

In North Carolina interest begins from the first day of the term in which the judgment is rendered. Reade v. Street, 122 N. C. 301, 30 S. E. 124.

Where an injunction was obtained by the judgment debtor against the payment of the judgment, but was afterwards dissolved, interest was allowed from the date of the judgment. Bartlett v. Blanton, 4 J. J. Marsh. (Ky.) 426.

[443] *United States:* Roberts v. Wheelen, 3 Dall. 506, 1 L. ed. 698 (judgment entered merely by way of security).

England: Phillips v. Homfray, [1892] 1 Ch. 465, 61 L. J. Ch. 210, 66 L. T. Rep. (N. S.) 657 (interlocutory decree).

In Shaller v. Brand, 6 Binn. (Pa.) 435, 6 Am. Dec. 482, it was held, that a judgment on which it is agreed that no execution shall issue until plaintiff has perfected title to certain land for which the bond supporting the judgment was given, will carry interest.

[444] *Kentucky:* Louisville Water Co. v. Clark, 16 Ky. L. Rep. 585, 29 S. W. 309.

Contra, Nebraska: Stuart v. Burcham, 62 Neb. 84, 86 N. W. 898, 89 Am. St. Rep. 739.

[445] *Arkansas:* Nevada County v. Hicks, 50 Ark. 416, 8 S. W. 180.

California: Huellmantel v. Huellmantel, 124 Cal. 583, 57 Pac. 582.

Georgia: National Bank v. Heard, 65 Ga. 189.

Indiana: Hull v. Butler, 7 Ind. 267.

Kentucky: Com. v. Bosley, 5 Bush, 221.

[446] *Illinois:* Aldrich v. Sharp, 4 Ill. 261 (but see Heffron v. Gage, 44 Ill. App. 147).

Nebraska: Stenger v. Carrig, 61 Neb. 753, 86 N. W. 475.

If the decree does not fix the amount due, interest does not run on the decree, but continues to run on the original debt:

United States: Shepherd v. Pepper, 133 U. S. 626, 10 Sup. Ct. 438, 33 L. ed. 706.

[447] *Alabama:* Kyle v. Mays, 22 Ala. 692.

California: Olvera's Estate, 70 Cal. 184, 11 Pac. 624.

Illinois: Randolph v. People, 40 Ill. App. 174.

Texas: Finley v. Carothers, 9 Tex. 517, 60 Am. Dec. 186.

No interest can be allowed on an award to a widow of a share in her husband's estate, at least until she elects to take the amount of the award in money. Stunz v. Stunz, 131 Ill. 210, 23 N. E. 407.

[448] Nuestra Senora de Regla, 108 U.S. 92, 107, 2 Sup. Ct. 287, 27 L. ed. 662.

verdict and judgment,[449] although it is sometimes held that the jury has the power to find a verdict for a certain amount "with interest." [450] In other jurisdictions, interest continues to accrue on an interest-bearing claim,[451] and in others still on any claim, of whatever nature,[452] but only on the principal amount, not on interest which may be included in the judgment.[453] And it would seem that in those States where points of law are carried up, not by an appeal from a judgment or by a writ of error from it, but by a bill of exceptions, interest should be allowed on the verdict as it would on a judgment appealed from. The same rules govern, and interest has been allowed upon an award of arbitrators [454] and upon a master's report.[455]

[449] *Arkansas:* Hallum *v.* Dickinson, 14 S. W. 477.
Colorado: Hawley *v.* Barker, 5 Colo. 118; Cody *v.* Filley, 5 Colo. 124.
Kentucky: Dawson *v.* Clay, 1 J. J. Marsh. 165.
Louisiana: Trimble *v.* Moore, 2 La. 577; Bonner *v.* Copeley, 15 La. Ann. 504.
Maryland: Baltimore C. P. Ry. *v.* Sewell, 37 Md. 443.
New York: Lord *v.* New York, 3 Hill, 426; Henning *v.* Van Tyne, 19 Wend. 101.
Pennsylvania: Kelsey *v.* Murphy, 30 Pa. 340; Norris *v.* Philadelphia, 70 Pa. 332.

[450] Irvin *v.* Hazelton, 37 Pa. 465.

[451] Dowell *v.* Griswold, 5 Sawy. 23; Swails *v.* Cissna, 61 Ia. 693.

[452] *United States:* Gibson *v.* Cincinnati Enquirer, 2 Flip. 88; Dowell *v.* Groswold, 7 Fed. Cas. No. 4,040, 5 Sawy. 23; Griffith *v.* Baltimore, etc., R. R., 44 Fed. 574.
California: Golden Gate Mill, etc., Co. *v.* Joshua Hendy Mach. Works, 82 Cal. 184, 23 Pac. 45.

Connecticut: Weed *v.* Weed, 25 Conn. 494.
Iowa: Carson *v.* German Ins. Co., 62 Iowa, 433, 17 N. W. 650. (See Shepard *v.* Brenton, 20 Iowa, 41.)
Massachusetts: Vail *v.* Nickerson, 6 Mass. 261; Com. *v.* Boston & M. R. R., 3 Cush. 25.
Nebraska: Fremont, etc., R. R. *v.* Root, 49 Neb. 914, 69 N. W. 397; Hilton *v.* State, 60 Neb. 421, 83 N. W. 354; Missouri Pacific R. R. *v.* Fox, 60 Neb. 531, 555, 83 N. W. 744.
New Hampshire: Johnson *v.* Atlantic & S. L. R. R., 43 N. H. 410.
Wisconsin: McLimans *v.* Lancaster, 65 Wis. 240.
Canada: Gordon *v.* Victoria, 7 Brit. Col. 339.

[453] *Massachusetts:* McKim *v.* Blake, 139 Mass. 593.
New York: Earle *v.* Earle, 73 App. Div. 300, 76 N. Y. Supp. 851.
Where by local law interest was allowed from the time of the verdict or report until judgment, the court (sitting without a jury) made a special finding of facts as a basis from which

[454] *Maine:* Cary *v.* Whitney, 50 Me. 337 (*contra*, in an earlier case, of a report of referees: Kendall *v.* Lewiston Water Power Co., 36 Me. 19).
Pennsylvania: Buckman *v.* Davis, 28 Pa. 211.

[455] Illinois Cent. R. R. *v.* Turrill, 110 U. S. 301, 4 Sup. Ct. 5, 28 L. ed. 154. But see Match *v.* Hunt, 38 Mich. 1.

If the giving of judgment on the verdict is delayed by fault of the plaintiff, interest will not be allowed.[456] The matter is almost everywhere regulated by statute.[457]

§ 336. In error.

* Interest is sometimes given in error, by way of damages. In an early case,[458] on affirmance of judgment in the King's Bench on error, a rule was obtained to show cause why the master should not compute interest, and add it to the costs, on the ground of an old statute,[459] which enacted that on a writ of error being brought, and judgment affirmed, the person against whom it is sued out shall recover his costs and damages. And it was held that "interest ought to be the measure of damages."

The principle of this statute has been fixed in American legislation. By the judiciary act of the United States,[460] the Supreme Court is authorized, in case of affirmance of any judgment or decree, to award to the respondent just damages for his delay. And by the rules of the same court,[461] in cases where the suit is defended for mere delay, damages are to be awarded at the rate of 10 per centum per annum on the amount of the judgment, to the time of the affirmance thereof. Where there is a real controversy, the damages are to be at the rate of 6 per cent. per annum only. And in both cases, the interest is to be computed as part of the damages. It is, therefore, entirely for the decision of the court, whether any damages, or interest as a part thereof, are to be allowed or not, in cases of affirmance.[462]

the amount due the plaintiff for principal and interest might be computed, but gave judgment for defendant. On reversal of this judgment, plaintiff was held entitled to recover interest from the date of the finding. Metcalf v. City of Watertown, 68 Fed. 859, 34 U. S. App. 107, 16 C. C. A. 37.

[456] *United States:* Redfield v. Ystalyfera Iron Co., 110 U. S. 174, 3 Sup. Ct. 570, 34 L. ed. 112.

New York: Williams v. Smith, 2 Cai. 253, Col. Cas. 403, Col. & C. Cas. 239.

[457] Thus in New York by the act of May 7, 1844, interest is to be taxed on all verdicts and reports of referees, as costs, from the time of obtaining them to that of perfecting the judgment. Co. Civ. Proc., § 1235.

[458] Zink v. Langton, 2 Douglass, 751, in notes.

[459] 3 Hen. VII., c. 10.

[460] 1789, c. 20, § 23.

[461] Made in February Term, 1803, and February Term, 1807.

[462] Boyce's Executors v. Grundy, 9 Pet. 275, 9 L. ed. 275; Himely v. Rose, 5 Cranch, 313, 3 L. ed. 313; Santa

The same principle was followed in New York, where it was provided by statute,[463] that "If upon writ of error, the judgment be affirmed, or the writ be discontinued or quashed, or the plaintiff in error be nonsuited, the defendant in error shall recover costs, and also *damages for the delay and vexation, to be assessed in the discretion of the court* before whom the writ was returnable." The limit of discretion under this statute was legal interest. The allowance of damages, however, in these cases, rests entirely in discretion; and so, where the action was in tort, the Court of Errors refused it.[464] It was allowed, however, in another case, on a judgment in trover.[465] But this branch of the subject rather belongs to the head of statutes regulating damages, which we shall elsewhere consider.**

It may be laid down as a general principle that where the defendant appeals or brings proceedings in error, and the judgment for the plaintiff is affirmed, he is entitled to interest; [466] and if it is affirmed in part, he may have interest on that portion of the judgment which is affirmed.[467] Where the plaintiff

Maria, 10 Wheat. 431, 442, 6 L. ed. 431; Hall v. Jordan, 19 Wall. 271, 22 L. ed. 47; West W. Ry. v. Foley, 94 U. S. 100, 24 L. ed. 71; Sire v. Ellithope A. B. Co., 137 U. S. 579, 34 L. ed. 80, 11 Sup. Ct. 195.

[463] 2 R. S. 618, § 32; superseded by the Code of Civil Procedure.

[464] Gelston v. Hoyt, 13 Johns. 561.

[465] Bissell v. Hopkins, 4 Cow. 53. In the same State it has been said that "the judicial doctrine of allowing and disallowing interest on judgments, whether on affirmance in error, or in other cases, seems in some respects to rest rather upon arbitrary discretion, practice, or precedent, than any principle which conforms to our general notions of justice." Klock v. Robinson, 22 Wend. 157, 160.

[466] *United States:* Fleckner v. Bank, 8 Wheat. 338, 5 L. ed. 338; Schell v. Cochran, 107 U. S. 625, 2 Sup. Ct. 827, 27 L. ed. 490; Kneeland v. American L. & T. Co., 138 U. S. 509, 11 Sup. Ct. 426, 34 L. ed. 1052.

Illinois: Atchison, T. & S. F. R. R. v.

Chicago, etc., R. R., 162 Ill. 632, 654, 44 N. E. 823, 35 L. R. A. 167.

Maryland: Contee v. Findley, 1 Harr. & J. 331; Butcher v. Norwood, 1 Harr. & J. 485 (on appeal bond).

Montana: Palmer v. Murray, 8 Mont. 312.

New York: Lord v. New York, 3 Hill, 426; Van Valkenburgh v. Fuller, 6 Paige, 10.

Pennsylvania: Respublica v. Nicholson, 2 Dall. 256, 1 L. ed. 371; McCausland v. Bell, 9 S. & R. 388.

Tennessee: Cowan v. Donaldson, 95 Tenn. 327, 32 S. W. 457.

Vermont: Smith v. Pike, 44 Vt. 61.

Canada: Trinity College v. Hill, 8 Ont. 286.

Australia: Smart v. O'Callaghan, 4 Vict. L. R. 448.

[467] *California:* Barnhart v. Edwards, 128 Cal. 572, 61 Pac. 176.

Louisiana: Black v. Carrollton R. R., 10 La. Ann. 33, 63 Am. Dec. 586.

See *Kentucky:* Beall v. Beall, 6 Ky. L. Rep. 516.

appeals from a judgment for the defendant, and succeeds, no interest can be given as on a prior judgment in his favor, since there was none.[468] Where the plaintiff gets a judgment and appeals from it himself, and the appeal is dismissed, he is entitled to no interest on the original judgment, since the delay is his own fault.[469] But where *both* parties appeal, interest is not allowed to the prevailing party.[470]

§ 337. Municipal corporations.

It is a controverted question whether municipal corporations are liable for interest except upon express contract or in consequence of a statute. It seems clear that municipal corporations are not required to seek their creditors; the creditor must seek the debtor if the debtor is a municipal body. A municipal body is therefore not in default till payment of the debt is demanded, and no interest can be recovered until that time.[471] In some States it is held that municipal corporations are not liable to pay interest at all, in the absence of agreement to do so or of other special circumstances.[472] And this is certainly the case where the claim is not a general obligation of the cor-

[468] *Kansas:* Kansas City R. R. v. Berry, 55 Kan. 186, 40 Pac. 288.

Montana: Priest v. Eide, 19 Mont. 53, 47 Pac. 206, 958.

[469] *United States:* New York, etc., Mail Steamship Co. v. The Express, 59 Fed. 476, 8 C. C. A. 182.

Illinois: Cook v. South Park Comm'rs, 61 Ill. 115.

New Hampshire: March v. Portsmouth, etc., R. R., 19 N. H. 372.

See *California:* Ferrea v. Tubbs, 125 Cal. 687, 58 Pac. 308.

[470] The Rebecca Clyde, 12 Blatch. 403.

[471] *Cities:*
New York: Paul v. New York, 7 Daly, 14; Wilson v. Troy, 60 Hun, 183, 14 N. Y. Supp. 721; Holihan v. City of New York, 33 Misc. 249, 68 N. Y. Supp. 148.

Pennsylvania: Mahanoy v. Comry, 103 Pa. 362.

Counties:
New Jersey: Curley v. Hudson

County, 66 N. J. L. 401, 49 Atl. 471.

North Carolina: Yellowly v. Pitt County, 73 N. C. 164.

Oregon: Grant County v. Lake County, 17 Ore. 453, 21 Pac. 447.

[472] *Cities:*
Illinois: Pekin v. Reynolds, 31 Ill. 529; Chicago v. People, 56 Ill. 327; Hobit v. Bloomington, 87 Ill. App. 479.

Pennsylvania: Snyder v. Boviard, 122 Pa. 442, 15 Atl. 910, 9 Am. St. Rep. 118 (unless there is unreasonable delay).

Counties:
Arkansas: Garland County v. Hot Spring County, 68 Ark. 83, 56 S. W. 636.

California: Beals v. Supervisors, 28 Cal. 449; Soher v. Supervisors, 39 Cal. 134; Hopkins v. Contra Costa County, 106 Cal. 556, 39 Pac. 933.

Illinois: Madison County v. Bartlett, 2 Ill. 67 (because creditors understand they must wait until the county is able to pay); Franklin County v.

poration, but is payable only out of a special assessment or tax.[473] But apart from statutory reasons, there seems to be no principle of law which should exempt municipal corporations from liability for interest; for they have in no sense sovereign rights, and are legally obliged to pay their debts like other debtors. Upon all debts of liquidated amount payable at a definite time a city or county is almost everywhere now held to pay interest from that time,[474] and in the case of warrants and other debts not payable at a definite time, from the time of presentment.[475]

Layman, 145 Ill. 138, 33 N. E. 1094 (unless there is unreasonable and vexatious delay).
Mississippi: Anderson v. Issaquena County, 75 Miss. 873, 896, 23 So. 310 (because county is agency of government); Warren County v. Klein, 51 Miss. 807; Clay County v. Chickasaw County, 64 Miss. 534.
Oregon: Seton v. Hoyt, 34 Ore. 266, 43 L. R. A. 634, 55 Pac. 967, 75 Am. St. Rep. 641.
Pennsylvania: Allison v. Juniata County, 50 Pa. 351.
South Carolina: Wheeler v. Newberry County, 18 S. C. 132.
Texas: Ashe v. Harris County, 55 Tex. 49.
District of Columbia: Gray v. District of Columbia, 1 App. Cas. (D. C.) 20.
[473] *Cities:*
Illinois: Vider v. Chicago, 164 Ill. 354, 45 N. E. 720.
Louisiana: Begue v. Herbert, 108 La. 119, 32 So. 333.
Minnesota: Keigher v. St. Paul, 69 Minn. 78, 72 N. W. 54.
Tennessee: Gas Light Co. v. Memphis, 93 Tenn. 612, 30 S. W. 25 (even though the tax has been collected).
Washington: Tacoma Bituminous Paving Co. v. Sternberg, 26 Wash. 84, 66 Pac. 121.
Counties:
Road Com'rs v. Hudson, 45 N. J. L. 173.

[474] *United States:* Genoa v. Woodruff, 92 U. S. 502, 23 L. ed. 586 (bonds); Graves v. Saline County, 43 C. C. A. 414, 104 Fed. 61 (bond coupons); Board of Commissioners of Ouray County v. Geer, 47 C. C. A. 450, 108 Fed. 478 (bonds).
Arkansas: Nevada Co. v. Hicks, 50 Ark. 416, 8 S. W. 180 (judgment).
Florida: Jefferson County v. Hawkins, 23 Fla. 223, 2 So. 362 (coupons on bonds).
Kentucky: Washington County Court v. McKee, 12 Ky. L. Rep. 102, 13 S. W. 909 (liquidated debt assumed by note).
Minnesota: J. D. Moran Mfg. & C. Co. v. St. Paul, 65 Minn. 300, 67 N. W. 1000.
Missouri: Neosho C. W. Co. v. Neosho, 136 Mo. 498, 38 S. W. 89 (water rent payable at stated times).
New York: Oswego C. S. Bank v. Board of Education, 70 App. Div. 538, 75 N. Y. Supp. 417 (bonds).
Pennsylvania: Port Royal v. Graham, 84 Pa. 426 (money borrowed).
Wisconsin: Pruyn v. Milwaukee, 18 Wis. 367 (bonds).
See Friend v. Pittsburgh, 131 Pa. 305, 17 Am. St. Rep. 811, 18 Atl. 1060, 6 L. R. A. 636.
[475] *Arkansas:* Jacks v. Turner, 36 Ark. 89.
California: O. Mills, etc., Nat. Bank v. Greenhaw, 134 Cal. 673, 66 Pac. 963.
Indiana: Sithin v. Shelby County Com'rs, 66 Ind. 109 (bounty).

§ 338.[a] The State.

The case is different with the State. Unlike a municipal corporation the State, being sovereign, is under no legal obligation to pay any claim against it; and if it can be sued, it is only by its own consent. Being under no legal obligation to pay at all, it is not legally in default for not paying, and unless by statute or express agreement it is not held to the payment of interest by way of damages for delay. It is almost universally held, therefore, that the State cannot be called upon to pay interest for delay in settling a claim,[476] or even upon its bonds, except so far as the interest is expressly provided for in the agreement.[477] In some jurisdictions, however, the State is, by statute or otherwise, held to pay interest [478] in certain cases.

Missouri: Robbins v. Lincoln County, 3 Mo. 57; Risley v. Andrew County, 46 Mo. 382.

New York: Paul v. New York, 7 Daly, 144.

North Carolina: Yellowly v. Pitt County, 73 N. C. 164.

Oregon: Monteith v. Parker, 36 Ore. 170, 59 Pac. 192, 78 Am. St. Rep. 767.

Washington: Williams v. Shoudy, 12 Wash. 362, 41 Pac. 169.

[a] For § 338 of the eighth edition, see § 339.

[476] THE CROWN OF ENGLAND: *In re* Gosman, 17 Ch. Div. 771 (*contra*, in Quebec, a province governed by the civil law: Reg. v. Henderson, 28 Can. 425).

THE UNITED STATES: Tillson v. United States, 100 U. S. 43, 47, 25 L. ed. 543; United States v. Bayard, 127 U. S. 251, 8 Sup. Ct. 1156, 32 L. ed. 159; Wightman v. United States, 23 Ct. of Cls. 144; Walton v. U. S., 61 Fed. 486; Bunton v. U. S., 62 Fed. 171; Marine v. Lyon, 62 Fed. 153, 13 C. C. A. 268; United States v. Sargent, 162 Fed. 81, 89 C. C. A. 81.

THE STATES:

California: Sawyer v. Colgan, 102 Cal. 23, 36 Pac. 580.

Indiana: Carr v. State, 127 Ind. 204, 26 N. E. 778 (*semble*).

Mississippi: State v. Mayes, 28 Miss. 706; Whitney v. State, 52 Miss. 732.

North Carolina: Attorney General v. Cape Fear Nav. Co., 2 Ired. Eq. 444.

Ohio: Ohio v. Board of Public Works, 36 Ohio St. 409.

Oregon: Young v. State, 36 Ore. 417, 59 Pac. 812, 47 L. R. A. 548.

[477] *United States:* U. S. v. N. Carolina, 136 U. S. 211, 222, 10 Sup. Ct. 920, 34 L. ed. 336 (no interest after maturity).

California: Davis v. State, 121 Cal. 210, 53 Pac. 555 (no interest on coupons).

Florida: Hawkins v. Mitchell, 34 Fla. 405, 16 So. 311 (no interest after maturity).

But see Gray v. State, 72 Ind. 567, where it is held that overdue coupons draw interest.

The State is of course bound to pay interest it has agreed to pay; and this obligation cannot be repudiated by the legislature. Carr v. State, 127 Ind. 204, 26 N. E. 778, 22 Am. St. Rep. 624, 11 L. R. A. 370.

[478] *Kentucky:* Com. v. Collins, 12 Bush, 386.

E.—RELIEF FROM PAYMENT OF INTEREST

§ 339.[a] **Interest after payment of the principal.**

Where interest is not stipulated for in the contract, but is recoverable merely as damages, a creditor is precluded from sustaining an action for its recovery after accepting the principal; [479] and protest at the time of the acceptance of the principal is of no avail.[480] But where interest is stipulated for in the contract, suit may be brought for it, although the principal has been paid.[481]

§ 339a. **Effect of partial payments upon interest.**

Where partial payments have been made in cash, or by rents and profits, or otherwise, the payments are to be first applied to the satisfaction of the interest then due, and the

New York: Coxe v. State, 144 N. Y. 396, 39 N. E. 400; Lakeside Paper Co. v. State, 45 App. Div. 112, 60 N. Y. Supp. 1081, 55 App. Div. 208, 66 N. Y. Supp. 959.

Pennsylvania: Respublica v. Mitchell, 2 Dall. 101.

[a] For § 339 of the eighth edition, see § 324a.

[479] *United States:* Stewart v. Barnes, 153 U. S. 456, 14 Sup. Ct. 849, 38 L. ed. 781; Pacific R. R. v. U. S., 158 U. S. 118, 16 Sup. Ct. 766, 39 L. ed. 918; Southern R. R. v. Dunlop Mills, 76 Fed. 505, 22 C. C. A. 302.

Connecticut: Canfield v. Eleventh School District, 19 Conn. 529.

District of Columbia: Potomac Co. v. Union Bank, 3 Cranch, C. C. 101.

Illinois: Keehner v. Kinder, 81 Ill. App. 23.

Louisiana: Succession of Mann, 4 La. Ann. 28; Succession of Anderson, 12 La. Ann. 95.

Maine: American Bible Society v. Wells, 68 Me. 572.

New York: Stevens v. Barringer, 13 Wend. 639; Jacot v. Emmett, 11 Paige, 142; Cutter v. New York, 92 N. Y. 166; Donnelly v. Brooklyn, 121 N. Y. 19, 24 N. E. 17; Devlin v. New

York, 131 N. Y. 123, 30 N. E. 45, affirming 60 Hun, 68, 14 N. Y. Supp. 251; Southern C. R. R. v. Moravia, 61 Barb. 180; Tenth Nat. Bank v. New York, 4 Hun, 429; Smith v. Buffalo, 39 N. Y. Supp. 881; Bonner Brick Co. v. M. M. Canada Co., 18 Misc. 681, 42 N. Y. Supp. 14; Brady v. Mayor, 14 App. Div. 152, 43 N. Y. Supp. 452; Bronx Gas & Elec. Co. v. N. Y., 29 Misc. 402, 60 N. Y. Supp. 58.

North Carolina: Moore v. Fuller, 2 Jones, 205.

South Carolina: St. Paul's Church v. Washington, 3 Rich. 380 (but see Fishburne v. Sanders, 1 Nott & M. 242).

In Los Angeles v. City Bank, 100 Cal. 18, 34 Pac. 510, interest was refused in such a case on another ground.

[480] Graves v. Saline Co., 104 Fed. 61, 43 C. C. A. 414.

[481] *Indiana:* Robbins v. Cheek, 32 Ind. 328.

Missouri: Stone v. Bennett, 8 Mo. 41.

New York: Fake v. Eddy, 15 Wend. 76.

North Carolina: King v. Phillips, 95 N. C. 245.

balance only is to go towards the reduction of the principal.[482] If the payment is not large enough to discharge the interest already accrued, it is said in a few jurisdictions that a balance is then struck and interest runs on the whole balance; [483] but the rule almost universally followed is that laid down in the leading case of Connecticut *v.* Jackson; [484] in which Chancellor Kent said that the rule for casting interest, when partial payments have been made, is to apply the payment, in the first place, to the discharge of the interest then due. If the payment exceeds the interest, the surplus goes towards discharging the principal, and the subsequent interest is to be computed on the balance of principal remaining due. If the payment be less than the interest, the surplus of interest must not be taken to augment the principal; but interest continues on the former principal until the period when the payments, taken together, exceed the interest due, and then the surplus is to be applied towards discharging the principal; and interest is to be computed on the balance, as aforesaid.[485] Where by

[482] *United States:* Massachusetts *v.* Western Union Tel. Co., 141 U. S. 40, 11 Sup. Ct. 889, 35 L. ed. 628; Russell *v.* Lucas, 21 Fed. Cas. No. 12,156a, Hempst. 91; Wittkowski *v.* Harris, 64 Fed. 712.

Alabama: Vaughan *v.* Smith, 69 Ala. 92; Hunt *v.* Stockton Lumber Co., 113 Ala. 387, 21 So. 454.

Illinois: Heartt *v.* Rhodes, 66 Ill. 351.

Iowa: Smith *v.* Coopers, 9 Iowa, 376; Bayliss *v.* Pearson, 15 Iowa, 279.

Maine: Leonard *v.* Wildes, 36 Me. 265.

Maryland: Lamott *v.* Sterett, 1 Harr. & J. 42.

Massachusetts: Dean *v.* Williams, 17 Mass. 417; Fay *v.* Bradley, 1 Pick. 194; Reed *v.* Reed, 10 Pick. 398.

Mississippi: Stewart *v.* Stebbins, 30 Miss. 66.

Nebraska: Mills *v.* Saunders, 4 Neb. 190.

New Hampshire: Townsend *v.* Riley, 46 N. H. 300.

New York: French *v.* Kennedy, 7 Barb. 452.

North Carolina: Overby *v.* Fayetteville Bldg., etc., Assoc., 81 N. C. 56.

Wisconsin: Reed *v.* Jones, 15 Wis. 40.

[483] *Minnesota:* Whittacre *v.* Fuller, 5 Minn. 508.

New Hampshire: Ross *v.* Russell, 31 N. H. 386.

Canada: Bettes *v.* Farewell, 15 Up. Can. C. P. 450.

[484] 1 Johns. (N. Y.) Ch. 13, 17.

[485] The rule in Connecticut *v.* Jackson was followed in these cases:

United States: Story *v.* Livingston, 13 Pet. 359, 10 L. ed. 200.

Alabama: Marr *v.* Southwick, 2 Port. 351.

Florida: Hart *v.* Dorman, 2 Fla. 445, 50 Am. Dec. 285.

Indiana: Wasson *v.* Gould, 3 Blackf. 180; McCormick *v.* Mitchell, 57 Ind. 248; Jacobs *v.* Ballenger, 130 Ind. 231, 29 N. E. 782, 15 L. R. A. 169.

Iowa: Huner *v.* Doolittle, 3 Greene, 76, 54 Am. Dec. 489.

Kentucky: Hawkins *v.* L., etc., Assoc., 89 S. W. 197.

Louisiana: Estebene *v.* Estebene, 5

agreement interest is payable at certain fixed times, payments are first to be applied on the arrears of the stipulated interest and interest on such arrears, next on interest accrued on the principal since the last interest day, and last on the principal itself.[486] Where the debt itself bears no interest, the payment is applied directly to the debt, and does not bear interest.[487] These rules may in any case be modified by agreement, and payments applied to the principal.[488]

§ 340. Laches or fault of creditor.

Since interest is given as damages for delay in payment, if the defendant was not chargeable with the delay, or if the plaintiff was to blame for it, interest will not run. So if the creditor himself is chargeable with the delay, he cannot recover compensation for it.[489] So where a plaintiff prosecuted

La. Ann. 738; Union Bank v. Lobdell, 10 La. Ann. 130; Bird v. Lobdell, 10 La. Ann. 159.

Maine: Pierce v. Faunce, 53 Me. 351.

Maryland: Williar v. B a l t i m o r e Butchers' Loan, etc., Assoc., 45 Md. 546.

Massachusetts: Downer v. Whittier, 144 Mass. 448, 11 N. E. 585.

Michigan: Payne v. Avery, 21 Mich. 524; McBride v. McIntire, 100 Mich. 302, 58 N. W. 994.

Minnesota: Betcher v. Hodgman, 63 Minn. 30, 65 N. W. 96, 56 Am. St. Rep. 447.

Mississippi: Brooks v. Robinson, 54 Miss. 272.

Missouri: Riney v. Hill, 14 Mo. 500, 55 Am. Dec. 119.

New Jersey: Meredith v. Banks, 6 N. J. L. 408; Baker v. Baker, 28 N. J. L. 13, 75 Am. Dec. 243; Stark v. Hunton, 3 N. J. Eq. 300. ˙

New York: Peyser v. Myers, 135 N. Y. 599, 32 N. E. 699.

North Carolina: Bunn v. Moore, 2 N. C. 279; Bratton v. Allison, 70 N. C. 498.

Ohio: Hammer v. Nevill, Wright, 169.

Wisconsin: Case v. Fish, 58 Wis. 56,

15 N. W. 808; Hill v. Durand, 58 Wis. 160, 15 N. W. 390.

Canada: Barnum v. Turnbull, 13 U. C. Q. B. 277.

See McGill v. U. S. Bank, 12 Wheat. 511, 6 L. ed. 711.

[486] *Arkansas:* Vaughan v. Kennan, 38 Ark. 114.

New Hampshire: Townsend v. Riley, 46 N. H. 300.

[487] *Maine:* Parker v. Moody, 58 Me. 70. *South Carolina:* Killilan v. Herndon, 4 Rich. 609.

[488] Tooke v. Bonds, 29 Tex. 419.

[489] *New York:* North American F. Ins. Co. v. Mowatt, 2 Sandf. Ch. 108.

Vermont: Gage v. McSweeney, 74 Vt. 370, 52 Atl. 960.

England: London, C. & D. Ry. v. South Eastern Ry., [1892] 1 Ch. 120, 61 L. J. Ch. 294, 65 L. T. Rep. 722.

See Pierce v. Lehigh V. C. Co. (Pa.), 81 Atl. 142.

So where the creditor is not ready to accept the goods, he cannot recover interest as damages for delay in delivering them. Wheelock v. Tanner, 39 N. Y. 481.

And where the creditor is unable to surrender the note or other document which the debtor is entitled to receive

a claim with such unreasonable delay as to amount to laches, it was held that the court might refuse him interest.[490] So where the creditor leaves the jurisdiction without notice to the debtor and cannot be found, the debtor is not chargeable with interest till demand.[491] And where the vendor of land is unwilling or unable to pass title at the time set, he cannot claim interest on the purchase-money.[492] So where the plaintiff agreed to submit the claim to arbitration, and unreasonably delayed the submission, he cannot recover interest during the period of delay.[493]

§ 340a. Death or insolvency.

Mere difficulty in making payment is not material. Thus the running of interest is not interrupted by the death of either the debtor[494] or the creditor,[495] the estate of the deceased being bound to pay or entitled to receive interest.

upon payment, he cannot claim interest for delay in payment.

New Jersey: Britton v. Supreme Council Royal Arcanum, 46 N. J. Eq. 102, 18 Atl. 675, 19 Am. St. Rep. 376.

New York: Bishop v. Sniffen, 1 Daly, 155.

Virginia: Farmers' Bank v. Reynolds, 4 Rand. 186.

But see *Missouri:* Rector v. Mark, 1 Mo. 288, 13 Am. Dec. 500.

[490] *United States:* Erskine v. Van Arsdale, 15 Wall. 75, 21 L. ed. 63; Redfield v. Ystalyfera Iron Co., 110 U. S. 174, 3 Sup. Ct. 570, 28 L. ed. 109; United States v. Sanborn, 135 U. S. 271, 10 Sup. Ct. 812, 34 L. ed. 112; Redfield v. Bartels, 139 U. S. 694, 11 Sup. Ct. 683, 35 L. ed. 310, affirming Bartells v. Redfield, 27 Fed. 286; Stewart v. Schell, 31 Fed. 65; see also Jourolmon v. Ewing, 80 Fed. 604; Borough v. Abele, 105 Fed. 366.

New York: Constable v. Colden, 2 Johns. 480.

Utah: Culmer v. Caine, 22 Utah, 216, 230, 61 Pac. 1008.

England: Anderton v. Arrowsmith, 2 P. & D. 408.

Though laches does not ordinarily apply as against a claim made by the United States, it does apply in a case of this sort to affect the recovery of interest. United States v. Sanborn, 135 U. S. 271, 10 Sup. Ct. 812, 34 L. ed. 112; United States v. Butler, 114 Fed. 582.

[491] *North Carolina:* Child v. Devereux, 5 N. C. 398.

Tennessee: Laura Jane v. Hagen, 10 Humph. 332.

Virginia: McCall v. Turner, 1 Call, 133.

[492] *Kentucky:* Hart v. Brand, 1 A. K. Marsh. 159, 10 Am. Dec. 715.

Tennessee: Williams v. Willhite, 3 Head, 344.

England: Roberts v. Massay, 13 Ves. 561.

[493] Schrepfer v. Rockford Ins. Co., 77 Minn. 291, 79 N. W. 1005.

[494] *Indiana:* Gale v. Corey, 112 Ind. 39, 13 N. E. 108, 14 N. E. 362.

Kentucky: Tatum v. Gibbs, 19 Ky. L. Rep. 665, 41 S. W. 565.

Ireland: Purcell v. Blannerhassett, 9 Ir. Eq. 103, 3 J. & L. 24.

[495] *New York:* Watts v. Garcia, 40 Barb. 656.

It has often been said that insolvency or at least an assignment by an insolvent debtor suspends interest; sometimes on the ground that the principal itself not being paid, it is of no use to consider interest, and sometimes on the ground that the delay is an act of the law.[496] These reasons do not seem convincing; for if the allowance of interest would make any difference at all in the amounts that would be received by the various creditors, it would seem that in justice it should be calculated. And this is the prevailing view.[497] But where a receiver of the debtor's property is appointed and the collection of debts enjoined interest will not be allowed.[498]

§ 340b. Tender.

The commonest case in which the defendant is not charged with delay, and is therefore relieved, is that of tender. When a debtor makes a legal tender of the amount of the debt, he is chargeable no longer with interest or any other damages.[499]

Canada: Stevenson v. Hodder, 15 Grant Ch. 570.

[496] Thomas v. Western Car Co., 149 U. S. 95, 37 L. ed. 663, 13 Sup. Ct. 824; New England R. R. v. Carnegie Steel Co., 75 Fed. 59, 39 U. S. App. 491; New York Security & Trust Co. v. Lombard Investment Co., 73 Fed. 537.

[497] Richmond v. Irons, 121 U. S. 27, 64, 30 L. ed. 864, 7 Sup. Ct. 788; Middaugh v. Wilson, 151 U. S. 333, 360, 88 L. ed. 183, 14 Sup. Ct. 356 (*semble;* interest was refused under the peculiar circumstances); Bain v. Peters, 44 Fed. 307; Nashua & L. R. R. v. Boston & L. R. R., 61 Fed. 250, 9 C. C. A. 468, 21 U. S. App. 50; Richmond & I. C. Co. v. Richmond, N. I. & B. R. R. R., 68 Fed. 105, 115, 15 C. C. A. 289, 31 U. S. App. 704. In Chemical Nat. Bank v. Armstrong, 59 Fed. 372, 8 C. C. A. 155, the recovery of interest was barred by laches.

[498] White v. Knox, 111 U. S. 784, 4 Sup. Ct. 686, 28 L. ed. 603; *infra,* § 341.

[499] *United States:* Dooley v. Smith, 13 Wall. 604, 20 L. ed. 547; Wilcox v. Richmond & D. R. R. R., 3 C. C. A. 73, 52

Fed. 264, 17 L. R. A. 804; Cheney v. Bilby, 74 Fed. 52, 20 C. C. A. 291.

Alabama: Rudulph v. Wagner, 36 Ala. 698; Park v. Wiley, 67 Ala. 310; Steele v. Hanna, 91 Ala. 190, 9 So. 174.

Arkansas: Turner v. Watkins, 31 Ark. 429.

California: Hidden v. Jordan, 39 Cal. 61; Patterson v. Sharp, 41 Cal. 133.

Connecticut: Loomis v. Knox, 60 Conn. 343, 22 Atl. 771.

Illinois: Stow v. Russell, 36 Ill. 18; Alle v. Woodruff, 96 Ill. 16.

Kentucky: January v. Martin, 1 Bibb, 586; Craig v. Penrick, 3 J. J. Marsh. 16; Fenwick v. Ratcliff, 6 T. B. Mon. 154.

Louisiana: Hill v. Place, 7 Rob. 389; Frey v. Fitzpatrick-Cromwell Co., 108 La. 125, 32 So. 437.

Massachusetts: Suffolk Bank v. Worcester Bank, 5 Pick. 106.

Michigan: Cowles v. Marble, 37 Mich. 158.

Missouri: Cockrill v. Kirkpatrick, 9 Mo. 697; Berthold v. Reyburn, 37 Mo. 586; Raymond v. McKinney, 58 Mo. App. 303.

Upon a similar principle, when in an action of tort it appears that the wrongdoer before trial offered to pay an amount greater than that found due by the jury, no interest will be allowed, though the case is otherwise a proper one for its recovery.[500] A tender of a portion of the claim, as a partial payment, will prevent interest running thereafter on the amount so tendered.[501] If it is tendered as full payment, and afterwards proves to be all that is due, it will prevent interest;[502] but if it proves insufficient, it will not affect interest.[503] Where, however, an award is made by the court and the amount tendered, though the award is increased on appeal, interest ceases on the amount tendered; as the defendant is there acting properly, in view of the award.[504] In order to stop the running of interest the tender must be to the proper party,[505] must be unconditional,[506] and must be made with the proper legal formalities.[507] Above all, the tender must be kept good; that is, the amount must always be kept on hand ready to deliver to the creditor on demand,[508] or, in jurisdictions where it is so required, must be paid into court.[509] If therefore after a ten-

Nebraska: Clark *v.* Colfax County, 2 Neb. (Unoff.) 133, 96 N. W. 607.

New Hampshire: McNeil *v.* Call, 19 N. H. 403, 51 Am. Dec. 188.

New Jersey: National D. & N. J. J. C. Ry. *v.* Pennsylvania R. R., 54 N. J. Eq. 142, 33 Atl. 860.

New York: Jackson *v.* Law, 5 Cow. 248; Harris *v.* Jex, 55 N. Y. 421, 14 Am. Rep. 285; Tuthill *v.* Morris, 81 N. Y. 94; Benkard *v.* Babcock, 27 How. Pr. 391.

North Carolina: Jeter *v.* Littlejohn, 3 Murph. 186.

Pennsylvania: Merrell *v.* Merrell, 5 Kulp, 125.

Tennessee: Gracy *v.* Potts, 4 Baxt. 395.

Virginia: Ross *v.* Keewood, 2 Munf. 141.

[500] Thompson *v.* Boston & M. R. R., 58 N. H. 524.

[501] Metropolitan Nat. Bank *v.* Commercial State Bank, 104 Iowa, 682, 74 N. W. 26.

[502] Budd *v.* Union Ins. Co., 4 McCord (S. C.), 1.

[503] *Texas:* San Antonio *v.* Campbell (Tex. Civ. App.), 56 S. W. 130.

Virginia: Shobe *v.* Carr, 3 Munf. 10.

[504] Shattuck *v.* Wilton R. R., 23 N. H. 269.

[505] King *v.* Finch, 60 Ind. 420.

[506] Heywood *v.* Hartshorn, 55 N. H. 476.

[507] Mudd *v.* Stille, 6 La. 17.

[508] *Illinois:* Thayer *v.* Meeker, 86 Ill. 470; Aulger *v.* Clay, 109 Ill. 487.

Kentucky: Lloyd *v.* O'Rear, 59 S. W. 483, 22 Ky. L. Rep. 1000; Woodland Cemetery Co. *v.* Ellison, 80 S. W. 169, 25 Ky. L. Rep. 2069.

Massachusetts: Donohue *v.* Chase, 139 Mass. 407, 2 N. E. 84.

New York: Nelson *v.* Loder, 132 N. Y. 288, 30 N. E. 369.

[509] *Arkansas:* Hamlett *v.* Tallman, 30 Ark. 505.

Kentucky: Tobin *v.* Wilson, 3 J. J. Marsh. 63.

der the debtor fails to pay the amount to the creditor on demand, the tender does not prevent interest running.[510] Where commercial paper is payable at a certain place, and at maturity the payor has funds there to pay it, he is not chargeable with interest so long as he keeps the funds there;[511] but if the funds were not at the place appointed when payment was due interest will run, even if the creditor failed to present the obligation for payment.[512]

§ 340c. War.

Where the debtor is forbidden by law to pay the debt, he is not chargeable with interest for delay in paying it. This happens in time of war, when a debtor is in one hostile country and the creditor in the other; interest is not given while that state of things continues.[513] This is true only of interest

New Jersey: Shields v. Lozear, 22 N. J. Eq. 447.

[510] Kentucky: Nantz v. Lober, 1 Duv. 304.

Maryland: Columbian Bldg. Assoc. v. Crump, 42 Md. 192.

West Virginia: Thompson v. Lyon, 20 S. E. 812.

[511] United States: Grand Trunk R. R. v. Central Vermont R. R., 105 Fed. 411.

Missouri: Mahan v. Waters, 60 Mo. 167.

New York: Locklin v. Moore, 57 N. Y. 360.

Pennsylvania: Miller v. Bank of Orleans, 5 Whart. 503; Emlen v. Lehigh Coal, etc., Co., 47 Pa. 76, 86 Am. Dec. 518.

Canada: McDonald v. Great Western R. R., 21 U. C. Q. B. 223.

[512] Missouri: Mahan v. Waters, 60 Mo. 167; Skinker v. Butler County, 112 Mo. 332, 20 S. W. 613.

New York: Mills v. Place, 48 N. Y. 520, 8 Am. Rep. 568; Kelley v. Phœnix Nat. Bank, 17 App. Div. 496, 45 N. Y. Supp. 533.

Utah: McCauley v. Leavitt, 10 Utah, 91, 37 Pac. 164.

[513] United States: Hoare v. Allen, 2 Dall. 102; Foxcroft v. Nagle, 2 Dall. 132, 1 L. ed. 319; Brown v. Hiatt, 15 Wall. 177, 21 L. ed. 128; Bigler v. Waller, Chase Dec. 316; Jackson Ins. Co. v. Stewart, 13 Fed. Cas. No. 7,152, 1 Hughes, 310; Chappelle v. Olney, 5 Fed. Cas. No. 2,613, 1 Sawy. 401.

Georgia: Mayer v. Reed, 37 Ga. 482.

Kentucky: Selden v. Preston, 11 Bush, 191.

Maryland: Bordley v. Eden, 3 H. & McH. 167.

South Carolina: Higginson v. Air, 1 Desauss. Eq. 427; Blake v. Quash, 3 McCord, 340.

Tennessee: McGaughy v. Berg, 4 Heisk. 695.

Virginia: Brewer v. Hastie, 3 Call, 22; McVeigh v. Old Dominion Bank, 26 Gratt. 188.

The suspension of interest is due entirely to the illegality of transactions between enemies. If both parties are resident in the same country, interest is not suspended.

Arkansas: Williams v. State, 37 Ark. 463.

Virginia: Hawkins v. Minor, 5 Call, 118.

given as damages, not of interest accruing on a contract. So, if a contract does not mature until after the war, interest may be recovered.[514] And if it matures during the war, interest runs to maturity.[515] But if the creditor has a known agent in the same country with the debtor it is the debtor's duty to pay such agent, and interest therefore does not cease.[516] And where the creditor and the sureties are in the same country, interest runs against the sureties, though not against the debtor.[517] And if a note is payable at a bank in the country of the debtor, interest runs in case of non-payment, since he may pay and ought to pay the amount to the bank.[518] Where a note was payable within the Union lines to a person in Confederate territory, and there were two makers, one on each side, it was held that interest would run during the war against both; one maker could pay the creditor, the other could make payment at the place of payment.[519]

§ 341.[a] Legal process.

Where a foreign attachment, trustee process, or injunction is laid on a party liable to pay interest, the interest ceases running till the legal impediment is removed.[520] So where

On the other hand, though the creditor in fact goes to the debtor and demands payment, yet if he continues resident in enemy country payment would be illegal, and interest is suspended. Tucker v. Watson, 6 Am. L. Reg. (N. S.) 220.

[a] For § 341 of the eighth edition, see § 342.

[514] Lash v. Lambert, 15 Minn. 416.

[515] Brown v. Hiatt, 15 Wall. 177, 21 L. ed. 128.

[516] Ward v. Smith, 7 Wall. 447, 19 L. ed. 217; Conn. v. Penn., Pet. C. C. 496; Denniston v. Imbrie, 3 Wash. C. C. 396.

[517] *Alabama:* Bean v. Chapman, 62 Ala. 58.

Maryland: Paul v. Christie, 4 Harr. & McH. 161.

[518] Gates v. Union Bank, 12 Heisk. (Tenn.) 325.

[519] Yeaton v. Berney, 62 Ill. 61.

[520] *United States:* Osborn v. U. S. Bank, 9 Wheat. 738, 6 L. ed. 738; Bainbridge v. Wilcocks, Bald. 536; Willings v. Consequa, Pet. C. C. 172, 301.

Alabama: Gunn v. Howell, 35 Ala. 144, 73 Am. Dec. 484.

California: Newport Wharf, etc., Co. v. Drew, 141 Cal. 103, 74 Pac. 697.

Connecticut: Candee v. Skinner, 40 Conn. 464.

Louisiana: Zimmerman v. Langles, 36 La. Ann. 65.

Maine: Norris v. Hall, 18 Me. 332.

Maryland: Clagett v. Hall, 9 Gill & J. 80. (But contra, Wallis v. Dilley, 7 Md. 237.)

Massachusetts: Oriental Bank v. Tremont Ins. Co., 4 Met. 1; Rennell v. Kimball, 5 Allen, 356; Bickford v. Rich, 105 Mass. 340; Huntress v. Burbank, 111 Mass. 213; Smith v. Flanders, 129 Mass. 322; Norris v. Massachu-

a fund is deposited in a bank [521] or in court [522] awaiting an order of the court for its payment, it does not bear interest. In some States it is held that a garnishee or party enjoined can relieve himself from the payment of interest only by bringing the money into court.[523] In any State, if the gar-

setts Mut. L. Ins. Co., 131 Mass. 294.
Michigan: Michigan & O. P. Co. *v.* White, 44 Mich. 25, 5 N. W. 1086.
Minnesota: Twohy Mercantile Co. *v.* Melbye, 83 Minn. 394, 86 N. W. 411.
New Hampshire: Swamscot Mach. Co. *v.* Partridge, 25 N. H. 369.
New Jersey: Le Branthwait *v.* Halsey, 9 N. J. L. 3.
New York: Kellogg *v.* Hickok, 1 Wend. 521; Stevens *v.* Barringer, 13 Wend. 639.
Pennsylvania: Fitzgerald *v.* Caldwell, 2 Dall. 215, 1 Yeates, 274; Stewart *v.* Stocker, 13 S. & R. 199, 15 Am. Dec. 588; Irwin *v.* Pittsburgh, etc., R. R., 43 Pa. 488; Jackson *v.* Lloyd, 44 Pa. 82.
Utah: Wilson *v.* Sullivan, 17 Utah, 341, 53 Pac. 994.
Vermont: Platt *v.* Continental Ins. Co., 62 Vt. 166, 19 Atl. 637.
England: Legrange *v.* Hamilton, 4 T. R. 613; Hamilton *v.* Legrange, 2 H. Black. 144; Farmer *v.* Farmer, 15 Wkly. Rep. 371.
Interest is suspended only on the amount actually tied up by the process. So where the claim is less than the amount due, the debtor can justify withholding no more than enough to cover the debt, with interest, costs, and expenses. Sickman *v.* Lapsley, 13 Serg. & R. (Pa.) 224, 15 Am. Dec. 596.
In Com. *v.* Ricks, 1 Gratt. 416, it was held that tenants holding property subject to controversy in a pending suit must pay interest on the rents, though it is not ascertained who the proper party is to receive them. It is obvious that a tenant must in such a case either pay the original lessor or

pay the money into court. And when the money is part of an estate held in trust, the trustee is not relieved by legal proceedings from the obligation of accounting for interest. Hawley *v.* Tesch, 88 Wis. 213, 50 N. W. 670.
Where a bank agreed to hold money for a certain purpose, and litigation arose between claimants, it was held that if the bank kept and used the money instead of paying it into court it must pay interest. Roussel *v.* Mathews, 171 N. Y. 634, 63 N. E. 1122, affirming 62 App. Div. 1, 70 N. Y. Supp. 886.
[521] Taylor *v.* Minor, 12 Ky. L. Rep. 479, 14 S. W. 544.
[522] *United States:* Bowman *v.* Wilson, 2 McCrary, 394; Groves *v.* Sentell, 13 C. C. A. 386, 69 Fed. 223 (interpleader).
Iowa: Van Gordon *v.* Ormsby, 60 Iowa, 510, 15 N. W. 306.
Michigan: Sager *v.* Tupper, 35 Mich. 134 (deposit with register, on bill to redeem mortgage); Lilley *v.* Mutual Ben. L. Ins. Co., 92 Mich. 153, 52 N. W. 631.
Nebraska: Cobbey *v.* Knapp, 28 Neb. 158, 44 N. W. 104.
Virginia: Daniel *v.* Wharton, 90 Va. 584, 19 S. E. 170.
If the fund is not brought into court on a bill for interpleader, interest is not interrupted. Spring *v.* South Carolina Ins. Co., 8 Wheat. 268, 5 L. ed. 61.
[523] *Alabama:* Kirkman *v.* Vanlier, 7 Ala. 217; Godwin *v.* McGehee, 19 Ala. 468; Bullock *v.* Ferguson, 30 Ala. 227.
Kentucky: Shackleford *v.* Helm, 1 Dana, 338; Curd *v.* Letcher, 3 J. J. Marsh. 443.

nishee is in collusion with either party, or denies his indebtedness and litigates the question, he is chargeable with interest; [524] and so if it can be shown that he used the money during the pendency of the case instead of keeping it on hand to pay over at any time.[525] And so if the debtor himself instituted the process which caused the delay,[526] or if he might safely and legally have paid the debt notwithstanding the legal proceedings,[527] interest runs. Even without actual legal proceedings, the defendant may be legally forbidden to pay over money, as for instance by notification by adverse claimants to hold the money; in such a case also interest is suspended.[528]

§ 342.[a] Interest not affected by intent.

The cases all depend upon the principle that where one party commits a wrongful act, he is liable in damages to the party injured. It is therefore unnecessary to the allowance of interest that there should have been any wrongful intent.

Maryland: Chase *v.* Manhardt, 1 Bland, 333.

Mississippi: Smith *v.* German Bank, 60 Miss. 69.

Ohio: Candee *v.* Webster, 9 Oh. St. 452.

Virginia: Templeman *v.* Fauntleroy, 3 Rand. 434.

[a] For § 342 of the eighth edition, see ch. lix, Conflict of Laws.

[524] *United States:* Albion Lead Works *v.* Citizens' Ins. Co., 3 Fed. 197 (unreasonable delay).

Mississippi: Work *v.* Glaskins, 33 Miss. 539.

Missouri: Stevens *v.* Gwathmey, 9 Mo. 628.

Pennsylvania: Rushton *v.* Rowe, 64 Pa. 63; Jones *v.* Manufacturers' Nat. Bank, 99 Pa. 317.

Virginia: Tazewell *v.* Barrett, 4 Hen. & M. 259 (unreasonable delay).

[525] *United States:* Mattingly *v.* Boyd, 20 How. 128, 15 L. ed. 845.

Connecticut: Woodruff *v.* Bacon, 35 Conn. 97.

Maine: Norris *v.* Hall, 18 Me. 332.

Contra, Pennsylvania: M i l l e r *v.* Rhodes, 3 Montg. Co. Rep. 133.

In Greenish *v.* Standard Sugar Refinery, 2 Low. 553, it was held that the garnishee, having had the use of the money, must pay interest at the actual market rate, but was not liable for the statutory rate.

[526] *California:* Pfister *v.* Wade, 69 Cal. 133, 10 Pac. 369.

Virginia: Shipman *v.* Fletcher, 95 Va. 585, 29 S. E. 325.

[527] *Massachusetts:* Watson *v.* Phœnix Bank, 8 Met. 217, 41 Am. Dec. 500 (debtor restrained from doing business only).

Michigan: Anderson *v.* Smith, 108 Mich. 69, 65 N. W. 615 (debtor previously sued by creditor).

New York: McKnight *v.* Chauncey, Seld. 97 (debtor enjoined by creditor from paying third party); New York, L. E. & W. R. R. *v.* Carhart, 1 N. Y. St. 426 (same case).

[528] *New York:* Gillespie *v.* Mayor, 3 Edw. 512.

Pennsylvania: In re Schneider, 11 Leg. Int. 122.

Thus, in Sumner *v.* Beebe [529] the happening of the event upon which the debt became due was unknown to the defendant. The court held, however, that as it was one not within the special knowledge of the plaintiff, the defendant was bound to discover when the event happened, and was liable, therefore, for interest.

F.—COMPOUND INTEREST

§ 343. Compound interest not originally allowed.

* In regard to compound interest, or interest on interest, there has existed much doubt and difference of opinion. It was rigorously prohibited by the Roman law: *Nullo modo usuræ insurarum a debitoribus exigantur.*[530] The English law followed in the same track. So, in an early case in chancery, Lord Cowper held a clause in a mortgage, that if the interest was behind six months, then it should be accounted principal and compound interest, was "void and of no use"; "that to make interest principal, it is requisite that it be grown due, and then an agreement concerning it may make it principal."[531] It is not regarded as within the statutory prohibition of usury, but as leading to oppression and abuse. So Lord Eldon has said, "There is nothing unfair or perhaps illegal in taking a covenant, originally, that if interest is not paid at the end of the year, it shall be converted into principal. But this court will not permit that, as tending to usury, though it is not usury."[532]

The cases were reviewed at length by Chancellor Kent, in an early case in New York; and it was said, "The cases and language in the books are clear in acknowledging the rule that even an agreement, made at the time of the original contract, to allow interest upon interest as it should become due is not to be supported";[533] and he placed the objection to the provision on the ground of its harsh and oppressive character. Again in a subsequent case, the same learned judge laid down the rule that "*compound interest cannot be demanded and taken,*

[529] 37 Vt. 562.
[530] Cod. 4, 32, 38.
[531] Ossulston *v.* Yarmouth, 2 Salk. 449; Daniell *v.* Sinclair, L. R. 6 App. Cas. 181.
[532] Chambers *v.* Goldwin, 9 Ves. 254, 271.
[533] Connecticut *v.* Jackson, 1 Johns. Ch. 13.

except upon a special agreement made after the interest has become due";[534] and the general principle has been generally
accepted.[535]   In this case it was said, however, that if compound interest be voluntarily paid, it cannot be recovered
back.[536]   So in ascertaining the amount due on a note made
payable with interest annually, simple interest only is to be
computed;[537] and interest on the interest will not be allowed.[538]

[534] Van Benschooten v. Lawson, 6
Johns. Ch. 313.

[535] *United States:* Burgess v. South-
bridge Savings Bank, 2 Fed. 500;
Gaines v. New Orleans, 17 Fed. 16, 4
Woods, 581.

Alabama: Paulling v. Creagh, 54
Ala. 646; Noble v. Moses, 81 Ala. 530,
1 So. 217, 60 Am. Rep. 175; Hunt v.
Stockton Lumber Co., 113 Ala. 387,
21 So. 454.

Illinois: Bowman v. Neely, 151 Ill.
37, 37 N. E. 840.

Kentucky: Breckenridge v. Brooks,
2 A. K. Marsh. 335, 12 Am. Dec. 401.

Maine: Lewis v. Small, 75 Me. 323.

Massachusetts: Lewin v. Folsom, 171
Mass. 188, 50 N. E. 523.

Michigan: Fosdick v. Van Husan, 21
Mich. 567; McVicar v. Denison, 81
Mich. 348, 45 N. W. 659.

Minnesota: Mason v. Callender, 2
Minn. 350.

Missouri: Sanguinett v. Webster, 153
Mo. 343, 54 S. W. 563; Clemens v.
Dryden, 6 Mo. App. 597.

Montana: Wilson v. Davis, 1 Mont.
183.

Nebraska: Hager v. Blake, 16 Neb.
12.

New Hampshire: Folsom v. Plumer,
43 N. H. 469.

New Jersey: Force v. Elizabeth, 28
N. J. Eq. 403.

New York: Mowry v. Bishop, 5 Paige,
98; Toll v. Hiller, 11 Paige, 228; For-
man v. Forman, 17 How. Pr. 255;
Barthgate v. Haskin, 5 Daly, 361;
Bennett v. Cook, 2 Hun, 526, 5 Th. &
C. 134.

Ohio: Averill C. & O. Co. v. Verner,

22 Oh. St. 372; Rosenbaum v. Pendle-
ton, 9 Ohio Dec. 642, 646.

Pennsylvania: Kennon v. Thompson, 34 Pa. 210.

Tennessee: Merrill v. Elam, 4 Baxt.
235.

West Virginia: Genin v. Ingersoll, 11
W. Va. 549; Lamb v. Cecil, 25 W. Va.
288; Boggess v. Goff, 47 W. Va. 139, 34
S. E. 741.

England: Waring v. Cunliffe, 1 Ves.,
Jr., 99.

New Zealand: Reeves v. Lane, 8 N.
Z. 44.

See *North Carolina:* Little v. Anderson, 71 N. C. 190.

[536] See also, as to demand of compound interest, Von Hemert v. Porter,
11 Met. 210.   In Connecticut, a contract for the payment of compound
interest, made before interest has accrued, is to that extent void, and will
not, unless in special cases, be enforced
either in law or in equity.   Camp v.
Bates, 11 Conn. 487; Rose v. Bridgeport, 17 Conn. 243.   In Louisiana,
compound interest is prohibited by the
Code: "Interest upon interest cannot
be recovered, unless it be added to
the principal and by another contract
made a new debt.   No stipulation to
that effect in the original contract is
valid."   Art. 1939.   The whole subject of interest is codified in that State.
In Indiana, see Niles v. Board of
Commis'rs, 8 Blackf. 158.

[537] Hastings v. Wiswall, 8 Mass. 455;
Dean v. Williams, 17 Mass. 417; Von
Hemert v. Porter, 11 Met. 210; Doe v.
Warren, 7 Me. 48.

[538] Ferry v. Ferry, 2 Cush. 92.

But if a new note is given for the interest, it is thereby converted into capital, and it may be given with interest.[539] And so generally if the parties make a new agreement, by the terms of which the debt and accrued interest is turned into the principal amount of a new debt, interest will then be allowed upon the entire new principal.[540]

§ 344. Except by mercantile custom, or for fraud.

An exception was, however, recognized as introduced by the usages of modern trade to the general rule which denies compound interest. As between merchants upon their mutual accounts, it is the custom to cast interest upon the several items, and to strike a balance at the end of the year of the items of principal and those of interest, and to carry the footing of the two to a new account, as forming the first item of principal for the ensuing year. In this manner, yearly rests, as they are called, have for a long time been made and acquiesced in by the mercantile world.[541] But after the mutual trade and dealings have ceased, the right to make annual rests ceases; and in the absence of any specific agreement, the creditor is allowed simple interest only on the balance of his account; the right to make the yearly rests growing out of the mutuality of the debits and credits, and the allowing of interest on each side.[542] ** This custom does not extend to ac-

[539] Wilcox v. Howland, 23 Pick. 167.
[540] *Illinois:* Thayer v. Star Mining Co., 105 Ill. 540.
Louisiana: Lee v. Goodrich, 21 La. Ann. 278.
Michigan: Ruloff v. Hazen, 124 Mich. 570, 83 N. W. 370.
Mississippi: Perkins v. Coleman, 51 Miss. 298.
Missouri: Gunn v. Head, 21 Mo. 432.
Ohio: Goodhart v. Rastert, 10 Ohio S. & C. Pl. Dec. 40, 7 Ohio N. P. 534.
See also the following:
Kentucky: Hatcher v. Kelly, 1 Bibb, 282 (replevin bond given).
Canada: Wellington County v. Widmot Twp., 17 U. C. Q. B. 82 (principal

and interest of defendant's debt paid for him at his request).
[541] *United States:* Barclay v. Kennedy, 3 Wash. C. C. 350.
Kentucky: Farmers' Bank v. Calk, 4 Ky. L. Rep. 617 (custom of banks).
Louisiana: Sentell v. Kennedy, 29 La. Ann. 679.
Massachusetts: Von Hemert v. Porter, 11 Met. 210.
New York: Stoughton v. Lynch, 2 Johns. Ch. 209; Reddington v. Gilman, 1 Bosw. 235.
Vermont: Langdon v. Castleton, 30 Vt. 285; Davis v. Smith, 48 Vt. 52.
England: Eaton v. Bell, 5 B. & Ald. 34.
[542] *United States:* Denniston v. Im-

counts between mortgagor and mortgagee, and in the absence of an express agreement compound interest cannot be recovered on a mortgage.[543] Another exception to the general rule denying compound interest grows out of the conduct of the defendant; where that is grossly delinquent or intentionally contrary to his duty, compound interest is sometimes inflicted by way of punishment.[544] Thus a trustee using the trust funds for his own profit is often held liable to pay compound interest.[545]

§ 345. Interest on arrears of stipulated interest.

Where interest is by the terms of the contract payable at a fixed day, interest should be recovered as damages for nonpayment of it. For this stipulated interest is not given by the law, but is a sum of money which is due because the debtor has agreed to pay it, just as he has agreed to pay the principal of the debt.   If he does not pay it at the agreed time, the creditor is thereby damaged; and there can be no valid public policy to prevent the payment of compensation for this damage. Thus where on a note or other agreement for the payment of money it is stipulated that a certain amount shall be paid as interest on a fixed day, upon default in payment interest on the stipulated amount may, by the better opinion, be recovered by way of damages; [546] though in many jurisdictions this

brie, 3 Wash. C. C. 396, Fed. Cas. No. 3,802.

Massachusetts: Von Hemert *v.* Porter, 11 Met. 210.

[543] Young *v.* Hill, 67 N. Y. 162.

[544] *United States:* New Orleans *v.* Fisher, 91 Fed. 574, 34 C. C. A. 15.

New York: Ackerman *v.* Emott, 4 Barb. 626.

[545] *California:* Merrifield *v.* Longmire, 66 Cal. 180.

Connecticut: Connecticut *v.* Howarth, 48 Conn. 207.

Massachusetts: Jennison *v.* Hapgood, 10 Pick. 77, 104.

New York: Schieffelin *v.* Stewart, 1 Johns. Ch. 620.

But one not occupying a fiduciary position, like a co-tenant, is not liable to compound interest because he min-

gles his co-tenant's funds with his own. Moers *v.* Bolton, 157 N. Y. 293, 401.

See *ante,* § 311c.

[546] *Arkansas:* Vaughan *v.* Kennan, 38 Ark. 114.

Georgia: Calhoun *v.* Marshall, 61 Ga. 275, 34 Am. Rep. 99; Tillman *v.* Morton, 65 Ga. 386; Wofford *v.* Wyly, 72 Ga. 863.

Iowa: Mann *v.* Cross, 9 Ia. 327; Hershey *v.* Hershey, 18 Ia. 24; Preston *v.* Walker, 26 Ia. 205; Burrows *v.* Stryker, 47 Ia. 477.

Kentucky: Talliaferro *v.* King, 9 Dana, 331; Graves *v.* Waller, 4 Ky. L. Rep. 452; Shanks *v.* Stephens, 4 Ky. L. Rep. 838; Hall *v.* Scott, 90 Ky. 340, 13 S. W. 249, 11 Ky. L. Rep. 819.

Massachusetts: Greenleaf *v.* Kellogg, 2 Mass. 468; Hayward *v.* Cain, 110 Mass.

is forbidden as an illegal compounding of interest.[547] So interest is usually allowed on arrears of an annuity,[548] though the annuity may be in form an obligation for the payment of interest on a certain sum.[549]

273 (but see Hastings v. Wiswall, 8 Mass. 455; Henry v. Flagg, 13 Met. 64). *Michigan:* Morris v. Hoyt, 11 Mich. 9; Rix v. Strauts, 59 Mich. 364, 26 N. W. 638 (but see Van Husan v. Kanouse, 13 Mich. 303).

New Hampshire: Pierce v. Rowe, 1 N. H. 179; Townsend v. Riley, 46 N. H. 300.

North Carolina: Kennon v. Dickins, Cam. & Norw. Conf. R. 357, 2 Am. Dec. 642; Bledsoe v. Nixon, 69 N. C. 89, 12 Am. Rep. 642.

Ohio: Anketel v. Converse, 17 Oh. St. 11; Cramer v. Lepper, 26 Oh. St. 59, 20 Am. Rep. 756; Cook v. Courtright, 40 Oh. St. 248, 48 Am. Rep. 681.

Rhode Island: Wheaton v. Pike, 9 R. I. 132; Lanahan v. Ward, 10 R. I. 299; Pearce v. Hennessy, 10 R. I. 223.

South Carolina: Henderson v. Laurens, 2 Dess. 170; Singleton v. Lewis, 2 Hill, 408; Gibbs v. Chisolm, 2 N. & McC. 38; Doig v. Barkley, 3 Rich. 125, 45 Am. Dec. 762; O'Neall v. Bookman, 9 Rich. 80; Wright v. Eaves, 10 Rich. Eq. 582; O'Neall v. Sims, 1 Strobh. 115; Wilson v. Kelly, 19 S. C. 160.

Tennessee: House v. Tennessee F. C., 7 Heisk. 128.

Texas: Lewis v. Paschal, 37 Tex. 315; Angel v. Miller, 90 Tex. 505, 39 S. W. 916; Robertson v. Parrish (Civ. App.), 39 S. W. 646; Stone v. Pettus (Civ. App.), 103 S. W. 413.

Vermont: Catlin v. Lyman, 16 Vt. 44.
[547] *Alabama:* Broughton v. Mitchell, 64 Ala. 210.

California: Montgomery v. Tutt, 11 Cal. 307; Doe v. Vallejo, 29 Cal. 385 (by statute).

Colorado: Denver B. & M. Co. v. McAllister, 6 Colo. 261.

Connecticut: Rose v. Bridgeport, 17 Conn. 243.

Illinois: Leonard v. Villars, 23 Ill. 377; Smith v. Luse, 30 Ill. App. 37.

Indiana: Niles v. Board, 8 Blackf. 158; Grimes v. Blake, 16 Ind. 160.

Maine: Doe v. Warren, 7 Me. 48; Bannister v. Roberts, 35 Me. 75; Farwell v. Sturdivant, 37 Me. 308; Kittredge v. McLaughlin, 38 Me. 513; Stone v. Locke, 46 Me. 445.

Maryland: Banks v. McClellan, 24 Md. 62 (*contra*, Fitzhugh v. McPherson, 3 Gill, 408).

Minnesota: Dyar v. Slingerland, 24 Minn. 267 (reluctantly following Mason v. Callender, 2 Minn. 350).

Missouri: Stoner v. Evans, 38 Mo. 461.

New Jersey: Corrigan v. Trenton D. F. Co., 5 N. J. Eq. 232, 245.

New York: Mowry v. Bishop, 5 Paige, 98; Young v. Hill, 67 N. Y. 162; Henderson v. Hamilton, 1 Hall, 314 (*contra*, Howard v. Farley, 3 Robt. 308, 19 Abb. Pr. 126).

Pennsylvania: Sparks v. Garrigues, 1 Binn. 152; Stokely v. Thompson, 13 Pa. 210 (but see Sherman v. Philadelphia & R. R. R., 13 Wkly. Notes Cas. 238).

Virginia: Pindall v. Bank of Marietta, 10 Leigh, 481.

Washington: Cullen v. Whitham, 33 Wash. 366, 74 Pac. 581.

West Virginia: Genin v. Ingersoll, 11 W. Va. 549.

[548] *Delaware:* Elliott v. Beeson, 1 Harr. 106; Houston v. Jamison, 4 Harr. 330.

But *contra, New York:* Isenhart v. Brown, 2 Edw. 341.

Virginia: Adams v. Adams, 10 Leigh, 527.

[549] *Pennsylvania:* Knettle v. Crouse, 6 Watts, 123; Addams v. Heffernan, 9 Watts, 529.

Since after the maturity of the obligation, interest, though secured by the obligation, accrues as damages, no interest can be recovered on account of the non-payment of stipulated interest after the maturity of the obligation, and no interest can be recovered for delay in paying interest on the overdue instalments of interest. Consequently at the maturity of the obligation interest runs upon the amount of the obligation itself with the interest secured by it and unpaid; the additional amount due as damages for non-payment of the stipulated interest does not bear interest, even after maturity of the obligation.[550] Even if the obligation provides that if the interest is not promptly paid it shall become principal and bear interest like the principal, no interest can be recovered on arrears of this secondary interest;[551] for it is interest payable after maturity, and by way of damages. In short, *compound* interest is never allowed by way of damages; but interest is allowed upon unpaid interest which is a part of the debt.

§ 346.ᵃ Interest on coupons or other separable obligations for interest.

Whenever a separate or separable obligation for interest is given it is to be treated as an ordinary obligation for the payment of money, and interest accrues on it as damages for non-payment at maturity. So interest runs upon a note,[552] bond,[553] or warrant[554] for the payment of interest. And upon this principle interest is almost universally allowed on the overdue coupons of a coupon bond, though they are obligations for the payment of interest.[555] It was thought necessary in the earlier

ᵃ For § 346 of the eighth edition, see § 324.

[550] *Iowa:* Aspinwall v. Blake, 25 Iowa, 319.
Maine: Whitcomb v. Harris, 90 Me. 206, 38 Atl. 138.
Michigan: Voigt v. Beller, 36 Mich. 140, 22 N. W. 270; Hoyle v. Page, 41 Mich. 533, 2 N. W. 665.
Rhode Island: Wheaton v. Pike, 9 R. I. 132.
[551] *Arkansas:* Vaughan v. Keenan, 38 Ark. 114.

North Carolina: Bledsoe v. Nixon, 69 N. C. 89.
[552] *Alabama:* Stickney v. Moore, 108 Ala. 590, 19 So. 76.
Contra, Louisiana: Compton v. Compton, 5 La. Ann. 615.
[553] Graeme v. Cullen, 23 Gratt. 266.
[554] *United States:* Aurora v. West, 7 Wall. 82, 19 L. ed. 42.
New Hampshire: Ashuelot R. R. v. Elliot, 57 N. H. 397.
Pennsylvania: Philadelphia & R. R. R. v. Smith, 105 Pa. 195.
[555] *United States:* Gelpcke v. Dubu-

cases to prove a demand for payment and refusal,[556] or at least that there was no money at the place of payment to pay

que, 1 Wall. 175, 17 L. ed. 520; Aurora v. West, 7 Wall. 82, 19 L. ed. 42; Clark v. Iowa City, 20 Wall. 583, 22 L. ed. 427; Genoa v. Woodruff, 92 U. S. 502, 23 L. ed. 586; Amy v. Dubuque, 98 U. S. 470, 25 L. ed. 228; Koshkonong v. Burton, 104 U. S. 668, 26 L. ed. 486; Pana v. Bowler, 107 U. S. 529, 27 L. ed. 424; U. S. Mortgage Co. v. Sperry, 138 U. S. 313, 343, 11 Sup. Ct. 321, 330, 34 L. ed. 969; Nesbit v. Independent Dist., 144 U. S. 610, 619, 12 Sup. Ct. 746, 748, 36 L. ed. 562; Cairo v. Zane, 149 U. S. 122, 13 Sup. Ct. 803, 37 L. ed. 673; Edwards v. Bates County, 163 U. S. 269, 16 Sup. Ct. 967, 41 L. ed. 155; Rich v. Seneca Falls, 19 Blatch. 558, 8 Fed. 852; Fauntleroy v. Hannibal, 5 Dill. 219; Hollingsworth v. Detroit, 3 McLean, 472, Fed. Cas. No. 6,613; Huey v. Macon County, 35 Fed. 481; New Eng. Mortg. Security Co. v. Vader, 28 Fed. 265; Skinner v. Franklin Co., 179 Fed. 862 (contra, Clarke v. Janesville, 1 Biss. 98).
Colorado: Lake County v. Linn, 29 Colo. 446, 68 Pac. 839.
Connecticut: Fox v. Hartford, etc., R. R., 70 Conn. 1, 38 Atl. 871 (but see Rose v. Bridgeport, 17 Conn. 243).
Illinois: Harper v. Ely, 70 Ill. 581; Humphreys v. Morton, 100 Ill. 592; Cook v. Illinois Trust & Savings Bank, 68 Ill. App. 478.
Indiana: Jeffersonville v. Patterson, 26 Ind. 15.
Kentucky: Kentucky Title Co. v. English, 50 S. W. 968, 20 Ky. L. Rep. 2024.
Louisiana: Forstall v. Louisiana Planters' Assoc., 34 La. Ann. 770.

Maryland: Virginia v. Ches. & Ohio Canal Co., 32 Md. 501.
Minnesota: Welsh v. First Div. of St. P. & P. R. R. R., 25 Minn. 314.
Mississippi: Lexington v. Union Nat. Bank, 75 Miss. 1, 22 So. 291.
North Carolina: Burroughs v. Richmond County, 65 N. C. 234; McLendon v. Anson County, 71 N. C. 38.
Ohio: Dunlap v. Wiseman, 2 Disney, 398.
Pennsylvania: North P. Ry. v. Adams, 54 Pa. 94; Philadelphia & Reading R. R. v. Knight, 124 Pa. 58, 16 Atl. 492; Moody v. Philadelphia & R. R. R., 13 Wkly. Notes Cas. 48; Fitchett v. North Pennsylvania R. R., 5 Phila. 132; Love v. Philadelphia & Reading R. R., 19 Phila. 304.
South Carolina: Langston v. S. C. Ry., 2 S. C. 248; Rice v. Shealy, 71 S. C. 161, 50 S. E. 868.
Tennessee: Nashville v. First Nat. Bank, 1 Baxt. 402.
Texas: San Antonio v. Lane, 32 Tex. 405.
Virginia: Arents v. Com., 18 Gratt. 750, 776; Gibert v. Washington, C. V. M. & G. S. R. R. R., 33 Gratt. 586, 598.
Wisconsin: Mills v. Jefferson, 20 Wis. 50.
Canada: London & Canadian Loan & Agency Co. v. Morris, 7 Manitoba, 128.
Contra, Massachusetts: Shaw v. Norfolk County R. R., 16 Gray, 407.
New Jersey: Force v. Elizabeth, 28 N. J. Eq. 403.
In *New York* interest is not allowed on overdue coupons so long as they are in the hands of the original owner, i. e.,

---

[556] *United States:* Phelps v. Lewiston, 15 Blatch. 131.
Pennsylvania: Beaver County v. Armstrong, 44 Pa. 63.

Rhode Island: Whitaker v. Hartford, P. & F. R. R., 8 R. I. 47; Nat. Exchange Bank v. Hartford, P. & F. R. R., 8 R. I. 375.

the coupons;[557] but it is now held that interest will be allowed, without proof of presentment. The debtor can avoid the payment of interest only by proving that the money to pay the coupons was ready at the time and place of payment.[558] Where a coupon bond was converted by the defendant, it was held that interest on the coupons could be recovered by the owner from the times they were payable.[559]

Where the creditor has the option, on default of any kind, to declare the entire debt due and payable, no interest will be allowed on coupons not due at the time such option is exercised.[560]

unless they have been detached and passed to another holder. Bailey v. Buchanan County, 115 N. Y. 297, 32 N. E. 155, 6 L. R. A. 562; Williamsburgh Sav. Bank v. Solon, 136 N. Y. 465, 32 N. E. 1058. It is difficult to see how this distinction can be supported on principle, as the coupon is payable to bearer; the same coupon will be refused interest if sued upon by the holder of the bond, while interest will be allowed if it has been deposited by him in a bank, though merely for collection. Klein v. East River Electric Light Co., 33 Misc. (N. Y.) 596, 67 N. Y. Supp. 922; Conn. Mut. Life Ins. Co. v. C., C. & C. R. R., 41 Barb. 9.

[557] Nashville v. First Nat. Bank, 1 Baxt. (Tenn.) 402.

[558] *United States:* Walnut v. Wade, 103 U. S. 683, 26 L. ed. 526; Grand Trunk Ry. v. Central Vermont Co., 105 Fed. 411.

Illinois: Humphreys v. Morton, 100 Ill. 592.

[559] Winona v. Minnesota Ry. C. Co., 29 Minn. 68.

[560] Stubbings v. O'Connor, 102 Wis. 352, 363, 78 N. W. 577.

CHAPTER XVI

EXEMPLARY DAMAGES

686

§ 347. Meaning of the term.

In actions of tort, when gross fraud, wantonness, malice, or oppression appears, the jury are not bound to adhere to the strict line of compensation, but may, by a severer verdict, at once impose a punishment on the defendant, and hold him up as an example to the community. It might be said, indeed, that the malicious character of the defendant's intent does, in fact, increase the injury, and the doctrine of exemplary damages might thus be reconciled with the strict notion of compensation; but it will appear from the cases we now proceed to examine that the idea of compensation is abandoned, and that of punishment introduced. Damages assessed upon this principle are called "exemplary," "punitive," or "vindictive" damages.[1]

§ 348. Origin of the doctrine of exemplary damages.

The term "exemplary damages" seems to have owed its origin to Lord Camden, the first reported case in which it occurs being that of Huckle v. Money,[2] one of the general warrant cases. It can hardly be said that the decisions in this

[1] *Georgia:* Batson v. Higginbothem, 7 Ga. App. 835, 68 S. E. 455.
Utah: Murphy v. Booth, 36 Utah, 285, 103 Pac. 768.
Since these damages are not given for compensation, and the plaintiff has no legal claim to them before verdict, he has no vested interest in them which is protected by any constitutional provision; and the legislature may therefore change the law so as to withhold them. Louisville & N. R. v. Street, 164 Ala. 155, 51 So. 306.
Other terms sometimes used are "punitory" or "punitive" damages, and "smart money." Such terms are usually employed indifferently in describing these damages.

Illinois: Hackett v. Smelsley, 77 Ill. 109; Roth v. Eppy, 80 Ill. 283.
Kentucky: Chiles v. Drake, 2 Met. 146; Louisville & P. R. R. v. Smith, 2 Duvall, 556.
Missouri: Stoneseifer v. Sheble, 31 Mo. 243; Kennedy v. North Missouri R. R., 36 Mo. 351; Green v. Craig, 47 Mo. 90.
In a few cases it was attempted to make a distinction between "exemplary" and "punitory" damages; but the cases were soon overruled. Freese v. Tripp, 70 Ill. 496; Meidel v. Anthis, 71 Ill. 241; Freidenheit v. Edmundson, 36 Mo. 226; McKeon v. Citizens' R. R., 42 Mo. 79.
[2] 2 Wils. 205; Sayer on Damages, 220.

case and those which are cited as following it established a new rule of damages. They were, on the contrary, cases where the court held to old precedent in the face of hard pressure to establish a novel doctrine. To understand this, it is only necessary to recall the original position of the jury in the assessment of damages.

§ 349. Original position of the jury in the assessment of damages.

Until comparatively recent times juries were as arbitrary judges of the amount of damages as of the facts. The court could review the finding of the jury only in cases of mayhem, and then it must be *super visum vulneris*.[3] The parties, by putting themselves upon the country, had agreed to abide by its decision. Thus, the jury having awarded enormous damages in an action of *scandalum magnatum*, the court was asked for a new trial. In refusing to grant this, North, C. J., said: "In *civil actions* the plaintiff is to recover by way of compensation for the damages he hath sustained, and the jury are the proper judges thereof."[4] This principle applied as well to actions of contract as to actions of tort. And in an action against an attorney for negligence, "the jury were told they might find what damages they pleased."[5] Even as late as the time of Lord Mansfield it was possible for counsel to state the law to be that "The court cannot measure the ground on which the jury find damages that may be thought large; they may find upon facts within their own knowledge. And in order to enable them to do this it was that the old common-law writ appointed them to be *de vicenet*. Twelve jurors are not to be supposed to give a verdict contrary to their conscience, and both parties put themselves upon the jury to abide their decision, as to the quantity of the damages, as well as whether any or not."[6] At the end of the eighteenth century, however, the present law regulating the measure of damages was settled so far as it concerned actions of contract; and in actions of tort where the injury was to property only,

---

[3] Hawkins *v.* Sciet, Palm. 314; Staneley's Case, Hetl. 93, Lit. 150; Delves *v.* Wyer, Brownl. 204.

[4] Townsend *v.* Hughes, 2 Mod. 150.
[5] Russel *v.* Palmer, 2 Wils. 325.
[6] Gilbert *v.* Berkinshaw, Lofft, 771.

there seems to have been an approach to fixed principles of compensation. But where personal suffering or outraged feelings complicated the estimate of damages, the court still held itself incompetent to review the verdict of the jury. The doctrine of exemplary damages is thus seen to have originated in a survival in this limited class of cases of the old arbitrary power of the jury.

§ 350. Development of the theory of exemplary damages.

It remains to consider the steps by which the rule of exemplary damages acquired its present form. As has already been said, nothing was further from the idea of the judges than that they were establishing a new doctrine; they founded their decision entirely on existing precedents.

The case generally cited as establishing the rule was, as has been already stated, an action for trespass, assault and imprisonment, the act complained of being an arrest of the plaintiff as printer of the "North Briton," under a general warrant issued by Lord Halifax, then Secretary of State, no actual illtreatment being alleged, and the jury having found a verdict for £300; on a motion for a new trial on the ground of excessive damages, Lord Chief Justice Pratt, afterwards Lord Camden, said:

"The personal injury done to the plaintiff was very small; so that if the jury had been confined by their oath to consider the mere personal injury only, perhaps £20 damages would have been thought damages sufficient; but the small injury done to the plaintiff, or the inconsiderableness of his station and rank in life, did not appear to the jury in that striking light in which the great point of law, touching the liberty of the subject, appeared to them at the trial; they saw a magistrate over all the king's subjects exercising arbitrary power, violating *Magna Charta*, and attempting to destroy the liberty of the kingdom, by insisting upon the legality of this general warrant before them; they heard the king's counsel, and saw the solicitor of the treasury endeavoring to support and maintain the legality of the warrant in a tyrannical and severe manner; these are the ideas which struck the jury on the trial; and I think they have done right in giving exemplary

44

damages. I cannot say what damages I should have given if I had been upon the jury; but I directed and told them they were not bound to any certain damages, against the solicitor-general's argument." [7]

And the motion for a new trial was denied. The same case, as reported in Sayer on Damages,[8] contains a further extract from the opinion of the Chief Justice: "Whenever an injury is done under the color of authority, as if an officer empowered to press exceed the authority given him by the press warrant; or if a master of a ship abuse the power by law vested in him over the sailors under his command; or if, as in the present case, a person is arrested upon a general warrant, the jury in assessing damages are not confined to the damages which have been actually sustained, but ought to assess exemplary damages." By the concurring opinion of Bathurst, J., it clearly appears that in his opinion the decision was only a refusal to restrict the jury to certain damages.

Beardmore v. Carrington [9] was an action also growing out of these general warrants, where a verdict was found for the plaintiff in £1,000. As he had been imprisoned but six days a motion was made for a new trial, on the ground of the excessiveness of the damages. But it was refused. Lord Campbell, in his *Lives of the Chancellors*, vol. v, p. 249, reports Lord Chief Justice Pratt to have said: "As to the damages, I continue of opinion that the jury are not limited to the injury received. Damages are designed not only as a satisfaction to the injured person, but likewise as a punishment to the guilty, and as a proof of the detestation in which the wrongful act is held by the jury." But this language cannot be found in the case as reported by Wilson. On the contrary, it is clear that the case was another refusal of the court to set aside the verdict of the jury, and that their reason was the lack of the court's power to do so. They cited Townsend v. Hughes in support of their decision; and said: "We desired to be understood that this court does not say, or lay down any rule that there can never happen a case of such excessive damages in *tort*, where the court may not grant a new trial; but in that case the damages

[7] Huckle v. Money, 2 Wils. 205. [9] 2 Wils. 244.
[8] At p. 220.

must be monstrous and enormous indeed, and such as all mankind must be ready to exclaim against, at first blush." [10]

In a later case the plaintiff brought an action for a blow on the face given him by the defendant. Pratt, C. J., said: "As a challenge and death may be the consequence of a blow given by one gentleman to another, I think the jury, who are in all cases the proper judges of damages, have done right in the present case in giving exemplary damages." [11]

In an action of trespass for entering the plaintiff's house and debauching his daughter, soon after decided, expressions were thrown out in passing which might give countenance to the doctrine. Thus on a motion for a new trial on the ground that the damages were excessive, Wilmot, Lord Chief Justice, said: "Actions of this sort are brought for example's sake; and although the plaintiff's loss in this case may not really amount to the value of twenty shillings, yet the jury have done right in giving liberal damages." [12]   That the court, however, desired as far as possible to reconcile this view with the rule of compensation appears from the opinion of Bathurst, J., who said: "In actions of this nature, and of assaults, the circumstances of time and place, when and where the insult is given, require different damages, as it is a greater insult to be beaten upon the Royal Exchange than in a private room."

In an action in the English Common Pleas, of trespass *quare clausum fregit*, it appeared that the plaintiff, a gentleman of fortune, was shooting on his own estate, when the defendant, a banker, magistrate, and member of parliament, forced himself on the plaintiff's land, fired at game several times, and used very intemperate language. The jury found a verdict for £500; and on a motion to set it aside for excess, Gibbs, C. J., said:

"I wish to know, in a case where a man disregards every principle which actuates the conduct of gentlemen, what is to restrain him except large damages? To be sure, one can hardly conceive worse conduct than this. What would be

[10] At p. 250.
[11] Grey *v.* Grant, C. B., Trin. 4 Geo. III.; Sayer on Damages, 227.
[12] Tullidge *v.* Wade, 3 Wils. 18.

said to a person in a low station of life who should behave himself in this manner? I do not know upon what principle we can grant a rule in this case, unless we were to lay it down that the jury are not justified in giving more than the absolute pecuniary damage that the plaintiff may sustain. Suppose a gentleman has a paved walk in his paddock, before his window, and that a man intrudes, and walks up and down before the window of his house, and looks in while the owner is at his dinner, is the trespasser to be permitted to say, 'Here is a half-penny for you, which is the full extent of all the mischief I have done'? Would that be a compensation? I cannot say that it would be.''

And Heath, J., said:

"I remember a case where the jury gave £500 damages, for merely knocking a man's hat off; and the court refused a new trial. There was not one country gentleman in a hundred who would have behaved with the laudable and dignified coolness which this plaintiff did. It goes to prevent the practice of duelling, if juries are permitted to punish insult by exemplary damages." [13]

In a case in the King's Bench, which was trespass for breaking the plaintiff's close, and laying poison upon it to destroy the plaintiff's poultry, the defendant contended that he was only liable for the value of the fowls destroyed; but Abbott, J., told the jury that they might consider not only the mere pecuniary damage, but also the intention, whether for insult or injury, and the verdict was £50.[14] So, the Court of Exchequer has said: [15] "In actions for malicious injuries, juries have been allowed to give what are called vindictive damages, and to take all the circumstances into consideration." So, in the Exchequer Chamber, Lord Denman said that the actions of trespass to real and personal property were an extension of that protection which the law throws around the person, and that substantial damages may be recovered in respect of such rights, though no loss or diminution in value of property may have occurred.[16]

---

[13] Merest v. Harvey, 5 Taunt. 442.
[14] Sears v. Lyons, 2 Stark. 317.
[15] Doe v. Filliter, 13 M. & W. 47.

[16] Rogers v. Spence, 13 M. & W. 571.
See, also, Williams v. Currie, 1 C. B. 841.

§ 351. History of the doctrine in America.

The rule was very early established in several jurisdictions of this country. Thus in New Jersey, in an action for breach of promise of marriage, brought at the end of the last century, the jury was charged "that they were not to estimate the damages by any particular proof of suffering or actual loss; but to give damages for *example's* sake, to prevent such offences in future." [17] So in New York, in an action for libel, it was urged, on a motion for a new trial, that the public character of the plaintiff as an officer of government, and the evil example of libels, were stated by the judge to the jury as considerations with them for increasing the damages; but Kent, C. J., delivering the opinion of the Supreme Court said: "Surely this is the true and salutary doctrine. The actual pecuniary damages in actions for defamation, as well as in other actions for torts, can rarely be computed, and are never the sole rule of assessment." And after reviewing the English cases, the court proceeded: "But it cannot be requisite to multiply instances in which the doctrine contained in this part of the charge has received the sanction of the English and of the American courts of justice. It is too well settled in practice, and is too valuable in principle, to be called in question." Spencer, J., held still stronger language: "In vindictive actions," he said, "such as for libels, defamation, assault and battery, false imprisonment, and a variety of others, it is always given in charge to the jury that they are to inflict damages for example's sake, and by way of punishing the defendant." [18]

So again, in another case,[19] where trespass was brought for beating a horse to death, the judge charged, that if they found for the plaintiff, it was a case in which, from the wantonness and cruelty of the defendant's conduct, the jury had a right to give smart money. A verdict was found for $75. A motion was made to set aside the verdict, for misdirection and for excessive damages; but the Supreme Court of New York said: "Great barbarity was proved on the part of the plain-

[17] Coryell *v.* Colbaugh, Coxe, 77.
[18] Tillotson *v.* Cheetham, 3 Johns.
56, 64.

[19] Woert *v.* Jenkins, 14 Johns.
352.

tiff; we think the charge of the judge was correct, and should have been better satisfied with the verdict if the amount of damages had been greater and more ·exemplary"; and the motion was denied.

So in Pennsylvania a sheriff was held liable in exemplary damages for the act of his deputy; [20] and it was afterwards laid down as a general rule that with a view to promote the peace and quiet of society, and to protect every one in the full enjoyment of his rights, the jury are at liberty to give vindictive or exemplary damages.[21]

These authorities were followed by such a multitude of cases that the principle became by the middle of the last century, as fully established by weight of authority as any doctrine of the law. In the first edition of this treatise, the doctrine was recognized as so established; and this opinion, in the face of able and persistent opposition, has prevailed.

§ 352. American cases.

The principle was recognized on the Massachusetts circuit, by Mr. Justice Story,[22] who said:

"In cases of marine torts, or illegal captures, it is far from being uncommon in the Admiralty to allow costs and expenses, and to *mulct the offending parties, even in exemplary damages,* when the nature of the case requires it. Courts of Admiralty allow such items, not technically as costs, but on the same principle that they are often allowed as damages in cases of torts by courts of common law; as a recompense for injuries sustained, as *exemplary damages,* or as a remuneration for expenses incurred, or losses sustained, by the misconduct of the other party."

So, again, the same learned judge, on the Maine circuit, in an action for malicious prosecution, used this language: "If, in the present case, there was, on the part of the defendant, a want of probable cause; yet, if he acted under a mistaken sense of duty and without any intention of oppression, it was, at most, a case for *compensatory* and not for *vindictive*

---

[20] Hazard *v.* Israel, 1 Binn. 240.   [22] Boston Manuf. Co. *v.* Fiske, 2
[21] Phillips *v.* Lawrence, 6 W. & S.   Mason, 119.
150.

damages." [23]   So in Connecticut, in an action on the case for gross negligence, it was said by Church, J., in delivering the opinion of the Supreme Court of Errors: "There is no principle better established and no practice more universal than that *vindictive damages or smart money* may be and are awarded by the verdict of juries, and whether the form of the action be trespass or case." [24]   So in Pennsylvania, Gibson, J., delivering the opinion of the court, said: "In cases of personal injury, damages are given not to compensate but to punish." [25]

So in a case of marine trespass, brought against the owners of a privateer for an illegal seizure, the Supreme Court of the United States said:

"This is a case of gross and wanton outrage. The honor of the country and the duty of the court equally require that a just compensation should be made to the unoffending neutrals, for all the injuries and losses actually sustained by them. And if this were a suit against the original wrongdoers, it might be proper to go yet farther, and visit upon them, in the shape of exemplary damages, the proper punishment which belongs to such lawless misconduct. But it is to be considered that this is a suit against the owners of the privateer; they are innocent of the demerit of the transaction. Under such circumstances, we are of opinion that they are bound to repair all the real injuries and personal wrongs sustained by the libellants, but they are not bound to the extent of vindictive damages." [26]

So in Connecticut, it has been said, that in actions for injuries to personal property, "the jury are not restricted to the pecuniary loss of the plaintiff." [27]

In Alabama it has been said, in reference to the action for malicious prosecution, that "the common law in such case allows the jury, if they choose, to make an example of the defendant when sued for redress, and will allow them to go beyond the actual damage the party has sustained." [28]

[23] Wiggin *v.* Coffin, 3 Story, 1, 11.
[24] Linsley *v.* Bushnell, 15 Conn. 225, 236; Huntley *v.* Bacon, 15 Conn. 267.
[25] Pastorius *v.* Fisher, 1 Rawle, 27; but it is to be noticed that the remark is *obiter.*

[26] Story, J., in the Amiable Nancy, 3 Wheaton, 546, 558.
[27] Merrills *v.* Tariff Manuf. Co., 10 Conn. 384.
[28] Donnell *v.* Jones, 13 Ala. 490, 502.

In New York the general rule has been repeatedly declared. So, in an action for libel, it was said by the chancellor, in the Court of Errors: "The jury may not only give such damages as they think necessary to compensate the plaintiff for his actual injury, but they may also give damages by way of punishment to the defendants. This is usually denominated exemplary damages, or smart money." [29] The subject was again examined in the same State, and the general principle very clearly stated. It was an action for assault and battery, where it was insisted that the fact that the defendant had been punished criminally for the offense should be received in evidence to mitigate damages in the civil suit. The court held otherwise, saying:

"In vindictive actions, and this is agreed to come within that class, jurors are always authorized to give exemplary damages, where the injury is attended with circumstances of aggravation; and the rule is laid down without the qualification, that we are to regard neither the possible or the actual punishment of the defendant by indictment and conviction at the suit of the people. . . . . We concede that smart money allowed by a jury, and a fine imposed at the suit of the people, depend on the same principle. Both are penal, and intended to deter others from the commission of the like crime. The former, however, becomes incidentally compensatory for damages, and at the same time answers the purposes of punishment." [30]

And again, in the Court of Errors of the same State, Mr. Senator Strong said: "In aggravated cases of this nature, are not jurors daily charged to give such damages as shall not only remunerate the plaintiff, but operate as a punishment to the defendant—as shall deter him and others in like cases offending, from the perpetration of similar enormities?" [31]

In an exceedingly well reasoned case on the Pennsylvania circuit, Mr. Justice Grier said:

[29] King v. Root, 4 Wend. 113, 139.

[30] Cook v. Ellis, 6 Hill, 466; see, also, Tifft v. Culver, 3 Hill, 180; Auchmuty v. Ham, 1 Denio, 495, and Brizsee v. Maybee, 21 Wend. 144, where it is suggested the jury may give smart money in replevin.

[31] Burr v. Burr, 7 Hill, 207, 217; and see the rule very strongly laid down, in cases of slander of title, in Kendall v. Stone, 2 Sandf. 269.

"It is a well-settled doctrine of the common law, though somewhat disputed of late, that a jury, in actions of trespass or tort, may inflict exemplary or vindictive damages upon a defendant, having in view the enormity of the defendant's conduct rather than compensation to the plaintiff. Indeed, in many actions, such as slander, libel, seduction, etc., there is no measure of damages by which they can be given as compensation for an injury, but are inflicted wholly with a view to punish and make an example of the defendant." [32]

So, also, it has been said in Illinois: "In vindictive actions the jury are always permitted to give damages for the double purpose of setting an example and of punishing the wrong-doer." [33] So, again, in an action of trespass for assault and battery, it was said: "In this class of cases the jury may give exemplary damages, not only to compensate the plaintiff, but to punish the defendant." [34]

In the Supreme Court of the United States, Mr. Justice Grier, in delivering the opinion of the court, laid down the following rule:

"It is a well-established principle of the common law, that in actions of trespass, and in all actions on the case for torts, a jury may inflict what are called exemplary, punitive, or vindictive damages upon a defendant, having in view the enormity of his offence rather than the measure of compensation to the plaintiff. We are aware that the propriety of this doctrine has been questioned by some writers; but if repeated judicial decisions for more than a century are to be received as the best exposition of what the law is, the question will not admit of argument. By the common as well as by statute law, men are often punished for aggravated misconduct or lawless acts by means of a civil action, and the damages, inflicted by way of penalty or punishment, given to the party injured. In many civil actions, such as libel, slander, seduction, etc., the wrong done to the plaintiff is incapable of being measured by a money standard; and the damages assessed depend on the circumstances showing the degree of moral turpitude or atroc-

[32] Stimpson v. The Railroads, 1 Wallace, Jr., 164, 170.
[33] Grabe v. Margrave, 4 Ill. 373; see, also, Johnson v. Weedman, 5 Ill. 495.
[34] McNamara v. King, 7 Ill. 432, 436.

ity of the defendant's conduct, and may properly be termed exemplary or vindictive rather than compensatory. In actions of trespass, where the injury has been wanton and malicious, or gross and outrageous, courts permit juries to add to the measured compensation of the plaintiff, which he would have been entitled to recover had the injury been inflicted without design or intention, something farther by way of punishment or example, which has sometimes been called 'smart money.' This has been always left to the discretion of the jury; as the degree of punishment to be thus inflicted must depend on the peculiar circumstances of each case." [35]

In the case of Voltz v. Blackmar,[36] the plaintiff brought an action for false imprisonment. The jury were told that they might "award damages to any extent by way of punishment to the defendant, and as a warning to others against committing like offences." This was held to be correct, Andrews, J., saying:

"In vindictive actions, as they are sometimes termed, such as libel, assault and battery, and false imprisonment, the conduct and motive of the defendant is open to inquiry, with a view to the assessment of damages; and if the defendant, in committing the wrong complained of, acted recklessly, or wilfully and maliciously, with a design to oppress and injure the plaintiff, the jury, in fixing the damages, may disregard the rule of compensation, and beyond that may, as a punishment to the defendant, and as a protection to society against a violation of personal rights and social order, award such additional damages as in their discretion they may deem proper. The same rule has been held to apply in the case of a wilful injury to property, and in actions of tort founded upon negligence, amounting to misconduct and recklessness."

§ 353. Objections to the doctrine.

The foremost place on the negative side of the discussion was taken by Professor Greenleaf in a familiar passage in his treatise on Evidence.[37] Later, one of the ablest judges of the Supreme Court of New Hampshire, in an exhaustive opinion

[35] Day v. Woodworth, 13 How. 363, 371, 14 L. ed. 181.

[36] 64 N. Y. 440, 444.

[37] 14th ed., vol. ii., § 253, n.

overruling former decisions of that court, held that exemplary damages could not be recovered.[38] The Supreme Court of New Jersey has characterized the doctrine graphically as "a sort of hybrid between a display of ethical indignation and the imposition of a criminal fine."[39] The opponents of the doctrine have maintained, what is perfectly true, that it is an exceptional or anomalous doctrine, at variance with the general rule of compensation; hence that, logically, it is wrong.

Again, it is urged that the practice of giving damages in order to punish the defendant is an unjust one. The two chief reasons given are—first, the defendant is deprived of his right to have the offence proved beyond a reasonable doubt, as should be done if he is to be punished for it; second, the amount of his punishment is left entirely to the mercy of a jury, untrained in determining the amount of punishment, who may assess, and frequently do assess, the damage at a sum far greater than the fine provided by law as a proper punishment for the act, considered as a criminal offence. Many jurisdictions restrict the allowance of exemplary damages to cases where the defendant's act is not a crime; but this allows the jury to decide that to be worthy of punishment which the State in its legislative capacity has not deemed it best to punish. Objections such as these have led to strong attempts to give the doctrine a quasi criminal basis; but these have not succeeded. Thus it has been held that the circumstances relied on to authorize exemplary damages need not be proved beyond a reasonable doubt,[40] and that the liability to exemplary damages and a criminal prosecution is not double jeopardy.[41] In the words of Ryan, C. J.: "Considered as strictly punitory, the damages are for the punishment of the private tort, not of the public crime."[42]

The opponents of the rule have attempted to explain away the authorities in its favor in a variety of ways, but without much success. It may be admitted that in many cases damages have been called exemplary which might have been granted as compensatory damages for mental suffering; but the fact

[38] Foster, J., in Fay v. Parker, 53 N. H. 342.

[39] Haines v. Schultz, 50 N. J. L. 481.

[40] St. Ores v. McGlashen, 74 Cal. 148.

[41] See § 386.

[42] Brown v. Swineford, 44 Wis. 282.

remains that damages were granted in these cases *in pœnam*. A vast body of decisions exists, in which the recovery could only be *in pœnam;* and the inquiry is always made, not as to the effect of the defendant's malice, but as to its motive. As the Supreme Court of North Carolina has well said, the inquiry is as to "the extent of the injury intended, and not that which was really inflicted." [43]

§ 354. The rule established by authority and convenience.

Upon the whole, the doctrine is to be supported (except in those few jurisdictions which have repudiated it) mainly upon the grounds of authority and convenience. The historical facts already referred to show that it has its roots in that jealousy of the exercise of arbitrary and malicious power, to which the jury in our system of law has always been so keenly alive; and if it is an anomalous survival of a part of the old rule that the jury were judges of the damages, it must be inferred that it has survived because of its inherent usefulness. Many anomalies which have far less authority behind them must be supported on this ground, and no anomaly supported by both authority and convenience can be eradicated simply by showing it to be illogical. The idea that it is unjust rests upon the assumption that there is something unfair in allowing the plaintiff's damages to be enhanced on account of the defendant's intent, but it is to be said in reply to this that although the intent cannot make a wrongful act *more wrongful*, it may make the consequences of it much more serious, and of the extent of these consequences the jury is the judge and the only possible judge. In support of this view the reasoning of the early cases seems thus far to have been convincing. It should be observed in conclusion that even in jurisdictions which discountenance the doctrine, juries are allowed to give, under the title of damages to feelings, verdicts quite as substantial as any which could be recovered under the head of exemplary damages. Hence it is not open to the opponents of exemplary damages to contend that the practical results of the application of the rule work any injustice, or that the rule bears more heavily upon the wrongdoer than

[43] Gilreath *v.* Allen, 10 Ired. (N. C.) 67.

the substitute of which they are advocates. In either case it is the jury and not the court which practically decides how much the plaintiff may recover.

§ 355. Exemplary damages in other systems of law.

* In the Roman and Civil Law exemplary damages seem to have been unknown. In Scotland the principle of compensation seems rigidly adhered to, even in cases of flagrant wrong. So, in an action of damages for defamation, sending a challenge, assault, and threatened battery, the Lord Chief Commissioner Adam, one of the most eminent judges of the last century, said: "In all cases of damage, a fair, unprejudiced discussion (*avoiding in civil cases the converting compensation for a civil injury into a matter of punishment*) will lead to a rational, conscientious, and fair compromise of your different opinions, and bring you to fix on one sum"; and the reporter adds: "In all cases of this sort, his lordship has been in the habit of repeating this doctrine." [44]

Again, in an action for defamation, the Lord Chief Commissioner said: "The question of damages, in case of an attack on the character of a professional man, must always include both a question of loss and *solatium*. You must consider it *as a question of reparation, not of punishment;* but if a person of perfectly pure character is assailed in this manner, you will consider whether a rich man ought not to pay a little more." [45]   The same rule was laid down by the same judge in actions of *crim. con.*   In Baillie *v.* Bryson,[46] an action of this class, the Lord Chief Commissioner said: "I cannot help thinking that Lord Kenyon introduced into cases of this sort a principle, as to damages, extremely dangerous in its consequences. He considered such questions, not merely as calculated to *repair the injury* done to the one party, but *as a punishment* of the other, and as intended to correct the morals of the country. The morals of the country have not been improved, and I am afraid its feeling has been much impaired. A civil court in matters of civil injury is a bad corrector of morals; it has only to do with the rights of parties." ** [47]

[44] Hyslop *v.* Staig, 1 Murr. 15, 24.

[45] Christian *v.* Lord Kennedy, 1 Murr. 419, 428.

[46] 1 Murr. 317, 337.

[47] It would seem that the introduction of Lord Kenyon's name in this

§ 356. **Exemplary damages and damages for mental suffering.**
It will at once appear that circumstances of aggravation,
such as give rise to exemplary damages, are frequently, if not
generally, of a nature to cause additional loss to the plaintiff
of an intangible sort, such as mental suffering or loss of reputation. As Foster, J., points out in Fay v. Parker,[48] the earliest
cases cited as allowing exemplary damages were of this sort;
the court refused to set aside the large verdicts found by the
jury, on the ground of the impossibility of saying that the
jury had estimated this element of loss too highly. But the
doctrine of exemplary damages as established has no relation
to the suffering of the plaintiff.

The allowance of exemplary damages gave rise for a time
to the notion that mental suffering was not a subject for compensatory damages. This notion has been generally abandoned; in Massachusetts and other jurisdictions where exemplary damages are not allowed, the right to recover damages
for mental suffering has always been recognized.

§ 357. **Exemplary damages in addition to compensatory.**
The similarity between exemplary damages and damages
for wounded feelings has been noticed by the Supreme Court
of Wisconsin, in the case of Brown v. Swineford.[49]

"The distinction between compensatory damages for
wounded feeling, sense of insult, etc., and punitory damages
is sometimes very vague. . . . And the vagueness of this
distinction, in practice as well as in theory, is illustrated by
the three reports of Bass v. Railway Co.[50] The case was three
times tried in different counties, twice upon instructions allowing exemplary damages, and once upon instructions disallowing
them. And yet the verdict on each trial was for the same
sum. Apparently what was allowed on two trials for exem-

connection is a mistake. In the only
reported case to be found where the
subject of excessive damages was discussed by him, he follows the language
of the older cases, and refuses to set
aside a verdict on the ground that in
actions of tort the court cannot control
the jury. There is not in his opinion
a hint of the right to punish the defendant. Duberley v. Gunning, 4 T. R.
651. Lord Camden is probable meant.
   [48] 53 N. H. 342.
   [49] 44 Wis. 282, 289, per Ryan, C. J.
   [50] 36 Wis. 450, 39 Wis. 636, 42 Wis.
654.

plary damages was allowed on the third trial for compensatory damages for wounded feelings, etc."

In spite of this similarity, however, the two sorts of damage are quite distinct. Damages for wounded feelings are compensatory in their nature, and are given, as has been seen, in all cases where the allowance is proper. Exemplary damages are given because of the motive of the defendant or the wanton or aggravated nature of the tort, and it is well settled that when they are allowed it is in addition to compensatory damages for either physical or mental suffering.[51] In Texas exemplary damages are to be demanded in the pleadings, and the jury must in their verdict find separately the compensatory and the exemplary damages.[52]

§ 358. In some States exemplary damages are not awarded.

As has been said, the doctrine of exemplary damages has never been established in Massachusetts.[53] In that State the "manner and manifest motive" of a tort may be shown, as tending to prove mental suffering.[54] In Hawes v. Knowles,[55] Gray, C. J., said: "In an action of tort for a wilful injury to the person, the manner and manifest motive of the wrongful act may be given in evidence as affecting the question of damages; for when the merely physical injury is the same, it may be more aggravated in its effect upon the mind if it is done in wanton disregard of the rights and feelings of the plaintiff, than if it is the result of mere carelessness"; and it was held that the wantonness must be such as to cause additional pain

---

[51] *Illinois:* Harrison v. Ely, 120 Ill. 83.

Iowa: Parkhurst v. Masteller, 57 Ia. 474; Root v. Sturdivant, 70 Ia. 55.

Mississippi: Bonelli v. Bowen, 70 Miss. 142, 11 So. 791.

New Jersey: Haines v. Schultz, 50 N. J. L. 481.

New York: Hamilton v. Third Avenue R. R., 35 N. Y. Super. Ct. 118.

South Carolina: Chiles v. Southern Ry., 69 S. C. 327, 48 S. E. 252, explaining Aaron v. Southern Ry., 68 S. C. 98, 46 S. E. 556.

Virginia: Norfolk & W. R. R. v.

Neely, 91 Va. 539, 22 S. E. 367, 44 Am. St. Rep. 884.

Wisconsin: Craker v. Chicago & N. W. Ry., 36 Wis. 657.

[52] Kaufman v. Wicks, 62 Tex. 234.

[53] Spear v. Hubbard, 4 Pick. 143, 145; Sampson v. Henry, 11 Pick. 379, 388; Barnard v. Poor, 21 Pick. 378; Burt v. Advertiser Newspaper Co., 154 Mass. 238, 28 N. E. 1, 13 L. R. A. 97; Ellis v. Brockton Pub. Co., 198 Mass. 538, 84 N. E. 1018.

[54] Smith v. Holcomb, 99 Mass. 552; Hawes v. Knowles, 114 Mass. 518.

[55] 114 Mass. 518.

to the plaintiff in body or mind. The same decision denying exemplary damages has been given in the new States of Colorado,[56] Nebraska,[57] and Washington,[58] where the court, treating the question as *res integra*, followed the Massachusetts decisions on principle. In New Hampshire the same result has been reached by overruling earlier cases allowing exemplary damages.[59]

In Wilson *v.* Bowen [60] the Supreme Court of Michigan said: "The purpose of an action of tort is to recover the damages which the plaintiff has sustained from an injury done him by the defendant; *compensation* to the plaintiff is the purpose in view; and, when that is accorded, anything beyond, by whatever name called, is unauthorized. It is not the province of the jury, after *full* damages have been found for the plaintiff, so that he is fully *compensated* for the wrong committed by the defendant, to mulct the defendant in an additional sum, to be handed over to the plaintiff as a *punishment* for the wrong he has done to the plaintiff." And after some fluctuation of opinion, this appears to be the present doctrine in that State.[61]

§ 359. In some States exemplary damages, so called, are in fact compensatory.

In West Virginia exemplary damages so called are allowed; but they are distinctly held to be compensatory damages,

[56] Murphy *v.* Hobbs, 7 Colo. 541; Greeley, St. L. & P. Ry. *v.* Yeager, 11 Colo. 345. A statute was passed in 1889 (Sess. Laws, p. 64) allowing the recovery of exemplary damages; but this statute does not apply to an action for a wrong done before its passage. Howlett *v.* Tuttle, 15 Colo. 454, 24 Pac. 921.

[57] Boyer *v.* Barr, 8 Neb. 68, 30 Am. Rep. 814; Riewe *v.* McCormick, 11 Neb. 261; Bee Pub. Co. *v.* World Pub. Co., 59 Neb. 713, 82 N. W. 28.

[58] Spokane Truck & D. Co. *v.* Hoefer, 2 Wash. 45, 25 Pac. 1072, 11 L. R. A. 689, 26 Am. St. Rep. 842; Woodhouse *v.* Powles, 43 Wash. 617, 86 Pac. 1063; Helland *v.* Bridenstine, 55

Wash. 470, 104 Pac. 626. In some cases exemplary damages are now allowed by statute.

[59] Fay *v.* Parker, 53 N. H. 342; Bixby *v.* Dunlap, 56 N. H. 456.

[60] 64 Mich. 133, 141, per Champlin, J.; following Stilson *v.* Gibbs, 53 Mich. 280.

[61] Durfee *v.* Newkirk, 83 Mich. 522, 47 N. W. 351; Ford *v.* Cheever, 105 Mich. 679, 63 N. W. 975; Haviland *v.* Chase, 116 Mich. 214, 74 N. W. 477, 72 Am. St. Rep. 519; Boydan *v.* Haberstumpf, 129 Mich. 137, 88 N. W. 386; McChesney *v.* Wilson, 132 Mich. 252, 93 N. W. 627; Hink *v.* Sherman, 129 N. W. 732.

"indeterminate" damages, as the court calls them.[62] The court divides damages into "determinate" damages, those for which there is an easily ascertained measure, and "indeterminate" damages, given for non-pecuniary loss, such as physical or mental pain or loss of reputation. Both classes of damages may be recovered, the court held, the latter under the name "exemplary" damages; but no damages can be recovered *in pœnam*.[63] Consequently though by the Civil Damage Act a wife was allowed to recover exemplary damages from one selling liquor to her husband, this was held to mean compensation for mental anguish.[64]

The doctrine of the West Virginia court appears to be law also in Nevada [65] and Wyoming.[66] In Lower Canada, a State deriving its jurisprudence from the Civil Law, the rule seems to be the same.[67] Damages have been allowed, called "exemplary" ("dommages exemplaires" as distinguished from "dommages reels"); but they are apparently compensatory damages for pain,[68] mental suffering,[69] or loss of reputation.[70]

In Texas a peculiar rule obtains. Exemplary damages seem to be regarded as compensatory, but as an award of compensation for losses which in ordinary cases are not to be compensated. The ordinary rules restricting compensation to proximate and natural loss are relaxed, and litigation expenses are also recovered. Thus where the injury was wilful and

[62] Pegram *v.* Stortz, 31 W. Va. 220; Beck *v.* Thompson, 31 W. Va. 459; Stevens *v.* Friedman, 58 W. Va. 78, 51 S. E. 132.

[63] The court followed the common authorities on exemplary damages, and as a result held that "indeterminate" damages are allowed only in case of an injury inflicted with vicious intention. Such losses are more likely to result from a wilful tort; but they may also result from a well-intended or even an involuntary act, and they are then to be compensated. This is notably true in the case of physical suffering, which may be compensated as well in an action for negligence as in an action for wilful trespass; but it is equally true in

some cases of mental suffering. Chapman, C. J., in Smith *v.* Holcomb, 99 Mass. 552, 554.

[64] Pegram *v.* Stortz, 31 W. Va. 220.

[65] Quigley *v.* Central P. R. R., 11 Nev. 350.

[66] Union P. R. R. *v.* Hause, 1 Wyo. 27.

[67] See, however, Guest *v.* Macpherson, 3 Leg. News, 84, where damages are divided into three sorts: nominal, compensatory, and punitive.

[68] Falardeau *v.* Couture, 2 L. C. J. 96.

[69] Mathieu *v.* Laflamme, 4 R. L. 371.

[70] Brossoit *v.* Turcotte, 20 L. C. J. 141.

malicious, damages (called exemplary) are allowed for mental anguish, for counsel fees, and for loss of credit in an action for the destruction of property, or for a wrongful attachment, or other tort.[71] And the same rule appears to prevail in Kansas.[72] But it is doubtful if in any case the damages can exceed compensation for the plaintiff's actual loss.

In some States the jury is allowed to consider the expenses of litigation in assessing exemplary damages.[73] This doctrine is similar to that held in Texas, though it does not go so far. Such damages are plainly compensatory, and have no proper connection with damages given for punishment.

In several States exemplary damages, when allowed, include compensation for the aggravation of the plaintiff's feelings.[74]

§ 360. In most jurisdictions exemplary damages are given for punishment.

In most jurisdictions it is settled that exemplary damages, as a warning to other wrongdoers and as a punishment to the defendant, may be recovered in addition to compensatory

[71] International & G. N. R. R. v. Telephone & Telegraph Co., 69 Tex. 277; Biering v. First Nat. Bank of Galveston, 69 Tex. 599; Trawick v. Martin-Brown Co., 79 Tex. 460, 14 S. W. 564.

[72] Duff & R. F. Co. v. Read, 74 Kan. 730, 88 Pac. 263.

[73] *Alabama:* Marshall v. Betner, 17 Ala. 833.

Arkansas: Patton v. Garrett, 37 Ark. 605 (*semble*).

Connecticut: Huntley v. Bacon, 15 Conn. 267; Ives v. Carter, 24 Conn. 392; Beecher v. Derby Bridge Co., 24 Conn. 491; St. Peter's Church v. Beach, 26 Conn. 355; Dibble v. Morris, 26 Conn. 416; Platt v. Brown, 30 Conn. 336; Welch v. Durand, 36 Conn. 182; Dalton v. Beers, 38 Conn. 529; Mason v. Hawes, 52 Conn. 12; Bennett v. Gibbons, 55 Conn. 450; Wynne v. Parsons, 57 Conn. 73; Maisenbacker v. Society, 71 Conn. 369, 42 Atl. 67, 71 Am. St. Rep. 213; Hanna v. Sweeney, 78 Conn. 492, 62 Atl. 785, 4 L. R. A.

(N. S.) 907; Shupack v. Gordon, 79 Conn. 298, 64 Atl. 740; Distin v. Bradley, 76 Atl. 991.

Kansas: Titus v. Corkins, 21 Kan. 722; Winstead v. Hulme, 32 Kan. 568.

Louisiana: Eatman v. New Orleans P. Ry., 35 La. Ann. 1018.

Mississippi: Northern, J. & G. N. R. R. v. Allbritton, 38 Miss. 243.

Ohio: Roberts v. Mason, 10 Oh. St. 277; Finney v. Smith, 31 Oh. St. 529; Stevenson v. Morris, 37 Oh. St. 10; Peckham Iron Co. v. Harper, 41 Oh. St. 100; Winters v. Cowen, 90 Fed. 99 (Ohio law). See § 234.

[74] *Georgia:* Chattanooga, R. & C. R. R. v. Liddell, 85 Ga. 482, 11 S. E. 853, 21 Am. St. Rep. 169; Jacobus v. Congregation, etc., 107 Ga. 518, 33 S. E. 853, 73 Am. St. Rep. 141; Wright v. Hollywood Cemetery Corp., 112 Ga. 884, 38 S. E. 94, 52 L. R. A. 621; Georgia Ry. & Elec. Co. v. Davis, 6 Ga. App. 645, 65 S. E. 785.

South Carolina: Gosa v. Southern Ry., 67 S. C. 347, 45 S. E. 810.

damages.[75]   The authorities in Oregon leave the question doubtful.   The Supreme Court of that State, in an elaborate opinion, refused to give exemplary damages in any case not

[75] *United States:* Day v. Woodworth, 13 How. 363, 14 L. ed. 181; Milwaukee & St. P. Ry. v. Arms, 91 U. S. 489, 23 L. ed. 374; Missouri P. Ry. v. Humes, 115 U. S. 512, 29 L. ed. 463, 6 Sup. Ct. 110; Denver & R. G. Ry. v. Harris, 122 U. S. 597, 30 L. ed. 1146, 7 Sup. Ct. 1286; Brown v. Evans, 8 Sawy. 488; U. S. v. Taylor, 35 Fed. 484; Scott v. Donald, 165 U. S. 58, 77, 41 L. ed. 632, 17 Sup. Ct. 265.

Alabama: Jefferson County Sav. Bank v. Eborn, 84 Ala. 529.

Arizona: Jaeger v. Metcalf, 11 Ariz. 283, 94 Pac. 1094.

Arkansas: Clark v. Bales, 15 Ark. 452; Ward v. Blackwood, 41 Ark. 295 (*semble*); Citizens' St. Ry. v. Steen, 42 Ark. 321.

California (by Code): St. Ores v. McGlashen, 74 Cal. 148; Waters v. Dumas, 75 Cal. 563; Bundy v. Maginess, 76 Cal. 532.

Connecticut: Linsley v. Bushnell, 15 Conn. 225; Dibble v. Morris, 26 Conn. 416; Dalton v. Beers, 38 Conn. 529.

Dakota: Bates v. Callender, 3 Dak. 256 (*semble*).

Delaware: Robinson v. Burton, 5 Harr. 335.

District of Columbia: Redwood v. M. R. R., 6 D. C. 302.

Florida: Smith v. Bagwell, 19 Fla. 117 (*semble*).

Georgia (by Code): Coleman v. Allen, 79 Ga. 637.

Illinois: Harrison v. Ely, 120 Ill. 83.

Indiana: Binford v. Young, 115 Ind. 174.

Iowa: Parkhurst v. Masteller, 57 Ia. 474; Root v. Sturdivant, 70 Ia. 55; Redfield v. Redfield, 75 Ia. 435; Thill v. Pohlman, 76 Ia. 638.

Kansas: Wheeler & Wilson Manuf. Co. v. Boyce, 36 Kan. 350; Cady v. Case, 45 Kan. 733, 26 Pac. 448.

Kentucky: Louisville & N. R. R. v. Ballard, 85 Ky. 307.

Louisiana: Daly v. Van Benthuysen, 3 La. Ann. 69.

Maine: Pike v. Dilling, 48 Me. 539; Webb v. Gilman, 80 Me. 177.

Maryland: Baltimore & Yorktown Turnpike v. Boone, 45 Md. 344; Philadelphia, W. & B. R. R. v. Larkin, 47 Md. 155.

Michigan: McPherson v. Ryan, 59 Mich. 33; Ross v. Leggett, 61 Mich. 445; Newman v. Stein, 75 Mich. 402 (but see another line of decisions *contra*, Stilson v. Gibbs, 53 Mich. 280; Wilson v. Bowen, 64 Mich. 133).

Minnesota: McCarthy v. Niskern, 22 Minn. 90; Peck v. Small, 35 Minn. 465.

Mississippi: Vicksburg & M. R. R. v. Scanlan, 63 Miss. 413; Higgins v. L., N. O. & T. R. R., 64 Miss. 80.

Missouri: Buckley v. Knapp, 48 Mo. 152; Joice v. Branson, 73 Mo. 28.

Montana: Bohm v. Dunphy, 1 Mont. 333.

New Jersey: Magee v. Holland, 27 N. J. L. 86; Haines v. Schultz, 50 N. J. L. 481.

New York: Bergmann v. Jones, 94 N. Y. 51.

North Carolina: Johnson v. Allen, 100 N. C. 131; Bowden v. Bailes, 101 N. C. 612; Knowles v. N. S. R. R., 102 N. C. 659.

Ohio: Atlantic & G. W. Ry. v. Dunn, 19 Oh. St. 162; Hayner v. Cowden, 27 Oh. St. 292.

Pennsylvania: Lake Shore & M. S. Ry. v. Rosenzweig, 113 Pa. 529; Phila. Traction Co. v. Orbann, 119 Pa. 37, 12 Atl. 816.

Rhode Island: Hagan v. Providence & W. R. R., 3 R. I. 88 (*semble*); Von Storch v. Winslow, 13 R. I. 23 (*semble*); Kenyon v. Cameron, 17 R. I. 116.

South Carolina: Quinn v. S. C. Ry.,

required by the authorities.[76] In an earlier case exemplary damages were allowed; but the defendant's counsel conceded the point.[77] The latest case recognizes the theory as law, but refuses to allow exemplary damages on the facts.[78] In Missouri it was at one time doubtful whether exemplary damages, so called, could ever go beyond a "good round compensation";[79] but it is now settled that true exemplary damages may be recovered.[80]

In States where exemplary damages are given in pœnam it is not permissible to prove, as bearing on their amount, any actual loss, such as the payment of counsel fees.[81]

§ 361. **Exemplary damages not allowed without actual loss.**
It is held in most jurisdictions that if the plaintiff has suffered no actual loss, he cannot maintain an action merely to recover exemplary damages.[82] A plaintiff has no right, the

29 S. C. 381; Griffin v. Ry., 65 S. C. 122, 43 S. E. 445.
Tennessee: Polk v. Fancher, 1 Head, 336; Jones v. Turpin, 6 Heisk. 181; Cox v. Crumley, 5 Lea, 529; Louisville, N. & G. S. R. R. v. Guinan, 11 Lea, 98.
Vermont: Rea v. Harrington, 58 Vt. 181; Camp v. Camp, 59 Vt. 667.
Virginia: Borland v. Barrett, 76 Va. 128; Harman v. Cundiff, 82 Va. 239.
Wisconsin: McWilliams v. Bragg, 3 Wis. 424; Spear v. Hiles, 67 Wis. 350; Templeton v. Graves, 59 Wis. 95, 17 N. W. 672.
Wyoming: Cosgriff v. Miller, 10 Wyo. 190, 68 Pac. 206.
England: Emblen v. Myers, 6 H. & N. 54; Bell v. Midland Ry., 4 L. T. (N. S.) 293. But see McArthur v. Cornwall, [1892] A. C. 75.
Canada: Gingras v. Desilets, Cass. Can. Dig. 116; Clissold v. Machell, 26 Up. Can. Q. B. 422; Silver v. Dom. Tel. Co., 2 R. & G. (N. Scot.) 17.
[76] Sullivan v. Ore. Ry. & Nav. Co., 12 Ore. 392.
[77] Heneky v. Smith, 10 Ore. 349.
[78] Day v. Holland, 15 Ore. 464.
[79] Freidenheit v. Edmundson, 36 Mo. 226; McKeon v. C. Ry., 42 Mo. 79.

[80] Buckley v. Knapp, 48 Mo. 152; Joice v. Branson, 73 Mo. 28.
[81] *Vermont:* Hoodley v. Watson, 45 Vt. 289, 12 Am. Rep. 197.
Wisconsin: Fairbanks v. Witter, 18 Wis. 287, 86 Am. Dec. 765.
[82] *Illinois:* Meidel v. Anthis, 71 Ill. 241; Martin v. Leslie, 93 Ill. App. 44; Duffy v. Frankenberg, 144 Ill. App. 103.
Iowa: Kuhn v. Chicago, M. & S. P. R. R., 74 Ia. 137, 37 N. W. 116; Boardman v. Marshalltown Grocery Co., 105 Ia. 445, 75 N. W. 343; International Harvester Co. v. Iowa Hardware Co., 146 Ia. 172, 122 N. W. 951.
Kansas: Schippel v. Norton, 38 Kan. 567, 16 Pac. 804 (but see Hefley v. Baker, 19 Kan. 9, allowed in case of wilful trespass on land); Adams v. Salina, 58 Kan. 246, 48 Pac. 918; First Nat. Bank v. Kansas Grain Co., 60 Kan. 30, 55 Pac. 277; Cole v. Gray, 70 Kan. 705, 79 Pac. 654; Sondegard v. Martin, 111 Pac. 442; Stonestreet v. Crandell, 10 Kan. App. 575, 62 Pac. 249.
Maine: Stacy v. Portland Pub. Co., 68 Me. 279.
Michigan: Ganssly v. Perkins, 30 Mich. 492.

courts say, to maintain an action *merely* to inflict punishment; exemplary damages are in no case a right of the plaintiff and cannot, therefore, become a cause of action. But in the lower Federal courts and a few other jurisdictions it is held, on the other hand, that if a right of action exists, though the loss is nominal, exemplary damages may be recovered in a proper case; for the plaintiff had a right to maintain his action apart from the privilege of recovering exemplary damages.[83] The rule generally followed, however, does not require the proof of a given amount of actual loss; if there was actual damage, though not so proved as to establish a definite amount of loss, exemplary damages may be recovered.[84]

Mississippi: Robinson v. Goings, 63 Miss. 500; Mississippi & T. R. R. v. Gill, 66 Miss. 39, 5 So. 393.

Missouri: Hoagland v. Forest Park Highlands Amusement Co., 170 Mo. 335, 70 S. W. 878, 94 Am. St. Rep. 740 (overruling Ferguson v. Evening Chronicle Pub. Co., 72 Mo. App. 462, and Mills v. Taylor, 85 Mo. App. 111; but where the failure to recover actual damages is due solely to defect in the pleadings exemplary damages may be recovered: Favorite v. Cottrill, 62 Mo. App. 119; or if it is due to a defect in the verdict: Adams v. St. Louis & S. F. R. R., 149 Mo. App. 278, 130 S. W. 48); Courtney v. Kneib, 131 Mo. App. 204, 110 S. W. 665.

Texas: Flanagan v. Womack, 54 Tex. 50; Jones v. Matthews, 75 Tex. 1; Frawick v. Martin-Brown Co., 79 Tex. 460, 14 S. W. 564; Girard v. Moore, 86 Tex. 675, 26 S. W. 945; Carson v. Texas Installment Co. (Tex. Civ. App.), 34 S. W. 762; Smith v. Dye, 21 Tex. Civ. App. 662, 51 S. W. 858; Lacy v. Gentry (Tex. Civ. App.), 56 S. W. 949; McCarthy v. Miller (Tex. Civ. App.), 57 S. W. 973; Rogers v. O'Barr (Tex. Civ. App.), 76 S. W. 593; Stewart v. Smallwood, 46 Tex. Civ. App. 467, 102 S. W. 159; Seal v. Holcomb, 48 Tex. Civ. App. 330; 107 S. W. 916, Beckham v. Collins, 117 S. W. 431, (Tex. Civ.

App.); Thouron v. Skirvin, (Tex. Civ. App.), 122 S. W. 55.

Washington: (In case of exemplary damages allowed by special statute); Hilfrich v. Meyer, 11 Wash. 186, 39 Pac. 455; Levy v. Fleischner, 12 Wash. 15, 40 Pac. 384.

[83] *United States:* Wilson v. Vaughn, 23 Fed. 229; Press Pub. Co. v. Monroe, 19 C. C. A. 429, 73 Fed. 196, 38 U. S. App. 410.

Alabama: Alabama G. S. R. R. v. Sellers, 93 Ala. 9, 9 So. 375, 30 Am. St. Rep. 17; Louisville & N. R. R. v. Smith, 141 Ala. 335, 37 So. 490.

Georgia: Seaboard A. L. R. R. v. O'Quin, 124 Ga. 357, 52 S. E. 427, 2 L. R. A. (N. S.) 472.

New York: Prince v. Brooklyn Daily Eagle, 37 N. Y. Supp. 250.

North Carolina: Gilreath v. Allen, 10 Ired. 67; Upchurch v. Robertson, 127 N. C. 127, 37 S. E. 157.

South Carolina: Doster v. Western U. T. Co., 77 S. C. 56, 57 S. E. 671; Fields v. Lancaster Cotton Mills, 77 S. C. 546, 58 S. E. 608, 11 L. R. A. (N. S.) 822, 122 Am. St. Rep. 593; Vlasservitch v. Augusta & A. Ry., 85 S. C. 291, 67 S. E. 306.

[84] McConathy v. Deck, 34 Colo. 461, 83 Pac. 135, 4 L. R. A. (N. S.) 358.

§ 362. Survival of exemplary damages.

When the wrongdoer dies before the action is brought to trial, and the action is brought or continued against his executor or administrator, only compensatory damages can be recovered: the liability to exemplary damages does not survive.[85] Nor, on the other hand, does the right survive in favor of an executor or administrator in a suit first brought by him; but if the action is brought by the injured party himself, and revived by his administrator after his death, it has been held that the administrator may recover exemplary damages.[86]

§ 363. Exemplary damages are allowed only for wilful, wanton or aggravated wrong.

The justification of exemplary damages lies in circumstances of aggravation; and the allowance of such damages is therefore restricted to such cases. There must usually be some wrong motive accompanying the wrongful act,[87] and in the absence of malice or some other circumstance of aggravation exemplary damages cannot be recovered in any form of action.[88]   This

[85] *Alabama:* Meighan v. Birmingham Terminal Co., 165 Ala. 591, 51 So. 775.
Georgia: Morris v. Duncan, 126 Ga. 467, 54 S. E. 1045.
Iowa: Sheik v. Hobson, 64 Ia. 146.
Louisiana: Edwards v. Ricks, 30 La. Ann. 926.
North Carolina: Rippey v. Miller, 11 Ired. L. 247.
Texas: Wright v. Donnell, 34 Tex. 291.
[86] Union Mill Co. v. Prenzler, 100 Iowa, 540, 69 N. W. 876.
[87] *Illinois:* Reeder v. Purdy, 48 Ill. 261; Farwell v. Warren, 70 Ill. 28; Toledo, W. & W. R. R. v. Roberts, 71 Ill. 540; Miller v. Kirby, 74 Ill. 242; Scott v. Bryson, 74 Ill. 420; Becker v. Dupree, 75 Ill. 167.
Indiana: Moore v. Crose, 43 Ind. 30.
Iowa: Brown v. Allen, 35 Ia. 306.
Kentucky: Tyson v. Ewing, 3 J. J. Marsh. 185; Courier Journal Co. v. Sallee, 104 Ky. 335, 47 S. W. 226.
Maryland: Philadelphia, B. & W. R. R. v. Green, 110 Md. 32, 71 Atl. 986.

Michigan: Elliott v. Herz, 29 Mich. 202.
New York: Prince v. Socialistic C. P. Assoc., 64 N. Y. Supp. 285, 31 Misc. 234.
North Carolina: Waters v. Greenleaf-Johnson Lumber Co., 115 N. C. 648, 20 S. E. 718.
South Carolina: Wingo v. Inman Mills, 76 S. C. 550, 57 S. E. 525.
Wisconsin: Beveridge v. Welch, 7 Wis. 465; Reed v. Keith, 99 Wis. 672, 75 N. W. 392.
[88] *Alabama:* Snedecor v. Pope, 39 So. 318, 143 Ala. 275 (trespass on land).
Arkansas: St. Louis S. W. Ry. v. Myzell, 87 Ark. 123, 112 S. W. 203 (assault).
Iowa: Wentworth v. Blackman, 71 Iowa, 255, 22 N. W. 666 (wrongful taking of personal property).
Kansas: McCormick H. M. Co. v. Drake, 5 Kan. App. 882, 48 Pac. 944 (replevin).
Kentucky: Andrews v. Singer Mfg. Co., 48 S. W. 976, 20 Ky. L. Rep. 1089

has been held even in an action on a Civil Damage Act which provided expressly that the plaintiff might recover exemplary damages.[89] So where a sheriff makes a levy or an attachment in good faith on an informal process, or otherwise unlawfully, exemplary damages cannot be recovered against him.[90] So in an action for wrongful suing out of attachment to entitle plaintiff to recover exemplary damages, there must be an intent to injure the debtor; lack of reasonable grounds for believing allegations made to procure attachment is not enough.[91] So in an action against a carrier for wrongful ejection of a passenger [92]

(trespass on personal property); Southern Ry. v. Thurman, 121 Ky. 716, 90 S. W. 240, 2 L. R. A. (N. S.) 1108 (compelling white woman to ride in car for colored persons); Bevis v. Vanceburg Tel. Co., 132 Ky. 385, 113 S. W. 811 (maintaining telephone pole where passer on highway ran into it); Louisville & N. R. R. v. Wilkins, 136 S. W. 1026 (defect in roadbed).

Maryland: Bernheimer v. Becker, 102 Md. 250, 62 Atl. 526, 3 L. R. A. (N. S.) 221 (illegal arrest).

Minnesota: Carli v. Union Depot, S. R. & T. Co., 32 Minn. 101, 20 N. W. 89 (trespass on land).

Mississippi: Yazoo & M. V. R. R. v. Christmas, 89 Miss. 686, 42 So. 169 (delay in delivering goods); Cumberland Telephone & Tel. Co. v. Paine, 94 Miss. 883, 48 So. 229 (refusal to give free county telephone service); Western U. T. Co. v. Jackson, 95 Miss. 471, 49 So. 737 (delay in delivering message); Western U. T. Co. v. Miller, 52 So. 701 · (delay in delivering message); Yazoo & M. V. R. R. v. Hardie, 55 So. 967 (carrying passenger past station). (But see Ill. Cent. R. R. v. Armstrong, 93 Miss. 583, 47 So. 427, where exemplary damages were allowed on the facts though it is hard to find in them any circumstances of aggravation.)

New York: Powers v. Manhattan Ry., 120 N. Y. 178, 24 N. E. 295 (running trains before instituting condemnation proceedings).

North Carolina: Wilson v. Atlantic Coast Line R. R., 142 N. C. 333, 55 S. E. 257 (personal injury by train); Stanford v. A. F. Messick Grocery Co., 143 N. C. 419, 55 S. E. 815 (malicious prosecution).

Pennsylvania: Cummings v. Gann, 52 Pa. 484 (replevin).

South Carolina: Matheson v. Southern Ry., 79 S. C. 155, 60 S. E. 437 (loss of freight).

South Dakota: Baxter v. Campbell, 17 S. Dak. 475, 97 N. W. 386 (personal injury).

Texas: International & G. N. Ry. v. Greenwood, 2 Tex. Civ. App. 76, 21 S. W. 559 (boycotting).

Exemplary damages cannot be given for an injury committed without circumstances of aggravation even if the injury constituted a misdemeanor. Warren v. Coharie Lumber Co., 154 N. C. 34, 69 S. E. 685.

[89] Jockers v. Borgman, 29 Kan. 109.

[90] *Kansas:* Dow v. Julien, 32 Kan. 576.

Maryland: Wanamaker v. Bowes, 36 Md. 42.

Missouri: Engle v. Jones, 51 Mo. 316.

New York: Wallace v. Williams, 14 N. Y. Supp. 180.

Texas: Wallis v. Chowning, 18 Tex. Civ. App. 625, 46 S. W. 45.

[91] Nordhaus v. Peterson, 54 Ia. 68.

[92] *Alabama:* Cook v. Southern Ry., 153 Ala. 118, 45 So. 156.

Kansas: Atchison, T. & S. F. R. R.

or for other injury to the passenger,[93] exemplary damages cannot be recovered where the act was done in good faith or without circumstances of aggravation.

An accidental injury, therefore, or one committed by mistake, does not give grounds for exemplary damages,[94] as, for instance, an accidental trespass on the plaintiff's chattels or land by the defendant, who believes it to be his own,[95] as where he acts under a *bona fide* claim of title,[96] or of right to enter land,[97]

v. Hogue, 50 Kan. 40, 31 Pac. 698; Schwartz *v.* Missouri, K. & T. Ry., 83 Kan. 30, 109 Pac. 767.

Kentucky: Louisville & N. R. R. *v.* Champion, 68 S. W. 143, 24 Ky. Law Rep. 87.

Minnesota: Du Laurans *v.* St. Paul R. R., 15 Minn. 49, 2 Am. Rep. 102; Pine *v.* St. Paul City R. R., 50 Minn. 144, 52 N. W. 392, 16 L. R. A. 543.

Mississippi: Ill. Cent. R. R. *v.* Dodds, 53 So. 409.

Missouri: Gardner *v.* St. Louis & S. F. R. R., 117 Mo. App. 138, 93 S. W. 917.

[93] *Arkansas:* St. Louis, I. M. & S. Ry. *v.* Wilson, 70 Ark. 136, 144, 66 S. W. 661.

Georgia: Southern Ry. *v.* O'Bryan, 119 Ga. 147, 45 S. E. 1000.

Maryland: Northern Central Ry. *v.* Newman, 98 Md. 507, 56 Atl. 973.

South Carolina: Tucker *v.* Southern Ry., 75 S. C. 85, 55 S. E. 154; Black *v.* Atlantic C. L. R. R., 82 S. C. 478, 64 S. E. 418.

[94] *Arkansas:* Walker *v.* Fuller, 29 Ark. 448.

California: Lyles *v.* Perrin, 119 Cal. 264, 51 Pac. 332.

Illinois: Tripp *v.* Grouner, 60 Ill. 474.

Iowa: Waller *v.* Waller, 76 Ia. 513.

Louisiana: Jackson *v.* Schmidt, 14 La. Ann. 806.

Vermont: Blodgett *v.* Brattleboro, 30 Vt. 579.

[95] *United States:* U. S. *v.* Taylor, 35 Fed. 484.

Arkansas: Walker *v.* Fuller, 29 Ark. 448.

Maine: Ames *v.* Hilton, 70 Me. 36.

Maryland: Sapp *v.* N. C. Ry., 51 Md. 115.

New York: Dyke *v.* National Transit Co., 22 App. Div. 360, 49 N. Y. Supp. 180.

North Carolina: Remington *v.* Kirby, 120 N. C. 320, 26 S. E. 915.

Rhode Island: Adams *v.* Lorraine Mfg. Co., 29 R. I. 333, 71 Atl. 180.

[96] *United States:* Murray *v.* Pannaci, 130 Fed. 529.

Georgia: Scott *v.* Mathis, 72 Ga. 119; Georgia R. R. & B. Co. *v.* Gardner, 115 Ga. 954, 42 S. E. 250.

Illinois: Sullivan *v.* Dee, 8 Ill. App. 263.

North Carolina: Hays *v.* Askew, 52 N. C. 272.

Pennsylvania: Blair Co. *v.* Lloyd, 1 Walk. 158.

South Carolina: Perry *v.* Jefferies, 61 S. C. 292, 39 S. E. 515.

Wisconsin: Hazelton *v.* Week, 49 Wis. 661, 6 N. W. 309, 35 Am. Rep. 796; Scheer *v.* Kriesel, 109 Wis. 125, 85 N. W. 138.

England: McArthur *v.* Cornwall, [1892] A. C. 75, 61 L. J. P. C. 1, 65 L. T. Rep. 718.

[97] *Illinois:* Leiter *v.* Day, 35 Ill. App. 248; Goldstein *v.* Miller, 93 Ill. App. 103.

Michigan: Allison *v.* Chandler, 11 Mich. 542.

Missouri: Franz *v.* Hillerbrand, 45 Mo. 121.

New Jersey: Hollister *v.* Ruddy, 66 N. J. L. 68, 48 Atl. 520.

or to take personalty.[98] The mere fact that the defendant had reason to believe his act an illegal one will not necessarily make the act so wilfully wrong as to justify the infliction of exemplary damages.[99] But circumstances of aggravation will subject a trespasser to exemplary damages even if he acted under claim of right; as where he acted after protest by the plaintiff [100] or to pay a private grudge,[101] or with gross negligence in ascertaining the extent of his right.[102]

Upon the general principle here considered, an idiot or person incapable of forming an evil intent cannot be subjected to exemplary damages.[103]

§ 363a. Exemplary damages allowed for aggravating circumstances.

Exemplary damages are allowed when the injury was accompanied by circumstances of aggravation.[104] Thus they may

Texas: Jackel v. Reiman, 78 Tex. 588, 14 S. W. 1001.

[98] Stell v. Paschal, 41 Tex. 640.

[99] *Iowa:* Inman v. Ball, 65 Ia. 543.

Minnesota: Anderson v. International Harvester Co., 104 Minn. 327, 116 N. W. 101, 16 L. R. A. (N. S.) 440.

[100] *Alabama:* Louisville & N. R. R. v. Smith, 141 Ala. 335, 37 So. 490.

Kentucky: Clinton v. Franklin, 26 Ky. Law Rep. 1053, 83 S. W. 142.

Maryland: Medairy v. McAllister, 97 Md. 488, 55 Atl. 461.

Mississippi: Cumberland T. & T. Co. v. Cassedy, 78 Miss. 666, 29 So. 762.

New York: Hammond v. Sullivan, 112 App. Div. 788, 99 N. Y. Supp. 472.

Wyoming: Cosgriff v. Miller, 10 Wyo. 190, 68 Pac. 206.

[101] Miller v. Rambo, 73 N. J. L. 726, 64 Atl. 1053.

[102] Beaudrot v. Southern Ry., 69 S. C. 160, 48 S. E. 106.

[103] *Illinois:* McIntire v. Sholty, 121 Ill. 660, 13 N. E. 239, 2 Am. St. Rep. 140.

New Hampshire: Jewell v. Colby, 66 N. H. 399, 24 Atl. 902.

New York: Ulrich v. New York Press

Co., 23 Misc. 168, 50 N. Y. Supp. 788 (*semble*).

[104] *Alabama:* Mitchell v. Billingsley, 17 Ala. 391; Burns v. Campbell, 71 Ala. 271; Garrett v. Sewell, 108 Ala. 521, 18 So. 737; Snedecor v. Pope, 143 Ala. 275, 39 So. 318.

California: Dorsey v. Manlove, 14 Cal. 553.

Illinois: Merrill v. Dibble, 12 Ill. App. 85; McCarty v. Gray, 95 Ill. App. 559.

Kentucky: Jennings v. Maddox, 8 B. Mon. 430.

Maryland: Scott v. Bay, 3 Md. 431; Moore v. Schultz, 31 Md. 418; Zimmerman v. Helser, 32 Md. 274.

Mississippi: Jackson Electric Ry., L. & P. Co. v. Lowry, 79 Miss. 431, 30 So. 634; Avera v. Williams, 81 Miss. 714, 33 So. 501; Yazoo & M. V. R. R. v. Mitchell, 83 Miss. 179, 35 So. 339.

Missouri: Milborn v. Beach, 14 Mo. 104, 55 Am. Dec. 91; Engle v. Jones, 51 Mo. 316; Prueitt v. Cheltenham Quarry Co., 33 Mo. App. 18.

New Hampshire: Towle v. Blake, 48 N. H. 92.

New York: Gilmore v. Wale, Anth. N. P. 64.

Pennsylvania: Reynolds v. Braith-

EXEMPLARY DAMAGES § 363a

be allowed when the act was wilfully wrong,[105] or done with excessive force,[106] rudely,[107] violently,[108] or cruelly,[109] with de-

waite, 131 Pa. 416, 18 Atl. 1110, 25 W. N. C. 269; Mayfield v. White, 1 Browne, 241; Greeney v. Pa. Co., 29 Pa. Super. Ct. 136.

Rhode Island: Herreshof v. Tripp, 15 R. I. 92, 23 Atl. 104.

Texas: Cook v. Garza, 9 Tex. 358; Rodgers v. Ferguson, 36 Tex. 544; Sinclair v. Stanley, 64 Tex. 67.

Virginia: Fishburne v. Engledore, 91 Va. 548, 22 S. E. 354.

[105] *Illinois:* Bull v. Griswold, 19 Ill. 631; Williams v. Reil, 20 Ill. 147; Stillwell v. Barnet, 60 Ill. 210; Illinois C. R. R. v. Cobb, 68 Ill. 53; Jones v. Jones, 71 Ill. 562; Illinois C. R. R. v. Ogle, 92 Ill. 353; West Chicago St. R. R. v. Morrison, 160 Ill. 288, 43 N. E. 393.

Louisiana: Marion v. Johnson, 23 La. Ann. 597; Nickerson v. Wadley, 110 La. 194, 34 So. 410.

Maryland: Ridgely v. Bond, 17 Md. 14; Barton Coal Co. v. Cox, 39 Md. 1, 17 Am. Rep. 525; Atlantic & G. C. C. C. Co. v. Maryland Coal Co., 62 Md. 135.

Minnesota: Lynd v. Pickett, 7 Minn. 184.

Missouri: Goetz v. Ambs, 27 Mo. 28; McKeon v. Citizens' Ry., 42 Mo. 87.

New Jersey: Trainer v. Wolff, 58 N. J. L. 381, 33 Atl. 1051.

New York: Tifft v. Culver, 3 Hill, 180; Ives v. Humphreys, 1 E. D. Smith, 196.

Pennsylvania: Huling v. Henderson, 161 Pa. 553, 29 Atl. 276; Gerwig v. W. J. Johnston Co., 207 Pa. 585, 57 Atl. 42; Greeney v. Pa. Co., 29 Pa. Super. Ct. 136; Reed v. Vastine, 1 Northumb. Co. Leg. N. 115.

South Carolina: Hall v. South Carolina Ry., 28 S. C. 261, 5 S. E. 623; Willoughby v. Northeastern R. R., 32

S. C. 410, 11 S. E. 339; Campbell v. Seaboard Air Line Ry., 83 S. C. 448, 65 S. E. 628.

Texas: Champion v. Vincent, 20 Tex. 811; Tignor v. Toney, 13 Tex. Civ. App. 518, 35 S. W. 881.

Vermont: Bragg v. Laraway, 65 Vt. 673, 27 Atl. 492; Whitney v. Adams, 66 Vt. 679, 30 Atl. 32, 44 Am. St. Rep. 875, 25 L. R. A. 598.

[106] *United States:* McAfee v. Crofford, 13 How. 447, 14 L. ed. 217.

Georgia: Shores v. Brooks, 81 Ga. 468; Henson v. Taylor, 108 Ga. 567, 33 S. E. 911; Seaboard A. L. R. R. v. O'Quin, 124 Ga. 357, 52 S. E. 427, 2 L. R. A. (N. S.) 472.

Mississippi: Bonelli v. Brown, 70 Miss. 142, 11 So. 791.

New Hampshire: Towle v. Blake, 48 N. H. 92.

Tennessee: Simpson v. Markwood, 6 Baxt. 340.

Texas: Sinclair v. Stanley, 69 Tex. 718, 7 S. W. 511; Gillett v. Moody (Tex. Civ. App.), 54 S. W. 35; Bollinger v. McMinn, 47 Tex. Civ. App. 89, 104 S. W. 1079.

[107] *Alabama:* Burns v. Campbell, 71 Ala. 271; Terry v. Williams, 148 Ala. 468, 41 So. 804.

Maryland: Gusdorff v. Duncan, 94 Md. 160, 50 Atl. 574.

Mississippi: Light, etc., Co. v. Compton, 86 Miss. 269, 38 So. 629.

Missouri: Engle v. Jones, 51 Mo. 316; McMenamy v. Cohick, 1 Mo. App. 529; Ickenroth v. St. Louis Transit Co., 102 Mo. App. 597, 77 S. W. 162.

North Carolina: Parrott v. Atlantic & N. C. R. R., 140 N. C. 546, 53 S. E. 432.

[108] *United States:* Denver & R. G. Ry. v. Harris, 122 U. S. 597, 7 Sup.

[109] *New York:* Ives v. Humphreys, 1 E. D. Smith, 196.

North Carolina: Duncan v. Stalcup, 18 N. C. 440.

sire to injure,[110] or in known violation of law,[111] against protest,[112] or where the injury is repeated after a former successful suit against the wrongdoer.[113] On the other hand, no exemplary damages can be allowed when there are no circumstances of aggravation.[114]

§ 364. Exemplary damages for malice.

Actual malice in the commission of a wrongful act is a cause for exemplary damages.[115] Thus exemplary damages

Ct. 1286, 30 L. ed. 1146; Berry v. Fletcher, 1 Dill. 67, Fed. Cas. No. 1,357.
Arkansas: St. Louis, I. M. & S. Ry. v. Davis, 56 Ark. 51, 19 S. W. 107.
Maryland: Thillman v. Neal, 88 Md. 525, 42 Atl. 242; Baltimore C. & A. Ry. v. Kirby, 91 Md. 313, 46 Atl. 975.
Missouri: Prueitt v. Cheltenham Quarry Co., 33 Mo. App. 18; Hickey v. Welch, 91 Mo. App. 4.

New Hampshire: Towle v. Blake, 48 N. H. 92.
New York: Walker v. Wilson, 8 Bosw. 586.
Pennsylvania: Greeney v. Pa. Co., 29 Pa. Super. Ct. 136.
Tennessee: Nashville St. Ry. v. Griffin, 104 Tenn. 81, 57 S. W. 153, 9 L. R. A. 451.
Texas: Smith v. Sherwood, 2 Tex. 460.
Canada: Lunn v. Turner, 4 Up. Can. Q. B. 282.

[110] *Georgia:* Darnell v. Columbus S. C. Co., 129 Ga. 62, 58 S. E. 631, 13 L. R. A. (N. S.) 333.
Missouri: Engle v. Jones, 51 Mo. 316.
Texas: Lesk v. Pollard, 1 W. & W. Ct. App. 117.
[111] *Alabama:* Hicks v. Swift Creek M. Co., 133 Ala. 411, 31 So. 947, 57 L. R. A. 720.
Louisiana: Bentley v. Fischer Co., 51 La. Ann. 451, 25 So. 262.
Missouri: Parker v. Shackelford, 61 Mo. 68.
Ireland: Reeves v. Penrose, 26 L. R. Ir. 141.
[112] *Louisiana:* Bright v. Bell, 113 La. 1078, 37 So. 976.
Minnesota: Heartz v. Klinkhammer, 39 Minn. 488, 40 N. W. 826.
Missouri: Milburn v. Beach, 14 Mo. 104.
[113] *Virginia:* Wood v. American Nat. Bank, 100 Va. 306, 40 S. E. 931.
West Virginia: Pickens v. Coal R.

B. & T. Co., 51 W. Va. 445, 41 S. E. 400.
[114] *Alabama:* Burns v. Campbell, 71 Ala. 271.
Georgia: Central of Ga. Ry. v. Sowell, 3 Ga. App. 142, 59 S. E. 323.
Iowa: Young v. Gormley, 119 Ia. 546, 93 N. W. 565.
Kentucky: Andrews v. Singer Co., 20 Ky. L. Rep. 1089, 48 S. W. 976.
Minnesota: Carli v. Union D. S. R. & T. Co., 32 Minn. 101, 20 N. W. 89.
Mississippi: Keystone L. & I. Co. v. McGrath, 21 So. 301.
Missouri: Ross v. New Home S. M. Co., 24 Mo. App. 353.
North Carolina: Gwaltney v. Southern Timber Co., 115 N. C. 579, 20 S. E. 465.
Texas: Nafe v. Hudson, 19 Tex. Civ. App. 381, 47 S. W. 675.
[115] *United States:* Day v. Woodworth, 13 How. 363, 14 L. ed. 181; Ralston v. The State Rights, Crabbe, 22; Spooner v. Daniels, 22 Fed. Cas. No.

may be given where an act is done with evil motive,[116] with intent to injure,[117] with malicious outrage,[118] with insult [119] or in revenge,[120] or out of ill-will [121] or desire to injure.[122]

13,244a; Berry v. Fletcher, Fed. Cas. No. 1,357, 1 Dill. 67.

Alabama: Burns v. Campbell, 71 Ala. 271; Garrett v. Sewell, 108 Ala. 521, 18 So. 737; Louisville & N. R. R. v. Smith, 141 Ala. 335, 37 So. 490; Snedecor v. Pope, 143 Ala. 275, 39 So. 318; Western Union Co. v. Dickens, 148 Ala. 480, 41 So. 469.

Arkansas: Barlow v. Lowder, 35 Ark. 492.

California: Dorsey v. Manlove, 14 Cal. 553.

Connecticut: Curtiss v. Hoyt, 19 Conn. 154, 48 Am. Dec. 149; Dibble v. Morris, 26 Conn. 416; Keane v. Main, 76 Atl. 269.

Delaware: Kennedy v. Woodrow, 6 Houst. 46.

District of Columbia: Kilbourn v. Thompson, 1 McA. & M. 401.

Hawaii: Coffin v. Spencer, 2 Hawaii, 23.

Illinois: Sherman v. Dutch, 16 Ill. 283; Stillwell v. Barnet, 60 Ill. 210; Illinois Cent. R. R. v. Cobb. 68 Ill. 53; Becker v. Dupree, 75 Ill. 167.

Indiana: Moore v. Crose, 43 Ind. 30; Moyer v. Gordon, 113 Ind. 282, 14 N. E. 476.

Iowa: Brown v. Alley, 35 Ia. 306; Curl v. Chicago, R. I. & P. Ry., 63 Iowa, 417, 16 N. W. 69, 19 Am. St. Rep. 308.

Kansas: Hefley v. Baker, 19 Kan. 9; Hess v. Sparks, 44 Kan. 465, 24

Pac. 979, 21 Am. St. Rep. 300; Walker v. Wickens, 49 Kan. 42, 30 Pac. 181; Martin v. Carlock, 82 Kan. 266, 108 Pac. 92.

Kentucky: Louisville & N. R. R. v. Ballard, 85 Ky. 307; Ohio V. T. Co. v. Meyer, 22 Ky. L. Rep. 36, 56 S. W. 673.

Maine: Webb v. Gilman, 80 Me. 177.

Maryland: Moore v. Schultz, 31 Md. 418; Smith v. Thompson, 55 Md. 5, 39 Am. Rep. 409; Fresh v. Cutter, 73 Md. 87, 20 Atl. 774, 25 Am. St. Rep. 575, 10 L. R. A. 67.

Minnesota: Lynd v. Pickett, 7 Minn. 184; Gardner v. Minea, 47 Minn. 295, 50 N. W. 199.

Mississippi: Yazoo & M. V. R. R. v. White, 82 Miss. 120, 33 So. 970.

Missouri: Engle v. Jones, 51 Mo. 316; Joice v. Branson, 73 Mo. 28; Callahan v. Ingram, 122 Mo. 355, 26 S. W. 1020, 43 Am. St. Rep. 583; Minter v. Bradstreet Co., 174 Mo. 444, 73 S. W. 668; Carp v. Queen Ins. Co., 203 Md. 295, 101 S. W. 78; McMenamy v. Cohick, 1 Mo. App. 529; Prueitt v. Cheltenham Quarry Co., 33 Mo. App. 18; Berlin v. Thompson, 61 Mo. App. 234.

New Hampshire: Towle v. Blake, 48 N. H. 92.

New Jersey: Miller v. Rambo, 73 N. J. L. 726, 64 Atl. 1053.

New York: Bergmann v. Jones, 94 N. Y. 51; Woert v. Jenkins, 14 Johns.

---

[116] Towle v. Blake, 48 N. H. 92.

[117] *Iowa:* Tyler v. Bowen, 124 Ia. 452, 100 N. W. 505.

Vermont: Newell v. Whitcher, 53 Vt. 589, 38 Am. Rep. 702.

[118] Smith v. Sherwood, 2 Tex. 460.

[119] Wilkins v. Gilmore, 2 Humph. (Tenn.) 140.

[120] Greenville Co. v. Partlow, 14 Rich. L. (S. C.) 237.

[121] Smith v. Thompson, 55 Md. 5, 39 Am. Rep. 409.

[122] *Missouri:* McMenamy v. Cohick, 1 Mo. App. 529.

Texas: First Bank of Mertens v. Steffens, 51 Tex. Civ. App. 211, 111 S. W. 782.

The existence of such malice as will justify the infliction of exemplary damages is of course a question of fact; and the malice must be actual, not constructive or, as it is often called, implied.[123]   In one class of cases, however—actions for defamation—it is held in many jurisdictions that malice may be implied from the mere fact of the false statement without probable cause.[124]   In other jurisdictions, however, malice in fact must exist, and implied malice will not supply its place; [125] and this seems to us to be the better opinion.

352; Ives v. Humphreys, 1 E. D. Smith, 196.
North Carolina: Duncan v. Stalcup, 18 N. C. 440; Ratliff v. Huntly, 27 N. C. 545; Wylie v. Smitherman, 30 N. C. 236; Sowers v. Sowers, 87 N. C. 303; Bowden v. Bailes, 101 N. C. 612, 8 S. E. 342; Upchurch v. Robertson, 127 N. C. 127, 37 S. E. 157.
Pennsylvania: Neeb v. Hope, 111 Pa. 145, 2 Atl. 568; Phila. Traction Co. v. Orbann, 119 Pa. 37, 12 Atl. 816; Pittsburgh, C. & S. L. Ry. v. Lyon, 123 Pa. 140; Hodgson v. Millward, 3 Grant Cas. 406; Greeney v. Pa. Co., 29 Pa. Super. Ct. 136; Blair Co. v. Lloyd, 1 Walk. 158.
Rhode Island: Herreshof v. Tripp, 15 R. I. 92, 23 Atl. 104.
South Carolina: Greenville R. R. v. Partlow, 14 Rich. L. 237 (see however *contra*, Stallings v. Corbett, 2 Speers, 613, 42 Am. Dec. 388, denying recovery of exemplary damages on account of malice except in actions for injury to character); McIntosh v. Augusta & A. Ry., 69 S. E. 159.
Tennessee: Cox v. Crumley, 5 Lea, 529.
Texas: Smith v. Sherwood, 2 Tex. 460; Sinclair v. Stanley, 69 Tex. 718, 7 S. W. 511; Mayer v. Duke, 72 Tex. 445, 10 S. W. 565; Lesk v. Pollard, 1 W. & W. Ct. App., § 117; Tignor v. Toney, 13 Tex. Civ. App. 518, 35 S. W. 881.
Utah: Marks v. Cumher, 6 Utah, 419, 24 Pac. 528.

Vermont: Newell v. Whitcher, 53 Vt. 589, 38 Am. Rep. 702.
Virginia: Harman v. Cundiff, 82 Va. 239; Fishburne v. Engledore, 91 Va. 548, 22 S. E. 354.
Wisconsin: Klewin v. Bauman, 53 Wis. 244, 10 N. W. 398.
Wyoming: Cosgriff v. Miller, 10 Wyo. 190, 68 Pac. 206.
[123] *Alabama:* Johnson v. Collier, 161 Ala. 204, 49 So. 761.
Iowa: Ahrens v. Fenton, 138 Ia. 559, 115 N. W. 233.
Maryland: Knickerbocker Ice Co. v. Gardiner Dairy Co., 107 Md. 556, 69 Atl. 405, 16 L. R. A. (N. S.) 746.
Missouri: Dunham v. Miller (Mo. App.), 133 S. W. 675.
Texas: Webb v. J. L. Wiginton & Co. (Tex. Civ. App.), 118 S. W. 856.
[124] *Illinois:* Schmisseur v. Kreilich, 92 Ill. 347; Schofield v. Baldwin, 102 Ill. App. 560.
Kentucky: Nicholson v. Merritt, 67 S. W. 5, 23 Ky. L. Rep. 2281.
Maryland: Coffin v. Brown, 94 Md. 190, 50 Atl. 567.
Missouri: Arnold v. Savings Co., 76 Mo. App. 159.
Pennsylvania: Regensperger v. Kiefer, 7 Atl. 724, 20 W. N. C. 97.
Texas: King v. Sassaman (Tex. Civ. App.), 54 S. W. 304.
[125] *United States:* Anstruc v. Starr Co., 182 Fed. 705.
Arkansas: Stallings v. Whittaker, 55 Ark. 494, 18 S. W. 829.

§ 365. For oppression, brutality, or insult.

Oppression, brutality, or insult in the infliction of a wrong is a cause for the allowance of exemplary damages.[126] Such, for instance, is abuse of process [127] or wilful refusal to perform

California: Gilman v. McClatch, 111 Cal. 606, 44 Pac. 241 (but see Childers v. San Jose M. P. & Co., 105 Cal. 284, 291, 45 Am. St. Rep. 40, 38 Pac. 903).

Colorado: Republicar Pub. Co. v. Conroy, 5 Colo. App. 262, 38 Pac. 423.

Indiana: Belck v. Belck, 97 Ind. 73.

New York: Southcombe v. Armstrong, 8 N. Y. Supp. 1, 361; Miller v. Donovan, 16 Misc. 453, 39 N. Y. Supp. 820; Butler v. Gazette Co., 104 N. Y. Supp. 637, 119 App. Div. 767; Amory v. Vreeland, 110 N. Y. Supp. 859, 125 App. Div. 850; Bingham v. Gaynor, 119 N. Y. Supp. 1010, 135 App. Div. 426 (but see Morrison v. Press Pub. Co., 59 N. Y. Super. Ct. 216, 14 N. Y. Supp. 131).

Wisconsin: Templeton v. Graves, 59 Wis. 95, 17 N. W. 672; Driessel v. Urkart, 132 N. W. 894.

[126] *United States:* Berry v. Fletcher, 1 Dill. 67, Fed. Cas. No. 1, 357.

Alabama: Burns v. Campbell, 71 Ala. 271.

Arkansas: Barlow v. Lowder, 35 Ark. 492.

California: Dorsey v. Manlove, 14 Cal. 553.

Illinois: Reeder v. Purdy, 48 Ill. 261; Cutler v. Smith, 57 Ill. 252; Smith v. Wunderlich, 70 Ill. 426; Drohn v. Brewer, 77 Ill. 280; West Chicago St. R. R. v. Morrison, etc., Co., 160 Ill. 288, 43 N. E. 393.

Indiana: Anthony v. Gilbert, 4 Blackf. 348; Moore v. Crose, 43 Ind. 30; Moyer v. Gordon, 113 Ind. 282.

Kansas: Hefley v. Baker, 19 Kan. 9; Cady v. Case, 45 Kan. 733, 26 Pac. 448.

Kentucky: Jennings v. Maddox, 8 B. Mon. 430; L. & N. R. R. v. Ballard, 85 Ky. 307; Weber-Stair Co. v. Fisher (Ky. L. Rep.), 119 S. W. 195.

Maine: Webb v. Gilman, 80 Me. 177.

Maryland: Thillman v. Neal, 88 Md. 525, 42 Atl. 242.

Michigan: Raynor v. Nims, 37 Mich. 34.

Minnesota: Gardner v. Minea, 47 Minn. 295, 50 N. W. 199.

Missouri: Engle v. Jones, 51 Mo. 316; Joice v. Branson, 73 Mo. 28; Newman v. St. Louis & I. M. R. R., 2 Mo. App. 402; Prueitt v. Cheltenham Quarry Co., 33 Mo. App. 18; Gildersleeve v. Overstolz, 90 Mo. App. 518; Baxter v. Magill, 127 Mo. App. 392, 105 S. W. 679.

New Hampshire: Towle v. Blake, 48 N. H. 92.

New York: Ives v. Humphreys, 1 E. D. Smith, 196.

North Carolina: Bowden v. Bailes, 101 N. C. 612.

Pennsylvania: Nagle v. Mullison, 34 Pa. 48; Phila. Traction Co. v. Orbann, 119 Pa. 37, 12 Atl. 816; Greeney v. Pa. Co., 29 Pa. Super. Ct. 136.

South Dakota: Bailey v. Walton, 24 S. D. 118, 123 N. W. 701.

Tennessee: Cox v. Crumley, 5 Lea, 529.

Texas: Smith v. Sherwood, 2 Tex. 460; Loftees v. Maxey, 73 Tex. 242, 11 S. W. 272; Lesk v. Pollard, 1 W. & W. Ct. App., § 117; Tignor v. Toney, 13 Tex. Civ. App. 518, 35 S. W. 881; Diamond v. Smith, 27 Tex. Civ. App. 558, 66 S. W. 141.

Virginia: Fishburne v. Engledore, 91 Va. 548, 22 S. E. 354.

[127] *California:* Nightingale v. Scannell, 18 Cal. 315; Foley v. Martin, 142 Cal. 256, 71 Pac. 165.

Kansas: Stonestreet v. Crandell, 10 Kan. App. 575, 62 Pac. 249.

North Carolina: Louder v. Hinson, 4 Jones L. 369.

an official duty.[128] A woman in delicate health is wrongfully turned out of her house at night in a storm; she may recover exemplary damages.[129] A passenger wrongfully ejected from a railroad train with rudeness and violence, may recover exemplary damages; [130] though mere indecorous conduct in expelling a passenger is held not to be sufficient cause for their infliction.[131] So exemplary damages may be recovered where the wrongful act is accompanied with circumstances of insult and outrage.[132] But insulting conduct to another passenger on the same occasion will not support exemplary damages to the plaintiff in an action for wrongful ejection from a railroad train.[133]

Texas: Rodgers v. Ferguson, 36 Tex. 544; Shaw v. Brown, 41 Tex. 446.

England: Huckle v. Money, 2 Wils. 205.

[128] *United States:* Wilson v. Vaughan, 23 Fed. 229.

Maryland: Elbin v. Wilson, 33 Md. 135.

[129] Redfield v. Redfield, 75 Ia. 435.

[130] *Indiana:* Citizens' St. R. R. v. Willoeby, 134 Ind. 563, 33 N. E. 627.

Kentucky: Louisville & N. R. R. v. Fowler, 107 S. W. 703, 32 Ky. L. Rep. 1021.

Maryland: Philadelphia, W. & B. R. R. v. Larkin, 47 Md. 155.

Missouri: Bolles v. Kansas City Southern Ry., 134 Mo. App. 696, 115 S. W. 459; Cathey v. St. Louis & S. P. R. R., 130 S. W. 130 (Mo. App.)

North Carolina: Knowles v. N. S. R. R., 102 N. C. 59.

South Carolina: Kibler v. Southern Ry., 64 S. C. 242, 41 S. E. 977.

And so of rude, insulting and oppressive conduct toward a passenger without expulsion:

Kentucky: Cincinnati, N. O. & T. P. Ry. v. Strosnider, 121 S. W. 971.

Mississippi: Yazoo & M. V. R. R. v. Fitzgerald, 50 So. 631.

[131] Louisville & N. R. R. v. Ballard, 85 Ky. 307.

[132] *United States:* Day v. Woodworth, 13 How. 363, 14 L. ed. 181.

Alabama: Burns v. Campbell, 71 Ala. 271.

Arkansas: Barlow v. Lowder, 35 Ark. 492.

Georgia: Atlantic Consolidated St. Ry. v. Keeny, 99 Ga. 266, 25 S. E. 629, 33 L. R. A. 824.

Indiana: Moore v. Cross, 43 Ind. 30.

Kentucky: Memphis & Cinc. Packet Co. v. Nagel, 97 Ky. 9, 29 S. W. 743; Hughes v. Louisville & N. R. R., 104 Ky. 768, 48 S. W. 671; Southern Ry. v. Thurman, 121 Ky. 716, 90 S. W. 240, 28 Ky. L. Rep. 699, 979, 2 L. R. A. (N. S.) 1108.

Michigan: Buggi v. Milburn, 40 Mich. 512.

Mississippi: Louisville & N. R. R. v. Maybin, 66 Miss. 83, 5 So. 401.

New Hampshire: Towle v. Blake, 48 N. H. 92.

New York: Adams v. Rivers, 11 Barb. 390.

North Carolina: Duncan v. Stalcup, 18 N. C. 440; Story v. Norfolk & S. R. R., 133 N. C. 59, 45 S. E. 349.

Pennsylvania: Greeney v. Pa. Co., 29 Pa. Super. Ct. 136.

[133] Louisville & N. R. R. v. Scott (Ky.), 133 S. W. 800.

§ 366. For wantonness of injury.

If the injury is wantonly inflicted, exemplary damages may be recovered; [134] as for instance where the act was done with reckless disregard of the rights of others, or of the consequences

[134] *United States:* Day v. Woodworth, 13 How. 363, 14 L. ed. 181; Downing v. Outerbridge, 51 U. S. App. 106, 79 Fed. 931, 25 C. C. A. 241; Cowen v. Winters, 96 Fed. 929, 37 C. C. A. 628; Friedly v. Giddings, 119 Fed. 438.

Alabama: Devaughn v. Heath, 37 Ala. 595; Burns v. Campbell, 71 Ala. 271; Garrett v. Sewell, 108 Ala. 521, 18 So. 737; Snedecor v. Pope, 143 Ala. 275, 39 So. 318; Western U. T. Co. v. Dickens, 148 Ala. 480, 41 So. 469; Terry v. Williams, 148 Ala. 468, 41 So. 804.

California: Dorsey v. Manlove, 14 Cal. 553.

Connecticut: Curtiss v. Hoyt, 19 Conn. 154, 48 Am. Dec. 149; Dibble v. Morris, 26 Conn. 416.

District of Columbia: Kilbourn v. Thompson, 1 McA. & M. 401.

Illinois: Sherman v. Dutch, 16 Ill. 283; Stillwell v. Barnet, 60 Ill. 210; Jones v. Jones, 71 Ill. 562; Browning v. Jones, 52 Ill. App. 597.

Kentucky: Louisville & N. R. R. v. Ballard, 85 Ky. 307.

Maine: Wellman v. Dickey, 78 Me. 29, 2 Atl. 133; Webb v. Gilman, 80 Me. 177, 13 Atl. 688.

Maryland: Moore v. Schultz, 31 Md. 418; Strasburger v. Barber, 38 Md. 103 ; Sapp v. North C. Ry., 51 Md. 115.

Minnesota: Lynd v. Picket, 7 Minn. 184 (Gil. 128), 82 Am. Dec. 79; Craig v. Cook, 28 Minn. 232, 9 N. W. 712; Matteson v. Monroe, 80 Minn. 340, 83 N. W. 153.

Mississippi: Yazoo & M. V. R. R. v. White, 82 Miss. 120, 33 So. 970.

Missouri: Goetz v. Ambs, 27 Mo. 28; Green v. Craig, 47 Mo. 90; Prueitt v. Cheltenham Quarry Co., 33 Mo. App. 18.

New Hampshire: Towle v. Blake, 48 N. H. 92.

New York: Voltz v. Blackmar, 64 N. Y. 440, 444; Farnsworth v. Western U. T. Co., 53 Hun, 636, 6 N. Y. Supp. 735; Sheldon v. Baumann, 19 App. Div. 61, 45 N. Y. Supp. 1016.

North Carolina: Duncan v. Stalcup, 18 N. C. 440; Ratliff v. Huntley, 27 N. C. 545; Wylie v. Smitherman, 30 N. C. 236.

Pennsylvania: Phila. Traction Co. v. Orbann, 119 Pa. 37, 12 Atl. 816; Kennedy v. Erdman, 150 Pa. 427, 24 Atl. 643; Huling v. Henderson, 161 Pa. 553, 29 Atl. 276; Sperry v. Seidel, 218 Pa. 16, 66 Atl. 853; Blair I. & C. Co. v. Lloyd, 1 Walk. 158.

South Carolina: Richardson v. Atlantic C. L. R. R., 71 S. C. 444, 51 S. E. 261; Thomasson v. Southern Ry., 72 S. C. 1, 51 S. E. 443; Bridges v. Mills Mfg. Co., 85 S. C. 520, 67 S. E. 738; Rhodes v. Granby Cotton Mills, 68 S. E. 824.

Tennessee: Cumberland T. & T. Co. v. Poston, 94 Tenn. 696, 30 S. W. 1040.

Texas: Lesk v. Pollard, 1 W. & W. Civ. App., § 117; Vincent v. Mayblum, 1 W. & W. Civ. App., § 763; Alderson v. Gulf, C. & S. F. Ry. (Tex. Civ. App.), 23 S. W. 617.

Utah: Marks v. Cumber, 6 Utah, 419, 24 Pac. 528.

Vermont: Hoadley v. Watson, 45 Vt. 289.

Virginia: Borland v. Barrett, 76 Va. 128.

Wisconsin: Gilman v. Brown, 115 Wis. 1, 91 N. W. 227.

Wyoming: Cosgriff v. Miller, 10 Wyo. 190, 68 Pac. 206.

Ontario: Douglas v. Fox, 31 Up. Can. C. P. 140.

of the act.[135] Thus in Baltimore & Yorktown Turnpike Road
v. Boone,[136] where the company exacted illegal fare and the
plaintiff, on his refusal to pay, was forcibly ejected, it was held
that he could recover exemplary damages on the ground that
the company had been guilty of a criminal indifference to
the obligations of public duty, which amounted to malice;
and so generally exemplary damages may be given against
a carrier for ejection of a passenger in wanton disregard of
his rights,[137] or for deliberate refusal to stop a train on sig-
nal.[138] Thus also exemplary damages may be recovered for

[135] *United States:* Scott *v.* Donald, 165 U. S. 58, 89, 17 Sup. Ct. 265, 41 L. ed. 632; Berry *v.* Fletcher, 1 Dill. 67, Fed. Cas. No. 1,357.
Alabama: Devaughn *v.* Heath, 37 Ala. 595; Burns *v.* Campbell, 71 Ala. 271; Gambill *v.* Schmuck, 131 Ala. 321, 31 So. 604; Terry *v.* Williams, 148 Ala. 468, 41 So. 804; Garden *v.* Houston Bros., 163 Ala. 300, 50 So. 1030; Sloss-Sheffield S. & I. Co. *v.* O'Neal, 52 So. 953.
California: Dorsey *v.* Manlove, 14 Cal. 553.
Colorado: Gray *v.* Linton, 38 Colo. 175, 88 Pac. 749.
Illinois: Illinois C. R. R. *v.* Cobb, 68 Ill. 53; Becker *v.* Dupree, 75 Ill. 167; Chicago Co. *v.* Core, 223 Ill. 58, 79 N. E. 108, affirming s. c. 126 Ill. App. 272.
Maryland: Moore *v.* Schultz, 31 Md. 418; Smith *v.* Thompson, 55 Md. 5, 39 Am. Rep. 409.
Minnesota: Gardner *v.* Minea, 47 Minn. 295, 50 N. W. 199; Berg *v.* R. R., 96 Minn. 513, 105 N. W. 191.
Mississippi: Vicksburg R. R. *v.* Marlett, 78 Miss. 872, 29 So. 62.
New Jersey: Trainer *v.* Wolff, 58 N. J. L. 381, 33 Atl. 1051.
New York: Ives *v.* Humphreys, 1 E. D. Smith, 196.
North Carolina: Tucker *v.* Winders, 130 N. C. 147, 41 S. E. 8.
Oregon: Hamerlynck *v.* Banfield, 36 Ore. 436, 59 Pac. 712.

Pennsylvania: Reynolds *v.* Braithwaite, 131 Pa. 416, 18 Atl. 1110, 25 W. N. C. 269; Sperry *v.* Seidel, 218 Pa. 16, 66 Atl. 853; Greeney *v.* Pa. Co., 29 Pa. Super. Ct. 136.
South Carolina: Griffin *v.* Southern Ry., 65 S. C. 122, 43 S. E. 445; Harrison *v.* Western U. T. Co., 75 S. C. 267, 55 S. E. 450.
Tennessee: Telephone & Tel. Co. *v.* Shaw, 102 Tenn. 313, 52 S. W. 163.
Utah: Thirkfield *v.* Mountain View Cemetery Assoc., 12 Utah, 76, 41 Pac. 564.
Vermont: Newell *v.* Whitcher, 53 Vt. 589, 38 Am. Rep. 702.
[136] 45 Md. 344; Cowen *v.* Winters, 37 C. C. A. 628, 96 Fed. 929; Summerfield *v.* St. Louis Transit Co., 108 Mo. App. 718, 84 S. W. 172.
[137] *Alabama:* Birmingham Ry. L. & P. Co. *v.* Lee, 153 Ala. 79, 45 So. 164.
Georgia: Atlanta & W. P. R. R. *v.* Potts, 57 S. E. 686, 128 Ga. 397.
Illinois: Chicago C. T. Co. *v.* Mahoney, 230 Ill. 562, 82 N. E. 868.
Mississippi: Illinois Cent. R. R. *v.* Gortikov, 90 Miss. 787, 45 So. 363, 14 L. R. A. (N. S.) 464.
Missouri: Graham *v.* Pacific R. R., 66 Mo. 536.
South Carolina: Tant *v.* Southern Ry., 69 S. E. 158.
[138] Yazoo & M. V. R. R. *v.* Mitchell, 83 Miss. 179, 35 So. 339.

46

an unprovoked and causeless battery,[139] and for reckless
defamation.[140]

§ 367. For fraud.

If the injury was inflicted through fraud, this alone affords
ground for exemplary damages; [141] and so where the injury is
done with corrupt motives; [142] since in such a case the injury
is necessarily malicious.[143] Thus the New York Court of Appeals has held that exemplary damages may be recovered in
an action brought by the husband against a third party, who
by means of fraud has brought about his marriage with an
unchaste woman.[144]

§ 368. For gross negligence.

In Wilson v. Brett,[145] Rolfe, B., said that he could see no
difference between *negligence* and *gross* negligence; that it was
the same thing with the addition of a vituperative epithet:
and this observation has been quoted with approval in later

[139] *Mississippi:* Lochte v. Mitchell, 28 So. 877.
Missouri: Shelby v. Metropolitan St. Ry., 141 Mo. App. 514, 125 S. W. 1189.
New York: Conners v. Walsh, 131 N. Y. 590, 30 N. E. 59.
North Carolina: White v. Barnes, 112 N. C. 323, 16 S. E. 922.
Texas: Sargent v. Carnes, 84 Tex. 156, 19 S. W. 378.

[140] Morrison v. Press Co., 14 N. Y. Supp. 131; Ullrich v. N. Y. Press Co., 23 Misc. 168, 50 N. Y. Supp. 788; Waltenberg v. Bernhard, 26 Misc. 659, 56 N. Y. Supp. 396.

[141] *Alabama:* Burns v. Campbell, 71 Ala. 271.
California: Dorsey v. Manlove, 14 Cal. 553.
Illinois: Chicago T. & T. Co. v. Core, 223 Ill. 58, 79 N. E. 108 (affirming 126 Ill. App. 272); Batmann v. Cook, 120 Ill. App. 203.
Indiana: Moyer v. Gordon, 113 Ind. 282.
Kentucky: L. & N. R. R. v. Ballard,

85 Ky. 307; but see *contra*, Singleton v. Kennedy, 9 B. Mon. 222.
Maryland: Baltimore & O. R. R. v. Boyd, 63 Md. 325.
Minnesota: Gardner v. Minea, 47 Minn. 295, 50 N. W. 199.
Tennessee: Cox v. Crumley, 5 Lea, 529.
Texas: Smith v. Sherwood, 2 Tex. 460; Lesk v. Pollard, 1 W. & W. Ct. App., § 117; Western C. P. Co. v. Anderson, 45 Tex. Civ. App. 513, 101 S. W. 1061; Werkheiser P. M. Co. v. Langford, 51 Tex. Civ. App. 224, 115 S. W. 89 (but see Williams v. Detroit O. & C. Co., 52 Tex. Civ. App. 243, 114 S. W. 167).
Virginia: Fishburne v. Engledore, 91 Va. 548, 22 S. E. 354.

[142] *New York:* Ives v. Humphreys, 1 E. D. Smith, 196.
Texas: Smith v. Sherwood, 2 Tex. 460.

[143] See Crane v. Schaefer, 140 Ill. App. 647.

[144] Kujek v. Goldman, 150 N. Y. 176, 44 N. E. 773.

[145] 11 M. & W. 113.

cases.[146]   In Railroad Co. v.•Lockwood,[147] Mr. Justice Bradley, after stating the distinctions commonly drawn between slight, ordinary and gross negligence, said: "In each case the negligence, whatever epithet we give it, is failure to bestow the care and skill which the situation demands; and hence it is more strictly accurate perhaps to call it simply 'negligence.' And this seems to be the tendency of modern authorities." In these cases, however, the question was not considered with reference to exemplary damages, but to the amount of care due from the defendants in their respective situations. Whether little or great care is due, a dereliction from that amount is, in each case, negligence, and creates a *liability;* but one upon whom a duty is imposed may fall a little or far below the line dividing liability from impunity, and it is not improper, when the latter is the case, to apply the term "gross" to the defendant's dereliction, having reference, however, merely to the character of his acts and not to his liability. The allowance of exemplary damages depends upon the bad motive of the wrongdoer as exhibited by his acts. Where, therefore, the acts fall short of wilful misconduct, or that entire want of care which would raise the presumption of a conscious indifference to consequences, exemplary damages should not be given. Gross negligence, so far as *right of action* is concerned, does not differ from any other wrong. But as malice, though not making the act legally more wrongful, may be a ground for exemplary damages, so may grossness of negligence in the sense explained above; and the term so explained is open to no objection, and accords with its use in common speech. The epithet, it should be said, which corresponds to the *crassa* of the Roman law, is not properly vituperative but both descriptive and condemnatory.

Gross negligence, then, in the sense of culpable indifference to consequences, is usually held to be a good ground for the allowance of exemplary damages; [148] in this sense it is there-

146 *United States:* Milwaukee & St. Paul Ry. *v.* Arms, 91 U. S. 489, 23 L. ed. 374; and see Steamboat New World *v.* King, 16 How. 469, 14 L. ed. 467.

Missouri: McPheeters *v.* Hannibal & St. J. R. R., 45 Mo. 22.

England: Grill *v.* General I. S. C. Co., 12 Jur. (N. S.) 727.

147 17 Wall. 357, 383, 21 L. ed. 627.

148 *United States:* U. S. *v.* Taylor, 35 Fed. 484; Mandeville *v.* Courtright, 142 Fed. 97, 73 C.

fore such negligence as evinces a conscious indifference to consequences and only in this sense will it be a ground for exemplary damages; [149] as, for instance, where the owner of

C. A. 321, 6 L. R. A. (N. S.) 1003.
Alabama: Mobile & M. R. R. *v.* Ashcraft, 48 Ala. 15; Lienkauf *v.* Morris, 66 Ala. 406; Burns *v.* Campbell, 71 Ala. 271; Alabama Great Southern R. R. *v.* Arnold, 80 Ala. 600, 2 So. 337; Alabama Great Southern R. R. *v.* Hill, 93 Ala. 514, 9 So. 722, 30 Am. St. Rep. 65, 90 Ala. 71, 8 So. 90, 24 Am. St. Rep. 764, 9 L. R. A. 442; Richmond & D. R. R. *v.* Greenwood, 99 Ala. 501, 14 So. 495.
Arkansas: C. S. Ry. *v.* Steen, 42 Ark. 321; Texarkana Gas & Electric Light Co. *v.* Orr, 59 Ark. 215, 27 S. W. 6, 43 Am. St. Rep. 30.
Colorado: W. U. Tel. Co. *v.* Eyser, 2 Colo. 141.
Connecticut: Linsley *v.* Bushnell, 15 Conn. 225.
District of Columbia: Kilbourn *v.* Thompson, 1 McA. & M. 401.
Iowa: Frink *v.* Coe, 4 Greene, 555, 61 Am. Dec. 141; Cochran *v.* Miller, 13 Ia. 128.
Kansas: Hefley *v.* Baker, 19 Kan. 9; Southern Kansas R. R. *v.* Rice, 38 Kan. 398, 16 Pac. 817, 5 Am. St. Rep. 755.
Kentucky: Bowler *v.* Lane, 3 Met. 311; Fleet *v.* Hollenkemp, 13 B. Mon. 219; Kountz *v.* Brown, 16 B. Mon. 577; Hughes *v.* Louisville & N. R. R., 104 Ky. 768, 48 S. W. 671.
Maine: Wilkinson *v.* Drew, 75 Me. 360.
Maryland: Atlantic & G. C. C. Coal Co. *v.* Maryland C. Co., 62 Md. 135.
Mississippi: Vicksburg & J. R. R. *v.* Patton, 31 Miss. 156; Memphis & C. R. R. *v.* Whitfield, 44 Miss. 466; Wilson *v.* New Orleans, etc., R. R., 63 Miss. 352; Keystone L. & I. Co. *v.* McGrath, 21 So. 301; R. R. *v.* Roberts, 88 Miss. 80, 40 So. 481.

New Hampshire: Hopkins *v.* A. & St. L. R. R., 36 N. H. 9, 72 Am. Dec. 287; Taylor *v.* G. T. Ry., 48 N. H. 304.
New York: Caldwell *v.* N. J. S. B. Co., 47 N. Y. 282.
Pennsylvania: Pittsburgh, C. & S. L. Ry. *v.* Lyon, 123 Pa. 140, 000 Atl. 000.
South Carolina: Hart *v.* Charlotte C. & A. R. R., 33 S. C. 427, 12 S. E. 9, 10 L. R. A. 794; Brasington *v.* South Bound R. R., 62 S. C. 325, 40 S. E. 665; Boyd *v.* Blue Ridge Ry., 65 S. C. 326, 43 S. E. 817; Thompson *v.* Seaboard A. L. Ry., 81 S. C. 333, 62 S. E. 396, 20 L. R. A. (N. S.) 426.
Tennessee: Byram *v.* McGuire, 3 Head, 530; Cox *v.* Crumley, 5 Lea, 529; Cumberland T. & T. Co. *v.* Poston, 94 Tenn. 696, 30 S. W. 1040; American Lead Pencil Co. *v.* Davis, 108 Tenn. 251, 256, 67 S. W. 864.
Texas: Smith *v.* Sherwood, 2 Tex. 460; Kolb *v.* Bankhead, 18 Tex. 228; Southern C. P. & M. Co. *v.* Bradley, 52 Tex. 587; San Antonio & A. P. Ry. *v.* Grier, 20 Tex. Civ. App. 148, 49 S. W. 148.
England: Emblen *v.* Myers, 6 H. & N. 54.
Contra, under the California Code: Yerian *v.* Linkletter, 80 Cal. 135.

[149] *United States:* Milwaukee & St. P. Ry. *v.* Arms, 91 U. S. 489, 23 L. ed. 374.
Alabama: Lienkauf *v.* Morris, 60 Ala. 406; Alabama G. S. R. R. *v.* Hill, 90 Ala. 71, 24 Am. St. Rep. 764, 8 So. 9, 9 L. R. A. 442.
Arkansas: Arkansas & L. Ry. *v.* Stroude, 77 Ark. 109, 91 S. W. 18.
California: Moody *v.* McDonald, 4 Cal. 297.
Florida: Florida R. & N. Co. *v.* Webster, 25 Fla. 394, 419, 5 So. 714.
Illinois: Kolb *v.* O'Brien, 86 Ill. 210.

a furious dog knowingly allowed it to run at large,[150] or where a libel was recklessly published.[151] Mere negligence, even though it may be called gross, without the element of conscious disregard of consequences, is not enough to justify the infliction of exemplary damages.[152] In Kentucky it has been intimated that gross negligence alone is not enough to justify

Indiana: Louisville N. A. & C. Ry. *v.* Shanks, 94 Ind. 598.

Kansas: Kansas P. Ry. *v.* Little, 19 Kan. 267; Kansas City, F. S. & G. R. R. *v.* Kier, 41 Kan. 661, 671, 21 Pac. 770, 13 Am. St. Rep. 311; Atchison, T. & S. F. Ry. *v.* Ringle, 71 Kan. 839, 80 Pac. 43.

Kentucky: Kentucky C. R. R. *v.* Dills, 4 Bush, 593; Jacobs *v.* L. & N. R. R., 10 Bush, 263.

Maryland: Bannon *v.* B. & O. R. R., 24 Md. 108.

Mississippi: Chicago, St. L. & N. O. R. R. *v.* Scurr, 59 Miss. 456.

New Hampshire: Hopkins *v.* Atlantic & S. L. R. R., 36 N. H. 9, 72 Am. Dec. 287.

New York: Cleghorn *v.* N. Y. C. & H. R. R. R., 56 N. Y. 44, 15 Am. Rep. 375; Fisher *v.* Met. El. Ry., 34 Hun, 433.

Oklahoma: Atchison, T. & S. F. R. R. *v.* Chamberlain, 4 Okla. 542, 46 Pac. 499.

South Carolina: Watts *v.* South Bound R. R., 60 S. C. 67, 38 S. E. 240; Southern Ry. *v.* Proctor, 61 S. C. 189, 39 S. E. 351; Boyd *v.* Seaboard Air Line Ry., 67 S. C. 218, 45 S. E. 186; Webb *v.* Atlantic C. L. R. R., 76 S. C. 193, 56 S. E. 954, 9 L. R. A. (N. S.) 1218.

Tennessee: East T. V. & G. Ry. *v.* Lee, 90 Tenn. 570, 18 S. W. 268.

Texas: Cotton Press Co. *v.* Bradley, 52 Tex. 587; Missouri Pac. Ry. *v.* Shuford, 72 Tex. 165, 10 S. W. 408; Foley *v.* Northrup, 47 Tex. Civ. App. 277, 105 S. W. 229.

Wisconsin: Pickett *v.* Crook, 20 Wis. 358.

[150] *Missouri:* Von Fragstein *v.* Windler, 2 Mo. App. 598.

Wisconsin: Meibus *v.* Dodge, 38 Wis. 300.

[151] *United States:* Malloy *v.* Bennett, 15 Fed. 371; Press Pub. Co. *v.* McDonald, 63 Fed. 238, 11 C. C. A. 155, 26 L. R. A. 53; Times Pub. Co. *v.* Carlisle, 94 Fed. 762, 36 C. C. A. 475; Duke *v.* Morning Journal Assoc., 120 Fed. 860.

Missouri: Lanius *v.* Druggist Pub. Co., 20 Mo. App. 12.

New York: Karwowski *v.* Pitass, 20 App. Div. 118, 46 N. Y. Supp. 691; Young *v.* Fox, 26 App. Div. 261, 49 N. Y. Supp. 634; Grant *v.* Herald Co., 42 App. Div. 354, 59 N. Y. Supp. 84; McMahon *v.* New York News Pub. Co., 51 App. Div. 488, 64 N. Y. Supp. 713; O'Brien *v.* Bennett, 59 App. Div. 623, 69 N. Y. Supp. 298; Saunders *v.* Post-Standard Co., 107 App. Div. 84, 94 N. Y. Supp. 993; Smith *v.* Matthews, 6 Misc. 162, 27 N. Y. Supp. 763.

[152] *Alabama:* Alabama G. S. R. R. *v.* Arnold, 84 Ala. 159, 5 Am. St. Rep. 354, 4 So. 359; Birmingham Ry. L. & P. Co. *v.* Wise, 149 Ala. 492, 42 So. 821.

Arkansas: Harris Lumber Co. *v.* Morris, 96 S. W. 1067, 80 Ark. 260; St. Louis, I. M. & S. Ry. *v.* Dysart, 89 Ark. 261, 116 S. W. 224; Greer *v.* White, 90 Ark. 117, 118 S. W. 258.

California: Wardrobe *v.* California Stage Co., 7 Cal. 118, 68 Am. Dec. 231; Spencer *v.* San Francisco Brick Co., 4 Cal. App. 265, 89 Pac. 851.

Georgia: Southern Ry. *v.* Davis, 127 Ga. 89, 65 S. E. 131.

Illinois: Chicago *v.* Martin, 49 Ill. 241, 95 Am. Dec. 590.

exemplary damages [153] unless human life is at stake,[154] as it would be in every case of gross neglect of the safety of passengers by a railroad company.[155]

§ 369. Circumstances preventing the allowance of exemplary damages.

As the ground of allowing exemplary damages is evil motive or wantonness, or aggravation, all circumstances showing the absence of these may be proved, to prevent the allowance of such damages: and if they show that the defendant's malice was slight, they may be proved to mitigate exemplary damages. Proof of such circumstances for either purpose will be more fully discussed later.[156]

§ 370. Exemplary damages not allowed in actions of contract.

Ordinarily exemplary damages are allowed only in actions of tort. In actions of contract, exemplary damages cannot be recovered.[157] An exception is the action for breach of promise

---

Kentucky: Henderson City Ry. *v.* Lockett, 98 S. W. 303, 30 Ky. L. Rep. 321; Southern Ry. *v.* Lee, 101 S. W. 307, 30 Ky. L. Rep. 1360, 10 L. R. A. (N. S.) 837; Louisville & N. R. R. *v.* Mount, 101 S. W. 1182, 31 Ky. L. Rep. 210.

Mississippi: Cumberland T. & T. Co. *v.* Allen, 89 Miss. 832, 42 So. 666; St. Louis & S. F. R. R. *v.* Garner, 51 So. 273.

South Carolina: Moore *v.* Cummings, 69 S. E. 154.

[153] McHenry Coal Co. *v.* Sneddon, 98 Ky. 684, 34 S. W. 288, 17 Ky. L. Rep. 1261; Ill. Cent. R. R. *v.* Lence, 100 S. W. 215, 30 Ky. L. Rep. 988; National Casket Co. *v.* Powar, 137 Ky. 156, 125 S. W. 279.

[154] Louisville & N. R. R. *v.* Kingman, 18 Ky. L. Rep. 82, 35 S. W. 264; Chesapeake & O. Ry. *v.* Satterfield, 100 S. W. 844, 30 Ky. L. Rep. 1168; Cleveland *v.* South C. & C. S. Ry., 30 Ky. L. Rep. 1072, 100 S. W. 283, 11 L. R. A. (N. S.) 853; Louisville & N. R. R. *v.*

Schroader, 113 S. W. 874; Buford *v.* Hopewell, 131 S. W. 502.

[155] Louisville & N. R. R. *v.* Earl, 94 Ky. 368, 22 S. W. 607; Louisville & N. R. R. *v.* Greer, 16 Ky. L. Rep. 667, 29 S. W. 337; Southern Ry. *v.* Barr, 55 S. W. 900, 12 Ky. L. Rep. 1615; Illinois Cent. R. R. *v.* Stewart, 63 S. W. 596, 23 Ky. L. Rep. 637; Louisville & N. R. R. *v.* Simpson, 64 S. W. 733, 23 Ky. L. Rep. 1044; Smith *v.* Middleton, 23 Ky. L. Rep. 2010, 66 S. W. 388; Louisville St. Ry. *v.* Brownfield, 29 Ky. L. Rep. 1097, 96 S. W. 912; Southern Ry. *v.* Lee, 101 S. W. 307, 30 Ky. L. Rep. 1360, 10 L. R. A. (N. S.) 837; Louisville & N. R. R. *v.* Marshall, 110 S. W. 885, 33 Ky. L. Rep. 639; Lexington Ry. *v.* Johnson, 139 Ky. 323, 122 S. W. 830.

[156] §§ 383–386.

[157] *United States:* Baumgarten *v.* Alliance Assur. Co., 159 Fed. 275.

Georgia: Ford *v.* Fargason, 120 Ga. 708, 48 S. E. 180; Hadden *v.* Southern Messenger Service, 69 S. E. 480.

of marriage. In that action it is held that if the engagement to marry was broken with circumstances of abruptness and humiliation, exemplary damages may be recovered.[158] It has been held in some cases that if the condition of a bond given in pursuance of a statute is broken by the commission of a tort, such as would be a proper cause for exemplary damages, such damages may be recovered in an action on the bond.[159] This is contrary, however, to the current of authority, which is to the effect that only compensatory damages can be recovered in an action on a statutory bond.[160]

§ 371. Not recoverable in equity.

Where a court of equity has power to award damages, it cannot go beyond compensation; by applying to such a court, the complainant waives all claim to exemplary damages.[161]

§ 371a. In actions against public-service companies.

Actions against public-service companies, even when they

Kentucky: Cumberland T. & T. Co. v. Cartwright C. T. Co., 128 Ky. 395, 108 S. W. 875.

Missouri: Trout v. Watkins L. & U. Co., 130 S. W. 136.

North Carolina: Richardson v. Wilmington & W. R. R., 126 N. C. 100, 35 S. E. 235.

Texas: Hooks v. Fitzenreiter, 76 Tex. 277, 13 S. W. 230; Southwestern T. & T. Co. v. Luckett (Tex. Civ. App.), 127 S. W. 856.

Canada: Guildford v. Anglo-French S. S. Co., 9 Can. 303.

It is immaterial that under the present system of pleading the action may be put in the form of an action of tort, if it arises out of breach of contract. Richardson v. Wilmington & W. R. R., 126 N. C. 100, 35 S. E. 235.

But exemplary damages may be recovered in South Carolina for a breach of contract if it is accompanied by circumstances of fraud or hardship. Welborn v. Dixon, 70 S. C. 108, 120, 49 S. E. 232; Prince v. State M. L. I. Co., 77 S. C. 187, 57 S. E. 766.

[158] McPherson v. Ryan, 59 Mich. 33;

Johnson v. Jenkins, 24 N. Y. 252; Thorn v. Knapp, 42 N. Y. 474; Chellis v. Chapman, 125 N. Y. 214, 26 N. E. 308, 11 L. R. A. 784; Jacobs v. Sire, 4 Misc. 398, 23 N. Y. Supp. 1063.

[159] *Alabama:* Lloyd v. Hamilton, 33 Ala. 235.

Iowa: Richmond v. Shickler, 57 Ia. 486.

Tennessee: Renkert v. Elliott, 11 Lea, 235.

Texas: Gross v. Hays, 73 Tex. 515, 11 S. W. 523.

Washington: Levy v. Fleischner, 12 Wash. 15, 40 Pac. 384.

[160] *Illinois:* Cobb v. People, 84 Ill. 511.

Kentucky: Johnson v. Williams, 23 Ky. L. Rep. 658, 63 S. W. 759.

South Carolina: McClendon v. Wells, 20 S. C. 514.

The sureties at least cannot be held for such damages:

Minnesota: North v. Johnson, 58 Minn. 242, 59 N. W. 1012.

Texas: Emerson v. Skidmore, 7 Tex. Civ. App. 641, 25 S. W. 671.

[161] *New York:* Witkop & Holmes Co.

are based on a failure to perform a duty and are therefor similar to actions for breach of contract, have a sufficient element of tortious wrongdoing to justify the infliction of exemplary damages is a proper case.[162] Therefore exemplary damages may be recovered for a breach of duty by a carrier or a telegraph company or other public-service company, whether the injury consists in the actual infliction of personal harm [163] or in the mere failure to perform a legal duty.[164]

§ 372. In actions for personal injury.

Exemplary damages may be recovered, in the proper case, in an action for assault and battery,[165] false imprison-

v. Great A. & P. T. Co. (Misc.), 124 N. Y. Supp. 956.

South Carolina: Bird v. W. & M. R. R., 8 Rich. Eq. 46.

[162] Trout v. Watkins L. & U. Co., 130 S. W. 136.

[163] See § 372.

[164] Delay in carrying passenger: Black v. Charlestown & W. C. Ry. (S. C.), 69 S. E. 230.

Wrongfully disconnecting plaintiff's premises from water mains: Vicksburg W. W. Co. v. Dutton (Miss.), 53 So. 537.

Delay in delivering telegram: *Mississippi:* Steinberger v. Western U. T. Co., 52 So. 691.

South Carolina (statutory): Bolton v. Western U. T. Co., 76 S. C. 529, 57 S. E. 543; Butler v. Western U. T. Co., 77 S. C. 148, 57 S. E. 757; Todd v. Western U. T. Co., 77 S. C. 522, 58 S. E. 433; Glover v. Western U. Tel. Co., 78 S. C. 502, 59 S. E. 526; Balderston v. Western U. Tel. Co., 79 S. C. 160, 60 S. E. 435; Sullivan v. Western U. T. Co., 82 S. C. 569, 64 S. E. 752; Strauss v. Postal T. C. Co., 83 S. C. 22, 64 S. E. 913; McIntosh v. Augusta & A. R. R., 69 S. E. 159, 30 L. R. A. (N. S.) 889.

Failure to wake, and haste in putting out, a person in a sleeping-car: Pullman Co. v. Lutz, 154 Ala. 517, 45 So. 675, 14 L. R. A. (N. S.) 907.

[165] *Arkansas:* Barlow v. Lowder, 35 Ark. 492.

California: Wade v. Thayer, 40 Cal. 578; Bundy v. Maginness, 76 Cal. 532.

Connecticut: Welch v. Durand, 36 Conn. 182, 4 Am. Rep. 55; Shupack v. Gordon, 79 Conn. 298, 64 Atl. 740; Bogudsky v. Backes, 76 Atl. 540.

Delaware: Watson v. Hastings, 1 Pennew. 47, 39 Atl. 587.

Florida: Smith v. Bagwell, 19 Fla. 117.

Hawaii: Coffin v. Spencer, 2 Hawaii, 23.

Illinois: McNamara v. King, 7 Ill. 432; Ously v. Hardin, 23 Ill. 403; Reeder v. Purdy, 48 Ill. 261; Mitchell v. Robinson, 72 Ill. 382; Drohn v. Brewer, 77 Ill. 280; Harreson v. Ely, 120 Ill. 83; Cummins v. Crawford, 88 Ill. 312, 30 Am. Rep. 558; Amann v. Chicago C. T. Co., 243 Ill. 263, 90 N. E. 673.

Iowa: Hendrickson v. Kingsbury, 21 Ia. 379; Ward v. Ward, 41 Ia. 686; White v. Spangler, 68 Ia, 222, 26 N. W. 85; Root v. Sturdivant, 70 Ia. 55, 29 N. W. 802.

Kansas: Titus v. Corkins, 21 Kan. 722.

Kentucky: Slater v. Sherman, 5 Bush, 206.

Louisiana: Scheen v. Poland, 34 La. Ann. 1107; Webb v. Rothschild, 49 La. Ann. 244, 21 So. 258; Turnbow v. Wimberly, 106 La. 259, 30 So. 747.

ment,[166] malicious prosecution,[167] or other injury to the person, as where the plaintiff was wrongfully and wantonly ejected from a railroad train.[168] So it has been held that a passenger may recover exemplary damages, when he is wilfully carried beyond his station,[169] or is capriciously refused passage.[170] An

Maine: Pike *v.* Dilling, 48 Me. 539; Webb *v.* Gilman, 80 Me. 177, 13 Atl. 688.

Maryland: Baltimore & Yorktown Turnpike *v.* Boone, 45 Md. 344.

Michigan: Elliott *v.* Van Buren, 33 Mich. 49; Fay *v.* Swan, 44 Mich. 544, 7 N. W. 215.

Missouri: Green *v.* Craig, 47 Mo. 90.

New Hampshire: Towle *v.* Blake, 48 N. H. 92.

New York: Cook *v.* Ellis, 6 Hill, 466; Clayton *v.* Keeler, 18 Misc. 488, 42 N. Y. Supp. 1051.

North Carolina: Causee *v.* Anders, 20 N. C. 320; Louder *v.* Hinson, 49 N. C. (4 Jones L.) 369.

Pennsylvania: Porter *v.* Seiler, 23 Pa. 424, 67 Am. Dec. 341.

Vermont: Earl *v.* Tupper, 45 Vt. 275; Newell *v.* Whitcher, 53 Vt. 589, 38 Am. Rep. 703.

Virginia: Borland *v.* Barrett, 76 Va. 128.

West Virginia: Smith *v.* Fahey, 63 W. Va. 346, 60 S. E. 250.

Wisconsin: McWilliams *v.* Bragg, 3 Wis. 424; Shay *v.* Thompson, 59 Wis. 540; Lamb *v.* Stone, 95 Wis. 254, 70 N. W. 72.

[166] *Colorado:* McConathy *v.* Deck, 34 Colo. 461, 83 Pac. 135, 4 L. R. A. (N. S.) 358.

North Carolina: Bradley *v.* Morris, Busbee, 395.

Pennsylvania: McCarthy *v.* DeArmit, 99 Pa. 63; McAleer *v.* Good, 216 Pa. 473, 65 Atl. 934, 10 L. R. A. (N. S.) 303.

Texas: Gold *v.* Campbell (Tex. Civ. App.), 117 S. W. 463.

Canada: Gingras *v.* Desilets, Cass.

Can. Dig. 116; Clissold *v.* Machell, 26 Up. Can. Q. B. 422.

England: Huckle *v.* Money, 2 Wils. 205.

[167] *Alabama:* Donnell *v.* Jones, 13 Ala. 490.

Georgia: Coleman *v.* Allen, 79 Ga. 637 (by code).

Iowa: Parkhurst *v.* Masteller, 57 Ia. 474.

Maryland: McWilliams *v.* Hoban, 42 Md. 56.

Minnesota: Peck *v.* Small, 35 Minn. 465.

Wisconsin: Winn *v.* Peckham, 42 Wis. 493; Spear *v.* Hiles, 67 Wis. 350.

[168] *Arkansas:* Little Rock R. & E. Co. *v.* Goerner, 80 Ark. 158, 95 S. W. 1007, 7 L. R. A. (N. S.) 97.

Connecticut: Dalton *v.* Beers, 38 Conn. 529.

Georgia: Georgia R. R. *v.* Olds, 77 Ga. 673.

Indiana (by code): Jeffersonville R. R. *v.* Rogers, 38 Ind. 116.

Maryland: Philadelphia W. & B. R. R. *v.* Larkin, 47 Md. 155.

Mississippi: Illinois Cent. Ry. *v.* Reid, 93 Miss. 458, 46 So. 146, 17 L. R. A. (N. S.) 344.

Missouri: Leyser *v.* Chicago B. & Q. R. R., 138 Mo. App. 34, 119 S. W. 1068.

North Carolina: Knowles *v.* N. S. R. R., 102 N. C. 59.

[169] *Alabama:* Alabama G. S. R. R. *v.* Sellers, 93 Ala. 9, 9 So. 375, 30 Am. St. Rep. 17.

Mississippi: Higgins *v.* L. N. O. & T. R. R., 64 Miss. 80; Dorrah *v.* I. C. R. R., 65 Miss. 14.

[170] Heirn *v.* McCaughan, 32 Miss. 17, 66 Am. Dec. 588.

action against an attorney for giving plaintiff false information that he had secured her a divorce, by reason of which plaintiff was led to marry again, thus contracting a bigamous marriage, was held a proper case for exemplary damages.[171]

§ 373. For injury to real estate.

Exemplary damages may in a proper case be recovered for a wilful injury to land; as for a malicious trespass [172] or flowing

[171] Hill v. Montgomery, 84 Ill. App. 300.

[172] *United States:* U. S. v. Taylor, 35 Fed. 484.

Alabama: Devaughn v. Heath, 37 Ala. 595; Coleman v. Pepper, 159 Ala. 310, 49 So. 310; Southern Ry. v. McEntire, 53 So. 158.

Arkansas: Clark v. Bales, 15 Ark. 452.

California: Waters v. Dumas, 75 Cal. 563 (by code).

Connecticut: Curtiss v. Hoyt, 19 Conn. 154.

Georgia: Shores v. Brooks, 81 Ga. 468.

Illinois: Cutler v. Smith, 57 Ill. 252; Chicago & I. R. R. v. Baker, 73 Ill. 316; Koester v. Cowan, 37 Ill. App. 252.

Iowa: Keirnan v. Heaton, 69 Ia. 136.

Kansas: Hefley v. Baker, 19 Kan. 9.

Kentucky: Jennings v. Maddox, 8 B. Mon. 430; Kentucky M. Ry. v. Stump, 12 Ky. L. Rep. 316; Louisville Gas Co. v. Kentucky Heating Co., 33 Ky. L. Rep. 912, 111 S. W. 374 (wasting natural gas so as to prevent plaintiff from getting it); Wilcox v. Alley, 140 Ky. 187, 130 S. W. 1115.

Louisiana: Ball v. Levin, 48 La. Ann. 359, 19 So. 118.

Maine: Ames v. Hilton, 70 Me. 36.

Michigan: Briggs v. Milburn, 40 Mich. 512.

Minnesota: Craig v. Cook, 28 Minn. 232.

Mississippi: Cumberland T. & T.

Co. v. Cassedy, 78 Miss. 666, 29 So. 762.

Missouri: Parker v. Shackelford, 61 Mo. 68; Newman v. St. L. & I. M. R. R., 2 Mo. App. 402.

New Hampshire: Perkins v. Towle, 43 N. H. 220, 80 Am. Dec. 149.

New Jersey: Winter v. Peterson, 24 N. J. L. 524; Trainer v. Wolff, 58 N. J. L. 381, 33 Atl. 1051; Miller v. Rambo, 73 N. J. L. 726, 64 Atl. 1053.

New York: Allaback v. Utt, 51 N. Y. 651; Steenburgh v. McRorie, 60 Misc. 510, 113 N. Y. Supp. 1118.

North Carolina: Brame v. Clark, 148 N. C. 364, 62 S. E. 418 (entry with purpose of seducing plaintiff's wife).

Oregon: Day v. Holland, 15 Ore. 464 (*semble*).

Pennsylvania: Kennedy v. Erdway, 150 Pa. 425, 24 Atl. 643; Huling v. Henderson, 161 Pa. 553, 29 Atl. 276.

South Carolina: Windham v. Rhame, 11 Rich. L. 283; Jefcoat v. Knotts, 11 Rich. L. 649; Greenville & C. R. R. v. Partlow, 14 Rich. L. 237; Dobson v. Postal T. C. Co., 79 S. C. 429, 60 S. E. 948.

Tennessee: Burson v. Cox, 6 Baxt. 360; Cox v. Crumley, 5 Lea, 529.

Texas: Cook v. Garza, 9 Tex. 358.

Vermont: Ellsworth v. Potter, 41 Vt. 685; Burnham v. Jenness, 54 Vt. 272; Camp v. Camp, 59 Vt. 667.

Wisconsin: Koenigs v. Jung, 73 Wis. 178.

England: Brewer v. Dew, 11 M. & W. 625.

of land.[173] Such damages were allowed for maliciously setting fire to the plaintiff's house; [174] in an action for damage to hedges; [175] in an action for defacing the walls and breaking the windows of the plaintiff's house; [176] and in an action for cutting and carrying away timber and hauling away sand; [177] so also in an action of forcible entry,[178] an action for entering a house to search without a search-warrant,[179] and an action by a tenant for injury to the premises by the landlord.[180] And in an action on the case for taking down plaintiff's furnace and leaving it down, by which he was injured, exemplary damages may be recovered in a proper case.[181] So exemplary damages may in a proper case be allowed for nuisance [182] or other injury to real estate; [183] and for interference with the exercise of the right of burial in land.[184]

§ 373a. For injury to personal property.

Exemplary damages may in a proper case be recovered for an injury to personal property. So exemplary damages have been allowed for a wrongful levy or attachment of personal property,[185] for wrongfully suing out an attachment writ,[186] or for a wrongful distraint; [187] for the vexatious or oppressive de-

---

[173] *Alabama:* Hughes *v.* Anderson, 68 Ala. 280.

Pennsylvania: Martin *v.* Riddle, 26 Pa. 415, *n.*

[174] Smalley *v.* Smalley, 81 Ill. 70.

[175] Parker *v.* Shackelford, 61 Mo. 68.

[176] Weston *v.* Gravlin, 49 Vt. 507.

[177] Rosser *v.* Bunn, 66 Ala. 89.

[178] Mosseller *v.* Deaver, 106 N. C. 494.

[179] McClurg *v.* Brenton, 123 Ia. 368, 98 N. W. 881.

[180] Hysore *v.* Quigley, 9 Houst. (Del.) 348, 32 Atl. 960.

[181] Vogel *v.* McAuliffe, 18 R. I. 791, 13 Atl. 1.

[182] Yazoo & M. V. R. R. *v.* Sanders, 87 Miss. 607, 40 So. 163, 3 L. R. A. (N. S.) 1119.

[183] Kentucky H. Co. *v.* Hood, 133 Ky. 383, 118 S. W. 337, 22 L. R. A. (N. S.) 588.

[184] Wright *v.* Hollywood Cemetery Corp., 112 Ga. 884, 38 S. E. 94.

[185] *Alabama:* Jefferson County Savings Bank *v.* Eborn, 84 Ala. 529.

Dakota: Bates *v.* Callender, 3 Dak. 256.

Illinois: Sherman *v.* Dutch, 16 Ill. 283.

Kansas: Western News Co. *v.* Wilmarth, 33 Kan. 510, 6 Pac. 786.

Minnesota: Lynd *v.* Picket, 7 Minn. 184.

Missouri: Carson *v.* Smith, 133 Mo. 606, 34 S. W. 855.

Pennsylvania: Nagle *v.* Mullison, 34 Pa. 48.

[186] *Alabama:* Floyd *v.* Hamilton, 33 Ala. 235.

Illinois: Lawrence *v.* Hagerman, 56 Ill. 68.

Kansas: Morris *v.* Shew, 29 Kan. 661.

[187] *Illinois:* Clevenger *v.* Dunaway, 84 Ill. 367.

Mississippi: Briscoe *v.* McElween, 43 Miss. 556.

tention of personal property,[188] as for instance the wanton refusal of a carrier to deliver goods seasonably; [189] for the malicious taking of personal property or injury to it,[190] as for the killing of a slave [191] or domestic animal.[192] So in an action for wrongful seizure and sale of mortgaged property by a mortgagee, exemplary damages may be recovered; [193] and they have also been allowed for an unlawful interference with trade.[194]

§ 374. In actions of trover.

In actions of trover the jury may go beyond the value and give exemplary damages when there has been outrage in the taking, or vexation or oppression in the detention.[195]

§ 375. Of replevin.

In New York and Pennsylvania, it has been declared that if the writ of replevin be sued out fraudulently, vexatiously, or

[188] Taylor v. Morgan, 3 Watts, 333.

[189] Silver v. Kent, 60 Miss. 124.

[190] *California:* Rubio Canon Land & Water Ass'n v. Everett, 154 Cal. 29, 96 Pac. 811.

Connecticut: Dibble v. Morris, 26 Conn. 416.

Delaware: Hysore v. Quigley, 9 Houst. 348, 32 Atl. 960.

Illinois: Bull v. Griswold, 19 Ill. 631; Johnson v. Camp, 51 Ill. 219.

Kentucky: Kountz v. Brown, 16 B. Mon. 577.

Maryland: Schindel v. Schindel, 12 Md. 108; Snively v. Fahnestock, 18 Md. 391; Young v. Mertens, 27 Md. 114.

New York: Smalling v. Jackson, 133 App. Div. 382, 117 N. Y. Supp. 268.

[191] Polk v. Fancher, 1 Head (Tenn.), 336.

[192] *Alabama:* Parker v. Mise, 27 Ala. 480.

Illinois: Dean v. Blackwell, 18 Ill. 336; Pearson v. Zehr, 138 Ill. 48, 29 N. E. 854, 32 Am. St. Rep. 113.

New York: Woert v. Jenkins, 14 Johns. 352.

Texas: Cole v. Tucker, 6 Tex. 266; Champion v. Vincent, 20 Tex. 811.

[193] Casey v. Ballou Banking Co., 98 Iowa, 107, 67 N. W. 98.

[194] Dunshee v. Standard Oil Co. (Ia.), 126 N. W. 342.

But in Lampert v. Judge & Dolph Drug Co., 119 Mo. App. 693, 100 S. W. 659, it was held that exemplary damages would not be allowed for infringement of a trade-mark.

[195] *Minnesota:* Vine v. Casmey, 86 Minn. 74, 90 N. W. 158 (*semble*).

Pennsylvania: Dennis v. Barber, 6 S. & R. 420; Harger v. McMains, 4 Watts, 418.

Texas: Frank v. Tatum (Tex. Civ. App.), 26 S. W. 900; Tignor v. Toney, 13 Tex. Civ. App. 518, 35 S. W. 881.

But see *contra*, that exemplary damages cannot be given in trover, Peterson v. Gresham, 25 Ark. 380; Berry v. Vantries, 12 S. & R. (Pa.) 89. In Jones v. Rahilly, 16 Minn. 320, it was said that exemplary damages cannot be given for a wilful withholding of property that came rightfully into the defendant's possession; but they were allowed in such a case in Silver v. Kent, 60 Miss. 124; Taylor v. Morgan, 3 Watts (Pa.), 333.

maliciously, or the defendant's proceedings be of the same character, the jury may give exemplary damages against either plaintiff or defendant, as in cases of wilful trespass.[196] And the same rule should apply in actions of detinue.[197]

§ 376. For loss of service.

Exemplary damages have been allowed in actions for loss of service either through enticement [198] or seduction; [199] and in actions for criminal conversation [200] and for harboring the plaintiff's wife [201] or enticing away the plaintiff's husband.[202] It has been held that exemplary damages cannot be recovered in an action for loss of service caused by physical injury to a

[196] *California:* Arzaga *v.* Villalba, 85 Cal. 191, 24 Pac. 656.

Dakota: Holt *v.* Van Eps, 1 Dak. 206.

Mississippi: Whitfield *v.* Whitfield, 40 Miss. 352 (*semble*).

New York: Cable *v.* Dakin, 20 Wend. 172; Brizsee *v.* Maybee, 21 Wend. 144.

Pennsylvania: McCabe *v.* Morehead, 1 W. & S. 513; McDonald *v.* Scaife, 11 Pa. 381; Schofield *v.* Ferrers, 46 Pa. 438; Herdic *v.* Young, 55 Pa. 176.

South Carolina: Lander *v.* Ware, 1 Strob. 15.

Wyoming: Knight *v.* Beckwith Commercial Co., 6 Wyo. 500, 46 Pac. 1094 (*semble*).

It is otherwise in this action in *Illinois:* Butler *v.* Mehrling, 15 Ill. 488; and *Indiana:* Hotchkiss *v.* Jones, 4 Ind. 260. And the mere fact that the wrongdoer acted wilfully does not justify such damages. There must be circumstances of fraud, malice, or wanton injury to entitle the plaintiff to recover them. Single *v.* Schneider, 30 Wis. 570.

[197] Whitfield *v.* Whitfield, 40 Miss. 352 (*semble*); but *contra*, McDonald *v.* Norton, 72 Ia. 652.

In *South Carolina* it has been held that in the statutory action for recovery of specific personal property (differing from the common-law action of replevin) no exemplary damages can

be recovered: Tittle *v.* Kennedy, 71 S. C. 1, 50 S. E. 544.

[198] *Georgia:* Smith *v.* Goodman, 75 Ga. 198.

Kentucky: Tyson *v.* Ewing, 3 J. J. Marsh. 185.

New Hampshire: Bixby *v.* Dunlap, 56 N. H. 456.

New Jersey: Magee *v.* Holland, 27 N. J. L. 86.

[199] *Delaware:* Robinson *v.* Burton, 5 Harr. 335.

Illinois: Grable *v.* Margrave, 4 Ill. 372.

Iowa: Stevenson *v.* Belknap, 6 Ia. 97.

Minnesota: Fox *v.* Stevens, 13 Minn. 272.

New York: Lawyer *v.* Fritcher, 130 N. Y. 239, 29 N. E. 267, 27 Am. St. Rep. 521, 14 L. R. A. 700.

Oregon: Anderson *v.* Aupperle, 51 Ore. 556, 95 Pac. 330.

Wisconsin: Lavery *v.* Crooke, 52 Wis. 612.

[200] *Michigan:* Johnston *v.* Disbrow, 47 Mich. 59.

Pennsylvania: Matheis *v.* Mazet, 164 Pa. 580, 30 Atl. 434.

[201] Johnson *v.* Allen, 100 N. C. 131.

[202] *Colorado:* Williams *v.* Williams, 20 Colo. 51, 37 Pac. 614.

Kentucky: Scott *v.* O'Brien, 129 Ky. 1, 110 S. W. 260, 16 L. R. A. (N. S.) 742.

child or servant. They are only given if the injured child or servant brings the action in his own name.[203]

§ 377. Exemplary damages for defamation.

In actions for libel or slander exemplary damages may be given in the proper case.[204] The evil intent that justifies exemplary damages in these cases is usually express malice,[205] of which the falsity of the defamation is evidence;[206] but it is

[203] *Georgia:* Augusta Factory *v.* Barnes, 72 Ga. 217, 53 Am. Rep. 838.

Louisiana: Black *v.* C. R. R., 10 La. Ann. 33.

Michigan: Hyatt *v.* Adams, 16 Mich. 180 (*semble*).

New York: Whitney *v.* Hitchcock, 4 Den. 461.

But *contra*, Klingman *v.* Holmes, 54 Mo. 304.

[204] *United States:* Philadelphia, W. & B. R. R. *v.* Quigley, 21 How. 202, 16 L. ed. 73.

California: Harris *v.* Zanone, 93 Cal. 59, 28 Pac. 845; Childers *v.* San Jose M. P. & P. Co., 105 Cal. 284, 38 Pac. 903.

Delaware: Smith *v.* Singles, 6 Pennew. 544, 72 Atl. 977.

Indiana: Binford *v.* Young, 115 Ind. 174.

Iowa: Thompson *v.* Rake, 140 Ia. 232, 118 N. W. 279, 18 L. R. A. (N. S.) 921.

Kansas: Hess *v.* Sparks, 44 Kan. 465, 24 Pac. 979; Walker *v.* Wickens, 49 Kan. 42, 30 Pac. 181.

Louisiana: Daly *v.* Van Benthuysen, 3 La. Ann. 69.

Maine: Harmon *v.* Harmon, 61 Me. 233.

Missouri: Buckley *v.* Knapp, 48 Mo. 152; Miller *v.* Dorsey, 149 Mo. App. 24, 129 S. W. 66.

New York: King *v.* Root, 4 Wend. 113; Bergmann *v.* Jones, 94 N. Y. 51; Holmes *v.* Jones, 121 N. Y. 461, 24 N. E. 701; Warner *v.* Press Pub. Co., 132 N. Y. 181, 30 N. E. 393; Shanks *v.* Stumpf, 23 Misc. 264, 51 N. Y.

Supp. 154; Burkhardt *v.* Press Pub. Co., 114 N. Y. Supp. 451, 130 App. Div. 22 (publishing plaintiff's picture under name of a disreputable woman).

North Carolina: Gilreath *v.* Allen, 10 Ire. 67; Sowers *v.* Sowers, 87 N. C. 303; Reeves *v.* Winn, 97 N. C. 246, 1 S. E. 448, 2 Am. St. Rep. 287; Logan *v.* Hodges, 146 N. C. 38, 59 S. E. 349.

Pennsylvania: Barr *v.* Moore, 87 Pa. 385. (*Contra*, by Act of July 1, 1897: Goebeler *v.* Wilhelm, 17 Pa. Super. Ct. 432.)

Rhode Island: Hopkins *v.* Drowne, 21 R. I. 20, 41 Atl. 567 (slander of title).

Vermont: Rea *v.* Harrington, 58 Vt. 181.

Virginia: Harman *v.* Cundiff, 82 Va. 239.

Wisconsin: Klewin *v.* Bauman, 53 Wis. 244.

Canada: Guest *v.* Macpherson, 3 Leg. News (Quebec), 84; Silver *v.* Dom. Tel. Co., 2 R. & G. (N. Scot.) 17.

[205] *United States:* Philadelphia, W. & B. R. R. *v.* Quigley, 21 How. 202, 16 L. ed. 73.

California: Davis *v.* Hearst, 116 Pac. 530.

Delaware: Kennedy *v.* Woodrow, 6 Houst. 46.

North Carolina: Bowden *v.* Bailes, 101 N. C. 612, 8 S. E. 342; Upchurch *v.* Robertson, 127 N. C. 127, 37 S. E. 157.

[206] *Michigan:* Hatt *v.* Evening News Assoc., 94 Mich. 114, 54 N. W. 766.

Missouri: Callahan *v.* Ingram, 122 Mo. 355, 26 S. W. 1020.

enough if the defamation was uttered with wilful indifference to the consequences, that is, in mere wantonness.[207] The fact that the words are slanderous in themselves may justify the presumption of malice; [208] so may an unsustained plea of justification,[209] and *a fortiori* such a plea known to be false, yet supported at the trial.[210]

The bad character of the plaintiff may be shown in mitigation of exemplary as well as of compensatory damage.[211]

§ 377a. Exemplary damages in statutory actions.

In actions based on statute, the statute itself may provide for or against the allowance of exemplary damages. If there is no such provision, exemplary damages are usually allowed in such cases. Thus they have been allowed in statutory actions for death,[212]

New York: Bergmann v. Jones, 94 N. Y. 51; Gray v. Sampers, 35 App. Div. 270, 55 N. Y. Supp. 3. Or absence of probable cause: *Texas:* King v. Sassaman (Tex. Civ. App.), 54 S. W. 304.

[207] *United States:* Morning Journal Assoc. v. Rutherford, 51 Fed. 513, 1 U. S. App. 296; Sun Printing Assoc. v. Smith, 55 Fed. 240, 14 U. S. App. 172, 5 C. C. A. 91; Press Pub. Co. v. McDonald, 63 Fed. 238, 11 C. C. A. 155, 26 L. R. A. 53; Times Pub. Co. v. Carlisle, 94 Fed. 762, 36 C. C. A. 475.
District of Columbia: Russell v. Washington Post Co., 31 App. D. C. 277.
Kentucky: Courier Journal Co. v. Sallee, 104 Ky. 335, 47 S. W. 226.
New York: Smith v. Matthews, 152 N. Y. 157, 46 N. E. 164; Karkowski v. Pitass, 20 App. Div. 118, 46 N. Y. Supp. 691; Young v. Fox, 26 App. Div. 261, 49 N. Y. Supp. 631.
North Carolina: Bowden v. Bailes, 101 N. C. 612; Fields v. Buinum, 72 S. E. 449.
[208] Conwisher v. Johnson, 127 Ill. App. 602.
[209] Coffin v. Brown, 94 Md. 190, 50 Atl. 567.

[210] Walker v. Wickens, 49 Kan. 42, 30 Pac. 181.
[211] Maxwell v. Kennedy, 50 Wis. 645.
[212] *United States:* Otto Kuehne Preserving Co. v. Allen, 148 Fed. 666, 78 C. C. A. 418.
Kentucky: Louisville & N. R. R. v. Kelly, 100 Ky. 421, 38 S. W. 852.
Missouri: Haehl v. Wabash R. R., 119 Mo. 325, 24 S. W. 737.
Montana: Olsen v. Montana O. P. Co., 35 Mont. 400, 89 Pac. 731.
Tennessee: Kansas City M. & B. R. R. v. Doughtry, 88 Tenn. 721, 13 S. W. 698.
West Virginia: Turner v. Norfolk & W. R. R., 40 W. Va. 675, 22 S. E. 83; Couch v. Chesapeake & O. Ry., 45 W. Va. 51, 30 S. E. 147.
Contra, Pennsylvania: Palmer v. Philadelphia, B. & W. R. R., 218 Pa. 114, 66 Atl. 1127.
South Carolina: Garrick v. Florida Central & P. R. R., 53 S. C. 448, 31 S. E. 334, 69 Am. St. Rep. 874 (but now such damages are authorized by statute: Osteen v. Southern Ry., 76 S. C. 368, 57 S. E. 196.
Washington: Atrops v. Costello, 8 Wash. 149, 35 Pac. 620.

upon the Civil Damage Act [213] and in other statutory actions. [214]

§ 377b. Exemplary damages because of judicial act.

It would seem that no exemplary damages can be recovered against anyone, when the wrong is done under due authority of any judgment, decree, or order of a court. Thus where one co-tenant evicted the other from land by a judgment of ejectment obtained in court, it was held that no exemplary damages could be recovered in such a case. [215] And no exemplary damages can be obtained upon dissolution of an injunction. [216]

§ 378. Liability of a principal to exemplary damages for the act of his agent or servant.

It is the better opinion that no recovery of exemplary damages can be had against a principal for the tort of an agent or servant, [217] unless the defendant expressly authorized the

[213] *Illinois:* Earp *v.* Lilly, 217 Ill. 582, 75 N. E. 552, affirming 120 Ill. App. 123; Leverenz *v.* Stevens, 124 Ill. App. 401.

Iowa: Miller *v.* Hammers, 93 Iowa, 746, 61 N. W. 1087 (by construction of the statute they may be recovered in any case, regardless of circumstances of aggravation).

Maine: Campbell *v.* Harmon, 96 Me. 87, 51 Atl. 801.

Michigan: Lafler *v.* Fisher, 121 Mich. 60, 79 N. W. 934; Merrinane *v.* Miller, 148 Mich. 412, 111 N. W. 1050, 14 Det. L. N. 242; Scahill *v.* Ætna Indemnity Co., 157 Mich. 310, 122 N. W. 78.

New York: Neu *v.* McKechnie, 95 N. Y. 632, 47 Am. Rep. 89; Wilber *v.* Dwyer, 69 Hun, 507, 23 N. Y. Supp. 395.

West Virginia: Pennington *v.* Gillaspie, 63 W. Va. 541, 61 S. E. 416, 66 W. Va. 643, 66 S. E. 1009.

[214] *United States:* Minneapolis & S. L., etc., Ry. *v.* Beckwith, 129 U. S. 26, 32 L. ed. 585, 9 Sup. Ct. 207 (killing stock).

Alabama: Southern Ry. *v.* Bunt, 131 Ala. 591, 32 So. 507 (employers' liability act).

Kentucky: Koestel *v.* Cunningham, 97 Ky. 421, 30 S. W. 970 (injury by biting dog).

Pennsylvania: Hendler *v.* Quigley, 38 Pa. Super. Ct. 39 (action to recover leased premises).

Contra, Kansas: Gripton *v.* Thompson, 32 Kan. 367, 4 Pac. 698 (crops destroyed by swine).

Vermont: Giffen *v.* Barr, 60 Vt. 599, 15 Atl. 190 (failure to discharge mortgage after payment).

[215] Stephens *v.* Taylor (Tex. Civ. App.), 36 S. W. 1083.

[216] Dempster *v.* Lansingh, 128 Ill. App. 388.

[217] *United States:* The Amiable Nancy, 3 Wheat. 546, 4 L. ed. 546.

Alabama: Pollock *v.* Gantt, 69 Ala. 373; Burns *v.* Campbell, 71 Ala. 271.

California: Wardrobe *v.* Stage Co., 7 Cal. 118; Mendelsohn *v.* Anaheim Lighter Co., 40 Cal. 657, overruling Wade *v.* Thayer, Ibid. 578; Davis *v.* Hearst, 116 Pac. 530.

act as it was performed or approved it,[218] or was grossly negligent in hiring the agent or servant,[219] or in not preventing
him from committing the act.[220] The burden of showing authorization or approval by the principal is on the plaintiff.[221]
In Cleghorn v. New York Central & Hudson River Railroad,[222]
Church, C. J., said:

"For injuries by negligence of the servant, however gross
or culpable, he (the master) is not liable to be punished in
punitive damages, unless he is also chargeable with gross
misconduct. Such misconduct may be established by showing
that the act of the servant was authorized or ratified, or that
the master employed or retained the servant knowing that he
was incompetent or, from bad habits, unfit for the position

Colorado: Page v. Yool, 28 Colo. 464,
65 Pac. 636; Ristine v. Blocker, 15
Colo. App. 224, 61 Pac. 486.

Connecticut: Haywood v. Hamm, 77
Conn. 158, 68 Atl. 695.

District of Columbia: Woodward v.
Ragland, 5 App. D. C. 220.

Illinois: Grund v. Van Vleck, 69 Ill.
478; Mead v. Pollock, 99 Ill. App. 151.

Kentucky: Patterson v. Waldman, 46
S. W. 17, 20 Ky. L. Rep. 514.

Louisiana: Keene v. Lizardi, 8 La.
26; Boulard v. Calhoun, 13 La. Ann. 445.

Missouri: McMenamy v. Cohick, 1
Mo. App. 529.

New Jersey: Haines v. Schultz, 50
N. J. L. 481, 14 Atl. 488.

New York: Craven v. Bloomingdale,
171 N. Y. 439, 64 N. E. 169 (see Davey
v. Davey, 22 Misc. 668, 50 N. Y. Supp.
161); Rose v. Imperial Engine Co., 112
N. Y. Supp. 8, 127 App. Div. 885.

Oklahoma: Chicago, R. I. & P. R. R.
v. Newburn, 27 Okla. 9, 110 Pac. 1065,
30 L. R. A. (N. S.) 432.

Rhode Island: Staples v. Scmid, 18 R.
I. 224, 19 L. R. A. 824, 26 Atl. 193.

Texas: Dillingham v. Russell, 73 Tex.
47, 11 S. W. 139, 15 Am. St. Rep. 753,
3 L. R. A. 634; Texas T. Ry. v. Johnson, 75 Tex. 158; Strange v. Dundon
(Tex. Civ. App.), 27 S. W. 503; Mutual
L. I. Co. v. Hargus (Tex. Civ. App.),
99 S. W. 580.

Wisconsin: Eviston v. Cramer, 57
Wis. 570, 15 N. W. 760; Mace v. Reed,
89 Wis. 440, 62 N. W. 186.

England: Robertson v. Wylde, 2 M.
& Rob. 101.

[218] *United States:* Kilpatrick v. Haley,
66 Fed. 133, 13 C. C. A. 480.

Alabama: Lienkauf v. Morris, 66
Ala. 406.

Connecticut: Wyeman v. Deady, 79
Conn. 414, 65 Atl. 129.

Illinois: Becker v. Dupree, 75 Ill.
167.

Kansas: Duff & R. Co. v. Read, 74
Kan. 730, 88 Pac. 263.

Texas: Strauss v. Dundon (Tex. Civ.
App.), 27 S. W. 503.

Wisconsin: Eviston v. Cramer, 57
Wis. 570.

[219] Burns v. Campbell, 71 Ala. 271;
Sawyer v. Sauer, 10 Kan. 466; Reed
v. New York Gas Co., 87 N. Y. Supp.
810, 93 App. Div. 453 (*semble*).

[220] *Alabama:* Burns v. Campbell, 71
Ala. 271.

Illinois: Freese v. Tripp, 70 Ill.
496.

Michigan: Kehrig v. Peters, 41
Mich. 475.

[221] Haines v. Schultz, 50 N. J. L.
481.

[222] 56 N. Y. 44.

he occupied. Something more than ordinary negligence is requisite; it must be reckless and of a criminal nature, and clearly established. If a railroad company knowingly and wantonly employs a drunken engineer or switchman, or retains one after knowledge of his habits is clearly brought home to the company, or to a superintending agent authorized to employ and discharge him, and injury occurs by reason of such habits, the company may and ought to be amenable to the severest rule of damages; but I am not aware of any principle which permits a jury to award exemplary damages in a case which does not come up to this standard, or to graduate the amount of such damages, by their views of the propriety of the conduct of the defendant, unless such conduct is of the character above specified."

The Chief Justice also said: "It is the exception and not the rule that, in this class of cases, exemplary damages are allowable."

In some jurisdictions, however, the principal, if liable for compensatory damages, is liable also for exemplary damages as the agent or servant would be.[223] Where one partner in the course of the partnership business commits a tort subjecting him to exemplary damages, such damages may be recovered from the firm.[224]

§ 379. Of a corporation for acts of agents.

A corporation is liable for exemplary damages for its own act, that is, for the act of its directors or other agents whose act is the act of the corporation.[225] Thus gross negligence in hiring servants will subject a corporation to exemplary damages,[226] and so will express authorization or ratification of the

---

[223] *United States:* Malloy v. Bennett, 15 Fed. 371; Bennett v. Salisbury, 78 Fed. 769, 24 C. C. A. 329.

Georgia: Jones v. Lamon, 92 Ga. 529, 18 S. E. 423.

Illinois: Nagle v. Keller, 141 Ill. App. 444, affirmed, 237 Ill. 431, 86 N. E. 694 (under dram shop act).

Maine: Wellman v. Dickey, 78 Me. 29, 2 Atl. 133.

Maryland: Boyer v. Coxen, 92 Md. 366, 48 Atl. 161; Gusdorff v. Duncan, 94 Md. 160, 50 Atl. 574.

Mississippi: Southern Express Co. v. Brown, 67 Miss. 260.

Pennsylvania: Hazard v. Israel, 1 Binn. 240; Bruce v. Reed, 104 Pa. 408.

[224] Robinson v. Goings, 63 Miss. 500.

[225] Bingham v. Lipman, 40 Ore. 363, 371, 67 Pac. 98.

[226] *United States:* Henning v. Western U. T. Co., 41 Fed. 864.

servant's acts.[227] Where the superintendent of a corporation with full knowledge of the damage being done persisted for a long time in using unusually heavy blasts of dynamite, thus injuring plaintiff's building, the corporation was held liable in exemplary damages.[228]

§ 380. For acts of servants.

It is held in many, perhaps in most, jurisdictions that a corporation is liable to exemplary damages, if to any, for an act of its servant which would subject the servant to exemplary damages.[229] It is argued that since a corporation can act only

Alabama: S. & N. A. R. R. v. McLendon, 63 Ala. 266.

Connecticut: Murphy v. N. Y. & N. H. R. R., 29 Conn. 277.

Illinois: I. C. R. R. v. Hammer, 72 Ill. 347.

New York: Cleghorn v. N. Y. C. & H. R. R. R., 56 N. Y. 44.

Oregon: Sullivan v. Ore. Ry. & Nav. Co., 12 Ore. 392.

Tennessee: Nashville & C. R. R. v. Starnes, 9 Heisk. 52.

[227] *Illinois:* Illinois C. R. R. v. Hammer, 72 Ill. 347.

Missouri: Malecek v. Tower G. & L. Ry., 57 Mo. 17; Doss v. Missouri, K. & T. R. R., 59 Mo. 27; Travers v. Kansas P. Ry., 63 Mo. 421.

New York: Murphy v. Central Park, N. & E. R. R., 48 N. Y. Super. Ct. 96; Kutner v. Fargo, 45 N. Y. Super. Ct. 753.

Tennessee: Nashville & C. R. R. v. Starnes, 9 Heisk. 52.

Wisconsin: Milwaukee & M. R. R. v. Finney, 10 Wis. 388; Craker v. Chicago & N. W. Ry., 36 Wis. 657; Bass v. Chicago & N. W. Ry., 42 Wis. 654.

[228] Funk v. H. S. Kerbaugh, 222 Pa. 18, 70 Atl. 953, 22 L. R. A. (N. S.) 296.

[229] *Alabama:* Jefferson County Sav. Bank v. Eborn, 84 Ala. 529, 4 So. 386; Alabama G. S. R. R. v. Frazier, 93 Ala. 45, 9 So. 303; Kansas City, etc., R. R. v. Phillips, 98 Ala. 159, 13 So.

65; Mobile & O. R. R. v. Seales, 100 Ala. 368, 13 So. 917; Highland Ave. & Belt R. R. v. Robinson, 125 Ala. 482, 28 So. 28; Kress v. Lawrence, 158 Ala. 496, 47 So. 574. (See City National Bank v. Jeffries, 73 Ala. 183.)

Arkansas: C. S. Ry. v. Steen, 42 Ark. 321; St. Louis, I. M. & S. Ry. v. Wilson, 70 Ark. 136, 66 S. W. 661.

Colorado: (before exemplary damages were dissallowed): W. U. Tel. Co. v. Eyser, 2 Colo. 141.

Delaware: Ford v. Charles Warner Co., 1 Marvel, 88, 37 Atl. 39.

District of Columbia: Flannery v. B. & O. R. R., 4 Mack. 111.

Georgia: Gasway v. A. & W. P. R. R., 58 Ga. 216; G. R. R. v. Olds, 77 Ga. 673; East Tenn., V. & G. Ry. v. Fleetwood, 90 Ga. 23, 15 S. E. 778; Williamson v. R. R., 127 Ga. 125, 56 S. E. 119.

Illinois (by code): I. C. R. R. v. Hammer, 72 Ill. 353; Singer Manuf. Co. v. Holdfodt, 86 Ill. 455, 29 Am. Rep. 43; Wabash, St. L. & P. Ry. v. Rector, 104 Ill. 296; Chicago T. & T. Co. v. Core, 223 Ill. 58, 79 N. E. 108, affirming 126 Ill. App. 272.

Indiana: J. R. R. v. Rogers, 38 Ind. 116; Baltimore & O. S. W. R. R. v. Davis, 44 Ind. App. 375, 89 N. E. 403.

Kansas: Wheeler & Wilson Manuf. Co. v. Boyce, 36 Kan. 350, 13 Pac. 609; Southern K. R. R. v. Rice, 38 Kan. 398, 16 Pac. 817, 5 Am. St. Rep. 755.

by its agents or servants it would altogether escape liability to exemplary damages unless it were subjected to them for its agents' or servants' acts. The corporation is therefore held liable although in most of these jurisdictions an individual principal would not be. In South Carolina this has been carried so far that a corporation is held liable in exemplary damages for the act of another corporation which was operating its railroad as lessee.[230] But it is more in the nature of exemplary damages, as punishment, to allow a recovery of them only against a defendant who has been personally in fault; the better opinion, therefore, seems to be that exemplary damages should be allowed against a corporation for the act of its servant only if it expressly authorized the act as it was

Kentucky: Bowler *v.* Lane, 3 Met. 311; Jacobs *v.* L. & N. R. R., 10 Bush, 263; L. & N. R. R. *v.* Ballard, 85 Ky. 307; Memphis & C. P. Co. *v.* Nagel, 97 Ky. 9, 29 S. W. 743; Louisville & N. R. R. *v.* Kelly, 100 Ky. 421, 38 S. W. 852; Lexington Ry. *v.* Cozine, 23 Ky. L. Rep. 1137, 64 S. W. 848; Louisville & N. R. R. *v.* Eaden, 93 S. W. 7, 29 Ky. L. Rep. 365, 6 L. R. A. (N. S.) 581.

Maine: Goddard *v.* G. T. Ry., 57 Me. 202; Hanson *v.* E. & N. A. R. R., 62 Me. 84.

Maryland: Baltimore & O. R. R. *v.* Blocher, 27 Md. 277; Baltimore & Yorktown Turnpike *v.* Boone, 45 Md. 344; Philadelphia, W. & B. R. R. *v.* Larkin, 47 Md. 155; Baltimore C. & A. Ry. *v.* Kirby, 91 Md. 313, 46 Atl. 975; Baltimore & O. R. R. *v.* Strube, 111 Md. 119, 73 Atl. 697.

Minnesota: Peterson *v.* Western U. Tel. Co., 75 Minn. 368, 77 N. W. 985, 74 Am. St. Rep. 502, 43 L. R. A. 581; Berg *v.* R. R. Co., 96 Minn. 513, 105 N. W. 191.

Mississippi: Vicksburg & J. R. R. *v.* Patton, 31 Miss. 156; New Orleans J. & G. N. R. R. *v.* Bailey, 40 Miss. 395; Pullman Palace Car Co. *v.* Lawrence, 74 Miss. 782, 22 So. 53 (as to Illinois law); Cumberland T. & T. Co.

v. Cassedy, 78 Miss. 666, 29 So. 762; Southern R. R. *v.* Lanning, 83 Miss. 161, 35 So. 417.

Missouri: Perkins *v.* M., K. & T. R. R., 55 Mo. 201; Travers *v.* K. P. Ry., 63 Mo. 421 (overruling McKeon *v.* C. Ry., 42 Mo. 79); Haehl *v.* Wabash R. R., 119 Mo. 325, 24 S. W. 737; Canfield *v.* Chicago, R. I. & P. Ry., 59 Mo. App. 354. See, however, Rouse *v.* Metropolitan St. R. R., 41 Mo. App. 298.

New Hampshire (before exemplary damages were disallowed): Belknap *v.* B. & M. R. R., 49 N. H. 358.

Ohio: Atlantic & G. W. Ry. *v.* Dunn, 19 Oh. St. 162, 2 Am. Rep. 382; Western U. T. Co. *v.* Smith, 64 Oh. St. 106, 59 N. E. 890; Scioto Valley Traction Co. *v.* Craybill, 29 Ohio Cir. Ct. R. 95.

South Carolina: Quinn *v.* S. C. Ry., 29 S. C. 381; Skipper *v.* Clifton Manuf. Co., 58 S. C. 143, 36 S. E. 509.

Tennessee: Louisville & N. R. R. *v.* Garrett, 8 Lea, 438 (explaining Nashville & C. R. R. *v.* Starnes, 9 Heisk. 52); Knoxville Traction Co. *v.* Lane, 103 Tenn. 376, 53 S. W. 557, 46 L. R. A. 549.

West Virginia: Davis *v.* Chesapeake & O. Ry., 61 W. Va. 246, 56 S. E. 400, 9 L. R. A. (N. S.) 993.

[230] Hart *v.* Charlotte, C. & A. R. R., 33 S. C. 427, 12 S. E. 9.

performed, or afterwards ratified it, or was negligent in hiring the servant or retaining him in its employ. And such is the law in many jurisdictions.[231] This view has received the support of the Supreme Court of the United States; [232] and, the question being regarded as one of general jurisprudence and not of local state law, this view must be followed in all the Federal courts.[233]

[231] *California:* Turner v. N. B. & M. R. R., 34 Cal. 594; Mendelsohn v. Anaheim Lighter Co., 40 Cal. 657; Trabing v. California Navigation & Imp. Co., 121 Cal. 137, 53 Pac. 644.
Delaware: McCoy v. P. W. & B. R. R., 5 Houst. 599.
Louisiana: Hill v. N. O. O. & G. W. R. R., 11 La. Ann. 292; Graham v. St. Charles St. R. R., 47 La. Ann. 1656, 49 Am. St. Rep. 436, 18 So. 707.
Michigan: Great W. Ry. v. Miller, 19 Mich. 305.
New Jersey: Ackerson v. Erie Ry., 32 N. J. L. 254; Forhmann v. Consolidated Traction Co., 63 N. J. L. 391, 43 Atl. 892; Peterson v. Middlesex & S. T. Co., 71 N. J. L. 296, 59 Atl. 456.
New York: Murphy v. Central Park, N. & E. R. R. R., 48 N. Y. Super. Ct. 96; Wright v. Glen Falls, S. H. & F. E. S. R. R., 24 App. Div. 617, 48 N. Y. Supp. 1026; Kastner v. Long Island R. R., 76 App. Div. 323, 78 N. Y. Supp. 469; Reed v. New York Gas Co., 93 App. Div. 453, 87 N. Y. Supp. 810; Samieloff v. New York & Q. C. Ry., 122 App. Div. 770, 107 N. Y. Supp. 774; Magagnos v. Brooklyn Heights R. R., 128 App. Div. 182, 112 N. Y. Supp. 637.
Oregon: Sullivan v. Ore. Ry. & Nav. Co., 12 Ore. 392.
Pennsylvania: Keil v. Chartiers V. C. Co., 131 Pa. 466, 19 Atl. 78 (but see Lake S. R. R. v. Rosenzweig, 113 Pa. 519; Philadelphia T. Co. v. Orbann, 119 Pa. 37, 12 Atl. 816; Artherholt v. Erie E. M. Co., 27 Pa. Super. Ct. 141).

Rhode Island: Hagan v. Providence & W. R. R., 3 R. I. 88, 62 Am. Dec. 377.
Texas: Hays v. H. G. N. R. R., 46 Tex. 272; G. H. & S. A. Ry. v. Donahoe, 56 Tex. 162; International & G. N. R. R. v. Garcia, 70 Tex. 207; Missouri Pacific R. R. v. Richmond, 73 Tex. 568, 11 S. W. 555, 15 Am. St. Rep. 794, 4 L. R. A. 280; Fort Worth & N. O. Ry. v. Smith, (Tex. Civ. App.), 25 S. W. 1039; Texas & P. Ry. v. Beezley, 46 Tex. Civ. App. 108, 101 S. W. 1051.
Vermont: Wells v. Boston & M. R. R., 82 Vt. 108, 71 Atl. 1103.
Virginia: Norfolk & W. R. R. v. Neely, 91 Va. 539, 22 S. E. 367, 44 Am. St. Rep. 884 (but see Norfolk & W. R. R. v. Anderson, 90 Va. 1, 17 S. E. 757, 44 Am. St. Rep. 884).
West Virginia: Ricketts v. Chesapeake & O. Ry., 33 W. Va. 433, 10 S. E. 801.
Wisconsin: M. & M. R. R. v. Finney, 10 Wis. 388; Bass v. C. & N. W. Ry., 36 Wis. 450, 39 Wis. 636, 40 Wis. 654, 24 Am. Rep. 437; Craker v. C. & N. W. Ry., 36 Wis. 657; Eviston v. Cramer, 57 Wis. 570; Rueping v. Chicago & N. W. Ry., 116 Wis. 625, 93 N. W. 843; Topolewski v. Plankington Packing Co., 143 Wis. 52, 126 N. W. 554.
[232] Lake Shore & M. S. Ry. v. Prentice, 147 U. S. 101, 37 L. ed. 97, 13 Sup. Ct. 261.
[233] Pittsburgh, C., C. & S. L. Ry. v. Russ, 57 Fed. 822, 18 U. S. App. 279, 6 C. C. A. 597; Bank of Palo Alto v. Pacific P. T. C. Co., 103 Fed. 841; Pacific P. & N. Co. v. Fielding, 136

§ 380a. Ratification or approval by the master.

In those jurisdictions which do not otherwise permit the allowance of exemplary damages against the master for his servant's tort, actual approval of the circumstances by the master will justify such damages against him. What constitutes such approval depends upon the circumstances of the case. Mere retention of the servant in the employment is not enough to constitute an approval of the act;[234] but retention after knowledge of the wrong, including its aggravating circumstances, is evidence of approval,[235] and where the master defends the servant upon a complaint brought against him for the act and upon conviction pays his fine the act is ratified.[236] Continuing in the wrong will constitute sufficient ratification; as where the master refuses upon demand to return property wrongfully taken by the servant,[237] or continues to maintain a fence without an opening after suit has been brought for wrongfully doing so.[238] If the injury is the result of a rule, custom, or system, maintained by the corporation, which tends to encourage wanton injury, the corporation may be held to exemplary damages. Thus when a newspaper maintains a system of publication under which despatches, though libellous, are likely to be published, with-

Fed. 577, 69 C. C. A. 325; Toledo, S. L. & W. R. R. v. Gordon, 143 Fed. 95. Fell v. Northern Pac. R. R., 44 Fed. 248, and Times Pub. Co. v. Carlisle, 36 C. C. A. 475, 487, 94 Fed. 762, which allowed such damages, are therefore overruled.

And this rule also prevails in Territorial courts, as in the Indian Territory before the admission of Oklahoma. Chicago, R. I. & P. Ry. v. Newburn, 27 Okla. 9, 110 Pac. 1065.

[234] Dillingham v. Russell, 73 Tex. 47, 15 Am. St. Rep. 753, 11 S. W. 139, 3 L. R. A. 634; McGown v. International & G. N. Ry., 85 Tex. 289, 20 S. W. 80; Gulf, C. & S. F. Ry. v. McFadden (Tex. Civ. App.), 25 S. W. 451.

[235] *District of Columbia:* Woodward v. Ragland, 5 D. C. App. Cas. 220.

Missouri: Tanger v. Southwest Missouri Electric Ry., 85 Mo. App. 28.

Virginia: Norfolk & W. R. R. v. Anderson, 90 Va. 1, 17 S. E. 757, 44 Am. St. Rep. 884.

Wisconsin: Pfister v. Milwaukee F. P. Co., 139 Wis. 627, 121 N. W. 938.

Mere suit on a note obtained by the agent in the transaction is not ratification:

Mutual L. I. Co. v. Hargus (Tex. Civ. App.), 99 S. W. 580.

[236] Denison & S. Ry. v. Randell, 29 Tex. Civ. App. 460, 69 S. W. 1013.

[237] *United States:* Kilpatrick v. Haley, 13 C. C. A. 480, 66 Fed. 133.

California: Avakian v. Noble, 121 Cal. 216, 53 Pac. 559.

[238] San Antonio & A. P. Ry. v. Grier, 20 Tex. Civ. App. 138, 49 S. W. 148.

out any effort to ascertain their accuracy, the corporation is responsible.[239]

§ 380b. For acts of municipal corporations.

Municipal corporations are not liable to exemplary damages.[240]

§ 381. For acts of an officer.

A ministerial officer acting in good faith is not liable to exemplary damages; but such an officer is liable to exemplary damages if he acts maliciously.[241] And this malice, though it must now be found as a fact by the jury, does not necessarily mean actual malice. Where primary constitutional rights are invaded, the malice seems to lie in this fact, and not in the manner of inflicting the oppression. Thus in Scott v. Donald,[242] and Huckle v. Money [243] there seems to have been no actual malice.

§ 382. For acts of one of two joint defendants.

When only one of two or more joint wrongdoers acted in

[239] Press Pub. Co. v. McDonald, 63 Fed. 238, 11 C. C. A. 155, 26 U. S. App. 167; cf. Davis v. Hearst (Cal.), 116 Pac. 530; Haines v. Schultz, 50 N. J. Law, 481, 14 Atl. 488; Daily Post Co. v. McArthur, 16 Mich. 447.

[240] Dakota: Larson v. Grand Forks, 3 Dak. 307.

Illinois: Chicago v. Martin, 49 Ill. 241, 95 Am. Dec. 590 (semble); Chicago v. Langlass, 52 Ill. 256; Chicago v. Jones, 66 Ill. 349; Chicago v. Kelly, 69 Ill. 475.

Iowa: Bennett v. Marion, 102 Iowa, 425, 63 Am. St. Rep. 454, 71 N. W. 360.

Missouri: Hunt v. Boonville, 65 Mo. 620.

Vermont: Willett v. St. Albans, 69 Vt. 330, 38 Atl. 72.

West Virginia: Wilson v. Wheeling, 19 W. Va. 350, 42 Am. Rep. 780.

Contra, Louisiana: McGary v. President, 12 Rob. 668, 43 Am. Dec. 239, 4 La. Ann. 440.

Contra, by express statute, Myers v. San Francisco, 42 Cal. 215.

The question was raised but not decided in

Alabama: Mayor v. Lewis, 92 Ala. 352, 357, 9 So. 242.

Kansas: Adams v. Salina, 58 Kan. 246, 48 Pac. 918.

New York: Costic v. Rochester, 68 App. Div. 623, 73 N. Y. Supp. 835.

Texas: In Ostrom v. San Antonio, 33 T. C. A. 683, 77 S. W. 829, the court said that such damages could not be recovered unless in an exceptional case.

[241] United States: Scott v. Donald, 165 U. S. 58, 77, 89, 41 L. ed. 632, 17 Sup. Ct. 265.

California: Nightingale v. Scannell, 18 Cal. 315.

Connecticut: Pratt v. Pond, 42 Conn. 318.

Iowa: Plummer v. Harbut, 5 Ia. 308.

Maine: Pierce v. Getchell, 76 Me. 216.

[242] 165 U. S. 58, 41 L. ed. 632, 17 Sup. Ct. 265.

[243] 2 Wils. 205.

such a way as to render himself liable to exemplary damages, the plaintiff may have judgment against him for exemplary damages and against the others for compensatory damages.[244] When, however, a husband and wife are sued jointly for the tort of the wife, a judgment for exemplary damages may be recovered against them jointly; for the husband is not really a joint defendant, but only a formal party.[245]

§ 383. Mitigation—Want of malice.

Since the cause for inflicting exemplary damages is a malicious intent or wantonness on the part of the defendant, and the amount is regulated according to the degree of wrong, all circumstances bearing on the defendant's intent may be shown to the jury, to be considered by them. All circumstances which negative the existence of malice, or show the malice to have been little, may be shown to mitigate the damages: such circumstances are good faith, the advice of counsel, and belief

[244] *New York:* Krug v. Pitass, 126 N. Y. 154, 56 N. E. 526, 76 Am. St. Rep. 317.

Ohio: Mauk v. Brundage, 68 Ohio St. 89, 67 N. E. 152.

Utah: Marks v. Culmer, 6 Utah, 419, 24 Pac. 528.

England: Clark v. Newsam, 1 Ex. 131.

Canada: Clissold v. Machell, 26 Up. Can. Q. B. 422.

If both defendants participated in the entire wrong, the fact that one was wealthy and the other not would not prevent the allowance of exemplary damages against both of them. White v. White, 140 Wis. 538, 122 N. W. 1051.

In Reizenstein v. Clark, 104 Iowa, 287, 73 N. W. 588, the court held that the condition of mind of one party would be attributed to the other and each would be liable in exemplary damages. The same view seems to have been taken in Ousley v. Hardin, 23 Ill. 403; but in later cases a lower court has held that exemplary damages cannot be recovered against the defendant who had no malice. Doug-

las v. Hoffman, 72 Ill. App. 110; Corkings v. Meier, 112 Ill. App. 655.

In a few jurisdictions it is held that if one of the defendants was not liable to exemplary damages, none could be given and that if all were liable, the jury should assess damages as against the least culpable defendant.

California: Hearne v. DeYoung, 119 Cal. 570, 52 Pac. 150; Davis v. Hearst, 116 Pac. 530.

Pennsylvania: McCarthy v. DeArmit, 99 Pa. 63.

Vermont: Boutwell v. Marr, 71 Vt. 1, 42 Atl. 607, 76 Am. St. Rep. 746, 43 L. R. A. 803; Moore v. Duke, 80 Atl. 194.

[245] *Missouri:* Munter v. Bande, 1 Mo. App. 484.

Texas: Patterson v. Frazer (Tex. Civ. App.), 93 S. W. 146.

Vermont: Lombard v. Batchelder, 58 Vt. 558.

In *Tennessee* it has been held that the joint judgment should be for compensatory damages only, with a separate judgment against the wife for exemplary damages. Price v. Clapp, 119 Tenn. 425, 105 S. W. 864.

of right. So where the cause of offence was discontinued by the defendant with reasonable promptness, that will rebut the presumption of malice, and prevent the recovery of exemplary damages.[246] In short, as exemplary damages are recoverable only upon a full view of the motive of the act, in the light of all the attendant circumstances, so too all circumstances going to show that the motive of the act was innocent must be taken into account also.[247] And of course the fact that the suit is an amicable suit will prevent the allowance of exemplary damages.[248]

§ 383a. Good faith.

If the defendant acted in good faith, he cannot be made liable to exemplary damages.[249] So in an action of libel, good faith may be shown to prevent exemplary damages.[250] And where a collector of customs while carrying out in good faith the orders of his superior officer committed a tort, it was held that he was not liable to exemplary damages;[251] nor is any ministerial officer acting in good faith.[252] So where a railway conductor acted honestly in ejecting the plaintiff from a car, exemplary damages cannot be recovered.[253]

[246] *Indiana:* White v. Sun Pub. Co., 164 Ind. 426, 73 N. E. 890.

Maryland: Oursler v. Baltimore & O. R. R., 60 Md. 358.

[247] *California:* Lamb v. Harbaugh, 105 Cal. 680, 39 Pac. 56.

Illinois: Merrifield v. Davis, 130 Ill. App. 162.

New York: Millard v. Brown, 35 N. Y. 297.

North Dakota: Galvin v. Tibbs, 17 N. Dak. 600, 119 N. W. 39.

Ohio: Henn v. Horn, 56 Oh. St. 442, 47 N. E. 248.

[248] Amer v. Longstreth, 10 Pa. 145.

[249] *Connecticut:* St. Peter's Church v. Beach, 26 Conn. 355.

Illinois: Gray v. Waterman, 40 Ill. 522.

Ohio: Western U. T. Co. v. Smith, 64 Oh. St. 106, 59 N. E. 890.

Texas: Kaufman v. Wicks, 62 Tex. 234; Erie Tel. & Tel. Co. v. Kennedy, 80 Tex. 71, 15 S. W. 704.

[250] *Alabama:* Burns v. Campbell, 71 Ala. 271.

Missouri: Flowers v. Smith, 214 Mo. 98, 112 S. W. 499.

New York: Bennett v. Smith, 23 Hun, 50.

[251] Tracy v. Swartwout, 10 Pet. 80, 9 L. ed. 354.

[252] *Alabama:* Boggan v. Bennett, 102 Ala. 400, 14 So. 742; Stephenson v. Wright, 111 Ala. 579, 20 So. 622.

California: Selden v. Cashman, 20 Cal. 57.

Indiana: Buntin v. Duchane, 1 Blackf. 56.

Iowa: Plummer v. Harbut, 5 Ia. 308.

Maine: Pierce v. Getchell, 76 Me. 216.

Texas: Wright v. Jones, 14 Tex. Civ. App. 423, 38 S. W. 249.

[253] *Iowa:* Fitzgerald v. Chicago, R. I. & P. Ry., 50 Ia. 79.

§ 383b. Advice of counsel.

If the defendant acted under the advice of counsel, the plaintiff cannot recover exemplary damages; [254] and the same is true where he acted upon the advice of one he supposed to be a lawyer, who in fact was not. [255] But the advice of a layman who made no pretence to being a lawyer will not relieve the defendant from liability to exemplary damages. [256] And the advice of counsel will be no protection if it is not exactly followed; so where the defendant's lawyer advised him that he could enter certain premises if the plaintiff's family were away, and in fact he entered them when they were not away, the advice could not protect him from exemplary damages. [257] Nor will the defendant be protected unless he shows that the advice was based upon a knowledge of all the facts of the case, [258] as where the defendant did not make a full statement of them to counsel; [259] nor unless his consultation with counsel and following advice was in good faith. [260]

Maryland: Philadelphia, W. & B. R. R. v. Hoeflich, 62 Md. 300.

Missouri: Logan v. Hannibal & S. J. R. R., 77 Mo. 663.

New York: Hamilton v. Third Ave. R. R., 53 N. Y. 25; Yates v. New York C. & H. R. R. R., 67 N. Y. 100.

North Carolina: Tomlinson v. Wilmington & S. C. R. R., 107 N. C. 327, 12 S. E. 138.

[254] *United States:* Chambers v. Upton, 34 Fed. 473.

Alabama: City Nat. Bank v. Jeffries, 73 Ala. 183.

California: Abbott v. Land & Water Co., 103 Cal. 607, 37 Pac. 527; Walker v. Chanslor, 153 Cal. 118, 94 Pac. 606.

Georgia: Shores v. Brooks, 81 Ga. 468.

Illinois: Cochrane v. Tuttle, 75 Ill. 361 (but see Jasper v. Purnell, 67 Ill. 358).

Indiana: Moyer v. Gordon, 113 Ind. 282.

Minnesota: Grimestad v. Lofgren,

105 Minn. 286, 117 N. W. 515, 17 L. R. A. (N. S.) 990.

New York: Brown v. McBride, 24 Misc. 235, 52 N. Y. Supp. 620.

Wisconsin: Bonesteel v. Bonesteel, 30 Wis. 511.

Ireland: Reeves v. Penrose, 26 L. R. Ir. 141.

In spite of the fact that defendant acted under advice of counsel, exemplary damages may be given if the jury choose. Parks v. Laurens Cotton Mills, 75 S. C. 560, 56 S. E. 234.

[255] Murphy v. Larson, 77 Ill. 172.

[256] Livingston v. Burroughs, 33 Mich. 511.

[257] Carpenter v. Barber, 44 Vt. 441.

[258] *Alabama:* Louisville & N. R. R. v. Smith, 141 Ala. 335, 37 So. 490.

Georgia: Shores v. Brooks, 81 Ga. 468.

[259] *Iowa:* Union Mill Co. v. Prenzler, 100 Ia. 540, 69 N. W. 876.

Texas: Rainey v. Kemp, 118 S. W. 630 (Tex. Civ. App.).

[260] *United States:* The Mascotte, 72 Fed. 684.

§ 383c. Belief of right: Mistake.

If the defendant honestly believed himself in the right, this may be shown to prevent or mitigate the allowance of exemplary damages;[261] and therefore a tort committed through a mistake as to the rights of the parties will not give a right to exemplary damages,[262] whether the mistake is one of law [263] or of fact.[264]

§ 384. Provocation.

The existence of provocation, though it may not be a defence, will prevent the allowance of exemplary damages.[265] Thus in an action of false imprisonment it appeared that the plaintiff had been arrested for contempt of court in not complying with an order to pay a claim against an estate of which he was administrator. The order turned out to be void. It was held that the defendant might show, in mitigation of exemplary damages, fraud on the part of the plaintiff in getting possession of the estate and the making false claims

---

Vermont: Carpenter *v.* Barber, 44 Vt. 441.

[261] *Alabama:* Wilkinson *v.* Searcy, 76 Ala. 176; Barrett *v.* Mobile, 129 Ala. 179, 30 So. 36.

Illinois: Farwell *v.* Warren, 70 Ill. 28.

Michigan: Allison *v.* Chandler, 11 Mich. 542.

South Carolina: Gwynn *v.* Citizens Tel. Co., 69 S. C. 434, 48 S. E. 460, 104 Am. St. Rep. 819, 67 L. R. A. 111.

South Dakota: Richardson *v.* Huston, 10 S. D. 484, 74 N. W. 234.

Tennessee: Cannon *v.* Overstreet, 2 Baxt. 464.

Texas: Hillman *v.* Baumbach, 21 Tex. 203.

[262] *Iowa:* Brown *v.* Allen, 35 Ia. 306.

Kansas: Schwartz *v.* Missouri, K. & T. Ry., 83 Kan. 30, 109 Pac. 767.

[263] *Kentucky:* Gerkins *v.* Kentucky Salt Co., 67 S. W. 821, 23 Ky. L. Rep. 2415.

New York: Dyke *v.* National Transit Co., 22 App. Div. 360, 49 N. Y. Supp. 180.

[264] *Virginia:* Burruss *v.* Hines, 94 Va. 413, 26 S. E. 875.

Wisconsin: Scheer *v.* Kriesel, 109 Wis. 125, 85 N. W. 138.

[265] *Arkansas:* Ward *v.* Blackwood, 41 Ark. 295.

California: Badostain *v.* Grazide, 115 Cal. 425, 47 Pac. 118.

Georgia: Grier *v.* Ward, 23 Ga. 145; City Electric R. R. *v.* Shropshire, 101 Ga. 33, 28 S. E. 508.

Maryland: Baltimore & O. R. R. *v.* Barger, 80 Md. 23, 30 Atl. 560, 45 Am. St. Rep. 319, 26 L. R. A. 220; Baltimore & O. R. R. *v.* Strube, 111 Md. 119, 73 Atl. 697.

Missouri: Wehmeyer *v.* Mulvihill, 150 Mo. App. 197, 130 S. W. 681.

New Jersey: Osler *v.* Walton, 67 N. J. L. 63, 50 Atl. 590.

New York: Gressman *v.* Morning Journal Assoc., 197 N. Y. 474, 90 N. E. 1131.

Vermont: Goldsmith *v.* Joy, 61 Vt. 488, 17 Atl. 1010, 15 Am. St. Rep. 923, 4 L. R. A. 500.

against it in order to escape payment of the legal claims.[266] So in an action of assault and battery the fact that the injury was inflicted during a mutual fight will prevent the allowance of exemplary damages.[267] So in an action of trespass *quare clausum* it has been held that it could be shown, in mitigation of exemplary damages, that the parties had had a difficulty in the morning, for, *per curiam*, "otherwise there would have been nothing to indicate to the jury but that the house was entered for the purpose of robbery and plunder, or something of the kind. The fact of a previous affray might have some weight upon the question of the amount of damages recoverable, and might legitimately be regarded as a part of the transaction to be investigated in this suit." [268]

In a case where the plaintiff was the aggressor, but the defendant in his defence used excessive force, the Court of Appeals of New York refused to allow exemplary damages.[269] In the course of the opinion Danforth, J., said:

"If the injury of which he complains came in part from his own act, there is less reparation demanded from the defendant, for the law seeks to do justice between the parties, and will not require one to atone for the other's error. If satisfaction is to be made for the breach of public order, it is not due to him, for his own wrong is the consideration upon which it stands, and for that he cannot be allowed to profit. Otherwise he would receive compensation for damages occasioned by himself. Yet we have this spectacle before us. A fine laid upon the defendant that the rights of others may be respected, and its payment ordered, not into the public treasury, but the hand of the first aggressor. The law is careful and exact in its dealings. It denies compensation to him who, by his own negligence, contributed to injuries from which he suffers. Much less will it allow one who excites public disorder to profit by punishment imposed upon his adversary for the protection of the community. In offending, the plaintiff came first. If he had kept the peace there would have been no

---

[266] Johnson v. Von Kettler, 66 Ill. 63.

[267] *California:* Badostain v. Grazide, 115 Cal. 425, 47 Pac. 118.

Indiana: Kinssly v. Hire, 2 Ind. App. 86, 28 N. E. 195.

Wisconsin: Shay v. Thompson, 59 Wis. 540.

[268] Currier v. Swan, 63 Me. 323.

[269] Kiff v. Youmans, 86 N. Y. 324, 331.

second. It would very much impair that sense of security which grows out of the legal right to hold and enjoy property, and defend by reasonable force its possession, if the owner, when his rights are invaded, was required to answer not only for a failure to measure with precision the degree of strength applicable to the aggressor, but respond to him in a civil action according to the estimate which a jury influenced by the impassioned appeals of private counsel might place upon the value of public order."

A provocation offered *some time* previously cannot be shown in mitigation. It must have been so recent that the act can be said to have been committed under the immediate influence of the feelings excited.[270] And it must have been sufficient to have stirred some degree of resentment in an ordinary man. Thus a simple trespass on land will not mitigate exemplary damages for a wanton assault on the trespasser.[271]

§ 384a. Aggravation.

Any fact which tends to show malice or to disprove matter of mitigation may be shown in aggravation of exemplary damages. Thus evidence tending to enhance the impression of malice may be shown;[272] so may an unsustained plea of justification in an action of libel.[273] Evidence in mitigation may be met by showing that in spite of the mitigating circumstances the defendant acted in a cruel and abusive manner;[274] thus, though the defendant honestly believed the slander he published to be true, yet if he published it in a wanton and reckless manner, or maliciously, the plaintiff may recover exemplary damages.[275]

---

[270] *Illinois:* Huftalin v. Misner, 70 Ill. 55.

New Hampshire: Perkins v. Towle, 43 N. H. 220, 80 Am. Dec. 149.

[271] Conners v. Walsh, 131 N. Y. 590, 30 N. E. 59.

[272] Langton v. Hagerty, 35 Wis. 150.

[273] Coffin v. Brown, 94 Md. 190, 50 Atl. 567.

A repetition of defamation by others cannot be shown in aggravation of damages for the original publication. Raines v. New York Press Co., 92 Hun, 515, 37 N. Y. Supp. 45.

[274] *Connecticut:* Dalton v. Beers, 38 Conn. 529.

Illinois: Johnson v. Camp, 51 Ill. 219; Bauer v. Gottmanhausen, 65 Ill. 499; Jasper v. Purnell, 67 Ill. 358.

Michigan: Raynor v. Nims, 37 Mich. 34.

[275] Hayner v. Cowden, 27 Oh. St. 292.

§ 385. Exemplary damages as affected by the pecuniary condition of the defendant.

The plaintiff may show the defendant's wealth, whether the defendant is an individual or a corporation, that the jury may judge what will be a sufficient punishment; [276] and in rebuttal the defendant may show his own poverty. [277] In Maine it is held that the defendant may show his poverty, even though the plaintiff has introduced no evidence on the

[276] *United States:* Brown *v.* Evans, 8 Sawy. 488.

California: Barclay *v.* Copeland, 74 Cal. 5, 15 Pac. 307, 5 Am. St. Rep. 413; Greenberg *v.* Western Turf Ass'n, 140 Cal. 358, 73 Pac. 1050; Tingley *v.* Times Mirror Co., 151 Cal. 1, 89 Pac. 1097.

Georgia: Tolleson *v.* Poset, 32 Ga. 372.

Illinois: Grable *v.* Margrave, 4 Ill. 372; Arasmith *v.* Temple, 11 Ill. App. 39; Brown *v.* Jones, 52 Ill. App. 597.

Kansas: White *v.* White, 76 Kan. 82, 90 Pac. 1087.

Kentucky: Jacobs *v.* L. & N. R. R., 10 Bush, 263.

Maryland: Sloan *v.* Edwards, 61 Md. 89.

Minnesota: M'Carthy *v.* Niskern, 22 Minn. 90; Peck *v.* Small, 35 Minn. 465.

Mississippi: Whitfield *v.* Westbrook, 40 Miss. 411; Pullman P. C. Co. *v.* Lawrence, 74 Miss. 782, 22 So. 53.

Missouri: Buckley *v.* Knapp, 48 Mo. 152; Schafer *v.* Ostmann, 148 Mo. App. 644, 129 S. W. 63.

New Hampshire: Belknap *v.* B. & M. R. R., 49 N. H. 358.

North Carolina: Reeves *v.* Winn, 97 N. C. 246, 2 Am. St. Rep. 287, 1 S. E. 448; Johnson *v.* Allen, 100 N. C. 131, 5 S. E. 666; Bowden *v.* Bailes, 101 N. C. 612, 8 S. E. 342; Tucker *v.* Winders, 130 N. C. 147, 41 S. E. 8.

North Dakota: King *v.* Hanson, 13 N. Dak. 85, 99 N. W. 1085.

Ohio: Hayner *v.* Cowden, 27 Oh. St. 292.

Pennsylvania: McBride *v.* McLaugh-

lin, 5 Watts, 375; Matheis *v.* Mazet, 164 Pa. 580, 30 Atl. 434.

Tennessee: Dush *v.* Fitzhugh, 2 Lea, 307; Cumberland Tel. & T. Co. *v.* Poston, 94 Tenn. 696, 30 S. W. 1040.

South 'Carolina: Elms *v.* Southern Power Co., 79 S. C. 502, 60 S. E. 1110; Calder *v.* Southern Ry., 71 S. E. 841.

Vermont: Rea *v.* Harrington, 58 Vt. 181.

Virginia: Harman *v.* Cundiff, 82 Va. 239.

Wisconsin: Birchard *v.* Booth, 4 Wis. 67; Meibus *v.* Dodge, 38 Wis. 300; Winn *v.* Peckham, 42 Wis. 493; Brown *v.* Swineford, 44 Wis. 282; Lavery *v.* Crooke, 52 Wis. 612; Hare *v.* Marsh, 61 Wis. 435, 21 N. W. 267; Draper *v.* Baker, 61 Wis. 450, 50 Am. Rep. 143, 21 N. W. 527; Spear *v.* Hiles, 67 Wis. 350, 30 N. W. 506; Gilman *v.* Brown, 115 Wis. 1, 91 N. W. 227; Thomas *v.* Williams, 139 Wis. 467, 121 N. W. 148.

Wyoming: Cosgriff *v.* Miller, 10 Wyo. 190, 68 Pac. 206.

Contra, United States: Western U. T. Co. *v.* Cashman, 132 Fed. 805.

Alabama: Southern C. & F. Co. *v.* Adams, 131 Ala. 147, 32 So. 503.

Illinois: Holmes *v.* Holmes, 64 Ill. 294.

Iowa: Guengerech *v.* Smith, 34 Ia. 348.

Kentucky: Givens *v.* Berkley, 21 Ky. L. Rep. 1653, 56 S. W. 158.

New York: Farnsworth *v.* Western U. T. Co., 53 Hun, 636, 6 N. Y. Supp. 735.

[277] Mullin *v.* Spangenberg, 112 Ill. 140; Rea *v.* Harrington, 58 Vt. 181.

point.[278] It has been held in a few cases that the plaintiff might show his own poverty or social condition to enhance exemplary damages.[279] This, however, has usually nothing to do with the proper punishment of the defendant, and the better view is that this cannot be shown.[280]

§ 386. Exemplary damages for injuries which are also crimes.

In some jurisdictions it is held that the doctrine of exemplary damages does not apply to actions for wrongs which are also criminal offences, on the ground that the defendant should not be twice punished for the same offence.[281] In some jurisdictions, evidence of a conviction and fine paid may be given for the purpose of mitigating exemplary damages, but does not bar the claim altogether as a matter of law;[282] in Quebec it is an absolute bar to exemplary damages.[283] Everywhere

[278] Johnson v. Smith, 64 Me. 553.

[279] *United States:* Press Pub. Co. v. McDonald, 63 Fed. 238, 11 C. C. A. 155, 26 L. R. A. 53.

Illinois: Grable v. Margrave, 4 Ill. 372; Schmitt v. Kurrus, 140 Ill. App. 132, affd., 234 Ill. 578, 85 N. E. 261.

Missouri: Beck v. Dowell, 111 Mo. 506, 20 S. W. 209, 33 Am. St. Rep. 547.

[280] *Kentucky:* Givens v. Berkley, 21 Ky. L. Rep. 1653, 56 S. W. 158.

Minnesota: Griser v. Schoenborn, 109 Minn. 297, 123 N. W. 823.

North Carolina: Robertson v. Conklin, 153 N. C. 1, 68 S. E. 899.

[281] *Colorado:* Murphy v. Hobbs, 7 Colo. 541.

District of Columbia: Huber v. Teuber, 3 McA. 484.

Georgia: Cherry v. McCall, 23 Ga. 193.

Indiana: Taber v. Hutson, 5 Ind. 322; Butler v. Mercer, 14 Ind. 479; Nossaman v. Rickert, 18 Ind. 350; Humphries v. Johnson, 20 Ind. 190; Meyer v. Bohlfing, 44 Ind. 238; Ziegler v. Powell, 54 Ind. 173; Koerner v. Oberly, 56 Ind. 284, 26 Am. Rep. 34; Stewart v. Maddox, 63 Ind. 51; Farman v. Lauman, 73 Ind. 568; State v.

Stevens, 103 Ind. 55, 53 Am. Rep. 482, 2 N. E. 214; Moyer v. Gordon, 113 Ind. 282, 14 N. E. 476; Wabash Printing Co. v. Crumrine, 123 Ind. 89, 21 N. E. 904; White v. Sun Publishing Co., 164 Ind. 426, 73 N. E. 890 (see, however, Tracy v. Hackett, 19 Ind. App. 133, 49 N. E. 185); Borkenstein v. Shrack, 31 Ind. App. 220, 67 N. E. 547; Hartford L. I. Co. v. Hope, 40 Ind. App. 354, 81 N. E. 595.

Massachusetts: Austin v. Wilson, 4 Cush. 273 (before it was decided that such damages can never be recovered).

New Hampshire: Fay v. Parker, 53 N. H. 342.

In Bendich v. Scobel, 107 La. 242, 31 So. 703, it was held that courts would be "slow to inflict" punitive damages where a prosecution had taken place.

[282] *North Carolina:* Smithwick v. Ward, 7 Jones, L. 64; Johnston v. Crawford, 62 N. C. (Phillips) 342; Sowers v. Sowers, 87 N. C. 303.

Pennsylvania: Wirsing v. Smith, 222 Pa. 8, 70 Atl. 906.

Texas: Flanagan v. Womack, 54 Tex. 45; Shook v. Peters, 59 Tex. 393.

[283] Guest v. Macpherson, 3 Leg. News, 84.

else it is held that the fact that the defendant is liable to a criminal prosecution or has actually paid a fine to the State can neither bar nor mitigate exemplary damages.[284] In the case of Fry v. Bennett,[285] which was an action of libel, Mr. Justice Hoffman maintained, with much force, that there was a clear difference between the particular injury to the plaintiff (independently of his pecuniary damage) by the defendant's wrongful act, and the injury caused by the same act to society at large, contending that penalties for each, although both pecuniary, might be inflicted without injustice to the defendant.

In Illinois an attempt was made at one time to distinguish between exemplary and punitive damages, and to hold that the former can, but the latter cannot, be given where the act is punishable as a crime.[286] The attempted distinction was, however, as will be seen from cases already cited, immediately abandoned by the court.

[284] *United States:* Brown v. Evans, 8 Sawy. 488.

Alabama: Phillips v. Kelly, 29 Ala. 628.

California: Wilson v. Middleton, 2 Cal. 54; Bundy v. Maginess, 76 Cal. 532.

Delaware: Jefferson v. Adams, 4 Harr. 321.

Florida: Smith v. Bagwell, 19 Fla. 117, 45 Am. Rep. 12.

Iowa: Hendrickson v. Kingsbury, 21 Ia. 379; Garland v. Wholeham, 26 Ia. 185; Guengerich v. Smith, 36 Ia. 587; Reddin v. Gates, 52 Ia. 210.

Kentucky: Chiles v. Drake, 2 Met. 146; Slater v. Sherman, 5 Bush, 206; Doerhoefer v. Shewmaker, 97 S. W. 7, 29 Ky. L. Rep. 1193.

Maine: Johnson v. Smith, 64 Me. 553.

Michigan: Elliott v. Van Buren, 33 Mich. 49.

Minnesota: Boetcher v. Staples, 27 Minn. 308.

Mississippi: Wheatley v. Thorn, 23 Miss. 62.

Missouri: Corwin v. Walton, 18 Mo. 71, 59 Am. Dec. 285; Baldwin v. Fries, 46 Mo. App. 288; Summers v. Keller, 152 Mo. App. 626, 133 S. W. 1180.

New York: Cook v. Ellis, 6 Hill, 466.

North Carolina: Sowers v. Sowers, 87 N. C. 303.

Ohio: Roberts v. Mason, 10 Oh. St. 277.

Pennsylvania: Barr v. Moore, 87 Pa. 385, 30 Am. Rep. 367; Rhodes v. Rodgers, 151 Pa. 634, 24 Atl. 1044.

South Carolina: Wolff v. Cohen, 8 Rich. L. 144.

Texas: Cole v. Tucker, 6 Tex. 266.

Vermont: Hoodley v. Watson, 45 Vt. 289, 12 Am. Rep. 197; Roach v. Caldbeck, 64 Vt. 593, 24 Atl. 989; Edwards v. Leavitt, 46 Vt. 126.

Wisconsin: Klopfer v. Bromme, 26 Wis. 372; Brown v. Swineford, 44 Wis. 282; Corcoran v. Harran, 55 Wis. 120.

Wyoming: Cosgriff v. Miller, 10 Wyo. 190, 68 Pac. 206, 216.

[285] 4 Duer, 247.

[286] Freese v. Tripp, 70 Ill. 496; Meidel v. Anthis, 71 Ill. 241.

§ 387. Relations of court and jury in awarding exemplary damages.

Whether there is any evidence to justify the assessment of exemplary damages is a question for the court, and if there is none, it is error to submit the question of exemplary damages to the jury.[287] Where there is evidence of circumstances sufficient to uphold a verdict for exemplary damages, the question whether they shall be given or not is one for the jury;[288] and it is error to instruct the jury to give exemplary damages, for the plaintiff can never claim them as a matter of law.[289] It is error, when the facts are in dispute, to instruct

[287] *Alabama:* Louisville & N. R. R. *v.* Hall, 87 Ala. 708, 6 So. 277.

California: Selden *v.* Cashman, 20 Cal. 56.

Colorado: Eisenhart *v.* Ordean, 3 Colo. App. 162, 32 Pac. 495.

Kansas: Chicago, K. & W. R. R. *v.* O'Connell, 46 Kan. 581, 26 Pac. 947.

Kentucky: Lexington Ry. *v.* Fain, 80 S. W. 463, 25 Ky. L. Rep. 2243; Louisville & N. R. R. *v.* Berry, 33 Ky. L. Rep. 850, 111 S. W. 370.

Maryland: Smith *v.* Phila., W. & B. R. R., 87 Md. 48, 38 Atl. 1072.

Mississippi: Chicago, S. L. & N. O. R. R. *v.* Scurr, 59 Miss. 456.

New Jersey: Bullock *v.* Delaware, L. & W. R. R., 61 N. J. L. 550, 40 Atl. 650.

North Carolina: Waters *v.* Greenleaf-Johnson Lumber Co., 115 N. C. 648, 20 S. E. 718.

Pennsylvania: Rose *v.* Story, 1 Pa. 190; Amer *v.* Longstreth, 10 Pa. 145; Pittsburgh S. Ry. *v.* Taylor, 104 Pa. 306; Phila. Traction Co. *v.* Orbann, 119 Pa. 37, 12 Atl. 816.

South Dakota: Baxter *v.* Campbell, 17 S. D. 475, 97 N. W. 386.

Texas: Bradshaw *v.* Buchanan, 50 Tex. 492.

Virginia: Norfolk & W. R. R. *v.* Neely, 91 Va. 539, 22 S. E. 367, 44 Am. St. Rep. 884.

If in spite of an instruction not to allow exemplary damages the jury allows them, the verdict will be set aside.

Anderson *v.* Western U. T. Co., 85 S. C. 252, 67 S. E. 232, 477.

[288] *Alabama:* Gambill *v.* Cargo, 151 Ala. 421, 43 So. 866; Alabama G. S. R. R. *v.* Arrington, 56 So. 78.

Connecticut: Pratt *v.* Pond, 42 Conn. 318.

Georgia: Dye *v.* Denham, 54 Ga. 224.

Maine: Johnson *v.* Smith, 64 Me. 553.

Maryland: Smith *v.* Thompson, 55 Md. 5.

Minnesota: Sneve *v.* Lunder, 100 Minn. 5, 110 N. W. 99.

Mississippi: Chicago, S. L. & N. O. R. R. *v.* Scurr, 59 Miss. 456; Burns *v.* Alabama & V. R. R., 93 Miss. 816, 47 So. 640.

Missouri: Graham *v.* Pacific R. R., 66 Mo. 536; Nicholson *v.* Rogers, 129 Mo. 136, 31 S. W. 260; Bosch *v.* Miller, 136 Mo. App. 482, 118 S. W. 506.

Pennsylvania: Nagle *v.* Mullison, 34 Pa. 48; Blair Iron & Coal Co. *v.* Lloyd, 1 Walk. 158.

Rhode Island: Kenyon *v.* Cameron, 17 R. I. 122, 20 Atl. 233.

[289] *Alabama:* Louisville & N. R. R. *v.* Bizzell, 131 Ala. 429, 437, 30 So. 777.

California: Davis *v.* Hearst, 116 Pac. 530.

Illinois: Hawk *v.* Ridgway, 33 Ill. 473; Wabash, St. L. & P. Ry. *v.* Rector, 104 Ill. 296; Consolidated Coal Co. *v.* Haenni, 146 Ill. 614, 35 N. E. 162; Brown *v.* Jones, 52 Ill. App. 597.

Kentucky: Louisville & N. R. R. *v.*

the jury that "this is one of the cases where they may give exemplary damages,"[290] or to leave the question to the jury without instructing them that the facts will warrant exemplary damages.[291] It is, however, held in Iowa that the Civil Damage Act gives the plaintiff a right to exemplary damages, and the court should therefore, in a proper case, instruct the jury to give them.[292] And in South Carolina and Texas, under the statutes, the plaintiff has a right to exemplary damages if the circumstances permit their allowance.[293]

In Wisconsin, in a case of assault and battery, an instruction to the jury that "if the assault was committed in an insulting manner, wilfully and maliciously, with an intent to injure the plaintiff's feelings, and disgrace him in the estimation of the public," they *ought* to give punitory damages, was held not to be error.[294] On the other hand, the jury must not be restricted by a direction not to give exemplary damages, if they believe from the evidence that the defendant's trespass was malicious.[295]

Brooks, 83 Ky. 129; Ryan v. Quinn, 24 Ky. L. Rep. 1513, 71 S. W. 872; Chesapeake & O. Ry. v. Conley, 136 Ky. 601, 124 S. W. 861.

Mississippi: Southern R. R. v. Kendrick, 40 Miss. 374; N. O., St. L. & C. R. R. v. Burke, 53 Miss. 200.

Missouri: Nicholson v. Rogers, 129 Mo. 136, 31 S. W. 260; Carson v. Smith, 133 Mo. 606, 34 S. W. 855.

New York: Jacobs v. Sire, 4 N. Y. Misc. 398, 23 N. Y. Supp 1063; Eupes v. Nephue, 120 App. Div. 621, 105 N. Y. Supp. 542.

Pennsylvania: Neeb v. Hope, 111 Pa. 145, 2 Atl. 568.

Vermont: Jerome v. Smith, 48 Vt. 230; Boardman v. Goldsmith, 48 Vt. 403; Snow v. Carpenter, 49 Vt. 426.

West Virginia: Fink v. Thomas, 66 W. Va. 487, 66 S. E. 650; Carpenter v. Hyman, 67 W. Va. 4, 66 S. E. 1078.

Wisconsin: Robinson v. Superior Rapid Transit Ry., 94 Wis. 345, 68 N. W. 961, 59 Am. St. Rep. 896, 34 L. R. A. 205; Haberman v. Gasser, 104 Wis. 98, 80 N. W. 105; Thomas v.

Williams, 139 Wis. 467, 121 N. W. 148; Tilton v. James L. Gates Land Co., 140 Wis. 197, 121 N. W. 331.

And therefore the court will not reverse if the jury, under proper instructions, fails to allow them. Simpson v. Markwood, 6 Baxt. (Tenn.) 340.

[290] Pickett v. Crook, 20 Wis. 358.

[291] *New York:* Kutner v. Fargo, 45 N. Y. Supp. 753.

North Dakota: Lindblorn v. Sonstelie, 10 N. Dak. 140, 86 N. W. 357.

Wisconsin: Haberman v. Gasser, 104 Wis. 98, 80 N. W. 105.

[292] Fox v. Wunderlich, 64 Ia. 187; Thill v. Pohlman, 76 Ia. 638.

[293] *United States:* Morgan v. Barnhill, 118 Fed. 24 (Texas statute).

South Carolina: Beaudrot v. Southern Ry., 69 S. C. 160, 48 S. E. 106.

Texas: Galveston, H. & S. A. R. R. v. Dunlavy, 56 Tex. 256; Mayer v. Duke, 72 Tex. 445, 10 S. W. 565; Nolan v. Mendere, 6 Tex. Civ. App. 203, 25 S. W. 28.

[294] Hooker v. Newton, 24 Wis. 292.

[295] Devaughn v. Heath, 37 Ala. 595.

Where the case is tried by the court, not by a jury, the allowance of exemplary damages is discretionary with the court.[296]

§ 388. Power of the jury over the amount of exemplary damages—Power of the court.

The amount of exemplary damages is generally said to be entirely within the discretion of the jury.[297] But this discretion is subject to review by the court.[298] So where the highest value of a house torn down and removed by the defendant, testified to by any witness, was $250, and the court instructed the jury that, if they found it a case for exemplary damages, they might find a verdict for any amount not exceeding the sum laid in the declaration, which was $2,000, and the jury found a verdict for $567, it was set aside on the ground that this instruction might have wrongly influenced them as to the amount of damages, as a verdict for the amount laid in the declaration would have warranted the inference of prejudice, partiality, or corruption on their part.[299] An instruction that they might give such damages as would satisfy the highly excited feelings of the plaintiff was held erroneous.[300]

The verdict can be set aside by the court only when it is grossly excessive, or evidently actuated by passion, prejudice, or undue influence.[301] The case of New Orleans, J. & G.

[296] Carter v. Ill. Cent. R. R., 17 Ky. L. Rep. 1352, 34 S. W. 907.

[297] Kentucky: Major v. Pulliam, 3 Dana, 582; Louisville & N. R. R. v. Donaldson, 13 Ky. L. Rep. 1384, 43 S. W. 439.

Mississippi: C. R. R. v. Scurr, 59 Miss. 456.

New Jersey: Allen v. Craig, 1 J. S. Green, 294.

New York: Weed v. Brush, 89 Hun 62, 34 N. Y. Supp. 1025.

Virginia: Borland v. Barrett, 76 Va. 128.

[298] Alabama: Cox v. Birmingham Ry. L. & P. Co., 163 Ala. 170, 50 So. 975.

Kentucky: Louisville & N. R. R. v. Roth, 130 Ky. 759, 114 S. W. 264.

[299] Georgia: Bryan v. Acee, 27 Ga. 87.

Texas: Willis v. McNeill, 57 Tex. 465.

[300] Jones v. Turpin, 6 Heisk. (Tenn.) 181.

[301] Colorado: Page v. Yool, 28 Colo. 464, 65 Pac. 636.

District of Columbia: Flannery v. Baltimore & O. R. R., 4 Mack. 111.

Illinois: Cutler v. Smith, 57 Ill. 252; Farwell v. Warren, 70 Ill. 28.

Iowa: Collins v. Council Bluffs, 35 Ia. 432; Saunders v. Mullen, 66 Ia. 728, 24 N. W. 529.

Kentucky: Louisville Southern R. R. v. Minogue, 90 Ky. 369, 14 S. W. 357, 12 Ky. L. Rep. 378, 29 Am. St. Rep. 378.

Missouri: Goetz v. Ambs, 27 Mo. 28.

N. R. R. v. Hurst [302] would seem to carry the principle of exemplary damages to its extreme limit. The jury having, in that case, found a verdict of $4,500 against a railroad company for the misconduct of a conductor in carrying the plaintiff four hundred yards beyond the station, and refusing to return, so that, to avoid being taken to the next station, he had to walk back, carrying his valise, the court, while regretting the rigor of the jury, refused to set aside the verdict, saying that the law in such cases furnished "no legal measurement save their discretion." In this case, we think, with deference, that the verdict might with great propriety have been set aside. The amount warranted the presumption of undue bias.

In Louisiana, in cases proper for exemplary damages, the jury are still under the control of the court in regard to the extent to which they may go, and, in an action for malicious arrest and imprisonment, the court said: "Exemplary damages should nevertheless be commensurate to the nature of the offence, and when extravagant damages are allowed, they will be reduced to their proper standard." [303] The damages should be in some degree proportioned to the amount of actual damages. [304]

The power of the court to set aside a verdict for exemplary damages is the same power, and is exercised upon the same principle, as in any case of excessive verdict. [305] Its effect upon the allowance of exemplary damages is to prevent the severe and arbitrary consequences that might otherwise result from the doctrine, and so to meet the principal objection to the allowance of exemplary damages: namely, that it gives the jury an arbitrary and unrestricted power over the property of defendants.

Virginia: Borland v. Barrett, 76 Va. 128.

Wisconsin: Rogers v. Henry, 32 Wis. 327.

[302] 36 Miss. 660.

[303] Burkett v. Lanata, 15 La. Ann. 337; acc., Fitzgerald v. Boulat, 13 La. Ann. 116.

[304] *Illinois:* Hildreth v. Hancock, 55 Ill. App. 572.

Texas: Flanary v. Wood, 32 Tex. Civ. App. 250, 73 S. W. 1072.

[305] See chapter upon Powers of Court and Jury.

CHAPTER XVII

LIQUIDATED DAMAGES

757

§ 389. Amount of damages stipulated by the parties.

We now come to a class of cases where the contracting parties fix or liquidate the amount that shall furnish the measure of compensation in case of non-fulfilment of the agreement, either in the shape of a penalty or of stipulated damages.

§ 390.[1] Refusal of courts to enforce a penalty.

Equity early relieved against forfeitures, and enjoined the collection of mere penalties. Thus, courts of law were forbidden by the chancellor to exact the penalty of a bond,[2] even though default had been made by the obligor; or to enforce the forfeiture of land conveyed in mortgage after default of the mortgagor. Courts of law themselves eventually came to enforce the same doctrines; and if parties to a contract provided that a penalty should be exacted for non-performance a court of law as well as a court of equity would refuse to give judgment for the amount of the penalty.

§ 391.[3] Liquidated damages and penalty.

* It is competent for parties entering upon an agreement to avoid all future questions as to the amount of damages which may result from the violation of the contract, and to agree upon a definite sum, as that which shall be paid to the party who alleges and establishes the violation of the agreement.[4] In this case the damages so fixed are termed *liquidated, stipulated, or stated* damages. But even where this course has been adopted, and a sum certain named in the contract, difficulty has arisen as to whether it should be considered as such liquidated damages, or only as a penalty.[5] It being settled by the courts, both of equity and law, that a penalty was only intended as a security for the principal sum due or the actual damages sustained, it became doubtful,

[1] For § 390 of the eighth edition, see § 675a.

[2] See *infra*, chap. 32.

[3] For § 391 of the 8th edition see § 675b.

[4] A provision of this nature has been engrafted on charter-parties, and is familiarly known as demurrage. See § 419.

[5] The word *penalty* is in this contradistinction not very correct or significant; the word designates a sum absolutely due in case of the non-performance of an agreement, quite as clearly as the phrase *liquidated damages*. But the term has now acquired a fixed and well-settled technical meaning.

even when a definite sum was named, whether the parties intended it for that purpose, or whether it was meant as liquidated damages, behind which the courts could not go; and on this subject various cases have been decided.**

If no actual damages have been sustained, a clause liquidating the damages will not avail the plaintiff: in such a case only nominal damages are recoverable.[6]

§ 392.[7] Classification of the subject.

*It is proper, however, before we examine these cases, to notice a distinction as to the way in which the question presents itself, growing out of the form of the contract, from want of a constant attention to which part of the confusion has arisen.

First. The agreement may, in the first place, be to do or refrain from doing some particular act, or in default thereof, to pay a given sum of money; and this was well known to the Roman law. So the imperial legislator advises his subjects in making contracts for the doing of anything, to fix the amount of damages by inserting a precise stipulation to that effect: *Non solum res in stipulationem deduci possunt, sed etiam facta: ut si stipulemur aliquid fieri vel non fieri. Et in hujusmodi stipulationibus optimum erit pœnam subjicere, ne quantitas stipulationis in incerto sit, ac necesse sit actori probare quid ejus intersit. Itaque si quis, ut fiat aliquid, stipuletur ita adjici pœna debet: si ita factum non erit, tunc pœnœ nomine decem aureos dare spondes.*[8] This, as Lord Kaims clearly points out[9] is properly an alternative obligation, and the sum stated cannot be correctly termed a penalty.

Secondly, the agreement may assume the technical form of the bond, containing a declaration of an absolute indebtedness in a given sum, conditioned to become void on the payment of a less sum, or the performance of some particular act. Here there is no express promise or undertaking to do anything. The indebtedness declared in the prior part of the

[6] McCann v. Albany, 158 N. Y. 634, 53 N. E. 673.

[7] For § 392 of the eighth edition, see § 675c.

[8] Inst. lib. iii, tit. xv, de Verb. Oblig., § 7. Vinnius, in his commentary on this section, discusses the subject of

the measure of damages, and its necessary uncertainty in many cases: *Est vero id quod interest incertum duplici ratione, ab eventu ipsius rei, et a probatione.* Vinn. Comm., p. 606.

[9] Kaims' Equity, book iii, ch. ii, p. 277.

instrument is not intended to be binding. The promise relied on is contained in or implied from the condition, and that is sanctioned by the penalty.

Thirdly, the agreement may bind the party absolutely to do, or refrain from doing, the particular act, and then proceed to declare that if the promise is not performed, the party stipulating shall pay a given sum of money as a *penalty*.

And *lastly*, the agreement may in all respects resemble the last, except that the fixed sum may be declared payable as *liquidated or stated damages*, or as a *forfeiture*.

§ 393.[10] General observations.

Whenever questions of the nature we are now considering present themselves, the attention of the courts is mainly fixed on three different points: First, the language employed; second, the subject-matter of the contract; and third, the intention of the parties. These are, indeed, the great elements of interpretation of all contracts. But in the case we are now examining, the courts, especially in this country, have generally shown a marked desire to lean toward that construction which excludes the idea of liquidated damages, and permits the party to recover only the damage which he has actually sustained. The language of the contract is not controlling.

And such, it seems, was the disposition of the civil law in the somewhat analogous case of the *stipulatio duplex: Quœ scrupulositates et differentiœ procedent propter odiositatem strictamque naturam stipulationis duplœ, quœ stricti juris est, contra quam etiam in dubio fit interpretatio. Contra, vero, actio ex empto bonœ fidei est, et etiam favorabilis, cum non competat ad veram pœnam, sed subsistere et probari oportet, verum et justum interesse, merito in ea plenior fit interpretatio.*[11]

The subject-matter of the contract, and the intention of the parties are the controlling guides. If, from the nature of the agreement, it is clear that any attempt to get at the actual damage would be difficult, if not vain, then the courts will incline to give the relief which the parties have agreed on. But if, on the other hand, the contract is such that the strict

---

[10] For § 393 of the eighth edition, see § 675d.

[11] Dumoulin, de Eo quod Int., § 123.

construction of the phraseology would work absurdity or oppression, the use of the term liquidated damages will not prevent the courts from inquiring into the actual injury sustained, and doing justice between the parties.[12]**

§ 394.[13] Early English cases.

The earliest notice of the general subject appears to be in Sir Baptiste Hixts' case,[14] which is as follows:

"In an action of covenant, if the plaintiff counts that in an agreement for certain lands between plaintiff and defendant, the defendant covenanted that if, on measurement, there was not found as many acres as the defendant had stated to the plaintiff at the time of sale, he would repay for each acre wanting £11 per acre, and avers that, on measurement, as many acres were wanting as would, at £11 per acre, amount to £700; and issue being joined whether they were wanting, and the jury find for the plaintiff, and give £400 damages, this issue is well found for the plaintiff; for although it were found that all the acres were wanting, still *they are chancellors*, and may give such damages as the case requires in equity, inasmuch as the whole consists in giving damages."

To this decision we have already referred, as being strikingly illustrative of the laxity of all the early cases on the subject of compensation.[15]

§ 395.[16] Decisions in the Court of Chancery.

In the next case in which the subject was discussed,[17] the

[12] It is to be observed that the plaintiff, as well as the defendant, has the right to show that the stipulated sum is a penalty, and to prove the actual damages, though they are greater than the penalty. In other words, when the performance of a contract is secured by a penalty the amount of damages upon breach is not limited to the penalty. Noyes v. Phillips, 60 N. Y. 408.

[13] For § 394 of the eighth edition, see § 391.

[14] 2 Rolle Abr. 703, tit. Trial.

[15] In a subsequent case, Lowe v. Peers, 4 Burr. 2225, 2229, Lord Mansfield said: "As to the case mentioned by Mr. Mansfield, from Rolle's Abr., it is impossible to support it; for it cannot be that a man should be obliged to take less than the liquidated sum. And the writ of error in that case was plainly brought by the defendant. Besides, the damages could never be taken advantage of upon a writ of error. How could the *quantum* of damages found by the *jury* be the subject of a *writ of error?*"

[16] For § 395 of the eighth edition, see § 392.

[17] Roy v. The Duke of Beaufort, 2 Atk. 190, decided in 1741. But on the

§ 395 LIQUIDATED DAMAGES

plaintiff had executed a bond in £100 penalty to the Duke of Beaufort, that his son should not poach on the duke's grounds without leave from the gamekeeper, or unless in company with a qualified person. The son afterward fished; the bond was put in suit, the penalty of £100 recovered, and paid by the plaintiff, with £40 costs of suit. This bill was filed for relief. It was insisted that the bond was only given as a security that the son should not poach; but Lord Chancellor Hardwicke said: "It is most absurd to think that bonds of this kind were intended merely as a security," and asked: "In what respect is the gentleman who has such a bond in a better condition than he was before, if after obtaining judgment at law, a court of equity will give him no other satisfaction than the bare value of the price of the game that is killed?"

In a case before the same great judge,[18] Aylet had charged certain lands by his will with an amount of ten pounds for the maintenance of a school-master, to be paid half-yearly; and if in arrear forty-two days after due, 5s. per week were allotted, *nomine pœnæ*. A commission of charitable uses issued from chancery summoned the owner of the land, who was in default, and awarded the arrears and the *pœna*. Exception was taken that, in a court of equity, the *pœna* would be relieved against on payment of the actual arrears. Lord Chancellor Hardwicke said that the *pœna* should stand, according to the *intention of the parties, as a security for the legal interest.* But he went on to say, that where there is a *" nomine pœnæ "* in a lease to prevent the tenant from breaking up pasture ground, it is otherwise; for the intention there is to give the landlord a compensation for the damage sustained, and in such case the whole *pœna* shall be paid.

And so in a subsequent case,[19] where an increased rent was declared payable, provided land should be plowed up, the agreement was held conclusive on the quantum of damages.[20]

---

ground that an ill use had been made of the bond, the chancellor relieved the plaintiff against the verdict, and decreed the duke to refund the £100 and £40 damages.

[18] Aylet v. Dodd, 2 Atk. 238, decided in the same year.

[19] Farrant v. Olmius, 3 B. & Ald. 692.

[20] But in Wilbeam v. Ashton, 1 Camp.

Again,[21] where a bond had been given by the plaintiff Benson, to the defendant, a hair merchant, as a security for his services in Flanders as an agent to buy hair, the plaintiff was to stay abroad a certain time; and as security for his performance he deposited £100 with the defendant. The plaintiff bought but five pounds' worth of hair, and returned to England before the time agreed on. The bill was filed for £50 per annum, agreed to be paid by the defendant to the plaintiff, and also to recover back the deposit. It was insisted that the plaintiff had committed a breach, that the £100 was stated damages; and the previous cases, of the *nomine pœnæ* in leases and the poaching bond, were cited: but Lord Hardwicke said that this was a bond for services only, and refused to decree the penalty, but directed an issue of *quantum damnificatus*.

In a subsequent case,[22] the plaintiff demised certain lands in Ireland, for three lives, at the yearly rent of £125, with a condition, that if the tenant should not live on the premises, the rent should be raised to £150. The tenant violated the condition by non-residence. The landlord distrained; the tenant replevied; the landlord avowed; and while the proceedings at law were going on, the tenant filed his bill for a perpetual injunction. The Irish court granted an injunction. An appeal was taken to the House of Lords, where it was insisted that the covenant was only inserted for the sake of improvement, and that it was admitted by the pleadings that the lands had been kept well stocked, and that the agreement had been substantially performed. But the bill was dismissed. No reason being assigned, the case is altogether unsatisfactory; and if it was intended to decide that the covenant should be considered as one for stipulated damages, it would seem incorrect.

Again,[23] where the appellant Rolfe demised certain lands,

78, where assumpsit was brought on an agreement to serve the plaintiff as a leather dresser, under a penalty of £50, Lord Ellenborough, at Nisi Prius, said: "The legal construction of such an agreement is this: *beyond* the penalty you shall not go; *within* it, you are to give the party any compensation which he can prove himself entitled to."

[21] Benson *v.* Gibson, 3 Atk. 395 (1647).

[22] Ponsonby *v.* Adams, 2 Bro. P. C. 431, case 35 (anno 1770).

[23] Rolfe *v.* Peterson, 2 Bro. P. C. 436, case 42 (anno 1772).

with a covenant on the part of the lessee, that if he, during
the term, should convert into tillage any part of the ancient
meadow ground that had not been in tillage within twenty
years, or if he should plow or sow out of course any of the
arable lands, then for such lands converted or sown out of
course a further rent of £5 should be paid. There were other
covenants against cutting trees, etc. The tenant converted
certain furze land, which had not been tilled within twenty
years, into tillage, and committed breaches of the other covenants; upon which the landlord brought an action of covenant,
and, default being made, on a writ of inquiry recovered £300.
The respondent (the tenant) filed a bill for relief against the
judgment; and Lord Chancellor Camden directed an issue of
quantum damnificatus, holding that the plaintiff was entitled
to relief against the judgment, on making a just and adequate
satisfaction for the damages sustained by breach of the covenant. On appeal to the House of Lords, the main question
was whether, on an action of covenant by landlord against
lessee, and damages assessed by a jury, a court of equity has
jurisdiction to direct an issue for reassessing those damages.
It was insisted that the estate had been really benefited by
the conversion of the furze land into tillage, and that the £300
verdict was outrageous; but the Lords reversed the decree,
and dismissed the bill, no reason, however, being assigned.
The decision plainly turned on the jurisdiction of chancery,
and so far seems evidently right. The true construction of the
contract, whether to be regarded as a penalty or liquidated
damages, was not passed upon.

Again,[24] where the plaintiff and defendant were partners,
and the plaintiff had given the defendant a bond in a penalty
of £500 that he, the defendant, should have the use of a particular room, the use of it being refused, the defendant brought
suit on the bond. This bill was thereupon filed, praying an
injunction, and an issue of *quantum damnificatus;* and the only
question, on a motion to dissolve the injunction before hear-
ing, was whether the penalty was merely intended as a security for the use of the room, or in the nature of assessed

---

[24] Sloman *v.* Walter, 1 Brown Ch. 418.

damages. Lord Chancellor Thurlow held that it belonged to the former class, and the injunction was retained.[25]

§ 396.[26] Lowe v. Peers.

In a case already referred to,[27] the defendant had made a contract, under seal, not to marry any person besides the plaintiff; and if he did, to pay her £1,000 within three months thereafter. The defendant married another woman, and this suit was brought. Under the direction of Lord Mansfield, the jury found a verdict for the £1,000. On a motion for a new trial, the question was raised, whether the jury could give more or less damages than the £1,000; and it was insisted for the defendant that they might, if they saw fit, give less. But Lord Mansfield remarked on the difference between covenants in general, and covenants secured by a penalty or forfeiture, and said: "In the latter case the obligee has his election. He may either bring an action of debt for the penalty, and recover the penalty, after which recovery of the penalty he cannot resort to the covenant, because the penalty is to be a satisfaction for the whole; or if he does not choose to go for the penalty, he may proceed upon the covenant, and recover more or less than the penalty, *toties quoties;* and upon this distinction they proceed in courts of equity." That, in the former, to which this case belonged, even equity would not interfere. "The £1,000 is the particular liquidated sum fixed and agreed upon between the parties, and is therefore the proper quantum of the damages." But the judgment was arrested on account of the invalidity and illegality of the instrument. The doctrine of this decision has been recognized in the English Court of Exchequer, in an action on a covenant not to lop trees, under a given penalty for each tree.[28] The case seems, however, rather that of an agreement to pay a

---

[25] In the case of Hardy *v.* Martin, cited in notes to this case, the same course was pursued in regard to a bond given by one partner, on the dissolution of a partnership, not to trade; and very rightly. In Astley *v.* Weldon, 2 B. & P. 346, this latter case was referred to by Chambre, J., who said that he

was concerned in it, and that Lord Mansfield, at the trial at law, inclined to think it a case of stipulated damages.

[26] For § 396 of the eighth edition, see § 393.

[27] Lowe *v.* Peers, 4 Burr. 2225 (1768).

[28] Hurst *v.* Hurst, 4 Ex. 571.

certain sum on a contingency, which contingency is itself dependent on the choice of the party himself, and belongs more properly to a class of alternative obligations of which we shall have occasion to speak later.

§ 397.[29] Fletcher v. Dyche.

Where [30] a bond had been given by the plaintiff to the defendant in £236, conditioned that certain iron-work should be done by himself and another party for £118 18s. within six weeks, and if not, they would *"forfeit and pay"* [31] £10 for every week, till it was finished, the plaintiff brought an action for work and labor against the defendant; and the latter pleaded the bond in question, averred that the work had not been performed within the time limited, nor until four weeks thereafter, and insisted on a set-off of £40. Upon demurrer, it was contended that the £10 was a mere penalty, and could not be set off. But the court said that the sums offered to be set off were liquidated damages, which a court of equity could not relieve against; and Buller, J., said, "It is as strongly a case of liquidated damages as can possibly exist, and is *like the case of demurrage*"; and the demurrer was overruled. It seems, however, to be rather like the case last cited, a conditional agreement, where the party had his election to do the act or pay the money, and not having done the act, he is to be held as having made his election to pay the money.

§ 398. Leading cases—Astley v. Weldon.

The case which is looked upon as settling the doctrine of

[29] For § 397 of the eighth edition, see §§ 394–397.

[30] Fletcher *v.* Dyche, 2 T. R. 32 (1787).

[31] In Tayloe *v.* Sandiford, 7 Wheat. 13, 5 L. ed. 384, Marshall, C. J., commented on these words, and said, they were not so strongly indicative of a penalty as the word *"penalty"* itself. But in Horner *v.* Flintoff, 9 M. & W. 678, where an agreement was entered into binding the parties in the sum of £100 "as liquidated and settled damages, to be paid and *forfeited*," the Court of Exchequer [Parke, B.] said that the case came within that of Kemble *v.* Farren, hereinafter cited, but was rather stronger; "as the word *'forfeited'* was used, which points to a penalty." And in Cheddick *v.* Marsh, 21 N. J. L. 463, the Supreme Court of New Jersey said: "When a contracting party stipulates upon a given event to *forfeit and pay* a specified sum, the natural and plain import of the language is, that upon the happening of the contingency he will pay that precise sum, not that it shall stand by way of penalty or escurity for damages incurred."

liquidated damages in England is Astley *v.* Weldon,[32] where an agreement was entered into by the defendant to perform for the plaintiff at a theatre, and attend all rehearsals, or pay the established fines for all forfeitures of any kind whatsoever, with a clause that either of the parties neglecting to perform the agreement should pay the other £200. The declaration averred a refusal to perform; plea, non-assumpsit. On trial, a verdict was had for £20, with leave to the plaintiff to enter a verdict for £200, if the court should consider the agreement one in the nature of liquidated damages. Here it will be noticed that the phrase *liquidated damages* was not used, and that if the sum of £200 was not construed as a penalty merely, the non-payment of any one of the fines would have forfeited the whole amount. Lord Eldon, then Lord Chief Justice of the Common Pleas, in delivering the judgment of the court, said that he had felt much embarrassment in ascertaining the principle of the decisions, and that "this appeared to him the clearest principle, that where a doubt is stated, whether the sum inserted be intended as a penalty or not, *if a certain damage, less than that sum, is made payable upon the face of the same instrument in case the act intended to be prohibited be done,* that sum shall be construed to be a penalty"; though the mere fact of the sum being apparently enormous and excessive, would not prevent it from being considered as liquidated damages. He went on to say: "*Prima facie,* this certainly is contract, and not penalty, but we must look to the whole instrument"; and it was held a penalty.

This case of Astley *v.* Weldon was subsequently cited with approbation;[33] and there is no doubt, according to the suggestion of Lord Eldon, that the form of the instrument may make some difference; as, if it be a bond, the presumption will be that the greater sum is intended merely as a penalty. This is not, however, the necessary construction of such an instrument.

§ 399. Kemble v. Farren.

The doctrine laid down in Astley *v.* Weldon was applied in a subsequent case,[34] to a very similar state of facts. The

[32] 2 B. & P. 346.
[33] Street *v.* Rigby, 6 Ves. 815.
[34] Kemble *v.* Farren, 6 Bing. 141, 147.

defendant had agreed with the plaintiff to act as principal comedian at Covent Garden, and to conform to its rules; the plaintiff was to pay £3 6s. 8d. every night that the theatre should be open; and the agreement contained a clause, that if either party failed to fulfil his agreement, or any part thereof, or any stipulation therein contained, such party was to pay the sum of £1,000; to which sum it was agreed that the damages should amount, and which sum was declared by the parties to be *liquidated and ascertained damages, and not a penalty or penal sum, or in the nature thereof.* The breach alleged, was a refusal to act during the second season, and the jury gave a verdict for £750. A motion was made to increase this verdict to £1,000, on the ground that that sum was the amount liquidated by the parties; but it was denied, and Tindal, C. J., said:

"It is undoubtedly difficult to suppose any words more precise or explicit than those used in the agreement; the same declaring not only affirmatively that the sum of £1,000 should be taken as liquidated damages, but negatively also, that it should not be considered as a penalty or in the nature thereof. And if the clause had been limited to breaches which were of an uncertain nature and amount, we should have thought it would have had the effect of ascertaining the damages upon any such breach at £1,000. For we see nothing illegal or unreasonable in the parties, by their mutual agreement settling the amount of damages, uncertain in their nature, at any sum upon which they may agree. In many cases such an agreeement fixes that which is almost impossible to be accurately ascertained, and in all cases it saves the expense and difficulty of bringing witnesses to that point. But in the present case, the clause is not so confined; it extends to the breach of any stipulation by either party. If, therefore, on the one hand, the plaintiff had neglected to make a single payment of £3 6s. 8d. per day, or on the other hand, the defendant had refused to conform to any usual regulation of the theatre, however minute or unimportant, it must have been contended that the clause in question, in either case, would have given the stipulated damages of £1,000. But that a very large sum should become immediately payable in consequence of the non-payment of a very small sum, and that the former should not be considered as a penalty, appears to be a contradiction in terms; the case being precisely that in which courts of equity have always relieved, and against which courts of law have, in modern times, endeavored to relieve by directing juries to assess the real damages sustained by the breach of the agreement. It has been argued at the bar, that the liquidated damages apply to those breaches of the agreement only, which are in their nature uncertain, leaving those which are certain to a distinct remedy, by the verdict of a jury; but we can only say, if such is the intention of the parties, they have not expressed it, but have made the clause relate, by express and positive terms, to all breaches of every kind. We cannot, therefore, distinguish this case in principle from that of Astley v. Weldon, in which it was stipulated that either of the parties neglecting to perform the agreement should pay to the other of them the full sum of £200, to be recovered in his Majesty's courts at Westminster."

The authority of this case has been repeatedly recognized. So in a case in the Court of Exchequer, where the sum named was held a penalty only, Parke, B., said:

"When parties say that the same ascertained sum shall be paid for the breach of any article of an agreement, however minute and unimportant, they must be considered as not meaning exactly what they say, and a contrary intention may be collected from the other parts of the agreement. The rule laid down in Kemble v. Farren, was, that when an agreement contains several stipulations of various degrees of importance and value, a sum agreed to be paid by way of damages for the breach of any of them, shall be construed as a penalty, and not as liquidated damages, even though the parties have in express terms stated the contrary." [35]

§ 400. Early New York cases.

* The decisions in this country are now to be examined. Our courts will be found generally to be inclined to treat a fixed sum as a penalty, and to hold that the real damages are

[35] Horner v. Flintoff, 9 M. & W. 678. See, also, Boys v. Ancell, 5 Bing. N. C. 390; Beckham v. Drake, 8 M. & W. 846; reversed on another ground, 11 M. & W. 315; Edwards v. Williams, 5 Taunt. 247.

to be inquired into. Thus,[36] where the plaintiff had agreed to convey to the defendant seven hundred acres of land in exchange for a farm, valued at $3,750, with a further covenant that in case of failing, the party not fulfilling the covenant "should pay to the other party the sum of $2,000 damages," the Supreme Court of New York held this to be a penalty; and stress was laid on the great discrepancy between the value of the property to be exchanged, and the damages for not fulfilling the contract.

Where an agreement had been made [37] by which the defendant covenanted, on the first of January then next, to convey certain lands, and the plaintiff agreed to pay the price, $1,250, on the delivery of the deed, and in case of failure, they bound themselves each to the other in the sum of $500, which they consented to fix and liquidate as the amount of damages to be paid by the failing party; in this case it was held to be too clear for question; and the sum of $500 was to be regarded as liquidated damages. The plaintiff having by parol enlarged the time for the delivery of the deeds (although to no fixed day), it was insisted that such extension was a waiver of the liquidated damages, and that the plaintiff could only recover his actual loss; but the court held otherwise, and that the stated sum was still to be the measure of compensation.

In all cases where a party relies on the payment of liquidated damages as a discharge, it must clearly appear from the contract that they were to be paid and received absolutely in lieu of performance; and it is also settled here, as in England,[38] that a covenant, on a certain contingency to pay to another person a sum of money, with a provision that if he fails, then to pay a larger sum as liquidated damages, might be wholly incompatible with our laws in restraint of usury.

Both these points were ruled in a case [39] already referred to, where the plaintiff had made a bond and mortgage to a third party in the sum of $5,000, which had been assigned to the defendant, and a covenant was then entered into between them,

[36] Dennis v. Cummins, 3 Johns. Cas. 297.

[37] Hasbrouck v. Tappen, 15 Johns. 200.

[38] In Orr v. Churchill, 1 H. Black. 227.

[39] Gray v. Crosby, 18 Johns. 219.

that three several farms belonging to the plaintiff and covered by the mortgage, should be appraised by arbitration; that if their value fell short of the defendant's claim he should have them (*i. e.*, the three farms); if they exceeded his demands, he should pay the balance, with a stipulation that either party failing should forfeit to the other $500 as liquidated damages. The farms were assessed, a balance found in favor of the plaintiff, and the defendant refused to pay. The sum of $500 was claimed; and the defendant admitted that he was bound to pay that sum as liquidated damages, but insisted that on such payment, the whole agreement was to be rescinded; and as his $5,000 bond remained due, he offered to offset the $500 against the $5,000 due on the bond, and asked that the balance should be certified in his favor. But the jury, under the charge of the court, found a verdict for the plaintiff for the balance fixed by the appraisers; and on a motion for a new trial, this was held right. It was held, so far as the defendant was concerned, that the stipulated damages were not intended in lieu of a performance of anything to be done, nor as an extinguishment of the appraisement itself; and that as to the plaintiff, he could only recover the exact balance due him.

In the same State,[40] a contract to pay three hundred and sixty dollars for twelve cows and twelve calves, in four years, was held to be in the nature of a penalty merely, and that the plaintiff could only recover the value of the cows and calves. And this on the same grounds as in the last two cases.[41]

In a subsequent case,[42] the following facts were presented: By articles of dissolution between the plaintiff's intestate and the defendant, the defendant agreed to pay $3,000 in various instalments, of which the last was one of $750, on the 1st of December, 1812. The articles then recited, that the object was for the intestate entirely to quit the business, and for the defendant to continue it, and that such intention was the basis of allowing the $3,000, and then declared, that in case the intestate should be concerned in or carry on the same kind of business within twenty miles from the present stand,

---

[40] Spencer *v.* Tilden, 5 Cowen, 44.

[41] In Nobles *v.* Bates, 7 Cowen, 307,

this decision was said to go on the oppressiveness of the contract.

[42] Nobles *v.* Bates, 7 Cowen, 307.

the last instalment should not be paid. The action was for the last instalment; in answer to which the defendant proved that the plaintiff's intestate had recommenced the partnership business within four miles. It was insisted that the contract was in the nature of a penalty; but the court said: "A more suitable case for the liquidation of damages by the parties themselves can scarcely be imagined"; and the nonsuit which was directed at the trial was sustained.

The rule laid down in Astley v. Weldon, and already stated, that when the agreement contains formal distinct covenants on which there may be divers breaches, some of an uncertain nature, and others certain, with one entire sum specified to be paid on breach of performance, then the contract will be treated as one for a penalty and not liquidated damages, was approved in New York,[43] where a bond was given in the penal sum of $10,000, conditioned that the defendant would not practice as a physician, and if he did, that he should pay $500 for every month that he so practiced. Here the $10,000 was held to be penalty, and the $500 stipulated damages. And the same rule has been laid down in New Jersey.[44]

In a case [45] where the plaintiff had entered into an agreement with the defendants to sell them two lots of ground on certain terms, upon compliance with which the plaintiff was to give a deed, and to this a clause was added, "that if the parties of the second part should fail to perform this contract, or any part therein specified, they will pay the said party of the first part $25, *as liquidated damages*, and give immediate possession to the said party of the first part," the plaintiff brought an action of covenant for breach of the condition. The defendant pleaded tender of $25. But the Supreme Court of New York said: "There is nothing in this case which authorizes us to say that it was in the contemplation of the parties that the defendants might relieve themselves from their covenant to pay the price of the land by paying the sum agreed upon as stipulated damages, and surrendering possession"; and the plea was, for this as well as for other reasons, held bad.

[43] Smith v. Smith, 4 Wend. 468. See also Spear v. Smith, 1 Denio, 464.

[44] Cheddick v. Marsh, 21 N. J. L. 463.

[45] Ayres v. Pease, 12 Wend. 393.

Again,[46] where the defendant covenanted to assign to the plaintiff a lease, and to deliver possession thereof, with the following provision: "And I further covenant that, in case of non-performance of any or either of the above covenants, I will forfeit the sum of five hundred dollars, as the liquidated damages to the said Knapp," the same court said: "It is a clear case of liquidated damages, if it is in the power of parties to liquidate them."

§ 401. Dakin v. Williams.

The subject was much considered in a subsequent case:[47] the defendant Williams, for $3,000, sold to the plaintiff a newspaper establishment, called the "Utica Sentinel," and all his interest in the subscription, good-will, and patronage of the paper, together with the types, etc., for $500. In consideration of this the plaintiffs on their part covenanted to pay to Williams $3,500, namely, $3,000 for the patronage and good-will, etc., and $500 for the types, etc. And then followed a covenant by which the defendants agreed that they would not establish any paper in the city of Utica, nor suffer any paper to be established in any building owned by them, nor aid nor assist in such publication; and to this was added a clause binding the defendants to the strict and faithful performance of this covenant, and every part thereof, in the sum of $3,000; and declaring that the said sum of $3,000 should be, and was thereby fixed and settled as liquidated damages, and not as a penal sum for any violation of the preceding covenant, or any of its terms or conditions. The breach alleged was the publication of another paper. The cases which we have been considering were reviewed, and the $3,000 was held to be liquidated damages, both by the Supreme Court and Court of Errors. The Supreme Court held that it was only the province of the court to inquire into the intent of the parties, and that whether the bargain was wise or foolish was not for them to decide.

And in the Court of Errors, the chancellor, in pronouncing his opinion,[48] laid stress on the fact that, without the stipu-

[46] Knapp v. Maltby, 13 Wend. 587.

[47] Dakin v. Williams, 17 Wend. 447; and s. c. in Error, 22 Wend. 201.

[48] 22 Wendell, 210.

lation, the damages were wholly uncertain, and incapable of estimation otherwise than by conjecture. In a case in the same State,[49] the preference of the law to construe the stated sum as a penalty, was very strongly declared.**

§ 402. Tayloe v. Sandiford.

In 1822 the subject was considered by the Supreme Court of the United States.[50] A written contract was entered into, by which the defendants in error, T. & S. Sandiford, agreed to build for the plaintiff three houses on Pennsylvania Avenue, in Washington. A subsequent contract, under seal, was entered into between the same parties, for the building of three additional houses, "the said houses to be completely finished on or before the 24th day of December next, *under a penalty of one thousand dollars,* in case of failure." The three houses were not finished at the day. The plaintiff in error retained the sum of $1,000, as stipulated damages, out of the money due the defendants in error. This suit was brought; and on the trial the plaintiff in error (the defendant below) offered to set off the $1,000 as stipulated damages, which was not allowed; and the Supreme Court held the charge on this point right, though a new trial was ordered on other grounds. Marshall, C. J., said:

"In general, a sum of money in gross to be paid for the non-performance of an agreement, is considered as a penalty. It will not, of course, be considered as liquidated damages. Much stronger is the inference in favor of its being a penalty, when it is expressly reserved as one. The parties themselves denominate it a penalty, and it would require very strong evidence to authorize the court to say that their own words do not express their own intention.[51]

§ 403. Streeper v. Williams.

In the case of Streeper *v.* Williams [52] the owner of a hotel had agreed to sell it for $14,000, of which $3,000 were to be

[49] Hoag *v.* M'Ginnis, 22 Wend. 163, 165, *per* Cowen, J.

[50] Tayloe *v.* Sandiford, 7 Wheaton, 13, 17, 5 L. ed. 384.

[51] And the court referred to Smith *v.* Dickenson, 3 B. & P. 630; and Fletcher *v.* Dyche, 2 T. R. 32.

[52] 48 Pa. 450, 454.

paid on a specified day, when the deed was to be signed. Possession of the bar-room was to be given immediately. The parties mutually agreed to "forfeit" $500 in case of failure to keep the agreement. The $500 was held to be liquidated damages, and not a penalty. The court, per Agnew, J., in reference to the question under consideration, says:

"Upon no question have courts doubted and differed more. It is unnecessary to examine the numerous authorities in detail, for they are neither uniform nor consistent. No definite rule to determine the question is furnished by them, each being determined more in reference to its own facts than to any general rule. In the earlier cases the courts gave more weight to the language of the clause designating the sum as a penalty or as liquidated damages. The modern authorities attach greater importance to the meaning and intention of the parties; yet the intention is not all-controlling, for in some cases the subject-matter and surroundings of the contract will control the intention where equity absolutely demands it. A sum expressly stipulated as liquidated damages will be relieved from, if it is obviously to secure payment of another sum capable of being compensated by interest. On the other hand, a sum denominated a penalty or forfeiture will be considered liquidated damages, where it is fixed upon by the parties as the measure of the damages because the nature of the case, the uncertainty of the proof, or the difficulty of reaching the damages by proof, have induced them to make the damages a subject of previous adjustment. In some cases, the magnitude of the sum, and its proportion to the probable consequence of a breach, will cause it to be looked upon as minatory only. Upon the whole, the only general observation we can make is, that in each case we must look at the language of the contract, the intention of the parties as gathered from all its provisions, the subject of the contract and its surroundings, the ease or difficulty of measuring the breach in damages, and the sum stipulated, and from the whole gather the view which good conscience and equity ought to take of the case. Equity lies at the foundation of relief in the case of forfeiture and penalties, and hence the difficulty of reaching any general rule to govern all cases."

§ 404. Bagley v. Peddie.

In the case of Bagley *v.* Peddie [53] the subject was very thoroughly discussed both by the court below and on appeal. The defendant in that case had entered into sealed articles of agreement with the plaintiff, by which he covenanted to abide with the plaintiff four years, and serve him during that time according to his best ability, keep the secrets of the business, not misappropriate any money or property of the plaintiff, keep just accounts of the business, and render such accounts when required.

The Superior Court, in their opinion, stated the following tests for distinguishing between liquidated damages and a penalty:

"1. Where it is doubtful, on the face of the instrument, whether the sum mentioned was intended to be stipulated damages or a penalty to cover actual damages, the courts hold it to be the latter.

"2. On the contrary, where the language used is clear and explicit to that effect, the amount is to be deemed liquidated damages, however extravagant it may appear, unless the instrument be qualified by some of the circumstances hereafter mentioned.

"3. If the instrument provide that a larger sum shall be paid on the failure of the party to pay a less sum in the manner prescribed, the larger sum is a penalty, whatever may be the language used in describing it.

"4. When the covenant is for the performance of a single act or several acts, or the abstaining from doing some particular act or acts which are not measurable by any exact pecuniary standard, and it is agreed that the party covenanting, shall pay a stipulated sum as damages for a violation of any of such covenants, that sum is to be deemed liquidated damages, and not a penalty.

"5. Where the agreement secures the performance or omission of various acts of the kind mentioned in the last proposition, together with one or more acts in respect of which the damages on a breach of the covenant are certain or readily ascertainable by a jury, and there is a sum stipulated as dam-

[53] 5 Sand. 192, 194, 16 N. Y. 469.

ages to be paid by each party to the other, for a breach of any one of the covenants, such sum is held to be a penalty merely."

And the court below considered that two of the covenants in the agreement, one against wrongfully detaining plaintiff's moneys or property, and one requiring the defendant to give a true account of things committed to his management, were clearly certain in their nature, and that damages for their breach might be readily ascertained by a jury. They held, therefore, that the sum payable by the agreement was a penalty. Without apparently disapproving the principles relied on by the Superior Court, the Court of Appeals did not consider these covenants as having the certainty necessary to avoid the stipulation liquidating the damages, but held that the damages to result from a breach of any of the covenants were "uncertain and conjectural," and therefore, maintaining the stipulation as to the damages, reversed the decision because of the erroneous application of a sound principle.

§ 405. General rule.

From the foregoing we derive the following as a general rule governing the whole subject. Whenever the damages were evidently the subject of calculation and adjustment between the parties, and a certain sum was agreed upon and intended as compensation, and is in fact reasonable in amount, it will be allowed by the court as liquidated damages.[54] This rule will be found to be applicable to all contracts, and really involves the consideration of the subject in the three following aspects—that of the intent of the parties; that of the reasonableness of the contract; and that of the weight allowed by the court to the language employed.

[54] *Iowa:* Howes *v.* Axtell, 74 Ia. 400.

Massachusetts: Wakefield *v.* Stedman, 12 Pick. 562.

New York: Manice *v.* Brady, 15 Abb. Pr. 173.

Oregon: Pengra *v.* Wheeler, 24 Ore. 532, 34 Pac. 354.

Pennsylvania: Westerman *v.* Means, 12 Pa. 97; Powell *v.* Burroughs, 54 Pa. 329.

South Carolina: Williams *v.* Vance, 9 S. C. 344.

Texas: Durst *v.* Swift, 11 Tex. 273; Eakin *v.* Scott, 70 Tex. 442; Fessman *v.* Seeley (Tex. Civ. App.), 30 S. W. 268.

It may be observed here that any liquidation of damages must have all the essential elements of a contract. "It must have the mutual assent of both parties, and be supported by a sufficient consideration; and if conditional, the condition must be shown to have been performed." Union L. & E. Co. *v.* Erie Ry., 37 N. J. L. 23, 27.

§ 406. Intent of the parties.

The courts will not go outside the contract to ascertain the intention of the parties in entering into it. To do this would often be to violate the elementary maxim that parol evidence cannot be introduced to vary or control a written instrument, and, accordingly, it is well settled that the character of the agreement is a matter of law to be decided by the court upon a consideration of the whole instrument.[55] It is indeed said, in a work of great authority,[56] that the "burden of proof" will be upon the party who contends that the sum named in the contract is stipulated damages "to show that it was intended as such by the parties," but the only case referred to in support of the proposition is Tayloe v. Sandiford,[57] where the point was certainly not involved or adjudicated upon. In Moore v. Anderson,[58] Prof. Greenleaf's language is cited with approval, but there seems to have been no doubt as to the character of the instrument sued upon. The interpretation of a written contract by the court is, of course, a matter wholly apart from the question of the burden of proof. It may be that the phrase "burden of proof" was used by Prof. Greenleaf to indicate that, in case of doubt, the court would treat the sum fixed by the parties as a penalty;[59] but such a rule would be one of interpretation, not of evidence. Since, therefore, the intention of the parties cannot be gone into as a matter of fact outside the contract, it remains to be considered whether that intention, as expressed *in the contract*, is invariably followed. If it were, there would be no difference between the law applicable to these contracts and any others. But it is clear, from the cases already considered, that the intention of the parties is not necessarily the guide, though it is the fundamental matter for inquiry, and as always will so far as is legally possible be carried into effect.[60] In Kemble

[55] 2 Taylor, Ev., 8th ed., p. 963, § 1132; Sainter v. Ferguson, 7 C. B. 716. See, however, Wright v. Dobie, 3 Tex. Civ. App. 194, 22 S. W. 66.

[56] 2 Greenl. Ev., 14th ed., p. 267, § 257.

[57] 7 Wheat. 13, 5 L. ed. 384.

[58] 30 Tex. 224.

[59] § 408.

[60] *Alabama:* Stratton v. Fike, 166 Ala. 203, 51 So. 874.

New York: Perley v. Schubert, 121 App. Div. 786, 106 N. Y. Supp. 593; Salzer v. Sheffield F. S. D. Co., 115 N. Y. Supp. 81.

Texas: Elmore v. Rugely (Tex. Civ. App.), 107 S. W. 151.

v. Farren, for instance, where a sum of money fixed by the parties as "liquidated and ascertained damages, and not a penalty or penal sum, or in the nature thereof," was held by the court to be a penalty, it seems an abuse of language to say that this was in accordance with the parties' intention. The only method of reasoning, by which such a conclusion could be justified, would be that the parties cannot intend to agree upon a sum as stipulated damages when a principle of law makes the agreement futile; but this really begs the question. Clearly, therefore, the intention of the parties does not govern in a large class of cases, and it will be necessary to find some other guide to decide these by. To ascertain this, we must refer to the original equitable doctrine by which the penalty of a bond was avoided. This rested upon the duty of equity to relieve from unjust, unconscionable, and oppressive agreements. This whole equitable jurisdiction, so far as it related to contracts of the class under consideration, is now exercised by courts of law, which under the guise of interpreting them actually enforces or refuses to enforce them, as justice requires.

And here we are brought back by a somewhat circuitous path to the great fundamental principle which underlies our whole system: that of compensation. The great object of this system is to place the plaintiff in as good a position as he would have had if his contract had not been broken. So long as parties themselves keep this principle in view, they will be allowed to agree upon such a sum as will probably be a fair equivalent of a breach of contract. But when they go beyond this, and undertake to stipulate, not for compensation, but for a sum out of all proportion to the measure of liability which the law regards as compensatory, then the law will not allow the agreement to stand. In all agreements, therefore, fixing upon a sum in advance as the measure or limit of liability, the final question is whether the subject of the contract is such that it violates this fundamental rule of compensation. If it does so, the sum fixed is necessarily a penalty. If it does not do so, the question arises, as in any other contract,

---

In *Colorado* it is said that the real intent of the parties to liquidate damages will always be carried into effect; but their words are not necessarily conclusive. Bilz *v.* Powell, 117 Pac. 344.

as to what agreement the parties have actually made, and here, as in all other cases, their intention, as ascertained from the language employed, is a guide. It is not, however, conclusive, and the mere use of the word "penalty," "penal," "forfeit," on one side, or "stipulated damages" on the other, will not decide the question. As to the effect of the use of these words, the decisions are often confusing; in most cases where the first class of words are used, the agreement will be found to be of that kind in which the law determines the character of the sum designated; but where the intention of the parties is allowed to govern, there is no reason why the use of a particular word should be of conclusive force.

§ 407. The liquidation must be reasonable.

The parties, then, must not only intend that the sum named shall be paid over to the plaintiff upon the breach; the sum must also be reasonable in itself.[61] In other words, in every case where a fixed sum is stipulated as damages, the court will look to see whether the stipulated compensation is a reasonable one; and if not, they will require damages to be assessed as if no stipulated sum were named in the contract. In the words of the Supreme Court of Michigan: "Just compensation for the injury sustained is the principle at which the law aims, and the parties will not be permitted, by express stipulation, to set this principle aside." [62] So firmly is this principle applied that the liquidation provided by a contract may, as the circumstances show to be equitable, in one case be upheld, and in another set aside. Thus in Hahn v. Horstman,[63] a case of a common building contract, with stipulated damages at the rate of twenty dollars a day for delay in completing the contract, the defendant left the work unfinished; and the plaintiff, more than a year after the time for completion, brought suit, claiming damages for the whole time at the stipulated rate. If the work had been finished, though a few

[61] *California:* People v. C. P. R. R., 76 Cal. 29.

New York: Perzell v. Shook, 53 N. Y. Super. Ct. 501; Mawson v. Leavitt, 37 N. Y. Supp. 1138; McCann v. Albany, 42 N. Y. Supp. 94.

Wisconsin: Gates v. Parmly, 93 Wis. 739, 66 N. W. 253.

Canada: Sleeman v. Waterous, 23 Up. Can. C. P. 195.

[62] Marston, J., in Myer v. Hart, 40 Mich. 517, 523.

[63] 12 Bush, 249.

days after the agreed time, it is well settled, as will be seen, that the stipulated sum could be recovered. In this case, however, to allow recovery at the stipulated rate would be grossly in excess of compensation; and the court refused to allow damages at the stipulated rate.[64]

Some courts say that the damages must not be "grossly excessive," [65] some that they must not be "unjust and oppressive," [66] "unreasonable," [67] "extravagant," [68] or "disproportionate"; [69] but all seem to agree upon the principle that the stipulated sum will not be allowed as liquidated damages unless it may fairly be allowed as compensation for the breach.[70] Thus where a contract of hiring provided that, on the servant leaving without notice, whatever was then due to him should be considered as liquidated damages for the breach of his contract, it was held that the forfeiture would not be enforced by the courts. Since the arrears of wages might be large or small, the principle of compensation was clearly departed from by the parties; [71] but the forfeiture of a fixed reasonable sum would be allowed.[72]   So in any case if the damages

[64] *Acc.*, Greer *v.* Tweed, 13 Abb. (N. S.) 427; Colwell *v.* Foulks, 36 How. Pr. 306.

[65] Parr *v.* Greenbush, 42 Hun, 232.

[66] *Illinois:* Scofield *v.* Tompkins, 95 Ill. 190; Mueller *v.* Kleine, 27 Ill. App. 473.

Massachusetts: Higginson *v.* Weld, 14 Gray, 165.

[67] *Georgia:* Hardee *v.* Howard, 33 Ga. 533; Sutton *v.* Howard, 33 Ga. 536.

Maine: Maxwell *v.* Allen, 78 Me. 32.

Pennsylvania: Daly *v.* Maitland, 88 Pa. 384.

South Carolina: Williams *v.* Vance, 9 S. C. 344.

Tennessee: Schrimpf *v.* Tenn. Manuf. Co., 86 Tenn. 219.

[68] Gammon *v.* Howe, 14 Me. 250.

[69] *Indiana:* Jaqua *v.* Headington, 114 Ind. 309.

Missouri: Hamaker *v.* Schroers, 49 Mo. 406.

New York: Staples *v.* Parker, 41 Barb. 648.

[70] *Kansas:* Tholen *v.* Duffy, 7 Kan. 405.

Massachusetts: Stearns *v.* Barrett, 1 Pick. 443.

Missouri: Gower *v.* Saltmarsh, 11 Mo. 271.

New York: Dennis *v.* Cummins, 3 Johns. Cas. 297.

North Carolina: Burrage *v.* Crump, 3 Jones, L. 330.

Pennsylvania: Pennypacker *v.* Jones, 106 Pa. 237.

Canada: Jones *v.* Queen, 7 Can. 570.

[71] *Michigan:* Richardson *v.* Woehler, 26 Mich. 90.

New York: Schmieder *v.* Kingsley, 6 Misc. 107, 26 N. Y. Supp. 31 (but see Fenster *v.* Bass, 107 N. Y. Supp. 872.

Tennessee: Schrimpf *v.* Tenn. Manuf. Co., 86 Tenn. 219; Tennessee Mfg. Co. *v.* James, 91 Tenn. 154, 18 S. W. 262, 30 Am. St. Rep. 865, 15 L. R. A. 211.

Canada: Jones *v.* Queen, 7 Can. 570.

[72] *Michigan:* Richardson *v.* Woehler, 26 Mich. 90.

are capable of estimate with reasonable certainty, a greater amount of stipulated damages will be regarded as a penalty.[73] A transaction was once common in certain parts of the country, whereby a debtor in embarrassed circumstances obtained an extension of time from his creditors by means of an agreement by them not to sue on their demands for a certain length of time, it being provided in the agreement that if suit were brought within the time limited, the debt should be wholly discharged. This provision was enforced by the Supreme Court of Massachusetts.[74] It will be seen that breach of the agreement by one creditor might defeat the whole transaction, and therefore that the stipulation was not at all unreasonable.

§ 408. Language not conclusive—Rule in case of doubt.

It follows from what has been said that the language of the contract is not conclusive.[75] The question whether a stipulated sum is to be allowed as liquidated damages is a question of law,[76] and no agreement of the parties to call it a penalty or liquidated damages can decide the question. It is expressly said in a well-considered case decided by the Supreme Court of Michigan, that even if it were admitted as a fact that the parties intended the sum to be considered as liquidated damages and not as a penalty, the admission could have no influence upon the decision of a court of law.[77] The mere use of the word "penalty," "penal," or "forfeit" on one side, or "stipulated damages" on the other, will therefore not decide the question.[78] The only inquiry as to intention is whether

New York: Salzer v. Sheffield F. S. D. Co., 115 N. Y. Supp. 81.

As where a week's wages are to be retained:

Georgia: Gleaton v. Fulton B. & C. Mills, 5 Ga. App. 420, 63 S. E. 520.

Michigan: Wilson v. Godkin, 136 Mich. 106, 98 N. W. 985.

Or a certain amount for each week of the unexpired term. Werner v. Finley, 144 Mo. App. 544, 129 S. W. 73.

So where a portion of the compensation was to be retained weekly until it amounted to a certain sum, which was to be held to secure performance, this was held a valid liquidation.

Bilz v. Powell (Colo.), 117 Pac. 344.

[73] *Indiana:* Walker v. Bement (Ind. App.), 94 N. E. 339; J. I. Case T. Co. v. Souders, 96 N. E. 177.

Nebraska: Haffke v. Coffin, 130 N. W. 1045.

[74] White v. Dingley, 4 Mass. 433.

[75] *United States:* Gay Mfg. Co. v. Camp, 65 Fed. 794, 13 C. C. A. 137.

Massachusetts: Leary v. Laflin, 101 Mass. 334.

[76] Sainter v. Ferguson, 7 C. B. 716; Reindel v. Schell, 4 C. B. (N. S.) 97.

[77] Jaquith v. Hudson, 5 Mich. 123, 136.

[78] *United States:* Bignall v. Gould, 119 U. S. 495, 30 L. ed. 491, 7 Sup. Ct. 294.

or not the parties intended the sum to be accepted *as compensation.* That is a question involving the interpretation of the contract, and of course no evidence on the question can be received *dehors* the instrument. The case of Bigony *v.* Tyson [79] is in conflict with the views expressed here. There the agreement was in the form of a common bond, binding Bigony not to practice medicine within a certain district. The court below charged the jury that the sum named in the bond was liquidated damages. This the court above decided to be error, but sent the case down for a new trial, on the ground that while there was nothing in the instrument itself which would enable the court to construe it as anything but a bond, the plaintiff was entitled to have the jury pass upon the intention of the parties outside the contract. The court even speaks of the "well established" rule that "the intention of the parties, gathered *extra* the written instrument, may control the technical rule as found upon the face of that instrument, and thus fix the sum therein mentioned as stipulated damages"; and adds, "it is obvious, then, that this dispute, involving, as it does, the character of the obligation in controversy, can be settled only by a jury." The court refers, however, to no authorities, and the decision cannot be supported on principle.

California: Pogue *v.* Keweah P. & W. Co., 138 Cal. 664, 72 Pac. 144.

Illinois: Scofield *v.* Tompkins, 95 Ill. 190.

Indiana: Duffy *v.* Shockey, 11 Ind. 70; Merica *v.* Burget, 36 Ind. App. 453, 75 N. E. 1083.

Iowa: Beard *v.* Delaney, 35 Ia. 16; Sanders *v.* McKim, 138 Ia. 122, 115 N. W. 917.

Massachusetts: Pierce *v.* Fuller, 8 Mass. 223.

Michigan: Jaquith *v.* Hudson, 5 Mich. 123; Ross *v.* Loescher, 152 Mich. 386, 116 N. W. 195.

Missouri: Basye *v.* Ambrose, 28 Mo. 39.

Montana: Wibaux *v.* Grinnell L. S. Co., 9 Mont. 154, 22 Pac. 492.

New York: Nobles *v.* Bates, 7 Cow. 307; Ward *v.* Hudson R. B. Co., 125 N. Y. 230, 26 N. E. 256; Brownold *v.*

Rodbell, 130 App. Div. 371, 114 N. Y. Supp. 846.

Oregon: Wilhelm *v.* Eaves, 21 Or. 194, 27 Pac. 1053, 14 L. R. A. 297.

Pennsylvania: Streeper *v.* Williams, 48 Pa. 450.

Texas: Eakin *v.* Scott, 70 Tex. 442, 7 S. W. 777; McMillan *v.* First Nat. Bank (Tex. Civ. App.), 119 S. W. 709.

Wisconsin: Yenner *v.* Hammond, 36 Wis. 277; Seeman *v.* Biemann, 108 Wis. 365, 84 N. W. 490.

Canada: Henderson *v.* Nichols, 5 Up. Can. Q. B. 398; Chatterton *v.* Crothers, 9 Ont. 683.

England: Parfitt *v.* Chambre, L. R. 15 Eq. 36; Fletcher *v.* Dyche, 2 T. R. 32; Sainter *v.* Ferguson, 7 C. B. 716; Jones *v.* Green, 3 Y. & J. 298.

[79] 75 Pa. 157. See to the same effect: Disisway *v.* Edwards, 134 N. C. 254, 46 S. E. 501.

The prevailing doctrine is that in interpreting the contract, the court when in doubt will presume the parties not to have meant the stipulated sum to be compensation, or in other words, will treat the sum fixed by the parties as a penalty; [80] but in a few jurisdictions, notably in the Supreme Court of the United States and in Massachusetts, the court is inclined to regard the sum named as an effective liquidating of damages unless the contrary is shown.[81]

§ 408a. Breach of contract necessary.

The parties may also use the term "liquidated damages," when what is really meant is neither such damages, nor a penalty. Thus when the right was reserved to terminate the contract by notice, and payment to the contractor for all labor performed, and $3,000 "liquidated damages," this was held not to be liquidated damages for breach of contract, but a power reserved in the contract of discharging it. Hence (this power not having been exercised) on an actual breach, the contractor was not restricted in his recovery by it, nor would he recover it in addition to his actual damages.[82]

§ 409. Rules of interpretation.

Having now stated the general rules applicable to all contracts, we proceed to examine the particular canons applicable in certain well-defined classes of cases. These, however, are derived from and are themselves no more than particular

[80] *Alabama:* Stratton *v.* Fike, 166 Ala. 203, 51 So. 874.

California: People *v.* C. P. R. R., 76 Cal. 29.

Georgia: Brunswick *v.* Ætna Indemnity Co., 4 Ga. App. 722, 62 S. E. 475.

Missouri: Thompson *v.* St. Charles County, 227 Mo. 220, 126 S. W. 1044.

North Carolina: Disisway *v.* Edwards, 134 N. C. 254, 46 S. E. 501.

South Carolina: Bearden *v.* Smith, 11 Rich. L. 554.

Tennessee: Baird *v.* Tolliver, 6 Humph. 186.

Texas: Moore *v.* Anderson, 30 Tex. 224; Kellam *v.* Hampton (Tex. Civ. App.), 124 S. W. 970; Stidham *v.* Laurie (Tex. Civ. App.), 133 S. W. 1082.

Vermont: Smith *v.* Wainright, 24 Vt. 97, 103.

Canada: Henderson *v.* Nichols, 5 Up. Can. Q. B. 398.

England: Davies *v.* Penton, 6 B. & C. 216; Crisdee *v.* Bolton, 3 C. & P. 240.

[81] *United States:* U. S. *v.* Bethlehem Steel Co., 205 U. S. 105, 25 Sup. Ct. 450, 51 L. ed. 731.

Minnesota: Lunt *v.* Egeland, 104 Minn. 351, 116 N. W. 653.

Missouri: Werner *v.* Finley, 144 Mo. App. 544, 129 S. W. 73.

New York: Peabody *v.* Richard Realty Co., 125 N. Y. Supp. 349, 69 Misc. 582.

[82] Curnan *v.* Delaware & Otsego R. R., 138 N. Y. 480, 34 N. E. 201.

applications of the general rules. It should be observed, also, that they are really artificial canons of interpretation, applied by the court to the construction of the contract, and are not formulated as positive rules of law for the guidance of the jury. They only express the experience of judges in applying a variety of tests to the contract in order to determine whether it conforms to a certain legal standard, or whether, falling short of this standard, it must be set aside.

§ 410. Penal sum collateral to object of contract.

Where the stipulated sum is wholly collateral to the object of the contract, being evidently inserted merely as security for performance, it will not be allowed as liquidated damages. In a contract for the sale of land for $8,000, payable, $5,000 on the 1st of January following, and the rest in three annual instalments, a clause stating that "in further confirmation of the said agreement, the parties bind themselves, each to the other, in the penal sum of $1,000," is not to be considered as liquidated damages for the breach of this agreement, but as a penalty superadded.[83]

The plaintiff drew up and delivered to the defendant a written lease of land of the plaintiff, and the defendant agreed to return the lease in ninety days or pay $3,000 on failure to do so. It was held that this sum was wholly collateral to the loan of the written instrument, and was not liquidated damages.[84] The defendant agreed to allow the plaintiff to use a certain building while it stood, and gave him a note payable on breach of the agreement. This note was held not to be enforceable, since it was in the nature of a penalty.[85] And where the plaintiff allowed the defendant to use electrotype plates for a certain purpose, and the defendant agreed to pay a fine to the owner equal to ten times the price of the plates in case of injury to the plates, this was held a penalty.[86]

[83] *District of Columbia:* Robinson *v.* Cathcart, 2 Cr. C. C. 590.

New York: Richards *v.* Edick, 17 Barb. 260.

South Carolina: Law *v.* House, 3 Hill, 268.

Virginia: Potomac Power Co. *v.* Burchell, 109 Va. 676, 64 S. E. 982.

West Virginia: Wilkes *v.* Bierne, 69 S. E. 366.

[84] Burrage *v.* Crump, 3 Jones, L. (N. C.) 330.

[85] Merrill *v.* Merrill, 15 Mass. 488.

[86] Meyer *v.* Estes, 164 Mass. 457, 41 N. E. 683, 32 L. R. A. 283.

50

A penal bond comes ordinarily under this rule. In some exceptional cases the penalty in a bond, as will be seen, is regarded as liquidated damages; but in general it is regarded as a penalty.[87] So of a bond to submit to arbitration,[88] or to convey land.[89] The rule is the same if such an arrangement is in the form of an ordinary contract. If an agreement to submit to arbitration is secured by a promise to pay a collateral sum of money on breach of the agreement, that sum is held to be a penalty, and payment of it is not enforced by the court.[90] And though the use of the words "penalty," "forfeiture," "liquidated damages" is not conclusive, it will be considered by the court as indicating the intention of the parties as to whether the sum named was or was not regarded by them as compensatory.[91] In fact, there has been a disposition to regard the word "penalty" as conclusive; and though this is not an absolute rule, yet great reluctance is shown in construing as liquidated damages a sum expressly called a penalty by the parties. But even the penal sum in

[87] *Illinois:* Doane *v.* Chicago City Ry., 51 Ill. App. 353.

Indiana: Dill *v.* Lawrence, 109 Ind. 564, 10 N. E. 573.

Iowa: Bolster *v.* Post, 57 Iowa, 698, 111 N. W. 637.

Kansas: Cimarron Land Co. *v.* Barton, 51 Kan. 554, 33 Pac. 317.

Mississippi: Coker *v.* Brevard, 90 Miss. 64, 43 So. 177.

Nebraska: Gillilan *v.* Rollins, 41 Neb. 540, 59 N. W. 893.

New Hampshire: Davis *v.* Gillett, 52 N. H. 126.

Pennsylvania: Keck *v.* Bieber, 148 Pa. 645, 24 Atl. 170, 33 Am. St. Rep. 846.

Utah: McIntosh *v.* Johnson, 8 Utah, 359, 31 Pac. 450.

[88] Henry *v.* Davis, 123 Mass. 345.

[89] *Kansas:* Cimarron Land Co. *v.* Barton, 51 Kan. 554, 33 Pac. 317.

Massachusetts: Brown *v.* Bellows, 4 Pick. 179.

Pennsylvania: Robeson *v.* White-sides, 16 S. & R. 320; Burr *v.* Todd, 41 Pa. 206.

So of a building and loan association contract: Tilley *v.* American B. & L. Assoc., 52 Fed. 618.

[90] *New York:* Spear *v.* Smith, 1 Den. 464.

North Carolina: Henderson *v.* Cansler, 65 N. C. 542.

[91] *United States:* Van Buren *v.* Digges, 11 How. 461, 13 L. ed. 771; Bignall *v.* Gould, 119 U. S. 495, 30 L. ed. 491, 7 Sup. Ct. 294; Nichols *v.* Haines, 96 Fed. 692, 39 C. C. A. 235.

Maryland: Dyer *v.* Dorsey, 1 G. & J. 440.

Massachusetts: Stearns *v.* Barrett, 1 Pick. 443.

New York: Salters *v.* Ralph, 15 Abb. Pr. 273; Colwell *v.* Foulks, 36 How. Pr. 306.

South Carolina: Williams *v.* Vance, 9 S. C. 344.

Vermont: Smith *v.* Wainwright, 24 Vt. 97.

England: Reilly *v.* Jones, 1 Bing. 302.

a bond may be shown really to be a proper liquidation of damages. So where the plaintiff conveyed unimproved property to defendant, taking back a bond in a penal sum equal to the value of the property, conditioned upon the building of a cable road, the property being part of a bonus to secure this, and the road was not built, the measure of damages on the bond is the penal sum without interest, this being the exact equivalent of the loss suffered.[92]

§ 411. Stipulated sum for non-payment of smaller sum.

Whenever an amount stipulated is to be paid on the non-payment of a less amount or on default in delivering a thing of less value, the sum will generally be treated as a penalty.[93] Thus where the defendant, as surety, bound himself in the sum of $240, for the performance by his principal of a contract to deliver two boat-loads of coal, the sum to be recoverable on failure to deliver either, the sum was not allowed as

[92] Blewett *v.* Front St. Ry., 49 Fed. 126, 7 U. S. App. 285, 2 C. C. A. 415.

[93] *United States:* White *v.* Arleth, 1 Bond, 319.

Arkansas: Haldeman *v.* Jennings, 14 Ark. 329.

Illinois: Tiernan *v.* Hinman, 16 Ill. 400; Peine *v.* Weber, 47 Ill. 41; Morris *v.* Tillson, 81 Ill. 607; Bryton *v.* Marston, 33 Ill. App. 211.

Iowa: Kuhn *v.* Myers, 37 Ia. 351.

Kentucky: Hahn *v.* Horstman, 12 Bush, 249.

Massachusetts: Fisk *v.* Gray, 11 All. 132; Kellogg *v.* Curtis, 9 Pick, 534.

Missouri: Morse *v.* Rathburn, 42 Mo. 594.

Nevada: Morris *v.* McCoy, 7 Nev. 399.

North Carolina: Lindsay *v.* Anesley, 6 Ired. 186; Thoroughgood *v.* Walker, 2 Jones, L. 15.

Vermont: Smith *v.* Wainwright, 24 Vt. 97.

Canada: Rutherford *v.* Stovel, 12 Up. Can. C. P. 9.

In Gowen *v.* Gerrish, 15 Me. 273, defendant entered into a bond with plaintiff for $7,000, conditioned that he should not become surety for any other person than plaintiff, until he should have paid him a debt of $6,000, for which a long credit had been given. The credit had been given upon a contract for the purchase of real estate, and the sum secured by the bond exceeded by one-sixth the price agreed. The court said that this must have been intended to *secure* the accruing interest, and held the measure of damages on breach to be the original price, with interest. This case is cited in an article contributed to the *American Law Review* by the late Mr. John Proffatt of the California Bar (12 Am. L. R. 286), as one in which the damages were held to have been liquidated, but we do not so understand the language of the court.

In Poppers *v.* Meager, 148 Ill. 192, 35 N. E. 805, it was said that the rules deducible from the cases were (1) that where a greater sum was to be paid for default in payment of a lesser sum at a given time the provision was a penalty; (2) where the damages are not difficult of ascertainment and the sum stipu-

liquidated damages.[94] But the larger sum may appear to be a fair compensation for the breach. Thus where the larger sum is a debt actually due, but the debtor may discharge the debt by the payment before a certain time of a less sum, the payment of the larger sum may be enforced after that date.[95] So a note for a sum certain at a future day, which may be discharged by the payment of a lesser sum on any earlier day, is valid, and the larger sum is not a penalty.[96] Damages for such delay will often be an equivalent for interest. So a stipulation that in case of non-payment of a note at maturity a certain additional sum should be paid as liquidated damages for delay was held reasonable, and the amount was allowed as liquidated damages.[97] On the same principle, a provision in a note that it shall bear interest at a certain rate from its date if the principal is not paid at maturity is valid, and the arrears of interest is liquidated damages for non-payment of the money.[98]

lated is unconscionable it will be regarded as a penalty; (3) within these rules parties may agree upon any sum as compensation for breach of contract. The action was to recover for a sum stipulated as damages for holding over leased premises. It was about 50% in excess of the rent. The court said that in view of the difficulty of renting after the season is passed the amount was not unreasonable.

[94] Curry v. Larer, 7 Pa. 470.

[95] *United States:* U. S. Mortgage Co. v. Sperry, 138 U. S. 313, 34 L. ed. 969, 11 Sup. Ct. 321.

England: Thompson v. Hudson, L. R. 4 H. L. 1.

[96] *Alabama:* Jordan v. Lewis, 2 Stew. 426; Carter v. Corley, 23 Ala. 612.

Ohio: Waggoner v. Cox, 40 Oh. St. 539.

Virginia: Campbell v. Shields, 6 Leigh, 517.

But *contra*, Moore v. Hylton, 1 Dev. Eq. 429.

[97] *Georgia:* Sutton v. Howard, 33 Ga. 536.

Texas: Yetter v. Hudson, 57 Tex. 604.

But *contra*, Taul v. Everet, 4 J. J. Marsh. 10; Brockway v. Clark, 6 Oh. 46.

[98] *California:* Main v. Casserly, 67 Cal. 127, 7 Pac. 426.

Georgia: Alexander v. Troutman, 1 Kelly, 469.

Illinois: Reeves v. Stipp, 91 Ill. 609.

Indiana: Hackenburg v. Shaw, 11 Ind. 392.

Iowa: Wilson v. Dean, 10 Ia. 432; Fisher v. Anderson, 25 Ia. 28.

Kansas: Parker v. Plymell, 23 Kan. 402.

Kentucky: Rumsey v. Matthews, 1 Bibb, 242.

Mississippi: Rogers v. Sample, 33 Miss. 310.

South Carolina: Satterwhite v. McKie, Harp. 397.

Tennessee: McNairy v. Bell, 1 Yerg. 502.

Contra, Virginia: Waller v. Long, 6 Munf. 71.

Washington: Krutz v. Robbins, 12 Wash. 7, 40 Pac. 415.

§ 411.ᵃ A stipulated sum obviously greater than the damage.

Whenever the stipulated sum is obviously greater than the damage could be, it will not be allowed as liquidated damages. So where the contract called for a recovery of twice the amount of the actual damages, the provision for such recovery is a penalty.[99] Where a purchaser agrees that if he does not pay for the thing bought at a certain time he will be liable for the payment, but the seller may keep the property, this is an agreement for a penalty, since the loss cannot equal the full value of the property.[100] And conversely where it is provided that upon default of the seller (either by failure to deliver or by breach of warranty) the property shall become the property of the buyer, and he need pay nothing for it, this is an agreement for a penalty.[101] Even where the sum named as damages for failure in the contract for sale· was five-sevenths of the purchase-money, this was held necessarily a penalty.[102] On this ground it has been held that where only nominal damages are suffered by a breach of contract, no liquidated damages will be allowed.[103]

§ 412. Stipulated sum not proportioned to injury.

Whenever the stipulated sum is to be paid on breach of a contract of such a nature that the loss may be much greater or much less than the sum, it will not be allowed as liquidated damages. In a contract providing for payment in instalments it is often provided that a certain proportion of the contract price shall

[99] Carruthers v. Gay (Tex. Civ.App.), 91 S. W. 593.

[100] *Illinois:* Scofield v. Tompkins, 95 Ill. 190.

Rhode Island: Bradstreet v. Baker, 14 R. I. 546.

[101] *California:* Greenleaf v. Stockton C. H. & A. Works, 78 Cal. 606, 21 Pac. 360.

Kentucky: Daniel v. Lumber Co., 85 S. W. 1092.

[102] Hurd v. Dunsmore, 63 N. H. 171.

But in Louis v. Brown, 7 Ore. 326, a contract to cut a certain number of cords of wood by a given time, a stip-

ulation that in case it was not cut by the time named, the defendant should forfeit 5 cents per cord and what wood he had cut, was held a reasonable stipulation fixing the damages.

[103] *Missouri:* Werner v. Finley (Mo. App.), 129 S. W. 73.

New York: Dunn v. Morgenthau, 73 App. Div. 147, 76 N. Y. Supp. 827, affirmed, 175 N. Y. 518, 67 N. E. 1081; Traut-Ditmar Const. Co. v. Hartman, 61 Misc. 173, 112 N. Y. Supp. 919; Fehlinger v. Boos, 118 N. Y. Supp. 167.

Wisconsin: Hathaway v. Lynn, 75 Wis. 187, 43 N. W. 956, 6 L. R. A. 553.

be retained at each payment; and upon breach of the contract the whole sum so retained shall be forfeited. It is held in some States, and this seems to be the correct view, that this sum bears no proportion to the actual damage, since the earlier (and presumably the more injurious) the breach, the less the stipulated damages are; and in these States the amount is therefore not allowed as liquidated damages.[104] In other States, however, the amount, if not excessive, is allowed.[105] A similar case arises where upon the sale of property to be paid for in instalments, the contract provides that upon failure to pay an instalment the seller shall keep the property, and the buyer forfeit the instalments already paid; this is an agreement for a forfeiture, and will not be enforced.[106] And where in a contract of employment it is provided that upon breach by the servant the master may retain the unpaid wages as damages, this is not a good liquidation of damages, since the amount that happened to be in the employer's hands at the time of the breach would bear no relation to the amount of actual loss.[107]

§ 413. One sum stipulated for breach of contract securing several things.

A sum fixed as security for the performance of a contract containing a number of stipulations of widely different importance, breaches of some of which are capable of accurate valuation,

---

[104] *Alabama:* Henderson-Boyd Lumber Co. *v.* Cook, 149 Ala. 226, 42 So. 838.

Georgia: Savannah & C. R. R. *v.* Callahan, 56 Ga. 331.

Iowa: Jemmison *v.* Gray, 29 Ia. 537.

Missouri: Potter *v.* McPherson, 61 Mo. 240.

Texas: Gulf, C. & S. F. Ry. *v.* Wards (Tex. Civ. App.), 34 S. W. 328.

Virginia: Stony Creek L. Co. *v.* Fields, 102 Va. 1, 45 S. E. 797.

Wisconsin: Dullaghan *v.* Fitch, 42 Wis. 679, explaining and affirming Jackson *v.* Cleveland, 19 Wis. 400; Kerslake *v.* McInnis, 113 Wis. 659, 89 N. W. 895.

[105] *Kentucky:* Elizabethtown & P. R. R. *v.* Geoghegan, 9 Bush, 56.

Maryland: Geiger *v.* W. M. R. R., 41 Md. 4.

Ohio: Easton *v.* P. & O. Canal Co., 13 Oh. 79.

[106] *Georgia:* Lytle *v.* Scottish American Mortg. Co., 122 Ga. 458, 50 S. E. 402.

South Dakota: Barnes *v.* Clement, 8 S. D. 421, 66 N. W. 810.

Contra, Keefe *v.* Fairfield, 184 Mass. 334, 68 N. E. 342; K. E. Mining Co. *v.* Jacobson, 30 Utah, 115, 83 Pac. 728, 4 L. R. A. (N. S.) 755.

[107] *Ante,* § 407.

for any of which the stipulated sum is an excessive compensation, is a penalty.[108] The rule is not always fully stated in the cases;

[108] *United States:* Watts *v.* Camors, 115 U. S. 353, 29 L. ed. 406, 6 Sup. Ct. 91; Charleston Fruit Co. *v.* Bond, 26 Fed. 18; East Moline Co. *v.* Weir Plow Co., 95 Fed. 250, 37 C. C. A. 62; Chicago House-Wrecking Co. *v.* U. S., 106 Fed. 385, 45 C. C. A. 343.

Arkansas: Stillwell *v.* Lumber Co., 73 Ark. 432, 84 S. W. 483, 108 Am. St. Rep. 42.

California: Nash *v.* Hermosilla, 9 Cal. 584; People *v.* C. P. R. R., 76 Cal. 29.

Florida: Smith *v.* Newell, 27 Fla. 147, 20 So. 249.

Georgia: Brunswick *v.* Ætna Indemnity Co., 4 Ga. App. 722, 62 S. E. 475; Florence Wagon Wks. *v.* Salmon (Ga. App.), 68 S. E. 866.

Illinois: Trower *v.* Elder, 77 Ill. 452; Steer *v.* Brown, 106 Ill. App. 361; Iroquois Furnace Co. *v.* Wilkin Mfg. Co., 181 Ill. 582, 54 N. E. 994.

Indiana: Carpenter *v.* Lockhart, 1 Ind. 434.

Iowa: Foley *v.* McKeegan, 4 Ia. 1, 66 Am. Dec. 101; Lord *v.* Gaddis, 9 Ia. 265; Hallock *v.* Slater, 9 Ia. 599; De Graff *v.* Wickham, 89 Ia. 720, 52 N. W. 503, 57 N. W. 420; Kelly *v.* Fejervary, 111 Ia. 693, 83 N. W. 791; Sanders *v.* McKim, 138 Ia. 122, 115 N. W. 917.

Kansas: St. Louis & S. F. Ry. *v.* Shoemaker, 27 Kan. 677; Heatwole *v.* Gorrell, 35 Kan. 692; Condon *v.* Kemper, 47 Kan. 126, 27 Pac. 829, 13 L. R. A. 671; Evans *v.* Moseley, 114 Pac. 874.

Maryland: Hough *v.* Kugler, 36 Md. 186.

Massachusetts: Heard *v.* Bowers, 23 Pick. 455; Higginson *v.* Weld, 14 Gray, 165.

Michigan: Daily *v.* Litchfield, 10 Mich. 29; First Orthodox Cong. Church *v.* Walrath, 27 Mich. 232.

Minnesota: Carter *v.* Strom, 41 Minn. 522, 43 N. W. 394.

Mississippi: Bright *v.* Rowland, 3 How. 398.

Missouri: Moore *v.* Platte County, 8 Mo. 467; Basye *v.* Ambrose, 28 Mo. 39; Hammer *v.* Breidenbach, 31 Mo. 49; Long *v.* Towl, 42 Mo. 545; Boulware *v.* Crohn, 99 S. W. 796, 122 Mo. App. 571.

Nevada: Morris *v.* McCoy, 7 Nev. 399.

New Jersey: Whitfield *v.* Levy, 35 N. J. L. 149; State *v.* Dodd, 45 N. J .L. 525; Monmouth Park Assoc. *v.* Warren, 55 N. J. L. 598, 27 Atl. 932.

New York: Jackson *v.* Baker, 2 Edw. Ch. 471; Niver *v.* Rossman, 18 Barb. 50; Staples *v.* Parker, 41 Barb. 648; Beale *v.* Hayes, 5 Sandf. 640; Brownold *v.* Rodbell, 130 App. Div. 371, 114 N. Y. Supp. 846.

North Carolina: Thoroughgood *v.* Walker, 2 Jones' L. 15.

North Dakota: Raymond *v.* Edelbrock, 15 N. D. 231, 107 N. W. 194.

Ohio: Berry *v.* Wisdom, 3 Oh. St. 241.

Oregon: Wilhelm *v.* Eaves, 21 Ore. 194, 27 Pac. 1053, 14 L. R. A. 297.

Pennsylvania: Shreve *v.* Brereton, 51 Pa. 175; March *v.* Allabough, 103 Pa. 335; Keck *v.* Bieber, 148 Pa. 645, 21 Atl. 170, 33 Am. St. Rep. 846.

Washington: Myers *v.* Ralston, 57 Wash. 47, 106 Pac. 474.

Wisconsin: Lyman *v.* Babcock, 40 Wis. 503.

England: Ex parte Capper, 4 Ch. D. 724; Davies *v.* Penton, 6 B. & C. 216; Edwards *v.* Williams, 5 Taunt. 247; Kemble *v.* Farren, 6 Bing. 141; Boys *v.* Ancell, 5 Bing. N. C. 390; Magee *v.* Lavell, L. R. 9 C. P. 107; Beckham *v.* Drake, 8 M. & W. 846; Horner *v.* Flintoff, 9 M. & W. 678.

Canada: McLean *v.* Tinsley, 7 Up. Can. Q. B. 40; Brown *v.* Taggart, 10 Up. Can. Q. B. 183; Rutherford *v.* Stovel, 12 Up. Can. C. P. 9.

the court usually states only that part of the rule which is forcibly brought out by the facts under consideration. Thus it is sometimes laid down in a more specific form, that where the agreement binds the parties to the performance of several matters of different degrees of importance, and one of the stipulations contemplates the payment of a sum of money less than the sum fixed as security, the latter is to be regarded as a penalty; [109] sometimes that where the agreement binds the parties to the performance of several matters of different degrees of importance, in a sum made payable for the non-performance of any or either of them, it must be regarded as a penalty.[110] But it is very difficult to see how a mere difference of degree in the importance of the stipulations can of itself affect the question, provided the damages are uncertain or difficult of computation, unless indeed the difference creates that glaring sort of disproportion between the injury likely to arise from a breach and the stipulated remedy, which enables the court to say at once that the parties could not have intended such a result, or that it would be unjust to allow this expressed intention of the parties to govern. The rule in its general form is that stated above.

The rule in its varying forms appears to be based upon the principle already stated, that when the court can see that the fundamental guide of compensation has been abandoned by the parties, and an arbitrary and unjust measure applied, they will not allow the intention of the parties to take effect. That this must frequently be the case in contracts covering a variety of stipulations differing from others in importance, provided the stipulations, or some of them, are such that the actual damages can be readily calculated, is obvious. Where a contract consists of several important stipulations, and damages cannot be adequately assessed for a breach of any of the stipulations, the court (except, no doubt, in case of great disproportion between the stipulated sum and the

---

[109] Cotheal v. Talmage, 9 N. Y. 551; Lampman v. Cochran, 16 N. Y. 275; Clement v. Cash, 21 N. Y. 253. A substantially identical interpretation was arrived at in Brewster v. Edgerly, 13 N. H. 275, where, however, the court refused to accede to the rule.

[110] Hahn v. Horstman, 12 Bush (Ky.), 249.

actual loss) will enforce the payment of the stipulated sum as liquidated damages.[111]

§ 414. Deposit and advance payments to be forfeited on default.

Where the instrument refers to a sum deposited as security for performance, or paid in advance to be forfeited on default, the forfeiture, if reasonable in amount, will be enforced as liquidated damages.[112] The intention is evident here that the money shall actually be paid over upon breach of the contract. So where in a contract for teaching plaintiff's son in a boarding school it was agreed that tuition should be paid in advance, and in case of withdrawal or expulsion during the term, the whole amount should be forfeited, this was held a good agreement for liquidated damages.[113] So where in the case of a contract to convey land a deposit is made to secure the bargain, or a part payment is made in advance of conveyance, to be forfeited on failure to complete the transaction, this is to be regarded as a valid liquidation of damages for breach.[114]

---

[111] *Indiana:* Merica *v.* Burgett, 75 N. E. 1083, 36 Ind. App. 453.

Missouri: Werner *v.* Finley, 144 Mo. App. 554, 129 S. W. 73.

Texas: Carruthers *v.* Gay (Tex. Civ. App.), 91 S. W. 593.

England: Wallis *v.* Smith, 21 Ch. Div. 243; Mercer *v.* Irving, E. B. & E. 563.

See Conried M. O. Co. *v.* Brin, 66 Misc. 282, 123 N. Y. Supp. 6, where one amount was stipulated for a specific partial breach, and a larger amount for a total breach, and the latter amount was allowed as liquidated damages.

[112] *Georgia:* Swift *v.* Powell, 44 Ga. 123.

Illinois: Moyses *v.* Schendorf, 238 Ill. 232, 87 N. E. 401.

Massachusetts: Garcin *v.* Pa. Furnace Co., 186 Mass. 405, 71 N. E. 793.

New York: Perzell *v.* Shook, 53 N. Y. Super. Ct. 501; Karnitzky *v.* Banwer, 119 N. Y. Supp. 661.

Pennsylvania: Mathews *v.* Sharp, 99 Pa. 560.

Texas: Eakin *v.* Scott, 70 Tex. 442; Halff *v.* O'Connor, 14 Tex. Civ. App. 191, 37 S. W. 238.

England: Wallis *v.* Smith, 21 Ch. Div. 243; Reilly *v.* Jones, 1 Bing. 302; Hinton *v.* Sparkes, L. R. 3 C. P. 161; Lea *v.* Whitaker, L. R. 8 C. P. 70.

This principle is the true explanation of Stillwell *v.* Temple, 28 Mo. 156.

See, however, Evans *v.* Mosely, (Kan.), 114 Pac. 874, where a provision that an advance payment of $3,000 on a $40,000 contract for the purchase of cattle should be forfeited on breach was held unenforceable as a provision for a penalty.

[113] Fessman *v.* Seeley (Tex. Civ. App.), 30 S. W. 268.

[114] *United States:* Hansbrough *v.* Peck, 5 Wall. 497, 18 L. ed. 520.

Georgia: Sanders *v.* Carter, 91 Ga. 450, 17 S. E. 345.

And where in a contract of lease it is provided that a certain amount, paid in advance by the lessee to secure performance, shall be taken as damages for breach by the lessee, this will be allowed.[115] In a case in New York,[116] however, this rule was said to apply only where the deposit was made in part performance of the contract, not where it was a mere security. In that case $1,500 were deposited by a lessee to secure payment of the rent of $500 a month. Upon default in the payment of one month's rent it was held that the whole deposit would not be forfeited. It will be noticed, however, that the decision itself is not in conflict with the rule as above stated, since the deposit was greatly in excess of the actual damage, as the court pointed out.

§ 415. Contracts performed in part.

If the contract is one in which the measure of damages for part performance is ascertainable and a sum is stipulated for entire breach of it, this sum will not be allowed as liquidated

Illinois: Pinckney v. Weaver, 216 Ill. 185, 74 N. E. 714.

Massachusetts: Donahue v. Parkman, 161 Mass. 412, 37 N. E. 205, 42 Am. St. Rep. 415.

Minnesota: Womack v. Coleman, 89 Minn. 17, 93 N. W. 663, 92 Minn. 328, 100 N. W. 9.

New Jersey: Moore v. Durnam, 63 N. J. Eq. 96, 51 Atl. 449.

New York: Lawrence v. Miller, 86 N. Y. 132; Van Kamen v. Roes, 65 Hun, 625, 20 N. Y. Supp. 548; Harris v. Snyder, 55 Misc. 306, 105 N. Y. Supp. 502; Beveridge v. West Side Const. Co., 130 App. Div. 139, 114 N. Y. Supp. 521; Levy v. Freiman, 115 N. Y. Supp. 996, 131 App. Div. 298; Brodfield v. Schlanger, 104 N. Y. Supp. 369.

Pennsylvania: Yoder v. Strong, 227 Pa. 432, 76 Atl. 176.

Texas: Talkin v. Anderson, 19 S. W. 852; Norman v. Vickery (Tex. Civ. App.), 128 S. W. 452; Lipscomb v. Fuqua, 131 S. W. 1061; Atwood v. Fagan (Tex. Civ. App.), 134 S. W. 765.

Contra, Drew v. Pedlar, 87 Cal. 443, 25 Pac. 749, 22 Am. St. Rep. 257, by interpretation of the provisions of the code.

Where the contract provides that the obligation shall continue, notwithstanding the forfeiture of the deposit, this is obviously a penalty. Tinkham v. Satori, 44 Mo. App. 659. And see Hall v. Middleby, 197 Mass. 485, 83 N. E. 1114; Kellam v. Hampton (Tex. Civ. App.), 124 S. W. 970.

[115] Rosenquist v. Canary, 20 Misc. 46, 45 N. Y. Supp. 342; Longobardi v. Yuliano (App. Div.), 67 N. Y. Supp. 902.

Contra, Carson v. Arvantes, 10 Colo. App. 382, 50 Pac. 1080.

And see Cunningham v. Stockton, 81 Kan. 780, 106 Pac. 1057.

[116] Chaude v. Shepard, 122 N. Y. 397, 25 N. E. 358.

damages in case of a partial breach; for what would be reasonable compensation in case of a total breach would not be such in case of a partial breach.[117] If it appears affirmatively from the language of the contract that the sum was meant to be payable only in case of total breach, the stipulated sum will not be considered at all in an action for a partial breach.[118] In Louisiana, by statute, if the obligation is partly executed the judge may modify the penalty.[119]

The contract may be of such a nature that the performance, though it consists of various acts or a series of acts, is yet one complex affair, and a failure to perform any part is really a total breach, defeating the entire object of the contract. In such a case the stipulated sum, if not unreasonable, may be recovered, although there has been a breach of only one stipulation. Thus the object of a contract by the defendant to refrain from intoxicating liquors during a term of service in the plaintiff's employ is entirely lost by a single breach, and the stipulated sum may be recovered.[120] The same decision has been reached in the case of a contract to marry and support a woman and give her no cause of divorce,[121] and of a contract between manufacturers of a certain article to employ no union men, use no union label, or buy and sell no article marked with a union label.[122] And where defendants,

[117] *United States:* Gay Mfg. Co. *v.* Camp, 65 Fed. 794, 13 C. C. A. 137; *Ex parte* Pollard, 2 Low. 411.

Alabama: McPherson *v.* Robertson, 82 Ala. 459, 2 So. 333; Watts *v.* Sheppard, 2 Ala. 425; Keeble *v.* Keeble, 85 Ala. 552, 2 So. 149 (*semble*).

Kansas: Heatwole *v.* Gorrell, 35 Kan. 692.

Massachusetts: Shute *v.* Taylor, 5 Met. 61.

Missouri: Gower *v.* Saltmarsh, 11 Mo. 271; Hamaker *v.* Schroers, 49 Mo. 406.

Montana: Wibaux *v.* Grinnell L. S. Co., 9 Mont. 154.

New York: Lampman *v.* Cochran, 16 N. Y. 275; Colwell *v.* Lawrence, 38 Barb. 643; Wheatland *v.* Taylor, 29 Hun, 70.

South Carolina: Owens *v.* Hodges, 1 McM. 106.

West Virginia: Wilkes *v.* Bierne, 69 S. E. 366.

Wisconsin: Fitzpatrick *v.* Cottingham, 14 Wis. 219.

Canada: Sleeman *v.* Waterous, 23 Up. Can. C. P. 195.

England: Charrington *v.* Laing, 6 Bing. 242.

[118] Cook *v.* Finch, 19 Minn. 407.

[119] Code, § 2127.

[120] Keeble *v.* Keeble, 85 Ala. 552, 2 So. 149; *acc.,* Henderson *v.* Murphree, 109 Ala. 556, 20 So. 45.

[121] Stanley *v.* Montgomery, 102 Ind. 102.

[122] Schrader *v.* Lillis, 10 Ont. 358.

who had agreed to deliver a certain number of cattle, tendered the agreed number, but some were imperfect; and upon plaintiff's objecting to the imperfect ones refused to deliver any unless all were taken, the liquidated damages agreed upon for an entire breach were allowed.[123]

§ 416. Stipulated sum in liquidation of uncertain damage.

Where, independently of the stipulation, the damages would be wholly uncertain, and incapable or very difficult of being ascertained, except by mere conjecture, there the damages will be usually considered liquidated.[124]

The uncertainty contemplated by the rule is an uncertainty as to the extent and amount, and not as to the proper measure of damages. If the views expressed above, however, are correct, the mere fact that the precise amount of damages cannot be anticipated will not be enough. It must also be clear that there will not be a glaring disproportion between the sum

[123] Frost *v.* Foote (Tex. Civ. App.), 44 S. W. 1071.

[124] *United States:* Harris *v.* Miller, 6 Sawy. 319.

Alabama: Keeble *v.* Keeble, 85 Ala. 552, 2 So. 149.

Arkansas: Williams *v.* Green, 14 Ark. 315.

California: Cal. Steam Nav. Co. *v.* Wright, 6 Cal. 258; Fisk *v.* Fowler, 10 Cal. 512; People *v.* Love, 19 Cal. 676.

Connecticut: Tingley *v.* Cutler, 7 Conn. 291.

District of Columbia: Goldsborough *v.* Baker, 3 Cranch C. C. 48.

Georgia: Newman *v.* Wolfson, 66 Ga. 764.

Indiana: Hamilton *v.* Overton, 6 Blackf. 206; Studabaker *v.* White, 31 Ind. 211.

Iowa: Wolf *v.* D. M. & F. D. Ry., 64 Ia. 380; Chicago & S. E. Ry. *v.* McEwen, 35 Ind. App. 251, 71 N. E. 926.

Maine: Dwinel *v.* Brown, 54 Me. 468.

Massachusetts: Leary *v.* Laflin, 101 Mass. 334.

New York: Williams *v.* Dakin, 22 Wend. 201; Holmes *v.* Holmes, 12 Barb. 137; Esmond *v.* Van Benschoten, 12 Barb. 366; Mundy *v.* Culver, 18 Barb. 336; DeGroff *v.* Amer. Linen Thread Co., 24 Barb. 375; Brinkerhoff *v.* Olp, 35 Barb. 27; Parr *v.* Greenbush, 42 Hun, 232; Peekskill S. C. & M. R. R. *v.* Peekskill, 21 App. Div. 94, 47 N. Y. Supp. 305.

North Carolina: Bingham *v.* Richardson, 1 Winston, 217.

Ohio: Lange *v.* Werk, 2 Oh. St. 519.

Pennsylvania: Powell *v.* Burroughs, 54 Pa. 329; Wolf Creek Diamond Coal Co. *v.* Schultz, 71 Pa. 180; Kunkle *v.* Wherry, 189 Pa. 198, 42 Atl. 112.

South Carolina: Williams *v.* Vance, 9 S. C. 344.

Texas: Indianola *v.* G. W. T. & P. Ry., 56 Tex. 594.

Wisconsin: Pierce *v.* Jung, 10 Wis. 30; Ryan *v.* Martin, 16 Wis. 57.

Wyoming: Ivinson *v.* Althrop, 1 Wyo. 71.

England: Reynolds *v.* Bridge, 6 E. & B. 528; Hurst *v.* Hurst, 4 Ex. 571.

Canada: Craig *v.* Dillon, 6 Ont. App. 116.

stipulated and the probable legal measure. The meaning and scope of the rule can best be learned by an examination of the cases.

The plaintiff and other landowners subscribed towards having a hotel built by the defendant near their land; the defendant agreed, in case he failed to build the hotel, to pay $20,000 to the subscribers. This sum was allowed as liquidated damages.[125] The plaintiff and defendant, manufacturers of cigars, in order to oppose the demands of their workmen, mutually agreed to employ no union workman, use no union label, and buy or sell no cigar marked with a union label. On any breach $500 were to be paid. This was allowed as liquidated damages.[126] In an agreement to extend streets through land sold by the defendants to the plaintiff the sum of $250 was named as liquidated damages in case of default. It was held that that amount might be recovered.[127] Where the plaintiff licensed the defendant to use his patent, with an agreement that the plaintiff might at any time inspect the work done under the license "under a penalty of $1,000 fixed as liquidated damages," it was held that the amount might be recovered.[128]

The contract of a railway company with its conductors provided that any conductor who took a fare directly from a passenger should be liable to a fine of $15. This was held to be a reasonable stipulation, and the fine was allowed as liquidated damages.[129] Where an assignor of a mortgage agreed with his assignee, that a decree foreclosing a prior mortgage on the same and other premises, should provide that the others be first sold, and their proceeds applied to the prior mortgage, stipulating in the agreement that if it were not performed, he should pay the assignee a specific sum (equal to the amount of the assigned mortgage), this stipulation, on account of the uncertainty of the damages, was held, by the New York Court of Appeals, to liquidate them, and not to be a penalty.[130]

In McIntire v. Cagley [131] the parties had stipulated for ten

125 Chase v. Allen, 13 Gray, 42.

126 Schrader v. Lillis, 10 Ont. 358.

127 Jaqua v. Headington, 114 Ind. 309.

128 Wooster v. Kisch, 26 Hun, 61.

129 Birdsall v. Twenty-third St. Ry., 8 Daly, 419.

130 Cowdrey v. Carpenter, 1 Abb. App. 445.

131 37 Ia. 676; acc., Tholen v. Duffy, 7 Kan. 405.

per cent. of the amount of a note as attorney's fees, if the note were collected by suit. It was held that the amount was to be considered as liquidated damages, on the ground of the impossibility of ascertaining with certainty beforehand the pecuniary measure of the injury. But where a mortgage note for a large amount stipulated that in case legal proceedings were necessary the mortgagee should be entitled to five per cent. of the note as an attorney's fee, the stipulated sum was held excessive.[132] In Michigan a lump sum as an attorney's fee was held a penalty,[133] but in Wisconsin, if it was reasonable in amount it was allowed as liquidated damages.[134] Upon breach of a covenant to discharge an incumbrance the amount stipulated may be recovered as liquidated damages.[135] In Berrinkott v. Traphagen[136] a bond had been given in the penal sum of $900, conditioned to pay to plaintiff the interest on $464 every year, and in case of default, that the principal should become due. It was held (Ryan, C. J., *dissenting*) that the real value of the annuity could not be determined by reference to tables of mortality; that the damages were therefore uncertain, and that the sum named must be regarded as liquidated damages. On an agreement by the defendant to buy all his meat of the plaintiff, a stipulated sum was allowed as liquidated damages for the breach.[137] And the general principle may be illustrated by numerous other cases.[138]

[132] Daly v. Maitland, 88 Pa. 384, overruling earlier cases.

[133] Myer v. Hart, 40 Mich. 517.

[134] Tallman v. Truesdale, 3 Wis. 443.

[135] *Minnesota:* Fasler v. Beard, 39 Minn. 32.
Washington: Herberger v. Orr, 114 Pac. 178.

[136] 39 Wis. 219; *acc.*, Waggoner v. Cox, 40 Oh. St. 539. But where the interest on the stipulated sum was greater than the annuity, it was held a penalty. Cairnes v. Knight, 17 Oh. St. 68.

[137] Lightner v. Menzel, 35 Cal. 452.

[138] *United States:* Gallo v. McAndrews, 29 Fed. 715 (to enter vessel at a port by a certain agent); Martin v. Berwind-White Coal Min. Co., 114 Fed. 553 (agreement by lessee of coal lands to mine certain amount or pay royalty on that amount); Brooks v. City of Wichita, 114 Fed. 297 (to furnish a city with electric lights); Blodget v. Columbia Live Stock Co., 164 Fed. 305, 90 C. C. A. 237 (to sink oil wells).
Arkansas: Nilson v. Jonesboro, 57 Ark. 168, 20 S. W. 1093 (with town, to complete street railway in certain time); Jonesboro L. C. & E. R. R. v. Crigger, 103 S. W. 1153.
California: Escondido O. & D. Co. v. Glaser, 144 Cal. 494, 77 Pac. 1040 (to sink oil well).
Illinois: Burk v. Dunn, 55 Ill. App. 25 (to give and take conveyance of land).
Indiana: Mondamin M. Dairy Co.

§ 416a. Forfeiture to State or city to secure contract of public interest.

In the case of a bond in a penal sum given to the State or to a city, not to secure it against actual ascertainable loss but in order to secure performance by means of a forfeit of a contract entered into for the public benefit, the recovery is for the full amount of the penalty; for the damages would usually be difficult or impossible of ascertainment, and the intention of the

v. Brudi, 163 Ind. 642, 72 N. E. 643 (to deliver 1,000 pounds of milk a day). *Kansas:* Illinois Trust & Savings Bank *v.* Burlington, 79 Kan. 797, 101 Pac. 649 (to furnish water for city purposes).

Massachusetts: Leary *v.* Laflin, 101 Mass. 334 (to deliver up leased premises in good repair); Tufts *v.* Atlantic Tel. Co., 151 Mass. 269, 23 N. E. 844 (to carry on business, employing the plaintiff).

Minnesota: Taylor *v.* Times Newspaper Co., 83 Minn. 523, 86 N. W. 760, 85 Am. St. Rep. 473 (not to use plaintiff's advertising plan).

New Hampshire: Houghton *v.* Pattee, 58 N. H. 326 (to build a hotel on certain land); State *v.* Corron, 73 N. H. 434, 62 Atl. 1044 (bond of liquor dealer to secure State against violation of license).

New Jersey: Gussow *v.* Beinson, 76 N. J. Law, 209, 68 Atl. 907 (to serve as manager of a business).

New York: Mawson *v.* Leavitt, 16 Misc. 289, 37 N. Y. Supp. 1138 (to furnish theatre for week); Pastor *v.* Solomon, 25 Misc. 322, 55 N. Y. Supp. 956 (not to perform at any theatre but plaintiff's); Conried M. O. Co. *v.* Brin, 66 Misc. 282, 123 N. Y. Supp. 6 (to sing at plaintiff's opera house); Shubert *v.* Sonheim, 123 N. Y. Supp. 529, 138 App. Div. 800 (to lease a theatre); Peabody *v.* Richard Realty Co., 69 Misc. 582, 125 N. Y. Supp. 349 (to carry out provisions of lease of several stores and a hotel).

Pennsylvania: Wolf Creek Diamond Coal Co. *v.* Schultz, 71 Pa. 180 (to allow plaintiff at agreed compensation to mine a certain amount of coal); Emery *v.* Boyle, 200 Pa. 249, 49 Atl. 779 (not to publish defamatory matter concerning plaintiff); Worrell *v.* Hurtig, 11 Pa. Dist. 788 (to present a play at plaintiff's theatre and nowhere else in the city).

Rhode Island: Darcey *v.* Darcey, 29 R. I. 384, 71 Atl. 595, 23 L. R. A. (N. S.) 886 (not to resume adulterous relations).

South Carolina: Lipscomb *v.* Seegers, 19 S. C. 425 (to prevent escape of convicts).

Texas: Santa Fe St. Ry. *v.* Schultz, 34 Tex. Civ. App. 14, 83 S. W. 39 (to operate street railway); Witherspoon *v.* Duncan (Tex. Civ. App.), 131 S. W. 660 (to sink oil wells).

Washington: Go Fun *v.* Fidalgo Island Canning Co., 37 Wash. 238, 76 Pac. 797 (to pack certain amount of fish per day); Sheard *v.* United States Fidelity & Guaranty Co., 58 Wash. 29, 107 Pac. 1024 (to furnish material and labor and erect a house); Yatsuyagi *v.* Shimamura, 59 Wash. 24, 109 Pac. 282 (to carry out a partnership agreement).

In Wilcox *v.* Walker (Tex. Civ. App.), 43 S. W. 579, a liquidation of damages which might well have been considered uncertain was disallowed because the stipulated sum was obviously disproportionately large.

parties is held to be that an absolute forfeiture is contemplated.[139] The same general principle is also illustrated by cases where one who contracts with a city to do a piece of work deposits a sum of money by way of security for performance. Where a street railway company deposited bonds to secure performance of its undertaking to build its road [140] or to keep it properly paved,[141] the deposit, not being unreasonable in amount, was regarded as liquidated damages. Where one in bidding upon a piece of work deposits with the city a certified check as guaranty for his entering into a formal contract if his bid is accepted, his check has in a few cases been held merely security for the payment of actual damages if he does not complete a contract,[142] but by the prevailing and better view it is to be retained by the city as liquidated damages for failure to complete the contract.[143]

§ 417. Breach of contract of sale.

Upon breach of a contract for the sale of property of uncertain

[139] *United States:* Clark v. Barnard, 108 U. S. 436, 27 L. ed. 780, 2 Sup. Ct. 878 (bond to secure the construction of a railroad); U. S. v. Pingree, 1 Spr. 339, Fed. Cas. No. 16,050 (bond for re-warehousing; U. S. v. Oteri, 67 Fed. 146, 14 C. C. A. 344 (bond on withdrawal for export); U. S. v. Hatch, 1 Paine, 335, Fed. Cas. No. 15,325 (to exhibit a certified copy of list of crew); U. S. v. Montell, Taney, 47, Fed. Cas. No. 15,798 (bond that certificate of registry of vessel shall not be sold or lent to be used for another vessel); Dieckerhoff v. U. S., 136 Fed. 545, 69 C. C. A. 255 (bond for return of imported merchandise).
Connecticut: New Britain v. New Britain Tel. Co., 74 Conn. 326, 50 Atl. 881, 1015 (to furnish telephone service).
Pennsylvania: York v. York Rys., 229 Pa. 236, 78 Atl. 128 (bond to complete and run railroad).
Texas: Marshall v. J. W. & W. S. Atkins (Tex. Civ. App.), 127 S. W.

1148 (bond to equip and extend gas plant).
[140] *Michigan:* Springwell v. Detroit P. & N. R. R., 140 Mich. 277, 103 N. W. 700.
New York: Peekskill S. C. & M. R. R. v. Peekskill, 47 N. Y. Supp. 305.
Texas: Whitcomb v. Houston (Tex. Civ. App.), 130 S. W. 215.
[141] Wight v. City of Chicago, 137 Ill. App. 240, affirmed, 84 N. E. 628, 234 Ill. 83.
[142] *Maryland:* Wilson v. Baltimore, 83 Md. 203, 34 Atl. 774, 55 Am. St. Rep. 339.
Texas: Lindsey v. Rockwall County, 10 Tex. Civ. App. 225, 30 S. W. 380.
[143] *United States:* Turner v. City of Fremont, 159 Fed. 221, 95 C. C. A. 455.
Massachusetts: Wheaton B. & L. Co. v. Boston, 204 Mass. 218, 90 N. E. 598.
Missouri: Coonan v. Cape Girardeau, 149 Mo. App. 609, 129 S. W. 745.
New York: Davin v. Syracuse, 126 N. Y. Supp. 1002.

value the stipulated sum is allowed as liquidated damages.[144]   In
Gobble *v.* Linder,[145] plaintiff and defendant had agreed to exchange farms. The contract contained a provision that either
party failing to make the deed in exchange, should "forfeit and
pay as damages" the sum of $1,500. Defendant failed to per-
form. By stipulation in the case, plaintiff argued that the actual damages did not exceed $50. The sum was decided to be
liquidated damages.[146]   The damages are often liquidated in
case of purchase of property in large quantities. In that case,
if the property cannot easily be procured in the market in such
quantities the damage by failure to deliver is obviously uncertain, even though there may be an easily ascertained market
price, and the stipulated sum may therefore be recovered.[147]   On
the other hand, if the goods are easily procurable in the market
the damages are not uncertain, and the liquidation is not allowed.[148]   The property is of uncertain value, and the liquidation is therefore allowed, in case of a contract for the sale of an
interest in a business,[149] or of personal property of uncertain
price.[150]

[144] *Maine:* Gammon *v.* Howe, 14 Me. 250.
Nebraska: Lorius *v.* Abbott, 49 Neb. 214, 68 N. W. 486.
New Hampshire: Chamberlain *v.* Bagley, 11 N. H. 234; Mead *v.* Wheeler, 13 N. H. 351.
New York: Main *v.* King, 10 Barb. 59.
Pennsylvania: Streeper *v.* Williams, 48 Pa. 450.
Texas: Durst *v.* Swift, 11 Tex. 273.
Wisconsin: Yenner *v.* Hammond, 36 Wis. 277.
In McCall Co. *v.* Deuchler, 174 Fed. 133, 98 C. C. A. 169, the stipulated damages were refused as unreasonable.
[145] 76 Ill. 157.
[146] *Acc.,* Calbeck *v.* Ford, 140 Mich. 48, 103 N. W. 516. *Contra,* Carlisle *v.* Green (Tex. Civ. App.), 131 S. W. 1140.
[147] *United States:* Davis *v.* Alpha P. C. Co., 134 Fed. 274 (cement).
Indiana: McCormick *v.* Mitchell, 57 Ind. 248 (hogs).

Louisiana: Gartner *v.* Richardson, 123 La. 194, 48 So. 886 (lumber: agree-
ment that vendee might buy elsewhere and charge vendor with cost).
England: Diestel *v.* Stevenson, 75 L. J. K. B. 797, [1906] 2 K. B. 345, 96 L. T. 10, 12 Com. Cas. 1, 22 T. L. R. 673 (steam coal).
[148] *Nebraska:* Squires *v.* Elmwood, 33 Neb. 126, 49 N. W. 939 (sheep).
Pennsylvania: Shreve *v.* Brereton, 51 Pa. 175 (oil).
[149] *Iowa:* Sanford *v.* Belle Plaine First Nat. Bank, 94 Iowa, 680, 63 N. W. 459.
Kentucky: Woodbury *v.* Turner D. & W. M. Co., 96 Ky. 459, 29 S. W. 295.
Maine: Maxwell *v.* Allen, 78 Me. 32.
Massachusetts: Lynde *v.* Thompson, 2 All. 456.
[150] Knowlton *v.* Mackay, 29 Up. Can. C. P. 601.

51

In New York it is held that in ordinary contracts for the sale of land the amount of loss is easily ascertained, and that therefore the stipulated sum will not be allowed as liquidated damages unless there is some other ground for so considering it. This is held both in cases of exchange[151] and of sale[152] of land. But if the parties clearly intended the sum to be paid as compensation, it will be allowed as liquidated damages if it is reasonable in amount,[153] but not otherwise.[154]   In Kentucky an agreement that in case of eviction from the granted premises the grantor should refund the consideration with interest was held to make that sum liquidated damages.[155]   When the sum agreed upon represents a *bona fide* valuation of property for the purposes of the contract, no reason is perceived why it should be construed to be a penalty.   In The Sun Printing and Publishing Association v. Moore [156] the suit was for the total loss of a yacht, valued in the charter at $75,000, and the Supreme Court of the United States, on an elaborate review of the authorities, held the valuation binding.

In case of breach by the buyer the principle is the same: and a liquidation of damages otherwise uncertain will be allowed.[157]

§ 418. Of agreement not to carry on business.

Where a party binds himself in a sum named not to carry on any particular trade, business, or profession, within certain limits, or within a specified period of time, the sum mentioned will be

[151] Noyes v. Phillips, 60 N. Y. 408.
[152] Richards v. Edick, 17 Barb. 260; Laurea v. Bernauer, 33 Hun, 307.
[153] *Arkansas:* Westbay v. Terry, 83 Ark. 144, 103 S. W. 160.
Indiana: Howard v. Adkins, 167 Ind. 184, 78 N. E. 665.
Missouri: Mores v. Rathburn, 42 Mo. 594, 97 Am. Dec. 359.
New York: Slosson v. Beadle, 7 Johns. 72; Hasbrouck v. Tappen, 15 Johns. 200; Knapp v. Maltby, 13 Wend. 587.
Oklahoma: Gavin v. Ball, 110 Pac. 1067.
Washington: Madler v. Silverstone, 55 Wash. 159, 104 Pac. 165.

[154] Dennis v. Cummins, 3 Johns. Cas. 297.
[155] Bradshaw v. Craycraft, 3 J. J. Marsh. 77.
[156] 183 U. S. 642, 46 L. ed. 366, 22 Sup. Ct. 240.
[157] *Arkansas:* Tidwell v. Southern E. & B. Works, 87 Ark. 52, 112 S. W. 152 (machinery).
Iowa: Selby v. Matson, 137 Ia. 97, 114 N. W. 609, 14 L. R. A. (N. S.) 1210 (land).
Texas: Cowart v. Walter Connally Co. (Tex. Civ. App.), 108 S. W. 973 (machinery).

regarded as liquidated damages and not a penalty.[158]   It is sometimes said that agreements of this sort are alternative in character; but in Stewart *v.* Bedell [159] the Supreme Court of Pennsylvania decided that this is not the case.   In Sparrow *v.* Paris [160] the defendant had guaranteed the plaintiff, a shipper, that no more than one ship should sail for Havana before that containing his goods, under penalty of forfeiting one-half the freight of the goods.   Although the word "penalty" was used, this was held to be liquidated damages, on the ground that the sum was to be paid on *one* event, and was not a security for the performance of several matters.   An attempt was made in this case to argue that several events were secured, viz., that the ship should not be the second, nor third, nor fourth, etc.   But the court (Bram-

[158] *Alabama:* McCurry *v.* Gibson, 108 Ala. 451, 18 So. 806, 54 Am. St. Rep. 177.

California: California S. N. Co. *v.* Wright, 6 Cal. 258; Streeter *v.* Rush, 25 Cal. 67; Potter *v.* Ahrens, 110 Cal. 674, 43 Pac. 388; Shafer *v.* Sloan, 85 Pac. 162, 3 Cal. App. 325.

Georgia: Newman *v.* Wolfson, 69 Ga. 764.

Illinois: Boyce *v.* Watson, 52 Ill. App. 361.

Indiana: Duffy *v.* Shockey, 11 Ind. 70; Spicer *v.* Hoop, 51 Ind. 365; Johnson *v.* Gwinn, 100 Ind. 466.

Iowa: Stafford *v.* Shortreed, 62 Iowa, 524, 17 N. W. 756.

Kentucky: Applegate *v.* Jacoby, 9 Dana, 206.

Maine: Holbrook *v.* Tobey, 66 Me. 410; Laundry Co. *v.* Debow, 98 Me. 496, 57 Atl. 845.

Massachusetts: Pierce *v.* Fuller, 8 Mass. 223; Cushing *v.* Drew, 97 Mass. 445.

Michigan: Jaquith *v.* Hudson, 5 Mich. 123; Geiger *v.* Cawley, 146 Mich. 550, 109 N. W. 1064.

Missouri: Wills *v.* Forester, 140 Mo. App. 321, 124 S. W. 1090.

New Hampshire: Clark *v.* Britton, 79 Atl. 494.

New Jersey: Cheddick *v.* Marsh, 21 N. J. L. 463; Hoagland *v.* Segur, 38 N. J. L. 230.

New York: Nobles *v.* Bates, 7 Cow. 307; Smith *v.* Smith, 4 Wend. 468; Dakin *v.* Williams, 17 Wend. 447, 22 Wend. 201; Dunlop *v.* Gregory, 10 N. Y. 241; Tode *v.* Gross, 127 N. Y. 480, 28 N. E. 469; Breck *v.* Ringler, 13 N. Y. Supp. 501; Mott *v.* Mott, 11 Barb. 127.

Ohio: Lange *v.* Werk, 2 Oh. St. 519; Grasselli *v.* Lowden, 11 Oh. St. 349.

Pennsylvania: Kelso *v.* Reid, 145 Pa. 606, 33 Atl. 323, 27 Am. St. Rep. 716; Stover *v.* Spielman, 1 Pa. Super. Ct. 526.

Tennessee: Muse *v.* Swayne, 2 Lea, 251.

Texas: Rucker *v.* Campbell, 35 Tex. Civ. App. 178, 79 S. W. 627.

Vermont: Barry *v.* Harris, 49 Vt. 392.

Washington: Canady *v.* Knox, 43 Wash. 567, 86 Pac. 930.

England: National Provincial Bank of England *v.* Marshall, 40 Ch. Div. 112; Reynolds *v.* Bridge, 6 E. & B. 528; Sainter *v.* Ferguson, 7 C. B. 716; Leighton *v.* Wales, 3 M. & W. 545; Crisdee *v.* Bolton, 3 C. & P. 240.

Contra, Perkins *v.* Lyman, 11 Mass. 76; Smith *v.* Wainwright, 24 Vt. 97, overruled.

[159] 79 Pa. 336.

[160] 7 H. & N. 594.

well, B.) said: "If this argument availed, it would equally have availed in those cases where liquidated damages have been held recoverable for carrying on trade within limited distances." Where the defendant on retiring from business had covenanted that he would not reside within the distance of two and a half miles from his then residence, and that if he did, he would pay £1,000, as liquidated damages, and not as penalty; and he fixed his new residence a few feet within the distance, it was held that the whole sum was recoverable; Parke, B., saying that Kemble v. Farren was "somewhat stretched," and that "if a party agrees to pay £1,000 on several events, all of which are capable of accurate valuation, the sum must be construed as a penalty, and not as liquidated damages. But if there be a contract consisting of one or more stipulations, the breach of which cannot be measured, then the parties must be taken to have meant that the sum agreed on was to be liquidated damages and not a penalty."[161]

So, again, where the defendant had contracted not to practice as a performer within a certain district, he bound himself to the plaintiff in the sum of £5,000, "as and by way of liquidated damages, and not of penalty;" the authority of Kemble v. Farren was invoked for the defendant; but the court said:

"Where the deed contains several stipulations of various degrees of importance, as to some of which the damages might be considered liquidated whilst for others they might be deemed unliquidated, and a sum of money is made payable upon a breach of any of them, the courts have held it to be a penalty only, and not liquidated damages. But where the damage is altogether uncertain, and yet a definite sum of money is expressly made payable in respect of it by way of liquidated damages, those words must be read in the ordinary sense, and cannot be construed to import a penalty."[162]

Where suit was brought on an agreement made between two coach proprietors, that, in consideration of a certain sum of money, the defendant would withdraw his stagecoach, and not concern himself in driving any other coach on that road; and the agreement contained a clause that for its due and punctual

[161] Atkyns v. Kinnier, 4 Ex. 776; acc., Galsworthy v. Strutt, 1 Ex. 659.   [162] Green v. Price, 13 M. & W. 695; Price v. Green, 16 M. & W. 346.

performance, each of the parties bound himself to the other " in the sum of £500, to be considered and taken as liquidated damages, or sum of money forfeited or due from the one party to the other, who shall neglect or refuse to perform his part of the agreement;" it was held not a penalty, but liquidated damages, from which the court would not depart.[163]   And the same point was decided in a very analogous case at an early day [164] by the Supreme Court of Massachusetts, where the opinion was delivered by Mr. Justice Sedgwick.

So where one sued the owner of a laboratory in the neighborhood for damages to his real estate from the operations of a laboratory, and the parties, pending the suit, entered into an agreement by which the plaintiff discontinued it, and the defendant agreed to stop the laboratory business within five years, or pay $3,000 as liquidated damages, and the defendant did not close the business within the time, the court held that the $3,000 were liquidated damages, refusing to consider the fact alleged by the defendant, that the mode of conducting the business had been so changed that it was thereby rendered entirely harmless and unobjectionable, as affecting the question.[165]   But where the parties mutually bound themselves in the sum of $300, one to pay $150 for a certain business, and the other to refrain from competition, it was held, in an action by the purchaser, that the sum stipulated would be regarded as a penalty.[166]   The court was influenced by the fact that the sum secured the plaintiff's payment of a less sum of money; and there is no doubt that as to him the amount is a penalty.   But there seems to be no reason why a stipulated sum, though a penalty so far as regards one of the parties, should not be regarded as liquidated damages when the other party is defendant.

Here, as elsewhere, the intention of the parties to liquidate the damage must be found,[167] and if the sum named is unreasonably large, the liquidation will not be allowed, no matter what the parties intended.[168]

[163] Barton v. Glover, 1 Holt, N. P. 43.
[164] Pierce v. Fuller, 8 Mass. 223.
[165] Grasselli v. Lowden, 11 Oh. St. 349.
[166] Moore v. Colt, 127 Pa. 289.
[167] Smith v. Brown, 164 Mass. 584, 42 N. E. 101.

[168] *New Mexico:* Thomas v. Gavin, 110 Pac. 841.
Pennsylvania: Wilkinson v. Colley, 164 Pa. 35, 30 Atl. 286, 14 Am. St. Rep. 845 (penalty twice the consideration of the sale).

§ 419. For delay in completing performance.

Parties may usually liquidate damages for delay in the perform-ance of a contract. This is one of the commonest instances of stipulated damages. When it is provided in a building con-tract that the work shall be completed on a certain day, and that the builder shall " forfeit " or " allow " a stipulated sum for every day or week the completion of the work is delayed beyond that time, the stipulated sum, if a reasonable one, may be re-covered as liquidated damages for the delay.[169] But if the work,

In the absence of evidence on the question of reasonableness the sum named was held a penalty in *Disoway v. Edwards*, 134 N. C. 254, 46 S. E. 501.

[169] *United States:* Chapman Dec. Co. *v.* Security Mut. L. Ins. Co., 149 Fed. 189, 79 C. C. A. 137.

Alabama: O'Brien *v.* Anniston Pipe Works, 93 Ala. 582, 9 So. 415; Stratton *v.* Fike, 166 Ala. 203, 51 So. 874.

Arkansas: Lincoln *v.* Little Rock Granite Co., 56 Ark. 405, 19 S. W. 1056.

Illinois: Mueller *v.* Kleine, 27 Ill. App. 473.

Indiana: Barber A. P. Co. *v.* Wabash, 43 Ind. App. 167, 86 N. E. 1034.

Iowa: Kelly *v.* Fejervary, 111 Ia. 693, 83 N. W. 791.

Kansas: St. Louis & S. F. R. R. *v.* Gaba, 78 Kan. 432, 97 Pac. 435.

Kentucky: Illinois Surety Co. *v.* Garrard Hotel Co., 118 S. W. 967, 34 Ky. L. Rep.

Louisiana: Hebert *v.* Weil, 115 La. 424, 39 So. 389.

Massachusetts: Curtis *v.* Brewer, 17 Pick. 513; Folsom *v.* McDonough, 6 Cush. 208; Hall *v.* Crowley, 5 All. 304, 81 Am. Dec. 745; Morrison *v.* Rich-ardson, 194 Mass. 370, 80 N. E. 468; Norcross Bros. Co. *v.* Vose, 199 Mass. 8, 85 N. E. 468.

Michigan: Western Gas Const. Co. *v.* Dowagiac Gas & Fuel Co., 146 Mich. 119, 109 N. W. 29, 13 Detroit Leg. N. 689; Germain *v.* Union School Dist., 158 Mich. 214, 123 N. W. 789, 16 De-troit Leg. N. 834.

New Jersey: Monmouth Park Ass'n *v.* Wallis Iron Works, 55 N. J. Law, 132, 26 Atl. 140, 19 L. R. A. 456, 39 Am. St. Rep. 626.

New York: Curtis *v.* Van Bergh, 161 N. Y. 47, 55 N. E. 398; Mosler Safe Co. *v.* Maiden Lane S. D. Co., 190 N. Y. 479, 93 N. E. 81; Bridges *v.* Hyatt, 2 Abb. Pr. 449; O'Donnell *v.* Rosen-berg, 14 Abb. (N. S.) 59; Farnham *v.* Ross, 2 Hall, 167; Weeks *v.* Little, 47 N. Y. Super. Ct. 1.

South Carolina: Worrell *v.* McClin-aghan, 5 Strobh. 115.

Tennessee: Railroad Co. *v.* Cabinet Co., 104 Tenn. 568, 58 S. W. 303, 50 L. R. A. 729, 78 Am. St. Rep. 933.

Virginia: Welch *v.* McDonald, 35 Va. 500.

England: Fletcher *v.* Dyche, 2 T. R. 32; Legge *v.* Harlock, 12 Q. B. 1015; Crux *v.* Aldred, 14 W. R. 656.

Canada: Jones *v.* Queen, 7 Can. 570; Gilmour *v.* Hall, 10 Up. Can. Q. B. 309; McPhee *v.* Wilson, 25 Up. Can. Q. B. 169; Scott *v.* Dent, 38 Up. Can. Q. B. 30; Gaskin *v.* Wales, 9 Up. Can. C. P. 314; Chatterton *v.* Crothers, 9 Ont. 683; Horton *v.* Tobin, 20 N. S. 169; Lefurgy *v.* McGregor, 1 Pr. Ed. Isl. 72.

Contra, Wilcus *v.* Kling, 87 Ill. 107, where no actual damage was shown; Patent Brick Co. *v.* Moore, 75 Cal. 205, and Seim *v.* Krause, 13 S. Dak. 530, 83 N. W. 583, according to the code, which allows liquidated damages only when it would be impracticable or extremely difficult to fix the actual damage;

instead of being delayed, is abandoned in an unfinished state by the defendant, it is evident that the stipulated sum cannot be recovered for an indefinite time; [170] it would be grossly oppressive to make the plaintiff "a pensioner upon the defendant *ad infinitum.*" Whether the courts would allow the plaintiff a reasonable time to complete the work himself, or whether they would refuse altogether to enforce the stipulation, has not been decided. In the former case we should have another illustration of the application of the rule of avoidable consequences, elsewhere discussed, and a consequence of this would be that the party injured would be allowed the stipulated damages for a reasonable period, after which, his natural course to cause the contract to be performed himself would interrupt further recovery of them. A large sum agreed to be paid at once if performance is delayed beyond a certain date is not allowed as liquidated damages,[171] unless it is reasonable in amount.[172]

And if the stipulated damages for delay, though proportioned to the time of delay, are greatly out of proportion to the actual damage, they are not allowed.[173] Thus where damages for delay

Brennan v. Clark, 29 Neb. 385, 45 N. W. 472.

In Otis v. Cottage Grove Mfg. Co., 121 Ill. App. 233, the contract, as construed, did not provide for liquidated damages, but only for the retention of the amount as security for the payment of actual damages.

[170] *California:* Bacigalupi v. Phœnix B. & C. Co., 11 Cal. App. 527, 112 Pac. 892.

Kentucky: Hahn v. Horstman, 12 Bush, 249.

New York: Greer v. Tweed, 13 Abb. (N. S.) 427; Colwell v. Foulks, 36 How. Pr. 306; Murphy v. U. S. F. & G. Co., 100 App. Div. 93, 91 N. Y. Supp. 582. But in Phaneuf v. Corey, 190 Mass. 237, 76 N. E. 718, where there was a dispute as to the completion of the building which lasted six months, the liquidated damages were allowed for the entire period.

[171] *United States:* Tayloe v. Sandiford, 7 Wheat. 13, 5 L. ed. 384.

Georgia: S. & C. R. R. v. Callahan, 56 Ga. 331.

Kansas: Condon v. Kemper, 47 Kan. 126, 27 Pac. 829, 13 L. R. A. 671.

[172] *New York:* Ward v. Hudson River Blg. Co., 125 N. Y. 230, 26 N. E. 256.

South Carolina: Allen v. Brazier, 2 Bail. 293.

[173] The following damages were held unreasonably large and the stipulation was not allowed:

Iowa: Coen v. Birchard, 124 Iowa, 394, 100 N. W. 48 ($5 a day for house of $25 per month rental value).

Michigan: Ross v. Loescher, 152 Mich. 386, 116 N. W. 193 ($20 a day on $825 porch).

Missouri: Cochran v. People's Ry., 113 Mo. 359, 21 S. W. 6 ($50 a day on $17,785 building).

North Carolina: Weedon v. American B. & T. Co., 128 N. C. 69, 38 S. E. 255 ($10 a day on building of $30 per month rental value).

Texas: Jennings v. Willer (Tex. Civ.

in finishing a house, the rental value of which was $25 a month, were stipulated at $150 a week, this was not allowed as liquidated damages.[174] In accordance with the general principle, where in case of the non-delivery of negroes at a certain time damages were to be paid at a stipulated rate per year, they were allowed at that rate.[175] A carrier agreed to deliver goods at a certain time, or to deduct a stipulated amount from the freight for every day's delay. This deduction was allowed.[176] It was provided in a lease that the lessee, on failure to surrender the premises at the end of the term, should pay double rent. This was allowed as liquidated damages.[177] In case of an agreement to furnish goods at a certain time, or to pay a stipulated amount per day

App.), 32 S. W. 24 ($25 a day for house of $150 per month rental value).

Wisconsin: J. G. Wagner Co. *v.* Cawker, 112 Wis. 532, 88 N. W. 599 ($50 a day on $16,458 contract).

The following damages were held reasonable:

United States: Simpson Bros. Corp. *v.* John R. White & Son, 187 Fed. 418 ($300 a week for coal pocket costing $29,000).

Colorado: Denver L. & S. Co. *v.* Rosenfield Constr. Co., 19 Colo. 539, 36 Pac. 146 ($5 a day for nine houses).

Illinois: Hennessy *v.* Metzger, 152 Ill. 505, 38 N. E. 1058, 43 Am. St. Rep. 267 ($50 a day for $15,000 mill).

Iowa: DeGraff *v.* Wickham, 89 Iowa, 720, 52 N. W. 503, 57 N. W. 420 ($10 a day for house).

Maryland: United Surety Co. *v.* Summers, 110 Md. 95, 72 Atl. 775 ($50 a day for $13,000 building; same amount to contractor for each day ahead of time).

Missouri: Thompson *v.* St. Charles County, 227 Mo. 220, 126 S. W. 1044 ($10 a day for $37,000 courthouse); Ramlose *v.* Dollman, 100 Mo. App. 347, 73 S. W. 917 ($10 a day for building renting at $300 a month).

New York: Macey Co. *v.* New York, 129 N. Y. Supp. 241 (App. Div.)

($10 a day for exhibition cases costing $7,245).

South Carolina: Carter *v.* Kaufman, 67 S. C. 456, 45 S. E. 1017 ($5 a day for 10 days, then $10 a day for brick storehouse renting for $35 a month).

Texas: Harris County *v.* Donaldson, 20 Tex. Civ. App. 9, 48 S. W. 791 ($10 a day for courthouse, rental value $200 to $300 a month); Brown Iron Co. *v.* Norwood (Tex. Civ. App.), 69 S. W. 253 ($5 a day for $2,200 house); Neblett *v.* McGraw, 41 Tex. Civ. App. 239, 91 S. W. 309 ($20 a day for store).

Virginia: Crawford *v.* Heatwole & Hedrick, 110 Va. 358, 66 S. E. 46 ($10 a day for $7,000 house much needed).

Washington: Reichenbach *v.* Sage, 13 Wash. 364, 43 Pac. 354 ($10 a day for a house); Clemons *v.* Gray's H. & P. S. Ry. (Wash.), 114 Pac. 865 ($1,000 a day for a railroad crossing).

Wisconsin: Davis *v.* La Crosse Hospital Assoc., 121 Wis. 579, 99 N. W. 332 ($20 a day for $24,000 hospital).

[174] Clements *v.* Schuylkill R. E. S. R. R., 132 Pa. 445.

[175] Tardeveau *v.* Smith, Hardin, 175.

[176] Harmony *v.* Bingham, 12 N. Y. 99.

[177] Walker *v.* Engler, 30 Mo. 130; *acc.,* Poppers *v.* Meager, 148 Ill. 192, 35 N. E. 805.

as damages for failure, the stipulated amount is enforced as liquidated damages.[178] Ordinary clauses for demurrage in charter parties are governed by the same general rule.[179] And the same principle applies to liquidated damages for delay in performing other contracts.[180]

§ 420. Stipulations to evade the usury laws.

* If the sum be evidently fixed to evade the usury laws or any other statutory provisions, the courts will relieve by treating it as a penalty.[181] So, in a case,[182] where a bond was given that if cer-

[178] Bergheim v. Blaenavon Iron & Steel Co., L. R. 10 Q. B. 319; Young v. White, 5 Watts, 460.

[179] Post, § 857.

[180] For building a railroad:
United States: Fruin-Bambrick Construction Co. v. Ft. Smith & W. R. R., 140 Fed. 465 (liquidated damages not recoverable after the company takes possession of the road before it is fully completed and operates it).
Iowa: Wolf v. Des Moines & F. D. Ry., 64 Iowa, 380, 20 N. W. 481.
Kentucky: Ford v. Ingles Coal Co., 102 S. W. 332, 31 Ky. L. Rep. 382.
Pennsylvania: Faunce v. Burke, 16 Pa. 469, 55 Am. Dec. 519.
Constructing other works:
United States: Stephens v. Bridge Co., 139 Fed. 248, 71 C. C. A. 374 (viaduct; $100 per day held a penalty).
Alabama: Hooper v. Savannah & M. R. R., 69 Ala. 529 (streets).
Georgia: Washington v. Potomac Eng. & Construction Co., 132 Ga. 849, 65 S. E. 80 (waterworks).
New York: McCann v. Albany, 11 App. Div. 378, 42 N. Y. Supp. 94 (sewer; $50 a day held a penalty).
Pennsylvania: Malone v. Philadelphia, 147 Pa. 416, 28 Atl. 628 (bridge).
Delivering machinery:
Alabama: Cleveland C. & C. Co. v. American C. I. P. Co. (Ala.), 53 So. 313 (electric crane).
Mississippi: Hardie-Tynes F. & M.

Co. v. Glen Allen Oil Mill, 84 Miss. 259, 36 So. 262.
West Virginia: Wheeling M. & F. Co. v. Wheeling S. & I. Co., 58 W. Va. 62, 51 S. E. 129, 130.
Wisconsin: Manistee I. W. Co. v. Shores Lumber Co., 92 Wis. 21, 65 N. W. 863.
Delivering fire boat:
Dist. of Columbia v. Harlan & Hollingsworth Co., 30 App. D. C. 270.
Furnishing steel work for roof:
Louisville Water Co. v. Youngstown Bridge Co., 16 Ky. L. Rep. 350.
And so of a stipulated rate for keeping animals:
Morris v. Wilson, 114 Fed. 74.
And of other contracts:
United States: U. S. v. Bethlehem Steel Co., 205 U. S. 105, 27 S. Ct. 450, 51 L. ed. 731 (to supply gun carriages).
Indiana: Barber Asphalt Pav. Co. v. City of Wabash, 86 N. E. 1034, 43 Ind. App. 167 (to pave a street).
Missouri: House Wrecking Co. v. Sonken, 152 Mo. App. 458, 133 S. W. 355 (to tear down buildings).
Washington: Erickson v. Green, 44 Wash. 613, 92 Pac. 449 (to remove soil from a lot).
[181] Georgia: Clark v. Kay, 26 Ga. 403.
Indiana: Brown v. Maulsby, 17 Ind. 10.
Kansas: Kurtz v. Sponable, 6 Kan. 395.

[182] Orr v. Churchill, 1 H. Black. 227, 232.

tain bills were not accepted, the obligors would pay the amount of them, with interest at ten per cent., by way of penalty, it was insisted that the damages were liquidated. But Lord Loughborough said: "There can only be an agreement for liquidated damages where there is an engagement for the *performance of certain acts* the not doing of which would be injurious to one of the parties, or to guard *against the performance of acts* which if done would also be injurious. But in cases like the present, the law, having by positive rules fixed the rate of interest, has bounded the measure of damages." And it was held that the amount of the bills, with legal interest only, could be recovered. And, in a similar case, this language was held by the Supreme Court of New York: "Such facts constitute no right to recover beyond the money actually due. Liquidated damages are not applicable to such case. If they were, they might afford a sure protection for usury, and countenance oppression under the form of law."[183] **

Probably, in some cases, agreements open to this objection would be wholly void. This depends upon the local statutes with regard to usury. It will be observed that whenever an agreement for stipulated damages is treated as a cover for usury, and therefore converted into a penalty, this is put on the ground of the violation of the statute law. The *intention* of the parties in cases of this sort may be, either to liquidate damages, or to evade the statute. If it is the latter case, the agreement is a nullity, as contrary to express law; if the former, intention is not allowed to prevail. In a Kansas case of the sort under consideration it was held that it must affirmatively appear that

---

Michigan: Davis *v.* Freeman, 10 Mich. 188.

Ohio: State *v.* Taylor, 10 Oh. 378; Shelton *v.* Gill, 11 Oh. 417.

In Illinois, an agreement in a promissory note made in good faith, without design to evade the usury laws, in case the note is not paid at maturity, to pay thereafter, by way of penalty, a rate exceeding the legal rate until paid, is not usurious. Lawrence *v.* Cowles, 13 Ill. 577; Gould *v.* The Bishop Hill Colony, 35 Ill. 324.

[183] Gray *v.* Crosby, 18 Johns. 219, 226. In Galsworthy *v.* Strutt, 1 Exch. 659, 665, Parke, B., is reported to have said, with, perhaps, less than his usual care and discrimination: "I take it that it would be competent for the parties to make a stipulation to pay a certain sum on the non-performance of a covenant to pay a smaller sum; but they must do so in express terms; and if that be done, I do not see how the courts can avoid giving effect to such a contract."

the stipulation was not an evasion of the usury law; and in case of doubt the stipulation would not be allowed.[184]

§ 420a. Valuation and pre-ascertainment.

The Supreme Court has recently had occasion to consider fully the subject of liquidated damages in a case construing part of an agreement for the charter of a yacht as a dispatch boat.[185] The libel was filed in the Southern District of New York to recover for the loss of the Yacht Kanapata while in the service of the defendant. The yacht was chartered during the Spanish-American war of 1898 to collect news for the defendants' newspaper, for $10,000 for four months from June 1 to October 1. The charter contained a provision that "for the purpose of this charter the value of the yacht" should "be considered and taken at the sum of $75,000," and that the hirer should "procure security or guaranty to and for the owner in the sum of $75,000 to secure any and all losses and damages which may occur to said boat or its belongings which may be sustained by the owner by reason of such loss or damage and by reason of the breach of any of the terms or conditions of this contract." By another agreement, termed "an agreement of suretyship," the defendant itself guaranteed performance, and stipulated that its liability should in no case exceed the sum of $75,000. The yacht was insured for $60,000. In the trial court [186] Brown, J., held that the libellants could recover $65,000—the whole sum arranged as the extreme liability, less $10,000 paid for the charter. On appeal,[187] the Circuit Court of Appeals took the view that no allowance should be made for the $10,000, but that libellant was entitled to recover $75,000 as the agreed value of the yacht. On appeal to the Supreme Court, that tribunal treated the agreement as two-fold, one part being to return the yacht, or pay $75,000, the agreed value, the other fixing a penalty for the non-payment of the hire, or failure to repair, etc.[188] It would seem that in this view of the contract, the conclusion of the Supreme Court, that the libellant was entitled to recover the whole sum as liquidated damages was inevitable.

---

[184] Foote v. Sprague, 13 Kan. 155.

[185] Sun Printing & Publishing Assn. v. Moore, 183 U. S. 642, 46 L. ed. 366, 22 Sup. Ct. 240.

[186] 95 Fed. 485.

[187] 101 Fed. 591.

[188] 183 U. S. at p. 658.

Such an agreement was not unreasonable, the value of a yacht is extremely uncertain, and therefore exactly that sort of property as to which parties may well stipulate the value in advance.[189]

But upon the trial, the defendant appears to have contended that if it could show that the yacht was actually worth less than $75,000, the recovery must be limited by this proof, on the ground that where "the amount is disproportioned to the loss" it is the duty of the court to treat the sum named as a penalty. This doctrine the Supreme Court declared to be "wrong in principle," "not warranted by the decisions of this court" and added that "it does not prevail in the courts of England at the present time." The support found for it, the court referred to as "embodied in the reasoning of the opinions" in Chicago House Wrecking Co. v. United States.[190] But it may be added that while some of the language made use of in these opinions may have been loose, the actual scope of the decisions was not to violate in any degree the principle justly reprobated by the Supreme Court, for both cases seem to have been decided by the application of the ordinary principle that a large sum of money made to secure *grossly* disproportionate matters is always a penalty. The actual point decided in this case by the Supreme Court of the United States is that the mere proof that the amount of actual damages is less than the amount stipulated, or that it is possible to ascertain the actual damages by the ordinary rules of law does not make the sum named a penalty, and that if the agreement itself shows the sum to be properly liquidated damages on the principles enumerated above, offers of such proof should be rejected.

The most recent English cases point in the same direction as that just considered. The House of Lords had before it a contract for a torpedo boat for the Spanish Government, containing a clause providing for a weekly payment of £500 for delay in delivery. This was held to be liquidated damages.[191] The Lord Chancellor said:

[189] 101 Fed. 591; see remarks of Wallace, C. J., on this point, p. 595. *Cf.* The H. F. Dimock, 23 C. C. A. 123, 77 Fed. 226. And see *ante*, § 417.
[190] 106 Fed. 385, 45 C. C. A. 343; Gay Mfg. Co. v. Camp, 65 Fed. 794, 25 U. S. App. 134, 13 C. C. A. 137.
[191] Clydebank E. & S. Co. v. Castaneda, [1905] A. C. 6.

"It is obvious on the face of it that the very thing intended to be provided against by this pactional amount of damages is to avoid that kind of minute and somewhat difficult and complex system of examination which would be necessary if you were to attempt to prove the damages. As I pointed out to the learned counsel during the course of his argument, in order to do that properly and to have any real effect upon any tribunal determining that question, one ought to have before one's mind the whole administration of the Spanish Navy—how they were going to use their torpedo boat destroyers in one place rather than in another, and what would be the relative speed of all the boats they possessed in relation to those which they were getting by this agreement. It would be absolutely idle and impossible to enter into a question of that sort unless you had some kind of agreement between the parties as to what was the real measure of damages which ought to be applied."

The payments agreed upon are declared by Lord Robertson, quoting one of the judges below, to be "a genuine pre-estimate of the creditor's probable or possible interest in the due performance of the principal obligation."[192] If not a real pre-estimate, the sum fixed will be a penalty.[193]

§ 420b. The canons of interpretation in the light of recent cases.

The various canons of interpretation adopted by the courts to distinguish between penalty and liquidation are not rules of law, for the guidance of the jury. They are binding on the court, but are not to be regarded as absolute tests.[194]

Taken together they form a peculiar code of hermeneutics, quite foreign to the ordinary principles governing in contract; the fundamental principle being that whenever the parties intended to liquidate damages in a way obnoxious to equity and fair dealing and departing widely from the common-law measure, they shall be held to have intended the opposite: and the language employed by them shall be held to have been

[192] Ib., p. 19. Lord Halsbury assumes the Scotch and English law to be the same.

[193] Com. of Public Works v. Hills, [1906] A. C. 368.

[194] Pye v. British Automobile Co., [1906] 1 K. B. 425.

used in a sense entirely opposed to the ordinary meaning of the terms employed; e. g., the most deliberate use of the terms "penalty" or "liquidated damages" is not conclusive.[195] While the recent English and American cases [196] do not professedly change the law, they seem to pave the way for its simplification in this respect, by undermining the foundation on which the hermeneutics of the canons of interpretation rest—that there can be two different *intentions*, one that of the parties as a matter of fact, and the other that of the parties as a matter of law. With the disappearance of this, a good deal of the difficulty in the cases would disappear, and on one side would remain cases of *penalty*, in which the contract measure of damages, no matter what its intention or language, is set aside as contrary to the rule that parties cannot be allowed to make unconscionable or extortionate contracts, and on the other contracts in which the contract measure of damages is allowed to stand, as a genuine pre-estimate or pre-ascertainment *inter partes*, of the probable or possible interest of one party in the performance by the other of his obligation.[197]

§ 420c. Stipulated damages and avoidable consequences.

The question has been raised whether by stipulating the amount of damages the rule of avoidable consequences can be itself avoided. In Schroeder *v.* California Yukon Trading Co.[198] the contract, which was one of service, contained a clause providing for the payment of a whole year's salary in case of breach by discharge in contravention of its terms. The court, however, construed this as a penalty, saying that if regarded otherwise, it would permit the plaintiff to recover more than compensation: the whole sum stipulated in addition to all his earnings meantime. The contract was held to belong to the class in which no difficulty as to the ordinary measure of damages exists.

[195] Diestal *v.* Stevenson, [1906] 2 K. B. 345.
[196] *United States:* Sun P. & P. Assoc. *v.* Moore, 183 U. S. 642, 46 L. ed. 366, 22 Sup. Ct. 240.
England: Clydebank E. & S. Co. *v.*
Castaneda, [1905] A. C. 6, 11; Com. of Public Works *v.* Hills, [1906] A. C. 368.
[197] Clydebank E. & S. Co. *v.* Castaneda, [1905] A. C. 6, 19.
[198] 95 Fed. 296.

§ 421. Alternative contract. Rule of least beneficial alternative.

In dealing with such contracts as provide for performance in the alternative, as, for instance, a contract to do a certain act or pay a certain sum of money, there is at the outset an important question of interpretation. The intention of the parties may have been really to give an option to the defendant. This is a true alternative contract. The rule which has been laid down in such cases, as will be seen, is that the plaintiff recovers compensation for the less valuable alternative, on the supposition that had the defendant performed, he would have taken upon himself the discharge of the least onerous obligation.[199]

A simple case will show the complicated character of the questions that may arise. J. S., an owner of horses, contracts to deliver, after a race, his horse A. or his horse B., both being entered for the race; he clearly has his election to deliver either. Looking at the contract at the time of its being entered into, it is impossible to say which is the least beneficial alternative. After the race, if A. makes better time than B., it will probably be for the owner's interest to deliver B., and on a breach, the measure of damages will be the value of B., and *vice versa*. If the owner enters his horse A., and the contract be to deliver A. or pay a sum of money, the rule of the least beneficial alternative, in the event of A.'s winning the race, might make the measure of damages the loss arising from the non-payment of the money; or, in other words, the money itself; but if A. lost the race, it might very likely be for the owner's interest to deliver him, rather than pay the money. If the rule as to the least beneficial alternative is applicable to cases of this kind, the measure of damages would, in such a case, be the value of A.

§ 422. Deverill v. Burnell.

This question has been discussed by the English Court of Common Pleas;[200] and though the judges differed upon the interpretation of the contract, they seem to have agreed upon the distinction above set forth. Plaintiff gave defendant for collection drafts drawn against bills of lading, on an agreement that if

[199] See Cockburn *v.* Alexander, 6 C. B. 791, 814, per Maule, J.

[200] Deverill *v.* Burnell, L. R. 8 C. P. 475.

the drafts should not be paid, the defendant should either return them or pay the amount of them. The jury found that the drafts were worthless. It was held by the majority of the judges that the measure of damages was the amount of the bills. Grove, J., put this on the ground that the contract was "not in the strictest sense an alternative promise," but "a promise that the defendant would return the bills,[201] and if he did not return them, he would pay the amount of them;" and Brett and Keating, JJ., seem to have taken the same view. Bovill, C. J., dissenting from this interpretation, said:

" The question, as it seems to me, turns entirely on the construction of the language in which the contract is alleged in the declaration. If the contract as there stated is simply in the alternative to do one of two things, it would be satisfied by the performance of either, and the damages would be the loss occasioned by the non-performance of that alternative which would be least beneficial to the plaintiff. If the true construction be that of the two things to be done, one depended upon the non-performance of the other; that is, if the defendant did not return the bills, then he should pay the amount of them, the damages would be the non-payment of that amount. The rule of law is clear that, in the case of alternative contracts, the person who has to perform the contract has the right to elect which branch of the alternative he will perform. On the other hand, it is equally clear, if the contract is to do a thing, and if not, to pay a sum of money, then the damages for not doing the thing are the sum of money."

And interpreting the contract as a simple alternative contract, he thought the measure of damages should be compensation for the less beneficial alternative, that is, for the non-delivery of the worthless drafts.

§ 423. Ordinary rule.

Generally, the courts have laid it down as a rule that when the alternative is to do some particular thing or pay a given sum of money, the court will hold the party failing to have had his election, and compel him to pay the money.[202] So, where, in

---

[201] i. e., bills of exchange.   [202] *Maryland:* Pennsylvania Ry. v. Reichert, 58 Md. 261.

consideration of the conveyance of certain city lots for $21,000 *only*, the defendant covenanted that he would erect, on or before the 1st of May, 1836, within two years, two brick houses thereon, or in default thereof, pay $4,000 after the 1st of May, 1836, Bronson, J., said: [203]

" This does not belong to the class of cases in which the question of liquidated damages has usually arisen. It will be found in most, if not all of those cases, that there was an absolute agreement to do or not to do a particular act, followed by a stipulation in relation to the amount of damages in case of a breach. But here there is no absolute engagement to build the houses. It was optional with the defendant whether he would build them or not."

And mainly on the ground that the defendant had made his election not to build, but to pay, and that the court would not modify or reform the agreement between the parties, the sum of $4,000 was held to be the measure of damages. [204] And this is the general rule. So where a lessee of oil land agreed to pay $2.00 per day for each well not completed, or forfeit ten acres of land, it was held that the lessee, in order to avail himself of the option, should have declared it and tendered a release of the land. Not having done that, he must pay damages, and in this case the $2.00 a day is liquidated damages. [205] Where it is agreed that a consumer of gas or electric light shall pay at a certain rate, or if he pays before a certain time then at a lower rate, this is neither a penalty nor liquidated damages, but an

---

Massachusetts: Hodges *v.* King, 7 Met. 583.

New York: Slosson *v.* Beadle, 7 Johns. 72.

South Carolina: Allen *v.* Brazier, 2 Bail. 293.

South Dakota: Russell *v.* Wright, 23 S. D. 338, 121 N. W. 842.

Texas: Levy *v.* Goldsoll, 131 S. W. 420 (Tex. Civ. App.).

England: Layton *v.* Pearce, 1 Doug. 15; Stevens *v.* Webb, 7 C. & P. 60.

[203] Bronson, J., in Pearson *v.* Williams, 24 Wend. 244; s. c. in error, 26 Wend. 630.

[204] When this came into the Court of Errors, Mr. Senator Ely moved to reverse the judgment, on the ground that the doctrine of liquidated damages ought never to apply to a case which admitted of partial performance, as here where the house might have been half built, but only where the contract must be wholly performed, or left wholly unperformed. It is plain that this consideration did not apply to this case. But there may be instances where the suggestion will be found not without weight.

[205] Steel *v.* People's Oil & Gas Co., 147 Ill. App. 133.

alternative price, and the consumer who does not pay at the time named must pay the higher rate; and so of any agreement to make a discount for advance payment.[206] And a provision in a promissory note that if it is not paid at maturity a higher rate of interest must be paid was upheld.[207] On sale of physician's practice, the seller agreed never to practice, provided he should have a right to do so at any time after five years by paying the purchaser $2,000. This is not liquidated damages or penalty, but a price fixed for what the contract permits; and upon the seller engaging in the business, he does not break the contract, but from that moment owes the agreed amount as the price of the privilege.[208] So on a grant of privilege to take clay from land for 12 years at so much a ton, and if less than a minimum amount was taken, then $150 a year, it was held that this is not liquidated damages but an alternative price to be paid for the privilege.[209] And so an agreement with an electric light company to pay so much a watt, but at any rate to pay one dollar per month whether or not enough is taken to make the price come to that amount, was held not an agreement for liquidated damages, but part of the contract, which was to pay one dollar per month, or more if necessary, for electric light; and it would be allowed at any rate as the actual alternative method of compensation fixed in the contract.[210] Upon a breach of a contract to deliver a certain number of logs each year at $6.25 per thousand, but if less than stipulated quantity is delivered in any one year, then the rate shall be $6.00, it was held that the parties had agreed on the amount as compensation for the shortage, and it was allowed.[211] And on an agreement to deliver a deed and abstract

[206] *United States:* United S. M. Co. v. Abbott, 158 Fed. 762, 86 C. C. A. 118.
Missouri: Missouri Edison Electric Co. v. M. J. Steinberg Hat & Fur Co., 94 Mo. App. 543, 68 S. W. 383.
But in *Illinois:* Goodyear Shoe Machinery Company v. Selz, Schwab & Co., 157 Ill. 187, 41 N. E. 625, 51 Ill. App. 390, the advanced rate was not allowed where the discount was not for prepayment, but for payment within a certain time *after* it was due.

[207] Bane v. Gridley, 67 Ill. 388.
[208] Smith v. Bergengren, 153 Mass. 236, 26 N. E. 690, 18 L. R. A. 768.
[209] Johnston v. Cowan, 59 Pa. 275. So of a lease of a coal mine at a rental of five cents per ton, with a minimum of 8,000 tons a year. Wilson v. Big Joe B. C. Co., 142 Ia. 521, 119 N. W. 604.
[210] Beck v. Indianapolis L. & P. Co., 36 Ind. App. 600, 76 N. E. 312.
[211] Jackson v. Hunt, 76 Vt. 284, 56 Atl. 1010.

of title or in lieu thereof pay $1,300, it was held that upon non-delivery of the deed and abstract the $1,300 must be paid.[212] That this rule, however, is not to be applied in every case, but depends to some extent upon the circumstances, is shown by the case of Kemp v. Knickerbocker Ice Co.,[213] decided by the New York Court of Appeals. The defendant contracted to deliver to the plaintiff a certain amount of ice at a fixed price, and in case of breach to forfeit one dollar a ton. The amount to be furnished was disputed by the defendant, who delivered a less amount than the contract called for; the plaintiff then purchased more ice of the defendant at the market price, which exceeded the contract price by more than one dollar a ton. It was held that though the stipulated amount would ordinarily be allowed as liquidated damages, yet in this case the court should allow the plaintiff the whole excess he had been forced to pay to the defendant.

In California the provision of the Code forbidding liquidated damages unless the amount of actual damage is uncertain is applied to alternative contracts. So where the defendant borrowed the plaintiff's lighter, and agreed to return it in good condition or pay $3,500, this was held to be a liquidation of the damages which the court would not allow.[214]

§ 424. Alternative contracts and liquidated damages.

The whole subject seems to be involved in a good deal of difficulty. If we are to understand that the question of liquidated damages is not involved at all, the cases must turn either on the rule of the least beneficial alternative or the still simpler rule laid down in Pearson v. Williams. But frequently a contract though expressed in the alternative must be designed as a liquidation of damages, and if the fundamental principle govern-

[212] Taylor v. Smith, 25 App. Div. 632, 49 N. Y. Supp. 41.
In Luntz v. Berry, 35 Pa. Super. Ct. 204, the purchaser of certain goods having refused to take them although they were in his possession, the seller then wrote offering a reduced price; and if that offer was refused, then the goods to be reshipped to the seller. The purchaser replied, declining the purchase, but did not reship, and the goods were eventually burned; it was held that the purchaser was liable for the value of the goods, and not for the reduced price at which the goods were offered to him, since he had refused that offer.
[213] 69 N. Y. 45.
[214] Wilmington Transp. Co. v. O'Neil, 98 Cal. 1, 32 Pac. 705.

ing the whole subject is, that the court will only follow the expressed intention of the parties to liquidate the damages, when this intention is not calculated to work injustice, or to substitute for the compensation, which the law regards as proper, an arbitrary and oppressive pecuniary fine, then the form which the agreement takes cannot be conclusive; and an alternative contract may obviously be as open to this objection as any other. It is said that in these cases the party has his election, and the law will hold him to it; but so, in any case, it may be said that a party has his election to perform his contract or to pay the sum fixed upon in case of breach; and it is clear that in every case in which an attempt is made to stipulate damages, the parties contemplate the alternative of performance or breach. Besides this, if the canon as to alternative contracts be invariable, all the safeguards contained in the other rules relating to liquidated damages may be swept away by a mere change in the phraseology of the agreement, and the sum fixed as security for the performance of the same covenant be treated as a penalty if it is found in a bond, but as conclusive if found in an alternative contract. In a case decided by the Supreme Court of North Carolina,[215] the plaintiff sued on a contract to pay $3,000 for a lease received from him, or return the lease within ninety days, and after proving its execution, rested. The defendant offered to prove that the lease was of little or no value, insisting that the sum mentioned in the instrument was a penalty. The evidence was rejected by the court, and the plaintiff recovered judgment for $3,000, with interest. On appeal it was held that there must be a new trial, on the ground that, "to consider the sum mentioned in the contract as liquidated damages, would be absurd and oppressive on the defendant." So, too, on a promise to return certain bonds or pay a price greatly in excess of their value, the Supreme Court of Tennessee held the sum to be a penalty.[216] Bell v. Truit [217] was an action on an alternative covenant contained in a lease of lands to be bored for oil, to commence operations within a fixed period or to pay to the lessor $25 per annum until the work should be commenced. On breach by lessee, this was held to be

[215] Burrage v. Crump, 3 Jones' L. 330.

[216] Baird v. Tolliver, 6 Humph. 186.
[217] 9 Bush, 257.

a penalty, and the plaintiff only allowed to recover nominal damages.

§ 424a. General conclusions. The "abnegated option."

As already explained in discussing the medium of payment, contracts embodying promises to pay a sum of money in commodities at a specified rate or price present the case, according to the usual interpretation, of an option, and the contract is sometimes referred to as one liquidating damages.[218] Other cases apply the rule of the least beneficial alternative.[219] We seem to have, therefore, thus far in cases of alternative contracts which are not obnoxious to the law as involving penalties, two rules: first, the rule that where the defendant has an option to do one thing or another, if he fails to do one the law holds him to the other, and that this furnishes the measure of damages; second, the rule of the least beneficial alternative, *i. e.*, that where he has an option between two courses, since he might have chosen the one most beneficial to himself, that, in the event of the breach, furnishes the measure of damages. Applications of the latter rule are certainly extremely rare, and there seems to be a very serious argument against its being ever applied except in the very unusual cases where the parties have expressly adopted it as the rule of their own contract. The objection to it in all cases but these is that it gives to the defendant a double option. This was pointed out in Brooks *v.* Hubbard; where the court said that the adoption of the rule would give the defendant the benefit of the "abnegated option" [220] in another shape. In every ordinary case where the defendant is given an option to do one of two things, he contracts to exercise the option. Consequently, if he fails to exercise it, he has broken the contract in its entirety, and not merely committed a breach as to an alternative. There seems no reason, therefore, why the plaintiff should suffer for this and be compelled to limit his rule of damages because the defendant has broken his contract. Suppose that the plaintiff has paid to the defendant $10,000, and has given the defendant the option to de-

[218] § 279c; Brooks *v.* Hubbard, 3 Conn. 58.

[219] *Kentucky:* Anderson *v.* Ewing, 3 Litt. 245.

Tennessee: Hixon *v.* Hixon, 7 Humph. 33.

[220] 3 Conn. 58, 62.

liver to him either a house according to certain specifications, or a yacht according to certain specifications. It turns out that it will be cheaper for the defendant to deliver the yacht, but by doing neither he breaks the contract. This and all cases like it would seem to be a *prevention of the performance of the contract by the defendant's own act,* and there seems no reason why the plaintiff should not on that ground, in a proper case, recover the money with which he has parted.

The plaintiff sold a locomotive to the defendant, who was to use it for a certain time and then either return it or pay the agreed price. At the end of the time defendant did neither. It was held that the plaintiff, upon proving the value of the locomotive to be greater than the agreed price, might recover the value; [221] thus rightly depriving the defendant of the benefit of the abnegated option.

§ 425. Stipulation of damages strictly construed.

A stipulation for liquidated damages in a contract is to be strictly construed. The defendant contracted to deliver coal in monthly instalments, with an agreement to pay twenty-five cents a ton liquidated damages in case of failure to deliver the agreed amount; but instead thereof the plaintiff might demand the instalment deliverable one month in the next succeeding month. The defendant having failed to deliver the coal, the plaintiff demanded delivery the following month; but the defendant still failed to deliver it. It was held that the stipulation as to damages did not apply in case of the latter breach. [222]

In a building contract the damages for delay were fixed at a certain sum per day. Owing to the fault of the owner the beginning of the work was delayed, and the builder therefore absolved from completing his contract at the agreed time; but he committed a breach of the contract by delaying unreasonably after he had an opportunity to complete the work. The court, however, refused to allow the owner damages for delay at the stipulated rate, and damages were assessed in the usual way. [223] And

[221] Fox *v.* Jones, 39 La. Ann. 929, 3 So. 95. See Hull *v.* Angus (Ore.), 118 Pac. 284.

[222] Grand Tower Co. *v.* Phillips, 23 Wall. 471, 23 L. ed. 71.

[223] Hamilton *v.* Moore, 33 Up. Can.

Q. B. 520. And so generally where the delay may in part be charged to the plaintiff, he cannot recover the stipulated damages.

United States: Jefferson Hotel Co. *v.*

the same thing is true where the actual breach was one obviously not contemplated by the parties when they agreed on the damages.[224]   So where the contractor abandoned a building and plaintiff finished it, he could not recover the stipulated damages for delay.[225]   And so where the plaintiff waived complete performance, only actual damages could be recovered for a subsequent partial breach.[226]   Nor will stipulated damages be allowed when the meaning of the clause which applies to the damages is uncertain.[227]

§ 426. Consequences of liquidating damages.

The consequences resulting from the construction of agreements, in this point of view, are complex and curious. On the one hand, it may be in many cases desirable to get rid of the stipulated damages, and to require an examination into the real loss sustained. But, on the other, a specific performance may be desirable; and this, it was formerly thought, could not be allowed if the damages were stipulated. The court inquired simply whether the stipulated sum was clearly meant as a penalty; so,[228] where articles were executed for the purchase of an estate, with a provision that if either should break the agreement, he should pay £100, Lord Hardwicke treated this as a mere penalty, and decreed a specific performance.[229]

Brumbaugh, 168 Fed. 867, 94 C. C. A. 279; Vilter Mfg. Co. v. Tygart's V. B. Co., 168 Fed. 1002; Caldwell & Drake v. Schmulbach, 175 Fed. 429.

Indiana: Geo B. Swift Co. v. Dolle, 80 N. E. 678, 39 Ind. App. 653.

New York: Heckmann v. Pinkney, 81 N. Y. 211; Weeks v. Little, 89 N. Y. 566.

Pennsylvania: Lilly v. Person, 168 Pa. 219, 32 Atl. 23; Focht v. Rosenbaum, 176 Pa. 14, 34 Atl. 1001.

Texas: Wilkens v. Wilkerson (Tex. Civ. App.), 41 S. W. 178.

[224] Moses v. Autuono, 56 Fla. 499, 47 So. 925.

[225] Gillett v. Young, 45 Colo. 562, 101 Pac. 766.

[226] *Montana:* Wibaux v. Grinnell L. S. Co., 9 Mont. 154, 22 Pac. 492.

New York: Mosler Safe Co. v. Maiden

Lane S. D. Co., 190 N. Y. 479, 93 N. E. 81; Holland Torpedo Boat Co. v. Nixon, 115 N. Y. Supp. 573.

[227] Robertson v. Grand Rapids, 96 Minn. 69, 104 N. W. 715.

[228] Howard v. Hopkyns, 2 Atkyns, 371.

[229] But, on the other hand, where defendant had underlet a church lease to the complainant, with a covenant to renew under a penalty of £70, it was held in the Irish Excehquer, and on appeal by the House of Lords, that this was not a covenant to renew, but that the party was at liberty to renew or pay the penalty. Unless the agreement was in the alternative, the decision may perhaps be questioned. Magrane v. Archbold, 1 Dow, 107. The rule is still maintained in some jurisdictions.

Iowa: Stafford v. Shortreed, 62 Ia. 524, 17 N. W. 756.

It is now settled, however, that specific performance may in a proper case be decreed, though the parties have agreed on a sum that a court of law would award as liquidated damages, if the plaintiff brought his action at law.[230] "It is not consistent with the bond or with the intention of the parties that the obligor should be free if he paid the penalty of £1,000. He could not acquire the right to break the agreement by paying the penalty. The plaintiffs have an alternative remedy to enforce the agreement if they do not bring an action."[231]

Another consequence flowing from the distinction between stipulated damages and a penalty, under the original English law of arrest, was that for the former the defendant might be held to bail, but not for the latter; and therefore an affidavit to hold to bail, which did not show what the agreement was, nor in what respects it was broken, but merely alleged an obligation to pay £50 in case of non-performance, and charged such non-performance, was held insufficient, and the defendant was released from custody.[232]

The stipulated damages are of course binding upon the plaintiff as well as upon the defendant, and the former can therefore recover nothing beyond the stipulation.[233] The jury may be

Maryland: Hahn v. Concordia Society, 42 Md. 460.

New York: Nessle v. Reese, 29 How. Pr. 382.

[230] *Alabama:* McCurry v. Gibson, 108 Ala. 451, 18 So. 806, 54 Am. St. Rep. 177; Harris v. Theus, 149 Ala. 133, 43 So. 131, 10 L. R. A. (N. S.) 204, 123 Am. St. Rep. 17.

Illinois: Koch v. Streuter, 218 Ill. 546, 75 N. E. 1049, 2 L. R. A. (N. S.) 210.

Iowa: Heinz v. Roberts, 110 N. W. 1034, 35 Ia. 748.

Maine: Augusta Steam Laundry Co. v. Debow, 98 Me. 496, 57 Atl. 845.

Massachusetts: Ropes v. Upton, 125 Mass. 258.

Michigan: Buckhout v. Witwer, 157 Mich. 406, 122 N. W. 184, 23 L. R. A. (N. S.) 506.

Nebraska: Hickey v. Brinkley, 129 N. W. 553.

New Jersey: Crane v. Peer, 43 N. J. Eq. 553.

New York: Diamond Match Co. v. Roeber, 106 N. Y. 473, 13 N. E. 419, 60 Am. Rep. 464.

Pennsylvania: Wilkinson v. Colley, 164 Pa. 35, 30 Atl. 286, 26 L. R. A. 114.

[231] Lindley, L. J., in National Provincial Bank of England v. Marshall, 40 Ch. Div. 112, 118. In using the word "penalty," the Lord Justice did not mean that the sum was not recognized as liquidated damages; all the judges agreed that the plaintiff might have recovered the stipulated amount if he had brought his action at law.

[232] Wildey v. Thornton, 2 East. 409; Edwards v. Williams, 5 Taunt. 247.

[233] *United States:* Catterlin v. Voney, 177 Fed. 527.

New York: Glick v. Wm. Horne Co., 110 N. Y. Supp. 918.

directed to find a verdict for the amount of the stipulated damages, since the exact amount must be allowed and there is no discretion in the jury to find more or less.[234]

If the plaintiff is entitled to liquidated damages, it is not necessary for him to allege or prove actual damages.[235] And evidence that by a fortunate sale of the property covered by the contract his loss was finally made up to him is not pertinent.[236]

§ 426a. Statutory regulations of liquidated damages.

In a few States the recovery of liquidated damages has been regulated by statute. Thus in Georgia it has been provided by law that the sum fixed shall be treated as a penalty whenever the damages are "capable of computation." Under this provision, a contract to furnish all the turpentine made on a plantation at a fixed price, and that "either party failing to perform their part forfeits to the other the sum of $1,000," is an agreement for a penalty.[237] It will be seen that this statutory provision is based on the principle of adhesion to the fixed legal standard of compensation, wherever that is possible. A similar statute in California is interpreted to cover all cases where it is practicable by evidence of values and by computation to arrive at the amount of damages.[238] And a similar interpretation is given to the statute in Montana.[239]

South Dakota: Woodford v. Kelley, 18 S. D. 615, 101 N. W. 1069.

Utah: Donovan v. Hanauer, 32 Utah, 317, 90 Pac. 569.

Washington: West Coast Mfrs. Agency v. Oregon Condensed Milk Co., 54 Wash. 247, 103 Pac. 4.

On the other hand, if the stipulated sum is found to be a penalty it does not limit the amount of damages, and the plaintiff may recover a greater amount of damages than the stipulated penalty. Sherman v. Gray, 11 Cal. App. 348, 104 Pac. 1004.

[234] Camp v. Pollock, 45 Neb. 771, 64 N. W. 231.

[235] *Indiana:* Howard v. Adkins, 167 Ind. 184, 78 N. E. 665.

West Virginia: Charleston Lumber Co. v. Friedman 64 W. Va. 151, 61 S. E. 815.

[236] Atwood v. Fagan, (Tex. Civ. App.), 134 S. W. 765.

[237] Lee v. Overstreet, 44 Ga. 507.

[238] Under this statute liquidation of damages has been disallowed in the following cases: Brick Co. v. Moore, 75 Cal. 205, 16 Pac. 890 (delay in completing building); Eva v. McMahon, 77 Cal. 467, 19 Pac. 872 (breach of contract to deliver possession at a certain day); Drew v. Pedlar, 87 Cal. 443, 25 Pac. 749 (failure to accept conveyance of land); Pacific Factor Co. v. Adler, 90 Cal. 110, 120, 27 Pac. 36, 25 Am. St. Rep. 102 (failure to deliver grain-bags); Transportation Co. v. O'Neil, 98 Cal. 1, 32 Pac. 705 (damage to lighter); Jack v. Sinsheimer, 125 Cal. 563, 58 Pac. 130 (failure to perform covenants of lease).

[239] Home Land and Cattle Co. v. McNamara, 111 Fed. 822, 49 C. C. A. 642

§ 427. Civil law.

*The French Code, like our law, enables the parties to liquidate the damages for the non-performance of the contract; and the tribunal cannot depart from the sum thus fixed.[240]**

(failure to deliver a certain number of cattle).

[240] *Lorsque la convention porte que celui qui manquera de l'exécuter paiera une certaine somme, à titre de dommages intérêts, il ne peut être alloué à l'autre partie une somme plus forte ni moindre.* Code Civil, § 1152.

The commissioners charged with preparing the codes proposed to retain the former jurisprudence in this respect, which permitted the judge to moderate the penalty in behalf of the debtor, if it evidently exceeded the damage sustained, but gave him no power to augment it in favor of the creditor, although it might be far short of the injury suffered. These views were, however, overruled. Toullier, vol. vi, 812, *des Obligations, ou Clauses Pénales;* see Domat, part i, book 3, tit. v, sec. 2, § 15.

The rejected provision is, however, adopted in Louisiana. There the judge may modify the penalty if the obligation has been partly performed. Code, § 2127.

CHAPTER XVIII

I.—General Considerations

§ 428. Torts in general.

Having thus considered the general rules which govern and limit compensation in all cases, we now proceed to consider the special rules applicable in actions of tort; deferring, however, the examination of such torts as affect real estate to a later chapter. The technical forms prescribed by the common law

827

for the redress of wrongs, or, as they are termed, actions *ex delicto*, were trespass, case, replevin, and detinue.[1] The divisions of the system in this respect were arbitrary; there being many actions nominally in tort, which in respect to the measure of relief, were treated as virtually actions *ex contractu;* and in these cases a fixed rule of damages has always been adhered to. In all cases of tort where no question of fraud, malice, or oppression intervenes, the measure of compensation is determined by fixed rules. So in an action of trespass without any circumstances of aggravation, the Supreme Court of the United States said that, the case not being one which called for vindictive or exemplary damages, the plaintiff was only entitled to recover for his actual injury.[2] So the Supreme Court of New Jersey said in an action of *trespass quare clausum fregit:* "In actions of trespass, where the plaintiff complains of no injury to his person or his feelings; where no malice is shown; where no right is involved beyond a mere question of property; where there is a clear standard for the measure of damages, and no difficulty in applying it, the measure of damages is a question of law, and is necessarily under the control of the court."[3] And so again in North Carolina, in an action for trespass for destroying a building by fire, the jury at Nisi Prius were directed that the measure of damages was not the value of the building, but the amount it would have taken to rebuild it if destroyed. But this, on review, was held wrong; and the court said: "The proper measure in actions of this kind, is the real value of the property destroyed, unless the trespass is committed wantonly or maliciously, when the jury may, if they think proper, give vindictive damages. But whether they should have been given or not was a question

[1] The old action of detinue is of comparatively rare occurrence, and is frequently abolished by statute.

Grotius thus begins his chapter: *De Damno. Supra diximus ejus quod nobis debetur fontes esse tres; pactionem—maleficium—legem. De pactionibus satis tractatum. Veniamus ad id quod ex maleficio naturaliter debetur.* Lib. ii, cap. 17, § 1, *De Jure Belli et Pacis.*

Grotius treats only of Damnum, under this head of Maleficium. *De Jure Belli et Pacis,* lib. ii, cap. 17.

[2] Conard *v.* The Pacific Ins. Co., 6 Peters, 262, 282, 8 L. ed. 262. See, also, Bell *v.* Cunningham, 3 Peters, 69, 7 L. ed. 69; Tracy *v.* Swartwout, 10 Peters, 80, 95, 9 L. ed. 80.

[3] Berry *v.* Vreeland, 21 N. J. L. 183.

which ought to have been submitted with proper instructions to the jury." [4]

§ 429. Measure of relief independent of form of action.

* It follows, from what has been said, that in the cases of wrongs such as we now proceed to consider, the measure of relief does not depend on the form of the action; whether case or trespass would have been the proper form of action at common law, if no aggravation be proved, the rule of damages is a question of law; though it is always competent to show those circumstances of evil motive which, as we have already seen, go to place the subject of relief largely within the control of the jury. In regard to this class of cases generally, it will be noticed that the object is to limit relief to compensation, as that term is legally understood; and we shall find, therefore, that while the power of the jury over the subject in cases of aggravation is fully recognized, still, even where such facts are presented, if evidence has been admitted or directions given at the trial, which, had the intention of the jury been to give compensatory and not vindictive damages, would have been incorrect, the court, assuming that such was the purpose of the jury, will exercise their control over the subject. "We consider the law," says the Superior Court of New York, "as properly and wisely settled, that the quantum of damages, with the exception of cases in which exemplary or vindictive damages may properly be given, is strictly a question of law; so that the jury are bound by the rule which the judge directs them to follow." [5] In an early case in Pennsylvania, for running down a ship, it was intimated that where the act complained of was purely fortuitous, the jury might give less than the value of the property; but if there be any right of action, the least compensation is certainly the value of property taken or destroyed.[6] **

In Milwaukee & St. Paul Railway v. Arms,[7] Mr. Justice Davis said: "It is undoubtedly true that the allowance of anything more than an adequate pecuniary indemnity for a wrong suf-

---

[4] Wylie v. Smitherman, 8 Ired. (N. C.) 236.

[5] Suydam v. Jenkins, 3 Sandf. (N. Y.) 614, 628, per Duer, J. See, also, Baker v. Wheeler, 8 Wend. (N. Y.) 505.

[6] Bussy v. Donaldson, 4 Dall. 206, 1 L. ed. 802.

[7] 91 U. S. 489, 23 L. ed. 374; acc., Swayne, J., in Oelrichs v. Spain, 15 Wall. 211, 230, 21 L. ed. 43.

fered is a great departure from the principle on which damages in civil suits are awarded. But although, as a general rule, the plaintiff recovers merely such indemnity, yet the doctrine is too well settled now to be shaken, that exemplary damages may, in certain cases, be assessed." This being so, the same rules of compensation should apply in contract and in tort. The decided cases are generally to this effect, and this is the tenor of Judge Rapallo's remarks, in Baker v. Drake.[8]

§ 430. Aggravation and mitigation.

We have already seen [9] that where the amount of compensation is wholly or in part in the discretion of the jury, the circumstances attending the injury may be shown for the purpose of enhancing or mitigating the damages. It is to be observed, however, that whether the action be in tort or in contract, if the damages are measured entirely by the value of property, or by the amount of injury to property, no circumstances can be shown for this purpose.

§ 431. Joint wrongdoers.[10]

In an action of tort the damages are not divisible. There can be but one verdict and for one amount against all of those found guilty. All are principals; and each defendant is liable for all the damages sustained, without regard to different degrees or shades of wrongdoing.[11] The fact that one of the defendants received only a small proportion of the proceeds of the tort, or none at all, does not lessen the recovery against him.[12] So, where all the defendants, in an action charging them with a joint trespass, are defaulted, and the case referred to an assessor to assess the damages, they are all liable for the

[8] 53 N. Y. 211, 216.

[9] § 51.

[10] See ante, § 36a.

[11] Georgia: Mashburn v. Danneberg, 117 Ga. 567, 44 S. E. 97.

Indiana: Peru Heating Co. v. Lenhart, 95 N. E. 680.

Kentucky: Hill v. Mudd, 9 Ky. L. Rep. 59.

New York: Beal v. Finch, 11 N.Y. 128; Posthoff v. Bauendahl, 43 Hun, 570.

Rhode Island: Heyer v. Carr, 6 R. I. 45.

Canada: Grantham v. Severs, 25 Up. Can. Q. B. 468; Barker v. Westover, 5 Ont. 116.

[12] Alabama: Stix v. Keith, 85 Ala. 465.

Massachusetts: White v. Sawyer, 16 Gray, 586.

Vermont: Crumb v. Oaks, 38 Vt. 566.

Canada: McMillan v. Fairley, 1 Han. 325.

Macklem v. Durrant, 32 Up. Can. Q. B. 98.

whole damage actually sustained by the plaintiff, although it appears, by the evidence before the assessor, that one of them did not participate in the trespass.[13] But where the tort is really made up of several tortious acts, each defendant is liable only for those in which he participated. In an action for the wrongful seizure of the plaintiff's cattle, it appeared that Fleming, one of the defendants, had recovered a judgment against a brother of the plaintiff, on which the execution was issued; Fleming, with her attorney in that suit, who had directed the wrongful seizure, were joined as defendants. A verdict was found against both defendants for £83 15s. 10d. Of this £25 was for the seizure; and the rest was the amount of the costs ordered against the defendant Fleming in an interpleader suit, which had been had to try the title to the cattle. An order had been made in that suit that Fleming pay those costs, and as this order was equivalent to a judgment, it was held that the judgment against Fleming must be reduced by that amount. And as the plaintiff could not recover these costs against her, and could not recover against her attorney any other damages than he was entitled to against her, the court reduced the verdict by the amount of the costs.[14] Where damage is done by cattle belonging to different owners, each owner is liable for the damage done by his own cattle, and for no more; and in the absence of all proof as to the amount of damage so done, the law will infer that the cattle did equal damage.[15]

II.—TAKING OR INJURING PERSONAL PROPERTY

§ 432. General rules.

We proceed now to notice the general rules which govern in trespass for taking or injuring personal property. Where personal property is taken or injured, the remedy at common law was by an action of trespass *de bonis asportatis*, or by an action on the case. As has been seen, however, the form of action should cause no difference in the measure of damages; and the distinction has in fact been very generally abolished under the modern systems of pleading. In this discussion injuries which

[13] Gardner *v.* Field, 1 Gray, 151.
[14] Power*v.*Fleming,4Ir.R.(C.L.)404.
[15] Wood *v.* Snider, 187 N. Y. 28,

79 N. E. 858, 12 L. R. A. (N. S.) 912; Partenheimer *v.* Van Order, 20 Barb. (N. Y.) 479; *ante* § 36a.

would formerly have been remedied by an action of trespass and those where case would have been brought have been grouped together, no distinction being noted.

The principal injury in this case being pecuniary, the damages are not capable of mitigation in the strict sense, as distinguished from reduction.[16] So where defendant killed a dog which was trespassing on his land and was about to do harm, the killing being illegal, the trespass could not be shown to mitigate the damages.[17]

Any pecuniary injury, however small, is regarded as entitling the injured party to recovery, for no real invasion of property rights is a proper case for the application of the maxim *de minimis non curat lex*. So where defendant as a practical joke took plaintiff's reins from his harness, in spite of the small amount of loss the plaintiff was held entitled to recover compensatory damages.[18]

§ 432a. Damages for destruction or total loss.

It has been often decided, that where trespass is brought for personal property, and no circumstances of aggravation are shown, the action is to be regarded as similar to one of conversion, and the value of the property, with interest, furnishes the measure of damages.[19] In a case in Massachusetts, tres-

---

[16] *Ante,* § 51.

[17] Ten Hopen *v.* Walker, 96 Mich. 236, 55 N. W. 657, 35 Am. St. Rep. 598.

[18] Wartman *v.* Swindell, 54 N. J. L. 589, 25 Atl. 356, 18 L. R. A. 44.

[19] *United States:* The Henry Buck, 39 Fed. 211.

Alabama: Louisville & N. R. R. *v.* Kelsey, 89 Ala. 287.

Arkansas: St. Louis, I. M. & S. Ry. *v.* Biggs, 50 Ark. 169.

California: Dorsey *v.* Manlove, 14 Cal. 553.

Colorado: Parks *v.* Sullivan, 46 Colo. 340, 104 Pac. 1035.

Connecticut: Oviatt *v.* Pond, 29 Conn. 479.

Delaware: Colbourn *v.* Wilmington, 4 Pennew. 443, 56 Atl. 605.

Illinois: Gilson *v.* Wood, 20 Ill. 37;

Toledo, P. & W. Ry. *v.* Johnston, 74 Ill. 83.

Kentucky: Schulte *v.* Louisville & N. R. R., 128 Ky. 627, 108 S. W. 941.

Louisiana: Yarborough *v.* Nettles, 7 La. Ann. 116.

Maryland: Schindel *v.* Schindel, 12 Md. 108.

Mississippi: Briscoe *v.* McElween, 43 Miss. 556.

Missouri: Walker *v.* Borland, 21 Mo. 289; Funk *v.* Dillon, 21 Mo. 294; State *v.* Smith, 31 Mo. 566.

New Hampshire: Felton *v.* Fuller, 35 N. H. 226.

New Jersey: Hopple *v.* Higbee, 23 N. J. L. 342.

New York: Campbell *v.* Woodworth, 26 Barb. 648.

Pennsylvania: Fernwood M. H. A. *v.* Jones, 102 Pa. 307.

pass was brought for destroying game-cocks, which had been taken by a public officer acting on an erroneous construction of the statute against gaming. It was held that, though cockfighting is in that State illegal, the sale of game-cocks is lawful; and that the measure of the plaintiff's damages was "what the cocks were worth to him as articles of merchandise or sale, whether the market for them was to be found in this commonwealth or elsewhere." [20] So where property of the plaintiff was sold by the defendant on an execution which was afterwards reversed on appeal, the measure of damages was the value of the property at the time of the sale.[21] From the value of the property is of course to be deducted any amount realized from the sale and returned to the plaintiff or applied to his benefit.[22]

§ 433. Value, how estimated.

The market value of the property, with interest from the time of the trespass, not its value to the plaintiff, is usually said to be the measure.[23] So where the defendant had carried off some corn belonging to the plaintiff, it was held that the market value at the time of taking was the measure of damages, and the plaintiff could not show that he had a contract to deliver that corn, and what it was worth to him under that contract, "especially in the absence of knowledge of such contract by defendant." [24] But this is subject to the qualifications heretofore pointed out that the *value* is the fundamental rule, that the market price is only one of the evidences of this value, and the value as between plaintiff and defendant may according to circumstances be higher or lower than the market.[25] So where the assignees of a bankrupt sold fixtures on leased premises belonging to the plaintiff, for £36, a fair price on such sale,

South Carolina: Josey v. Wilmington & M. R. R., 11 Rich. 399.

Tennessee: Burke v. Louisville & N. R. R., 7 Heisk. 451.

Texas: Gulf, C. & S. F. Ry. v. Keith, 74 Tex. 287.

Vermont: Gray v. Stevens, 28 Vt. 1.

Canada: Maxwell v. Crann, 13 Up. Can. Q. B. 253; Sweeney v. Port Burwell Harbour, 17 Up. Can. C. P. 574.

[20] Coolidge v. Choate, 11 Met. (Mass.) 79.

[21] Smith v. Zent, 83 Ind. 86.

[22] Gilliam v. Globe Tailoring Co., 152 Mo. App. 414, 133 S. W. 628. See *ante*, §§ 59–62.

[23] *United States:* Pacific Ins. Co. v. Conard, 1 Bald. 138.

Massachusetts: Gardner v. Field, 1 Gray, 151.

New York: Marcus v. Stein (Misc.), 84 N. Y. Supp. 970.

[24] Brown v. Allen, 35 Ia. 306.

[25] *Ante*, § 252.

but it was shown that, as between incoming and outgoing tenant, the value would have been £80, it was held that the plaintiff was entitled to recover the latter sum.[26] So where a horse was specially fitted for the business in which he was being used, its value for such use could be recovered.[27] And where it was shown that a horse could not have been sold for more than twenty dollars, but was doing work for which another horse could not be bought for less than thirty-five dollars, the latter amount should be recovered for its destruction.[28] And, in general, the value of a thing is its value for the most valuable use for which it is adapted.[29]

§ 434. Value, when and where estimated.

The question as to the time when the value is to be computed, whether at the time of the illegal act, or at any subsequent period, if the value has fluctuated, presents itself in actions of trespass. In Crouch v. London & North Western Railway,[30] it seems to have been assumed that the period fixing the right of the parties was that of the trespass, and it has been so stated by the Supreme Court of New York;[31] and this is now the established rule.[32] Where defendant's cattle destroyed plaintiff's corn, the measure of damages was held to be the value of the corn at the time of the trespass, and not the value it would have had if it had matured.[33] And where ice in an ice-house was destroyed, the value of the ice at that time is recoverable, though a large part of it would have melted before use.[34]

The value is to be taken at the place of injury; and if there is

[26] Thompson v. Pettitt, 10 Q. B. 101.

[27] Farrel v. Colwell, 30 N. J. L. 123.

[28] Seavey v. Dennett, 69 N. H. 479, 45 Atl. 247.

[29] Indiana: Loesch v. Koehler, 144 Ind. 278, 41 N. E. 326, 43 N. E. 129, 35 L. R. A. 682 (work horse).

Montana: Parrin v. Montana Cent. Ry., 22 Mont. 290, 56 Pac. 315 (dairy stock).

Nevada: Watt v. Nevada Central R. R., 23 Nev. 154, 44 Pac. 423 (hay kept against a hard winter).

[30] 2 C. & K. 789.

[31] Brizsee v. Maybee, 21 Wend. (N. Y.) 144.

[32] United States: Pacific Ins. Co. v. Conard, 1 Bald. 138.

Connecticut: Hubbard v. New York, N. H. & H. R. R., 70 Conn. 563, 40 Atl. 533.

Kentucky: Schulte v. Louisville & N. R. R., 128 Ky. 627, 108 S. W. 941.

Maine: Brannin v. Johnson, 19 Me. 361.

[33] Richardson v. Northrup, 66 Barb. (N. Y.) 85.

[34] Hubbard v. New York, N. H. & H. R. R., 70 Conn. 563, 40 Atl. 533.

there no market, the basis of value is its value at the nearest market. To this should be added the cost of transportation, if the article is needed for use at the place of injury, or from it should be subtracted such cost if the article was to be sent away and sold.[35]

§ 435. Injury less than destruction.

Where a trespass upon the property of the plaintiff results in a less injury than destruction or deprivation of the property, the rule stated does not apply; the difference in value of the property before and after the injury is usually the measure.[36] Thus where the goods of the plaintiff were seized by the defendant, but the plaintiff's possession was not disturbed and he continued to have the use of them, his damages are the amount of his injury.[37] Where the plaintiff's property was taken out of his possession, and afterwards returned to him, he may recover compensation for injury to the property.[38] So if the plaintiff's animal is killed by the defendant, since the carcass remains the plaintiff's property, his recovery is limited to the difference in value between the live animal and the carcass.[39]

So where the defendant's bull entered plaintiff's pasture and covered plaintiff's heifer, which was a blooded animal and was

[35] *Illinois:* Chicago G. W. Ry. v. Gitchell, 95 Ill. App. 1.

Nevada: Watt v. Nevada C. R. R., 23 Nev. 154, 44 Pac. 423.

See *ante*, § 247.

[36] *Arkansas:* St. Louis, I. M. & S. Ry. v. Biggs, 50 Ark. 169, 6 S. W. 724.

Michigan: Davidson v. Michigan C. R. R., 49 Mich. 428.

Missouri: Cottrell v. Russell, 21 Mo. App. 1.

Nebraska: Chicago, B. & Q. R. R. v. Metcalf, 44 Neb. 848, 63 N. W. 51, 28 L. R. A. 824; Hespen v. Union Pac. R. R., 82 Neb. 495, 118 N. W. 98.

New Hampshire: Sinclair v. Tarbox, 2 N. H. 135.

Oklahoma: Tuttle v. Kent, 12 Okla. 674, 73 Pac. 310.

[37] Bayliss v. Fisher, 7 Bing. 153.

[38] *Iowa:* Turner v. Younker, 76 Ia. 258.

Michigan: Haviland v. Parker, 11 Mich. 103.

New York: Barber v. Dewes, 101 App. Div. 432, 91 N. Y. Supp. 1059.

Pennsylvania: Hyde v. Kiehl, 183 Pa. 414, 38 Atl. 998.

Wisconsin: Anderson v. Sloane, 72 Wis. 566, 40 N. W. 214.

Canada: Benson v. Connor, 6 Up. Can. C. P. 356.

[39] *Alabama:* Georgia P. R. R. v. Fullerton, 79 Ala. 298; Memphis & C. R. R. v. Hembres, 84 Ala. 182.

Missouri: Case v. St. Louis & S. F. R. R., 75 Mo. 668; Harrison v. Missouri P. Ry., 88 Mo. 625.

North Carolina: Roberts v. Richmond & D. R. R., 88 N. C. 560; Boing v. Raleigh & G. R. R., 91 N. C. 199; Godwin v. Wilmington & W. R. R., 104 N. C. 146.

to have been covered by a high-bred bull, the measure of damages for trespass on the heifer was the difference in her value before and after the trespass; in which was to be considered the difference in value of the calf, and the effect, if any, on her future calves.[40] And where a mare with foal was so injured as to drop her foal prematurely, the measure of damages was the reduction in value of the mare by loss of her foal.[41]

When, however, the injury is capable of repair at a reasonable expense, that is, at an expense less than the diminution in value of the property as injured, the diminution in value cannot be recovered, but plaintiff's damages are limited to the cost of repair.[42]

§ 435a. Loss of use and expense of maintenance.

Where an injury to plaintiff's property which does not cause its total destruction results in his losing the use of it for a time, either because it is rendered unfit for use or because he is temporarily deprived of the possession of it, he may in addition to the deterioration in value recover the value of the use of it during the time he lost the use,[43] and the expense of its maintenance, if he was at such expense.[44] But if the plaintiff recovers the full value of the property, as for a complete destruction, he cannot also recover the value of the use.[45]

[40] Kopplin v. Quade, 145 Wis. 454, 130 N. W. 511.

So where defendant's ram covered plaintiff's ewe, so that she was got with lamb out of season, the measure of damages was the difference in her value for breeding and other purposes before and after the trespass. Stearns v. McGinty, 8 N. Y. Supp. 216, 55 Hun, 101.

[41] Baker v. Mims, 14 Tex. Civ. App. 413, 37 S. W. 190.

[42] *Mississippi:* Cue v. Breeland, 78 Miss. 864, 29 So. 850.

Washington: West v. Martin, 51 Wash. 85, 97 Pac. 1102.

[43] *Georgia:* Atlanta & W. P. R. R. v. Hudson, 62 Ga. 679.

Iowa: Turner v. Younker, 76 Ia. 258.

Michigan: Haviland v. Parker, 11 Mich. 103.

Missouri: Streett v. Laumier, 34 Mo. 469; Missouri R. P. Co. v. Hannibal & St. J. R. R., 79 Mo. 478.

Washington: West v. Martin, 51 Wash. 85, 97 Pac. 1102.

Wisconsin: Wright v. Mulvaney, 78 Wis. 89, 46 N. W. 1045, 23 Am. St. Rep. 393, 9 L. R. A. 807.

Canada: Benson v. Connor, 6 Up. Can. C. P. 356.

As an alternative, plaintiff may show the cost of a substitute necessarily hired to take the place of the property injured. Chaperon v. Portland G. E. Co., 41 Ore. 39, 67 Pac. 928.

[44] Gould v. Merrill Ry. & L. Co., 139 Wis. 433, 121 N. W. 161.

[45] *United States:* Ft. Pitt Gas Co. v. Evansville Contract Co., 123 Fed. 63, 59 C. C. A. 281.

§ 436. Consequential damages.

As a rule, when interest is given, this represents the sum total of redress for the *consequences* of the loss, and hence consequential damages, as such, are not recoverable.[46]

In Maine, in an action of trespass *de bonis asportatis*, it was ruled, at the trial, that the jury should give the value of the property at the time it was taken, and *something for the detention*. But, on motion for a new trial, the court said: "For an injury done to property, such as is this case, the value of the property at the time of the injury is the measure of damages. There may be circumstances enhancing that value to the party injured, which may be properly taken into account. To the value here, interest might be added as a part of the plaintiff's indemnity. But as the term *interest* was not used, and probably not intended as the limit of damages for *detention*, the jury were at liberty to go into an estimate of the probable or speculative loss the plaintiff might have sustained on this ground. In our judgment, the instruction was too vague and loose, and had a tendency to mislead the jury." [47]

So, in Texas, in an action for tortious conversion analogous to that of trover, where, although there was no other evidence of damage than the value of the property, and no proof of fraud, violence, or malice, yet the jury had given double the value, the verdict was set aside.[48]

So, in trespass for taking corn, it will not be permitted the plaintiff to show that, in consequence of the alleged illegal act, he was obliged to work as a day laborer, to obtain the means to purchase more corn. "Such testimony," says the Supreme Court of Alabama, "tends to establish a criterion of damages too remote and disconnected with the act done, and supposes the rule to fluctuate according to the poverty of the plaintiff." [49]

So, again, in trespass for taking the plaintiff's goods in execution under a warrant of attorney and judgment, which were afterwards set aside as illegal, it was held in the English Queen's Bench, that the plaintiff could not claim, as part of the damage,

Alabama: Fail v. Presley, 50 Ala. 342. *Wisconsin:* Page v. Sumpter, 53 Wis. 652, 11 N. W. 60.

[46] *United States:* Pacific Ins. Co. v. Conard, 1 Bald. 138.

Iowa: Thomas v. Isett, 1 Greene, 470.

[47] Brannin v. Johnson, 19 Me. 361.

[48] Smith v. Sherwood, 2 Tex. 460.

[49] Sims v. Glazener, 14 Ala. 695.

his costs incurred in vacating the warrant of attorney and judgment; Lord Denman saying: "The plaintiff might have recovered these costs in a proper form of proceeding, but he cannot sue the defendant for a trespass *per quod* he was put to expense in removing the cause of the trespass." [50]

A verdict for profits which might have been made on the goods wrongfully taken, in addition to their value, is erroneous.[51] Nor can the plaintiff recover for injury to his business caused by loss of use of the property destroyed.[52]

Where, however, the property was actually in use at the time it was destroyed, the plaintiff may recover compensation for the damage caused by the loss of it up to the time when he could replace it. So where the driver of a street-car negligently attempting to pass the horse and wagon of an expressman, which had been temporarily left in the city street near the curbstone, the car was brought into contact with the wagon, and the horse, having been thrown in consequence on the curbstone and against a tree, received a fatal injury, compensation for the loss of the profits of the plaintiff's business during the time reasonably necessary to enable him to select another horse, was allowed to be included in the damages recovered by him.[53] And where a wagon in which plaintiff was actually on his way to market to buy goods with which to fill orders for customers was disabled by defendant's fault, it was held that plaintiff might recover what he lost by his inability to fill the orders in time.[54]

Mental suffering does not ordinarily result from a wrongful

[50] Holloway *v.* Turner, 6 Q. B. 928.

[51] *California:* Butler *v.* Collins, 12 Cal. 457.

Kentucky: Ludlow *v.* Steffen, 19 Ky. L. Rep. 1671, 44 S. W. 1119.

Michigan: Quay *v.* Duluth, S. I. & A. Ry., 153 Mich. 567, 116 N. W. 1101, 18 L. R. A. (N. S.) 250.

But see *Oklahoma:* Tootle *v.* Kent, 12 Okla. 674, 73 Pac. 310.

[52] *Alabama:* Nelms *v.* Hill, 5 So. 344.

Maine: McLaughlin *v.* Bangor, 58 Me. 398.

Montana: Parrin *v.* Montana Cent. Ry., 22 Mont. 290, 56 Pac. 315.

Nevada: Watt *v.* Nevada C. R. R., 23 Nev. 154, 44 Pac. 423.

See, however, Parks *v.* Sullivan, 46 Colo. 340, 104 Pac. 1035, where the refusal of recovery in such a case was placed on the ground that the loss was not proved with sufficient certainty.

[53] *Michigan:* Quay *v.* Duluth, S. I. & A. Ry., 153 Mich. 567, 116 N. W. 1101, 18 L. R. A. (N. S.) 250.

New York: Albert *v.* Bleecker St. R. R., 2 Daly, 389.

[54] Graves *v.* Baltimore & N. Y. Ry., 76 N. J. L. 362, 69 Atl. 971.

seizure of personal property, and in an action for such a seizure compensation for mental suffering cannot be recovered.[55] But in an exceptional case mental suffering may naturally result, and compensation for it may be recovered; as where defendant maliciously hit plaintiff's mare with an axe.[56]

§ 437. Expense of avoiding consequences.

The reason of this rule does not, however, apply in all cases. It will often happen where the injury is less than a total destruction, or where there is a doubt whether it will amount to total destruction, that consequential damages will be allowed. Under this head would fall all allowances for expenses incurred by the plaintiff in an attempt to avoid the consequences of the trespass.[57]

So in New York it has been held that in an action on the case for the wrongful detention of personal property, the plaintiff might recover damages for the time lost and expenses incurred in pursuit of the property.[58] In an action for injury to cattle which necessitated their being killed, it was held that the plaintiff was entitled to a reasonable allowance for his time and trouble in disposing of them, and should be charged with the net proceeds realized, or which might have been realized, after deducting such allowance.[59] And so the cost of selecting a part of cotton bales which was not injured and shipping the same to market should be added to the difference in value.[60]

Where the expense incurred results in diminishing the loss, the defendant, being chargeable with the expense, is of course

[55] *Nebraska:* Henderson v. Weidman, 88 Neb. 813, 130 N. W. 579.
North Carolina: Chappell v. Ellis, 123 N. C. 259, 31 S. E. 709, 68 Am. St. Rep. 822.
[56] Kimball v. Holmes, 60 N. H. 163.
[57] *Indiana:* Sullivan County v. Arnett, 116 Ind. 438, 19 N. E. 299 (expense of cure of animal).
New Hampshire: Seavey v. Dennett, 69 N. H. 479, 45 Atl. 247 (expense of care of animal).
Pennsylvania: Hyde v. Kiehl, 183 Pa. 414, 38 Atl. 998 (expense of recovery.)

Wisconsin: Plunkett v. Minneapolis, S. S. M. & A. Ry., 79 Wis. 222, 48 N. W. 519 (expense of curing animal); Anderson v. Sloane, 72 Wis. 566, 40 N. W. 214 (expense of recovery).
[58] Bennett v. Lockwood, 20 Wend. (N. Y.) 223; *acc.,* Watson v. Boswell, 25 Tex. Civ. App. 377, 61 S. W. 407.
[59] Dean v. Chicago & N. W. Ry., 43 Wis. 305.
[60] Texas & P. Ry. v. Levi, 59 Tex. 674.

entitled to the benefit of it; and if he is still called upon to make compensation for a diminution in value, it is for the difference between the value before the injury and after the final recovery of the property.[61]

§ 438. Damages may exceed entire value of property.

Since consequential damages may in some cases be recovered, it is obvious that the damages may in some cases exceed the entire value of the property injured or destroyed, with interest.[62] This not infrequently happens in cases of attempts to avoid loss. The rule that the expense of a reasonable attempt to repair the injury may be recovered is not limited to cases where the attempt was successful; if the attempt was a reasonable one, the expense of it may be recovered, although in spite of it the property proved a total loss. In that case, the expense of the attempted repair or cure is recoverable in addition to the value of the property.[63]

III.—FRAUD

§ 439. False representations.

Where the plaintiff suffers pecuniary injury through the loss of personal property by the fraud of the defendant, instead of by force, the general principles are the same. The damages recoverable are those which naturally flow from the fraud.[64] Here as in other cases of torts the rule of compensation is to put the party defrauded back into the condition in which he was before the wrong was done. Hence, in case of false repre-

[61] Solomon v. New York City Ry., 56 Misc. 502, 107 N. Y. Supp. 744.

[62] Shibley v. Gendron, 25 R. I. 519, 57 Atl. 304.

See, however, a contrary intimation in Atlanta I. & C. Co. v. Mixon, 126 Ga. 457, 55 S. E. 237.

[63] *United States:* The Henry Buck, 39 Fed. 211.

Georgia: Atlanta & W. P. R. R. v. Hudson, 62 Ga. 679; Central R. R. v. Warren, 84 Ga. 329.

Illinois: Hey v. Hawkins, 120 Ill. App. 483.

Maine: Watson v. Lisbon Bridge Co., 14 Me. 201.

Massachusetts: Gillett v. Western R. R. Corp., 8 All. 560; Atwood v. Forwarding, etc., Co., 185 Mass. 557, 71 N. E. 72.

Missouri: Streett v. Laumier, 34 Mo. 469; Missouri R. P. Co. v. Hannibal & S. J. R. R., 79 Mo. 478.

Texas: Gulf, C. & S. F. Ry. v. Keith, 74 Tex. 287.

Canada: Sweeney v. Port Burwell Harbour, 17 Up. Can. C. P. 574.

See *ante*, § 226a.

[64] *Maryland:* Buschman v. Codd, 52 Md. 202.

Mississippi: Estell v. Myers, 54 Miss. 174.

sentations, relied on by the plaintiff to his detriment, the measure of recovery is not the difference between the plaintiff's pecuniary condition if the representations had been true and his condition under the actual facts, but rather the difference between what the plaintiff had before he acted on the representation and what he had afterward. This represents his actual loss. The action is for the recovery of pecuniary damages. Thus in an action for a false representation, by which the plaintiff was alleged to have been compelled to pay £2,000, and thereby became bankrupt, and suffered great annoyance and inconvenience, the only damage recoverable was the direct pecuniary loss, the right to which passed to the assignees.[65]

The general rule that damages must be actual, and not contingent, or speculative, may prevent recovery in actions for deceit. Thus for false representations in a transfer of property where the only consideration was the payment by the plaintiff of an existing debt, recovery was denied on the ground that he had suffered no certain loss.[66] Where one was induced to indorse a note, in ignorance of the legal effect of an indorsement, but failed to show that he had been compelled to pay the note, the court denied a recovery on the ground that the damages were contingent.[67]

It is, however, to be remembered that in equity fraud is a sufficient cause for setting aside a transaction, and giving the defrauded party his choice of recovering a consideration that he has paid or of claiming the benefit of any profit the defendant may have made by means of his fraud; and this profit may sometimes be given by way of damages.

The varieties of fraud are infinite; and numerous examples are necessary in order to follow the operation of the principles just examined. We now proceed to consider such examples.

§ 439a. Fraud in procuring a contract.

The general rule is that where a fraud is perpetrated in procur-

[65] Hodgson v. Sidney, L. R. 1 Ex. 313.

[66] Brown v. Blunt, 72 Me. 415.

[67] Freeman v. Venner, 120 Mass. 424.

It is to be observed that in all actions for deceit, damage, to be recoverable, must be produced by the deceit. Falsehood or deception are not in themselves actionable. Ansbacher v. Pfeiffer, 13 N. Y. Supp. 418. Cf. Bigelow on Torts (7th Ed.), 110.

ing the execution of a contract the defrauded party may either rescind and recover the consideration, or may affirm the contract, perform it on his side, and maintain an action for the damages suffered through the fraud. Thus where the owner of property is induced by false representations as to its quality or value, etc., to sell it to the defendant, he may affirm the sale and recover from the vendee the difference between the price paid by the vendee and the actual value of the property in its real condition.[68] It has been held in Massachusetts, in an action on the case, where the defendant, being part owner of a vessel, by fraudulent representations persuaded the attorney of the plaintiff, during his absence, to sell him the vessel at a less price than its value, and he afterwards himself sold it for a greater price, that if the latter sale was an actual sale, the sum realized at it would be the proper measure of damages; "because it would be unjust to permit the fraudulent party to retain the fruits of his fraud," and because the plaintiff, if not deceived, might have obtained the larger sum. But the court allowed the defendants to show that the price which they paid was the true and full value of the plaintiff's share, both in order to disprove the fraud, and as proper for the consideration of the jury on the question of damages.[69]

The general rule may, however, be varied by special circumstances. The owner of shares in a corporation received two offers, of which the defendant had notice, one of eighty dollars cash per share, the other of fifty dollars cash and fifty dollars additional if the corporation should pay a certain divi-

[68] *Arkansas:* McDonough *v.* Williams, 77 Ark. 261, 92 S. W. 783.

Colorado: Vivian *v.* Allen, 9 Colo. App. 147, 47 Pac. 844.

Massachusetts: Matthews *v.* Bliss, 22 Pick. 48.

Michigan: McMillan *v.* Reaume, 137 Mich. 1, 100 N. W. 166.

Nevada: Gruber *v.* Baker, 20 Nev. 453, 23 Pac. 858, 9 L. R. A. 302.

New York: Bench *v.* Sheldon, 14 Barb. 66.

Pennsylvania: Weaver *v.* Cone, 12 Pa. Super. Ct. 143.

Texas: Ellis *v.* Barlow (Tex. Civ. App.), 26 S. W. 908.

Wisconsin: Potter *v.* Necedah Lumber Co., 105 Wis. 25, 80 N. W. 88, 81 N. W. 118.

Nominal damages at least may be recovered. Isman *v.* Loring, 115 N. Y. Supp. 933, 130 App. Div. 845.

[69] Matthews *v.* Bliss, 22 Pick. (Mass.) 48. This decision assumes that the object of the jury was merely to give compensatory damages: because, as we have already said, fraud is a case for vindictive or exemplary damages, where such damages are allowed.

dend, and, relying on the defendant's representations as to the financial condition of the company, accepted the second offer; the expected dividend was not declared, and consequently the second fifty dollars was not paid: in an action for the deceit the seller recovered the difference between eighty and fifty dollars.[70]

In a case in Illinois, where the owner of land was induced to sell it for a price less than its actual value, by a false representation of the buyer that the seller's interest was only a life estate, the court held the measure of damages to be the difference between the value of the interest actually conveyed and the value of a life estate in the property conveyed. The court said, "if the defendant purchased the life estate for less than it was actually worth he is entitled to the benefit of his bargain." [71] Such a holding does not accord with the general rule of damages for fraud. The defrauded plaintiff is entitled to be put back into as good a position as he was in before the wrong. The alternative remedies of rescission and an action of deceit are the methods of accomplishing this result, but the compensation under either remedy should be substantially the same; otherwise one remedy would not exactly compensate the injured person. The nearest possible equivalent to getting the property back is to realize its actual value; hence it would seem to be the correct rule, in an action of deceit, to award the difference between the value and the amount already received. Though the rule of damages adopted in the Illinois case has been accepted by the weight of American authority in case of false representations by the vendor, the reasons which sustain it in such a case do not apply where the vendee was fraudulent, as will appear later.[72]

When the misrepresentation does not relate to the quality of the thing sold, but is confined to a collateral matter, the general rule for measuring damages is not so difficult of application. Thus when the vendee induced the sale of a slave at a special price by a fraudulent promise to take the slave out of the State, and where the facts sustained an action of deceit, the vendor

[70] Rothmiller v. Stein, 143 N. Y. 581, 38 N. E. 718, 26 L. R. A. 148.

[71] Hicks v. Deemer, 187 Ill. 164, 58 N. E. 252.

[72] Ch. xxxv, §§ 777 et seq.

recovered the difference between the actual value of the slave and the reduced price.[73]

§ 439b. Fraud in effecting a sale.

Where one is induced to purchase property by the false representations of the vendor, he may either rescind the sale, or retain the property and sue for the fraud. If the form of action were respected, the measure of damages in the latter case would be the difference between the price paid and the actual value of the thing sold. This would put the vendee in substantially the same position in which he was before the tort was committed. By the weight of authority, however, the measure of recovery is the difference in value between the thing sold in its actual condition and if it had been as represented.[74] When a lease was effected through false representations as to the furnace and the requirements for heating, it was held that the plaintiff has a right to continue in occupation, paying the rent, and then sue for his damages, which would be the difference in the rental value of the premises as they were, and as they would have been if as represented; in all such cases the plaintiff may waive his right to damages by acquiescence, but this will generally be a question of fact.[75]

§ 439c. Fraud in inducing a contract of insurance.

Where by the defendant's fraudulent representations the plaintiff was induced to take out a policy of insurance, which he surrendered upon discovering the fraud, the measure of damages is the amount of premiums paid, without deduction.[76] In

[73] Oldham v. Bentley, 6 B. Mon. (Ky.) 428.

But see McCready v. Phillips, 56 Neb. 446, 76 N. W. 885.

[74] The subject is more fully treated in ch. xxxv on Sales of Personalty at §§ 777 et seq., and in ch. xliii on Sales of Real Estate at §§ 1027 et seq.

[75] Pryor v. Foster, 130 N. Y. 171, 29 N. E. 123.

[76] Iowa: Van Werden v. Equit. Life Assur. Soc., 99 Ia. 621, 68 N. W. 892.

Massachusetts: Hedden v. Griffin, 136 Mass. 229, 49 Am. Rep. 25 (semble).

New York: Rohrschneider v. Knickerbocker L. I. Co., 76 N. Y. 216, 32 Am. Rep. 298; May v. N. Y. S. R. F. Soc., 14 Daly, 389, 13 N. Y. St. 66.

North Carolina: Sykes v. Life Ins. Co., 148 N. C. 54, 61 S. E. 610; Caldwell v. Ins. Co., 140 N. C. 100, 52 S. E. 252; Briggs v. Life Ins. Co. (N. C.), 70 S. E. 1068.

England: Kettleworth v. Refuge Assur. Co., [1908] 1 K. B. 545.

See also Butler v. Prentiss, 158 N. Y. 49, 64, 52 N. E. 652.

a recent Vermont case,[77] it was held that from this amount should be deducted the value of the insurance to the plaintiff between the date of the policy and the date when he elected to rescind. The court said:

"The general rule is that the party who would rescind a contract on account of fraud practiced upon him by the other party must seasonably return the property to him and put him *in statu quo*. If the plaintiff in this case has received dividends upon his policy the law would not permit him to recover the premiums and retain the dividends for then the other party would not be placed *in statu quo*. The plaintiff had received no dividends to be returned, but he had been insured for a year and a half before he rescinded the contract, and if he had died within that time his estate would have received $5,000 from the insurance company; so it cannot be held as a matter of law that he had received no benefit from the contract."

The dispute seems to turn on the question of what *"in statu quo"* means. If it means that the plaintiff must surrender or give an equivalent for, whatever benefit he has received under the contract which he seeks to rescind, the Vermont case is right. If, however, as seems to be the better view, it means that the defendant must be put back into his original position, the other rule is correct. The fact that the defendant was under a contingent liability is thus immaterial, since upon rescission such liability is wiped out and the defendant's pecuniary condition unchanged thereby.

§ 439d. Fraud in procuring a conveyance.

Where the defendant secured by fraud a conveyance of the plaintiff's land, the measure of damages is the value of the land at the time of the conveyance,[78] or if value was given for the land, the difference between the actual value of the land conveyed and the consideration received.[79] Where the defendant

[77] McKinley v. Drew, 69 Vt. 210, 71 Vt. 138, 37 Atl. 285.

[78] *Michigan:* Woolenslagle v. Runals, 76 Mich. 545.

Texas: Butler v. Anderson (Tex. Civ. App.), 107 S. W. 656.

[79] *Kentucky:* Campbell v. Kerrick, 134 S. W. 186.

Missouri: Boyce v. Gingrich (Mo. App.), 134 S. W. 79.

Wisconsin: Potter v. Necedah Lumber Co., 105 Wis. 25, 80 N. W. 88.

So of fraud in procuring a sale of personalty. Johnson v. Culver, 119 Ind. 277, 19 N. E. 129.

fraudulently induced the plaintiff to mortgage his farm to one A for a certain sum, and the defendant agreed with A to have the amount applied on an old indebtedness from the defendant to A, so that the plaintiff got nothing, the measure of damages was the amount of the mortgage, with interest.[80]   And where the grantee's agent fraudulently induced the plaintiff to sign a deed by the false representation that certain timber was excepted from the grant, the measure of damages was the value of the timber.[81]

§ 439e. Fraud in securing a loan.

Where by the fraud of a bank officer plaintiff was induced to deposit money in an insolvent bank, the measure of recovery is the amount of the deposit, less the value of his claim against the bank.[82]   And the same rule applies where a private loan was fraudulently induced.[83]

Where the plaintiff was defrauded into making a loan on a mortgage of land which was worth less than the loan, the measure of damages is the difference between the loan and the value of the land.[84]

Where one had been induced by the fraudulent representations of another's creditor to take from the debtor certain goods and give the creditor his own note for the debt, and it proved that the goods were worth much less than represented, but it did not appear whether the defendant had received them by way of absolute purchase or as collateral security only, the instruction of the judge to the jury to find for the defendant if the difference in value between the goods as represented and their actual value equalled the balance due on the note, which would have been the rule in the case of an absolute sale, was held inapplicable and therefore erroneous, because if the goods were taken as security only, the defendant should have been

[80] Forbes v. Thomas, 22 Neb. 541. The plaintiff was not allowed to recover the value of his farm, though the mortgage had been foreclosed.

[81] Griffin v. Roanoke R. & L. Co., 140 N. C. 514, 53 S. E. 307, 6 L. R. A. (N. S.) 463.

[82] New Jersey: Westervelt v. Dema-

rest, 46 N. J. L. 37, 50 Am. Rep. 400.

Texas: Baker v. Ashe, 80 Tex. 356, 16 S. W. 36.

[83] Browning v. Nat. Capital Bank, 13 D. C. App. Cas. 1.

[84] Briggs v. Brushaber, 43 Mich. 330.

held to account on the note for what they were worth.[85] Where, by false representations as to the value of the security, the plaintiff was induced to loan money to the defendant, and the defendant in fact had no title to the property given as security, the measure of recovery is the amount of the loan with interest.[86]

§ 439f. Misrepresentation of credit of a third party.

Where the defendant falsely represented a third party to be of good credit, whereupon the plaintiff sold him goods on credit and was unable to recover the price, the measure of damages is the value of the goods supplied,[87] less the value of any collateral security.[88] The rule is not varied by the fact that the plaintiff was a manufacturer and that the market value of the goods included a manufacturer's profits.[89]

§ 439g. Fraud in obtaining payment of debt owed another.

A judgment debtor was induced to give a note for the amount of the judgment to one who represented himself to be the owner of the judgment. This note was negotiated and paid. The plaintiff recovered from the fraudulent person the amount paid on the note, though the rightful owner of the judgment did not attempt to enforce it.[90] The defendant represented that he was the owner of a bond and mortgage given by the plaintiff which was then overdue. Plaintiff paid defendant one hundred and twenty dollars upon his agreeing to carry the bond and mortgage for a year. Defendant did not own the mortgage, but by paying the owner one hundred dollars induced him to carry it for a year. The plaintiff was held entitled to recover the twenty dollars which he had paid the defendant over and above what the defendant had paid the creditor.[91]

[85] Stevenson v. Greenlee, 15 Ia. 96, and see, Briggs v. Brushaber, 43 Mich. 330, 5 N. W. 383.

[86] Horne v. Walton, 117 Ill. 130, 141, 7 N. E. 100, 103; Schwitters v. Springer, 236 Ill. 271, 86 N. E. 102. Cf. Emmerson v. Dardanelle Bank, 66 Ark. 646, 52 S. W. 274.

[87] Massachusetts: Kidney v. Stoddard, 7 Met. 252.

New York: Bean v. Wells, 28 Barb. 466; Von Bruck v. Peyser, 4 Rob. 514.

[88] American Nat. Bank v. Hammond, 25 Colo. 367, 55 Pac. 1090.

[89] Shaw v. Gilbert, 111 Wis. 165, 86 N. W. 188.

[90] Goring v. Fitzgerald, 105 Iowa, 507, 75 N. W. 358. See also Lahay v. City Nat. Bank of Denver, 15 Colo. 339, 25 Pac. 704.

[91] Saunders v. Chamberlain, 13 Hun (N. Y.), 568.

§ 439h. Fraud in dealings with corporate stock.

Where by the defendant's false representations the plaintiff is induced to subscribe to bank stock and to give his bond to secure the subscription, the bank being insolvent and the bond having been assigned for value, the measure of damages is the amount of the subscription, though it is as yet unpaid.[92] A corporation issued stock to the defendant upon a forged power of attorney; the owner sued the corporation, which notified the defendant, and the owner recovered. The corporation now sued the defendant, and the measure of damages was held to be the value of the stock at the termination of the former suit, the expenses of that suit, and the dividends which had been paid to the defendant.[93] In case of a fraudulent overissue of stock by the defendant's agent, the measure of damages is the value of the stock at the time the defendant refused to recognize it as valid.[94] Where the plaintiff in such a case is a broker who had sold the stock for the agent of the defendant and had been obliged to take it up on the customary broker's guaranty of genuineness, he may recover the amount he received upon the sale.[95] And where defendant made a fraudulent invoice of stock for the purpose of incorporation, he was liable to a purchaser of the stock for the difference between the actual value of the stock and the value as he represented it.[96]

§ 439i. Fraud by promoter of a joint enterprise.

Where the defendant proposed to the plaintiff a joint purchase of land and falsely represented that the price was $8,000, whereas it was in fact but $3,000, and the plaintiff paid $4,000 for a half interest, the plaintiff in an action for the fraud recovered the amount paid in excess of his share of the actual price; and the fact that the land was actually worth more than the represented price was held immaterial.[97] So, where one

[92] Hubbard v. Briggs, 31 N. Y. 518.
[93] Boston & A. R. R. v. Richardson, 135 Mass. 473.
[94] Allen v. South Boston R. R., 150 Mass. 200, 22 N. E. 917.
[95] Jarvis v. Manhattan B. Co., 53 Hun (N. Y.), 362.
[96] Smith v. Owsley, 102 S. W. 277, 31 Ky. L. R. 432.

[97] *Colorado:* Mayo v. Wahlgreen 9 Colo. App. 506, 5 Pac. 40.
Illinois: Bunn v. Schnellbacher, 163 Ill. 328, 45 N. E. 227.
Iowa: Johnson v. Gavitt, 114 Iowa, 183, 86 N. W. 256.
Wisconsin: Bergeron v. Miles, 88 Wis. 397, 60 N. W. 783, 43 Am. St. Rep. 911.

party to a joint purchase got a secret rebate from the seller, the other party was entitled to recover his share of the rebate.[98] And where a promoter of a corporation, who sold its property for stock, realized secret profits, the measure of damages is the difference between the value of the stock issued to him and the property conveyed.[99]

§ 439j. Fraud in procuring marriage.

If a marriage is induced by the fraud of a third person, suit may be maintained for the damages occasioned. When the fraud consists of false representations as to the financial condition of the other spouse the usual rule of damages for torts is difficult to apply, for, from the nature of the case, it is not possible to put the plaintiff *in statu quo*, and the monetary equivalent of that status cannot be ascertained with any degree of accuracy. It has, accordingly, been held that the fraudulent person is bound to make good his representations, and the difference between the actual and represented finances of the other spouse is the measure of damages.[100] Where, by a conspiracy between a woman and one who had debauched her and made her pregnant, the plaintiff was induced to marry her in ignorance of the facts, the damages were held to include, not only loss of services, but also loss of *consortium*, because though the formal right to *consortium* may remain, the essential value of it is taken away. And the jury may of course give exemplary damages.[101]

§ 439k. Assignments in fraud of creditors.

Upon a fraudulent assignment of goods to a creditor, the measure of damages is the value of the goods at that time,[102] not what the defendant sold them for.[103] In an action brought

---

[98] Jones *v.* Kinney (Wis.), 131 N. W. 339.

[99] Old Dominion, C. M. & S. Co. *v.* Bigelow, 203 Mass. 159, 89 N. E. 193.

[100] *New York:* Piper *v.* Hoard, 107 N. Y. 73, 76, 13 N. E. 626.

   England: Montefiori *v.* Montefiori, 1 Wm. Black, 363.

[101] Kujek *v.* Goldman, 150 N. Y. 176, 44 N. E. 773, 55 Am. St. Rep. 670, 34

L. R. A. 156, affirming 9 Misc. 34, 29 N. Y. Supp. 294.

[102] Burpee *v.* Sparhawk, 97 Mass. 342.

   See Hamilton Nat. Bank *v.* Halsted, 134 N. Y. 520, 31 N. E. 900.

[103] *Michigan:* Robinson *v.* Boyd, 17 Mich. 128.

   Texas: Oppenheimer *v.* Halff, 68 Tex. 409.

by plaintiffs as judgment creditors of defendant Cavanaugh, who had conspired with defendant Strauss to put his property out of reach of his creditors by transferring it to defendant Strauss, it was held that damages to the full amount of plaintiff's claim were proper.[104] The defendant "was a wrongdoer, and it lies not in his mouth to say that the property may still be taken under execution. It exceeds in value the plaintiff's judgment, and has been fraudulently appropriated by the defendant to his own use. It is just that he should pay the creditor whose claim he sought to defeat."

§ 440. Other frauds.

In Kentucky, where suit was brought for fraud in assigning a note for which the plaintiff had given certain property, the court held that the value of the property, and not the amount of the note, was the proper measure of damages; though they considered the precise amount to be recovered by the plaintiff a matter for the consideration and decision of the jury.[105] Where the defendant assigned a note and mortgage, and then fraudulently filed a certificate of satisfaction of the mortgage, the plaintiff's damages were held to be the value of the security, not exceeding the amount of the note.[106] Where defendant assigned a note secured by a mortgage, and then released the mortgage to one who had bought the land subject to the mortgage, and who then sold it to a bona fide purchaser, it was held in an action by the mortgagor that he could recover the amount of the note, although at the time of the commencement of the action the note had not been paid, the court saying that the defendant had fraudulently destroyed the security set apart by the plaintiff for the payment of the note.[107] If the owner of a promissory note of an insolvent maker by fraud sells it to an innocent purchaser he is liable to refund the money received for it with interest.[108]

At a sheriff's sale of the plaintiff's land, the defendant represented that he held an equitable mortgage on the land for $1,500. In fact the mortgage was for only $1,000. Defendant

---

[104] Quinby v. Strauss, 90 N. Y. 664.
[105] Crews v. Dabney, 1 Littell (Ky.), 278.
[106] Fox v. Wray, 56 Ind. 423.
[107] Ely v. Stannard, 46 Conn. 124.
[108] Clayton v. O'Connor, 35 Ga. 193.

in consequence of his misrepresentation was able to bid in the property at a figure lower than its actual value. Held, that the measure of damage is the difference between the price at which the land was bid in and what it would have brought but for the misrepresentation, with interest up to the time of trial.[109]

In an action to recover damages for fraudulently inducing the plaintiff to manufacture boxes, the measure of damages is the cost of manufacture.[110] Where by the representation of defendant that he was owner of a certain wood-lot plaintiff was induced to construct a logging road across the lot, and the road was obstructed, the plaintiff could recover the cost of building the road across the lot, and, it seems, of any other portion of road built to connect with it and rendered useless by the obstruction.[111] In an action by a sheriff against parties whose fraudulent representations had induced him wrongfully to seize the property of T, it was held that the measure of damages was the amount of T's judgment against the sheriff, with interest.[112] Where a creditor is fraudulently induced to compromise a claim he may recover the difference between the sum acutally received and the sum he would have received if he had not compromised.[113] Where an attorney by false representations induces a client to bring a useless suit, the damages recoverable are the expenses of the litigation.[114] Similarly, when a physician induces a patient to expend money for medical treatment by falsely representing his disease to be curable, the patient may recover, not the damages arising from not being cured, but the expenditures thus unnecessarily incurred.[115]

Where an employer represented to his workmen that in consideration of a deduction from their wages he was carrying accident insurance for their benefit, whereas in fact he was carrying indemnity insurance for his own, a workman in an action

[109] Denham v. Kirkpatrick, 64 Ga. 71.
[110] Rabinowitz v. Cohen, 17 N. Y. Supp. 502.
[111] Storseth v. Folsom, 50 Wash. 456, 97 Pac. 492.
[112] Kenyon v. Woodruff, 33 Mich. 310: the defendants defended T's suit for the sheriff.
[113] *Maine:* Buck v. Leach, 69 Me. 484.

Texas: Grabenheimer v. Blum, 63 Tex. 369.
But see *Michigan:* Walsh v. Sisson, 49 Mich. 423, 13 N. W. 802.
[114] Loof v. Lawton, 97 N. Y. 478.
[115] Hedin v. Minneapolis, M. & S. Inst., 62 Minn. 146, 64 N. W. 158, 54 Am. St. Rep. 628, 35 L. R. A. 417.

for deceit is entitled to recover the amount so deducted, with interest.[116] Where a mortgagee of chattels fraudulently represented to the mortgagor that if the latter would allow him to bid in the goods at foreclosure sale at a nominal price he would dispose of the goods at private sale and give the mortgagor the benefit of this sale, and the mortgagor in consequence allowed the goods to be sold, the measure of damages was the difference between the actual value of the goods and the price bid.[117] It was alleged that the defendant by fraud induced plaintiff, a mortgagor, not to pay interest on the debt, whereupon, the mortgagee having brought foreclosure, the plaintiff, not being able to pay the mortgage debt, sold the property at a sacrifice; it was held that he could at most recover the amount of foreclosure costs and attorney's fee, but not his loss by the sale.[118]

§ 441. Consequential damages.

The rules governing consequential damages are uniformly applied in cases of fraud as well as all others. So, in a case in England, where the defendant was sued for false representations in regard to the credit of his son, where it appeared that the plaintiffs had trusted the son for a length of time, and to an amount which might be considered ill-judged and excessive, even if the representations had been true, Tindal, C. J., charged the jury: "As to the damages, the verdict must be for such damage as is justly and immediately referable to the falsehood of the statement. The goods first purchased have been paid for, but six hundred pounds' worth since have not, and the son was made a bankrupt by the plaintiff in the month of October. You must say how much of this is justly and immediately referable to the false statement. That is a problem which you must solve for yourselves. I will only make an observation, and that is, if they give the son an indiscreet and ill-judging credit, they cannot, in fairness, call on the father to be answerable for the loss occasioned by it." [119]   The language of the

---

[116] Williams v. Detroit, O. & C. Co. (Tex.), 123 S. W. 405.

[117] Cerny v. Paxton & Gallagher Co., 78 Neb. 134, 110 N. W. 882.

[118] Nearing v. Hathaway, 128 App. Div. 745, 113 N. Y. Supp. 318.

[119] Corbett v. Brown, 5 C. & P. 363; see Collins v. Cave, 6 H. & N. 131; affirming 4 H. & N. 225.

eminent judge is particularly deserving of notice; for if, in cases of this kind, the principles that exclude remote damages are not adhered to, the whole subject of remuneration would be in the hands of the jury.

Where the vendor of live-stock falsely represented that they were free from a certain infectious disease, he is liable for the value of other animals in the herd which caught the disease and died,[120] and for medical treatment for the same,[121] and, if the disease is communicated to a human being who dies, the vendor is liable for such death.[122] It has also been held that he is liable for the value of a stable which the vendee had to burn to prevent further contagion.[123] Where the plaintiff, a livery-stable keeper, had taken the defendant's horse to keep in his stable, relying on the defendant's representation that the horse was well, which was untrue, and the horse having the distemper, communicated it to two stallions of the plaintiff, who were thereby incapacitated for service during the season, it was held that evidence of what would have been their probable earnings during the season, but for the distemper, was proper for the consideration of the jury in estimating the damages.[124] In Sellar v. Clelland [125] it was held that the plaintiff could recover for cattle lost on a journey which he had been induced to take through the defendant's false representations, and could recover an exceptionally high price he had to pay to replace the cattle lost. The defendant fraudulently concealed the fact that a bull sold to the plaintiff was without the power of propagation, the purpose for which it was sold. Damages in an action of deceit were awarded for the diminution in value of the plaintiff's dairy resulting from the use of the bull, i. e., the inferior quantity of butter in consequence of the cows not having been gotten with calf.[126] When the defendant falsely represented that he had authority to sell land, and the plaintiff, relying on the contract, converted into money a number of

[120] *Indiana:* Rose v. Wallace, 11 Ind. 112.
Kentucky: Faris v. Lewis, 2 B. Mon. 375.
[121] Merguire v. O'Donnell, 103 Cal. 50, 36 Pac. 1033.
[122] State v. Fox, 79 Md. 514, 527, 29 Atl. 601, 47 Am. St. Rep. 424, 24 L. R. A. 679.
[123] Merguire v. O'Donnell, 103 Cal. 50, 36 Pac. 1033.
[124] Fultz v. Wycoff, 25 Ind. 321.
[125] 2 Colo. 532.
[126] Maynard v. Maynard, 49 Vt. 297.

interest-bearing securities, in order to pay for the land on a certain day, the measure of damages was the legal rate of interest on the money, not the rate of interest which the converted securities bore.[127] In Fitzsimmons v. Chapman [128] the defendant represented to the plaintiff that a firm, having a large capital and business, could be induced, by the payment of a certain sum, to remove to the plaintiff's town, and, by their business, enhance the value of property in that place. The plaintiff subscribed a certain sum, and the firm moved. It turned out to be insolvent. It was held that damages from the fact that it did not enhance the value of property were too remote. The purchaser of a vessel, falsely and fraudulently represented by the seller as eighteen instead of twenty-eight years old, having sent her to sea before he had knowledge that such representation was false, and the vessel being afterwards condemned in a foreign port, it was held that the purchaser was entitled to recover his actual damages occasioned by sending her to sea, not exceeding her value.[129] Where a horse sold is represented as not being afraid of the cars, compensation may be recovered for property injured by the horse in running away from the cars.[130]

In the Normannia [131] the action was by a passenger for damages caused by false representations as to a voyage to the effect that the vessel would carry no steerage passengers, cholera contagion and detention in quarantine being at the time a natural consequence of carrying such passengers. Cholera did appear in the steerage and the owners were held liable for the ensuing damages. After detention for some days on the Normannia, the passenger was transferred to another vessel. For damages ensuing, the owners of the Normannia were held not responsible, other causes than the original deceit having intervened.

§ 442. Expenses.

Whether expenses incurred by the plaintiff are recoverable depends on the doctrine of proximate cause. Where the fraud

[127] Place v. Dodge, 54 Ill. App. 167.
[128] 37 Mich. 139.
[129] Tuckwell v. Lambert, 5 Cush. (Mass.) 23.
[130] Allen v. Truesdell, 135 Mass. 75.
[131] Beers v. Hamburg-American Packet Co., 62 Fed. 469.

was intended to induce the expenditure the plaintiff may recover.[132] Where a vendor by fraud induced the plaintiff to purchase a stallion for breeding purposes, and it proved to be sterile, the damages were held to include the cost of keeping the stallion a reasonable time for the purpose of testing him.[133] Where a draft was, by fraud, procured from a bank, and on discovery of the fraud the bank incurred expenses in attempting to stop payment in an action for the fraud, such expenses were held recoverable.[134]

On the other hand, where, as in Slingerland v. Bennett,[135] the defendant made fraudulent representations as to the responsibility of the maker of a note given by the defendant to the plaintiff in payment of a debt, it was held that the plaintiff could not recover the costs of an action against the maker, as these were not the proximate result of the fraud. So in Connecticut, in an action against the vendor of a horse for false representations, the plaintiff could not recover the expenses of keeping, previous to an offer to return the horse.[136] Where the defendant falsely represented that his horse had been damaged by reason of a defect in the highway, and the town thereupon incurred expenses in investigating the claim, in an action by the town for the fraud, recovery for such expenses was denied.[137]

[132] Norae v. Lonsley, 130 Fed. 17.
[133] Peak v. Frost, 162 Mass. 298, 38 N. E. 518.
[134] First Nat. Bank v. Williams, 62 Kan. 431, 63 Pac. 744.
[135] 66 N. Y. 611.
[136] West v. Anderson, 9 Conn. 107.
[137] Enfield v. Colburn, 63 N. H. 218.

CHAPTER XIX

MALICIOUS TORTS

I.—SLANDER AND LIBEL

§ 443. General rule.

We now come to a class of torts in which the injury is malicious, and the degree of injury, and therefore the measure of damages, depends to a great extent upon the nature and extent of the malice displayed by the defendant; and matters of aggravation and of mitigation become important. The first actions of this nature to be considered are actions for defamation—slander and libel.

* A very important line of demarcation exists in actions of slander between those defamatory words which are actionable *per se*, and from which damage is presumed to result, and those where, to sustain a suit, special damage must be averred and proved. As, for instance, damage is presumed if a clergyman is charged with intemperance or profligacy, a lawyer with dishonesty, a merchant with bankruptcy, or a physician with ignorance; while, on the other hand, if a charge of want of chastity is made against a woman, no action lies unless she can prove special damage.[1] But in this latter case slight damages have been held sufficient, and the loss of marriage is enough.[2] Into this distinction it is not proper more fully here to enter; but it is well to remark with reference to the subject of this treatise, that where the plaintiff undertakes to show special damage by the loss of customers in trade, he ought to state in his declaration the names of such customers,[3] and he cannot prove that any persons not named in his declaration left off dealing with him in consequence of the words spoken.[4] ** The direct injury suffered from slander or libel is to the reputation; and compensation for injured reputation is therefore the principal item of damages in an action for such an injury.[5] But

[1] Bradt *v.* Towsley, 13 Wend. (N. Y.) 253.

[2] *New York:* Moody *v.* Baker, 5 Cow. 351.

Texas: Linney *v.* Maton, 13 Tex. 449. Expensive illness caused by the charge, and resultant loss of time, have been held special damage.

New York: Fuller *v.* Fenner, 16 Barb. 333.

Texas: McQueen *v.* Fulghan, 27 Tex. 463.

Vermont: Underhill *v.* Welton, 32 Vt. 40.

Contra, England: Allsop *v.* Allsop, 5 H. & N. 534.

[3] Hartley *v.* Herring, 8 T. R. 130.

[4] Hallock *v.* Miller, 2 Barb. (N. Y.) 630.

[5] *Delaware:* Todd *v.* Every Evening Pr. Co., 6 Pennew. 233, 66 Atl. 97.

another direct result of defamation is mental suffering on the part of the person defamed; and in an action for slander or libel a plaintiff may recover compensation for mental suffering.[6] Where partners sue jointly for an attack upon them as such, damages will include only the loss sustained in trade, and not injury to their private feelings;[7] and where a corporation sues for libel, since a corporation cannot suffer mentally, it can recover nothing for mental suffering.[8]

There is but one recovery for all damages in libel or slander; the jury may, accordingly, properly include compensation for losses suffered after the date of the writ[9] or likely to be sustained in the future.[10]

Substantial damages may and ordinarily are found, though there is no evidence as to the amount of damage, since the non-pecuniary elements of recovery are not susceptible of proof by direct evidence.[11]

Maryland: Blumhardt v. Rohr, 70 Md. 328.

Massachusetts: Markham v. Russell, 12 All. 573.

[6] *United States:* Shattuc v. M'Arthur, 29 Fed. 136.

Alabama: Johnson v. Robertson, 8 Port. 486.

California: Graybill v. DeYoung, 140 Cal. 523, 73 Pac. 1067.

Colorado: Republican Publishing Co. v. Mosman, 15 Colo. 399, 24 Pac. 1051.

Connecticut: Swift v. Dickerman, 31 Conn. 285.

Delaware: Todd v. Every Evening Pr. Co., 6 Pennew. 233, 66 Atl. 97.

Kentucky: Louisville Press Co. v. Tennelly, 105 Ky. 365, 49 S. W. 15, 20 Ky. L. Rep. 1231.

Louisiana: Dufort v. Abadie, 23 La. Ann. 280.

Maryland: Blumhardt v. Rohr, 70 Md. 328.

Massachusetts: Lombard v. Lennox, 155 Mass. 70, 28 N. E. 1125, 31 Am. St. Rep. 528.

Michigan: Newman v. Stein, 75 Mich. 402, 42 N. W. 956.

New Jersey: Marsh v. Edge, 68 N. J. L. 661, 54 Atl. 834.

South Dakota: Bedtkey v. Bedtkey, 15 S. D. 310, 89 N. W. 479.

Texas: Houston Printing Co. v. Moulden, 15 Tex. Civ. App. 574, 41 S. W. 381.

Vermont: Rea v. Harrington, 58 Vt. 181.

It is not essential to recovery for mental suffering from a libel that the plaintiff's reputation should be injured. McArthur v. Sault News Printing Co., 148 Mich. 556, 112 N. W. 126, 14 Detroit Leg. N. 265.

[7] Haythorn v. Lawson, 3 C. & P. 196, 14 E. C. L. 523.

[8] Farbenfabriken of Elberfeld Co. v. Beringer, 158 Fed. 802, 86 C. C. A. 62.

[9] Weston v. Barnicoat, 175 Mass. 454, 56 N. E. 619, 49 L. R. A. 612.

[10] *Maine:* True v. Plumley, 36 Me. 466.

England: Gregory v. Williams, 1 C. & K. 568, 47 E. C. L. 568.

Contra, New York: Halstead v. Nelson, 24 Hun, 395 (*semble*).

[11] *Arkansas:* Taylor v. Gumpert (Ark.), 131 S. W. 968.

§ 444. Consequential damages.

In Georgia v. Kepford [12] the defendant charged the plaintiff with larceny and adultery. The plaintiff endeavored to show that, in consequence of the slander, his wife left him and began an action for divorce on the ground of inhuman treatment. It was held that the desertion of his wife and the expenses of defending the divorce suit were too remote to be considered as damages from the slander. It seems, however, that if the plaintiff had proved, as he had alleged, that the words were uttered to induce his wife to leave him, damages for this could have been recovered; and in Case v. Case [13] the plaintiff, who had been grossly slandered in respect of her chastity by her mother-in-law, was allowed to include in her recovery damages for alienation of her husband's affections.

Loss of business resulting from defamation may be a proper subject of recovery,[14] provided it is proved with reasonable certainty.[15]   It seems that writing of the plaintiff that he "was the ringleader of the nine-hours' system," cannot be considered likely to produce any damage to the plaintiff.[16] In this case, the plaintiff alleged that, by reason of the libel, he was prevented from obtaining employment at his trade. In a Texas decision [17] one libelling a public officer in his capacity as such was held liable for damages proximately resulting from the publication; but such damages were declared not to include the loss of financial credit, the expense of borrowing money, or other injuries unconnected with his official position.   In Scotland, in Leven v. Young,[18] an action for defamation, in consequence of which the plaintiff was removed from his office, which was one dependent on the will of his superiors, it was held that the jury must take into consideration both the nature and tenure of the office, and not give the value of an annuity certain.

Iowa: Dorn v. Cooper, 139 Ia. 742, 117 N. W. 1.

But see Woodhouse v. Powles, 43 Wash. 617, 86 Pac. 1063, 8 L. R. A. (N. S.) 783.

[12] 45 Ia. 48.

[13] 45 Neb. 493, 63 N. W. 867.

[14] Smith v. Hubbell, 151 Mich. 59, 114 N. W. 865.

[15] Gattis v. Kilgo, 128 N. C. 402, 38 S. E. 931.

[16] Miller v. David, L. R. 9 C. P. 118.

[17] Cotulla v. Kerr, 74 Tex. 89, 11 S. W. 1058, 15 Am. St. Rep. 819; *acc.,* Cranfill v. Hayden, 22 Tex. Civ. App. 656, 55 S. W. 805.

[18] 1 Murray, 350, 384.

In Butler *v.* Hoboken Printing Co.[19] the New Jersey court declared illness produced by mental suffering following the attacks not to be an element in the plaintiff's recovery.

In one or two cases, presumably on the theory that the vindication of character is a natural consequence of attacks upon it, the plaintiff has been allowed to recover reasonable counsel fees,[20] but this is not the general rule.[21]

§ 444a. Repetition by a third person.

It must be regarded as an established general principle that the repetition by others of the defendant's charge is not an element of recovery in the action against him.[22] And where, in an action by a surgeon for a slander imputing that a female servant had a bastard child by him, in consequence of which one who had engaged him as accoucheur would not employ him, and the plaintiff was otherwise injured in his business, it was held that although his damages should not be confined to the fee lost in the special instance, he could not recover for a general loss of business caused by repetition of the slander by third persons, which could not have arisen directly from the speaking of the words by the defendant.[23] But where the repetition could have been anticipated by the defendant he is responsible. So a newspaper publisher who in fact knows that the defamation will be copied in other newspapers is probably liable for the repetition; [24] and where references by third parties to the charge are not actionable, the original author is liable in damages for loss sustained through them.[25] The circulation of a letter by the recipient increases

[19] 73 N. J. L. 45, 62 Atl. 272.

[20] *Louisiana:* Guice *v.* Harvey, 14 La. 198.

Ohio: Finney *v.* Smith, 31 Ohio St. 529, 27 Am. Rep. 524.

[21] Hicks *v.* Foster, 13 Barb. (N. Y.) 663; Halstead *v.* Nelson, 24 Hun, 395; *ante,* § 233.

[22] *Iowa:* Prime *v.* Eastwood, 45 Iowa, 640.

New York: Austin *v.* Bacon, 49 Hun, 386, 3 N. Y. Supp. 587.

Contra, Maine: Davis *v.* Starrett, 97 Me. 568, 55 Atl. 516.

[23] Dixon *v.* Smith, 5 H. & N. 450.

Acc., California: Turner *v.* Hearst, 115 Cal. 394, 47 Pac. 129.

Massachusetts: Parker *v.* Republican Co., 181 Mass. 392, 63 N. E. 931.

[24] Whitney *v.* Moingnard, 24 Q. B. Div. 630.

[25] *New York:* Keenholts *v.* Becker, 3 Denio, 346.

Rhode Island: Rice *v.* Cottrel, 5 R. I. 340.

Vermont: Nott *v.* Stoddard, 38 Vt. 25, 88 Am. Dec. 633.

the liability of the author only where it is a natural consequence of the act of sending it.[26]

§ 445. Aggravation—Social and pecuniary position of the parties.

Evidence may be given of the defendant's pecuniary circumstances, and his position and influence in society. The defendant's wealth is an element in his social rank and influence, and therefore tends to show the extent of the injury from his slanderous speech.[27] In Brown v. Barnes[28] it was said that the jury should be cautioned against considering it except as bearing on the injury likely to flow from slanders uttered by a man of the defendant's standing. The fact that a communication reflecting on the plaintiff's solvency was made by a banker has been held to be an element in the determina-

[26] Merchants' Ins. Co. v. Buckner, 98 Fed. 222, 39 C. C. A. 9.

[27] *United States:* Broughton v. McGrew, 39 Fed. 672.

Connecticut: Barber v. Barber, 33 Conn. 335.

Illinois: Hintz v. Crauper, 138 Ill. 158, 27 N. E. 935.

Indiana: Wilson v. Shepler, 86 Ind. 275.

Iowa: Bailey v. Bailey, 94 Iowa, 598, 63 N. W. 341.

Maine: Stanwood v. Whitmere, 63 Me. 209.

Massachusetts: Bodwell v. Osgood, 3 Pick. 379, 15 Am. Dec. 228.

Michigan: Loranger v. Loranger, 115 Mich. 681, 74 N. W. 228.

Minnesota: Burch v. Bernard, 107 Minn. 210, 120 N. W. 33.

Missouri: Taylor v. Pullen, 152 Mo. 434, 53 S. W. 1086.

New York: Lewis v. Chapman, 19 Barb. 252.

Ohio: Mauk v. Brundage, 68 Oh. St. 89, 67 N. E. 152.

Pennsylvania: M'Almont v. M'Clelland, 14 S. & R. 359.

Virginia: Harman v. Cundiff, 82 Va. 239.

Contra, Alabama: Ware v. Cartledge, 24 Ala. 622.

Delaware: Morris v. Barker, 4 Harr. 520; Nailor v. Ponder, 1 Marv. 408, 41 Atl. 88.

Florida: Jones v. Greeley, 25 Fla. 629, 6 So. 448.

And see Palmer v. Haskins, 28 Barb. 90; Austin v. Bacon, 49 Hun, 386.

In a few states such evidence has been admitted as bearing on the question of exemplary damages only.

Maryland: Wilms v. White, 26 Md. 380.

Missouri: Buckley v. Knapp, 48 Mo. 152.

New Hampshire: Knight v. Foster, 39 N. H. 576.

North Carolina: Adcock v. Marsh, 8 Ired. 360.

Ohio: Hayner v. Cowden, 27 Oh. St. 297 (but see Alpin v. Morton, 21 Oh. St. 536, where it is said it shows the plaintiff's injury).

In Taylor v. Pullen, 152 Mo. 434, 53 S. W. 1086, one suing a husband and wife for slander by the latter was allowed to prove the financial condition of both defendants.

[28] 39 Mich. 211; *acc.*, Buckstaff v. Hicks, 94 Wis. 34, 68 N. W. 403.

tion of his damages.[29] Where a libel is published in a newspaper, the circulation of the paper, and its character and standing, may be shown; but not the wealth of the defendant, its proprietor, where no exemplary damages are to be given.[30] In Storey v. Early [31] the court says:

"The extent of the circulation of the newspaper of defendant, and the character and standing of that newspaper for fairness, justice, and truth, might well be considered upon that question. The wealth of the publisher might be great, and his social standing high, and yet the paper might be of such character as to exert but little influence upon the public mind. On the other hand, the publisher might be insolvent, and his position in society very low, and yet the paper might be very attractive and have a very large circulation, and enjoy the confidence of the public to such a degree, for justice and truth, that statements in its columns might carry great weight."

In an action for defamation against a corporation evidence of its financial standing is inadmissible.[32] Where several individuals are joined as defendants, the financial standing of some of them may be proved.[33]

Evidence of the defendant's resources is clearly of a nature to tempt the jury into giving excessive damages; and much opposition has been shown toward the doctrine which admits it. It is urged with force that the slander receives its added force not from the defendant's wealth, but from his character, and that the latter, not the former, should be shown. In Palmer v. Haskins [34] Marvin, J., said:

"The question, so far as principle is concerned, hinges upon the assumption that wealth influences the rank in society of its possessor, and that the slander of a man of rank and influence is more injurious than the slander of one of less

[29] Lewis v. Chapman, 19 Barb. (N. Y.) 252.
[30] Illinois: Storey v. Early, 86 Ill. 461. Nebraska: Rosewater v. Hoffman, 24 Neb. 222.
[31] 86 Ill. 461, 465.
[32] United States: Western Union Tel. Co. v. Cashman, 132 Fed. 805.

Michigan: Randall v. Evening News Assoc., 97 Mich. 136, 56 N. W. 361. Virginia: Sun L. Assur. Co. v. Bailey, 101 Va. 443, 44 S. E. 692.
[33] Mauk v. Brundage, 68 Ohio St. 89, 67 N. E. 152, 62 L. R. A. 477.
[34] 28 Barb. 90, 92.

influence. It may be admitted that the slander of a man of high character and influence would be more destructive to the character of the party slandered than the slander of one without character and influence. Hence the character and standing in society of the defendant have long been admitted in evidence in this class of cases. But I am not satisfied that wealth is a necessary ingredient to constitute character, standing, and influence in society. It may form an element in fixing character and influence, but not necessarily. Why not limit the inquiry, then, to the question, what are the character, standing, and influence of the defendant in the society where the slander was uttered?'' [35]

Since it is the influence of the defendant's wealth on the minds of the hearers that aggravates the offense, rather than the mere possession of wealth, it has been held in Maine that proof should be made of the general reputation of the defendant for wealth *in the place where the slander was uttered*, rather than the amount of property he in fact possesses.[36] But perhaps the best solution of the question is that all facts bearing on character, standing, and influence should go to the jury, subject to a charge that they must only consider them *in this bearing*. The poverty of the plaintiff cannot be shown in aggravation;[37] but his social position and standing may be shown, that the jury may properly estimate compensation for injury to them.[38]

---

[35] *Acc.*, Justice *v.* Kirlin, 17 Ind. 588.
[36] Stanwood *v.* Whitmore, 63 Me. 209.
[37] *Alabama:* Pool *v.* Devers, 30 Ala. 672.
Connecticut: Case *v.* Marks, 20 Conn. 248.
Iowa: Perrine *v.* Winter, 73 Ia. 645.
North Carolina: Reeves *v.* Winn, 97 N. C. 246.
Contra, Pennsylvania: M'Almont *v.* M'Clelland, 14 S. & R. 359 (*semble*).
[38] *United States:* Press Pub. Co. *v.* McDonald, 63 Fed. 238, 11 C. C. A. 155, 26 L. R. A. 53.
Illinois: Peltier *v.* Mict, 50 Ill. 511.

Indiana: Wilson *v.* Shepler, 86 Ind. 275.
Missouri: Clements *v.* Maloney, 55 Mo. 352.
Ohio: Alliance R. P. Co. *v.* Valentine, 9 Ohio C. Ct. 387.
Contra, New York: Prescott *v.* Tousey, 50 N. Y. Super. Ct. 12.
In Gassely *v.* Humphries, 35 Ala. 617, it was laid down that in slander for imputing larceny, the fact that the plaintiff was a clergyman cannot be considered by the jury in enhancement of the damages, where there is no averment on his part in the pleadings to that effect, and no claim or proof of special damages on that ground.

The fact of plaintiff's being a married man and having children may be shown as a circumstance enhancing mental suffering, at least in the case of a charge of sexual immorality.[39] The intellectual and moral quality of the hearer of a slander has been declared irrelevant to the determination of the injury sustained through it.[40]

In a few cases the plaintiff to enhance recovery has been allowed to prove the excellence of his reputation, although the defendant has not attacked it,[41] in others his right to do so has been denied.[42]

§ 446. Other charges by the defendant than that alleged.

There is great confusion in the authorities as to the admissibility and effect of earlier or later expressions of the defamation sued upon or of other defamations. In a number of jurisdictions even charges of other offences published at earlier or later dates are admitted to prove the character of the original transaction, and the motives of the defendant and, by so establishing express malice, to enhance damages;[43] but such wrongs are not to be in themselves substantive elements of the damages recovered. In Louisiana[44] proof of distinct defamations seems to be confined to attacks upon the plaintiff's character within the year preceding the inception of the suit. In most cases evidence of this sort has taken the form

[39] *California:* Cahill *v.* Murphy, 94 Cal. 29, 30 Pac. 195, 28 Am. St. Rep. 88.
New York: Morey *v.* Morning Journal Assoc., 123 N. Y. 207, 25 N. E. 161, 20 Am. St. Rep. 730, 9 L. R. A. 621; Enos *v.* Enos, 135 N. Y. 609, 32 N. E. 123; Weber *v.* Butler, 81 Hun, 244, 30 N. Y. Supp. 713.

[40] Sheffill *v.* Van Deusen, 15 Gray (Mass.), 485, 77 Am. Dec. 377.

[41] *Kentucky:* Williams *v.* Greenwade, 3 Dana, 432.
Virginia: Adams *v.* Lawson, 17 Gratt. 250, 94 Am. Dec. 455.

[42] *California:* Davis *v.* Hearst, 116 Pac. 530.
Delaware: Parke *v.* Blackiston, 3 Harr. 373.

Pennsylvania: Chubb *v.* Gsell, 34 Pa. 114.

[43] *United States:* Post Pub. Co. *v.* Hallam, 59 Fed. 530, 8 C. C. A. 201.
Alabama: Scott *v.* McKinnish, 15 Ala. 662.
Kentucky: Smith *v.* Lovelace, 1 Duv. 215.
Maine: Davis *v.* Starrett, 97 Me. 568, 55 Atl. 516.
New Hampshire: Symonds *v.* Carter, 32 N. H. 458.
Wisconsin: Hacker *v.* Heiney, 111 Wis. 313, 319, 87 N. W. 249.
And see Rustell *v.* Macquister, 1 Campb. 49; Pearson *v.* Lemaitre, 5 Mann. & G. 700.

[44] Kendrick *v.* Kemp, 6 Mart. (N. S.) 500.

of antecedent or subsequent expressions in the same or similar language of the principal charge;[45] a few of the cases have denied to such the testimony all bearing upon the matter of damages, accordingly giving to it the effect merely of cumulative evidence of the malice which the law itself implies in the making of defamatory statements.[46]   In Howell v. Chatham[47] evidence was rejected of an attack upon the plaintiff's character after the commencement of suit; in a New Jersey decision, the admissibility of any defamations themselves actionable was denied.[48]   The New York courts for a while showed a tendency to restrict evidence of this character to charges that, as barred by the statute of limitations[49] or by a release,[50] could never be of themselves subjects of recovery, and words spoken[51] or written[52] after the inception of the action were of necessity excluded; but more recent decisions have put the State in accord with the weight of authority on the point.[53]

A Connecticut decision[54] admitted in evidence a charge itself the subject of an earlier successful action by the plain-

[45] *Alabama:* Parmer v. Anderson, 33 Ala. 78.
California: Westerfield v. Scripps, 119 Cal. 607, 51 Pac. 958.
Connecticut: Swift v. Dickerman, 31 Conn. 285.
Illinois: Ransom v. McCurley, 140 Ill. 626, 31 N. E. 119.
Indiana: Barker v. Prizer, 150 Ind. 4, 48 N. E. 4.
Maine: Conant v. Leslie, 85 Me. 257, 27 Atl. 147.
Maryland: Gambrill v. Schooley, 93 Md. 48, 52 Atl. 500.
Massachusetts: Markham v. Russell, 12 Allen, 573, 90 Am. Dec. 169.
Michigan: Leonard v. Pope, 27 Mich. 145.
North Dakota: Lauder v. Jones, 13 N. D. 525, 101 N. W. 907.
Oregon: Upton v. Hume, 24 Ore. 420, 33 Pac. 810, 21 L. R. A. 493, 41 Am. St. Rep. 863.
Pennsylvania: Shock v. McChesney, 2 Yeates, 473.

Virginia: Lincoln v. Chrisman, 10 Leigh, 338.
[46] *Indiana:* Meyer v. Bohlfing, 44 Ind. 238.
Iowa: Hinkle v. Davenport, 38 Iowa, 355.
[47] Cooke (Tenn.), 247; acc., Defries v. Davis, 7 C. & P. 112.
[48] Schenck v. Schenck, 20 N. J. L. 208.
[49] Inman v. Foster, 8 Wend. 602; Titus v. Sumner, 44 N. Y. 266.
[50] Glanders v. Graff, 25 Hun (N. Y.), 553.
[51] Distin v. Rose, 69 N. Y. 122.
[52] Eccles v. Radam, 75 Hun, 535, 27 N. Y. Supp. 486.
[53] Enos v. Enos, 135 N. Y. 609, 32 N. E. 123; Turton v. New York Recorder Co., 144 N. Y. 144, 38 N. E. 1009.
[54] Swift v. Dickerman, 31 Conn. 285.

55

tiff. A Maine case [55] accepted words spoken on a qualifiedly privileged occasion; but words absolutely privileged have been twice rejected.[56] A few cases have differentiated the proof of other libellous publications than that alleged from the proof of earlier or later spoken slanders. In Mix v. Woodward [57] the court rejected such evidence altogether in the case of written defamation; in Fisher v. Patterson [58] it was admitted only to explain the intent, in itself doubtful, of the principal publication; and in Finnerty v. Tipper [59] only where the charges adduced in terms referred to that alleged.

§ 447. Plea of justification.

It has been held that an unsuccessful plea of justification is a good ground for increasing the damages. But the inclination of the later cases is against this idea; which, in truth, leads to an effort to punish what may be a perfectly innocent act. So, in Indiana, in slander for perjury, if the defendant plead the truth of the words in justification, and fail to prove the plea, the filing of that plea is not an aggravation; and, on the contrary, if, from the evidence, it appear that the defendant, though he cannot strictly justify, had reason to believe, from the plaintiff's conduct, that the charge was true, such fact may go to the jury in mitigation of damages.[60] And, in Tennessee, an invalid and insufficient plea of justification in an action of slander upon which no judgment could have been entered, is entitled to no weight in aggravation of damages under the plea of not guilty.[61]

The decisions upon this point are, however, not in harmony. In some jurisdictions it is held that such a plea is evidence of actual malice, and a high aggravation of the offence.[62] So, in

[55] Davis v. Starrett, 97 Me. 568, 58 Atl. 516.

[56] *Massachusetts:* Watson v. Moore, 2 Cush. 133, 141.

New York: McLaughlin v. Charles, 60 Hun, 239, 14 N. Y. Supp. 608.

[57] 12 Conn. 262.

[58] 14 Ohio, 418; *acc.,* Saunders v. Baxter, 6 Heisk. (Tenn.) 369.

[59] 2 Camp. 72.

[60] *Indiana:* Sanders v. Johnson, 6 Blackf. 50; Byrket v. Monohon, 7 Blackf. 83; Shortly v. Miller, Smith, 395.

West Virginia: Sweeney v. Baker, 13 W. Va. 158, 31 Am. Rep. 757.

England: Chalmers v. Shackell, 6 C. & P. 475.

[61] Braden v. Walker, 8 Humphreys, 34.

[62] *Alabama:* Pool v. Devers, 30 Ala. 672.

Vermont, it is competent for the jury, on the question of damages, to take into consideration the fact that the defendant, in his pleadings, has repeated and attempted to justify his statements.[63] On the other hand, in other jurisdictions, such a plea, interposed in good faith, is no ground for increasing the damages.[64] As just stated, we think the last rule is the true one, and that the plea should not, as matter of law, carry with it any effect of aggravation. The necessity of such a consequence may prevent an honest defence. As was said, in Rayner v. Kinney,[65] the motive with which the justification is pleaded, should be "for the consideration of the jury. If they find that it was done with the intention to injure the plaintiff, they may rightly consider it an aggravation of the damages; but where no wrongful intention is found, there is no just ground for the punishment of the defendant." In New York, the severer rule formerly obtained,[66] although, before the Code of Procedure, it had perhaps been modified by a limitation of the increase of the damages to the extent of the injury sustained by the repetition.[67] But it would seem to have been wholly superseded by that act, which permits the defendant, in his answer, to allege both the truth of the matter charged as defamatory, and any mitigating circumstances, and whether he

Colorado: Downing v. Brown, 3 Colo. 571.

Georgia: Henderson v. Fox, 83 Ga. 233.

Louisiana: Weil v. Israel, 42 La. Ann. 955, 8 So. 826.

Maine: Sawyer v. Hopkins, 22 Me. 268.

Maryland: Coffin v. Brown, 94 Md. 190, 50 Atl. 567.

Massachusetts: Jackson v. Stetson, 15 Mass. 48; Clark v. Binney, 2 Pick. 113, 121.

Mississippi: Doss v. Jones, 5 How. 158.

Pennsylvania: Gorman v. Sutton, 32 Pa. 247.

South Carolina: Burckhalter v. Coward, 16 S. C. 435.

Tennessee: Wilson v. Nations, 5 Yerg. 211.

England: Simpson v. Robinson, 12 Q. B. 511.

[63] Cavanaugh v. Austin, 42 Vt. 576.

[64] *Connecticut:* Ward v. Dick, 47 Conn. 300.

Illinois: Cummerford v. McAvoy, 15 Ill. 311; Sloan v. Petrie, 15 Ill. 425; Thomas v. Dunaway, 30 Ill. 373; Corbley v. Wilson, 71 Ill. 209.

Indiana: Murphy v. Stout, 1 Ind. 372.

New Hampshire: Pallet v. Sargent, 36 N. H. 496.

Ohio: Rayner v. Kinney, 14 Oh. St. 283, overruling the dictum *contra* in Dewit v. Greenfield, 5 Oh. 225.

Canada: Corridan v. Wilkinson, 20 Ont. App. 184.

[65] 14 Oh. St. 283.

[66] Fero v. Ruscoe, 4 N. Y. 162.

[67] Fulkerson v. George, 3 Abb. Pr. 75.

prove the justification or not, to give in evidence the mitigating circumstances.[68] And it is now held by the New York Court of Appeals, that where the defendant, in an action of libel or slander, pleads under this section, facts both in justification and mitigation, the allegations in justification, though unproved, are no longer evidence of malice to be considered by the jury, or taken as enhancing the plaintiff's damages.[69] In every jurisdiction, however, the *malicious* filing of a plea in justification may be considered in aggravation of damages, since it furnishes a ground for exemplary damages.[70] So, too, the filing of a plea in justification merely to uphold a newspaper policy of insisting upon the truth of every statement appearing in the defendant's columns.[71] That an objectionable pleading was withdrawn was held in Illinois [72] not to prevent its being used to enhance the plaintiff's recovery; but the opposite result was reached in California.[73] In Lamb *v.* West,[74] where the defendant's attorney conducted the case with obvious malice toward the plaintiff, the latter was held entitled to punitive damages.

§ 448. Mitigation.

Since the damages for defamation are in general nonpecuniary, evidence may be given in mitigation of compensatory damages as well as of exemplary damages. As in other cases, however, nothing should be received in mitigation of compen-

[68] N. Y. Co. Civ. Proc., § 535; Bush *v.* Prosser, 11 N. Y. 347.
[69] Klinck *v.* Colby, 46 N. Y. 427; Decker *v.* Gaylord, 35 Hun, 584. The remarks, therefore, of Mr. Justice E. D. Smith, to the contrary, in delivering the opinion of the Supreme Court of New York, in Bennett *v.* Matthews, 64 Barb. 410, are at variance with the settled law.
[70] *California:* Pink *v.* Catanich, 51 Cal. 420; Dauphiny *v.* Buhne, 153 Cal. 757, 96 Pac. 880; Davis *v.* Hearst, 116 Pac. 530, and cases cited.
Illinois: Spencer *v.* McMasters, 16 Ill. 405.
Missouri: Browning *v.* Powers, 38 S. W. 943, 946.

New York: Marx *v.* Press Pub. Co., 134 N. Y. 561, 31 N. E. 918.
Oregon: Shartle *v.* Hutchinson, 3 Ore. 337.
Rhode Island: Tillinghast *v.* McLeod, 17 R. I. 208, 21 Atl. 345.
Utah: Lowe *v.* Herald Co., 6 Utah, 175.
[71] Kansas City Star Co. *v.* Carlisle, 108 Fed. 344, 47 C. C. A. 384, 393.
[72] Beasley *v.* Meigs, 16 Ill. 139.
[73] Morris *v.* Lachman, 68 Cal. 109, 8 Pac. 799.
[74] 15 N. S. W. L. Rep. 120; *acc.,* Struthers *v.* Peacock, 11 Phila. (Pa.) 287.

satory damages unless it tends to show what those damages actually were. When actual damages are once ascertained they cannot be mitigated; though they are to be determined in view of all mitigating circumstances.[75] The case of exemplary damages is of course different; and there any circumstance which has a bearing on the defendant's malice may be shown.

Thus where compensatory damages only are to be given, defendant cannot, to mitigate damages, show that he is poor.[76] Nor may he show that the plaintiff has already brought suit for libel against another defendant who published an identical statement.[77] Nor should the good faith of the defendant be shown to affect compensatory damages,[78] though on this point the authorities are in conflict.[79] But this conflict may be in great part explained by the fact that exemplary damages were recoverable (though this fact is not always brought out), and such evidence is clearly admissible in mitigation of exemplary damages. So, where it appears that the defendant was drunk when he uttered the words, this may go in mitigation of damages as tending to rebut malice.[80] But where it is proved that he repeated the charge both when drunk and sober, on public and private occasions, his being drunk at the particular time alleged is no reason for abating the damages.[81] The insanity of the defendant may be shown.[82] It has apparently been allowed as a complete defence,[83] but that is not to be approved in a civil suit.

§ 448a. Disproof of actual malice.

Damages may be mitigated by disproof of actual malice.[84]

[75] Keller v. American B. P. Co., 140 App. Div. 311, 125 N. Y. Supp. 212.

[76] Harter v. Whitebread, 38 Pa. Super. Ct. 10.

[77] *United States:* Printing Assoc. v. Smith, 55 Fed. 240, 5 C. C. A. 91.

New York: Palmer v. Matthews, 162 N. Y. 100, 56 N. E. 501; Palmer v. New York News Pub. Co., 31 App. Div. 210, 52 N. Y. Supp. 539.

[78] Schattler v. Daily Herald Co., 162 Mich. 115, 127 N. W. 42, 17 Det. L. N. 481.

[79] See the cases cited in the following sections.

[80] *Indiana:* Gates v. Meredith, 7 Ind. 440.

England: Wakelin v. Morris, 2 F. & F. 26.

[81] Howell v. Howell, 10 Ired. (N. C.) 84.

[82] Brown v. Brooks, 3 Ind. 518; Yeates v. Reed, 4 Blackf. 463.

[83] Bryant v. Jackson, 6 Humph. (Tenn.) 199.

[84] *United States:* Erber v. Dun, 12

The damages so mitigated are regularly, and in some jurisdictions solely,[85] punitive; but there are cases holding the defendant's attitude of mind relevant upon the plaintiff's mental suffering and, accordingly, upon his actual damages.[86] In an action for libel, it is proper to admit evidence of what was said by the defendant in directing the printing, in order to disprove actual malice in the publication, and to influence the question of damages. The terms and conditions on which the defendant requested the printing and publication to be done, and on which the witness agreed to do it, are admissible in evidence as pertinent and material in respect to the *motives* of the defendant in procuring the publication complained of.[87]

§ 448b. Imperfect privilege.

That the charges were made in good faith to a person interested in receiving the information may be shown in mitiga-

Fed. 526, 4 McCrary, 160; Palmer *v.* Mahin, 120 Fed. 737, 57 C. C. A. 41.

Arkansas: Patton *v.* Cruce, 72 Ark. 421, 81 S. W. 380, 65 L. R. A. 937, 105 Am. St. Rep. 46.

California: Lick *v.* Owen, 47 Cal. 252.

Delaware: Donahoe *v.* Star Pub. Co., 4 Pennew. 166, 55 Atl. 337; Todd *v.* Every Evening Printing Co., 6 Pennew. 233, 66 Atl. 97.

Iowa: Fountain *v.* West, 23 Iowa, 9, 92 Am. Dec. 405.

Louisiana: Germann *v.* Crescioni, 105 La. 496, 29 So. 968; Levert *v.* Daily States Pub. Co., 123 La. 594, 49 So. 206.

Michigan: Davis *v.* Marxhausen, 103 Mich. 315, 61 N. W. 504.

Minnesota: Quinn *v.* Scott, 22 Minn. 456.

Missouri: Jones *v.* Murray, 167 Mo. 25, 66 S. W. 981.

Nevada: Thompson *v.* Powning, 15 Nev. 195.

New York: Hawk *v.* American News Co., 33 N. Y. Supp. 848, 24 N. Y. Civ. Proc. 255; Collis *v.* Press. Pub. Co., 68 App. Div. 38, 74 N. Y. Supp. 78.

Ohio: Henn *v.* Horn, 56 Ohio St. 442, 448, 47 N. E. 248.

Pennsylvania: Updegrove *v.* Zimmerman, 13 Pa. 619.

Wisconsin: Adamson *v.* Raymer, 94 Wis. 243, 68 N. W. 1000.

[85] *United States:* Times Pub. Co. *v.* Carlisle, 94 Fed. 762, 36 C. C. A. 475; Kansas City Star Co. *v.* Carlisle, 108 Fed. 344, 47 C. C. A. 397; Post Pub. Co. *v.* Butler, 137 Fed. 723, 71 C. C. A. 309.

Arkansas: Murray *v.* Galbraith, 95 Ark. 199, 128 S. W. 1047.

Kentucky: Nicholson *v.* Rust, 21 Ky. L. R. 645, 52 S. W. 934.

New Jersey: Knowlden *v.* Guardian Printing, etc., Co., 69 N. J. L. 670, 55 Atl. 287; Neafie *v.* Hoboken P. & P. Co., 75 N. J. L. 564, 68 Atl. 146.

New York: Robinson *v.* Evening Post Pub. Co., 39 App. Div. 525, 57 N. Y. Supp. 303.

Wisconsin: Pellardis *v.* Journal Printing Co., 99 Wis. 156, 74 N. W. 99.

[86] *Massachusetts:* Markham *v.* Russell, 12 Allen, 573, 90 Am. Dec. 169.

Michigan: Detroit Daily Post Co. *v.* McArthur, 16 Mich. 447; Scripps *v.* Reilly, 38 Mich. 10.

[87] Taylor *v.* Church, 8 N. Y. 452.

tion, though the circumstances were not such as to make the communication privileged in the technical sense. Thus, the fact that charges against an officer of state or candidate for office were made from a genuine desire to enlighten the public will be received in mitigation of damages.[88] A defendant has been allowed to prove that the charge of unchastity was made to a young man who seemed to be courting the plaintiff.[89] The circumstance that a reflection on the plaintiff's commercial credit was telegraphed in confidence by a company engaged in supplying information on the topic goes in mitigation.[90] One whose defamation was uttered in order to give warning against an undesirable neighbor is entitled to some leniency from the jury;[91] and in assessing damages the fact that the defendant did not seek the interview may properly be considered.[92]

§ 448c. Belief in truth of charge.

Matters which induced a belief of the truth of the charge in the defendant may be shown to disprove malice;[93] for example, that the plaintiff was seen in a suspicious situation,[94] or that his conduct was equivocal.[95] Where the defendant accused the plaintiff of unchastity, evidence is admissible of an increase in the plaintiff's size resembling pregnancy, which in fact was from another cause.[96] In an action for a libel the receipt by the de-

[88] *Illinois:* Rearick v. Wilcox, 81 Ill. 77.

Maryland: Negley v. Farrow, 60 Md. 158, 45 Am. Rep. 715.

Michigan: Bailey v. Kalamazoo Pub. Co., 40 Mich. 251; Bronson v. Bruce, 59 Mich. 467, 26 N. W. 671, 60 Am. Rep. 307.

[89] Blocker v. Schoff, 83 Iowa, 265, 48 N. W. 1079.

[90] Jeffras v. McKillop, 2 Hun, 351.

[91] Beggarly v. Craft, 31 Ga. 309, 76 Am. Dec. 687.

[92] Davis v. Sladden, 17 Ore. 259, 21 Pac. 140.

[93] *Illinois:* Moore v. Mauk, 3 Ill. App. 114.

Kansas: Miles v. Harrington, 8 Kan. 425.

Kentucky: Evening Post Co. v. Rhea, 31 S. W. 273, 26 Ky. L. Rep. 375.

Pennsylvania: Petrie v. Rose, 5 Watts & S. 364.

Sickra v. Small, 87 Me. 493, 33 Atl. 9, 47 Am. St. Rep. 344, *contra*, is perhaps best to be explained on the theory that punitive damages were on principles apart from this topic disallowed.

[94] Haywood v. Foster, 16 Ohio, 88.

[95] *New York:* Spooner v. Keeler, 51 N. Y. 527.

Ohio: Wilson v. Apple, 3 Ohio, 270; Reynolds v. Tucker, 6 Oh. St. 516.

Pennsylvania: Minesinger v. Kerr, 9 Pa. 312.

Shepard v. Merrill, 13 Johns. 475, reached an opposite result partly, it would seem, on a point of pleading.

[96] Doe v. Roe, 32 Hun, 628.

fendant of forged letters containing statements upon which
the charge was founded may be shown in mitigation; [97] and so,
too, evidence has been admitted that the charge was founded
on information obtained from the journal of Congress [98] or
from the police [99] or from newspapers.[100] And generally if the
defendant can establish his *bona fide* belief in the truth of the
charge this may be shown in mitigation; [101] though in some
jurisdictions it cannot be shown in mitigation of actual damages, but only of exemplary damages.[102]

§ 448d. Repetition of earlier charge made by another.

In actions of slander and libel, it has been much discussed
how far the fact of the slander or libel complained of being a
mere repetition or republication can be set up, either in justification or mitigation.[103]   In some early actions of slander
proof that the words were first spoken by another person,
whom the defendant in his statement named as author, barred
the plaintiff's action; [104] and though this is not now law, later
decisions almost uniformly admit such evidence in mitigation
of damages, alike in actions of libel and of slander.[105] And it

[97] *Illinois:* Storey *v.* Early, 86 Ill. 461.
Kentucky: FosterMilburn Co. *v.* Chinn, 137 Ky. 834, 120 S. W. 364.
[98] Romayne *v.* Duane, 3 Wash. C. C. 246, Fed. Cas. No. 12,028.
[99] Evening Post Co. *v.* Hunter, 18 Ky. L. Rep. 726, 38 S. W. 487.
[100] *United States:* Printing Assoc. *v.* Smith, 55 Fed. 240, 5 C. C. A. 91.
Michigan: Hay *v.* Reid, 85 Mich. 296, 48 N. W. 507.
Minnesota: Hewitt *v.* Pioneer-Press Co., 23 Minn. 178, 23 Am. Rep. 680.
New York: Gray *v.* Brooklyn Union Pub. Co., 35 App. Div. 286, 52 N. Y. Supp. 35.
[101] Republican Pub. Co. *v.* Mosman, 15 Colo. 409, 24 Pac. 1055; Rocky Mountain N. P. Co. *v.* Fridborn, 46 Colo. 440, 104 Pac. 956, 24 L. R. A. (N. S.) 891.
[102] Garrison *v.* Robinson (N. J. L.), 79 Atl. 278.

[103] Bennett *v.* Bennett, 6 C. & P. 588, and cases cited.
[104] *Maine:* Haynes *v.* Leland, 29 Me. 233.
Pennsylvania: Binns *v.* McCorkle, 2 Browne, 79; Hersh *v.* Ringwalt, 3 Yeates, 508, 2 Am. Dec. 392.
South Carolina: Miller *v.* Kerr, 2 McCord, 285, 13 Am. Dec. 722.
Tennessee: Larkins *v.* Tarter, 3 Sneed, 681.
England: Davis *v.* Lewis, 7 T. R. 17.
[105] *Indiana:* Kelley *v.* Dillon, 5 Ind. 426.
Iowa: Beardsley *v.* Bridgman, 17 Iowa, 290.
Kentucky: Williams *v.* Greenwade, 3 Dana, 432.
Missouri: Baldwin *v.* Boulware, 79 Mo. App. 5.
Pennsylvania: Follett *v.* Jewett, 1 Am. L. Reg. 600, 11 N. Y. Leg. Obs. 193; Stepp *v.* Croft, 18 Pa. Super. Ct. 101; Kennedy *v.* Gregory, 1 Bin. 85.

is now well established that a defendant, in order to show the absence of bad motive for the publication, may prove that his charge was repeated from some reliable source, whether or not the authority was named.[106] Some cases have declared the existence of common rumor of the truth of the charge relevant, upon the question of malice, but other cases have denied its admissibility.[107]

In order to afford evidence of the defendant's motives the defamation of others must have been known to him; [108] and even where the authority for the charge is mentioned, further facts, such as lack of belief in its truth, may show actual malice.[109] In Hayes v. Tibbits [110] the fact that a libel was published at the request and on the information of a third person was held not to be a mitigating circumstance.

§ 449. Provocation.

In Louisiana verdicts for the defendant have been allowed to stand where the facts showed a war of slanderous words between the parties.[111] In other jurisdictions it is agreed that

Rhode Island: Rice v. Cottrel, 5 R. I. 340.

South Carolina: Easterwood v. Quin, 2 Brev. 64, 3 Am. Dec. 700.

[106] *United States:* McDonald v. Woodruff, 16 Fed. Cas. No. 8,770, 2 Dill. 244.

Connecticut: Arnott v. Standard Assoc., 57 Conn. 86, 17 Atl. 361, 3 L. R. A. 69 (see Treat v. Browning, 4 Conn. 408, 10 Am. Dec. 156).

Iowa: Morse v. Times Republican Printing Co., 124 Iowa, 707, 100 N. W. 867.

Kentucky: Evans v. Smith, 5 T. B. Mon. 363, 17 Am. Dec. 74.

Missouri: Hawkins v. Globe Printing Co., 10 Mo. App. 174.

Oregon: Upton v. Hume, 24 Ore. 420, 33 Pac. 810, 21 L. R. A. 493, 41 Am. St. Rep. 863.

Pennsylvania: Regensperger v. Kiefer, 4 Pa. Cas. 541, 7 Atl. 724; Morris v. Duane, 1 Bin. 90.

Rhode Island: Folwell v. Providence Journal Co., 19 R. I. 551, 37 Atl. 6.

South Carolina: Galloway v. Courtney, 10 Rich. 414.

England: Creevy v. Carr, 7 C. & P. 64.

Contra, Missouri: Moberly v. Preston, 8 Mo. 462.

Pennsylvania: Good v. Grit Pub. Co., 36 Pa. Super. Ct. 238.

[107] Post, § 451.

[108] *Michigan:* Wolff v. Smith, 112 Mich. 359, 70 N. W. 1010.

Minnesota: Larrabee v. Minnesota Tribune Co., 36 Minn. 141, 39 N. W. 462.

New York: Hatfield v. Lasher, 81 N. Y. 246; Palmer v. Matthews, 162 N. Y. 100, 56 N. E. 501; Witcher v. Jones, 17 N. Y. Supp. 491; Carpenter v. N. Y. Evening Journal Pub. Co., 96 App. Div. 376, 89 N. Y. Supp. 263.

[109] Jones v. Chapman, 5 Blackf. (Ind.) 88.

[110] 2 Abb. Pr. (N. Y.), N. S. 97.

[111] Fulda v. Caldwell, 9 La. Ann. 358; Goldberg v. Dobbertine, 46 La. Ann. 1303, 1308, 16 So. 192, 28 L. R. A. 721.

the defendant in actions of slander may show in mitigation the plaintiff's speaking or writing of irritating words or other provocation.[112] The defendant's passion not founded on the plaintiff's acts or words will not reduce damages.[113] There must, accordingly, be some connection between the provocation and the defamation.[114] In some cases it has been said that the test in slander is the same as in assault and that the plaintiff's wrongdoing is inadmissible if so remote from the defendant's as to afford an opportunity for hot blood to cool.[115] In other decisions, both in libel and slander, evidence of the plaintiff's charges has been declared inadmissible unless a part of the controversy or transaction which included the defendant's publication.[116] Testimony will not be received to show the plain-

---

[112] *Alabama:* Moore *v.* Clay, 24 Ala. 235, 60 Am. Dec. 461.
Arkansas: Patton *v.* Cruce, 72 Ark. 421, 81 S. W. 380, 105 Am. St. Rep. 46, 65 L. R. A. 937.
Georgia: Pugh. *v.* McCarty, 40 Ga. 444.
Illinois: Freeman *v.* Tinsley, 50 Ill. 497; Thomas *v.* Fischer, 71 Ill. 576.
Indiana: Brown *v.* Brooks, 3 Ind. 518; Mousler *v.* Harding, 33 Ind. 176.
Iowa: McClintock *v.* Crick, 4 Iowa, 453; Emerson *v.* Miller, 115 Iowa, 315, 88 N. W. 803.
Kentucky: Craig *v.* Catlet, 5 Dana, 323; Duncan *v.* Brown, 15 B. Mon. 186.
Maryland: Botelar *v.* Bell, 1 Md. 173; Shockey *v.* McCauley, 101 Md. 461, 61 Atl. 583; Davis *v.* Griffith, 4 Gill & J. 342.
Michigan: Ritchie *v.* Stenius, 73 Mich. 563, 41 N. W. 687; Newman *v.* Stein, 75 Mich. 402, 42 N. W. 956, 13 Am. St. Rep. 447.
Minnesota: Warner *v.* Lockerby, 31 Minn. 421.
Mississippi: Powers *v.* Presgroves, 38 Miss. 227.
Missouri: Israel *v.* Israel, 109 Mo. App. 366, 84 S. W. 453.
New York: Xavier *v.* Oliver, 80 App. Div. 292, 80 N. Y. Supp. 225; Else *v.*

Ferris, Anth. N. P. 36; Maynard *v.* Beardsley, 7 Wend. 560.
Oregon: Shartle *v.* Hutchinson, 3 Ore. 337.
Tennessee: Haws *v.* Stanford, 1 Tenn. Cas. 80.
Wisconsin: Rogers *v.* Henry, 32 Wis. 327; Massuere *v.* Dickens, 70 Wis. 83; Candrian *v.* Miller, 98 Wis. 164, 73 N. W. 1004.
England: Watts *v.* Fraser, 7 C. & P. 369.
Canada: Downey *v.* Stirton, 1 Ont. 186; Stirton *v.* Gummer, 31 Ont. 227.
[113] *Illinois:* Flagg *v.* Roberts, 67 Ill. 485; Miller *v.* Johnson, 79 Ill. 58.
Louisiana: Bonnin *v.* Elliott, 19 La. Ann. 322.
Maryland: Shockey *v.* McCauley, 101 Md. 461, 61 Atl. 583.
New York: Gould *v.* Weed, 12 Wend. 12.
[114] Battell *v.* Wallace, 30 Fed. 229.
[115] *Massachusetts:* Sheffill *v.* Van Deusen, 15 Gray, 485, 77 Am. Dec. 377; Child *v.* Homer, 13 Pick. 503.
Minnesota: Quinby *v.* Minn. Tribune Co., 38 Minn. 528, 38 N. W. 623, 8 Am. St. Rep. 693.
[116] *Indiana:* Swann *v.* Rary, 3 Blackf. 298.
New York: Lister *v.* Wright, 2 Hill, 320.

tiff's habit of defaming the defendant; [117] nor to prove general hostile relations between the parties,[118] even though the neighborhood knew of them.[119] And the publication of a slander by way of deliberate reprisal has been regarded as evidence of malice in fact.[120]

It was held in North Carolina that mental distress of the defendant at the time he uttered the slander, caused by his belief in the truth of it, was admissible in mitigation.[121] But the defendant cannot prove in mitigation of damages, irritating language addressed to him by the father of the plaintiff immediately previous to the uttering of the slanderous words to another person.[122]

§ 450. Disproof of damage.

Another class of facts is received in mitigation as proving that the amount of damage caused to the plaintiff by the defamation was less than would at first seem to be the case.[123] Since the principal element of damage is injury to the plaintiff's character, it is pertinent to show that this character was not at all or very little injured in the minds of the hearers. This may be done in one of two ways: by showing that the words were not believed, or by showing that the plaintiff's character was so bad as not to be injured. The latter method is not encouraged by the courts, because in adopting it the defendant is obliged to defame himself. Thus in Massachusetts it was held that the defendant could not show that he was in the habit of talking

Pennsylvania: Steever *v.* Beehler, 1 Miles, 146.

Virginia: Bourland *v.* Eidson, 8 Gratt. 27.

England: May *v.* Brown, 3 B. & C. 113; Tarpley *v.* Blabey, 2 Bing. N. C. 437.

[117] *Michigan:* Porter *v.* Henderson, 11 Mich. 20, 82 Am. Dec. 59.

North Carolina: Goodbread *v.* Ledbetter, 1 Dev. & Bat. L. 12.

England: Wakley *v.* Johnson, R. & M. 422, 27 Rev. Rep. 767, 21 E. C. L. 787.

[118] Andrews *v.* Bartholomew, 2 Met. (Mass.) 509.

In Craig *v.* Catlet, 5 Dana, 323, it was pointed out that if evidence of enmity between the parties were admissible, its normal effect would seem to be to prove rather than to disprove express malice.

[119] Swann *v.* Rary, 3 Blackf. (Ind.) 298.

[120] Gray *v.* Elzroth, 10 Ind. App. 587.

[121] McDougald *v.* Coward, 95 N. C. 368.

[122] Underhill *v.* Taylor, 2 Barb. (N. Y.) 348.

[123] Morgan *v.* Lexington Herald Co., 138 Ky. 637, 128 S. W. 1064.

too much about persons and things, so that what he said was not regarded in the community as worthy of notice.[124] Yet the evidence would bear directly on the degree of the plaintiff's injury. The defendant may prove, in mitigation of damages, a declaration of the plaintiff that he was not injured by the words complained of. But evidence that the witnesses who heard the words uttered did not believe them, is not admissible.[125] The fact that a libel will not be believed has been held in Massachusetts,[126] where exemplary damages are not allowed, not to deprive the plaintiff of his right to substantial damages.

§ 451. Bad character and reputation of plaintiff.

The general bad character and reputation of the plaintiff at the time of the alleged slander is admissible in mitigation of damages, not merely with a view to disprove malice, but upon the broader ground that a person of already disparaged reputation is not entitled to the same measure of damages as one with an unblemished fame. The evidence is admitted to show the value of what is alleged to be injured, and is, therefore, not to be restricted to the particular traits of character involved in the slanderous words.[127] So a charge to the jury

[124] Howe v. Perry, 15 Pick. 506; Hastings v. Stetson, 130 Mass. 76.

Acc. Young v. Slemons, Wright (Ohio), 124.

[125] Richardson v. Barker, 7 Ind. 567.

[126] Bishop v. Journal Newspaper Co., 168 Mass. 327, 47 N. E. 119.

[127] United States: Whitney v. Janesville Gazette, 5 Biss. 330; Wright v. Schroeder, 2 Curt. 548.

Alabama: Commons v. Walters, 1 Port. 323.

California: Edwards v. San Jose Printing Assoc., 99 Cal. 431, 34 Pac. 128, 37 Am. St. Rep. 70.

Indiana: McCabe v. Platter, 6 Blackf. 405.

Iowa: Fletcher v. Burroughs, 10 Ia. 557; Hanners v. McClelland, 74 Ia. 318.

Kansas: Haag v. Cooley, 33 Kan. 387, 6 Pac. 585.

Maine: Sickra v. Small, 87 Me. 493, 33 Atl. 9, 47 Am. St. Rep. 344.

Massachusetts: Larned v. Buffinton, 3 Mass. 546.

Michigan: Proctor v. Houghtaling, 37 Mich. 41; Randall v. Evening News Assoc., 97 Mich. 136, 56 N. W. 361; Fowler v. Fowler, 113 Mich. 575, 71 N. W. 1084; Georgia v. Bond, 114 Mich. 196, 72 N. W. 232.

Minnesota: Warner v. Lockerby, 31 Minn. 421.

New York: Calkins v. Colburn, 10 N. Y. 778; Wuensch v. Morning Journal Assoc., 4 App. Div. 110, 38 N. Y. Supp. 665; Dinkelspiel v. New York Evening Journal Pub. Co., 42 Misc. 74, 85 N. Y. Supp. 570; Paddock v. Salisbury, 2 Cow. 811; Hamer v. McFarlin, 4 Denio, 509; Stiles v. Comstock, 9 How. Pr. 48; King v. Root, 4 Wend. 113, 21 Am. Dec. 102.

North Carolina: Goodbread v. Ledbetter, 1 Dev. & Bat. L. 12; Vick v.

that if the plaintiff by her own dissolute conduct had so destroyed her character as to receive no injury from the words they should give nominal damages is good.[128]   But bad character of the plaintiff after he is defamed by the defendant will of course not be admissible in mitigation.[129]   The bad character of the plaintiff in the particular trait involved in the defamation may be shown.[130]

Whitfield, 2 Hayw. 222; Sowers *v.* Sowers, 87 N. C. 303.

Ohio: Dewit *v.* Greenfield, 5 Oh. 225; Fisher *v.* Patterson, 14 Oh. 418; Duval *v.* Davey, 32 Oh. St. 604.

Pennsylvania: Conroe *v.* Conroe, 47 Pa. 198; Moyer *v.* Moyer, 49 Pa. 210 (overruling Steinman *v.* McWilliams, 6 Pa. 170, on this point); Drown *v.* Allen, 91 Pa. 393; Fitzgerald *v.* Stewart, 53 Pa. 343; Henry *v.* Norwood, 4 Watts, 347.

Rhode Island: Folwell *v.* Providence Journal Co., 19 R. I. 551, 37 Atl. 6.

South Carolina: Sawyer *v.* Eifert, 2 N. & McC. 511.

Wisconsin: B. *v.* I., 22 Wis. 372; Maxwell *v.* Kennedy, 50 Wis. 645; Campbell *v.* Campbell, 54 Wis. 90.

England: Scott *v.* Sampson, 8 Q. B. D. 491, 46 J. P. 408, 51 L. J. Q. B. 380, 46 L. T. Rep. (N. S.) 412, 30 Wkly. Rep. 451.

Ireland: Bell *v.* Parke, 11 Ir. C. L. Rep. 413.

Contra, Tennessee: Lambert *v.* Pharis, 3 Head, 622; Bell *v.* Farnsworth, 11 Humph. 608.

Vermont: Smith *v.* Shumway, 2 Tyler, 74.

Virginia: Dillard *v.* Collins, 25 Gratt. 343.

Canada: Williston *v.* Smith, 3 Kerr, 443.

And see *New York:* Foot *v.* Tracy, 1 Johns. 45.

[128] Flint *v.* Clark, 13 Conn. 361.

[129] *Alabama:* Scott *v.* McKinnish, 15 Ala. 662.

New York: Douglass *v.* Tousey, 2 Wend. 352.

[130] *Alabama:* Pope *v.* Welsh, 18 Ala. 631; Fuller *v.* Dean, 31 Ala. 654; Waters *v.* Jones, 3 Port. 442.

Connecticut: Treat *v.* Browning, 4 Conn. 408, 10 Am. Dec. 156; Swift *v.* Dickerman, 31 Conn. 285; Brunson *v.* Lynde, 1 Root, 354; Seymour *v.* Merrills, 1 Root, 459.

District of Columbia: Turner *v.* Foxall, 24 Fed. Cas. No. 14,255, 2 Cranch, C. C. 324.

Illinois: Young *v.* Bennett, 5 Ill. 43; Sheahan *v.* Collins, 20 Ill. 325; Adams *v.* Smith, 58 Ill. 417.

Indiana: Woods *v.* Anderson, 5 Blackf. 598; Burke *v.* Miller, 6 Blackf. 155.

Iowa: Armstrong *v.* Pierson, 8 Ia. 29; Fletcher *v.* Burrows, 10 Ia. 557.

Kentucky: Eastland *v.* Caldwell, 2 Bibb, 21.

Maine: Sickra *v.* Small, 87 Me. 493, 33 Atl. 9, 47 Am. St. Rep. 344.

Maryland: Shilling *v.* Carson, 27 Md. 175.

Massachusetts: Clark *v.* Brown, 116 Mass. 504; Peterson *v.* Morgan, 116 Mass. 350; Mahoney *v.* Belford, 132 Mass. 393; Parkhurst *v.* Ketchum, 6 Allen, 406, 83 Am. Dec. 639; Leonard *v.* Allen, 11 Cush. 241; Stone *v.* Varney, 7 Met. 86; Bodwell *v.* Swan, 3 Pick. 376.

Minnesota: Davis *v.* Hamilton, 88 Minn. 64, 92 N. W. 512.

Missouri: Anthony *v.* Stephens, 1 Mo. 254.

New Hampshire: Lamos *v.* Snell, 6 N. H. 413.

New Jersey: Sayre *v.* Sayre, 25 N. J. L. 235; Pier *v.* Speer, 73 N. J. L. 633, 64 Atl. 161.

There is a conflict of opinion upon the question whether a general rumor of the truth of the fact charged by the defendant is admissible in mitigation of damages. The weight of authority favors the admission of the evidence,[131] but some courts exclude it.[132] The objection to its admission is that

Pennsylvania: Good *v.* Grit Pub. Co., 36 Pa. Super. Ct. 238.

Texas: Schulz *v.* Jalonick, 18 Tex. Civ. App. 296, 44 S. W. 580.

Vermont: Bowen *v.* Hall, 20 Vt. 232; Bridgman *v.* Hopkins, 34 Vt. 532.

Virginia: Dillard *v.* Collins, 25 Gratt. 343; M'Nutt *v.* Young, 8 Leigh, 542.

Wisconsin: B. *v.* I., 22 Wis. 372; Campbell *v.* Campbell, 54 Wis. 90; Nellis *v.* Cramer, 86 Wis. 337, 56 N. W. 911; Earley *v.* Winn, 129 Wis. 291, 109 N. W. 633.

England: Anon. *v.* Moor, 1 M. & S. 284.

Contra, New York: Root *v.* King, 7 Cow. 613; Van Benschoten *v.* Yaple, 13 How. Pr. 97.

England: Jones *v.* Stevenson, 11 Price, 235.

Ireland: Bell *v.* Park, 11 Ir. C. L. Rep. 413.

[131] *United States:* Broughton *v.* Mc-Grew, 39 Fed. 672.

Alabama: Fuller *v.* Dean, 31 Ala. 654.

Colorado: Republican Pub. Co. *v.* Mosman, 15 Colo. 399, 24 Pac. 1051.

Connecticut: Case *v.* Marks, 20 Conn. 248 (*semble*).

Delaware: Morris *v.* Barker, 4 Harr. 520; Nailor *v.* Ponder, 1 Marv. 408, 41 Atl. 88.

Florida: Montgomery *v.* Knox, 23 Fla. 595, 3 So. 211.

Indiana: Brown *v.* Brooks, 3 Ind. 518; Gray *v.* Elzroth, 10 Ind. App. 587, 37 N. E. 551.

Iowa: Hinkle *v.* Davenport, 38 Ia. 355; Barr *v.* Hack, 46 Ia. 308.

Kentucky: Calloway *v.* Middleton, 2 A. K. Marsh. 372, 12 Am. Dec. 406; McIntyre *v.* Bransford, 13 Ky. L. Rep. 454, 17 S. W. 359; Morgan *v.* Lexing-

ton Herald Co., 138 Ky. 637, 128 S. W. 1064.

Michigan: Farr *v.* Rasco, 9 Mich. 353, 80 Am. Dec. 88; Fowler *v.* Fowler, 113 Mich. 575, 71 N. W. 1084; Brewer *v.* Chase, 121 Mich. 526, 80 N. W. 575, 80 Am. St. Rep. 527, 46 L. R. A. 397.

New Hampshire: Wetherbee *v.* Marsh, 20 N. H. 561; Wier *v.* Allen, 51 N. H. 177 (see Dame *v.* Kenney, 25 N. H. 318).

New Jersey: Hoboken Printing, etc., Co. *v.* Kahn, 58 N. J. L. 359, 33 Atl. 382, 1060, 55 Am. St. Rep. 609; Stuart *v.* News Pub. Co., 67 N. J. L. 317, 51 Atl. 709.

New York: Springstein *v.* Field, Anth. N. P. 252; Matson *v.* Buck, 5 Cow. 499; Skinner *v.* Powers, 1 Wend. 451 (see Inman *v.* Foster, 8 Wend. 602).

North Carolina: McCurry *v.* Mc-Curry, 82 N. C. 296.

Ohio: Wilson *v.* Kenyon, Wright, 651; Hilbrant *v.* Simmons, 18 Ohio C. Ct. 123 (see Fisher *v.* Patterson, 14 Ohio, 418; McCoy *v.* Crawford, Tapp. 238).

Pennsylvania: Pease *v.* Shippen, 80 Pa. 513, 21 Am. Rep. 116 (see Fitzgerald *v.* Stewart, 53 Pa. 343).

Tennessee: Hancock *v.* Stephens, 11 Humph. 507.

Texas: Patten *v.* Belo, 79 Tex. 41, 14 S. W. 1037; Schultz *v.* Jalonick, 18 Tex. Civ. App. 296, 44 S. W. 580.

Canada: Edgar *v.* Newall, 24 Up. Can. Q. B. 215.

The court in Nelson *v.* Wallace, 48 Mo. App. 193, admitted the existence of general rumor, as bearing upon express malice, to reduce exemplary damages, but denied its relevancy upon the point of actual damages.

[132] *California:* Chamberlin *v.* Vance, 51 Cal. 75; Preston *v.* Frey, 91 Cal. 107,

if the truth is not pleaded in justification the plaintiff is not prepared to disprove the fact. Yet, on the other hand, if a general rumor already prevailed of the same tenor as the defendant's words, the latter would clearly not damage the plaintiff to so great a degree as if no such rumor prevailed. So far as any principle of the law of damages is concerned, therefore, the evidence should be received. If rejected, it should be upon the ground that the line of defense is not open under the pleadings.

By the great weight of authority, no evidence can be received of particular acts not charged in the defendant's words, nor of rumors of them, even though the charge was of a general bad character which the particular acts would tend to prove; [133] but in a few cases the defendant has been allowed to prove particular forms of wrongdoing of the same char-

27 Pac. 533; Edwards *v.* San Jose Printing, etc., Co., 99 Cal. 431, 34 Pac. 128, 37 Am. St. Rep. 70; Davis *v.* Hearst, 116 Pac. 530.

Illinois: Young *v.* Bennett, 5 Ill. 43; Lehning *v.* Hewett, 45 Ill. 23; Strader *v.* Snyder, 67 Ill. 404.

Iowa: Marker *v.* Dunn, 68 Iowa, 720, 28 N. W. 38.

Massachusetts: Peterson *v.* Morgan, 116 Mass. 350; Mahoney *v.* Belford, 132 Mass. 393.

Missouri: Anthony *v.* Stephens, 1 Mo. 254.

Utah: Fenstermaker *v.* Tribune Pub. Co., 13 Utah, 532, 43 Pac. 112.

England: Scott *v.* Sampson, 8 Q. B. D. 491, 46 J. P. 408, 51 L. J. Q. B. 380, 46 L. T. Rep. (N. S.) 412, 30 Wk'ly Rep. 451; Saunders *v.* Mills, 6 Bing. 213; Waithman *v.* Weaver, 11 Price, 257, *n.* (See Earl of Leicester *v.* Walter, 2 Camp. 251; Mills *v.* Spencer, 1 Holt, 533.)

Ireland: Bell *v.* Park, 11 Ir. C. L. Rep. 413.

[133] *United States:* Sun Printing & Pub. Assoc. *v.* Schenck, 98 Fed. 925, 40 C. C. A. 163; Tribune Assoc. *v.* Follwell, 107 Fed. 646, 46 C. C. A. 526.

Alabama: Bradley *v.* Gibson, 9 Ala. 406.

Connecticut: Seymour *v.* Merrills, 1 Root, 459.

Illinois: Hosley *v.* Brooks, 20 Ill. 115, 71 Am. Dec. 252.

Indiana: Hallowell *v.* Guntle, 82 Ind. 554; Burke *v.* Miller, 6 Blackf. 155.

Iowa: Hanners *v.* McClelland, 74 Ia. 318.

Massachusetts: McLaughlin *v.* Cowley, 131 Mass. 70; Parkhurst *v.* Ketchum, 6 Allen, 406, 83 Am. Dec. 639.

Michigan: Randall *v.* Evening News Assoc., 97 Mich. 136, 56 N. W. 361.

New Hampshire: Lamos *v.* Snell, 6 N. H. 413.

New Jersey: Pier *v.* Speer, 73 N. J. L. 633, 64 Atl. 161.

New York: Willover *v.* Hill, 72 N. Y. 36; Wuensch *v.* Morning Journal Association, 4 App. Div. 110, 38 N. Y. Supp. 605; Dinkelspiel *v.* New York Evening Journal Pub. Co., 42 Misc. 74, 85 N. Y. Supp. 570.

North Carolina: Vick *v.* Whitfield, 2 Hayw. 222.

Ohio: Dewit *v.* Greenfield, 5 Oh. 225; Duval *v.* Davey, 32 Oh. St. 604.

acter as that charged,[134] or even entirely independent trans-
gressions; [135] and where the defendant's defamation involved
two charges, proof of the truth of one has been allowed to
diminish the amount of damages for the other.[136] These decisions are difficult to sustain on principle; for, as was pointed
out in the case of Sun Printing & Publishing Co. v. Schenck,[137]
it cannot diminish the injury sustained through defendant's
charge that the plaintiff's actual conduct was bad, so long as
his reputation remained good. It has been held in New York
that evidence of the plaintiff's reputation as a common libel-
ler may be shown in mitigation.[138]

In a case in the United States Circuit Court, it was said
that the high and established character of the plaintiff could
be shown in mitigation, since there was less chance of such a
character being injured.[139] This doctrine, if established,
would lead to the curious result that only a person of no
character at all, either good or bad, could resist the introduction of evidence by the defendant as to his character. Yet,
on the whole, the doctrine seems to be sound; and if so, either
party can introduce evidence of good or bad character, that
the jury, having all the facts, may the better estimate the
amount of damage.

§ 452. Truth.

Originally in slander under the general issue, the defendant
might avail himself of any defence. But it was decided in

Rhode Island: Folwell v. Providence
Journal Co., 19 R. I. 551, 37 Atl. 6.

South Carolina: Sawyer v. Eifert, 2
N. & McC. 511.

Vermont: Bowen v. Hall, 20 Vt.
232.

[134] New York: Heaton v. Wright, 10
How. Pr. 79.

Texas: Knapp v. Campbell, 14 Tex.
Civ. App. 199, 36 S. W. 765.

Virginia: Dillard v. Collins, 25
Gratt. 343.

So where defendant had charged
plaintiff with entering a house and
stealing, defendant was allowed to
show in mitigation that plaintiff had

entered the house to commit statutory
rape upon the owner's minor daughter.
O'Connor v. Press Pub. Co., 34 Misc.
564, 70 N. Y. Supp. 367.

[135] Brinkmann v. Taylor, 105 Fed.
773; Edwards v. Kansas City Times
Co., 32 Fed. 813.

[136] Maine: True v. Plumley, 36 Me.
466.

New York: Holmes v. Jones, 147 N.
Y. 59, 41 N. E. 409.

[137] 98 Fed. 925, 40 C. C. A. 163.

[138] Maynard v. Beardsley, 7 Wend.
(N. Y.) 560.

[139] Broughton v. McGrew, 39 Fed.
672.

England at an early day,[140] that if the defendant intended to justify, he should plead his justification, in order that the plaintiff might know what defence he was to meet. In New York it was held that if the defendant justified he admitted the malice, and could not resort to any defence based upon the absence of malice. So, mitigating circumstances having a tendency to prove the truth of the charge could not be given in evidence under the general issue in diminution of damages; but any circumstances which disprove malice, but do not tend to prove the truth of the charge, are admissible.[141] This rule, that facts tending to prove the truth of the charge cannot be shown in mitigation of damages, has been abrogated in New York by the Code of Procedure.[142] A similar relaxation of the rule obtains also in some other jurisdictions.[143] But in most of the cases the rule that nothing which tends to prove the truth of the charge can be received in mitigation, is adhered to.[144]

---

[140] Underwood v. Parks, Strange, 1200.

[141] Gilman v. Lowell, 8 Wend. 573.

[142] Code. Civ. Proc., § 535. Since that act the defendant may give in evidence any circumstances tending to disprove malice although they also tend to prove the charge. Bush v. Prosser, 11 N. Y. 347 (reversing s. c. 13 Barb. 221), and Bisbey v. Shaw, 12 N. Y. 67.

[143] *Alabama:* Advertiser Co. v. Jones, 53 So. 759 (see Scott v. McKinnish, 15 Ala. 662).

District of Columbia: Cooke v. O'Brien, 2 D. C. (2 Cr. C . C.) 17.

Florida: Jones v. Townsend, 21 Fla. 431.

Georgia: Ransone v. Christian, 49 Ga. 491 (but see Richardson v. Roberts, 23 Ga. 215).

Maryland: Wagner v. Holbrunner, 7 Gill, 296.

Michigan: Huson v. Dale, 19 Mich. 17, 2 Am. Rep. 66.

New York: Mattice v. Wilcox, 147 N. Y. 624, 42 N. E. 270; W. T. Hanson Co. v. Collier, 119 App. Div. 794, 104 N. Y. Supp. 787.

Vermont: Hutchinson v. Wheeler, 35 Vt. 330.

England: Knobell v. Fuller, Peake's Add. Cas. 139.

[144] *Connecticut:* Swift v. Dickerman, 31 Conn. 285 (see Bailey v. Hyde, 3 Conn. 463, 8 Am. Dec. 202).

Illinois: Storey v. Early, 86 Ill. 461; Nolte v. Herter, 65 Ill. App. 430.

Indiana: Abshire v. Cline, 3 Ind. 115.

Kentucky: Samuel v. Bond, Litt. Sel. Cas. 158 (*semble*).

Massachusetts: Alderman v. French, 1 Pick. 1; Brickett v. Davis, 21 Pick. 407.

New Hampshire: Knight v. Foster, 39 N. H. 576.

Pennsylvania: Updegrove v. Zimmerman, 13 Pa. 619; Stees v. Kemble, 27 Pa. 112; Smith v. Smith, 39 Pa. 441; Porter v. Botkins, 59 Pa. 484, 11 Am. Dec. 130.

Tennessee: Bank v. Bowdre, 92 Tenn. 723, 23 S. W. 131 (but see West v, Walker, 2 Swan, 32).

Virginia: Bourland v. Eidson, 8 Gratt. 27; McAlexander v. Harris, 6 Munf. 465.

In Indiana, although the same evidence is required to establish the plea of justification of slander, consisting in charging the plaintiff with a criminal offence, as would be necessary to convict him of the offence in a criminal prosecution,[145] evidence insufficient to establish the plea may be considered in mitigation of damages.[146]

§ 453. Retraction.

In an action of slander, a *recantation* of the slanderous charge may be admissible in evidence, in mitigation of damages;[147] and so too the publication of an exculpatory letter of the plaintiff's attorney.[148] A retraction must be in public, or in a mode to qualify the slander, in order to be of any avail.[149] And it must be so seasonable as really to lessen the damage. In Evening News Association v. Tryon [150] the court said: "After the libellous article has run its course, a retraction could in no sense mitigate the injury sustained. Indeed, at such a late day, a retraction would but revive the scandal and might be an aggravation rather than otherwise." Failure, despite reasonable opportunity, to publish a retraction has been deemed evidence upon the point of punitive damages.[151]

§ 454. Rule in Louisiana.

* It has been distinctly declared in Louisiana that no proof of damage is necessary to entitle the plaintiff to recover in

[145] Landis v. Shanklin, 1 Ind. 92; Shoulty v. Miller, 1 Ind. 544; Swails v. Butcher, 2 Ind. 84.
[146] Landis v. Shanklin, 1 Ind. 92; Shoulty v. Miller, 1 Ind. 544.
[147] *Alabama:* Bradford v. Edwards, 32 Ala. 628.
California: Taylor v. Hearst, 107 Cal. 262, 40 Pac. 392.
Georgia: Constitution Pub. Co. v. Way, 94 Ga. 120, 21 S. E. 139.
Illinois: Storey v. Wallace, 60 Ill. 51.
Indiana: White v. Sun Pub. Co., 164 Ind. 426, 73 N. E. 890.
Iowa: Hulbert v. New Nonpareil Co., 111 Iowa, 490, 82 N. W. 928.
Kentucky: Morgan v. Lexington

Herald Co., 138 Ky. 637, 128 S. W. 1064.
New York: Turton v. New York Recorder Co., 144 N. Y. 144, 38 N. E. 1009; Hotchkiss v. Oliphant, 2 Hill, 510.
Canada: Auburn v. Berthiaume, 23 Quebec Super. Ct. 476.
[148] Cass v. New Orleans Times, 27 La. Ann. 214.
[149] Kent v. Bonzey, 38 Me. 435.
[150] 42 Mich. 549, 550.
[151] *North Carolina:* Knott v. Burwell, 96 N. C. 272, 2 S. E. 588.
Pennsylvania: Clark v. North American Co., 203 Pa. 346, 53 Atl. 237.

actions of libel, and that the pecuniary damage is never the sole rule of assessment.[152] **

§ 455. Slander of title.

* It is also necessary to notice the action of slander of title of real estate. A false statement made maliciously with reference to the title to real estate, is a good cause of action; but the malice cannot be inferred from the falsehood: in order to recover substantial damages, they must be proved to have resulted from the false statement.[153] **

To maintain an action for slander of title to lands, the words spoken must not only be false, but they must be uttered maliciously, and be followed, as a natural and legal consequence, by a pecuniary damage to the plaintiff, which must be specially alleged and proved. Where the plaintiff, before the speaking of the words, had entered into a written contract with a third person, for the sale to him of the lands in relation to which the words were spoken; and the purchaser afterwards, in consequence of these words, having become dissatisfied with his purchase, the contract was, at his request, cancelled by the plaintiff, and part of the purchase-money which had been paid returned to him (the loss of a sale to that person being the only special damage alleged); it was held that the action could not be maintained; that the damages (if any) sustained by the plaintiff were the consequence of his own voluntary act, and not of the words spoken by the defendant.[154] And in Burkett v. Griffith [155] it was laid down that while a slanderer of title might be liable for a third party's failure to enter upon a contract, the latter's refusal to execute one gave rise to an action against himself alone. But for damage proximately caused by the falsehood, including injury to business [156] and the expenses of litigation, even, according to Chesebro v. Powers,[157] beyond taxable costs, the defendant is accountable.

---

[152] Daly v. Van Benthuysen, 3 La. Ann. 69; Levert v. Daily States Pub. Co., 123 La. 594, 49 So. 206; Jozsa v. Moroney, 125 La. 813, 51 So. 908.

[153] Brook v. Rawl, 4 Exch. 521; Pitt v. Donovan, 1 M. & S. 639; Malachy v. Soper, 3 Bing. N. C. 371.

[154] Kendall v. Stone, 5 N. Y. 14.

[155] 90 Cal. 532, 27 Pac. 527, 25 Am. St. Rep. 151, 13 L. R. A. 707.

[156] Ryan v. Hower Brewing Co., 13 N. Y. Supp. 660.

[157] 78 Mich. 472, 44 N. W. 290.

II.—MALICIOUS PROSECUTION AND FALSE IMPRISONMENT

§ 456. Malicious prosecution—Elements of damage.

We next consider a class of actions where the defendant wrongfully caused the arrest and imprisonment of the plaintiff, or otherwise maliciously set in motion the machinery of the law, to his damage. Where the defendant himself was concerned in the arrest, an action for false imprisonment lies; otherwise the action must be one of those actions upon the case, the gist of which is malice, such as malicious prosecution, malicious attachment, etc.; and first of malicious prosecution.

Three sorts of damage will support an action for a malicious indictment: first, to a man's fame; second, to his person, as where he is put in danger of losing his life, or limb, or liberty; third, to his property, as where he is forced to expend money to acquit himself of the crime charged.[158] It has been held in New York that the jury in this action cannot, upon the question of malice and in determining the amount of damages, take into consideration facts which establish against some of the defendants a case of false imprisonment, as such facts constitute a distinct cause of action, for which those defendants may be rendered liable in another suit.[159] It is intimated by Cockburn, C. J., that in estimating damages in an action for false imprisonment and malicious prosecution, the jury must consider not only the sufferings and loss of the plaintiff, but also the necessity which exists for the occasional prosecution of innocent persons in order to prevent the escape of criminals from justice.[160] If the observation of this very eminent judge be sound, it introduces into the rule of damages a principle neither based on the notion of compensation nor on those of example and punishment, and one which we think has never been distinctly recognized.

Compensatory damages could not properly be affected by evidence that plaintiff's wife was dead, and he had four children to support.[161]

[158] Savile *v.* Roberts, 1 Ld. Raym. 374.
[159] Carpenter *v.* Shelden, 5 Sand. (N. Y.) 77.
[160] Tulley *v.* Corrie, 16 L. T. R. N. S. 796.
[161] Reisan *v.* Mott, 42 Minn. 49, 43 N. W. 691.

§ 457. Physical injury.

Compensation may be recovered for injury to the person by being imprisoned upon the defendant's charge,[162] such as injury to the health.[163] So compensation may be recovered for being rendered insane by the imprisonment.[164] In a few jurisdictions it is held that the plaintiff cannot recover for any effects of imprisonment such as being confined in filthy or unhealthy quarters, and for physical suffering caused by cold, want of a bed, and deprivation of food, because these were the acts of persons over whom defendant had no control, and whose conduct he had no knowledge of and no occasion to anticipate.[165] But by the better doctrine the condition of the jail and the treatment of the prisoners in the ordinary course may be shown, since the circumstances of the imprisonment are the natural results of the prosecution.[166] But where the loss complained of is really remote from the prosecution damages cannot be recovered for it; as where plaintiff's name was entered in a book open to inspection, an indignity neither required by law nor by known custom.[167]

§ 458. Injury to feelings, reputation, and liberty.

Compensation may be recovered for the wrong and indig-

[162] *Arkansas:* Lavender *v.* Hudgens, 32 Ark. 763.
Massachusetts: Morrow *v.* Wheeler & W. Mfg. Co., 165 Mass. 349, 43 N. E. 105 (*semble*).
[163] *Indiana:* Lytton *v.* Baird, 95 Ind. 349.
New York: Fagnan *v.* Knox, 40 N. Y. Super. Ct. 41.
Wisconsin: Plath *v.* Braunsdorff, 40 Wis. 107.
[164] Plath *v.* Braunsdorff, 40 Wis. 107.
[165] *Connecticut:* Seidler *v.* Burns, (Conn.), 79 Atl. 53.
Pennsylvania: Zebley *v.* Storey, 117 Pa. 478, 12 Atl. 569 (in which the case of Abrahams *v.* Cooper, cited in the next note, was not referred to).
In *Iowa* the case of Flam *v.* Lee, 116

Iowa, 289, 90 N. W. 70, 93 Am. St. Rep. 242, has been cited as taking this view, but it is there held that the condition of the jail may be shown to enhance the damages though the defendant would not be responsible for intentional acts of abuse by the officers.
[166] *Iowa:* Flam *v.* Lee, 116 Ia. 289, 90 N. W. 70, 93 Am. St. Rep. 242.
Kansas: Drumm *v.* Cessnum, 61 Kan. 467, 59 Pac. 1078.
Pennsylvania: Abrahams *v.* Cooper, 81 Pa. 232.
Texas: San Antonio & A. P. Ry. *v.* Griffin, 20 Tex. Civ. App. 91, 48 S. W. 542.
Wisconsin: Spear *v.* Hiles, 67 Wis. 350, 30 N. W. 506.
[167] Garvey *v.* Wayson, 42 Md. 178.

nity,[168] and for injury to the reputation.[169]   In Michigan it has been said that the plaintiff could recover compensation for the loss of society of his family, injury to his fame, personal mortification and the smart and injury of the malicious arts and acts of oppression of the defendant.[170]   But where the plaintiff had been arrested for theft, he was not allowed to show that his name was entered in the detective's book, and publicity thus given to it, without showing that this was done in accordance with law, or that the defendant knew it would be done.[171]   Compensation may also be recovered for the deprivation of liberty [172] and for the risk of conviction,[173]

[168] *Arkansas:* Lavender *v.* Hudgens, 32 Ark. 763.

Delaware: Herbener *v.* Crossan, 4 Pennew. 38, 55 Atl. 223.

Indiana: Lytton *v.* Baird, 95 Ind. 349.

Maine: Tompson *v.* Mussey, 3 Me. 305.

Maryland: McWilliams *v.* Hoban, 42 Md. 56.

Oklahoma: Ten Cate *v.* Fansler, 10 Okla. 7, 65 Pac. 375.

[169] *United States:* Blunk *v.* Atchison, T. & S. F. R. R., 38 Fed. 311; Ambs *v.* Atchison, T. & S. F. R. R., 114 Fed. 317.

Arkansas: Lavender *v.* Hudgens, 32 Ark. 763.

Delaware: Herbener *v.* Crossan, 4 Pennew. 38, 55 Atl. 223.

Indiana: Lytton *v.* Baird, 95 Ind. 349.

Michigan: Fine *v.* Navarre, 104 Mich. 93, 62 N. W. 142.

Nebraska: Miles *v.* Walker, 66 Neb. 728, 92 N. W. 1014.

New York: Sheldon *v.* Carpenter, 4 N. Y. 578; Fagnan *v.* Knox, 40 N. Y. Super. Ct. 41.

Oklahoma: Ten Cate *v.* Fansler, 10 Okla. 7, 65 Pac. 375.

South Dakota: Jackson *v.* Bell, 5 S. D. 257, 58 N. W. 671.

Washington: Jones *v.* Jenkins, 3 Wash. 17, 27 Pac. 1022.

To show injury to reputation, publication of the fact of prosecution in the newspapers may be shown. Cooney *v.* Chase, 81 Mich. 203, 41 N. W. 833. So may any comment on the prosecution by a newspaper. Minneapolis Threshing Mach. Co. *v.* Regier, 51 Neb. 402, 70 N. W. 934.

In *Texas,* however, it has been held that loss of reputation is not an element in compensatory damages, and can be shown only to affect the amount of exemplary damages. Curlee *v.* Rose, 27 Tex. Civ. App. 259, 65 S. W. 197.

[170] Hamilton *v.* Smith, 39 Mich. 222.

[171] Garvey *v.* Wayson, 42 Md. 178.

[172] *Delaware:* Herbener *v.* Crossan, 4 Pennew. 38, 55 Atl. 223.

Michigan: Hamilton *v.* Smith, 39 Mich. 222.

New York: Sheldon *v.* Carpenter, 4 N. Y. 578.

North Dakota: Merchant *v.* Piekle, 10 N. D. 48, 84 N. W. 574.

Oklahoma: Ten Cate *v.* Fansler, 10 Okla. 7, 65 Pac. 375.

Pennsylvania: Abrahams *v.* Cooper, 81 Pa. 232.

Contra, Shipman *v.* Fletcher, 20 D. C. 245, where it is held that the arrest is a separate cause of action, and is not caused by the prosecution.

[173] *Arkansas:* Lavender *v.* Hudgens, 32 Ark. 763.

and for the mental suffering and sense of humiliation,[174] and for the loss of social standing.[175]

§ 459. Pecuniary loss.

The pecuniary loss resulting from the prosecution may be recovered. So the plaintiff may get compensation for loss of credit and injury to his business.[176] The attorney's fees in the previous action can generally be recovered.[177] And it has been held that the plaintiff can recover the charges sustained by him in defending the original suit, in excess of his taxable costs.[178] In fact, the court usually says merely that the reasonable expense of defending the criminal action is recoverable.[179]

Pennsylvania: Abrahams v. Cooper, 81 Pa. 232.

[174] *United States:* Ambs v. Atchison, T. & S. F. R. R., 114 Fed. 317.

California: Shatto v. Crocker, 87 Cal. 629, 25 Pac. 921.

Iowa: Rule v. McGregor, 115 Ia. 323, 88 N. W. 814.

Montana: Martin v. Corscadden, 34 Mont. 308, 86 Pac. 33.

North Dakota: Merchant v. Piekle, 10 N. D. 48, 84 N. W. 574.

Oklahoma: Ten Cate v. Fansler, 10 Okla. 7, 65 Pac. 375.

South Dakota: Jackson v. Bell, 5 S. D. 257, 58 N. W. 671.

Washington: Jones v. Jenkins, 3 Wash. 17, 27 Pac. 1022.

The plaintiff may therefore show that he was arrested in the presence of his family. Flam v. Lee, 116 Ia. 289, 90 N. W. 70, 93 Am. St. Rep. 242.

The prolongation of the mental suffering during a continuance of the criminal case for the purpose of enabling the present plaintiff to prepare his defense may be shown, as that was the proximate result of the prosecution. Cramer v. Barmon, 136 Mo. App. 653, 118 S. W. 1179.

[175] *United States:* Ambs v. Atchison, T. & S. F. R. R. 114 Fed. 317.

Iowa: Flam v. Lee, 116 Ia. 289, 90 N. W. 70, 93 Am. St. Rep. 242.

[176] *Illinois:* Lawrence v. Hagerman, 56 Ill. 68.

Oklahoma: Ten Cate v. Fansler, 10 Okla. 7, 65 Pac. 375.

South Dakota: Jackson v. Bell, 5 S. D. 257, 58 N. W. 671.

Wisconsin: Magmer v. Renk, 65 Wis. 364.

[177] *Arkansas:* Harr v. Ward, 73 Ark. 437, 84 S. W. 496.

Illinois: Krug v. Ward, 77 Ill. 603.

Indiana: Walker v. Pittman, 108 Ind. 341, 9 N. E. 175.

Minnesota: Mitchell v. Davies, 51 Minn. 168, 53 N. W. 863 (if value is proved).

North Dakota: Kolka v. Jones, 6 N. D. 461, 71 N. W. 558, 66 Am. St. Rep. 615 (if proved to be reasonable).

Texas: Hurlbut v. Boaz, 4 Tex. Civ. App. 371, 23 S. W. 446.

Contra, however, in the Federal courts. Stewart v. Sonneborn, 98 U. S. 187, 25 L. ed. 116.

[178] Closson v. Staples, 42 Vt. 209.

[179] *United States:* Blunk v. Atchison, T. & S. F. R. R., 38 Fed. 311; Ambs v. Atchison, T. & S. F. R. R., 114 Fed. 317.

Arkansas: Lavender v. Hudgens, 32 Ark. 763; Harr v. Ward, 73 Ark. 437, 84 S. W. 496.

Delaware: Herbener v. Crossan, 4 Pennew. 38, 55 Atl. 223.

The loss of the plaintiff's time is also an element of recovery,[180] but not profits as such, although their average amount may be considered by the jury as a fact tending to show the magnitude of the injury.[181]

§ 460. Mitigation.

Evidence of the plaintiff's bad character is admissible in mitigation of damages.[182] In Georgia the advice of counsel is of itself no defence to an action of malicious prosecution; but, if given *bona fide*, it is a circumstance to be considered on the question of probable cause and in mitigation of damages.[183] But in Illinois it seems that advice of counsel is a defence, and it has been held that the advice of a detective may be shown in mitigation.[184]

It may be shown in mitigation of damages that the plain-

Kansas: Drumm *v.* Cessnum, 61 Kan. 467, 59 Pac. 1078.

Massachusetts: Wheeler *v.* Hanson, 161 Mass. 370, 37 N. E. 382, 42 Am. St. Rep. 408.

Michigan: Hamilton *v.* Smith, 39 Mich. 222.

Minnesota: Hlubek *v.* Pinske, 84 Minn. 363, 87 N. W. 939.

New York: Sheldon *v.* Carpenter, 4 N. Y. 578; Fagnan *v.* Knox, 40 N. Y. Super. Ct. 41.

South Dakota: Jackson *v.* Bell, 5 S. D. 257, 58 N. W. 671.

Texas: Hurlbut *v.* Boaz, 4 Tex. Civ. App. 371, 23 S. W. 446.

In Mitchell *v.* Davies, 51 Minn. 168, 53 N. W. 863, it was held that no evidence of such expenses could be introduced until the reasonable value was proved; but in Blazek *v.* McCartin, 106 Minn. 461, 119 N. W. 215, it was said that "the Mitchell case proceeds along technical lines, and should not be extended."

In Aldrich *v.* Island E. T. & T. Co. (Wash.), 113 Pac. 264, it was held that while the expense of defending the criminal suit may be recovered, the expense of obtaining a transcript of the evidence in that suit may not be.

The plaintiff had already been discharged and the prosecution ended when that expense was incurred.

[180] *United States:* Blunk *v.* Atchison, T. & S. F. R. R., 38 Fed. 311; Ambs *v.* Atchison, T. & S. F. R. R., 114 Fed. 317.

Michigan: Hamilton *v.* Smith, 39 Mich. 222.

South Dakota: Jackson *v.* Bell, 5 S. D. 257, 58 N. W. 671.

Texas: Hurlbut *v.* Boaz, 4 Tex. Civ. App. 371, 23 S. W. 446.

Washington: Jones *v.* Jenkins, 3 Wash. 17, 27 Pac. 1022.

Anticipated loss of time in the future from failure to obtain employment cannot ordinarily be recovered, as it could not be proved with sufficient certainty. Missouri, K. & T. Ry. *v.* Groseclose, 50 Tex. Civ. App. 525, 110 S. W. 477.

[181] Sturgis *v.* Frost, 56 Ga. 188.

[182] *Illinois:* Rosenkrans *v.* Barker, 115 Ill. 331.

Maine: Fitzgibbon *v.* Brown, 43 Me. 169.

Massachusetts: Bacon *v.* Towne, 4 Cush. 217.

[183] Fox *v.* Davis, 55 Ga. 298.

[184] Hirsch *v.* Feeney, 83 Ill. 548.

tiff voluntarily surrendered himself to the officer and was really never arrested at all, except in a technical sense; since this shows that no damages should be allowed for the ignominy and disgrace of arrest.[185]

§ 461. False imprisonment—loss of time.

The action for false imprisonment lies, as has been seen, where the defendant himself made the arrest. It is not necessary to the maintenance of this action that there has been a real or pretended arrest; it also lies where the plaintiff was restrained of his liberty, without any pretence that it was done in pursuance of legal authority. The plaintiff in this action may recover for his loss of time,[186] and the interruption to his business,[187] or loss of employment.[188]

§ 462. Bodily and mental suffering.

The plaintiff may recover compensation for the bodily and mental suffering caused by the imprisonment,[189] and for the

[185] Chatfield v. Bunnell, 59 Conn. 511, 37 Atl. 1074.

[186] United States: Jay v. Almy, 1 W. & M. 262.
Delaware: Petit v. Colmery, 4 Pennew. 266, 55 Atl. 344.
District of Columbia: Kilbourn v. Thompson, McA. & M. 401.
Louisiana: Wentz v. Bernhardt, 37 La. Ann. 636.
Massachusetts: Morgan v. Curley, 142 Mass. 107.
Mississippi: Hewlett v. Ragsdale, 68 Miss. 703, 9 So. 885, 13 L. R. A. 682.
Missouri: State v. Evans, 83 Mo. App. 301.
Pennsylvania: Duggan v. Baltimore & O. R. R., 159 Pa. 248, 28 Atl. 182, 39 Am. St. Rep. 672; Mihalyik v. Klein, 22 Pa. Super. Ct. 193.
Texas: Hays v. Creary, 60 Tex. 445; Gold v. Campbell (Tex. Civ. App.), 117 S. W. 463.
Virginia: Parsons v. Harper, 16 Gratt. 64; Bolton v. Vellines, 94 Va. 393, 26 S. E. 847, 64 Am. St. Rep. 373.

[187] District of Columbia: Kilbourn v. Thompson, McA. & M. 401.
Pennsylvania: Duggan v. Baltimore & O. R. R., 159 Pa. 248, 28 Atl. 182, 39 Am. St. Rep. 672; Butler v. Stockdale, 19 Pa. Super. Ct. 98; Mihalyik v. Klein, 22 Pa. Super. Ct. 193.
See Texas: Gold v. Campbell (Tex. Civ. App.), 117 S. W. 463.

[188] Wentz v. Bernhardt, 37 La. Ann. 636.

[189] Alabama: Shannon v. Simms, 146 Ala. 673, 40 So. 574.
California: Neves v. Costa, 5 Cal. App. 111, 89 Pac. 860, 865; Gomez v. Scanlon, 155 Cal. 528, 102 Pac. 12.
Delaware: Petit v. Colmery, 4 Pennew. 266, 55 Atl. 344.
Indiana: Golibart v. Sullivan, 30 Ind. App. 428, 66 N. E. 188.
Iowa: Young v. Gormley, 120 Ia. 372, 94 N. W. 922.
Kentucky: Johnson v. Collins, 89 S. W. 253, 28 Ky. L. Rep. 375.
Massachusetts: Paine v. Kelley, 197 Mass. 22, 83 N. E. 8.

indignity,[190] and humiliation, shame and disgrace.[191] Evidence may be given of the circumstances of plaintiff's family as bearing on the mental suffering resulting from the imprisonment.[192] So compensation may be recovered for the deprivation of liberty.[193]

§ 463. Expense of release.

The expense of obtaining release from imprisonment may be recovered.[194] So costs actually paid in the former action and

Michigan: Ross v. Leggett, 61 Mich. 445.
Missouri: State v. Evans, 83 Mo. App. 301.
New Jersey: Cone v. Central R. R., 62 N. J. L. 99, 40 Atl. 780.
Pennsylvania: Duggan v. Baltimore & O. R. R., 159 Pa. 248, 28 Atl. 182, 39 Am. St. Rep. 672; Butler v. Stockdale, 19 Pa. Super. Ct. 98.
Texas: Hays v. Creary, 60 Tex. 445; Coffin v. Varila, 8 Tex. Civ. App. 417, 27 S. W. 956; Gold v. Campbell (Tex. Civ. App.), 117 S. W. 463.
Virginia: Parsons v. Harper, 16 Gratt. 64; Bolton v. Vellines, 94 Va. 393, 26 S. E. 847, 64 Am. St. Rep. 373.
So recovery may be had for impairment of health. Johnson v. Collins, 89 S. W. 253, 28 Ky. L. R. 375.
For nervous prostration. Bailey v. Warner, 118 Fed. 395, 55 C. C. A. 329.
Publication of the facts in a newspaper may be shown to enhance damages: Scott v. Flowers, 50 Neb. 675, 84 N. W. 81.
[190] *California:* Gomez v. Scanlan, 155 Cal. 528, 102 Pac. 12.
Massachusetts: Morgan v. Curley, 142 Mass. 107, 7 N. E. 726.
Missouri: State v. Evans, 83 Mo. App. 301.
Virginia: Bolton v. Vellines, 94 Va. 393, 26 S. E. 847, 64 Am. St. Rep. 373.
[191] *California:* Neves v. Costa, 5 Cal. App. 111, 89 Pac. 860; Gomez v. Scanlan, 155 Cal. 528, 102 Pac. 12.

Delaware: Petit v. Colmery, 4 Pennew. 266, 55 Atl. 344.
Indiana: Harness v. Steele, 159 Ind. 286, 64 N. E. 875; Golibart v. Sullivan, 30 Ind. App. 428, 66 N. E. 188.
Iowa: Young v. Gormley, 120 Iowa, 372, 94 N. W. 922.
Mississippi: Hewlett v. Ragsdale, 68 Miss. 703, 9 So. 885, 13 L. R. A. 682.
Missouri: State v. Evans, 83 Mo. App. 301.
New York: Ball v. Horrigan, 19 N. Y. Supp. 913.
Pennsylvania: Duggan v. Baltimore & O. R. R., 159 Pa. 248, 28 Atl. 182, 39 Am. St. Rep. 672; Butler v. Stockdale, 19 Pa. Super. Ct. 98.
Utah: Vanderberg v. Connoly, 18 Utah, 112, 54 Pac. 1097.
[192] Fenelon v. Butts, 53 Wis. 344.
[193] *District of Columbia:* Kilbourn v. Thompson, McA. & M. 401.
Utah: Vanderberg v. Connoly, 18 Utah, 112, 54 Pac. 1097.
[194] *California:* Neves v. Costa, 5 Cal. App. 111, 89 Pac. 860.
Delaware: Petit v. Colmery, 4 Pennew. 266, 55 Atl. 344.
Louisiana: Wentz v. Bernhardt, 37 La. Ann. 636.
Mississippi: Hewlett v. Ragsdale, 68 Miss. 703, 9 So. 885, 13 L. R. A. 682.
Pennsylvania: Duggan v. Baltimore & O. R. R., 159 Pa. 248, 28 Atl. 182, 39 Am. St. Rep. 672.
Utah: Vanderberg v. Connoly, 18 Utah, 112, 125, 54 Pac. 1097.

properly alleged are recoverable.[195] And in Wisconsin it is held that under a proper averment, counsel fees in procuring the plaintiff's discharge may be recovered if the plaintiff was liable for them, although they had not been actually paid.[196] "Where a party," said Erle, C. J., in the case of Bradlaugh v. Edwards,[197] "has been illegally imprisoned, and has been put to expense in procuring his discharge, he may very well urge that fact before the jury as an aggravation, but he has no *right* to demand to be reimbursed *ex debito justitiæ.*" And the court refused to grant a new trial, which was demanded on the ground that the plaintiff had incurred an expense of £7 14s. in procuring his discharge from custody at a police station where he had been detained on a charge of assault which proved unfounded. It has been held, however, in New York, in an action for false imprisonment, that the plaintiff may recover damages for the time spent, and expenses incurred, in procuring his discharge upon habeas corpus, where the application for the discharge was not palpably unnecessary. It does not appear, from the opinion, that these damages were specially alleged.[198] So where the plaintiff, who had been committed to jail for manslaughter, by a coroner's warrant, was afterwards admitted to bail, and subsequently got the inquisition under which he had been committed quashed, it was held, in an action against the coroner for false imprisonment, in which was alleged as special damage that plaintiff had been obliged to pay money in procuring his discharge from

Virginia: Parsons v. Harper, 16 Gratt. 64; Bolton v. Vellines, 94 Va. 393, 26 S. E. 847, 64 Am. St. Rep. 737.

Even where a valid debt was paid to secure a discharge from the unlawful imprisonment, the amount so paid may be recovered. Taylor v. Coolidge, 64 Vt. 506, 24 Atl. 656.

Expenses incurred after the imprisonment has ceased, as in defending the prosecution commenced by the illegal imprisonment, should not be recovered, as these expenses were not caused by the imprisonment. Worden v. Davis, 108 N. Y. Supp. 221, 123 App. Div. 193.

But see Gold v. Campbell, 117 S. W. 463, (Tex. Civ. App.).

[195] Pritchett v. Boevey, 1 Cr. & M. 775.

[196] Bonesteel v. Bonesteel, 30 Wis. 511.

[197] 11 C. B. (N. S.) 377, 384.

[198] Blythe v. Tompkins, 2 Abb. Pr. 468. But in another case in New York it was held that fees paid to an attorney for getting rid of an illegal arrest were special damages, and must be laid in the declaration. Strang v. Whitehead, 12 Wend. 64.

custody, that he was entitled to recover the costs of quashing the inquisition.[199]

§ 464. Consequential damages.

In an action of false imprisonment, the defendant had given the plaintiff into custody on a charge of felony. The magistrate heard the charge, and remanded the prisoner. It subsequently appearing that the charge had been made under a mistake, the plaintiff was released. The declaration charged the first arrest and the remand as distinct acts of trespass, and damages were given for both, although the latter was the act of the magistrate, on the ground that the wrongdoer was responsible for it as the consequence of his wrongful act; but this was held erroneous, and a new trial was granted, on the ground that the defendant was not responsible for the act of the magistrate.[200] This decision must be supported, if at all, upon the particular facts of the case. The natural consequences of the arrest are subjects of compensation, and the remand may surely be a natural result of the arrest. By the better view, the condition of the jail in which the plaintiff is confined and the circumstances of the imprisonment may be shown to enhance the damages, as the confinement is a proximate consequence of the original imprisonment.[201] So compensation may be recovered for having been manacled and compelled to labor in common with other prisoners.[202]

[199] Foxall v. Barnett, 2 E. & B. 928.

[200] Lock v. Ashton, 12 Q. B. 871. The decision perhaps turns on the form of action; the court suggesting that consequential damages should be recovered in case, not in trespass. See to the same effect Lyden v. McGee, 16 Ont. 105.

[201] *Alabama:* Fuqua v. Gambill, 140 Ala. 464, 37 So. 235.

California: Miller v. Fano, 134 Cal. 103, 66 Pac. 183.

District of Columbia: Kilbourn v. Thompson, MacA. & M. 401.

Mississippi: Hewlett v. Ragsdale, 68 Miss. 703, 9 So. 885, 13 L. R. A. 682.

Texas: San Antonio & A. P. Ry. v. Griffin, 20 Tex. Civ. App. 91, 48 S. W.

542; Southwestern P. C. Co. v. Reitzen (Tex. Civ. App.), 135 S. W. 237.

Wisconsin: Fenelon v. Butts, 53 Wis. 344, 10 N. W. 501.

Contra, in *New York*, on the ground that the subsequent detention and circumstances of the imprisonment are not chargeable to the defendant. Baker v. Secor, 4 N. Y. Supp. 303; Newman v. N. Y., L. E. & W. R. R., 54 Hun, 335, 7 N. Y. Supp. 560.

Plaintiff cannot recover compensation for injury to his feelings by reason of a mock trial held by his fellow prisoners in jail. Southwestern P. C. Co. v. Reitzen (Tex. Civ. App.) 135 S. W. 237.

[202] McCall v. McDowell, Deady, 233.

So it was held in Illinois that the defendant, who secured the plaintiff's arrest, must compensate him for being taken into another county and confined in a filthy jail.[203]   And where a seaman was wrongfully imprisoned in a foreign port by his master, and his vessel sailed without him, he was allowed compensation for the loss of his effects and the cost of his passage home.[204]   A publication in a newspaper of a fair account of the arrest is a proximate consequence for which recovery may be had,[205] and so is an illness, such as nervous prostration, caused by the arrest.[206]

On the other hand, no compensation can be recovered for a remote consequence of the arrest, or one that was avoidable. So where the plaintiff might have procured his discharge by giving a bond, as he could easily have done, he cannot recover for his subsequent confinement in jail; [207] and where a person illegally arrested on poor debtor process was discharged on his own recognizance, afterwards appeared, was examined, and took the poor debtor's oath, he was not allowed to recover the expense of the examination; his recognizance did not bind him, and the effect of the arrest was spent.[208]   Where plaintiff was arrested on a criminal process, but by subsequent abuse the officer became a trespasser *ab initio*, and plaintiff was discharged and the prosecution dropped, it was held that he could not recover for the injurious effect of the suppression of prosecution, but only for the effect of the arrest itself.[209] And where after an illegal arrest the plaintiff is again arrested legally, he is entitled to compensation only for the first arrest.[210]

§ 465. Aggravation.

An action of trespass being brought for false imprisonment, and a plea that the defendant had committed a felony being put in, it was held not to be a misdirection, that the judge

[203] Kindred *v.* Stitt, 51 Ill. 401.
[204] Jay *v.* Almy, 1 W. & M. 262.
[205] Filer *v.* Smith, 96 Mich. 347, 55 N. W. 999, 35 Am. St. Rep. 603.
[206] Bailey *v.* Warner, 118 Fed. 395, 55 C. C. A. 329.
[207] Yost *v.* Tracy, 13 Utah, 431, 45 Pac. 346.

[208] Lane *v.* Holman, 145 Mass. 221, 13 N. E. 602.
[209] Clark *v.* Tilton, 74 N. H. 330, 68 Atl. 335.
[210] *Michigan:* McCullough *v.* Greenfield, 133 Mich. 463, 95 N. W. 532, 62 L. R. A. 906.
Texas: Cabell *v.* Arnold (Tex. Civ. App.), 22 S. W. 62.

told the jury that the putting of such a plea on the record was a persisting in the charge contained in it, and was to be taken into account by them in estimating the damages.[211] Plaintiff may not show the mere fact that he was a married man and has a family in aggravation of compensatory damages, as that does not affect the actual damage;[212] but he may show that the arrest was made in the presence of his family as increasing his mental suffering.[213]

§ 466. Mitigation.

It has been held in Pennsylvania, that in trespass against a constable for arresting and imprisoning the plaintiff on suspicion of a felony, the bad character of the plaintiff cannot be given in evidence in mitigation of damages.[214] The fact that the defendant was advised to make the arrest by an ignorant and inexperienced attorney may be considered in mitigation.[215] And generally the information under which the defendant acted may be shown as bearing on the question of intent.[216] Evidence of good faith and want of malice is not proper where exemplary damages are not claimed.[217] In an action to recover damages of the defendant for having illegally procured the plaintiff's arrest and imprisonment for discouraging enlistments, which was done by a Federal officer on the defendant's affidavit, the defendant was allowed to prove in mitigation that the plaintiff had in fact discouraged enlistments.[218] It was held in Prentiss v. Shaw,[219] in an action

[211] Warwick v. Foulkes, 12 M. & W. 507.

[212] Young v. Gormley, 120 Iowa, 372, 94 N. W. 922.

[213] Bergeron v. Peyton, 106 Wis. 377, 82 N. W. 291, 80 Am. St. Rep. 33.

[214] Russell v. Shuster, 8 W. & S. 308.

[215] Mortimer v. Thomas, 23 La. Ann. 165.

[216] *United States:* Barnes v. Viall, 6 Fed. 661 (mistaken computation of time).

Alabama: Sanders v. Davis, 153 Ala. 375, 44 So. 979 (good faith).

Maine: Palmer v. Maine Cent. R. R., 92 Me. 399, 42 Atl. 800, 69 Am. St.

Rep. 513, 44 L. R. A. 673 (unreasonable and suspicious conduct of plaintiff).

Michigan: Livingston v. Burroughs, 33 Mich. 511.

Wisconsin: Grace v. Dempsey, 75 Wis. 313, 43 N. W. 1127 (good faith).

[217] *Kansas:* Comer v. Knowles, 17 Kan. 436.

Wisconsin: Fenelon v. Butts, 53 Wis. 344, 10 N. W. 501.

Such circumstances may of course be shown in mitigation of exemplary damages. Petit v. Colmary, 4 Pennew. (Del.) 266, 55 Atl. 344.

[218] Roth v. Smith, 54 Ill. 431.

[219] 56 Me. 427.

for an unlawful arrest, that the declarations of a plaintiff prior to the arrest and tending to provoke it, could not be admitted to reduce his compensation for the actual injury, but were admissible to mitigate the damages for the indignity and the punitive damages. During the Civil War the plaintiff, having publicly and indecently exulted at the assassination of the President of the United States, was arrested pursuant to a general order of the defendant, who commanded a military department. The order was illegal, but was issued without malice, and was intended as a means of preserving the public peace. The plaintiff was held not entitled to exemplary damages. On the other hand, the provocation of his language was allowed in mitigation.[220] And evidence that the plaintiff went to jail voluntarily may be admitted for the same purpose.[221] Where the arrest was upon a charge which involved damage to reputation, it may be shown that plaintiff had frequently been charged with the same offence before the arrest, as that fact tends to diminish the injury to the reputation.[222]

III.—OTHER MALICIOUS TORTS

§ 467. Malicious attachment.

An action lies for maliciously attaching the plaintiff's property. In Alabama it has been decided that in an action for wrongfully and vexatiously suing out an attachment auxiliary to the main suit to enable the plaintiff to obtain a lien on property for the satisfaction of whatever judgment he might recover, the costs incurred in defending the original suit constitute no part of the plaintiff's damages;[223] though the counsel fees in the suit may be proven and considered by the jury.[224] Nor can expenses incurred in attending or damages for loss of time incurred in defending the principal suit be recovered.[225] The measure of damages is said to be the actual loss from being deprived of use of property, injury to it, and expenses incurred in defending attachment proceedings.[226]

[220] McCall v. McDowell, Deady, 233.
[221] Yost v. Tracy, 13 Utah, 431, 45 Pac. 346.
[222] Texas M. R. R. v. Dean, 98 Tex. 517, 85 S. W. 1135.

[223] White v. Wyley, 17 Ala. 167.
[224] Marshall v. Betner, 17 Ala. 832.
[225] Craddock v. Goodwin, 54 Tex. 578.
[226] Boatwright v. Stewart, 37 Ark. 614.

Where wheat wrongfully attached advanced considerably in value pending the proceeding, but at the time of its redelivery to the defendant in the attachment had declined to about the price it bore when the process was levied, it was held that he could not recover the difference between its highest market value pending the attachment and its value at the time of the redelivery, without proof that he could or would have sold it at the advanced rate.[227] Where, however, bonds and notes belonging to a bank were wrongfully attached, and declined in value pending the attachment, the defendants were held liable for the actual loss resulting from the sale at a price lower than would have been realized but for the attachment.[228] So, in Mississippi, the depreciation in the value of wheat pending an attachment was held to be the measure of damages for the wrongful suing out of the attachment.[229] In this action evidence of the plaintiff's profits alleged to be lost by injury to his credit has been admitted, not as a measure of damages, but as an ingredient in the cause, or to guide the discretion of the jury.[230] Damages for destruction of business may be recovered.[231] A shopkeeper has been allowed, where his goods had been wrongfully attached, to recover for loss of business during the time it was suspended, and evidence was admitted as to the value of the use of such goods where the amount received per day was stated.[232] Where, in Louisiana,

[227] Meshke v. Van Doren, 16 Wis. 319.
[228] Horn v. Bayard, 11 Rob. (La.) 259.
[229] Fleming v. Bailey, 44 Miss. 132.
In Pratt v. Hampe, 114 Iowa, 237, 86 N. W. 292, an action for the malicious attachment of sweet potatoes in the ground not matured at the time of the attachment, and not dug or marketed until after the attachment was released, it was held that the measure of damages was the difference in value of the crop as it lay in the ground at the time of the attachment and at the time it was released; but query as to this, because it would seem that no use could have been made of the crop until after the release of the attachment, and if the crop had deteriorated in value during that time it would not

have been by reason of the attachment, but from some other cause.
[230] Donnell v. Jones, 17 Ala. 689.
[231] *Massachusetts:* Zinn v. Rice, 161 Mass. 571, 37 N. E. 747.
Michigan: Haynes v. Knowles, 36 Mich. 407.
It was said in Reidhar v. Berger, 8 B. Mon. (Ky.) 160, that these could only be recovered in an action on the case, and not in an action on the attachment bond. See, further, Wallace v. Finberg, 46 Tex. 35.
In Brown v. Master, 104 Ala. 451, 16 So. 443, damages were allowed for closing plaintiff's store and for unlawfully detaining the attached goods.
[232] Alexander v. Jacoby, 23 Oh. St. 358.

an attachment against a vessel was released on the execution
of a mortgage on her by her master, which mortgage was void
by the laws of the State, and pending the suit in which the
attachment was issued the vessel passed into the hands of
bona fide purchasers, but was not registered in the custom-
house, and there was no record evidence of the change of
ownership, and after final judgment decreeing her to be liable
she was again seized by her attaching creditors, but released
in four days without being delayed in the prosecution of her
next voyage, it was held in an action by the owners for the
wrongful seizure that they were entitled to nominal damages
only.   The court said that they had no cause to complain
that they were called to make proof of ownership in a thing
apparently bound for the claim of the seizing creditor.[233]

It has been held that compensation may be recovered for injury to the feelings.[234]

Recovery may be had for the proximate consequences of
the malicious attachment, as for the suing out of other attachments.[235] But in an action for malicious garnishment of wages,
plaintiff cannot recover compensation for being discharged
from his employment because of the attachment,[236] nor in
an action for the malicious garnishment of money can plaintiff recover for loss of business caused by his want of the
money to pay the expenses of the business.[237]

§ 468.[a] Malicious prosecution of a civil suit.

When an action is allowed to lie for the malicious prosecution of a civil suit against the plaintiff, compensation may be
recovered for the pecuniary loss;[238] but generally that is all
that can be recovered, since there was no imprisonment of
the plaintiff.[239] The expenses incurred by the present plain-

[a] For § 468 of the eighth edition,
see §§ 486a, 486c.

[233] Hunter v. Bennett, 15 La. Ann.
715.

[234] Friel v. Plumer, 69 N. H. 498, 43
Atl. 618, 76 Am. St. Rep. 189.

Contra, Trawisk v. Martin-Brown
Co., 79 Tex. 460, 14 S. W. 564.

[235] Grimes v. Bowerman, 92 Mich.
258, 52 N. W. 751.

[236] Cooper v. Scyoc, 104 Mo. App.
414, 79 S. W. 751.

[237] O'Neill v. Johnson, 53 Minn. 439,
55 N. W. 601, 39 Am. St. Rep. 615.

[238] *Kentucky:* Woods v. Finnell, 13
Bush, 628.

Wisconsin: Magmer v. Renk, 65 Wis.
364.

[239] In *Louisiana*, however, in an
action for the malicious prosecution

tiff in the maliciously prosecuted proceeding may be recovered; [240] and where the process involved deprivation of the use of property compensation may be recovered for that loss. [241] In a proper case, damages may also be recovered for injury to credit and reputation. [242]   In Sonneborn v. Stewart, [243] it was said that in an action for maliciously instituting bankruptcy proceedings compensation might be recovered for the actual damage to the defendant's goods, and damages for the breaking up of his business and destruction of his credit.

§ 469. Enticement of servant.

In the action for enticing a servant from his employment, it was said that the general rule of damages is the value of the servant's time during the period he was in the defendant's employment; but that, in cases of aggravation, the jury may give the whole value of the servant; [244] this, however, referred rather to slaves than to servants.   In a case of this kind in Illinois, for enticing a registered servant, it was held that the plaintiff was entitled to recover the value of the services

of an action of ejectment, it was held that plaintiff might recover for mortification, mental distress and humiliation. Deslonde v. O'Hern, 39 La. Ann. 14, 1 So. 286.

[240] *United States:* Sonneborn v. Stewart, 2 Woods, 599 (bankruptcy; but see the same case on appeal, Stewart v. Sonneborn, 98 U. S. 187).

Georgia: Slater v. Kimbro, 91 Ga. 217, 18 S. E. 296, 44 Am. St. Rep. 19.

Indiana: Whitesell v. Study, 37 Ind. App. 429, 76 N. E. 1010 (personal action).

New York: Gerken v. Ruppert, 33 Misc. 382, 67 N. Y. Supp. 589 (replevin).

In an action for malicious prosecution of garnishment proceedings it appeared that plaintiff, instead of appearing in those proceedings himself, sent an agent to answer for him; while the court held that a garnishee could not answer by agent but must appear personally. It was held that the cost of the answer by agent would not be

allowed in this action.   Cornell v. Payne, 115 Ill. 63, 3 N. E. 718.

[241] *Colorado:* Lord v. Guyot (Colo.), 70 Pac. 683 (property tied up by attachment).

Georgia: Farrar v. Brackett, 86 Ga. 463, 12 S. E. 686 (plaintiff dispossessed of mill); Slater v. Kimbro, 91 Ga. 217, 18 S. E. 296, 44 Am. St. Rep. 19 (plaintiff dispossessed of boarding-house).

Ohio: Newark Coal Co. v. Upson, 40 Ohio St. 17 (injunction against mining).

In Gerken v. Ruppert, 33 Misc. 382, 67 N. Y. Supp. 589, a suit for the malicious prosecution of a replevin action, damages for the wrongful taking having already been recovered in the replevin suit could not be recovered again in this action.

[242] Lord v. Guyot, (Colo.), 70 Pac. 683.

[243] 2 Woods, 599.

[244] Dubois v. Allen, Anthon's N. P. 128.

lost up to the time of the commencement of the suit, the reasonable expenses necessarily incurred in getting the servant back again, and damages for the loss of time, trouble, and injury sustained until the commencement of the suit; and that, if the plaintiff lost the entire service in consequence of the defendant's act, then he was entitled to the value of the term of service.[245] So it has been held that the reasonable expenses of searching for an abducted child may be recovered by the parent.[246] And where the enticement was at the time the servants were engaged in getting in a crop, recovery may be had for damage to the crop caused by lack of hands to get it in.[247]

§ 470. Consequential damages.

In an action on the case for enticing the plaintiff's servants (who were not hired by the plaintiff for a limited or constant period, but worked by the piece), by inviting them to dinner, and inducing them to sign an agreement not to work for him; it being proved that the plaintiff, a pianoforte maker, realized about £800 per annum by the sale of his instruments, the jury found a verdict for £1,600. The plaintiff was nearly, if not absolutely, ruined. On a motion for a new trial, it was insisted that, as the men worked by the piece, each of them was justified in leaving the plaintiff when he had completed the work in hand; and that, in point of fact, the plaintiff could only be entitled to recover damages for the half-day for which his workmen accepted the defendant's invitation. The court refused to interfere on the ground that the damages were excessive; and Richardson, J., said: "The measure of damages he is entitled to receive from the defendant is not necessarily to be confined to the servants he might have in his employ at the time they were so enticed, or for that part of the day on which they absented themselves from his service, but he is entitled to recover damages for the loss he sustained by their leaving him at that critical period."[248] So where the defendant entices away the farm hand of the plaintiff, the

[245] Hays v. Borders, 6 Ill. 46.
[246] Rice v. Nickerson, 9 All. 478.
[247] McCutchin v. Taylor, 11 Lea (Tenn.), 259.
[248] Gunter v. Astor, 4 Moore, 12.

latter may recover the expense of an unsuccessful attempt to replace him, and the net profits made by men of fair business capacity out of the labors of such a hand during the period for which the hand was hired.[249]

§ 470a. Maliciously procuring discharge or other breach of contract.

In an action for maliciously procuring the discharge of the plaintiff, all damages may be recovered which the plaintiff could have recovered if he had been wrongfully discharged by his master, including compensation for loss of time.[250] But even if the plaintiff could not have sued his master, as for instance if the employment was at will, he may nevertheless recover substantial damages against one who maliciously procures his discharge.[251]

And so for maliciously procuring the breach of any contract the measure of damages is ordinarily the same as it would be in an action for breach of the contract itself.[252]

§ 470b. Conspiracy.

In an action for conspiracy in restraint of trade, the plaintiff may recover his loss of profits and also the diminution in value of his property by the conspiracy.[253] And in general the measure of damages in an action for a conspiracy is what the plaintiff lost as a result of the conspiracy. So where one employed a broker to sell his land, and the broker got an offer of a cash price and certain other lots of land, but the broker and others conspired to defraud the seller by keeping him ignorant of the fact that land was offered in exchange, and as a result of the conspiracy he sold his land for the cash payment, while the defendants got title to the other land offered in exchange, the measure of damages was the value of such land, since the plaintiff would have got it but for the

[249] Lee v. West, 47 Ga. 311; Smith v. Goodman, 75 Ga. 198.

[250] *Missouri:* Lally v. Cantwell, 40 Mo. App. 44.

New York: Connell v. Stalker, 20 Misc. 423, 45 N. Y. Supp. 1048.

[251] Chipley v. Atkinson, 23 Fla. 206, 1 So. 934, 11 Am. St. Rep. 367.

[252] Knickerbocker Ice Co. v. Gardiner Dairy Co., 107 Md. 556, 69 Atl. 405.

[253] Bratt v. Swift, 99 Wis. 579, 75 N. W. 411.

defendant's conspiracy.[254] And in an action for conspiracy to procure from a corporation a contract to construct buildings for it at a high price, the difference between the price asked and the real price to be divided between an officer of the corporation and the other conspirators, where the conspiracy succeeded, the contract was made and performed and the price paid, the measure of damages was the excess of the contract price over the real cost of the work.[255]

IV.—SEDUCTION AND ALIENATION OF AFFECTION

§ 471. Seduction.

* The common-law action of case, by the father or master, for seducing a daughter or female servant, is one of a peculiar character. It is eminently a legal fiction: the demand is based upon the mere loss of service; but the damages are very much at large, and in the discretion of the jury. It is very curious to see how the practice of giving damages beyond the mere value of the service has grown up. As late as the latter part of the 18th century, in a case tried before Mr. Justice Chambre, the action being brought by the father for the seduction of his natural daughter, the judge charged the jury that they must consider the female merely in the character of a servant, and award the plaintiff compensation for the loss of service only.[256] In the year 1800, Lord Eldon, then chief justice of the Common Pleas, in an action tried before him, told the jury that they were to look, not merely to the loss of service, but to the *wounded feelings* of the party.[257] In 1805, Lord Ellenborough, in a case before him, told the jury that "damages might be given for the loss which the father sustained by being deprived of the *society* and *comfort* of his child, and by the *dishonor* which he receives." [258] And finally, the same learned judge on a motion to set aside an inquisition in a case of seduction, on the ground of excessive damages, said that this proceeding was one *sui generis*, where, in estimating the damages, the parental feelings and the feelings of those who

[254] Emmons v. Alvord, 177 Mass. 466, 59 N. E. 126.
[255] St. Paul Distilling Co. v. Pratt, 45 Minn. 215, 47 N. W. 789.
[256] Selwyn's Nisi Prius, 7th ed., 1116.
[257] See note to Andrews v. Askey, 8 C. & P. 7.
[258] See same note.

stood in *loco parentis*, had always been taken into consideration; and although it was difficult to conceive on what legal
principles the damages could be extended ultra the injury
arising from the loss of service, yet the practice was now
inveterate, and could not be shaken.[259] "The action for seduction," says the Supreme Court of New York, "is peculiar,
and would seem to form an exception to the rule that actual
damages only can be recovered when the action is for loss of
service consequential upon a direct injury; but there the party
directly injured cannot sustain an action, and the rule of damages has always been considered as founded upon special
reasons only applicable to it." [260]   In a case brought by the
mother, in 1837, Tindal, Chief Justice of the English Common Pleas, directed the jury that they might give damages
for the *distress* and *anxiety* of the plaintiff.[261] As to the right
of recovery, however, the English cases adhere to the original
idea on which the action is founded.   So, if there is no proof
of loss of service whatever, there can be no relief.[262] So, although the defendant be guilty of the seduction, but the jury
are of opinion that the child is not his, the plaintiff cannot
recover.[263]   In other words, without some damage to the
plaintiff or master, occasioned by the illness of the female,
and resulting from the illicit intercourse, the plaintiff is without relief.**

§ 472. Damages governed by legal rules.

* Where the jury were directed, or supposed they were directed, that damages might be given for bringing up the child,
the fruit of the illicit connection, the Supreme Court of New
York granted a new trial, on the ground that the plaintiff,
the master, was under "no legal obligation to support and
educate the child; that he could not be compelled to appro-
priate the proceeds of the verdict to that purpose; and that
the verdict would not afford the defendant any exemption
from his liability to provide for the child, when called on in
the regular course of the law." [264]   This, in effect, declares

[259] Irwin *v.* Dearman, 11 East, 23.
[260] Whitney *v.* Hitchcock, 4 Den.
461.
[261] Andrews *v.* Askey, 8 C. & P. 7.

[262] Grinnell *v.* Wells, 7 M. & G. 1033.
[263] Eager *v.* Grimwood, 1 Ex. 61.
[264] *New York:* Hitchman *v.* Whitney,
9 Hun, 512.

that the damages are to be measured by strict legal rules, or at least asserts the principle already stated, that even in cases of aggravation, where it appears that the jury did not intend to give vindictive, but only compensatory damages, and on that point were wrongly instructed, such course will be taken as to restrict the compensation within legal limits.[265] **

§ 473. General rule.

In an action for the seduction of his daughter, the father, or one who stands in his place, recovers not only for the actual loss of his daughter's services and the medical expenses of her illness,[266] but also for his wounded feelings and affections,[267] his sense of shame, humiliation and disgrace,[268] for the wrong done him in his social and family relations,[269] and for the

Vermont: Haynes *v.* Sinclair, 23 Vt. 108.

But see *England:* Terry *v.* Hutchinson, L. R. 3 Q. B. 599, 9 B. & S. 487.

[265] Sargent *v.* ———, 5 Cow. 106. See, also, Edmondson *v.* Machell, 2 T. R. 4.

[266] *Arkansas:* Simpson *v.* Grayson, 54 Ark. 404, 16 S. W. 4, 26 Am. St. Rep. 52.

Illinois: Garretson *v.* Becker, 52 Ill. App. 255.

Indiana: Pruitt *v.* Cox, 21 Ind. 15.

New Jersey: Coon *v.* Moffitt, 3 N. J. L. 436; Middleton *v.* Nichols, 62 N. J. L. 636, 43 Atl. 575.

New York: Akerley *v.* Haines, 2 Cai. 292; Hogan *v.* Cregan, 6 Robt. 138.

West Virginia: Riddle *v.* McGinnis, 22 W. Va. 253.

One not a parent, but standing *in loco parentis*, recovers damages of the same character as a parent. Tittlebaum *v.* Boehmcke (N. J.), 80 Atl. 323.

[267] *Delaware:* Herring *v.* Jester, 2 Houst. 66.

Georgia: Kendrick *v.* McCrary, 11 Ga. 603.

Illinois: Garretson *v.* Becker, 52 Ill. App. 255.

Indiana: Pruitt *v.* Cox, 21 Ind. 15; Felkner *v.* Scarlet, 29 Ind. 154; Taylor *v.* Shelkett, 66 Ind. 297.

Massachusetts: Hatch *v.* Fuller, 131 Mass. 574.

New Hampshire: Lunt *v.* Philbrick, 59 N. H. 59.

New Jersey: Coon *v.* Moffitt, 3 N. J. L. 436; Middleton *v.* Nichols, 62 N. J. L. 636, 43 Atl. 575.

Pennsylvania: Hornketh *v.* Barr, 8 S. & R. 36.

Virginia: Clem *v.* Holmes, 33 Gratt. 722.

For a father's loss of the comfort and consolation in the virtue of his daughter, and for the loss of hope in her future. Barbour *v.* Stephenson, 32 Fed. 66.

[268] *Arkansas:* Simpson *v.* Grayson, 54 Ark. 404, 16 S. W. 4, 26 Am. St. Rep. 52.

Illinois: Garretson *v.* Becker, 52 Ill. App. 255.

New Jersey: Middleton *v.* Nichols, 62 N. J. L. 636, 43 Atl. 575.

West Virginia: Riddle *v.* McGinnis, 22 W. Va. 253.

[269] *Delaware:* Herring *v.* Jester, 2 Houst. 66.

Oregon: Parker *v.* Monteith, 7 Ore. 277.

Virginia: Clem *v.* Holmes, 33 Gratt. 722.

stain and dishonor brought on the family.[270] And in order
to estimate such injuries, the general good character of the
plaintiff's family may be shown.[271]

§ 474. Exemplary damages.

As a general rule, exemplary damages may always be given.[272]
Even where the relation of master and servant exists by convention only, as where the plaintiff's daughter is of age, the
recovery will not necessarily be restricted to compensatory
damages.[273] Nor although the statute authorizes the daughter
to sue in her own name, will they be thus restricted in an action
brought by the father.[274]

§ 475. Aggravation.

Evidence of the pecuniary condition of both plaintiff and
defendant has been held admissible, not for the purpose of
ascertaining how much the defendant can pay, but how much
the plaintiff has been injured.[275] Evidence of an abortion

[270] *Delaware:* Herring *v.* Jester, 2 Houst. 66.

Georgia: Kendrick *v.* McCrary, 11 Ga. 603.

Illinois: Mighell *v.* Stone, 175 Ill. 261, 51 N. E. 906; Garretson *v.* Becker, 52 Ill. App. 255.

Indiana: Felkner *v.* Scarlet, 29 Ind. 154; Taylor *v.* Shelkett, 66 Ind. 297.

Kentucky: Wilhoit *v.* Hancock, 5 Bush, 567.

New Jersey: Coon *v.* Moffitt, 3 N. J. L. 436; Middleton *v.* Nichols, 62 N. J. L. 636, 43 Atl. 575.

Oregon: Parker *v.* Monteith, 7 Ore. 277.

Pennsylvania: Hornketh *v.* Barr, 8 S. & R. 36.

Virginia: Clem *v.* Holmes, 33 Gratt. 722.

Canada: Paterson *v.* Wilcox, 20 Up. Can. C. P. 385.

[271] *Oregon:* Parker *v.* Monteith, 7 Ore. 277.

Pennsylvania: Wilson *v.* Sproul, 3 Pen. & W. 49.

West Virginia: Riddle *v.* McGinnis, 22 W. Va. 253.

[272] *Illinois:* Ball *v.* Bruce, 21 Ill. 161.

New York: Bartley *v.* Richtmyer, 4 N. Y. 38, 44; Ingersoll *v.* Jones, 5 Barb. 661.

England: Edmondson *v.* Machell, 2 T. R. 4; Irwin *v.* Dearman, 11 East, 23.

[273] Lipe *v.* Eisenlerd, 32 N. Y. 229; Badgley *v.* Decker, 44 Barb. 577.

[274] Stevenson *v.* Belknap, 6 Ia. 97.

[275] *Delaware:* Herring *v.* Jester, 2 Houst. 66.

Illinois: White *v.* Murtland, 71 Ill. 250.

North Carolina: McAulay *v.* Birkhead, 13 Ind. 28; so to affect exemplary damages.

Virginia: Clem *v.* Holmes, 33 Gratt. 722.

Wisconsin: Lavery *v.* Crooke, 52 Wis. 612.

But *contra:*

Michigan: Watson *v.* Watson, 53 Mich. 168.

New York: Dain *v.* Wycoff, 7 N. Y. 191.

produced by the defendant is not inadmissible on the ground that the damages it tends to prove are too remote.[276] It has been held that in this action no evidence can be given as to any promise of marriage, either with reference to the right of action or measure of damages; the remedy for the breach of that contract belonging to the female in her own name.[277] Thus, in the King's Bench, Lord Ellenborough said: "The daughter may be asked whether the defendant paid his addresses to her in an honorable way; further than that you can on no account go." [278] So in New York, in such a case, it has been held incorrect to admit this description of evidence, whether the judge instructs the jury that they may give damages for the seduction and also for the breach of the promise, or whether he admits it only to prove the seduction, but not to enhance the damages.[279]

§ 476. Mitigation.

Proof of indifference on the plaintiff's part, in affording opportunities of criminal intercourse between his daughter and the defendant, may be admitted in mitigation of damages,[280] but not of a seeming insensibility on the part of the father to his daughter's disgrace.[281] Nor is it competent for the defendant to show that the daughter consented willingly to the seduction, nor even that she, in fact, seduced the defendant, her consent not depriving the plaintiff of his right of action.[282] But the unchastity of the daughter previous to the defendant's act will mitigate the damages, and may reduce them to mere compensation for loss of service and expense of lying in.[283] Nor can an offer to marry the female

---

[276] *Illinois:* Whiter v. Murtland, 71 Ill. 250.

Wisconsin: Klopfer v. Bromme, 26 Wis. 372.

[277] Whitney v. Elmer, 60 Barb. 250. *Contra,* Parker v. Monteith, 7 Ore. 77.

[278] Dodd v. Norris, 3 Camp. 519. See, also, Tullidge v. Wade, 3 Wils. 18.

[279] Foster v. Scoffield, 1 Johns. 297; Clark v. Fitch, 2 Wend. 459; Gillet v. Mead, 7 Wend. 193. See, also, Brown-

ell v. M'Ewen, 5 Denio, 367; Wells v. Padgett, 8 Barb. 323.

[280] Zerfing v. Mourer, 2 Greene (Ia.), 520.

[281] Bolton v. Miller, 6 Ind. 262.

[282] McAulay v. Birkhead, 13 Ired. 28.

[283] *Arkansas:* Simpson v. Grayson, 54 Ark. 404, 16 S.W. 4, 26 Am. St. Rep. 52.

Michigan: Stoudt v. Shepherd, 73 Mich. 588, 41 N. W. 696.

New York: Akerley v. Haines, 2 Cai. 292; Hogan v. Cregan, 6 Robt. 138.

be given in evidence to mitigate the damages;[284] but actual marriage may be.[285] In an action for the seduction of the plaintiff's daughter, the defendant can show that the plaintiff was not, in fact, married to his reputed wife, as it shows that the plaintiff was not entitled to the services of his daughter.[286] A recovery by the daughter for the seduction, where such an action can be maintained, does not mitigate the damages recoverable by the father.[287]

§ 477. Action by party seduced.

Where the woman is allowed (by statute) to recover in her own name for seduction, the measure of her recovery is subject to the same rules. Thus a woman may recover for wounded feelings and dishonor,[288] for loss of social standing,[289] and for consequences such as pregnancy, childbirth, sickness, and the like.[290] Prior unchastity may be shown in mitigation;[291] and the pecuniary condition of the defendant may be shown.[292]

§ 478. Criminal conversation.

In the assessment of damages against a co-respondent in this action, the measure of damages is the value of the wife of whom the husband has been deprived.[293] This is the value of her services, conjugal aid, society, affection and comfort, less a sum represented by his obligation to clothe, support, cherish and care for her.[294] The wife's wealth is important only if it is shown that she was contributing from it toward the support of the family, thus relieving her husband from that amount of burden.[295] The husband may also recover for his suffering and dishonor.[296] So it has been said that the

[284] *Illinois:* White *v.* Murtland, 71 Ill. 250.
New York: Ingersoll *v.* Jones, 5 Barb. 661.
[285] Eichar *v.* Kistler, 14 Pa. 282.
[286] Howland *v.* Howland, 114 Mass. 517.
[287] Pruitt *v.* Cox, 21 Ind. 15.
[288] Simons *v.* Bushy, 119 Ind. 13.
[289] Hawn *v.* Banghart, 76 Ia. 683, 39 N. W. 251.
[290] McCoy *v.* Trucks, 121 Ind. 292.

[291] Stowers *v.* Singer, 24 Ky. L. Rep. 395, 68 S. W. 637.
[292] White *v.* Gregory, 126 Ind. 95, 25 N. E. 806.
[293] Cowing *v.* Cowing, 33 L. J. N. S. Prob. 149.
[294] Jenness *v.* Simpson, 81 Vt. 109, 78 Atl. 886.
[295] Jenness *v.* Simpson, 81 Vt. 109, 78 Atl. 886.
[296] *Illinois:* Browning *v.* Jones, 58 Ill. App. 597.

husband can recover more than nominal damages, even if
he had not lost the affection of his wife by the act, nor had
his family broken up, nor his domestic relations impaired.[297]
In a case at Nisi Prius, where the husband was unaware of
his wife's dishonor till she made the disclosure to him on her
dying bed, and he continued to treat her with great kindness
till her death, which occurred in the same month, Mr. Justice
Coleridge, while instructing the jury against the allowance
of vindictive damages, told them to give damages for the
shock to the husband's feelings and *the loss of his wife's society*
down to the time of her death.[298]   In Yundt *v.* Hartrunft [299]
Walker, C. J., said:
"The degradation which ensues, the distress and mental
anguish which necessarily follow, are the real causes of recovery.   It has not been the policy of the law to confine the
recovery by the injured party to the precise amount of money
which he has proved he has lost by the deprivation of labor
ensuing from the injury.   But the law has, in a more just
spirit, allowed a recovery for injury to family reputation and
anguish growing out of the injury.   Nor is it true that because
appellee was absent from home he therefore could have sustained no loss of service by reason of his wife being debauched.
He had a right to her services in the nurture of his children,
as well as a virtuous example to them by her.   He had the
right to the teachings of a virtuous, and not of a depraved
mother to his children.   If he intrusted their care to a virtuous
and undefiled mother, and appellant corrupted and debased
her, he thereby became liable to appellee for the neglect to
her family and her example to her children."

§ 479. Aggravation.

If the co-respondent's fortune was used by him as a means
of the seduction, it is said, in England, that it may be taken
into account, but not otherwise.[300]   In Peters *v.* Lake [301] it

Pennsylvania: Matheis *v.* Mazet, 164
Pa. 580, 30 Atl. 434.
  [297] Stumm *v.* Hummel, 39 Ia. 478.
  [298] Wilton *v.* Webster, 7 C. & P. 198.
  [299] 41 Ill. 9, 12.

  [300] Cowing *v.* Cowing, 33 L. J. (N. S.)
Prob. 149.
  [301] 66 Ill. 206.
  Acc., Matheis *v.* Mazet, 164 Pa. 580,
30 Atl. 434.

was held that evidence of the defendant's pecuniary ability was admissible as affecting the question of exemplary damages.

§ 480. Mitigation.

Proof of the ill-treatment of the wife by the husband before the criminal intercourse may be received in mitigation;[302] so may the fact that the plaintiff is dissolute and immoral;[303] or that the general character of the wife is bad.[304] In Conway v. Nicol[305] it was held proper to show that the wife, before her marriage, had given birth to a child; but this must be taken in connection with the fact that the defendant was the father of the child, and that the plaintiff's wife had been true to her marriage vows, except with the defendant. In Stumm v. Hummel[306] it was held competent to show, for the purpose of ascertaining the amount of damages, that the plaintiff's wife had, before marriage, lived in the defendant's family, when he had intercourse with her; and that he had induced her to marry the plaintiff on the ground that the latter would make a good husband, and that he (the defendant) would continue to have intercourse with her. It was also held that, if the wife's bad conduct was confined to her intimacy with the defendant, and the plaintiff was induced to marry her on his recommendation that she was a good girl, then her intercourse with the defendant before marriage could not be considered in mitigation of damages. It has been held competent to show, in mitigation of damages, that the plaintiff's wife was an actress; that he concealed his marriage from his wife's mother, and very seldom saw his wife, but suffered his wife to remain living with her mother as if

[302] *Indiana:* Coleman v. White, 43 Ind. 429.
Iowa: Dance v. McBride, 43 Ia. 624.
Massachusetts: Palmer v. Crook, 7 Gray, 418.
New Hampshire: Cross v. Grant, 62 N. H. 675, 13 Am. St. Rep. 607.
[303] *Illinois:* Browning v. Jones, 52 Ill. App. 597.
New Hampshire: Cross v. Grant, 62 N. H. 675, 13 Am. St. Rep. 607.

New York: Bennett v. Smith, 21 Barb. 439.
Or that the wife had lost her affection for her husband. Browning v. Jones, 52 Ill. App. 597.
[304] *Indiana:* Clouser v. Clapper, 59 Ind. 548.
New Hampshire: Sanborn v. Neilson, 4 N. H. 501.
[305] 34 Ia. 533.
[306] 39 Ia. 478.

she were a single woman, and allowed her to continue her theatrical performances in her maiden name.[307] And so connivance by the husband may be shown in mitigation.[308]

§ 480a. Alienation of affection of a wife.

In an action for alienation of the affection of a wife the husband may recover compensation for loss of the services, society, and comfort of the wife,[309] and for the injury to his feelings and affections, and to his family pride.[310] It may be shown in mitigation that the husband had abused his wife [311] and that she did not love him,[312] and had obtained a divorce since the defendant's wrongful act; [313] or that he had no affection for his wife, that his own immoral conduct and relations with other women established the fact, and that his violence and cruelty had driven her from his home.[314]

§ 480b. Alienation of affection of a husband.

In an action for alienation of the affection of a husband the wife may recover for the loss of her husband's society and of his support and maintenance,[315] and to establish the value of these items she may show his position in life, occupation, etc.[316] Having shown these things, she may recover the cost of her separate maintenance; and this without deducting the amount she may have made by her own services after the separation.[317] She may also recover for her mental anguish,

[307] Calcraft v. Earl of Harborough, 4 C. & P. 499.

[308] Sanborn v. Neilson, 4 N. H. 501.

[309] Hartpence v. Rogers, 143 Mo. 623, 45 S. W. 650; Modisett v. McPike, 74 Mo. 636.

The expense of her support should be subtracted from the value of her services. Rudd v. Rounds, 64 Vt. 432, 25 Atl. 438.

[310] *Alabama:* Long v. Booe, 106 Ala. 570, 17 So. 716.

Missouri: Hartpence v. Rogers, 143 Mo. 623, 632, 45 S. W. 650.

[311] *Kentucky:* Peck v. Taylor, 17 Ky. L. Rep. 1312, 34 S. W. 705.

New York: Millspaugh v. Potter, 62 App. Div. 521, 71 N. Y. Supp. 134.

[312] Millspaugh v. Potter, 62 App. Div. 521, 71 N. Y. Supp. 134.

[313] McNamara v. McAllister (Ia.), 130 N. W. 26.

[314] Allen v. Besecker, 55 Misc. 366, 105 N. Y. Supp. 416.

[315] *Kentucky:* Scott v. O'Brien, 129 Ky. 1, 110 S. W. 260.

Michigan: Rice v. Rice, 104 Mich. 371, 62 N. W. 833.

New York: Wilson v. Coulter, 29 App. Div. 85, 51 N. Y. Supp. 804.

[316] Bailey v. Bailey, 94 Iowa, 598, 606, 63 N. W. 341. It was also held in this case that she cannot show the defendant's wealth.

[317] Bowersox v. Bowersox, 115 Mich. 24, 72 N. W. 986.

mortification, and wounded feelings.[318] It may be shown in mitigation that the plaintiff did not love her husband or desire his affection,[319] or that she married him only because he was rich.[320] Her unfaithfulness to him may also be shown in mitigation, as it indicates that she did not feel affection for him.[321]

[318] *Kentucky:* Scott *v.* O'Brien, 129 Ky. 1, 110 S. W. 260.
Michigan: Rice *v.* Rice, 104 Mich. 371, 381, 62 N. W. 833.
[319] *California:* Humphrey *v.* Pope, 1 Cal. App. 374, 82 Pac. 223.

New York: Van Olinda *v.* Hall, 88 Hun, 452, 34 N. Y. Supp. 777.
[320] Derham *v.* Derham, 125 Mich. 109, 83 N. W. 1005.
[321] Wolf *v.* Frank, 92 Md. 138, 145, 48 Atl. 132.

CHAPTER XX

§ 481. General rule.

We now proceed to consider another class of cases, namely, actions for personal injuries. And here, too, though malice is not the gist of the action, the circumstances of the injury have much bearing upon the amount of loss, and matters of aggravation and mitigation become important. In actions for personal injury, therefore, much latitude is necessarily given the jury. The Supreme Court of California, in enlarging upon the sound and familiar rule that courts will not disturb the verdict in cases of personal tort, unless it is obviously not the result of cool and dispassionate deliberation, broadly declares that in such actions "the law does not attempt to fix any precise rules for the admeasurement of damages, but, from the necessity of the case, leaves their assessment to the good sense and unbiassed judgment of the jury." [1]

[1] Aldrich *v.* Palmer, 24 Cal. 513.
All the authorities are to the same effect:
Alabama: Southern Ry. *v.* McGowan, 149 Ala. 440, 43 So. 378.
Arkansas: Ward *v.* Blackwood, 48 Ark. 396, 3 S. W. 624.
California: Scally *v.* W. T. Garratt & Co. (Cal. App.), 104 Pac. 325.
Illinois: Scott *v.* Hamilton, 71 Ill. 126.
Indiana: Little *v.* Tingle, 26 Ind. 168.
Kansas: Salina M. & E. Co. *v.* Hoyne, 10 Kan. App. 579, 63 Pac. 660.

So the Supreme Court of the United States say that in these actions "there can be no fixed measure of compensation for the pain and anguish of body and mind, nor for the loss of time and care in business, or the permanent injury to health and body." [2] The damages are not, however, wholly at large, but must be controlled by the evidence. [3] The price at which one would voluntarily undergo pain and disfigurement is not the measure of recovery for such injury. [4] The damages for a personal injury in cases of simple trespass free from malice, or of simple negligence (where the rule seems to be the same), should, as far as a money standard is applicable, be such as to compensate the injured party for such loss of time, medical and other expenses, physical pain and mental distress, as are fairly and reasonably the plain consequences to him of the injury. [5] Where the health of the plaintiff, already impaired,

Maine: Wadsworth v. Treat, 43 Me. 163.

Massachusetts: Coffin v. Coffin, 4 Mass. 1; Com. v. Sessions of Norfolk, 5 Mass. 435.

Mississippi: Bell v. Gulf & C. R. R., 76 Miss. 71, 23 So. 268.

In Ackerson v. Erie R. R., 32 N. J. L. 254, it was suggested that for permanent injury the jury might multiply the annual loss by the probable duration of life; but this mathematical method was held improper in Denver v. Sherret, 88 Fed. 226, 31 C. C. A. 499.

[2] *United States:* Illinois C. R. R. v. Barron, 5 Wall. 90, 105, 18 L. ed. 591, per Nelson, J.

Louisiana; Armstrong v. Jackson, 37 La. Ann. 219.

Rhode Island: McGowan v. Interstate Consolidated St. R. R., 20 R. I. 264, 30 Atl. 497.

Virginia: Richmond R. & E. Co. v. Garthright, 92 Va. 627, 24 S. E. 267, 32 L. R. A. 220.

[3] *Georgia:* Davis v. Central R. R., 60 Ga. 329.

Iowa: Johnson v. Tillson, 36 Ia. 89.

Vermont: Drown v. New England Tel. & Tel. Co., 81 Vt. 358, 70 Atl. 599.

Plaintiff should recover the present

cash value of the injury. Coley v. North Carolina R. R., 128 N. C. 534, 542, 39 S. E. 43.

[4] *Kansas:* Union P. Ry. v. Milliken, 8 Kan. 647, per Brewer, J.

Pennsylvania: Dooner v. Delaware & H. C. Co., 164 Pa. 17, 30 Atl. 269; Willis v. Second Ave. Traction Co., 189 Pa. 430, 43 Atl. 1.

But while there can be no market value for pain and suffering, nor can damages be given from a sentimental or benevolent standpoint, the jury must find such reasonable sum as is a fair compensation for the injury. Schenkel v. Pittsburg & B. Tr. Co., 194 Pa. 182, 44 Atl. 1072.

[5] *United States:* Wade v. Leroy, 20 How. 34, 15 L. ed. 813; Vicksburg & M. R. R. v. Putnam, 118 U. S. 545, 30 L. ed. 257, 7 Sup. Ct. 1; Hanson v. Fowle, 1 Sawy. 539; Bowas v. Pioneer Tow Line, 2 Sawy. 21; Potts v. Chicago C. Ry., 33 Fed. 610; Saldana v. Galveston, H. & S. A. Ry., 43 Fed. 862.

Alabama: South & N. A. R. R. v. McLendon, 63 Ala. 266.

Arkansas: St. Louis, I. M. & S. R. R. v. Cantrell, 37 Ark. 519.

Colorado: Wall v. Cameron, 6 Colo. 275; Wall v. Livezay, 6 Colo. 465.

was further injured by the defendant, the measure of damages is compensation for the additional impairment of health, and for obstruction to recovery.[6] For any assault the plaintiff

Delaware: Wallace *v.* Wilmington & N. R. R., 8 Houst. 529, 18 Atl. 818.
Hawaii: Coffin *v.* Spencer, 2 Hawaii, 23.
Illinois: Peoria Bridge Association *v.* Loomis, 20 Ill. 235; Pierce *v.* Millay, 44 Ill. 189; Chicago & A. R. R. *v.* Wilson, 63 Ill. 167; Chicago *v.* Jones, 66 Ill. 349; Chicago *v.* Langlass, 66 Ill. 361; Chicago *v.* Elzeman, 71 Ill. 131; Sheridan *v.* Hibbard, 119 Ill. 307.
Indiana: Indianapolis *v.* Gaston, 58 Ind. 224.
Iowa: Lucas *v.* Flinn, 35 Ia. 9; Muldowney *v.* Illinois C. Ry., 36 Ia. 462; McKinley *v.* Chicago & N. W. Ry., 44 Ia. 314; Morris *v.* Chicago, B. & Q. R. R., 45 Ia. 29; Stafford *v.* Oskaloosa, 64 Ia. 251.
Kansas: Tefft *v.* Wilcox, 6 Kan. 46; Kansas P. Ry. *v.* Pointer, 9 Kan. 620; Missouri, K. & T. Ry. *v.* Weaver, 16 Kan. 456 (*semble*).
Kentucky: Central P. Ry. *v.* Kuhn, 86 Ky. 578; Carson *v.* Singleton, 65 S. W. 821, 23 Ky. L. Rep. 1626; Beavers *v.* Bowen, 80 S. W. 1165, 26 Ky. L. Rep. 291.
Louisiana: Donnell *v.* Sandford, 11 La. Ann. 645.
Maine: Mason *v.* Ellsworth, 32 Me. 271; Blackman *v.* Gardiner & P. Bridge, 75 Me. 214.
Maryland: Bannon *v.* Baltimore & O. R. R., 24 Md. 108.
Michigan: Huizega *v.* Cutler & S. Lumber Co., 51 Mich. 272; Power *v.* Harlow, 57 Mich. 107; Sherwood *v.* Chicago & W. M. Ry., 82 Mich. 374, 46 N. W. 773.
Mississippi: Memphis & C. R. R. *v.* Whitfield, 44 Miss. 466.
Missouri: West *v.* Forrest, 22 Mo. 344; Russell *v.* Columbia, 74 Mo. 480; Steiner *v.* Moran, 2 Mo. App. 47.

Nebraska: Chicago, B. & Q. R. R. *v.* Starmer, 26 Neb. 630.
Nevada: Quigley *v.* Central P. R. R., 11 Nev. 350; Cohen *v.* Eureka & P. R. R., 14 Nev. 376.
New York: Ransom *v.* New York & E. Ry., 15 N. Y. 415; Morse *v.* Auburn & S. Ry., 10 Barb. 621; Quinn *v.* Long Island R. R., 34 Hun, 331; Rown *v.* Christopher & T. S. R. R., 34 Hun, 471; Harding *v.* New York, L. E. & W. R. R., 36 Hun, 72; Keyes *v.* Devlin, 3 E. D. Smith, 518; Brignoli *v.* Chicago & G. E. R. R., 4 Daly, 182.
Oregon: Oliver *v.* North P. T. Co., 3 Ore. 84.
Pennsylvania: Pennsylvania & O. C. Co. *v.* Graham, 63 Pa. 290; Scott *v.* Montgomery, 95 Pa. 444.
Texas: Houston & T. C. Ry. *v.* Boehm, 57 Tex. 152.
Utah: Giblin *v.* McIntyre, 2 Utah, 384.
Virginia: Daingerfield *v.* Thompson, 33 Gratt. 136.
West Virginia: Wilson *v.* Wheeling, 19 W. Va. 323; Beck *v.* Thompson, 31 W. Va. 459, 7 S. E. 447, 13 Am. St. Rep. 870.
Wisconsin: Goodno *v.* Oshkosh, 28 Wis. 300; Stewart *v.* Ripon, 38 Wis. 584; Hulehan *v.* Green Bay, W. & S. P. R. R., 68 Wis. 520; King *v.* Oshkosh, 75 Wis. 517.
England: Phillips *v.* Southwestern Ry., 4 Q. B. D. 406.
But in Beach *v.* Hancock, 27 N. H. 223, 59 Am. Dec. 373, the jury were told to consider the effect of trivial damages in an action for assault and battery in encouraging disregard of law and disturbance of the public peace.
[6] *Georgia:* Bray *v.* Latham, 81 Ga. 640.
Plaintiff suffered two successive in-

may recover at least nominal damages,[7] but no more than nominal damages, if in fact there was no damage.[8]

§ 482. Loss of time.

Plaintiff who suffers a loss of time by reason of a personal injury may recover the value of the time lost.[9] It is often said that the plaintiff may recover for his loss of wages or of employment,[10] which is certainly much the same thing as

juries by the same defendant. Having already recovered damages for the first, which included damages for permanent injury, she now claimed damages from the second accident, including permanent injury to her earning power. It was held that she could not recover in the second action for anything that was caused by the first injury, but might recover where old injuries were increased or aggravated by the second accident. She cannot recover for disability to carry on profession where she has already recovered for such disability in the first action. If she was disabled in some other way and so incapacitated from doing something else that she could have done before the second and subsequent to the first accident, she might recover for that in the action for the second. Brooks v. Rochester Ry., 156 N. Y. 244, 50 N. E. 945.

[7] *Ante,* § 98.

[8] Shaffer v. Austin, 68 Kan. 234, 74 Pac. 1118.

[9] *Alabama:* Birmingham R. L. & P. Co. v. Wright, 153 Ala. 99, 44 So. 1037; Alabama Steel & Wire Co. v. Tallant, 165 Ala. 521, 51 So. 835.

Arkansas: St. Louis, I. M. & S. R. R. v. Cantrell, 37 Ark. 519, 40 Am. Rep. 105; Dunbar v. Cowger, 68 Ark. 444, 59 S. W. 951.

Delaware: File v. Wilmington City Ry., 80 Atl. 623; Coyle v. People's Ry., 80 Atl. 638.

Indiana: Cox v. Vanderkleed, 21 Ind. 164; Linton C. & M. Co. v. Persons, 11 Ind. App. 264, 39 N. E. 214;

Evansville H. & S. Co. v. Bailey, 43 Ind. App. 153, 84 N. E. 549; Whiteley M. C. Co. v. Wishon, 42 Ind. App. 517, 85 N. E. 832; Singer S. N. Co. v. Phipps (Ind. App.), 94 N. E. 793.

Iowa: Martin v. Murphy, 85 Ia. 669, 52 N. W. 662; Haden v. Sioux City & P. R. R., 92 Ia. 226, 60 N. W. 537.

Kentucky: Cross v. Illinois C. R. R., 33 Ky. L. Rep. 432, 110 S. W. 290; Louisville & N. R. R. v. Crow, 118 S. W. 365; Georgetown v. Groff, 136 Ky. 662, 124 S. W. 888; West Ky. C. Co. v. Davis, 138 Ky. 667, 128 S. W. 1074.

Missouri: Happy v. Prichard, 111 Mo. App. 6, 85 S. W. 655.

New Mexico: Schmidt v. Southwestern Brewery & Ice Co., 107 Pac. 677.

North Carolina: McCracken v. Smathers, 122 N. C. 799, 29 S. E. 354.

Oregon: Jones v. Peterson, 44 Ore. 161, 74 Pac. 661.

Pennsylvania: Goodhart v. Pennsylvania R. R., 177 Pa. 1, 35 Atl. 191, 55 Am. St. Rep. 705.

Texas: Houston E. Co. v. Seegar (Tex. Civ. App.), 117 S. W. 900.

[10] *Delaware:* Hendle v. Geiler, 50 Atl. 632; Heinel v. People's Ry., 6 Pennew. 428, 67 Atl. 173; Walls v. People's Ry., 80 Atl. 355; Tobias v. People's Ry., 80 Atl. 358.

Kentucky: Cincinnati, N. O. & T. P. Ry. v. Fortner, 113 S. W. 847.

Michigan: Abbott v. Detroit, 150 Mich. 245, 113 N. W. 1121.

Pennsylvania: Hawes v. O'Rielly, 126 Pa. 440, 17 Atl. 642.

loss of time; but, as was said by the Supreme Court of Massachusetts, "the wages which the plaintiff might have earned, if not injured, are not strictly recoverable; the value of his time, while prevented from working by reason of the negligence of the defendant, is a proper element to be considered in fixing the damages." [11]

In order to show the value of time lost plaintiff may show what plaintiff's trade or profession was, and the value of his services therein.[12] For that purpose the compensation he was receiving at the time of the injury may be shown.[13] If he has a trade the wages of which are greater than those he was receiving at the time of the accident, this may be proved as bearing on the value of his time;[14] but not matters having a remote bearing only, such as a political office held several years before,[15] or wages paid at a distant city.[16]

Where the butler of a London club brought his action against an architect employed to make repairs on the club-house, and his agents, and averred that they put in gas so negligently that it exploded, and crippled the plaintiff for life, and he was discharged for incapacity to perform the duties of his place, it was insisted for the plaintiff that the measure of damages was the amount of money which would be required to purchase an annuity for the plaintiff equal to the sum which he

[11] Sibley v. Nason, 196 Mass. 125, 81 N. E. 887.

[12] *Michigan:* Welch v. Ware, 32 Mich. 77.

Missouri: Griveaud v. St. Louis Cable & W. Ry., 33 Mo. App. 458, 466.

[13] *California:* Bonneau v. North Shore R. R., 152 Cal. 406, 93 Pac. 106.

Connecticut: Finken v. Elm City Brass Co., 73 Conn. 423, 47 Atl. 670.

Georgia: Broyles v. Prosock, 97 Ga. 643, 25 S. E. 389.

Illinois: Wabash Western Ry. v. Friedman, 146 Ill. 583, 30 N. E. 353, 34 ib. 1111; Illinois Steel Co. v. Ryska, 200 Ill. 280, 65 N. E. 734.

Missouri: Paul v. Omaha & S. L. Ry., 82 Mo. App. 500.

Oklahoma: Chicago, R. I. & P. Ry. v. Stibbs, 17 Okla. 97, 87 Pac. 293.

So he may prove a contract of employment, though not yet entered upon. Dunbar v. Cowger, 68 Ark. 444, 59 S. W. 951.

[14] *United States:* Northern Pac. Ry. v. Wendel, 156 Fed. 336, 84 C. C. A. 232.

Michigan: Sias v. Reed City, 103 Mich. 312, 61 N. W. 502.

Texas: Chicago, R. I. & T. Ry. v. Long, 26 Tex. Civ. App. 601, 65 S. W. 882.

[15] Houston & T. C. R. R. v. Gee, 27 Tex. Civ. App. 414, 66 S. W. 78.

[16] Omaha & R. V. R. R. v. Ryburn, 40 Neb. 87, 58 N. W. 541; Omaha & R. V. Ry. v. Chollette, 41 Neb. 578, 592, 59 N. W. 921.

was receiving from the club; but Lord Abinger ruled otherwise; and after commenting on the fact that neither party was in actual fault, said: "If it be asked that the jury are to give damages equal to an annuity, it may be demanded, what right has the plaintiff to calculate that he would have continued in office to the end of his life? I think it would be absurd to make the value of the annuity the measure of damages."[17] The plaintiff can recover the expense of hiring labor while unable to perform work which he, when well, performed himself,[18] but the expenses of living cannot be included in the damages in addition to the value of the plaintiff's time.[19]

§ 482a. Loss of business.

When a man engaged in business is injured, he is of course entitled to compensation for his loss of time resulting from the injury; and the nature and extent of his business may be shown as bearing on the value of his time.[20] If the injury caused not only loss of time, but also loss of profits of the business, this might be shown in a proper case.[21] This point is distinctly held in Hanover Railroad v. Coyle.[22] The plaintiff in that case was a peddler, and on the trial below offered to prove the nature and character of his business, the extent of his loss of time, also of the percentage on the goods sold by him in his usual course of business and the loss of interest

[17] Rapson v. Cubitt, 1 Car. & M. 64.
[18] Connecticut: Ashcraft v. Chapman, 38 Conn. 230.
Illinois: North Chicago St. R. R. v. Zeiger, 182 Ill. 9, 54 N. E. 1006, 74 Am. St. Rep. 157, 78 Ill. App. 463.
Iowa: Kendall v. Albia, 73 Iowa, 241, 34 N. W. 833.
Pennsylvania: Willis v. Second Ave. Tr. Co., 189 Pa. 430, 43 Atl. 1.
[19] Graeber v. Derwin, 43 Cal. 495.
[20] United States: Nebraska v. Campbell, 2 Black, 590, 17 L. ed. 271.
California: Union D. & Ry. v. Londoner, 114 Pac. 316.
Kansas: Chicago, R. I. & P. Ry. v. Scheinkoenig, 62 Kan. 57, 61 Pac. 414.
Michigan: Silsby v. Michigan Car Co., 95 Mich. 204, 54 N. W. 761.

Pennsylvania: McLean v. Pittsburg Railways, 230 Pa. 291, 79 Atl. 237.
[21] California: Castino v. Ritzman, 156 Cal. 587, 105 Pac. 739.
Pennsylvania: Wallace v. Pennsylvania R. R., 195 Pa. 127, 45 Atl. 685.
Wisconsin: Kinney v. Crocker, 18 Wis. 74.
But see Missouri: Paquin v. St. Louis & S. Ry., 90 Mo. App. 118, 128.
In Haas v. St. Louis & S. F. R. R., 128 Mo. App. 79, 106 S. W. 599, where plaintiff was paid a fixed salary and also a percentage on his sales, he was confined in his recovery to the loss of his fixed salary.
[22] 55 Pa. 396.

of money received for the same, in consequence of the injuries received, and the annual amount of sales made by him. The evidence was admitted against the objection of the defendant, who excepted. On error it was held by the Supreme Court that the evidence had been correctly admitted as bearing directly upon the question of damages, in affording a means of computing the plaintiff's loss for the time he was confined by his injuries, and prevented from carrying on his business. Of course, when damages are claimed for loss of business, and no proof is offered of the value of the business, no damages on that account can be given.[23]

Recovery can be had for loss of profits only when the profits were the result of the personal exertions of the injured person, not where they were the result of invested capital or of the good will of an established business; and evidence of the profits of the plaintiff's business can be given only when it is shown that such profits were the result of his personal efforts. The character of the business or occupation and of the income derived therefrom must determine the admissibility of such evidence in this class of actions. If the asserted loss consists of profits which are essentially the uncertain and fluctuating increment of invested capital, proof thereof is inadmissible, no matter how small it may be; and, conversely, if the loss is due to the destruction or impairment of one's personal earning capacity, the evidence thereof is not to be excluded simply because it may be large.[24] Where the facts disclose such a preponderance of the business element over the personal equation, or such an admixture of the two, that the question of personal earnings could not be safely or properly segregated from the returns upon capital invested, the income or profits from a business should not be considered[25] in deter-

[23] *Missouri:* Mannerberg v. Metropolitan St. Ry., 62 Mo. App. 563.
New Jersey: Mason v. Erie R. R., 75 N. J. Law, 521, 68 Atl. 105.
New York: Klein v. Second Avenue R. R., 54 N. Y. Super. Ct. 164.
[24] Gombert v. New York C. & H. R. R. R., 195 N. Y. 273, 88 N. E. 382.
[25] *United States:* Chicago, R. I. & P. Ry. v. Hale, 186 Fed. 626.

California: Lombardi v. California St. Ry., 124 Cal. 311, 57 Pac. 66.
Michigan: Silsby v. Michigan Car Co., 95 Mich. 204, 54 N. W. 761.
Missouri: Pryor v. Metropolitan St. R. R., 85 Mo. App. 367.
New York: Weir v. Union Ry., 188 N. Y. 416, 81 N. E. 168; Gombert v. New York C. & H. R. R. R., 195 N. Y. 273, 88 N. E. 382.

mining the amount of the damages to which the plaintiff is entitled. But where the investment of capital is insignificant, and a mere incident to the performance of personal services, recovery may be had for the loss of business earnings.[26] This general subject has been discussed at length in a previous chapter.[27]

§ 483. Medical expenses.

The medical expenses, including the cost of medicine and nursing, may always be recovered,[28] including such future expenses as can be proved with reasonable certainty.[29] The expenses may be recovered though they have not yet been

[26] *Colorado:* Rio Grande Western Ry. *v.* Rubenstein, 5 Colo. App. 121, 38 Pac. 76 (physician).
Georgia: Macon Ry. & L. Co. *v.* Mason, 123 Ga. 773, 51 S. E. 569 (dentist).
Iowa: Escher *v.* Carroll County, 146 Ia. 738, 125 N. W. 810 (farmer).
New Jersey: Schwartz *v.* North Jersey St. Ry., 66 N. J. Law, 437, 49 Atl. 676 (builder).
New York: Masterton *v.* Mt. Vernon, 58 N. Y. 391 (tea merchant); Kronold *v.* New York, 186 N. Y. 40, 78 N. E. 572 (importer of laces); Fraser *v.* Buffalo, 123 App. Div. 159, 108 N. Y. Supp. 127 (tailor).

[27] *Ante,* §§ 180, 181.

[28] *United States:* Beardsley *v.* Swann, 4 McLean, 333.
Alabama: Alabama Great Southern R. R. *v.* Siniard, 123 Ala. 557, 26 So. 689.
Arkansas: St. Louis, I. M. & S. R. R. *v.* Cantrell, 37 Ark. 519, 40 Am. Rep. 105.
Delaware: Heidelbaugh *v.* People's Ry., 6 Pennew. 209, 65 Atl. 587; Tobias *v.* People's Ry., 80 Atl. 358; File *v.* Wilmington C. Ry., 80 Atl. 623; Evans *v.* Wilmington C. Ry., 80 Atl. 634; Coyle *v.* People's Ry., 80 Atl. 638.
Indiana: Cox *v.* Vanderkleed, 21 Ind. 164.

Iowa: Martin *v.* Murphy, 85 Ia. 669, 52 N. W. 662.
Kentucky: Cross *v.* Illinois C. R. R., 33 Ky. L. Rep. 432, 110 S. W. 290; Louisville & N. R. R. *v.* Crow, 118 S. W. 365.
Massachusetts: McGarrahan *v.* New York, N. H. & H. R. R., 171 Mass. 211, 50 N. E. 610.
Michigan: Sherwood *v.* Chicago & W. M. Ry., 82 Mich. 374, 46 N. W. 773.
Missouri: Happy *v.* Prichard, 111 Mo. App. 6, 85 S. W. 655.
New Hampshire: Emery *v.* Boston & M. R. R., 67 N. H. 434, 36 Atl. 367.
New York: Metcalf *v.* Baker, 57 N. Y. 662; Sheehan *v.* Edgar, 58 N. Y. 631; Feeney *v.* Long Island R. R., 116 N. Y. 375, 22 N. E. 402, 5 L. R. A. 544.
North Carolina: Rushing *v.* Seaboard A. L. Ry., 149 N. C. 158, 62 S. E. 890.
Pennsylvania: Hayes *v.* O'Reilly, 126 Pa. 440, 17 Atl. 642.

[29] *Illinois:* Chicago C. Ry. *v.* Henry, 218 Ill. 92, 75 N. E. 758.
Pennsylvania: Baker *v.* Hagey, 177 Pa. 128, 35 Atl. 705, 55 Am. St. Rep. 712; Amos *v.* Delaware R. F. Co., 228 Pa. 362, 77 Atl. 12.
Washington: Webster *v.* Seattle R. & S. Ry., 42 Wash. 364, 85 Pac. 2.

paid, at least if the plaintiff has become liable for them.[30] But it is not enough to show the amount paid for medical expenses; it must also appear that the amount is a reasonable one.[31] If the plaintiff's living expenses were increased by the injury and the medical treatment, he may recover the amount of such increase.[32] The amount reasonably paid for going to a distant city for special medical treatment may be recovered.[33] Medical expenses may be recovered, though not specially named in the declaration.[34]

The authorities are in conflict as to whether the jury may find a value for medical services, the nature of them having been shown, without affirmative evidence of such value.[35] In many cases the jury are allowed to find the value of such services on their general knowledge,[36] while in other cases this power is denied.[37]

[30] *United States:* Denver & R. G. R. R. *v.* Lorentzen, 79 Fed. 291, 24 C. C. A. 592.
Alabama: Lunsford *v.* Walker, 93 Ala. 36, 8 So. 386.
California: Donnelly *v.* Hufschmidt, 79 Cal. 74.
Illinois: Chicago & E. R. R. *v.* Cleminger, 178 Ill. 536, 53 N. E. 320; Mueller *v.* Kuhn, 59 Ill. App. 353; Chicago & Alton R. R. *v.* Harrington, 77 Ill. App. 499; Wilson *v.* Chicago C. Ry., 144 Ill. App. 604.
Kansas: Abilene *v.* Wright, 4 Kan. App. 708, 46 Pac. 715; Hutchinson *v.* Van Cleve, 7 Kan. App. 676, 46 Pac. 715.
Missouri: Wilbur *v.* Southwest M. E. Ry., 110 Mo. App. 689, 85 S. W. 671.
Nebraska: Friend *v.* Ingersoll, 39 Neb. 717, 58 N. W. 281; Omaha St. Ry. *v.* Emminger, 57 Neb. 240, 77 N. W. 675.
South Carolina: Parker *v.* South Carolina & G. R. R., 48 S. C. 364, 382, 26 S. E. 669.
Utah: Wilson *v.* Southern Pacific Co., 13 Utah, 352, 360, 44 Pac. 1040, 57 Am. St. Rep. 766.

[31] *Nebraska:* Golder *v.* Lund, 50 Neb. 867, 70 N. W. 379.
New York: Gumb *v.* 23d St. Ry., 114 N. Y. 411, 21 N. E. 993; Meade *v.* Goldman, 129 N. Y. Supp. 899.
[32] *California:* Irrgang *v.* Ott, 9 Cal. App. 440, 99 Pac. 528.
Massachusetts: McGarrahan *v.* New York & N. H. R. R., 171 Mass. 211, 50 N. E. 610.
[33] *Michigan:* Sherwood *v.* Chicago & W. M. Ry., 82 Mich. 374, 46 N. W. 773.
Oklahoma: Ayers *v.* Macoughtry, 117 Pac. 1088 (Pasteur treatment).
South Carolina: Hart *v.* Charlotte, C. & A. R. R., 33 S. C. 427, 12 S. E. 9, 10 L. R. A. 794 (trip to healing springs).
[34] Folsom *v.* Underhill, 36 Vt. 580.
[35] *Ante,* § 171a.
[36] *Illinois:* Chicago & E. R. R. *v.* Holland, 122 Ill. 461, 13 N. E. 145.
Massachusetts: McGarrahan *v.* New York & N. H. R. R., 171 Mass. 211, 50 N. E. 610.
New York: Feeney *v.* Long Island R. R., 116 N. Y. 375, 22 N. E. 402, 5 L. R. A. 544. (See Gumb *v.* 23d St. R., 114 N. Y. 411, 21 N. E. 993).
[37] *Missouri:* Duke *v.* Missouri Pac. R. R., 99 Mo. 347, 12 S. W. 636.

By the better view the plaintiff may recover compensation for physician's or nurses' services even though such services were rendered gratuitously,[38] or for any other reason the plaintiff is not legally bound to pay for them.[39]

§ 484. Mental and physical suffering.

The plaintiff may recover for all suffering, both mental and physical, which results from the injury.[40] Future suffering

Nebraska: Friend *v.* Ingersoll, 39 Neb. 717, 727, 58 N. W. 281.

Pennsylvania: Brown *v.* White, 202 Pa. 297, 51 Atl. 962.

Texas: Fry *v.* Hillan (Tex. Civ. App.), 37 S. W. 359.

[38] Dean *v.* Wabash R. R., 229 Mo. 425, 129 S. W. 953.

Ante, § 67.

[39] So where the surgeon's bill is outlawed by the statute of limitations the plaintiff may recover the amount of it; he cannot be required to set up the statute of limitations for defendant's benefit, as a bar to an honest debt. Mueller *v.* Kuhn, 59 Ill. App. 353. But see *ante,* § 483, note 50.

[40] *United States:* Peterson *v.* Roessler & H. C. Co., 131 Fed. 156.

Alabama: Louisville & N. R. R. *v.* Binion, 107 Ala. 645, 18 So. 75; Alabama G. S. R. *v.* Bailey, 112 Ala. 167, 177, 20 So. 313; Birmingham R. L. & P. Co. *v.* Wright, 153 Ala. 99, 44 So. 1037.

Arkansas: St. Louis, etc., R. R. *v.* Cantrell, 37 Ark. 519, 40 Am. Rep. 105.

California: Zibbell *v.* Southern Pac. Co., 116 Pac. 513.

Delaware: Hendle *v.* Geiler, 50 Atl. 632; Heidelbaugh *v.* People's Ry., 6 Pennew. 209, 65 Atl. 587; Reiss *v.* Wilmington City Ry. — Pennew. —, 67 Atl. 153; Walls *v.* People's Ry., 80 Atl. 355; Tobias *v.* People's Ry., 80 Atl. 358; File *v.* Wilmington C. Ry., 80 Atl. 623; Ewans *v.* Wilmington C. Ry., 80 Atl. 634; Coyle *v.* People's Ry., 80 Atl. 638.

Illinois: Chicago, B. & Q. R. R. *v.*

Warner, 108 Ill. 538; Mueller *v.* Kuhn, 59 Ill. App. 353.

Indiana: Taber *v.* Hutson, 5 Ind. 322, 61 Am. Dec. 96; Elkhart *v.* Ritter, 66 Ind. 136; Evansville H. & S. Co. *v.* Bailey, 43 Ind. App. 153, 84 N. E. 549.

Iowa: Martin *v.* Murphy, 85 Iowa, 669, 52 N. W. 662.

Kansas: Ft. Scott, W. & W. Ry. *v.* Lightburn, 9 Kan. App. 642, 58 Pac. 1033.

Kentucky: Faulkner *v.* Davis, 18 Ky. L. Rep. 1004, 38 S. W. 1049; Dorris *v.* Warford, 100 S. W. 312, 20 Ky. L. Rep. 963, 9 L. R. A. (N. S.) 1090; Cross *v.* Illinois C. R. R., 33 Ky. L. Rep. 432, 110 S. W. 290; Louisville & N. R. R. *v.* Crow, — Ky. L. Rep. —, 118 S. W. 365; West Ky. C. Co. *v.* Davis, 138 Ky. 667, 128 S. W. 1074.

Louisiana: Donnell *v.* Sandford, 11 La. Ann. 645.

Maryland: Thillman *v.* Neal, 88 Md. 525, 42 Atl. 242; Zell *v.* Dunaway, 80 Atl. 215.

Michigan: Sherwood *v.* Chicago & W. M. Ry., 82 Mich. 374, 46 N. W. 773.

Mississippi: Hollinshed *v.* Yazoo & M. V. R. R., 55 So. 40.

Missouri: Stuppy *v.* Hof, 82 Mo. App. 272; Happy *v.* Prichard, 111 Mo. App. 6, 85 S. W. 655; Diel *v.* Ferguson (Mo. App.), 138 S. W. 545.

Montana: Hosty *v.* Moulton Water Co., 39 Mont. 310, 102 Pac. 568.

New Hampshire: Cooper *v.* Hopkins, 70 N. H. 271, 279, 46 Atl. 100.

New York: Caldwell *v.* Central Park, etc., R. R., 7 Misc. 67, 27 N. Y. Supp. 397, 57 N. Y. St. 489.

is to be considered.[41] Where a surgeon is sued for malpractice compensation is not to be recovered for the whole amount of suffering, but only such additional suffering as was caused by the malpractice.[42] Where a man who was suffering from hernia was wrongfully expelled from a railroad train, it was held that the fact of his hernia might be shown, though no aggravation of his injury was proved; for it tended to show increased mental suffering.[43] Thomas J., said:

"The conductor put the plaintiff in fear by compelling him to accept the alternative of jumping from the platform or being pushed off in the dark, while the train was moving very fast, as it appeared to the plaintiff, and his fear must naturally have been greatly intensified by reason of his physical condition; and it was proper to put the jury in possession of all the facts relating to his physical condition, for the purpose of ascertaining the extent of his mental suffering as a element of damage."

Recovery may be had for any kind of physical or mental suffering, as has already been seen in a previous chapter.[44] So compensation may be recovered for insult and indignity,[45]

North Carolina: McCracken *v.* Smathers, 122 N. C. 799, 29 S. E. 354; Rushing *v.* Seaboard A. L. Ry., 149 N. C. 158, 62 S. E. 890.

Pennsylvania: Goodhart *v.* Pennsylvania R. R., 177 Pa. 1, 35 Atl. 191, 55 Am. St. Rep. 705; Foote *v.* American Product Co., 201 Pa. 510, 51 Atl. 364.

Texas: Gulf W. T. & P. Ry. *v.* Holzheuser (Tex. Civ. App.), 45 S. W. 188; Kirby Lumber Co. *v.* Lloyd (Tex. Civ. App.), 126 S. W. 319.

[41] *Delaware:* Murphy *v.* Hughes, 1 Pennew. 250, 40 Atl. 187; Heinel *v.* People's Ry.,6 Pennew.428, 67 Atl.173.

Illinois: Chicago & M. E. Ry. *v.* Ullrich, 213 Ill. 170, 72 N. E. 815; Chicago City Ry. *v.* Carroll, 206 Ill. 318, 68 N. E. 1087.

Iowa: Fry *v.* Dubuque & S. W. R. R., 45 Ia. 416.

Kentucky: Georgetown *v.* Groff, 136 Ky. 662, 124 S. W. 888.

Michigan: Langworthy *v.* Green, 88 Mich. 207, 50 N. W. 130; Howell *v.* Lansing E. Ry., 136 Mich. 432, 99 N. W. 406.

Missouri: Maguire *v.* Transit Co., 103 Mo. App. 459, 78 S. W. 838.

New York: Aaron *v.* Second Ave. R. R., 2 Daly, 127.

Oregon: Smitson *v.* Southern Pacific Co., 37 Ore. 74, 60 Pac. 907.

Texas: Houston Electric Co. *v.* Seegar, 117 S. W. 900.

Washington: Gallamore *v.* Olympia, 34 Wash. 379, 75 Pac. 978.

Wisconsin: Stewart *v.* Ripon, 38 Wis. 584; Stutz *v.* Chicago & N. W. Ry., 73 Wis. 147, 40 N. W. 653; Heddles *v.* Chicago & N. W. Ry., 77 Wis. 228, 46 N. W. 115.

[42] Wenger *v.* Calder, 78 Ill. 275.

[43] Fell *v.* Northern P. R. R., 44 Fed. 248.

[44] *Ante,* §§ 41, 44.

[45] *Illinois:* Von Reeden *v.* Evans, 52 Ill. App. 209.

for sense of shame and humiliation,[46] for mortification and distress caused by disfigurement,[47] for apprehension of future disease or suffering,[48] and for similar feelings.[49] But the suffering must be real, not imaginary or the result of over-sensitive or over-refined feelings.[50]

§ 485. Impairment of physical capacity.

Compensation should be given for permanent disability or loss of capacity for labor.[51] Since the recovery is for a future

Kentucky: Faulkner v. Davis, 18 Ky. L. Rep. 1004, 38 S. W. 1049.

[46] *California:* Thomas v. Gates, 126 Cal. 1, 58 Pac. 315.

Illinois: Von Reeden v. Evans, 52 Ill. App. 209.

Indiana: Wolf v. Trinkle, 103 Ind. 355, 3 N. E. 110; Kelley v. Kelley, 8 Ind. App. 606, 34 N. E. 1009; Singer S. M. Co. v. Phipps (Ind. App.), 94 N. E. 793.

Louisiana: Carrick v. Joachim, 126 La. 5, 52 So. 173.

Texas: Leach v. Leach, 11 Tex. Civ. App. 699, 33 S. W. 703.

Washington: Caldwell v. Northern Pac. Ry., 56 Wash. 223, 105 Pac. 625.

Wisconsin: Schmitt v. Milwaukee St. Ry., 89 Wis. 195, 61 N. W. 834.

[47] *Indiana:* American Strawboard Co. v. Foust, 12 Ind. App. 421, 431, 39 N. E. 891.

Pennsylvania: Rockwell v. Eldred, 7 Pa. Super. Ct. 95.

Washington: Gray v. Washington Water Power Co., 30 Wash. 665, 71 Pac. 206.

Wisconsin : Heddles v. Chicago & N. W. Ry., 77 Wis. 228, 46 N. W. 115.

Contra, United States: Chicago R. I. & P. Ry. v. Caulfield, 63 Fed. 396, 11 C. C. A. 552.

Illinois: Chicago City Ry. v. Mauger, 105 Ill. App. 579.

[48] *New Hampshire:* Walker v. Boston & M. R. R., 71 N. H. 271, 51 Atl. 918 (apprehension of insanity).

But see *Illinois:* Illinois Cent. R. R. v. Cole, 165 Ill. 334, 46 N. E. 275.

So of apprehension of hydrophobia from the bite of a dog:

Ohio: Heintz v. Caldwell, 16 Ohio C. Ct. 630.

Vermont: Godeau v. Blood, 52 Vt. 251, 36 Am. Rep. 751.

See *Texas:* Trinity & S. Ry. v. O'Brien, 18 Tex. Civ. App. 690, 46 S. W. 389.

[49] *District of Columbia:* Washington T. Co. v. Downey, 26 App. D. C. 258 (shock).

Indiana: Kline v. Kline, 158 Ind. 602, 64 N. E. 9, 58 L. R. A. 397 (fright); Louisville & N. R. R. v. Williams, 20 Ind. App. 576, 588, 51 N. E. 128 (peril).

Washington: Cole v. Seattle R. & S. Ry., 42 Wash. 462, 85 Pac. 3 (impairment of mental faculties).

[50] *Ante,* § 46a.

Thus no recovery can be had for regret at inability to work. Linn v. Duquesne, 204 Pa. 551, 54 Atl. 341.

Nor for loss of enjoyment of the pleasures of life. Locke v. International & G. N. Ry., 25 Tex. Civ. App. 145, 60 S. W. 314.

Nor for mere inconvenience. Jensen v. Chicago, S. P. M. & O. Ry., 86 Wis. 589, 57 N. W. 359, 22 L. R. A. 680.

Except such as is actual physical inconvenience, so that it may be comprehended in the term physical discomfort or physical suffering. Texas Tr. Co. v. Hanson (Tex. Civ. App.), 124 S. W. 494.

[51] *United States:* Vicksburg & M. R. R. v. Putnam, 118 U. S. 545, 30 L. ed.

loss, allowance must be made for the fact that the plaintiff
will receive his damages before he would, if uninjured, have

257, 7 Sup. Ct. 1; Potts v. Chicago C.
Ry., 33 Fed. 610; Campbell v. Pullman
P. C. Co., 42 Fed. 484.
  Alabama: South & N. A. R. R. v.
McLendon, 63 Ala. 266; Mobile & O.
R. R. v. George, 94 Ala. 199, 10 So. 145.
  Arkansas: Cameron v. Vandegriff,
53 Ark. 381, 13 S. W. 1092.
  California: Zibbell v. Southern Pac.
Co., 116 Pac. 513.
  Delaware: Wallace v. Wilmington &
N. R. R., 1 Marv. 25, 8 Houst. 529, 18
Atl. 818; Murphy v. Hughes, 1 Pen-
new. 250, 40 Atl. 187; Heidelbaugh v.
People's Ry., 6 Pennew. 209, 65 Atl.
587; Heinel v. People's Ry., 6 Pennew.
428, 67 Atl. 173; Walls v. People's Ry.,
80 Atl. 355; Tobias v. People's Ry., 80
Atl. 358; File v. Wilmington C. Ry., 80
Atl. 623; Ewans v. Wilmington C. Ry.,
80 Atl. 634; Coyle v. People's Ry., 80
Atl. 638.
  District of Columbia: Washington &
G. R. R. v. Patterson, 9 D. C. App.
423, 436.
  Illinois: Frink v. Schroyer, 18 Ill.
416; Pierce v. Millay, 44 Ill. 189;
Chicago v. Langlass, 52 Ill. 256, 66
Ill. 361; Toledo, W. & W. Ry. v. Bad-
deley, 54 Ill. 19; Chicago & A. R. R.
v. Wilson, 63 Ill. 167; Chicago v. Jones,
66 Ill. 349; Chicago v. Elzeman, 71 Ill.
131; Chicago, B. & Q. R. R. v. Warner,
108 Ill. 538; Sheridan v. Hibbard, 119
Ill. 307.
  Indiana: Indianapolis v. Gaston, 58
Ind. 224; Evansville H. & S. Co. v.
Bailey, 43 Ind. App. 153, 84 N. E. 549;
Holcomb v. Norman (Ind. App.), 91
N. E. 625.
  Iowa: McKinley v. Chicago & N. W.
Ry., 44 Ia. 314; Morris v. Chicago, B.
& Q. R. R., 45 Ia. 29; Stafford v.
Oskaloosa, 64 Ia. 251; Knapp v. Sioux
City & P. Ry., 71 Ia. 41.
  Kansas: Tefft v. Wilcox, 6 Kan. 46;
Kansas P. Ry. v. Pointer, 9 Kan. 620;

Missouri, K. & T. Ry. v. Weaver, 16
Kan. 456 (semble).
  Kentucky: Central P. Ry. v. Kuhn,
86 Ky. 578; Dorris v. Warford, 124
Ky. 768, 100 S. W. 312, 20 Ky. Law
Rep. 963, 9 L. R. A. (N. S.) 1090; Cross
v. Ill. Cent. R. R., 110 S. W. 290, 33
Ky. L. Rep. 432; West K. C. Co. v.
Davis, 138 Ky. 667, 128 S. W. 1074.
  Louisiana: Donnell v. Sandford, 11
La. Ann. 645.
  Maine: Blackman v. Gardiner & P.
Bridge, 75 Me. 214.
  Maryland: McMahon v. Northern
C. Ry., 39 Md. 438; Zell v. Dunaway,
80 Atl. 215.
  Massachusetts: McGarrahan v. New
York, N. H. & H. R. R., 171 Mass. 211,
50 N. E. 610.
  Michigan: Geveke v. Grand Rapids
& I. R. R., 57 Mich. 589, 24 N. W. 675;
Sherwood v. Chicago & N. W. Ry., 82
Mich. 374, 46 N. W. 773; Abbott v. De-
troit, 150 Mich. 245, 113 N. W. 1121.
  Mississippi: Memphis & C. R. R.
v. Whitfield, 44 Miss. 466.
  Missouri: Whalen v. St. Louis, K.
C. & N. Ry., 60 Mo. 323; Ridenhour
v. Kansas City C. Ry., 102 Mo. 270,
13 S. W. 889; Steiner v. Moran, 2 Mo.
App. 47; McNeill v. Cape Girardeau,
153 Mo. App. 424, 134 S. W. 582; Diel
v. Ferguson (Mo. App.), 138 S. W.
545.
  Nebraska: Chicago, B. & Q. R. R.
v. Starmer, 26 Neb. 630.
  Nevada: Cohen v. Eureka & P. R. R.,
14 Nev. 376.
  New Hampshire: Holyoke v. Grand
T. Ry., 48 N. H. 541.
  New York: Filer v. New York C. R.
R., 49 N. Y. 42.
  North Carolina: Rushing v. Seaboard
A. L. Ry., 149 N. C. 158, 62 S. E.
290.
  Oregon: Oliver v. North P. T. Co., 3
Ore. 84.

earned the money for which they stand; in other words, he is entitled not to the entire amount which he has been prevented from earning, but the present worth of such amount.[52] So in Fuls me v. Concord,[53] it was held correct to instruct the jury that in estimating the plaintiff's prospective damages they should reduce his losses to their present worth, or to such a sum as, being put at interest, would amount to the sum they found the plaintiff would lose in the future by the injuries. In actions for personal injury where the basis of damages is the reduced capacity to earn money, it is error to instruct the jury to give the plaintiff a sum which put at interest will produce annually a sum equal to the difference between what he could earn before and after the injury. They should be instructed to give an amount which would purchase an annuity equal to the difference during the probable life of the plaintiff, calculated upon a reliable estimate of the average duration of human life.[54] In estimating this amount, life

Pennsylvania: Pennsylvania & O. C. Co. v. Graham, 63 Pa. 290; Pittsburg, A. & M. P. Ry. v. Donahue, 70 Pa. 119; Scott v. Montgomery, 95 Pa. 444; Willis v. Second Ave. Traction Co., 189 Pa. 430, 42 Atl. 1.

Texas: Houston & T. C. R. R. v. Willie, 53 Tex. 318; Houston & T. C. Ry. v. Boehm, 57 Tex. 152; Gulf, W. T. & P. Ry. v. Holzheuser (Tex. Civ. App.), 45 S. W. 188; Kirby Lumber Co. v. Lloyd, 126 S. W. 319 (Tex. Civ. App.).

Utah: Giblin v. McIntyre, 2 Utah, 384.

Vermont: Lincoln v. Central Vermont Ry., 82 Vt. 187, 72 Atl. 821.

Wisconsin: Weisenberg v. Appleton, 26 Wis. 56; Goodno v. Oshkosh, 28 Wis. 300; Hulehan v. Green Bay, W. & S. P. R. R., 68 Wis. 520; King v. Oshkosh, 75 Wis. 517.

England: Phillips v. Southwestern Ry., 4 Q. B. D. 406; Fair v. London & N. W. Ry., 21 L. T. Rep. 326.

To give damages for loss of time and in addition for impairment of earning capacity is not to give double damages,

since the former recovery applies to the period during which the plaintiff was totally incapacitated by the injury, and the latter to the permanent impairment of capacity after recovery from the immediate injury.

Colorado: Denver v. Hyatt, 28 Colo. 129, 63 Pac. 403.

Iowa: Haden v. Sioux C. & P. R. R., 92 Ia. 226, 60 N. W. 537.

[52] *United States:* Peterson v. Chemical Co., 131 Fed. 156.

Iowa: Williams v. Clarke County, 143 Ia. 328, 120 N. W. 306; Greenway v. Taylor County, 144 Ia. 332, 122 N. W. 943.

New York: Gregory v. New York, L. E. & W. Ry., 55 Hun, 303, 8 N. Y. Supp. 525; Morrison v. Long Island R. R., 3 App. Div. 205, 38 N. Y. Supp. 393.

Pennsylvania: Wilkinson v. Northeast Borough, 215 Pa. 486, 64 Atl. 734.

[53] 46 Vt. 135.

[54] *United States:* Baltimore & O. R. R. v. Henthorne, 73 Fed. 634, 19 C. C. A. 623.

Montana: Bourke v. Butte Electric

tables may be used,[55] but are not conclusive; [56] and other evidence of the probable duration of life may be introduced.[57] Damages for permanent deformity, resulting from an injury, may be allowed; though, it has been said, not the expenses of surgical operations undertaken after the wound is healed, for the purpose of removing the blemish.[58] So compensation may be had for lost usefulness and enjoyment of life,[59] and for loss of capacity to have offspring.[60]

§ 485a. Amount of loss by physical impairment.

In ascertaining the proper amount in case of disability, the jury may take into consideration the nature of the plaintiff's previous occupation,[61] and the kind and amount of physical

& P. Co., 33 Mont. 267, 83 Pac. 470; Moyse v. Northern Pac. Ry., 41 Mont. 272, 108 Pac. 1062.

Texas: Houston & T. C. R. R. v. Willie, 53 Tex. 318.

[55] *United States:* Vicksburg & M. R. R. v. Putnam, 118 U. S. 545, 30 L. ed. 257, 7 Sup. Ct. 1.

Alabama: Birmingham Ry., L. & P. Co. v. Wright, 153 Ala. 99, 44 So. 1037.

Indiana: Indianapolis v. Marold, 25 Ind. App. 428, 58 N. E. 512.

Iowa: Knapp v. Sioux City & P. Ry., 71 Ia. 41.

[56] Robinson v. Helena L. & Ry. Co., 38 Mont. 222, 99 Pac. 837.

[57] *Maine:* Haynes v. Waterville & O. St. Ry., 101 Me. 335, 64 Atl. 614.

Wisconsin: Waterman v. Chicago & A. R. R., 82 Wis. 613, 52 N. W. 247.

[58] *United States:* The Oriflamme, 3 Sawy. 397.

California: Karr v. Parks, 44 Cal. 46.

[59] Haynes v. Waterville & O. St. Ry., 101 Me. 335, 64 Atl. 614.

Damages may be recovered for impairment of the power of speech. Garbaczewski v. Third Ave. R. R., 5 App. Div. 186, 39 N. Y. Supp. 33.

But not, it has been held, for the shortening of life. Richmond Gas Co. v. Baker, 146 Ind. 600, 609, 45 N. E. 1049, 36 L. R. A. 683.

And in Kentucky it has been said that

no compensation can be had for permanent impairment of health, in addition to impairment of physical powers. Georgetown v. Groff, 136 Ky. 662, 124 S. W. 888.

[60] *Illinois:* Postal T. C. Co. v. Likes, 225 Ill. 249, 80 N. E. 136.

New York: Devine v. Brooklyn H. R. R., 131 App. Div. 142, 115 N. Y. Supp. 263.

See *ante,* § 41a.

[61] *United States:* Nebraska City v. Campbell, 2 Black, 590, 17 L. ed. 271; Southern Pac. R. R. v. Hall, 100 Fed. 760, 41 C. C. A. 50.

Alabama: Alabama G. S. R. R. v. Yarborough, 83 Ala. 238, 3 So. 447, 3 Am. St. Rep. 715.

California: Shaw v. Southern Pac. R. R., 157 Cal. 240, 107 Pac. 108; Zibbell v. Southern Pac. Co., 116 Pac. 513.

Colorado: Denver v. Hyatt, 28 Colo. 129, 63 Pac. 403.

Indiana: Elkhart v. Ritter, 66 Ind. 136; Linton Coal & M. Co. v. Persons, 11 Ind. App. 264, 273, 38 N. E. 214.

Iowa: Moore v. Central R. R., 47 Ia. 688.

Missouri: Batten v. Transit Co., 102 Mo. App. 285, 76 S. W. 727.

New York: Caldwell v. Murphy, 11 N. Y. 416.

North Carolina: Wilkie v. Raleigh & C. F. R. R., 127 N. C. 203, 37 S. E. 204.

Pennsylvania: Goodhart v. Pennsyl-

and mental labor to which he has been accustomed.[62] For that purpose the previous earnings of the plaintiff may be shown, as compared with his earnings in his present condition.[63] Any particular aptitude, talent, or training which the plaintiff possessed may also be shown,[64] and the plaintiff is not confined to the employment in which he was actually

vania R. R., 177 Pa. 1, 35 Atl. 191, 55 Am. St. Rep. 705; McKenna v. Citizens' Natural Gas Co., 201 Pa. 146, 50 Atl. 922.

Vermont: Nones v. Northouse, 46 Vt. 587.

Wisconsin: Ripon v. Bittel, 30 Wis. 614.

The income derived from an illegal employment cannot be shown. Murray v. Interurban St. Ry., 118 App. Div. 35, 102 N. Y. Supp. 1026.

[62] Ballou v. Farnum, 11 All. (Mass.) 73.

If there is no evidence of the pecuniary value of such services, the plaintiff is entitled to at least nominal damages for a permanent injury. Sloss-Sheffield S. & I. Co. v. Stewart (Ala), 55 So. 785.

[63] *United States:* Parshall v. Minneapolis & S. L. Ry., 35 Fed. 649; Illinois Cent. R. R. v. Davidson, 76 Fed. 517, 22 C. C. A. 306.

Alabama: Seaboard Mfg. Co. v. Woodson, 94 Ala. 143, 11 So. 733; Elba v. Bulard, 152 Ala. 237, 44 So. 412.

California: Bonneau v. North Shore R. R., 152 Cal. 406, 93 Pac. 106.

Illinois: Chicago & E. R. R. v. Meech, 163 Ill. 305, 45 N. E. 290; Chicago U. Tr. Co. v. Brethauer, 223 Ill. 521, 79 N. E. 287.

Indiana: Carthage Turnpike Co. v. Andrews, 102 Ind. 138, 1 N. E. 364, 52 Am. Rep. 653.

Massachusetts: Murdock v. New York & B. D. E. Co., 167 Mass. 549, 46 N. E. 57.

Michigan: Welch v. Ware, 32 Mich. 77; Van Dusen v. Letellier, 78 Mich. 492, 44 N. W. 572; Moore v. Kalamazoo, 109 Mich. 176, 66 N. W. 1089.

Minnesota: Palmer v. Winona R. & L. Co., 78 Minn. 138, 80 N. W. 869, 83 Minn. 85, 85 N. W. 941.

Ohio: Mt. Adams & E. P. I. Ry. v. Isaacs, 18 Ohio C. Ct. 177.

In the absence of evidence to the contrary, the wages actually obtained by the plaintiff after the injury will be taken as the highest he could reasonably obtain. Roth v. Buettel Bros. Co., 142 Ia. 212, 119 N. W. 166.

See, however, Mt. Adams & E. P. I. Ry. v. Isaacs, 18 Oh. C. Ct. 177.

[64] *California:* Doolin v. Omnibus Cable Co., 140 Cal. 369, 73 Pac. 1060 (ability to play musical instruments and sing); Scally v. W. T. Garratt & Co., 9 Cal. App. 194, 104 Pac. 325 (musical talent and ability to play violin).

New Jersey: Rhinesmith v. Erie R. R., 76 N. J. Law, 783, 72 Atl. 15 (well-trained voice).

In District of Columbia v. Woodbury, 136 U. S. 450, 459, 10 Sup. Ct. 990, 993, 34 L. ed. 472, it was held that plaintiff may show that he, being a medical man, had in the past written for medical journals upon various medical subjects, and that since the injury he had not been able to do so. This shows the serious and permanent character of the injuries received by him, and that his capacity to pursue his studies was impaired, in spite of the fact that it did not appear that the plaintiff had derived any income from these contributions. He was entitled to recover for this impairment though his contributions were made without compensation.

engaged at the time of the injury. He may recover compensation based upon what he could have earned in any employment for which he was fitted,[65] or was in process of becoming fitted.[66] So a person retired from business at the time of the injury may recover compensation based upon what he might have earned in business;[67] and one who happened to be idle or at work in a less lucrative trade at the time of the injury may show his earnings before the time of the injury in a more lucrative trade.[68] Other circumstances which tend to establish the amount of loss may be shown;[69] but the loss of special opportunities will not ordinarily be either proximate or certain enough for recovery.[70]

Certain personal qualities or habits of the plaintiff may be shown, so far as they have a bearing on the actual amount

[65] *California:* Zibbell v. Southern Pac. Co., 116 Pac. 513.

Texas: Pecos & N. T. Ry. v. Blasengame (Tex. Civ. App.), 93 S. W. 187.

[66] Howard Oil Co. v. Davis, 76 Tex. 630, 13 S. W. 665.

[67] *Illinois:* Fisher v. Jansen, 128 Ill. 549, 21 N. E. 598.

Texas: El Paso Electric Ry. v. Murphy, 49 Tex. Civ. App. 586, 109 S. W. 489.

[68] *Illinois:* West Chicago St. Ry. v. Dougherty, 209 Ill. 241, 70 N. E. 586.

Texas: Missouri, K. & T. Ry. v. St. Clair, 21 Tex. Civ. App. 345, 51 S. W. 666; Chicago, R. I. & T. Ry. v. Long, 26 Tex. Civ. App. 601, 65 S. W. 882.

Washington: Peterson v. Seattle Traction Co., 23 Wash. 615, 643, 63 Pac. 539.

Plaintiff cannot show his earnings many years before in a special position quite different from his present employment. Chicago & J. E. R. R. v. Spence, 213 Ill. 220, 72 N. E. 796.

Where there is no evidence that plaintiff could have obtained or exercised any other employment than that in which he was engaged at the time of the injury, his earnings in that employment alone will be taken as

the measure of his loss. O'Connor v. Chicago, R. I. & P. Ry., 144 Ia. 289, 117 N. W. 979.

[69] *Alabama:* Helton v. Alabama Midland R. R., 97 Ala. 275, 12 So. 276 (plaintiff being disabled from manual labor may show that he has not sufficient education to earn money in a clerical calling).

Illinois: Hamilton v. Pittsburgh, C. C. & S. L. Ry., 104 Ill. App. 207 (defendant may show that by the use of an artificial leg plaintiff will be able to earn money).

Michigan: Ostrander v. Lansing, 115 Mich. 224, 73 N. W. 110 (defendant may not show that by reason of the injury plaintiff may be compelled to educate himself, and will then be able to secure a better income than before).

[70] *Georgia:* Richmond & D. R. R. v. Allison, 86 Ga. 145, 12 S. E. 352 (probability of promotion to a higher political office).

Illinois: Chicago & E. R. R. v. Meech, 163 Ill. 305, 45 N. E. 290 (particular contract of employment).

Massachusetts: Brown v. Cummings, 7 Allen, 507 (application for position of surgeon's mate).

of his loss; as that one of his hands was previously crippled; [71] or that he was a tramp.[72] So evidence of the plaintiff's habitual drunkenness, incapacitating him for labor, is proper in reference to the amount of the compensatory damages he should receive for a permanent disability.[73] But matters which have no bearing on the actual amount of loss cannot be shown.[74]

§ 486. Recovery by married woman.

Where the suit is by a married woman, her loss of time is no part of the injury for which compensation can be given. Her time and services belong to the husband, and for a loss of them he must sue alone.[75] And for the same reason she cannot recover the amount of medical expenses, unless actually paid out of her separate estate.[76] She may recover compensa-

[71] Townsend v. Briggs, 99 Cal. 481, 32 Pac. 307, 34 Pac. 116.

[72] Central of Georgia Ry. v. Moore, 5 Ga. App. 562, 63 S. E. 642.

[73] Cleveland & P. R. R. v. Sutherland, 19 Oh. St. 151.

[74] *Alabama:* Louisville & N. R. R. v. Woods, 115 Ala. 527, 22 So. 33 (amount plaintiff had been able to save from his wages).

Michigan: Van Dusen v. Letellier, 78 Mich. 492, 44 N. W. 572 (that plaintiff had no means of support except by his own exertions).

[75] *Illinois:* Joliet v. Conway, 119 Ill. 489, 10 N. E. 223.

Indiana: Ohio & M. Ry. v. Cosby, 107 Ind. 32.

Iowa: Thomas v. Brooklyn, 58 Ia. 438, 10 N. W. 849; Hall v. Manson, 90 Ia. 585, 58 N. W. 881; Frohs v. Dubuque, 109 Ia. 219, 80 N. W. 341.

Kansas: Holton v. Hicks, 9 Kan. App. 179, 58 Pac. 998.

Massachusetts: Jordan v. Middlesex R. R., 138 Mass. 425.

Michigan: Tunnicliffe v. Bay Cities C. Ry., 102 Mich. 624, 61 N. W. 11.

Missouri: Plummer v. Milan, 70 Mo. App. 598; Wallis v. Westport, 82 Mo. App. 522.

New Jersey: Klein v. Jewett, 26 N. J. Eq. 474.

Wisconsin: Barnes v. Martin, 15 Wis. 240.

Therefore it is error to instruct the jury that the damages under statutes giving an action for causing death, are the same in the case of a married and an unmarried woman. An unmarried woman is entitled to her whole earnings. The time of a married woman is not exclusively her own, but a portion of it must be devoted to the care of the family and aiding her husband. Stulmuller v. Cloughly, 58 Ia. 738.

[76] *Connecticut:* Tompkins v. West, 56 Conn. 478, 16 Atl. 237.

Delaware: Louth v. Thompson, 1 Pennew. 149, 39 Atl. 1100.

Georgia: Lewis v. Atlanta, 77 Ga. 756.

Indiana: Ohio & M. Ry. v. Cosby, 107 Ind. 32.

Massachusetts: Jordan v. Middlesex R. R., 138 Mass. 425.

Michigan: Cousins v. Lake Shore & M. S. Ry., 96 Mich. 386, 56 N. W. 14; Rogers v. Orion, 116 Mich. 324, 74 N. W. 463.

Minnesota: Belyea v. Minneapolis, S. P. & S. S. M. Ry., 61 Minn. 224, 63 N. W. 627.

New Jersey: Klein v. Jewett, 26 N. J. Eq. 474.

tion for her pain and suffering,[77] and for inability to perform services personal to herself, such as dressing and eating.[78] It has also been held that she may recover for permanent impairment of her earning capacity.[79]

Under the married women's property acts, now passed in almost every jurisdiction, the case is different. Under these acts her domestic services are still performed on her husband's account, but if she performs other services for hire, the proceeds are her own; and if she carries on business on her own account, she is entitled to the profits. Consequently, if she was in fact carrying on business for herself at the time of the injury, or was in fact earning money on her own account, she may recover compensation for the loss of capacity to earn money as she had been doing,[80] which must not include any compensation for loss of ability to do housework or perform ordinary domestic services, since that is still her husband's loss.[81] In some jurisdictions she is allowed to recover com-

New York: Burnham v. Webster, 54 N. Y. Super. Ct. 30; Moody v. Osgood, 50 Barb. 628.

[77] *United States:* Green v. Pennsylvania R. R., 36 Fed. 66.
Connecticut: Tompkins v. West, 56 Conn. 478.
Delaware: Louth v. Thompson, 1 Pennew. 149, 39 Atl. 1100.
District of Columbia: Johnson v. Baltimore & P. R. R., 17 D. C. (6 Mack.) 232.
Indiana: Ohio & M. Ry. v. Cosby, 107 Ind. 32.
Massachusetts: Jordan v. Middlesex R. R., 138 Mass. 425.
New Jersey: Klein v. Jewett, 26 N. J. Eq. 474.
Texas: Missouri Pac. Ry. v. Martino, 2 Tex. Civ. App. 634, 18 S. W. 1066.
Washington: Hawkins v. Front St. Cable Ry., 3 Wash. 592, 28 Pac. 1021, 28 Am. St. Rep. 72, 16 L. R. A. 808.
So she may recover compensation for being marred in her personal appearance. Chicago & M. E. Ry. v. Krempel, 103 Ill. App. 1.
[78] *District of Columbia:* Johnson v.

Baltimore & P. R. R., 17 D. C. (6 Mack.) 232.
Illinois: Chicago & M. E. Ry. v. Krempel, 103 Ill. App. 1.
[79] *Delaware:* Louth v. Thompson, 1 Pennew. 149, 39 Atl. 1100.
Georgia: Southern Ry. v. Hutcheson, 71 S. E. 802.
Indiana: Ohio & M. Ry. v. Cosby, 107 Ind. 32.
Massachusetts: Jordan v. Middlesex R. R., 138 Mass. 425.
[80] *United States:* Texas & P. Ry. v. Humble, 97 Fed. 837, 38 C. C. A. 502.
Missouri: Nelson v. Metropolitan St. Ry., 113 Mo. App. 659, 88 S. W. 781.
Montana: Hamilton v. Woodworth Ry., 17 Mont. 334, 42 Pac. 860, 43 Pac. 713.
New Jersey: Healey v. Ballentine, 66 N. J. L. 339, 49 Atl. 511.
New York: Brooks v. Schwerin, 54 N. Y. 343; Minick v. Troy, 19 Hun, 253; Blaechinska v. Howard Mission, etc., 56 Hun, 322, 9 N. Y. Supp. 679.
[81] Hall v. Manson, 90 Iowa, 585, 58 N. W. 881.

pensation for the impairment of her ability to earn money, outside of her domestic service, even if she has never engaged in any gainful occupation, since she is entitled to do so;[82] but in other jurisdictions the right to recover is confined to cases where she was actually earning money at the time of the injury.[83] Since under these statutes she has power to contract, she may make a valid agreement to pay for medical services and expenses; and if she does so, she may recover the amount for which she is liable.[84]

§ 486a. Husband's action for injury to wife.

In an action by a husband for the loss of his wife's services through the defendant's fault, he may recover the value of her services which he has lost.[85] This includes not only the

[82] *Kentucky:* Louisville & N. R. R. v. Dick, 78 S. W. 914, 25 Ky. L. Rep. 1831.

Massachusetts: Harmon v. Old Colony R. R., 165 Mass. 104, 105, 42 N. E. 505, 30 L. R. A. 658, 52 Am. St. Rep. 499; Millmore v. Boston Elevated Ry., 198 Mass. 370, 84 N. E. 468.

[83] *Missouri:* Kroner v. Transit Co., 107 Mo. App. 41, 80 S. W. 915; Becker v. Lincoln R. E. & B. Co., 118 Mo. App. 74, 93 S. W. 291.

New York: Uransky v. Dry Dock, E. B. & B. R. R., 118 N. Y. 304, 23 N. E. 451, 16 Am. St. Rep. 759.

Virginia: Richmond R. & E. Co. v. Bowles, 92 Va. 738, 24 S. E. 388.

Even where she was employed and paid by her husband as a sempstress, it was held that she could not recover for impairment of her earning capacity, as if she had been working for a stranger, since she could not make a valid contract with her husband for payment for such services. Blaechinska v. Howard Mission, 130 N. Y. 497, 29 N. E. 755, 15 L. R. A. 215.

[84] *Alabama:* Southern R. R. v. Crowder, 135 Ala. 427, 33 So. 335; Elba v. Bullard, 152 Ala. 237, 44 So. 412.

Illinois: Mueller v. Kuhn, 59 Ill. App. 353.

Indiana: Shelby County v. Castetter, 7 Ind. App. 309, 33 N. E. 986, 34 N. E. 687.

Michigan: Lacas v. Detroit City Ry., 92 Mich. 412, 52 N. W. 745.

Nebraska: Struble v. De Witt, 132 N. W. 124.

North Dakota: Chacey v. Fargo, 5 N. D. 173, 64 N. W. 932.

Oklahoma: Willet v. Johnson, 13 Okla. 563, 76 Pac. 174.

[85] *Alabama:* Alabama C. G. & A. Ry. v. Appleton, 54 So. 638.

Colorado: Union Pac. Ry. v. Jones, 21 Colo. 340, 40 Pac. 891.

Connecticut: Comstock v. Connecticut R. & L. Co., 77 Conn. 65, 58 Atl. 465.

District of Columbia: Washington & G. R. R. v. Hickey, 12 D. C. App. 269.

Indiana: Citizens' S. Ry. v. Twiname, 121 Ind. 375, 23 N. E. 159.

Nebraska: Riley v. Lidtke, 49 Neb. 139, 68 N. W. 356.

North Carolina: Kimberly v. Howland, 143 N. C. 398, 55 S. E. 778, 7 L. R. A. (N. S.) 545.

Pennsylvania: Henry v. Klopfer, 147 Pa. 178, 23 Atl. 337; Hewitt v. Pennsylvania R. R., 228 Pa. 397, 77 Atl. 623.

ordinary domestic services, but also the comfort of her society and companionship, and her capacity for usefulness, aid and comfort as a wife,[86] and her parental care for his children.[87] Even under the married women's property acts the husband may recover for the value of her domestic services and her assistance in his business, as well as the loss of her society.[88] No special evidence need be offered as to the value of such services, which the jury may find on their own knowledge.[89] But in such an action it is proper to admit evidence of what the plaintiff had paid a third person to do the work his wife usually performed.[90] The husband may recover the medical expenses of his wife's illness.[91] So, also, he can recover something for his own services in attending on her; [92] but only the amount which such services are worth in nursing, not the value

Wisconsin: Keller *v.* Gilman, 93 Wis. 9, 66 N. W. 800.

Canada : Fox *v.* Saint John, 23 N. B. 244.

[86] *District of Columbia:* Washington & G. R. R. *v.* Hickey, 12 D. C. App. 269.

Iowa: Hutcheis *v.* Cedar Rapids & M. C. Ry., 128 Iowa,· 279, 103 N. W. 779.

Missouri: Furnish *v.* Missouri Pac. R. R., 102 Mo. 669, 22 Am. St. Rep. 800, 15 S. W. 315.

Nebraska: Omaha & R. V. Ry. *v.* Ryburn, 40 Neb. 87, 58 N. W. 541.

Pennsylvania: Hewitt *v.* Pa. R. R., 228 Pa. 397, 77 Atl. 623.

Wisconsin: Selleck *v.* Janesville, 104 Wis. 570, 80 N. W. 944, 76 Am. St. Rep. 892, 47 L. R. A. 691.

[87] Indianapolis & M. R. T. Co. *v.* Reeder, 42 Ind. App. 520, 85 N. E. 1042.

[88] *Illinois:* Blair *v.* Bloomington & N. R. E. & H. Co., 130 Ill. App. 400.

Nebraska: Omaha & R. V. Ry. *v.* Ryburn, 40 Neb. 87, 58 N. W. 541; Riley *v.* Lidtke, 49 Neb. 139, 68 N. W. 356.

Pennsylvania: Standen *v.* R. R., 214 Pa. 189, 63 Atl. 467.

[89] Ft. Worth & R. H. St. Ry. *v.* Hawes, 48 Tex. Civ. App. 487, 107 S. W. 556.

[90] *Nebraska:* Riley *v.* Lidtke, 49 Neb. 139, 68 N. W. 356.

Vermont: Lindsey *v.* Danville, 46 Vt. 144.

But he cannot recover both the value of her services and also the expense of hiring a substitute. Indianapolis & M. R. T. Co. *v.* Reeder, 42 Ind. App. 520, 85 N. E. 1042.

[91] *Alabama:* Alabama C. G. & A. Ry. *v.* Appleton, 54 So. 638.

Colorado: Union Pacific Ry. *v.* Jones, 21 Colo. 340, 40 Pac. 891.

Indiana: Indianapolis & M. R. T. Co. *v.* Reeder, 85 Ind. App. 520, 85 N. E. 1042.

Pennsylvania: Henry *v.* Klopfer, 147 Pa. 178, 23 Atl. 337.

But only if he is liable for them. Birmingham R. L. & P. Co. *v.* Humphries, 55 So. 307.

[92] *Alabama:* Louisville & N. R. R. *v.* Quinn, 145 Ala. 657, 39 So. 616.

Missouri: Smith *v.* St. Joseph, 55 Mo. 456.

Texas: Dallas *v.* Moore, 32 Tex. Civ. App. 230, 74 S. W. 95.

of his time in his business.[93] The husband cannot recover for his wife's suffering,[94] nor for the loss of her unborn child.[95] Evidence of the pecuniary condition of the plaintiff is inadmissible.[96]

§ 486b. Recovery by minor.

A minor cannot recover for loss of time or earning capacity during his minority, since his earnings during that time belong to his parent;[97] unless he has been emancipated, when his earnings belong to himself and he may therefore recover for loss of time even during minority,[98] or unless his parent waives his right to his earnings.[99] Since the parent is obliged to support the child during minority, and therefore to furnish

[93] *United States:* Hazard Powder Co. *v.* Volger, 58 Fed. 152, 7 C. C. A. 130.
Colorado: Salida *v.* McKinna, 16 Colo. 523, 27 Pac. 810.
Washington: Howells *v.* North American Transportation & T. R. Co., 24 Wash. 689, 64 Pac. 786.
Wisconsin: Selleck *v.* Janesville, 104 Wis. 570, 80 N. W. 944, 76 Am. St. Rep. 892, 47 L. R. A. 691.

[94] Indianapolis T. & T. Co. *v.* Menze, 173 Ind. 31, 89 N. E. 370.

[95] Butler *v.* Manhattan Ry., 143 N. Y. 417, 37 N. E. 826, 42 Am. St. Rep. 738, 26 L. R. A. 46.

[96] *Texas:* Dallas *v.* Moore (Tex. Civ. App.), 74 S. W. 95.
Wisconsin: Rooney *v.* Milwaukee C. Co., 65 Wis. 397.

[97] *Arkansas:* St. Louis, I. M. & S. Ry. *v.* Warren, 65 Ark. 619, 48 S. W. 222.
Georgia: Western & A. R. R. *v.* Young, 81 Ga. 397, 7 S. E. 912, 12 Am. St. Rep. 320; Atlanta & W. P. R. R. *v.* Smith, 94 Ga. 107, 20 S. E. 763.
Illinois: Richardson *v.* Nelson, 221 Ill. 254, 77 N. E. 583; Western U. Tel. Co. *v.* Woods, 88 Ill. App. 375; Chicago City Ry. *v.* Schaefer, 121 Ill. App. 334.
Iowa: Wilder *v.* Great Western Cereal Co., 134 Ia. 451, 109 N. W. 789.
Kentucky: Cincinnati, N. O. & T. P. Ry. *v.* Troxell, 137 S. W. 543.

Michigan: Braasch *v.* Michigan Stove Co., 153 Mich. 652, 118 N. W. 366.
New Jersey: Clark Mile-End Spool Cotton Co. *v.* Shaffery, 58 N. J. L. 229, 33 Atl. 284.
Tennessee: Burke *v.* Ellis, 105 Tenn. 702, 58 S. W. 855.
Texas: Gulf, C. & S. F. Ry. *v.* Evansich, 63 Tex. 54; Texas & P. Ry. *v.* Morin, 66 Tex. 225; Freeman *v.* Mireles (Tex. Civ. App.), 127 S. W. 1162.
Wisconsin: Peppercorn *v.* Black River Falls, 89 Wis. 38, 61 N. W. 79, 46 Am. St. Rep. 818.

[98] *Georgia:* Atlanta & West Point R. R. *v.* Smith, 94 Ga. 107, 20 S. E. 763 (*semble*).
Illinois: Manufacturers' Fuel Co. *v.* White, 228 Ill. 187, 81 N. E. 841, affirming 130 Ill. App. 29.

[99] *Vermont:* Judd *v.* Ballard, 66 Vt. 668, 30 Atl. 96.
Wisconsin: Kucera *v.* Merrill Lumber Co., 91 Wis. 637, 65 N. W. 374 (*semble*).
In *Washington* it has been held that a parent waives his right to compensation for loss of the minor's time by suing as next friend, and that the minor can therefore recover for it. Donald *v.* Ballard, 34 Wash. 576, 76 Pac. 80; Hammer *v.* Caine, 47 Wash. 475, 92 Pac. 441.

medical attendance, the minor cannot recover medical expenses resulting from the injury,[100] unless, as may happen, the minor's estate has become responsible for them.[101] A minor may however recover compensation for strictly personal loss, such as pain and suffering [102] and disfigurement; [103] and he may also recover in case of any permanent injury compensation for all effects of such injury as will be felt after he becomes of age.[104]

§ 486c. Parent's action for injury to child.

If the parent sues for an injury to his child, the ground of action being the loss of service, the measure of damages is the actual pecuniary loss which the parent has sustained,[105]

[100] Iowa: Newbury v. Getchel & M. L. & M. Co., 100 Ia. 441, 69 N. W. 743, 62 Am. St. Rep. 582.

Tennessee: Burke v. Ellis, 105 Tenn. 702, 58 S. W. 855.

Texas: Bering Mfg. Co. v. Peterson, 28 Tex. Civ. App. 194, 67 S. W. 133.

Wisconsin: Peppercorn v. Black River Falls, 89 Wis. 38, 61 N. W. 79, 46 Am. St. Rep. 818.

[101] Alabama: Forbes v. Loftin, 50 Ala. 396 (minor emancipated).

Vermont: Judd v. Ballard, 66 Vt. 668, 30 Atl. 96 (incurred by minor himself and necessary).

[102] Arkansas: St. Louis, I. M. & S. Ry. v. Warren, 65 Ark. 619, 48 S. W. 222.

Delaware: Linthicum v. Truitt, 80 Atl. 245.

Kentucky: Cincinnati, N. O. & T. P. Ry. v. Troxell, 137 S. W. 543.

Missouri: McMillan v. Union P. B. W., 6 Mo. App. 434.

[103] Arkansas: St. Louis, I. M. & S. Ry. v. Warren, 65 Ark. 619, 48 S. W. 222.

Iowa: Newbury v. Getchel & M. L. & M. Co., 100 Iowa, 441, 69 N. W. 743, 62 Am. St. Rep. 582.

[104] United States: Delaware, L. & W. R. R. v. Devore, 114 Fed. 155, 52 C. C. A. 77.

Arkansas: St. Louis, I. M. & S. Ry. v. Warren, 65 Ark. 619, 48 S. W. 222.

Delaware: Linthicum v. Truitt, 80 Atl. 245.

Kentucky: Cincinnati, N. O. & T. P. Ry. v. Troxell, 137 S. W. 543.

Missouri: Rosenkrantz v. Lindell Ry., 108 Mo. 9, 18 S. W. 892, 32 Am. St. Rep. 588; McMillan v. Union P. B. W., 6 Mo. App. 434. In Brown v. St. Louis & S. Ry., 127 Mo. App. 499, 106 S. W. 83, evidence of such loss was held too speculative; but the prevailing view in that State is that the jury may find compensation for such loss even without evidence of its amount. Ferrier v. Shoenberg Mercantile Co., 138 S. W. 893; Buckry-Ellis v. Missouri Pac. Ry., 138 S. W. 912.

In Western & A. R. R. v. Young, 81 Ga. 397, 7 S. E. 912, 12 Am. St. Rep. 320, it was held that the jury should estimate loss of the minor's probable future earnings, having in view his degree of intelligence, and his opportunities to equip himself for the race of life, according to his present condition, in view of the pursuits he might have applied himself to if he had not been injured.

[105] New York: Werbolovsky v. New York & B. D. E. Co., 63 Misc. 329, 117 N. Y. Supp. 150.

Pennsylvania: Pennsylvania R. R. v. Kelly, 31 Pa. 372; Pennsylvania R. R. v. Zebe, 33 Pa. 318; Woeckner v. Erie E. M. Co., 182 Pa. 182, 37 Atl. 936.

without compensation for loss of society of the child,[106] or for grief of the parent because of the injury,[107] or for loss or inconvenience to other members of the family.[108] In the ordinary case of loss of service through a physical injury to the child or other servant the injuries to the master and to the servant are distinct, and recovery by one of them cannot affect the amount recoverable by the other.[109] The measure of damages in such cases is compensation for loss of the minor's time,[110] the expenses sustained by the injury, such as those for surgical and medical attendance, and the increased expense of maintaining the child during minority.[111] A parent can recover for the expenses incurred,

Rhode Island: McGarr v. National & P. W. Mills, 24 R. I. 447, 53 Atl. 320, 60 L. R. A. 122.

[106] Werbolovsky v. New York & B. D. E. Co., 63 Misc. 329, 117 N. Y. Supp. 150.

[107] *Colorado:* Union Pac. Ry. v. Jones, 21 Colo. 340, 347, 40 Pac. 891.

Louisiana: Brinkman v. St. Landry C. O. Co., 118 La. 835, 43 So. 458.

Rhode Island: McGarr v. National & P. W. Mills, 24 R. I. 447, 53 Atl. 320, 60 L. R. A. 122.

[108] Woeckner v. Erie E. M. Co., 182 Pa. 182, 37 Atl. 936.

[109] *Texas:* Evansich v. Gulf, C. & S. F. Ry., 57 Tex. 123.

Vermont: Bradley v. Andrews, 51 Vt. 525.

[110] *United States:* Netherland A. S. N. Co. v. Hollander, 59 Fed. 417, 8 C. C. A. 169.

Kansas: Sawyer v. Sauer, 10 Kan. 519.

Missouri: Buck v. People's St. R. E. L. & P. Co., 46 Mo. App. 555, 568.

New York: Cuming v. Brooklyn City R. R., 109 N. Y. 95, 16 N. E. 65; Lang v. New York, L. E. & W. R. R., 51 Hun, 603; Gilligan v. New York & H. R. R., 1 E. D. Smith, 453.

Pennsylvania: Oakland Ry. v. Fielding, 48 Pa. 320.

Texas: Houston & G. N. R. R. v.

Miller, 49 Tex. 322; Texas & P. Ry. v. Morin, 66 Tex. 133.

[111] *United States:* Netherland A. S. N. Co. v. Hollander, 59 Fed. 417, 8 C. C. A. 169.

Illinois: Seltzer v. Saxton, 71 Ill. App. 229.

Louisiana: Brinkman v. St. Landry Cotton Oil Co., 118 La. 835, 43 So. 458.

Massachusetts: Keating v. Boston El. Ry., 95 N. E. 840.

New York: Barnes v. Keene, 132 N. Y. 13, 20 N. E. 1090.

Rhode Island: Galligan v. Woonsocket R. R., 27 R. I. 376, 62 Atl. 376. In Heater v. R. R., 90 App. Div. 495, 85 N. Y. Supp. 524, it was said that the father could not recover the amount of the medical expenses without evidence that he was under a legal liability to pay them.

In Cuming v. Brooklyn City R. R., 109 N. Y. 95, 16 N. E. 65, it was said that speculative medical or surgical expenses likely to be incurred at some time during the child's minority cannot be recovered, as it is too uncertain whether the parent will be called upon to pay them, since either the child or parent might die or the parent be pecuniarily unable to pay for the services rendered. If anyone can recover for such services it must be the minor himself on the ground that if the money

although the child was too young to render any service.[112] If the parent himself renders services to the child, as, for instance, nursing, beyond what he would have rendered if there had been no injury, he may recover the value of such services.[113] No recovery can be had for the cost of supporting the child during minority, since the parent is bound to do that at any rate.[114]

In addition to these items of loss, the parent is entitled to compensation for the diminished earning capacity of the child during his minority,[115] but not for any loss of support that might have come to the parent after the child became of age.[116] As no allowance is to be made for cost of supporting the child, since the parent must support him during minority at any rate, he is therefore damaged by the entire amount by which the child's earning capacity is diminished.[117] Definite evidence of such diminution in earning power cannot be expected, especially in case of a young child, and need not be produced.[118]

§ 487. Mitigation.

Circumstances which show that the damage was not as

is not obtained for that purpose, it will really be the child who will suffer.

[112] Sykes v. Lawlor, 49 Cal. 236.

[113] *Louisiana:* Brinkman v. St. Landry C. O. Co., 118 La. 835, 43 So. 458.

Missouri: Schmitz v. St. Louis, I. M. & S. Ry., 46 Mo. App. 380.

New Hampshire: Connell v. Putnam, 58 N. H. 534.

Rhode Island: Simone v. R. I. Co., 28 R. I. 186, 66 Atl. 202, 9 L. R. A. (N. S.) 740.

The amount recoverable is the value of the parent's services as nurse, not his loss in his own business by reason of his loss of time in nursing.

Alabama: Woodard Iron Co. v. Curl, 153 Ala. 205, 44 So. 974.

New York: Barnes v. Keene, 132 N. Y. 12, 29 N. E. 1090; Ceigler v. Hopper-Morgan Co., 90 App. Div. 379, 85 N. Y. Supp. 656.

[114] Birkel v. Chandler, 26 Wash. 241, 66 Pac. 406.

[115] *Illinois:* Seltzer v. Saxton, 71 Ill. App. 229.

Iowa: Goodrich v. Burlington C. R. & N. Ry., 97 Ia. 521, 66 N. W. 770.

New York: Traver v. Eighth Ave. R. R., 3 Keyes, 497.

[116] *New York:* Ceigler v. Hopper-Morgan Co., 90 App. Div. 379, 85 N. Y. Supp. 656.

Texas: Pacific Express Co. v. Watson (Tex. Civ. App.), 124 S. W. 127.

[117] *Missouri:* Mauerman v. St. Louis, I. M. & S. Ry., 41 Mo. App. 348; Schmitz v. St. Louis, I. M. & S. Ry., 46 Mo. App. 380.

Rhode Island: Galligan v. Woonsocket St. R. R., 27 R. I. 363, 62 Atl. 376.

[118] *Missouri:* Blackwell v. Hill, 76 Mo. App. 45, 54.

Nebraska: Vanderveer v. Moran, 112 N. W. 581, 79 Neb. 431.

Tennessee: Central Mfg. Co. v. Cotton, 108 Tenn. 63, 65 S. W. 403.

great as the evidence of the plaintiff appears to indicate may be introduced in mitigation. This is usually allowed in two cases. Where (as may always happen in cases of personal injury) a part of the damages consists in physical and mental suffering, non-pecuniary damage, circumstances of mitigation may be shown;[119] and where, as often happens in such cases, exemplary damages are allowed, circumstances of mitigation may always be shown.[120] In allowing evidence to be introduced in mitigation the courts are not always careful to state whether compensatory or exemplary damages are in question; and this fact has caused some confusion as to what may be admitted in mitigation. But the safe rule to follow is that any circumstance which tends to qualify the amount of pain, physical or mental, suffered by the plaintiff, may be shown in mitigation of compensatory damages; while any evidence which tends to qualify the malice of the defendant, or his desert to suffer punishment, may be shown in mitigation of exemplary damages.

The fact that parties fought by mutual agreement, or voluntarily engaged in a mutual affray, may be shown to mitigate at least exemplary damages,[121] but has been held not to mitigate compensatory damages.[122] The fact that the plaintiff was the aggressor may be shown to mitigate actual damages,[123] and so may the fact that plaintiff was making a great disturbance on defendant's land, and refused to leave when requested.[124] In an action for an assault and battery, where the altercation grew out of a question of veracity between the parties, the defendant was allowed to show that the *truth* of the matter in dispute was with him, in mitigation of damages.[125] But in an action by a husband and wife for an assault and battery on the wife, previous misconduct of the husband cannot be received in mitigation. Nor, it seems, where the misconduct consisted in fraudulently obtaining pos-

[119] *Ante,* § 51.
[120] *Ante,* §§ 383 *et seq.*
[121] Barholt *v.* Wright, 45 Oh. St. 177.
[122] *Maine:* Grotton *v.* Glidden, 84 Me. 589, 24 Atl. 1008, 30 Am. St. Rep. 413.
Wisconsin: Shay *v.* Thompson, 59

Wis. 540, 18 N. W. 473, 48 Am. Rep. 538.
[123] Kiff *v.* Youmans, 86 N. Y. 324, 40 Am. Rep. 543.
[124] Robison *v.* Rupert, 23 Pa. 523.
[125] Marker *v.* Miller, 9 Md. 338.

session of premises, and the assault and battery were perpetrated in forcibly turning out the fraudulent occupant, could such fraud be shown in mitigation of any real damages sustained by him. It could be received in mitigation of exemplary damages only, and then only where the fraud or its discovery was very recent and the defendant acted under the consequent excitement of the moment.[126]

The good character of the defendant is not admissible in mitigation of damages.[127]

§ 487a. Provocation.

One of the simplest forms of mitigatory evidence is always provocation. "In actions for personal wrongs and injuries," says Lord Abinger,[128] at Nisi Prius, "a defendant who does not deny that the verdict must pass against him, may give evidence to show that the plaintiff in some degree brought the thing upon himself." This was an action for assault and battery; and it was held that a libel published by the plaintiff on the defendant may be given in evidence in mitigation of damages, even though it be at the time the subject of a cross-action; but that being so, the defendant ought not to derive much advantage from it in mitigating the damages. Provocation may be given in evidence in mitigation of damages, provided it be so recent and immediate as to induce a presumption that the violence done was committed under the immediate influence of the feelings and passions excited by it.[129] In most

[126] Jacobs v. Hoover, 9 Minn. 204.

[127] Elliott v. Russell, 92 Ind. 526; Sturgeon v. Sturgeon, 4 Ind. App. 232, 30 N. E. 805.

[128] Fraser v. Berkeley, 7 C. & P. 621.

[129] *Delaware:* Hendle v. Geiler, 50 Atl. 632.

Illinois: Murphy v. McGrath, 79 Ill. 594; Chicago & A. R. R. v. Randolph, 65 Ill. App. 208.

Iowa: Ireland v. Elliott, 5 Ia. 478; Gronan v. Kukkuck, 59 Ia. 18, 12 N. W. 748.

Maine: Turner v. Footman, 71 Me. 218.

Maryland: Gaither v. Blowers, 11 Md. 536; Byers v. Horner, 47 Md. 23.

Massachusetts: Tyson v. Booth, 100 Mass. 258.

Mississippi: Martin v. Minor, 50 Miss. 42.

Missouri: Collins v. Todd, 17 Mo. 537.

New York: Corning v. Corning, 6 N. Y. 97; Willis v. Forrest, 2 Duer, 310.

North Carolina: Johnston v. Crawford, 62 N. C. (Phillips) 342; Palmer v. Winston-Salem R. & E. Co., 131 N. C. 250, 42 S. E. 604.

South Carolina: Hayes v. Sease, 51 S. C. 534, 29 S. E. 259.

of the cases cited it does not appear whether the damages to be mitigated were compensatory or exemplary; but in some jurisdictions evidence of provocation can be shown to mitigate exemplary damages only.[130]   So in Cushman v. Waddell,[131] which was an action by a schoolmaster against a parent for a severe beating, the court held that no provocation could excuse the defendant from making full compensation for all the injury the plaintiff had suffered by the unlawful attack on his person.   But if the jury were satisfied that, without any previous malice towards the plaintiff or any deliberate design to injure him in person or the estimation of the public, he acted in the heat of passion, caused by the appearance and account of his son, it was a circumstance which ought to operate powerfully to reduce the damages to such as were compensatory.

The provocation must be sufficient.[132]   Mere words may be proved in mitigation;[133] but words uttered by the plaintiff

Tennessee: Daniel v. Giles, 108 Tenn. 242, 66 S. W. 1128.

[130] *Delaware:* Armstrong v. Rhoades, 4 Pennew. 151, 53 Atl. 435.

Illinois: Donnelly v. Harris, 41 Ill. 126.

Missouri: Burley v. Menefee, 129 Mo. App. 518, 108 S. W. 120.

Nebraska: Mangold v. Oft, 63 Neb. 397, 88 N. W. 507.

New Jersey: Osler v. Walton, 67 N. J. L. 63, 50 Atl. 590.

New York: Genung v. Baldwin, 75 App. Div. 195, 77 N. Y. Supp. 679.

Vermont: Goldsmith v. Joy, 61 Vt. 488, 17 Atl. 110, 4 L. R. A. 500, 15 Am. St. Rep. 424.

Wisconsin: Wilson v. Young, 31 Wis. 574; Brown v. Swineford, 44 Wis. 282, 28 Am. Rep. 582; Corcoran v. Harran, 55 Wis. 120, 12 N. W. 468.

In *Pennsylvania,* Robinson v. Rupert, 23 Pa. 523, a peculiar distinction is taken; provocation by a third person may mitigate exemplary damages only, but provocation by the plaintiff may mitigate compensatory damages as well.

[131] 1 Bald. 57.

[132] Refusal of plaintiff to return defendant's salutation is not sufficient. Turnbow v. Wimberly, 106 La. 259, 30 So. 747.

The more violent and wanton the attack, the greater must be the provocation to mitigate (exemplary) damages.

Illinois: Drohn v. Brewer, 77 Ill. 280.

Minnesota: Crosby v. Humphreys, 59 Minn. 92, 60 N. W. 843.

[133] *California:* Bundy v. Maginess, 76 Cal. 532, 18 Pac. 668.

Delaware: Tatnall v. Courtney, 6 Houst. 434; Hendle v. Geiler, 50 Atl. 632.

Georgia: Berkner v. Danneberg, 116 Ga. 954, 43 S. E. 463, 60 L. R. A. 559.

Illinois: Donnelly v. Harris, 41 Ill. 126.

Kentucky: Doerhoefer v. Shewmaker, 97 S. W. 7, 29 Ky. L. Rep. 1193 (obscene language).

Louisiana: Munday v. Landry, 51 La. Ann. 303, 25 So. 66.

Minnesota: Crosby v. Humphreys, 59 Minn. 92, 60 N. W. 843.

against the defendant in the absence of the latter, and reported to him by a third person, are not admissible in mitigation.[134]

§ 488. Bad character of the plaintiff.

The plaintiff's bad character and association with persons of ill repute does not usually palliate an assault, and cannot mitigate the damages.[135]   Nor can a person guilty of wilful assault and battery show that, from the intemperate habits of the other party, the injury was more aggravated than it would have been upon a person of temperate habits.[136]   Yet evidence of character and habits may be admissible in many cases where it would have a special bearing on the damages claimed.[137]   So in an action for assault with intent to ravish, the plaintiff's character for modesty may be shown, since it would have a bearing on the amount of injury to her feelings; [138] and for the same reasons the plaintiff's quarrelsome character may be considered in an action for assault and battery.[139] So it has been held that in an action for personal injuries caused by the defendant's negligence the unchastity of the plaintiff may be considered on the question of her loss of wages for domestic service.[140]

New York: Keyes v. Devlin, 3 E. D. Smith, 518; Roades v. Larson, 21 N. Y. Supp. 855, 50 N. Y. St. 551.

In a case in Maine it appeared that plaintiff gave provocation for an assault by the use of insulting language, but this was the result of intoxication by liquors furnished plaintiff by the defendant. It was held that defendant could not take advantage of the state of mind which he himself had caused, and while the general rule is that provocation could be shown to mitigate the damages for such an injury, that could not be done in this case. Robichaud v. Maheux, 104 Me. 524, 72 Atl. 334.

[134] Jarvis v. Manlove, 5 Harr. (Del.) 452.

[135] *Massachusetts:* Bruce v. Priest, 5 All. 100.

Nevada: Johnson v. Wells, 6 Nev. 224.

New York: Corning v. Corning, 6 N. Y. 97.

Texas: Shook v. Peters, 59 Tex. 393.

[136] Littlehale v. Dix, 11 Cush. (Mass.) 364.

[137] So in Abbott v. Tolliver, 71 Wis. 64, 70, 36 N. W. 622, Cole, C. J., said: "The fact of chastity, as well as other personal virtues and business qualifications, would be proper matters for a jury to consider in making up their verdict as to what damages should be given as a compensation for the injury."

[138] *Vermont:* Parker v. Coture, 63 Vt. 155, 21 Atl. 494, 25 Am. St. Rep. 750.

Wisconsin: Barton v. Bruley, 119 Wis. 326, 96 N. W. 815.

[139] Lowe v. Ring, 123 Wis. 107, 101 N. W. 381.

[140] Carlton v. St. Louis & Suburban Ry., 128 Mo. App. 451, 106 S. W. 1100.

§ 489. Criminal conviction.

Nor can the defendant in a civil action for an assault and battery be permitted to prove in mitigation of damages that he had been indicted, convicted, and fined for the same offence. An indictment is intended as a vindication of public justice; an action is brought for compensation for private injury. The object of the two proceedings is entirely distinct, and the one should not interfere with the course of the other.[141] In Texas, however, the payment of a fine is admissible in mitigation of exemplary damages.[142] And in England the fact that defendant had been convicted on complaint of the plaintiff, who had received part of the fine, could be shown in mitigation.[143]

§ 489a. Aggravation.

Proper evidence may be introduced in aggravation of damages. Thus evidence of the defendant's malice may be given to aggravate damages for assault and battery, since it affects plaintiff's mental suffering.[144] And plaintiff may prove that he was sober and industrious, as affecting his earning power, in an action for personal injury.[145] But where defendant has already been prosecuted criminally for a battery, the fact that only a nominal fine was inflicted and paid will not increase the damages.[146]

§ 490. Circumstances of the parties.

The amount of compensatory damages is not affected by the wealth or poverty of the plaintiff.[147] Nor can he augment damages by proving that he has a wife and several small

[141] *Delaware:* Armstrong v. Rhoades, 4 Pennew. 151, 53 Atl. 435.
Illinois: Hanson v. Urbana & C. El. St. Ry., 75 Ill. App. 474.
Iowa: Lucas v. Flinn, 35 Ia. 9; Reddin v. Gates, 52 Ia. 210, 2 N. W. 1079.
Mississippi: Wheatley v. Thorn, 23 Miss. 62.
New York: Cook v. Ellis, 6 Hill, 466, 41 Am. Dec. 757.
South Carolina: Wolff v. Cohen, 8 Rich. L. 144; Edwards v. Weissinger, 65 S. C. 161, 43 S. E. 518.
Vermont: Roach v. Caldbeck, 64 Vt. 593, 24 Atl. 989.
[142] Flanagan v. Womack, 54 Tex. 45; Jackson v. Wells, 13 Tex. Civ. App. 275, 35 S. W. 528.
[143] Jacks v. Bell, 3 C. & P. 316, 14 E. C. L. 586.
[144] Webb v. Gilman, 80 Me. 177, 13 Atl. 688.
[145] Metropolitan St. Ry. v. Kennedy, 82 Fed. 158, 27 C. C. A. 136.
[146] Honaker v. Howe, 19 Gratt. (Va.) 50.
[147] *United States:* Alabama G. S. R.

children.[148] And the wealth of the defendant should not be considered in estimating compensatory damages.[149] For this reason the fact that defendant is a rich corporation cannot be considered by the jury. So in Illinois Central Railroad v. Nelson,[150] an action for being wrongfully put off a train, it

R. v. Carroll, 84 Fed. 772, 28 C. C. A. 207.

Alabama: Barbour Co. v. Horn, 48 Ala. 566.

California: Shea v. R. R., 44 Cal. 414; Malone v. Hawley, 46 Cal. 409.

Georgia: Georgia R. & B. Co. v. Benton, 117 Ga. 785, 45 S. E. 70.

Kansas: City of Parsons v. Lindsay, 26 Kan. 426; Bank of LeRoy v. Harding, 1 Kan. App. 389, 41 Pac. 680; Fort Scott, W. & W. Ry. v. Lightburn, 9 Kan. App. 642, 58 Pac. 1033.

Missouri: Berryman v. Cox, 73 Mo. App. 61.

Texas: Belton v. Lockett (Tex. Civ. App.), 57 S. W. 687; Dallas C. E. St. Ry. v. Summers, 48 Tex. Civ. App. 474, 106 S. W. 891.

Vermont: Roach v. Caldbeck, 64 Vt. 593, 24 Atl. 989.

Wisconsin: Vosberg v. Putney, 78 Wis. 84, 47 N. W. 99, 14 L. R. A. 226 (wealth of father of minor plaintiff).

Contra, Illinois: McNamara v. King, 7 Ill. 432; Cochran v. Ammon, 16 Ill. 316, where Skinner, J., said: "The pain and suffering may be much greater where, from his pecuniary condition, the husband is unable to furnish medical aid, remedies, apartments, and nursing, such as ample means would afford," and therefore the pecuniary condition of the husband "tended to show the extent of the injury to the wife."

Indiana: Taber v. Hutson, 5 Ind. 322, 61 Am. Dec. 96.

Mississippi: Eltringham v. Earhart, 67 Miss. 488, 7 So. 346, 19 Am. St. Rep. 319.

[148] *United States:* Pennsylvania R. R. v. Roy, 102 U. S. 451, 26 L. ed. 141; Baltimore & O. R. R. v. Camp, 81 Fed.

807, 26 C. C. A. 626; Alabama G. S. R. R. v. Carroll, 84 Fed. 772, 28 C. C. A. 207.

Alabama: Louisville & N. R. R. v. Binion, 107 Ala. 645, 18 So. 75.

Georgia: Georgia R. & B. Co. v. Benton, 117 Ga. 785, 45 S. E. 70.

Illinois: Chicago v. O'Brennan, 65 Ill. 160; Pittsburg, F. W. & C. Ry. v. Powers, 74 Ill. 341 (but see McNamara v. King, 7 Ill. 432).

Kansas: Kansas City, F. S. & M. R. R. v. Eagan, 64 Kan. 421, 67 Pac. 887; Union Pac. Ry. v. Hammerlund, 70 Kan. 888, 79 Pac. 152.

Maryland: Stockton v. Frey, 4 Gill, 406, 45 Am. Dec. 138.

Tennessee: Louisville & N. R. R. v. Gower, 85 Tenn. 465.

Texas: City of Belton v. Lockett (Tex. Civ. App.), 57 S. W. 687.

Virginia: Southern Ry. v. Simmons, 105 Va. 651, 55 S. E. 459.

West Virginia: More v. Huntington, 31 W. Va. 842, 8 S. E. 512; Sesler v. Rolfe Coal & C. Co., 51 W. Va. 318, 41 S. E. 216.

Contra, South Carolina: Youngblood v. South Carolina & G. R. R., 60 S. C. 9, 38 S. E. 232.

Australia: Devir v. Curley, 3 N. S. W. L. R. 322.

[149] Taber v. Hutson, 5 Ind. 322, 61 Am. Dec. 96.

But in a few cases, where the damages appear to have been compensatory, the wealth of the defendant was shown:

Illinois: McNamara v. King, 7 Ill. 432.

Mississippi: Etringham v. Earhart, 67 Miss. 488, 7 So. 346, 19 Am. St. Rep. 319.

[150] 59 Ill. 110.

was held error to charge the jury that they were "not confined to the same amount of damages or the same rules as if the suit was between individuals, as the public have an interest in such cases which may be considered and looked to in assessing the damages." In Toledo, Wabash & Western Railway v. Smith [151] it was held to be error to tell the jury that in assessing damages against a company and a conductor, for expelling the plaintiff from the cars, they could consider the ability of the company to pay. And in an action against a town for personal injury to the plaintiff, the assessed value of the town cannot be shown.[152]

Where exemplary damages are permissible, the pecuniary condition of the defendant may be shown,[153] as has been seen in a previous chapter.[154]

§ 491. Avoidable consequences.

The fact that plaintiff might by proper care have avoided part of the consequences of the defendant's tort may, as has already been seen,[155] be shown to limit recovery. So where the plaintiff was injured by a train, but did not employ a physician for a week after the injury, it was held that she was bound to take ordinary care to make the damages as small as possible, and if she did not, she could not recover for the damages resulting.[156] But the failure to obey the orders of his physician does not bar the plaintiff from his action; it simply goes in mitigation.[157]

[151] 57 Ill. 517.

[152] Madigan v. Schaghticoke, 128 N. Y. Supp. 800 (App. Div.).

[153] United States: Brown v. Evans, 8 Sawy. 488, 17 Fed. 912.

Illinois: Alcorn v. Mitchell, 63 Ill. 553.

Maryland: Zell v. Dunaway, 80 Atl. 215.

Mississippi: Bell v. Morrison, 27 Miss. 68.

Missouri: Beck v. Dowell, 40 Mo. App. 71; Johnston v. Wells, 112 Mo. App. 557, 87 S. W. 70.

Ohio: Hendricks v. Fowler, 16 Ohio C. Ct. 597, 9 Ohio Cir. Dec. 209.

South Carolina: Rowe v. Moses, 9 Rich. 423, 67 Am. Dec. 560.

If evidence of defendant's wealth is admitted, defendant may in reply introduce evidence of his own poverty to meet it.

Illinois: Mullin v. Spangenberg, 112 Ill. 140, 145.

Maine: Johnson v. Smith, 64 Me. 553.

[154] Ante, § 385.

[155] Ante, § 214a.

[156] Allender v. Chicago, R. I. & P. R. R., 37 Ia. 264.

[157] New York: DuBois v. Decker, 130 N. Y. 325, 29 N. E. 313, 14 L. R. A. 429.

Owing to the condition of plaintiff, caused by indulgence in intoxicating liquors, although he was then in good health, the shock of the injury produced delirium tremens, which retarded his recovery. It was held that the general rule, that where injury develops a latent disease the person responsible for the injury is responsible for such disease,[158] applies here, although the tendency was caused by the defendant's voluntary indulgence in liquor.[159]

North Carolina: M c C r a c k e n *v.* Smathers, 122 N. C. 799, 29 S. E. 354. *Texas:* Trinity & S. Ry. *v.* O'Brien, 18 Tex. Civ. App. 690, 46 S. W. 389.

[158] *Ante,* § 121b.

[159] Maguire *v.* Sheehan, 117 Fed. 819, 54 C. C. A. 642.

CHAPTER XXI

§ 492. Forms of action.

* Trover is the form of action prescribed by the common law, where damages are demanded for specific personal property which has been wrongfully appropriated, or, in more technical language, converted to the use of any other than its rightful owner. It was often brought at the option of the plaintiff in cases where assumpsit, and in others where trespass, or replevin, would lie.[1] The consequences flowing from

[1] Barker v. Cory, 15 Oh. 9. And so, to-day, facts showing conversion may justify an action of contract. Fifth Nat. Bk. v. Providence Warehouse, 17 R. I. 112, 20 Atl. 203, 9 L. R. A. 260; Anderson v. First Nat. Bk., 5 N. D. 451, 67 N. W. 821.

the election of assumpsit are well stated in the language of Lord Ellenborough, C. J.:

"In bringing an action for money had and received, instead of trover, the plaintiff does no more than waive any complaint, with a view to damages, of the tortious act by which the goods were converted into money, and takes to the net proceeds of the sale as the value of the goods,[2] subject, of course, to all the consequences of considering the demand in question as a *debt*, and, amongst others, to that of the defendants having a right of set-off, if they should happen to have any counter-demand against the plaintiff." [3] **

Assumpsit for money had and received is the proper form of action when the defendant has received money, or what is to be treated as such, to the use of the plaintiff; but it will not lie for stocks, goods, or other articles, unless by the understanding of the parties they were to be treated as money. Accordingly, where the plaintiff sued in this form of action, at a time when gold had risen to a premium, to recover a sum of gold which had been deposited with the sheriff's deputy as bail, the recovery was limited to the value of the gold as money, with interest.[4] But in an action of trover, for the value of certain special deposits in coin, it was held, by the Supreme Court of Missouri, that the measure of damages was the *value* of the coin at the date of its conversion.[5] In Stevens *v.* Low [6] where goods having been sold at an agreed price, to be paid in notes, and delivered conditionally, and the condition being broken, trover was brought for the goods, the court said that if assumpit had been brought, the plaintiff would have been entitled to the *agreed* value; but that in trover the *value* and interest was the true measure, and that the defendant was at liberty to show that the value of the property was much less than the agreed price. And this is in accordance with

[2] DeClerq *v.* Mungin, 46 Ill. 112.

[3] Hunter *v.* Prinsep, 10 East, 378, 391.

[4] Frothingham *v.* Morse, 45 N. H. 545.

[5] Coffey *v.* National Bank of Missouri, 46 Mo. 140, 2 Am. Rep. 488. If plaintiff waives the conversion, and

sues in *assumpsit* for money had and received, he can recover only what the defendant actually received. Howell *v.* Greaves, 27 Ark. 365. *Cf.* Murray *v.* Pate, 6 Dana (Ky.), 335; Thomas *v.* Waterman, 7 Met. (Mass.) 227.

[6] 2 Hill (N. Y.), 132.

60

the analogous cases brought on implied or express warranties of chattels, which will be considered later.

§ 492a. The modern action for conversion.

Any interference or intermeddling with the property of another, or the exercise of dominion over it, in denial of the owner's right, constitutes a conversion, for which an action for the value of the property converted can be maintained.[7] Since by our law a purchaser gets no better title than his vendor had, the plaintiff may recover not only from the original wrongdoer, but from anyone claiming title under him however innocent; e. g., the person who originally committed the wrong or his vendee or an officer attaching and selling at the suit of one having no title, or his vendee.

The transfer of a promissory note by indorsement to a *bona fide* holder, who enforces it against plaintiff (a prior indorser) may involve a conversion, though having been negotiated for a purpose not intended by the first indorser; and the latter may recover the amount he has had to pay.[8]

If the plaintiff has been deprived of property, it will constitute a conversion, though there be no acquisition of property to defendant.[9] Conversion may be either direct or constructive, and may be proved, directly or by inference.[10]

---

[7] Milner & Kettig Co. v. DeLeach Mill. Mfg. Co., 139 Ala. 645, 36 So. 765.

[8] Comstock v. Hier, 73 N. Y. 269, 29 Am. Rep. 142.

[9] Keyworth v. Hill, 5 E. C. L. 422, 3 B. & Ald. 685 (book burnt by wife, by order of husband).

[10] Every *unlawful taking* with intent to apply the goods to the use of the taker, or of some other persons than the owner, or having the effect of destroying or altering their nature, is a conversion. But if it does not interfere with the owner's dominion over the property, nor alter its condition, it is not. Upon these principles, it has been held that if a ferryman wrongly put the horses of a passenger out of the boat, without farther intent concerning them, it may be a trespass, but it is not a conversion; but if he make any further disposition of them, inconsistent with the owner's rights, it is a conversion. 2 Greenl. Ev., § 642. These are the principles to be deduced from the numerous cases on this subject. If there is no intent to interfere with the owner's dominion of property, there can be no conversion. The bare removing of one's chattel from one spot to another, without denying his ownership, but on the contrary acknowledging it, cannot be a conversion. It is neither a deprivation of the owner's right, nor is it the use, enjoyment, change or destruction of the property:

Alabama: King v. Franklin, 132 Ala. 559, 31 So. 467.

Conversion is the gist of the action; and an unqualified refusal after demand is evidence which, combined with proof of title in the plaintiff, is conclusive. The return of the property after conversion is no bar, but is admissible in mitigation of damages. In such a case, of course, the plaintiff recovers the actual damages sustained. Under ordinary circumstances, the defendant cannot compel plaintiff to accept a return, but sometimes, e. g., when the property came lawfully into the defendant's possession, and no actual damages are suffered, the plaintiff recovers only nominal damages for a technical conversion. The term conversion is used in two senses; one denoting the legal cause of action, the other the substantive acts, causing or not causing damage, but still adequate to bring the cause of action into existence.[11] For a purely technical conversion (i. e., where there is a conversion in law but no damage is done), nominal damages only are recoverable. The title does not vest in the defendant until either judgment, or satisfaction of judgment, and if before the title leaves the plaintiff the property is taken from defendant on a writ against the plaintiff, of which he must ultimately have the benefit, nominal damages only can be allowed.[12]

Under the modern system of pleading, a complaint for the conversion of property must, it is said, still contain the *material* allegations necessary in a common-law action of trover. This does not mean that the fictitious allegation of the finding of the property is retained; the gist of the modern action is the unlawful conversion, that is, assumption of ownership, of goods coming lawfully or unlawfully into the defendant's possession. The property must have value, but the value need not be alleged. Damages, however, must be alleged. It is no defence that the conversion was by mistake. There must have been possession, actual or constructive, and there must be some act of dominion (not necessarily manual) in denial of the owner's right or inconsistent with it. Demand and refusal of the property, originally in trover probably indis-

Missouri: Sparks *v.* Purdy, 11 Mo. 219, 225.

[11] Bigelow Co. *v.* Heintze, 53 N. J. L. 69, 21 Atl. 109.

[12] Jones *v.* Cobb, 84 Me. 153, 24 Atl. 798.

pensable, are evidence of conversion, but the fact of conversion is capable of proof by any adequate evidence. Possession, or the right to it at the time of the conversion, must be alleged. The measure of damages (running from the time of the conversion) is, in the absence of special circumstances, the value of the property or property rights converted, at the time of the conversion, with interest. Special damages may be recovered; if accepted, the return in such a case goes in mitigation of damages.[13] And so, too, if the return and acceptance is by operation of law. A destruction of the property, after conversion, does not affect the measure of damages.[14]

Where defendant knowing another to be mentally incompetent, induces the other by fraud or undue influence to transfer property to him, this is conversion.[15]

Conversion is not trespass and they must be carefully distinguished.[16] Trespass does not necessarily import anything in derogation or denial of title.

After the plaintiff acquires a claim for the amount of money representing the measure of damages involved, the ordinary rate of interest is allowed upon it.[17]

§ 492b. Conversion by demand and refusal.

It frequently happens that the measure of damages in the action for conversion begins to run from the time of demand for the property by the plaintiff and refusal by the defendant, and where there is no actual demand, from the time of judicial demand or suit brought; but it is important to notice that refusal to restore goods on demand is only evidence of the conversion and is not necessary whenever a conversion can

[13] *Colorado:* Sigel-Campion Live Stock Com. Co. *v.* Holly, 44 Colo. 580, 101 Pac. 68.

Indiana: B. L. Blair Co. *v.* Rose, 26 Ind. App. 487, 60 N. E. 10.

Massachusetts: Iasigi *v.* Shea, 148 Mass. 538, 20 N. E. 110.

Montana: Babcock *v.* Coldwell, 22 Mont. 460, 56 Pac. 1081.

New York: Suffus *v.* Bangs, 15 N. Y. Supp. 444; Gleason *v.* Morrison, 20 Misc. 320, 45 N. Y. Supp. 684.

[14] Burney *v.* Pledger, 3 Rich. L. (S. C.) 191.

[15] Hagar *v.* Norton, 188 Mass. 47, 73 N. E. 1073. *Cf.* Cone *v.* Ivinson, 4 Wyo. 203, 35 Pac. 933.

[16] *Michigan:* Mattice v. Brinkman, 74 Mich. 705, 42 N. W. 172.

Oregon: Lee Tung *v.* Burkhart, 116 Pac. 1066.

[17] Scollans *v.* Rollins, 173 Mass. 275, 60 N. E. 983, 73 Am. St. Rep. 284.

otherwise be proved.[18] Hence it is not necessary to allege a demand and refusal.[19] Thus in a case where goods were converted and there was afterwards demand and refusal, defendant claimed that the measure of damages was the value at the time of demand and refusal; but it was held that the conversion having been prior to that time, he could recover damages from the time of conversion.[20] On the other hand, the purchaser of property in good faith from one who is not the owner has been held in Louisiana to be only liable for the fruits from the time of suit brought.[21]

The following cases may serve as illustrations of the necessity of finding out by the circumstances of the case the precise point in time at which the conversion takes place. In California, the measure of damages being by the Code, the value of the property at the time of the conversion with interest, plaintiff cannot in an action for the conversion of stock based on the refusal of the corporation to register a transfer recover as part of the damages dividends declared prior to the conversion. Recovery of the dividends after demand would be a separate cause of action.[22]

In another suit in the same State, where plaintiff alleged placing in the hands of defendant as agent a sum of money to be loaned and the agency is denied, it has been held that plaintiff need not allege or prove demand. By denying the agency, the defendant rendered unnecessary allegation and proof of demand.[23]

The commencement of an action for an accounting between partners has been held to be equivalent to a demand by the plaintiff for his share of the partnership property. The defendant by resisting recovery converts it.[24]

Proof of demand is said to be necessary where defendant had an interest in the property and came into lawful posses-

[18] *Georgia:* Scarborough *v.* Goethe, 118 Ga. 543, 45 S. E. 413.

Minnesota: Hogan *v.* Atlantic Elevator Co., 66 Minn. 344, 69 N. W. 1.

[19] Baltimore & O. R. R. *v.* O'Donnell, 49 Ohio St. 489, 32 N. E. 476.

[20] Zindorf *v.* Western American Co., 26 Wash. 695, 67 Pac. 355.

[21] Dyson *v.* Phelps, 14 La. Ann. 722; *cf.* Rideau *v.* Bornet, 1 La. Ann. 408.

[22] Ralston *v.* Bank of California, 112 Cal. 208, 44 Pac. 476.

[23] Becker *v.* Feizenbaum (Cal.), 46 Pac. 837.

[24] Continental Divide Mining Inv. Co. *v.* Bliley, 23 Cal. 160, 46 Pac. 633.

sion of it, and a mere allegation of demand without proof, of course, will not do.[25] Between tenants in common, if one takes property against the other's protest, the latter being present and forbidding the conversion, demand before suit is not necessary.[26] If personal property is taken from the true owner by a wrongdoer and by him sold to an innocent purchaser, the true owner's action, he having been guilty of no wrong or negligence, may be brought without previous demand.[27] And generally, wherever demand would be a useless ceremony, it is unnecessary.[28]

The rule often laid down that one who comes lawfully into possession of property cannot be charged with conversion until after demand and refusal, should probably be qualified by the addition—unless he is guilty of some act of dominion in contradiction to the title or property of the owner. If he commits an overt and positive act of conversion, the character of his possession changes and becomes tortious. The object of securing the refusal by means of the demand is the same, that is, to change the character of possession.[29]

An officer, levying on property (if he knows nothing to rebut the presumption that, being in the possession of the defendant in execution, it is his) cannot be charged with conversion, unless after notice, he insists on retaining possession, and refuses to restore to the owner. In all such cases demand and refusal becomes of great importance.[30]

§ 493. General rule in cases of conversion.

We now come to the examination of the rules which govern damages in the common-law action of trover, or in actions where redress is demanded for the wrongful conversion of specific articles of personal property. In an action for the conversion of personal property, the measure of damages is the value of the property at the time of the conversion, with

[25] Moynahan v. Prentiss, 10 Colo. App. 295, 51 Pac. 94.

[26] Wallor v. Bowling, 108 N. C. 289, 12 S. E. 990.

[27] Rosum v. Hodges, 1 S. D. 308, 47 N. W. 140.

[28] E. F. Hallock Lumber & Mfg. Co. v. Gray, 19 Colo. 149, 34 Pac. 1000.

[29] MacDonnell v. Buffalo L. T. & S. D. Co., 193 N. Y. 92, 85 N. E. 801.

[30] Pilcher v. Hickman, 132 Ala. 574, 31 So. 469.

interest.[31]   And if the conversion of part of an article renders the rest worthless for all purposes, the value of the whole may be recovered.[32]

[31] *United States:* Watt v. Potter, 2 Mass. 77; Scull v. Briddle, 2 Wash. C. C. 150.
Alabama: Williams v. Crum, 27 Ala. 468 (*semble*); Massey v. Fain (Ala. App.), 55 So. 936.
Arkansas: Ryburn v. Pryor, 14 Ark. 505; Jefferson v. Hale, 31 Ark. 286.
California: Cassin v. Marshall, 18 Cal. 689; Barrante v. Garratt, 50 Cal. 112.
Colorado: Sutton v. Dana, 15 Colo. 98, 25 Pac. 90.
Connecticut: Lewis v. Morse, 20 Conn. 211; Swift v. Barnum, 23 Conn. 523 (*semble*); Hurd v. Hubbell, 26 Conn. 389; Cook v. Loomis, 26 Conn. 483.
Delaware: Vaughan v. Webster, 5 Harr. 256; Layman v. F. F. Slocomb & Co., 76 Atl. 1094.
Florida: Robinson v. Hartridge, 13 Fla. 501; Skinner v. Pinney, 19 Fla. 42, 45 Am. Rep. 1.
Georgia: Riley v. Martin, 35 Ga. 136; Hilton v. Sylvania & G. R. R., (Ga. App.), 68 S. E. 746.
Illinois: Keaggy v. Hite, 12 Ill. 99; Sturges v. Keith, 57 Ill. 451, 11 Am. Rep. 28; Tripp v. Grouner, 60 Ill. 474; Schwitters v. Springer, 236 Ill. 271, 86 N. E. 102.
Indiana: Yater v. Mullen, 24 Ind. 277.
Iowa: Cutter v. Fanning, 2 Ia. 580; Robinson v. Hurley, 11 Ia. 410, 79 Am. Dec. 497; Russell v. Huiskamp, 77 Ia. 727, 42 N. W. 525.
Kentucky: Sanders v. Vance, 7 T. B. Mon. 209, 18 Am. Dec. 167; Freeman v. Luckett, 2 J. J. Marsh. 390; Daniel v. Holland, 4 J. J. Marsh. 18; Justice v. Mendell, 14 B. Mon. 12.
Louisiana: Chamberlain v. Worrell, 38 La. Ann. 347; Jennings H. O. Synd.

v. Housserie-Latreille Oil Co., 127 La. 971, 54 So. 318.
Maine: Hayden v. Bartlett, 35 Me. 203; Robinson v. Barrows, 48 Me. 186.
Maryland: Stirling v. Garritee, 18 Md. 468; Hopper v. Haines, 71 Md. 64, 18 Atl. 29, 20 Atl. 159.
Massachusetts: Beecher v. Denniston, 13 Gray, 354.
Michigan: Symes v. Oliver, 13 Mich. 9; Ripley v. Davis, 15 Mich. 75, 90 Am. Dec. 262; Allen v. Kinyon, 41 Mich. 281, 1 N. W. 863.
Minnesota: Chase v. Blaisdell, 4 Minn. 90; Murphy v. Sherman, 25 Minn. 196.
Missouri: Carter v. Feland, 17 Mo. 383; Polk v. Allen, 19 Mo. 467; Spencer v. Vance, 57 Mo. 427; Charles v. St. Louis & I. M. R. R., 58 Mo. 458.
Nevada: Carlyon v. Lannan, 4 Nev. 156; Newman v. Kane, 9 Nev. 234.
New York: Andrews v. Durant, 18 N. Y. 496, 62 Am. Dec. 55; Griswold v. Haven, 25 N. Y. 595, 82 Am. Dec. 380; McCormick v. Pennsylvania C. R. R., 49 N. Y. 303; Mechanics' & T. Bank v. Farmers' & M. Nat. Bank, 60 N. Y. 40; Wehle v. Haviland, 69 N. Y. 448; Prince v. Conner, 69 N. Y. 608; Cutler v. James Goold Co., 43 Hun, 516; King v. Orser, 4 Duer, 431; Devlin v. Pike, 5 Daly, 85.
Ohio: Dixon v. Caldwell, 15 Oh. St. 412, 86 Am. Dec. 487.
Oregon: Singer v. Pearson-Page Co., 115 Pac. 158; Lee Tung v. Burkhart, 116 Pac. 1066.
Pennsylvania: Perrin v. Wells, 155 Pa. 299, 26 Atl. 543.
Texas: Hillebrant v. Brewer, 6 Tex. 45, 55 Am. Dec. 757; Hatcher v. Pelham, 31 Tex. 201; Schoolher v. Hutchins, 66 Tex. 324, 1 S. W. 266; Smith

[32] Walker v. Johnson, 28 Minn. 147.

§ 493a. Elasticity of the rule—Reduction of damages.

There is no other way of stating the normal rule in conversion than the foregoing, but as the great advantage of the action is its elasticity, the great advantage of the rule is that it can be stretched to cover the facts of any case as it presents itself, and hence the action has been called equitable in character. The normal conversion must be imagined as consisting of a wrongful transfer of title at a given instant of time, and in this case, the rule as it is given applies.[33]

In an action in Pennsylvania for the conversion of three rafts of timber, the defendant asked the court to instruct the jury that "In no event can the plaintiff in this action of trover recover more than the actual value of the three rafts of timber and interest thereon—the value to be fixed by the market value of the timber at the time when and the place where the alleged trover and conversion took place." It was held that it was error to refuse so to instruct.[34]

Ordinarily the plaintiff cannot recover the value of the use, because he recovers the value of the property as of the time when it was taken from his possession, very much as if it were the case of a forced sale.[35] Consequently it is error to render judgment for rent or hire.[36] So in a case of bonds bearing

v. Bates (Tex. Civ. App.), 27 S. W. 1044.

Vermont: Grant v. King, 14 Vt. 367; Thrall v. Lathrop, 30 Vt. 307, 73 Am. Dec. 306; Crumb v. Oaks, 38 Vt. 566.

Wisconsin: Tenney v. Bank of Wisconsin, 20 Wis. 152; Ingram v. Rankin, 47 Wis. 406, 2 N. W. 755, 32 Am. Rep. 762.

England: Watson v. McLean, 1 E. B. & E. 75; Mulliner v. Florence, 3 Q. B. Div. 484; Ried v. Fairbanks, 13 C. B. 692; Johnson v. Lancashire & Y. Ry., 3 C. P. D. 499.

Canada: Rankin v. Mitchell, 1 Han. 495.

[33] *Colorado:* Hannan v. Connett, 10 Colo. 171, 50 Pac. 214; Sylvester v. Craig, 18 Colo. 44, 31 Pac. 387.

Georgia: Dorsett v. Frith, 25 Ga. 537.

Illinois: Wenham v. Wilson, 129 Ill. App. 553.

Kansas: Simpson v. Alexander, 35 Kan. 225, 11 Pac. 171.

Kentucky: Greer v. Powell, 1 Bush, 489.

Maryland: Thomas v. Sternheimer, 29 Md. 268.

Nevada: Carlyon v. Lannan, 4 Nev. 156.

Pennsylvania: Backentoss v. Stahler, 33 Pa. 251, 75 Am. Dec. 592.

[34] Hill v. Canfield, 56 Pa. 454.

[35] *New York:* Cutler v. James Goold Co., 43 Hun, 516.

Oregon: Singer v. Pearson-Page Co., (Ore.), 115 Pac. 158.

[36] Texarkana Water Co. v. Kizer, 2 Tex. Ct. Rep. 1056, 63 S. W. 913. But see Moore v. King, 4 Tex. Civ. App. 400, 23 S. W. 481.

interest at 4% and worth par, the measure of damages was the value of the bonds with legal interest, not 4% interest, from the date of conversion.[37] Reduction of damages becomes of great importance in case of title to personal property derived from illegal process and sale. The principle is familiar that the moment illegal process is set aside for irregularity, the party in fault becomes a trespasser *ab initio*. The return of the property only goes in reduction of damages. It is no bar to an action for the wrong.[38] In such cases, the fact that the defendant is a creditor of the plaintiff does not reduce damages.[39] On the other hand, where there was a seizure of goods on a void writ, and the defendant procured the goods subsequently to be seized on a valid writ, when they were sold and the proceeds paid in on the claim, this could be shown in reduction. The law here makes the application.[40] So amount due for taxes may be applied in reduction.[41] In an action for conversion of cattle by delivery to one not entitled, defendant may show in reduction of damages that plaintiff has received payment for the cattle and has not been damnified, or that his damages are merely nominal.[42] And it has been said that the measure of damages is the actual value at the date of conversion minus any claim which the defendant had on the property.[43] But ordinarily mere possession is a sufficient title on which to recover, and the action cannot be defeated, nor damages mitigated, by proof of ownership in some one else, unless he shows connection with the owner, so that he can stand upon his right; or that the property has gone to his use.[44]

Where the goods have been returned, the reduction is ordinarily the net receipts, taking the expense out of the value of the goods as returned; but here again the elasticity of the rule is shown, and if it is for any reason not proper in this action to make allowance for such expense, it will not be

[37] Govin *v.* DeMiranda, 140 N. Y. 474, 35 N. E. 626.

[38] Kerr *v.* Mount, 28 N. Y. 659; Johnson *v.* Marks, 66 Misc. 153, 121 N. Y. Supp. 294.

[39] Kelley *v.* Archer, 48 Barb. (N. Y.) 68.

[40] Mississippi Mills *v.* Meyer, 83 Tex. 433, 18 S. W. 748.

[41] Clements *v.* Eisely, 63 Neb. 651, 88 N. W. 871.

[42] Stone *v.* Chicago, M. & S. P. Ry., 3 S. D. 330, 53 N. W. 189.

[43] Merchants' Nat. Bank *v.* Williams, 110 Md. 334, 72 Atl. 1114.

[44] Wooley *v.* Edson, 35 Vt. 214.

done. So in an action for conversion of oxen, when the oxen were taken into New York and there the plaintiff obtained possession of them by legal process, and he now brings this action, in which he seeks to recover the expenses of regaining the property, it is held that he cannot recover, having chosen to resort to a form of action in which he got possession of the goods. He is restricted to the costs allowed in that action and cannot bring trover to recover the expenses not there allowed.[45]

Where the articles are returned and accepted, it is obvious that the title does not finally change. Hence interest cannot always be the proper measure of damages. The plaintiff may claim damages for the use and deterioration.[46] And when the property has been sold and the proceeds applied to the plaintiff's debt, the reason for the ordinary rule forbids its application.[47] On the other hand, if the whole proceeding is void, as on a void execution, defendant's offer to apply the amount on the judgment goes for nothing if plaintiff does not consent.[48] When the thing converted is reduced to money in the hands of the defendant, the smallest measure of damages must be the amount received, with interest.[49]

Statutory changes or a local judicial divergence from the general view of the character of the action make the rule of damages still more elastic in many jurisdictions. Thus in Texas, judgment in conversion may be for the return of the property, or for its value; and during the existence of slavery, the recovery might be not only for the value of a slave, but for damages equal to the value of his services,[50] the court going so far as to say that the old rule for the measure of damages in trover had no application to the remedial system prevailing in Texas. In Missouri by statute, interest is within the discretion of the jury.[51] Under this statute it is error to

[45] Harris v. Eldred, 42 Vt. 39.
[46] Shotwell v. Wendover, 1 Johns. (N. Y.) 65.
[47] Pierce v. Benjamin, 14 Pick. (Mass.) 356, 361, 25 Am. Dec. 396.
[48] Isaacs v. McLean, 106 Mich. 79, 64 N. W. 2.

[49] United States: Ewart v. Kerr, 2 McMill. 141.
Minnesota: Nininger v. Banning, 7 Minn. 274.
[50] Pridgin v. Strickland, 8 Tex. 427, 435, 58 Am. Dec. 124.
[51] State v. Hope, 121 Mo. 34, 25 S. W. 893.

direct the jury to give interest.[52]   In Georgia it has been said that where the action is for the conversion of a mule and the recovery of hire, interest as such is not recoverable in the action, this appearing to be a transposition of the opposites, on the ordinary rule that the allowance of interest excludes the recovery of hire.[53]

§ 494. Conversion by temporary wrongful use.

Although the conversion generally deprives the owner of the property, it does not necessarily do so. The property may, on return by the wrongdoer, be accepted. In that case, of course, the measure of damages is not the whole value of the property, but compensation for the injury done to the property,[54] which would usually be the value of the use or interest on the value of the property while it was withheld from the plaintiff [55] together with the deterioration in its market value if any.[56]

So where the defendant withheld possession of a certificate of stock belonging to the plaintiff, the court held that since that act could not deprive the plaintiff of his property in the stock the measure of damages was not the value of the stock.[57] Where the plaintiff's stock in trade was seized upon an execution which afterward proved void, and after several days he bought it back by paying the amount of the execution and costs, the measure of damages was held to be, first, the expense of securing the goods, which would include the costs and counsel fees included in the execution; second, the depreciation in value of the goods during detention; and third, interest on the value of the goods during detention, or at the plaintiff's option the value of his business during the time he was deprived of

[52] Hawkins v. Kansas City H. P. B. Co., 63 Mo. App. 64.
[53] Martin v. Oslin, 94 Ga. 658, 19 S. E. 988.
[54] Williams v. Crum, 27 Ala. 468.
[55] Kinnear v. Robinson, 2 Han. (N. Brun.) 73.
[56] United States: Hoyt v. Fuller, 43 C. C. A. 466, 104 Fed. 192.
Alabama: Renfro v. Hughes, 69 Ala. 581.

Illinois: Davenport v. Ledger, 80 Ill. 574.
Massachusetts: Lucas v. Trumbull, 15 Gray, 306.
Texas: Carter v. Roland, 53 Tex. 540.
Canada: Kinnear v. Robinson, 2 Han. 73. The defendant cannot avail himself to diminish the damages of anything which lessens the value while in his wrongful possession.
[57] Daggett v. Davis, 53 Mich. 35, 18 N. W. 548, 51 Am. Rep. 91.

his stock in trade.[58] There is no reason why, when the title does not change, damages should not in the case of particular species of property be allowed for the value of the use, but, the title once vested in the defendant, interest does not take its place.[59] In National Bank v. Rush [60] it was held that where the owner recovers the property, the measure of damages is the expense necessarily incurred, together with the value of the time spent in recovering it, and the value of the use— not exceeding the total value of the property at the time of the conversion.

Where the conversion is by temporary wrongful use, the action takes the place of *detinue*, and the measure of damages changes so as to fit the circumstances of the particular case. The property has been returned but the plaintiff is not entitled to merely nominal damages. One of the cases most often cited is that of an action for the conversion of a horse driven by the hirer beyond the agreed destination. Here the plaintiff is entitled to recover the difference between the value of the property at the time of its conversion and when it was returned; it is competent to show the value of the horse when it left the stable and before it arrived at the place where it was converted. The plaintiff having testified that the horse was worthless when it was returned, and on cross-examination that he had afterwards traded it off, it was competent to ask him on re-direct examination what he got for the horse and what expense he had been put to. The defendant having testified that the horse was permanently lame before he hired it, plaintiff was permitted, although he had previously shown the condition of the horse, to show in rebuttal that it was not lame.[61] The same measure has been held to apply in a case of seizure and return of liquor by a military officer.[62] And in that of unauthorized temporary use of oxen by an agister.[63]

[58] Anderson v. Sloane, 72 Wis. 566, 40 N. W. 214, 7 Am. St. Rep. 885.

[59] Endel v. Norris, 15 Tex. Civ. App. 140, 39 S. W. 608.

[60] 56 U. S. App. 556, 565, 29 C. C. A. 333, 85 Fed. 539. *Cf.* Dodson v. Cooper, 37 Kan. 346, 349, 350, 15 Pac. 200; Sprague v. Brown, 40 Wis. 612, 619, 621; Curtis v. Ward, 20 Conn. 204,

206; Hurlburt v. Green, 41 Vt. 490, 492, 494; United States v. Pine R. L. & I. Co., 49 U. S. App. 24, 24 C. C. A. 101, 78 Fed. 319.

[61] Stillwell v. Farewell, 64 Vt. 286, 24 Atl. 243.

[62] Bates v. Clark, 95 U. S. 204, 24 L. ed. 471.

[63] Gove v. Watson, 61 N. H. 136.

On the other hand, where machinery was taken and returned after ten days, the measure of damages was held to be the value of the use or rental value for that time.[64] In another case, of conversion by a sheriff, plaintiff having bought at the sheriff's sale and not having been deprived of the use at all, the measure of damages is what he paid to get the property back.[65] Where corn in the crib was converted by a wrongful levy and the value of the use was nothing, plaintiff demanded damages equal to the intermediate highest market value on the ground that he might have sold it at that time. The question was not decided, as it was proved that the value remained as high for some time after the recovery of the property.[66]

§ 494a. Return and acceptance—Reduction.

A cause of action for conversion having been established, a return of the property is no bar to the action, but is admissible in mitigation of damages.[67] This is the rule generally laid down, but in connection with it it should be noticed, as pointed out by Bramwell, L. J.,[68] that the term *conversion* is used in two different senses, one, as simply describing the cause of action, and the other, as conversion in its effect on the measure of damages. The conversion, as a cause of action, may be complete, but the quantum of damages varies in every case. The measure of damages in conversion, therefore, may be anything from nominal damages up to the full value of the property, and, as we shall see, special damages may be added.

In a leading case in New Jersey [69] the plaintiffs delivered to one G a drying machine under a conditional sale. The machine weighed seven tons and may or may not have been a fixture. The defendant, as sheriff, made a levy on the factory and lands under an execution against G. On the 24th of June, plaintiffs demanded in writing the delivery of the machine. The defendant immediately erased the machine from

[64] Baldwin v. G. M. Davidson & Co., 127 S. W. 562 (Tex. Civ. App.).
[65] Fields v. Williams, 91 Ala. 502, 8 So. 808.
[66] Hoyt v. Fuller, 104 Fed. 192, 43 C. C. A. 466.

[67] Aylesbury Mercantile Co. v. Fitch, 22 Okla. 475, 99 Pac. 1089.
[68] Hiort v. London & N. W. Ry., 4 Ex. Div. 188.
[69] Bigelow Co. v. Heintze, 53 N. J. L. 69, 21 Atl. 109.

his inventory and levy on personal property, intending to hold it, if at all, as part of the realty, but on June 30th wrote "by direction of counsel we will hold the dryer." An action of trover was brought July 2d. On July 9th defendant wrote to plaintiffs' attorney disclaiming title except in connection with the levy on realty, and therefore tendered $15 to cover costs. A verdict for the plaintiffs for the full value of the machine having been directed by the trial court, the Supreme Court set the verdict aside on the ground, first, that the letter of June 30th was sufficient evidence to sustain the action; second, that the refusal of the defendant to disclaim a lien on the machine in virtue of his levy on the lands was no evidence of a conversion; third, that the renunciation by him of any claim upon the machine as personal property effected a complete restoration of the property, supposing it to be personal property, to the plaintiffs; and fourth, that the defendant never having taken possession of the property, and the machine not having deteriorated in value in the interval between June 30th and July 9th, plaintiffs could recover only nominal damages.

In a case in Wisconsin [70] where the action was for the conversion of a certificate of stock, the certificate was returned to and accepted by the plaintiff, and a verdict was directed in his favor for nominal damages. The plaintiff had previously attempted to amend his complaint by alleging consequential damages to the amount of upwards of $1,000, owing to his having been subjected to great trouble and expense in order to regain repossession of the certificate. But the court held that the return and acceptance extinguished the whole cause of action, and that the plaintiff, by taking back the property, had waived the entire conversion. Under the circumstances of the case it was held also that even his right to costs was gone, and the defendant had judgment for costs and disbursements. In another case in the same State [71] where the goods sued for were returned to and accepted by the plaintiff pending the trial, and no special damages were shown, it was held also that the plaintiff was entitled to nominal

---

[70] Collins v. Lowry, 78 Wis. 629, 47 N. W. 612.

[71] Cernahan v. Chrisler, 107 Wis. 645, 83 N. W. 778.

damages; and this was said to be a sufficient foundation for costs. The court repudiates the rule laid down in Collins *v.* Lowry, and the result of the case seems to be that had special damages been shown, the plaintiff could have recovered for them. This would seem to be the true rule.

When return and tender, kept good, are set up in mitigation, all the facts must be called to the attention of the jury under proper instructions.[72]

In some cases, where the facts are clear, an agreement on the part of the plaintiff to accept may be dispensed with, *e. g.*, if the property be shown to have gone, subsequently to the conversion, into the possession or under the control of the plaintiff who is suing, or to his use, this will go in mitigation of damages, though not in bar of the action, without proof of any express agreement to receive it.[73] The measure of damages in this class of cases is generally laid down as being the difference in value of the property at the time of conversion and when returned.[74] This, of course, covers deterioration; but the plaintiff is also entitled to the value of the use.[75]

Where the plaintiff took legal steps to get the property back the case is otherwise. If he merely attached the property, this of itself gives him no beneficial right in it, and does not amount to a return nor result in a diminution of damages.[76]

§ 494b. Return by order of court.

Both in England and in some of the United States the power of the court to compel a return and acceptance of the property in any proper case, has long been recognized. The cases usually mentioned as not adapted to this relief are where the original taking was wilful, where the property has deteriorated in value, or where there was a wilful refusal to surrender on demand. In the first and last cases the question of exemplary damages may be raised, and in the second, a verdict would generally be necessary upon the question of

[72] Seaboard A. L. R. R. *v.* Phillips, 108 Md. 285, 70 Atl. 232.

[73] Yale *v.* Saunders, 16 Vt. 243.

[74] Stillwell *v.* Farewell, 64 Vt. 286, 24 Atl. 243.

[75] *United States:* Coulson *v.* Pan-

handle Nat. Bk., 54 Fed. 855, 4 C. C. A. 616.

Kentucky: Louisville & N. R. R. *v.* Young, 1 Bush, 401.

[76] Lewis *v.* Morse, 20 Conn. 211.

value. The existence of the power is of great importance; it supplements the effect of voluntary return and acceptance in adjusting the measure of damages to the real value of the rights lost or injured, by direct judicial control analogous to that of a Court of Chancery. The origin and development of the practice in England is lucidly analyzed and explained by Redfield, J., in a Vermont case,[77] in an opinion in substance as follows:—Of the right of the defendant in actions of trover and trespass *d. b. a.* in English courts, to surrender the property taken in specie, in mitigation, or in many cases in satisfaction of damages, there can be no manner of doubt. While the action of detinue continued in use, no such right of return was allowed in trover or trespass, except by the consent of the plaintiff; but later on, after detinue fell into disuse, the courts were almost constantly pressed to receive the surrender of the thing claimed, as had been practised in detinue. Their ingenuity was taxed to find some good excuse for refusal, but the absurdity of the reason given served but to show more clearly the fallacy of the conclusion. They answered that they did not "keep a warehouse," and so could not order a surrender of the property except in case of money *in numero.* But it seems soon to have been perceived that in making this concession they had yielded the whole ground. Accordingly, the rule acknowledged in the case of money was extended to pictures and other goods not cumbrous or perishable. So the matter remained until after the middle of the 19th century.[78]

The rule seems fully to have been established in King's Bench in Fisher *v.* Prince[79] where Lord Mansfield put the matter in this way:

"Such motions are neither to be refused nor granted as *of course;* they must depend on their own circumstances. No injury is done the plaintiff if the court should think he ought not to proceed for damages beyond a specified point, because he may still proceed for more *at the peril of costs.*"

In the case at bar Lord Mansfield declined to apply the rule, the goods having been altered and their value changed.

[77] Hart *v.* Skinner, 16 Vt. 138, 141, 42 Am. Dec. 500. This power is, of course, merely an exception to the general rule; see *ante,* § 53.

[78] Buller's N. P. 49; 6 Bac. Abr. 483, 484, 708.

[79] 3 Burr. 1363.

The rule was extended to the case of goods taken by way of trespass, where the defendants, officers of the excise or revenue on leather, by mistake, made the seizure, and where the goods had suffered no damage.[80]

The rule seems to have been recognized as the settled law in Westminster Hall.[81] In this country the practice is recognized in a few jurisdictions and regulated by the courts, or by statute, or both.

In an action for the conversion of bonds, plaintiffs alleged special damages in raising funds to relieve their property from attachment. Before trial the defendants offered in court to deliver the bonds to the plaintiff and pay their costs already accrued, and the County Court made an order to allow them to bring bonds and costs into court for the plaintiffs, and that if the latter refused to receive them, they must proceed at their peril as to further costs, unless they succeeded in recovering more than nominal damages above the face of the bonds. This was decided to be a proper exercise of the power of the court, and the defendant having complied with the order, and the plaintiffs having failed in an attempt to prove any case differing materially from that which was already in proof, was held to be entitled only to nominal damages.[82]

In Georgia, it has been held that a verdict may be rendered for damages with the condition that it may be discharged on returning the property sued for. The defendant in such cases must elect to do one or the other. He cannot restore a part and pay a part.[83]

§ 494c. Property bought back by owner.

If goods are wrongfully seized and sold, and the plaintiff buys the property in at the sale, the measure of damages is the amount he pays to get it back, whether that is more or less than the real value.[84] This is really a recovery of the

---

[80] Pickering v. Trustees, 7 T. R. 53.

[81] Earle v. Holderness, 4 Bing. 462, 15 E. C. L. 41; Cook v. Hartle, 8 Car. & P. 568, 34 E. C. L. 528.

[82] Rutland R. R. v. Bank of Middlebury, 32 Vt. 639.

[83] Foster v. Brooks, 6 Ga. 287; Mitchell v. Printup, 19 Ga. 579.

[84] *Pennsylvania:* Kline v. McCandless, 139 Pa. 223, 20 Atl. 1045.

Texas: Muenster v. Fields, 89 Tex. 102, 33 S. W. 852 (*overruling* Hart v. Blum, 76 Tex. 113, 13 S. W. 181).

expense of getting the property back; and if the property has depreciated in value, he should also get the loss in value as special damages. So where, upon conversion of goods by a sheriff who attaches and sells as goods of third person, plaintiff buys them back from the purchaser, in an action for the conversion, his measure of damages is the amount paid to purchase the goods, not exceeding the value.[85] And where a sheriff seized and sold property of plaintiff's intestate, some of which was exempt, and plaintiff in the attachment suit bought it in and sold it to plaintiff's intestate, it was held that the measure of damages for the exempt property was the amount paid to get it, which would be arrived at by apportioning the entire amount paid between the exempt and the non-exempt property, in proportion to its value as shown by the evidence.[86] In the case of a horse wrongfully distrained for taxes, where it was sold and bid off by the plaintiffs, his measure of damages is the amount of his bid.[87] So the owner may recover the amount of a reasonable reward paid to get the property back.[88]

§ 495. Value, how determined.

The value of anything is not limited to the immediate cash value, that is, the price it would bring cash down.[89] Nor to its value for a particular use, if it has a more valuable use. Logs of cedar fit for paving are not to be valued as firewood.[90]

Defendant sold plaintiff's slaves. Held that he was accountable for the proceeds, in spite of the fact that subsequent emancipation would have made them valueless if he had retained them; but for slaves which were emancipated but which he did not sell he was not liable.[91]

[85] Dodson v. Cooper, 37 Kan. 346, 15 Pac. 200.

[86] Blewett v. Miller, 131 Cal. 149, 63 Pac. 157.

[87] Hurlburt v. Green, 41 Vt. 490.

[88] Greenfield Bank v. Leavitt, 17 Pick. (Mass.) 1; see Pierce v. Benjamin, 14 Pick. 356, 25 Am. Dec. 396.

[89] Kasper v. Walla, 49 Neb. 288, 68 N. W. 476.

So where a fence was converted, the measure of damages, in the absence of a market for standing fences, was the actual value at the time and place. Harrison v. McGehee (Tex. Civ. App.), 139 S. W. 613.

[90] LaChappelle v. Warehouse & B. S. Co., 95 Wis. 518, 70 N. W. 589; ante, § 252.

[91] Craufurd v. Smith, 93 Va. 623, 23 S. E. 235, 25 S. E. 657. The liability of a person to pay the value of slaves wrongfully appropriated is not affected by the fact of the subsequent abolition

The value recovered is usually the market value, not the cost of production,[92] nor the consideration paid.[93] Where goods were wrongfully sold on execution, it was held that the price obtained at the auction sale was competent evidence of their value.[94] In an early case,[95] Abbott, C. J., said that the plaintiff was not *bound* by the sum at which goods were sold by the defendant at auction, "but where the plaintiff is an assignee, who must have sold the goods if they had come to his hands before any sale by the sheriff, it *often happens that a jury considers* the sum at which the goods were actually sold at auction, as a fair measure of damages." Where the goods are contained in a number of packages the value is not what could be obtained on a sale of the entire number of packages, but the aggregate market value of the separate packages at the time.[96] In the case of household furniture, the original cost having been proved, deterioration, through wear and tear, etc., may be shown.[97]

§ 496. Value, where to be estimated.

As a general rule, the value of the property is to be taken at the place of conversion.[98] So for the conversion of a piano in Alaska the measure of damages is the value of the piano there.[99] And where plaintiff shipped lilies from Bermuda by express to customers in New York, and the goods were delivered to defendant, a florist, the measure of damages was held to be the value of the flowers at the time and place of conversion; that is, in New York just before Easter.[100] It seems to have been held by the New York Court of Appeals, that the value of foreign goods in an action of trover should be ascertained by the custom-house valuation of them in this

of slavery.   Calhoun *v.* Burnett, 40 Miss. 599.

[92] Gunn *v.* Burghart, 47 N. Y. Super. Ct. 370; *acc.*, Sigel-Campion Live Stock Com. Co. *v.* Holly, 44 Colo. 580, 101 Pac. 68.

[93] Kingsbury *v.* Smith, 13 N. H. 109.

[94] Heinmuller *v.* Abbott, 34 N. Y. Super. Ct. 228.

[95] Whitehouse *v.* Atkinson, 3 C. & P. 344.

[96] Miller *v.* Jannett, 63 Tex. 82.

[97] Hannan *v.* Connett, 10 Colo. App. 171, 50 Pac. 214.

[98] *California:* Hamer *v.* Hathaway, 33 Cal. 117.
Massachusetts: United S. M. Co. *v.* Holt, 185 Mass. 97, 69 N. E. 1056.

[99] Lines *v.* Alaska Commercial Co., 29 Wash. 133, 69 Pac. 642.

[100] Downing *v.* Outerbridge, 79 Fed. 931, 25 C. C. A. 244.

country, if made nearly at the time of the conversion.[101]   But where the plaintiffs, lumber dealers doing business at Troy, bought lumber to be sold in their lumber-yard there, in an action for its conversion, it was held error to charge that if the lumber was to be taken to Troy to be sold there, the plaintiffs were entitled to recover the value at Troy, less the expenses of transportation.[102]

A distinction must be noticed between the value of a thing and the evidence of its value.   When there is a market for the chattel at the place where its value is to be shown, the market value establishes its actual value; but where there is no market at the place, its value must be established by other evidence, which is ordinarily its value in the nearest market.[103]   So where logs are converted in a river the measure of damages is the value of the logs at the nearest market less the cost of moving the logs there; [104] and so in an action for the conversion of plows of a peculiar kind made for sale in Nebraska, the market value of the plows in Nebraska may be shown, with the expense of getting them there and selling them, to indicate their value in Wisconsin where there was no sale for them.[105]

§ 497. Value, when to be estimated.

Upon general principles, the value of the property at the time of the conversion should be the measure of damages, and that is the rule generally adopted.[106]   If the conversion is established by a demand and refusal, the value should be estimated at the time of the refusal.[107]

[101] Caffe v. Bertrand, 1 How. App. 224.

[102] Spicer v. Waters, 65 Barb. 227.

[103] Ante, §§ 244, 246, 247.

Iowa: Gensburg v. Marshall Field & Co., 104 Ia. 599, 74 N. W. 3.

Massachusetts: Selkirk v. Cobb, 13 Gray, 313.

New York: Tiffany v. Lord, 65 N. Y. 310; Fleischman v. Samuel, 18 App. Div. 97, 45 N. Y. Supp. 404.

North Carolina: Boylston Ins. Co. v. Davis, 70 N. C. 485.

Tennessee: Fort v. Saunders, 5 Heisk. 487.

[104] Hodson v. Goodale, 22 Ore. 68, 29 Pac. 70.

[105] Lathers v. Wyman, 76 Wis. 616, 45 N. W. 669.

[106] United States: Sedgwick v. Place, 12 Blatch. 163.

Louisiana: Arrowsmith v. Gordon, 3 La. Ann. 105.

Michigan: Greeley v. Stilson, 27 Mich. 153.

Texas: Norwood v. Cobb, 37 Tex. 141.

England: France v. Gaudet, L. R. 6 Q. B. 199; Falk v. Fletcher, 18 C. B. (N. S.) 403.

[107] United States: Dows v. National

Where the defendants, holding certain bonds of the plaintiff's as security for a loan void for usury, sold them first at auction where they purchased them themselves, and subsequently resold them at private sale, the private sale was held to be the conversion, and the value at that time was held to furnish the measure of damages.[108] And where property attached on mesne process remains in the plaintiff's possession until judgment and execution in the attachment suit, the measure of his damages is the value of the property at the time it was taken on execution, with interest.[109] Where bonds of the plaintiff were stolen from the defendant by its negligence, the measure of damages is the value of the bonds at the time of the theft, not at the time of a demand by the plaintiff.[110] So, where an officer had wrongfully taken from the plaintiff a promissory note, the maker of which was then solvent, but who became insolvent before the officer offered to return it, the measure of damages was held to be the value of the note at the time of the conversion, and interest.[111] Where property was attached by plaintiff, a deputy sheriff, and held under attachment, an outstanding leasehold interest could not be seized; but the lease came to an end during the attachment, and before the conversion. Plaintiff was held entitled to recover the value of the property when converted by the assignee of the owner taking it out of his hands.[112] In an action against a director for wrongfully taking a gift of shares from the company, the measure of damages is the

Exchange Bank, 91 U. S. 618, 23 L. ed. 214.

Illinois: Northern Transportation Co. *v.* Sellick, 52 Ill. 249.

Massachusetts: Eastern R. R. *v.* Benedict, 10 Gray, 212, 66 Am. Dec. 384.

Minnesota: Dolliff *v.* Robbins, 83 Minn. 498, 86 N. W. 772, 85 Am. St. Rep. 466.

Missouri: Carter *v.* Feland, 17 Mo. 383.

Tennessee: Fort *v.* Saunders, 5 Heisk. 487.

Utah: Walley *v.* Deseret Nat. Bank, 14 Utah, 305, 47 Pac. 147.

[108] Tyng *v.* Commercial Warehouse Co., 58 N. Y. 308.

[109] Henshaw *v.* Bank of Bellows Falls, 10 Gray (Mass.), 568.

[110] Third National Bank *v.* Boyd, 44 Md. 47, 22 Am. Rep. 35.

[111] King *v.* Ham, 6 All. (Mass.) 298. In the case of goods on hand for sale, this value may include the expected profit of the sale. Ebenreitter *v.* Dahlman, 41 N. Y. Supp. 559, 18 Misc. 351, 75 N. Y. St. Rep. 948; Rheinfeldt *v.* Dahlman, 43 N. Y. Supp. 281, 19 Misc. 9.

[112] Pond *v.* Baker, 58 Vt. 293, 2 Atl. 164.

actual value of the shares at the time of the gift being accepted by the director.[113] For the conversion of stock in which plaintiff owns a remainder after a life interest, his measure of damages is the value of the stock at the death of the life tenant.[114] Evidence may, of course, be competent as bearing on the value at the time of conversion though it relates to facts of a different time. Thus in an action for the conversion of a judgment, though the judgment debtors were insolvent at the time of conversion, they afterwards became solvent. Evidence of this showed what the judgment was worth to the plaintiff.[115] The general principle may be modified by the circumstances considered in the next section.

§ 497a. Result of following the property.

In Ingram v. Rankin,[116] Taylor, J., said that damages higher than the value at the time of conversion might be recovered in two cases: first, if it appears that the defendant, in case of a wrongful taking or conversion, has sold the chattels, the plaintiff may, at his election, recover as his damages the amount for which the same were sold, with interest from the time of the sale to the day of trial; and second, if it appears that the chattels wrongfully taken or converted are still in the possession of the defendant at the time of trial, the plaintiff may, at his election, recover the present value of the same at the place where the same were taken or converted, in the form they were in when so taken or converted. It would seem, however, that even in these cases the principle of damages *in the action of trover* should not be changed. The result indicated is obtained by invoking the principle of following the property in the hands of the wrongdoer. If the property remains in the possession of the wrongdoer, the owner may obtain it in an action of replevin, or he may demand it, and in case of refusal bring an action of trover founded upon the demand and refusal and recover the value of the property at the time and place of the demand. If the wrongdoer has disposed of the property the owner has the option of waiving the

---

[113] Montgomerie's Brewery Co. v. Blyth, 26 Vict. L. R. 612.

[114] Caulkins v. Gaslight Co., 85 Tenn. 683, 4 S. W. 287, 4 Am. St. Rep. 786.

[115] Rivinus v. Langford, 75 Fed. 959, 21 C. C. A. 581, 33 L. R. A. 250.

[116] 47 Wis. 406, 420, 2 N. W. 755, 32 Am. Rep. 762.

tort and recovering the proceeds of the property in an action for money had and received. In Texas it seems that this doctrine will be applied, at least in case of conversion by a fiduciary, even though the property may not remain in the hands of the defendant. Thus it has been held in an action for the conversion of money that plaintiff is not limited to the principal sum and interest, but may recover the total amount of money gained through the conversion.[117] And where an assignee for creditors wrongfully appropriated property belonging to the estate, the creditors were allowed to recover the value of the property at the time of trial.[118] The procedure in such a case is in substance equitable.

§ 497b. Recovery by owner of a limited interest.

Where an action for the conversion of a chattel is brought by one having a limited interest in it, he should recover no more than the value of his interest, unless he was in possession at the time of conversion and the defendant was a stranger to the title, in which case he should recover the entire value of the chattel.[119]

This principle is illustrated by cases where the goods of a partnership are converted. Each partner is in possession of such goods, and may recover the entire value against a stranger. So upon a wrongful sale of partnership goods on writ against one partner, in a suit by the other partner, the entire value of the goods converted can be recovered.[120] But against the other partner or one entitled to his rights, a partner can recover only half, that being the amount of his legal interest in the property. So in an action by the assignee of one partner for the conversion of the firm property by a sale of it by the other partner, it was held that the measure of damages was the value of plaintiff's undivided interest, without regard to insolvency or the state of the partnership accounts.[121] But where in an action against a partner, partnership property was attached, and the

---

[117] Black v. Black, 4 Tex. Ct. Rep. 178, 67 S. W. 928.

[118] McCord v. Nabours, 101 Tex. 494, 109 S. W. 913.

[119] Ante, §§ 76, 78.

[120] Summers v. Heard, 66 Ark. 550, 562, 50 S. W. 78.

[121] Carrie v. Cloverdale Banking & C. Co., 90 Cal. 84, 27 Pac. 58. Cf. Doll v. Hennessy Mercantile Co., 33 Mont. 80, 81 Pac. 625.

partner being insolvent, the attaching officer delivered the property to his assignee, it was held that the solvent partner could recover the full value of the property, without reduction on account of delivery to the assignee, since the solvent partner was entitled to the property to close up the partnership.[122]

Receiptors are chargeable with the valuation adopted, and are responsible if they let any portion of the goods go back into the possession of the debtor. Goods attached were given to a receiptor valued at $150, and a small part of the goods were taken by a paramount title. It was held that he was not responsible for this, but that the actual value of these goods would be deducted from the value in the receipt and he would be held for the balance, although this was greatly in excess of the actual value.[123]

Plaintiff, having by contract an interest in railway ties to the amount of ten cents each, in an action for conversion is entitled to the amount reserved to him under the contract, with interest, and not the value of the ties.[124] By an agreement for the curing of prunes, plaintiff was to have two per cent of the value. The owner converted. It was held that the measure of plaintiff's recovery was the value of his interest in the prunes, that is, two per cent.[125]

The principle is also illustrated by actions for the conversion of garnished or trusteed property. Defendants attaching and converting garnished property, with knowledge of the garnishment proceedings, are liable for the amount which plaintiffs would have realized.[126] In the case of conversion of trusteed property taken from the possession of the trustee by the defendant, he is liable in damages to the amount of the judgment in the trustee suit not exceeding the value of the property.[127]

Some of the commoner classes of cases illustrating this general principle will be considered in the following sections.

[122] Russell v. Cole, 167 Mass. 6, 44 N. E. 1057, 57 Am. St. Rep. 432.

[123] Healey v. Hutchinson, 66 N. H. 316, 20 Atl. 332; see Cross v. Brown, 41 N. H. 283.

[124] Harvey v. Morse, 69 N. H. 475, 45 Atl. 239.

[125] California Cured Fruit Assoc. v. Ainsworth, 134 Cal. 461, 66 Pac. 586.

[126] Focke v. Blum, 82 Tex. 440, 17 S. W. 770.

[127] Deno v. Thomas, 64 Vt. 358, 24 Atl. 140.

§ 497c. Conversion of pledged property: action by pledgor.

In an action by the pledgor against the pledgee for conversion of the pledged goods the measure of damages is the value of the property, minus the debt.[128] So where a pledgee converts a bond and mortgage held as security, the measure of recovery is the actual, not the face value of the security, minus the debt;[129] and the same is true where a pledged note is converted.[130] Where a pledge of stock, having an option to buy at a specified price, converted the stock, it was held that if the stock was worth more than the option the plaintiff could not recover any more, because that was the extent of the damage. If on the other hand it was worth less, the plaintiff might consider the conversion an election to purchase the stock and hold the defendant for the agreed price. The option price was therefore held to be the measure of damages.[131]

If the debt has been paid, the pledgor may recover the entire value of the property converted. So where a mortgagee deposited a chattel mortgage in pledge for a debt of his own, and the pledgee collected his own debt out of the goods and then gave up the mortgage to the mortgagor, who destroyed it, the measure of damages for this conversion was held to be the value of the mortgage at the time of conversion.[132] Tender of payment will have the same effect as actual payment. So where a pledgee sold the property after a tender to him of the whole amount of the debt, the tender discharged the lien, and the pledgor could recover the full value of the property.[133]

§ 497d. Action by pledgee.

Where the pledgor converts the pledged goods, the pledgee cannot recover the full value of the goods, but is limited to the amount of the debt secured by the pledge.[134] If a stranger converts the goods, the pledgee recovers the full value, being

---

[128] First Nat. Bank v. Boyce, 78 Ky. 42, 39 Am. Rep. 198; ante, § 78.

[129] Barber v. Hathaway, 47 App. Div. 165, 62 N. Y. Supp. 329.

[130] Hallack Lumber & Manuf. Co. v. Gray, 19 Colo. 149, 34 Pac. 1000.

[131] Upham v. Barbour, 65 Minn. 364, 68 N. W. 42.

[132] Nesbitt v. Moore, 39 S. C. 351, 17 S. E. 798.

[133] Hyams v. Bamberger, 10 Utah, 3, 36 Pac. 202.

[134] Bradley v. Burkett, 82 Ga. 255, 11 S. E. 492; Bell v. G. Ober & Sons Co., 96 Ga. 214, 23 S. E. 7.

answerable to the pledgor for the balance over the amount of the debt;[135] but where the act, though wrongful as against him, is good so far as the pledgor is concerned, the measure of damages is the same as that in an action against the pledgor, that is, the amount of the debt. So in an action by the pledgee to recover from a sheriff for the seizure of goods under process sued out by creditors of the pledgor, the amount recovered is the value of the interest of the pledgee in the goods.[136] And so in a suit against a company for calling in and cancelling shares without notice to him, the pledgee recovers only the amount due from the pledgor, with interest.[137]

§ 497e. Conversion of mortgaged property; action by mortgagor.

In an action by the mortgagor against the mortgagee for a conversion of the mortgaged property, the measure of damages is the value of the goods over and above the amount required to satisfy the mortgage.[138] So in the case of mortgaged goods wrongfully taken and sold by the mortgagee, together with other goods, the mortgagor recovers the value of the mortgaged goods less the amount of the mortgage, and the full value of the goods not mortgaged.[139]

In an action by a mortgagor in possession against a stranger the plaintiff recovers the entire value of the property.[140] If however after the conversion the mortgagee takes possession, this is an application of the property to the use of the mortgagor, and the recovery must be for the value as reduced by it.[141]

[135] Cramer v. Marsh, 5 Col. App. 302, 38 Pac. 612; ante, § 76.
[136] Cramer v. Marsh, 5 Col. App. 302, 38 Pac. 612; ante, § 78. But see Einstein v. Dunn, 171 N. Y. 648, 63 N. E. 1116, 32 Civ. Proc. 64, 61 App. Div. 195, 70 N. Y. Supp. 520.
[137] Brown v. Union S. & L. Assoc., 28 Wash. 657, 69 Pac. 383.
[138] United States: Kohn v. Dravis, 94 Fed. 288, 36 C. C. A. 253.
Arkansas: Jones v. Horn, 51 Ark. 19, 9 S. W. 309, 14 Am. St. Rep. 17.

Iowa: Howery v. Hoover, 97 Iowa, 581, 66 N. W. 772.
Kansas: Burton v. Randall, 4 Kan. App. 593, 46 Pac. 326.
Ante, § 82.
[139] Kearney v. Clutton, 101 Mich. 106, 59 N. W. 419, 45 Am. St. Rep. 394.
[140] Vandiver v. O'Gorman, 57 Minn. 64, 58 N. W. 831.
[141] Dahill v. Booker, 140 Mass. 308, 5 N. E. 496, 54 Am. Rep. 465.

§ 497f. Action by mortgagee.

The mortgagee of chattels is ordinarily out of possession, and his interest in the goods is merely as security for the debt. Even against a stranger, therefore, his recovery is limited to the amount of the mortgage debt.[142] Whether he is in possession of the goods or not, if his action is against the mortgagor or one claiming under him his recovery, while of course it cannot exceed the value of the goods, is limited to the amount due on the mortgage debt. So in an action against a purchaser from the mortgagor the mortgagee can recover no more than the amount of his debt; [143] and in an action against a sheriff attaching at the suit of a creditor he is also limited to the amount of the debt.[144] If, however, the illegal attachment involved a denial of the mortgagee's right in the goods, the mortgagee is allowed in some jurisdictions to recover the full value of the chattel.[145]

The mortgagee's recovery of the amount due on the mortgage is reduced by the value of any portion of the mortgaged goods which were not converted,[146] or by any portion of the goods or their proceeds which was returned to him.[147] Where part of the goods were returned to the mortgagee, who at once sold them on foreclosure, and bid them in, and afterwards resold them for a much larger amount than he had bid, the recovery for the conversion is to be reduced by the amount which he bid at the sale, and not by the amount which he

---

[142] Roberts v. Kain, 6 Rob. (N. Y.) 354 (action by assignee of mortgagee).

[143] *Alabama:* Seibold v. Rogers, 101 Ala. 438, 18 So. 312.

Massachusetts: West v. White, 165 Mass. 258, 43 N. E. 103.

[144] *California:* Irwin v. McDowell, 91 Cal. 119, 27 Pac. 601.

Michigan: Ganong v. Green, 71 Mich. 1, 38 N. W. 661.

Montana: Rocheleau v. Boyle, 12 Mont. 590, 31 Pac. 533.

Nebraska: Watson v. Coburn, 35 Neb. 492, 53 N. W. 477.

Contra, Kansas: Jones v. Kellogg, 51 Kan. 263, 284, 33 Pac. 997, 37 Am.

St. Rep. 278, where it is said that the sheriff is a stranger, and except so far as the proceeds of the attachment have actually been turned over to the mortgagor or his benefit the mortgagee recovers the full value of the property.

[145] *Connecticut:* Aldrich v. Higgins, 77 Conn. 370, 59 Atl. 498.

Massachusetts: Hanly v. Davis, 166 Mass. 1, 43 N. E. 523. *Cf.* Rund v. Blatt, 170 Mass. 469, 49 N. E. 642.

[146] Ganong v. Green, 71 Mich. 1, 38 N. W. 661.

[147] Watson v. Coburn, 35 Neb. 492, 53 N. W. 477.

afterwards realized at private sale.[148] But since he is entitled to the entire security, his recovery is not to be reduced either by the value of other property held as security, or by the fact that the mortgagor is solvent,[149] nor by the fact that the proceeds were applied to other debts of the mortgagor.[150]

These rules may be affected by the existence of a junior mortgage. Where there is a mortgage senior to plaintiff's, the amount of his recovery cannot exceed the value of the property, less the amount of the senior mortgage.[151] Where the first mortgagee sues the second mortgagee for conversion, the extent of the recovery is the amount of plaintiff's claim.[152] And where the first mortgagee converts, and is sued by the second mortgagee, the measure of damages is the value of the second mortgagee's interest in the property.[153]

§ 497g. Conversion of property sold conditionally.

Where the title to goods sold has been reserved and the property partly paid for, the general rule is that the seller in an action for the conversion of the goods may recover the unpaid balance of the purchase price, with interest.[154] But where the entire right has revested in the seller, and he has an immediate right to take the goods, free from any claim whatever on the part of the buyer, he may recover the entire value of the goods converted. So on such a sale of a bicycle delivered to the buyer, on failure of the buyer to redeliver

---

[148] Hull v. Bernatz, 106 Mich. 551, 64 N. W. 473.

[149] Huellmantel v. Vinton, 112 Mich. 47, 70 N. W. 412.

[150] Watson v. Coburn, 35 Neb. 492, 53 N. W. 477.

[151] *Dakota:* Straw v. Jenks, 6 Dakota, 414, 43 N. W. 941.

Michigan: Huellmantel v. Vinton, 116 Mich. 621, 74 N. W. 1004.

[152] *Colorado:* Stanley v. Citizens' Coal & Coke Co., 24 Colo. 103, 49 Pac. 35.

Georgia: Harris v. Grant, 96 Ga. 211, 23 S. E. 390.

[153] Lovejoy v. Merchants' State Bank, 5 N. D. 623, 625, 67 N. W. 956.

[154] *Georgia:* Ross v. McDuffie, 91 Ga. 120, 16 S. E. 648.

Maine: Town v. Harlam, 82 Me. 84, 24 Atl. 587.

Rhode Island: Woods v. Nichols, 21 R. I. 537, 45 Atl. 548, 48 L. R. A. 773, 22 R. I. 225, 47 Atl. 211.

In *Georgia,* the vendor after obtaining a judgment against the vendee for the price, and collecting a portion of it, may maintain an action of bail trover for the purpose of collecting the balance of the purchase money, with interest. Jones v. Snider, 99 Ga. 276, 25 S. E. 668. *Cf.* Fussell v. Heard, 119 Ga. 527, 48 S. E. 621.

it on demand, after breach of the promise to pay, the seller may recover the entire value of the property.[155] If the condition fixes a time for payment, after the time has expired, the price not being paid, in an action brought by the seller against the attaching creditor of the buyer, the rule of damages is the value of the property at the time of the attachment.[156] This seems entirely clear under the rule that the general property remains in the vendor subject to be divested by performance of the condition. In this case the attempted enforcement of the creditor's right was based entirely on the erroneous idea that the plaintiff's interest was a mere lien. The case is entirely different where the vendee has acquired a special property, as where he has already paid part and the condition has not lapsed.[157]

This vital distinction, which runs through all the cases, seems to have been overlooked by the New York Court of Appeals in a recent case,[158] in which the seller after breach of condition was allowed to recover only the amount of the unpaid purchase-money. That court is undoubtedly entirely right in saying that the weight of authority is in favor of limiting the conditional seller to the amount unpaid, but this is on the assumption that part performance by the buyer has vested an interest in the latter. This is often the case where no time is fixed; but where a time fixed runs out, without any payment, nothing has vested in the buyer.

§ 498. Natural increase.

The natural increase of the property accruing before the conversion belongs to the owner, and he may recover compensation for the loss of it,[159] but he has no claim for increase after the conversion. Thus, where mares were converted, it was said by the Court of Common Pleas of Upper Canada: "If they had been in foal at the time of their wrongful conversion, that would form an ingredient in the estimate of their

[155] *Maine:* Hawkins v. Hersey, 86 Me. 394, 30 Atl. 14.

New York: Gormully & Jeffery Mfg. Co. v. Catharine, 25 Misc. 336, 55 N. Y. Supp. 475.

[156] Buckmaster v. Smith, 22 Vt. 203.

[157] Rose v. Story, 1 Pa. 190.

[158] Davis v. Bliss, 187 N. Y. 77, 79 N. E. 851, 10 L. R. A. (N. S.) 458, n.

[159] Arkansas V. L. & C. Co. v. Mann, 130 U. S. 69, 9 Sup. Ct. 458, 32 L. ed. 854.

value, but it would not give the plaintiff a right to recover independently for foals dropped after the conversion of the mares."[160] The question in such cases is, how far the claim is speculative.[161] When it can be proved in the sufficient certainty that, but for the conversion, the plaintiff would have had the increase, the claim seems warranted.

§ 499. Property increased in value by the defendant.

Where the property has been increased in value by the defendant, and the plaintiff attempts to get the benefit of the increase, the decisions are in conflict; some cases allowing recovery of the value of the property at the time it was taken, others allowing recovery of the full value. In the simplest case, the defendant has expended labor upon personal property after he got it into his possession. In this case, if the plaintiff has not lost his title to the property, he will often be allowed to follow the property and recover it. But by bringing the action of trover he demands damages for the conversion. By the conversion he was deprived of the property, and a claim for the value of it took its place; consequently, that value at the time of conversion, with interest, should be the limit of his recovery. It should make no difference that the plaintiff by another form of action might perhaps have obtained the property itself; having the choice, he chose to bring trover, and his damages must be measured by the principles applying to that action, if, as in this case, they afford full and equitable compensation. Nor should it make any difference in this action that the conversion was wilful, and the labor was bestowed upon the property with full knowledge of the facts.

This appears to be the principle generally adopted in the cases. Thus where goods were sent to a dyer,[162] who dyed them, and then insisted on a right to retain them, not only for the charges on them, but for a debt due for dyeing other goods, the Court of King's Bench held that he had no lien but

[160] Draper, C. J., in Scott v. McAlpine, 6 Up. Can. C. P. 302, 306.

[161] See Drenner v. Charles, 12 Pa. Super. Ct. 476 (conversion of cow);

Kohai v. MacDonald, 9 N. Z. L. R. 221 (wool growing on lambs dropped after the conversion).

[162] Green v. Farmer, 4 Burr. 2214.

for the price of dyeing the particular goods, and the plaintiff recovered; but the report adds: "The price of dyeing was deducted at the time of taking the verdict, the value of the goods in white being only thereby given to the plaintiff." And the principle of this decision has been followed in Massachusetts, in a case where the plaintiffs made a conditional sale of brown cotton goods to a printing company, who, after printing them, transferred them to the defendant, but did not comply with the conditions; and it was held that the plaintiffs could recover in trover, but the court was of opinion "that the plaintiffs were not entitled to recover the full value of the goods in the printed state." The value of them in their brown state was taken as a more just and equitable measure of damages, under all the circumstances of the case.[163] So where the plaintiffs contracted with R. to build a ship for them, and made advances from time to time in respect of her; and R. gave them, as security for the advances, a bill of sale of the ship, which stated that he thereby did sell, transfer, etc., to the plaintiffs a certain ship in process of building (describing her), to have and to hold the ship, etc., to the plaintiffs forever, when she should be completed; the defendant having converted the vessel before she was finished, and having finished her, the plaintiffs were held entitled to recover as damages in trover, the value of the vessel at the time of her conversion, but not her value at a subsequent time, nor as special damage the value of freight which the plaintiffs might have earned with her if R. had completed her and delivered her to them.[164] Where the defendant took the plaintiff's logs at one place and transported them to another, the measure of damages is the value of the logs where they were taken.[165] So where the plaintiff's logs were sawed into

---

[163] Dresser Manuf. Co. v. Waterston, 3 Met. 9. In Alabama, where wood had been converted and made into coal by the defendant, the owner was held entitled to bring trover for the coal. As to the question we are now considering, it was said: "It is possible the jury might consider the value of the defendant's labor on the rough mate-rial;" but as this point had not been presented, it was not decided. Riddle v. Driver, 12 Ala. 590.

[164] Reid v. Fairbanks, 13 C. B. 692.

[165] *New Hampshire:* Beede v. Lamprey, 64 N. H. 510, 15 Atl. 133, 10 Am. St. Rep. 426.

Pennsylvania: Hill v. Canfield, 56 Pa. 454.

boards by the defendant, the measure of damages should be the value of the logs, not of the boards.[166] Where yarn was converted by the defendant during the process of manufacture, the measure of damages was the value of the yarn, not the value of the finished product.[167] Indeed, it is difficult to see what other rule could be adopted consistently with the general principles of compensation. Any other rule would give the plaintiff more than compensation for his loss, which was a loss of the chattel unchanged by the labor of the defendant.[168]

It may be claimed for the plaintiff that he has a right to say at what time the conversion took place; and that he may therefore allege a conversion after the labor of the defendant had been expended upon the property. Thus in Final v. Backus,[169] where the plaintiff's logs were taken to a distant mill and there made into boards, it was held that the plaintiff could elect to treat nothing as a conversion until the logs were cut into boards, and the value of the logs at the mill was held to be the measure of damages. This supposed principle is based on the right of the plaintiff to retake his property by means of an action of replevin at any time until its form was so changed as to divest him of his title. But this right of the plaintiff should not change the measure of

Vermont: Tilden v. Johnson, 52 Vt. 628, 36 Am. Rep. 769.
So of ore: Omaha & G. S. & R. Co. v. Tabor, 13 Colo. 41, 21 Pac. 925, 16 Am. St. Rep. 185. And of hay: Carpenter v. Lingenfelter, 42 Neb. 728, 60 N. W. 1022.
[166] Morton v. McDowell, 7 Up. Can. Q. B. 338. But *contra,* Eastman v. Harris, 4 La. Ann. 193 (*semble*); Baker v. Wheeler, 8 Wend. 505, 25 Am. Dec. 66; Rice v. Hollenbeck, 19 Barb. 664, where the taking seems not to have been in good faith. And in Stuart v. Phelps, 39 Ia. 14, where standing corn was wilfully converted, the defendant was obliged to pay its value *after he had husked and cribbed it.* These cases seem to have been influenced by the rule in the case of severance from the realty, *infra.*

[167] Aborn v. Mason, 14 Blatch. 405. The market value of the yarn as such was not given, but the value of the cloth less the cost of finishing it; that is, the value of the yarn *on the frames* as it was at the time of conversion.
[168] In Hendricks v. Evans, 46 Mo. App. 313, plaintiff was allowed to recover the value of a horse, only on the condition he was in at the time of the demand, not as improved by defendant's care. For an action for the conversion of mortgaged cotton, defendant was allowed his rent and expenses incident to gathering and preparing the cotton for market. McDaniel v. Staples, 113 S. W. 596. *Cf.* Walthur v. Wetmore, 1 E. D. Smith, 7, and cases cited.
[169] 18 Mich. 218; *acc.,* Everson v. Seller, 105 Ind. 266, 4 N. E. 854.

damages; for the principles upon which damages are given are quite distinct from the principles governing the protection of property. When the property is taken from the plaintiff by the tort, its place is taken by a right to compensation of equal value. If after that the plaintiff by accretion or otherwise becomes entitled to claim his property as enhanced in value by the results of the defendant's labor, that fact does not affect the right to compensation for the conversion, a right which accrued before the labor was performed.[170] Indeed, even in an action of replevin the rule seems to be that the innocent trespasser is to be allowed compensation for his labor.[171]

But where the labor of the defendant was of no value to the owner, he is entitled to no consideration. Thus where the wrongdoer bestowed labor in securing and transporting the property, and thereby increased its value, yet if the owner could and would have done the same thing without cost to himself he may recover the entire value at the place to which it was carried, without deducting the cost of transportation.[172]

§ 500. Severance from the freehold.

Where the property is severed from the freehold the conversion takes place after the labor has been expended upon the property, and the value of the property at the time of its conversion includes the labor. The amount of recovery in an action of trover would therefore seem at first sight to be the value of the property after the labor has been expended upon it.

There are, however, certain facts to be considered which tend to modify the general rule in this case. In the first place, this rule results in the recovery of a greater amount than actual compensation, for the owner is enabled to secure the whole

---

[170] See to this effect, Gates v. Rifle Boom Co., 70 Mich. 309, 38 N. W. 245.

[171] § 534. The case of Isle Royale Mining Co. v. Hertin, 37 Mich. 332, 26 Am. Rep. 520, seems at first sight opposed to this view; there the plaintiff carried the defendant's wood to the landing, where the defendant took possession of it; and the plaintiff was refused compensation for his labor in an action of trover. But there is in that case an important distinction, that is, the defendant could not get his wood, to which he had a right, without availing himself of the plaintiff's labor.

[172] Taber v. Jenny, Sprague, 315.

benefit of the defendant's labor. In the second place, although the defendant's wrongful act was in reality a trespass upon real estate, the plaintiff recovers a greater amount than the damage to the realty, and a greater amount than he could recover in an action of trespass, unless indeed (as is the case in a few jurisdictions) he is allowed to recover in the action of trespass the full amount the technical rule would give him in an action of trover.[173] Still further, where the distinction between the forms of action is abolished, as is very generally the case, and the plaintiff recovers upon the case stated in his pleadings, since he could gain no advantage from the form of action, he should clearly be entitled only to actual compensation, though he alleged a conversion. As we shall see, the result of these considerations has been a great conflict of authority.

§ 501. The rule in England.

The rule which was at first adopted in England allowed the plaintiff in all cases to recover the value of the property at the time of the conversion, that is, after it was severed from the soil. This was laid down in a case in the English Exchequer,[174] and the doctrine of this case was recognized in the Queen's Bench.[175] But in the case of Wood v. Morewood where a similar trespass was complained of, Parke, B., at Nisi Prius, told the jury that if there was fraud or negligence on the part of the defendant, they might give as damages under one of the counts, which was in trover, the value of the coals at the time they first became chattels, on the principle laid down in Martin v. Porter; but if they thought that the defendant was not guilty of fraud or negligence, but acted fairly and honestly in the full belief that he had a right to do what he did, they might give the fair value of the coals, as if the coal fields had been purchased from the plaintiff; which latter estimate was adopted by the jury.[176] This conflict of opinion continued for some time,[177] but the rule laid down by Baron Parke in Wood v. Morewood was finally adopted in Chan-

---

[173] For the rule in an action of trespass *quare clausum*, see the chapter on Injuries to Real Property.

[174] Martin v. Porter, 5 M. & W. 352.

[175] Morgan v. Powell, 3 Q. B. 278.

[176] Wood v. Morewood, 3 Q. B. 440, n.

[177] See Hilton v. Woods, L. R. 4 Eq. 432; Llynvi Co. v. Brogden, L. R. 11 Eq. 188.

cery,[178] and by the House of Lords in the case of Livingstone *v.* Rawyards Coal Co.,[179] a Scotch appeal.

§ 502. Technical rule followed in some jurisdictions.

The technical rule, allowing recovery of the whole value of the property after its severance, was at first followed in this country. So in New York,[180] where certain logs had been cut on the plaintiff's land, drawn to the defendant's mill, and converted into boards (the value of the logs being $187.56; of the boards, $309.46, and the difference, $121.90); and the judge charged that the measure of damages would be the value of the boards without reference to the price of the defendant's labor, and the jury gave $309.46. It was insisted, on a motion for a new trial, that in trover, where the conversion was the gist of the action, and the character of the original taking not inquired into, the damages should be confined to the value of the thing as taken, or the value of the defendant's labor deducted; and that even if the rule laid down at the trial were sound in *trespass*, it could not apply here, because the plaintiff had elected to bring trover. The court held otherwise, on the authority of previous cases. But Sutherland, J., dissented. He admitted that where the taking was *wilful and tortious*, this rule would not be oppressive or unjust. But that as the mode of taking could not, in trover, be inquired into, no such general rule could be laid down. He put the case of jewels lodged with a banker for safe custody, and pawned by him, and set at great expense by the pawnee; could the rightful owner in trover against the pawnee obtain the jewels as set, without deduction for the labor of setting? But a new trial was denied.

This rule has been followed in several jurisdictions in this country. So it is held, in the case of coal wrongfully mined, that the measure of damages is the value of the coal at the pit's mouth, less the expense of bringing it there, but allowing nothing for the expense of mining; [181] and in the case of timber wrongfully cut, that the measure of damages is the value of

---

[178] Jegon *v.* Vivian, L. R. 6 Ch. 742.

[179] 5 App. Cas. 25, 39.

[180] Brown *v.* Sax, 7 Cow. (N. Y.) 95.

[181] *United States:* Cheeney *v.* Nebraska & C. S. Co., 41 Fed. 740.

Alabama: Ivy C. & C. Co. *v.* Alabama C. & C. Co., 135 Ala. 579, 33 So. 547.

the logs just after they are felled.[182] So in Indiana it was held
in an action for the conversion of wheat, of which the defendant had forcibly taken possession, as it stood in his field, that
proof of the value of the defendant's labor in harvesting and
threshing the crop, for the purpose of reducing the damages,
had been erroneously admitted.[183] In Winchester v. Craig,[184]
an action for the conversion of timber, by cutting it by mistake
from the land of the plaintiff, it was said that the jury could
fix the measure of damages either at the value when taken,
together with profits that might have been derived in the ordinary market, or the market value at the place where it was
tortiously sold by the defendant, less his expenses in the transportation and preparation for sale, with interest from the date
of the conversion. In some jurisdictions the rule is held to be
different according to the form of action; the plaintiff in trover
being allowed the whole value of the property, as increased by
the defendant's labor, while in trespass he is confined to the
damage done to the realty.[185] While under this rule the cost

Illinois: McLean C. C. Co. v. Long, 81 Ill. 359; McLean C. C. Co. v. Len-non, 91 Ill. 561, 33 Am. Rep. 64.

Maryland: Franklin C. Co. v. Mc-Millan, 49 Md. 549, 33 Am. Rep. 280; Blaen Avon C. Co. v. McCulloh, 59 Md. 403, 43 Am. Rep. 560.

The amount to be deducted from the value at the pit's mouth is not what the defendant spent in getting it there, but what it would have cost the plaintiff. In re United Merthyr Collieries Co., L. R. 15 Eq. 46.

[182] *United States:* Bly v. U. S., 4 Dillon, 464.

Alabama: White v. Yawkey, 108 Ala. 270, 19 So. 360, 54 Am. St. Rep. 159, 32 L. R. A. 199.

Florida: Skinner v. Pinney, 19 Fla. 42, 45 Am. Rep. 1.

Georgia: Milltown L. Co. v. Carter, 3 Ga. App. 344, 63 S. E. 270.

Maine: Moody v. Whitney, 38 Me. 174, 61 Am. Dec. 239.

Michigan: Winchester v. Craig, 33 Mich. 205, 5 Am. Rep. 189.

New Hampshire: Beede v. Lamprey, 64 N. H. 510, 15 Atl. 133, 10 Am. St. Rep. 426.

[183] Ellis v. Wire, 33 Ind. 127; acc., Foley v. Southwestern Land Co., 94 Wis. 329, 68 N. W. 994.

[184] 33 Mich. 205, 5 Am. Rep. 189.

[185] *Alabama:* White v. Yawkey, 108 Ala. 270, 19 So. 360, 54 Am. St. Rep. 159, 32 L. R. A. 199.

Colorado: Omaha G. S. & R. Co. v. Tabor, 13 Colo. 41, 21 Pac. 925, 16 Am. St. Rep. 185.

Florida: Skinner v. Pinney, 19 Fla. 42, 45 Am. Rep. 1.

New Hampshire: Foote v. Merrill, 54 N. H. 490, 20 Am. Rep. 151.

But in other jurisdictions the rule in trespass is the same as in trover:

Georgia: Smith v. Gonder, 22 Ga. 353.

Illinois: Illinois & St. L. R. R. v. Ogle, 82 Ill. 627, 25 Am. Rep. 342.

New York: Firmin v. Firmin, 9 Hun, 571.

North Carolina: Bennett v. Thomp-son, 13 Ired. L. 146.

of severance accrues to the owner, the same is not true of expense subsequently incurred. The measure of damages is the value of the chattel at the moment of severance, at least in case of an innocent trespass; the additional value given it by change of form [186] or by transportation to market [187] cannot be recovered.

§ 503. Defendant generally allowed value of his labor.

But by the prevailing view the defendant, if he acted in good faith, is allowed the value of his labor; that is, the measure of damages is the value of the property as it was just before the defendant's wrongdoing began.

The leading case upon the subject in this country is Forsyth v. Wells,[188] which was decided before the present rule was established in England. That case was an action of trover for mining and carrying away coal from the plaintiff's lands. On the trial, the Court of Common Pleas, having decided against the argument of the defendant that trover would lie, held further that the measure of the plaintiff's damages was not simply the value of the coal in the ground, but its value after it had been "dug," or what was called "knocked down," the difference having been about as one to eight. On error the Supreme Court agreed that the action was properly brought, since the defendant below, as it appeared, had not claimed a line which would include the coal taken out, but had gone beyond the proper limit by mistake. But the court sent the case back for a new trial, on the ground that the measure of damages should have been the same as in trespass for mesne profits, and that if, as the jury appeared to have found, the defendant below had been guilty of no intentional wrong, he ought to have been charged, not with the value of the coal after he had been at the expense of mining it, but only with its value in place, and with such other damage to the land "as his mining may have caused. Such would manifestly be the measure in trespass for mesne profits."

[186] Brooks v. Rogers, 101 Ala. 111, 13 So. 386.

[187] Florida: Wright v. Skinner, 34 Fla. 453, 463, 16 So. 335.

New Hampshire: Beede v. Lamprey, 64 N. H. 510, 15 Atl. 133, 10 Am. St. Rep. 426.

[188] 41 Pa. 291, 294.

This case is generally followed. So in trover for wrongfully mining ore or coal, the measure of damages is the value of the ore or coal *in situ;* [189] for cutting trees, the value of the trees standing, [190] often measured by the difference in value of the land before and after cutting. [191] But this applies only when the defendant's trespass was in good faith. Where he knowingly converted property severed from the plaintiff's land, there can be no allowance for the expense of severing it. [192] Where a railroad company rightfully made a cut through the plaintiff's land, thereby excavating coal, and wrongfully sold the coal, the measure of damages was the value of the coal at the time of the sale. [193] This differs from the cases just considered. Technically, there was no wrongdoing till the sale, consequently compensation must be estimated at that time. As a matter of justice, the labor should not be deducted from the recovery because it was performed by the defendant for his own benefit, in making the cut.

[189] *California:* Goller *v.* Fett, 30 Cal. 481.

Iowa: Chamberlain *v.* Collinson, 45 Ia. 429.

Massachusetts: Stockbridge Iron Co. *v.* Cone Iron Works, 102 Mass. 80.

Mississippi: Illinois Cent. R. R. *v.* LeBlanc, 74 Miss. 626, 21 So. 748.

Montana: Maloney *v.* King, 30 Mont. 158, 76 Pac. 4.

Nevada: Waters *v.* Stevenson, 13 Nev. 157.

Pennsylvania: Irwin *v.* Nolde, 176 Pa. 504, 35 Atl. 217.

Tennessee: Coal Creek M. & M. Co. *v.* Moses, 15 Lea, 300, 54 Am. Rep. 415.

So of oil: Dyke *v.* National Transit Co., 22 App. Div. 360, 49 N. Y. Supp. 180.

Cf. Colorado C. C. M. Co. *v.* Turck, 70 Fed. 294, 17 C. C. A. 128.

[190] *Michigan:* Thompson *v.* Moiles, 46 Mich. 42, 8 N. W. 577; Gates *v.* Rifle Boom Co., 70 Mich. 309, 38 N. W. 245; Ayres *v.* Hubbard, 71 Mich. 594, 40 N. W. 10.

Minnesota: Whitney *v.* Huntington, 37 Minn. 197, 33 N. W. 561; King *v.* Merriman, 38 Minn. 47, 35 N. W. 570.

Mississippi: Heard *v.* James, 49 Miss. 236 (*semble*).

Nevada: Ward *v.* Carson R. W. Co., 13 Nev. 44.

New Hampshire: Foote *v.* Merrill, 54 N. H. 490, 20 Am. Rep. 151.

New York: Whitbeck *v.* New York C. R. R., 36 Barb. 644; Clark *v.* Holdridge, 12 App. Div. 613, 43 N. Y. Supp. 115.

Tennessee: Ross *v.* Scott, 15 Lea, 479.

Vermont: Tilden *v.* Johnson, 52 Vt. 628, 36 Am. Rep. 769.

[191] Chipman *v.* Hibberd, 6 Cal. 162.

[192] *United States:* Wooden Ware Co. *v.* U. S., 106 U. S. 432, 27 L. ed. 230, 1 Sup. Ct. 398; Cheeney *v.* Nebraska & C. S. Co., 41 Fed. 740; United States *v.* Teller, 106 Fed. 447, 45 C. C. A. 416.

Pennsylvania: Foster *v.* Weaver, 118 Pa. 42, 12 Atl. 313, 4 Am. St. Rep. 573.

[193] Lyon *v.* Gormley, 53 Pa. 261; *acc.,* Genet *v.* Delaware & H. C. Co., 14 App. Div. 177, 43 N. Y. Supp. 589. *Cf.* Lehigh V. C. Co. *v.* Wilkesbarre & E. R. R., 187 Pa. 145, 41 Atl. 37.

§ 504. Damages recoverable from purchaser.

Where a wanton trespasser severs property from the soil and sells it to the defendant, the measure of damages is the whole value of the property at the time of the sale.[194] In several jurisdictions it has been held or intimated that no more can be recovered from the purchaser than from the original trespasser, and if the original trespass was *bona fide* the plaintiff may recover from the purchaser only the value *in situ* or immediately after severance, according to the rule prevailing in the particular jurisdiction.[195] But in other jurisdictions it is held that the rule should be applied in all cases, irrespective of the good faith of the defendant himself; [196] on the ground that the defendant committed a tort at the time of purchase, and should pay compensation for that tort, not for the earlier tort of the trespasser, and that if the other rule were adopted it would in some way enure to the benefit of the undeserving trespasser. Of course if the purchaser had knowledge of the

---

[194] *Arkansas:* Central Coal & C. Co. v. John Henry Shoe Co., 69 Ark. 302, 63 S. W. 49.

Maine: Powers v. Tilley, 87 Me. 34, 32 Atl. 714, 47 Am. St. Rep. 304.

Minnesota: Hoxsie v. Empire Lumber Co., 41 Minn. 548, 43 N. W. 476.

Tennessee: Godwin v. Taenzer, 122 Tenn. 101, 119 S. W. 1133.

Where X., under a contract to purchase logs from the plaintiff, took the logs and sold them to defendants, with an agreement that the title should pass at the time of sale, but that X. should manufacture them into lumber, and advances were made by the defendants in good faith at the time the logs were skidded, it was held that, defendants being innocent purchasers, the measure of damages should be fixed at the time when they made the first advances, that is, at the time the logs were skidded, and should not include the subsequent increase in value by the logs being cut into lumber. Fisher v. Brown, 70 Fed. 570, 17 C. C. A. 225.

[195] *Arkansas:* Central Coal & C. Co. v. John Henry Shoe Co., 69 Ark. 302, 63 S. W. 49 (*semble*).

Colorado: Omaha & G. S. & R. R. Co. v. Tabor, 13 Colo. 41, 56, 21 Pac. 925, 16 Am. St. Rep. 185, 5 L. R. A. 236.

Minnesota: Hastay v. Bonness, 84 Minn. 120, 86 N. W. 896 (*semble*).

Ohio: Railway Co. v. Hutchins, 32 Oh. St. 571, 30 Am. Rep. 629.

Ontario: Smith v. Baechler, 18 Ont. 293 (*semble*).

[196] *United States:* Wooden Ware Co. v. United States, 106 U. S. 432, 27 L. ed. 230, 1 Sup. Ct. 398; United States v. Hielner, 11 Sawy. 406.

Georgia: Parker v. Waycross & F. R. R., 81 Ga. 387, 8 S. E. 871.

Maine: Wing v. Milliken, 91 Me. 387, 40 Atl. 138, 64 Am. St. Rep. 238.

Michigan: Tuttle v. White, 46 Mich. 485, 9 N. W. 528, 41 Am. Rep. 175; Saltmarsh v. Chicago & G. T. Ry., 122 Mich. 103, 80 N. W. 981.

Wisconsin: Tuttle v. Wilson, 52 Wis. 643, 9 N. W. 822.

trespass he would in any jurisdiction be held responsible for the entire value of the chattel at the time he bought it.[197]

§ 505. Confusion.

* The action of trover, as well as that of trespass, often presents interesting questions connected with what is technically termed confusion.[198] "If," says Blackstone,[199] "one wilfully intermixes his money, corn, or hay, with that of another man, without his approbation or knowledge, or casts gold in like manner into another's melting-pot or crucible, our law to guard against fraud gives the entire property, without any account, to him whose original dominion is invaded, and endeavored to be rendered uncertain without his own consent." [200] **

In Maine this doctrine of confusion of goods has been applied to a case where the defendant had taken the plaintiff's logs, and manufactured them into boards, and intermixed these boards with a pile of his own, so that they could not be distinguished, with the *fraudulent* intent of depriving the plaintiff of his property. And it was held that the owner of the logs might maintain replevin for the whole pile.[201] If, however, the mixture be accidental or not wrongfully made, each party will be entitled to his own property or to its value, provided the separation can be made, or the values be apportionable. If by the intermixture the property be destroyed, the loss falls on him whose fault occasioned the destruction.[202]

* The civil law does not in any case appear to recognize the severe rule of our system: *Quod si frumentum Titii frumento tuo mistum fuerit, siquidem voluntate vestrâ, commune est, quia singula corpora, id est, singula grana, quœ cujusque propria fuerint, consensu vestro communicata sunt. Quod si casu id mistum fuerit, vel Titius id miscuerit sine tuâ voluntate, non*

[197] Smith *v.* Baechler, 18 Ont. 293.
[198] Confusion, Lat. *Confusio. Confundi dicitur, quod aliis ita commiscetur ut deduci et se parari non possit, aut certe difficilis sit ejus separatio. Vicat. Vocab. Utriusque Furis in voc.* The term is applied also to the merger of different interests, and in this sense the analogous word is used in the French law.—*Crivelli, in voc.*
[199] 2 Comm., ch. 26, p. 405.
[200] *Anon.,* Popham, 38, pl. 2; Warde *v.* Aeyre, 2 Bulst. 323. See Stephenson *v.* Little, 10 Mich. 433.
[201] Wingate *v.* Smith, 20 Me. 287.
[202] Ryder *v.* Hathaway, 21 Pick. (Mass.) 298.

videtur commune esse, quia singula corpora in suâ substantiâ durant. Sed nec magis, istis casibus, commune sit frumentum quam grex intelligitur esse communis, si pecora Titii tuis pecoribus mista fuerint.[203]   Nor should the analogous case in regard to real property be overlooked. In trespass for mesne profits, the *bona fide* occupant of lands without notice, who has improved them, is allowed to set off or recoup the value of his improvements.**   Why should not the same equity be extended to this case?

It is clearly necessary to protect the innocent party; and so far as that requires the title to the entire mass to be put in him it must be done. When the goods cannot be identified, even if the mixture was an innocent one, the owner is entitled to the entire mixture, but only until he recovers the value of his own property.[204]   Where, however, the elements of the mixture are distinguishable, the owner is entitled to his own property only, and has no claim upon the entire mass.[205]

§ 506. Consequential and special damages.

It was suggested [206] by Parke, B., at Nisi Prius, that the plaintiff could recover special damages if laid in the declaration; as in trover for the conversion of a horse, that the plaintiff could recover for money paid for the hire of other horses. And it has been so since decided by the Queen's Bench, in trover brought by a carpenter for his tools; the declaration containing an allegation, that by reason of the conversion the plaintiff was prevented from working at his trade.[207]   In this country, it has been doubted; the doubt arising from the technical form of the action, as well as from the question as to remoteness.[208] It is hardly necessary to say that, wherever special damages

---

[203] Inst. lib. ii, tit. i, § 28. A different rule necessarily prevailed where separation was impossible. *Sed et id quod in charta mea scribitur aut in tabula pinxitur, statim meum fit; licet de pictura quidam contra senserint propter pretium picturæ; sed necesse est ei rei cedi quod sine illa esse non potest.* Dig. lib. vi, De Rei Vindi, p. 23, § 3.

[204] *Iowa:* Alger v. Farley, 19 Ia. 518.

Maryland: Gittings v. Winter, 101 Md. 194, 60 Atl. 630.

North Carolina: Lance v. Butler, 135 N. C. 419, 47 S. E. 488.

[205] McKnight v. United States, 65 C. C. A. 37, 130 Fed. 659.

[206] Davis v. Oswell, 7 C. & P. 804.

[207] Bodley v. Reynolds, 8 Q. B. 779.

[208] *Connecticut:* Hurd v. Hubbell, 26 Conn. 389; Seymour v. Ives, 46 Conn. 109.

are allowed, the special damage demanded must be distinctly alleged in the declaration.[209]

The case of Bodley *v.* Reynolds was followed in Reilley *v.* McMinn.[210] This was an action for the conversion of a blacksmith's tools; the blacksmith being unable to procure other tools, owing to his remote situation, was thrown out of employment. It was held that the jury might consider this in addition to the value of the tools. So in Shotwell *v.* Wendover,[211] the court said the plaintiff has a right to claim damages for the use of the articles (tools, etc.), and for their deterioration while in the possession of the defendant. In Stollenwerck *v.* Thacher [212] it appeared that the plaintiffs had sent certain goods to G. for sale. G. was to receive a certain commission on the sales. G. sold them to the defendant without requiring cash payment, as he had been ordered to do. In trover against the vendee, it was held that the damages should not include a commission to G. for the sale, because the plaintiff was not obliged to allow G. a commission for doing an act which was not shown to have been for the interest or according to the intent of the plaintiffs. In Leffingwell *v.* Gilchrist,[213] an action for the conversion of a file of the newspaper of which the plaintiff was editor, evidence of the inconvenience an editor would suffer from the destruction of a file of his newspaper was excluded. In France *v.* Gaudet [214] it appeared that the plaintiff had bought champagne at fourteen shillings per dozen, and resold it at twenty four-shillings to the captain of a ship about to leave England. The defendant, at whose wharf the wine was lying, refused to deliver it, and the plaintiff

Missouri: Saunders *v.* Brosius, 52 Mo. 50.

New York: Brizsee *v.* Maybee, 21 Wend. 144.

Pennsylvania: Farmers' Bank *v.* McKee, 2 Pa. 318.

[209] Moon *v.* Raphael, 2 Bing. N. C. 310; Tindall, C. J., said: "The injury of which the plaintiffs complain not being a damage necessarily consequent on the wrongful conversion of the goods, if it could in any shape fall within the remedy of an action of trover, ought at least to have formed the subject of a special allegation."

[210] 2 Pugs. (N. B.) 370.

[211] 1 Johns. (N. Y.) 65.

[212] 115 Mass. 224.

[213] 40 Ia. 416.

[214] L. R. 6 Q. B. 199, 204. *Cf.* Avery *v.* Catlin, 12 Wash. 322, 41 Pac. 55, where a contract of sale had been made which was put an end to by a wrongful attachment. The contract price was taken as the value of the goods.

could not fulfil the contract, there being no other champagne in the market of the same quality. It was held that the plaintiff was entitled to recover the price at which he had sold the champagne. Mellor, J., in delivering the opinion of the court, and in reference to the argument of the defendant's counsel, that "in analogy to the cases of special damages arising out of the breach of contract, notice of the special circumstances ought to have been given to the defendants, in order to entitle the plaintiff to recover anything beyond the ordinary value of the goods converted," used the following language:

"We are not prepared to say that there is any analogy between the case of contract alluded to, in which two parties making a contract for the sale and delivery of a specific chattel, the vendee gives notice to the vendor of the precise object of the purchase, and a case like the present. In the case of contract, special damages reasonably resulting from the breach of it may be considered within the contemplation of the parties. In case of trover, it is not in general special damage which can be recovered, but a special value attached by special circumstances to the article converted; the conversion consists in withholding from another property to the possession of which he is *immediately* entitled, and the circumstances which affix the value are then determined; no notice to the wrongdoer could then *affect the value*, although it might affect his conduct; but upon what principle is a notice necessary to a man who *ex hypothesi* is a wrongdoer? In such a case as the present, the actual value is fixed by circumstances at the time of the demand, and no notice of the special circumstances could then affect the actual value of the goods withheld from their rightful owner, who thereby sustains 'an actual present loss,' which appears to us to be a convertible term with 'actual value.' "

§506a. Proximate and remote damages.

The line of distinction which runs through the cases, separating those in which consequential damages are refused from those in which consequential damages, if specially alleged, are allowed, is the same which runs through the whole field of consequential, as distinguished from direct, damages in tort; that is, the cases are governed by the general principle that proxi-

mate damages may be recovered, while remote damages may
not.

Thus in Cernahan *v.* Chrisler [215] it is said:
"It is true that in actions for conversion of property the
measure of damages is generally the value of the property at the
time and place of the conversion, with interest; but when the
circumstances show special damage over and above the value
of the property, the almost universal current of authority is
that such damage may be recovered in such action." And it is
added that in case the property is returned, in the absence of
evidence showing special damage, the recovery must be limited
to nominal damages. So, in an action for taking and converting, the proof must show the value of the property taken, or
that the plaintiff sustained some special damage, in order to
entitle him to recover more than nominal damages. [216]   In
Massachusetts, in an action for conversion of plumbing fixtures
wrongfully taken from a house which was being built to be let
to tenants, it was held that the plaintiff might recover the
rental value of the house during the delay in completion caused
by the removal of the fixtures. [217]   In an action for converting a
ship, plaintiff can recover special damages beyond the value of
the property. [218]   And in an action for seizing a mortgaged
horse, it was held in North Carolina that plaintiff was not entitled to damages for the suffering he endured from cold on the
trip home; as the court very justly observes, such special or
consequential damages as these would not be recoverable in
any sort of action. [219]

To begin with cases excluding consequential damages, it has
been held that in trover by the vendee, the profits which might
have been made by the use of the chattel, or loss from incapacity to employ men and horses by reason of its detention, are
speculative. [220]   Where a vessel was converted by the defendants before she was finished, and they having afterwards finished her, the plaintiffs were not allowed to recover as a special

[215] 107 Wis. 645, 83 N. W. 778.
[216] Lay *v.* Bayles, 4 Cold. (Tenn.)
246.
[217] Munroe *v.* Armstrong, 179 Mass.
165, 60 N. E. 475.

[218] Spanish & P. S. S. S. Co. *v.* Bell,
34 Eng. L. & Eq. 178.
[219] Hinson *v.* Smith, 118 N. C. 503,
24 S. E. 541.
[220] Farmers' Bank *v.* McKee, 2 Pa.
(2 Barr) 318.

damage the value of freight which they might have earned with her.[221] In an action for the wrongful sale of tools which were exempt, plaintiff tried to recover on the ground of his having a contract to build certain bridge pillars, of which the attaching officer had no notice. It was held that he could not recover.[222] In an action for conversion, plaintiff claimed expenses incurred by him in recovering the property. The property was not in fact recovered. It was held that his damages could not exceed the actual value of the property, with interest.[223] In an action by the maker for conversion of a note, the plaintiff cannot recover costs of unsuccessful defence to note in the hands of holder.[224] In California, and perhaps in some other States, the Code provides that the detriment caused by the wrongful conversion of personal property is presumed to be, among other things, a fair compensation for the time and money properly expended in the pursuit of the property.[225] This provision is held not to authorize the recovery of attorneys' fees.[226] On the other hand, under a statute providing that damages for wrongful conversion shall include a fair compensation for the time and money properly expended "in pursuit of the property," attorney's fees paid out in recovering money lost through the fraud of another agent (the principal being liable), are recoverable as an element of compensatory damages against the principal.[227] In Vermont, in an action of trover, the plaintiff may recover the actual damage caused him by the defendant's wrongful conduct in respect to the property, but the expenses of the suit, beyond taxable costs, cannot be included in this. Damage outside the ordinary measure can be recovered only by special action on the case or by special averments in the declaration.[228]

In the following cases, on the other hand, the right to recover is recognized under the general principle stated above:

[221] Reid v. Fairbanks, 13 C. B. 692, 24 Eng. L. & Eq. 220.

[222] McKnight v. Carmichael, 7 Tex. Civ. App. 270, 27 S. W. 150.

[223] United States v. Pine River L. & I. Co., 89 Fed. 907, 32 C. C. A. 406.

[224] Dean v. Nichols & Shepard, 95 Ia. 89, 97, 63 N. W. 582.

[225] Inzaga v. Villaba, 85 Cal. 191, 24 Pac. 656.

[226] Nicholls v. Mapes, 1 Cal. App. 349, 82 Pac. 265.
Contra, Bank of Palo Alto v. Pac. P. T. C. Co., 103 Fed. 841.

[227] Bank of Palo Alto v. Pacific P. T. C. Co., 103 Fed. 841.

[228] Park v. McDaniels, 37 Vt. 594.

In an action of trover for a slave, brought by the administrator of an estate, damages have been given to the amount of the value of the slave and her descendants, together with damages for their detention for the time of demand and refusal.[229] In Wisconsin, plaintiff is allowed the reasonable expenses of seeking to recover the property.[230] In an action for the conversion of grain, time and money expended in pursuit thereof was allowed under the California Code.[231] In a case in Missouri, the innocent agent of a thief sold plaintiff's cattle. Plaintiff recovered them in replevin from the vendee. In an action of trover plaintiff was allowed the expenses of getting the cattle back by means of the action of replevin.[232] In Texas, in an action for the conversion of a wagon, the value of the wagon, and also the value of its use up to the time of trial, was allowed.[233] In New Jersey, in an action for the conversion of a railroad ticket taken up by the conductor after public altercation with passenger, it was held that the plaintiff could recover damages for the indignity and ignominy.[234] Where damages of this sort are claimed, they must be properly alleged.[235]

§ 506b. Avoidable consequences.

In the action for conversion as elsewhere, the rule of avoidable consequences will be applied in proper cases. Thus, when animals are not killed nor so injured as to be worthless for food, the owner will be expected to dispose of them to the best advantage. He cannot abandon them wantonly and then claim their full value.[236]

[229] Fishwick v. Sewell, 4 Har. & J. (Md.) 393.

[230] Parroski v. Goldberg, 80 Wis. 339, 50 N. W. 191. See remarks of the court at page 343 on the decision in Collins v. Lowry, 78 Wis. 329, 47 N. W. 612.

[231] Lothrop v. Golden (Cal.), 57 Pac. 394.

[232] Laughlin v. Barnes, 76 Mo. App. 258.

[233] Moore v. King, 4 Tex. Civ. App. 397, 23 S. W. 484.

[234] Harris v. Delaware, L. & W. R. R., 77 N. J. L. 278, 72 Atl. 50.

[235] Fish v. Nethercutt, 14 Wash. 582, 45 Pac. 44, 53 Am. St. Rep. 892.

[236] Illinois C. R. R. v. Finnigan, 21 Ill. 646.

CHAPTER XXII

THE RULE OF HIGHER INTERMEDIATE VALUE

§ 507. Higher intermediate value.

It has been held by many courts of high authority that in actions for the conversion, not only of stock, but of any personal property of fluctuating value, the measure of the damages is the highest market price which the property may have had from the date of the conversion to the end of the trial, provided the action be brought and pressed with due diligence. The same rule is also applied by these courts in other actions, namely, in actions of detinue and replevin, in actions for refusal to transfer or to deliver stock in corporations, and in actions for refusal by the vendor to deliver goods, the price of which has been paid in advance. It is impossible to consider the application of this rule in actions for conversion apart from its application in other forms of action. The rule will therefore here be discussed generally.

It is to be understood that even in jurisdictions in which the

991

rule of higher intermediate value is recognized, it is subordinate
to the general principle of compensation. Thus, in the case of
a detention of personal property through a levy of attachment,
where the plaintiff demands the highest price obtainable during the period of detention, the defendant may show that
within thirty days after its return, and while plaintiff still held
it, and before the action was brought, the property had as high
a market value, and its sale had been as possible as during the
detention.[1]

§ 508. English cases.

The early English cases can hardly be said to have established
any definite rule. The leading case [2] was on a writ of inquiry
to assess damages on a bond given by the defendant, conditioned to replace, on the 1st of August, 1799, a quantity of stock
lent him by the testator. The only question was whether the
damages should be calculated at the price of the stock on the
1st of August, or at the price on the day of trial; and the latter
sum was held the true rule of damages. Grose, J., said: "The
true measure of damages in all these cases is that which will
completely indemnify the plaintiff for the breach of the engagement." It was objected to this rule by counsel that it gave
the plaintiff the power either by hastening or delaying his suit
to take advantage of the rise in the market, without any risk
in case of a fall. And Lawrence, J., said: "Suppose a bill were
filed in equity, for a specific performance of an agreement to
replace stock on a given day, which had not been done at the
time, would not a court of equity compel the party to replace
it at the then price of the stock, if the market had risen in the
meantime?"

But in a later case in the Court of Exchequer,[3] the defendants,
in 1833, agreed to sell and deliver, on board the plaintiff's vessel, a certain quantity of Odessa linseed, at that place, at 30s.
per quarter. The plaintiff's vessel arrived at Odessa, and they
paid the defendants £1,575 in October, 1833, being a moiety of
the purchase-money of the expected cargo. The defendants

[1] Hoyt v. Fuller, 104 Fed. 192, 43   [3] Startup v. Cortazzi, 2 C. M. & R.
C. C. A. 466.   165.
[2] Shepherd v. Johnson, 2 East, 211.

gave notice that they could not comply with the contract. In
February, 1834, when the cargo would have arrived in England if it had been delivered to the plaintiffs at Odessa, the price
was from 47s. to 50s. per quarter; at the time of trial it would
have been about 56s. The defendants paid into court, in September, 1835, £2,072, which was at the rate of 47s., and which
was paid over to the plaintiffs, who contended that, as they had
paid a portion of the purchase-money and lain out of it for a
long time, they were entitled to damages according to the
price at which the seed was selling at the time of the trial.
Lord Abinger, at the trial, charged: "That in his opinion the
plaintiffs were not entitled to treat this as a case resembling
contracts for the replacing of stock where the damages are
estimated at the price of the funds, and they were not entitled
to damages according to the then price of the seed, and that
taking the price at the time the cargo would arrive, it appeared to him that enough had been paid into court; but with
these observations he left the case to the jury for their deliberation," who, designing, as Lord Abinger remarked, to give no
more than the *money advanced and interest on it*, found a verdict
for the defendants. A motion was made for a new trial, on the
ground of misdirection; but the rule was discharged.

In another case,[4] of a bond to retransfer stock, the same
principle was laid down. It was contended for the plaintiff,
that he was entitled, at his option, to the best of three prices:
either the value of the stock on the day fixed for the transfer;
or, secondly, the price at the day of trial; or, thirdly, the highest price which the stock had borne between the day of delivery
and the day of trial. But the court held, on the particular circumstances of the case, that the third claim could not be sustained. It seems difficult, however, in reason, to say why, if
the plaintiff is entitled to a subsequent rise, provided it maintain itself to the day of trial, he should be prejudiced by a fall
that may be due only to the delays of litigation.

Two later decisions in the English books held substantially
the same doctrine. In an action on a bond conditioned to replace stock at a particular day, the defendant not having
replaced it, Lord Ellenborough held, at Nisi Prius, that the

[4] M'Arthur *v.* Seaforth, 2 Taunt. 257.

63

plaintiff was entitled to claim according to the value upon the day of the trial.[5] In an action on a bond to replace stock, Best, C. J., at Nisi Prius, held that the price of the stock should be taken as at the time of the trial, saying: "When the defendant had the money, he promised to restore the stock. Justice is not done if he does not place the plaintiff in the same situation in which he would have been if the stock had been replaced at the stipulated time. We cannot act on the possibility of the plaintiff's not keeping it there. All we can say is, that the defendant has effectually prevented him from doing so." [6]

The subject was again examined, and the rule adhered to in Owen v. Routh.[7]

In a case of detinue for railway shares, the plaintiff demanded the shares on the 17th of May, 1845, when they were worth £3 5s. per share, and they were not delivered till the 25th of November of the same year, when they had fallen to £1. The measure of damages was held to be the difference between these two sums.[8]

These cases left the English law in an unsettled state; and it seems still to remain undetermined.[9] It is, however, beyond doubt that in actions for non-delivery of corporate stock the value at the time of trial may be recovered.[10] But in an action against a corporation for refusal to transfer stock on its books, the measure of damages is the value of the stock at the time it should have been transferred, with interest.[11] The distinction, if any there is, between these cases is a very unsatisfactory one. In actions for the conversion of chattels of a fluctuating value the general rule seems to be established, and the value at the time of conversion is the measure.[12]

§ 508a. No invariable rule in England.

The most important point to be gathered from the English

[5] Downes v. Back, 1 Stark. 318.
[6] Harrison v. Harrison, 1 C. & P. 412.
[7] 14 C. B. 327.
[8] Williams v. Archer, 5 C. B. 318; Archer v. Williams, 2 Car. & Kir. 26.
[9] Mayne on Damages, 8th ed., p. 220.
[10] Ibid., p. 220; Owen v. Routh, 14 C. B. 327.

[11] In re Bahia & S. F. Ry., L. R. 3 Q. B. 584.
[12] Mercer v. Jones, 3 Camp. 477; Loder v. Kekulé, 3 C. B. (N. S.) 128. But contra, Greening v. Wilkinson, 1 C. & P. 625.

cases seems to be that the measure of damages is regarded as very much at large, and dependent upon the particular circumstances of the case, and that there is no unalterable rule of the highest market value between the date of conversion or breach, and that of trial. When the action is one of contract, the terms of the contract become of the utmost importance, and in the case of a continuing contract, the right of the plaintiff may be to the value of the stock during a certain period of time, which may not embrace the time of action brought or trial at all. In Michael v. Hart,[13] the contract was to carry stocks over to a fortnightly settlement on the stock exchange. Wills, J., below, was of opinion that the plaintiff was entitled to the highest prices which were obtainable during the period during which *"he had the option of selling"* (*i. e.* under the contract), while on appeal it was held that at least the prices at the end of the settlement ought to govern.

§ 509. New York cases.

The question has been elaborately considered in New York. The leading case adopting the rule of higher intermediate value is Romaine v. Van Allen,[14] an action for the wrongful conversion of railway shares pledged with the defendant as collateral security for a loan. In this case, which was decided in 1863, Mr. Justice Rosekrans, delivering the opinion of the court, said: "Independent of the authorities, the rule appears to me to be reasonable and necessary to protect the rights of the owners and pledgors of stock against the tortious acts of pledgees, if the plaintiff commences his action within a reasonable time after conversion, and prosecutes it with reasonable diligence." The reasoning, however, on which the decision is based, applies broadly to all cases of the conversion of chattels, the learned justice using the following language: "Although the general rule of damages in trover may be the value of the chattel at the time of its conversion, with interest, or that value when the chattel has a determinate or fixed value, yet,

---

[13] [1902] 1 K. B. 482; [1901] 2 K. B. 867.

[14] 26 N. Y. 309, 311, 315. The rule had already been adopted in the case of failure to deliver goods paid for in ad-

vance, without much consideration. Cortelyou v. Lansing, 2 Cai. Cas. 200; West v. Wentworth, 3 Cow. 82; Wilson v. Matthews, 24 Barb. 295.

when there is any uncertainty or fluctuation attending the value, and the chattel afterwards rises in value, the plaintiff can only be indemnified by giving him the price of it, at some period subsequent to the conversion; and the necessary result of all the decisions, in my judgment, is that in such cases the plaintiff is entitled to recover the highest market value of the property at any time intermediate the conversion and the trial." In the case of Brass v. Worth,[15] a somewhat different rule was applied. This was also an action for the conversion, by a wrongful sale, of stock which, by special arrangement of the parties, had been purchased, and, as was adjudged, should have been held by the defendant for the plaintiff's account. The measure of damages was held to be, in reference to certain stock, its value on the day when the plaintiff demanded a return of it, and in reference to certain other stock, which had not been demanded, the difference between its market value on a certain day, which was "a reasonable time after the sale, and the cost price of the defendant's purchase thereof, with the interest." But the case of Romaine v. Van Allen was adhered to by the court of last resort in Burt v. Dutcher,[16] which was an action for the conversion of hops, and was followed by the Supreme Court of the State, in an action for the conversion of grain.[17] The same rule was also applied, by the Superior Court of the city of New York, to the case of a railroad bond lent by the plaintiff to the defendant, by whom it was converted to his own use.[18] The main question now before us was again very fully considered by the New York Court of Appeals, in an action by a principal against his factor, for the conversion of wheat by a sale, in violation of instructions.[19] In this case the plaintiff, who resided in Cleveland, Ohio, having certain wheat in the defendant's store at Buffalo, on the 12th day of July, 1853, telegraphed to the defendants at that city to sell it the same day at $1.08 a bushel, and if it were not sold on that day, to ship it to New York. The defendants accordingly offered the wheat the same day to a person who desired to be

---

[15] 40 Barb. 648.

[16] 34 N. Y. 493.

[17] Morgan v. Gregg, 46 Barb. 183; acc., Lawrence v. Maxwell, 6 Lans. 469.

[18] Nauman v. Caldwell, 2 Sweeney, 212.

[19] Scott v. Rogers, 31 N. Y. 676, 681, 4 Abb. App. 157.

allowed until the following morning to inspect it and decide on the purchase. To this the defendants assented, provided no news were received in the meantime affecting the value, and at eight o'clock the next morning he took the wheat at the price named. The case having been tried by the court without a jury, the sale was found to have been in good faith, but not having been made on the day to which the defendants were limited by their instructions, was adjudged a conversion of the wheat by them. The court fixed the 29th of November, in the same year, as the time within which the plaintiff might reasonably have brought the action. In the Court of Appeals the case was twice argued. On the first argument the court was equally divided. On a reargument before a court differently constituted, the four judges who opposed the severer rule being no longer on the bench, the following conclusions were adopted in an opinion delivered in September, 1864. Hogeboom, J., said:

"In the absence of any definite means for ascertaining the period when the owner of the property would have disposed of it, we are necessarily more or less in the dark as to the amount of injury which he has sustained by the illegal act of the defendants, and are driven to resort more or less to conjecture, or to fix upon some arbitrary period for determining the price of the property. It is obviously a rule of doubtful justice to give to the plaintiff the whole period until the statute of limitations would attach, for the commencement of this action, and the whole period intervening between the conversion and the trial to select his standard of price, without ever having given notice of his intention to adopt the price of any particular period. A much more just and equitable rule, independent of adjudications upon this question, would seem to be, to allow to the plaintiff some reasonable period, within the statute of limitations, for fixing the price of the property, provided he notifies the adverse party *at the time* of such act on his part; but never to allow him unlimited liberty of selection as to the price of which he will avail himself at the trial of the cause. If he does not make and notify his election of time, then to fix the time by the day of commencing the action, provided the action be commenced within a reasonable time after the conversion. . . . This seems to me the just and equitable rule. It is not, however, perhaps quite the rule which has obtained in the law for settling the question of damages in the case of an illegal conversion of property. . . . I think the rule of damages applicable to cases of this description is reasonably well settled to be as liberal as this in favor of the plaintiff, to wit: to allow to the plaintiff the highest price for the property prevailing between the time of conversion and a reasonable time afterwards for the commencement of the action. Some of the cases carry the period up to the time of trial of a suit commenced within a reasonable time; and as between these two periods, the time of commencing the suit and the time of trial, the rule is somewhat fluctuating. What this reasonable time shall be has never been definitely settled, and may, perhaps, fluctuate to some extent, according to the circumstances of the particular case. In the case at bar, it was held to be four months after the conversion, which terminated before the close of navigation in that year; which latter circumstance might perhaps be supposed to have some probable influence in raising the market price of the property in New York, and therefore as not unlikely to induce the plaintiff to retain the property until that time. I think the adjudications allow at least so much latitude in cases similarly circumstanced. For reasons before stated, the limit of time is necessarily, to some extent, arbitrary, for the want of available means to determine when the plaintiff would have sold his property, and, by consequence, the damages he has sustained. But it has been supposed, and I think reasonably, that a liberal allowance of time should be made in favor of the plaintiff, and against the defendant, inasmuch as the latter is the defaulting party."

The judge then compared the rule in trover to that in the case of an executory sale, where the plaintiff had paid the price in advance, and held the two cases to be analogous. He said that in the case of a sale, the highest value between the breach of contract and the commencement of an action, or of the trial of one brought within a reasonable time thereafter, was allowed on the ground that it might be impossible, and was certainly unjust, for the plaintiff to pay the price a second time, in order to procure a similar article to that of which he has been deprived; he held that the same reasoning applied to the action of trover, and that the only difficulty lay in fixing the period when the value of the property should be estimated. He added:

"Even if the evidence is satisfactory that the plaintiff intended to retain the property, I do not think that he should be permitted to roam through the entire period between the conversion and the time when the statute of limitations would attach, for the purpose of discovering the highest price at which the property sold in market. This gives to the transaction the color of a mere speculation, and not of a just ascertainment of damages actually sustained."

The rule in this case allows the plaintiff to fix his own damages after a retrospect of the market since the conversion, by selecting the highest market rate of the property during that time, provided within a reasonable time after the conversion he, by bringing the action or otherwise, gives the defendant notice of the day thus selected. But the court simply approved the measure adopted in that case by the judge before whom it was tried, as not unreasonable in itself and not unjust to the defendant. They considered that they could not say that four months after the time when the wheat, if duly forwarded, would have reached its destination, was, as matter of law, an unreasonable time for bringing the suit, and that, on questions of fact, they had no power to review the finding of the judge. But the decision did not reverse the still wider rule previously adopted in the case of Romaine v. Van Allen. That rule, in the later case of Burt v. Dutcher, was, as has been seen, reaffirmed by the same court. The latter case, as we have observed, was an action for the conversion of merchandise; and in the former, as we have also noticed, the court does not proceed upon the ground of any distinction between stocks and other personal property, in the application of the rule.

In the case of Suydam v. Jenkins [20] the English cases giving the value of stock at the time of trial were justified on the ground, "first, that as chancery may decree a specific execution of a contract for replacing stock, and the defendant, when such a decree is made, to enable himself to perform it, must, of ne-

[20] 3 Sandf. 614, 633, an action of replevin.

cessity, purchase the stock at its then market price, he can have no right to complain when he is compelled to pay the same sum as damages, by the judgment of a court of law; and, second, that as stock is usually held not for sale, but as a permanent investment, it is a reasonable presumption that had it not been replaced at the stipulated time, the plaintiff would have retained its possession until the day of trial, and hence its price at that time, whatever it might be, is no more than an indemnity." [21] The objections to the general application of the rule

[21] These are, doubtless, the reasons commonly assigned for the distinction. But it may be observed that it is more than questionable whether a decree can be had for the specific performance of an agreement for the delivery of shares in the public funds, or such other stocks as, from their well-known and permanent character, are usually sought for investment. Breaches of such contracts are readily compensated in damages, and are not, therefore, the subject of equitable relief. Story, Eq. Jur. §§ 717, 717a; Buxton v. Lister, 3 Atk. 383; Sullivan v. Tuck, 1 Md. Ch. Decisions, 59. And in regard to such stocks as are of fluctuating value, the presumption may be at least quite as applicable to them as to any other property, that they were bought for speculative purposes rather than to hold for investment and it must be added that there seems no justification for any *presumption* on the subject. To enable the plaintiff to recover damages on account of the *object* of his purchase, there must be *proof*, and *notice*, not presumption. In Romaine v. Van Allen the stock between the time of the conversion and the beginning of the trial rose from $3,937.50, which was its full market price on the day of the conversion, to $5,962.50 before trial began. The trial, which was before a referee, was a protracted one, and during its progress the stock happened to rise in the market to the price of $8,175, which was the highest

reached before the trial ended, and was the amount allowed. Here we have this remarkable result of the application of the rule adopted, that from the circumstance that the trial was had before a referee, instead of the court, or a court and jury, the plaintiff gained upwards of $2,000 in the amount of the judgment. It is difficult to see how the principle of compensation could justify this windfall. Again, if the action were brought in the city of New York, where the courts are often oppressed with business, it might be that the suit, although prosecuted with proper diligence, could not be tried within a much longer time than if it were in a contiguous county. On the principle of this case, the verdict for the same conversion, although obtained with proper diligence, might be double if the suit were brought in one county what it would be in another, where the same obstacles to an immediate or speedy trial did not exist. Another serious objection to the rule is, that the reason of it does not apply where the goods were purchased for use, or for some other purpose than for sale, nor even when they were bought for sale, unless the advance occurred within the period during which they would have been sold in the ordinary course of business. In the case in which the rule is least objectionable, that of goods intended for sale, indemnity would require that it be confined to such as were or may be presumed

were, however, stated in a masterly manner by Duer, J., in his celebrated opinion in this case: [22] "Our objections to considering an intermediate higher value as an invariable rule of damages, have already been stated, and need not be repeated. It is perfectly just, when the enhanced price has been realized by the wrongdoer, or it is reasonable to believe would have been realized by the owner, had he retained the possession; but, in all other cases, damages founded upon such an estimate, are either purely speculative, or plainly vindictive. They are conjectural and speculative, when it is barely possible that the owner, had he retained the possession, would have derived a benefit from the higher value. They are vindictive, when it is certain that no such benefit could have resulted to him."

In Markham v. Jaudon,[23] an action for the conversion of stock, it was held by the Court of Appeals that the plaintiff could recover the highest value between the time of the conversion and the time of the trial; that is, the "fluctuating rule" laid down in Romaine v. Van Allen was adopted, Grover and Woodruff, JJ., however, dissenting. The same rule was adopted by the Commission of Appeals of New York, in Lobdell v.

to have been meant for sale indefinitely in point of time. Where goods were to have been sold either immediately or within a certain fixed period, the range of the plaintiff's right of selection should, on the same principle, be narrowed to the time of the intended sale. So in the case of property which from its nature would have perished, or in the case of articles intended for consumption which would have been consumed within a limited period, the time of the fluctuation of the market, within which the price is to be determined, ought not on any principle of compensation to go beyond such period. In each case, the facts and circumstances showing what would have been the probable disposition of the property by the owner, would seem material in showing his actual loss, and, therefore, in ascertaining the proper indemnity. It is grossly in-

equitable that the owner should have the advantage of a chance rise in value, which it is certain he had never contemplated, and would not have taken advantage of had the property remained in his possession. The want of uniformity in the rule, and the numerous exceptions which must be engrafted on it, seem grave objections. Whenever the plain and definite rule of the value at the time of conversion or non-delivery is to be enlarged, that modification of it laid down in the case of Suydam v. Jenkins, 3 Sandf. 614, *supra*, by which damages beyond the value of the property and interest are allowed only where they are proved, and not merely presumed, to have been sustained, is the most satisfactory which has been suggested. See Meshke v. Van Doren, 16 Wis. 319.

[22] P. 629.

[23] 41 N. Y. 235.

Stowell.[24] The Court of Appeals later, however, took a different view, and both these decisions were overruled. In Matthews v. Coe,[25] which was an action to recover for an alleged conversion of warehouse receipts of corn, pledged by the plaintiff's assignor as security for advances made by the defendant, decided by that court in March, 1872, it appeared that the defendant had acted in good faith, and moreover that the plaintiff had intended to sell the corn at a dollar a bushel. The price, however, allowed by the referee before whom the action was tried, was fixed by him at the market rate prevailing a year and a half after the action was brought, which was a dollar and forty-five cents a bushel. Church, C. J., delivering the opinion of the court, observed that whatever might be the propriety of a rule giving the plaintiff the benefit of the highest market price between the conversion and the trial, in a case not exceptional in its circumstances, such a rule could have no application to one like that before the court. The learned chief judge closed with the significant intimation that the rule referred to was not so firmly settled as to be beyond the reach of review whenever necessary.

§ 510. Baker v. Drake.

Such a necessity arose in an action decided by the same court in September, 1873, concerning a speculation in stocks like that in Markham v. Jaudon, and in which the precise questions there presented were again raised.[26] In this case the plaintiff had advanced but $4,240 on account of the purchase of various railway shares, which, in November, 1868, had cost the defendants upwards of $66,300 beyond the plaintiff's advances. In that month the shares, at a sale of them made by the defendants in good faith, but without authority, at the market rates, to pay their advances, produced less than $67,000. Between this time and that of the trial the stock fluctuated heavily, and in August, 1870, rose in the market to 170, which was its culminating point, and from which it declined. The jury, instructed in accordance with the rule in Markham v. Jaudon, found a verdict for the plaintiff of $18,000, which was the dif-

[24] 51 N. Y. 70.
[25] 49 N. Y. 57.

[26] Baker v. Drake, 53 N. Y. 211, 217, 13 Am. Rep. 507.

ference between the average price, at which the defendant sold, and 170. This was held error on appeal to the Court of Appeals, where it was said that the proper rule in such a case, was the market price of the stock within a reasonable time after the plaintiff received notice of the conversion. Rapallo, J., in a very learned opinion, said that the supposition that a plaintiff who had failed to keep his margin good up to the sale, would have continued to supply it during the time necessary to carry the stock to its highest point, and then have been fortunate enough to sell it at that precise point, was an unreasonable one, and that the award of a measure of damages based on such a conjecture was a wide departure from that rule of simple indemnity which should control the damages, except in cases where punitive damages are allowable. The learned judge then pointed out, that as he had not paid for his stocks, and did not hold them as an investment, the loss, if any, which he sustained was simply that of the chance of their subsequent rise in the market, and this chance was accompanied by the corresponding one of their decline, and, also, by the further contingency in case of a rise of his not availing himself of it. He added:

"A continuation of the speculation also required him to supply further margin, and involved a risk of ultimate loss. If, upon becoming informed of the sale, he desired further to prosecute the adventure, and take the chances of a future market, he had the right to disaffirm the sale and require the defendants to replace the stock. If they failed, or refused to do this, his remedy was to do it himself, and charge them with the loss reasonably sustained in doing so. The advance in the market price of the stock, from the time of the sale up to a reasonable time to replace it, after the plaintiff received notice of the sale, would afford a complete indemnity. Suppose the stock, instead of advancing, had declined after the sale, and the plaintiff had replaced it, or had full opportunity to replace it, at a lower price, could it be said that he sustained any damage by the sale? Would there be any justice or reason in permitting him to lie by and charge his broker with the result of a rise at some remote subsequent period?"

Under the rule in Markham v. Jaudon, as he proceeded to show, the plaintiff is "in a position incomparably superior to that of which he has been deprived." It leaves him relieved both from risk and from the necessity of supplying "margin," "with his venture out for an indefinite period, limited only by what may be deemed a reasonable time to bring a suit and conduct it to its end." Meanwhile, obstacles and delays in the progress of the suit are for the interest of the suitor, since they extend the period for his retrospective selection of the rate of his own damages. He pointed out that the reasoning of those decisions which sanction the rule of a higher intermediate value, being founded on the idea that the plaintiff, having been wrongfully deprived of his property or the price agreed to be paid for it, cannot be justly expected to procure it a second time, is necessarily inapplicable to the case of property purchased for speculation, not with his funds, but the defendant's. It is to be noticed that, in this decision, the usual rule in trover, viz., the value of the goods at the time of the conversion, was not adopted, the court proceeding on the theory that the plaintiff should have a reasonable time to replace himself in the market, after notice of the wrong. The rule laid down as the proper one by Rapallo, J., in this case, was distinctly affirmed in a second appeal taken in the above case.[27] It appeared that, at the second trial, the judge charged the jury that the plaintiffs were entitled to recover as damages what it would have cost them to replace the stocks on a day within a reasonable time after the sale, deducting the sum due to the defendants, and the recovery was based upon the market value of the stock on a day between the sale and the commencement of the action. This was held to be correct.

§ 511. Wright v. Bank of the Metropolis.

The case of Baker v. Drake was approved, and the rule laid down by Rapallo, J., extended, in the later case of Wright v. Bank of the Metropolis,[28] an action for the wrongful sale of pledged stock. In that case Peckham, J., said:

"In such a case as this, whether the action sounds in tort or is based altogether upon contract, the rule of damages is the same. . . . There is no material distinction in the fact of

[27] Baker v. Drake, 66 N. Y. 518, 23 Am. Rep. 80.

[28] 110 N. Y. 237, 246, 18 N. E. 79, 6 Am. St. Rep. 356, 1 L. R. A. 289. The rule was again sustained in Griggs v. Day, 158 N. Y. 1, 52 N. E. 692.

ownership of the whole stock which should place the plaintiff outside of any liability to repurchase after notice of sale, and should render the defendant continuously liable for any higher price to which the stock might rise after conversion and before trial. As the same liability on the part of defendant exists in each case to replace the stock, and as he is technically a wrong-doer in both cases, but in one no more than in the other, he should respond in the same measure of damages in both cases, and that measure is the amount which, in the language of Rapallo, J., is the natural, reasonable, and proximate result of the wrongful act complained of, and which a proper degree of prudence on the part of the plaintiff would not have averted. The loss of a sale of the stock at the highest price down to trial, would seem to be a less natural and proximate result of the wrongful act of the defendant in selling it when plaintiff had the stock for an investment, than when he had it for a specula-tion, for the intent to keep it as an investment is at war with any intent to sell it at any price, even the highest. But in both cases the qualification attaches that the loss shall be only such as a proper degree of prudence on the part of the complainant would not have averted, and a proper degree of prudence on the part of the complainant consists in repurchasing the stock after notice of its sale, and within a reasonable time. If the stock then sells for less than the defendant sold it for, of course the complainant has not been injured, for the difference in the two prices inures to his benefit. If it sells for more, that differ-ence the defendant should pay.

"It is said that, as he had already paid for the stock once, it is unreasonable to ask the owner to go in the market and re-purchase it. I do not see the force of this distinction. In the case of the stock held on margin, the plaintiff has paid his margin once to the broker, and so it may be said that it is unreasonable to ask him to pay it over again in the purchase of the stock. Neither statement, it seems to me, furnishes any reason for holding a defendant liable to the rule of damages stated in this record. The defendant's liability rests upon the ground that he has converted, though in good faith and under a mistake as to his rights, the property of the plaintiff. The defendant is, therefore, liable to respond in damages for the value. But the duty of the plaintiff to make the damages as light as he reasonably may, rests upon him in both cases, for there is no more legal wrong done by the defendant in selling the stock, which the plaintiff has fully paid for, than there is in selling the stock which he has agreed to hold on a margin, and which agreement he violates by selling it. All that can be said is that there is a difference in amount, as in one case the plaintiff's margin has gone, while in the other the whole price of the stock has been sacrificed. But there is no such difference in the legal nature of the two transactions as should leave the duty resting upon the plaintiff in the one case to repurchase the stock, and in the other case should wholly absolve him therefrom. A rule which requires a repurchase of the stock in a reasonable time, does away with all questions as to the highest price before the commencement of the suit, or whether it was commenced in a reasonable time or prosecuted with reasonable diligence, and leaves out of view any question as to the presumption that plaintiff would have kept his stock down to the time when it sold at the highest mark before the day of trial, and would then have sold it, even though he had owned it for an investment. Such a presumption is not only of quite a shadowy and vague nature, but is also, as it would seem, entirely inconsistent with the fact that he was holding the stock as an investment. If kept for an investment, it would have been kept down to the day of trial, and the price at that time there might be some degree of propriety in awarding under certain circumstances, if it were higher than when it was converted. But to presume, in favor of an investor, that he would have held his stock during all of a period of possible depression, and would have realized upon it when it reached the highest figure, is to indulge in a presumption which, it is safe to say, would not be based on fact once in a hundred times. To formulate a legal liability based upon such presumption, I think is wholly unjust in such a case as the present. Justice and fair dealing are both more apt to be promoted by adhering to the rule which imposes the duty upon the plaintiff to make his loss as light as possible, notwithstanding the unauthorized act of the defendant, assuming of course, in all cases, that there was good faith on the part of the defendant.

"It is the natural and proximate loss which the plaintiff is to be indemnified for, and that cannot be said to extend to the highest price before trial, but only to the highest price 'reached within a reasonable time after the plaintiff has learned of the conversion of his stock within which he could go in the market and repurchase it. What is a reasonable time when the facts are undisputed and different inferences cannot reasonably be drawn from the same facts, is a question of law." [29]

§ 512. Result of the New York cases.

The result of the New York cases is that the rule of the higher intermediate value is applied in stock transactions, but in a very limited form; the highest value being allowed only between the time of injury and the time when the plaintiff by due diligence might have replaced himself in the market. The rule is applicable to all cases of conversion or breach of contract to deliver stocks. Subsequent decisions have only strengthened and extended it.[30] So, where a broker improperly closed out a speculation whereby he had sold stock short for a customer, the measure of damages is the difference between the price at which the short stock was bought in and the lowest market price of the stock within a reasonable time after the sale, less broker's commission.[31] The rule also applies to dealings in contracts for the future delivery of tangible chattels of a fluctuating value, i. e., *cotton futures*.[32] If no evidence is given by which the value of the article within a reasonable time after notice can be determined, only nominal damages can be recovered.[33]

Gruman v. Smith [34] was a stockbroker's action for balance of account on stock carried. A stockbroker sells, without due notice, stock bought and carried for a customer, on margin.

[29] As already explained (see chap. XI) the editors of the present edition are not of opinion that the measure of *cost of replacement* rests on a *duty* to replace, but on its being the natural and normal measure, in accordance with the custom of the market, under the rule of avoidable consequences.
[30] Minor v. Beveridge, 141 N. Y. 399, 36 N. E. 404, 38 Am. St. Rep. 804 (conversion by broker); Griggs v. Day, 158 N. Y. 1, 52 N. E. 692 (conversion by pledgee). See also Flagler v. Hearst, 91 App. Div. 12, 86 N. Y. Supp. 308; Corn Exchange Bank v. Peabody, 111 App. Div. 553, 98 N. Y. Supp. 78.
[31] Barber v. Ellingwood, 137 App. Div. 704, 129 N. Y. Supp. 414.
[32] Hurt v. Miller, 120 App. Div. 833, 105 N. Y. Supp. 775.
[33] Griggs v. Day, 158 N. Y. 1, 52 N. E. 692.
[34] 81 N. Y. 25.

This is a conversion, although the sale is on account of the failure of the customer to put up additional margin called for. It was held that this does not extinguish the entire claim of the broker, and hence his complaint cannot be dismissed. He is liable in damages, but whether they would equal the amount of the claim depends on the facts developed. The title of the stock purchased was in the customer, and the stock carried and margins put up constituted a pledge to secure the debt. The stock sold at 90. If it went down to 50 and remained there, the defendant would be benefited by the sale. The defendant might be able to show that the market value of the stock at the time of sale exceeded the price for which it was sold; and he was entitled to a reasonable time *after notice*, to replace himself; and if meantime it had advanced in price, the defendant would be entitled to the difference; beyond that he is not injured. In other words, he has a right to notice for the purpose of replacing himself, and the value of that right is the actual measuring of the injury.

In Colt *v.* Owens [35] defendants purchased and agreed to carry stock for plaintiff, until instructed to sell, for a period of six months. No money was paid by plaintiff, but he furnished the defendants the guaranty of a third person against loss. The defendants sold the stock without authority, and gave the plaintiff notice. In an action to recover damages, it appeared that for thirty days after the sale, the stock could have been bought in the market for the price of which it was sold, or less. It was held that the plaintiff, having had a reasonable time to replace the stock, could only recover nominal damages.

§ 512a. Notice and reasonable time under the New York rule.

The limit of reasonable time, and the point of time from which it begins to run, must depend upon circumstances. There must be either actual or constructive notice. [36] The plaintiff is entitled only to the highest price within a reasonable time after "he has learned of the conversion." When the facts are undisputed, the question is one of law, [37] but prece-

---

[35] 90 N. Y. 368.
[36] Smith *v.* Savin, 141 N. Y. 315, 329, 36 N. E. 388.

[37] Wright *v.* Bank of Metropolis, 110 N. Y. 237, 18 N. E. 79, 6 Am. St. Rep. 356, 1 L. R. A. 289; Burnham *v.* Law-

dents are of little value.[38] For a person living near the stock market, it has been intimated that forty days after notice is too long a period [39] and that thirty days is the limit.[40] In Rosenbaum *v.* Stiebel [41] the referee on whose opinion judgment was affirmed said:

"In the absence of evidence of special circumstances showing other elements of necessity for further time, we think it may be stated as a general rule that the customer is entitled to a reasonable opportunity to consult counsel, to employ other brokers, and to watch the market for the purpose of determining whether it is advisable to purchase on a particular day, or when the stock reaches a particular quotation, and to raise funds if he decides to repurchase. Doubtless the customer's financial ability would not enter into a determination of the question; but, assuming that he had property or securities, he should be given a reasonable time to convert them into money or to raise money on their security. Perhaps the most important of these elements is time to reflect and consider what is the tendency of the market and at what price it is advisable to purchase, in view of all the facts and circumstances." [42]

§ 513. Cases in the Supreme Court of the United States.

The question has been considered by the Supreme Court of the United States. Where a contract was made [43] to redeliver to the plaintiffs flour left with the defendants and not paid for, the plaintiff claimed damages only at the rate of the price of flour on the day fixed for delivery; and though the case went up to Washington, nothing was decided.

In an action brought in Louisiana,[44] by petition or libel, the forms of action of the English law being there unknown, on a contract for the delivery of cotton at 10 cents per pound, on or before the 15th day of February, when the article was 12 cents per pound, it appeared that it had risen to 30 cents before the

son, 103 N. Y. Supp. 482, 118 App. Div. 389.

[38] Burham *v.* Lockwood, 71 App. Div. 301, 75 N. Y. Supp. 828.

[39] Smith *v.* Savin, 141 N. Y. 315, 36 N. E. 338.

[40] Burham *v.* Lockwood, 71 App. Div. 301, 75 N. Y. Supp. 828.

[41] 137 App. Div. 912, 122 N. Y. Supp. 131.

[42] 122 N. Y. Supp. 135.

[43] Douglass *v.* McAllister, 3 Cranch, 298, 2 L. ed. 446.

[44] Shepherd *v.* Hampton, 3 Wheat. 200, 204, 4 L. ed. 369.

suit was brought; the plaintiffs insisted that they were entitled to the highest market price up to the rendition of the judgment. But the unanimous opinion of the court was, "that the price of the article at the time it was to be delivered was the measure of damages." Marshall, C. J., said: "For myself only, I can say that I should not think the rule would apply *to a case where advances of money* had been made by the purchaser under the contract. But I am not aware what would be the opinion of the court in such a case."

The New York rule, so far at least as stock transactions are concerned, has been adopted by the Supreme Court of the United States. In Galigher v. Jones,[45] Bradley, J., said:

"It has been assumed, in the consideration of the case, that the measure of damages in stock transactions of this kind is the highest intermediate value reached by the stock between the time of the wrongful act complained of and a reasonable time thereafter, to be allowed to the party injured to place himself in the position he would have been in had not his rights been violated. This rule is most frequently exemplified in the wrongful conversion by one person of stocks belonging to another. To allow merely their value at the time of conversion would, in most cases, afford a very inadequate remedy, and, in the case of a broker, holding the stocks of his principal, it would afford no remedy at all. The effect would be to give to the broker the control of the stock, subject only to nominal damages. The real injury sustained by the principal consists not merely in the assumption of control over the stock, but in the sale of it at an unfavorable time, and for an unfavorable price. Other goods wrongfully converted are generally supposed to have a fixed market value at which they can be replaced at any time; and hence with regard to them, the ordinary measure of damages is their value at the time of conversion, or, in case of sale and purchase, at the time fixed for their delivery. But the application of this rule to stocks would, as before said, be very inadequate and unjust. The rule of highest intermediate value as applied

[45] 129 U. S. 193, 200, 9 Sup. Ct. 335, 32 L. ed. 658; *acc., In re* Swift, 114 Fed. 947. Where there is no proof of difference in value at the respective dates the question cannot arise. Logan Co. Nat. Bank *v.* Townsend, 139 U. S. 67, 35 L. ed. 107, 11 Sup. Ct. 496.

to stock transactions has been adopted in England and in several of the States in this country, whilst in some others it has not obtained. The form and extent of the rule have been the subject of much discussion and conflict of opinion. . . . It would be a herculean task to review all the various and conflicting opinions that have been delivered on this subject. On the whole it seems to us that the New York rule, as finally settled by the Court of Appeals, has the most reasons in its favor, and we adopt it as a correct view of the law."

§ 514. Pennsylvania.

In Pennsylvania the rule of the highest intermediate value is not applied in actions for the non-delivery of chattels generally, though the price has been paid in advance,[46] nor in actions for the conversion of personal property.[47] In the case of the conversion of stock, the general rule is to some extent modified. Where the consideration for the stock has been paid, its highest market value between the breach and the trial, together with the bonus and dividends received in the meantime, is the rule; where the consideration has not been paid, the plaintiff is allowed the difference between it and the value of the stock, together with the difference between the interest on the consideration and the dividends on the stock.[48] The general rule in trover is said not to apply "where the article could not be obtained elsewhere, or where from restrictions on its production or other causes its price is necessarily subject to very considerable fluctuations." In the case of bank stock which is within this exception, the ordinary rule would hold out temptations to acts of wrongful conversion, by making them profitable to the wrongdoer, since the bank or any other trustee might deprive the owner of the very advantage he had in view when he made the investment. So, in an action to replace borrowed stock, where the value of the stock was highest at the time of the trial, that value was held in an early case to be the proper measure of damages.[49] But the principle of these decisions applies only to the case of a refusal to perform the contract,

[46] Smethurst v. Woolston, 5 W. & S. 106.

[47] Neiler v. Kelley, 69 Pa. 403.

[48] Bank of Montgomery v. Reese, 26 Pa. 143.

[49] Musgrave v. Beckendorff, 53 Pa. 310.

whereby the plaintiff suffers the loss in the advance of the price of the stock.[50] In Neiler *v*. Kelley [51] Sharswood, J., said that in cases of trover for stock the ordinary rule, "is not changed, but only modified to this extent, that wherever there is a duty or obligation devolved upon a defendant to deliver such stocks or securities at a particular time, and that duty or obligation has not been fulfilled, then the plaintiff is entitled to recover the highest price in the market between that time and the time of the trial. The grounds of this exception are that such securities are limited in quantity—are not always to be obtained at any price, and are of very fluctuating value. These are supposed to constitute sufficient reasons for the distinction." But it has finally been held that the rule in Pennsylvania does not apply to ordinary stock contracts, but only to trusts, and cases where justice could not be reached by the ordinary measure of damages.[52] In a case where a plaintiff, who had paid for stock, formally tendered it back to the defendant, and demanded the return of the money, or the defendant's note for the amount, pursuant to one of the terms of sale, the measure of damages was held to be the amount paid, and not the market price at the time of the refusal.[53]

The Pennsylvania courts make a broad distinction between cases involving conscious wrong and all others. "In all cases not involving an actually wrongful conversion or breach of trust, the old and well-established rule still prevails that the value of the stock at the time of the technical conversion, with interest thereon, is the true measure of damages." Hence when stock is wrongfully transferred under a forged power, the measure of damages in an action against the company is the market price of the stock at the time of the transfer; [54]

[50] Phillips' Appeal, 68 Pa. 130. See also Reitenbaugh *v*. Ludwick, 31 Pa. 131.

[51] 69 Pa. 403, 408.

[52] Bank of Montgomery *v*. Reese, 26 Pa. 143; Work *v*. Bennett, 70 Pa. 484; Huntingdon & B. T. R. R. & C. Co. *v*. English, 86 Pa. 247; North *v*. Phillips, 89 Pa. 250; Pennsylvania Co. for Insurance *v*. Philadelphia, G. & N. R. R., 153 Pa. 160, 25 Atl. 1043.

And so it is held to-day that the measure of damages for breach of contract to return borrowed stock is the value of the stock at the time of demand for return. Jennings *v*. Loeffler, 184 Pa. 318, 39 Atl. 214.

[53] Laubach *v*. Laubach, 73 Pa. 387.

[54] Penna. Co. for Insurance *v*. Phila., G. & R. R. R., 153 Pa. 160, 25 Atl. 1043.

while on the other hand in an action against a broker for conversion by a prema'ture sale of the stock he was carrying the highest price between the conversion and the trial was allowed.[55]

§ 515. Alabama, South Carolina, Wyoming.

In Alabama the latest cases hold it proper to give evidence of the highest value between the time of the conversion and that of the trial, and it is in the discretion of the jury to give the value they judge proper between this highest value and the value at the time of conversion, with lawful interest from that time;[56] but the jury has no discretion to give a lower value than that at the moment of conversion, so that the defendant cannot show that the value has diminished after the date of conversion.[57]   The rule is not confined to commercial securities of fluctuating value, but extends to other personal property as well; e. g., a mare.[58]   In Burks v. Hubbard [59] the court said: "This discretion of the jury in selecting the exact period of valuation should be exercised in such a manner as to prevent the defendant from reaping pecuniary profit through his wrongful act, and at the same time, in proper cases, to permit the special equities or hardships of the particular case so to operate in the mitigation of damages as exact justice may' require." [60]

The rule in South Carolina [61] and in Wyoming [62] seems to be the same as in Alabama. If the tort is committed under a

[55] Learock v. Paxson, 208 Pa. 602, 57 Atl. 1097.

[56] Loeb v. Flash, 65 Ala. 526; Street v. Nelson, 67 Ala. 504; Renfro v. Hughes, 69 Ala. 581; Ryan v. Young, 147 Ala. 660, 41 So. 954; Henderson v. Hollind (Ala. App.), 55 So. 323. See Calhoun v. Art Metal Constr. Co., 152 Ala. 607, 44 So. 877.

In the earlier cases the court appears to have laid down the rule in the more common form, without leaving it to the discretion of the jury.

Conversion: Tatum v. Manning, 9 Ala. 144; Ewing v. Blount, 20 Ala. 694; Jenkins v. McConico, 26 Ala. 213.

Detinue: Johnson v. Marshall, 34 Ala. 522. But in case of non-delivery of goods sold, higher intermediate value was disallowed. Rose v. Bozeman, 41 Ala. 678.

[57] Boutwell v. Parker, 124 Ala. 341, 27 So. 309.

[58] McGowan v. Lynch, 151 Ala. 458, 44 So. 573.

[59] 69 Ala. 379, 384.

[60] But see § 517.

[61] Gregg v. Bank, 72 S. C. 458, 52 S. E. 195. See an earlier case, Kidd v. Mitchell, 1 N. & McC. 334.

[62] Hilliard Flume Co. v. Woods, 1 Wyo. 396.

bona fide claim of right, the jury, it is said, ought not to give a very high verdict based on subsequent rise in value; but the remedy for a capricious exercise by the jury of its discretion is a new trial.[63]

§ 516. Florida, Arkansas, Mississippi.

In Florida the rule of the highest market value was approved by the court, in Moody *v.* Caulk,[64] as the proper one in the case of stock held for investment, of rare pictures, jewels, and like articles, provided the jury be satisfied that the plaintiff would have held the property up to the time of the advance. In Peterson *v.* Gresham,[65] the rule in Arkansas was said to be "in cases where there is an increase in value after the taking and before the demand, suit, or actual conversion," the highest market value during this time; but it was said, when the property was actually converted and passed beyond the possible reach of the plaintiff, then, in trover, its value and the interest is the fixed measure of damages.

In Mississippi,[66] the Court of Errors and Appeals, while rejecting the fluctuating rule, maintained the following exceptions to the fixed rule of the value and interest: First, where the original act was wrongful; second, where it was *bona fide*, but the defendants subsequently disposed of the property wrongfully, and with knowledge of the plaintiff's claim; third, where the taking and disposition of the property were both in good faith, but the defendant seeks to retain the excess of the proceeds of the sale over the market value at the time of the conversion "as a speculation"; and fourth, where the property has some peculiar value to the plaintiff, and is wilfully taken or withheld by the defendant. In the several classes of cases thus excepted by the learned court, the rule of compensation, in its opinion, is abandoned, and the damages are left at large to the jury. The last exception, however, as we think, with deference, might be properly included in the preceding ones.[67]

[63] Carter *v.* Du Pre, 18 S. C. 179, 44 Am. Rep. 569.
[64] 14 Fla. 50.
[65] 25 Ark. 380, 388, per Gregg, J. In an action for the conversion of scrip, the measure of damages is obviously not "the highest price" at which it would have been sold "at the time of conversion." Hamburg Bank *v.* George, 92 Ark. 472, 123 S. W. 654.
[66] Whitfield *v.* Whitfield, 40 Miss. 352.
[67] *Acc.*, Bickell *v.* Colton, 41 Miss. 368.

§ 516a. Indiana.

In Indiana the rule laid down in New York and in the Supreme Court of the United States is followed, and the measure of damages allowed is the highest intermediate value between the injury and a reasonable time after notice for replacement in the market.[68]

§ 516b. Iowa.

In Iowa, in case of the conversion of goods in general, the plaintiff is restricted to the value of the property at the time of conversion, with interest.[69] But in the case of corporate stock the plaintiff may recover the highest value which it attains between the time of conversion and a reasonable time for replacing it, if the purchase price has not been paid; or, if the purchase price has been paid, then the highest value between the conversion and the time of the bringing of the action, providing the bringing of the action is not unreasonably delayed; and in addition to this, there may also be recovery of interest and dividends.[70]

§ 516c. Texas, Australia.

In Texas and in Australia the rule of highest intermediate value between the injury and the time of trial is adhered to;[71] subject, however, to the limitation that the action must be brought seasonably, otherwise the plaintiff is restricted to the value at the time of the injury.[72]

---

[68] Citizens' Street R. R. v. Robbins, 144 Ind. 671, 42 N. E. 916, 43 N. E. 649, 25 Am. St. Rep. 445.

See the earlier cases: Kent v. Ginter, 23 Ind. 1; Ellis v. Wire, 33 Ind. 127.

[69] Gensburg v. Marshall Field & Co., 104 Iowa, 599, 74 N. W. 3, and cases cited.

[70] Loetscher v. Dillon, 119 Ia. 202, 93 N. W. 101; Doyle v. Burns, 123 Ia. 488, 99 N. W. 195. See the earlier cases: Cannon v. Folsom, 2 Ia. 101; Davenport v. Wells, 3 Ia. 242; Harrison v. Charlton, 37 Ia. 134; Myer v. Wheeler, 65 Ia. 390; Gilman v. Andrews, 66 Ia. 116; Gravel v. Clough, 81 Ia. 272, 46 N. W. 1092.

[71] *Texas:* Stephenson v. Price, 30 Tex. 715; Witliff v. Spreen, 51 Tex. Civ. App. 544, 112 S. W. 98; Randon v. Barton, 4 Tex. 289; Calvit v. McFadden, 13 Tex. 324; Brasher v. Davidson, 31 Tex. 190; Gregg v. Fitzhugh, 36 Tex. 127.

Australia: Amoretty v. City of Melbourne Bank, 13 Vict. L. R. 431; Vicary v. Foley, 17 Vict. L. R. 407.

[72] *Texas:* Heilbroner v. Douglass, 45 Tex. 402.

Australia: Amoretty v. City of Melbourne Bank, 13 Vict. L. R. 431 (*semble*).

§ 517. California.

In California, although the "highest value" rule was for a time adopted,[73] it was soon said that "some qualification of the rule may be found necessary where there has been an unreasonable delay in bringing suit, or under certain special circumstances."[74] And in a later case the rule was accordingly seriously modified. In May, 1863, the defendant had wrongfully replevied hay crops, then not worth over $2,500. The following year, in consequence of a drought, the price of hay rose enormously, and the jury, having been allowed to assess the plaintiff's damages at any market rate prevailing after the conversion, with interest, found a verdict for $25,763.37. The court, after reviewing the history of the fluctuating rule, say that it is an exceptional one of American origin, and that, if unqualified, it is unjust. Rejecting, however, as illogical and unreasonable the particular qualification of it sometimes adopted as to diligence in bringing and prosecuting the suit, they conclude that, in the class of cases in which it has been applied, the correct measure is the highest market value within what, under the circumstances of each case, is a reasonable time after the property was taken, with interest "from the time when the value was estimated." As the action had not been brought till 1869, they thought that too wide a range had been allowed the jury, and therefore set aside the verdict.[75] But soon after this decision a statute was passed,[76] to the effect that the detriment caused by the wrongful conversion of personal property is presumed to be the value of the property at the time of the conversion, with interest, or, where action has been prosecuted with reasonable diligence, the highest market value at any time between the conversion and the verdict, without interest at the option of the injured party, and a fair compensation for time and money properly expended in pursuit of the property.[77]

---

[73] Douglass v. Kraft, 9 Cal. 562; acc., Dabovich v. Emeric, 12 Cal. 171.

[74] Hamer v. Hatheway, 33 Cal. 117.

[75] Page v. Fowler, 39 Cal. 412, 2 Am. Rep. 462.

[76] Cal. Civ. Code, § 3336.

[77] Fromm v. Sierra Nevada S. M. Co., 61 Cal. 629; Niles v. Edwards, 90 Cal. 10, 27 Pac. 296; Ralston v. Bank of California, 112 Cal. 208, 44 Pac. 476; Lynch v. McGhan, 7 Cal. App. 132, 93 Pac. 1044.

§ 517a. Other jurisdictions having a statutory rule.

The California statute has been adopted in several of the western States. It was early adopted in Dakota [78] and reaffirmed in North Dakota.[79] It has also been adopted in Oklahoma.[80] A similar statute was passed independently in Georgia.[81]

§ 518. New Hampshire.

The rule of highest intermediate value was disapproved in New Hampshire in the important case of Pinkerton v. Manchester and Lawrence Railroad,[82] after a review of the cases, and the value of the articles which should have been delivered at the time of the failure to deliver them, is held to be the just and convenient measure of damages. Bellows, J., said:

"The general rule here and elsewhere is, that in an action on a contract to deliver goods, stocks, and other personal property, the measure of damages is the value of the property at the time and place of delivery. But a distinction has been made in some jurisdictions, by which, where the price has been paid in advance, the plaintiff has been allowed to elect the value at the time when the property ought to have been delivered, or at the time of trial, or, as some cases hold, the value at any intermediate period. Such a distinction has been recognized in England, in New York, and in the courts of some other States in the Union, upon the ground that the seller, having got the money of the plaintiff, the latter may be deprived of the means, by the seller's act, of going into the market and purchasing the same property at the then market prices.

"There being, then, much conflict in the authorities, the question is to be settled upon principle; and it may be assumed that the plaintiff is entitled to such damages as will be a full indemnity for withholding the stock. The general rule is, undoubtedly, that he shall have the value of the property at the

[78] Dak. Comp. L., § 4603.

[79] Pickert v. Rugg, 1 N. D. 230, 46 N. W. 446 (in this case Corliss, C. J., said that it would "work out absurd results"); First Nat. Bank v. Red River Valley Nat. Bank, 9 N. D. 319, 83 N. W. 221.

The statute is to be strictly construed. First Nat. Bank v. Minneapolis & N. E. Co., 8 N. D. 430, 79 N. W. 874.

[80] Funk v. Hendricks, 24 Okla. 837, 105 Pac. 352.

[81] Barnett v. Thompson, 37 Ga. 335.

[82] 42 N. H. 424, 457, 461.

time of the breach; and this is a plain and just rule and easy of application, and we are unable to yield to the reasons assigned for the exception which has been sanctioned in New York and elsewhere. It is true that, in some cases, the plaintiff may have been injured to the extent of the value of the property at the highest market price between the breach and the time of trial. But it is equally true that, in a large number of cases, and perhaps generally, it would not be so. In that large class of cases where the articles to be delivered entered into the common consumption of the country, in the shape of provisions, perishable or otherwise, horses, cattle, raw material, such as wool, cotton, hides, leather, dyestuffs, etc., to hold that the plaintiff might elect, as the rule of damages in all cases, the highest market price between the time fixed for the delivery and the day of trial, which is often many years after the breach, would, in many cases, be grossly unjust, and give to the plaintiff an amount of damages disproportioned to the injury. For, in most of these cases, had the articles been delivered according to the contract, they would have been sold or consumed within the year, and no probability of reaping any benefit from the future increase of prices. So there may be repeated trials of the same cause, by review, new trial, or otherwise. Shall there be a different measure of value at each trial? In the case of stocks, in regard to which the rule in England originated, there are, doubtless, cases, and a great many, where they are purchased as a permanent investment, and to be held without regard to fluctuations; and to hold that the damages should be the highest price between the breach and the trial, when there is no reason to suppose that a sale would have been made at that precise time, would also be unjust. But it may be fairly assumed that a very large portion of the stocks purchased are purchased to be sold soon; and to give the purchaser, in case of a failure to deliver such stock, the right to elect their value at any time before the trial, which might often be several years, would be giving him, not indemnity merely, but a power, in many instances of unjust extortion, which no court could contemplate without pain."

This case was followed later in Frothingham *v.* Morse.[83]

[83] 45 N. H. 545.

§ 519. Other jurisdictions following the general rule.

The rule of highest intermediate value is disapproved and the general rule, giving the value at the time of the loss, or, in case of stock carrying contracts, the New York rule, followed in most jurisdictions.[84] In Georgia this rule was followed where the conversion was not a continuing one, but began and ended in a single act, as a sale.[85]

In a case in Michigan [86] Cooley, J., said:

[84] *Connecticut:* Hurd v. Hubbell, 26 Conn. 389. *Contra,* in case of non-delivery when the price was paid in advance: West v. Pritchard, 19 Conn. 212.

District of Columbia: Non-delivery of stock: Tayloe v. Turner, 2 D. C. (2 Cr. C. C.) 203.

Illinois: Smith v. Dunlap, 12 Ill. 184; Otter v. Williams, 21 Ill. 118; Sturges v. Keith, 57 Ill. 451; Brewster v. Van Liew, 119 Ill. 554, 59 Am. Rep. 623; Shaefer v. Dickinson, 141 Ill. App. 234. *Non-delivery of goods sold:* Cushman v. Hayes, 46 Ill. 145.

Kentucky: Sproule v. Ford, 3 Litt. 25; Lillard v. Whittaker, 3 Bibb, 92.

Louisiana: Vance v. Tourne, 13 La. 225.

Maine: Freeman v. Harwood, 49 Me. 195, 77 Am. Dec. 254. *Failure to return borrowed stock:* McKenney v. Haines, 63 Me. 74.

Maryland: Third Nat. Bank v. Boyd, 44 Md. 47, 22 Am. Rep. 35. *Refusal to transfer stock:* Baltimore Marine Ins. Co. v. Dalrymple, 25 Md. 269, 306, 80 Am. Dec. 779, n. (*semble*); Baltimore C. P. Ry. v. Sewell, 35 Md. 238, 6 Am. Rep. 402; Andrews v. Clark, 72 Md. 396, 20 Atl. 429.

Massachusetts: Conversion: Kennedy v. Whitwell, 4 Pick. 466; Greenfield Bank v. Leavitt, 17 Pick. 1, 28 Am. Dec. 268; Johnson v. Sumner, 1 Met. 172. *Refusal to issue or transfer stock:* Gray v. Portland Bank, 3 Mass. 364, 390, 3 Am. Dec. 156; Sargent v. Franklin Ins. Co., 8 Pick. 90, 19 Am. Dec. 306; Hussey v. Manufacturers' & M.

Bank, 10 Pick. 415; Wyman v. American Powder Co., 8 Cush. 168. In Maynard v. Pease, 99 Mass. 555, in the case of a sale by a factor below a limit fixed by principal, the rule in Baker v. Drake was adopted as at least one of which defendant could not complain.

Michigan: Bates v. Stansell, 19 Mich. 91; Chadwick v. Butler, 28 Mich. 349, 352, per Cooley, J. (*semble*); Jackson v. Evans, 44 Mich. 510.

Missouri: Conversion: Walker v. Borland, 21 Mo. 289.

Nevada: Conversion: O'Meara v. North American M. Co., 2 Nev. 112, 90 Am. Dec. 306; Boylan v. Huguet, 8 Nev. 345.

North Carolina: Conversion: Arrington v. Wilmington & W. R. R., 6 Jones L. 68, per Ruffin, J. (*semble*).

Ohio: Failure to return borrowed stock: Fosdick v. Greene, 27 Oh. St. 484, 22 Am. Rep. 328.

Tennessee: Non-delivery of goods sold: Coffman v. Williams, 4 Heisk. 233, 240.

Vermont: Non-delivery: Hill v. Smith, 32 Vt. 433; Copper Co. v. Copper Mining Co., 33 Vt. 92; Austin v. Langlois, 83 Vt. 104, 74 Atl. 489.

Wisconsin: Ingram v. Rankin, 47 Wis. 406, 2 N. W. 755, 32 Am. Rep. 762, explaining Weymouth v. Chicago & N. W. Ry., 17 Wis. 550, 84 Am. Dec. 763; Webster v. Moe, 35 Wis. 75.

Canada: McMurrich v. Bond H. H. Co., 9 Up. Can. Q. B. 333 (*semble*); Glenn v. Schaffer, 17 W. L. Rep. 273.

[85] Dorsett v. Frith, 25 Ga. 537.

[86] Chadwick v. Butler, 28 Mich. 349, 352.

"A party's right of recovery must be deemed fixed at some time, and he cannot wait for an indefinite period and speculate upon the changes in the market while taking upon himself none of the risks of decline. This would put him in a better position than if he had the property in possession; for then, if he would realize upon it, he must select a particular time for making sale, and accept the price at that time; while under the rule relied upon he may have the highest price for a series of years by simply postponing the bringing of suit."

§ 520.ᵃ Time of breach or tort.

When it is said that the measure of damages is fixed by the time of the conversion, trespass, or breach, or other wrong, it must not be overlooked that this does not necessarily mean the moment at which the act is done which becomes the foundation of the suit. As the plaintiff frequently has a choice of remedies, *e. g.*, to ratify the act done, as in the case of a wrongful sale, or to call upon the wrongdoer to replace him, or to replace himself, the time at which the cause of action becomes complete, by no means necessarily coincides with the initial moment of wrong. In all such cases, the time cannot be fixed until the plaintiff has had notice or acquired knowledge of the wrong. Under the rule of highest intermediate value he may select a date arbitrarily from a period of time; under the rule of Baker *v.* Drake, he has a reasonable period of time to determine his course of action. The question of time may be also complicated by the agreement between the parties. Where negotiable securities are pledged for a time loan, it is the duty of the pledgor to keep the securities on hand at all times ready to be delivered to the pledgee on payment of the debt. An unauthorized sale is a conversion, but the pledgor may elect to treat the sale as a breach of the continuing duty to keep the securities till maturity; and if this is so, he can sue for the market value of the securities *at the time of the maturity of the contract*. He may, in other words, select one of two points of time.[87] And in the simple case of conversion, the election of

ᵃ For § 520 of the eighth edition, see § 522.

[87] Dimock *v.* U. S. Nat. Bank, 55

N. J. L. 296, 25 Atl. 926, 39 Am. St. Rep. 643.

the plaintiff may be made manifest by a *demand* for the stock pledged, and if this demand comes in the form of an action, the time of conversion coincides with that of the action and the time of its commencement fixes the initial point of liability.[88]

§ 521.[a] Importance and limitations of the New York rule.

The importance of the New York rule comes, as has been noticed by one of the courts which has had the matter under consideration, from the fact that the market for the greater part of all the speculative stock transactions in the country is the New York Stock Exchange. The rule laid down in the leading case of Baker *v.* Drake [89] may be described as the one rule which has survived the struggle for an expression of the principle underlying the allowance of a higher intermediate value.

It must not be forgotten, as is too often the case, that the rule in Baker *v.* Drake was limited by its learned author to the case which he had before him. Judge Rapallo never laid it down as a general measure of damages in all cases of conversion of stock. The case before him was that of a pledge of stock purchased on a margin, and pledged as security for a continuing contract to carry it with a view to profits through a rise in the market. There were two wrongs, one a tort—the conversion of the stock—the other a breach of the contract between pledgee and pledgor *not to sell without notice.* In either case there was room for the recovery of something more than the value of the stock at the time of the conversion: in one case, the "probable profits"; in the other the actual enhancement in the value of the stock down to the end of the reasonable time within which the plaintiff might, had he not been kept in ignorance of the sale, have fixed the amount of the loss by replacement.[90] Thus limited, the rule has stood the test of time. But it must not be mistaken for an universal rule, in all cases of conversion of stock. This fact is illustrated by the most recent cases. In

[a] For § 521 of the eighth edition, see § 523.

[88] Continental Divide M. I. Co. *v.* Bliley, 23 Colo. 160, 46 Pac. 633.

[89] 66 N. Y. 518, 23 Am. Rep. 80.

[90] See this case fully explained *ante,* chap. XI.

McIntyre *v.* Whitney [91] brokers converted stock purchased for a customer, on a margin. It was at the time worth $45,125. Without any knowledge of this, the customer deposited with the pledgees additional "margin," amounting to $25,000. Between the time of the discovery by him of the conversion, and a reasonable time to replace, the highest market value was $26,625; he then still owed $15,000, balance unpaid on the loan; this he tendered, and demanded his stock; defendants were unable to deliver it. The referee to whom the case was referred, applied the rule in Baker *v.* Drake and gave the plaintiff the difference between the highest market prices and $15,000. But on appeal the judgment was not allowed to stand; Miller, J., saying that, by that rule, the plaintiff could recover about one-third of what he had paid in cash, while the defendants would pocket as profits the amount of the decline in the market value of the stock, or $18,500. On appeal the judgment was modified so as to give the plaintiff the difference between the actual value of the stock converted, or $45,125, less the unpaid balance of $15,000, or $30,125, with interest on balances. [92]

This case, together with another recent decision in the same court, [93] gives a very complete view of the present state of the law in New York, and probably most other American jurisdictions in which stock-carrying contracts are treated as involving a pledge of stock owned by the customer. The rule may be stated as follows:

1. Whether the action is regarded as sounding in contract or tort, the customer is entitled at least to the benefit of the price actually realized.

2. Owing to the purpose of the contract itself having a reference to the fluctuations of the market, he is entitled in addition to the rise in the market within a reasonable time after he has knowledge of the sale, for replacement, either by the broker, or by himself.

3. All this is based on the assumption that the broker has

[91] 139 App. Div. 557, 124 N. Y. Supp. 234.

[92] The Court of Appeals affirmed the judgment as modified, no opinion being written. McIntyre *v.* Whitney, 201 N. Y. 526, 94 N. E. 1096.

[93] Barber *v.* Ellingwood, No. 2, 137 App. Div. 704, 122 N. Y. Supp. 131.

fully accounted to the customer for the money received by him, and that the customer is suing only for the profits of the venture, or the full damages occasioned by the tort.

4. If the securities have been *paid* for, the customer is entitled to their full value as ascertained by the highest price under the Baker *v.* Drake rule.[94]

5. If the broker was not reimbursed by the unauthorized sale for his advances he will be entitled to interpose a counterclaim for the balance.

6. When the stock has steadily declined in value, the rule in Baker *v.* Drake is necessarily inapplicable, and the plaintiff recovers the price for which the stock was sold less any balance due the broker, with interest.

§ 522. The New York rule and avoidable consequences.

The rule in Baker *v.* Drake, like some other variations from the ordinary rule of the *value* at the time of the act complained of, and which deprives the plaintiff of his property, must be considered with reference to the rule of avoidable consequences. It has been already pointed out [95] that the rule of avoidable consequences is a branch of the rule excluding *remote* damages. What the plaintiff would (acting as prudent men usually act) do, on notice of a breach of contract or tort, in order to reduce the loss, the law expects him to do in the ordinary course of things. If he does not take such steps, and the loss is thereby enhanced, this is the result of his own independent volition or negligence, and is only related to the defendant's act as a consequence of that remote class of which the law cannot take cognizance. For instance, in contracts of personal service, the plaintiff earns his living by the work. Hence, it is reasonable to assume that, if thrown out of work by defendant's act, he will reduce the loss as soon as possible by a new contract of service. If he lies by, his subsequent loss of money is the result of his own choice, not of the defendant's act. So, if a roof leaks, it is reasonable to assume that the person whose health and safety are endangered by the leak will repair. If an owner of a

---

[94] Wright *v.* Bk. of Metropolis, 110 N. Y. 237, 246, 18 N. E. 79, 6 Am. St. Rep. 356, *n.*, 1 L. R. A. 289.

[95] See chap. **X.**

boat looking for freight loses it through defendant's act, it is only natural that he should try to get other freight. And so in a multitude of other cases in which the rule has been applied. But it does not follow that because all contracts are founded on the expectation of benefit of some kind, all parties contracting must be expected on a breach to proceed to replace themselves.[96]

§ 523. Nature of the contract to carry stock.

The contract which the New York courts have had principally in view is the agreement by stock brokers *to carry stock for a customer.* The broker buys for the customer a certain number of shares, against which the customer makes a deposit, called a "margin." The intention of the agreement is that if the stock rises the broker shall, on notice, sell the stock for the customer, the latter getting the benefit of the rise. If it falls, the broker is also entitled to demand, by proper notice, additional margin, and on failure to make the margin good he may sell the stock. The broker is said to carry the stock because he advances the whole purchase-money (except the margin), charging the customer with interest and commissions. In New York a transaction of this kind is held to make the relation between the customer and broker that of pledgor and pledgee;[97] and if the broker sells without demand to supply additional margin, or without notice, this amounts to conversion.[98] Whatever the nature of the relation is held to be, it is obvious that the object of the agreement is always to secure a profit from a rise in the market value. It is also, a continuing contract. The broker agrees to carry the stock, not for a definite time, but for an indefinite time, he being not only pledgee, but selling agent as well, and the stock being left in his hands for sale. Both parties contemplate a sale, either at a profit or at a loss. If an unauthorized sale by the broker is regarded as a conversion, according to the ordinary rule the measure of damages would be simply the value of the stock at the time of the sale; if it is looked upon as a breach of a con-

[96] See *ante,* chap. XI.
[97] Gillett *v.* Whiting, 120 N. Y. 402, 24 N. E. 790.
[98] Ib.

tinuing agreement to carry the stock, and have it ready for the plaintiff if he wishes to sell it, there being no fixed time for performance, and the defendant having put performance wholly out of his power, there is no hardship in charging him with all the profits that might with reasonable certainty have been made within the period during which the contract would have continued. But, it has been contended in opposition to the New York rule, there is usually no certainty whatever that any profits would have been made, because the contract might at any moment have been brought to an end by the plaintiff himself. Nor is there in the ordinary case any certainty that he would have directed a sale on a rising market. There is consequently no way of proving with that certainty required by the first principles of the law of damages that he would have had anything but the value of the stock at the time and place of conversion. From this conclusion the New York courts have escaped by a limited application of the rule of avoidable consequences. Discarding from consideration *obiter dicta* in those cases in which a general *duty* of replacement is insisted on,[99] the law in New York, as evolved from Baker v. Drake, is quite consistent with itself and with general principles. If the action be regarded as one of contract, the necessary certainty is found in the circumstance that it is a continuing contract to *carry*, and cannot be brought to an end *ipso facto* by a wrongful sale; if as one of tort, the plaintiff has a *right* within a reasonable time after discovery to replacement. What he has been cut off from is the right to be replaced by the broker, or to replace himself, within a reasonable time after he comes to knowledge of the wrongful act, and the value of this right, which on a falling market is worth nothing, on a rising market is worth *something*, and the only way to measure it is that applied in Baker v. Drake. Hence it follows that the New York rules as they stand to-day, are not at war with the elementary principles of damages either in contract or tort. The plaintiff is entitled, *at least*, to the value at the time of conversion or failure to deliver. But whenever he has lost with reasonable certainty more than this, he recovers what, in contract, are reasonable

---

[99] Wright v. Bk. of Metropolis, 110 N. Y. 237, 18 N. E. 79, 1 L. R. A. 289, 6 Am. St. Rep. 356, n.; Weld v. Postal T. C. Co., 199 N. Y. 88, 92 N. E. 415.

profits, and in tort are *special* or *consequential damages*. This right again is limited by the rule of avoidable consequences. Whatever, after the expiration of a reasonable time for replacement, he might have made is remote, or uncertain. The reasonable time measures the extent of the right, and its length depends on all the circumstances of the case. The reason why these rules have little or no application in the ordinary case of sales of chattels is not that chattels do not ordinarily fluctuate in price, but because there is not usually any interval between the breach and the time when it comes to the knowledge of the customer. In Illinois, the New York rule is in force [100] as to stock contracts; and contracts to *carry* wheat or corn in that jurisdiction would seem to fall under the same principles.

§ 524. Contract to hold for a rise in the market—Principal and agent.

We have just seen that when a conversion is committed by a broker, selling the plaintiff's stock prematurely, the act may be not only a tort, but also the breach of a continuing contract. Upon principles that will be considered in a later chapter, the measure of damages for breach of such a contract would be regulated by the value of the stock *at the time of performance*.

If, for instance, the broker had directions to sell at a certain price, and that price was reached after the wrongful sale, but before notice to the plaintiff, he should recover damages measured by the value of the stock at that price. If the broker was to hold until ordered to sell, and the plaintiff, after the sale, but before notice of it, gave orders to sell, the value of the stock at the time such orders were given should be taken as the measure of damages. If no orders were given by the plaintiff until after notice of the sale, it is certain that he would have held the stock for a reasonable time after the time at which he had notice of the sale; long enough, at least, for him to send selling orders to the broker and for such orders to be carried out. And though it is impossible to prove that he would have *sold* at that time, it is certain that *he would have had the stock* then; and since, through breach of the broker's

---

[100] Brewster *v.* Liew, 119 Ill. 555, 59   Am. Rep. 823; Schaeffer *v.* Dickinson, 141 Ill. App. 234.

contract, he did not have it, he would seem entitled to the value of it at that time. This reasoning applies not only to brokers, but to factors, and other agents who hold the property of their principals with power of sale. Accordingly where a factor sells property contrary to his instructions he may, in a proper action, be held liable for the highest market value for a reasonable time after the sale.[101] This principle was approved in a case in North Carolina.[102] In that case a carrier was directed to deliver the plaintiff's goods to a certain factor of his who had instructions as to the sale of the goods. The carrier misdelivered the goods to another factor of the plaintiff, who having no instructions sold the goods. It was held that the same measure of damages should be adopted that would apply in the case of a wrongful sale by the factor to whom the goods were to be delivered; and this was the difference between the price obtained and the highest market price of the goods between the time of the sale and the receipt of notice by the plaintiff.

§ 525.[a] General conclusions.

We have gone into the subject of higher intermediate value in detail, and with liberal extracts from the cases, because otherwise it is involved in great confusion to which there is no apparent key. Arranged historically, however, the cases illustrate curiously the metamorphosis of the law in freeing itself from the old fetters of formal actions. While the forms of action lasted, the effort of the courts was to discover a measure of damages suitable for each form. Now, in trover, this was, owing to a number of causes, peculiarly difficult. It was easy to say that the measure of damages was the value at the time of the conversion, with interest, and that a demand and refusal were evidence of the conversion,[103] but this was no sooner done than it became evident that special circumstances must modify the application of the rule in different cases. The conversion by no means necessarily fixed the actual date

[a] For § 525 of the eighth edition, see § 497a.

[101] Loraine v. Cartwright, 3 Wash. C. C. 151; Maynard v. Pease, 99 Mass. 555; Milbank v. Dennistown, 21 N. Y. 386.

[102] Arrington v. Wilmington & W. R. R., 6 Jones L. (N. C.) 68.

[103] Gould's Pleading, 4th ed. 52, 53.

of the wrong, for the plaintiff might have had no knowledge of it at the time; the value might have fluctuated greatly before demand and refusal; the property might have had a special value; the plaintiff might be deprived of the opportunity to replace himself; the thing converted might be returned before trial. In the development of the action, it was natural that the courts should at first attempt to establish some more comprehensive rule of damages which should let in all the special circumstances. The rule of highest intermediate value between conversion and verdict was an attempt of this sort. Under it the greatest possible latitude was given the plaintiff, both as to time and value, and many years were wasted before it was settled that such a rule was entirely in conflict with the elementary principles of compensation. Since then, the courts have worked out the theory of a *higher* intermediate value in certain cases, and numerous cases have been found where the plaintiff must be allowed to prove special or consequential damages. At the end we reach what may be called the only general modern rule, the value of the property or property rights lost with interest; increased by special circumstances within the limits fixed by the rules governing consequential damages, and limited by the rule of avoidable consequences. And this, obviously, must have been the modern principle, had the action of trover never been heard of.[104]

[104] See chap. X.

CHAPTER XXIII

ACTIONS FOR THE RECOVERY OF SPECIFIC PERSONAL PROPERTY

§ 526. Actions for the recovery of personal property.

Two forms of action were prescribed by the common law for the recovery of specific personal property—detinue and replevin; the first being generally used where there was a tortious detention only, the latter where there was a tortious taking. The action of detinue has become obsolete except in a few jurisdictions. The action of replevin, on the other hand, or a statutory action of a similar nature, is still in force, and is the action ordinarily resorted to for the purpose of securing the possession of personal property.

The procedure in this form of action is peculiar. Where not modified by local practice, the action is begun by the sheriff taking possession of the property under the writ and delivering it to the plaintiff, who is required to execute a bond conditioned to return the property if he proves not to be entitled to it, and to pay such damages as may be suffered. The question of right to the property is then litigated, and a judgment given for one party or the other; if for the plaintiff, judgment is only for damages in taking and detaining the property; if

1029

for the defendant, it is for a return of the property, and damages for taking and detaining it under the writ. By a modern modification often adopted, judgment in the latter case is, as we shall see, in the alternative, either for a return or for the value of the goods.

If judgment is given for the defendant, two courses are open to him. He may take out a writ of execution on the judgment, as in an ordinary case. But he has also the bond given by the plaintiff upon taking the goods under the replevin writ, and he may bring action upon that. If he choose the latter alternative, his measure of recovery is, first, the amount of the judgment in the replevin suit; second, any further compensation secured to him by the bond. It is therefore clear that in an action on the replevin bond questions involving the measure of damages in actions of replevin may be involved, and some cases of actions upon replevin bonds will necessarily be considered in this chapter. The questions ordinarily involved in actions on such bonds will be considered later. What has been said of replevin bonds applies equally to detinue bonds.

§ 527. Detinue.

* In detinue, as in debt, no damages were generally given for the thing itself, that being recoverable in specie; but merely for its detention. If, however, the property was not finally returned, then damages might be given for its value.[1] "The action of detinue," says the Supreme Court of Tennessee, "is for the thing detained and damages for detention: the value of the property is ascertained by the jury; and the judgment is in the alternative for the sum so found, as the value in case the thing recovered cannot be had." [2] The question on the issue of *non detinet* was whether the chattel were detained, and if so, what was its value and what the damages for its detention; and so the ordinary modern form of verdict in detinue finds the value of the property and damages for its detention.

But, as has been said, if for any reason the property cannot be returned, the plaintiff is entitled to its full value.[3] So, in

---

[1] Sayer on Damages, 69, 70.

[2] Waite *v.* Dolby, 8 Humph. (Tenn.) 406.

[3] The value is to be taken as of the time of finding the verdict. Penny *v.* Davis, 3 B. Mon. (Ky.) 313. And

the early cases, where we often find detinue brought for charters or title-deeds, if the charters were destroyed or made way with (eloigned), the plaintiff recovered all in damages.[4]** Damages for the detention may, without proof of a demand, be recovered in this action from the commencement of the defendant's unlawful possession.[5] If the property were destroyed while in the defendant's possession, and without his fault, no part of its value should be included by the jury in their estimate of damages; but if the destruction resulted from the defendant's fault or culpable neglect, the jury may include that value in their estimate of damages.[6] In detinue, deterioration by use is an element of damage[7] in addition to the annual rent or hire of the property.[8] In detinue for slaves, it has been said that emancipation is no defence.[9] In Robinson v. Richards,[10] judgment in detinue (for mules) having been entered "that defendant recover of plaintiff (and appellant) the property sued for, or the value as assessed, at his election, and also the damages as assessed," etc., etc., it was held that the words "at his election" should be stricken out, the court further saying that damages in detinue go with the recovery whether of the chattel or of its value. In Holly v. Flournoy[11] it was said that the jury might, in their discretion, assess the highest value between the commencement of the suit and the time of trial.

In a case where detinue was brought for stock certificates, which had been returned *pendente lite*, it was held that the jury might confine themselves to an assessment of damages.[12]

where the defendant had an interest in the property (*e. g.*, was a mortgagor), plaintiff recovers the value of his interest only. Hundley v. Calloway, 45 W. Va. 516, 31 S. E. 937.

[4] So held where the property, a slave, died after judgment; but the court intimated that in case of death before judgment only nominal damages could have been given. May v. Jameson, 11 Ark. 368.

[5] Gardner v. Boothe, 31 Ala. 186; Whitfield v. Whitfield, 44 Miss. 254.

[6] Bethea v. McLennon, 1 Ired. L. (N. C.) 523.

[7] Freer v. Cowles, 44 Ala. 314.

[8] *Alabama:* Carroll v. Pathkiller, 3 Port. 279; Fralick v. Presley, 29 Ala. 457, 65 Am. Dec. 413.

Kentucky: Glascock v. Hays, 4 Dana, 58.

[9] Wilkerson v. McDougal, 48 Ala. 517.

[10] 45 Ala. 354.

[11] 54 Ala. 99.

[12] Williams v. Archer, 5 C. B. 318. See Archer v. Williams, 2 Car. & Kir. 26; Crossfield v. Such, 8 Ex. 825, 22 L. J. Ex. 325.

Where the plaintiff claims title to the property under a mortgage, evidence of the sale of the property under

In this case the property was demanded; the stock was worth
£3 5s.; when it was delivered it had fallen to £1, and the plaintiff was held entitled to recover the difference. A plaintiff in
detinue, whose title to the property sued for is legally divested
before the trial of the cause, can recover nothing beyond his
damages for its detention to the time when his title was divested, and the costs of suit.[13]

§ 528. Replevin.

* The action of detinue has, however, fallen into great disuse,
and in some of the States of the Union it is abolished by statute.
We proceed, therefore, to the action of replevin. And this
action, also, has been so much altered and modified by special
statutes, that it will only be proper here to treat of it very suc-
cinctly. As to the character of this action, we have already
stated that the plaintiff, by his writ, seizes the specific property,
and at the same time gives a bond with proper sureties, conditioned to return it, or its value, provided it shall finally appear that he has no right of action. The bond, however, is
only a cumulative security to the defendant; and if the plaintiff fails to establish his right, the court may proceed in the
action itself to award damages against him, as the result of a
claim declared to be unfounded, for the value of the property
taken by him.

The nature of the proceeding is well and briefly stated by
Parsons, C. J.:

"The plaintiff having by the service of the writ obtained the
possession of the goods replevied, prosecutes it to obtain judgment for damages and costs against the defendant for the caption and detention. These are the objects of his suit. The
defendant not only resists the plaintiff's claims, but he also
complains of an injury arising from the service of the writ. He
demands back the chattels, with damages occasioned by the
replevin, and his costs in the defense. . . . The distinction
between replevin and other actions in which the plaintiff de-

the mortgage by the plaintiff and its
purchase by the defendant, after the
plaintiff had acquired the possession
under the statutory bond given by him
in the action, is not competent evi-

dence for the purpose of mitigating the
defendant's damages. Foster v. Chamberlain, 41 Ala. 158.

[13] Cole v. Conolly, 16 Ala. 271.

mands a debt, or damages, or lands, is very clear, because the magnitude of the debt or damages, and the quantity of the land, is involved in the plaintiff's original demand, as well as his title to recover anything. But in replevin, the demand of the defendant is founded on the legal process sued and prosecuted by the plaintiff."[14] **

The essential distinction between trover and replevin as regards the rule of damages, aside from the element of wilfulness in the taking or detention, is briefly this: In trover, the title to the property is regarded as having passed to the defendant, who is therefore liable for its value simply with interest. In replevin, the title is treated as still in the plaintiff, who is therefore to recover not only the chattel itself or its value, but also damages for its detention, of which interest may be the measure but is not in all cases the necessary limit.[15]

Either plaintiff or defendant may have a judgment for the value of the property or for damages for detention; but the principles regulating the measure of damages will generally be the same, whether the judgment is in favor of the plaintiff or the defendant. Unless a distinction is expressly made, therefore, the principles stated and the authorities cited will apply equally to judgments for plaintiff or defendant.

Replevin will lie only against one in actual possession of the property at the time suit is instituted.[16]

§ 528a. Separate action by defendant.

It is to be observed that in replevin the plaintiff proceeds on the strength of his own title. The defendant may have (as in New York by statute[17]) the right, in case he prevails, to have his damages assessed in the same action; or he may afterwards bring a separate action for damages.[18] In such a suit the question of title is presumptively *res adjudicata*.[19]

§ 529. Nominal damages.

If the party really entitled to the property fails in the action,

[14] Bruce *v.* Learned, 4 Mass. 614, 617.
[15] McGavock *v.* Chamberlain, 20 Ill. 219.
[16] Bowen *v.* King, 146 N. C. 385, 59 S. E. 1044.

[17] L. 1882, chap. 410, § 1342.
[18] Brady *v.* Beadleton, 17 N. Y. Supp. 42.
[19] Brady *v.* Beadleton, 17 N. Y. Supp. 42, 43.

on account of a technicality, such as failure to prove a formal demand for the property, the prevailing party recovers nominal damages only.[20] So when the detention was momentary only, nominal damages for detention will be recovered.[21] And where a verdict is given for the plaintiff, this entitles him to nominal damages for the detention if no actual damages are proved.[22]

§ 530. Early English statutes.

* In this action the plaintiff had damages at common law; and, by the statute of Gloucester, costs, as a consequence of such damages; but the avowant or defendant in replevin had no costs, although in many cases where an avowry or conusance was made, and a return prayed, the defendant was an actor.[23] In consequence of this hardship two statutes were passed [24] giving such damages and costs to the defendant as the plaintiff would have had at common law.[25] These statutes have been generally re-enacted in this country; and where the statutes, or the decisions founded on them, do not apply, a reasonable rule may generally be deduced from the analogous cases decided upon the actions of trover, trespass *de bonis asportatis*, case for injury to personal property, and on sales of chattels.**

§ 531. Value of the property.

Where the chattel is not returned by the unsuccessful party, the damages must cover its value as well as the injuries done by the detention.[26] If there is no evidence on the record of

[20] *United States:* Treat *v.* Staples, 1 Holmes, 1.
Iowa: Harman *v.* Goodrich, 1 Greene, 13.
Maryland: Belt *v.* Worthington, 3 G. & J. 247.
New York: Pierce *v.* Van Dyke, 6 Hill, 613.
[21] Whitman *v.* Merrill, 125 Mass. 127.
[22] Starkey *v.* Waite, 69 Vt. 193, 37 Atl. 292.
[23] Bacon's Abr. Costs, F. of Costs in Replevin.
[24] 7 Hen. VIII, chap. 4; 21 Hen. VIII, chap. 19.
[25] James *v.* Tutney, Cro. Car. 497;

Rowley *v.* Gibbs, 14 Johns. 385; Caldwell *v.* West, 21 N. J. L. 411.
[26] *Indiana:* Peters, B. & L. Co. *v.* Lesh, 119 Ind. 98, 20 N. E. 291, 12 Am. St. Rep. 367.
Iowa: Neeb *v.* McMillan, 98 Ia. 718, 68 N. W. 438.
Maryland: Benesch *v.* Weil, 69 Md. 276.
Mississippi: Pearce *v.* Twichell, 41 Miss. 344; Woolner *v.* Spalding, 65 Miss. 204, 3 So. 583.
Missouri: Hohenthal *v.* Watson, 28 Mo. 360; Frei *v.* Vogel, 40 Mo. 149; Hinchey *v.* Koch, 42 Mo. App. 230.
Nebraska: Heidiman-Benoist Sad-

the value of the property or of its use, only nominal damages are allowed.[27] In Washington Ice Co. v. Webster [28] the property taken was ice. On assessment of damages for the defendant the jury were told that the defendant was entitled to the value of the ice at the time it was taken and where it was situated, for any lawful use to which it could be put. If it was valuable to use there, he is entitled to its value for use. If it was valuable for sale, he is entitled to its value for sale. If it was valuable to send to market he is entitled to whatever value it had at the time and place for any market—its value for any purpose to which it might be put. It was held that this charge was correct, and that if at the place of taking there were no sales, the value should be determined by sales made at the nearest point affording a market. So where the entire machinery of a cloth manufactory, including steam engines and apparatus, had been wrongfully replevied from a manufacturer, it was held in his suit on the replevin bond, the condition of which was, that the plaintiff in replevin should pay all such costs and damages as the defendant in replevin should recover against him, and should also return the goods in like order as when taken, in case such should be the final judgment, that the measure of damages was the same which under ordinary circumstances attending a sale and purchase might reasonably be agreed on as a fair price

dlery Co. v. Schott, 59 Neb. 20, 80 N. W. 47.

New Hampshire: Kendall v. Fitts, 22 N. H. 1; Messer v. Bailey, 31 N. H. 9.

New Jersey: Frazier v. Fredericks, 24 N. J. L. 162.

New York: Dows v. Rush, 28 Barb. 157; Tracy v. New York & Harlem R. R., 9 Bosw. 396.

Oklahoma: Jackson v. Glaze, 3 Okla. 143, 41 Pac. 79.

Pennsylvania: Swope v. Crawford, 16 Pa. Super. Ct. 474.

Tennessee: Sayers v. Holmes, 2 Cold. 259.

Canada: Deal v. Potter, 26 Up. Can. Q. B. 578; Lewis v. Teale, 32 Up. Can. Q. B. 108; Graham v. O'Callaghan, 14 Ont. App. 477.

As to the valuation of separate items, see Blakeley v. Duncan, 4 Tex. 184.

[27] *Alabama:* Hensley v. Orendorff, 152 Ala. 599, 44 So. 869.

Arkansas: Smith v. Houston, 25 Ark. 183.

Colorado: Sopris v. Webster, 1 Colo. 507.

Illinois: Seabury v. Ross, 69 Ill. 533.

Michigan: Phenix v. Clark, 2 Mich. 327.

[28] 68 Me. 449. But it is said that in replevin for goods, where there is no claim that they have fluctuated in value or advanced in price, testimony cannot be allowed as to their value *in view of the hazards of the plaintiff's business,* or what they are worth *to him* in the ordinary course of his business. Bonesteel v. Orvis, 22 Wis. 522.

for the property between a vendor desirous of selling and a purchaser desirous of purchasing the property as a whole, to be
used in the place where it was situated, and for the purpose for
which it was intended and arranged.[29]   In replevin for a fence,
the plaintiff can only recover the value of the materials after
removal, not the value of the fence as it stood on the land.[30]
In Texas, in an action for the recovery of specific property or
its value, a valuation by the jury higher than the evidence warranted, with the view of inducing a surrender of the property,
was sustained.[31]   Where goods are of special value to the owner,
such value may be recovered, though the value to the party in
the wrong is much less; so in case of "half-breed scrip"[32] or of
vouchers, statement of expenditures upon a building, and an
affidavit of their correctness.[33]

§ 531a. Recovery by owner of a special interest.

If the successful party is a special owner, and the other the
general owner, recovery can be only for the interest of the special owner.[34]   Thus a distraining landlord can recover only the
amount of his rent;[35] one holding on a lien can recover no
more than the amount of his lien;[36] and a sheriff who has attached or levied upon goods can recover no more than the
amount of the debt or execution, with costs and interest.[37]   So,

[29] Stevens v. Tuite, 104 Mass. 328;
acc., Roth v. Felt, 111 N. Y. Supp. 649,
60 Misc. 116.

[30] Pennybecker v. McDougal, 48 Cal.
160.

[31] Cochrane v. Winburn, 13 Tex. 143.
We know of no warrant for such a doctrine elsewhere.

[32] Bradley v. Gamelle, 7 Minn. 331.

[33] Drake v. Auerbach, 37 Minn. 505.

[34] *Kansas:* Wolfley v. Rising, 12 Kan.
535; Shahan v. Smith, 38 Kan. 474, 16
Pac. 749; Friend v. Green, 43 Kan. 167,
23 Pac. 93.

Michigan: Weber v. Henry, 16 Mich.
399.

Nebraska: Kersenbrock v. Martin, 12
Neb. 374; Cruts v. Wray, 19 Neb. 581;
Jameson v. Kent, 42 Neb. 412, 60 N. W.
879.

[35] Hart v. Tobias, 2 Bay (S. C.), 408.

[36] *Indian Territory:* George R. Barse
Live Stock Commission Co. v. Adams,
2 Ind. Ty. 119, 48 S. W. 1023.

Nebraska: Creighton v. Haythorn, 49
Neb. 526, 68 N. W. 934.

So of pledgee: Holmes v. Langston,
110 Ga. 861, 36 S. E. 251.

[37] *Colorado:* Whitkowski v. Hill, 17
Colo. 372, 30 Pac. 55.

Iowa: Hayden v. Anderson, 17 Ia.
158.

Minnesota: Dodge v. Chandler, 13
Minn. 114.

Missouri: Hall v. Bramell, 87 Mo.
App. 285.

Nebraska: Merrill v. Wedgwood, 25
Neb. 283, 41 N. W. 149; Gates v. Parrott, 31 Neb. 581, 48 N. W. 387; Gamble v. Wilson, 33 Neb. 270, 50 N. W. 3.

where the parties have different interests of any sort in the same property, one can recover against the other no more than the value of his interest.[38] Thus in case of a lease of rolling stock to a railroad, with agreement that the rental should be applied in payment of a purchase price, and all property of the railroad afterwards was mortgaged; this mortgage was foreclosed, the purchaser having notice of the lease; the lessor replevied, defendant gave bond and retained the property, and plaintiff had judgment; the court held that defendant was not answerable for the whole value, since he had a qualified interest in the property, that is, the interest under the lease. The amount of rent paid under the lease, since it went toward the purchase money of the property, was to be deducted from the value.[39] So, where a person wrongfully appointed receiver replevied the goods from the owner and got possession, and was afterwards rightly appointed receiver, it was held that though he must fail in the replevin suit this should be considered in the amount of damages, since the recovery must be proportioned to the actual interest of the successful party.[40]

On this principle, where a mortgagee succeeds against the mortgagor or a person claiming under him, he can recover no

Wisconsin: Battis v. Hamlin, 22 Wis. 669.

The sheriff cannot get the amount of executions which came to his hands after the goods had been taken from his possession by the replevin writ. Merrill v. Wedgwood, 25 Neb. 283, 41 N. W. 149; Sloan v. Coburn, 26 Neb. 607, 42 N. W. 726.

Where the sheriff has levied upon partnership property for the individual debt of a partner, and the property is replevied, the extent of his recovery is the value, at the time of the levy, of the beneficial interest of the execution defendant in such property, on accounting and settlement of the partnership business. Donellan v. Hardy, 57 Ind. 393; Ferguson v. Day (Ind. App.), 33 N. E. 213.

[38] *Iowa:* Peck v. Bonebright, 75 Ia. 98, 39 N. W. 213 (purchaser and seller of goods).

North Carolina: Barham v. Massey, 5 Ire. 192 (tenant for life of slave and remainderman).

Pennsylvania: Woods v. Klein, 223 Pa. 257, 72 Atl. 523 (owner subject to liens).

Wisconsin: Lillie v. Dunbar, 62 Wis. 198, 22 N. W. 467, 51 Am. Rep. 718 (vendor and purchaser).

Where one partner wrongfully by replevin took the property from the hands of the other, the full value of the property should be assessed against him, since to assess the value of his interest would involve a full partnership accounting. Jenkins v. Mitchell, 40 Neb. 664, 59 N. W. 90.

[39] Collins v. Bellefonte Central R. R., 171 Pa. 243, 33 Atl. 331.

[40] Guy v. Doak, 47 Kan. 366, 27 Pac. 968.

more than the amount of the mortgage debt;[41] and where he fails, he is liable for no more than the excess of the value of the property over his claim.[42] Where on the other hand the controversy is between the possessor of goods and a stranger the mere possessor, whatever his interest, is entitled to the full value of the goods.[43]

§ 532. Plaintiff bound by valuation in writ.

It has been held in England and in the United States, that the plaintiff in the replevin suit is bound by the estimate of the property made by himself.[44] The defendant, however, is not bound by the valuation in the writ,[45] nor in an action on a replevin bond is the value of the property fixed by the value stated in the undertaking given by the party replevying.[46]

[41] Against mortgagor:
Missouri: Dillard v. McClure, 64 Mo. App. 488.
Wisconsin: Smith v. Philips, 47 Wis. 202, 2 N. W. 285.
Against junior mortgagee:
Montana: Schwab v. Owens, 10 Mont. 381, 25 Pac. 1049.
Wisconsin: Klinkert v. Fulton, S. & M. Co., 113 Wis. 493, 89 N. W. 507.
Against purchaser from mortgagor:
Hundley v. Calloway, 45 W. Va. 516, 31 S. E. 937.
Contra, however, of an attaching creditor of the mortgagor, who appears to have been treated as a stranger: Stevenson v. Lord, 15 Colo. 131, 25 Pac. 313.
[42] Recovery by mortgagor: Deal v. Osborne, 42 Minn. 102, 43 N. W. 835.
By attaching sheriff in suit against mortgagor:
Kansas: Moore v. Shaw, 1 Kan. App. 103, 40 Pac. 929.
Wisconsin: Saxton v. Williams, 15 Wis. 292.
[43] *Dakota:* Madison Nat. Bank v. Farmer, 5 Dak. 282, 40 N. W. 345 (mortgagee).
Nebraska: Merchants' Bank v. Mc-

Donald, 63 Neb. 363, 377, 88 N. W. 492 (sheriff).
New York: Hanover Nat. Bank v. American D. & T. Co., 14 App. Div. 255, 43 N. Y. Supp. 544 (pledgee).
[44] *California:* Schmidt v. Nunan, 63 Cal. 371.
Maine: Tuck v. Moses, 58 Me. 461; Washington Ice Co. v. Webster, 62 Me. 341, 16 Am. Rep. 462.
Nebraska: Gamble v. Wilson, 33 Neb. 270, 50 N. W. 3.
New York: Tiedman v. O'Brien, 36 N. Y. Super. Ct. 539.
Oklahoma: Brook v. Bayless, 5 Okla. 568, 52 Pac. 738.
England: Middleton v. Bryan, 3 M. & S. 155.
But in Briggs v. Wiswell, 56 N. H. 319, it was said the value in the writ of replevin is *prima facie* evidence against the plaintiff on the trial.
[45] *Maine:* Thomas v. Spofford, 46 Me. 408; Tuck v. Moses, 58 Me. 461.
Tennessee: Goodman v. Floyd, 2 Humph. 59.
[46] *United States:* Sweeney v. Lomme, 22 Wall. 208, 22 L. ed. 727.
New Jersey: West v. Caldwell, 23 N. J. L. 736.

§ 533. Value, when to be estimated.

The value of the property is to be found in some cases at the time of the wrongful taking, in others at the time of the trial, according to whether damages are given for the conversion, or a sum of money is named as a substitute for the property.

In some jurisdictions it is in the option of the defendant by giving a bond to answer for damages to keep the property and turn the action into a mere action for damages for the conversion of the goods. Where this practice prevails, the value of the property is allowed as damages for the conversion, and is therefore to be found as of the time of the conversion by the defendant. So, in actions in the *detinet*, as it is called, that is, actions in which the property was eloigned or put by the defendant out of the sheriff's reach, so that it could not be restored by the sheriff to the plaintiff at the outset of the proceedings, the judgment cannot be for the property, since that is eloigned; it can only be for its value. The action becomes one for the conversion of property. Finally, when the plaintiff himself elects not to have the property taken on the writ though he is entitled to have it so taken, the action is in substance an action for the conversion of the property. In all these cases the measure of damages is the value of the property at the time of the demand by the sheriff,[47] or, in those jurisdictions following that rule, the highest value between that time and the trial.[48]

But where the property was taken by the plaintiff at the beginning of the suit, and judgment is in favor of the defendant

---

[47] *California:* Hisler *v.* Carr, 34 Cal. 641.

Georgia: Smith *v.* Duke, 6 Ga. App. 75, 64 S. E. 292.

Indiana: Yelton *v.* Slinkard, 85 Ind. 190; Peters B. & L. Co. *v.* Lesh, 119 Ind. 98, 20 N. E. 291, 12 Am. St. Rep. 367.

Iowa: Neeb *v.* McMillan, 98 Ia. 718, 68 N. W. 438.

Kansas: Garrett *v.* Wood, 3 Kan. 231; Werner *v.* Graley, 54 Kan. 383, 38 Pac. 482.

Minnesota: Sherman *v.* Clark, 24 Minn. 37; McLeod *v.* Capehart, 49 Minn. 187, 52 N. W. 381.

Missouri: Pope *v.* Jenkins, 30 Mo. 528 (but *contra*, Miller *v.* Bryden, 34 Mo. App. 602, value at time of trial).

Nebraska: Honaker *v.* Vesey, 57 Neb. 413, 77 N. W. 1100.

New Jersey: Maguire *v.* Dutton, 54 N. J. L. 597, 25 Atl. 254.

Pennsylvania: Woods *v.* Klein, 223 Pa. 257, 72 Atl. 523.

Texas: Norwood *v.* Interstate Nat. Bank, 92 Tex. 268, 48 S. W. 3.

Wisconsin: Findlay *v.* Knickerbocker Ice Co., 104 Wis. 375, 80 N. W. 436.

[48] Tully *v.* Harloe, 35 Cal. 302, 95 Am. Dec. 102.

for a return, the value is found as an alternative for the property in case the plaintiff fails to return it. For instance, in those jurisdictions permitting such a practice, where the defendant, upon proving his right, is allowed to elect between a return of the goods or their value, or, in any jurisdiction where, upon a judgment for a return of the property, it cannot be found by the sheriff, the value of the property stands for the property itself. If the defendant elects to take the value, or if the verdict is given in the alternative for the property or its value, the value is to be assessed at the time of the trial; [49] if judgment is given for a return, and, the sheriff not being able to find the property, damages are assessed on the bond, the value is to be taken at the time of the demand under the writ of restitution. [50] The same rule prevails where under the procedure of the jurisdiction the plaintiff is not entitled to be given the possession at the beginning of the suit, but eventually obtains judgment. [51]

In a few jurisdictions, where judgment is given for a return,

[49] *Iowa:* Bonnot Co. *v.* Newman, 109 Ia. 580, 80 N. W. 655.

Maryland: Hepburn *v.* Sewell, 5 H. & J. 211, 9 Am. Dec. 512.

Mississippi: Selser *v.* Ferriday, 13 S. & M. 698.

Missouri: Miller *v.* Whitson, 40 Mo. 97, 93 Am. Dec. 299; Chapman *v.* Kerr, 80 Mo. 158; Mix *v.* Kepner, 81 Mo. 93; Kreibohm *v.* Yancey, 154 Mo. 67, 87, 55 S. W. 260; Hutchins *v.* Buckner, 3 Mo. App. 595; Hinchey *v.* Koch, 42 Mo. App. 230; Trimble *v.* Keer R. M. Co., 56 Mo. App. 683; Schnabel *v.* Thomas, 98 Mo. App. 197, 71 S. W. 1076.

New York: Brewster *v.* Silliman, 38 N. Y. 423; New York G. & I. Co. *v.* Flynn, 55 N. Y. 653 (but Brizsee *v.* Maybee, 21 Wend. 144, is *contra*); Ditmars *v.* Sackett, 81 Hun, 317, 30 N. Y. Supp. 721.

North Carolina: Scott *v.* Elliott, 63 N. C. 215; Holmes *v.* Goodwin, 69 N. C. 467, 12 Am. Rep. 657.

Texas: Morris *v.* Coburn, 71 Tex. 406, 10 Am. St. Rep. 753; Avery *v.*

Dickson (Tex. Civ. App.), 49 S. W. 662. See, however, a different rule in Michigan and Nebraska, § 764, *infra.*

Where, however, the defendant in his answer did not ask for a return, but only for damages for the taking, he is confined to the value at the time of taking, *i. e.*, at the date of the writ. John Blaul & Sons *v.* Wandel, 137 Ia. 301, 114 N. W. 899.

[50] *Maine:* Howe *v.* Handley, 28 Me. 241; Washington Ice Co. *v.* Webster, 62 Me. 341, 16 Am. Rep. 462.

Massachusetts: Swift *v.* Barnes, 16 Pick. 194.

[51] *Missouri:* Jennings *v.* Sparkman, 48 Mo. App. 246.

Nevada: Gardner *v.* Brown, 22 Nev. 156, 158, 37 Pac. 240.

New York: National Cash Register Co. *v.* Agne, 43 App. Div. 605, 60 N. Y. Supp. 348.

North Carolina: Hall *v.* Tillman, 110 N. C. 220, 14 S. E. 745.

Oklahoma: Wade *v.* Gould, 8 Okla. 690, 59 Pac. 11.

the damages are to be estimated as of the date of taking.[52] In Tennessee the value of the property is estimated at the time of the replevin writ. In addition, if the property have increased in value since the seizure, and remain at the time of the trial at a higher point than when seized, the difference must be allowed the defendant as damages for the detention; if the value be greater at the trial than it had been at the seizure, but the increase be temporary, it will be left to the jury to allow the temporary increase as damages or not.[53]

§ 534. Value increased by labor of defeated party.

Where a return of the chattels in their condition at the time of the taking cannot be had—their original value having been increased through labor of the defendant bestowed on them in good faith—the measure of the plaintiff's recovery does not now usually include the additional value.[54] So in replevin for a yacht, a defendant who claimed her under a purchase was allowed, in Massachusetts, to show the amount of his expenditures in improving her after his purchase and before the service of the writ.[55] But if the wrongful taking was wilful, the increased value is the measure of damages.[56] So in replevin

[52] *Iowa:* Neeb v. McMillan, 98 Iowa, 718, 68 N. W. 438; Becker v. Staab, 114 Iowa, 319, 86 N. W. 305.
New Jersey: Schintzer v. Russell, 80 Atl. 938.
Oklahoma: George R. Barse L. S. C. Co. v. McKinster, 10 Okla. 708, 64 Pac. 14. (See Jackson v. Glaze, 3 Okla. 143, 41 Pac. 79.)
[53] Mayberry v. Cliffe, 7 Cold. (Tenn.) 117.
[54] *Arkansas:* Eaton v. Langley, 56 Ark. 448, 47 S. W. 123, 42 L. R. A. 474; Randleman v. Taylor, 94 Ark. 511, 127 S. W. 723.
Indiana: Peters B. & L. Co. v. Lesh, 119 Ind. 98, 20 N. E. 291, 12 Am. St. Rep. 367.
Kentucky: Strubbee v. Cincinnati Ry., 78 Ky. 481, 39 Am. Rep. 251.
Mississippi: Heard v. James, 49 Miss. 236; Acre v. Bufford, 80 Miss. 565, 31 So. 899.

Nebraska: Baker v. Meisch, 29 Neb. 227, 45 N. W. 685; Carpenter v. Lingenfelter, 42 Neb. 728, 60 N. W. 1022.
Nevada: Buckley v. Buckley, 12 Nev. 423.
New York: Sommer v. Adler, 36 App. Div. 107, 55 N. Y. Supp. 483.
Pennsylvania: Herdic v. Young, 55 Pa. 176, 93 Am. Dec. 739.
Wisconsin: Single v. Schneider, 30 Wis. 570, 24 Wis. 299; Hungerford v. Redford, 29 Wis. 345.
[55] Veazie v. Somerby, 5 All. (Mass.) 280.
[56] *Arkansas:* Nashville Lumber Co. v. Barefield, 93 Ark. 353, 124 S. W. 758.
Michigan: Nitz v. Bolton, 71 Mich. 388, 39 N. W. 15.
Mississippi: Heard v. James, 49 Miss. 236; Peterson v. Polk, 67 Miss. 163, 6 So. 615.

against a purchaser of logs from a homestead claimant, the
purchase being made with knowledge that the title is in controversy, the purchaser cannot be allowed for his expenses in
cutting the logs.[57]

§ 535. Damages for detention.

Damages for detention are assessed to the time of the verdict,[58] and they may be given in an action on the replevin bond,
although not previously assessed.[59]   In Illinois it has been held,
where there was no proof of actual damage, to be error for a
jury to assess the damages at $50.   In such a case only nominal
damages can be recovered.[60]   In a case in Texas it was held that,
as a general rule, no damages could be given for detention, the
value of the property at the time of the "conversion," with interest, being the measure of damages.[61]   In this case the court
obviously confused the action with the action of trover.   The

[57] Cunningham v. Metropolitan S.
Co., 110 Fed. 332.

[58] *Arkansas:* Lesser v. Norman, 51
Ark. 301.

California: Ryan v. Fitzgerald, 87
Cal. 345, 25 Pac. 546; Harris v. Smith,
132 Cal. 316, 64 Pac. 409.

Iowa: McIntire v. Eastman, 76 Ia.
455, 41 N. W. 162; Newberry v. Gibson,
125 Ia. 575, 101 N. W. 428.

Kansas: Chase County Nat. Bank v.
Thompson, 54 Kan. 307, 38 Pac. 274.

Kentucky: Cooper v. Ratliff (Ky.
L. Rep.), 116 S. W. 748.

Missouri: Reno v. Kingsbury, 39 Mo.
App. 240.

Nebraska: Schrandt v. Young, 62
Neb. 254, 86 N. W. 1085 (explaining
earlier cases).

New Hampshire: Kendall v. Fitts, 22
N. H. 1; Messer v. Bailey, 31 N. H. 9.

New Jersey: Maguire v. Dutton, 54
N. J. L. 597, 25 Atl. 254.

New Mexico: Hyde v. Elmer, 14
N. Mex. 39, 88 Pac. 1132.

North Carolina: Hall v. Tillman, 110
N. C. 220, 14 S. E. 745.

North Dakota: Nichols & Shepard
Co. v. Paulson, 10 N. D. 440, 87 N. W.
977.

Pennsylvania: Harrisburg E. L. Co.
v. Goodman, 129 Pa. 206, 19 Atl. 844.
Swope v. Crawford, 16 Pa. Super. Ct.
474.

Contra, California: Compressed A.
M. Co. v. West, S. P. L. & W. Co., 9
Cal. App. 361, 99 Pac. 531 (to date of
writ only).

Oklahoma: George R. Barse L. S. C.
Co. v. McKinster, 10 Okla. 708, 64
Pac. 14. (But see Jackson v. Glaze, 3
Okla. 143, 41 Pac. 79.)

Where the right of the successful
party ended during the litigation (as
by foreclosure of a mortgage) damages
for detention can be obtained only up
to the time when the right came to an
end. Gaar Scott & Co. v. Lyon, 99 Ky.
672, 37 S. W. 73.

Of course, no damages for detention
can be allowed unless there is a finding
that the party claiming them is entitled to possession. J. E. McMillan
Hardware Co. v. Ross, 24 Okla. 696,
104 Pac. 343.

[59] Smith v. Dillingham, 33 Me. 384;
Washington Ice Co. v. Webster, 62
Me. 341.

[60] Seabury v. Ross, 69 Ill. 533.

[61] Gillies v. Wofford, 26 Tex. 76.

rules governing the measure of damages in the two are, however, entirely different.

In Michigan and Nebraska it is held that if the prevailing party elects to take the value of the property instead of asking for a return, he can have no damages for detention of the property, but only the value at the time of the taking, with interest.[62]   In Romberg v. Hughes [63] the court said:

"It is only in cases where a return of the property is had that the party to whom the property is returned is entitled to damages for the detention. The rule allowing the value of the use is peculiar to replevin, and grows out of the fact that the party to whom the property is awarded seeks to recover the property itself and not its value. In such case when the property is returned, the party to whom the return is made is entitled to the damages awarded for the detention. If, however, a verdict is rendered for the value of the property, the action in that regard being one for damages only, the measure of damages is the value of the property as proved, together with lawful interest thereon." But in the later case of Schrandt v. Young [64] this rule was restricted to claims for deterioration or depreciation after the taking.

Where this rule is adopted, the peculiar action of replevin becomes, upon the election of the prevailing party to take the value of the property, exactly like an action of trover, and the same rule of damages is adopted.

§ 536. Decrease in value.

Where the goods depreciated in value or suffered injury during the period of detention, the successful party can always recover the amount of the depreciation in value as damages for detention.[65]   It is unimportant whether such depreciation arise

[62] *Michigan:* Hanselman v. Kegel, 60 Mich. 540; Just v. Porter, 64 Mich. 565; Nitz v. Bolton, 71 Mich. 388.

Nebraska: Hainer v. Lee, 12 Neb. 452; Aultman v. Stichler, 21 Neb. 72.

[63] 18 Neb. 579, 582.

[64] 62 Neb. 254, 86 N. W. 1085.

[65] *Colorado:* Rice v. Cassells, 47 Cal. 72, 108 Pac. 1001.

Illinois: Dalby v. Campbell, 26 Ill.

App. 502; Glow v. Yount, 93 Ill. App. 112; McDonough v. Reilly, 131 Ill. App. 553.

Indiana: Yelton v. Slinkard, 85 Ind. 190.

Kansas: Russell v. Smith, 14 Kan. 366; Bowersock v. Adams, 59 Kan. 779, 54 Pac. 1064.

Maine: Washington Ice Co. v. Webster, 62 Me. 341, 16 Am. Rep. 462.

from the defendant's act or default, or not; [66] nor need there be a special averment of this cause of damage to sustain a recovery on this ground.[67]   But the plaintiff who retains the articles replevied till judgment in the suit, cannot, if he succeed, claim damages for the depreciation in their value; because he may always convert them into money.[68]   •

In accordance with the general principle, where plaintiff replevied a cat which at the time defendant took it was in good health, but when he recovered possession it was dying, he could recover the difference in value between the cat in good health and the cat dying.[69]

§ 536a. Loss of the property pending litigation.

In case of death during the pendency of the litigation without the fault of the holder, it is held that the successful litigant

Michigan: Aber v. Bratton, 60 Mich. 357.

Missouri: Baldridge v. Dawson, 39 Mo. App. 527; Hinckey v. Koch, 42 Mo. App. 230; Trimble v. Keer, Rountree Mercantile Co., 56 Mo. App. 683; Cummings v. Badger Lumber Co., 130 Mo. App. 557, 109 S. W. 68.

Nebraska: Hooker v. Hammill, 7 Neb. 231; Moore v. Kepner, 7 Neb. 291; Schrandt v. Young, 62 Neb. 254, 86 N. W. 1085.

New York: Rowley v. Gibbs, 14 Johns. 385; Crossley v. Hojer, 11 Misc. 57, 31 N. Y. Supp. 837; Pabst Brewing Co. v. Rapid S. F. Co., 56 Misc. 445, 107 N. Y. Supp. 163.

North Carolina: Boylston Ins. Co. v. Davis, 70 N. C. 485; Harrison v. Chappell, 84 N. C. 258; Hall v. Tillman, 110 N. C. 220, 14 S. E. 745.

Wisconsin: Zitske v. Goldberg, 38 Wis. 216; Klinkert v. Fulton Storage & M. Co., 113 Wis. 493, 89 N. W. 507; Wadleigh v. Buckingham, 80 Wis. 230, 49 N. W. 745; Findlay v. Knickerbocker Ice Co., 104 Wis. 375, 80 N. W. 436.

So of notes of third parties. Sullivan v. Sullivan, 20 S. C. 509.

In Commerce Exchange Nat. Bank v.

Blye, 123 N. Y. 132, 25 N. E. 208, where defendant kept the property on giving a bond, he was held not responsible for deterioration in value during the litigation, without his fault, since his possession under the bond was legally valid.

[66] Depreciation from the fault of the party may of course always be recovered. Riley v. Littlefield, 84 Mich. 22, 47 N. W. 576.

[67] Young v. Willet, 8 Bosw. 486; but in Odell v. Hole, 25 Ill. 204, an action for the replevin of a mare, it was said that damages for *natural* depreciation could not be recovered where damages for use of the property were given; but even in that case damages could be recovered for depreciation caused by the default of the party in the wrong. And see Rosecrans v. Asay, 49 Neb. 512, 68 N. W. 627.

[68] Gordon v. Jenney, 16 Mass. 465.

[69] Taylor v. Welsh, 138 Ill. App. 190. The condition of the cat appears presumably to have been chargeable to the defendant; if it were dying from natural causes without the defendant's fault this would result in giving greater damages where the cat was returned dying than when it was already dead. *Post,* § 536a.

cannot recover damages for such loss.[70] If the loss happened through the default of the defendant, he is of course responsible.[71] There seems no reason why the same rule should not apply to the loss of other property by inevitable accident; but it has been held in such a case that the possessor must answer for its value, though the loss happened without his fault.[72] At any rate, where the goods are taken from the possession of the unsuccessful party by a valid legal process for salvage, he is responsible to the successful party for the value of the goods.[73]

§ 537. Value of use.

If the owner of the goods was deprived of the use of them pending the replevin proceedings, he is entitled to the value of the use, if any.[74]

[70] Haile v. Hill, 13 Mo. 612 (slave); Pope v. Jenkins, 30 Mo. 528 (slave); Jennings v. Sparkman, 48 Mo. App. 246 (mule).

[71] Jennings v. Sparkman, 48 Mo. App. 246.

[72] Suppiger v. Gruaz, 137 Ill. 216, 27 N. E. 22. In this case the plaintiff was eventually unsuccessful. The court said that though the goods were taken on legal process, yet the plaintiff acted at his peril, since he had no valid claim.

[73] Three States Lumber Co. v. Blanks, 133 Fed. 479. And see Ackerman v. King, 29 Tex. 291.

[74] Alabama: Mobile E. L. Co. v. Rust, 131 Ala. 484, 31 So. 486.

Arkansas: Dunnahoe v. Williams, 24 Ark. 264; Minkwitz v. Steen, 36 Ark. 260.

Illinois: Butler v. Mehrling, 15 Ill. 488; Odell v. Hole, 25 Ill. 204.

Iowa: Turner v. Younker, 76 Ia. 258, 41 N. W. 10.

Kansas: Yandle v. Kingsbury, 17 Kan. 195, 22 Am. Rep. 275; Ladd v. Brewer, 17 Kan. 204; Bell v. Campbell, 17 Kan. 211; Kennett v. Fickel, 41 Kan. 211.

Maine: Washington Ice Co. v. Webster, 62 Me. 341, 16 Am. Rep. 462;

Crabtree v. Clapham, 67 Me. 326, 24 Am. Rep. 31.

Massachusetts: Boston Loan Co. v. Myers, 143 Mass. 446.

Michigan: Burt v. Burt, 41 Mich. 82; Aber v. Bratton, 60 Mich. 357.

Minnesota: Nash v. Larson, 80 Minn. 478, 83 N. W. 451, 81 Am. St. Rep. 278.

Missouri: Reno v. Kingsbury, 39 Mo. App. 240.

Montana: Morgan v. Reynolds, 1 Mont. 163; Chauvin v. Valiton, 8 Mont. 451, 20 Pac. 658, 3 L. R. A. 194.

New York: Allen v. Fox, 51 N. Y. 562, 10 Am. Rep. 641.

North Carolina: Scott v. Elliott, 63 N. C. 215.

North Dakota: Northrup v. Cross, 2 N. D. 433, 51 N. W. 718.

Oregon: Coffin v. Taylor, 16 Ore. 375, 18 Pac. 658.

Tennessee: Stanley v. Donoho, 16 Lea, 492.

Texas: Robbins v. Walters, 2 Tex. 130.

Wisconsin: Williams v. Phelps, 16 Wis. 81; Zitske v. Goldberg, 38 Wis. 216.

Contra, New York: Twinam v. Swart, 4 Lans. 263.

In a few cases where under local practice the action becomes one for conversion the rule in trover is fol-

This doctrine is often applied in the case of animals which are of use,[75] but it extends as well to all articles which have an actual usable value.[76] It is sometimes said that the value of the use is normally measured by interest on the value of the goods, but if there is an actual usable value exceeding this, the successful party has the option of demanding it.[77] This however seems to be an inversion of thought; the party has lost the use of his property, and should recover compensation for such loss, but if he cannot prove the actual value of the use the rule of certainty provides for measuring the use by interest on the value.[78]

lowed, and the value of the use refused.

Iowa: Colean Implement Co. *v.* Strong, 126 Ia. 598, 102 N. W. 506.

Nebraska: Honaker *v.* Vesey, 57 Neb. 413, 77 N. W. 1100.

Texas: Huckins *v.* Lightner, 4 Tex. Civ. App. 38, 14 S. W. 1016.

[75] *Horse:*
Indiana: Farrar *v.* Eash, 5 Ind. App. 238, 31 N. E. 1125.

Iowa: Hartley State Bank *v.* McCorkell, 91 Ia. 660, 60 N. W. 197.

Michigan: Hutchinson *v.* Hutchinson, 102 Mich. 635, 61 N. W. 60.

Missouri: Cook *v.* Clary, 48 Mo. App. 166.

Colt: Van Horn *v.* Redman, 75 Ia. 421, 39 N. W. 679.

Mule:
Kentucky: Roach *v.* Houston, 15 Ky. L. Rep. 61.

Missouri: Jennings *v.* Sparkman, 48 Mo. App. 246.

Cow: Smith *v.* Stevens, 33 Colo. 427, 81 Pac. 35.

Slave:
Kentucky: Hall *v.* Edrington, 8 B. Mon. 47.

Texas: Clapp *v.* Waters, 2 Tex. 130.

[76] *Connecticut:* Adams *v.* Wright, 74 Conn. 551, 51 Atl. 53 (lunch wagon).

Florida: Ocala F. & M. Works *v.* Lester, 49 Fla. 199, 38 So. 51 (dummy engine).

Minnesota: Williams *v.* Wood, 61 Minn. 194, 63 N. W. 492 (threshing machine).

Missouri: Baldridge *v.* Dawson, 39 Mo. App. 527 (furniture).

Montana: Chauvin *v.* Valiton, 8 Mont. 451, 466, 20 Pac. 658, 3 L. R. A. 194 (piano).

New York: Crossley *v.* Hojer, 11 Misc. 57, 32 N. Y. Supp. 837 (furniture).

Texas: Stell *v.* Paschall, 41 Tex. 640 (cotton press); Mineralized Rubber Co. *v.* Cleburne, 22 Tex. Civ. App. 621, 56 S. W. 220 (fire hose).

Utah: Farrand & V. O. Co. *v.* Board of Church Extension, 17 Utah, 469, 54 Pac. 818, 70 Am. St. Rep. 810 (organ).

[77] *Missouri:* Reno *v.* Kingsbury, 39 Mo. App. 240.

Nebraska: Schrandt *v.* Young, 62 Neb. 254, 86 N. W. 1085.

Utah: Farrand & V. O. Co. *v.* Board of Church Extension, 17 Utah, 469, 474, 54 Pac. 818.

This is especially emphasized and the distinction drawn in the case of work-horses:

Colorado: Johnson *v.* Bailey, 17 Colo. 59; Smith *v.* Stevens, 14 Colo. App. 491, 60 Pac. 580.

Iowa: Hartley State Bank *v.* McCorkell, 91 Iowa, 660, 60 N. W. 197.

[78] *Ante,* § 171*b.*

No compensation will be given except upon proof that the owner was actually deprived of the use by the replevin proceedings;[79] but it is not necessary to show that he procured a substitute for the property taken from him.[80] Where, however, a pledgee succeeds in his action of replevin against the pledgor he can recover no compensation for use, since he has no right to use the pledged property;[81] and the same is true where the prevailing party is a mortgagee after default.[82]

When the property was not used by the possessor, the deterioration which it would have suffered by use must be considered in determining the value of the use, and only the net loss will be allowed.[83]

§ 538. Interest as damages for detention.

Where property is held by the owner, not for continuing use, but for consumption or sale, it is evident that no compensation can be recovered for use of the property; yet he has suffered damage by the detention of the property from him. This damage, in cases where the value of the use cannot be recovered, is measured by interest on the value of the property detained.[84]

---

[79] *Colorado:* Smith v. Stevens, 14 Colo. App. 491, 60 Pac. 580 (cow in pasture).
Massachusetts: Bartlett v. Brickett, 14 All. 62.
Wisconsin: Barney v. Douglass, 22 Wis. 464; Klinkert v. Fulton S. & M. Co., 113 Wis. 493, 89 N. W. 507.

[80] Boston Loan Co. v. Myers, 143 Mass. 446.

[81] McArthur v. Howett, 72 Ill. 358, 22 Am. Rep. 149.

[82] Thompson v. Scheid, 39 Minn. 102, 38 N. W. 801, 12 Am. St. Rep. 619.

[83] *Alabama:* White v. Sheffield & T. S. Ry., 90 Ala. 253, 7 So. 910.
Minnesota: Peerless Machine Co. v. Gates, 61 Minn. 124, 63 N. W. 260.
Montana: Brunell v. Cook, 13 Mont. 497, 34 Pac. 1015, 40 Am. St. Rep. 459.

[84] *United States:* Sleppy v. Bank of Commerce, 8 Sawy. 17.
Arkansas: Kelly v. Altemus, 34 Ark. 184, 34 Am. Rep. 6.

Colorado: Hanauer v. Bartels, 2 Colo. 514.
Iowa: Hurd v. Gallaher, 14 Ia. 394 (see Bonnot Co. v. Newman, 109 Ia. 580, 80 N. W. 655).
Kansas: Yandle v. Kingsbury, 17 Kan. 195 (semble); Ladd v. Brewer, 17 Kan. 204; Bell v. Campbell, 17 Kan. 211; Palmer v. Meiners, 17 Kan. 478.
Maine: Washington Ice Co. v. Webster, 62 Me. 341, 16 Am. Rep. 462.
Massachusetts: Wood v. Braynard, 9 Pick. 322; Stevens v. Tuite, 104 Mass. 328.
Minnesota: Berthold v. Fox, 13 Minn. 501, 97 Am. Dec. 243.
Missouri: Woodburn v. Cogdal, 39 Mo. 222; Reno v. Kingsbury, 39 Mo. App. 240.
Nevada: Blackie v. Cooney, 8 Nev. 41.
New York: Brizsee v. Maybee, 21 Wend. 144; Redmond v. American Mfg. Co., 121 N. Y. 415, 24 N. E. 924; Earle

The presumption is that damages for detention are to be so measured.[85] But if damages by way of compensation for use are recovered, there can be no recovery of interest.[86] So in replevin for grain, the measure of damages is interest on the value.[87] It is said that in replevin for certified bank checks, the damages are confined to interest on the amount.[88] So of a county warrant for the plaintiff's services.[89] But where the goods attached were subject to duties and the plaintiff paid them, it was held in an action on the replevin bond that the interest should be computed only on the difference between the amount so paid and the valuation in the writ of replevin.[90] Interest should be at the statutory rate; and this was held to be the case even where the property detained was a savings-bank book, and the bank paid less than the statutory rate of interest.[91] The value of the use of money is not limited by the

v. Gorham Manuf. Co., 2 App. Div. 460, 473, 37 N. Y. Supp. 1037.

North Carolina: Hall v. Tillman, 110 N. C. 220, 14 S. E. 745 (departing after a statutory change of procedure from the earlier practice *contra*, as shown in Scott v. Elliott, 63 N. C. 215; Potapsco v. Magee, 86 N. C. 350; but see Penny v. Ludwick, 152 N. C. 375, 67 S. E. 919).

Pennsylvania: McCabe v. Morehead, 1 W. & S. 513, 37 Am. Dec. 477; Collins v. Houston, 138 Pa. 481, 21 Atl. 234.

Tennessee: Mayberry v. Cliffe, 7 Cold. 117.

Wisconsin: Bigelow v. Doolittle, 36 Wis. 115; Wadleigh v. Buckingham, 80 Wis. 230, 49 N. W. 745; Klinkert v. Fulton S. & M. Co., 113 Wis. 493, 89 N. W. 507.

England: Dreyfus v. Peruvian Guano Co., 42 Ch. D. 66.

Contra, that no interest can be given in absence of proof of actual value of the use: Miller v. Jones, 26 Ala. 247 (detinue). In Indiana it was said that interest on the value of the property might be allowed by way of damages in an action on the replevin bond. Walls v. Johnson, 16 Ind. 374.

[85] *Colorado:* Johnson v. Bailey, 17 Colo. 59, 28 Pac. 81; Smith v. Stevens, 14 Colo. App. 491, 60 Pac. 580.

Missouri: Reno v. Kingsbury, 39 Mo. App. 240.

Nebraska: Schrandt v. Young, 62 Neb. 254, 86 N. W. 1085.

New York: New York G. & I. Co. v. Flynn, 55 N. Y. 653; Earle v. Gorham Mfg. Co., 2 App. Div. 460, 37 N. Y. Supp. 1037.

[86] *California:* Freeborn v. Norcross, 49 Cal. 313; Garcia v. Gunn, 119 Cal. 315, 51 Pac. 689, 63 Am. St. Rep. 131.

Kansas: McCarty v. Quimby, 12 Kan. 494.

Missouri: Reno v. Kingsbury, 39 Mo. App. 240.

Tennessee: Smith v. Roby, 6 Heisk. 546.

[87] Machette v. Wanless, 2 Colo. 169.

[88] Merchants' S. L. & T. Co. v. Goodrich, 75 Ill. 554. So of a note: Weaver v. Williams, 75 Miss. 945, 23 So. 649.

[89] McCoy v. Cornell, 40 Ia. 457.

[90] Huggeford v. Ford, 11 Pick. (Mass.) 223. See, also, Mattoon v. Pearce, 12 Mass. 406, 7 Am. Dec. 85.

[91] Wegner v. Second W. S. Bank, 76 Wis. 242, 44 N. W. 1096.

savings-bank rate, for the holder can withdraw his deposit at any time.

§ 539. Increase or income of the property.

The owner recovers not only the property, but any increase or income from it during the period of detention, as young born during the detention of a slave or animal,[92] wool clipped from sheep,[93] or dividends collected on stock while it was retained.[94] But it has been held in Nevada that the value of the wool from the sheep while detained could not be recovered unless pleaded as special damage.[95] And where compensation is recovered for the income from property, the specific cost of obtaining such income should be deducted.[96]

§ 540. Consequential damages.

It has been intimated, in Massachusetts, that if special damage were shown to have been suffered by the defendant, it might be allowed.[97] And where machinery in actual use in a factory was wrongfully replevied from the manufacturer, his damages were held [98] to include compensation for the general inconvenience and loss resulting from the interruption of his possession; [99] and compensation for the expense, trouble, and delay of restoring the property to its former condition.[100] So where a machine is taken to prevent the plaintiff from using it as a model for the construction of other machines, he may recover its value to him.[101] So, it has been held by the English

---

[92] *Mississippi:* Jordan v. Thomas, 31 Miss. 557.

Nevada: Buckley v. Buckley, 12 Nev. 423.

Oklahoma: Wade v. Gould, 8 Okla. 690, 59 Pac. 11.

Texas: Morris v. Coburn, 71 Tex. 406, 8 Am. St. Rep. 611.

But see Houston v. Bibb, 5 Jones, (N. C.) Law 83.

[93] Harrison v. Ilgner, 74 Tex. 86.

[94] Bercich v. Marye, 9 Nev. 312.

[95] Buckley v. Buckley, 12 Nev. 423.

[96] Cunningham v. Stoner, 10 Idaho, 549, 79 Pac. 228 (cost of clipping wool from sheep).

[97] Barnes v. Bartlett, 15 Pick. 71; but in New York, the right of recovering special damages in this action has been doubted. Briszee v. Maybee, 21 Wend. 144; although if the analogy of trover be followed, they would probably now be allowed to a limited extent. See McDonald v. North, 47 Barb. 530.

[98] Stevens v. Tuite, 104 Mass. 328.

[99] *Acc.*, Davenport v. Ledger, 80 Ill. 574.

[100] *Acc.*, Zitske v. Goldberg, 38 Wis. 216.

[101] Berry v. Vantries, 12 S. & R. (Pa.) 89. This is really recovering the value of the use.

Court of Common Pleas, that special damages may be recovered in this action. "When the goods were not redelivered by the sheriff, according to the books, it would appear that the plaintiff could recover the full amount of the damages that he had sustained. . . . I see no reason in principle, why there should be any limitation as to the amount of the damages recoverable in such a case. I do not know any ground in law, for confining the damages to the amount of the expenses of the replevin bond. In practice, these expenses are all that are recovered, merely because there is generally no other damage. . . . Whatever damages have been actually sustained may be recovered." [102] Where a plaintiff wrongfully replevied ice belonging to the defendant, it was held that the latter could recover the expense of procuring teams and appurtenances for the purpose of removing the ice, it having been actually incurred, and the teams, etc., having been rendered useless by the suing out the writ of replevin. It was held in this case that the defendant could not recover damages arising from a possible loss of customers, that being too indefinite, remote, and contingent to become an element of damage. It was said, also, that the plaintiff could not recover for a liability on outstanding contracts, since he could have replaced himself in the market. [103] Nor can he recover for loss of the profits of contracts which he has been unable to fulfil because his property was taken. [104]

It has been held that the owner may recover the expense of a reasonable attempt to recover the property, [105] but he cannot recover the expense of an ill-advised and ineffectual journey,

[102] Bovill, C. J., in Gibbs v. Cruikshank, L. R. 8 C. P. 454, 459.

[103] Washington Ice Co. v. Webster, 62 Me. 341, 16 Am. Rep. 462.

[104] *Minnesota:* Williams v. Wood, 55 Minn. 323, 56 N. W. 1066, 61 Minn. 194, 63 N. W. 492.

Nebraska: Schrandt v. Young, 62 Neb. 254, 86 N. W. 1085.

[105] *California:* Cain v. Cody, 29 Pac. 778.

New York: Bennett v. Lockwood, 20 Wend. 223, 32 Am. Dec. 532; Davis S. M. Co. v. Best, 50 Hun, 76.

Wisconsin: Parroski v. Goldberg, 80 Wis. 339, 50 N. W. 191.

Contra, that travelling expenses are not allowed:

Dakota: Jandt v. South, 2 Dak. 46, 47 N. W. 779.

Illinois: Taylor v. Welsh, 138 Ill. App. 190.

Mississippi: Taylor v. Morton, 61 Miss. 24.

New York: Hampton & B. R. R. v. Sizer, 35 Misc. 391, 71 N. Y. Supp. 990.

South Carolina: Loeb v. Mann, 39 S. C. 465, 18 S. E. 1.

taken with the object of repossessing himself of the property after it was in the sheriff's hands without being prepared to take it by legal proceedings.[106] On the same principle it has been held that he may recover the expense of securing the return of the property,[107] of replacing it in its former position,[108] or of finding a necessary substitute for it.[109] But counsel fees and expenses of litigation undertaken for the purpose of securing the property cannot be recovered.[110] In Riley v. Littlefield [111] replevin was brought for a race-horse. It appeared that the horse had been entered in races, and on account of the seizure had not been able to race. By regulation of the association which carried on horse-racing, the owner of the horse was obliged to pay certain fines on account of the non-appearance of the horse at the races, or he would be allowed to enter in no more races. This, however, was held to be too remote for compensation.

§ 541. Sequestration proceeding in Louisiana.

In Louisiana, proceeding by sequestration is strongly analogous to the replevin or attachment of the common law, and the party plaintiff gives a bond with sureties "to pay all damages that may accrue in case it shall appear that the sequestration was wrongfully sued out." In a suit on such a bond, it has been decided in that State that the counsel fees of the first suit can be recovered on such bond; nor is it material to show that such

[106] *California:* Kelley v. McKibben, 53 Cal. 13.

Wisconsin: Barney v. Douglass, 22 Wis. 46.

[107] Leonard v. Maginnis, 34 Minn. 506.

[108] Byrnes v. Palmer, 113 Mich. 17, 71 N. W. 331.

[109] Adams v. Wright, 74 Conn. 551, 51 Atl. 53.

[110] *California:* Black v. Hilliker, 130 Cal. 190, 62 Pac. 481; Hays v. Windsor, 130 Cal. 230, 62 Pac. 395; Harris v. Smith, 132 Cal. 316, 64 Pac. 409.

Dakota: Jandt v. South, 2 Dak. 46, 47 N. W. 779.

Florida: Gregory v. Woodbury, 53 Fla. 566, 43 So. 504.

Missouri: Trimble v. Keer R. M. Co., 56 Mo. App. 683; Howard v. Haas, 139 Mo. App. 591, 123 S. W. 1048.

New York: Cook v. Gross, 60 App. Div. 446, 69 N. Y. Supp. 924; Hampton & B. R. R. v. Sizer, 35 Misc. 391, 71 N. Y. Supp. 990; Sinskie v. Brust, 66 App. Div. 34, 72 N. Y. Supp. 922.

South Carolina: Loeb v. Mann, 39 S. C. 465, 18 S. E. 1.

Wyoming: Knight v. Beckwith Commercial Co., 6 Wyo. 500, 46 Pac. 1094.

So the expense of securing a surety on the replevin bond cannot be recovered. Wilson v. Hillhouse, 14 Ia. 199, 81 Am. Dec. 465, n.

[111] 84 Mich. 22, 47 N. W. 576.

fees have been actually paid; it is enough that the plaintiff has incurred a liability for them.[112]

§ 542. Reciprocal damages.

* It is the peculiarity of this action, that both parties may be actors; and so if it is found that a part of the property claimed is the plaintiff's, and a part not, both plaintiff and defendant may recover damages against each other; [113] ** and also costs.[114]

[112] Jones v. Doles, 3 La. Ann. 588.
[113] *Kansas:* Jones v. Annis, 47 Kan. 478, 28 Pac. 156.

Massachusetts: Powell v. Hinsdale, 5 Mass. 343.
[114] Knowles v. Pierce, 5 Houst. (Del). 178.

CHAPTER XXIV

ACTIONS AGAINST OFFICERS

§ 543. Ministerial officers responsible for violations of duty.

* We shall now consider that class of cases which arise out of the acts of the public officers who are charged with the ministerial portion of the administration of government. It is well settled under the English system, that sheriffs and other ministerial officers in case of neglect or violation of duty, are responsible to the party aggrieved in a civil action.[1] The mode prescribed is usually one of the great class of actions on the

[1] Clark v. Miller, 47 Barb. 38, 54 N. Y. 528. Public officers, however, vested by law with discretionary authority, and acting within its scope, are not answerable in damages for the consequences of their acts, unless done maliciously and with intent to injure. Burton v. Fulton, 49 Pa. 151.

case; but the proceeding often takes the form of trespass. To this general remedy, which flows from the principles of the common law, is frequently superadded some special statutory relief, enforced by some particular penalty; but the addition of such particular remedy does not interfere in any way with the right of the party to his compensation for the actual injury done in a suit of trespass, or on the case.[2] ** Every public officer is required to give bonds with sureties for the proper discharge of his duties, and in some jurisdictions an action against an officer for wrongful acts in the discharge of his duties may be brought upon his bond, and often is so brought. It is evident that the measure of damages should in general be the same, whether the injured party brings an action of tort or resorts to the bond, the real cause of action being a tort in either case; and therefore actions brought upon official bonds are frequently authorities upon the subjects discussed in this chapter, and many such actions will be found herein. The peculiar questions which arise by reason of the action being brought upon the bond will be discussed later.[3]

§ 544. Actual injury furnishes the general rule.

* The ordinary cases in which the questions arise which we are now about to examine, are presented in suits against sheriffs or other ministerial officers, either for negligence, as the escape of parties arrested on mesne or final process, for taking insufficient security, for neglect to seize or preserve property on execution, or omission to make a true return to the writ; or, on the other hand, for an excess of their powers, as for levying upon property which they are not authorized to do so by the process, excessive distress, etc. And in these cases we shall find the general principle to be, although the form of the action

---

[2] As a general principle, it is well settled, in regard to all public officers, that although created by statute, and although liable to the infliction of penalties for violation of official duty, they are still equally responsible to the aggrieved party, in an action on the case. "Where the law," says the Supreme Court of Maine, "has affixed forfeitures for certain infractions thereof, or for neglects in not conforming to its requirements, whereby individuals are injured, they are not in consequence thereof deprived of the remedy which would exist if no penalties were prescribed." Hayes v. Porter, 22 Me. 371, 376; Beckford v. Hood, 7 T. R. 620; Farmers' Turnpike v. Coventry, 10 Johns. 389.

[3] See chap. xxxii, Bonds.

be in tort, that the party aggrieved is entitled, independent of any statutory relief, to recover only to the extent of his actual injury.[4]

It is not correct, however, says the Supreme Court of Vermont, to hold "that in actions of trespass for taking personal property, when the defendant is an officer acting under legal process, no damages can in any case be recovered beyond the actual value of the property. Courts usually in such cases instruct the jury that they ought to confine themselves within those limits. It is a rule of practice merely. Circumstances may require a departure from it." [5]

The rule is, indeed, subject to many modifications; partly arising from the vagueness that we have often had occasion to notice in the early cases; [6] partly from the variety of the forms of action employed; and partly from the application of the rules of evidence; and partly from the general principle that in actions of tort the intent, disposition, and conduct of the defendant always bear largely on the question of damages.[7]

---

[4] Pierce v. Strickland, 2 Story, 292; Dyer v. Woodbury, 14 Me. 546.

[5] Joyal v. Barney, 20 Vt. 154, 159; acc., Dobbs v. The Justices, etc., 17 Ga. 624.

[6] Ravenscroft v. Eyles, Warden of the Fleet, 2 Wils. 294 (1776), is very strong to show the power which the courts originally gave in these cases to the jury. It was case for a voluntary escape; and the question being whether the action lay, the debtor having returned to custody before suit brought, and judgment having been recovered against him, Lord C. J. Wilmot said: "The quantum of damages is nothing to the purpose; for if the jury had power in this case to give damages, we must now take it that they have done right; and I am of opinion that the jury were not confined to give the exact damages in the final judgment, but had a power and discretion to assess what damages they thought proper; for this being an action upon the case, the damages were totally uncertain and at large."

In Sayer on Damages, 56, this case is stated to have been tried before Lord Camden, C. J.; that it was proved at the trial that the debt was sperate; and that on the argument, Bathurst, J., said: "Whether the debt was sperate or not, I take it to be a settled point, if the escape is a voluntary one, that it is the duty of the jury to assess damages to the amount of the whole debt." But by the report in 2 Wilson, above cited, no such point was made before the court on the subject of damages.

In Kent v. Kelway, case for rescue from arrest (Lane, 70; Sayer on Damages, 55), it is said that damages may be recovered to the amount of the debt for which the arrest was.

[7] In Bayley v. Bates, 8 Johns. 185, the Supreme Court of New York said: "An action for a false return sounds in tort and fraud, and it draws into consideration, in a greater or less degree, the quo animo of the defendant."

And these various questions we shall better understand by an examination of the cases.**

§ 545. General rule.

* As a general rule, however, it is settled that the measure of damages in suits of this class, brought against a public officer by a creditor plaintiff, whose remedy against his debtor has been impaired by the neglect or other misconduct of the officer, is the actual injury sustained, this actual injury being measured by the amount of the original debt due the plaintiff, or the value of the property, which has been lost or prejudiced by the neglect of the officer,** unless it is shown that the plaintiff's actual loss was less.[8]

§ 546. Burden of proof.

* It is an important question, where the breach of duty is clear, on whom does the proof of damage rest? Is the plaintiff to prove that he is damnified, or is the officer to disprove the fact? Our law, proceeding on a principle of evidence, throws the burden of proof on the negligent party, and assumes that the plaintiff is injured until the contrary appear. It might be urged that this should not be so, where there is mere ordinary negligence unaccompanied by any criminal intention; but as with common carriers, so with public officers, there are reasons, of controlling weight, why the party to whom a great trust is confided, and in whose hands usually all the testimony must

---

[8] *United States:* Jerman *v.* Stewart, 12 Fed. 266.

Alabama: Marcum *v.* Burgess, 67 Ala. 556.

California: Phelps *v.* Owens, 11 Cal. 22; Pelberg *v.* Gorham, 23 Cal. 349.

Georgia: Spain *v.* Clements, 63 Ga. 786.

Illinois: French *v.* Snyder, 30 Ill. 339, 83 Am. Dec. 193.

Iowa: Plummer *v.* Harbut, 5 Ia. 308.

Kansas: Crane *v.* Stone, 15 Kan. 94.

Kentucky: Commonwealth *v.* Lightfoot, 7 B. Mon. 298.

Louisiana: Marshall *v.* Simpson, 13 La. Ann. 437; Bogel *v.* Bell, 15 La. Ann. 163.

Massachusetts: Whitaker *v.* Sumner, 9 Pick. 308.

Missouri: State *v.* Cobb, 64 Mo. 586.

Montana: Randall *v.* Greenhood, 3 Mont. 506.

New Hampshire: Goodrich *v.* Foster, 20 N. H. 177.

New York: Clark *v.* Miller, 54 N. Y. 528.

Pennsylvania: Hamner *v.* Griffith, 1 Grant, 193.

Texas: Hogan *v.* Kellum, 13 Tex. 396.

Vermont: Briggs *v.* Gleason, 29 Vt. 78; Blodgett *v.* Brattleboro, 30 Vt. 579; Parker *v.* Peabody, 56 Vt. 221.

Wisconsin: Beveridge *v.* Welch, 7 Wis. 465.

be, should be compelled to exculpate himself after a *prima facie* case of negligence is made out against him.[9]

There appears, however, to be a discrepancy on this point between the English and American rule. In England, it would seem, though it is by no means clear, that the plaintiff must show affirmatively that he could have collected his debt but for the negligence of the defendant.

The earliest case on this subject [10] runs thus: "An action upon the case against a sheriff, upon an escape suffered by his bailee upon a mesne process, and it was in evidence, as is necessary to make this case, that there was such a debt, that such a process and warrant was, and a due debt, and lastly, that the party arrested was become insolvent; otherwise he should not have recovered damages to the value of his debt, as he here did upon all this proved in evidence as aforesaid."

On the authority of this case, Mr. Peake [11] lays down the rule thus: "In order to show the amount of damages he has sustained, the plaintiff should also prove the circumstances of the defendant at the time of the arrest, and that he has since absconded, or become insolvent; for if the defendant were originally in bad circumstances, or he may be met with every day, and the plaintiff has not, in fact, been injured by the negligence of the defendant, the damages will be merely nominal." Mr. Starkie briefly says: [12] "The plaintiff must prove his debt and the damages which he has sustained from the sheriff's negligence."

In this country, it appears to be settled that the plaintiff, after proving his debt against the prisoner, the custody, and escape, is entitled to recover as his damages the amount of his debt, unless the officer can show that the defendant was insolvent, or in any other way prove that the plaintiff has sustained no actual loss.[13] "The body," says Mr. J. Cowen, in a case in New York,[14] "is considered the highest satisfaction in the law;

[9] Sheldon *v.* Upham, 14 R. I. 493.

[10] Tempest *v.* Linley, Clayton, 34.

[11] Norris' Peake, 608.

[12] Evidence—Sheriff—Escape. Vol. ii, 1016.

[13] *Indiana:* State *ex rel.* Shirk *v.* Mullen, 50 Ind. 598.

Maryland: State use of Goddard *v.* Baden, 11 Md. 317.

New York: Loosey *v.* Orser, 4 Bosw. 391.

[14] Patterson *v.* Westervelt, 17 Wend. 543, 548.

that is, for the time, gone by the sheriff's negligence, and it is doing no violence to say, that a defendant who would escape had *prima facie* secreted himself, or otherwise placed himself and property beyond the reach of execution."

In this case the question as to the burden of proof was distinctly presented. The sheriff of New York was sued for the escape of one Kelly, against whom the plaintiff had recovered a judgment for $10,722.98; the debt and escape being proved, Edwards, C. J., charged, that to entitle the plaintiff to recover beyond nominal damages, it was incumbent on him to show the extent of the injury sustained by him; and a verdict for such damages only, was accordingly rendered. On motion for a new trial, the court held the burden to be on the defendant, and granted a new trial; admitting, however, that their decision was at variance with the English rule; but insisting that it was not unreasonable to assume that the plaintiff had lost his debt by the defendant's negligence, until the contrary should be proved.**

§ 547. Nominal damages.

* It would seem, on the general principles which we have already considered, that even if it affirmatively appear that the plaintiff has sustained no damage, the officer guilty of a technical violation of duty would still be liable for nominal damages.** But a distinction was taken at a comparatively early day in England, between the liability of officers for default in the execution of writs of mesne and of final process, and which is sustained by a series of decisions. Where the writ relates to mesne process, it is held that, as it is uncertain whether the aggrieved party would recover at all against the original defendant, he can recover from the officer such damages only, as he can show he has sustained. But in an action on the case for the sheriff's omission to arrest the debtor, on final process, or for an escape on such process, although no actual damage be proved, he is held liable, in any event, to nominal damages. His negligence in this case deprives the plaintiff of the satisfaction which, after judgment, is in law imported by the possession of the debtor's body.[15] So in case

---

[15] Planck *v.* Anderson, 5 T. R. 37;   Lewis *v.* Morland, 2 B. & Ald. 56; Scott *v.* Henley, 1 M. & Rob. 227.

for not executing a *ca. sa.*, the jury found that the sheriff was in default, but that the plaintiff had sustained no damage; and a verdict was entered for the defendant. But on argument, verdict was entered for the plaintiff, with nominal damages; Lord Denman saying: "When the clear right of a party is invaded in consequence of another's breach of duty, he must be entitled to an action against that party for some amount. There is no authority to the contrary." [16]

With the above exceptions of actions for not arresting a debtor on final process, or for allowing him to escape when held on such process, it seems to be settled in England, that civil actions against ministerial officers for neglect of duty, cannot be maintained, unless damage thereby accrues to the plaintiff, although the neglect affords a presumption of damage which must be disproved to entitle the defendant to a verdict. This has been held in actions against sheriffs, for the omission to seize goods to which the plaintiff has a present right of possession, or to execute a *capias*, or to levy under a *fi. fa.*, or for his making a false return. [17] The distinction thus

---

[16] Clifton *v.* Hooper, 6 Q. B. 468, 14 L. J. N. S. Q. B. 1. In an early case, where the sheriffs of Norwich sued the defendant, who had escaped by a rescue, on the ground of their liability over to I. S., at whose suit they arrested him, it was objected that the plaintiffs had not shown that they were charged, or in any way damnified; but the objection was held ill. Sheriffs of Norwich *v.* Bradshaw, Cro. Eliz. 53.

In Crompton *v.* Ward, 1 Str. 429, 436, it is said that the plaintiff has an interest, a sort of property, in the body of the prisoner, and sustains a damage by a rescue. But *what* damage is not said.

[17] Randell *v.* Wheble, 10 A. & E. 719; Hobson *v.* Thelluson, L. R. 2 Q. B. 642; Stimson *v.* Farnham, L. R. 7 Q. B. 175; Tancred *v.* Allgood, 4 H. & N. 438, 28 L. J. N. S. Ex. 362. The earlier cases were in conflict. In Powel *v.* Hord, 1 Strange, 650, an action for a false return on mesne process, the court held:

"That if the defendant were a man of estate, and could still be taken, and so no damage, they should think the debt too much to give; but that *not being this case*," the jury found the whole debt as damages, with the opinion of the chief justice. And in Planck *v.* Anderson, 5 T. R. 37, it was held that the sheriff is not liable to an action for an escape on mesne process, if the jury find that the plaintiff has not been delayed or prejudiced in his suit. In Barker *v.* Green, 2 Bing. 317, case for not arresting J. W., it was held that though the plaintiff had sustained no actual damage, it was still a case for nominal damages, and the court refused to enter a nonsuit. But in Williams *v.* Mostyn, 4 M. & W. 145, where case was brought for the voluntary escape of one Langford, taken on mesne process, and *it was admitted* that the plaintiff had sustained no *actual damage or delay*, the defendant having returned to the custody of the plaintiff, a verdict was found for

established in England, by which no liability attends the neglect of official duty unless the neglect results in positive loss to the person aggrieved, is founded on the assumption that the right of a suitor (or other person in a corresponding relation) to the officer's services, is in fact a right only to such pecuniary benefit as can be derived from them, and that if no such benefit can be obtained, no right exists. The exception has apparently been recognized in New York, in other cases than actions against sheriffs, and which seem to proceed upon such a distinction, though it was not in terms adverted to.[18] But although, owing to the abolition of imprisonment for a simple debt, the question loses its importance in reference to actions for the sheriff's neglect of duty, in those cases in which the defendant could formerly have been arrested as of course, we think the exception is to be regretted, both as anomalous, and as tending to laxity in the discharge of official duty. Under circumstances giving an officer no discretion, his failure to fulfil a positive duty for the benefit or protection of others should always be, in a legal sense, a wrong to the person in whose behalf the duty should have been discharged; and where there is a legal wrong there should always be a legal remedy. A right of action should accrue when the breach of duty is committed; and once existing, should not be destroyed by the circumstance that it afterwards proves to inflict no pecuniary damage.[19]

the plaintiff, with *nominal damages.* And on motion the court directed a *nonsuit* to be entered, saying, "that there had been *no damage in fact or law;*" and they disapproved of Barker *v.* Green. In Bales *v.* Wingfield, 4 Q. B. 580, where case was brought against the sheriff for neglecting to sell under a *fi. fa.* the writ was delivered to the sheriff, who seized on the 24th, and advertised a sale for the 6th of May; he did not, in fact, sell till the 27th. On the 15th of May a fiat in bankruptcy issued, and so the sheriff returned "no goods." The Q. B. held, that it lay on the plaintiff to show damage; and a verdict for nominal damages being entered, they refused to set it aside. But in Wylie *v.*

Birch, 4 Q. B. 566, case for a false return, Lord Denman, C. J., assumed the principle, that the action could not be maintained against the sheriff for breach of duty, unless damage accrued thereby to the plaintiff, and cited the above cases; but said, also, that the breach of duty afforded presumption of some damage to the party who sets the sheriff in motion; and in such a case it seems still in England, that if the plaintiff offered no proof of actual injury, he would be entitled to nominal damages.

[18] Commercial Bank *v.* Ten Eyck, 48 N. Y. 305; Bridge *v.* Mason, 45 Barb. 37.

[19] Pelham *v.* Way, 15 Wall. 196, 21

In this country nominal damages at least are usually given for every breach of duty by a public officer.[20] So in case of neglect to return an execution, although no injury appear to have resulted, judgment will still be given for nominal damages.[21] So in a case in Massachusetts, against a sheriff for neglecting to return an execution, the Supreme Court of that State said: "The plaintiff is entitled to nominal damages for the officer's neglect. No actual damages are proved, but where there is a neglect of duty, the law presumes damages." [22]

§ 548. Mitigation.

* Where the plaintiff proceeds on account of the loss of a debt the original debt is, of course, the gist of the action, and it is perfectly well settled that the existence of such debt must be proved by the plaintiff.[23] But if that fact is established, the equally important inquiry remains, whether the recovery of the debt has been prejudiced by the acts of the defendant. In other words, whether, under any circumstances, it could have been collected of the defendant's property.[24] The question sometimes arises on mesne, and sometimes on final process.**

It also presents itself in other actions of this class. An officer who has attached property and taken a receipt for it, cannot show mitigation of damages, in an action brought for his not delivering the property or the receipt, that the property was worth less than the value alleged in his return.[25] But in case against a sheriff for illegally selling goods lawfully seized and held by him, and which had deteriorated without his default, the measure of damages is said, by the Supreme Court of Vermont, not to be their value when taken, but at the time of the sale.[26]

§ 549. Failure to levy.

For failure to levy the defendant is liable *prima facie* for the

L. ed. 55; Dow *v.* Humbert, 91 U. S. 294, 23 L. ed. 368.
[20] Metzner *v.* Graham, 66 Mo. 653. But *contra*, Dwyer *v.* Woulfe, 40 La. Ann. 46; Amperse *v.* Winslow, 75 Mich. 234, 13 Am. St. Rep. 432.
[21] Kidder *v.* Barker, 18 Vt. 454.
[22] Laflin *v.* Willard, 16 Pick. 64, 26

Am. Dec. 629. See also Goodnow *v.* Willard, 5 Met. 571.
[23] Gunter *v.* Cleyton, 2 Lev. 85; Alexander *v.* Macauley, 4 T. R. 611.
[24] Crooker *v.* Melick, 18 Neb. 227; Hellman *v.* Spielman, 19 Neb. 152.
[25] Allen *v.* Doyle, 33 Me. 420.
[26] Walker *v.* Wilmarth, 37 Vt. 289.

whole debt,[27] and conclusively so unless he can mitigate the amount by showing that he was unable to collect it by an exercise of proper diligence,[28] as, if the defendant in the execution was insolvent,[29] or the plaintiff himself have been the cause why the whole was not collected.[30] If, however, the land on which the defendant should have levied is worth less than the debt, the measure of damages is the value of the land,[31] and that value is to be measured by what the land would bring at a forced sale,[32] and not the amount agreed upon by the appraisers, as shown in the officer's return.[33] The sheriff may show in mitigation of damages, that the defendant in the execution had no property upon which he could have levied,[34] but *not* that the judgment is still collectible.[35] And in such an action the sheriff may show in mitigation that other executions in his hands would have taken the proceeds of a sale.[36] Where, in Ohio, the sheriff refused to levy on and sell under an execution in his hands, at the request of the plaintiff in the execution, certain personal property, which was wholly covered by mort-

[27] *Alabama:* Bondurant ɐ Lane, 9 Port. 484.

Maryland: Maccubbin *v.* Thornton, 1 Har. & McH. 194.

Massachusetts: Fairfield *v.* Baldwin, 12 Pick. 388.

New Hampshire: Sanborn *v.* Emerson, 12 N. H. 57.

New York: Bank of Rome *v.* Curtiss, 1 Hill, 275; People *v.* Lott, 21 Barb. 130; Humphrey *v.* Hathorn, 24 Barb. 278; Carpenter *v.* Doody, 1 Hilt. 465.

Pennsylvania: Commonwealth *v.* Contner, 18 Pa. 439.

Vermont: Hall *v.* Brooks, 8 Vt. 485, 30 Am. Dec. 485.

And see *Ireland:* Simmonds *v.* Henchy, 16 L. R. Ire. 467.

But it is also held, that in declaring against a constable for failing to levy an execution, it is necessary to allege that the defendant in the execution had property on which the levy might have been made. The court says the officer was under no legal obligation to make the levy, unless the defendant had

property at the time upon which to make it, and it was incumbent on the plaintiff to allege the fact in the declaration; and this correctly, for no such presumption exists on executions against property before levy, as on mesne process after arrest. State, use of Brooks *v.* Kirby, 6 Ark. 453.

[28] Dunphy *v.* People, 25 Mich. 10.

[29] Varril *v.* Heald, 2 Me. 91; *contra,* Crawford *v.* Word, 7 Ga. 445.

[30] Pardee *v.* Robertson, 6 Hill (N. Y.), 550.

[31] Hurlock *v.* Reinhardt, 41 Tex. 580. See Hamner *v.* Griffith, 1 Grant (Pa.), 193.

[32] Harris *v.* Murfree, 54 Ala. 161.

[33] Parker *v.* Peabody, 56 Vt. 221.

[34] *Alabama:* Abbot *v.* Gillespy, 75 Ala. 180.

New York: Ledyard *v.* Jones, 7 N. Y. 550.

[35] Ledyard *v.* Jones, 7 N. Y. 550.

[36] Forsyth *v.* Dickson, 1 Grant (Pa.), 26. But see Crawford *v.* Word, 7 Ga. 445.

gages to an amount far more than its value, it was held that there should be a verdict for nominal damages only.[37]   The measure of damages in an action against a sheriff, for not selling a tract of land levied on under the foreclosure, is said to be the value of the land or the amount of the foreclosure, whichever was the less amount.[38]   And where the sheriff levied upon a special interest in the land, instead of the fee, he was liable in damages for the entire amount of the execution or value of the land less the actual value of the execution, measured by the amount received from sale of the special interest.[39]   But in an action for insufficient levy of execution on specific property, we have a different case.   The loss is merely the loss to the creditor of the benefit of the specific property in question, which is obviously a mere question as to the value of specific property. As in every case, however, the plaintiff, suing for injury to specific property, must prove the value of the property; and in the absence of evidence of value he is entitled to nominal damages only.[40]

§ 550. Failure to attach.

Attachments are governed by the same rule as executions, and if the sheriff, knowing of property enough to satisfy the demand, fails to levy to that extent, he is liable for the deficiency as ascertained by the result of the sale.   It does not excuse him that the property levied on was appraised at a sum sufficient to satisfy the debt.[41]   In an action against the sheriff for neglect to levy an attachment, or levy and return an execution, the amount of the judgment or execution, or so much thereof as the value of the property which the officer neglected to attach would have been sufficient to satisfy, is the measure.[42]   And where the value of the property lost by the neglect of the

[37] Coe v. Peacock, 14 Oh. St. 187; Coopers v. Wolf, 15 Oh. St. 523.
[38] Baker v. Bower, 44 Ga. 14; Blackman v. Clements, 45 Ga. 292.
[39] Richards v. Gilmore, 11 N. H. 493.
[40] Farmers' & M. Bank v. Maines, 183 Fed. 37.
[41] Ransom v. Halcott, 18 Barb. (N. Y.) 56.

[42] Michigan: People v. Colerick, 67 Mich. 362, 34 N. W. 683.
New Hampshire: Perkins v. Pitman, 34 N. H. 261.
New York: Bowman v. Cornell, 39 Barb. 69.
But see Maine: Wolfe v. Dorr, 14 Me. 104.

sheriff to execute the attachment equals or exceeds the amount of the plaintiff's demand, such amount becomes the measure of damages for which the sheriff and his sureties are liable.[43] So the damages should be reduced by the amount of property owned by the debtor at the time of the judgment, upon which the plaintiff might have levied.[44]

In Connecticut, it was originally decided that an officer who had been guilty of neglect in not serving mesne process should be liable for the whole debt; a rule which has been there characterized "as one of stern policy, rather than of exact justice;" and it is now well settled that the plaintiff can only recover the damages he has sustained. "But these damages it is peculiarly the duty of the jury to assess, and in so doing they are not limited to any precise sum; they may even give more than the plaintiff's original debt. Where that debt has been lost by the wilful misconduct or negligence of the officer, they may add to it the costs of a second suit; and as the jury may give more than the debt, so they may give less. If it should be found by them that the failure of the officer to return a writ was owing to a mere mistake, in consequence of which the party had suffered nothing, they might give, and indeed it would be their duty to give, only nominal damages."[45]

In North Carolina, in regard to mesne process, it has been said that the true inquiry is whether the debtor had any property which might, by due process, have been subject to execution, and whether the sheriff by his negligence has deprived the plaintiff of his remedy. But it is no answer for the sheriff to say that the debtor, even after being imprisoned, might pay, or secure to be paid by assignment, other *bona fide* debts, to the disappointment of the plaintiff.[46] Nor on such process is the reputation of the defendant as an insolvent any excuse; the officer is bound to ascertain for himself whether there is any property to satisfy the writ.[47]

[43] Smith v. Tooke, 20 Tex. 750.
[44] Townsend v. Libbey, 70 Me. 162.
[45] Palmer v. Gallup, 16 Conn. 555, 41 Am. Dec. 158; Duryee v. Webb, cited in notes to this case. See Clark v. Smith, 9 Conn. 379, 23 Am. Dec. 361, as to previous rule. Gleason v. Chester,

1 Day, 152; Hubbard v. Shaler, 2 Day, 195.
[46] Sherrill v. Shuford, 10 Ired. (N. C.) 200.
[47] Parks v. Alexander, 7 Ired. (N. C.) 412; The State v. Edwards, 10 Ired. 242.

§ 551. Failure to arrest.

Where the sheriff fails to take the debtor's body on execution, he may show in mitigation of damages the insolvency of the debtor.[48]   The actual loss must be proved.[49]   Where a constable, having received a writ, with directions to arrest the defendant named in it, returned it unexecuted, under a mistaken idea that he was entitled to indemnity, and the defendant remained publicly living in the State for some months, and the plaintiff might have issued another writ and arrested him, it was held, in Vermont, that these facts should have been submitted to the jury in mitigation of damages.[50]

§ 552. Escape from arrest on execution.

* In England, a remedy was originally given by statute, in an action of debt against the sheriff for the escape of prisoners charged in execution; and this statute has been re-enacted to some extent in this country.   But under it no question could arise as to the measure of damages; for, the action being debt, and the provisions of the statute being peremptory, the officer was charged with the whole amount of the plaintiff's original claim, as ascertained by his judgment.   Our present inquiry is directed to the measure of damages in the action on the case, or in trespass.[51] **   And the only remedy that existed in England prior to the abolition of forms of action against a sheriff for escape on final process, was an action on the case for such damages as the plaintiff may have sustained by reason of such escape.[52]

* When a prisoner for debt makes an escape [53] (says Lord Kaims), "the creditor is hurt in his interest, but sustains no actual damage; for it is not certain that he could have recovered his money by detaining the debtor in prison, and it is possible he may yet recover it, notwithstanding the escape.   But it is undoubtedly a hurt or prejudice to be deprived of his expectation to obtain payment by the imprisonment; and the common

[48] Dinninny v. Fay, 38 Barb. (N. Y.) 18.

[49] *Alabama:* Pugh v. McRae, 2 Ala. 393.

    Canada: Chapman v. Doherty, 25 N. B. 271.

[50] Blodgett v. Brattleboro, 30 Vt. 579.

[51] Bonafous v. Walker, 2 T. R. 126; Rawson v. Dole, 2 Johns. 454.

[52] 5 & 6 Vict., chap. 98, § 31; Arden v. Goodacre, 11 C. B. 371.

[53] Prin. of Equity, book i, chap. iv, § 5, ed. of 1767, p. 159.

law gives reparation by making the negligent jailor liable for the debt, precisely as equity doth in similar cases. A messenger who neglects to put a caption in execution, affords another instance of the same kind." This appears, Lord Kaims observes, to be the infliction of uncertain consequential damage.**

§ 553. Value of custody the rule in England.

* In a case in England, the Court of Common Pleas said, that they had not been able to find any decision in which the rule as to the measure of damages was clearly defined. The principal case was one in which it was endeavored to reduce the liability of the sheriff by showing, where an escape from final process had taken place, that the plaintiff might, by diligence, have re-arrested or detained the defendant, and recovered his debt. But this was denied; and it was declared that the true measure of damages is the value of the custody of the debtor at the moment of the escape; [54] that if, at the time of the escape, the debtor had not the means of satisfying the judgment, the plaintiff loses only the security of the debtor's body, and the damage may be small. If, on the other hand, at the time of the escape, the debtor could pay, and has wasted his means since then, it being clear that the loss of the debt is owing to the sheriff's neglect, the jury would be justified in giving the full amount of the execution.[55]

But it is plain that this still leaves the whole subject at very loose ends. What is meant by the value of the security of the body of a debtor? Are his physical and mental qualifications to be gone into, and the chance of his subsequently acquiring property, to be estimated? Are the chances of his friends being induced or coerced, by reason of his imprisonment, into paying the debt, to be inquired of? Again, what can be more vague than, in a matter of this kind, to say that *"the damages may be small."* Nor, on the other hand, even if the debtor is solvent, is the liability of the sheriff to pay the debt declared as matter of law. It is simply said that the jury would be *"justified in giving the full amount of the execution."* And the question on whom the burden of proof as to the debtor's pecuniary condition falls, is not alluded to.**

[54] McRae *v.* Dunlop, 3 Russ. & Gel. (N. S.) 315.   [55] Arden *v.* Goodacre, 11 C. B. 371.

In a case in chancery, it was said that the burden was on the defendant to show that the loss was not the amount of the debt.[56] In a case in the English Common Pleas, it was held that the jury might, in estimating the value of the custody, consider "the value to the plaintiff of the chance that the debt, or any part of it, would have been extracted by the debtor's remaining in prison," and the fact of an offer of the debtor's solicitor, some time before his arrest, to pay a certain amount in composition of his debts.[57]

§ 554. American rule.

In this country there has been particularly in the older cases, a tendency to hold the sheriff responsible for the full amount of the execution.[57a] So in New York, where one was arrested on a precept of the surrogate's court for failure to account, and was suffered to escape, the measure of damages under the Code was held to be the sum awarded by the surrogate's decree, with interest, and the insolvency of the delinquent could not be shown in mitigation.[58] It has long been well understood and universally recognized in Vermont that an officer who holds penal process against a debtor upon whom he may serve it, but who omits to do so, or having once had an opportunity to arrest the debtor, neglects to do it, and the debtor afterwards absconds, becomes *fixed with the debt;* and, of course, no evidence as to the debtor's insolvency is admissible.[59] So, in the same State, in an action against the sheriff for the escape of the debtor from the liberties of the jail, he having taken insufficient security, the rule of damages is the amount of the debt.[60] So, in Connecticut, in the sheriff's action for an escape on the security taken by him for the jail liberties, the rule is the debt and costs on the execution with

[56] Moore *v.* Moore, 25 Beav. 8.

[57] Macrae *v.* Clarke, L. R. 1 C. P. 403.

[57a] *Connecticut:* Bowen *v.* Huntington, 3 Conn. 423.

Maryland: State *v.* Lawson, 4 Gill, 62.

Massachusetts: Whitehead *v.* Varnum, 14 Pick. 523.

New York: Barnes *v.* Willett, 35 Barb. 514; Renick *v.* Orser, 4 Bosw. 384; McCreery *v.* Willett, 4 Bosw. 643,

9 Bosw. 600. See, however, Kellogg *v.* Manro, 9 Johns. 300; Rawson *v.* Dole, 2 Johns. 454.

[58] Dunford *v.* Weaver, 84 N. Y. 445.

[59] Goodrich *v.* Starr, 18 Vt. 222.

[60] Wheeler *v.* Pettes, 21 Vt. 398. See, in the same State, Vilas *v.* Barker, 20 Vt. 603, an action against a sheriff for refusing to assign a jail bond to the creditor.

interest.[61] So it is held that if the marshal fail to bring in the body of the defendant on the return of the writ, he will be amerced in the full amount of the debt or damages and costs.[62] So, in North Carolina, where the remedy of debt is given by statute against the sheriff who shall wilfully or negligently suffer a debtor charged in execution to escape; it has been held that the sheriff is fixed with the debt.[63] Later cases, however, appear to have established the English rule in this country; and it is now generally agreed that the true measure of damages is the value of the custody at the moment of the escape. That value must depend on the circumstances of each case.[64] So in Georgia, in an action of debt upon the sheriff's official bond for an escape on mesne process, it has been held that the insolvency of the original debtor may be given in evidence by the defendant in mitigation of damages.[65] In Massachusetts, it was said in an early case that in actions of this kind, "It is peculiarly the right of the jury to assess the damages, and in this they are not restricted to any precise sum." [66] And so again, "that the jury have the subject of damages at their discretion." [67] But notwithstanding this general language, the rule was settled that the amount of the plaintiff's debt is, *prima facie*, the measure of damages;[68] that it was competent for the defendant to show, in mitigation of damages, any circumstances which go to prove that the plaintiff has, in truth, not suffered any actual injury from the loss complained of,[69] and that, on the other hand, it was competent, if the wrong be a wilful one, for the jury to give more than the actual loss.[70] But

[61] Seymour v. Harvey, 8 Conn. 63.
[62] Winter v. Simonton, 2 D. C. (2 Cr. C. C.) 585.
[63] Adams v. Turrentine, 8 Ired. 147.
[64] *Connecticut:* Swan v. Bridgeport, 70 Conn. 143, 39 Atl. 110.
Indiana: State v. Caldwell, 115 Ind. 6, 17 N. E. 185.
Pennsylvania: Shuler v. Garrison, 5 W. & S. 455.
[65] Crawford v. Andrews, 6 Ga. 244.
[66] Weld v. Bartlett, 10 Mass. 470, and Colby v. Sampson, 5 Mass. 310.
[67] Rich v. Bell, 16 Mass. 294. See, also, Burrell v. Lithgow, 2 Mass. 526.

[68] Young v. Hosmer, 11 Mass. 89; Porter v. Sayward, 7 Mass. 377, 5 Am. Dec. 50.
[69] Brooks v. Hoyt, 6 Pick. 468; Shakford v. Goodwin, 13 Mass. 187; Nye v. Smith, 11 Mass. 188.
[70] Weld v. Bartlett, 10 Mass. 470. Though in this case it was intimated that the limit of the discretion of the jury, even in case of wilful wrong, is merely "expenses and costs not taxable." See, also, Selfridge v. Lithgow, 2 Mass. 374.

in Chase v. Keyes,[71] an action on the case founded upon the statute giving the plaintiff "such damages as he shall have suffered," it was held that the plaintiff must prove his loss, and the measure of damages was not even *prima facie* the amount of the debt.

In accordance with this doctrine now well established, if a party is in custody on process for contempt, and is to be held in custody only till he pay a pecuniary fine, and is utterly insolvent, the damages must be merely nominal. If he is ordered to stand committed till he perform a specified act which he has the power to perform, the value of the custody must depend on the nature of the act, and the consequences to the aggrieved party of a failure to secure its performance.[72] In the case of Jenkins v. Troutman,[73] the court, while again recognizing the rule of mitigation already acquiesced in, in that State,[74] by allowing the defendant to show that the effect of his wrongful act was not so great because the escaped debtor could not pay the debt, or any part of it, rejected as irrelevant, proof that the defendant was "largely indebted," which was offered with a view to establish the probability that the debtor would, if arrested, have assigned his property to secure the payment of those debts, thereby diminishing the plaintiff's chances of satisfaction. So, in the case of Sherrill v. Shuford,[75] the court say: "The true inquiry is, has the defendant, by his negligence, deprived the plaintiff of any legal means of securing the payment of his debt? If he has, and the debtor had property which might by due process have been subject to it, he shall answer to the full amount of the debt." Where, however, a defendant is arrested by the sheriff, and gives bail, and is discharged, but the bail do not justify, the sheriff becomes bail, and is liable to the same extent to which the bail would have been had they justified. In such case, therefore, after the return of the execution unsatisfied, the sheriff is liable for the judgment and interest, and the insolvency of the judgment debtor will not go in mitigation of the damages.[76] In an action against a former

[71] 2 Gray, 214.
[72] Hootman v. Shriner, 15 Oh. St. 43.
[73] 7 Jones, L. 169.
[74] Murphy v. Troutman, 5 Jones, L. 379.

[75] 10 Ired. 200.
[76] Metcalf v. Stryker, 31 N. Y. 255; Bensel v. Lynch, 44 N. Y. 162.

sheriff, as for an escape, on the ground of his neglect to assign over at the end of his term to his successor in office a debtor taken in execution, who is on the jail limits, the plaintiff's omission to cause the prisoner to be retaken, by issuing a new execution, may be considered in mitigation of the damages.[77] Where after an escape the sheriff rearrests the judgment debtor and holds him on the old execution, the plaintiff can recover only such expenses as the escape caused him.[78]

§ 554a. Escape from arrest on mesne process.

Whatever be the rule adopted in case of escape from arrest on execution, where the arrest was upon mesne process the actual damages must be proved, and the amount of a judgment subsequently recovered or of the damages named in the writ is at most only a *prima facie* measure of damages. Even in New York, where the liability for escape on execution is most stringent, the actual damages only can be recovered where the arrest was on mesne process;[79] and the same rule prevails elsewhere. So, in Arkansas, it has been held, that in actions for escape from mesne process, the presumption is that the plaintiff lost the entire debt by the escape; and the measure of damages against the officer is the amount of the original debt; but the defendant is at liberty to prove in mitigation of damages that the debt could not have been made out of the debtor,[80] and the same is the rule in Maryland.[81] So, in North Carolina, in debt, on a sheriff's bond for an escape, where the sheriff's return was, "The defendant arrested; signed the appearance bond; refused to give surety; and·made his escape by jumping on his horse and running, there being no one present to assist," the measure of damages was recently held to be, not the debt and interest, but such actual damages as the plaintiff had sustained.[82] It follows from this general rule that the plaintiff in order to recover must show the validity of the debt;[83]

---

[77] French v. Willet, 10 Bosw. 566.
[78] State v. Newcomer, 109 Ind. 243; State v. Caldwell, 115 Ind. 6.
[79] Potter v. Lansing, 1 Johns. 215, 3 Am. Dec. 310; Patterson v. Westervelt, 17 Wend. 543; Russell v. Turner, 7

Johns. 189, 5 Am. Dec. 254; Latham v. Westervelt, 26 Barb. 256.
[80] Faulkner v. Bartley, 6 Ark. 150.
[81] State v. Baden, 11 Md. 317.
[82] State v. Falls, 63 N. C. 188.
[83] Lewis v. Morland, 2 B. & Ald. 56; Scott v. Henley, 1 M. & Rob. 227.

and if it was outlawed he can recover only nominal damages.[84]

§ 555. Insufficient bail or surety.

In an action on the case, brought against a sheriff for not taking sufficient bail, the principal debtor being sued to judgment and the execution returned unsatisfied, this language was held: "Although the amount of the judgment is *prima facie* evidence of the measure of damages, yet this may be controlled by evidence showing the entire inability of the debtor to pay, and the actual injury therefrom to be less than the amount of the judgment against him." And although the principal debtors had left the State, and could not be found on the execution, evidence as to their poverty was held admissible, the court saying: "The fact that the principal debtors were out of the commonwealth, and could not be arrested on execution, may be important in its bearing upon the amount of damages sustained by the default of the sheriff, but it does not affect the general rule of damages, or the competency of evidence tending to show the entire inability of the debtor to satisfy the demand. In all actions on the case, the question is, what is the amount of damages sustained?" [85] So in an action on the case against the sheriff, for taking insufficient bail, it is competent for the defendant to prove, in mitigation of damages, the inability of the original debtor to pay the judgment which has been obtained against him in the suit upon which he was arrested. The true measure of damages is the injury actually sustained by the judgment creditor; and, therefore, evidence tending to show that the debtor was poor or insolvent, so that his arrest on execution would not have enabled the creditor to realize his debt, also tends to prove that the plaintiff suffered no essential injury by the negligence of the officer.[86] It is a general principle that, in an action against a sheriff for taking insufficient sureties, no more can be recovered against him than the party

---

[84] Slocum *v.* Riley, 145 Mass. 370, 14 N. E. 174.

[85] West *v.* Rice, 9 Met. (Mass.) 564.

[86] Danforth *v.* Pratt, 9 Cush. (Mass.) 318. *Contra,* Gerrish *v.* Edson, 1 N. H. 82; Jones *v.* Blair, 4 McCord (S.C.) 281.

The measure of damages is the full amount of the debt where there is no evidence of the debtor's insolvency. Crane *v.* Warner, 14 Vt. 40, 39 Am. Dec. 205.

could have recovered against sufficient sureties.[87] And in an action against the sheriff for taking insufficient sureties in replevin, the assignee of the replevin bond cannot recover as special damage, beyond the limits of the bond, the expenses of a fruitless action against the pledgees, unless he gave the sheriff notice of his intention to sue them.[88]

Where the sheriff took an informal replevin bond, and the defendant in replevin had judgment for a return, the measure of his damages in an action against the sheriff is the value of the goods at the time of taking, with interest;[89] and he may also recover the costs and expenses of the replevin suit, and of a fruitless action on the bond; but his recovery is limited to the penalty of the bond.[90] But if the goods were the property of the plaintiff in replevin, and the defendant in replevin had no right to a return, he can recover only nominal damages from the sheriff.[91]

§ 556. Failure to return.

For failure to return an execution, the measure of damages is the actual loss sustained,[92] which is *prima facie* the amount of the execution.[93]

In an action brought against a sheriff for neglecting to return a *fi. fa.*, an omission of duty for which the Revised Statutes of

[87] *Massachusetts:* Carter v. Duggan, 144 Mass. 32, 10 N. E. 486.
Missouri: Mortland v. Smith, 32 Mo. 225, 82 Am. Dec. 128.
England: Yea v. Lethbridge, 4 T. R. 433; Evans v. Brander, 2 H. Bl. 547. By this case, Concanen v. Lethbridge, 2 H. Bl. 36, was overruled. See, also, Jeffery v. Bastard, 4 A. & E. 823.
[88] Baker v. Garratt, 3 Bing. 56. See Gibbs v. Bull, 20 Johns. 212, a suit for taking insufficient pledges in replevin.
[89] O'Grady v. Keyes, 1 All. (Mass.) 284.
[90] Norman v. Hope, 13 Ont. 556, 14 Ont. 287.
[91] Case v. Babbitt, 16 Gray (Mass.), 278.
[92] *Kentucky:* Williams v. Hall, 2 Dana, 97; Shippen v. Curry, 3 Met. 184; Hill v. Turner, 3 Bush, 27, 96 Am.

Dec. 192, n. See O'Bannon v. Huffman, 1 B. Mon. 212.
Maine: Ware v. Fowler, 14 Me. 183.
Massachusetts: Waterhouse v. Waite, 11 Mass. 207.
New Hampshire: Grafton Bank v. White, 17 N. H. 389.
Texas: Hamilton v. Ward, 4 Tex. 356.
Vermont: Woolcott v. Gray, Brayt. 91; Hamilton v. Marsh, 2 Tyler, 403.
Contra, Alabama: Reid v. Dunklin, 5 Ala. 205.
Mississippi: Helm v. Gridley, Walk. 511.
[93] *Michigan:* Dunphy v. Whipple, 25 Mich. 10.
New York: Smith v. Geraty, 112 N. Y. Supp. 1100, 61 Misc. 101.
Texas: Smith v. Perry, 18 Tex. 510, 70 Am. Dec. 295.

New York declared that the officer shall be liable for *the damages sustained* by any party aggrieved, the measure of damages was held to be the amount of the execution, subject, however, to mitigation upon showing that the whole or any part of it could not be collected.[94] For refusal to hand over a bail bond, the measure of damages is the amount the bail must pay, which might be reduced by proof of the insolvency of the bail,[95] but not of the debtor.[96] For failure to return an order of sale of mortgaged property, the measure of damages is the actual value of the property.[97] For failure to hand over to the plaintiff in replevin the goods replevied, the measure of damages would ordinarily be the value of the goods; but the defendant may show that the plaintiff was not in fact entitled to the goods.[98] For failure to produce either attached property or the receipt he had taken for it, the sheriff is holder for the value of the property as returned in the writ.[99]

§ 557. False return.

For a false return of *nulla bona*, the measure of damages is the value of the property which the plaintiff would have been enabled to apply in satisfaction of the execution.[100] Where there is property enough to satisfy the amount directed to be collected on the execution, that amount, with interest, is the measure. The sheriff may show, in mitigation, that there was not property enough to satisfy the demand, or that it would have been absorbed by prior executions, but not that the amount directed to be levied was not due on the judgment.[101] In Ireland, for a false return of *non est inventus*, the analogy of escapes was followed, and the value of the custody was said to be the rule.[102] And in Beckford *v.* Montague,[103] case for a false

[94] Ledyard *v.* Jones, 7 N. Y. 550, modifying or confirming the earlier cases; Hinman *v.* Borden, 10 Wend. 367, 25 Am. Dec. 568; Stevens *v.* Rowe, 3 Den. 327; Persons *v.* Parker, 3 Barb. 249; Dolson *v.* Saxton, 11 Hun, 565.
[95] Bradt *v.* Holden, 12 R. I. 335.
[96] Seeley *v.* Brown, 14 Pick. 177; Bradt *v.* Holden, 12 R. I. 335.
[97] Boyd *v.* Desmond, 79 Cal. 250.
[98] Robinson *v.* Shirreff, 25 N. B. 68.
[99] Allen *v.* Doyle, 33 Me. 420.

[100] *Maine:* Thayer *v.* Roberts, 44 Me. 247.
England: Mullett *v.* Challis, 16 Q. B. 239, 2 Eng. L. & Eq. 260.
[101] *New York:* Bacon *v.* Cropsey, 7 N. Y. 195.
Pennsylaania: Forsyth *v.* Dickson, 1 Grant, 26.
[102] Cahill *v.* Verner, 2 Ir. C. L. 549.
[103] 2 Esp. 475; see also White *v.* Jones, 5 Esp. 160.

return of mesne process, the original defendant being still within the reach of process, Lord Kenyon told the jury that they were not called on to give the plaintiff the whole extent of the debt, if the original debtor was still solvent. In Massachusetts, where a sheriff returned to the original writ that he had taken bail, and then refused to deliver the bail-bond, the fact being that no bail had been taken, he was not permitted to show in mitigation that the original defendant was insolvent.[104] Pelham v. Way [105] was an action against a United States marshal for a false return, in returning that he had taken a note. In fact he had not taken the note, but had sold the debt of which the note was evidence. It was held that the plaintiff could only recover nominal damages, for the sale of the debt had not injured him, as it did not extinguish the note or the debt, for the libel under which the return was made was not against the debt. Where suit is brought against a sheriff for a false return of *nulla bona* to an execution, it seems that an inquisition finding the property out of the original defendant is a bar to the action; but in a suit against the officer in trespass by the true owner, an inquisition finding the other way is only to be received in mitigation.[106]

§ 558. Miscellaneous breaches of duty.

It is held in Indiana, that, on a sale of land in execution, the sheriff is bound to tender a deed to the purchaser; and where, without doing so, he resells for omission of the purchaser to pay the purchase-money, the sheriff is himself liable to the execution defendant for the amount of the difference between the two sales.[107] Where a sheriff, without the direction of the creditors, made sales of property on credit, on some of which sales he received interest before the return day of the executions, and on others, the purchasers proved insolvent, he was

[104] Simmons v. Bradford, 15 Mass. 82. In Indiana, by statute, in case of a false return to a writ of *fieri facias*, the constable and his sureties are liable on the bond for the full amount which the officer might have collected and paid over, with interest and ten per cent damages. R. S. 1881, § 784; Limpus v. The State, 7 Blackf. 43.

[105] 15 Wall. 196, 21 L. ed. 55.

[106] *New York:* Bayley v. Bates, 8 Johns. 185; Townsend v. Phillips, 10 Johns. 98.
England: Farr v. Newman, 4 T. R. 621, 633, 648; Roberts v. Thomas, 6 T. R. 88; Wells v. Pickman, 7 T. R. 174, 177.

[107] State v. Lines, 4 Ind. 351.

held bound to account to the creditors, on the executions, to the full amount of the sales, but not for the interest.[108] And where the sheriff having levied on sufficient property, it is wrongfully replevied, and he without excuse neglects to prosecute the sureties in the replevin bond, he will not be allowed his expenses in the replevin suit, though they are within the terms of the bond to indemnify him.[109] In an action against a sheriff, by the surety of a defendant in an elder execution, for applying the proceeds of such defendant's property upon a junior execution, whereby such surety's property was taken upon the elder, the officer is only liable for so much of the surety's property as sold for the sum so misapplied.[110]

§ 559. Magistrate.

Where a judicial officer is acting ministerially, he is liable for the damage directly resulting from his negligence. In such case, the rules of liability and mitigation are the same with those applicable to ministerial officers. And a magistrate liable for the damages directly resulting from his negligence in issuing an irregular or invalid execution, may, in an action brought for the recovery of such damage, show that the judgment debtor had no property, and that the debt could not have been collected on a valid execution.[111] And the same decision was reached in an action against a justice of the peace for neglecting to issue an execution.[112] In California, where, because of a defect in a notary's certificate of acknowledgment to a mortgage, it was held not to import notice to subsequent incumbrancers, and the lien of the plaintiff's mortgage was in consequence postponed to that of a later one, and his debt thereby lost, in an action by the mortgagee against the notary on his official bond, the plaintiff was held entitled to recover the mortgage debt and interest.[113]

[108] Chase v. Monroe, 30 N. H. 427.

[109] Swezey v. Lott, 21 N. Y. 481, 78 Am. Dec. 160.
   In an action against a sheriff for unauthorized release of the attached property, he may show that prior attachments were sufficient to exhaust the property. Lowenberg v. Jeffries, 74 Fed. 385.

[110] Staton v. Com., 2 Dana (Ky.), 397.

[111] Noxon v. Hill, 2 All. (Mass.) 215.

[112] Carpenter v. Warner, 38 Oh. St. 416; Gaylor v. Hunt, 23 Oh. St. 255.

[113] Fogarty v. Finlay, 10 Cal. 239. It should be mentioned that by statute the notary was liable on his official bond to parties injured by his official misconduct for "all damages sustained."

§ 559a. Clerk of court.

In Baltimore and Ohio Railroad *v.* Weedon [114] the action was against a clerk of court for failure to issue process to review a judgment against plaintiff. The measure of damages was held to be the amount of the judgment unless the officer could reduce it as by showing that the plaintiff must have been defeated in any case. In an action against prothonotary for negligence in issuing a writ, where he failed to inspect the record of plaintiff's judgment and the writ issued did not conform to it in every particular, in consequence of which part of the claim was lost, the measure of damages is the amount of the claim thus lost. [115]

§ 559b. Receiver.

Where a receiver takes goods wrongfully, but in *bona fide* exercise of the power conferred upon him by the court, he is not liable for damages to the owner, whose remedy lies in an application to the court. [116] If the applicant for the appointment of a receiver gave a bond, action will lie upon the bond for the entire damages caused by the receiver and chargeable to such applicant. [117]

§ 560. County clerk.

In an action in New York against a county clerk, who, by statute in that State (Laws 1853, ch. 142), was made liable for all damages for mistakes in searches made by him in his office, it appeared that in a search made by him at the request of an attorney who had been employed to examine the title to a house and lot belonging to the plaintiff's intestate, and paid by the plaintiff, a judgment of about twenty-seven dollars, which was a lien on the premises, had been omitted. The examination of the title was made for the purpose of procuring a loan by mortgage on the property. The money was obtained and applied, as far as necessary, to the satisfaction of such liens as were returned on the search. It was more than enough to satisfy them

---

[114] 78 Fed. 584, 47 U. S. App. 360, 24 C. C. A. 249. See Cohen *v.* Marchant, 1 Disney (Ohio), 113.

[115] Wilson *v.* Arnold, 172 Pa. 264, 33 Atl. 552.

[116] Tapscott *v.* Lyon, 103 Cal. 297, 37 Pac. 225.

[117] Haverly *v.* Elliott, 39 Neb. 201, 57 N. W. 1010.

and also the omitted judgment. The premises, which were worth $6,000, were afterwards sold on an execution on that judgment, and were bought in by the plaintiff in the execution for $60. By a compromise arrangement, in consideration of $400, he conveyed the premises to the plaintiff as executor and trustee of the deceased owner. In a judgment, which was affirmed by the Court of Appeals, the county clerk was held not responsible for the loss sustained, as it was directly caused by the non-payment of the judgment, and not by his omission.[118]

§ 561. Treasurer.

In McHaney v. Trustees,[119] it appeared that a note with two sureties came into the hands of the defendant as county treasurer. The principal died. In an action on his official bond for his failure to present the note for payment against the estate, it was held that, as there was no evidence to show that, if it had been presented, it would have been paid, or that the sureties were insolvent, only nominal damages could be recovered.

§ 562. Town officers.

In an action against the supervisors of a town for refusing to place on the tax list two judgments recovered against the town, evidence was admitted to show that, subsequently to the commencement of this action, one of the judgments had been placed on the tax list, and it was held that, such being the case, the defendants were not liable for the whole amount of the plaintiff's judgments. It was also said that, such being the case, it was proper to instruct the jury that the plaintiff could only recover nominal damages where he failed to show any special injury, Clifford, J., dissenting, and holding that the plaintiff was entitled to recover the actual damage sustained in view of the whole evidence.[120] In such an action a plaintiff can recover the expenses incurred in the employment of counsel.[121] In an action against the supervisor of a town for refusing to present to the board of supervisors of the county a reassessment of damages in the plaintiff's favor, the plaintiff can

[118] Kimball v. Connolly, 3 Keyes (N. Y.), 57, 2 Abb. App. 504.
[119] 68 Ill. 140.

[120] Dow v. Humbert, 91 U. S. 294, 23 L. ed. 368.
[121] Newark Savings Inst. v. Panhorst, 7 Biss. 99.

recover the amount of the reassessment, with interest, and he can recover the full interest, although he might have gone before another board and thus reduced the damage, the court saying, that he was not obliged to go before another board.[122]

In an action against a collector of taxes for a wrongful sale of the property for taxes, the amount recovered by the amount of the tax validly paid from the proceeds of the sale,[123] and if the plaintiff bid in the goods, his recovery is restricted to the amount he paid for them.[124] So, where it was made the duty of a town by statute to make good to a purchaser of land at a tax sale all damages by reason of the collector's neglect, in an action for such neglect, the measure was held to be, not the value of the land, but the amount paid and interest.[125] Where selectmen wrongfully but in good faith refused to allow plaintiff to vote, exemplary damages were refused.[126] Where a town clerk inadvertently gave a defendant a false certificate, attested as a copy of record, in order to support his plea of infancy, by reason of which the plaintiff was obliged to obtain a continuance of his cause to the next term, prior to which the debtor died,— it was holden that the town clerk was liable to pay the plaintiff the damages occasioned by the delay and continuance of the action.[127]

§ 563. Collector of customs.

In an action against a collector of customs, for refusing to sign a bill of entry for landing a cargo of foreign wheat, in consequence of which the plaintiff was obliged to pay duty on it when, in fact, no duty was by law payable, the proper measure of damages has been held, by the King's Bench in England, to be, not merely the amount of duties paid, but the amount of loss sustained by the plaintiff in consequence of a subsequent fall in the price of the article.[128]

In an action by the United States against a collector on his official bond, for not returning paid treasury notes to the proper department at Washington, it has been held that the rule of

[122] Clark v. Miller, 54 N. Y. 528.
[123] Maul v. Drexel, 55 Neb. 446, 76 N. W. 163.
[124] Hurlburt v. Green, 41 Vt. 490.
[125] Saulters v. Victory, 35 Vt. 351.
[126] Pierce v. Getchell, 76 Me. 216.
[127] Maxwell v. Pike, 2 Me. 8.
[128] Barrow v. Arnaud, 8 Q. B. 595, 10 Jur. 319.

damages would be the amount of the notes, unless it was shown that they were cancelled, and that the United States had suffered, or was likely to suffer, less than their amount; and that the jury were to take into consideration the amount of damage, from the risk of the notes getting into circulation again; from the delay and inconvenience in obtaining vouchers to settle the accounts; and from the want of evidence at the department that the notes had been redeemed.[129] Where trespass was brought against the collector of customs for New York [130] for illegally seizing the plaintiff's vessel, it appeared that she was seized on the 2d of October, 1801, and retained in custody till the 25th August, 1802, when she was restored. Six months before the seizure, the plaintiff had purchased her for $12,474; and the day previous to the trespass, he made a contract to sell her for $9,500. On the 2d September, 1802, eight days after her restoration, she was finally sold at public sale for $4,288; the plaintiff claimed the sum of $9,500 (the contract price), with interest and marshal's fees deducting the price actually obtained at the sale, $4,288; and this was held right by the Supreme Court of New York. This recognizes the principle that where an actual bargain is interfered with by the defendant's tortious act, he shall be made responsible for the loss sustained. It is not a case of mere contingent damages or speculative profits; it is an actual contract broken up by an unauthorized act.

§ 563a. Notary.

In an action against a notary, for failing to give notice of the dishonor of paper, according to his undertaking, the measure of damages must be the injury sustained by the neglect; in estimating which, the solvency of the party to whom notice should have been given, is a material element.[131] And where a notary falsely certified the acknowledgment of a mortgage, the measure of damages is the value of the security that would have been given by the mortgage, considering the value of the property and the amount of prior liens on it, not exceeding the amount of the mortgage debt.[132]

---

[129] U. S. v. Morgan, 11 How. 154, 13 L. ed. 643.

[130] Woodham v. Gelston, 1 Johns. (N. Y.) 134.

[131] Bank of Mobile v. Marston, 7 Ala. 108.

[132] Mahoney v. Dixon, 31 Mont. 107, 77 Pac. 519.

§ 563b. Other officers.

Where a letter was sent by the managers of a lottery to a vendor of tickets, enclosing a prize list, or statement of the drawing, which the postmaster unlawfully refused to deliver to such vendor, but delivered it to another, who, availing himself of the information it contained, purchased of such vendor a ticket which had drawn a prize,—the injury was holden to be the immediate consequence of such unlawful withholding of the letter, and consequently the true measure of damages would be the net amount of the prize.[133] And where a military officer wrongfully seized liquor supposed to be in the Indian country when in fact it was not, the measure of damages was the difference in value of the property at the time and place where it was seized and at the time and place where it was returned to the plaintiff.[134]

§ 564. Trespass by officer.

* We have been examining cases where the public officer is charged with neglect in not executing process confided to him. There is another large class of cases, where the complaint is that he has overstepped his powers, and abused the process of the court. In these cases we shall find, that where the acts of public officers are illegal, they are very narrowly watched, and often, by the infliction of vindictive damages, severely punished for the abuse of their trust; so, where trespass was brought for breaking and entering the plaintiff's house, and taking his goods, it appearing that judgment had been obtained in a court of local jurisdiction, and that execution was illegally levied on property of the plaintiff *out* of the jurisdiction, it was held that the plaintiff was entitled to recover the amount paid by him to release the levy. It was insisted that, as the plaintiff clearly owed the debt, this rule could not apply. But Lord Denman, C. J., said: "A person who takes upon himself to extort money by an authority which he does not possess, must repay the money which he raises thereby." And Patterson, J., said: "I am afraid of admitting the principle contended for, that where money has been extorted by means of an illegal authority,

[133] Bishop *v.* Williamson, 11 Me. 495.   [134] Bates *v.* Clark, 95 U. S. 204, 24 L. ed. 471.

the measure of damages is to be merely the amount of injury actually sustained." [135] ** Where the sheriff unlawfully and maliciously executed a search warrant, it was held that the plaintiff might recover for his sense of humiliation.[136]

* So, in a case, where the defendants, under color of process, illegally broke into the plaintiff's house to levy an execution, and the plaintiff paid the amount due on the writ, under protest, to induce the defendants to withdraw, the jury gave the amount so paid and £500 besides, as damages; a motion was made to reduce the damages; but the court said: "The trespasses were of a very serious nature, having been committed by officers of the law, under color of the law, breaking open the outer door with great violence. Such conduct is calculated to lead to dangerous conflicts; and the proper amount of damages must depend so much on the general circumstances, that it is very difficult to discover any standard by which to measure the amount; much must be left to the discretion of the jury." [137] So, in an action of trespass *de bonis asportatis*, for an illegal levy, it was held, "that the jury might give vindictive damages, if they should find that the trespass was committed maliciously, and in a wanton and aggravated manner, and with a design to vex and injure the plaintiff." [138] **

But exemplary damages can, of course, only be given for aggravated trespass; where there are no circumstances of aggravation compensatory damages only can be given.[139] And in such a case no damages can be recovered for mental anguish and humiliation.[140]

[135] Sowell *v.* Champion, 2 Nev. & P. 627, 6 A. & E. 407; *acc.,* Von Storch *v.* Winslow, 13 R. I. 23, 43 Am. Rep. 10.

[136] Melcher *v.* Scruggs, 72 Mo. 406.

[137] Duke of Brunswick *v.* Slowman, 8 C. B. 317.

[138] *Connecticut:* Huntley *v.* Bacon, 15 Conn. 267, 273.

Missouri: Central C. & L. Co. *v.* Welborn, 134 S. W. 2.

Texas: Rodgers *v.* Ferguson, 32 Tex. 533, 36 Tex. 544, 14 Am. Rep. 380; Railey *v.* Hopkins (Tex. Civ. App.), 131 S. W. 624.

[139] *California:* Van Pelt *v.* Littler, 14 Cal. 194; Spooner *v.* Cady 44 Pac. 1018.

Louisiana: Hollingsworth *v.* Atkins, 46 La. Ann. 515, 15 So. 77.

Nebraska: Murray *v.* Mace, 41 Neb. 60, 59 N. W. 387.

New Hampshire: Moore *v.* Bowman, 47 N. H. 494.

Pennsylvania: Rose *v.* Story, 1 Pa. 190, 44 Am. Dec. 121.

Utah: Marks *v.* Culmer, 6 Utah, 419, 24 Pac. 528.

[140] *Iowa:* Tisdale *v.* Major, 106 Ia. 1, 75 N. W. 663, 68 Am. St. Rep. 263.

Nothing can be recovered for the expense of defending the attachment suit.[141]

§ 565. Wrongful attachment or levy of execution.

In an action for the illegal seizure of goods, if there be no circumstances of aggravation, the measure of damages is the value of the goods, with interest from the time of the taking to that of the trial.[142] So in Vermont, in an action brought against an officer who had attached the plaintiff's goods, it has been said: "That no case can be found where damages have been given for trespass to *personal property*, when no unlawful intent or disturbance of a right or possession is shown, and where not only all *probable* but all *possible* damage is expressly disproved."[143] So, in an action on the sheriff's official bond, for the conversion of notes taken by him for property sold on partition, the measure is the value of the notes.[144] This value cannot be reduced

Nebraska: Murray *v.* Mace, 41 Neb. 60, 59 N. W. 387.

New Hampshire: Ahearn *v.* Connell, 72 N. H. 238, 56 Atl. 189.

North Carolina: Chappell *v.* Ellis, 123 N. C. 259, 31 S. E. 709.

Texas: Trawick *v.* Martin-Brown Co., 79 Tex. 460, 14 S. W. 564; Morris *v.* Wilford (Tex. Civ. App.), 70 S. W. 228; Ainsa *v.* Moses (Tex. Civ. App.), 100 S. W. 791.

Washington: Fish *v.* Nethercutt, 14 Wash. 582, 45 Pac. 44; McGill *v.* W. P. Fuller & Co., 45 Wash. 615, 88 Pac. 1038.

[141] Central C. & L. Co. *v.* Welborn, 134 S. W. 2. By statute in some jurisdictions such expense may be recovered from the plaintiff in the attachment suit. Talbott *v.* Great W. P. Co., 151 Mo. App. 538, 132 S. W. 15.

[142] *Alabama:* Ellis *v.* Allen, 80 Ala. 515, 2 So. 676.

Arkansas: Blass *v.* Lee, 55 Ark. 329, 18 S. W. 186; Perkins *v.* Ewan, 66 Ark. 175, 49 S. W. 569.

Colorado: Brasher *v.* Holtz, 12 Colo. 201; Cornforth *v.* Maguire, 12 Colo. 432.

Kansas: Dow *v.* Julien, 32 Kan. 576.

Maine: Smith *v.* Putney, 18 Me. 87.

Maryland: Wanamaker *v.* Bowes, 36 Md. 42.

Massachusetts: Mitchell *v.* Stetson, 7 Cush. 435.

Missouri: Walker *v.* Borland, 21 Mo. 289.

New York: Parker *v.* Conner, 44 N. Y. Super. Ct. 416.

Tennessee: Reeves *v.* John, 43 S. W. 134.

Texas: Erwin *v.* Bowman, 51 Tex. 513, 32 Am. Rep. 632; Willis *v.* Whitsitt, 67 Tex. 673; Willis *v.* McNatt, 75 Tex. 69, 12 S. W. 478; Richardson *v.* Jankofsky, 23 S. W. 815; Yarborough *v.* Weaver, 6 Tex. Civ. App. 215, 25 S. W. 468; Morris *v.* Williford (Tex. Civ. App.), 70 S. W. 228; Avindino *v.* Beck (Tex. Civ. App.), 73 S. W. 539; Railey *v.* Hopkins (Tex. Civ. App.), 131 S. W. 624.

Virginia: Crawford *v.* Jarrett, 2 Leigh, 630.

Wisconsin: Stanley *v.* Carey, 89 Wis. 410, 62 N. W. 188.

[143] Paul *v.* Slason, 22 Vt. 231, 54 Am. Dec. 75.

[144] Brobst *v.* Skillen, 16 Oh. St. 382, 88 Am. Dec. 456.

by showing that plaintiff bought the goods at a nominal price,[145] or that he had contemplated selling them at a low price,[146] nor can the plaintiff be limited to the price for which the officer sold the goods,[147] or to the invoice value.[148] But where plaintiff had sold the goods before the attachment, he could recover the price at which he had sold them.[149]

Where goods are illegally seized by the sheriff *in transitu*, the measure of damages is analogous to that in the case of a carrier failing to deliver, and is said to be their value at the place of destination, deducting the necessary expenses of transportation thither.[150] And where a sheriff, under color of an attachment, had seized the plaintiff's books of account and returned them as attached in a suit against another person, in consequence of which they were delivered to that person's receiver, who collected the accounts, the measure of damages was held to be the amount collected, with interest from the time of the collection.[151] Interest on the value of the property taken by the sheriff, from the time it was taken until its restitution, may be recovered;[152] and where there is no restitution, in accordance with the American doctrine as to interest, it should be added to the amount of the debt or the value of the property.[153]

A mortgagee or pledgee of personal property recovers the value of the goods taken, with interest, up to the amount of the mortgage or pledge.[154] In trespass brought by the assignee

---

[145] Beaman v. Stewart, 19 Colo. App. 222, 74 Pac. 342. But see Forsyth v. Palmer, 14 Pa. 96, 53 Am. Dec. 519.

[146] Estes v. Chesney, 54 Ark. 463, 16 S. W. 267.

[147] *Idaho:* Cowden v. Finney, 9 Ida. 619, 75 Pac. 765.

Pennsylvania: Rogers v. Fales, 5 Pa. 154.

[148] Reeves v. John (Tenn. Ch.), 43 S. W. 134.

[149] Curry v. Catlin, 12 Wash. 332, 41 Pac. 55.

[150] Eby v. Schumacher, 29 Pa. 40.

[151] Woodborne v. Scarborough, 20 Oh. St. 57.

[152] Beveridge v. Welch, 7 Wis. 465. So where money is garnished wrongfully, interest may be recovered as

damages. Biering v. Galveston First Nat. Bank, 69 Tex. 599, 7 S. W. 90. And where shares of stock were wrongfully attached, and dividends declared during the period of attachment were held up by the attachment, interest on the dividends was allowed. Jacobus v. Monongahela Nat. Bank, 35 Fed. 395.

[153] Hessing v. McClosky, 37 Ill. 341.

[154] *California:* Irwin v. McDowell, 91 Cal. 119, 27 Pac. 601.

Indiana: Slifer v. State, 114 Ind. 291; Collins v. Hutchinson, 3 Ind. App. 542, 30 N. E. 12.

Iowa: Crawford v. Nolan, 72 Ia. 763, 34 N. W. 754, 2 Am. St. Rep. 263.

Minnesota: Becker v. Dunham, 27 Minn. 32, 6 N. W. 406.

of a mortgage of personal property, against an officer for taking the property on an execution against the mortgagor, and holding it till the assignee paid the execution and officer's fees, the measure of damages is the amount paid and interest, besides a reasonable compensation for the taking and detention.[155] The mortgagor may recover for the wrongful attachment, but his damages for detention of the goods cannot be allowed after a foreclosure of the mortgage,[156] and the proceeds of the goods which were applied on the mortgage debt are to be deducted.[157]

§ 565a. Recovery of the goods or their proceeds.

Where the goods are returned, this fact can be shown in reduction of damages;[158] and in such case the measure of damages is their deterioration in value,[159] and the expense of bidding it in at the sale, repurchasing it, or otherwise securing a re-

Vermont: Chaffer *v.* Sherman, 26 Vt. 237.

But it is sometimes said that the sheriff is a stranger to the mortgagor's rights and cannot take advantage of them; and therefore that a mortgagee in possession at the time of the illegal attachment may recover the full value from the sheriff.

California: Dubois *v.* Spinks, 114 Cal. 289, 46 Pac. 95 (pledgee).

Michigan: Densmore *v.* Mathews, 58 Mich. 616, 26 N. W. 146.

[155] *Dakota:* Lander *v.* Propper, 6 Dak. 64, 50 N. W. 400.

New Hampshire: Carpenter *v.* Cummings, 40 N. H. 158.

[156] *Kentucky:* Gaar *v.* Lyons, 99 Ky. 672, 37 S. W. 73, 148.

Texas: Koyer *v.* White, 6 Tex. Civ. App. 381, 25 S. W. 46 (unless the wrongful attachment caused the foreclosure).

[157] Cooper *v.* Newman, 45 N. H. 339.

[158] *Arkansas:* Norman *v.* Fife, 61 Ark. 33, 31 S. W. 740.

North Carolina: Jones *v.* Alsbrook, 115 N. C. 46, 20 S. E. 170.

Pennsylvania: Graham *v.* McCreary, 40 Pa. 515.

Texas: Seal *v.* Holcomb (Tex. Civ. App.), 107 S. W. 916.

See Davis *v.* Gott, 130 Ky. 486, 113 S. W. 826.

The officer cannot insist on returning the goods to reduce the damages. Carpenter *v.* Dresser, 72 Me. 377, 39 Am. Rep. 337.

[159] *Arkansas:* Patton *v.* Garrett, 37 Ark. 605; Estes *v.* Chesney, 54 Ark. 463, 16 S. W. 267.

District of Columbia: Palmer *v.* Augenstein, 18 D. C. App. Cas. 511.

Georgia: Holton *v.* Taylor, 80 Ga. 508.

Illinois: MacVeagh *v.* Bailey, 29 Ill. App. 606; Smith *v.* Miller, 145 Ill. App. 606.

Iowa: Lowenstein *v.* Monroe, 55 Ia. 82; Chesmore *v.* Barker, 101 Ia. 576, 70 N. W. 701; Lord *v.* Wood, 120 Ia. 303, 94 N. W. 842.

Kansas: Sanford *v.* Willetts, 29 Kan. 647; Dow *v.* Julien, 32 Kan. 576; Dodson *v.* Cooper, 37 Kan. 346.

Nebraska: Schars *v.* Brand, 27 Neb. 94, 42 N. W. 906.

Texas: Girard *v.* Moore, 86 Tex. 675, 26 S. W. 945; Wilson *v.* Manning (Tex. Civ. App.), 35 S. W. 1079.

Wisconsin: Union Nat. Bank *v.* Cross, 100 Wis. 174, 79 N. W. 992.

turn,[160] together with compensation for loss of use of the goods during the period of detainer.[161] If the goods were sold by the sheriff and the proceeds applied to the satisfaction of the debt or judgment, the amount so applied will usually be deducted from the value,[162] but no allowance will be made for the expenses of the sale.[163] Attorneys' fees or other expenses of litigation for securing the return cannot be recovered.[164]

[160] *Alabama:* Fields v. Williams, 91 Ala. 502, 8 So. 808; Mitchell v. Corbin, 91 Ala. 599, 8 So. 810.

Georgia: Holton v. Taylor, 80 Ga. 508; Jones v. Lamon, 92 Ga. 529, 18 S. E. 423.

Kansas: Sanford v. Willetts, 29 Kan. 647; Dow v. Julien, 32 Kan. 576; Dodson v. Cooper, 37 Kan. 346.

New Hampshire: Felton v. Fuller, 35 N. H. 226.

New York: Baker v. Freeman, 9 Wend. 36; Clark v. Hallock, 16 Wend. 607.

Pennsylvania: McInroy v. Dyer, 47 Pa. 118; Kline v. McCandless, 139 Pa. 223, 20 Atl. 1045; Sensinger v. Boyer, 153 Pa. 628, 26 Atl. 222.

Texas: Munster v. Fields (Tex.), 33 S. W. 852; R. F. Scott Grocery Co. v. Kelly, 14 Tex. Civ. App. 136, 36 S. W. 140; Scott v. Childers (Tex. Civ. App.), 60 S. W. 775.

Where part of the property is rightly attached, and the remainder illegally attached, and the whole is repurchased by the owner, he may recover the proper proportion of the amount he paid. Blewett v. Miller, 131 Cal. 149, 63 Pac. 157. And where the property is bought in for the owner not with his money, but with the money of another, the amount cannot be shown in reduction, but the entire value of the property may be recovered. Rogers v. McDowell, 134 Pa. 424, 21 Atl. 166.

The right to repurchase the property and charge the wrongdoer with the amount paid must be exercised reasonably. One cannot fix the measure of his own damages by his voluntary act in paying money to recover back from

the execution purchaser the property sold. Duncan v. Matney, 29 Mo. 368.

[161] *United States:* Jacobus v. Monongahela Nat. Bank, 35 Fed. 395; Coulson v. Panhandle Nat. Bank, 54 Fed. 855, 13 U. S. App. 39, 4 C. C. A. 616.

Georgia: Jones v. Lamon, 92 Ga. 529, 18 S. E. 423.

Illinois: Smith v. Miller, 145 Ill. App. 606.

Iowa: Turner v. Younker, 76 Iowa, 258, 41 N. W. 10; Lord v. Wood, 120 Ia. 303, 94 N. W. 842.

Kansas: Adams v. Gillam, 53 Kan. 131, 36 Pac. 51.

Texas: R. F. Scott Grocery Co. v. Kelly, 14 Tex. Civ. App. 136, 36 S. W. 140.

Washington: McGill v. W. P. Fuller & Co., 45 Wash. 615, 88 Pac. 1038.

Wisconsin: Union Nat. Bank v. Cross, 100 Wis. 174, 79 N. W. 992.

[162] *Alabama:* Mitchell v. Corbin, 91 Ala. 599, 8 So. 810; Grisham v. Bodman, 111 Ala. 194, 20 So. 514.

Arkansas: Blass v. Lee, 55 Ark. 329, 18 S. W. 186; Norman v. Fife, 61 Ark. 33, 31 S. W. 740; Scanlan v. Guiling, 63 Ark. 540, 39 S. W. 713.

Louisiana: Fush v. Egan, 48 La. Ann. 60, 19 So. 108.

Texas: Avindino v. Beck (Tex. Civ. App.), 73 S. W. 539; Hillman v. Edwards (Tex. Civ. App.), 74 S. W. 787; Landes v. Eichelberger, 2 Tex. Civ. Cas. 127. But *contra*, where the goods were exempt. Wilson v. Manning (Tex. Civ. App.), 35 S. W. 1079.

[163] Perkins v. Ewan, 66 Ark. 175, 49 S. W. 569.

[164] *Kansas:* Adams v. Gillam, 53 Kan. 131, 36 Pac. 51.

§ 565b. Failure to keep safely the property taken.

In a suit against a sheriff for not safely keeping property attached on mesne process, if the owner is entitled to recover the value of the property seized, the damages could not be mitigated by deducting the expenses which would have necessarily attended the keeping, had it been kept safely.[165] And if the property is so carelessly kept that it suffers a deterioration in value, he is responsible for the amount of deterioration.[166] So where one had purchased certain premises on the foreclosure of a mortgage, executed to him by the occupants, and the sheriff neglected for two days to execute a writ of assistance, placed in his hands to put the purchaser in possession, and in the intervening time the occupants greatly injured the premises, the sheriff was held liable for the damage thus sustained. Called on to discharge a duty which the law enjoined of giving possession of property which could only be obtained through such official action by him, it was considered by the court just and legal that he should be held responsible to the full extent of the injury.[167] So, where through the negligence of the officer, a slave arrested by him for a criminal offence, escaped and was drowned, the damages recoverable by the plaintiff, who had but a life estate in the slave, was limited to the value of such estate.[168] In New York, it has been held that where the sheriff so negligently conducts himself in regard to personal property levied on that it is lost, and in consequence the real estate of the defendant is sold, and the security of a mortgage creditor is impaired, no action lies by such mortgage creditor against the sheriff, unless the conduct of the sheriff be explicitly

Texas: Yarborough v. Weaver, 6 Tex. Civ. App. 215, 25 S. W. 468; Lang v. Fritz (Tex. Civ. App.), 38 S. W. 233. *Contra* in *Louisiana:* State Bank v. Martin, 52 La. Ann. 1628, 28 So. 13.

[165] *Maine:* Lovejoy v. Hutchins, 23 Me. 272.

Massachusetts: Tyler v. Ulmer, 12 Mass. 163.

And see *New Hampshire:* Stevens v. Sabin, 20 N. H. 529.

The value of the property attached, as stated in the officer's return, and in a receipt taken for it, in the absence of all contradictory proof, may be taken as the true value of the property for which the officer is liable. Willard v. Whitney, 49 Maine, 235.

[166] *Alabama:* Vandiver v. Waller, 143 Ala. 411, 39 So. 136.

Michigan: Stilson v. Gibbs, 53 Mich. 280, 18 N. W. 815.

Wisconsin: Union Nat. Bank v. Cross, 100 Wis. 174, 79 N. W. 992.

[167] Chapman v. Thornburgh, 17 Cal. 87, 76 Am. Dec. 571.

[168] Tudor v. Lewis, 3 Met. (Ky.) 378.

charged to be *fraudulent and with intent* to diminish the security of the mortgage creditors.[169]

§ 565c. Consequential damages.

In an action against the sheriff for wrongful seizure of a stock of goods, their retail value cannot be given in evidence, as it includes profits.[170] Whether damages to the plaintiff's business from such seizure are to be taken into account is a question on which the authorities are at variance;[171] but loss of credit is too remote.[172] Damages may be recovered for detention of goods kept for sale until the season for sale is lost.[173] In an action of replevin against a sheriff, damages sustained from depositing a

[169] Bank of Rome v. Mott, 17 Wend. 554. See Yates v. Joyce, 11 Johns. 136.

[170] *Colorado:* Crymble v. Mulvaney, 21 Colo. 203, 40 Pac. 499.

Idaho: Sears v. Lydon, 5 Ida. 358, 49 Pac. 122.

Kansas: Bradley v. Borin, 53 Kan. 628, 36 Pac. 977 (at least when not alleged in the petition).

New Mexico: Cunningham v. Sugar, 9 N. Mex. 105, 49 Pac. 910.

[171] In the following cases damages were not allowed for injury to business: *California:* Nightingale v. Scannell, 18 Cal. 315.

Wisconsin: Union Nat. Bank v. Cross, 100 Wis. 174, 187, 79 N. W. 992.

In the following cases such damages were allowed:

Maryland: Moore v. Schultz, 31 Md. 418.

Michigan: McCausey v. Hock, 159 Mich. 570, 124 N. W. 570.

Nebraska: Meyer v. Fagan, 34 Neb. 184, 51 N. W. 753; Kyd v. Cook, 56 Neb. 71, 76 N. W. 524, 71 Am. St. Rep. 661.

New York: Kane v. Johnston, 9 Bosw. 154 (*semble*).

Texas: Deleshaw v. Edelen, 31 Tex. Civ. App. 416, 72 S. W. 413.

In McGill v. W. P. Fuller & Co., 45 Wash. 615, 88 Pac. 1038, damages for injury to business were refused because

the business was already disorganized and no damages were shown with sufficient certainty.

In Halcomb v. Stubblefield, 76 Tex. 310, 13 S. W. 231, the plaintiff was allowed to recover for loss of use of a mill which was caused by an attachment of the machinery.

Loss of profits, not from interruption of the business while it was interrupted but because of the effect of the attachment after resumption of the business, is too remote for recovery. Crymble v. Mulvaney, 21 Colo. 203, 40 Pac. 499. Therefore, where the attachment did not interrupt the business no damages can be recovered for loss of profits. Charles City Plow Co. v. Jones, 71 Ia. 234, 32 N. W. 280.

[172] *Colorado:* Crymble v. Mulvaney, 21 Colo. 203, 40 Pac. 499.

New Mexico: Cunningham v. Sugar, 9 N. M. 105, 49 Pac. 910.

Texas: R. F. Scott Grocery Co. v. Kelly, 14 Tex. Civ. App. 136, 36 S. W. 140; Neese v. Radford, 83 Tex. 585, 19 S. W. 141.

Wisconsin: Chicago Union Nat. Bank v. Cross, 100 Wis. 174, 75 N. W. 992.

Contra in *Nebraska:* Meyer v. Fagan, 34 Neb. 184, 51 N. W. 753; Kyd v. Cook, 56 Neb. 71, 76 N. W. 524, 71 Am. St. Rep. 661.

[173] Knapp v. Barnard, 78 Ia. 347.

sum of money with a third party to induce him to become surety in the replevin bond, are altogether too remote and consequential to be considered.[174] In Mississippi the damages for wrongful attachment are declared by statute to be attorney's fees, hotel bills, travelling expenses, loss of trade, and special injury to business. No allowance for counsel fee can be made except for defending the attachment suit, i. e., none for defending the main action, and no damage can be given for loss of trade where it appears that the parties were winding up their business, and none for credit where they were insolvent.[175] The sheriff has no ground for objection in an action against him for a wrongful attachment by his deputy, to an instruction to the jury that the plaintiff is entitled to recover the value of such property exempt from attachment as was attached and thereby wholly lost to him, with interest from the time of the attachment. And if the plaintiff thereby lost the temporary use only of such property, or of the property of other persons, to the use of which he was entitled, then he should recover for the injury from such loss of use. Where attached property was kept in the plaintiff's barn, it was held that if the custody of it had been such as wholly or partially to exclude him from the barn, he was entitled to indemnity for such loss of the use of the barn, so far as it was not occupied by the attached property. But where the plaintiff occupied such barn under a lease, in which he had covenanted to "spend or consume all the hay or other fodder on the premises" produced thereon during the term, he could not recover from the sheriff, who wrongfully executed an attachment obtained by the lessor, damages for being disabled from the fulfilment of this covenant, since the plaintiff could not be answerable to his lessor, who caused the attachment, for not performing the covenant.[176]

If other creditors are induced to attach by the wrongful act of the defendant, no damages can be recovered for the resulting harm.[177] And so where after the attachment a newspaper announced the failure of the plaintiff, whereupon a wholesale

---

[174] Wilson v. Hillhouse, 14 Ia. 199.
[175] Roach v. Brannon, 57 Miss. 490; Marqueeze v. Sontheimer, 59 Miss. 430; see Comer v. Mackintosh, 48 Mich. 374;

Neese v. Radford, 83 Tex. 585, 19 S. W. 141.
[176] Clapp v. Thomas, 7 All. 188.
[177] Goodbar v. Lindsley, 51 Ark. 380, 11 S. W. 577, 14 Am. St. Rep. 54.

dealer refused to forward goods to the plaintiff, it was held that the wrongful attachment was not the cause of this publication, and therefore the defendant was not responsible for the failure to get the goods.[178] In an action for the wrongful attachment of horse and wagon, plaintiff cannot recover the loss of corn in the field which he was unable to gather because he was deprived of the use of the horse and wagon; that was too remote.[179] Where an attachment was enjoined, but it nevertheless was issued, attorney's fees and costs incurred in the injunction proceedings cannot be recovered.[180]

A wife cannot recover for her husband's being thrown out of employment in her business, because of its interruption by the illegal attachment.[181]

§ 565d. Wrongful attachment of land or levy of execution.

An attachment of land, since it does not affect the possession or use of it, does not generally cause actual damages; [182] even if the value depreciates during the attachment, this cannot be recovered.[183] Nor can recovery be had for loss of a sale, where such sale is only contemplated,[184] as where a conditional offer was pending, but the plaintiff was not able to satisfy the condition.[185] Especially where the land was attached on a writ against a third party no damages can be recovered, since the attachment does not even cause a cloud on the title.[186]

Where the land was illegally sold on execution, the owner may waive the invalidity of the sale and recover the entire value of his interest in the land.[187]

---

[178] Tynberg v. Cohen (Tex. Civ. App.), 24 S. W. 314.

[179] Lang v. Fritz (Tex. Civ. App.), 38 S. W. 233.

[180] Neese v. Radford, 83 Tex. 585, 19 S. W. 141.

[181] Rains v. Herring, 68 Tex. 468, 5 S. W. 369.

[182] Adoue v. Wettermark, 36 Tex. Civ. App. 585, 82 S. W. 797.

[183] California: Heath v. Lent, 1 Cal. 410.

Iowa: Tisdale v. Major, 106 Iowa, 1, 75 N. W. 663, 68 Am. St. Rep. 263.

Louisiana: Brandon v. Allen, 28 La. Ann. 60.

Pennsylvania: Muldoon v. Rickey, 103 Pa. 110, 49 Am. Rep. 117.

Texas: Drew v. Ellis, 6 Tex. Civ. App. 507, 26 S. W. 95.

[184] Trawick v. Martin-Brown Co., 79 Tex. 460, 14 S. W. 564.

[185] Drew v. Ellis, 6 Tex. Civ. App. 507, 26 S. W. 95.

[186] Duncan v. Citizens' Nat. Bank, 20 Ky. L. Rep. 237, 45 S. W. 774.

[187] Pope v. Benster, 42 Neb. 304, 60 N. W. 561, 47 Am. St. Rep. 703.

§ 566. Suits between different officers.

* Questions of the kind we are now considering frequently arise in suits brought by one officer against another, to test the relative priority of different processes; and in such a case it has been said, in Vermont, that damages are never given beyond the actual value of the property.[188] **

§ 567. Receiptors.

* In some of the States of the Union, property, when levied on, is sometimes delivered by the attaching officer to a third party, called a receiptor, who holds it during the litigation, and promises to redeliver it to the officer on demand. In a case of this kind, in Vermont, the plaintiff, whose property had been unduly levied on, instead of that of the real debtor, brought his action of trespass, and, *pendente lite*, assigned his claim to the receiptor. Judgment was afterwards obtained and execution issued in the suits in which the attachment had been issued, and the officer demanded the property of the receiptor; but he refused to deliver it. It was held that the defendants, on the trial of the action of trespass, were not entitled to give in evidence, in mitigation of damages, such refusal on the part of the receiptor, they never having offered to surrender to him his receipt, or discharge him from his liability thereon;[189] and the same point has been similarly decided in Massachusetts.[190]

In another case of this kind, it has been decided in Vermont, that where the value of all the property attached and receipted for is expressed in the receipt at one entire sum, and a portion of it has been withdrawn from the custody of the receiptor, so as to discharge his liability, the damages in an action on the receipt are to be determined by assuming the whole value of the property receipted for to be the sum specified in their receipt, and by then ascertaining, on the basis of that assumed value, the just proportion which the property retained by the receiptor would bear to the property for which he is not liable.[191] **

---

[188] Goodrich v. Church, 20 Vt. 187.
[189] Ellis v. Howard, 17 Vt. 330.
[190] Robinson v. Mansfield, 13 Pick. 139.
[191] Parsons v. Strong, 13 Vt. 235, 37

Am. Dec. 592; Allen v. Carty, 19 Vt. 65, 46 Am. Dec. 177. In Connecticut, where the plaintiff, an officer who had, by virtue of an execution, levied on goods belonging to the judgment

So, in New Hampshire where property attached by the sheriff in two suits was delivered to a third party, who gave two receipts for it at the same value, which did not, however, state that one was subject to the other, and the receiptor, after judgment and execution, on a demand in the first suit, paid the amount due on the execution, it was held, after a subsequent judgment in the second suit against the owner, that the receiptor was liable to the officer only for the amount of the value receipted for over that paid in the first suit.[192] Where the receiptor has allowed the attached property to go into the owner's possession, and judgment is recovered against him, in an action by the officer on the receipt, the amount of the judgment and interest, with the fees on execution, not exceeding the value of the property, are the usual measure of damages.[193] But if, while the action is pending, the receiptor refuses to deliver the property to the officer, the latter may recover its full value, with interest from the demand.[194] Where, in an action of trover, the goods for the value of which the action was brought had been attached and delivered to the defendant on his receipt, and he had retained them, this was held no reason for reducing the damages below their value.[195] The valuation stated in the receipt is usually conclusive on the receiptor;[196] but where the goods were returned to the sheriff and sold by him for a less sum than that stated in the receipt, and he brought action, alleging that they were damaged, it was held that the valuation in the receipt was not conclusive, and the sheriff must prove the amount of his loss.[197] Where the property receipted for is an animal which dies in the receiptor's possession without his default, he is not liable for its value.[198]

debtor, and delivered them to the defendants on their receipt or promise to redeliver, which not being done, suit was brought; it was objected that, as it was not stated in the declaration that the officer was commanded, in the writ against the original debtor, to attach to any certain amount, the plaintiff could only recover nominal damages; but the Supreme Court held otherwise, and that the omission did not preclude the plaintiff from a recovery to the amount

of the execution. Jones v. Gilbert, 13 Conn. 507.
[192] Haynes v. Tenney, 45 N. H. 183.
[193] Foss v. Norris, 70 Me. 117.
[194] Clement v. Little, 42 N. H. 563.
[195] Luckey v. Roberts, 25 Conn. 486.
[196] Healy v. Hutchinson, 66 N. H. 316, 20 Atl. 332.
[197] Bancroft v. Parker, 13 Pick. 192.
[198] Shaw v. Laughton, 20 Me. 266.

§ 568. Illegal sale on execution.

Where a legal execution is levied upon property, but the sheriff's sale is for any reason illegal, the owner is entitled to compensation for the wrong thus done him. If the sale itself could not legally be made, the measure of damages is the value of the property, not at the time of the original attachment and levy but at the time of the sale.[199]   If, however, the sale was permitted, but irregularly conducted, as a result of which the goods were sold under their fair value, the sheriff is responsible for the difference between such value and the price realized at the sale.[200]

§ 569. Exclusion from office.

Where a public officer is wrongfully excluded from his office, the measure of damages is the amount of his salary during the period of exclusion,[201] deducting, however, if the defendant acted in apparent right and good faith, his reasonable expense in earning it.[202]   In United States v. Addison [203] it was contended that the rule requiring diligence in seeking employment ought to be extended to the case of a public officer wrongfully ousted from his office. But the court held that "no such rule can be applied to public offices of personal trust and confidence." Where, however, an officer wrongfully excluded from office brings mandamus for reinstatement, and is entitled after reinstatement to the entire salary, his damages in the writ of mandamus will be nominal only.[204]

[199] Walker v. Wilmarth, 37 Vt. 289.
[200] Daggett v. Adams, 1 Me. 198.
[201] *Kansas:* Rule v. Tait, 38 Kan. 765.
New York: People v. Nolan, 32 Hun, 612.
England: Arris v. Stukely, 2 Mod. 260.

[202] Mayfield v. Moore, 53 Ill. 428, 5 Am. Rep. 52.
[203] 6 Wall. 291, 18 L. ed. 919.
[204] Hill v. Fitzgerald, 193 Mass. 569, 79 N. E. 825.

CHAPTER XXV

ACTIONS FOR THE DEATH OF A HUMAN BEING

§ 570. No recovery for death at common law.[1]

* At common law, and independently of statutory provision, the death of a human being is not the ground of an action for damages.[2] In a case where the plaintiff brought an action against the proprietors of a stagecoach for negligent driving, by which his wife was killed, Lord Ellenborough said that, "in a civil court, the death of a human being cannot be complained of as an injury."[3] And so it has been held in Massachusetts, in a case where a widow sued a railroad company for negligence, by which her husband had been killed.[4]

In New York, in an action on the case [5] for negligently running over and killing the plaintiff's son, a lad of ten years of

---

[1] It is scarcely necessary to say that what is said here did not apply during the existence of slavery to an action for the death of a slave.

[2] Insurance Co. v. Brame, 95 U. S. 754, 24 L. ed. 580, and cases cited.

[3] Baker v. Bolton, 1 Camp. 493.

[4] Carey v. Berkshire R. R., 1 Cush. 475, 48 Am. Dec. 616.

[5] Ford v. Monroe, 20 Wend. 210.

age, the judge charged that the plaintiff was entitled to recover such sum by way of damages as they would be of the opinion the services of the child would have been worth, until he became twenty-one years of age. The case was carried up, but no question seems to have been distinctly made as to the correctness of this direction.[6] And in a subsequent case in the same State, where the plaintiff's infant child died within an hour and a half after the injury, Bronson, J., delivering the opinion of the Court of Appeals, said: "I have a strong impression that the father could recover nothing on account of the injury to the child, beyond the physician's bill and funeral expenses"; but the point was not decided.[7] ** It is, however, now well settled that no action will lie at common law for the tortious killing of a human being,[8] even for the payment of the funeral expenses,[9] or for loss of service.[10] The rule is the same in admiralty, in the absence of an Act of Congress or a State statute giving a right of action.[11] In Louisiana, however, a State governed by the civil law, an action will lie for pecuniary and other damages caused by death.[12]

But it seems that where there is a cause of action entirely independent of the act of killing, damages, at least pecuniary damages, may be recovered for death that proximately follows as a result of the injury. So where the defendant sold to the plaintiff tinned salmon, with the warranty that they were fit for food, and the plaintiff's wife was poisoned by eating the salmon and died, it was held in England that the husband in

---

[6] *Acc.*, Drew v. Sixth Ave. R. R., 26 N. Y. 49.

[7] Pack v. New York, 3 N. Y. 489.

[8] *Indiana:* Mayhew v. Burns, 103 Ind. 330, 2 N. E. 793.

Michigan: Hyatt v. Adams, 16 Mich. 179.

England: Osborn v. Gillett, L. R. 8 Ex. 88.

[9] Jackson v. Pittsburgh, C., C. & S. L. Ry., 140 Ind. 241, 39 N. E. 664, 49 Am. St. Rep. 192.

[10] Gulf, C. & S. F. Ry. v. Beall, 91 Tex. 310, 42 S. W. 1054.

[11] The Harrisburg, 119 U. S. 199, 30 L. ed. 358, 7 Sup. Ct. 140; Rundell v.

Compagnie Gen. Transatlantique, 100 Fed. 665, 40 C. C. A. 625; La Bourgogne, 117 Fed. 261. If such a statute exists, but no lien is expressly created by it, a libel *in rem* will not be entertained. The Corsair, 145 U. S. 335, 36 L. ed. 727, 12 Sup. Ct. 949. Whether a libel against the owners *in personam* will lie, *query*. *Ib.* 343, 347; *cf. Ex parte* McNiel, 13 Wall. 236, 20 L. ed. 624.

[12] McCubbin v. Hastings, 27 La. Ann. 713; LeBlanc v. Sweet, 107 La. 355, 31 So. 766, 90 Am. St. Rep. 303. See Rice v. Crescent City R. R., 51 La. Ann. 108, 24 So. 791.

an action for breach of warranty might recover for the loss of her services.[13]

§ 570a. Recovery for injury which finally results in death.

There may, of course, be an action at common law for an injury finally resulting in death, apart from any statute. Thus, a father may recover if the death was not instantaneous, for loss of service from the injury to the time of the death; [14] and a husband may maintain an action for the loss of his wife's services, caused by an injury done her by the defendant's malpractice, notwithstanding the injury resulted in her death; but the recovery should be only for the loss of her services between the injury and the death, and without including damages for her mental suffering; [15] and he may also recover for her funeral expenses.[16] So a father may recover for the medical expenses incurred by him on account of his minor child, injured by the defendant, between the injury and the death; [17] and an executor may recover the damage to the personal estate to the deceased by medical expenses and loss of time.[18]

§ 570b. Survival by statute of right of deceased.

In some States, by statute, actions for personal injuries survive to the representatives of the injured person, and in such cases the damages recoverable are those which the injured person could have recovered had he survived, being such dam-

---

[13] Jackson v. Walton, [1899] 2 K. B. 193. In a case in Massachusetts, however, in an action against a physician for breach of contract to render medical services to the plaintiff's wife, where the defendant's breach of contract resulted in the wife's death, the court, though allowing for the additional expenditures during her lifetime that resulted from the breach refused all damages for the death itself. Knowlton, C. J., said: "The decisions exclude, as a ground of recovery, all elements of damage which arise solely from death, and as to such damage they are applicable to actions of contract as to actions of tort." Sherlag v.

Kelley, 200 Mass. 232, 86 N. E. 293.

[14] *Arkansas:* Davis v. Ry., 53 Ark. 117, 13 S. W. 801, 7 L. R. A. 283 (no recovery for services after date of death).

Indiana: Pennsylvania Co. v. Lilly, 73 Ind. 252.

[15] Hyatt v. Adams, 16 Mich. 180.

[16] Philby v. Northern Pac. R. R., 46 Wash. 173, 89 Pac. 469, 9 L. R. A. (N. S.) 1193, and cases cited.

[17] Binford v. Johnston, 82 Ind. 431; Mayhew v. Burns, 103 Ind. 329, 2 N. E. 793.

[18] Bradshaw v. Lancashire & Y. Ry., L. R. 10 C. P. 189.

ages as he suffered up to the time of his death.[19]   In New Hampshire, in such an action, it is said that the administrator may recover for distress and anxiety of mind experienced by the deceased while in imminent danger, in view of impending death.[20]   Under the Kentucky statute, it is held that an appreciable interval must elapse between the injury and the death for the action to survive;[21] and the same interpretation is given to the statute in other jurisdictions.[22]   But in other States still this interpretation has been rejected, and recovery allowed though the death was instantaneous.[23]

In Michigan, the representative of the deceased may recover the amount decedent would have earned during the period of his expectancy of life, without deduction of the probable expense of living.[24]

[19] *Connecticut:* Goodsell v. Hartford & N. H. R. R., 33 Conn. 51.
Iowa: Muldowney v. Illinois C. Ry., 36 Ia. 462.
Massachusetts: Dickinson v. Boston, 188 Mass. 595, 75 N. E. 68.
Michigan: Oliver v. Houghton C. S. Ry., 134 Mich. 367, 96 N. W. 434; Davis v. Michigan Cent. R. R., 147 Mich. 479, 111 N. W. 76.
Montana: Beeler v. Butte & L. C. D. Co., 41 Mont. 465, 110 Pac. 528.
New Hampshire: Clark v. Manchester, 62 N. H. 577.
Tennessee: Freeman v. Illinois C. R. R., 107 Tenn. 340, 64 S. W. 1.
The same measure of damages prevails in Louisiana where action is brought by the representative of a deceased person (as it may there be brought without the aid of a statute) for a personal injury to the deceased. Payne v. Georgetown Lumber Co., 117 La. 893, 42 So. 475.
[20] Corliss v. Worcester, N. & R. R. R., 63 N. H. 404.
[21] Hansford v. Payne, 11 Bush (Ky.), 380.
[22] *United States:* The Corsair, 145 U. S. 335, 348, 36 L. ed. 727, 12 Sup. Ct. 949.
Massachusetts: Kearney v. Boston &

W. R. R., 9 Cush. 108; Hollenbeck v. Berkshire R. R., 9 Cush. 478; Kennedy v. Standard Sugar Refinery, 125 Mass. 90, 28 Am. Rep. 214; Moran v. Holling, 125 Mass. 93.
Mississippi: Illinois C. R. R. v. Pendergrass, 69 Miss. 425, 12 So. 954.
Montana: Dillon v. Great Northern Ry., 38 Mont. 485, 100 Pac. 960.
South Dakota: Belding v. Black Hills & Ft. P. R. R., 3 S. D. 369, 53 N. W. 750.
[23] *New Hampshire:* Clark v. Manchester, 62 N. H. 577.
Tennessee: Nashville & C. R. R. v. Prince, 2 Heisk. 580; Foulkes v. Nashville & D. R. R., 9 Heisk. 829.
Cf. Murphy v. New York & N. H. R. R., 30 Conn. 184; Broughel v. Southern N. E. Tel. Co., 72 Conn. 621, 45 Atl. 437, 49 L. R. A. 404.
Under a Tennessee statute giving damages for death to the next of kin (see § 571) and also for the mental and bodily suffering to the deceased, it has been said that even if the proof showed instantaneous 'death, it would still be a question for the jury whether some intermediate suffering was not caused. Western & A. R. R. v. Robinson, 61 Fed. 592, 601.
[24] Olivier v. Houghton C. S. Ry., 138

This action, allowed to survive by statute, exists independdently of, and in addition to, the action for death, commonly called Lord Campbell's Act.[25]

§ 571. Statutes.

* The remissness of the common law in this respect has been cured by various statutes. In England, the 9 & 10 Vict., c. 93, commonly known as Lord Campbell's act, provides, that whenever the death of a person shall be caused by a wrongful act, and which would, if death had not ensued, have entitled the party injured to maintain an action, the party offending shall be liable, notwithstanding the death. So, in Massachusetts,[26] if the life of any passenger is lost by the negligence, etc., of the proprietors of a railroad, etc., or of their servants, the proprietors shall be liable to a fine, not exceeding five thousand dollars, nor less than five hundred dollars, to be recovered by indictment for the benefit of the widow and heirs.

And in New York, a statute [27] provides, that whenever the death of any person shall be caused by any wrongful act or neglect, the party who would have been liable if death had not ensued, shall be liable to an action for damages, notwithstanding the death of the party injured, and although the act be felonious. This statute is taken from the English statute above cited, and the second section provides that the action is to be brought by the personal representatives of the deceased, and that "in every such action the jury may give such damages as they deem a fair and just compensation, not exceeding five thousand dollars, with reference to the injuries resulting from such death, to the person." ** These statutes are the basis of legislation in probably every jurisdiction where the ·common law prevails. The action for damages for negligently causing death is usually given by statute to the personal representatives of the deceased for the benefit of the "widow or next ·of kin," or, as in New York, of the "husband or wife and next ·of kin," although, in some of the States, the wording of the English

Mich. 242, 101 N. W. 530, 11 Det. Leg. N. 559.
[25] Stewart *v.* United E. L. & P. Co., 104 Md. 332, 65 Atl. 49, 8 L. R. A. (N. S.) 384.

[26] Stat. 1840, c. 80; Pub. Stats., c. 112, § 212.
[27] Laws of 1847, c. 450.

statute, "wife, husband, parent, child," is followed. The damages are usually limited to compensation for the "pecuniary injuries" resulting from the death.

§ 571a. Limitation of amount of recovery.

In many of the earlier statutes the amount that could be recovered was arbitrarily limited to $5,000, which in later statutes has often been increased to $10,000.[28] This arbitrary limitation of the amount of recovery was no doubt due to the same feeling which led the courts to refuse an action for death: the difficulty of estimating in money the value of a life. But any such arbitrary limitation is of course diametrically opposed to the fundamental nature of damages: that they are a judicially ascertained compensation for wrong. Any such effort on the part of the legislature to fetter the courts in the assessment of compensation is a return to the methods of the Anglo-Saxons; and the tendency is, and must be, to abolish the statutory limitation. In a considerable number of States there is now no limitation on the amount of compensation. The removal of this limit does not change the rule for the assessment of damages, which are still to be measured by the loss to the relatives.[29] It has, however, been intimated in the Federal courts that these statutory limits may be taken as a guide to the permissible amount of damages, even in States where there is no limitation in the statute.[30]

§ 571b. Varying types of statute.

For the specific provision of the statute as it exists in the various States reference must be had to the laws of those States. Several types of statutes have been passed, and should be distinguished. The commonest form is that giving to some one representing the relatives a right to recover the pecuniary loss to them from the death. In a few States the suit may be brought for the loss to the estate.[31] In several States there is no

[28] Tobin v. Missouri Pac. Ry. (Mo.), 18 S. W. 996; Lee v. Mo. Pac. Ry., 195 Mo. 400, 92 S. W. 614.

[29] Howell v. Rochester Ry., 49 N. Y. Supp. 17.

[30] Cheatham v. Red River Line, 56 Fed. 248; The Oceanic, 61 Fed. 338;

Farmers' L. & T. Co. v. Toledo A. A. & N. M. Ry., 67 Fed. 73.

[31] *United States:* Linss v. Chesapeake & O. Ry., 91 Fed. 964 (Kentucky); Jennings v. Alaska Treadwell Gold Mining Co., 170 Fed. 146, 95 C. C. A. 388 (Oregon & Alaska).

pecuniary measure, but the jury is authorized to award such damages as are "fair and just,"[32] or "proportionate to the injury."[33] In Alabama they are punitive, and not measured by the pecuniary loss,[34] and this is also the case in other States, where the jury is allowed to award a sum, under a certain limit, in proportion to the wrong.[35] In Georgia a statute allowing the jury to give the full value of the life, without making any deduction for the expense of living, is constitutional.[36]

§ 571c. Election of remedies.

The statute may furnish an alternative remedy to that given by the common law, and in that case a plaintiff must make an election between the two. So, where as in New York, a father can recover damages for the loss of service of his son, from a person who negligently caused his death, independent of the statute, it is held that a recovery under the statute will bar an action on the former ground.[37] And so it has been held that a recovery under the statute will bar an action by the husband to recover damages for the loss of the wife's society between the injury and the death.[38] In these cases the damages sought

Connecticut: McElligott *v.* Randolph, 61 Conn. 157, 22 Atl. 1094, 29 Am. St. Rep. 181; Wilmot *v.* McPadden, 79 Conn. 367, 65 Atl. 157.

New Hampshire: Carney *v.* Concord St. R. R., 72 N. H. 364, 57 Atl. 218.

[32] *Illinois:* Ohio & M. Ry. *v.* Wangelin, 152 Ill. 138, 38 N. E. 760; Brennen *v.* Chicago & Carterville Coal Co., 147 Ill. App. 263.

Michigan: Wynning *v.* Detroit L. & N. R. R., 59 Mich. 257, 26 N. W. 514.

Montana: Butte E. R. R. *v.* Jones, 164 Fed. 308, 18 L. R. A. (N. S.) 1205.

Virginia: Simmons *v.* McConnell, 86 Va. 494, 10 S. E. 838; Norfolk & W. Ry. *v.* Cheatwood, 103 Va. 356, 49 S. E. 489.

West Virginia: Turner *v.* Norfolk & W. R. R., 40 W. Va. 675, 22 S. E. 83. See Parker *v.* Lumber Co., 115 La. 463,39 So. 445; Chesapeake & O. Ry. *v.* Hawkins, 174 Fed. 579, 98 C. C. A. 443 (W. Va.).

[33] Strother *v.* South C. & G. R. R., 47 S. C. 375, 25 S. E. 272; Mason *v.* Southern Ry., 58 S. C. 70, 36 S. E. 440.

[34] Sloss-Sheffield Steel & Iron Co. *v.* Drane, 160 Fed. 780, 88 C. C. A. 34 (Ala.); Savannah, etc., R. R. *v.* Shearer, 58 Ala. 672; Richmond, etc., R. R. *v.* Freeman, 97 Ala. 289, 11 So. 800; Kansas City, etc., R. R. *v.* Sanders, 98 Ala. 293, 13 So. 57.

[35] Childress *v.* Southwest Missouri R. R., 126 S. W. 169, 141 Mo. App. 667; O'Connell *v.* Mo. Pac. Ry, 131 S. W. 117, 149 Mo. App. 501; Erwin *v.* St. L. I. M. & S. Ry. (Mo. App.), 139 S. W. 498; Dale *v.* Atchison, T. & S. F. R. R., 57 Kan. 601, 47 Pac. 521 (New Mexico).

[36] Clay *v.* Central R. & B. Co., 84 Ga. 345, 10 S. E. 967.

[37] McGovern *v.* New York C. & H. R. R. R., 67 N. Y. 417.

[38] Louisville & N. R. R. *v.* McElwain, 98 Ky. 700, 34 S. W. 236, 34 L. R. A. 788, 56 Am. St. Rep. 385.

in the common-law action are included in the damages recovered for the death. In a few cases it is held that a voluntary
settlement with the wrongdoer by the person injured bars a
subsequent action for the homicide.[39] These decisions, however, seem to be of questionable soundness; for the cause of
action of the deceased, even if by statute it is allowed to survive, is entirely distinct from that given by the statutes for
causing death, and settlement for one should not bar action
upon the other right.[40] So judgment in an action for the death
does not bar an action by the estate for the personal injury
which survives by statute.[41]

§ 572. General principles.

The decisions in cases arising under the statutes are not in
entire harmony, and many of them go farther in the allowance
of damages than a correct interpretation of the statutes would
seem to justify. The courts have found difficulty in giving to
the jury any satisfactory rule under which the damages in a
given case could be estimated. Loose directions have in consequence been often given to the jury, who, influenced as it would
seem by sentimental considerations, have in many cases awarded
damages where the life destroyed was without present or prospective value. In Pennsylvania Railroad v. Keller [42] it is said
that the life is to be regarded as property to be compensated for,
"without regard to past earnings or capacity to earn at the
time of death," and that the controversies which would arise, if
the opposite rule were adopted, would be "repugnant and of-

[39] Georgia: Southern Bell Tel. Co. v.
Cassin, 111 Ga. 575, 36 S. E. 881, 50
L. R. A. 694.
    Vermont: Legg v. Britton, 64 Vt. 652.
    England: Read v. Great Eastern Ry.,
L. R. 3 Q. B. 555.
    [40] Minnesota: Mageau v. Great No.
Ry., 106 Minn. 375, 115 N. W. 651, 15
L. R. A. (N. S.) 511, and cases cited.
    Wisconsin: Brown v. Chicago & N.
W. Ry., 102 Wis. 137, 78 N. W. 771, 44
L. R. A. 579. See ante, § 570b.
    The fact that there is pending an ac-
tion by a father for causing death of
a minor son will not operate to reduce
damages in an action by the mother for

the death of same child. Augusta R.
R. v. Glover, 92 Ga. 132, 18 S. E. 406.
The supposed incompatibility of the
two species of remedy has been much
discussed, and the weight of authority
is as stated in the text. See Sweetland
v. Chicago & G. T. R. R., 117 Mich.
329, 75 N. W. 1066, 43 L. R. A. 568;
Sedg. El. of Dam. 177.
    [41] Arkansas: St. Louis, I. M. & S. Ry.
v. Sweet, 63 Ark. 563, 40 S. W. 463.
    Vermont: Needham v. Grand Trunk
Ry., 38 Vt. 294.
    England: Leggott v. Great N. Ry., 1
Q. B. D. 599.
    [42] 67 Pa. 300.

fensive to the sensibilities of every person." [43]   It is submitted, with great deference, that this reasoning is unsound. Life, by the common law, was not property; its loss, however injurious, was not the subject of a civil action for damages. The former rule has only been modified by this statute, under which juries are allowed to give, in most of the States, damages for *pecuniary injuries* only; and all considerations as to the results of this view to the sensibilities of individuals are purely sentimental, and can have no weight in determining the proper scope of the statute. It would seem, in the absence of judicial construction, that the term "pecuniary injury" meant an injury resulting in the loss of money, either present or prospective, and proximate. A somewhat wider signification has been given to it by Denio, J., in Tilley *v.* The N. Y. C. & H. R. R.,[44] and embodies the interpretation which seems to have been generally adopted by the courts. In this case the action was brought to recover damages for the death of a mother, leaving surviving her children of tender years. The learned judge said: "The word pecuniary was used in distinction to those injuries to the affections and sentiments which arise from the death of relatives, and which, though most painful and grievous to be borne, cannot be measured or recompensed by money. It excludes, also, those losses which result from the deprivation of the society and companionship of relatives, which are equally incapable of being defined by any recognized measure of value." The learned judge regarded the loss of nurture, of intellectual, moral, and physical training, and of "such instruction as can only proceed from a mother," as essential to the future well-being of the children, and as, therefore, falling within the term "pecuniary," as used in the statute.[45] Under this interpretation of the word, three classes of cases would be embraced: (1) Those where there is a present pecuniary loss; (2) those where there is a prospective pecuniary loss; and (3) those in which the death deprives the claimant of services which would, in the ordinary course of events, result in a pecuniary value to him. A given case may embrace any or all of these elements.

[43] See, also, North P. R. R. *v.* Robinson, 44 Pa. 175.

[44] 24 N. Y. 471, 476.

[45] See, also, McIntyre *v.* New York C. R. R., 37 N. Y. 287.

Definite instructions should be given to the jury as to the true measure of damages under the statute; [46] although much must be left, it is said, to their sound discretion.[47] This is inevitable in the case of damages incapable of definite pecuniary measurement.[48]

Since the action by the statute is given only to a person damaged by the death, the action will not lie where there is no damage, and nominal damages therefore cannot be recovered.[49]

§ 573. Pecuniary loss.

The plaintiff on the common form of statute can recover the pecuniary loss only.[50] The rule governing the jury in their estimate of the pecuniary loss is, of course, the ordinary one, that the injured person shall receive compensation for the loss sustained; when it becomes necessary to determine the particular items of that loss, the question arises whether the principle of liability under the statute is the same as if the injured party had survived and brought the action. In Whitford v. The Panama Railroad [51] the court said:

[46] *United States:* Hunt v. Kile, 98 Fed. 49, 38 C. C. A. 641.
Idaho: Holt v. Spokane & P. Ry., 3 Ida. 703, 35 Pac. 39.
Iowa: Coates v. B. C. R. & N. Ry., 62 Ia. 486, 17 N. W. 760.
Kentucky: Louisville & N. R. R. v. Case, 9 Bush, 728.
Missouri: McGowan v. St. Louis O. & S. Co., 109 Mo. 518, 19 S. W. 199.
Pennsylvania: Pennsylvania R. R. v. Vandever, 36 Pa. 298; Philadelphia & R. R. R. v. Adams, 89 Pa. 31.
Texas: Galveston v. Barbour, 62 Tex. 172, 50 Am. Rep. 519.
[47] *Missouri:* Stoher v. St. Louis, I. M. & S. Ry., 91 Mo. 509, 4 S. W. 389.
Pennsylvania: Pennsylvania R. R. v. Ogier, 35 Pa. 60, 78 Am. Dec. 322.
[48] Countryman v. Fonda, 166 N. Y. 201, 59 N. E. 822, 82 Am. St. Rep. 640.
[49] Bader v. Galveston, H. & S. A. Ry. (Tex. Civ. App.), 137 S. W. 718.
[50] *United States: In re* California N. & I. Co., 110 Fed. 678.

Illinois: Consolidated Coal Co. v. Maehl, 130 Ill. 551, 22 N. E. 715; Ill. Cent. R. R. v. Whiteaker, 122 Ill. App. 333.
Indiana: Louisville & N. R. R. v. Gollihur, 40 Ind. App. 480, 82 N. E. 492.
Michigan: Van Brunt v. Cincinnati, J. & M. R. R., 78 Mich. 530, 44 N. W. 321.
New Mexico: Cerrillos Coal R. R. v. Deserant, 9 N. M. 49, 49 Pac. 307.
Texas: St. Louis, A. & T. Ry. v. Johnston, 78 Tex. 536, 15 S. W. 104; McGown v. International & G. N. R. R., 85 Tex. 289, 20 S. W. 80; Texas & N. O. Ry. v. Brown, 14 Tex. Civ. App. 697, 39 S. W. 140.
Ireland: Bourke v. Cork & M. Ry., 4 L. R. Ire. 682; Holleran v. Bagnell, 6 L. R. Ire. 333.
[51] 23 N. Y. 465, 469. But see dissenting opinion of Comstock, J.

"Although the action can be maintained only in the cases in which it could have been brought by the deceased, if he had survived, the damages are, nevertheless, given upon different principles and for different causes. In an action brought by a person injured, but not fatally, by the negligence of another, he recovers for his pecuniary loss and, in addition, for his pain and suffering of mind and body; while, under the statute, it is not the recompense which would have belonged to him which is awarded to his personal representative, but the damages are to be estimated with reference to the pecuniary injuries resulting from such death to the wife and next of kin."

This case has been generally followed. The same view is taken by Mr. Justice Coleridge, in Blake v. The Midland Railway [52] where he says: "The measure of damages is not the loss or suffering of the deceased, but the injury resulting from his death to his family." [53] The statute contemplates compensation to the widow, next of kin, etc., *from the death*, not for the injuries to the deceased from the *wrongful act*. The same reasoning leads to the conclusion that expenses for medical attendance, funeral expenses, etc., are not proper items of damages under the statute,[54] although in this country generally the medical expenses and the funeral expenses attendant upon the burial of the deceased may be recovered, where any of those for whose benefit the action is brought are legally bound to pay such expenses.[55] But as these expenses would be necessarily incurred

[52] 18 Q. B. 93.
[53] See *acc.*, Cleveland & P. R. R. v. Rowan, 66 Pa. 393.
[54] *United States:* Holland v. Brown, 35 Fed. 43; Hutchinson v. West. J. & S. R. R., 170 Fed. 615.
Arkansas: St. Louis, etc., R. R. v. Sweet, 57 Ark. 287, 21 S. W. 587.
California: Gay v. Winter, 34 Cal. 153; Salmon v. Rathjens, 152 Cal. 290, 92 Pac. 733.
Delaware: Wilcox v. Wilmington City Ry., 2 Pennew. 157, 44 Atl. 686.
New Jersey: Consolidated Traction Co. v. Hone, 60 N. J. L. 444, 38 Atl. 759.
England: Boulter v. Webster, 13 W.

R. 289; Dalton v. Southeastern Ry., 4 C. B. (N. S.) 296. They may be recovered in an action of *contract*. Pulling v. Great Eastern Ry., 9 Q. B. D. 110.
[55] *Arkansas:* Little Rock & F. S. Ry. v. Barker, 33 Ark. 350, 34 Am. Rep. 44.
California: Cleary v. City R. R., 76 Cal. 240, 18 Pac. 269.
District of Columbia: Bunyea v. Metropolitan R. R., 19 D. C. 76.
Georgia: Augusta Factory v. Davis, 87 Ga. 648, 13 S. E. 577; Southern R. R. v. Covenia, 100 Ga. 46, 29 S. E. 219, 62 Am. St. Rep. 312, 40 L. R. A. 253.
Kentucky: Eden v. Lexington R. R., 14 B. Mon. 204.
Missouri: Owen v. Brockschmidt, 54

at some time for the deceased, the reason for charging them as items of damage, under the statute, is not apparent. Nor can recovery be had for any injury to the plaintiff except what results directly from the death.[56] So no damages can be recovered for injuries to the widow's health caused by overwork.[57] And where the plaintiff was the partner as well as next of kin to the deceased, no compensation could be recovered for dissolution of the partnership.[58] As the court said in the last case, the statute gives damages "for injuries resulting from the severance of a relation of kinship and not of contract."

§ 573a. Non-pecuniary loss.

Since the pecuniary loss alone may be recovered, consideration of all non-pecuniary injuries is forbidden. So damages for the mental and physical sufferings of the deceased cannot be recovered under the statute.[59] And for the same reason no damages

Mo. 285; Rains v. St. Louis, I. M. & S. Ry., 71 Mo. 164, 36 Am. Rep. 459.

New York: Murphy v. New York C. & H. R. R. R., 88 N. Y. 445.

Pennsylvania: Pennsylvania R. R. v. Bantom, 54 Pa. 495; Cleveland & P. R. R. v. Rowan, 66 Pa. 393.

South Carolina: Petrie v. Columbia & G. R. R., 29 S. C. 303, 7 S. E. 515.

Texas: Gulf, C. & S. F. Ry. v. Southwick (Tex. Civ. App.), 30 S. W. 592.

Washington: Dean v. Oregon R. & Nav. Co., 44 Wash. 564, 87 Pac. 824; Philby v. Northern Pac. Ry., 46 Wash. 173, 89 Pac. 468, 9 L. R. A. (N. S.) 1193.

In Kentucky, by statute, the funeral expenses are to be taken out of the amount recovered. O'Malley v. McLean, 113 Ky. 1, 23 Ky. L. Rep. 2258, 67 S. W. 11.

[56] East Tenn., V. & G. R. R. v. Toppins, 10 Lea (Tenn.), 58.

[57] Elshire v. Schuyler, 15 Neb. 561.

[58] Demarest v. Little, 47 N. J. L. 28.

[59] *United States:* Illinois Central Ry. v. Barron, 5 Wall. 90, 18 L. ed. 591; Holland v. Brown, 35 Fed. 43; Hall v. Galveston, H. & S. A. Ry., 39 Fed. 18; Kelley v. Central R. R., 48 Fed. 663, 5

McCr. 653; St. Louis & S. F. Ry. v. Hicks, 79 Fed. 262, 24 C. C. A. 563; McLaughlin v. Hebron Mfg. Co., 171 Fed. 269.

Alabama: James v. Richmond & D. R. R., 92 Ala. 231, 9 So. 335.

California: Cleary v. City R. R., 76 Cal. 240, 18 Pac. 269.

District of Columbia: Bunyea v. Metropolitan R. R., 19 D. C. 76.

Florida: Florida, C. & P. R. R. v. Foxworth, 41 Fla. 1, 25 So. 338, 79 Am. St. Rep. 149.

Illinois: Spaulding v. Chicago, St. P. & K. C. R. R., 98 Ill. 205, 67 N. W. 227; Holton v. Daly, 106 Ill. 131; Maney v. Chicago, etc., R. R., 49 Ill. App. 105; West Chicago St. R. R. v. Foster, 74 Ill. App. 414; St. Louis E. S. R. R. v. Burns, 77 Ill. App. 529; Wetherell v. Chicago City R. R., 104 Ill. App. 357.

Indiana: Long v. Morrison, 14 Ind. 595, 77 Am. Dec. 72.

Iowa: Donaldson v. Mississippi & M. R. R., 18 Ia. 280, 87 Am. Dec. 391; Dwyer v. Chicago, S. P. M. & O. Ry., 48 Ia. 479, 51 N. W. 244, 35 Am. St. Rep. 342.

Kentucky: Louisville & N. Ry. v. Coniff, 90 Ky. 560, 14 S. W. 543; Louis-

can be given, under the statute, for mental suffering and grief occasioned by the death of the deceased to the plaintiff, or for his wounded affections.[60] Nor can damages be recovered for the

ville & N. R. R. v. Graham, 98 Ky. 688, 34 S. W. 229, 17 Ky. L. Rep. 1229. *Maine:* McKay v. New England Dredging Co., 92 Me. 454, 43 Atl. 29; Oakes v. Maine Cent. R.R.,95 Me. 103, 49 Atl. 418. *Michigan:* Mynning v. Detroit, L. & N. R. R., 59 Mich. 257. *Minnesota:* Hutchins v. St. Paul, M. & M. Ry., 44 Minn. 5, 46 N. W. 79. *New Jersey:* Telfer v. N. R. R., 30 N. J. L. 188. *New York:* Whitford v. Panama R. R., 23 N. Y. 465. *Oregon:* Carlson v. Oregon, S. L. & U. N. Ry., 21 Ore. 450, 28 Pac. 497. *Rhode Island:* McCabe v. Narragansett E. L. Co., 26 R. I. 427, 59 Atl. 112. *South Carolina:* Stuckey v. Atlantic C. L. R. R., 60 S. C. 237, 38 S. E. 416. *Texas:* Cotton Press Co. v. Bradley, 52 Tex. 587. *England:* Blake v. Midland Ry., 18 Q. B. 93, 16 Jur. 562, 21 L. J. Q. B. 233. *Contra,* under the *Tennessee* statute: Louisville & N. R. R. v. Stacker, 86 Tenn. 343, 6 S. W. 737, 6 Am. St. Rep. 840; Railroad Co. v. Wyrick, 99 Tenn. 500, 42 S. W. 434. Query under the *Virginia* statute: Baltimore & O. R. R. v. Wightman, 29 Gratt. 431, 26 Am. Rep. 384.

[60] *United States:* Holland v. Brown, 35 Fed. 43 (Ore. Stat.); Kelley v. Central R. R., 48 Fed. 663, 4 McCr. 653. *Alabama:* James v. Richmond & D. R. R., 92 Ala. 231, 9 So. 335. *Arkansas:* Little Rock & F. S. Ry. v. Barker, 33 Ark. 350, 34 Am. Rep. 418; Helena Gas Co. v. Rodgers, 135 S. W. 904. *California:* Munro v. Pacific C. D. & R. R., 84 Cal. 515, 24 Pac. 303, 18 Am. St. Rep. 248 (explaining Cleary v. City R.R.,76 Cal. 240, 18 Pac. 269); Morgan v. Southern Pac. Co., 95 Cal. 510, 30

Pac. 603, 29 Am. St. Rep. 143, 17 L. R. A. 71; Bond v. United Railroads, — Cal. —, 113 Pac. 366. *District of Columbia:* Bunyea v. Metropolitan R. R., 19 D. C. 76. *Florida:* Florida, C. & P. R. R. v. Foxworth, 41 Fla. 1, 25 So. 338, 79 Am. St. Rep. 149. *Illinois:* Chicago v. Major, 18 Ill. 349, 68 Am. Dec. 553; Chicago & R. I. R. R. v. Morris, 26 Ill. 400; Chicago, B. & Q. R. R. v. Harwood, 80 Ill. 88; Chicago City R. R. v. Gillam, 27 Ill. App. 386; Chicago Consol. Bottling Co. v. Tietz, 37 Ill. App. 599; Chicago & W. I. R. R. v. Ptacek, 62 Ill. App. 375; West C. S. R. R. v. Dooley, 76 Ill. App. 424; St. Louis E. S. R. R. v. Burns, 77 Ill. App. 529. *Indiana:* Ohio & M. R. R. v. Tindall, 13 Ind. 366, 74 Am. Dec. 259; Indianapolis C. Club v. Hilliker, 20 Ind. App. 239, 50 N. E. 578; Hunt v. Conner, 26 Ind. App. 41, 59 N. E. 50. *Iowa:* Spaulding v. Chicago, St. P. & K. C. R. R., 98 Ia. 205, 67 N. W. 227. *Kentucky:* Covington St. R. R. v. Packer, 9 Bush, 455, 15 Am. Rep. 725; Louisville & N. R. R. v. Graham,. 98 Ky. 688, 34 S. W. 229; Louisville & N. R. R. v. Creighton, 106 Ky. 42, 50 S. W. 227. *Maine:* McKay v. New England Dredging Co., 92 Me. 454, 43 Atl. 29; Oakes v. Maine Cent. R. R., 95 Me. 103, 49 Atl. 418. *Maryland:* Agricultural & M. Assoc. v. State, 71 Md. 86, 18 Atl. 37, 17 Am. St. Rep. 507; Baltimore & R. T. v. State, 71 Md. 573. *Michigan:* Mynning v. Detroit, L. & N. R. R., 59 Mich. 257, 26 N. W. 514. *Minnesota:* Hutchins v. St. Paul, M. & M. Ry., 44 Minn. 5, 46 N. E. 79. *Missouri:* Barth v. Kansas City El. Ry., 142 Mo. 535, 44 S. W. 778; Cal-

loss of the society of the deceased.[61]   Thus a husband cannot

caterra v. Iovaldi, 123 Mo. App. 347, 100 S. W. 675.

Nebraska: Anderson v. Chicago, B. & Q. R. R., 35 Neb. 95, 52 N. W. 840; Johnson County v. Carmen, 71 Neb. 682, 99 N. W. 502.

New York: Smith v. Lehigh V. R. R., 177 N. Y. 379, 69 N. E. 729.

North Carolina: Byrd v. Southern Exp. Co., 139 N. C. 273, 51 S. E. 851.

Ohio: Steel v. Kurtz, 28 Oh. St. 191; Cincinnati St. Ry. v. Altemeier, 60 Oh. St. 10, 53 N. E. 300.

Oregon: Carlson v. Oregon S. L. & U. N. Ry., 21 Ore. 450, 28 Pac. 497.

Pennsylvania: Pennsylvania R. R. v. Vandever, 36 Pa. 298; Caldwell v. Brown, 53 Pa. 453; Pennsylvania R. R. v. Butler, 57 Pa. 335; Pennsylvania R. R. v. Goodman, 62 Pa. 329; McHugh v. Schlosser, 159 Pa. 480, 28 Atl. 291, 39 Am. St. Rep. 669, 23 L. R. A. 574.

Rhode Island: Schnable v. Providence Public Market, 24 R. I. 477, 53 Atl. 634; McCabe v. Narragansett E. L. Co., 26 R. I. 427, 59 Atl. 112.

Tennessee: Nashville & C. R. R. v. Stevens, 9 Heisk. 12; Knoxville, C. G. & L. R. R. v. Wyrick, 99 Tenn. 500, 42 S. W. 434.

Texas: Storrie v. Marshall (Tex. Civ. App.), 27 S. W. 224; Gulf, C. & S. F. Ry. v. Finley, 11 Tex. Civ. App. 64, 32 S. W. 51; Houston & T. C. R. R. v. Loeffler (Tex. Civ. App.), 51 S. W. 536; Houston & T. C. R. R. v. Bowen, 36 Tex. Civ. App. 165, 81 S. W. 80; International & G. N. Ry. v. McVey, 99 Tex. Civ. App. 28, 87 S. W. 328 (see International & G. N. Ry. v. Boykin, 32 Tex. Civ. App. 72, 74 S. W. 93).

Utah: Webb v. Denver & R. G. W. Ry., 7 Utah, 17, 24 Pac. 616, 26 Pac. 981; Corbett v. Oregon S. L. R. R., 25 Utah, 449, 71 Pac. 1065.

Washington: Walker v. McNeill, 17 Wash. 582, 50 Pac. 518.

Wisconsin: Rudiger v. Chicago, S. P.

M. & O. Ry., 101 Wis. 292, 77 N. W. 169.

England: Blake v. Midland Ry., 18 Q. B. 93, 16 Jur. 562, 21 L. J. Q. B. 233.

Canada: Canadian P. Ry. v. Robinson, 14 Can. 105.

Under the statutes of a few States, however, a *solatium* may be recovered.

Louisiana: Parker v. Lumber Co., 115 La. 463, 39 So. 445; Bourg v. Brownell-Drews Lumber Co., 120 La. 1009, 45 So. 972 (common law).

South Carolina: Nohrden v. Northeastern R. R., 59 S. C. 87, 105, 37 S. E. 228; Stuckey v. Atlantic Coast L. R. R., 60 S. C. 237, 38 S. E. 416.

Virginia: Baltimore & O. R. R. v. Wightman, 29 Gratt. 431, 26 Am. Rep. 384; Baltimore & O. R. R. v. Noell, 32 Gratt. 394; Norfolk & W. R. R. v. Stevens, 97 Va. 631, 34 S. E. 525, 46 L. R. A. 367; Portsmouth St. R. R. v. Reed, 102 Va. 662, 47 S. E. 850.

West Virginia: Turner v. Norfolk & W. R. R., 40 W. Va. 675, 22 S. E. 83; Kelley v. Ohio R. R. R., 58 W. Va. 216, 52 S. E. 520, 2 L. R. A. (N. S.) 898.

No recovery can he had for nervous illness of the plaintiff. Norfolk & W. Ry. v. Stevens, 97 Va. 631, 34 S. E. 525, 46 L. R. A. 367.

And for negligent or wanton exposure of the dead body by the defendant no compensation can be recovered. Pinson v. Southern Ry., 85 S. C. 355, 67 S. E. 464.

[61] *United States:* Hall v. Galveston, H. & S. A. Ry., 39 Fed. 18.

Arkansas: Little Rock & F. S. Ry. v. Barker, 33 Ark. 350, 34 Am. Rep. 44.

California: Morgan v. Southern Pac. Co., 95 Cal. 510, 30 Pac. 603, 29 Am. St. Rep. 143, 17 L. R. A. 71; Pepper v. Southern Pac. Co., 105 Cal. 401, 38 Pac. 974; Fox v. Oakland C. S. R. R., 118 Cal. 55, 50 Pac. 25, 62 Am. St. Rep. 216; Wales v. Pacific E. M. Co., 130 Cal. 521, 62 Pac. 932 (explaining and

recover for the loss of his wife's society, [62] nor a wife for that of her husband.[63]

§ 574. Prospective pecuniary loss.

Where there is a prospective pecuniary loss resulting from the death, damages may be recovered in compensation for such loss.[64] It may be difficult, from the nature of the case, to lay

modifying Beeson v. Green Mountain G. M. Co., 57 Cal. 20; Cook v. Clay St. H. R. R., 60 Cal. 604; Munro v. Pacific C. D. & R. R., 84 Cal. 515, 24 Pac. 303, 18 Am. St. Rep. 248).

Illinois: West Chicago St. R. R. v. Dooley, 76 Ill. App. 424; East St. Louis E. S. R. R. v. Burns, 77 Ill. App. 529.

Indiana: Hunt v. Conner, 26 Ind. App. 41, 59 N. E. 50.

Maine: McKay v. New England Dredging Co., 92 Me. 454, 43 Atl. 29.

Minnesota: Hutchins v. St. Paul, M. & M. Ry., 44 Minn. 5, 46 N. W. 79.

Mississippi: Mobile & O. R. R. v. Watly, 69 Miss. 145, 12 So. 558, 13 So. 825.

Nebraska: Kerkow v. Bauer, 15 Neb. 150.

New Jersey: Telfer v. Northern R. R., 30 N. J. L. 188.

New York: Tilley v. New York C. & H. R. R. R., 24 N. Y. 471.

Pennsylvania: Caldwell v. Brown, 53 Pa. 453.

Rhode Island: Schnable v. Providence Public Market, 24 R. I. 477, 53 Atl. 634.

Texas: International & G. N. Ry. v. McVey, 99 Tex. Civ. App. 28, 87 S. W. 328.

Vermont: Lazelle v. Newfane, 70 Vt. 440, 41 Atl. 511.

England: Blake v. Midland Ry., 18 Q. B. 93, 16 Jur. 562, 21 L. J. Q. B. 233, 83 E. C. L. 93; Pym v. Great Northern Ry., 4 B. & S. 306.

[62] *Indiana:* Howard Co. v. Legg, 93 Ind. 523, 47 Am. Rep. 390.

Kentucky: Eden v. Lexington R. R., 14 B. Mon. 204.

Maryland: Baltimore & O. R. R. v. State, 63 Md. 135.

Canada: St. Lawrence & O. Ry. v. Lett, 11 Can. 422.

Contra, Cregin v. Brooklyn C. R. R., 19 Hun, 341.

[63] *United States:* Atchison, T. & S. F. R. R. v. Wilson, 48 Fed. 57.

Arkansas: Helena Gas Co. v. Rodgers, 135 S. W. 904.

Florida: Florida, C. & P. R. R. v. Foxworth, 41 Fla. 1, 25 So. 338, 79 Am. St. Rep. 149.

Missouri: Knight v. Sadtler, L. & Z. Co., 75 Mo. App. 541.

Pennsylvania: McHugh v. Schlosser, 159 Pa. 480, 28 Atl. 291, 39 Am. St. Rep. 669, 23 L. R. A. 574.

Rhode Island: McCabe v. Narragansett E. L. Co., 26 R. I. 427, 59 Atl. 112.

Texas: Schaub v. Hannibal & St. J. R. R. 16 S. W. 924; Houston & T. C. R. R. v. Loeffler (Tex. Civ. App.), 51 S. W. 536.

Wisconsin: Rudiger v. Chicago, S. P. M. & O. Ry., 101 Wis. 292, 77 N. W. 169.

Contra in California, as to the widow only: Munro v. Pacific C. D. & R. Co., 84 Cal. 515, 24 Pac. 303, 18 Am. St. Rep. 248.

[64] *California:* Keast v. Santa Ysabel G. M. Co., 136 Cal. 256, 68 Pac. 771.

Maryland: Balt. & O. R. R. v. State, 33 Md. 542.

Mississippi: Vicksburg v. McLain, 67 Miss. 4, 6 So. 774.

Missouri: Barth v. Kansas City El. Ry., 142 Mo. 535, 44 S. W. 778.

down more than a general rule to govern the jury in their award of prospective damages.[65] There should be, at least, a *reasonable expectation* of pecuniary benefit from the life of the deceased to entitle the plaintiff to recover;[66] but the damages are necessarily more or less speculative, and reasonable certainty only can be required.[67] The expectation of benefit need not be based on legal obligation.[68] It is to be based on circumstances showing a probability of such benefit.[69] The amount of compensation for this prospective pecuniary loss rests in the discretion of the jury.[70] In estimating the prospective pecuniary loss through loss of expected accumulations of the •deceased, no account can be taken of income from investments

New York: Oldfield *v.* N. Y. & H. R. R., 14 N. Y. 310; O'Mara *v.* Hudson R. R., 38 N. Y. 445; Ihl *v.* 42d St. R. R., 47 N. Y. 317.

Pennsylvania: Pennsylvania R. R. *v.* Adams, 55 Pa. 499.

Texas: March *v.* Walker, 48 Tex. 372.

[65] Chicago & N. W. R. R. *v.* Sweet, 45 Ill. 197.

[66] *United States:* Swift *v.* Johnson, 138 Fed. 867, 71 C. C. A. 619.

Illinois: Chicago & A. R. R. *v.* Kelly, 182 Ill. 267, 272, 54 N. E. 979, 80 Ill. App. 675; Cleveland, C., C. & S. L. Ry. *v.* Keenan, 190 Ill. 217, 60 N. E. 107; Consol. Coal Co. of St. Louis *v.* Stein, 220 Ill. 123, 77 N. E. 133, affirming 122 Ill. App. 310.

Kansas: Atchison, T. & S. F. Ry. *v.* Ryan, 62 Kan. 682, 64 Pac. 603.

Maryland: Baltimore & O. R. R. *v.* State, 24 Md. 271; Baltimore & O. R. R. *v.* State, 60 Md. 449.

New Jersey: Graham *v.* Consolidated Tr. Co., 64 N. J. L. 10, 44 Atl. 964.

North Carolina: Kesler *v.* Smith, 66 N. C. 154.

Texas: Fort Worth & D. C. Ry. *v.* Hyatt, 12 Tex. Civ. App. 435, 34 S. W. 677.

Wisconsin: Kaspari *v.* Marsh, 74 Wis. 562; Bauer *v.* Richter, 103 Wis. 412, 79 N. W. 404.

England: Franklin *v.* Southeastern

Ry., 3 H. & N. 211; Dalton *v.* Southeastern Ry., 4 C. B. (N. S.) 296.

Reasonable expectation of increased earning capacity may be shown. Central Foundry Co. *v.* Bennett, 144 Ala. 184, 39 So. 574. But not mere speculative chance of promotion. Bonnet *v.* Galveston, H. & S. A. Ry. (Tex.), 33 S. W. 334.

[67] *Ohio:* New York, C. & S. L. Ry. *v.* Roe, 25 Ohio Circ. Ct. 628.

Canada: Rombough *v.* Balch, 27 Ont. App. 32.

[68] *California:* Sneed *v.* Marysville Gas & Electric Co., 149 Cal. 704, 87 Pac. 376.

New York: Carpenter *v.* Buffalo, N. Y. & P. R. R., 38 Hun, 116.

Vermont: Eames *v.* Brattleboro, 54 Vt. 471.

[69] *Nebraska:* Johnson *v.* Missouri P. Ry., 18 Neb. 690.

Wisconsin: Tuteur *v.* Chicago & N. W. R. R., 77 Wis. 505, 46 N. W. 897.

[70] *United States:* St. Louis, I. M. & S. Ry. *v.* Needham, 52 Fed. 371, 3 C. C. A. 129, 3 U. S. App. 339.

Arkansas: Little Rock & F. S. Ry. *v.* Barker, 39 Ark. 491.

Louisiana: Dobyns *v.* Yazoo & M. V. R. R., 119 La. 72, 43 So. 934.

Missouri: Frick *v.* St. Louis, K. C. & N. Ry., 75 Mo. 542.

already made.[71] Nor can the jury consider profits from the business of deceased which in no way depended upon his skill and services.[72]

§ 574a. General rule for damages.

Under the ordinary form of the statute, where damages are restricted to pecuniary compensation for the loss, the amount to be recovered is the amount which would with reasonable probability have been contributed by the deceased either during his lifetime or at his death to the use of the beneficiary,[73] not its gross amount but at its present value,[74] taking into consider-

[71] *New Jersey:* Demarest v. Little, 47 N. J. L. 28.
Rhode Island: Underwood v. Old Colony St. Ry., 80 Atl. 390.
[72] *New York:* Read v. Brooklyn Heights R. R., 32 App. Div. 503, 53 N. Y. Supp. 209.
Utah: Spiking v. Consolidated Ry. & P. Co., 13 Utah, 313, 93 Pac. 838.
[73] *Alabama:* Louisville & N. R. R. v. Brown, 121 Ala. 221, 25 So. 609.
Colorado: Denver & R. G. R. R. v. Woodward, 4 Colo. 1.
Delaware: Reed v. Queen Anne's R. R., 4 Pennew. 413, 57 Atl. 529; Wood v. Philadelphia, W. & B. R. R., 76 Atl. 613.
Florida: Jacksonville E. Co. v. Bowden, 54 Fla. 461, 45 So. 755, 15 L. R. A. (N. S.) 451.
Illinois: Chicago v. Keefe, 114 Ill. 222.
Indiana: Lake Erie & W. R. R. v. Mugg, 132 Ind. 168, 31 N. E. 564; Consolidated Stone Co. v. Staggs, 164 Ind. 331, 73 N. E. 695.
Maine: McKay v. New England Dredging Co., 92 Me. 454, 43 Atl. 29.
Minnesota: Phelps v. Winona & S. P. R. R., 37 Minn. 485, 35 N. W. 273, 5 Am. St. Rep. 867.
Missouri: Jones v. Kansas City, F. S. & M. Ry., 178 Mo. 528, 77 S. W. 890.
Montana: Soyer v. Great Falls Water Co., 15 Mont. 1, 37 Pac. 838.

Pennsylvania: Catawissa R. R. v. Armstrong, 52 Pa. 282; Irwin v. Pennsylvania R. R., 226 Pa. 156, 75 Atl. 19.
Texas: Louisiana Extension Ry. v. Carstens, 19 Tex. Civ. App. 190, 47 S. W. 36; Houston Ry. v. White, 23 Tex. Civ. App. 280, 56 S. W. 204.
Utah: English v. Southern Pac. Co., 13 Utah, 407, 45 Pac. 47, 57 Am. St. Rep. 772, 35 L. R. A. 155.
Wisconsin: Tuteur v. Chicago & N. W. R. R., 77 Wis. 505, 46 N. W. 897; Bauer v. Richter, 103 Wis. 412, 79 N. W. 404.
No exact mathematical formula can be given. It is not necessarily limited to a sum which would produce an annual income equal to one-half the annual income of decedent, who was husband of plaintiff. Harkins v. Pullman P. C. Co., 52 Fed. 724.
[74] *United States:* Florida, C. & P. R. R. v. Sullivan, 120 Fed. 799, 57 C. C. A. 167, 61 L. R. A. 410.
Alabama: McAdory v. Louisville & N. R. R., 94 Ala. 272, 10 So. 507; Alabama Mineral R. R. v. Jones, 114 Ala. 519, 21 So. 507, 62 Am. St. Rep. 121; Decatur Car Wheel Co. v. Mehaffey, 128 Ala. 242, 29 So. 646.
Arkansas: St. Louis, I. M. & S. Ry. v. Sweet, 60 Ark. 550, 31 S. W. 571; Kansas City S. Ry. v. Hewie, 87 Ark. 443, 112 S. W. 967.
Iowa: Andrews v. Chicago, etc., R. R., 86 Iowa, 677, 686, 53 N. W. 399.

ation the age and expectation of life of the deceased, his ability and disposition to labor, his capacity to earn, and his habits of spending and saving.[75] This is sometimes stated as his prob-

Mississippi: Mississippi C. O. Co. v. Smith, 48 So. 735.
New Jersey: Hackney v. Delaware & A. T. & C. Co., 69 N. J. L. 335, 55 Atl. 252.
North Carolina: Pickett v. Wilmington & W. R. R., 117 N. C. 616, 23 S. E. 264, 53 Am. St. Rep. 611, 30 L. R. A. 257.
Pennsylvania: Burns v. Pennsylvania R. R., 219 Pa. 225, 68 Atl. 704; Irwin v. Pennsylvania R. R., 226 Pa. 156, 75 Atl. 19.
Rhode Island: McCabe v. Narragansett E. L. Co., 26 R. I. 427, 59 Atl. 112.
Texas: San Antonio T. Co. v. White, 94 Tex. 468, 61 S. W. 706; Fort Worth & D. C. Ry. v. Morrison (Tex. Civ. App.), 56 S. W. 931; R. R. v. Linthicum, 33 Tex. Civ. App. 375, 77 S. W. 40; San Antonio & A. P. Ry. v. Brock, 35 Tex. Civ. App. 155, 80 S. W. 422; St. Louis S. W. Ry. v. Shiflet (Tex. Civ. App.), 81 S. W. 524.
Utah: Evans v. Oregon Short Line R. R., — Utah, —, 108 Pac. 638.
England: Grand Trunk Ry. v. Jennings, 13 App. Cas. 800.
Such sum, as being put to interest, by taking part of the principal and adding it to the interest yields the amount of the deceased's yearly contribution to his family less his personal expenses; so that the whole remaining principal at the end of his expectancy of life added to the interest on this balance for that year will equal the amount of his yearly contribution to his family, less his personal expenses. Reiter-Conley Mfg. Co. v. Hamlin, 144 Ala. 192, 40 So. 280.
A sum not larger than would be exhausted at the end of deceased's expectancy by expending each year a sum equal to his net earnings. Atlantic & W. P. Ry. v. Newton, 85 Ga. 517, 11 S. E. 776.

Such sum as placed at legal interest for time of deceased's expectancy of life would produce the amount he would have accumulated over and above his liabilities at his death, had he lived out his expectancy. Lowe v. Chicago, B. & Q. R. R., 89 Ia. 420, 56 N. W. 519.
Such a sum as being put to interest, will each year, by taking part of the principal and adding to the interest, yield an amount sufficient for her support during the time deceased would probably have lived, together with such other sum as the evidence showed there was reasonable expectation she would receive from his earnings. Rudiger v. Chicago, S. P., M. & O. Ry., 101 Wis. 292, 77 N. W. 169.
[75] *United States:* Kelley v. Central R. R., 5 McCr. 653; Southern Pac. Co. v. Lafferty, 57 Fed. 536; Northern Pac. R. R. v. Freeman, 83 Fed. 82, 27 C. C. A. 457; Florida C. & P. R. R. v. Sullivan, 120 Fed. 799, 57 C. C. A. 167, 61 L. R. A. 410.
Alabama: Tutwiler C. C. & I. Co. v. Enslen, 129 Ala. 336, 30 So. 600; McGhee v. Willis, 134 Ala. 281, 32 So. 301; Woodstock Iron Works v. Kline, 144 Ala. 391, 43 So. 362.
Arkansas: St. Louis, I. M. & S. Ry. v. Sweet, 60 Ark. 550, 31 S. W. 571.
California: Taylor v. West P. R. R., 45 Cal. 323.
Colorado: Kansas Pac. R. R. v. Lundin, 3 Colo. 94; Pierce v. Conners, 20 Colo. 178, 37 Pac. 721, 46 Am. St. Rep. 279.
Connecticut: Howey v. New England Nav. Co., 83 Conn. 278, 76 Atl. 469.
Delaware: Neal v. Wilmington R. R., 3 Pennew. 467, 53 Atl. 338; MacFeat v. Philadelphia, W. & B. R. R., 5 Pennew. 52, 62 Atl. 898; Lenkewicz v. Wilmington City Ry., 74 Atl. 11.

able earnings during his life, less what he would have devoted or what would have been devoted to his personal use.[76] The

Florida: Jacksonville Electric Co. v. Bowden, 54 Fla. 461, 45 So. 755.

Georgia: Macon & Western R. R. v. Johnson, 38 Ga. 409.

Hawaii: Kake v. Horton, 2 Hawaii, 209.

Indiana: Ohio & M. Ry. v. Voight, 122 Ind. 288, 23 N. E. 774.

Iowa: Wheelan v. Chicago, M. & S. P. Ry., 85 Ia. 167, 52 N. W. 119; Lowe v. Chicago, S. P. M. & O. Ry., 89 Ia. 420, 56 N. W. 519.

Maine: Welch v. Maine Cent. R. R., 86 Me. 552, 570, 30 Atl. 116.

Maryland: Baltimore & R. T. v. State, 71 Md. 573.

Minnesota: Shaber v. St. Paul, M. & M. Ry., 28 Minn. 103, 9 N. W. 575; Opsahl v. Judd, 30 Minn. 126, 14 N. W. 575.

Missouri: Chambers v. Kupper-Benson Hotel Co., 154 Mo. App. 249, 134 S. W. 45.

New York: Etherington v. Prospect P. & C. I. R. R., 88 N. Y. 641; De Luna v. Union Ry., 130 App. Div. 386, 114 N. Y. Supp. 893.

North Carolina: Burton v. Wilmington & W. R. R., 82 N. C. 504.

Oregon: Skottowe v. Oregon Short Line Ry., 22 Ore. 430, 451, 30 Pac. 222, 16 L. R. A. 593.

Pennsylvania: Catawissa R. R. v. Armstrong, 52 Pa. 282; Mansfield Coal Co. v. McEnery, 91 Pa. 185, 36 Am. Rep. 662; McHugh v. Schlosser, 159 Pa. 480, 28 Atl. 291, 39 Am. St. Rep. 669, 23 L. R. A. 574.

Rhode Island: Reynolds v. Narragansett E. L. Co., 26 R. I. 457, 59 Atl. 393.

Tennessee: Louisville & N. R. R. v. Stacker, 86 Tenn. 343, 353.

Texas: International & G. N. Ry. v. Kuehn, 2 Tex. Civ. App. 210, 21 S. W. 58.

Utah: Pool v. Southern Pac. R. R., 7 Utah, 303, 26 Pac. 654.

Virginia: Norfolk & W. Ry. v. Cheatwood, 103 Va. 356, 49 S. E. 489.

Wisconsin: Castello v. Landwehr, 28 Wis. 522.

"What the deceased would have probably earned by his intellectual or bodily labor in his business or profession during the residue of his lifetime, and which would have gone for the benefit of his children, taking into consideration his age, ability, and disposition to labor, and his habits of living and expenditure." Pennsylvania R. R. v. Butler, 57 Pa. 335, 358.

"The jury is not confined to any procrustean rule in measuring the value of a life. Age, health, habits, the money he is making, are all data from which the jury may argue his length of life and ability to work, and thus what that life is worth to his wife." Central R. R. v. Thompson, 76 Ga. 770, 782. "The probable earnings of the deceased, taking into consideration the age, business capacity, experience and habits, health, energy and perseverance of the deceased, during what would probably have been his lifetime if he had not been killed." Baltimore & O. R. R. v. Wightman, 29 Gratt. (Va.) 431, 443, 26 Am. Rep. 384.

[76] *California:* Harrison v. Sutter St. R. R., 116 Cal. 156, 47 Pac. 1079.

Colorado: Denver & R. G. R. R. v. Spencer, 27 Colo. 313, 61 Pac. 606, 51 L. R. A. 121.

Delaware: Short v. Philadelphia, B. & W. R. R., 76 Atl. 363.

North Carolina: Pickett v. Wilmington & W. R. R., 117 N. C. 616, 23 S. E. 264, 53 Am. St. Rep. 611, 30 L. R. A. 257; Russell v. Windsor S. B. Co., 126 N. C. 961, 36 S. E. 191.

Pennsylvania: Peters v. Bessemer & L. E. R. R., 225 Pa. 307, 74 Atl. 61.

circumstances of the plaintiff must also be considered, as his age and expectation of life during which he might receive benefits from the deceased, his need of assistance, and any other circumstances which might indicate what he would receive.[77] These general rules may of course be modified by reason of some peculiarity in the statute. Thus in Kentucky the loss to the estate by the destruction of the earning power ·of the ·deceased is the only thing to be considered.[78]

§ 575. Services of a child.

A parent may recover the value of the services of a minor child during the minority.[79] But it should be made to appear

[77] *Indiana:* Louisville, N. A. & C. Ry. *v.* Wright, 134 Ind. 509, 34 N. E. 314. *Michigan:* Richmond *v.* Chicago & W. M. Ry., 87 Mich. 374, 49 N. W. 621. *Missouri:* Chambers *v.* Kupper-Benson Hotel Co., 154 Mo. App. 249, 134 S. W. 45.

[78] Louisville & N. R. R. *v.* Morris, 14 Ky. L. Rep. 466, 20 S. W. 539; Louisville & N. R. R. *v.* Berry, 96 Ky. 604, 29 S. W. 449; Chesapeake & O. Ry. *v.* Lang, 100 Ky. 221, 40 S. W. 451, 41 S. W. 271; Louisville & N. R. R. *v.* Kelly, 100 Ky. 421, 40 S. W. 452; Louisville & N. R. R. *v.* Milet, 20 Ky. L. Rep. 532, 46 S. W. 498; Louisville & N. R. R. *v.* Taafe, 21 Ky. L. Rep. 64, 50 S. W. 850; Southern Ry. *v.* Evans, 63 S. W. 445, 23 Ky. L. Rep. 568; Louisville & N. R. R. *v.* Sullivan, 76 S. W. 525, 25 Ky. L. Rep. 854; Big Hill Coal Co. *v.* Abney, 125 Ky. 355, 101 S. W. 394, 30 Ky. L. Rep. 1304. Therefore his family circumstances are not admissible. Louisville & N. R. R. *v.* Eakin's Adm'r, 103 Ky. 465, 479, 45 S. W. 529, 46 S. W. 496, 47 S. W. 872, 20 Ky. L. Rep. 933.

[79] *Arkansas:* Little Rock & F. S. Ry. *v.* Barker, 33 Ark. 350, 34 Am. Rep. 44. *California:* Cleary *v.* City R. R., 76 Cal. 240, 18 Pac. 269; Fox *v.* Oakland C. S. R. R., 118 Cal. 55, 50 Pac. 25, 62 Am. St. Rep. 216.

Delaware: Baldwin *v.* People's Ry., 76 Atl. 1088. *Georgia:* Augusta Factory *v.* Davis, 87 Ga. 648, 13 S. E. 577; Southern R. R. *v.* Covenia, 100 Ga. 46, 29 S. E. 219, 62 Am. St. Rep. 312, 40 L. R. A. 253. *Illinois:* Rockford, R. I. & S. L. R. R. *v.* Delaney, 82 Ill. 198, 25 Am. Rep. 308; Illinois C. R. R. *v.* Slater, 129 Ill. 91, 21 N. E. 575. *Indiana:* Louisville, N. A. & C. Ry. *v.* Rush, 127 Ind. 545, 26 N. E. 1010; Cleveland, C., C. & St. L. R. R. *v.* Miles, 162 Ind. 646, 70 N. E. 985; Southern I. Ry. *v.* Moore, 34 Ind. App. 154, 72 N. E. 479, 71 N. E. 516; City of Elwood *v.* Addison, 26 Ind. App. 28, 59 N. E. 47. *Iowa:* Hopkinson *v.* Knapp & Spaulding Co., 92 Ia. 328, 60 N. W. 653; Benton *v.* Chicago, R. I. & P. Ry., 55 Ia. 496, 8 N. W. 330. *Kansas:* Union Pac. R. R. *v.* Dunden, 37 Kan. 1, 14 Pac. 501. *Kentucky:* Covington St. R. R. *v.* Packer, 9 Bush, 455, 15 Am. Rep. 725. *Maryland:* Agricultural & M. Assoc. *v.* State, 71 Md. 86. *Michigan:* Hurst *v.* Detroit City Ry., 84 Mich. 539, 48 N. W. 44. *Minnesota:* Robel *v.* Chicago, M. & St. P. Ry., 35 Minn. 84, 27 N. W. 305. *Missouri:* Rains *v.* St. Louis, I. M. & S. Ry., 71 Mo. 164, 36 Am. Rep. 459;

to the jury that there is at least a *reasonable* expectation that the services of the child will be of pecuniary value to the plaintiff; [80] and the complaint should allege that the father has suf-

Barnes *v.* Columbia Lead Co., 107 Mo. App. 608, 82 S. W. 203.

New York: Oldfield *v.* New York & H. R. R., 14 N. Y. 310; O'Mara *v.* Hudson R. R. R., 38 N. Y. 445; Ihl *v.* 42d St. R. R., 47 N. Y. 317; Gill *v.* Rochester & P. R. R., 37 Hun, 107; Schaffer *v.* Baker Transfer Co., 29 App. Div. 459, 51 N. Y. Supp. 1092.

Pennsylvania: Pennsylvania R. R. *v.* Zebe, 33 Pa. 318; Pennsylvania R. R. *v.* Bantom, 54 Pa. 495.

Texas: Cole *v.* Parker, 27 Tex. Civ. App. 563, 66 S. W. 135; Freeman *v.* Carter, 28 Tex. Civ. App. 571, 67 S. W. 527; Galveston, H. & N. Ry. *v.* Olds, 112 S. W. 787.

Utah: Corbett *v.* Oregon Short Line R. R., 25 Utah, 449, 71 Pac. 1065.

Wisconsin: Ewen *v.* Chicago & N. W. Ry., 38 Wis. 613; Luessen *v.* Oshkosh E. L. & P. Co., 109 Wis. 94, 85 N. W. 124.

England: Duckworth *v.* Johnson, 4 H. & N. 653.

Ireland: Condon *v.* Great Southern R. R., 16 Ir. Com. L. 415.

In Louisiana a different rule prevails. The parent can recover only for his personal loss, the pecuniary loss to the child's estate being recoverable in another suit. Bourg *v.* Brownell-Drews Lumber Co., 120 La. 1009, 45 So. 972. In some States, notably in Kentucky, the damages must be recovered for the estate of the deceased child through loss to his earning power; and his earnings during minority, not enuring to the benefit of his estate, are not considered. Lines *v.* Chesapeake & O. Ry., 91 Fed. 964; Louisville & N. R. R. *v.* Creighton, 106 Ky. 42, 50 S. W. 227, 20 Ky. L. Rep. 1691.

So in *Iowa:* Lawrence *v.* Birney, 40 Iowa, 377.

But *contra* in *Illinois:* Illinois Cent.

R. R. *v.* Slater, 129 Ill. 91, 21 N. E. 575, 15 Am. St. Rep. 242, 6 L. R. A. 418.

In Telfer *v.* Northern R. R., 30 N. J. L. 188, 209, Van Dyke, J., said: "It is simply an action to recover, in dollars and cents, a compensation for the loss and damages which have actually been sustained. As the father of his children, the plaintiff was entitled to their services until they should arrive at the age of twenty-one years; and what those services might reasonably have been expected to be worth, he was entitled to recover, and nothing more, unless it be expenses growing out of the injuries, subject to the burdens and encumbrances which that relationship imposed upon him."

The cases of Ihl *v.* 42d St. R. R., 47 N. Y. 317; Oldfield *v.* New York & H. R. R., 14 N. Y. 310, and O'Mara *v.* Hudson R. R. R., 38 N. Y. 445, which are sometimes quoted as authorities for the position that the statute does not limit the recovery to the actual pecuniary loss proved on the trial, can only be regarded as correctly decided if the word *actual* is used as synonymous with the word *present;* and this would seem to be the case from the language used by Wright, J., in Oldfield *v.* The N. Y. & H. R. R. R. Yet in Gorham *v.* New York C. & H. R. R. R., 23 Hun (N. Y.), 449, the court said:

"It was held in an action to recover damages for death of a child, three years old, under provision of chap. 450, L. 1847, as amended by chap. 256, L. 1849, that absence of proof of special pecuniary damage resulting from death of the child will not justify the court in nonsuiting the plaintiff or in directing the jury to find only nominal damages."

[80] *Kansas:* Atchison, T. & S. F. R. R. *v.* Brown, 26 Kan. 443.

fered damage by the loss of service, or has been put to expense.[81] Since the jury must be satisfied by proof of the *probability* of actual loss resulting to the plaintiff from the death of the minor, the condition of the parents, the occupation of the father, etc., are admissible in evidence in this class of cases, when not in others under the statute, to enable the jury to determine the actual loss which will, in all probability, result from the death of the child.[82] The expense of providing for the child, had he lived, should be estimated and deducted from the estimated earnings of the child.[83] These elements are necessarily uncertain, and any verdict must to a considerable extent be based on speculation; but the jury may nevertheless in the exercise of its best judgment find substantial damages to have been suffered by the parent.[84] If the advice of the minor was valuable, compensation may be recovered for the loss of it.[85]

North Dakota: Scherer v. Schlaberg, 18 N. D. 421, 122 N. W. 1000, 24 L. R. A. (N. S.) 520.

Wisconsin: Potter v. Chicago & N. W. Ry., 21 Wis. 372, 94 Am. Dec. 548.

[81] Edgar v. Castello, 14 S. C. 20.

[82] *United States:* Barley v. Chicago & A. R. R., 2 Fed. Cas. No. 997, 4 Biss. 430.

Georgia: Crawford v. Southern R. R., 106 Ga. 870, 33 S. E. 826.

Illinois: Chicago v. Powers, 42 Ill. 169; Chicago City Ry. v. Riddick, 139 Ill. App. 160.

New York: Roger v. Rochester R. R., 2 App. Div. 5, 37 N. Y. Supp. 520.

Texas: Galveston, H. & S. A. Ry. v. Pigott (Tex. Civ. App.), 116 S. W. 841.

Washington: Atrops v. Costello, 8 Wash. 149, 35 Pac. 620.

Wisconsin: Ewen v. Chicago & N. W. Ry., 38 Wis. 613; Luessen v. Oshkosh, E. L. & P. Co., 109 Wis. 94, 85 N. W. 124.

[83] *Arkansas:* St. Louis, I. M. & S. Ry. v. Freeman, 36 Ark. 41.

California: Fox v. Oakland C. S. R. R., 118 Cal. 55, 50 Pac. 25, 62 Am. St. Rep. 216.

Illinois: Rockford, R. I. & S. L. R. R. v. Delaney, 82 Ill. 198, 25 Am. Rep. 308.

Indiana: Cleveland, C. C. & S. L. R. R. v. Miles, 162 Ind. 646, 70 N. E. 985; Elwood v. Addison, 26 Ind. App. 28, 35, 59 N. E. 47; Southern I. Ry. v. Moore, 34 Ind. App. 154, 70 N. E. 479, 71 N. E. 516.

Iowa: Hopkinson v. Knapp & Spaulding Co., 92 Ia. 328, 60 N. W. 653.

Michigan: Hurst v. Detroit City Ry., 84 Mich. 539, 48 N. W. 44.

Missouri: Barnes v. Columbia Lead Co., 107 Mo. App. 608, 82 S. W. 203.

New York: Schaffer v. Baker Transfer Co., 29 App. Div. 459, 51 N. Y. Supp. 1092.

Texas: Cole v. Parker, 27 Tex. Civ. App. 563, 66 S. W. 135; Freeman v. Carter, 28 Tex. Civ. App. 571, 67 S. W. 527.

[84] *New York:* Howell v. Rochester Ry., 24 App. Div. 502, 49 N. Y. Supp. 17.

Rhode Island: Schnable v. Providence Public Market, 24 R. I. 477, 53 Atl. 634.

[85] Gill v. Rochester & P. R. R., 37 Hun (N. Y.), 107.

The fact that the father of a deceased minor prior to the accident had relinquished to him the right to his time and services is not a bar to the action,[86] but may be taken into account in reduction.[87] The weight of authority is that the jury may take into account the reasonable expectation of pecuniary benefit from the continuance of the life beyond the minority.[88] Thus Earl, J., said in Birkett v. Knickerbocker Ice Co.: [89]

[86] *United States:* Swift v. Johnson, 138 Fed. 867, 71 C. C. A. 619.

Maryland: Agricultural & M. Assoc. v. State, 71 Md. 86, 18 Atl. 37, 17 Am. St. Rep. 507.

Wisconsin: Luessen v. Oshkosh E. L. & P. Co., 109 Wis. 94, 85 N. W. 124.

[87] *Illinois:* Quincy Coal Co. v. Hood, 77 Ill. 68.

Kansas: St. Joseph & W. R. R. v. Wheeler, 35 Kan. 185, 10 Pac. 461.

But a mother may recover for the value of her son's services lost to her though he intended to go back to school. His services and learning are one of the things that a parent has a right to. Clark v. Tulare L. D. Co., 11 Cal. App. 481, 112 Pac. 564.

[88] *United States:* Texas & P. Ry. v. Wilder, 92 Fed. 953, 35 C. C. A. 105 (and see the dissenting opinion for the proper limits of the doctrine); Southern Pac. Co. v. Lafferty, 57 Fed. 536, 6 C. C. A. 474, 15 U. S. App. 193.

Arkansas: Fordyce v. McCants, 51 Ark. 509, 11 S. W. 694, 14 Am. St. Rep. 69, 4 L. R. A. 296.

California: Munro v. Pacific C. D. & R. R., 84 Cal. 515, 24 Pac. 303, 18 Am. St. Rep. 248; Quill v. Southern Pac. Ry., 140 Cal. 268, 73 Pac. 991; Bond v. United Railroads, 113 Pac. 366.

Illinois: Baltimore & O. S. W. Ry. v. Then, 159 Ill. 535, 42 N. E. 971; Chicago, etc., R. R. v. Beaver, 199 Ill. 34, 65 N. E. 144; United States Brewing Co. v. Stoltenberg, 211 Ill. 531, 71 N. E. 1081, 133 Ill. App. 435; McLean

County Coal Co. v. McVey, 38 Ill. App. 158.

Indiana: Southern I. R. R. v. Moore, 34 Ind. App. 154, 72 N. E. 479.

Kansas: St. Joseph & W. R. R. v. Wheeler, 35 Kan. 185, 10 Pac. 461; Atchison, etc., R. R. v. Cross, 58 Kan. 424, 49 Pac. 59.

Minnesota: Scheffler v. Minneapolis & St. L. Ry., 32 Minn. 518, 21 N. W. 711; Gunderson v. Northwestern Elevator Co., 47 Minn. 161, 49 N. W. 694.

Nebraska: Draper v. Tucker, 69 Neb. 434, 95 N. W. 1026.

New York: Birkett v. Knickerbocker Ice Co., 100 N. Y. 504, 18 N. E. 108.

Texas: Houston & T. C. Ry. v. Cowser, 57 Tex. 293; Galveston, H. & S. A. Ry. v. Davis, 4 Tex. Civ. App. 468, 23 S. W. 301; Cole v. Parker, 27 Tex. Civ. App. 563, 66 S. W. 135; Freeman v. Carter, 28 Tex. Civ. App. 571, 67 S. W. 527; Texas, etc., R. R. v. Harby, 28 Tex. Civ. App. 24, 67 S. W. 541; San Antonio St. Ry. v. Mechler (Tex. Civ. App.), 29 S. W. 202; Galveston, H. & N. Ry. v. Olds, (Tex. Civ. App.), 112 S. W. 787.

Utah: Beaman v. Martha Washington Min. Co., 23 Utah, 139, 63 Pac. 631.

Wisconsin: Potter v. Chicago & N. W. R. R., 21 Wis. 372, 94 Am. Dec. 548; Thompson v. Johnston Bros. Co., 86 Wis. 576, 57 N. W. 298.

Such damages cannot extend beyond the lifetime of the parents. Fidelity

[89] 110 N. Y. 504, 508, 18 N. E. 108.

"The jury were not bound, in estimating the compensation to be made for the death of the child, to confine their considerations to her minority. It is true that the plaintiff, as father, could command her services only during her minority. But in certain circumstances she might, after her majority, owe him the duty of support, which could, by legal proceedings, be enforced; and after that event she might, in many ways, be of great pecuniary benefit to him. In estimating the pecuniary value of this child to her next of kin, the jury could take into consideration all the probable, or even possible, benefits which might result to them from her life, modified, as in their estimation they should be, by all the chances of failure and misfortune. There is no rule but their own good sense for their guidance, and they were not in this case bound to assume that no pecuniary benefits would come to the next of kin from this child after her majority."

In some jurisdictions, however, nothing can be recovered on account of loss of services after majority where the child was a minor when he died.[90] "The chances of survivorship, his ability and willingness to support her, are matters too vague to enter into an estimate of damages merely compensatory."[91] In Cooper v. Lake Shore & M. S. Ry. [92] the court said:

"Here was a broad field of chance and probabilities laid open before the jury through which they could roam without limit. They were permitted to speculate upon the future, and consider the probabilities or the possibilities of its unknown and unknowable contingencies; to consider and guess at what might

L. & I. Co. v. Buzzard, 69 Kan. 330, 76 Pac. 832. And so where the statute provides that the action shall be in favor of "the estate of the deceased," it is held that damages are not limited to the minority of the child. Pennsylvania R. R. v. Lilly, 73 Ind. 252; Walters v. Chicago, R. I. & P. R. R., 36 Ia. 458, 41 Ia. 71.

[90] United States: Deninger v. American Locomotive Co., 185 Fed. 22, (Pennsylvania statute).

Maryland: State v. Baltimore & O. R. R., 24 Md. 84, 87 Am. Dec. 600; Agricultural & M. Assoc. v. State, 71 Md. 86, 18 Atl. 37, 17 Am. St. Rep. 507.

Michigan: Cooper v. Lake Shore & M. S. Ry., 66 Mich. 261, 33 N. W. 306, 11 Am. St. Rep. 482.

New Jersey: Telfer v. Northern R. R., 30 N. J. L. 188.

Pennsylvania: Pennsylvania R. R. v. Kelly, 31 Pa. 372; Pennsylvania R. R. v. Zebe, 33 Pa. 318; Caldwell v. Brown, 53 Pa. 453; Lehigh Iron Co. v. Rupp, 100 Pa. 95.

[91] State v. Baltimore & O. R. R., 24 Md. 84, 107, 87 Am. Dec. 600.

[92] 66 Mich. 261, 33 N. W. 306, 11 Am. St. Rep. 482, per Champlin, J.

occur had the daughter not been killed, and had lived to an age measured by the probable duration of the life of a person 11 years of age. They were given the *data* of a healthy girl of 11 years of age, born of poor parents, living with and being cared for by her grandmother; and from this they were required to solve the mighty problem of a life whose future was unknown, and from its unfathomable depths to figure out the chances of pecuniary benefits the parents of that child would have received had she lived past the age of majority."

§ 576. Loss of an adult child.

In case of the killing of an adult child who is at the time actually rendering services, recovery may be had even in all jurisdictions.[93] So a parent may recover for loss of the advice of his adult son in pecuniary matters, if the probability of such loss is shown,[94] and for loss of the attentions and kindness of the child, adding as they do to the ease and physical comfort of the parent's life.[95] In Houston & Texas Central Railway v. Cowser,[96] it is suggested that the best measure of damages would, perhaps, be such a sum as would produce an annuity equal to the value of the pecuniary aid that the plaintiff would have derived from his deceased son, calculated on the basis of all accessible facts, including probable duration of life. But the amount of recovery is not necessarily restricted to such a sum,[97] but extends to the actual loss caused by the termination of the domestic relations.[98]

A reasonable probability of pecuniary advantage from the continuance of the life must be shown;[99] if it is shown the parent

[93] *California:* Hildebrand v. Standard Biscuit Co., 139 Cal. 233, 73 Pac. 163.

Maryland: Agricultural & M. Assoc. v. State, 71 Md. 86, 18 Atl. 37, 17 Am. St. Rep. 507.

Texas: Missouri Pac. Ry. v. Lee, 70 Tex. 496, 7 S. W. 857.

[94] *Pennsylvania:* North Pennsylvania R. R. v. Kirk, 90 Pa. 15.

Texas: Missouri Pac. Ry. v. Lee, 70 Tex. 496, 7 S. W. 857.

[95] *California:* Hildebrand v. Standard Biscuit Co., 139 Cal. 233, 73 Pac. 163.

Maine: McKay v. New England Dredging Co., 92 Me. 454, 43 Atl. 29.

[96] 57 Tex. 293.

[97] *New Jersey:* Jackson v. Consolidated Tr. Co., 59 N. J. L. 25, 35 Atl. 754.

Texas: International & G. N. R. R. v. Kindred, 57 Tex. 491.

[98] Rogers v. Rio Grande Western Ry., 90 Pac. 1075, 32 Utah, 367.

[99] *United States:* Scofield v. Pennsylvania Co., 149 Fed. 601.

Arkansas: St. Louis, M. & S. E. R. R. v. Garner, 76 Ark. 555, 89 S. W. 550.

may recover; if not, there can be no recovery.[100]   So where at and before the time of his death the deceased was not contributing to the parent's support there can be no recovery.[101]   The expectation of life of the deceased is ordinarily immaterial, since that of the parent is less, and the loss cannot extend beyond the parent's lifetime.[102]   But all circumstances bearing on the amount of loss are to be shown and considered.[103]

§ 577. Care and services of a parent.

The case of the death of the parents, where the death occasions actual pecuniary loss to the child, present or prospective, falls within the class of cases already considered; and a minor may recover for loss of support during minority.[104]   Where there is no present pecuniary loss, but where the services of the parent are such as to place the children in a better position in life, damages may be recovered under the rule as laid down in Tilley v. Hudson River Railroad.[105]   Thus the probable earnings of the parent which would have enured to the benefit of the child may be recovered; [106] and he may also be compensated

Texas: Winnt v. International G. N. Ry., 74 Tex. 32, 11 S. W. 907, 5 L. R. A. 172; Galveston, H. & S. A. Ry. v. Power (Tex. Civ. App.), 54 S. W. 629.

[100] *Illinois:* Huff v. Peoria & E. Ry., 127 Ill. App. 242.

Kansas: Cherokee & P. C. & M. Co., v. Limb, 47 Kan. 469, 28 Pac. 181.

Nebraska: Greenwood v. King, 82 Neb. 11, 116 N. W. 1128.

[101] *Georgia:* Smith v. Hatcher, 102 Ga. 158, 29 S. E. 162 (deceased in prison at time of death).

Texas: Light, etc., Co. v. Munsey, 33 Tex. Civ. App. 416, 76 S. W. 931 (deceased married and not contributing). But where the child had agreed to make a loan to the parent, this may be shown.   Mollie Gibson C. M. & M. Co. v. Sharp, 5 Colo. App. 321, 38 Pac. 850.

[102] Ill. Cent. R. R. v. Crudup, 63 Miss. 291.

[103] *Colorado:* Colorado C. & I. Co.

v. Lamb, 6 Colo. App. 255, 40 Pac. 251.

Indiana: Chicago & E. I. R. R. v. Vestor, 93 N. E. 1039.

[104] *California:* Simoneau v. Pac. E. Ry., 115 Pac. 320.

Georgia: Atlanta & W. P. R. R. v. Venable, 67 Ga. 697.

Maryland: Baltimore & R. T. v. State, 71 Md. 573.

Missouri: McPherson v. St. Louis, I. M. & S. Ry., 97 Mo. 253, 10 S. W. 846.

Texas: International & G. N. Ry. v. Kuehn, 2 Tex. Civ. App. 210, 21 S. W. 58; International & G. N. Ry. v. Culpepper, 19 Tex. Civ. App. 182, 46 S. W. 922.

[105] 24 N. Y. 471.

[106] *Missouri:* Jones v. Kansas City, F. S. & M. Ry., 178 Mo. 528, 77 S. W. 890.

Vermont: Lazelle v. Newfane, 70 Vt. 440, 41 Atl. 511. But see Wiest v. Electric Tr. Co., 202 Pa. 1, 49 Atl. 891.

S§ 577§§ 577   CARE AND SERVICES OF A PARENT   1119

for the value of the parent's services in the superintendence, attention to, and care of his family and the education of his children, of which they have been deprived by his death,[107] for as was said in Howard Co. v. Legg: [108] "The care, training, and education which a father can give his children may justly be regarded as increasing their capacity to make their way in the world, and this capacity, surely, may be valuable even in a pecuniary sense." But a child can recover for the loss of such advice only as would have had pecuniary value, in estimating

[107] *United States:* Duke v. St. Louis & S. F. R. R., 172 Fed. 684.
Arkansas: St. Louis, I. M. & S. Ry. v. Maddry, 57 Ark. 306, 21 S. E. 472; St. Louis, I. M. & S. Ry. v. Sweet, 60 Ark. 550, 31 S. W. 571; St. Louis, I. M. & S. Ry. v. Haist, 71 Ark. 258, 72 S. W. 893; St. Louis, I. M. & S. Ry. v. Hitt, 76 Ark. 227, 88 S. W. 908; St. Louis & N. A. R. R. v. Mathis, 76 Ark. 185, 91 S. W. 763, 113 Am. St. Rep. 85; St. Louis, I. M. & S. Ry. v. Standifer, 81 Ark. 275, 99 S. W. 81.
California: Dyas v. Southern Pac. Co., 140 Cal. 296, 73 Pac. 972; Johnson v. Southern Pac. R. R., 154 Cal. 285, 97 Pac. 520; Valenti v. Sierra Ry., 111 Pac. 95; Simoneau v. Pac. E. Ry., 115 Pac. 320.
Idaho: Anderson v. Great No. Ry., 15 Ida. 513, 99 Pac. 91.
Illinois: Anthony Ittner Brick Co. v. Ashby, 198 Ill. 562, 64 N. E. 110; Goddard v. Enzler, 222 Ill. 462, 78 N. E. 805, affirming 123 Ill. App. 108; Baltimore & O. R. R. v. Stanley, 54 Ill. App. 215.
Indiana: Howard County v. Legg, 93 Ind. 523, 47 Am. Rep. 390; Hunt v. Conner, 26 Ind. App. 41, 59 N. E. 50.
Missouri: Stoher v. St. Louis, I. M. & S. Ry., 91 Mo. 509, 4 S. W. 389.
New York: Tilley v. Hudson R. R. R., 29 N. Y. 252, 86 Am. Dec. 297; Sternfels v. Metropolitan St. Ry., 73 App. Div. 494, 77 N. Y. Supp. 309.
Pennsylvania: Mansfield Coal & Coke Co. v. McEnery, 91 Pa. 185.

Texas: International & G. N. Ry. v. McVey, 99 Tex. 28, 87 S. W. 328; Chicago, R. I. & T. Ry. v. Porterfield, 19 Tex. Civ. App. 225, 46 S. W. 919; Houston & T. C. R. R. v. Rutland, 45 Tex. Civ. App. 621, 101 S. W. 529; Gray v. Phillips, 117 S. W. 870, (Tex. Civ. App.).
Utah: Wells v. Denver & R. G. W. Ry., 7 Utah, 482, 27 Pac. 688; Chilton v. Union Pac. Ry., 8 Utah, 47, 29 Pac. 963.
Virginia: Baltimore & O. R. R. v. Wightman, 29 Gratt. 431, 26 Am. Rep. 384; Norfolk & W. Ry. v. Cheatwood, 103 Va. 356, 49 S. E. 489.
Vermont: Hoadley v. International Paper Co., 72 Vt. 79, 84, 47 Atl. 169.
West Virginia: Searle v. Kanawha & O. Ry., 32 W. Va. 370, 9 S. E. 248.
Washington: Walker v. McNeill, 17 Wash. 582, 50 Pac. 518.
Wisconsin: Castello v. Landwehr, 28 Wis. 522.
Canada: St. Lawrence & O. Ry. v. Lett, 11 Can. 422.
Contra, Michigan: Walker v. Lake Shore & M. S. Ry., 111 Mich. 518, 69 N. W. 1114.
North Carolina: Bradley v. Ohio River R. R., 122 N. C. 972, 30 S. E. 8.
Of course, nothing can be recovered on this account in a State where the measure of damages is the loss to the estate of the deceased. McCabe v. Narragansett E. L. Co., 27 R. I. 272, 61 Atl. 667.
[108] 93 Ind. 523, 530, 47 Am. Rep. 390.

which the age and situation of the parties is to be considered,[109] and nothing can be included for the merely sentimental loss; [110] and where there is no proof that the deceased was fitted by nature or education, or by disposition, to furnish to his children instruction, or moral, physical, or intellectual training, it has been said that it is erroneous to allow the jury to consider the loss of instruction and moral training by the children.[111] Since the father is bound to support a minor child, it is not material whether he has or has not done so in fact.[112] The recovery is not confined to losses suffered during minority; a child may recover for probable pecuniary loss after he reaches his majority.[113] So a married adult daughter with whom the deceased mother lived may recover the value of the services which the deceased was in the habit of performing.[114] But to justify recovery in such a case, evidence must be given to show that there was in fact a reasonable expectation of pecuniary benefit.[115]

§ 578. Services of a wife or husband.

A husband may recover the net value to him of the services of his deceased wife, though he can recover nothing for the loss of her companionship,[116] and the amount is to be found by

[109] Demarest v. Little, 47 N. J. L. 28.

[110] United States: Felt v. Puget S. E. Ry., 175 Fed. 477.

Texas: Gulf, C. & S. F. Ry. v. Finley, 11 Tex. Civ. App. 64, 32 S. W. 51.

[111] Illinois C. R. R. v. Weldon, 52 Ill. 290; Chicago, R. I. & P. R. R. v. Austin, 69 Ill. 426. It would seem that proof of such unfitness should come from the defendant; but see St. Louis & S. F. Ry. v. Townsend, 69 Ark. 380, 63 S. W. 994.

[112] International & G. N. Ry. v. Culpepper, 19 Tex. Civ. App. 182, 46 S. W. 922.

[113] United States: Butte Electric Ry. v. Jones, 164 Fed. 308.

Arkansas: Kansas City S. Ry. v. Frost, 93 Ark. 183, 124 S. W. 748.

California: Redfield v. Oakland C. S. R. R., 110 Cal. 277, 42 Pac. 822; Peters v. Southern Pac. Co., 116 Pac. 400.

Texas: Tyler S. E. Ry. v. Rasberry, 13 Tex. Civ. App. 185, 34 S. W. 794; Paris & G. N. Ry. v. Robinson (Tex.), 127 S. W. 294.

Contra, Michigan: Rouse v. Detroit Electric Ry., 128 Mich. 149, 87 N. W. 68.

[114] Baltimore & O. R. R. v. State, 63 Md. 135; acc., Omaha Water Co. v. Schamel, 147 Fed. 502, 78 C. C. A. 68.

[115] District of Columbia: Baltimore & O. R. R. v. Golway, 6 D. C. App. Cas. 143, 178.

Pennsylvania: Schnatz v. Phila. & R. R. R., 160 Pa. 602, 28 Atl. 952.

Texas: International & G. N. R. R. v. Bajligethy, 9 Tex. Civ. App. 108, 28 S. W. 829; San Antonio & A. P. Ry. v. Long, 19 Tex. Civ. App. 649, 48 S. W. 599.

[116] California: Green v. Southern C. Ry., 132 Cal. 254, 67 Pac. 4.

taking the excess of the value of the services over the cost of suitably maintaining her.[117] It has been held that it is incumbent upon the husband to prove that the wife's services actually had a value, and what the value was;[118] but it has been sensibly remarked that it is not necessary for him to prove that she possessed any special or exceptionally good qualities, as with propriety he might have done if the subject of his loss had been a horse or a cow.[119]

A widow may recover compensation for loss of support of her deceased husband.[120] She may recover for loss of support though separated from her husband at the time of his death. He still owed her his support; and an inquiry into the question whether he meant to support her is irrelevant.[121] Not only the amount that she would have received from year to year, but his probable accumulations during his life may be considered,[122] By the better view she may recover compensation for the loss of the care and counsel of her husband, so far as it had an actual pecuniary value,[123] though not for her grief at his loss, or for the

Canada: St. Lawrence & O. Ry. v. Lett, 11 Can. 422.

[117] *Colorado:* Denver & R. G. Ry. v. Gunning, 33 Colo. 280, 80 Pac. 727.

Michigan: Gorton v. Harmon, 116 N. W. 443, 15 Detroit Leg. N. 250, 152 Mich. 473.

Texas: Gulf, C. & S. F. Ry. v. Southwick (Tex. Civ. App.), 30 S. W. 592.

[118] Nelson v. Lake Shore & M. S. Ry., 104 Mich. 582, 62 N. W. 993. In Simmons v. McConnell, 86 Va. 494, 10 S. E. 838, it was permitted the defendant to show that the husband had been in better condition since the death of his wife than before, as bearing on the amount of his loss.

[119] Delaware, L. & W. R. R. v. Jones, 128 Pa. 308, 18 Atl. 330.

[120] *Delaware:* Cox v. Wilmington City Ry., 4 Pennew. 162, 53 Atl. 569.

Maryland: Baltimore & R. T. v. State, 71 Md. 573.

Michigan: Rouse v. Detroit Electric Ry., 128 Mich. 149, 87 N. W. 68.

Missouri: Nichols v. Winfrey, 90 Mo. 403, 2 S. W. 305.

Wisconsin: Keeley v. Great No. Ry., 139 Wis. 448, 121 N. W. 167.

The fact that the widow was left with children dependent upon her for support would be considered. Abbot v. McCadden, 81 Wis. 563, 51 N. W. 1079, 29 Am. St. Rep. 910.

[121] *Delaware:* Wood v. Philadelphia, B. & W. R. R., 76 Atl. 613.

Georgia: Georgia Cent. R. R. v. Bond, 111 Ga. 13, 36 S. E. 299.

Maryland: Baltimore & O. R. R. v. State, 81 Md. 371, 32 Atl. 201.

Texas: Dallas & W. Ry. v. Spicker, 61 Tex. 427.

[122] Ryan v. Oshkosh G. L. Co., 138 Wis. 466, 120 N. W. 264.

[123] *United States:* Kountz v. Toledo S. L. & W. R. R., 189 Fed. 494.

Alabama: Richmond & D. R. R. v. Freeman, 97 Ala. 289, 11 So. 800.

California: Munro v. Pacific C. D. Co., 84 Cal. 515, 24 Pac. 303; Morgan v. Southern Pac. Co., 95 Cal. 510, 30 Pac. 603, 17 L. R. A. 71, 29 Am. St. Rep. 143; Dyas v. Southern Pac. Co., 140 Cal. 296, 73 Pac. 975; Evarts v.

loss of his society; [124] but in some jurisdictions no recovery is allowed on this account. [125]

The Georgia statute [126] gives to the widow the right to recover the full value of her husband's life. This statute was meant to alter the rule that the family could only recover the value of the life to it, *i. e.*, the support they would derive from it. Hence the jury is to give, under the new statute, the entire prospective value of the life; the sum which would produce an annuity corresponding to the probable prospective income and earnings of the deceased. [127] In a State where the damages recoverable are the damages to the estate of the deceased, a recovery by the administrator of a married woman must be limited by the fact that a married woman's time is not her own; and no recovery can be had for the husband's loss. [128]

§ 579. Next of kin.

Where, as formerly in the New York statute, it is provided that the amount recovered shall be for the exclusive benefit of the widow and next of kin, questions arise which do not need to be considered where the action is given, as in the English

Santa Barbara C. R. Co., 3 Cal. App. 463, 86 Pac. 830; Jones *v.* Leonardt, 10 Cal. App. 284, 101 Pac. 811; Peters *v.* Southern Pac. Co., 116 Pac. 400.

Florida: Florida C. & P. R. R. *v.* Foxworth, 41 Fla. 1, 25 So. 338, 79 Am. St. Rep. 149.

Hawaii: Kake *v.* Horton, 2 Hawaii, 209.

Maryland: Baltimore & O. R. R. *v.* State, 24 Md. 271. ·

Missouri: Haines *v.* Pearson, 107 Mo. App. 481, 81 S. W. 645.

Montana: Mize *v.* Rocky Mountain Bell Tel. Co., 38 Mont. 521, 100 Pac. 971.

South Carolina: Petrie *v.* Columbia & G. R. R., 29 S. C. 303, 7 S. E. 515.

Texas: Paris & G. N. Ry. *v.* Robinson, 127 S. W. 294.

Utah: Wells *v.* Denver & R. G. W. Ry., 7 Utah, 482, 27 Pac. 688; Chilton *v.* Union Pac. Ry., 8 Utah, 47, 29 Pac. 963.

Virginia: Simmons *v.* McConnell, 86 Va. 494, 10 S. E. 838; Norfolk & W. Ry. *v.* Cheatwood, 103 Va. 356, 49 S. E. 489.

Wisconsin: Keeley *v.* Great No. Ry., 139 Wis. 448, 121 N. W. 167.

[124] *United States:* Kountz *v.* Toledo S. L. & W. R. R., 189 Fed. 494.

California: Green *v.* Southern Pacific Co., 122 Cal. 563, 55 Pac. 577.

Missouri: Knight *v.* Sadtler L. & Z. Co., 75 Mo. App. 541, 550.

Texas: Gulf, C. & S. F. Ry. *v.* Finley, 11 Tex. Civ. App. 64, 32 S. W. 51.

Utah: Wells *v.* Denver & R. G. W. Ry., 7 Utah, 482, 27 Pac. 688.

[125] *Indiana:* Howard County *v.* Legg, 93 Ind. 523, 47 Am. Rep. 390.

Tennessee: Illinois C. R. R. *v.* Bentz, 108 Tenn. 670, 69 S. W. 317.

[126] Code, § 2972.

[127] Georgia R. R. *v.* Pittman, 73 Ga. 325.

[128] Stulmuller *v.* Cloughly, 58 Iowa, 738, 13 N. W. 55.

statute, for the benefit of "the wife, husband, parent, and child." Thus it was held in New York, prior to the amendment of 1870 (L. of 1870, c. 78), by which the husband was included among those entitled to recover, that under the wording "next of kin," the husband could not recover.[129] Under what circumstances the "next of kin" may recover for the death of a relative under the statute is considered in Chicago & A. R. R. v. Shannon,[130] where the court says: "If the next of kin are collateral kindred of the deceased and have not been receiving from him pecuniary assistance, and are not in a situation to require it, it is immaterial how near the degree of relationship may be, only nominal damages can be given, because there has been no pecuniary injury. If, on the other hand, the next of kin have been dependent upon the deceased for support, in whole or in part, it is immaterial how remote the relationship may be, there has been a pecuniary loss, for which compensation under the statute must be given." The damages are therefore such as may fairly and reasonably be proved to have been suffered by the next of kin, either by depriving them of support during the life of the deceased or of an inheritance at his death.[131] The actual probability of advantage to the next of kin from the continuance of the life must be shown by the evidence; no such advantage will be presumed.[132] But to entitle the plaintiff to recover, it is not necessary that he should have

[129] Dickins v. New York C. R. R., 23 N. Y. 158; Drake v. Gilmore, 52 N. Y. 389; Green v. Hudson R. R. R., 2 Keyes, 294; Lucas v. New York C. R. R., 21 Barb. 245. A contrary view of this question is taken in Steel v. Kurtz, 28 Oh. St. 191.

[130] 43 Ill. 338.

[131] *United States:* The O. L. Hallenbeck, 119 Fed. 468.

Alabama: Bessemer, L. & I. Co. v. Campbell, 121 Ala. 50, 25 So. 793; Louisville & N. R. R. v. Jones, 130 Ala. 456, 30 So. 586.

Delaware: Coughlan v. Phila., B. & W. R. R., 6 Pennew. 242, 67 Atl. 148.

Nebraska: Anderson v. Chicago, B. & Q. R. R., 35 Neb. 95, 52 N. W. 840.

New York: Conklin v. Central New

York Telephone & Tel. Co., 114 N. Y. Supp. 190, 130 App. Div. 308.

Tennessee: Davidson-Benedict Co. v. Severson, 109 Tenn. 572, 12 S. W. 967.

In an action for the benefit of the next of kin of a married woman it was held that since her services belonged to her husband, they could not be of pecuniary benefit to her next of kin during his life; and whether she might have outlived the husband and her services become a pecuniary benefit to her kin is too remote to be considered. May v. West Jersey & S. R. R., 62 N. J. L. 63, 42 Atl. 163.

[132] *California:* Burk v. Arcata & M. R. R. R., 125 Cal. 364, 57 Pac. 1065, 73 Am. St. Rep. 52.

Indiana: Cleveland, C., C. & S. L. R.

had a legal claim for support on the deceased.[133] It would seem that nominal damages at least may, whenever the action is given, be recovered.[134]

§ 580. Evidence—Family circumstances.

In a few jurisdictions the doctrine appears to be established that the conditions and circumstances of the plaintiff cannot be shown to increase or diminish the damages.[135] That view is ably considered by Cooley, C. J., in Chicago & Northwestern Railway *v.* Bayfield,[136] where the learned judge said: "The damages recoverable in a case of this nature are by the statute to be assessed with reference to the pecuniary injuries resulting from such death to the wife and next of kin of such deceased person. They have no regard to the needs of the person designated, or to any moral obligation which may have rested upon the deceased to supply their wants. . . . What the family would lose by the death would be, what it was accustomed to receive, or had reasonable expectation of receiving, in his lifetime; and to show that the family was poor has no tendency towards showing whether this was or was likely to be large or small." In Illinois C. R. R. *v.* Baches [137] it was held erroneous for the court below to refuse to instruct the jury that the pecuniary circumstances of the plaintiff and her infant

R. *v.* Drumm, 32 Ind. App. 547, 70 N. E. 286.

[133] *United States:* Ill. Cent. R. R. *v.* Barron, 5 Wall. 90, 18 L. ed. 591.

Indiana: Smith *v.* R. R., 35 Ind. App. 188, 73 N. E. 928; Henry *v.* Prendergast, 94 N. E. 1015.

New Jersey: Paulmier *v.* Erie R. R., 34 N. J. L. 151.

Ohio: Grotenkemper *v.* Harris, 25 Oh. St. 510.

[134] *Illinois:* Chicago *v.* Scholten, 75 Ill. 468.

Kansas: Atchison, T. & S. F. R. R. *v.* Weber, 33 Kan. 543, 6 Pac. 877.

Ohio: Johnston *v.* Cleveland & T. R. R., 7 Oh. St. 336. See *In re* California, N. & I. Co., 110 Fed. 670, 678, in which nominal damages were disal-

lowed, but only because such damages are never given in admiralty.

[135] *Illinois:* Chicago & N. W. R. R. *v.* Moranda, 93 Ill. 302; Pennsylvania Co.*v.* Keane, 143 Ill. 172, 32 N. E. 260; Chicago, etc., R. R. *v.* Woolridge, 174 Ill. 330, 335, 51 N. E. 701; St. Louis, etc., R. R. *v.* Rawley, 90 Ill. App. 653. In North Chicago St. R. R. *v.* Brodie, 156 Ill. 317, 40 N. E. 942, it was shown that deceased was an habitual drunkard.

Pennsylvania: Pennsylvania R. R. *v.* Butler, 57 Pa. 335; Mansfield Coal Co. *v.* McEnery, 91 Pa. 185, 36 Am. Rep. 662. And see Wilcox *v.* Wilmington C. By., 2 Pennew. (Del.) 157, 44 Atl. 686.

[136] 37 Mich. 205, 214.

[137] 55 Ill. 379, 389.

daughter, and the fact that the plaintiff had a deformity of her hand, could not increase or diminish the amount of damages under the statute, the court saying: "How she has lost more money by being crippled than if she had not been, by the death of her husband, is not to our minds in any wise apparent. The question is how much has she lost in a pecuniary view, and the jury should be required to assess damages in this class of cases alone on that basis."

This view, however, is not usually held; for all circumstances which throw any light on the amount of loss suffered by the death should be shown. So all evidence bearing on the habits and the condition of the plaintiff may be introduced, if it would tend to show what assistance would have been furnished by the deceased.[138] Thus a widow, suing as administratrix of her deceased husband, may show the number of children dependent upon her,[139] and that she had no other means of support than the deceased.[140] So in the case of the death of minors, the con-

[138] *Iowa:* Donaldson v. Mississippi & Mo. R. R., 18 Ia. 280; Eginoire v. Union County, 112 Ia. 558, 84 N. W. 758.

Kansas: Kansas P. Ry. v. Cutter, 19 Kan. 83.

Tennessee: Davidson-Benedict Co. v. Severson, 109 Tenn. 572, 12 S. W. 967.

Texas: Houston & T. C. R. R. v. Loeffler (Tex. Civ. App.), 51 S. W. 536.

Wisconsin: Thoresen v. La Crosse City Ry., 94 Wis. 129, 133, 68 N. W. 548.

Family expenses may be shown. Hudson v. Houser (Ind.), 24 N. E. 243.

The fact that widow is a prostitute who had long lived apart from deceased may be shown. Orendorf v. New York C. & H. R. R. R., 119 App. Div. 638, 104 N. Y. Supp. 222.

[139] *United States:* Atchison, T. & S. F. R. R. v. Wilson, 48 Fed. 57.

Kansas: Coffeyville Mining Co. v. Carter, 65 Kan. 565, 70 Pac. 635.

Missouri: Tetherow v. St. Joseph & D. M. R. R., 98 Mo. 74, 11 S. W. 310, 14 Am. St. Rep. 617; O'Mellia v. Kan-

sas City, S. J. & C. B. R. R., 115 Mo. 205, 21 S. W. 503.

Nebraska: Kerkow v. Bauer, 15 Neb. 150.

Wisconsin: Mulcairns v. Janesville, 67 Wis. 24, 29 N. W. 565.

Contra, Louisville & N. R. R. v. Banks, 132 Ala. 471, 31 So. 573.

In Spiro v. Felton, 73 Fed. 91, the court allowed the evidence on the ground that the children were distributees.

In O'Mellia v. Kansas City, S. J. & C. B. R. R., 115 Mo. 205, 21 S. W. 503 (*supra*) the court made a distinction between a surviving mother and a surviving father, intimating that the latter could not show the number of children. Yet surely such evidence would be admissible, as showing the value of the mother's services in bringing up the children, which he has lost by the death.

[140] *California:* Kerrigan v. Market St. R. R., 138 Cal. 506, 71 Pac. 621.

Wisconsin: Annas v. Milwaukee & N. R. R., 67 Wis. 46, 30 N. W. 282, 58 Am. Rep. 848.

dition of the parents may be given in evidence; [141] and in the case of the death of a parent, that he left minor children, [142] and that they were in poor health. [143] Such evidence is admitted to assist the jury in determining the probability of pecuniary loss to the plaintiff: thus, if the father is poor, the probability is great that he would have required the services of the son; if well-to-do, the probability is equally great that he would have derived no pecuniary benefit from the service of his son; and if the children are in poor health the parent's services are the more requisite. [144]

§ 580a. Character and capacity of deceased.

For the purpose of showing the amount of loss, evidence may also be introduced of anything in the character or capacity of the deceased person which would have any bearing on the pecuniary loss resulting from his death. [145] So the earning ability of deceased and his skill in his profession may be shown, as well as his personal income; [146] but not the income of his

Contra in Nebraska: Gundy v. Nye-Schneider-Fowler Co., 131 N. W. 968 (*semble*).

[141] *United States:* Barley v. Chicago & A. R. R., 2 Fed. Cas. No. 997, 4 Biss. 430.

Illinois: Chicago v. Powers, 42 Ill. 169.

Maine: McKay v. New England Dredging Co., 92 Me. 454, 43 Atl. 29.

Michigan: Cooper v. Lake Shore & M. S. Ry., 66 Mich. 261, 33 N. W. 306.

Minnesota: Opsahl v. Judd, 30 Minn. 126, 14 N. W. 575.

Nebraska: Crabtree v. Missouri Pac. R. R., 86 Neb. 33, 124 N. W. 932.

New York: Pressman v. Mooney, 5 App. Div. 121, 39 N. Y. Supp. 44.

Pennsylvania: Hoon v. Beaver V. T. Co., 204 Pa. 369, 54 Atl. 270.

Texas: Gulf, C. & S. F. Ry. v. Younger, 90 Tex. 387, 38 S. W. 1121; Galveston, H. & S. A. Ry. v. Davis, 4 Tex. Civ. App. 468, 23 S. W. 301; Sills v. Fort Worth & D. C. Ry. (Tex. Civ. App.), 28 S. W. 908; Citizens' R. R. v.

Washington, 24 Tex. Civ. App. 422, 58 S. W. 1042.

Wisconsin: Ewen v. Chicago & N. W. Ry., 38 Wis. 613.

[142] Brinkman v. Gottenstroeter, 151 Mo. App. 153, 134 S. W. 584.

[143] *Indiana:* Hunt v. Conner, 26 Ind. App. 41, 59 N. E. 50.

Wisconsin: McKeigue v. Janesville, 68 Wis. 50, 31 N. W. 298.

[144] And see the remarks of Cooley, C. J., upon the admission of this kind of evidence in this class of cases, in Chicago & N. W. Ry. v. Bayfield, 37 Mich. 205, 215.

[145] Evidence of the personal beauty of a deceased wife cannot be shown, since it did not affect the pecuniary loss of the husband. Smith v. Lehigh V. R. R., 177 N. Y. 379, 69 N. E. 729.

[146] *United States:* Louisville & S. L. R. R. v. Clarke, 152 U. S. 230, 242, 14 Sup. Ct. 579, 38 L. ed. 425.

Tennessee: Louisville & N. R. R. v. Howard, 90 Tenn. 144, 19 S. W. 116.

Wisconsin: Wiltse v. Tilden, 77 Wis. 152, 46 N. W. 234.

business, since that might not be affected by his death.[147]
Chance of promotion may be shown in a proper case,[148] and it
may also be shown that deceased had previously earned more
than he was earning at the time of his death; [149] on the other
hand, the diminution of earning power with advancing age
may be considered.[150] Personal habits of the deceased which
would affect his value to his family may be shown, as for instance habits of intoxication, which might make his life a
burden rather than a benefit; [151] on the other hand, it is not
material to show the good character of the deceased, as that
he was a member of the church and did not use profane language.[152]

In Gregory v. R. R., 126 Iowa, 230, 101 N. W. 761, an action for negligently causing death of a girl of 2, wages of female school teachers in the locality were held admissible to show the value of the life. But in Atlanta & West Point R. R. v. Newton, 85 Ga. 517, 11 S. W. 776, evidence was held inadmissible which was offered to show the value of the services of the deceased in occupations in which he had never engaged. In Alabama, S. & W. Co. v. Griffin, 149 Ala. 423, 42 So. 1034, plaintiff was allowed to show probable earnings in several trades, in all of which deceased had engaged.

[147] Pennsylvania: McCracken v. Traction Co., 201 Pa. 384, 50 Atl. 832.

Tennessee: Louisville & N. R. R. v. Howard, 90 Tenn. 144, 19 S. W. 116 (income from farm).

Nor expected profits from particular business transactions. Karan v. Pease, 45 Ill. App. 382, 388.

[148] Iowa: Brown v. Chicago, R. I. & P. R. R., 64 Iowa, 652, 21 N. W. 193.

Texas: St. Louis, A. & T. Ry. v. Johnston, 15 S. W. 104.

[149] Georgia: Central of Georgia R. R. v. Perkerson, 112 Ga. 923, 38 S. E. 365.

Iowa: Grimmelman v. Union Pac. R. R., 101 Iowa, 74, 70 N. W. 90.

[150] Western, etc., R. R. v. Moore, 94 Ga. 457, 20 S. E. 640.

[151] Illinois: North Chicago St. R. R. v. Brodie, 156 Ill. 317, 40 N. E. 942.

Indiana: Wright v. Crawfordsville, 142 Ind. 636, 42 N. E. 227.

Texas: Standlee v. St. Louis S. W. Ry., 25 Tex. Civ. App. 340, 60 S. W. 781.

In Boswell v. Barnhart, 96 Ga. 52, 23 S. E. 414, however, defendant was not allowed to show that deceased was always in criminal scrapes, and that his family was better off after his death than before. And in Texas & P. Ry. v. Moody (Tex. Civ. App.), 23 S. W. 41, defendant was not allowed to show that deceased was a negro, for the purpose of arguing that family ties are not strong among negroes. In Galveston, H. & S. A. Ry. v. Harris (Tex. Civ. App.), 36 S. W. 776, testimony that the deceased expended his earnings upon a certain prostitute was held admissible for the purpose of contradicting the testimony of the plaintiff that he expended most of his wages in support of herself and his children. On the other hand, good qualities may be shown, as that he was in the habit of working about the house. International G. N. R. R. v. McVey (Tex. Civ. App.), 81 S. W. 991.

[152] Lipscomb v. Houston & T. C. Ry., 95 Tex. 5, 64 S. W. 923, 93 Am. St. Rep. 804, 55 L. R. A. 869.

For the same reason evidence may be introduced of the feeling of the deceased toward his surviving relatives, whether favorable [153] or unfavorable; [154] and, as bearing on the probability of pecuniary assistance, what he had been in the habit of doing for them [155] and what he had promised them to do or had represented to others that he intended to do.[156]

§ 581. Probable duration of life.

As the probable duration of the life of the deceased is one of the elements to be considered by the jury in their award of damages under the statute, mortality tables may be introduced in evidence.[157] But they must be allowed no more effect than to

[153] Cincinnati St. Ry. v. Altemeier, 60 Ohio St. 10, 53 N. E. 300.

[154] Disbrow v. Ulster T. (Pa.), 8 Atl. 912.

[155] Evidence that deceased had contributed to support of survivors:

Indiana: Lake Erie & W. R. R. v. Mugg, 132 Ind. 168, 31 N. E. 564.

Minnesota: Kerling v. G. W. Van Dusen & Co., 108 Minn. 51, 124 N. W. 235.

But see Bridge, etc., Co. v. La Mantia, 112 Ill. App. 43.

Evidence that deceased had not so contributed:

Georgia: Smith v. Hatcher, 102 Ga. 58, 29 S. E. 162.

Maryland: Baltimore & O. R. R. v. State, 81 Md. 371, 32 Atl. 201.

[156] *Indiana:* Southern Indiana R. R. v. Moore, 34 Ind. App. 154, 72 N. E. 479 (had bought and was paying for home for his mother, who survived).

Texas: Houston, etc., R. R. v. White, 23 Tex. Civ. App. 280, 56 S. W. 204 (son said he would support mother in future); Atchison, T. & S. F. R. R. v. Van Belle, 26 Tex. Civ. App. 511, 64 S. W. 397 (son had said he would give his parents all the money he earned); Freeman v. Carter (Tex. Civ. App.), 81 S. W. 81 (boy of ten said he should support his parents in after life); St. Louis S. W. Ry. v. Huey (Tex. Civ. App.),

130 S. W. 1017 (son said he should aid his father pecuniarily).

Washington: Dean v. R., etc., Co., 38 Wash. 565, 80 Pac. 842 (son who had run away said he should return and support his parents).

Wisconsin: Bright v. Barnett & Record Co., 88 Wis. 299, 60 N. W. 418 (son had said he should not marry, but would support his parents).

[157] *Georgia:* David v. Southwestern R. R., 41 Ga. 223; Georgia R. R. v. Pittman, 73 Ga. 325.

Iowa: Donaldson v. Mississippi & M. R. R. R., 18 Ia. 280, 87 Am. Dec. 391.

Kentucky: Louisville & N. R. R. v. Kelly, 100 Ky. 421, 38 S. W. 852.

Minnesota: Scheffler v. Minneapolis & St. L. Ry., 32 Minn. 518, 21 N. W. 711; Diesen v. Chicago, S. P., M. & O. Ry., 43 Minn. 454, 45 N. W. 864.

Missouri: O'Mellia v. Kansas City, S. J. & C. B. R. R., 115 Mo. 205, 21 S. W. 503.

New York: Sauter v. New York C. & H. R. R. R., 66 N. Y. 50.

Pennsylvania: Emery v. Phila., 208 Pa. 492, 57 Atl. 977.

Texas: Gulf, C. & S. F. Ry. v. Compton, 75 Tex. 667, 13 S. W. 667 (*semble:* the jury may find expectancy without the aid of tables); Missouri, K. & T. Ry. v. Hines, 18 Tex. Civ. App. 580, 40 S. W. 152.

prove the probable continuance of life. In Central Railroad *v.* Thompson, [158] Jackson, C. J., said: "The tables prepared for life insurance do not contemplate at all ability to work, and how long that ability will continue, and how much it will decrease as age increases, but those tables only calculate life's duration, however feeble and incapable of labor that life will be in old age." So any disease of the deceased that would tend to shorten his life, may be shown upon the question of the probable continuance of life. [159] Thus it may be proved that the deceased was suffering from a pulmonary disease. [160] And it may also be shown that the deceased was employed in an extra-hazardous occupation. [161]

§ 582. Excessive verdicts.

While the jury has great discretion in determining the amount of the recovery the discretion is not altogether unlimited, even in jurisdictions where "the jury may give such damages as they shall deem fair and just." "The jury are not warranted in giving damages not founded upon the testimony or beyond the measure of compensation for the injury inflicted. They cannot give damages founded upon their fancy, or based upon visionary estimates or probabilities or chances. [162] If the ver-

Virginia: Norfolk & W. Ry. *v.* Spencer, 104 Va. 657, 52 S. E. 310.

Wisconsin: Mulcairns *v.* Janesville, 67 Wis. 24, 29 N. W. 565; McKeigue *v.* Janesville, 68 Wis. 50, 31 N. W. 298.

England: Rowley *v.* London & N. W. Ry., L. R. 8 Ex. 221.

The jury is not obliged to follow the tables when the deceased was engaged in a hazardous employment. Western & A. R. R. *v.* Clark, 117 Ga. 548, 44 S. E. 1.

In Mississippi the tables are not admissible when the deceased was suffering from disease which might shorten his life, as the tables are not applicable to such a person. Mississippi Cotton Oil Co. *v.* Smith, 95 Miss. 528, 48 So. 735.

[158] 76 Ga. 770, 783.

[159] *New Jersey:* Williams *v.* Camden & A. R. R., 61 N. J. L. 646, 37 Atl. 1107.

North Carolina: Meekins *v.* Norfolk & S. Ry., 134 N. C. 217, 46 S. E. 493.

Wisconsin: Schaidler *v.* Chicago & N. W. Ry., 102 Wis. 564, 78 N. W. 732.

For the general scope of a proper charge in such cases, see St. Louis, I. M. & S. Ry. *v.* Needham, 10 U. S. App. 339, 52 Fed. 371, 3 C. C. A. 129.

[160] Columbus & W. Ry. *v.* Bridges, 86 Ala. 448, 5 So. 864.

[161] *Georgia:* Western, etc., R. R. *v.* Clark, 117 Ga. 548, 44 S. E. 1.

North Carolina: Watson *v.* Seaboard A. L. Ry., 133 N. C. 188, 45 S. E. 555.

Tennessee: Illinois Cent. R. R. *v.* Spence, 93 Tenn. 173, 23 S. W. 211, 42 Am. St. Rep. 907.

[162] Cooper *v.* Railway, 66 Mich. 271, 33 N. W. 306.

dict is clearly excessive it will be set aside by the court.[163] We shall consider later what verdicts have been held excessive.[164]

§ 583. Reduction of damages.

That the acquisition of property by the plaintiff from the death of the deceased cannot be shown in diminution of damages is apparent, from the consideration that there is no advantage obtained, since the property would ultimately vest in the plaintiff on the natural death of the deceased, and that it is for the intermediate pecuniary loss that the action is given by the statute.[165] In Sherlock v. Alling,[166] an action brought under the statute, the question was raised whether the receipt of a sum of money by the persons for whose benefit the action was prosecuted, on account of a policy of insurance on the life of the deceased, could be shown to reduce the amount of the recovery, and it was held that it could not, the court saying: "To allow such a defense would defeat actions, under the law, when the party killed had, by his prudence and foresight, made provision or left means for the support of his wife and children; and the wrongdoer would thus be enabled to protect himself against the consequences of his own wrongful act." And this is the universal rule.[167] Nor can the damages recoverable by a husband for the death of his wife be reduced by showing that he has married a second wife who performs the services formerly performed by the first wife,[168] or the damages recoverable by a wife for loss of services of the husband be reduced by showing that she has married a second husband,[169] who is a better provider than the first.[170]

[163] Walker v. Lake Shore & M. S. Ry., 104 Mich. 606, 62 N. W. 1032.

[164] Post, chap. lvii.

[165] Alabama: Sloss-Sheffield S. & I. Co. v. Holloway, 144 Ala. 280, 40 So. 211.

New York: Terry v. Jewett, 78 N. Y. 338.

Pennsylvania: Stahler v. Philadelphia & R. R. R., 199 Pa. 383, 49 Atl. 273, 85 Am. St. Rep. 791.

Texas: San Antonio & A. P. Ry. v. Long (Tex. Civ. App.), 26 S. W. 114.

[166] 44 Ind. 184, 200.

[167] Ante, § 67a.

[168] Indiana: Consolidated Stone Co. v. Morgan, 160 Ind. 241, 66 N. E. 696.

Ohio: Davis v. Guarnieri, 45 Oh. St. 470, 15 N. E. 350, 4 Am. St. Rep. 548.

Texas: Gulf, C. & S. F. Ry. v. Younger, 90 Tex. 387, 38 S. W. 1121.

[169] Illinois: Chicago & E. I. R. R. v.

[170] Georgia R. & B. Co. v. Garr, 57 Ga. 277, 24 Am. Rep. 492.

§ 584. Exemplary damages.

Exemplary damages cannot generally be recovered in actions for death.[171] So in Conant v. Griffin [172] it was said to be erroneous to admit evidence as to the wealth of the defendant, with a view to giving exemplary damages in an action under the statute. In some States, however, such damages are expressly allowed by the statute.[173]

Driscoll, 207 Ill. 9, 69 N. E. 620; O. S. Richardson F. Co. v. Peters, 82 Ill. App. 508.

Nebraska: Chicago, S. P., M. & O. Ry. v. Lagerkrans, 65 Neb. 566, 91 N. W. 358.

A *fortiori* the fact that she is left free to get a better husband if she can may not be considered. Rafferty v. Buckman, 46 Iowa, 195.

[171] *United States:* Swift v. Johnson, 138 Fed. 867, 71 C. C. A. 619.

Alabama: Louisville & N. R. R. v. Orr, 91 Ala. 548, 8 So. 360; Thompson v. Louisville & N. R. R., 91 Ala. 496, 8 So. 406, 11 L. R. A. 146; Williams v. South. etc., R. R., 91 Ala. 635, 9 So. 77.

California: Burk v. Arcata & Mad River R. R., 125 Cal. 364, 57 Pac. 1065, 73 Am. St. Rep. 52.

Colorado: Kansas P. R. R. v. Miller, 2 Colo. 442; Moffatt v. Tenney, 17 Colo. 189, 30 Pac. 348.

Delaware: Tully v. Philadelphia, etc., R. R., 3 Pennew. 455, 50 Atl. 95.

Illinois: West Chicago St. R. R. v. Dooley, 76 Ill. App. 424. (But exemplary damages for death may be recovered under the civil damage act. Belting v. Hobbett, 142 Ill. 72, 30 N. E. 1048.)

Iowa: Spaulding v. Chicago, etc., R. R., 98 Iowa, 205, 67 N. W. 227.

Kansas: Atchison, T. & S. F. Ry. v. Townsend, 71 Kan. 524, 81 Pac. 205.

Maine: McKay v. New England Dredging Co., 92 Me. 454, 43 Atl. 29; Oakes v. Maine Cent. R. R., 95 Me. 103, 49 Atl. 418.

Ohio: Cincinnati St. Ry. v. Altemeier, 60 Ohio St. 10.

Pennsylvania: Pennsylvania R. R. v. Henderson, 51 Pa. 315.

South Carolina: Garrick v. Florida Cent. & P. R. R., 53 S. C. 448, 31 S. E. 334, 69 Am. St. Rep. 874; Nohrden v. North Eastern R. R., 54 S. C. 492, 32 S. E. 524.

England: Smith v. London & N. W. Ry., 2 E. & B. 69.

[172] 48 Ill. 410.

[173] *California:* Myers v. San Francisco, 42 Cal. 215.

Kentucky: Chiles v. Drake, 2 Met. 146, 74 Am. Dec. 406; Bowler v. Lane, 3 Met. 311; Kentucky C. R. R. v. Gastineau, 83 Ky. 119; Owensboro & N. Ry. v. Barclay, 102 Ky. 16, 43 S. W. 177; Louisville & N. R. R. v. Ward, 44 S. W. 1112, 19 Ky. L. Rep. 1900.

New Mexico: Cerrillos Coal R. R. v. Deserant, 9 N. M. 49, 49 Pac. 807.

Tennessee: Kansas City, F. S. & M. R. R. v. Daughtry, 88 Tenn. 721.

Texas: March v. Walker, 48 Tex. 372.

In some States, the damages are made entirely punitive. Thus in Alabama the statute is an act "to prevent homicides," and the compensation of the next of kin is regarded only as a "fortuitous result of the punishment." The damages being entirely exemplary, their admeasurement depends on the degree of negligence or culpability shown and not the loss occasioned to the living.

United States: Louisville & Nashville R. R. v. Lansford, 42 C. C. A. 160, 102 Fed. 62.

So in *Missouri:* Haehl v. Wabash R. R., 119 Mo. 325, 24 S. W. 737.

§ 584a. Presumptions and pleading.

Under the Illinois statute certain presumptions are made as to damage following death. The law presumes pecuniary loss to a parent, and for such loss, without express proof of damage, substantial damages may be recovered.[174] So loss is presumed to a lineal descendant.[175] But there is no such presumption in the case of collateral kin, even brother or sister,[176] and actual loss must be shown to justify a verdict.[177]

In Indiana pecuniary loss will be presumed to a widow and a child.[178]

Whatever the presumption, no special damage to the next of kin need be pleaded, as the statute is held to contemplate some damage.[179]

§ 585. Contributory negligence.

* In England it has been held that the rule of the common law is applicable to this statute; that the action is to be treated as if the injured party had brought it; and that, if his negligence contributed to the disaster, the plaintiff cannot recover.[180] Such, too, is the doctrine in this country. So, in New York, where a lunatic, in charge of his father, was killed by being run over by a railway car; but it appeared that his death was owing, not to the negligence of the railway company or its agents, but to the carelessness of the father of the lunatic, it was held that no recovery could be had.[181] ** But in Texas it has been held that killing a man by making him drink three pints of whisky was actionable, though the experiment was made with the con-

[174] Bradley v. Sattler, 156 Ill. 603, 41 N. E. 171; Chicago, etc., R. R. v. Huston, 196 Ill. 480, 63 N. E. 1028; Grace & Hyde Co. v. Strong, 127 Ill. App. 336.

[175] Chicago, P. & S. L. R. R. v. Woolridge, 174 Ill. 330, 51 N. E. 701; Chicago, etc., R. R. v. Gunderson, 174 Ill. 495, 51 N. E. 708; Dukeman v. Cleveland, C., C. & St. L. Ry., 237 Ill. 104, 86 N. E. 712.

[176] Bridge Co. v. La Mantia, 112 Ill. App. 43.

[177] Rhoads v. Chicago & A. Ry., 227 Ill. 328, 81 N. E. 371, affirming s. c.

130 Ill. App. 145; Huff v. Peoria & Eastern R. R., 127 Ill. App. 242.

[178] Louisville & N. R. R. v. Buck, 116 Ind. 566, 19 N. E. 453, 2 L. R. A. 520, 9 Am. St. Rep. 883.

[179] *Illinois:* Chicago v. Hesing, 83 Ill. 204, 35 Am. Rep. 378; Stafford v. Rubens, 115 Ill. 196, 3 N. E. 568.

Minnesota: Barnum v. Chicago, M. & St. P. Ry., 30 Minn. 461; Johnson v. St. Paul & D. R. R., 31 Minn. 283.

[180] Tucker v. Chaplin, 2 Car. & Kir. 730.

[181] Willetts v. Buffalo & R. R. R., 14 Barb. (N. Y.) 585.

sent of the deceased.[182] If contributory negligence does not bar the action, it has been held that it may be shown in mitigation of damages.[183]

[182] McCue v. Klein, 60 Tex. 168, 48 Am. Rep. 260.

[183] Western & A. R. R. v. Roberson, 61 Fed. 592, 9 C. C. A. 646.

CHAPTER XXVI

§ 586. Rules adopted in admiralty.

At common law, if the plaintiff is not in fault, he recovers substantial damages, but if, on the other hand, the defendant can show him to have been guilty of contributory negligence, he covers nothing. There is no attempt to apportion the loss. In courts of admiralty, on the other hand, where both parties are in fault, the rule is wholly different; though not strictly within the scope of this treatise, it may be advantageous here, having disposed of the subject of torts at common law, to consider briefly the effect of a different system of rules.

§ 587. Collision—Division of loss.

In cases of collision, where both vessels are in fault the sums representing the damage sustained by each, are added together and the aggregate divided between the two.[1] This is in effect deducting the lesser from the greater, and dividing the re-

---

[1] *United States:* The Catharine v. Dickinson, 17 How. 170, 15 L. ed. 233; Chamberlain v. Ward, 21 How. 548, 16 L. ed. 211; Union S. S. Co. v. New York S. S. Co., 24 How. 307, 16 L. ed. 699; The Morning Light, 2 Wall. 550, 17 L. ed. 862; The Gray Eagle, 9 Wall. 505, 19 L. ed. 741; The Continental, 14 Wall. 345, 20 L. ed. 801; The Sapphire, 18 Wall. 51, 21 L. ed. 814; The Teutonia, 23 Wall. 77, 23 L. ed. 44; The Sunnyside, 91 U. S. 208, 215, 23 L. ed. 302; The America, 92 U. S. 432, 23 L. ed. 724; The Stephen Morgan, 94 U. S.

mainder. The effect of this rule is that the vessel least injured contributes to the extent of half this remainder to the loss of the other vessel. Thus if one vessel is injured to the extent of $25,000, and the other to the extent of $75,000, the first will contribute $25,000 to the loss of the latter. If the vessel in fault has sustained no injury, it is liable for half the damage sustained by the other, though that other was also in fault.

Where several vessels independently operated are all in fault, the loss is to be divided equally between all the vessels,[2] even though one owner owns two or more of them.[3]

The rule of division of damages prevails also when the collision is occasioned by inscrutable fault,[4] but if the collision

599, 24. L. ed. 266; The Connecticut, 103 U. S. 710, 26 L. ed. 467; The Manitoba, 122 U. S. 97, 30 L. ed. 1095, 7 Sup. Ct. 1158; The Magenta, 2 Abb. U. S. 495; The Kolon, 9 Ben. 197; The Brothers, 2 Biss. 104; The Phœnix, 3 Blatch. 273, Fed. Cas. No. 11,111; The Pavonia, 23 Blatch. 403; The Frisia, 24 Blatch. 40; Ralston v. The State Rights, Crabbe C. C. 22; The Monticello, 1 Lowell, 184; The Clover, 1 Lowell, 342; The Neil, 3 McCr. 177; Memphis Packet Co. v. Yaeger Transp. Co., 3 McCr. 259; Foster v. The Miranda, 6 McLean, 221; Lucas v. The Thomas Swann, 6 McLean, 282; Cannon v. The Potomac, 3 Woods, 158; The Alabama, 4 Woods, 48; The Ant, 10 Fed. 294; The Monticello, 15 Fed. 474; The B. & C., 18 Fed. 543; La Champagne, 43 Fed. 444; The Oregon, 45 Fed. 62; The Oneida, 84 Fed. 716; The Paoli, 92 Fed. 944; Jacobson v. Dalles P. & A. N. Co., 106 Fed. 428; The Hanson H. Keyes, 107 Fed. 537; The S. A. McCauley, 116 Fed. 107; The Itaska, 117 Fed. 885; The Hoyt, 136 Fed. 671; The Bellingham, 138 Fed. 619; The Depew, 139 Fed. 236; Ross v. Cornell Steamboat Co., 149 Fed. 196; The Dreamland, 149 Fed. 910; The Aries, 165 Fed. 514; The Director, 180 Fed. 606.

Louisiana: Brickell v. Frisby, 2 Rob. 204.
Washington: Puget Sound Com. Co. v. The Taylor, 2 Wash. Terr. 93.
England: The Agra & Elizabeth Jenkins, 4 Moore P. C. (N. S.) 435; The Singapore and Hebe, 4 Moore P. C. (N. S.) 271.
A few cases, however, have declined to make an equal division of the loss, and have apportioned the damage in proportion to the fault. Thompson v. The Great Republic, 23 Wall. 20, 23 L. ed. 55; The Rival, 1 Sprague, 128; The Mary Ida, 20 Fed. 741; The Anerly, 58 Fed. 744; The Victory, 68 Fed. 395; The Chattahoochee, 74 Fed. 899.
[2] The Manhattan, 181 Fed. 229.
[3] The Moran, 212 U. S. 466, 53 L. ed. 600, 29 Sup. Ct. 339.
[4] The Comet, 1 Abb. C. C. 451; The Bronson, 3 Ben. 341, 24 Fed. Cas. No. 14,131; Lucas v. The Swann, 6 McLean, 282; The John Henry, 3 Ware, 264; The Nautilus, 1 Ware, 2d ed., 529; The David Dows, 16 Fed. 154. But contra, that where there is a reasonable doubt as to which vessel was to blame there can be no recovery. The Breeze, 6 Ben. 14, per Blatchford, J.; The Summit, 2 Curt. 150, per Curtis, J.; The Worthington v. Davis, 19 Fed. 836; The Jemina, 149 Fed. 171.

is the result of inevitable accident, each vessel, in this country, must bear her own loss.[5] In some cases although there is no fault, so far as the collision is concerned, on the part of the damaged vessel, but the damage is largely caused by the unseaworthiness of the vessel, the fault is treated as mutual and the loss is divided;[6] or if the unseaworthiness of the damaged vessel alone is responsible for the loss, no recovery is allowed.[7]

In dividing the damages under this rule, no regard is paid to the difference in value between the vessels.[8]

§ 588. Liability to third parties.

Where both vessels are in fault, a party whose goods are injured can recover all the damages against the vessel libelled by him, i. e., the principle of the division of the loss applies only as between the colliding vessels.[9] So where a collision occurred between The Atlas and The Kate, whereby a canalboat in the tow of the latter was injured and goods were destroyed, which the libellant had insured, he was allowed to recover the whole amount of the loss against The Atlas, the only vessel he libelled.[10]. In the case of The Juniata,[11] it appeared that there had been a collision between The Juniata, a steamship, and a tug-boat, by which property of the United States, in the tug-boat's tow, was destroyed. Both the steamship and the tug were at fault. A libel was filed against The Juniata alone. It was held that the United States could recover full damages against it, and that The Juniata's claim against the tug-boat must be settled in other proceedings.

[5] Stainback v. Rae, 14 How. 532, 14 L. ed. 530; The Grace Girdler, 7 Wall. 196, 19 L. ed. 113; The Sunnyside, 91 U. S. 208, 215, 23 L. ed. 302; The J. L. Hasbrouck, 14 Blatch. 30; The City of Paris, 14 Blatch. 531; Ward v. The Fashion, Newb. Adm. 8; The Nautilus, 1 Ware, 2d ed., 529.

[6] The Syracuse, 18 Fed. 828; The Reba, 22 Fed. 546; The Starbuck, 29 Fed. 797. But see Boston T. B. Co. v. Pettie, 49 Fed. 464, 1 C. C. A. 314, 1 U. S. App. 57, 63.

[7] Mould v. The New York, 40 Fed. 900; The Gen. George G. Meade, 8 Ben. 481; The Charles R. Stone, 9 Ben. 182.

[8] The Nautilus, 1 Ware, 2d ed., 529.

[9] The Bernina, 13 App. Cas. 1; Holland v. Brown, 35 Fed. 43; The Britannic, 39 Fed. 395; The Eagle Point, 136 Fed. 1010.

[10] The Atlas, 93 U. S. 302, 23 L. ed. 863. In Scotland, the loss is apportioned in such a case. Hay v. LeNeve, 2 Shaw H. L. 395; The Washington, 5 Jur. 1067.

[11] 93 U. S. 337, 23 L. ed. 930.

Swayne, J., said: "We should adjudge that half the amount should be paid by the tug, and the other half by the steamer; but that the libel of the United States is against the steamer alone. The tug, therefore, cannot be reached in this proceeding. But the offence being a marine tort, and both being guilty, they are liable severally, as well as jointly, for the entire amount of the damages." In The Alabama and The Gamecock,[12] on the other hand, it appeared that the libellant's vessel had been injured by a collision between the tow-boat of his vessel, The Gamecock, and the steamer Alabama, both being in fault. The Alabama was bonded in $100,000, The Gamecock in $10,000. Both offending vessels being before the court, it was held that judgment should be entered against each for a half; but if the libellant could not recover against one all the damage, he could then proceed against the other.[13]

If one vessel is obliged to pay damages to a third party resulting from a collision in which another vessel is also at fault, the first vessel has the right to sue the other vessel subsequently for its portion of such damages.[14] In such cases, since the wrongdoers are sureties towards each other as respects claims of third parties, if one of them pending suit purchases such claims below their value the other is responsible only for his portion of the amount actually paid out with interest. One cannot speculate in the liability so as to make a profit out of the other.[15]

[12] 92 U. S. 695, 23 L. ed. 763. The cases of The Milan, 1 Lush. 388, and The Atlas, 4 Ben. 27, 10 Blatch. 459, which adopt the rule of division of loss, were cited. The court said of them: "It does not appear that any difficulty arose from the inability of either of the condemned parties to pay their share of the loss. No such inability seems to have existed. And when it does not exist, the application of the moiety rule operates justly as between the parties in fault, and works no injury to others. It is only when such inability exists that a different result takes place. The cases quoted, therefore, may have been well decided and yet furnish no precedent for the case under consideration."

[13] See to the same effect: The George Washington, 9 Wall. 513, 19 L. ed. 787; The Virginia Ehrman, 97 U. S. 309, 24 L. ed. 890; The Hartford v. Rideout, 97 U. S. 323, 24 L. ed. 930; The Civilta v. Perry, 103 U. S. 699, 26 L. ed. 599; The Monitor & Hill, 3 Biss. 24; The Frisia, 24 Blatch. 40; The Queen, 40 Fed. 694; The Mariska, 107 Fed. 989.

[14] Erie R. R. v. Erie & W. T. Co., 204 U. S. 220, 51 L. ed. 450, 27 Sup. Ct. 246; The Connemaugh, 135 Fed. 240.

[15] The Gulf Stream, 64 Fed. 809, 12 C. C. A. 613, 26 U. S. App. 409.

In a few cases it has been held (contrary to the usual rule) that where one vessel is more at fault than the other they should contribute unequally in proportion to their respective faults, to pay damage suffered by a third party.[16]

§ 589. General principles of recovery—Consequential damages.

In general the same rules of damages apply in Admiralty as at common law. As far as practicable the party who has sustained an injury by collision is entitled to the amount as damages which will put him in the same condition as before the injury.[17] Conjectural damages must be excluded.[18] But necessary incidental expenses and losses are allowed, such as loss of wages, and damage to the vessel from efforts to save her at the time of the collision,[19] salvage expenses,[20] charges for wharfage while repairing,[21] and the time of those employed in raising and clearing out the vessel.[22] The owner of the vessel injured by the collision can recover the expenses incurred in retaining his crew,[23] and in attempting to save and in storing

---

[16] The Chattahoochee, 74 Fed. 899, 21 C. C. A. 162.

In The Victory, 68 Fed. 395, 15 C. C. A. 491, it was held that where there was great damage to the cargo the entire proceeds of the vessel most in fault would first be applied to the loss, any deficiency to be supplied by the other vessel. In The Maling, 110 Fed. 227, where three vessels were concerned, but the fault of one of the three was held to be due to the act of one of the two others, it was at first held that the damages must be divided between the two last, in the proportion of one and two-thirds; but on a rehearing, it was decided that the damages and costs must be divided equally between the three. The S. A. McCauley, 116 Fed. 107. In Jacobson v. Dalles P. & A. N. Co., 103 Fed. 428, the court said that "the rule in admiralty does not admit of such an apportionment" between two vessels "as would correspond to the

negligence of the two respectively." See to the same effect The Hanson H. Keyes, 107 Fed. 537.

[17] The Baltimore v. Rowland, 8 Wall. 377, 19 L. ed. 463; The Minnie, 26 Fed. 860.

[18] The Blossom, Olcott, 188; The Narragansett, Olcott, 246.

[19] The Nautilus, 1 Ware, 2d ed., 529; Greenwood v. The Fletcher, 42 Fed. 504; The Switzerland, 67 Fed. 617.

[20] La Champagne, 53 Fed. 398; The Alaska, 44 Fed. 498; The Cepheus, 24 Fed. 507.

[21] The Dumont, 34 Fed. 428.

[22] Vantine v. The Lake, 2 Wall., Jr., 52.

[23] Hoffman v. Union Ferry Co., 68 N. Y. 385; Leonard v. Whitwell, 19 Fed. 547; The Switzerland, 67 Fed. 617; New Haven Steamboat Co. v. New York, 36 Fed. 716. Detaining crew and expenses thereof must be necessary. The Thorp, 46 Fed. 816.

and caring for cargo,[24] the expenses of a tug to tow the vessel to a port of safety,[25] expenses of the owner in going to view the wreck, if reasonable,[26] and of surveys, if proper,[27] superintendence of the repairs,[28] necessary readjusting of compass [29] and the expense of a new rating if necessary to effect insurance,[30] and the offending vessel is not exonerated from full damages, because after the wreck a part of the cargo was injured or lost through the efforts of a third party to save it.[31] The loss of the charter may sometimes be recovered,[32] and in certain cases commission paid to agents on the outlay for repairs is allowed.[33] There can be no recovery, however, for loss on account of disorganization of business resulting from the collision nor for lawyer's fees nor for forwarding the freight where the vessel did not give up the voyage, but only delayed it.[34]

The ordinary rules of avoidable consequences apply in admiralty. The owner of a vessel sunk through the negligence of another must endeavor to save her and if he does not cannot profit by his own remissness.[35]

Where the full value of the vessel is allowed, as upon a total loss, nothing further will be awarded for demurrage,[36] or other expenses.[37] But where the vessel was only a partial loss, it was held otherwise by a very able judge, in a case where the repairing of the vessel had been a prudent course, and the necessary repairs and demurrage together exceeded the value of the vessel at the time of the loss.[38] And even when the loss is

[24] The City of New York, 23 Fed. 616.
[25] The Benjamin F. Hunt, Jr., 34 Fed. 816; The Bulgaria, 83 Fed. 312.
[26] The Alaska, 44 Fed. 498; The California, 54 Fed. 404.
[27] The Alaska, 44 Fed. 498; The Golden Rule, 20 Fed. 198; The Venus, 17 Fed. 925.
[28] New Haven Boat Co. v. New York, 36 Fed. 716.
[29] The Belgenland, 36 Fed. 504.
[30] The Belgenland, id.; but if repairs make a radically different boat, contra, The Gilkey v. The Beta, 44 Fed. 389.
[31] The Narragansett, Olcott, 246.
[32] The Belgenland, 36 Fed. 504; The

Star of India, 3 Aspin. 261; The Argentine, 13 P. D. 191.
[33] The Dorchester, 134 Fed. 564.
[34] The Glenogle, 122 Fed. 503.
[35] The Boston Towboat Co. v. Pettie, 49 Fed. 464, 1 C. C. A. 314, 1 U. S. App. 57; Pennsylvania Railroad Co. v. Washburn, 50 Fed. 335; In re Merritt and Chapman D. & W. Co., 103 Fed. 988; The Abby M. Deering, 105 Fed. 400, and cf. The Havilah, 50 Fed. 331, 1 C. C. A. 519, 1 U. S. App. 138. He does enough if he takes what seems the reasonable course. The City of Macon, 121 Fed. 686, 58 C. C. A. 434.
[36] The Columbus, 3 W. Rob. 158.
[37] The Reno, 134 Fed. 555.
[38] The Glaucus, 1 Lowell, 366.

total, expenses necessarily incurred to ascertain the extent of the injury, *e. g.*, in raising the vessel, may be recovered.[39]

§ 590. Limitation of liability.

By American law [40] the liability of the owner in case of collision, when free from personal fault, only extends to the value of his interest after collision, including the freight then pending; [41] so that if the ship is a total loss, further liability is extinguished.[42]

The principle of liability, when both vessels are in fault, is not that the owners of one are liable to the owners of the other for one-half the loss sustained by the latter (and *vice versa*), but that the entire damage is added together in one common mass, and equally divided between them so as to be equally borne.[43] In the North Star [44] both vessels were in fault, and one was lost. The owners of the latter claimed that they were not liable at all, because of the statutory limitation, but since the other vessel was liable they were entitled to recover half their damage, without any deduction for the half of the damages incurred by the other. But it was held that the usual rule applied, and that the vessel which had been lost was entitled to a claim against the other vessel (which suffered least) for half the difference between the amounts of their respective losses. The former "by her loss discharged her portion of the common burden, and so much more as the amount that would thus be decreed in her favor. Her delivery to the waves was tantamount to her surrender into court in case she had survived. It extinguished the personal liability of her owners by the mere operation of the maritime rule itself. As there was no decree against her owners for the payment of money, there was no room for the application in their favor of the statute of limited liability."

---

[39] The Venus, 17 Fed. 925; The Oneida, 84 Fed. 716.

[40] U. S. Rev. Stat., § 4283; The North Star, 106 U. S. 17, 28, 27 L. ed. 96, 1 Sup. Ct. 41. In England liability is maintained to the extent of £8 per ton, and in some cases to £15 per ton.

[41] The Harter Act does not cover

losses which happen before the voyage begins: Ralli *v.* New York & T. S. S. Co., 154 Fed. 286, 82 C. C. A. 290.

[42] La Bourgogne, 117 Fed. 261; Van Eyken *v.* Erie R. R., 117 Fed. 712.

[43] The North Star, 106 U. S. 17, 22, 27 L. ed. 96, 1 Sup. Ct. 41.

[44] 106 U. S. 17, 28, 27 L. ed. 961, Sup. Ct. 41.

By the Revised Statutes and the Rules in Admiralty [45] all competing claims in collision cases are to be raised and adjusted in one suit.[46] In the Job T. Wilson [47] both vessels were in fault, one was a total loss, and an innocent sufferer from the collision was entitled to recover his whole claim from the survivor; it was held that the latter should be allowed to recoup himself, out of the money payable to the other vessel in fault. It was urged that this would permit a claim for contribution by one wrongdoer against another. But the court said that in collision cases in Admiralty, the object of the proceeding was a contribution between wrongdoers.[48] If the other vessel cannot be brought in because not within the jurisdiction this cannot defeat the right to contribution and an independent suit may be brought.[49] When innocent cargo owners are entitled to full recovery, and one vessel is entitled to recoup against the other one-half the cargo loss, and all parties are before the court, recoupment may be had even though no cross libel has been filed under such. So, in all such cases the subrogated insurer stands in the place of the party to whose rights he is subrogated and when the latter is entitled to recover only half the loss, the insurer is likewise restricted to one-half. On the other hand, the insurer subrogated to the rights of the innocent cargo-owner, recovers in full.[50]

§ 591. Reduction of damages.

It is no defense to a suit for collision that the loss has been paid by the underwriters. The trespasser has no concern with the contract with the insurer.[51] Where, in a case of collision, a decree has been obtained abroad against the offending vessel, but for an amount less than the actual loss, in an action here for the rest of the loss, against the insurance company in which the in-

[45] U. S. Rev. Stat., § 941; Admiralty Rule 59, 112 U. S. App. 743.

[46] For an account of the difficulties arising out of a contrary practice in England, see The North Star, 106 U. S. 17, 25, 27 L. ed. 96, 1 Sup. Ct. 41.

[47] 84 Fed. 209. See acc., The Hercules, 20 Fed. 205; Jakobson v. Springer, 87 Fed. 948.

[48] Cf. The Virginia Shoman, 97 U. S. 309, 24 L. ed. 890; The Sterling, 106 U. S. 647, 27 L. ed. 98, 1 Sup. Ct. 89.

[49] The Mariska, 107 Fed. 989, 47 C. C. A. 115; cf. The New York, 108 Fed. 102, 47 C. C. A. 232; The Maine, 161 Fed. 401.

[50] The Livingstone, 104 Fed. 919.

[51] Yates v. Whyte, 4 Bing. N. C. 272; The Monticello v. Mollison, 17 How. 152, 15 L. ed. 68; The Atlas, 93 U. S. 302, 310, 23 L. ed. 863. See ante, § 588.

jured vessel was insured, the amount recovered abroad is to be deducted from the gross damage only, and not from the loss adjusted as a partial loss by deducting one-third new for old.[52]

§ 592. Partial loss.

The general principle followed by the admiralty courts in cases of collision is, that the damages to be assessed against the offending vessel must be sufficient to restore the other to the condition she was in at the time of collision, if restoration is practicable. The reasonable expense of repairing the vessel is therefore recoverable in case of partial loss, even if the vessel is in some respects stronger and more valuable after the repairs than she was before the collision.[53] The rule of one-third new for old does not apply in case of collision.[54] The owner cannot sell the vessel as she lies, deduct the price from her value before the collision, and recover the difference.[55] But the permanent depreciation in value is an item of compensation, in addition to the cost of repairs.[56] If the cost of raising and repairing the vessel exceeds the value, only the value can be recovered.[57]

[52] Dunham v. New England M. I. Co., 1 Lowell, 253.

[53] *United States:* The Catharine v. Dickinson, 17 How. 170, 15 L. ed. 233; The Granite State, 3 Wall. 310, 18 L. ed. 179; The Baltimore, 8 Wall. 377, 19 L. ed. 463; The Atlas, 93 U. S. 302, 307, 23 L. ed. 863 (*semble*); The Blossom, Olcott, 188; The Lotty, Olcott, 329; The Narragansett, Olcott, 388; The New Jersey, Olcott, 444; The Rhode Island, Olcott, 505; The City of Chester, 34 Fed. 429; Seabrook v. Raft of R. R. Cross-ties, 40 Fed. 596; Comerford v. The Melvina, 43 Fed. 77; The Alaska, 44 Fed. 501; The Starin, 116 Fed. 443; The Brailsbery, 127 Fed. 1005; and see The Providence, 98 Fed. 133.

Louisiana: Minor v. The Picayune, 13 La. Ann. 564.

Missouri: Atchison v. The Doctor Franklin, 14 Mo. 63.

New York: Mailler v. Express Propeller Line, 61 N. Y. 312.

England: Heard v. Holman, 19 C. B. (N. S.) 1; The Black Prince, Lush.

Adm. 568; The Gazelle, 2 W. Rob. 279; The Clyde, Swabey, 23; The Inflexible, Swabey, 200.

An excessive amount paid for repairs is not recoverable, The Clark, 22 Fed. 752; The Newman, 68 Fed. 1017; and the contract price is not conclusive as to the reasonableness of the amount. The Venus, 17 Fed. 87.

[54] *United States:* The Catharine v. Dickinson, 17 How. 170, 15 L. ed. 233; The Baltimore, 8 Wall. 377, 19 L. ed. 463 (*semble*).

England: The Pactolus, Swabey, 173.

[55] The Catharine v. Dickinson, 17 How. 170, 15 L. ed. 233; The Way, 28 Fed. 526; The Havilah, 50 Fed. 331, 1 C. C. A. 519; Scott v. Cornell S. B. Co., 59 Fed. 638.

[56] The Favorita, 4 Ben. 132; The Transit, 4 Ben. 138; The McIlvane, 126 Fed. 434. *Cf.* The Loch Trool, 150 Fed. 429.

[57] The Venus, 17 Fed. 925; The Havilah, 50 Fed. 331, 1 C. C. A. 519; The Hamill, 100 Fed. 509.

§ 593. Earnings of the vessel.

No compensation can be recovered for the loss of uncertain and contingent profits; [58] but the net earnings of which the vessel is certainly deprived during the repairs, may be considered, [59] for the value of the use of the vessel during her detention is the measure of damages on account of the detention. [60] This may be measured by the cost of substituting a similar vessel; [61] and though this may be a spare vessel owned by the

[58] *United States:* Smith v. Condry, 1 How. 28, 11 L. ed. 35; The Vaughan and Telegraph, 2 Ben. 47; The Ocean Queen, 5 Blatch. 493; The Saginaw, 95 Fed. 403 (no loss); Fisk v. City of New York, 117 Fed. 885; The Loch Trool, 150 Fed. 429.

Delaware: Steamboat Co. v. Whilldin, 4 Harr. 228; Cummins v. Presley, 4 Harr. 315.

Louisiana: Minor v. The Picayune, 13 La. Ann. 564.

England: The Clarence, 3 W. Rob. 283.

[59] *United States:* Williamson v. Barrett, 13 How. 101, 14 L. ed. 68; The Conqueror, 166 U. S. 110, 41 L. ed. 937, 17 Sup. Ct. 510; The Rhode Island, 1 Abb. Adm. 100, 2 Blatch. 113; The M. M. Caleb, 10 Blatch. 467; The Narragansett, Olcott, 388; Vantine v. The Lake, 2 Wall., Jr., 52; The Venus, 17 Fed. 925; The James A. Dumont, 34 Fed. 428; Coffin v. Osceola, 34 Fed. 921; New Haven S. B. Co. v. Mayor of New York, 36 Fed. 716; The Cayuga, 59 Fed. 483; The Armonia, 81 Fed. 227; The Providence, 98 Fed. 133, 38 C. C. A. 670; The Cumberland, 135 Fed. 234. See, however, Orhanovich v. The America, 4 Fed. 337; The Silica v. The Lord Warden, 30 Fed. 845; The Columbia, 109 Fed. 660, 48 C. C. A. 596.

England: Heard v. Holman, 19 C. B. (N. S.) 1; The Argentino, 14 App. Cas. 519; The Black Prince, Lush. Adm. 568; The Gazelle, 2 W. Rob. 279; The Inflexible, Swabey, 200.

A similar rule prevails in the com-

mon law courts, Shelbyville L. B. R. R. v. Lewark, 4 Ind. 471; as also in the analogous case of the detention of a vessel by an unlawful obstruction to the navigation. Jolly v. Terre Haute D. B. Co., 6 McLean, 237.

In The Cayuga, 59 Fed. 483, 8 C. C. A. 188, 16 U. S. App. 577, 585, the case of a barge towed by a tug owned by the same owners, it was alleged that there was a custom to deduct the towage expenses one-third the gross earnings in order to find the net earnings; but the court held that only the actual expense should be deducted, since such a custom would apply only to towage by a stranger.

[60] *United States:* Williamson v. Barrett, 13 How. 101, 14 L. ed. 69; The Gorgas, 10 Ben. 666; The Mayflower, 1 Bro. Adm. 376; The Colorado, 1 Bro. Adm. 411; The Stromless, 1 Low. 153; The Belgenland, 36 Fed. 504; The Sanford, 37 Fed. 148; American-Hawaiian S. S. Co. v. Morse D. D. & R. Co., 169 Fed. 678.

New York: Mailler v. Express Propeller Line, 61 N. Y. 312.

England: The Star of India, 1 P. D. 466.

[61] *United States:* The Cayuga, 14 Wall. 270, 20 L. ed. 828; The Favorita, 18 Wall. 598, 21 L. ed. 856; The Emma Kate Ross, 50 Fed. 845; The North Star, 140 Fed. 263.

England: The Marpessa, [1907] A. C. 241, 76 L. J. P. 128, 97 L. T. 1, 10 Asp. M. C. 464 (*semble*).

libellant, the fact is no reason for withholding the value of its use.[62] The average net earnings of the injured vessel may be shown, as evidence of the value of her use,[63] and so may the amount paid for her use in an existing charter-party; [64] but the rate of demurrage named in the charter-party being *res inter alios* is not evidence of the value of her use.[65] In the absence of direct evidence of earnings, it has been said that interest on value of the vessel may be allowed for the time occupied in repairing.[66]

The allowance must not extend beyond the time necessarily lost; [67] but if the damage was such as to make it reasonable to go into port for repairs before proceeding with the voyage, the loss of time thereby caused may be compensated.[68]

§ 594. Total loss.

If the injured vessel is a total loss, her market value at the time will be the criterion of damages.[69] Where the vessel was a total loss, and was raised at an expense of $1,000, it was held that this sum, less the amount for which the wreck was sold, could be recovered, as it could only be ascertained by raising the vessel that she was a total loss.[70] But if it would cost more to raise a sunken vessel than the wreck would be worth, the plaintiff can recover as for a total loss without raising her.[71] Freight which the injured ship is deprived of earning

[62] See *ante*, § 243a. But see The William M. Hoag, 101 Fed. 846.

[63] Williamson *v.* Barrett, 13 How. 101, 14 L. ed. 69; The Potomac *v.* Cannon, 105 U. S. 630, 26 L. ed. 1194; The State of California, 54 Fed. 404; The Bulgarian, 83 Fed. 312; The North Star, 140 Fed. 263; The Tremont, 161 Fed. 1.

[64] The Providence, 98 Fed. 133, 38 C. C. A. 670; Christie *v.* Fane S. S. Co., 159 Fed. 648.

[65] The James A. Dumont, 34 Fed. 428; The Hermann, 4 Blatch. 441; The Silica *v.* The Warden, 30 Fed. 845. But see The America, 4 Fed. 337; The Columbia, 109 Fed. 660; Société des Voiliers *v.* Oregon R. & N. Co., 178 Fed. 324.

[66] The Rhode Island, 2 Blatch. 113; Great Lakes Towing Co. *v.* Kelley I. L. & T. Co., 176 Fed. 492, 100 C. C. A. 108.

[67] The Thomas Kiley, 3 Ben. 228; Seabrook *v.* Raft of R. R. Cross-ties, 40 Fed. 596.

[68] Comerford *v.* The Melvina, 43 Fed. 77.

[69] The Ann Caroline, 2 Wall. 538, 17 L. ed. 833; The Umbria, 166 U. S. 404, 41 L. ed. 1053, 17 Sup. Ct. 610; The Rebecca, Blatch. & H. 347; The New Jersey, Olcott, 444.

[70] The Mary Eveline, 14 Blatch. 497; *acc.,* The Empress Eugenie, Lush. Adm. 138; The Oneida, 84 Fed. 716.

[71] Blanchard *v.* New Jersey S. B. Co. 59 N. Y. 292.

on account of the collision, less the charges and expenses which would have been incurred in order to earn it, may always be recovered;[72] but nothing is allowed in case of total loss for loss of use or of profits, interest on the value of the vessel alone being recoverable.[73]

§ 595. Value of the vessel.

In The Granite State [74] it was said that there is no established market value for boats, barges, and other articles of that description, as in the case of grain, cotton, or stock, and their loss cannot be measured by the ratio of their profits, since the loss of an old hulk of little value, which was making or might make considerable profits, might be supplied at a price much less than one proportioned to such profits. In the absence of a market, resort may be had to the judgment of persons acquainted with the business and values involved;[75] if there is a market value, that governs.[76] In Blanchard v. New Jersey Steamboat Co.[77] it was held, that evidence of the value of other vessels, with which the plaintiff's vessel could be compared, was not admissible to prove the value of the plaintiff's vessel. In The City of Alexandria [78] it was held that, there being no market value, the cost of the vessel might be shown as some evidence of value.[79] Ability to earn a statutory bounty is an element of value to be considered.[80]

§ 596. Damage to cargo.

The damages to the cargo are to be made good.[81] Where it

[72] The Golden Grove, 13 Fed. 674; The Utopia, 16 Fed. 507; La Champagne, 53 Fed. 398. Cf. The Havener, 50 Fed. 232; The Belgenland, 36 Fed. 504.

[73] The Umbria, 166 U. S. 404, 41 L. ed. 1053, 17 Sup. Ct. 610; The Roby, 103 Fed. 328; Smith v. Booth, 112 Fed. 553. Cf. Pennell v. The United States, 162 Fed. 64.

[74] 3 Wall. 310, 18 L. ed. 179.

[75] The Transit, 4 Ben. 138; The Emilie, 4 Ben. 235.

[76] The Colorado, 1 Bro. Adm. 411; The Hall, 128 Fed. 815; The Mobila, 147 Fed. 882.

[77] 59 N. Y. 292.

[78] 40 Fed. 697.

[79] The Lee, 24 Fed. 483; The Ant, 13 Fed. 91; The Bell, 5 Hughes, 172, 3 Fed. 581; The Gazelle, 33 Fed. 301; The Dimmock, 77 Fed. 226; The Trudeau, 54 Fed. 907, 4 C. C. A. 654, 2 U. S. App. 596; The Lucille, 169 Fed. 719; La Normandie, 58 Fed. 427, 7 C. C. A. 285.

[80] The Bell, 5 Hughes, 172, 3 Fed. 581; The Gazelle, 33 Fed. 301; Cunard S. S. Co. v. Fabre, 53 Fed. 288, 3 C. C. A. 534, 1 U. S. App. 614; The Dimmock, 77 Fed. 226.

[81] The Narragansett, Olcott, 388; La Normandie, 58 Fed. 427, 7 C. C. A. 285 (personal baggage of a passenger).

is a total loss, its value is the measure.[82] This value, it has been held in a comparatively early case, in analogy to the rule in the case of carriers, was to be estimated at the port of destination, at the time when, in the ordinary course of things, it would have been delivered.[83] But by the rule now prevailing, it seems settled that the value must be taken at the port of shipment, and on this sum interest may be allowed;[84] also the expense of lading the cargo and transporting it to the place of collision.[85] This corresponds to the rule in prize cases.[86] So in Dyer v. The National Steamship Co.,[87] the Republic of Peru, as co-libellant, claimed damages for the loss of a cargo of guano through the collision of the libellant's vessel with a vessel belonging to the respondent. The sale of guano was a monopoly belonging to the government of Peru. The guano was exported by the government, and its exportation by other parties was prohibited. Peruvian subjects were allowed to dig the guano for use in Peru alone. A little of it so dug was sold in Peru for $12 a ton, gold, but subject to the limitation that it should not be exported. Beyond this, there was no market for it in Peru. The cargo was lost just outside the harbor of New York. If it had arrived in New York, it would have sold for $60 a ton, in gold. Benedict, J., admitting the general rule above stated, held the principle of indemnity was a higher law to which the general rule must yield; that resort to the latter in this case would violate the former, and that, therefore, the value at New York, less the costs and charges which would have been incurred from the time and place of the loss to its arrival in New York, must be taken in determining the loss to the Republic of Peru. But on appeal to the Circuit Court, this de-

[82] Porter v. Allen, 8 Ind. 1.
[83] The Joshua Barker, Abb. Adm. 215.
[84] Smith v. Condry, 1 How. 28, 11 L. ed. 35; The Scotland, 105 U. S. 24, 26 L. ed. 1001; The Bell, 3 Fed. 581; The City of New York, 23 Fed. 616; The Umbria, 59 Fed. 489, 11 U. S. App. 612, 8 C. C. A. 194.
[85] The Vaughan & Telegraph, 2 Ben. 47; The Ocean Queen, 5 Blatch. 493.
If a vessel carrying her owner's goods is lost, he cannot recover, as for freight; because if expectation of enhanced value cannot be considered as to goods, the same is true as regards the loss of the ship. Crowell v. The Beatrice Havener, 50 Fed. 232.
[86] The Amiable Nancy, 3 Wheat. 546, 560, 4 L. ed. 456; The Lively, 1 Gall. 315; Atlas S. S. Co. v. The Colon, 4 Fed. 469, 18 Blatch. 277.
[87] 7 Ben. 395. See also The Aleppo, 7 Ben. 120; The Hugo, 61 Fed. 860.

cision was reversed, on the ground, as stated by Blatchford, J., that the value at the place of loss should not include the profits to be realized by transmitting the cargo to the point of destination.[88] Expenses incurred by the master in minimizing the damage cannot be recovered, since they enure to his own advantage.[89]

§ 596a. Negligent injury to cargo—The Harter Act.

Prior to the passage of the Harter Act [90] the responsibility of the ship for due care in relation to the cargo was governed by principles substantially the same as in the case of any other carrier. In recent times, however, it had become usual to insert in bills of lading stipulations limiting the liability of the vessel for negligence, in the case of losses caused by unseaworthiness, bad stowage, negligence in navigation, etc.; and these stipulations had been held in England, if not in this country, to be valid contracts, in some cases even when they exempted the ship from the consequences of her own negligence.[91] Under these circumstances Congress passed the act of Feb. 13, 1893, entitled "an act relating to navigation of vessels, bills of lading, and to certain obligations, duties and rights in connection with the carriage of property." It may be regarded as a compromise between the attempt on the one

[88] 14 Blatch. 483, 490. Two cases in which the value at the port of destination was allowed were distinguished, on the ground that there was no value at the place where the cargo had been taken on board. Bourne v. Ashley, 1 Low. 27 (whale converted in Okhotsk Sea); Swift v. Brownell, 1 Holmes, 467 (oil and bone lost by collision in Arctic Ocean).

[89] Ralli v. New York & T. S. S. Co., 154 Fed. 286, 82 C. C. A. 290.

[90] 27 U. S. Stat. 445, c. 105.

[91] The Delaware, 161 U. S. 459, 471, 40 L. ed. 771, 16 Sup. Ct. 516. Cf. Compania de Nav. La Flecha v. Brauer, 168 U. S. 104, 117, 42 L. ed. 399, 18 Sup. Ct. 12; Knott v. Botany Mills, 179 U. S. 68, 71, 45 L. ed. 90, 21 Sup. Ct. 30.

In The Delaware, supra, at p. 472, the court said:

"As decisions were made by the courts from time to time, holding the vessel for non-excepted liabilities, new clauses were inserted in the bills of lading to meet these decisions until the common-law responsibility of carriers by sea had been frittered away to such an extent that several of the leading commercial associations, both in this country and in England, had taken the subject in hand and suggested amendments to the maritime law in line with those embodied in the Harter Act." The opinion contains extracts giving illustrations of the burdensome character of these stipulations.

hand to exempt the vessel from all liability, and the strict rule of liability on the other. The first section makes null and void stipulations relieving the vessels engaged in foreign trade or their owners from liability in case of negligence, fault or failure in proper loading, stowage, custody, care or proper delivery of goods. The second section declares it to be unlawful to avoid, or limit the obligation of the owner to exercise due diligence to properly equip, man, provision and outfit the vessel, to make her seaworthy, to carefully handle and stow her cargo, and to care for and properly deliver the same. The third section, introducing a wholly new principle, provides that, if the owner shall exercise due diligence to make her seaworthy, "neither the vessel, her owner or owners, agent or charterers shall become or be held responsible for damage or loss resulting *from faults or errors in navigation or in the management of said vessel,* nor shall they be liable for losses arising from damages of the sea or other navigable waters, acts of God or public enemies, or the inherent defect, quality or vice of the thing carried, or from insufficiency of packages, or service under legal process, or for loss resulting from any act or omission of the shipper or owner of the goods, his agent or representative, or from saving or attempting to save life or property at sea, or from any deviation in rendering such service.[92] In The Viola [93] this statute came before the District Court for the Southern District of New York. Brown, J., held that there was no intention on the part of Congress to legislate generally with reference to rights and liabilities growing out of collisions, and that the act was designed to deal solely with the carrying vessel and her own cargo. The two fundamental principles already established, that the innocent cargo owner may recover in full from either vessel, and that each vessel in fault shall bear an equal portion of the whole loss, must still be applied, so far as compatible with the new act. The statute imposes modifications upon both sides as applied in particular instances. "The owner of the carrier vessel being no longer liable for the losses sustained by her own

---

[92] For the proper construction of the act, see Knott *v.* Botany Mills, 179 U. S. 68, 45 L. ed. 90, 21 Sup. Ct. 30; Int.

Nav. Co. *v.* Farr & Barley Mfg. Co., 181 U. S. 218, 45 L. ed. 830, 21 Sup. Ct. 591.
[93] 59 Fed. 632, 634, 60 Fed. 296.

cargo through faults in her navigation, is not bound to admit, in case of her total loss, of any offset in favor of the other vessel for the half of what the latter may be bound to pay on account of the cargo of the former, and this introduces an important modification of the moiety rule as heretofore administered."

On the other hand, there is no reason to suppose that it was the intention of Congress to relieve the carrier vessel of the expense of the other vessel in collision cases, that is, to add to the liability of the latter. To avoid this, the act must be held to mean that so much of the cargo loss as would previously have been charged against the carrier vessel, shall now be borne by the cargo owner.

According to this decision the adjustment of loss in cases of collision by mutual fault is to be made upon the principle that neither vessel is to be charged with any greater aggregate since this Act than she would have been charged before, under like circumstances; that the losses of the two vessels themselves are first to be made even,[94] (including personal effects, which are treated as part of the vessel); that the carrying vessel cannot be charged with any part of the loss suffered by her own cargo directly, or indirectly, nor can any offset against her claim to damages be made by the other vessel on account of what the latter vessel must pay for that cargo damage; but that the same offset which would have been formerly allowed against the carrying vessel, or the moneys payable to her, must now be deducted from the claim of her cargo. "Under this construction the cargo owner, whenever the surviving vessel is of sufficient value, will always be paid at least one-half his loss, and sometimes in full; as when the damages to the cargoes of both vessels are equal."

Illustrations are given by the court. Vessels A and B are each damaged $10,000, and only A's cargo damaged—say $5,000. B pays $2,500. If A's loss were $2,000, and her cargo's $4,000; B's $8,000, and her cargo's $6,000, then B, after receiving $3,000 from A, should pay A's cargo in full, since that would not exceed half the aggregate loss; while A should pay B's cargo but $5,000, as this would reach A's limit of half the entire loss, and A could not offset against B's claim any further payment

---

[94] The North Star, 106 U. S. 17, 27 L. ed. 96, 1 Sup. Ct. 41.

to B's cargo. If the cargo losses had been $5,000 each, each would be paid in full.

If A and her cargo were each damaged $10,000, while B and her cargo sustained no damages, A's cargo loss might be required to be paid in full by B before equalizing the losses between the two vessels alone, if such payment could be lawfully offset by B against A's loss of $10,000. But as A is in no way responsible for any part of her own cargo loss, such payment by B cannot be availed of as an offset against A's claim for half her damage, and since B's aggregate liability should not be increased under the Act of 1893, the mode indicated in the case of The North Star [95] should be followed in such cases. These principles were applied in the case of The Viola. The loss of the libellants' vessel including freight and personal effects was about $5,930, of her cargo about $1,300 and these were total losses; the damage to The Viola was about $260, to her cargo nothing. The Viola had been sold, and her net proceeds amounted to about $3,440. On an adjustment of costs and fees, the claim of the libellant on his vessel's account against The Viola amounted to about $2,723, to equalize the loss between the two vessels. As no part of the cargo loss could be offset against the libellant, the cargo must bear one-half that loss itself; and the defendants the other half, this making up the amount the defendants would previously have been called upon to pay. The surplus, about $70, was decreed to belong to the defendant. In The Niagara [96] the principles laid down were still further explained by Brown, J., who said, "Upon any complication, the first inquiry is, to what amount was each vessel, or her owner, liable under the previous law, upon the particular facts of the case? Under the Harter Act, if it is applicable, that liability cannot be exceeded, and it will remain the same, if necessary to make good the damage to the cargo of the other ship. In getting at the amount which either vessel is to pay under the Harter Act, her own cargo is to be treated as non-existent, because when the Harter Act is oper-

---

[95] 106 U. S. 17, 27 L. ed. 96, 1 Sup. Ct. 41. As to the effect of the Harter Act on adjustments in general average, see The Irrawaddy, 171 U. S. 187, 43

L. ed. 130, 18 Sup. Ct. 831; The Jason, 178 Fed. 414, 101 C. C. A. 628.

[96] 77 Fed. 329; acc., The Rosedale, 88 Fed. 324.

ative the carrier vessel (A) is not liable for that item of damage. But the other ship (B) is bound to pay that item of cargo loss, as well as one-half the damage to the two ships up to the limit previously ascertained, as above stated, if the remaining value of the ship (B) and her pending freight are sufficient for that purpose. When this value is not sufficient, and the damage to the first vessel (A) is greater than the damage to the other ship (B) two conflicting claims arise, one in favor of the ship (A) for the purpose of equalizing the loss of the two vessels, and another claim for the loss on (A's) cargo. As those claims arise at the same time and are of equal merit, the remaining value of the ship (B) and her pending freight should be apportioned *pro rata*, according to the amount of the two claims." [97]

When both vessels are in fault, and one is sunk, with her cargo, the cargo owner has the superior lien for reparation; that of the owner, or charterer is subordinate.[98] Claims of officers and crew of a vessel in fault are also subordinate to those of the cargo owner.[99]

§ 597. Costs.

Costs in Admiralty are under the control of the court.

They are sometimes, on equitable considerations, denied to the party who prevails, and they are sometimes given to an unsuccessful libellant, who has been misled by the other party. Generally, they follow the decree, but circumstances of equity, of hardship, of oppression, or of negligence lead the court to depart from that rule in a great variety of cases.[100]

§ 597a. Interest.

The general principles governing the allowance of interest do not differ from those applied by courts of law.[101] Rule 23 of

---

[97] Injuries to passengers, and claims for loss or damage to their personal baggage are not within the exemptions of the first clause of the third section of the act. Such claims, therefore, can be proved against both vessels. The Rosedale, 88 Fed. 324; *In re* California N. & I. Co., 110 Fed. 678.

[98] The George W. Roby, 103 Fed. 328, 49 C. C. A. 481.

[99] The George W. Roby, 103 Fed. 328, 336, 49 C. C. A. 481.

[100] The Sapphire, 18 Wall. 51, 21 L. ed. 814. For recovery of premium for bond to secure discharge of vessel see The Europe, 175 Fed. 596.

[101] *United States:* The Swallow, Olcott, 334; The James A. Dumont, 34 Fed. 428; The John H. Starin, 116 Fed. 433; The Hamilton, 95 Fed. 844; The

the Supreme Court provides that "in cases in Admiralty, damages and interest may be allowed if specially directed by the court," and it has been said [102] that this "leaves the matter to the sound discretion of the court." [103] But there is nothing arbitrary about this discretion. The main difference between the allowance of interest at law and in Admiralty is that in the latter there is no question of the jurisdiction over the matter respectively by court and jury. In collision cases, when damages are given for detention, interest may be allowed as damages, though the demand is evidently unliquidated before suit brought.[104] Where demurrage is stipulated for day by day, and daily demanded for every day's detention, interest on it must be allowed.[105] In collision cases, however, notwithstanding the decision in The Alexandria [106] there would seem to be ordinarily no reason for allowing interest.[107]

In Hemmenway v. Fisher [108] it was said that the rate of interest in Admiralty should be uniform, and not vary with the law of the States.[109]

§ 598. Stipulations.

The judgment in Admiralty cannot generally exceed the amount of the stipulation given for the discharge of the vessel, for that is all that is within the jurisdiction of the court.[110]

Oregon, 89 Fed. 697; The Rabboni, 53 Fed. 948; The Illinois, 84 Fed. 697; The Celestial Empire, 11 Fed. 761; The Switzerland, 67 Fed. 617.

England: The Hebe, 2 W. Rob. 530.

[102] New Zealand Ins. Co. v. Parnmoor S. Co., 79 Fed. 368, 24 C. C. A. 644, 48 U. S. App. 245.

[103] Dyer v. National S. N. Co., 118 U. S. 507, 30 L. ed. 154, 6 Sup. Ct. 1174; The North Star, 44 Fed. 492; The Syracuse, 97 Fed. 978; The Alaska, 44 Fed. 697; The Itaska, 117 Fed. 885; The Mahoney, 127 Fed. 773; The Eagle Point, 136 Fed. 1010; The Rickmers, 142 Fed. 305; The North Star, 140 Fed. 263.

[104] The Natcher, 78 Fed. 183, 24 C. C. A. 49, 41 U. S. App. 708; The Kalbfleisch, 59 Fed. 198; The Gilchrist, 173 Fed. 666. In salvage cases,

when exaggerated claims are made, interest may be disallowed. Merritt & C. D. & W. Co. v. Chubb, 113 Fed. 173, 51 C. C. A. 119.

See, however, The Strong, 156 Fed. 427.

[105] 35,000 boxes of Oranges and Lemons, 14 U. S. App. 562, 57 Fed. 236, 16 C. C. A. 317.

[106] 10 Ben. 101.

[107] Johanson v. The Bark Storia, 4 Fed. 573.

[108] 20 How. 255, 15 L. ed. 799.

[109] This view was adhered to, and six per cent allowed, in The Oregon, 89 Fed. 520. And this is the rate of interest usually allowed in the Southern District of New York. The Aleppo, 7 Ben. 120.

[110] The Webb, 14 Wall. 406, 20 L. ed. 774.

And a stipulator, unless personally guilty of default or contumacy, cannot be held liable for more than the amount of his stipulation; even on appeal, the costs recoverable are limited to the stipulation for costs and the appeal bond.[111] The stipulated sum cannot be increased by the allowance of interest.[112] The stipulation may, however, expressly provide for interest. in which case it is reasonable.[113]

§ 599. Personal injury—Division of loss.

A vessel is liable for personal injuries (including loss of life, within Lord Campbell's act), which are the natural and proximate consequence of a collision.[114] So where the plaintiff's wife is killed by a collision between two vessels, he can recover against the vessel in fault by proceeding *in rem*.[115] The common law rule that no action lies for the death of a human being is held in the United States to be a rule of general maritime law.[116] Action may, however, be brought in a United States court on a State statute; but the damages for death, though unlimited by the State Constitution, may in collision cases be limited by Federal statutes, proportioning recovery to the owner's interest in the vessel—and the State courts will enforce the Federal limitation.[117]

The rule of division of loss is now held to apply to the case of personal torts.[118] As a result, a party suing in an admiralty court for any tort, though he was guilty of contributory negligence, is allowed to recover for a portion of his loss.

So in McCord *v.* The Tiber,[119] The Tiber having got aground,

[111] The Wanata, 95 U. S. 600, 24 L. ed. 461.

[112] Hemmenway *v.* Fisher, 20 How. 255, 15 L. ed. 799; The Ann Caroline, 2 Wall. 538, 17 L. ed. 833; The Favorite, 12 Fed. 213; *In re* Harris, 57 Fed. 243, 6 C. C. A. 320; The Battler, 58 Fed. 704; Smith *v.* Booth, 112 Fed. 553.

A few cases sometimes cited to the contrary: The Ann Caroline, 2 Wall. 538, 17 L. ed. 833; The Wanata, 95 U. S. 600, 24 L. ed. 461; The Manitoba, 122 U. S. 97, 30 L. ed. 1095, 7 Sup. Ct. 1158: are distinguished by Lacombe, J. in his learned opinion, *In re* Harris, 57 Fed. 243, 6 C. C. A. 322.

[113] The George W. Roby, 111 Fed. 601, 49 C. C. A. 481.

[114] The George and Richard, L. R. 3 Adm. 466, 24 L. T. R. 717.

[115] The Sea Gull, Chase, 145.

[116] The Harrisburg, 119 U. S. 199, 30 L. ed. 358, 7 Sup. Ct. 140; Rundell *v.* C. G. Transatlantique, 100 Fed. 655, 49 L. R. A. 92.

[117] Loughin *v.* McCauley, 186 Pa. 517, 40 Atl. 1020, 48 L. R. A. 33.

[118] The Oregon, 45 Fed. 62; The City of Norwalk, 55 Fed. 98; The Wilson, 84 Fed. 204; Jakobson *v.* Springer, 87 Fed. 948.

[119] 6 Biss. 409. In this case, the

a line was stretched across the main channel of the river to aid in getting her off. The plaintiff was piloting a raft down the river, and was struck in the back by the rope, and injured. It was held that both parties were in fault. The court said: "When both parties are in fault, the court apportions the damages between them, according to justice and equity, having due regard to the degree of negligence imputable to each; so that, in admiralty, a party in fault may recover of another party whose negligence contributed to cause the injury, a portion of the damages, while, at common law, a defendant must pay all damages, or none." So where by a collision between vessels mutually at fault a seaman or officer on one of the vessels is injured, he may recover compensation from the other vessel, but only for half his loss.[120]

But though the right of the injured party to recover a portion of his loss is settled, the application of the rule of equal division, which prevails in collision cases, is doubtful. It has often been decided that "the damages should be divided," as has been seen; but this phrase does not necessarily mean that the division must be equal. The whole subject has been recently reviewed by the Supreme Court of the United States in an exhaustive opinion of Blatchford, J.[121]

The suit was brought in the District Court for the Southern District of New York by the libellant against the steamer Max Morris, to recover damages for a personal injury while employed on the vessel in loading coal. In the District Court, Brown, J., entered a decree for the libellant, and on appeal, the opinions of the judges being in conflict, the question whether the libellant was entitled to "divided damages" was certified to the Supreme Court. The court found, as a matter of fact, that the injuries to the libellant were occasioned partly through his own negligence and partly through the negligence of the officers of the vessel.

The Supreme Court in deciding the case, refused to entertain the question whether the damages were to be equally

plaintiff was 47 years old, and had a family of five children. The accident disabled him from following his business as a pilot. It was held that he was entitled to $2,500.

[120] The Queen, 40 Fed. 694.
[121] The Max Morris, 137 U. S. 1, 34 L. ed. 586, 11 Sup. Ct. 29, affirming 24 Fed. 860, 28 Fed. 881, 24 Blatch. 124.

divided, holding that the only question presented by the certificate was whether the libellant was debarred from the recovery of any sum of money by reason of the fact that his own negligence contributed to the accident, although there was negligence also on the other side, and this question was decided in favor of the libellant, the court adding, "whether in a case like this the decree should be for exactly one-half of the damages sustained or might in the discretion of the court, be for a greater or less proportion of such damages, is a question not presented for our determination upon this record, and we express no opinion upon it."

The court refers to several cases in which the rule of the equal division of damages has been extended to claims other than those for damages to vessels in fault in collision,[122] and on the question before it refers to a number of cases in the lower courts of the United States, all of them cases in Admiralty, as showing "an amelioration of the common law rule, and an extension of the admiralty rule in a direction which is eminently just and proper. . . . As stated by the district judge in his opinion in the present case, the more equal distribution of justice, the dictates of humanity, the safety of life and limb and the public good will be best promoted by holding vessels liable to bear some part of the actual pecuniary loss sustained by the libellant, in a case like the present, when their fault is clear, provided the libellant's fault, though evident, is neither wilful, nor gross, nor inexcusable, and when the other circumstances present a strong case for his relief. We think this rule is applicable to all like cases of marine tort founded upon negligence and presented in admiralty, as in harmony with the rule for the division of damages in cases of collision. The mere fact of the negligence of the libellant as partly occasioning the injuries to him, when they also occurred partly through the negligence of the officers of the vessel, does not debar him entirely from a recovery."[123]

---

[122] The Washington, 9 Wall. 513, 19 L. ed. 787; Atlee v. Packet Co., 21 Wall. 389, 22 L. ed. 619; The Alabama, 92 U. S. 695, 23 L. ed. 763; The Atlas, 93 U. S. 302, 23 L. ed. 863; The Juniata, 93 U. S. 337, 23 L. ed. 930.

[123] Acc., The Frey, 113 Fed. 1003. Cf. The Explorer, 20 Fed. 135; The Wanderer, 20 Fed. 140; The Truro, 31 Fed. 158; The Eddystone, 33 Fed. 925; Olson v. Flard, 34 Fed. 477; Keiley v. The Cypress, 55 Fed. 332; William

As to the question, assuming that the loss is to be divided, what the rule of division is to be, the court refers to the ground of the rule for an equal division being the difficulty of determining in such cases, the degree of negligence on one side or the other. It is called by Cleirac [124] a *rusticum judicium i. e.,* a sort of rule of thumb. But either this rule must be adopted, or the whole matter must be left to the discretion of the court. This seems to be the rule adopted by the District Court of Oregon, which holds that the court will apportion the damages "according to principles of equity and justice, considering all the circumstances of the case." [125]

In the absence of an authoritative decision by the court of last resort, the rule cannot be yet regarded as definitely settled, though all the considerations in favor of the equal division of the loss in one class of cases would seem to apply in all.

§ 599a. Nominal damages in admiralty.

It is said that in Admiralty, a decree for nominal damages is never given, for the following reasons: 1st, because costs being discretionary, nominal damages cannot be requisite to support them; 2d, because they are not called for, as in some cases they are at common law to establish the existence of a right in the plaintiff. [126]

§ 599b. Exemplary damages.

Exemplary damages are awarded in Admiralty, as in other jurisdictions. [127]

In The William H. Bailey [128] it is said that they do not seem to have been allowed in any case in a proceeding *in rem;* and that in the English Admiralty the fact that the damage was caused by the wilful act of the master is sufficient reason for dismissing the libel. Generally, of course, when the dam-

Johnson & Co., Ltd., *v.* Johanson, 30 C. C. A. 675, 86 Fed. 886.

[124] Us et Coutumes de la Mer, 68.

[125] Olson *v.* Flard, 34 Fed. 477.

[126] Barnet *v.* Luther, 1 Curt. 434; Herbst *v.* The Asiatic Prince, 97 Fed. 343, 345; Munson *v.* Straits of Dover I. S. Co., 99 Fed. 787, 792; *In re* California N. & I. Co., 110 Fed. 670, 678.

[127] The Amiable Nancy, 3 Wheat. 546, 4 L. ed. 456; Gallagher *v.* The Yankee, 9 Fed. Cas. No. 5,196, Hoff. 456; The Yankee *v.* Gallagher, 30 Fed. Cas. No. 18,124, McAll. 467. Such damages cannot be awarded unless the owner is personally in fault. The Seven Brothers, 170 Fed. 126.

[128] 103 Fed. 799.

age is caused by a wilful act, it will be that of those engaged in the actual navigation of the vessel, and not that of the owner, who is the person responsible in a proceeding *in rem;* but if the owner himself is master, or authorizes the act, no reason is perceived why he should not be responsible in exemplary damages, whether the proceeding is *in rem* or *personam.*

§ 599c. Salvage.

Salvage is a claim peculiar to the law of Admiralty. It is never awarded in a court of common law, in which the nearest analogy is recovery on a *quantum meruit.*[129] It is an allowance made to persons by whose assistance a ship or boat, cargo, or other property is saved from danger or loss at sea. It is not prize-money, nor is it mere compensation for services; but is a reward for the hazard undertaken.

The elements on which the amount of salvage is based are generally stated as follows:[130]

1. The enterprise of the salvors in assisting a vessel in distress and the risk they take with their own lives and property of others.

2. The degree of danger and distress from which property is rescued, whether it was in imminent peril and almost certainly lost if not at the time rescued.

3. The degree of labor and skill shown, the time occupied.

4. The amount of property saved.

In order to justify the allowance of salvage, two elements must have been present; the absence of either prevents the allowance of salvage, and restricts the libellant to compensation for services rendered. These elements are danger [131] and success.[132] If the services were rendered at request salvage may be given, but it will be on a less liberal scale.[133]

[129] *Georgia:* Anthanissen v. Dart, 94 Ga. 543, 20 S. E. 124.
New York: Sturgis v. Law, 3 Sandf. 451.
[130] Taylor v. The Friendship, Bee, 175; McGinnis v. The Pontiac, 5 McLean, 359; Murphy v. Ship Suliote, 5 Fed. 99; Murray v. U. S., 55 Fed. 829, 5 C. C. A. 283; The Lamington, 86 Fed. 675, 30 C. C. A. 271; Wilder's Co. v. Lurline, 11 Hawaii, 83.

[131] Murray v. U. S., 55 Fed. 829. Cf. U. S. v. Morgan, 99 Fed. 570, where the risk existed, though it was slight, and salvage was awarded.
[132] Clark v. The Dodge Healey, 4 Wash. C. C. 651; Anderson v. The Edam, 13 Fed. 135.
[133] Wilmington Transportation Co. v. The Old Kensington, 39 Fed. 496.

The amount of salvage is entirely within the discretion of the court, and no rules can be laid down for its measure. At one time it was said that it should never exceed one-half the value of the property salved: [134] but in extreme cases salvage has been allowed at a higher rate.[135] It is often said that one-half the value is to be allowed for salving a derelict; [136] but even in this case there is no absolute rule beyond "enlarged discretion." [137] Where the danger to the property salved was great, and the services were attended with risk, or great exertions, the allowance is usually from one-third to one-half; [138] where the salvage is of a "low order" less than one-third is customary.[139] The amount of salvage is sometimes regulated by statute.[140]

[134] Cross v. The Bellona, Bee, 193; British Consul v. Smith, Bee, 178; Smith v. The Stewart, Crabbe, 218.

[135] Llewellyn v. Two Anchors, 1 Ben. 80.

[136] Hindry v. The Priscilla, Bee, 1; Sprague v. Barrels of Flour, 2 Story, 195. And see Coast Wrecking Co. v. Phœnix Ins. Co., 13 Fed. 127; Gardner v. Ninety-nine Gold Coins, 111 Fed. 552.

[137] Post v. Jones, 19 How. 150, 15 L. ed. 618.

[138] See Tyson v. Pryor, 1 Gall. 133 (1/3); Montgomery v. The T. P. Leathers, 1 Newb. 421 (1/3); Bearse v. Pigs of Copper, 1 Story, 314 (2/5). In Serviss v. Ferguson, 84 Fed. 202, 28 C. C. A. 327, the vessel was salved and brought into the dock, and while there she was destroyed by the negligence of the salvors. The salvors were awarded one-third of the value, and were then decreed to pay her whole value less the amount of salvage.

[139] See Crowell v. The Brothers, Bee, 136 (about 3/16); Blagg v. The Bicknell, 1 Bond, 270 (15%); Mattingly v. Colton, 2 Flip. 288, Fed. Cas. No. 9,294 (1/3 set aside); Bowley v. Goddard, 1 Low. 154 (51/2%); Studley v. Baker, 2 Low. 205 (1/4); Lee v. The Alexander, 2 Paine, 465 (1/15); United States v. Morgan, 99 Fed. 570.

[140] Talbot v. Seeman, 1 Cr. 1, 2 L. ed. 1 (1/8 to 1/2 for recapture).

CHAPTER XXVII

DAMAGES IN ACTIONS ON CONTRACTS

I.—General Principles

II.—Rules of Damages in Particular Cases

I.—GENERAL PRINCIPLES

§ 600. Actions upon contracts.

Having thus considered the general rules which govern and limit compensation in all cases, and the particular rules applicable in actions founded on tort, we now proceed to consider the great class of cases relating to actions founded on breach of contract. These actions generally grow out of negotiable paper, policies of insurance, the sale and warranty of chattels, contracts of agency, service, suretyship, or other express executory agreements, written or verbal, as well as those implied contracts where the law implies a quasi-contractual liability from the acts of the parties. These subjects will be considered separately; but before doing so, it will be necessary to state the general rules upon which the English and American law proceed in all cases *ex contractu*—rules which are themselves dependent upon and will be frequently found to throw additional light upon those great general principles as to certainty, remoteness, and other limits of recovery which lie at the root of our whole system of compensation.

In the present chapter contracts relating to real estate will not be considered. Although these are governed by the same general principles which affect all contracts, these principles are in the field of real estate more obscured by rules drawn from or affected by the feudal law. Understanding first the broad principles by which damages on any ordinary breach of contract are measured, we shall be the better prepared to comprehend a more complex and arbitrary system.

§ 601. Distinction between tort and contract.

* It was the constant and sedulous object of the common law to draw a distinct line between actions of contract and those of tort, *ex contractu* and *ex delicto;* and the rigor with which this distinction was maintained in regard to joinder of counts, causes of action, and election of actions, is familiar learning.**

* Again, as to the rules of evidence, while it is perfectly true that in actions of tort every attendant circumstance of aggravation can be given in evidence: on the other hand, nothing is better settled than that in actions of contract the parties are limited to the mere evidence of the breach of contract. But if damages are to be awarded on account of the oppressive, malicious, or fraudulent conduct of the defendant, it is manifest that this rule cannot be maintained; if one party gives evidence of such a character, it is plain that the other must have the right to rebut the testimony, and in this way the form of the action, the issue *ex contractu*, and the rules of testimony, would be completely lost sight of. If, at the trial, the evidence of a breach of contract were complete, certainly an offer to show that the defendant's act was dictated by a malicious, fraudulent, or oppressive spirit, would not be allowed; and it is very clearly inadmissible to consider, as in evidence for the purpose of regulating the damages, testimony incidentally introduced, which could not be directly given.**

§ 602. Distinction not destroyed by new system of pleading.

The modern system of pleading under which the old forms of action have disappeared might perhaps be expected in time to destroy the distinction between tort and contract. But there are many reasons for not anticipating this. No doubt in many cases,—*e. g.*, cases against carriers,—it is now often

impossible to tell from the pleadings whether the proceeding
sounds in tort or contract; but the breach of the contract here
is of a peculiar kind. The contract is one made in pursuance
of a public duty imposed upon the carrier; his breach of contract is therefore here in a certain sense a tort, at least in many
cases. But the inherent difference between a breach of an
agreement between parties, and that sort of a breach of duty
which we call a tort, is as old as the law itself. It is believed,
too, that as a general rule the measure of damages in one case
is necessarily different from the measure of damages in the
other. To put the plaintiff in the same position as if the contract has not been broken is the object in cases of contract;
whether the contract is broken by accident or by fraud can
make no difference. As long as the action is brought to obtain
compensation for the *loss of the contract*, the circumstances
attending the breach cannot affect the result. But if the cause
of action is a tort, the plaintiff must obtain full compensation
for an *act* or *series of acts*, the full effect of which cannot even
be understood unless we know every circumstance of aggravation and mitigation. The action for breach of promise of
marriage is an undoubted exception to the truth of this general observation; but this action is an anomaly in every respect, and unknown to other systems of law. It may be said
that redress should be given for bringing about a breach of
contract through duress, or fraud, or other oppression, and so
we conceive it would; but in such an action, the damages for
the loss of the contract would be one thing, and the damages
for the wrong another.[1]

§ 603. Motive not considered: Exemplary damages.

It may be considered then to be established that the motives
of the defendant in breaking his contract are to be disregarded. It follows from this principle that exemplary damages

[1] The rule of intervening cause pro-
duces a different result in tort and contract. In the former, the operation of
the intervening cause may affect the
right of action, and prevent any recovery; in the latter, where there is a
breach of contract, but the intervening
cause is the one to which loss is due, the
plaintiff still recovers, though only
a nominal sum. For an example, *cf.*
Lowery *v.* W. U. T. Co., 60 N. Y. 198,
19 Am. Rep. 154, with First Natl.
Bank of Barnesville *v.* W. U. T. Co.,
30 Oh. St. 555, 27 Am. Rep. 485.

cannot be recovered in an ordinary action for breach of contract.[2]

Like many other rules for determining the measure of damages, this has not always been recognized as law. At the beginning of the last century Chitty in his very valuable work on contracts [3] said that in certain cases, where the defendant might be regarded in the light of a wrongdoer in breaking his contract, great latitude might be allowed the jury in assessing the damages. The authority referred to by him [4] did not support the doctrine thus broadly stated; and although it received some support in American cases [5] it has been effectively disapproved in later cases.[6]

§ 604. Common law principles in cases of contract.

* "Damages are recoverable in every personal action which lies at the common law." [7] The language of the civil law is, *Loco facti impræstabilis succedit damnum et interesse.* We have already considered the subject of nominal damages and seen how far the courts go for the mere purpose of declaring a right. We are now to examine those cases of contract where substantial relief is demanded; and the two cardinal principles which will be found to pervade and regulate this branch of our

[2] *United States:* Grand Tower Co. *v.* Phillips, 23 Wall. 471, 23 L. ed. 71.
Georgia: Ford *v.* Fargason, 120 Ga. 606, 48 S. E. 180.
Illinois: Toledo, W. & W. Ry. *v.* Roberts, 71 Ill. 540.
Massachusetts: Magnolia Metal Co. *v.* Gale, 189 Mass. 124, 75 N. E. 219.
Michigan: Johnson *v.* Henry, 127 Mich. 548, 86 N. W. 1027.
New York: Duche *v.* Wilson, 37 Hun, 519.
Pennsylvania: Westfall *v.* Mapes, 3 Grant, 198 (but see McDowell *v.* Oyer, 21 Pa. 417).
Wisconsin: Kelley, Maus & Co. *v.* La Crosse Carriage Co., 120 Wis. 84, 97 N. W. 674.
England: Bain *v.* Fothergill, L. R. 7 H. L. 158.
The rule appears to be otherwise in the following states:

Louisiana (a civil law jurisdiction). Green *v.* Farmers' Consol. Dairy Co., 113 La. 869, 37 So. 858.
South Carolina: Welborn *v.* Dixon, 70 S. C. 108, 49 S. E. 232; Prince *v.* State M. L. I. Co., 77 S. C. 187, 57 S. E. 766.
Texas: Westfall *v.* Perry (Tex. Civ. App.), 23 S. W. 740; Ball *v.* Britton, 58 Tex. 57 (*cf.* Houston & T. C. R. R. *v.* Shirley, 54 Tex. 125).
[3] Page 684.
[4] Lord Sondes *v.* Fletcher, 5 B. & Ald. 835.
[5] Rose *v.* Beatie, 2 N. & McC. (S. C.) 538, 542; Garrett *v.* Stuart, 1 McC. (S. C.) 514; Ferrand *v.* Boushel, Harper (S. C.), 83.
[6] Hawkins *v.* Coulthurst, 5 B. & S. 343.
[7] Sayer on Damages, chap. 1, p. 6.

subject, are, *First*, that the plaintiff must show himself to have sustained damage, or, in other words, that actual compensation will only be given for actual loss; and, *Secondly*, that the contract itself furnishes the measure of damages. These two rules are closely interwoven with each other and it is impossible to consider them altogether separately. The first rule is one of great importance. It excludes a large class of cases in which relief is often sought before an injury has occurred; and we shall have frequent occasion to refer to it.** * This rule is, however, not without exception, as we shall hereafter see. The second rule, that the contract itself furnishes the measure of damages, is of equal importance. We have already adverted to it generally, but we have now to consider it more fully, and at the same time to notice such exceptions to it as may be found to exist.**

§ 605. Vague discretion of jury formerly.

* We have already had occasion to observe the vague discretion that in the early books is attributed to the jury in the matter of damages. Thus, as late as the reign of James I, where the plaintiff sued the defendant on a covenant that if certain land conveyed to him by the defendant fell short of a specified measurement, he, the defendant, would pay a fixed sum for every deficient acre, and alleged that the number of acres wanting would have amounted to the sum of £700, and the jury gave but £400 damages,—it was held, that this was well found; and it was said, "If *all* the land was wanting, *still the jury are chancellors*, and can give such damages as the case requires in equity." [8]

So even as late as the middle of the 18th century, in an action for escape against the sheriff, Lord C. J. Wilmot said that in actions on the case, the damages are "totally uncertain and at large." [9] So, a standard text-writer [10] uses this language:

"In all actions which sound in damages, the jury seem to have a discretionary power of giving what damages they think proper; for though in contracts the very sum specified and agreed on is *usually* given, yet if there are any circumstances of

---

[8] Sir Baptist Hixt's Case, 2 Roll. Abr. 703 (Trial pl. 9).

[9] Ravenscroft *v.* Eyles, 2 Wils. 295.

[10] Bacon Abr. Tit. Damages, D.

hardship, fraud, or deceit, though not sufficient to invalidate the contract, the jury may consider of them, and proportion and mitigate the damages accordingly; as in case upon a policy of assurance, which was a cheat, for an old vessel was painted, and goods of no value put in the vessel, and about £1,500 insured on it, and then the ship was voluntarily sunk."

There can be no stronger proof of the revolution that has been effected in this branch of our law, than is furnished by this citation. Here, even on promissory notes, the jury are said to have power to give a sum less than that expressed in them; and a contract which now the law would pronounce utterly void, is declared to be a matter for the mere discretion of the jury.**

§ 606. Compensation now a question of law.

* It is, in truth, but slowly and at comparatively a recent period that the jury has relinquished its control over actions even of contract, and that any approach has been made to a fixed and legal measure of damages. But, by degrees, the salutary principle has been recognized, and it is now well settled, that in all actions of contract, subject to the exception already noticed, and in all cases of tort where no evil motive is charged, the amount of compensation is to be regulated by the direction of the court, and the jury cannot substitute their vague and arbitrary discretion for the rules which the law lays down.[11]

It is, in fact, indispensable that it should be so: the measure of damages is the gist of the remedy; the remedy is no part of the facts of the cause, while, on the other hand, it so completely controls the rights of the parties, that, if any absolute discretion be given to the jury over the amount of compensation, the power of the court over questions of law would be most emphatically a barren sceptre. The measure of damages in all cases, then, where no complaint is made of evil motive, is a pure question of law; in all cases of contract, the sole object of the

[11] It is therefore error in an action of contract to charge the jury that they may use their discretion in assessing damages. Jenkins *v.* Kirtley, 70 Kan. 801, 79 Pac. 671; Union Pac. Ry. *v.* Shook, 3 Kan. App. 710, 44 Pac. 685.

Or that they may allow what they believe to be just and right.
Michigan: Howe *v.* North, 69 Mich. 272, 37 N. W. 213.
Missouri: Kick *v.* Doerste, 45 Mo. 134.

court is to ascertain the agreement of the parties, and that agreement, as a general rule, controls the measure of remuneration. "In contracts," said the Supreme Court of Massachusetts,[12] "where the precise sum is fixed amd agreed on by the parties, as in many actions of assumpsit and of covenant, the jury are confined to that sum." **

* It is urged, says the Supreme Court of Pennsylvania, that the standard furnished by the contract "may be resorted to as a measure of damages, but not as the measure. If it be not the exclusive measure, it must be disregarded altogether. If it be but one of many standards, then there is no standard at all, or as good as none. The jury are without a rule when they have their choice between different rules." [13]   "There are certain established rules," says the Court of Exchequer in England, "according to which the jury ought to find. And here there is a clear rule, that the amount which would have been received if the contract had been kept, is the measure of damages if the contract is broken." [14]

"It is desirable," says the Supreme Court of Massachusetts, "to have as definite and precise rules upon the subject of damages as are practicable." [15]   "A proper administration of justice requires that the rules established by law for the assessment of damages should be adhered to," says the Supreme Court of Louisiana.[16] **

606a. Amount of the consideration not recoverable.

The amount of the consideration is not the measure of recovery.[17]   * So, where the plaintiff had forborne a debt, in consideration that the defendant would build a house and give a lease of it, the value of the lease was the standard.[18] So, where a wagon was transferred in consideration that the de-

[12] Leland v. Stone, 10 Mass. 459.
[13] McDowell v. Oyer, 21 Pa. 417.
[14] Alder v. Keighley, 15 M. & W. 117.
[15] Batchelder v. Sturgis, 3 Cush. (Mass.) 201.
[16] Arrowsmith v. Gordon, 3 La. Ann. 105.
[17] Arkansas: Manuel v. Campbell, 3 Ark. 324.

California: Norddeutschen F. V. G. v. Bertheau, 79 Cal. 495; Rayner v. Jones, 90 Cal. 78, 27 Pac. 24.
Michigan: Pierson v. Spaulding, 61 Mich. 90.
Tennessee: Singleton v. Wilson, 85 Tenn. 344.
Texas: Bell v. Keays (Tex. Civ. App.), 100 S. W. 813.
[18] Strutt v. Farlar, 16 M. & W. 249.

fendant would break up certain land, the value of the labor, and not of the wagon, was held to be the measure of damages.[19] So again, if the rent of mills is to be paid in repairs, the measure of damages is the value of the repairs agreed to be made.[20] ** On the same principle, where the plaintiff agreed to work for a man till she was 21 or married, and he agreed to leave her in his will a portion of his estate equal to that left to any of his children, it was held, in an action against his executors, that the measure of her damages was the value of the portion promised, and not the value of her services.[21]

In Homesly v. Elias [22] it appeared that the plaintiff sold yarn to the defendant to be paid for in cotton, the deliveries to be made before a certain day. Before that time the defendant refused to complete the contract. The plaintiff had then delivered more than enough yarn to pay for the cotton delivered. It was held that the plaintiff's damages were the value at the time of refusal of the cotton not delivered, less the value at the limit of time fixed for delivery of the yarn not delivered. Where one agreed with a surviving partner that he would pay the firm's debts, if the partner would apply the firm's property to his debts, it was held, in an action brought on this agreement by the surviving partner, that the measure of damages was the amount the other should have paid.[23] The measure of damages in an action by the father to recover the earnings of his minor son, is not what the son's labor would have been worth to the father, but what the son, had he been of age to contract, would have been entitled to from the employer.[24] So for breach of contract to teach a slave a trade, the measure of damages was held to be the additional value he would have had from knowing the trade.[25]

So where a town gave the defendant $1,000, for his agreement to run a factory employing twenty workmen in the town for ten years, and the defendant ran the factory for six years only the town could not, in an action for breach of the agree-

[19] Ellison v. Dove, 8 Blackf. (Ind.) 571.

[20] Baldwin v. Lessner, 8 Ga. 71.

[21] Frost v. Tarr, 53 Ind. 390.

[22] 75 N. C. 564.

[23] Weddle v. Stone, 12 Ind. 625.

[24] Weeks v. Holmes, 12 Cush. (Mass.) 215.

[25] Bell v. Walker, 5 Jones, L. (43 N. C.) 43.

ment, recover a proportional part of the $1,000,[26] and so for breach of a contract by which the defendant agreed to employ the plaintiff as its manager, in consideration of a conveyance of certain property to the defendant, the measure of damages is not the value of the property.[27]

This principle was lost sight of in a Missouri case.[28] The plaintiff agreed to help cut the defendant's wheat, for which the defendant was to help cut the plaintiff's oats; the plaintiff performed his part of the contract, the defendant did not perform his part. The plaintiff sued on a *quantum meruit* for the value of his services, and also for damages for failure to help cut the oats. It was held that damages for failure to help cut the oats could not be recovered, but the value of the plaintiff's services was allowed as the measure of damages. This was an allowance of the consideration.[29]

§ 606b. Inadequacy of consideration.

* It is to be observed that mere inadequacy of consideration is no objection to a contract. Some consideration is requisite, but the sufficiency of the consideration cannot be inquired into. So it has been contended that a guarantor of negotiable paper receiving a trifling percentage for his guaranty, could not be held liable for the whole face of the paper; but on the same ground he was held liable;[30] and the rule has been repeatedly declared, that the value of the services or the amount of the consideration is of no importance, where a stipulated sum is agreed to be paid for the performance of a specific service.[31] It is only where fraud, mistake, illegality, or oppression intervenes, that the consideration can, in this respect, be inquired into.**

§ 606c. Unconscionable agreements.

* There is a class of decisions which may at first sight appear

[26] Brighton v. Auston, 19 Ont. App. 305. *Contra*, Fort Wayne E. L. Co. v. Miller, 131 Ind. 499, 30 N. E. 23.

[27] Marston v. Singapore Rattan Co., 163 Mass. 296, 39 N. E. 1113.

[28] Otis v. Koontz, 70 Mo. 183.

[29] The claim to recover the consideration paid is ordinarily put on the ground that the plaintiff has the right

to rescind the contract. It is sometimes recovered where the profits are uncertain. Missouri, K. & T. Ry. v. Fort Scott, 15 Kan. 435.

[30] Oakley v. Boorman, 21 Wend. (N. Y.) 588.

[31] Hamilton College v. Stewart, 1 N. Y. 581.

to be opposed to the general rule, that the contract furnishes the measure of damages. In an early case, brought on an assumpsit to pay for a horse a barley-corn a nail, doubling it every nail, with an averment that there were thirty-two nails in the shoes of the horse, which, being so doubled every nail, came to five hundred quarters of barley, the judge who tried the cause directed the jury to disregard the contract, and to give the value of the horse in damages, which was £8, and so they did.[32] The principle of this decision is, that if the agreement be unconscionable, the court will render such damages as may appear reasonable, without being bound by the terms of the contract. So in Massachusetts, where a note had been given to stay execution, payable in oats at twenty cents per bushel, when in fact they were worth thirty-seven cents, it was held that the jury might disregard the contract on the ground that it was unconscionable, and fix the value of the oats at twenty cents.[33] So in an action brought on a promise of £1,000

[32] James v. Morgan, 1 Levintz, 111. In another case, a somewhat similar contract came up on demurrer. The plaintiff declared on an agreement that the defendant, in consideration of 2s. 6d. in hand paid, and of £4 17s. 6d. to be paid on performance, agreed to deliver two grains of rye corn on Monday, the 29th of March, and four grains on the next Monday, and so doubling *quolibet alio die Lunæ* for one year. The defendant demurred, saying, "that the agreement appeared, upon the face of it, to be impossible, the rye to be delivered amounting to such a quantity as all the rye in the world was not so much; and being impossible, was void, and the defendant not bound to perform it." But after argument the court thought otherwise, Powell, J., saying: "That though the contract was a foolish one, it would hold in law, and the defendant ought to pay something for his folly;" whereupon the reporter adds: "The counsel for the defendant perceiving the opinion of the court to be against his client, offered the plaintiff his half crown and his costs, which

was accepted of, and so no judgment given in the case."

A question arose on the meaning of the contract—the defendant insisting that *quolibet alio die Lunæ* meant *every* Monday, but Lord Holt said it must be construed "*every other Monday.*" This made a material difference in the possibility of executing the contract; for if the quantity were doubled thirty times, it would have reached 125 quarters; if fifty-two, it would have amounted to 524,288,000 quarters. Thornborow   v. Whitacre, 2 Lord Raym. 1164.

And the principle of James v. Morgan was approved of by Lord Chancellor Hardwicke, in Earl of Chesterfield v. Jansen, 1 Wils. 286, 295.

[33] Cutler v. How, 8 Mass. 257; Cutler v. Johnson, 8 Mass. 266; Baxter v. Wales, 12 Mass. 365; Leland v. Stone, 10 Mass. 459. And Lord Mansfield used analogous language in regard to the action for money had and received. "Shall a man," said his lordship, "in an action for money had and received, which is an equitable action, and

if the plaintiff should find the defendant's owl, the court declared, though the promise was proved, that the jury might mitigate the damages.[34] ** And where the building of a jail was let to the lowest bidder, and the defendant took the contract at less than a fourth part of a fair price, and, upon his subsequent failure to perform, the contract was let to another contractor, it was held that the measure of damages was not the difference between the two bids, but the difference between a fair price at the first and at the second letting; the court remarking that "equity" will permit no more recovery than the actual loss caused by the defendant's foolish bidding.[35]

On this principle must be rested the decision in a New York case.[36] The defendants being engaged in a flour commission business, hired of the plaintiff for one night a canvas cover, fifty feet in length by twenty-five feet wide, to be spread over flour on board a canal boat lying at a wharf in the city of New York. The price to paid be for the use of the canvas was the "customary charge," which for twenty-four hours or less was proved to be one dollar. Through some oversight the cover was not returned until the lapse of about five weeks. The action was brought for the use of the canvas during the whole period last mentioned. The plaintiff insisted upon a recovery of one dollar for each day of the detention. It was held that defendants were not liable to be charged at the contract rate per day for every day during which the canvas was detained. The recovery should have been limited to the value of the use for the entire period of the detention. It will be noticed that this is the result of a fair interpretation of the contract; for the "customary charge" for one night was not the customary charge for five weeks.

But in a later case in Massachusetts, the earlier cases cited above are overruled, and the right of a court of law to modify an unconscionable contract has been denied.[37] The assertion of the right to sever the contract, to declare a part of it uncon-

founded in conscience, recover such an unmeasurable and exorbitant demand? Most clearly he shall not." Jestons v. Brooke, 2 Cowp. 793; and Floyer v. Edwards, 1 Cowp. 112.

[34] Bacon Abr. Damages, D.

[35] Chambers v. Fort Bend County, 14 Tex. 34.

[36] Russell v. Roberts, 3 E. D. Smith, 318.

[37] Lamprey v. Mason, 148 Mass. 231, 19 N. E. 350.

scionable and oppressive, and to decree performance of the remainder, is the exercise of an equitable power of a high order, the incautious exercise of which might lead to very dangerous results. These cases might more properly be brought within the rule governing cases of fraud and oppression. If the contract is on its face so extortionate and unjust as to bear evident marks of deceit, then, instead of wasting time in trying to reduce the relief to the standard of strict justice, the whole agreement should be pronounced void. Under the modern system of pleading and the fusion of the two systems of Law and Equity, either party is usually able, in cases of unconscionable agreements, to obtain such equitable relief as he may be entitled to, either in the way of reforming or avoiding the contract.

§ 607. Preparations to perform.

As we shall presently see, the general rule is that the plaintiff recovers the sum total of the benefits or gains of a contract *less* the expenses. Hence he cannot recover for the expenses of preparations to commence performance of the contract, for he would have equally incurred those expenses if the defendant had performed his part.[38] Where, however, the plaintiff cannot recover the profits he would have made by his contract, as, when they are uncertain, he is in the ordinary case allowed to recover the expenses incurred by him in his preparations to perform.[39] So where the plaintiff agreed to supply laborers

[38] *Alabama:* Benziger *v.* Miller, 50 Ala. 206; Mason *v.* Ala. Iron Co., 73 Ala. 270.

Georgia: Fontaine *v.* Baxley, 90 Ga. 416, 17 S. E. 1015.

Indiana: Williams *v.* Oliphant, 3 Ind. 271.

Massachusetts: Noble *v.* Ames Mfg. Co., 112 Mass. 402.

Utah: Hawley *v.* Corey, 9 Utah, 175, 33 Pac. 695.

Vermont: Curtis *v.* Smith, 48 Vt. 116.

West Virginia: Patton *v.* Elk River Nav. Co., 13 W. Va. 259.

[39] *United States:* Ellithorpe Air-Brake Co. *v.* Sire, 41 Fed. 662 (to install elevator; no profits being proved, plaintiff recovers outlay on parts of elevator prepared for installing); Griffen *v.* Sprague Electric Co., 115 Fed. 749 (contract by defendant to test patent and use it if successful; plaintiff recovers expense of preparing for test); Curran *v.* Smith, 149 Fed. 945, 81 C. C. A. 537 (contract to investigate project for pipe line; expenditures made after contract signed in preparation for performance recoverable).

Alabama: Worthington *v.* Gwin, 119 Ala. 44, 24 So. 739, 43 L. R. A. 382 (contract to mine and deliver iron ore;

for the defendant at $1.25 per day, and expended money in procuring laborers, but the defendant refused to hire them, no

if profits uncertain, reasonable expenses of preparation recoverable). *California:* Cederberg *v.* Robison, 100 Cal. 93, 34 Pa. 625 (to harvest grain; plaintiff recovers outlay on faith of the contract). *Florida:* Brent *v.* Parker, 23 Fla. 200, 1 So. 780 (to cut and haul timber; expense of making causeways and landings recoverable). *Georgia:* McKenzie *v.* Mitchell, 123 Ga. 72, 51 S. E. 34 (to submit a claim to arbitration; necessary expenses in preparing for arbitration may be recovered). *Illinois:* Southern Pac. Co. *v.* American Well Works, 172 Ill. 9, 49 N. E. 575 (to sink wells; plaintiff gets value of materials for work which were prepared and wasted). *Iowa:* Dean *v.* White, 5 Ia. 266 (to give use of defendant's mill; plaintiff recovers expense of preparing engine and boiler for use of mill). *Kansas:* Arkansas V. T. & L. Co. *v.* Lincoln, 56 Kan. 145, 42 Pac. 706 (to build railroad through town; purchaser of land from the defendant recovers loss of profits of established business which he relinquished to move to the town); Paola Gas Co. *v.* Paola Glass Co., 56 Kan. 614, 44 Pac. 621, 54 Am. St. Rep. 598 (to supply fuel for factory; plaintiff recovers expense of attempt to operate factory). *Kentucky:* Courier Journal Co. *v.* Millen, 20 Ky. L. Rep. 1811, 50 S. W. 46 (to employ plaintiff as agent in certain county; plaintiff recovers expense of hiring room, etc., in preparation). *Massachusetts:* Johnson *v.* Arnold, 2 Cush. 46 (to employ plaintiff to take charge of a business; plaintiff recovers loss of time and expense of removal). *Mississippi:* New Orleans, J. & G. N. R. R. *v.* Echols, 54 Miss. 264 (to

buy water from plaintiff at certain station; plaintiff recovers expense of erecting water-tank there). *New York:* People *v.* Flynn, 189 N. Y. 180, 82 N. E. 169 (holder of theatre ticket refused admission; recovers necessary expenses incurred to attend performance); Meylert *v.* Gas Consumers' Ben. Co., 14 N. Y. Supp. 148 (contract that plaintiff should introduce a patent burner; plaintiff recovers expense of preparation, and also amount he would have earned in his profession as physician); Abbey *v.* Mace, 19 N. Y. Supp. 375 (contract for decorating; plaintiff recovers expense of preparing machinery and value of time lost); Nelson *v.* Hatch, 70 App. Div. 206, 75 N. Y. Supp. 389 (contract by defendant to carry on litigation; advances and expenditures recoverable); Luxenberg *v.* Keith & P. A. Co., 64 Misc. 69, 117 N. Y. Supp. 979 (holder of theatre ticket refused admission; recovers necessary expenses incurred to attend performance). *North Carolina:* Jones *v.* Mial, 89 N. C. 89 (to provide money for plaintiff to carry on business; plaintiff recovers time lost and expense of hiring assistance). *Pennsylvania:* Rogers *v.* Davidson, 142 Pa. 436, 21 Atl. 1083 (to saw defendant's timber; plaintiff recovers cost of preparation to run the saw-mill). *South Carolina:* Martin *v.* Seaboard A. L. Ry., 70 S. C. 8, 48 S. É. 616 (to run spur-track to plaintiff's mill; plaintiff recovers expenditures in expectation of having track). *Tennessee:* Taylor *v.* Hunnicut, 42 S. W. 225 (to enter into partnership; plaintiff recovers value of time put into the business, also of time during which he remained idle in expectation of the partnership being formed). *Texas:* Smith *v.* Crosby, 47 Tex. 121

damages being provable for loss of profits of the contract, the plaintiff was allowed to recover the expense of procuring the laborers.[40] So in an action for breach of contract to submit the claims of the parties to arbitrators, although it was found that the plaintiff had no claim, and, therefore, that the right was probably of very small value, he was allowed to recover "expenses to which he has been subjected by reason of his necessary preparations for a trial before the arbitrators, on account of his own loss of time and trouble, and in employing counsel, taking depositions, payments to witnesses and arbitrators," and other expenses, his recovery, however, being limited to these expenses only so far as these preparations would not be available for the trial of his cause before the ordinary tribunals.[41] So where it was found impossible to estimate the profits of a contract to build a railroad, the plaintiff was allowed to recover for the abrupt termination, for loss of material, for shanties put up, travel of hands, depreciation in value of tools, materials, etc.[42] And where the defendant agreed to set up a machine for the plaintiff, and give him the exclusive use of such machines in his county, the plaintiff, upon breach of the contract, may recover the loss incurred by procuring a boiler.[43] And upon breach of an agreement that the plaintiff shall have the exclusive sale of the defendant's goods in a certain territory, the plaintiff may recover the advertising expenses and other expenditures in preparation for sale.[44] So

(to locate land for defendant; plaintiff recovers value of time and labor in locating); Withers v. Edwards, 26 Tex. Civ. App. 189, 62 S. W. 795 (to cooperate in buying stock to secure control of a bank; plaintiff recovers premiums paid for stock above its actual value); Peacock v. Coltrane (Tex. Civ. App.), 116 S. W. 389 (to teach school; plaintiff recovers expense of hiring assistant).

England: Herring v. Tomlin, 28 Eng. L. & Eq. 142 (to enter into partnership; profits being uncertain, plaintiff recovers expense of journeys on the business of the firm).

Canada: Mandia v. McMahon, 17

Ont. App. 34 (to bring laborers from a distant place to work for defendant; plaintiff recovers expense of journey and of bringing the men).

[40] Mandia v. McMahon, 17 Ont. App. 34.

[41] *Georgia:* McKenzie v. Mitchell, 123 Ga. 72, 51 S. E. 34.

Maine: Call v. Hagar, 69 Me. 521.

Massachusetts: Pond v. Harris, 113 Mass. 114; New Haven & N. Co. v. Hayden, 117 Mass. 433.

[42] Phillips & C. C. Co. v. Seymour, 91 U. S. 646, 23 L. ed. 341.

[43] Dean v. White, 5 Ia. 266.

[44] *United States:* Taylor Mfg. Co. v. Hatcher Mfg. Co., 39 Fed. 440.

where the defendant agrees to provide plaintiff with a place for a public performance; since the profits of the business are too speculative for recovery, the plaintiff may recover the expenses of preparation for the performance.[45]

The case of Curtis *v.* Smith [46] may seem to be opposed to these views. In that case the plaintiff, a builder, had agreed to furnish stone and to build some wing walls for the defendant's bakery, to be commenced when the stagings were taken down. Before they were taken down, the defendant terminated the contract. The plaintiff had performed some labor in getting out stone. The court said, that if the intention was that the quarrying should not be commenced till after the staging had been taken down, then the plaintiff could only recover the excess of the contract price over what it would have cost him to perform, but that if the stone was to be quarried previous to the taking down of the staging, the plaintiff should recover the difference between the value of the stone and the value of the plaintiff's services in getting it out. In this case it appears that the decision turned upon the interpretation of the contract; and no allowance was made for mere *preparations* to perform, because the profits of the contract were given as damages. And in the case of Curran *v.* Smith [47] the legal expenses of preparing the contract for signature were not allowed, on the ground that they were quite independent of performance or of preparation to perform.

In another class of cases, where the expenses incurred by the plaintiff had no relation to the defendant's performance, it has been said they could not be recovered, though the profits of the contract were too uncertain for recovery. So where plaintiff undertook to put down at an agreed price per foot a well

---

Ohio: Smith *v.* Weed S. M. Co., 26 Oh. St. 562.

West Virginia: Sterling O. Co. *v.* House, 25 W. Va. 64.

See, however, Carroll-Porter B. & T. Co. *v.* Columbus Mach. Co., 55 Fed. 451, 5 C. C. A. 190.

[45] *Arkansas:* O'Connell *v.* Rosso, 56 Ark. 603, 29 S. W. 531 (providing apparatus, procuring license, getting performers to the place).

Missouri: Athletic Baseball Assoc. *v.* St. Louis S. P. Assoc., 67 Mo. App. 653 (traveling expenses); Claudius *v.* West End H. A. Co., 109 Mo. App. 346, 84 S. W. 354.

New York: Bernstein *v.* Meech, 130 N. Y. 354, 29 N. E. 255.

[46] 48 Vt. 116.

[47] 149 Fed. 945, 81 C. C. A. 537.

which could not be pumped dry, and after several unsuccessful borings he was stopped in the midst of another boring, it was held that he could not recover the cost of the abandoned borings. The labor, as the court said, had been expended in vain, and no part of the cost could have been recovered if they had completed the contract.[48] So where three persons covenanted jointly to buy a set of boring tolls and each sink an oil well on his own land, and at his own expense, and if successful to deliver to the others one-twentieth of the oil taken, and one sunk his well but obtained no oil, and there was no evidence that any could be obtained, the court held that he could not recover in an action against one of the others the expense of sinking his own well.[49]

It is submitted that the real reason for the distinction in these cases is the speculative nature of the contract. If the whole matter is a speculation there can be no presumption that the plaintiff would have realized from performance an amount equal to the cost of preparation; in these cases it is quite clear that he would not have done so.

If there is an express contract to pay any expenses incurred, of course the defendant is liable to the plaintiff for the amount.[50] So where a lessor had agreed to pay the lessee for any damage sustained in consequence of fitting up the premises if he ousted him, the lessee was allowed to recover the expense of fitting them up, *less* the use which he had had for two years. In the estimate should be included, it was said, the injury to the carpets by being cut.[51] So, also, where there is an implied contract, for instance, where the United States had agreed to pay the defendant for services, and to give him due notice beforehand of the time when performance would be required. Notice was given, but performance was not required. The plaintiff was not allowed to recover the profits he would have made, but was allowed to recover for injury suffered by making ready to meet the requirements of the contract, which would include damages for "loss of time," "trouble and expense." The no-

---

[48] Reynolds *v.* Levi, 122 Mich. 115, 80 N. W. 999.

[49] Hutchinson *v.* Snider, 137 Pa. 1, 20 Atl. 510.

[50] Tufts *v.* Plymouth G. M. Co., 14 All. (Mass.) 407.

[51] Pratt *v.* Paine, 119 Mass. 439.

tice seems to have been treated as an implied promise to pay for expenses incurred if performance was not required.[52]

§ 607a. Expense of removal.

Expense of removal to leased premises, of which the landlord fails to give possession, may be recovered. Thus where an agreement had been made to let certain premises as a tavern stand, and the plaintiff had removed his family to take possession, which was refused, it was held that the plaintiff was entitled to recover, not only the value of the lease, but also his expenses in removing his family and furniture, and this without any allegation of special damage in the declaration.[53]

Where the agreement is that the plaintiff shall come from a distance and take employment with the defendant, in an action for breach of the contract of employment, the plaintiff may recover the expense of removal. Thus where a defendant had engaged the plaintiff to remove to Indiana, to carry on business there, and failed to furnish the stock necessary for so doing, the court allowed the plaintiff as damages compensation for the loss of his time in removing to Indiana and back again to his original domicile.[54]

So, in New Hampshire, where the defendant proposed by letter to the plaintiff that the latter should come to that State from Minnesota; agreeing, if he would do so, to give him and his wife a year's board, and allow him to carry on the defendant's farm; it was held that the expenses incurred by the plaintiff in removing his family, and probably compensation for his necessary loss of time, might be recovered.[55] So where the defendant agreed to support plaintiff if plaintiff would live with him, plaintiff may recover the expenses of removal.[56]

A Massachusetts decision seems difficult to reconcile with

[52] Bulkley v. U. S., 19 Wall. 37, 22 L. ed. 62.

[53] Driggs v. Dwight, 17 Wend. (N. Y.) 71; Lawrence v. Wardwell, 6 Barb. (N. Y.) 423; acc., Giles v. O'Toole, 4 Barb. (N. Y.) 261.

But he may not recover the expense of packing and storing his goods a long time in advance. Lowenstein v. Chappell, 30 Barb. (N. Y.) 241.

[54] Johnson v. Arnold, 2 Cush. (Mass.) 46; acc., McLean v. News Pub. Co., (N. D.) 129 N. W. 93.

[55] Woodbury v. Jones, 44 N. H. 206.

[56] Kentucky: McDaniel v. Hutcherson, 136 Ky. 412, 124 S. W. 384.

Nebraska: Bryant v. Barton, 32 Neb. 613, 49 N. W. 331.

New Hampshire: Woodbury v. Jones, 44 N. H. 206.

this general doctrine.[57] In that case the offer was: "I am ready to offer you a foreman's situation as soon as you may get here." It was held that the plaintiff could not recover the expenses of his journey from the Sandwich Islands to Massachusetts, nor the value of his time in the journey. Morton, J., said: "The expenses of the removal were incurred before the contract took effect." Though this may be technically true, the removal was contemplated by the parties as a consequence of the offer, and it is difficult to distinguish the case from others in which the expense of removal was allowed. In a later case in the same State [58] in which it appeared that the plaintiff, on the promise of the defendant to give property to plaintiff's wife, after defendant's death, if plaintiff would move "from his residence" to defendant's home, and take care of her, accepted the offer, and actually removed his buildings to defendant's land, he was not allowed to recover the cost of moving the buildings, since this was not called for by the contract.

§ 607b. Stock of goods purchased on faith of lease or conveyance.

Loss on a stock of goods bought on faith of a lease of business premises of which the lessor refuses to give possession is, it would seem, too remote. Nevertheless, in an early case, in which the plaintiff declared for breach of an agreement to let the plaintiff have the use of certain mills for six months, in consideration of £10, it appeared that the mills were worth but £20 per annum, and yet damages were given to £500, by reason of the stock laid in by the plaintiff; and, *per curiam*, "the jury may well find such damages, for they are not only bound to give the £10, but also all the special damages." [59] The Supreme Court of New York, commenting on this case, said: "Very likely it appeared that the breach of contract was committed to favor some particular interest of the defendant, or his friend, though the case mentions a simple refusal to perform;" [60] but perhaps it may rather be brought within the rule of Hadley v. Baxendale, which will be presently stated, both parties know-

[57] Noble *v.* Ames Manufacturing Co., 112 Mass. 492.

[58] Kenerson *v.* Colgan, 164 Mass. 166, 41 N. E. 122.

[59] Nurse *v.* Barns, T. Raym. 77.

[60] Blanchard *v.* Ely, 21 Wend. 342.

ing the object to which the mills were to be applied, and the loss of the plaintiff's stock being considered as contemplated by them.

Recent authorities hold such a loss not to be compensated, in the absence of notice. Thus, where the leased premises consisted of a farm, the plaintiff was not allowed to recover the loss he suffered by a purchase of stock for it.[61]

In a similar action, where machinery of a less capacity than that bargained for was furnished for a new mill, it was held that loss on large purchases of stock for running a mill of the agreed capacity and loss caused by abandoning the planting for the milling business, were both too remote.[62] Where the defendant broke his contract to convey land to the plaintiff, the latter cannot recover compensation for money paid an architect for plans for a proposed building on the premises.[63] But he may recover for expense of examining title.[64]

§ 608. Reduction of damages: Rule of avoidable consequences.

The rule of avoidable consequences is fully applicable to actions for breach of contract. So for breach of a contract to repair, the plaintiff cannot recover consequential damages resulting to his property from a failure to repair, except for such damage as happened before he could reasonably make the repairs himself,[65] and for failure properly to construct waterworks the plaintiff could not recover for damage caused by leaking after he should have repaired the leaks himself;[66] so on breach of an agreement that plaintiff might store secondhand brick on a lot adjoining that upon which he was building a house, the plaintiff could not recover the value of the brick but only the cost of removing them and storing them elsewhere.[67] On this principle it was held that for a breach of the contract to remove the plaintiff's hotel the plaintiff could not

[61] Robrecht v. Marling, 29 W. Va. 765.

[62] Willingham v. Hooven, 74 Ga. 233, 58 Am. Rep. 435.

[63] Chamberlain v. Brady, 49 N. Y. Super. Ct. 484.

[64] Walker v. Moore, 10 B. & C. 416.

[65] Louisiana: Cable v. Leeds, 6 La. Ann. 293.

Tennessee: Fort v. Orndoff, 7 Heisk. 167.

[66] Hensen v. Beebe, 111 Iowa, 534, 82 N. W. 942.

[67] Zinn v. N. J. Steamboat Co., 49 N. Y. 442, 10 Am. Rep. 402.

recover the profits which he could have made from the hotel, but only the expense of procuring its removal by another.[68] For a defect in part of a machine the plaintiff could not recover for loss of use of the machine if the part could have been replaced.[69] Where the defendant contracted to take and pasture cattle and the contract was terminable at any time at the will of the plaintiff and the plaintiff claimed damages for injury to the cattle by reason of poor pasturage it was held that if he discovered that the animals were not being properly pastured and nevertheless allowed them to remain in the defendant's possession, he could not recover damages for injury to the cattle by the poor pasturage.[70]

On this principle again where the defendant had agreed to furnish power, and the power was to the knowledge of the plaintiff insufficient, the latter cannot recover the value of raw materials spoiled in an unwise attempt to manufacture.[71] On the other hand, where logs were badly sawed by the defendant in the performance of a contract, but the damages could have been reduced by resawing this should be done.[72]

Attempts have been made to reduce the measure of recovery by showing that the plaintiff made or might have made another contract, to be performed at the same time in which the contract in suit was to have been performed. Thus where the plaintiff sued on a contract for driving piles, the court intimated that the defendant might reduce the damages by showing that the plaintiff could have gotten other contracts, immediately upon the defendant's breach, and might have made a profit from them.[73]

But the better opinion is, as we have already seen,[74] that no such reduction should be allowed.[75] In the first place, it sel-

[68] Sherman Center Town Co. v. Leonard, 46 Kan. 354, 26 Pac. 717.

[69] D. N. Osborne & Co. v. Carpenter, 37 Minn. 331, 34 N. W. 163.

[70] Loomer v. Thomas, 38 Neb. 277, 56 N. W. 973. The same principle applies in case of a contract to supply feed for cattle. Kentucky D. & W. Co. v. Lillard, 160 Fed. 34, 87 C. C. A. 191.

[71] Russell v. Giblin, 16 Daly, 258, 10 N. Y. Supp. 315.

[72] Grice v. Noble, 66 Mich. 700, 33 N. W. 768.

[73] Cincinnati, I. St. L. & C. Ry. v. Lutes, 112 Ind. 276, 11 N. E. 784, 14 N. E. 706.

[74] See chapter on Avoidable Consequences.

[75] Iowa: Klingman v. Racine Sattley Co. (Ia.), 128 N. W. 1109 (to sell defendant's goods).

Missouri: Black River L. Co. v.

dom appears that both contracts might not have been entered into and a profit made upon both by the plaintiff. In the second place, the defendant has no claim, legal or equitable, to have the benefit of the second contract. The seeming analogy of contracts of service is not sound, for in such contracts the measure of damages is the loss of the wages of service, and if another employment can be obtained the defendant does not cause a loss of wages. To state it in another way, the profits of a contract of service consist in the difference between the wages that can be earned under the contract and the wages that can be earned elsewhere, and there is no possibility of the plaintiff's obtaining double employment at the same time. In an ordinary contract the profits are measured by the difference between the price to be obtained for the plaintiff's performance under the contract and the cost at which the plaintiff can perform. Accordingly where the plaintiff agreed to barb the defendant's wire at a certain price the defendant cannot reduce the damages by showing that the plaintiff might have procured other contracts for barbing wire.[76] So when the plaintiff contracted to clear the defendant's field of stumps for a certain sum in gross, it was held that the defendant could not reduce the damages by showing the amount the plaintiff earned elsewhere;[77] and where the defendant refused the plaintiff possession of a farm he had agreed to lease, damages could not be reduced by showing that the plaintiff had engaged in hauling at a profit.[78]

In some cases, however, it has been shown that the plaintiff after breach of contract by the defendant made profits which could properly be regarded as a substitute for the profits the plaintiff would have received by the performance of the defendant's contract and which, therefore, the plaintiff could not have

Warner, 93 Mo. 374, 6 S. W. 210, 3 Am. St. Rep. 544 (to saw lumber).

New York: Durkee v. Mott, 8 Barb. 423 (to raft lumber).

Texas: Western U. T. Co. v. Williams (Tex. Civ. App.), 137 S. W. 148.

Washington: Watson v. Gray's H. B. Co., 3 Wash. 283, 28 Pac. 527 (to sink a well).

Wisconsin: Nilson v. Morse, 52 Wis.

240, 9 N. W. 1 (to pull stumps); Cameron v. White, 74 Wis. 425, 43 N. W. 408, 5 L. R. A. 493 (to saw lumber); Allen v. Murray, 87 Wis. 41, 57 N. W. 979 (to cut and deliver logs).

[76] Crescent Mfg. Co. v. Nelson Mfg. Co., 100 Mo. 325, 13 S. W. 503.

[77] Nilson v. Morse, 52 Wis. 240, 9 N. W. 1.

[78] Wolf v. Studebaker, 65 Pa. 459.

made if the defendant's breach of contract had not put him in a position to do so. In a case of this sort, if such profits can be made after breach of contract by the defendant the rule of avoidable consequences would require the plaintiff to make them and thus relieve the defendant from a portion of the loss caused by his breach. Such case arises where the defendant had chartered space in the plaintiff's vessel and then failed to provide a cargo. If the space thus left unfilled could have been filled by the plaintiff the amount of freight he could thus have realized should be deducted from the damages to be paid by the defendant.[79] So where the defendant broke his contract to supply a certain amount of advertising to the plaintiff, but the plaintiff filled all the space reserved for the defendant with equally profitable advertising matter, it was held that this fact could be shown in reduction of damages.[80] And where upon breach of a contract by plaintiff to manufacture a number of automobile parts for defendant at a certain price, the plaintiff obtained another contract with another company to manufacture automobile parts, which occupied the plaintiff's entire time and force employed, and the profits of the second contract offset the entire loss of the first, it was held that this could be shown to diminish damages.[81] It will be noticed that in such cases the subtraction of this amount is necessary in order to arrive at the real profit of the contract, since the sacrifice of the substituted profit would be necessary in order to earn the payment due under the contract and therefore as an expense of performance it must be subtracted from the contract price in order to arrive at the profit.

On this principle, on breach of a contract which calls for the use of plaintiff's property or the expenditure of a certain amount of plaintiff's time the use of the property or the time may be saved to the plaintiff, and for the value of the property or time thus saved an allowance must be made. Such value may be most easily proved by showing what the plaintiff realized, or

[79] Medberry v. Sweet, 3 Chand. (Wis.) 231, 3 Pinn. 210.

[80] Savage v. Medical and Surgical Association, 59 Mich. 400. The court said that no action would lie; but the plaintiff was clearly entitled, at the least, to nominal damages.

[81] Harrington-Wiard Co. v. Blomstrom Mfg. Co. (Mich.), 131 N. W. 559.

might have realized, by the use of the property or time.[82]   And on the same principle it has been held that where the plaintiff agreed to manufacture steel rails for the defendant at a certain price, and the defendant refused to receive them, the trial court allowed profits made from the sale to another party of rails made from the steel procured to fill the defendant's order, to be subtracted from the profits of the contract with the defendant; and the judgment was affirmed in the Supreme Court of the United States; the court saying that the defendant thereby received the benefit of all profits made by the plaintiff which could properly be regarded as a substitute for the profits it would have received had the contract been carried out.[83]

Where the plaintiff contracted to saw in his saw-mill the defendant's logs, and the logs were not supplied, it has been held that the profits made by using the mill to saw other logs should be deducted.[84]   The correctness of this decision may be questioned.   The value of the steel and of the use of the saw-mill should of course be deducted in order to arrive at the profits of the contract broken; but the defendant should not be entitled to the profits of the other contract.

In such cases if the substituted profits can be deducted the

[82] Plaintiff's time required for performance: deduct income from time saved.

Nebraska: Jewett v. Wilmot, 57 Neb. 700, 71 N. W. 775.

Texas: Joske v. Pleasants, 15 Tex. Civ. App. 433, 39 S. W. 586.

Plaintiff's property to be used in performance; deduct income from use of that specific property which was made possible only by the breach. Dunn v. Allen, 59 App. Div. 561, 67 N. Y. Supp. 218; Baker Transfer Co. v. Merchants' R. & I. M. Co., 12 App. Div. 260, 42 N. Y. Supp. 76.

It should be noticed in these cases that the rule in certain contingencies is one which does not cut down but one which enlarges recovery. The profit of the contract would be arrived at by subtracting from the contract price the cost of performance, and the value of the property or time would be sub-

tracted as part of the cost of performance. If, however, there were no other demand for the use of the property or the time, a loss of this profitable employment of them would be a consequence of the breach. The true doctrine would therefore seem to be that the value of the use of property or time should in these cases be deducted, unless it can be shown by the plaintiff that by the breach they were left on his hands without any chance of employing them usefully.

[83] Hinckley v. Pittsburgh B. S. Co., 121 U. S. 264, 276, 30 L. ed. 967, 7 Sup. Ct. 875; acc., Diamond State I. Co. v. San Antonio & A. P. Ry., 11 Tex. Civ. App. 587, 33 S. W. 987.

[84] *Kentucky:* Frazier v. Clark, 88 Ky. 260, 10 S. W. 806.

Michigan: Petrie v. Lane, 67 Mich. 454, 35 N. W. 70.

burden is on the defendant of establishing the fact that they were or should have been earned.[85]

§ 609. General principles of recovery.

A contract is conceived as a valuable right owned by the parties of it and a breach of the contract is regarded as depriving the owner of his contract right. The damage caused by the breach is therefore the damage caused by the destruction of a right of property and is measured by the value of the property. The measure of damages for breach of contract then is the value of the contract right destroyed by the breach. In the case of many contracts there is no market value, since contracts generally are not bought and sold in the market. There are, to be sure, many contracts which are so bought and sold; among these are contracts for the future delivery of articles dealt with in the market. Of such contracts we shall speak later. A contract, as such, however, has no market value and damages for its breach must therefore be measured by its actual value. This value is most readily found by showing what would be the benefit of having the contract performed, that is, what would have been received upon performance of the contract, over and above what must be given to secure performance. If the performance of a contract would be profitable to the plaintiff, that is, if upon its performance by the defendant the plaintiff would have left in his hands more than it would have cost him to perform on his side, then the contract itself, entirely apart from the effect of the performance upon his other property, would have a certain pecuniary value measured by the amount of such profit remaining in his hands. This is the direct profit of the contract. If by reason of non-performance on the part of the defendant the plaintiff loses his contract he is entitled on the general principles of recovery to its value and this value as has been seen is the direct profit. Such direct profit of a contract is therefore always recoverable in an action for the breach.

On the other hand, the value of the contract is not the value

[85] *Indiana:* Cincinnati & C. Ry. *v.* Lutes, 112 Ind. 276, 11 N. E. 784. *New York:* Railway Advertising Co. *v.* Standard R. C. Co., 83 App. Div. 191, 83 N. Y. Supp. 338; affirmed, 178 N. Y. 570, 70 N. E. 1108.

of what the plaintiff was to receive from the performance of it, unless there is nothing to be done on his part to secure the benefit of it. He cannot, for instance, recover the contract price for work he was to do without first deducting the cost of the work not yet done.[86]

§ 610.[a] Nominal damages.

The right to the performance of a contract is an absolute right and any breach of the contract is a wrong to the other party, whether actual damage follows or not. As a consequence of this principle, the plaintiff may always recover for breach of a contract at least nominal damages even though he is unable by evidence to establish that any particular loss has been suffered.[87] But where there is no sufficiently certain proof of the amount of the damages, nominal damages only are recoverable;[88] the burden being on the plaintiff to prove the amount of damages.[89] So for breach of a contract by the purchaser of land to build houses on the land within a year only nominal damages can be recovered, the amount of the loss being too speculative to be proved.[90] And in Finney v. Cad-

---

[a] For § 610 of the 8th edition see § 606a.

[86] Brown v. Mader, 120 App. Div. 15, 105 N. Y. Supp. 705.

[87] *Louisiana:* Judice v. Southern Pac. Co., 47 La. Ann. 257, 16 So. 816; Bourdette v. Sieward, 107 La. 264, 31 So. 630; Green v. Farmers' Consol. Dairy Co., 113 La. 869, 37 So. 858.

Nebraska: Kreamer v. Irwin, 46 Neb. 827, 65 N. W. 885.

New Jersey: Rockwell v. American L. B. Co., 76 Atl. 334.

New York: Hopedale Electric Co. v. Electric S. B. Co., 96 App. Div. 344, 89 N. Y. Supp. 325; American S. S. Co. v. Rush, 100 N. Y. Supp. 1019.

North Carolina: Clinton v. Mercer, 3 Murph. 119.

[88] *United States:* Chesapeake T. Co. v. Walker, 158 Fed. 850.

Colorado: Patrick v. Colorado Smelting Co., 20 Colo. 268, 38 Pac. 236, 46 Am. St. Rep. 288.

Georgia: Shaw v. Jones, 133 Ga. 446, 66 S. E. 240.

Maryland: Lanahan v. Heaver, 79 Md. 413, 29 Atl. 1036.

Michigan: Shaw-Walker Co. v. Fitzsimmons, 148 Mich. 626, 112 N. W. 501.

New York: Independent T. Y. M. B. Assoc. v. Somach, 52 Misc. 538, 102 N. Y. Supp. 495.

Texas: Drumm S. & F. Co. v. J. Horace McFarland Co. (Tex. Civ. App.), 30 S. W. 93; Albertype Co. v. Gust Feist Co., 114 S. W. 791.

Washington: Church v. Wilkeson-Tripp Co., 58 Wash. 262, 108 Pac. 596.

[89] *Alabama:* Taylor v. Howard, 110 Ala. 468, 18 So. 311.

New York: Benner v. Phœnix Towing & Transp. Co., 80 Hun, 412, 30 N. Y. Supp. 290.

Pennsylvania: Lentz v. Choteau, 42 Pa. 435.

[90] McConaghy v. Pemberton, 168 Pa. 121, 31 Atl. 996.

wallader[91] an agreement was made to establish a bank and make the defendant its manager, and to establish a line of steamers and make the defendant its agent. It was held that damages for a breach of this contract were too remote and uncertain to be estimated.

It is, however, to be noticed that in such a case every reasonable presumption is to be made against the wrongdoing defendant, and if by the aid of such presumption the damages can be fixed the plaintiff may recover substantial damages.[92]

Since the profits are found by subtracting the cost of doing the work from the contract price, it is clear that if the cost of doing the work is equal to or greater than the contract price, the damages are nominal.[93] The same is true if for lack of evidence it is impossible to prove what the profit of the contract would have been. So when it is impossible to estimate the profit of doing the work because the cost of performance cannot be proved, and no money has been expended, nominal damages only can be recovered;[94] as where the amount of work is left uncertain.[95] So if the performance by the defendant would have given something other than money to the plaintiff, nominal damages only can be recovered if the value of performance cannot be proved.[96]

§ 611.ᵃ Executed contracts.

If the contract on the plaintiff's side has been entirely performed before breach by the defendant, the plaintiff may recover the entire value of the defendant's performance; since he is entitled to the performance without further expense on his

ᵃ For § 611 of the 8th edition see § 606b.

[91] 55 Ga. 75.

[92] Wilson v. Northampton & B. J. Ry., L. R. 9 Ch. 279.

[93] United States: Harvey v. United States, 8 Ct. Cl. 501.
Connecticut: Beattie v. New York, N. H. & H. R. R., 80 Atl. 709.
Kentucky: O'Connor v. Henderson Bridge Co., 95 Ky. 633, 27 S. W. 251.
New York: Durkee v. Mott, 8 Barb. 423.

Ohio: Toledo v. Libbie, 19 Ohio C. Ct. 704.

[94] Florida: Sullivan v. McMillan, 26 Fla. 543, 8 So. 450.
New Jersey: Harrison v. Clarke, 78 N. J. L. 236, 73 Atl. 43.

[95] Wakeford v. Commissioner of Railways, 2 N. S. W. L. R. 258.

[96] Illinois: Tribune Co. v. Bradshaw, 20 Ill. App. 17.
Missouri: Gibson v. Whip Pub. Co., 28 Mo. App. 450.
Pennsylvania: Kenderdine H. C. F. Co. v. Plumb, 182 Pa. 463, 38 Atl. 480.

own part.[97] If the performance by the defendant consisted in the payment of a certain sum of money, this must be paid upon full execution of the plaintiff's side. Thus where an owner of logs agreed with the plaintiff to pay him a certain amount for hauling the logs, and a creditor of the owner attached the logs and agreed to pay the plaintiff upon their delivery, the plaintiff, having hauled the logs, may recover from the attaching creditor the agreed compensation, though the plaintiff had received a partial payment upon the original contract.[98] So where a father agreed to pay his son a fixed sum per week for board, and then left to the son certain property in lieu of payment, the son, renouncing the legacy, could not claim the value of the board, but only the contract price.[99] And where defendant, as part consideration for the purchase of a machine, agreed to test it with another machine and if it were better to pay an additional amount, and then refused to make the test, plaintiff, upon proving that his machine was better than the other machine, was allowed the additional amount agreed to be paid.[100] And so where a contract has been fully performed, the plaintiff cannot recover the value of performance on a *quantum meruit*, but is restricted to the contract price.[101]

Where the contract has been fully performed on the plaintiff's part, and by the terms of the contract the defendant was to give the plaintiff something else than money, or was to perform services for him, the plaintiff may recover the value of the

[97] Defendant in return for permission to cut wood on the plaintiff's lot, agrees to deliver an equal amount of wood to the plaintiff on demand; on breach of this agreement the plaintiff may recover the value of the wood at the time of demand. Mitchell *v.* Gile, 12 N. H. 390. In return for conveyance of plaintiff's land defendant agreed to give warrants for other land; on breach, plaintiff recovers value of the warrants. Rayner *v.* Jones, 90 Cal. 78, 27 Pac. 24. Defendant agrees to convey land in return for services to be rendered by the plaintiff; plaintiff having performed the services may recover

the value of the land. McDowell *v.* Oyer, 21 Pa. 417.

[98] Miller *v.* Ward, 2 Conn. 494.

[99] Laird *v.* Laird, 127 Mich. 24, 86 N. W. 436.

[100] Hopedale Electric Co. *v.* Electric S. B. Co., 132 App. Div. 348, 116 N. Y. Supp. 859; affirmed, 198 N. Y. 588, 92 N. E. 1086.

[101] *Indiana:* Kentucky & I. C. Co. *v.* Cleveland, 4 Ind. App. 171, 30 N. E. 802.

New Jersey: Weart *v.* Hoagland, 22 N. J. L. 517.

Texas: Kocher *v.* Mayberry, 15 Tex. Civ. App. 342, 39 S. W. 604.

thing or the services.[102] So where the defendant guaranteed
that the plaintiff should realize ten per cent profit on certain
goods, but, in fact, the goods, though sold at the market price,
were sold at a loss, the measure of damages was the difference
between the cost of the goods, plus ten per cent, and the
amount realized from the sale of them.[103] So where the plaintiff purchased a house of the defendant, who, as part consideration for the price paid, agreed to keep the house rented at a
certain rental for a given period, but failed to do so, the plaintiff, on obtaining the best rental he could, was allowed to recover the deficit.[104] Plaintiff was to serve defendant in his
business, and as soon as the profits amounted to $800 plaintiff
was to be entitled to a half interest in the business. When the
profits had reached $780, defendant wrongfully terminated
the arrangement. It was held that the measure of damages
was the value of the half interest in the business, making allowance for the amount which had not been earned.[105] Plaintiff contracted to furnish ballast to a railroad, which was to
furnish the stone-crusher. They furnished a crusher which
was insufficient. The measure of damages was the difference
between the cost of manufacturing with the crusher furnished
and what it would have cost with a proper crusher.[106] The
plaintiff transferred his stock of goods to the defendant, on the
agreement of the latter to pay certain debts of the plaintiff, and
if he could sell the stock for more than the amount of the debts,
to return the net balance to the plaintiff. The plaintiff afterwards secured an offer to give certain land for the stock of

[102] *Missouri:* Ramsey *v.* Maberry, 135 Mo. App. 569, 116 S. W. 1066 (to allow mortgagor to remove mortgaged cattle to another market for sale; on breach plaintiff recovers difference between market price in the other market and what they actually sold for); Kansas City *v.* Davidson, 154 Mo. App. 269, 133 S. W. 365 (in return for dirt taken from plaintiff's lot, defendant agreed to grade the lot; on breach plaintiff recovers cost of grading).
New York: May *v.* Poluhoff, 65 Misc. 546, 120 N. Y. Supp. 827 (defendant granted advertising privilege,

and it proved he had no title to it; plaintiff recovers value of privilege).
[103] Morris *v.* Barrett, 24 Oh. St. 201; *acc.*, of a guaranty to sell the plaintiff's property at a certain price, Dunn *v.* Mackey, 80 Cal. 104.
[104] Williams *v.* Arnold, 139 Wis. 177, 120 N. W. 824. And so of a contract to sell plaintiff's land for a certain price. George *v.* Lane, 80 Kan. 94, 102 Pac. 55.
[105] Gilbert *v.* Grubel, 82 Kan. 476, 108 Pac. 798.
[106] El Paso & S. W. R. R. *v.* Eichel & Weikel (Tex. Civ. App.), 130 S. W. 922.

goods, which the defendant accepted. The defendant finally refused to carry out the transaction. In an action for breach of the original contract plaintiff may recover the amount of the debts which the defendant agreed to pay, together with the excess, if any, of the value of the land for which defendant had agreed to exchange the goods over the amount of the debts and the expenses.[107]

Upon this ground, if plaintiff performs services upon an agreement to receive in payment stock in a corporation, and he performs the services but does not receive the stock, the measure of damages is the actual value of the stock.[108]

§ 612.[a] Entire contract price recoverable in some cases.

In some cases the plaintiff may recover the whole contract price. A common case is that of a schoolmaster. If a scholar is removed from the school during the quarter the schoolmaster may recover the tuition fee for the whole quarter.[109] So upon an agreement to pay the plaintiff a certain amount for his legal services in a pending litigation he may recover the agreed amount, though the controversy is brought to an end by compromise.[110] Where it was agreed that the plaintiff should weigh all the grain carried over the defendant's road at a stipulated price, and the defendant allowed another to weigh grain, the plaintiff was allowed to recover at the contract price for all grain thus weighed by the other.[111]

The principle upon which these cases rest seems to be, that the whole contract price is to be given, because it is impossible

[a] For § 612 of the 8th edition see § 606c.

[107] Doolittle v. Murray, 134 Ia. 536, 111 N. W. 999.

[108] Ware v. McMurray, 74 N. J. L. 37, 64 Atl. 967.

[109] England: Collins v. Price, 5 Bing. 132.
Alabama: Sprague v. Morgan, 7 Ala. 952.
See, however, Michigan: International T. B. Co. v. Schulte, 151 Mich. 149, 114 N. W. 1031; International T. B. Co. v. Jones, 131 N. W. 98; International T. B. Co. v. Marvin, 132 N. W. 437.

[110] Alabama: Hunt v. Test, 8 Ala. 713, 42 Am. Dec. 659.
California: Baldwin v. Bennett, 4 Cal. 392.

[111] Lake Shore & M. S. Ry. v. Richards, 126 Ill. 448.
So where, in a contract for work on a building, the work is almost completed, so that it would be impracticable for the laborer to secure employment elsewhere during the short time required for completion, he may upon discharge recover the entire contract price for the labor. Danley v. Williams, 16 Wis. 581.

to show with the required certainty any pecuniary outlay which the plaintiff has been saved by the breach. The school must continue in session, with its entire corps of instructors, although a scholar is withdrawn; the office of a weigher of grain must still be kept open, and at the same expense, though part of the anticipated custom fails. So far as the evidence shows, it would have cost the plaintiff nothing, in addition to the expense he had already been put to, if he had fully performed on his side. If, in such a case, the plaintiff is put to the same expense in time and money as if he had fully performed, the contract price of the whole work is the measure of damages.[112]

So where plaintiff agreed to guaranty defendant against loss in a certain business for a year for a percentage of the total sales, and defendant sold the business during the year, plaintiff at the end of the year could recover the agreed percentage on the sales made by the purchaser of the business.[113] So where the plaintiff engages transportation for his goods, and at the time for delivering the goods he fails to provide them, the carrier, if he is unable to obtain other goods to carry, may recover the agreed freight.[114] And where a lodger engages a room for a certain term and fails to occupy the room, the landlord, if unable to let the room to another, may recover the agreed rent.[115] And in case of breach of an agreement to take advertising space, the plaintiff, in the absence of evidence to show less damage, recovers the contract price.[116] In such cases the burden is on the defendant to show that the damage is less than the agreed compensation.[117]

§ 612a. Readiness to perform or tender of performance.

In the ordinary case the plaintiff cannot by showing readiness to perform or a tender of performance, recover the contract price.[118] So on a contract to transport horses in a canal-

[112] Wood v. Schettler, 23 Wis. 501.
[113] Wilson v. Wernwag, 217 Pa. 82, 66 Atl. 242.
[114] Burrow v. Pound, 29 Mo. 435, 77 Am. Dec. 579; Hardy v. United States, 9 Ct. Cl. 244.
[115] Wilkinson v. Davies, 146 N. Y. 25, 40 N. E. 501.
[116] Post, § 633f

[117] Missouri: Simpson v. Ball, 145 Mo. App. 268, 129 S. W. 1017 (agreement to pay architect).
New York: Beattie v. New York & L. I. C. Co., 196 N. Y. 346, 89 N. E. 831 (agreement to quarry and shape stone; labor completed).
[118] Indiana: Lindley v. Dempsey, 45 Ind. 246.

boat for a given sum of money, the plaintiffs averred a readiness and offer to perform on their part, and a neglect and refusal on the part of the defendants to furnish the freight, and claimed to recover the entire sum specified in the agreement. But the Supreme Court of New York held that they were only entitled to recover what they had actually lost by the defendants' non-performance, saying: "Suppose the plaintiffs had the next hour been furnished with freight entirely adequate to the voyage at the same sum, they then would have been entitled to the damage arising from detention for that time, but no more. A tender and offer to perform is equivalent to performance, but merely for the purpose of sustaining an action; it is not performance, though in one respect it resembles it consequentially. It is *quasi performance*, but it does not regulate the amount of damages." [119]

* So, in Kentucky it has been held, that a plaintiff contracting to do work for a stipulated price, and who is ready to perform his agreement, but is prevented by the other party, cannot recover the price named in the contract for the whole work, but only the actual damages sustained by him. And as "the amount of compensation which the plaintiffs had recovered exceeded the value of the work they had done, and as, moreover, they did not attempt to prove any special loss or damage, they were not entitled to recover anything." ** [120]

The same rule applies where the consideration is paid by an employer in advance. The mechanic is not entitled in such case to retain the full price, even if the work is stopped by the default of his employer, but so much only as will compensate his actual damage.[121]

§ 612b. Settlement of amount due on contract prevented by defendant.

Where a sum is to be paid the ascertainment of which is con-

Kentucky: Powers v. Walker, 39 S. W. 256.

Michigan: Hosmer v. Wilson, 7 Mich. 294, 74 Am. Dec. 716.

New York: Dunham v. Hastings P. Co., 95 App. Div. 390, 88 N. Y. Supp. 835.

[119] Shannon v. Comstock, 21 Wend. (N. Y.) 457, 460, 34 Am. Dec. 262.

[120] Chamberlin v. McCallister, 6 Dana (Ky.), 352. See, also, Caldwell v. Reed, Littell Sel. Cas. 366.

[121] Hood v. Raines, 19 Tex. 400.

tingent upon some action of the party who is to pay the money, and he refuses to co-operate in the ascertainment and is sued for such refusal, a difficulty arises in fixing the amount of damages. So where H, an inventor, sold certain inventions to the defendant, the consideration being one hundred shares of the defendant's stock, paid on the transfer of title; and its additional stock, not to exceed four hundred shares, to be paid defendant upon the award of arbitrators as to the value of the inventions as compared with those then in use. The defendant withdrew its submission, and H brought suit, claiming that the subsidiary contract embodied a condition subsequent, and that this having failed, the obligation to deliver the four hundred shares became absolute. But the Supreme Court held that the company had only agreed to pay the excess in value of the property (if any) to be ascertained in a particular way; that, having made this ascertainment impossible by their own act, they were liable on a *quantum valebat*, the value to be fixed by the jury.[122] The measure of damages was therefore what the jury should determine to be the excess, if any, of the value of the property, under the terms of the contract, when sold and delivered, over the value of the stock already received under it, with interest from the date of the revocation of the submission.[123] In Hopedale Electric Co. *v.* Electric Storage Battery Co.[124] the vendee purchased some electric properties (including a storage system) for a certain price, agreeing to pay an additional sum of $100,000, provided vendor's system should on a competitive test prove equal to that of the vendee; if five per cent better, $150,000; if ten per cent better, $350,000; if twenty per cent better, $500,000. The vendee prevented the application of the test. The vendor was held entitled to recover the *value of the contract.* On proof of equality between the two systems a verdict for $100,000 and interest was sustained. In

[122] This is the rule in sales. Benjamin on Sales, 7th ed. 558; Clark *v.* Westrope, 18 C. B. 765, where an outgoing tenant sold the straw on his farm to the incomer, at a price to be fixed by a valuation by two indifferent persons, but pending the valuation the buyer consumed the straw.

[123] Humaston *v.* Telegraph Co., 20 Wall. 20, 22 L. ed. 279.

[124] 39 App. Div. 491, 57 N. Y. Supp. 422, 132 N. Y. 348, 30 N. E. 381, 96 App. Div. 344, 89 N. Y. Supp. 325, 184 N. Y. 356, 77 N. E. 394, 198 N. Y. 588, 92 N. E. 1086.

the first case, performance having been rendered impossible, the only question was the value of the *property*, with which the vendor had parted under the contract; in the second, how much, under the stipulations of the contract, would the defendant have been obliged to pay on account of the equality or superiority of plaintiff's system.

§ 613. Recovery of the profits of a contract.

Whenever it can be proved that the performance of the contract would have been beneficial to the plaintiff, he may recover the profits of the contract in an action for the breach of it.[125] For the purpose of determining the application of this

[125] *United States:* Philadelphia, W. & B. R. R. *v.* Howard, 13 How. 307, 14 L. ed. 157; United States *v.* Speed, 8 Wall. 77, 19 L. ed. 449; United States *v.* Smith, 94 U. S. 214, 24 L. ed. 115; Hinckley *v.* Pittsburgh B. S. Co., 121 U. S. 246, 30 L. ed. 967, 7 Sup. Ct. 875; Cook *v.* Hamilton County, 6 McLean, 612; Greenwell *v.* Ross, 34 Fed. 656; Kingman *v.* Western Mfg. Co., 92 Fed. 486, 34 C. C. A. 489; Safety I. W. & C. Co. *v.* Baltimore, 66 Fed. 140, 25 U. S. App. 166, 13 C. C. A. 375.

Alabama: Lecroy *v.* Wiggins, 31 Ala. 13; Mason *v.* Alabama Iron Co., 73 Ala. 270; George *v.* Cahawba & M. R. R., 8 Ala. 234.

California: Cunningham *v.* Dorsey, 6 Cal. 19; Coffee *v.* Meiggs, 9 Cal. 363; Hale *v.* Trout, 35 Cal. 229.

Colorado: Baldwin *v.* Central Sav. Bk., 17 Colo. App. 7, 67 Pac. 179.

Georgia: Atlanta & L. G. R. R. *v.* Hodnett, 29 Ga. 461; Willingham *v.* Hooven, 74 Ga. 233, 58 Am. Rep. 435.

Idaho: Harris *v.* Faris-Kesl Const. Co., 13 Ida. 211, 89 Pac. 760.

Illinois: Brigham *v.* Hawley, 17 Ill. 38; McClelland *v.* Snider, 18 Ill. 58; Springdale C. A. *v.* Smith, 24 Ill. 480; Evans *v.* Chicago & R. I. R. R., 26 Ill. 189; Chicago *v.* Sexton, 115 Ill. 230, 2 N. E. 263.

Indiana: Herbert *v.* Stanford, 12 Ind.

503; Fairfield *v.* Jeffreys, 68 Ind. 578; Cincinnati, I., St. L. & C. Ry. *v.* Lutes, 112 Ind. 276, 11 N. E. 784, 14 N. E. 706.

Iowa: Richmond *v.* Dubuque & S. C. R. R., 40 Ia. 264.

Kentucky: Thompson *v.* Jackson, 14 B. Mon. 114; Elizabethtown & P. R. R. *v.* Pottinger, 10 Bush, 185.

Maryland: Eckenrode *v.* Chemical Co., 55 Md. 51.

Massachusetts: Fox *v.* Harding, 7 Cush. 516; Somers *v.* Wright, 115 Mass. 292; Jewett *v.* Brooks, 134 Mass. 505.

Michigan: Burrell *v.* New York & S. S. S. Co., 14 Mich. 34; Loud *v.* Campbell, 26 Mich. 239; Grand Rapids & B. C. R. R. *v.* Van Dusen, 29 Mich. 431; Goodrich *v.* Hubbard, 51 Mich. 62, 16 N. W. 232; Leonard *v.* Beaudry, 68 Mich. 312, 36 N. W. 88, 13 Am. St. Rep. 344.

Minnesota: Morrison *v.* Lovejoy, 6 Minn. 319; Ennis *v.* Buckeye Pub. Co., 44 Minn. 105, 46 N. W. 314.

Missouri: Crescent Mfg. Co. *v.* Nelson Mfg. Co., 100 Mo. 325.

Nebraska: Hale *v.* Hess, 30 Neb. 42, 46 N. W. 261.

New Jersey: Boyd *v.* Meighan, 48 N. J. L. 404, 4 Atl. 778; Holt *v.* United Security L. I. & T. Co., 76 N. J. L. 585, 72 Atl. 301, 21 L. R. A. (N. S.) 691.

New York: Masterton *v.* Mayor, 7

rule contracts may be divided into two classes; first, where the contract secured the doing of work or the giving of property on the one hand for a contract price to be paid in money on the other; second, where there is an exchange of property or of services, no contract price being payable in money on either side. These two classes of cases will be considered separately.

§ 614. Contracts in which a contract price is fixed: plaintiff to perform an act:

Where a contract price is fixed in the contract, this becomes the standard of value of the contract, the profit being the difference between the contract price and the cost or value of performance. The application of this rule may be examined in cases of several sorts.

In the first class of cases the plaintiff on his side undertakes to perform some act for the defendant and in return the defendant agrees to pay money for the plaintiff's act. In such

Hill, 61, 42 Am. Dec. 38; Cramer v. Metz, 57 N. Y. 659; Cahen v. Platt, 69 N. Y. 348, 25 Am. Rep. 203; Reed v. McConnell, 101 N. Y. 270.

North Carolina: Wilkinson v. Dunbar, 149 N. C. 20, 62 S. E. 748.

Pennsylvania: Hoy v. Gronoble, 34 Pa. 9, 75 Am. Dec. 628; Addams v. Tutton, 39 Pa. 447; Imperial C. & C. Co. v. Port Royal C. & C. Co., 138 Pa. 45, 20 Atl. 937.

Rhode Island: Collyer v. Moulton, 9 R. I. 90, 98 Am. Dec. 370.

Tennessee: Singleton v. Wilson, 85 Tenn. 344.

Texas: Porter v. Burkett, 65 Tex. 383; Osborne v. Ayres (Tex. Civ. App.), 32 S. W. 73.

Vermont: Curtis v. Smith, 48 Vt. 116; Morey v. King, 49 Vt. 304.

Virginia: Kendall B. N. Co. v. Commissioners of Sinking Fund, 79 Va. 563.

Washington: Perolin Co. v. Young, 118 Pac. 1.

West Virginia: Barrett v. Raleigh, C. & C. Co., 55 W. Va. 395, 47 S. E. 154.

Wisconsin: Nash v. Hoxie, 59 Wis. 384, 18 N. W. 408; Cameron v. White, 74 Wis. 425, 43 N. W. 155; Muenchow v. Roberts, 77 Wis. 520, 46 N. W. 802.

In a few cases it is said that the recovery of profits of a contract should not be allowed, on the ground that profits are not generally recoverable. This is confusing two separate things; collateral profits of another undertaking, claimed to have been lost through breach of the contract, and profits of the contract itself. The loss of collateral profits is always consequential, and cannot be recovered if it is either remote, unforeseen, or uncertain; the loss of the profits of the contract is direct loss, and is always recoverable if it can be proved with sufficient certainty. "Wherever profits are spoken of as not a subject of damages it will be found that something contingent upon future bargains, or speculations, or states of the market, is referred to, and not the difference between the agreed price of something contracted for and its ascertainable value or cost." Curtis, J., in Philadelphia, W. & B. R. R. v. Howard, 13 How. 307, 344, 14 L. ed. 307.

a case the profit of the contract is represented by the contract price less the cost of performing the act to be done by the plaintiff.[126] In estimating the cost of performance there should,

[126] *Construction contracts:* Contract price less cost of construction recoverable.

Buildings:

Illinois: Allphin v. Working, 132 Ill. 484, 24 N. E. 54.

Louisiana: Seaton v. New Orleans Second Municipality, 32 La. Ann. 44.

Minnesota: Swanson v. Andrus, 83 Minn. 505, 86 N. W. 465.

Nebraska: Kreamer v. Irwin, 46 Neb. 827, 65 N. W. 885.

New Jersey: Boyd v. Meighan, 48 N. J. L. 404, 4 Atl. 788.

New York: Danolos v. State, 89 N. Y. 36, 42 Am. Rep. 277 (public buildings); Baker v. State, 77 App. Div. 528, 78 N. Y. Supp. 922.

South Carolina: Feaster v. Richland Cotton Mills, 51 S. C. 143, 28 S. E. 301.

Texas: Joske v. Pleasants, 15 Tex. Civ. App. 433, 39 S. W. 586.

Work on or about buildings:

Alabama: Peck-Hammond Co. v. Heifner, 136 Ala. 473, 33 So. 807 (to put heating apparatus in building).

Arkansas: Gibney v. Turner, 52 Ark. 117, 12 S. W. 201.

Indiana: Richter v. Meyers, 5 Ind. App. 33, 31 N. E. 582.

Louisiana: Lynch v. Sellers, 41 La. Ann. 375, 6 So. 561.

Nebraska: Jewett v. Wilmot, 51 Neb. 700, 71 N. W. 775.

New York: Wieser v. Times R. & C. Co., 110 N. Y. Supp. 963 (to build floor); Goldstein v. Godfrey Co., 61 Misc. 64, 113 N. Y. Supp. 123 (to install fixtures); Kenny v. Knickerbocker B. & Y. Co., 136 App. Div. 568, 121 N. Y. Supp. 59 (to install machinery); Miller v. Loncao, 127 N. Y. Supp. 90 (to paint).

Wisconsin: Spafford v. McNally, 130 Wis. 537, 110 N. W. 387 (to do brickwork and plastering).

Railroads:

United States: Phila., W. & B. R. R. v. Howard, 13 How. 307, 14 L. ed. 307; Myers v. York & C. R. R., 2 Curt C. C. 28.

Alabama: George v. Cahawba & M. R. R., 8 Ala. 234; Danforth v. Tennessee & C. R. R., 93 Ala. 614, 11 So. 60.

Indiana: Chicago & S. E. Ry. v. Yawger, 24 Ind. App. 460, 56 N. E. 50.

Kentucky: Williams v. Yates, 113 S. W. 503 (to set piling).

Michigan: Grand Rapids & B. C. R. R. v. Van Dusen, 29 Mich. 431.

Tennessee: Smith v. O'Donnell, 8 Lea, 468.

Bridges:

United States: Insley v. Shepard, 31 Fed. 869; Harvey v. United States, 8 Ct. Cl. 501.

Indiana: Cincinnati & C. Ry. v. Lutes, 112 Ind. 276, 11 N. E. 784.

Other structures:

United States: Myerle v. United States, 31 Ct. Cl. 105 (vessel); Safety I. W. & C. Co. v. Baltimore, 66 Fed. 140, 13 C. C. A. 375 (conduits for cables).

California: McConnell v. Corona City Water Co., 149 Cal. 60, 85 Pac. 929, 8 L. R. A. (N. S.) 1171 (tunnel).

Wisconsin: Conway v. Mitchell, 97 Wis. 290, 72 N. W. 752 (monument).

Logging contracts: Plaintiff recovers contract price less cost of getting out, transporting or sawing the timber.

Contracts to cut and deliver:

Arkansas: Ingham L. Co. v. Ingersoll, 93 Ark. 447, 125 S. W. 139.

Kentucky: Blood v. Herring, 22 Ky. L. Rep. 1725, 61 S. W. 273; Horn v. Carroll, 25 Ky. L. Rep. 2305, 80 S. W. 518.

Michigan: Atkinson v. Morse, 63 Mich. 276, 29 N. W. 711; Rayburn v. Comstock, 80 Mich. 448, 45 N. W.

§ 614   PRICE FIXED: PLAINTIFF TO PERFORM AN ACT   1195

according to the better view, be included a reasonable allowance for the risk and responsibility of performing; and a reasonable deduction from the contract price to cover such risk

378; Lee v. Briggs, 99 Mich. 487, 58 N. W. 477; Greenwood v. Davis, 106 Mich. 230, 64 N. W. 26.
New Hampshire: Hutt v. Hickey, 67 N. H. 411, 29 Atl. 456.
North Carolina: Hawk v. Pine L. Co., 149 N. C. 10, 62 S. E. 752.
Texas: Carrico v. Stevenson (Tex. Civ. App.), 135 S. W. 260.
West Virginia: Patton v. Elk R. N. Co., 13 W. Va. 259.
Wisconsin: Salvo v. Duncan, 49 Wis. 151, 4 N. W. 1074.
Contracts to transport:
Alabama: Bonifay v. Hassell, 100 Ala. 269, 14 So. 46; Griffin v. Ogletree, 114 Ala. 343, 21 So. 488.
Minnesota: Pevey v. Schulenberg & B. L. Co., 33 Minn. 45, 21 N. W. 844; Glaspie v. Glassow, 28 Minn. 158, 9 N. W. 669.
New York: Durkee v. Mott, 8 Barb. 423.
Texas: Long v. McCauley, 3 S. W. 689.
Vermont: Gibson v. Wheldon, 82 Vt. 175, 72 Atl. 909.
Wisconsin: Corbett v. Anderson, 85 Wis. 218, 54 N. W. 727.
Contracts to saw:
Alabama: Robinson v. Bullock, 66 Ala. 548.
Arkansas: Beekman L. Co. v. Kittrell, 80 Ark. 228, 96 S. W. 988 (to plane); Hurley v. Oliver, 91 Ark. 427, 121 S. W. 920; Singer Mfg. Co. v. Reeves L. Co., 129 S. W. 805.
California: Winans v. Sierra Lumber Co., 66 Cal. 61, 4 Pac. 952.
Kentucky: Blood v. Herring, 61 S. W. 273, 22 Ky. L. Rep. 1725.
Louisiana: Barnette S. M. Co. v. Fort Harrison L. Co.,126 La. 75, 52 So. 222 (to take output of mill).
Michigan: Leonard v. Beaudry, 68 Mich. 312, 26 N. W. 88, 13 Am. St.

Rep. 344; Fell v. Newberry, 106 Mich. 542, 64 N. W. 474; Barrett v. Grand Rapids Veneer Works, 110 Mich. 6, 67 N. W. 976.
New York: Snell v. Remington Paper Co., 102 App. Div. 138, 92 N. Y. Supp. 343.
Wisconsin: Nash v. Hoxie, 59 Wis. 384, 18 N. W. 408.
Contracts to do work on land: contract price less cost of work recovered.
To mine coal:
Kentucky: Sagamore Coal Co. v. Clark, 109 S. W. 349, 33 Ky. L. Rep. 134.
West Virginia: Smith v. Atlas P. C. Co., 66 W. Va. 599, 66 S. E. 746.
To drill for oil or gas:
Kansas: Fredonia Gas Co. v. Bailey, 77 Kan. 296, 94 Pac. 258.
Kentucky: New Domain O. & C. Co. v. Feeley, 107 S. W. 1185, 32 Ky. L. Rep. 1181.
Ohio: Leffler v. Witten, 76 Oh. St. 632, 81 N. E. 1189, affirming 28 Oh. C. Ct. 533.
To do other work:
Colorado: McClair v. Austin, 17 Colo. 576, 31 Pac. 225, 31 Am. St. Rep. 340 (to grade lawns and plant shade trees).
Delaware: Truitt v. Fahey, 3 Penn. 573, 52 Atl. 339 (to build road).
Michigan: Burrell v. New York & S. Salt Co., 14 Mich. 34 (to construct vats).
New Jersey: Ryan v. Remmey, 57 N. J. L. 474, 31 Atl. 766 (to remove clay from defendant's beds).
New York: Riley v. Black, 1 N. Y. Misc. 288, 20 N. Y. Supp. 695 (to remove rock).
Tennessee: Singleton v. Wilson, 85 Tenn. 344, 2 S. W. 801 (to build dam).
Texas: Campbell v. Howerton (Tex. Civ. App.), 87 S. W. 370 (to clear land).
Washington: Watson v. Gray's H. B.

and responsibility should be made wherever the amount of risk and responsibility would have been appreciable.[127]   The profit is to be arrived at by considering what the cost would be to the plaintiff, not to any ordinary person nor to the defendant. If the plaintiff was in a position to perform the contract at a very small cost, the profit of the contract is larger on that account.[128]   So where the plaintiff agreed to furnish

Co., 3 Wash. 283, 28 Pac. 527 (to sink well).

Wisconsin: Nilson *v.* Morse, 52 Wis. 240, 9 N. W. 1 (to pull stumps).

Contract for board and lodging: plaintiff recovers contract price less value of lodging and cost of board. Wilkinson *v.* Davies, 146 N. Y. 25, 40 N. E. 501; Wetmore *v.* Jaffray, 9 Hun, (N. Y.), 140; Lydecker *v.* Valentine, 71 Hun, 194, 24 N. Y. Supp. 567; Strakosch *v.* Wray, 6 Misc. 207, 26 N. Y. Supp. 537; Crane *v.* Powell, 19 N. Y. Supp. 220; Thayer *v.* Hamlin, 59 Misc. 171, 110 N. Y. Supp. 244; Ashton *v.* Margolies, 129 N. Y. Supp. 617.

Contract for work: contract price less cost of doing the work recoverable.

United States: United States *v.* Speed, 8 Wall. 77, 9 L. ed. 449 (to pack hogs); The Gazelle & Cargo, 128 U. S. 487, 32 L. ed. 496, 9 Sup. Ct. 139 (to transport goods); Dalbeattie S. Co. *v.* Card, 59 Fed. 159 (*ibid*); Lincoln *v.* Orthwein, 120 Fed. 880 (to do stevedore work).

Arkansas: St. Louis, A. & T. Ry. *v.* Beard, 56 Ark. 309, 29 S. W. 146 (to print time-tables).

Georgia: Pope *v.* Graniteville Mfg. Co., 1 Ga. App. 176, 57 S. E. 949 (to finance and store a cotton crop).

Massachusetts: Magnolia Metal Co. *v.* Gale, 189 Mass. 124, 75 N. E. 219 (to maintain office: office expenses deducted from contract price).

Mississippi: Friedlander *v.* Pugh, 43 Miss. 111, 5 Am. Rep. 478 (to do work).

Missouri: Wiggins Ferry Co. *v.* Chicago & A. R. R., 73 Mo. 389, 39 Am. Rep. 519 (to do all defendant's ferrying); Hume *v.* Hale, 146 Mo. App. 659, 125 S. W. 811 (to pay rent in work).

New York: Cramer *v.* Metz, 57 N. Y. 659 (to manufacture goods); Baker Transfer Co. *v.* Merchants' R. & I. M. Co., 12 App. Div. 260, 42 N. Y. Supp. 76 (to deliver defendant's ice to his customers); Ashkanazy *v.* Sachs, 110 N. Y. Supp. 929 (to press clothing); Thacke *v.* Hernsheim, 115 N. Y. Supp. 216 (to do iron work).

Pennsylvania: Nixon *v.* Myers, 141 Pa. 477, 21 Atl. 670 (to do hauling).

Texas: Porter *v.* Burkett, 65 Tex. 383 (to use mule teams in work for defendant).

Vermont: Parker *v.* McKannon, 76 Vt. 96, 56 Atl. 536 (to make and supply musical instruments for sale by defendant).

Virginia: Kendall B. N. Co. *v.* Commissioners of Sinking Fund, 79 Va. 563 (to engrave bonds).

Washington: General L. & P. Co. *v.* Washington Rubber Co., 55 Wash. 461, 104 Pac. 650 (to print).

West Virginia: Electric S. & C. Co. *v.* Consolidated L. & R. Co., 42 W. Va. 583, 26 S. E. 188 (to repair machinery).

[127] *United States:* United States *v.* Speed, 8 Wall. 77, 19 L. ed. 449; Insley *v.* Shepard, 31 Fed. 869.

Alabama: Danforth *v.* Tennessee & C. R. R., 93 Ala. 614, 11 So. 60.

New York: McMaster *v.* State, 108 N. Y. 542, 15 N. E. 417.

[128] Campbell *v.* Howerton (Tex. Civ. App.), 87 S. W. 370.

and set up a motor for the defendant he was allowed to show the price at which he had secured a second-hand motor which would have answered the purpose of the contract.[129]

Therefore when the plaintiff has made an advantageous sub-contract by which he was to secure the performance by another at a cost much below the contract price, it would seem that he should be allowed to show this, and to recover the difference between the contract price and the sub-contract price, allowing, however, a fair amount on account of his relief from the responsibility and trouble of himself performing.[130]

In several cases, however, it has been said that the cost to the plaintiff of sub-contracts could not be shown.[131] In these decisions the courts intended to follow the rule laid down in the leading case of Masterton v. Mayor of Brooklyn.[132] In that case, however, the court was not dealing with an offer by the plaintiff to show the sub-contract price as evidence of the cost to the plaintiff of performing his own contract. The plaintiff was endeavoring to recover from the defendant the damages he would be obliged to pay to the sub-contractor for breach of the sub-contract. Allowing this the trial court had charged that the plaintiff could recover the difference between the contract price and the cost to the sub-contractor, of performance, thus giving both the profits of the contract in suit and of the sub-contract. This was held error on two grounds: first, that the sub-contract was not within the contemplation of the parties; second, that it was not certainly proved that the consequence of defendant's breach of contract was a breach of the sub-contract. If the view of the matter stated above is correct, cases denying the admissibility of the sub-contract price are wrongly decided.

When the defendant not only refuses to allow the plaintiff to do the work, but also secures another to do it at a less price,

---

[129] Silberstein v. Duluth News-Tribune Co., 68 Minn. 430, 71 N. W. 622.

[130] *United States:* Floyd v. U. S., 2 Ct. Cl. 429; affirmed, U. S. v. Floyd, 8 Wall. 77, 19 L. ed. 449.

Alabama: Tennessee & C. R. R. v. Danforth, 112 Ala. 80, 20 So. 502.

[131] *United States:* Stout v. United States, 27 Ct. Cl. 385; Barlow v. United States, 35 Ct. Cl. 514.

New York: Levenson v. Bollowa, 42 Misc. 201, 85 N. Y. Supp. 386; Story v. New York & H. R. R., 6 N. Y. 85.

[132] 7 Hill (N. Y.), 61, 42 Am. Dec. 38.

the plaintiff may, it would seem, recover as the value of the contract the difference between the price he was to receive and the cost to the defendant of the substituted work.[133]

§ 615. Cost of partial performance.

When the contract has been partly performed, the plaintiff upon a breach of it loses more than the mere value of the contract; he has not only lost the benefit of the contract, but he has also lost the expense of partial performance on his own part. He may gain some benefit from this partial performance, as by the value of the material left on his hands; but this loss is greater than the profits of the contract by an amount equal to the net expense of the partial performance, after deducting the benefit of such partial performance to himself. So if the plaintiff on completion was to receive payment of a contract price, he may recover upon breach the profits of the contract (that is, the contract price less the cost of complete performance), and in addition the net cost of the partial performance.[134]

[133] *Georgia:* Chattahoochee Brick Co. *v.* Sullivan, 86 Ga. 50, 12 S. E. 216 (to build a railroad).

New Jersey: Ryan *v.* Remmey, 57 N. J. L. 474, 31 Atl. 766 (to remove clay from defendant's beds).

In Michigan Paving Co. *v.* Detroit, 34 Mich. 201, the plaintiff contracted with the defendant city to pave a street. The city under a right reserved in the contract declared it forfeited after part performance. Plaintiff claimed he was entitled to all of the original contract price except what the city paid another contractor for completing the work; but *held,* this was not so since the city might have made a more beneficial contract the second time.

[134] *Contracts of construction:* plaintiff recovers profits plus cost of labor and materials furnished.

Houses:

Georgia: L. Campbell & Co. *v.* Mion, 6 Ga. App. 134, 64 S. E. 571.

Louisiana: Dugue *v.* Levy, 114 La. 21, 37 So. 995

Maryland: Black *v.* Woodrow, 39 Md. 194.

Nebraska: Van Dorn *v.* Mengedoht, 41 Neb. 525, 59 N. W. 800.

Railroads:

United States: Hambly *v.* Delaware, M. & V. R. R., 21 Fed. 541.

Alabama: Danforth *v.* Tennessee & C. R. R., 93 Ala. 614, 11 So. 60.

Kentucky: Elizabethtown & P. R. R. *v.* Pottinger, 10 Bush, 185.

Maryland: Bush *v.* Baltimore & C. Constr. Co., 88 Md. 665, 41 Atl. 1092.

Other structures:

Mississippi: Vicksburg Water Supply Co. *v.* Gorman, 70 Miss. 360, 11 So. 680 (waterworks).

Contracts to do work: Plaintiff recovers profits plus cost of the work done.

California: Cunningham *v.* Dorsey, 6 Cal. 19 (to deliver logs at mill) Cederberg *v.* Robinson, 100 Cal. 93, 34 Pac. 625 (to harvest grain).

Kentucky: Haggin *v.* Price, 8 Dana, 48 (to board the plaintiff).

Minnesota: Glaspie *v.* Glassow, 28 Minn. 158, 9 N. W. 669 (to drive logs).

The simplest method of finding the damages in such a case is to subtract from the contract price the cost of completing performance by the plaintiff;[135] subtracting, however, from this amount the value of the partial performance to the plaintiff.[136]

If some portion of the contract had been so far completed that the contract itself furnishes a price for such partial performance, the plaintiff should recover the contract price for this completed portion and the profits lost on the remainder of the contract.[137]   And it is sometimes held that where a

Texas: Dunham *v.* Orange L. Co. (Tex. Civ. App.), 125 S. W. 89 (to save stranded logs).
Washington: Anderson *v.* Hilker, 38 Wash. 632, 80 Pac. 848 (to move building).
[135] *United States:* Altoona E. E. & S. Co. *v.* Kittanning & F. C. St. Ry., 126 Fed. 559 (to equip electric railway; plaintiff prevented from equipping a portion; recovers contract price less cost of equipping such portion).
Kentucky: Blood *v.* Herring, 22 Ky. L. Rep. 1725, 61 S. W. 273 (to saw lumber; subtract cost of sawing the remainder from contract price).
Maine: Morgan *v.* Hefler, 68 Me. 131 (to build a stable).
Maryland: Baltimore & O. R. R. *v.* Stewart, 79 Md. 487, 29 Atl. 964 (to build bridge; plaintiff recovers contract price less cost of completion).
Minnesota: Ennis *v.* Buckeye Pub. Co., 44 Minn. 105, 46 N. W. 314 (to do work).
Missouri: Hammond *v.* Beeson, 112 Mo. 190, 20 S. W. 646 (to build section of railroad; subtract cost of completion from contract price); Park *v.* Kitchen, 1 Mo. App. 357 (to construct a building).
New York: Devlin *v.* Mayor of New York, 63 N. Y. 8 (to clean streets); Dunn *v.* Allen, 59 App. Div. 561, 67 N. Y. Supp. 218 (to use boats and horses in work on canal; subtract expense of complete performance from contract price).

Ohio: Toledo *v.* Libbie, 19 Ohio C. Ct. 704 (to build sidewalks; plaintiff recovers contract price less cost of completing).
Wisconsin: Allen *v.* Murray, 87 Wis. 41, 57 N. W. 979 (to cut and deliver logs; contract price less cost of cutting and hauling remaining logs recoverable.
[136] *Arkansas:* Gibney *v.* Turner, 52 Ark. 117, 12 S. W. 201 (to build house; plaintiff recovers contract price less labor and material required to complete the contract, subtracting, however, the value of the material on hand).
Georgia: Mimms *v.* J. L. Betts Co. (Ga. App.), 72 S. E. 271.
New York: Thomas *v.* Cauldwell, 26 N. Y. Supp. 785 (to build printing press of unusual size, of no value to anyone but defendant: contract price recoverable, less cost of completion, subtracting value of press as old metal).
Vermont: Allen *v.* Thrall, 36 Vt. 711 (to manufacture machines; subtract cost of completion, together with the value of unfinished machines left on plaintiff's hands, from contract price).
So when plaintiff contracted to furnish five brown stone stoops for houses of the defendant, and after cutting the stone defendant prevented performance, plaintiff was not entitled to recover the cost of repairing the stoops without evidence that the work of preparation was useless. Miller *v.* Hahn, 23 App. Div. 48, 48 N. Y. Supp. 346.
[137] *United States:* Moore *v.* U. S., 17

single contract has been partially performed the plaintiff may recover a portion of the contract price proportional to the amount performed plus the proportional part of the profit upon the portion unperformed.[138]

§ 616. Cost of partial performance where no profits proved: doctrine of United States v. Behan.

If the plaintiff cannot or does not prove that any profits would have been earned by a full performance, he may nevertheless recover the expense of the partial performance.[139] So

Ct. Cl. 17 (to manufacture and supply 600,000 brick; plaintiff recovers difference between contract price of brick manufactured and what they could be sold for plus difference between contract price of the remainder and what they could be manufactured for); Ferris v. U. S., 27 Ct. Cl. 542 (to dredge, at fixed price per cubic yard; contract price of amount dredged plus profits on work not done recoverable).

California: Hale v. Trout, 35 Cal. 229 (to deliver lumber at certain price; contract price of lumber delivered plus profits on lumber not accepted recoverable); Upstone v. Weir, 54 Cal. 124 (to manufacture and deliver iron work; plaintiff recovers contract price of part delivered plus profits on the balance).

Connecticut: Leonard v. Dyer, 26 Conn. 172, 68 Am. Dec. 382 (to transport lumber).

Iowa: Dibol v. Minott, 9 Ia. 403 (to paint ten houses for $70 each; broken after several houses painted. Plaintiff recovers $70 for each house painted, and profits on houses not painted).

Missouri: Gabriel v. Akinsville Pressed Brick Co., 57 Mo. App. 520 (to drive a well at a fixed price per foot; plaintiff recovers agreed price for distance driven, and difference between contract price and cost for the remaining distance).

New Jersey: Kehoe v. Rutherford, 56 N. J. L. 23, 27 Atl. 912 (to grade and build a road; plaintiff recovers con-

tract price for the portion graded, plus the profits of remaining work); Sullivan v. Moffatt, 70 N. J. L. 4, 56 Atl. 304 (to supply and set marble in a building; proper proportion of the contract price plus profits of remaining work recoverable).

Texas: Houston & T. C. Ry. v. Mitchell, 38 Tex. 85 (to cut and deliver hay); Duncan v. Johnson (Tex. Civ. App.), 59 S. W. 46 (to build house; plaintiff recovers contract price for part done plus profit on remainder).

[138] *Illinois:* Demme & Dierkes Furniture Co. v. McCabe, 49 Ill. App. 453.

Iowa: McCausland v. Cresap, 3 Greene, 161.

Nebraska: Thompson v. Gaffey, 52 Neb. 317, 72 N. W. 314 (to do plumbing in house).

New Jersey: Wilson v. Borden, 68 N. J. L. 627, 54 Atl. 815 (to build a house).

Washington: Noyes v. Pugin, 2 Wash. 653, 27 Pac. 548 (to serve as architect).

[139] *United States:* Sperry & Hutchinson Co. v. O'Neill Adams Co., 185 Fed. 231, 000 C. C. A. 000.

Missouri: Ragland v. Conqueror Zinc Cos., 136 Mo. App. 631, 118 S. W. 1194 (to sublease land for mining).

New Jersey: Holt v. United S. L. I. & T. Co., 76 N. J. L. 585, 72 Atl. 301.

Pennsylvania: In re Carroll's Estate, 219 Pa. 440, 68 Atl. 1038 (to adopt).

Texas: Ball v. Britton, 58 Tex. 57 (to enter into partnership).

where the plaintiff agreed to drive a well at an agreed price per
foot, but the number of feet was not agreed upon, and the contract was broken after partial performance, he was allowed
to recover the cost of partial performance.[140] And where plaintiff agreed to take care of deceased during life and deceased
agreed to leave him property by will, the latter agreement being
too indefinite to enforce, the plaintiff may recover the value of
his services.[141]

This principle is illustrated by the leading case of United
States *v.* Behan.[142] In this case the claimant was the surety
for one Roy upon a contract between Roy and the United
States to improve the harbor of New Orleans, and later, upon
the contract with Roy being annulled, the claimant was authorized to fulfil the contract. He went to expense in providing
machinery and materials and did a portion of the work and
after this part performance the government finally cancelled
the contract. The claimant thereupon sold the materials on
hand. The Court of Claims allowed him for his actual expenditures in the prosecution of the work together with the unavoid-
able losses on materials. It did not appear whether a profit
would have been made or not by a performance of the contract.
The government appealed on the ground that by making a claim
for profits the claimant asserted the existence of the contract
and could recover only nominal damages if he was unable to
show that a profit would have been made. The Supreme Court,
however, speaking by Justice Bradley, affirmed the decision
of the Court of Claims on the ground that in a case of this sort
the claimant should at least be made whole for his losses even
though he did not prove what the profits of the contract would
be.

"The *prima facie* measure of damages for the breach of a
contract is the amount of the loss which the injured party has
sustained thereby. If the breach consists in preventing the
performance of the contract, without the fault of the other
party, who is willing to perform it, the loss of the latter will

[140] *Iowa:* Thompson *v.* Brown, 106
Ia. 367, 76 N. W. 819.

Minnesota: Olson *v.* Nonenmacher,
63 Minn. 425, 65 N. W. 642.

[141] Shakespeare *v.* Markham, 10 Hun
(N. Y.), 311.

[142] 110 U. S. 338, 28 L. ed. 168, 4 Sup.
Ct. 81.

consist of two distinct items on grounds of damage, namely: first,what he has already expended toward performance (less the value of materials on hand); secondly, the profits that he would realize by performing the whole contract. The second item, profits, cannot always be recovered. They may be too remote and speculative in their character, and therefore incapable of that clear and direct proof which the law requires. But when, in the language of Chief Justice Nelson, in the case of Masterson *v.* Mayor of Brooklyn,[143] they are 'the direct and immediate fruits of the contract,' they are free from this objection; they are then 'part and parcel of the contract itself, entering into and constituting a portion of its very elements; something stipulated for, the right to the enjoyment of which is just as clear and plain as to the fulfillment of any other stipulation.' Still in order to furnish a ground of recovery in damages, they must be proved. If not proved, or if they are of such a remote and speculative character that they cannot be legally proved, the party is confined to his loss of actual outlay and expense. This loss, however, he is clearly entitled to recover in all cases, unless the other party, who has voluntarily stopped the performance of the contract, can show the contrary.

"The rule as stated in Speed's case is only one aspect of the general rule. It is the rule as applicable to a particular case. As before stated, the primary measure of damages is the amount of the party's loss; and this loss, as we have seen, may consist of two heads or classes of damages—actual outlay and anticipated profits. But failure to prove profits will not prevent the party from recovering his losses for actual outlay and expenditure. If he goes also for profits, then the rule applies as laid down in Speed's case, and his *profits* will be measured by 'the difference between the cost of doing the work and what he was to receive for it,' etc. The claimant was not bound to go for profits, even though he counted for them in his petition. He might stop upon showing of losses. The two heads of damage are distinct, though closely related. When profits are sought, a recovery for outlay is included and something more. That something more is the profits. If the outlay equals or exceeds the amount to be received, of course there can be no profits."

[143] 7 Hill (N. Y.), 69.

If the cost of partial performance is recovered there can be no recovery for profits, and if the profits can be proved with sufficient certainty for recovery the cost of partial performance cannot be allowed. In no case can both be recovered.[144]

§ 617. Contracts in which a contract price is fixed: plaintiff to deliver property.

If the plaintiff agrees to deliver something to the defendant and the defendant on his part agrees to pay money for it, then the profit of the contract is to be measured by the contract price less the value of the property to be delivered by the plaintiff.[145]

[144] Tygart *v.* Albritton, 5 Ga. App. 412, 63 S. E. 521.

[145] The typical example of this sort of contract is a sale of chattels by the plaintiff to the defendant, which will be considered in a separate chapter. *Post*, chap. xxxv. And where there is not a technical contract of sale but the plaintiff contracts for a certain sum of money to do work in making or procuring property and then to deliver the property to defendant, the plaintiff recovers as the profits of the contract the contract price less the cost of procuring and delivering the property.

Contract to supply an article: Contract price less cost of supplying recoverable.

United States: Floyd *v.* United States, 8 Wall. 77, 19 L. ed. 449 (affirming 2 Ct. Cl. 429); United Engineering & C. Co. *v.* Broadnax, 136 Fed. 351, 69 C. C. A. 177; H. T. Smith Co. *v.* Minetto-Meriden Co., 168 Fed. 777 (to let teams); Stout *v.* United States, 27 Ct. Cl. 385 (material for building).

Alabama: Peck-Hammond Co. *v.* Heifner, 136 Ala. 473, 33 So. 807 (to put in heating apparatus); Wheeler *v.* Cleveland, 54 So. 277 (to sell standing timber).

California: Tahoe Ice Co. *v.* Union Ice Co., 109 Cal. 242, 41 Pac. 1020 (to supply annual ice crop).

Colorado: Kilpatrick *v.* Inman, 46 Colo. 514, 105 Pac. 1080, 26 L. R. A.

(N. S.) 188 (to let "livery rig" with driver).

Indiana: Indiana Canning Co. *v.* Priest, 16 Ind. App. 445, 45 N. E. 618 (to supply plaintiff's crop of tomatoes).

Kentucky: Hollerbach & M. C. Co. *v.* Wilkins, 130 Ky. 51, 112 S. W. 1126 (to supply broken stone).

Louisiana: Avery *v.* Segura Sugar Co., 111 La. 891, 35 So. 967 (to supply plaintiff's sugar crop).

Maryland: Furstenburg *v.* Fawsett, 61 Md. 184 (defendant to cut and carry away plaintiff's standing wood).

Minnesota: Silberstein *v.* Duluth News-Tribune Co., 68 Minn. 430, 71 N. W. 622 (to set up electric motor).

Missouri: Chapman *v.* Kansas City, C. & S. Ry., 146 Mo. 481, 48 S. W. 646 (to deliver railroad ties).

Nebraska: Hale *v.* Hess, 30 Neb. 42, 46 N. W. 261 (to provide and set up furnace).

New York: McMaster *v.* State, 108 N. Y. 542, 15 N. E. 417 (to provide material for building).

Oregon: American B. & C. Co. *v.* Bullen B. Co., 29 Ore. 549, 46 Pac. 138 (to provide material for building).

Texas: Watkins *v.* Junker, 4 Tex. Civ. App. 629, 23 S. W. 802 (to supply boats for dredging canal; plaintiff recovers difference between rental value and contract price).

Contracts to manufacture: Plaintiff

§ 618. Contracts in which a contract price is fixed: defendant to perform an act or deliver property.

If the plaintiff was to pay an agreed price for work to be done or property to be delivered by the defendant, the profit of the contract to the plaintiff is measured by the value of defendant's performance less the contract price; [146] or if he has paid part of the price, he recovers the difference plus the partial pay-

recovers contract price less cost of manufacture.

United States: Hinckley *v.* Pittsburgh B. S. Co., 121 U. S. 264, 30 L. ed. 967, 7 Sup. Ct. 875.

Missouri: Crescent Mfg. Co. *v.* N. O. Nelson Mfg. Co., 100 Mo. 325, 13 S. W. 503 (barbed wire).

South Carolina: Millar *v.* Hilliard, Cheves, 149 (bread: deduct value of bread left on plaintiff's hands).

Virginia: Worrell *v.* Kinnear Mfg. Co., 103 Va. 719, 49 S. E. 988 (steel doors).

Wisconsin: Walsh *v.* Myers, 92 Wis. 397, 66 N. W. 250 (lye cans).

In Brazell *v.* Cohn, 32 Mont. 556, 81 Pac. 339, the defendant contracted to purchase the plaintiff's entire supply of milk; and the measure of damages for the breach was held to be the contract price less the wholesale price of milk, rather than the cost of production. For if the contract had been carried out, since his whole supply was contracted for, he could have sold none at the wholesale price; and any profit he might make after breach by selling at wholesale is earned only as a result of the breach, and should therefore reduce by that amount the damages which would otherwise be recoverable.

[146] This is the rule of damages for breach by the seller of a contract for the sale of chattels. *Post,* chap. xxxv. And the same rule may be applied in the case of other contracts for delivery of property.

Alabama: Northen *v.* Tatum, 164 Ala. 368, 51 So. 17 (to cut plaintiff's timber and manufacture it into shin-

gles; difference between value of the timber when cut and made into shingles, less cost of doing so, and its value standing).

Arkansas: Ford H. L. Co. *v.* Clement, (Ark.), 135 S. W. 343 (to supply lumber for plaintiff's mill; profits of the contract).

Connecticut: Cohn *v.* Norton, 57 Conn. 480, 5 L. R. A. 572, 18 Atl. 595 (to lease a building; difference between the agreed rent and value of the term).

Illinois: World's Columbian Exposition Co. *v.* Pasteur-Chamberland Filter Co., 82 Ill. App. 94 (to allow defendant to advertise in plaintiff's park; value of advertising minus the contract price).

New York: Bean *v.* Carleton, 51 Hun, 318 (to publish book for plaintiff; recovers loss through not having book published); Nash *v.* Thousand Islands S. B. Co., 123 App. Div. 148, 108 N. Y. Supp. 336 (to let plaintiff the exclusive checking, news, confectionery, and view privileges on defendant's fleet of steamers; difference between actual value of the privileges and the contract price); Hirsh *v.* Press Pub. Co., 141 App. Div. 357, 126 N. Y. Supp. 298 (breach of contract by which plaintiff was to remove iron from a building for a certain price; defendant refused to allow him to remove it. Measure of damages, difference between the value of the iron after removal and the contract price plus the cost of removal. Cannot recover damages based on favorable contracts plaintiff might have made with other parties).

ment.[147] If no profits can be shown he recovers at least his partial payments and other expenditures.[148] In such a case, however, the value of the performance by the defendant can ordinarily be established only by showing the cost of securing preformance elsewhere. The measure of damages, as ordinarily stated, is the cost of securing performance of the work elsewhere, less the contract price.[149] If the contract

[147] Barr v. Henderson, 105 La. 691, 30 So. 158.

[148] *Kansas:* King v. Perfection B. M. Co., 81 Kan. 809, 106 Pac. 1071 (to supply machinery; partial payment, prepayment of freight, and expense of special construction of building to receive machinery).

Kentucky: Corbin O. & G. Co. v. Mull, 123 Ky. 763, 30 Ky. L. Rep. 91, 97 S. W. 385 (to drill oil well; no profits being proved, partial payments).

New York: Deluise v. Long Island R. R., 65 App. Div. 487, 72 N. Y. Supp. 988 (lease of boot-blacking privilege; rent paid in advance); Tabak v. Fettner, 139 App. Div. 248, 123 N. Y. Supp. 982 (actual value of ice-box given by plaintiff at an arbitrary valuation as part payment of contract price).

[149] *United States:* Goldsboro v. Moffett, 49 Fed. 213 (to build waterworks; plaintiff recovers price at which the contract was let on a second bidding less the original price).

Alabama: O'Brien v. Anniston Pipe Works, 93 Ala. 582, 9 So. 415 (to do excavation and grading. The fact that part of the work was done at a cheaper rate than the agreed rate is immaterial; the result of securing performance of the whole contract fixes the damages).

Delaware: Hartnett v. Baker, 4 Pennew. 431, 56 Atl. 672 (to grow and supply tomatoes).

Illinois: Tribune Co. v. Bradshaw, 20 Ill. App. 17 (to insert advertisement in a newspaper; difference between cost of inserting a similar advertisement in another paper and the contract price recoverable).

Kentucky: Corbin O. & G. Co. v. Mull, 123 Ky. 763, 97 S. W. 385, 30 Ky. L. Rep. 91 (to drill oil well).

Massachusetts: Weed v. Draper, 104 Mass. 28 (to build machines); Florence M. Co. v. Daggett, 135 Mass. 582 (to make castings for stoves).

New Hampshire: Lamoreaux v. Rolfe, 36 N. H. 33 (to haul lumber).

New York: Cody v. Turn Verein, 48 App. Div. 279, 64 N. Y. Supp. 219, affirmed, 167 N. Y. 607, 60 N. E. 1108 (to excavate land); Jacobs v. Mandel, 104 N. Y. Supp. 721 (to furnish labor and materials); New York M. C. Co. v. City H. I. Co., 94 App. Div. 439, 88 N. Y. Supp. 233 (to put in metal cornice); Samuels v. Fidelity, etc., Co., 49 Hun 122, 1 N. Y. Supp. 850 (to become surety for the plaintiff on a bond; plaintiff recovers increased expense of getting another surety); Eagle Tube Co. v. Edward Barr Co., 16 Daly, 212, 10 N. Y. Supp. 113 (to weld tubes in boiler; increased expense of having the work done later by another recoverable).

North Carolina: State v. Ingram, 5 Ire. 441 (to keep a bridge in repair).

Ohio: Cincinnati & S. Ry. v. Carthage, 36 Oh. St. 631 (to grade streets).

Oregon: Haskins v. Scott, 52 Ore. 271, 96 Pac. 1112 (to furnish engine for threshing machine: plaintiff recovers cost of hiring from others).

Pennsylvania: Collins v. Baumgardner, 52 Pa. 461 (to carry coal; plaintiff recovers cost of getting coal carried by others, including expense of finding other carriers, less contract price).

price has been paid by the plaintiff, or his part of the contract
fully performed, the cost of getting the defendant's work done
elsewhere is recoverable.[150] So where a contractor gave a bond

Texas: Watson *v.* De Witt County,
19 Tex. Civ. App. 150, 46 S. W. 1061
(to build courthouse); A. J. Anderson
Electric Co. *v.* Cleburne W. I. & L. Co.,
23 Tex. Civ. App. 74, 57 S. W. 575 (to
erect a building); Osborne *v.* Ayers
(Tex. Civ. App.), 32 S. W. 73 (to keep
a repair plant for a machine; plaintiff
recovers cost of going to a greater distance to get it repaired).

Vermont: Royalton *v.* Royalton & W.
T. Co., 14 Vt. 311 (to repair bridge);
Forsyth *v.* Mann, 68 Vt. 116, 34 Atl.
481, 32 L. R. A. 788 (to cut and furnish
a granite monument).

Washington: Carroll *v.* Caine, 27
Wash. 402, 67 Pac. 993 (to transport
lumber from vessel to plaintiff's yard).

Wisconsin: Eastern Ry. *v.* Tuteur,
127 Wis. 382, 105 N. W. 1067 (to
handle all the freight at plaintiff's station; plaintiff recovers cost of such
handling by others less the contract
price).

[150] *Arkansas:* Sullivant *v.* Reardon, 5
Ark. 140, 39 Am. Dec. 368 (to clear
land); Neale *v.* Smith, 61 Ark. 564, 33
S. W. 1058 (to teach plaintiff book-
keeping, price being paid in advance;
plaintiff recovers cost of the course);
Plunkett *v.* Meredith, 72 Ark. 3, 77
S. W. 600 (to dig a well until it would
give a certain supply of water).

California: Taylor *v.* North P. C.
R. R., 56 Cal. 317 (to build a wagon
road in place of one destroyed by railroad and to fence the road).

Connecticut: Hawley *v.* Belden, 1
Conn. 93 (to build a road; it was so
defectively built that part of it required to be repaired; cost of repairing recoverable).

Illinois: St. Louis, J. & C. R. R.
v. Lurton, 72 Ill. 118 (to build a
bridge).

Indiana: Howe M. Co. *v.* Reber, 66

Ind. 498 (to keep a sewing machine in
repair); Seavey *v.* Shurick, 110 Ind.
494, 11 N. E. 597 (to clear land).

Iowa: Great W. P. Co. *v.* Tucker, 73
Ia. 755, 34 N. W. 205 (to print posters;
plaintiff recovers cost of equivalent
advertising).

Maryland: Broumel *v.* Rayner, 68
Md. 47 (to build a street).

Minnesota: Carli *v.* Seymour, 26
Minn. 276, 3 N. W. 348 (to grade a
road).

Missouri: Hirt *v.* Hirn, 61 Mo. 496
(to build a house); Woodworth *v.* Mc-
Lean, 97 Mo. 325, 11 S. W. 43 (to sink a
shaft in mine 500 feet); Wright *v.* Sanderson, 20 Mo. App. 534 (to build
foundation of house; improperly built;
cost of putting it into proper shape recoverable); Spink *v.* Mueller, 77 Mo.
App. 85 (to build a house, finishing
woodwork with certain varnish. Defendant used a different and inferior
varnish. Plaintiff recovers sum necessarily expended to put on required
varnish).

Nebraska: Orr W. Co. *v.* Reno W.
Co., 19 Neb. 60 (to repair a ditch).

New York: Mayor of New York *v.*
Second Ave. R. R., 102 N. Y. 572, 55
Am. Rep. 839, 7 N. E. 905 (to keep
street in repair); Haist *v.* Bell, 24 App.
Div. 252, 48 N. Y. Supp. 405 (to build
a house and put in pine finish; some
finish was put in of hemlock. Plaintiff
recovers cost of replacing the hemlock
by pine); Morrell *v.* Long Island R. R.,
15 Daly, 127, 3 N. Y. Supp. 928 (to fill
in depot site on plaintiff's land); May *v.*
Georger, 21 Misc. 622, 47 N. Y. Supp.
1052 (to fit for plaintiff a sealskin coat,
price paid in advance; plaintiff recovers cost of making it suitable to
wear); Whitehouse *v.* Staten I. W. S.
Co., 101 App. Div. 112, 91 N. Y.
Supp. 544 (to supply water; plaintiff

to the plaintiff for the performance of his contract, and upon breach of contract the plaintiff had the right to complete the work and the plaintiff exercised this right, he was allowed to recover the increased expense of the work, and damages paid for injuries naturally and necessarily incurred by workmen in the course of the work.[151] The cost of completion is not shown on the ground that this amount has actually been expended by the plaintiff; it is merely the evidence of the value of performance, and one of the factors entering into the profit of the contract. This profit is the same in amount whether the plaintiff actually secures performance of the contract by another or leaves it incomplete. Consequently if the work is left incomplete by the defendant, the plaintiff may under this rule recover the cost of completion, whether he actually has had the work completed or not.[152] If, however, the completion of the contract is actually secured by the plaintiff, the amount paid by him for such completion is, if reasonable, the best evidence of the value or cost of performance, and it is therefore *prima facie* to be taken as the value of performance; [153] but it is always open to the de-

recovers cost of labor employed in getting a supply elsewhere).

Pennsylvania: Morse *v.* Arnfield, 15 Pa. Super. Ct. 140 (to supply elevator; elevator supply was defective; plaintiff recovers what it would cost to make it conform to specifications); Colburn *v.* Chicago, S. P. M. & O. Ry., 109 Wis. 377, 85 N. W. 354 (to leave plaintiff's land in a smooth condition, contract price paid. Plaintiff recovers cost of putting the land into condition).

Vermont: Clifford *v.* Richardson, 18 Vt. 620 (to repair mill); Keyes *v.* Western V. S. Co., 34 Vt. 81 (to repair drain).

Wisconsin: Ashland L. S. & C. Co. *v.* Shores, 105 Wis. 122, 81 N. W. 136 (to construct building. Plaintiff recovers cost of remedying defects in construction); Colburn *v.* Chicago, S. P. M. & O. Ry., 109 Wis. 377, 85 N. W. 354 (to leave plaintiff's land in a smooth condition, contract price paid. Plaintiff recovers cost of putting the land into condition).

England: Fletcher *v.* Gillespie, 3 Bing. 635 (to load vessel); Portman *v.*

Middleton, 4 C. B. (N. S.) 322 (to repair a machine).

[151] Newton *v.* Devlin, 134 Mass. 490.

[152] *Connecticut:* Hawley *v.* Belden, 1 Conn. 93, 6 Am. Dec. 206.

Maryland: Davis *v.* Ford, 81 Md. 333, 32 Atl. 280.

Minnesota: King *v.* Nichols, 53 Minn. 453, 55 N. W. 604.

Ohio: Cincinnati & S. Ry. *v.* Carthage, 36 Oh. St. 631.

Texas: Sherman *v.* Connor, 88 Tex. 35, 29 S. W. 1053; Hill *v.* Leigh (Tex. Civ. App.), 100 S. W. 351.

Contra, American Surety Co. *v.* Woods, 105 Fed. 41, 45 C. C. A. 282 (a sporadic case).

[153] *Minnesota :* Anderson *v.* Nordstrom, 60 Minn. 231, 61 N. W. 1132.

New Hampshire: Lamoreaux *v.* Rolfe, 36 N. H. 33.

New York: Mayor of New York *v.* Second Ave. R. R., 102 N. Y. 572, 7 N. E. 905, 55 Am. Rep. 839.

fendant to show that the amount paid was greater than reasonable.[154] And a mere contract for the work with a third party if the work has not in fact been done under the contract, is not evidence at all; [155] still less a bid from a person who did not do the work, higher than the bid of the person who eventually did it.[156]

§ 619. Cost of substituted performance useless to plaintiff.

The cost of substituted performance is only one way of arriving at the value of the contract; and if it appears that the contract is worth less than the cost of performance, the latter cannot be recovered.

Thus where the defendant agreed to take stock in a corporation and give it to the plaintiff and failed to do so, and it then appeared that while to get the stock would require the payment of the par value, the stock when procured would have been worthless, the plaintiff could not recover the par value of the stock, but was restricted to nominal damages.[157] And where a railroad agreed to build its repair shops within the limits of the plaintiff's city, the measure of damages for failure so to do is not the cost of building the shops.[158]

So where defendant agreed to draw out the casing from a well, and failed to do so, the measure of damages is not the cost of drawing out the casing (the well not being benefited thereby) but the (less) value of the casing when drawn out.[159]

In return for the grant of a right of way across plaintiff's land, defendant agreed to grade and curb a street along the location of its track. Neither the railway nor the street was built. In an action for not grading and curbing the railway only nominal damages were given. If the right of way had been used and the railway built, the plaintiff could have recovered the cost of grading and curbing. But here the injury consisted in leaving the land as it was, without *either* railway or street and no damage appears as a result of the injury.[160]

---

[154] State *v.* Ingram, 5 Ire. (N. C.) 441.

[155] Lamoreaux *v.* Rolfe, 36 N. H. 33.

[156] Gorham Co. *v.* United E. & C. Co. (N. Y.), 95 N. E. 805.

[157] Barnes *v.* Brown, 130 N. Y. 372, 29 N. E. 760.

[158] Missouri, K. & T. Ry. *v.* Fort Scott, 15 Kan. 435.

[159] Elmendorf *v.* Classen, 92 Tex. 472, 49 S. W. 1043.

[160] Hays *v.* Wilkinsburg & E. P. S. Ry., 204 Pa. 488, 54 Atl. 332.

And in general if the thing done is worth less than the cost of doing it, the measure of damages is not the cost but the value of it.[161]   So for breach of contract to fill land to a certain grade the measure of damages is not the cost of filling the land to the agreed grade, but the (less) difference in value of the land so filled and the land as it was left.[162]

And so where defendant agreed to sink an oil well on his own land, so that no one else could have been pecuniarily interested in it, the plaintiff cannot recover the cost of sinking the well.[163] He should recover what he can show with reasonable certainty would have come to him from the performance.[164]   In a grant of land there was a covenant that a defendant should sink upon the demised premises a pit to the depth of 130 yards in search of coal, and, in case a marketable vein should be reached, pay the plaintiff £2,500.   In an action by the plaintiff for breach of this covenant, evidence being given to show that if the defendants had sunk the pit, marketable coal might have been found, it was held that the plaintiff was entitled to more than nominal damages, and that the true measure of damage was the amount which he had lost by being deprived of the opportunity of finding marketable coal.[165]   If, however, the thing agreed was to build a structure on the plaintiff's land, the mere fact that the

[161] *Michigan:* Archer v. Milwaukee, A. E. & S. Co. (Mich.), 129 N. W. 598 (to put a new engine in plaintiff's boat; plaintiff recovers difference between value of boat as it would have been and as it was).

North Carolina: Winston C. M. Co. v. Wells-Whitehead T. Co., 144 N. C. 421, 57 S. E. 148 (to exhibit machine at exposition: cost of securing exhibition of it by another, this not having been done, cannot be recovered).

Pennsylvania: Kenderdine Hydro-Carbon Fuel Co. v. Plumb, 182 Pa. 463, 38 Atl. 480 (to expend $9,000 in manufacturing a patented article; $3,000 only spent. Measure of damages not the remaining $6,000 where the value of the article would be less).

[162] Bigham v. Wabash-Pittsburg T. Ry., 223 Pa. 106, 72 Atl. 318.

[163] Chamberlain v. Parker, 45 N. Y. 569.

[164] *Pennsylvania:* Bradford Oil Co. v. Blair, 113 Pa. 83, 57 Am. Rep. 442.

England: Pell v. Shearman, 10 Ex. 766.

[165] *California:* Taylor v. North Pacific Coast R. R., 56 Cal. 317 (to grade a road and build a fence).

Texas: Sherman v. Connor, 88 Tex. 35, 29 S. W. 1053 (to build waterworks supplying more water than plaintiff had use for).

See, however, *Kentucky:* Louisville & P. C. Co. v. Rowan, 4 Dana, 606, where upon failure by defendant to perform his agreement to excavate a basin on plaintiff's land it was held that evidence to show that the basin would have been useless to the plaintiff is admissible, in mitigation of damages.

plaintiff personally might not have used the structure does not affect the recovery. The cost of building the structure may be recovered at least in the absence of evidence that the structure would not be of such value to anyone.

§ 620. Performance deficient in quantity or quality.

If the work was actually done, but fell short of the agreement in quality, quantity, or circumstances of performance, the measure of damages is the cost of remedying the defect; [166] or if the defect cannot be remedied by a reasonable expenditure, then the difference between the value of the property if the work had been done properly and its value as the work was actually done.[167] So upon the breach of a contract to store

[166] *United States:* Stillwell & B. M. Co. *v.* Phelps, 130 U. S. 520, 32 L. ed. 1035, 9 Sup. Ct. 601; North Chicago St. Ry. *v.* Burnham, 42 C. C. A. 584, 102 Fed. 669.

Illinois: Chase *v.* Heaney, 70 Ill. 268.

Louisiana: Leathers *v.* Sweeney, 41 La. Ann. 287, 5 So. 662.

New York: Parmalee *v.* Wilks, 22 Barb. 539.

[167] *Florida:* Griffing Bros. Co. *v.* Winfield, 53 Fla. 589, 43 So. 687 (to cultivate fruit trees on land).

Indiana: Sunman *v.* Clark, 120 Ind. 142, 22 N. E. 113 (to saw lumber in certain dimensions. It was sawed in other dimensions. Plaintiff recovers difference between market value as sawed and what the value would have been, sawed as it should); Elwood Planing Mills Co. *v.* Harting, 21 Ind. App. 408, 52 N. W. 621 (to furnish lumber for use in a house. Inferior quality furnished. Measure of damages, difference between actual value of the house as built and as it would have been if built of proper materials).

Iowa: Duggleby Bros. *v.* Lewis Roofing Co., 139 Ia. 432, 116 N. W. 711 (to roof a building).

Massachusetts: Wiley *v.* Athol, 150 Mass. 426, 23 N. E. 311, 6 L. R. A. 342 (to furnish a supply of water to the town; less than agreed amount fur-

nished; plaintiff recovers difference in value between the supply actually furnished and that agreed to be furnished).

Michigan: White *v.* Brockway, 40 Mich. 209 (to put in steam boiler; not up to specifications; recover difference in value); Sinker *v.* Diggins, 76 Mich. 557, 43 N. W. 674 (to supply saw-mill to cut a certain amount per day; it cut less; difference in value of mill to be supplied and that actually supplied may be recovered).

Minnesota: Whalon *v.* Aldrich, 8 Minn. 346 (to drive and deliver logs during a certain year; part were not delivered until next year; plaintiff recovers difference in value of logs in first and second year).

New York: Barretts P. & H. D. E. Co. *v.* Wharton, 101 N. Y. 631, 4 N. E. 344 (to dye bunting; unskilfully done; difference in value recoverable); Emmerich *v.* Chegnay, 46 Misc. 456, 92 N. Y. Supp. 336 (to dye ribbons; unskilfully done; difference in value recoverable).

Oregon: Chamberlain *v.* Hibbard, 26 Ore. 428, 38 Pac. 437 (to plaster building; quality of plastering poor; difference in value of plaster which was and of plaster which should have been put on recoverable.)

Texas: Hardin *v.* Newell (Tex. Civ.

fruit at a certain temperature, the measure of damages is the diminution in value of the fruit.[168] And the value that would have been added to a slave, by a trade which he was apprenticed to learn, is the measure of damages for a breach of the covenant to teach him properly.[169] So where the plaintiff, a water company, furnished hydrants to the defendant town, and agreed to furnish a certain amount of water, and the supply fell short, in an action for the agreed price, the town was allowed to recoup the difference between the value of the water which should have been furnished and of that actually furnished.[170] The defendant agreed to furnish to the plaintiff, the publisher of a country newspaper, "patent outsides," containing no more than three columns of advertisements. The "outsides" furnished did, in fact, contain more than three columns, and the plaintiff claimed compensation for the excess at his own advertising rates. It was held, however, that the measure of damages was the difference between the value of "outsides" with three columns of advertising and the value of those furnished.[171]

Upon this general principle where the contract secures some act for the benefit of land, the measure of damages is the difference between the value of the land without the act done and its value if the act had been done.[172] Upon a similar principle

App.), 40 S. W. 331 (to pasture cattle; water and pasturage furnished insufficient; plaintiff recovers diminution in value of cattle).

Utah: Farr v. Griffith, 9 Utah, 416, 35 Pac. 506 (to keep ice-pond flooded so as to make ice; on breach plaintiff recovers value of the ice which would have been made).

Vermont: Laurent v. Vaughn, 30 Vt. 90, 72 Am. Dec. 288 (to carry peas to New York; by defendant's improper delay they were frozen in the lake at Burlington. Owner, acting reasonably, took the peas and sent them to Boston and there sold them. Measure of damages is difference between net value of peas in New York and amount realized in Boston).

Wisconsin: Ashland Lime, Salt & Cement Co. v. Shores, 105 Wis. 122, 81 N. W. 136 (to construct a building; not properly done. Plaintiff recovers diminished value of building on account of defects not remediable); Noble v. Libby, 144 Wis. 632, 129 N. W. 791 (to locate certain land; inferior land located; plaintiff recovers difference in value of the land).

[168] Hyde v. Mechanical Refr. Co., 144 Mass. 432, 11 N. E. 673. So of contract to keep chickens frozen: Beeman v. Banta, 118 N. Y. 538, 23 N. E. 837, 16 Am. St. Rep. 779.

[169] Bell v. Walker, 5 Jones' (N. C.) L. 43.

[170] Wiley v. Athol, 150 Mass. 426, 23 N. E. 311.

[171] Baltzell v. Moritz, 85 Ala. 123, 4 So. 835.

[172] *To build a station on or near the land:*

in Mine Hill & S. H. Railroad v. Lippincott,[173] a railroad company agreed on notice to remove its road from over certain coal beds, so as to allow them to be mined. The measure of damages for a breach was held to be the value of the coal in the mine.

§ 621. Contracts in which no contract price is fixed.

When the contract is for the exchange of labor or of property, or of one for the other, the profit of the contract is found by

Alabama: Mobile & M. Ry. v. Gilmer, 85 Ala. 422, 5 So. 138.

Indiana: Louisville, N. A. & C. Ry. v. Sumner, 106 Ind. 55, 55 Am. Rep. 719, 5 N. E. 404.

Kentucky: Louisville A. & P. E. Ry. v. Whipple, 25 Ky. L. Rep. 2312, 80 S. W. 507 (overruling Louisville & N. R. R. v. Neafus, 93 Ky. 53, 18 S. W. 1030).

Pennsylvania: Watterson v. Allegheny Valley R. R., 74 Pa. 208.

Texas: Houston & T. C. Ry. v. Malloy, 64 Tex. 607.

England: Wilson v. Northampton, etc., Ry., L. R. 9 Ch. 279.

See *post,* § 630.

To build and maintain railroad crossings on plaintiff's land:
Martin v. Monongahela R. R., 48 W. Va. 54, 37 S. E. 563.

To build and operate a railroad through the land:
California: Smith v. Los Angeles & P. Ry., 98 Cal. 210, 33 Pac. 53.

District of Columbia: Eckington & S. H. Ry. v. McDevitt, 18 D. C. App. Cas. 497.

Oregon: Blagen v. Thompson, 23 Ore. 239, 31 Pac. 647, 18 L. R. A. 315 (where plaintiff did not own the land, but had a contract for its purchase, the measure of damages is the difference between the contract price and its value if the road had been built; the defendant having had notice of the contract).

South Carolina: Lipscomb v. South Bound R. R., 65 S. C. 148, 43 S. E. 388 (loss of rental value for delay).

To build and maintain a side track on or connected with the land. Amsden v. Dubuque & S. C. R. R., 28 Iowa, 542.

To supply water to irrigate the land. Pallett v. Murphy, 131 Cal. 192, 63 Pac. 366, 82 Am. St. Rep. 341 (difference in rental value, since the supply is an annual one).

To establish business on the land. Ironton Land Co. v. Butchart, 73 Minn. 39, 75 N. W. 749 (contract by an owner of 165 acres of land with the defendant that defendant should erect and operate a steel plant of certain capacity. Measure of damages for breach of agreement is difference between value of land with and without the plant. If agreement was partly performed then measure of damages is difference between value of land as it would have been if the contract had been wholly performed and as it actually was with the partial performance).

To plant vines on the land. Waldteufel v. Pacific Vineyard Co., 5 Cal. App. 465, 92 Pac. 747 (inferior vines planted; plaintiff recovers difference in value of land at time of discovery of the inferiority).

To put street and sidewalks adjacent to land in good condition. King v. Hudson R. R. R., 141 App. Div. 346, 126 N. Y. Supp. 536.

To maintain dams in connection with mill. Hurxthal v. St. Lawrence, B. & M. Co., 65 W. Va. 346, 64 S. E. 355.

[173] 86 Pa. 468.

subtracting the cost or value of the plaintiff's performance from the value of the defendant's performance.

So if the defendant agreed to do some act for the plaintiff and the plaintiff on his side was to do some act for the defendant, then the profit of the contract is measured by subtracting the cost of the plaintiff's act from the value of the defendant's act.[174]

So where the plaintiff agreed to convey a house and lot to defendant on defendant's promise to erect a house for plaintiff; the profit is found by subtracting the value of the house to be conveyed from the value of the house to be built.[175] And where the parties exchanged land and defendant agreed to erect a building on the property conveyed by him, the plaintiff upon breach of the contract may recover the value of such building.[176] Where a creditor of a corporation accepted bonds in payment of his debt, on the agreement that $50,000 should be invested in additions to the plant, the measure of damages for failures to invest the amount is the additional value which would have been given to the bonds by the investment.[177]

II.—RULES OF DAMAGES IN PARTICULAR CASES

§ 622. Agreements to loan money.

Having now stated the general rules applicable in actions of contract, we proceed to give some instances of their application in special classes of cases; and first, an agreement to loan money.

Upon breach of a contract to loan money, if no special damage is shown, the recovery is only nominal.[178] For though by

[174] So where the defendant employed plaintiff to build an extension to a water tower and agreed to keep the water inside the tower at such a height as the plaintiff might need to support his workmen, but the water was not furnished and the plaintiff was obliged to place a scaffolding outside the tower for his workmen to stand on, it was held that the measure of damages was not the entire cost of the scaffolding, but only the amount by which the cost was increased by the breach; and what it would have cost him to build a float on the water inside the tower must be deducted. Mason Manuf. Co. v. Stephens, 127 N. Y. 602, 28 N. E. 411.

[175] Laraway v. Perkins, 10 N. Y. 371.

[176] Braddy v. Elliott, 146 N. C. 578, 60 S. E. 507, 16 L. R. A. (N. S.) 1121.

[177] South Texas Tel. Co. v. Huntington (Tex.), 138 S. W. 381.

[178] *Indiana:* Turpie v. Lowe, 114 Ind. 37, 15 N. E. 834; Lowe v. Turpie, 147 Ind. 652, 44 N. E. 25, 5 Am. St. Rep. 578.

New York: Bradford E. & C. R. R. v. New York, L. E. & W. R. R., 123 N. Y. 316, 25 N. E. 499, 20 Am. St. Rep. 748. See § 829.

the contract the plaintiff would receive the amount of the loan, it would be saddled with an obligation of exactly equal amount, so that the profit of the contract would be nothing. It is clear, however, that a contract to loan money at less than the current rate of interest would give the right to substantial damages, equal to the difference between the current rate and the agreed rate.[179]

If the borrower could get the money elsewhere, no consequential damages can be recovered for breach of the agreement,[180] except the actual cost of obtaining another loan, which may be recovered.[181] And of course no consequential damages can be recovered unless the lender had notice of the purpose of the loan.[182] But if the money could not be obtained elsewhere, and the lender had notice of the purpose of the loan, he must make compensation for the failure of that purpose by reason of his breach of contract.[183] Thus if the defendant

---

[179] New York Life Co. *v.* Pope, 24 Ky. L. Rep. 485, 68 S. W. 851.

[180] *Alabama:* Gooden *v.* Moses, 99 Ala. 230, 13 So. 765.

Texas: Equitable Mortgage Co. *v.* Thorn (Tex. Civ. App.), 26 S. W. 276.

[181] Bohemian-American W. G. Assoc. *v.* Northern Bank, 120 N. Y. Supp. 134.

[182] *California:* Savings Bank of Southern California *v.* Asbury, 117 Cal. 96, 48 Pac. 1081.

Texas: Equitable Mortgage Co. *v.* Thorn (Tex. Civ. App.), 26 S. W. 276.

Where defendant, sued as guarantor of the debt of a third party, desired to offset damages for plaintiff's breach of agreement to extend the debtor further credit, it was held that damages to the defendant because the debtor, lacking the credit, was closed out of business and rendered unable to pay a debt to defendant were "too remote, speculative and contingent." Leftovits *v.* First Nat. Bank, 152 Ala. 521, 44 So. 613.

[183] *Alabama:* Bixby-Theison Lumber Co. *v.* Evans, 167 Ala. 431, 52 So. 843 (contract to loan money to build

concrete dam to run a saw-mill. Breach after part of dam built. Plaintiff entitled to such damages as would replace him in *statu quo;* but profits expected from the operation of the mill could not be recovered as they were speculative).

New York: Treanor *v.* New York Breweries Co., 51 Misc. 607, 101 N. Y. Supp. 189 (contract to loan money to set up plaintiff in saloon business. Plaintiff hired premises, and paid for good will of business and two months' rent; after breach, paid a bonus for release from terms of lease. On defendant failing to furnish money, plaintiff allowed to recover cost of good will and bonus paid for release, but not the rent paid, in absence of evidence that the rental value of premises was not equal to rent); Pardee *v.* Douglas, 122 App. Div. 395, 106 N. Y. Supp. 775 (plaintiff having a contract with S. to bore an oil well, in order to get funds to pay for boring the well, entered into a contract with the defendant whereby the latter agreed to furnish the money and pay it to the said S. as their payments came due for the work, and the plaintiff agreed to deposit certificates

agreed to advance money to buy certain land, and by reason of the breach the borrower, not being able to get the money elsewhere, lost the value of his purchase, the borrower must pay the value of the bargain lost.[184] So where the defendant agreed to advance the money to take up a mortgage, and because of his default the mortgage was foreclosed and the borrower lost his equity of redemption he may recover the value of the equity.[185] And upon breach of an agreement to loan money for the express purpose of discharging debts by means of a composition with creditors, the measure of damages is the difference between the amount of the debts and the amount for which they could have been discharged in composition.[186]

Where the defendant agreed to advance money in order to enable the plaintiff to get out and market certain logs the measure of damages for failure to advance the money (which the plaintiff could not obtain elsewhere) was the difference between the value of the logs that could have been marketed with the money and the value of the smaller number of logs actually marketed, less the cost of getting out and marketing the additional logs.[187]

for 100,000 shares of its stock with a specified bank to be transferred from time to time by said bank to the defendant at the rate of $5 a share in payment of the money they should pay to S. Defendant failed to pay the money. The measure of damages was the excess of the cost of boring the well agreed upon over the value of the 100,000 shares of stock).

[184] *New York:* Goldsmith v. Holland Trust Co., 5 App. Div. 104, 38 N. Y. Supp. 1032.

Texas: Equitable Mortgage Co. v. Thorn (Tex. Civ. App.), 26 S. W. 276 (*semble*).

[185] Doushkess v. Burger Brewing Co., 20 App. Div. 375, 47 N. Y. Supp. 312.

[186] Banewur v. Levenson, 171 Mass. 1, 50 N. E. 10. In this case Field, C. J., dissenting, said: "For a breach of promise to lend or advance money when the plaintiffs have parted with nothing as the consideration for the promise,

but only have made certain promises in return, the damages often are merely nominal. The reasonable cost of procuring another similar loan, or, where another loan has not been obtained, the value of the contract to the plaintiffs, or what it would have cost to procure a similar one on the same terms, usually has been allowed as damages. This, I think, is the correct rule. See Greene v. Goddard, 9 Met. (Mass.) 212, 232, 233; Prehn v. Bank, L. R. 5 Exch. 92; Property Co. v. West, [1892] 1 Ch. 271, 277; South African Territories v. Wallington, [1897] 1 Q. B. 692; Dodd v. Jones, 137 Mass. 322; 2 Sedg. Meas. Dam. (5th ed.) 622. Under this rule, I think, it is obvious that the damages never can be more than the amount agreed to be lent, with interest, and usually would be much less."

[187] Graham v. McCoy, 17 Wash. 63, 48 Pac. 780.

In the case of Duckworth v. Ewart,[188] Messrs. Ratledge, the owners of building land on which they were erecting houses, having become unable to proceed with the building, and having mortgaged it to a building society for £4,300, and in lesser amounts to three mortgagees, of whom the plaintiff was one, entered into an indenture with the plaintiff and the other mortgagees and other creditors, in which it was agreed that the plaintiff should have power to sell the land, subject to the mortgage to the building society, and out of the proceeds pay the expenses of the trust and the other mortgages, and the surplus to the owners. It also empowered the plaintiff to enter on the land and finish the buildings, and also to raise any sum not exceeding £5,000 for carrying into effect the trust of the indenture by a mortgage on the premises, which should have priority over all the other mortgages except that to the building society. In the same instrument the defendant covenanted to execute all assurances for enabling the plaintiff to execute the trusts of the deed. The plaintiff entered on the execution of the trusts and incurred an expense of £1,100 on the land. He also arranged with the building society to accept £4,100 in satisfaction of their debt, and contracted with certain persons for a loan of £5,000 on the land, by a mortgage which was prepared, and was agreed to by all parties. At the last moment, when the parties had met to close the transaction, the defendant refused to execute the mortgage; whereupon the building society, acting on a power of sale contained in their mortgage, foreclosed it, and sold the property at a forced sale, for £4,510, which was exhausted in paying their debt and expenses. Martin, B., was of the opinion that, in addition to the costs of the proposed mortgage, the defendant was liable for the difference between £5,000 and the value of the land as building land, such as it was contemplated as being by the indenture, or at all events that plaintiff was entitled to £900, the residue of £5,000, after paying £4,100, agreed to be taken for the first mortgage. But the majority of the court per Pollock, C. B., and Bramwell, B.,

But see Bixby-Theison L. Co. v. Evans, 167 Ala. 431, 52 So. 84, where upon breach of contract to loan money to build a dam to create power for a mill no recovery was allowed for loss of profits of the mill.

[188] 2 H. & C. 129, 33 L. J. N. S. Ex. 24.

held that the plaintiff was entitled to recover only the costs of the abortive mortgage.

§ 622a. For settlement or security of a debt.

For breach by the creditor of a contract that the debtor should be allowed to work out the debt by services, or by sale of goods, the measure of damages is the profit which would have been made by performing services or selling goods the value of which would amount to the debt. So for breach of a contract to allow plaintiff to work out his debt by grinding corn at eight cents per bushel the measure of damages was the profit that would have been made by grinding corn enough to pay the debt at the agreed price.[189]

Where such a contract for the settlement of a debt is broken by the debtor, the measure of damages is the amount of the debt.[190] The measure of damages for breach of contract to give a mortgage or other security for a debt is *prima facie* the amount of the debt still unpaid.[191]

§ 622b. To pay money.

For breach of a contract to pay money, the measure of damages is the amount of money to be paid, with interest.[192] And where a debtor, being unable to pay in cash, gave interest-bearing certificates of indebtedness, which could be sold only at a discount, the creditor could not claim from the debtor to be reimbursed for the discount.[193]

[189] Oldham*v.* Kerchner, 79 N. C. 106, 28 Am. Rep. 302.

In Toomey *v.* Atyoe, 95 Tenn. 373, 32 S. W. 254, the court appears to have allowed the whole amount of the debt as damages in such a case; but clearly the cost of performance by the debtor should have been subtracted from the amount of the debt.

[190] Vallens *v.* Tillman, 103 Cal. 187, 37 Pac. 213.

[191] *Minnesota:* Dye *v.* Forbes, 34 Minn. 13.

New York: Schmaltz *v.* Weed, 27 App. Div. 309, 50 N. Y. Supp. 168.

So for breach of contract to give a mortgage to secure a loan from a third party to the plaintiff, the damages are *prima facie* the amount of the loan. Rider *v.* Pond, 19 N. Y. 262.

[192] *Connecticut:* Tyler *v.* Marsh, 1 Day, 1.

Kentucky: Federal Lumber Co. *v.* Reece, 116 S. W. 783.

Texas: Close *v.* Fields, 13 Tex. 623.

Virginia: Bethel *v.* Salem Imp. Co., 93 Va. 354, 25 S. E. 304, 57 Am. St. Rep. 803, 33 L. R. A. 602.

Washington: Arnott *v.* Spokane, 6 Wash. 442, 33 Pac. 1063.

[193] Looney *v.* District of Columbia, 113 U. S. 258, 5 Sup. Ct. 463, 28 L. ed. 974; Board of Directors *v.* Roach, 174 Fed. 949, 99 C. C. A. 453.

§ 622c. To make a contract.

A contract to enter into a contract subjects the defendant upon breach to the same damages as if he had made and broken the second contract.[194] Thus for breach of a contract to give a promissory note the measure of damages is the amount of the note.[195] If plaintiff is obliged to go to expense in order to procure another to enter into the contract, he may recover the expense. So where defendant agreed to become surety on plaintiff's bond the latter, upon breach, may recover the expense of supplying a new bond.[196]

§ 623. To insure, or to assign a policy of insurance.

For breach of a contract to insure a house the plaintiff, if the house is burnt without his knowledge of the breach, is entitled to recover the amount which would have been recovered on the policy, that is, in general, the amount of the policy (not exceeding however, the amount of the loss), less the premiums.[197] The same rule applies in the case of a contract to insure goods against fire.[198] In the case of a valued policy, the measure of damages is the face of the policy less the premiums; as in case of a contract to insure a vessel.[199] And so for breach of an agreement to keep alive a policy of life insurance the measure of damages is the face of the policy, less the premiums.[200] If the insurance company in which the defendant

[194] Pratt v. Hudson R. R. R., 21 N. Y. 305.

[195] *Minnesota:* American Mfg. Co. v. Klarquist, 47 Minn. 344, 50 N. W. 243; Deering v. Johnson, 86 Minn. 172, 90 N. W. 363.

New York: Hanna v. Mills, 21 Wend. 90.

North Dakota: Kelly v. Pierce, 16 N. D. 234, 112 N. W. 995.

Ohio: Stephenson v. Repp, 47 Oh. St. 551, 25 N. E. 803, 10 L. R. A. 620.

Texas: Young v. Dalton, 83 Tex. 497, 18 S. W. 819.

England: Robinson v. Robinson, 29 Eng. L. & Eq. 212.

[196] Samuels v. Fidelity & C. Co., 49 Hun, 122, 1 N. Y. Supp. 850.

[197] *United States:* DeTaslet v. Crou-sellat, 1 Wash. C. C. 504, Fed. Cas. No. 3827; Morris v. Summerl, 2 Wash. C. C. 203, Fed. Cas. No. 9837.

New Jersey: Lehneis v. Egg Harbor Commercial Bank, 26 Atl. 797.

Wisconsin: Campbell v. American F. I. Co., 73 Wis. 100, 40 N. W. 661; Franck v. Stout, 139 Wis. 223, 120 N. W. 867.

Canada: Douglass v. Murphy, 16 U. C. Q. B. 113.

[198] *New Hampshire:* Ela v. French, 11 N. H. 356.

England: Ex parte Bateman, 8 D. M. & G. 263, 268; Smith v. Price, 2 F. & F. 748.

[199] Miner v. Tagert, 3 Binn. (Pa.) 205.

[200] *Missouri:* Scheele v. Lafayette Bank, 120 Mo. App. 611, 97 S. W. 621.

should have taken out or kept alive a policy was insolvent at the time when the loss should have been paid, the measure of damages is the amount which could have been realized from the policy.[201] So where a defendant had agreed to procure insurance for the plaintiff, but before the insurance was effected, the property was destroyed in the Chicago fire of 1872, it was held that the defendant was not liable for the face value of the policy, that he was only liable for the amount of dividends which the company would have declared on a policy of that face value.[202]

If, however, the plaintiff was informed of the breach a sufficient time before the loss to place the insurance himself, he cannot recover the amount which would have been recoverable on the policy; for by the rule of avoidable consequences he should have insured himself. The measure of damages is the value of the policy at the time the failure to insure or the lapse is discovered; which would be the cost of a policy.[203] In an English case the defendant assigned a policy of insurance for £1,000, on which he was to pay the premiums, to trustees for his creditors by a deed containing a covenant that he would do nothing to avoid the policy, which was subject to a condition that if the assured should go beyond the limits of Europe, it should be void. He violated this covenant, thereby avoiding the policy. It was held that the measure of damages was the value of the policy at the time of the judgment, taking into consideration the fact that the defendant had covenanted to pay and should pay the premiums thereon.[204]

The same principle applies to an agreement to assign a policy.

New York: Toplitz *v.* Baur, 161 N. Y. 325, 55 N. E. 1059; Gray *v.* Murray, 3 Johns. Ch. 167; Soule *v.* Union Bank, 45 Barb. 111, 30 How. Pr. 105; Bailey *v.* American D. & L. Co., 52 App. Div. 402, 65 N. Y. Supp. 330.

[201] Sawyer *v.* Mayhew, 51 Me. 398.

[202] Chicago Building Society *v.* Crowell, 65 Ill. 453.

[203] *Illinois:* Brant *v.* Gallup, 111 Ill. 487, 53 Am. Rep. 638.

Kentucky: Vaughan *v.* Reddick, 32 Ky. L. Rep. 531, 106 S. W. 292.

Maine: Grindle *v.* Eastern Express Co., 67 Me. 317, 24 Am. Rep. 31.

New York: Ainsworth *v.* Backus, 5 Hun, 414 (but see Douglass *v.* Murphy, 16 Up. Can. Q. B. 113, where the contrary seems to be assumed).

On this ground must be explained: National Mahaiwe Bank *v.* Hand, 80 Hun, 584, 30 N. Y. Supp. 508, 1133, 89 Hun, 329, 35 N. Y. Supp. 449.

[204] Hawkins *v.* Coulthurst, 5 B. & S. 343.

1220 DAMAGES IN ACTIONS ON CONTRACTS § 624

So where the defendant sold the plaintiff a house, and agreed to assign the policy of insurance upon it, the measure of damages upon a breach of the agreement is the cost of insurance for the unexpired term of the policy; in other words, the value of the policy. If the house is burned without insurance, the plaintiff can recover nothing for loss of the insurance money, for he should have insured himself; but is restricted in his recovery to the actual value of the policy at the time of breach.[205] Where defendant agreed with an agent to take from him an insurance policy to take effect several months later, and then refused to take the policy it was held that the agent could not recover the entire amount of his commissions on the supposition that the policy would take effect at the later date and would continue in effect throughout the term.[206]

§ 624. To work a farm on shares.

In an action for breach of a contract by which the defendant agrees to cultivate a farm on shares, the measure of damages is the profit which the plaintiff would have made if the contract had been fulfilled.[207] Where such an agreement was broken by the owner of the farm, the fact that the plaintiff got another farm to work was held immaterial.[208] The value of the probable crop has been held not too uncertain to form the basis of recovery between the parties; and the due proportion of the probable net profit from cultivation may be recovered,[209] whether the breach was by the owner [210] or by the laborer.[211]

[205] *Massachusetts:* Dodd v. Jones, 137 Mass. 322.

New *York:* Elfenbeim v. Abbondanza, 64 Misc. 176, 118 N. Y. Supp. 1073.

[206] Weingrad v. Kletzky, 52 Misc. 129, 101 N. Y. Supp. 588.

[207] *California:* Shoemaker v. Acker, 116 Cal. 239, 48 Pac. 62.

Michigan: McClure v. Thorpe, 68 Mich. 33.

Missouri: Smock v. Smock, 37 Mo. App. 56.

New York: Ecker v. Cottrell, 24 App. Div. 496, 48 N. Y. Supp. 1031.

Pennsylvania: Hoy v. Grenoble, 34 Pa. 9, 75 Am. Dec. 628.

[208] *New York:* Taylor v. Bradley, 4 Abb. App. 363, 100 Am. Dec. 415.

Pennsylvania: Wolf v. Studebaker, 65 Pa. 459.

[209] In New York the rule appears to be, to estimate the value of the chance at the time the contract was made, by estimating the probable profits and the probable cost: Taylor v. Bradley, 39 N. Y. 129; Ecker v. Cottrell, 24 App. Div. 496, 48 N. Y. Supp. 1031.

[210] Shoemaker v. Acker, 116 Cal. 239, 48 Pac. 62.

[211] Zachary v. Swanger, 1 Ore. 92.

§ 625. To share the profits of a business.

For breach of a contract to share the profits of a business the measure of damages is the amount of profits, if this can be ascertained with sufficient certainty since that is the amount which the plaintiff would have realized by performance.[212] So where the defendant agreed to supply steers for plaintiff to fatten for market, profits to be divided, the measure of damages is the probable profits.[213] In estimating future profits there is of course an element of uncertainty, but the jury must do its best to estimate them. If the business has been disposed of by the defendant to a third party, profits realized by him may be shown.[214]

§ 626. For forbearance.

* Contracts for forbearance are often entered into by creditors for certain considerations, on which they forbear to pursue their debtor during a given time. In a case of this kind, where the plaintiff had recovered judgment against his debtor, the defendant, in consideration that the plaintiff would forbear to sue out execution for a certain time, agreed to erect a house and lease it to the plaintiff; such erection and lease to be in full satisfaction of the judgment. The agreement not being performed, it was held that the value of the house was the measure of damages, and not the difference between the amount of the judgment and value of the house.[215] ** For breach of a contract to forbear committed by the creditor damages are nominal merely, where a case for consequential damages is not

[212] *Colorado:* Beckwith *v.* Talbot, 2 Colo. 639 (to sell cattle on joint account); Ramsay *v.* Meade, 37 Colo. 465, 86 Pac. 1018 (to engage in mercantile business as partners).

Iowa: Dockstader *v.* Young M. C. Assoc., 109 N. W. 906 (to fit up athletic ground, to be paid out of revenue).

New York: Crittenden *v.* Johnston, 7 App. Div. 258, 40 N. Y. Supp. 87 (to manage a hotel on shares).

Pennsylvania: Kenderdine H. C. F. Co. *v.* Plumb, 182 Pa. 463, 38 Atl. 480 (to manufacture goods, plaintiff to have half the profits of sale).

Texas: Gordon *v.* Sanborn (Tex. Civ. App.), 35 S. W. 291 (to buy in land on foreclosure and sell for benefit of mortgagee).

Washington: Belch *v.* Big Store Co., 46 Wash. 1, 89 Pac. 174 (to conduct plumbing business for half profits).

[213] Rule *v.* McGregor, 117 Ia. 419, 90 N. W. 811.

[214] Treat *v.* Hiles, 81 Wis. 280, 50 N. W. 896.

[215] Strutt *v.* Farlar, 16 M. & W. 249. See Ellison *v.* Dove, 8 Blatchf. 571.

made out,[216] and the creditor can recover only the amount forborne, with interest and costs to the sale. Damages sustained by a forced sale of the property levied on are too remote.[217] The plaintiff cannot recover compensation for the expense of raising money to pay the debt.[218]

Where, however, consequential damages are within the contemplation of the parties they may be recovered. So, if the contract includes an agreement to vacate an attachment, and upon breach of this agreement the property is sold at judicial sale, the measure of damages is the true value of the property less the amount realized on the sale.[219] And where the defendant had the plaintiff arrested, the latter may also recover the expense of obtaining a discharge.[220]

§ 627. Actions against stockholders.

* The measure of damages in actions brought by incorporated companies against stockholders, upon calls made for payment of stock, furnishes us with another subject of inquiry. Where the defendant subscribed for stock which had been forfeited by the company, it has been held in New York that the forfeiture was not a bar to the action, but that the nominal value of the stock forfeited, less the actual cash value at the time it was declared forfeited, was the measure of compensation.[221] And unless the value of the stock reaches the whole debt and interest,[222] the plaintiff must have judgment for the balance.[223] ** Where, in such actions, all the money subscribed is necessary for the purpose intended, the recovery is of course measured and limited by the amount subscribed; but if an amount less than the amount subscribed is all that is in fact required, it is held, in Illinois, that the recovery should be *pro rata*.[224] A promise to subscribe for a certain amount of stock in a plank-road company, to induce the selection of a particular

[216] Reid v. Johnson, 132 Ind. 416, 31 N. E. 1107.

[217] Indiana & I. C. Ry. v. Scearce, 23 Ind. 223.

[218] Deyo v. Waggoner, 19 Johns. (N. Y.) 241.

[219] Cole v. Stearns, 23 App. Div. 446, 48 N. Y. Supp. 318.

[220] Smith v. Way, 6 All. (Mass.) 212.

[221] Herkimer Man. & H. Co. v. Small, 21 Wend. 273.

[222] s. c. 2 Hill, 127.

[223] Johnson v. Stear, 15 C. B. (N. S.) 330.

[224] Miller v. Ballard, 46 Ill. 377.

route, if accepted, is valid, and may be enforced. The measure of damages is the difference between the value of the stock at the time of the trial, and the amount agreed to be paid for it.[225] On the other hand, on a breach of an agreement to give land for stock, if a specific performance cannot be decreed, in estimating the damages, reference should be had not to the nominal value of the stock, but to the land which ought to have been conveyed.[226]

§ 627a. To buy, sell or transfer stock.

For breach of an agreement to buy stock, the seller may recover the difference between the contract price and the market value of the stock; [227] or, if he is able to secure a transfer to the purchaser on the books of the company the entire contract price.[228] He is also entitled to recover back assessments levied on him after the date at which the defendant agreed to buy the stock.[229] Where one sells stock to plaintiff with an agreement to buy it back after a certain time or to secure a purchaser for it at a certain price, and fails to keep his contract, the measure of damages, upon tender of the stock, has been held to be the agreed price,[230] together with a subsequent assessment on the stock which the plaintiff was obliged to pay.[231] The damages cannot be reduced by showing that plaintiff might have sold the shares during the period at the agreed price, since he might keep them during that period if he desired; [232] but after breach he should take reasonable means by sale of the stock to reduce the damages.[233] In an action against a corporation for failure to transfer stock on its books

[225] Rhey v. Ebensburg & S. P. R. Co., 27 Pa. 261.

[226] Dayton & C. R. R. Co. v. Hatch, 1 Disney (Oh.), 84.

[227] Herd v. Thompson, 149 Pa. 434, 24 Atl. 282.

[228] Orr v. Bigelow, 20 Barb. (N. Y.) 21.

[229] California: Gay v. Dare, 103 Cal. 454, 37 Pac. 466.

New York: Orr v. Bigelow, 20 Barb. (N. Y.) 21.

[230] Campbell v. Woods, 122 Mo. App. 719, 99 S. W. 468. The reason given was that any other rule would defeat the object of the contract. This hardly seems sufficient, since a breach necessarily defeats the object of the contract, and the allowance of damages is not to secure the object of the contract but to give compensation for the defeat of such object.

[231] Gay v. Dare, 103 Cal. 454, 37 Pac. 466.

[232] Aken v. Clark, 146 Ia. 436, 123 N. W. 379.

[233] Davidor v. Bradford, 129 Wis. 524, 109 N. W. 576.

to the plaintiff, the measure of damages is the value of the stock; the plaintiff losing his ownership in the stock by the act of the company.[234] And where a corporation failed to give a stockholder an opportunity to subscribe to new stock at a certain price, which he had a right to do, the measure of damages is the difference between the actual value of the stock and the price at which he had the right to subscribe for it.[235]

In an action for breach of a contract to pay plaintiff for his services by a certain amount of preferred stock in a corporation, it appeared that the corporation never issued such stock; the plaintiff was nevertheless allowed to recover its estimated value, if issued.[236]

§ 628. By assignees of bankrupts.

* Interesting questions are often presented in suits by assignees seeking to enforce contracts made by the bankrupt. In a case in assumpsit in the English Exchequer, the facts were that the bankrupt had, previous to his bankruptcy, delivered to the defendant a bill of exchange for £600, which he promised to discount, retaining £100 and the discount. He kept the bill, however, and paid nothing to the bankrupt. On this state of facts, the judge who tried the cause told the jury that they were bound to give the £600, less the £100 and the discount. An effort was made to set the verdict aside, on the ground that the cause should have been left to the jury

---

[234] *United States:* Tayloe v. Turner, 23 Fed. Cas. No. 13,770, 2 Cranch C. C. 203; Crosby Lumber Co. v. Smith, 51 Fed. 63.

New York: Commercial Bank v. Kortwright, 22 Wend. 348 (affirming Kortwright v. Commercial Bank, 20 Wend. 91) (highest value between refusal and suit).

Pennsylvania: German U. B. & S. F. Assoc. v. Sendmeyer, 50 Pa. 67 (value at time of refusal).

So where a corporation issued bonds with the agreement that at maturity they might be converted into preferred stock, and at maturity it failed on demand to deliver the stock, the measure of damages is the value of the stock at the time of the demand. Bratten v. Catawissa R. R., 211 Pa. 21, 60 Atl. 319.

In one case where the refusal was by a building society, the plaintiff was allowed to recover the amount paid on the stock from time to time, as dues, with interest from the times of payment. North America Bldg. Assoc. v. Sutton, 35 Pa. 463, 78 Am. Dec. 349.

[235] Stokes v. Continental Trust Co., 186 N. Y. 285, 78 N. E. 1090, 12 L. R. A. (N. S.) 969.

[236] Crichfield v. Julia, 147 Fed. 65, 77 C. C. A. 297.

at large, and that the judge erred in telling them, as *a point of law*, that the sum above stated was the measure of damages. But the charge was held right, and the court said: "No doubt all questions of damage are, strictly speaking, for the jury, and however clear and plain may be the rule of law on which the damages are to be found, the act of finding is for them. But there are certain established rules according to which they ought to find; and here there is a clear rule that the amount which would have been received if the contract had been kept, is the measure of damages if the contract is broken." [237] **

§ 629. Agreements for arbitration and award.

Where the defendant broke his contract to submit a dispute to arbitrators, it was held that the plaintiff could recover substantial damages, although it was found that he had no valid claim. The damages would include "expenses to which he had been subjected by reason of his necessary preparation for a trial before the arbitrators, on account of his own loss of time and trouble, and in employing counsel, taking depositions, payments to witnesses and arbitrators," and other expenditures; but he could only recover these so far as they were not available for the trial of his cause before the court, for he had to repair to the latter, and the only result of the defendant's act was to make him incur the extra expenses. It was said that the counsel fees were recoverable, for they were suitable and properly incurred, and the plaintiff was deprived of their benefit by the wrongful act of the defendant.[238] If, however, no extra expenses were incurred by reason of the agreement, nominal damages only may be recovered.[239]

§ 630. To construct stations, etc.

Where a railroad company breaks an agreement to build a

[237] Alder *v.* Keighley, 15 M. & W. 117. The equitable assignee in this class of cases has no greater right than the plaintiffs in the record. Griffiths *v.* Perry, 1 E. & E. 680. But his right is equal to theirs: Ashdown *v.* Ingamells, 5 Ex. Div. 280.

[238] *Georgia:* McKenzie *v.* Mitchell, 123 Ga. 72, 51 S. E. 34.

Maine: Call *v.* Hagar, 69 Me. 521.

Massachusetts: Pond *v.* Harris, 113 Mass. 114; New Haven & N. Co. *v.* Hayden, 117 Mass. 433.

Ante, § 607.

[239] Munson *v.* Straits of Dover S. S. Co., 43 C. C. A. 57, 102 Fed. 926.

station at any given place, the measure of damages is the enhanced value of the land had the depot been erected.[240] In Missouri, Kansas & Texas Railway v. Fort Scott [241] the company broke its contracts to extend its line to Fort Scott. It was held that plaintiff could recover either the value of the improvements for purposes of taxation, or, as the contract was entire, the whole consideration paid in advance; but evidence to show a decline in population and depreciation in real estate was inadmissible as being too speculative. Where a subscription was made to the stock of a railway company on the condition that the railway should pass by a certain place, which condition the company failed to comply with, but before their failure the subscriber had paid his subscription by a transfer of land to the company: in an action by the subscriber against the company for breach of the agreement, the measure of damages was held the value of the land at the time of the transfer.[242] Where plaintiff conveyed to street railway a right of way across her land and agreed to pay certain money in consideration of which the railway agreed to extend its road over

[240] *Alabama:* Mobile & M. Ry. v. Gilmer, 85 Ala. 422, 5 So. 138.

Florida: Atlanta S. A. B. Ry. v. Thomas (Fla.), 53 So. 510.

Indiana: Louisville, N. A. & C. Ry. v. Sumner, 106 Ind. 55, 5 N. E. 404, 55 Am. Rep. 719.

Iowa: Varna v. St. L. & C. R. Ry., 55 Ia. 677, 8 N. W. 624.

Kentucky: Louisville A. & P. V. E. Ry. v. Whipps, 18 Ky. 121, 80 S. W. 507; Louisville H. & St. L. Ry. v. Baskett, 121 S. W. 957.

Mississippi: Yazoo & M. V. R. R. v. Baldwin, 78 Miss. 57, 29 So. 763.

Oregon: Blagen v. Thompson, 23 Ore. 239, 31 Pac. 647, 18 L. R. A. 315.

Pennsylvania: Watterson v. Alleghany V. R. R., 74 Pa. 208.

Texas: Houston & T. C. Ry. v. Molloy, 64 Tex. 607.

Washington: Belt v. Washington W. P. Co., 24 Wash. 387, 64 Pac. 525.

Contra, on the ground that such increase is too uncertain:

Arkansas: St. Louis, I. M. & S. Ry. v. Berry, 86 Ark. 309, 110 S. W. 1049 (distinguishing St. Louis & N. A. R. R. v. Crandell, 75 Ark. 89, 86 S. W. 855, 112 Am. St. Rep. 42, where upon the wrongful discontinuance of an established station the diminution in value of buildings was allowed).

Illinois: Rockford, R. I. & St. L. R. R. v. Beckemeier, 72 Ill. 267.

Canada: Grand Tronc C. E. v. Black, 17 Rev. Leg. 669.

And see *South Carolina:* Standard Supply Co. v. Carter, 81 S. C. 181, 62 S. E. 50, 19 L. R. A. (N. S.) 155.

Ante, § 194.

Depreciation of adjacent land not naturally resulting from failure to build the station cannot be recovered. Atlanta & S. A. B. Ry. v. Thomas (Fla.), 53 So. 510.

[241] 15 Kan. 435.

[242] Jewett v. Lawrenceburgh & U. M. Ry., 10 Ind. 539.

the right of way granted, and to run cars at stated intervals, without designating any period, and the extension was made and operated for several years, then abandoned because not profitable, the tracks taken up, and the right of way restored, and plaintiff relieved from paying money, the court held that the difference in value with road and expectation of continuing to run in the future over the value without the road was the proper measure of damages; but the present value must be the value in consideration of the possibility of getting the connection in some other way than through the action of the defendant.[243]   And where defendant sold a site for a lumber mill with an agreement that the plaintiff should get track connections with the railroad, and connections were not furnished, the measure of damages is the difference between the value of the plant with and without the guaranteed connection.[244] The expense of hauling freight to a more distant point may also be recovered.[245]

§ 631. To build fences, walls, etc.

For breach of an agreement to build fences and cattle-guards, the measure of damages is the cost of building them.[246]   But where a sea-wall, built by the defendant, had not been constructed according to his agreement, and he had promised the plaintiff to rebuild it, but failed to do so, and in reliance on such promise, the plaintiff himself delayed rebuilding; the loss of the use of the wharf, during the period of delay thus caused, was held the direct and immediate consequence of the defendant's failure, for which he was liable.[247]   Where the grantee failed to build a wall on his own land, according to agreement, the grantor's measure of damages is not the cost of the wall, but the difference in value of his own adjoining land with and without the wall.[248]

In an action for a breach of contract by a railroad to construct

[243] Eckington & S. H. Ry. v. McDevitt, 191 U. S. 103, 24 Sup. Ct. 36, 48 L. ed. 112.

[244] South Memphis L. Co. v. McLean H. L. Co., 179 Fed. 417.

[245] Atlanta & S. A. B. Ry. v. Thomas (Fla.), 53 So. 510.

[246] Logansport, C. & S. W. Ry. v. Wray, 52 Ind. 578.

[247] Willey v. Fredericks, 10 Gray (Mass.), 357.

[248] Wigsell v. School, 8 Q. B. D. 357.

a farm crossing over a railroad it appeared that it would be necessary in building approaches to the crossing to take some of plaintiff's land. It was held that this was part of the expense of constructing the crossing, since the railroad would have to take the land and pay for it; and therefore in an action for breach of contract, the plaintiff could recover not merely the cost of building the crossing itself, but also the value of the land which would be occupied by the approaches.[249]

§ 631a. Negative agreements.

For breach of a negative agreement, the plaintiff may recover the damage caused him by the doing of the act contracted against. In Harrison v. Charlton,[250] the plaintiff purchased a lumber-yard. The lumber was to be measured, and in the meantime no lumber was to be added. For breach of the contract in adding lumber, the difference between the market and contract prices of the additional lumber was held to be the measure of damages. Where no actual damage can be proved to have resulted from the act, the plaintiff on general principles may recover the amount he has paid to secure the promise, or the proportionate part of his expense which is due to the promise. So where a printer, having contracted to print for his employer a thousand copies of a book, and no more, printed from the same types, while set up at the expense of his employer, five hundred other copies, for his own disposal, he was held liable to refund to his employer one-third part of the expense of setting up the types, no actual damage having been proved.[251]

§ 632. Not to engage in business.

The measure of damages upon breach of a contract not to engage in business is so difficult to estimate that the damages are usually liquidated. If no damages are stipulated in the agreement the plaintiff can, of course, recover only such as he proves he has sustained by the breach.[252] In the ordinary case

[249] Pittsburg, C., C. & St. L. Ry. v. Wilson (Ind. App.), 91 N. E. 725.

[250] 37 Ia. 134.

[251] Williams v. Gilman, 3 Me. 276.

[252] Georgia: Jenkins v. Temples, 39 Ga. 655, 99 Am. Dec. 482.

Ohio: Burckhardt v. Burckhardt, 36 Oh. St. 261, 42 Oh. St. 474, 51 Am. Rep. 842.

the profit realized by competitors in a transaction may be allowed on the ground that this profit presumably would have been realized by the plaintiff if it had not been for the competition. So where a borough contracted with a water company not to furnish water itself to its inhabitants and thereafter did furnish the water, the measure of damages was held to be equal to the water rents received by the borough less the additional expense the water company would have been at to supply these takers.[253] So where the defendant sells the good will of a business and engages not to enter into competition with the purchaser the measure of damages if he does so enter into competition will ordinarily be the profit on the sales which it can be shown the plaintiff would have made but for the competition.[254] And so where the plaintiff was granted the exclusive right to sell cigars on a fair ground, and other persons were then allowed to sell cigars on the same ground, he was entitled to recover as damages the profits he would have made on the cigars sold by the other people unless it is likely that he himself would not have been able to sell the cigars.[255] Of course in any case of this sort the facts may be such that sales by the plaintiff, if the defendant had not broken his contract, would be entirely conjectural.[256]

But the breach of contract may cause not only a loss of the profits from the actual business done by defendant, but an injury to the value of the plaintiff's business. In such a case the amount of depreciation may be recovered, and therefore evidence of the extent of business after the competition, and

[253] Bennett Water Co. v. Millvale, 200 Pa. 613, 50 Atl. 155, 202 Pa. 616, 51 Atl. 1098.

[254] Long v. O'Bryan, 91 S. W. 659, 28 Ky. L. Rep. 1062.

.Strictly speaking the profit of the competitor is not the measure of damages but merely evidence of the plaintiff's loss; the true measure of damages being the loss of sales which plaintiff was prevented from making by defendant's act. Gregory v. Spieker, 110 Cal. 150, 42 Pac. 576.

[255] Whorley v. Tenn. C. E. Co. (Tenn. Ch.), 62 S. W. 346.

But in Montgomery C. U. A. Soc. v. Harwood, 126 Ind. 440, 26 N. E. 182, such damages were held too speculative on the ground that it could not be proved with certainty that the plaintiff would have sold the goods which the other person did in fact sell.

[256] Bradford v. Montgomery F. Co., 115 Tenn. 610, 92 S. W. 1104, 9 L. R. A. (N. S.) 979.

Of course in such a case nominal damages may be recovered. Raymond v. Yarrington, 96 Tex. 443, 73 S. W. 800.

even after suit brought, is admissible as tending to show the amount of injury done to the business by competition.[257] So where the defendant sold a tavern-stand, with the agreement not to compete, and afterwards opened a competing tavern, the purchaser was allowed to recover the amount by which the value of his tavern was depreciated by the defendant's act; the court holding that this was an actual, certain, present loss.[258]

Where the defendant by breach of the contract so increased the demand for labor that the rate of wages was increased, it was held that the plaintiff might recover compensation for the increased wages he had to pay, and also for his loss by reason of workmen enticed away by the defendant.[259]

In Peltz v. Eichele [260] the defendant had covenanted not to manufacture certain articles. It was said that what the defendant had gained might be evidence of what the plaintiff had lost, but the plaintiff must show that he has suffered the loss, as, for example, in the decrease of his business, the stoppage of his factory, etc. In an action against a physician for breach of an agreement not to practice, the measure of damages was held to be such sum as the jury might find to have been the value of the practice which the plaintiff lost between the time when the defendant resumed practice and the time of instituting the suit.[261] Where a combination is formed to raise or depress the price of an article, the measure of damages for the breach of the agreement is the difference in price which would have been produced by the combination.[262]

§ 633. For exclusive agency.

Where the plaintiff was constituted sole agent of the defendant for sale of his goods, and the defendant allowed those to be sold by another, the plaintiff may recover as damages the profit which he would have made upon the sales actually made by the other.[263] So where the plaintiff was given exclusive

---

[257] Calucha v. Naso, 147 Ia. 309, 126 N. W. 146.

[258] Evans v. Elliott, 20 Ind. 283, 83 Am. Dec. 319.

[259] Whittaker v. Welch, 2 Pugs. (N. B.) 436.

[260] 62 Mo. 171.

[261] Warfield v. Booth, 33 Md. 63.

[262] Havemeyer v. Havemeyer, 43 N. Y. Super. Ct. 506.

[263] United States: Cincinnati S. L. G. I. Co. v. Western S. L. Co., 152 U. S. 200, 38 L. ed. 411, 14 Sup. Ct. 523.

territory for securing members for the defendant benefit society, and another person was allowed to secure members within the plaintiff's territory, the plaintiff was entitled to recover the profits which he would have made on the members actually secured within the territory.[264] And so upon breach of a contract by which defendant agreed to give the ferrying of all its passengers to the plaintiff, the plaintiff could recover the profit he would have made on ferrying the passengers.[265]

Where it is impossible to determine the exact amount of business the plaintiff would have obtained by showing the amount of business done by another in his place, recovery for loss of profits depends upon the certainty with which it can be proved that the profits would have been realized. Recovery can be had for the loss of such profits only as can be proved with reasonable certainty.[266] If the plaintiff's business was sufficiently established and supplied a sufficiently steady demand, he may recover not only commissions on sales actually made but also the probable profits of future sales.[267]

When the contract secures the right to exclusive territory, but owing to the newness or to the nature of the business it cannot be said that the business is an established one, many

California: Schiffman v. Peerless M. C. Co., 10 Cal. App. 913, 110 Pac. 460.

Michigan: Mueller v. Bethesda M. S. Co., 88 Mich. 390, 50 N. W. 319.

Minnesota: Emerson v. Pacific C. & N. B. Co., 96 Minn. 1, 104 N. W. 573.

New York: Wakeman v. Wheeler & W. Mfg. Co., 101 N. Y. 205, 4 N. E. 264, 54 Am. Rep. 676; Carr v. Hills Archimedean Lawn Mower Co., 12 Daly, 332.

South Carolina: Cofield v. E. A. Jenkins Motor Co., 71 S. E. 969.

Wisconsin: The Dr. Harter Medicine Co. v. Hopkins, 83 Wis. 309, 53 N. W. 501.

This is of course the net profit, subtracting the value of the services which the defendant would have been obliged to render in order to make the sales. Dunham v. Hastings Pavement Co., 95 App. Div. 360, 88 N. Y. Supp. 835;

Napier v. Spielmann, 54 Misc. 96, 103 N. Y. Supp. 982.

In the case of Carlson v. Stone-Ordean-Wells Co., 40 Mont. 434, 107 Pac. 419, the court thought it necessary for the plaintiff to prove that he would have made the sales if the defendant had not sold through another. But as the defendant's act has made it impossible to prove this (if it is in fact impossible) it would seem clear that the defendant and not the plaintiff should suffer from the impossibility of proving the amount of loss. *Ante,* § 170a.

[264] Hitchcock v. Supreme Tent of Knights of Maccabees, 100 Mich. 40, 58 N. W. 640.

[265] Wiggins Ferry Co. v. Chicago & A. R. R., 73 Mo. 389, 39 Am. Rep. 519.

[266] Federal I. & B. Bed Co. v. Hock, 42 Wash. 668, 85 Pac. 418.

[267] Kenney v. Knight, 127 Fed. 403.

authorities deny the right to damages for loss of expected profits. The defendant, a manufacturer of organs, agreed to sell the plaintiff organs, and that the plaintiff alone should sell organs at retail within a certain territory. The plaintiff went to expense to advertise and sell organs, and sold or could at once have sold a certain number of organs, which he ordered of the defendant. The defendant refused to supply them. It was held, in the first place, that no damages could be recovered on account of profits exepcted from future sales; for not only the uncertainty of the trade, but also the fact that the defendants could not prevent, and evidently were not expected to prevent the entire sale of the defendant's organs by others, made the general profits of the agreement entirely conjectural. The plaintiff was allowed, in the second place, the general expense for advertising and sale of the organs, on the principle that when the expected profits of an agreement cannot be recovered the expenses of the plaintiff in preparing to do his part may be recovered. In the third place, the plaintiff was allowed the profits on the sale of so many organs, as it was shown with reasonable certainty that he had sold or was on the point of selling.[268]

It would seem that the true rule in such a case is to find whether the exclusive agency has any value, and if so, to allow that. It would seem fair to infer that the agency was worth at least what the plaintiff had expended in time and money.[269]

In an Iowa case action was brought for breach of a contract by which plaintiffs were to have the right for five years to make use of defendant's warerooms without rent, and carry on the retail business of selling defendant's machinery within a certain territory, and also of selling their own goods. Plaintiffs were to receive the difference between the wholesale price of

[268] *West Virginia:* Sterling O. Co. v. House, 25 W. Va. 64.

See to the same effect the following cases:

United States: Taylor Mfg. Co. v. Hatcher Mfg. Co., 39 Fed. 440, 3 L. R. A. 587.

Georgia: Fontaine v. Baxley, 90 Ga. 416, 17 S. E. 1015.

Iowa: Howe Machine Co. v. Bryson, 44 Ia. 159, 24 Am. Rep. 735.

Wisconsin: Ramsey v. Holmes Electric Protective Co., 85 Wis. 174, 55 N. W. 391.

[269] Taylor v. Spencer, 75 Kan. 152, 88 Pac. 544.

the machinery and the retail price at which they should sell it, and were to pay defendant a percentage of the actual profit on the other goods which they should sell. The contract was broken by the defendant, and plaintiffs excluded from the building at the end of two years. The receipts and profits of the business for these two years being shown, it was held that the plaintiffs could recover for loss of profits during the remaining three years of the term.[270]

§ 633a. To support.

For breach of a contract to support the plaintiff during his life the measure of damages is the present value of the plaintiff's support during the probable duration of his life; that is, such an amount as, properly invested, will from its income and principal furnish an amount annually during his life sufficient for his support, and leave nothing remaining at his death.[271]

Where the defendant agreed to support and care for the plaintiff's child, but neglected to give proper support, the measure of damages was held to be the difference in value between the care and treatment called for by the contract and what was actually received.[272] Where the condition of a bond for the plaintiff's maintenance required the defendant to furnish the plaintiff with "money necessary for him to spend whenever he thinks proper to visit his friends;" the defendant was held bound to furnish a sum proper for such expenses to the extent of reasonable visits. In an action of debt upon such a bond, there having been previously a demand and refusal of the sum necessary for a visit, the plaintiff's measure of damages was held to be the amount of money required for the visit, with interest.[273] On a breach of a contract by which plaintiff agreed

[270] Klingman v. Racine Sattley Co., 143 Ia. 435, 128 N. W. 1109.

[271] *Indiana:* Baughan v. Brown, 122 Ind. 115, 23 N. E. 695 (when death occurs before trial, take the amount required for support during actual duration of life); Shover v. Myrick, 4 Ind. App. 7, 30 N. E. 207.

Maine: Fales v. Hemenway, 64 Me. 373; Freeman v. Fogg, 82 Me. 408, 19 Atl. 907.

New York: Schnell v. Plumb, 55

N. Y. 592; Carpenter v. Carpenter, 66 Hun, 177, 20 N. Y. Supp. 928.

Oregon: Morrison v. McAtee, 23 Ore. 530, 32 Pac. 400 (where plaintiff was to furnish his own labor, deduct what he can earn by his labor during his life).

[272] Vancleave v. Clark, 118 Ind. 61, 20 N. E. 527, 3 L. R. A. 519. See Ottoway v. Milroy, 144 Ia. 631, 123 N. W. 467.

[273] Berry v. Harris, 43 N. H. 376.

to live with deceased and take care of her during life, and deceased agreed to give her house and lot at her death to plaintiff or one of the members of the family, and deceased did not give the house and lot at her death either to plaintiff or to a member of the family, it was held that on account of the uncertainty as to the beneficiary the value of the house and lot could not be recovered; but the plaintiff should recover the value of her services.[274] And so where for any other reason the house or its value cannot be recovered, the value of the services may be recovered, less the value of any benefit which the plaintiff received while the agreement was being carried out.[275]

Where the contract to support another is made with or for the benefit of the plaintiff, who is already under an obligation to support the person in question, the plaintiff for breach of the contract may recover the amount he was thereby compelled to pay out for the support of the person.[276]

§ 633b. Of bailment.

Upon a lease of personal property, if the lessee fails to return the property in good condition the measure of damages is the amount of the rent and the diminished value of the property;[277] or if the property is not returned at all, the rent plus the value of the property.[278]

On a bailment for repairs or other work on the property by the bailee, where the bailee injures the property the measure of damages is the diminished value of the property less the cost of the work.[279]

---

[274] Stanton v. Miller, 14 Hun (N. Y.), 383. Qu.: it would seem that the contract having been executed, plaintiff, who had the right to sue, should have recovered the value of the house and lot, even though the deceased might, if she had chosen, have given it to another member of the family.

[275] Bovee v. Barrett, 101 N. Y. Supp. 322, 116 App. Div. 20.

[276] Case v. Case, 137 App. Div. 393, 121 N. Y. Supp. 746.

[277] *Connecticut:* Cadwell v. Town of Canton, 81 Conn. 288, 70 Atl. 1025 (steam roller).

Minnesota: Langhren v. Barnard, 132 N. W. 301.

Texas: Phillips v. Hughes (Tex. Civ. App.), 33 S. W. 157.

[278] Robinson v. Varnell, 16 Tex. 382.

[279] *New York:* May v. Georger, 21 Misc. 622, 47 N. Y. Supp. 1057, reversing May v. Gunther, 20 Misc. 659, 46 N. Y. Supp. 379; Miller v. Levy, 104 N. Y. Supp. 368 (injury to cloth while being sponged); Mayer v. La Piemme, 110 N. Y. Supp. 263 (damage to dress

For wrongful delay in returning property bailed the measure of damages, if the property is not injured, is the rental value of the property,[280] or if no rental value can be shown, interest on its value.[281] For wrongful failure to return, the value may be recovered.[282]

§ 633c. To collect a claim.

Where a claim is sent to a bank for collection and it negligently fails to collect, or to take necessary steps to preserve the claim or its security, it is liable for the loss thereby occasioned. Thus where a note is sent for collection, and the collecting bank fails at maturity to present it or to protest it, or to give due notice of protest, the measure of damages is *prima facie* the face of the note [283] which may be reduced by showing either inability to collect at maturity or continued possibility of collecting after its return to plaintiff.[284] So for delay in returning the note, by reason of which it became uncollectible, the bank is responsible for the face of the note.[285] Where a bank to which a secured note was sent for collection negligently lost the collateral security, which was land certif-

in cleaning it); Chaityn *v.* Stock, 120 N. Y. Supp. 89 (failure to dye skins according to sample); Gutschneider *v.* Pirosnick, 123 N. Y. Supp. 190 (damage to skins in dyeing).

Oklahoma: Southwestern C. S. O. Co. *v.* Stribling, 18 Okla. 417, 89 Pac. 1129 (injury to cattle bailed by failure to water).

[280] In Rollins *v.* Sidney B. Bowman Cycle Co., 96 App. Div. 365, 89 N. Y. Supp. 289, plaintiff left his bicycle with defendant to be repaired under an agreement that, when finished, it should be shipped to him at a certain place, where he intended to go to begin a bicycle trip, and that the repairs should be charged to him. Defendant afterwards refused to ship the wheel unless the repairs were first paid for. It was held that plaintiff's measure of damages was the difference between the price he was compelled to pay for a

wheel to take the place of one wrongfully withheld by defendant and the value of such wheel after he returned from his contemplated trip.

[281] Porter *v.* Duval Co., 60 Misc. 122, 111 N. Y. Supp. 825.

[282] Carll *v.* Goldberg, 59 Misc. 172, 110 N. Y. Supp. 318.

[283] *Arkansas:* Second Nat. Bank *v.* Bank of Alma, 138 S. W. 472.

New York: First Nat. Bank *v.* Fourth Nat. Bank, 77 N. Y. 320, 33 Am. Rep. 678.

[284] *Alabama:* Hendrix *v.* Jefferson Co. Sav. Bk., 153 Ala. 636, 45 So. 136, 14 L. R. A. (N. S.) 686.

Arkansas: Second Nat. Bank *v.* Bank of Alma, 138 S. W. 472.

New York: Howard *v.* Bank of Metropolis, 95 App. Div. 342, 88 N. Y. Supp. 1070.

[285] Lord *v.* Hingham Nat. Bank, 186 Mass. 161, 71 N. E. 312.

icates, the owner, being able to replace them, was entitled to recover the necessary expenses of replacing them.[286]

§ 633d. To expend labor on property.

In a very large class of contracts, such as provide for manufacture, construction, repairs, and transportation, the benefit to be derived from performance is the addition of value to property through the expenditure of labor. The consideration on the other side may, or may not, be pecuniary. The plaintiff in these cases recovers, as his measure of damages, the difference between the value of the property, as left by the defendant, and the value it would have had if the labor had been expended. There are cases where the plaintiff would be held obliged to reduce this loss if on breach he might have procured the performance of the contract by some other person and neglected to do so; but this subject is fully treated elsewhere. The difference in value may be got at in different ways, as has been well explained by the New York Court of Appeals in the case of Kidd v. McCormick.[287] This was an action brought by plaintiff to reach a trust fund deposited with the Union Trust Co. of New York. Plaintiff entered into a contract with defendants, T. and J. McCormick, by which it was agreed that plaintiff should sell seven lots of land to defendant J. McCormick, who should give back his bond and mortgage thereon for the purchase-money. The McCormicks further agreed to erect a dwelling upon each lot to be completed on July 1, 1877, plaintiff making to them certain advances to aid in their erection, and to be repaid to him when the houses had reached a certain stage of completion.

After the land had been conveyed, and the erection of the buildings commenced, the vendees procured a loan from defendants, C. B. & G. H. Granniss, secured by mortgages on four of the lots, and an agreement was made between all par-

---

[286] First Nat. Bank v. First Nat. Bank, 116 Ala. 520, 22 So. 976. After loss of the collateral, the debtor gave a mortgage as additional security which the plaintiff was eventually obliged to foreclose; but it was held that the expense of foreclosure was too remote.

[287] 83 N. Y. 391.

ties that a certain portion of the moneys loaned by said Grannisses should be deposited in a trust company as collateral security for the completion of the dwelling-houses, and that said mortgages should have priority of plaintiff's mortgages on said lots. The vendees proceeded with the work till September 1, 1877, when they abandoned the houses in an unfinished condition and declined to complete them. Whereupon the plaintiffs went on and finished the buildings. The question was, what was the measure of plaintiff's damages?

Folger, J., said that the plaintiff's damages were the difference in the value of the premises, as they were with the houses unfinished, at the date of their abandonment, from what the value of them would have been had the houses been finished on that day according to the contract.[288] So where the defendant agreed to tow the plaintiff's coal from Pittsburg to Oil City, and failed to do so, and it was impossible to secure other means of transportation, the plaintiff was allowed the difference in the value of the coal at Pittsburg and at Oil City.[289] The plaintiff loaned money on a mortgage of certain uncompleted houses, which the defendant covenanted should be built in a certain manner; they were not so completed. The houses were sold on foreclosure, and it became impossible, therefore, to complete them. The measure of damages was held to be the difference in value of the houses as completed and as they should have been completed, at the time the plaintiff had notice of their deficient construction; not exceeding, however, the mortgage debt and interest at that time.[290] And where the work of repairing a house was not done according to the contract, but the work having been completed, it would be impossible to have the errors rectified except at enormous expense, the cost of such rectification was not allowed to be shown as evidence of the difference in value between the house as it was and as it should have been.[291]

---

[288] Acc., Morton v. Harrison, 52 N. Y. Super. Ct. 305.

[289] McGovern v. Lewis, 56 Pa. 231, 94 Am. Dec. 60.

[290] Norway Plains Bank v. Moors, 134 Mass. 129.

[291] Morton v. Harrison, 52 N. Y. Super. Ct. 305.

§ 633e. To furnish water for irrigation.

For breach of contract to furnish water for irrigation purposes, if the water could be obtained elsewhere at a reasonable expense, the cost of obtaining it is the measure of damages.[292] If other water cannot be obtained, and no crop is raised, the measure of damages is the difference in value of the land with the water and without,[293] together, of course, with any expenditure made on the faith of obtaining the water and rendered valueless by failure to obtain it. If a crop is raised, but is damaged by the lack of water, the amount of damage, if proved with sufficient certainty, may be recovered;[294] and even if the crop is destroyed before reaching maturity, it has been held that the value if it reached maturity less the necessary expense of maturing and placing it on the market may be recovered.[295]

§ 633f. To take or furnish advertising.

For breach of a contract to take and pay for certain advertising space in the defendant's newspaper the measure of damages is *prima facie* the contract price, and the burden is on the defendant to diminish this amount.[296] And so for breach of contract to pay a certain sum for the privilege of placing advertisements on the roof of plaintiff's building, the measure of damages is the balance unpaid of the contract price, since the plaintiff is to be under no trouble or expense in the mat-

[292] Gagnon v. Molden, 15 Ida. 727, 99 Pac. 965.

[293] *California:* Pallett v. Murphy, 131 Cal. 192, 63 Pac. 366, 82 Am. St. Rep. 341.
Nebraska: Wade v. Belmont, I. C. & W. P. Co., 87 Neb. 732, 128 N. W. 514. See *ante,* § 620.

[294] Hutchinson v. Mt. Vernon W. & P. Co., 49 Wash. 469, 95 Pac. 1023.

[295] Smith v. Hicks (N. Mex.), 95 Pac. 138, 19 L. R. A. (N. S.) 938.
Idaho: Rios v. Azcuenaga (Ida.), 115 Pac. 922.

[296] *Indiana:* Hamilton v. Love, 152 Ind. 641, 53 N. E. 181, 54 N. E. 437, 71 Am. St. Rep. 384.

Massachusetts: Maynard v. Royal Worcester Corset Co., 200 Mass. 1, 85 N. E. 877 (*semble*).
Michigan: Tradesman Co. v. Superior Mfg. Co., 147 Mich. 702, 111 N. W. 343.
New Jersey: McDermott v. De Meridor Co. (N. J. L.), 76 Atl. 331.
New York: Ware Bros. Co. v. Cortland C. & C. Co., 192 N. Y. 439, 85 N. E. 666, 22 L. R. A. (N. S.) 272, 127 Am. St. Rep. 914.
Washington: Starr Pub. Co. v. Charles Knosher & Co. (Wash.), 113 Pac. 569.

ter.[297] The fact that the plaintiff could get other advertisements would reduce damages only if he could not have received the compensation for such advertisements except for breach of the contract.[298] If for instance the defendant contracted to take all the advertising space in the paper, or all the space for display on the building, upon breach of the contract he should be allowed for what others would pay for the space; and so if the defendant's advertisement would in fact have filled the available space. But if the advertising space was in fact unlimited, defendant clearly should obtain no benefit from other advertisements.[299]

For breach of contract for accepting advertisements from plaintiff, who was to take the advertising space at an agreed price, the measure of damages is the value of the space to plaintiff; [300] if the parties contemplated his securing contracts from advertisers for the space, and he did so, he could recover the profits of such contracts.[301]   If the defendant himself obtained advertisements for the space, this may be shown to indicate plaintiff's loss.[302]   So in the case of Gardner v. The Roycrofters,[303] the publishers of periodicals sold to plaintiff the advertising privileges of the periodicals, reserving only a specified space for their own use, and they actually used more than the reserved space, the plaintiff was entitled to recover the profit he could have realized on the extra space.

§ 634. Assignments of judgment.

* In the case of an assignment of a judgment containing a warranty that the sum specified remained due and unpaid, when in fact no judgment had ever been entered up, the Supreme Court of New York held, in an action of covenant, that the measures of damages was not the amount recovered

[297] United M. R. & I. Co. v. American Bill Posting Co., 128 N. Y. Supp. 666.

[298] Ante, § 608.

[299] See, however, Tradesman Co. v. Superior Mfg. Co., 147 Mich. 702, 111 N. W. 343, where the court apparently allowed only the difference between the contract price and the price at which other advertisements could have

been obtained, even by cutting the price.

[300] Patten v. Lynett, 133 App. Div. 746, 118 N. Y. Supp. 185.

[301] May v. Breunig (Misc.), 120 N. Y. Supp. 98.

[302] Patten v. Lynett, 133 App. Div. 746, 118 N. Y. Supp. 185.

[303] 134 App. Div. 45, 118 N. Y. Supp. 703.

as stated in the assignment of the judgment, but the amount of property owned by the judgment debtor, and which might have been taken in execution intermediate the time of assignment and the commencement of the suit.[304] It is worthy of notice here, that the amount of consideration or value paid did not appear on the face of the assignment, and that it is not stated in the report whether the evidence in regard to the amount of property owned by the alleged judgment debtor came from the plaintiff or defendant; although, as the declaration is stated to have averred that the plaintiff had property enough to satisfy the demand, the pleader seems to have thought that, regularly, it should have come from the plaintiff. It would seem that, *prima facie*, either the amount appearing to have been paid for the judgment, or the amount recovered by it, should be the measure of damages. If the assignment were treated as a chattel, then the price paid would again be the rule, subject to the plaintiff's right to show that the whole amount could have been recovered, and then for its value beyond the price; and also subject to the further right of the defendant to show that, owing to the judgment debtor's insolvency, it was worthless. If the analogy in the case of sheriffs were adopted, then the amount recovered by the judgment would be the *prima facie* measure, subject to the defendant's right to reduce the sum by showing that, owing to the judgment debtor's circumstances, its whole amount could not be collected.** It is well settled that the measure of damages is not the consideration. So where, in assigning a judgment, the defendants covenanted that there was then due a certain sum, and that they would not discharge the judgment, and it appeared that they had previously discharged one judgment debtor, it was held that the plaintiffs could recover the difference between the present value and the value it would have had if that debtor had not been discharged. In this case the price paid was only ten per cent of the judgment.[305] Where one of three judgment debtors had been released, it was held, in an action by the assignee of the judgments against the assignor for breach of covenant, that, neither of the others having been released, in the absence of proof that the judgment was wholly valueless, the assignee could not, while retaining it, recover as if there had been a total failure of consideration. He would be entitled in such a case to the expenses of attempting to enforce the judgment against the released debtor.[306]

§ 635. Alternative contracts.

Contracts are sometimes in the alternative, that is, the promisee agrees to perform one of two things; for instance, to deliver an article or to pay a sum of money. This sometimes gives him his election, and the damages are measured by the rule most beneficial to him. The whole subject of alternative contracts is fully discussed in an earlier chapter.[307] It is important, however, to notice that a contract which was originally in the alternative may have ceased to be so, through the exercise of the option by one party or the other. As soon as the option is exercised, and one alternative chosen, the other falls entirely out of the case; and, if the contract is thereafter broken, the damages are to be determined as upon an ordinary contract to do what has been chosen by the party exercising the option. So where an insurance company after a fire, elected to rebuild a house, this converted the contract into a contract to build; and the amount of the policy no longer furnished any measure of damages. The house having been partially rebuilt and then left by the company, the measure of damages was the cost of completing the building so as to make it like the original house.[308] When the contract is broken while the alternative is still alive, the measure of damages, where the defendant has the alternative, is the value of the less valuable alternative.[309] So on a contract to deliver slaves between eight and ten years old the measure of damages is the value of slaves eight years old, since they are less valuable.[310] On a contract to pay a certain sum of money in

[306] Weston v. Chamberlain, 56 Barb. (N. Y.) 415.
[307] §§ 421–424.
[308] Morrell v. Irving F. Ins. Co., 33 N. Y. 429, 88 Am. Dec. 396.
[309] W. J. Holliday & Co. v. Highland

I. & S. Co., 43 Ind. App. 342, 87 N. E. 249.
[310] Mudd v. Phillips, Litt. Sel. Cas. (Ky.) 50; Pope v. Campbell, Hardin (Ky.), 31.

paper or specie, the measure of damages is the value of the least valuable medium.[311] And on a contract to pay a certain amount "in Georgia, Alabama, or Tennessee bank notes or notes on any good men" the measure of damages is the same.[312]

Where, however, the performance of one alternative becomes impossible before the time for performance, this destroys the alternative, and the measure of damages is the value of the remaining alternative. Thus on a contract to give certain property or a fixed sum of money, if the property is destroyed or taken by title paramount the measure of damages is the amount of money named.[313]

What seems at first sight to be an alternative may be in reality an option to defendant to discharge a contract by the performance of some act; if the option is not accepted, the contract must be performed. Thus on a contract to break up certain land by the first of July, with an agreement that the contract may be discharged by the payment of $75.00 by the first of December, the contract becomes an absolute one to break up the land as soon as the first of December passes without a payment of the money; and upon breach on the first of July the measure of damages is the cost of breaking up the land.[314] And so where a machine was hired, to be paid for according to the amount of work done, of which the lessee was to keep an account, and if the lessee did not keep such account the lessor might, at his option, either himself keep the account, or charge the lessee in lien thereof five dollars per day, and the lessee did not keep the account, the lessor might insist on the payment of five dollars a day.[315]

III.—WAIVER OF PERFORMANCE AND REPUDIATION

§ 636. Express waiver by acceptance of partial performance.

When full performance by the plaintiff is expressly waived by the defendant, it is really the waiver of a condition, and the undertaking of the defendant thereupon becomes unconditional. If the undertaking is not then performed, the plain-

[311] White v. Green, 3 T. B. Mon. (Ky.) 155.
[312] Hixon v. Hixon, 7 Humph. (Tenn.) 33.
[313] Wolfe v. Parham, 18 Ala. 441.
[314] Wilson v. Graham, 14 Tex. 222.
[315] Standard B. F. Co. v. Breed, 163 Mass. 10, 39 N. E. 346.

tiff's loss is the whole benefit which was to come to him by the contract. So where there is an acceptance of partial performance in lieu of complete performance of an entire contract by one party to it, the other being ready to complete it on his part, compensation may be recovered for the whole benefit secured to the plaintiff by the contract.[316]

§ 636a. Repudiation of the contract.

Notice of repudiation of a contract by one of the parties may be relied upon by the other party as a waiver of performance on his side, and the latter may sue for a breach of the contract when the time comes for performance without himself doing any more acts in performance of his part of the contract.[317] Such waiver nevertheless does not entitle the plaintiff to any greater compensation than he would get if the notice of repudiation had not been given before the breach. The repudiating party must, of course, compensate the other for such damage as he inflicts; but he does not by his wrongdoing subject himself to a forfeiture. The measure of damages recoverable against him for non-performance is the ordinary measure for breach of such a contract: the value of the contract at the time for its performance, or in other words the

[316] *New York:* Ellis *v.* Willard, 9 N. Y. 529.

North Carolina: Ashcraft *v.* Allen, 4 Ired. L. 96.

[317] Cort *v.* Ambergate, N. & B. & J. Ry., 17 Q. B. 127. This is the case even in jurisdictions not accepting the doctrine of anticipatory breach of contract. Ripley *v.* McClure, 4 Ex. 345 (decided before the doctrine of anticipatory breach had been established in England); P. P. Emory Mfg. Co. *v.* Saloman, 178 Mass. 582, 60 N. E. 377.

In order to constitute an anticipatory breach the repudiation by defendant must in some way be accepted by the plaintiff. If he insists on the performance, the repudiation is not a breach.

Kentucky: Louisville Pk. Co. *v.* Crain, 141 Ky. 379, 132 S. W. 575.

Texas: Carlisle *v.* Green (Tex. Civ. App.), 131 S. W. 1140.

England: Michael *v.* Hart, [1902] 1 K. B. 482.

In such a case, the repudiating party is entitled to perform when the time for performance comes. B. B. Ford & Co. *v.* Lawson, 133 Ga. 237, 65 S. E. 444. And if the other party tenders performance at the time set in the contract, the repudiating party may retract his notice and accept performance and there will then be no breach. Ripley *v.* McClure, 4 Ex. 345. Consequently if the market value has altered between the notice of repudiation and the time for performance, the other party's damages may be less than they would have been if he had accepted the notice as an anticipatory breach. Rhodes *v.* Cleveland R. M. Co., 17 Fed. 426. The contract, to use the phrase commonly employed, is kept alive for the benefit of both parties.

profit of the contract. This, generally speaking, is the difference between the contract price and the cost of full performance;[318] in case of a contract for the sale of goods this will be equal to the difference between the contract price for the goods and their actual value at the time for delivery.[319] In the case of a contract for the manufacture and sale of goods, when the breach consists in a refusal to accept the goods, it will amount to the difference between the contract price and the cost of manufacture.[320] In many cases, however, the result of the notice of repudiation will be to stop performance by the plaintiff and in that way to cause a waste of his labor and materials. Whenever the result of the defendant's repudiation is to cause a waste of this sort to the plaintiff, compensation for this waste may be recovered in addition to the profit of the contract.[321]

§ 636b. Repudiation of contract performable in instalments.

Where a contract is performable in instalments, such, for instance, as a contract for the delivery of goods in stated amounts from time to time, and there is a repudiation during

[318] *Illinois:* Long v. Conklin, 75 Ill. 32.

Michigan: Goodrich v. Hubbard, 51 Mich. 62.

New York: McMaster v. State, 108 N. Y. 488, 15 N. E. 417.

England: Brown v. Muller, L. R. 7 Ex. 319.

[319] *Cases where the seller repudiated:*
Massachusetts: P. P. Emory Mfg. Co. v. Saloman, 178 Mass. 582, 60 N. E. 377.

Michigan: Leo Austrian & Co. v. Springer, 94 Mich. 343, 54 N. W. 50, 34 Am. Rep. 350.

England: Leigh v. Patterson, 8 Taunt. 540.

Cases where the buyer repudiated:
United States: Rhodes v. Cleveland R. M. Co., 17 Fed. 426.

Illinois: Kadish v. Young, 108 Ill. 170, 48 Am. Rep. 548.

Michigan: Simons v. Ypsilanti Paper Co., 77 Mich. 185, 43 N. W. 864.

England: Philpot v. Evans, 5 M. & W. 475.

[320] *United States:* Hinckley v. Pittsburgh Steel Co., 121 U. S. 264, 30 L. ed. 967, 7 Sup. Ct. 875.

Virginia: Worrell v. Kinnear Mfg. Co., 103 Va. 719, 49 S. E. 988.

[321] *Nebraska:* Hale v. Hess, 30 Neb. 42, 46 N. W. 261.

New York: Dunn v. Allen, 55 App. Div. 637, 67 N. Y. Supp. 218.

So where the defendant contracted with the plaintiff for ten-inch leather hose to be manufactured by the plaintiff, and repudiated the contract after the leather had been cut, and there was no sale for larger than nine-inch hose, the plaintiff was entitled to recover not only the profit that would have been made on the contract if it had been fully performed, but also the waste caused by cutting the leather down for nine-inch hose. City of Chicago v. Greer, 9 Wall. 726, 19 L. ed. 769.

the progress of the performance, the damages¯for a breach
consisting of the non-performance of subsequent instalments
is to be estimated as at the time for the performance of each,
and not as at the time for the performance of the last instalment. If, for instance, between the time of the first breach
and of the final breach the value of goods to be delivered
fluctuates, the buyer who has failed to receive the instalments due him cannot demand damages based on the value
of the goods at the time the last instalment should have
been delivered, but he must be content with a basis of compensation which will give him the value of each instalment
at the time it should have been delivered.[322]   If, however,
when delay occurs in the course of delivery, the parties by
mutual agreement extend the time for delivery, so that when
a breach finally happens, it is a breach of what has come to
be an obligation at that time to deliver all the overdue instalments, the damages are of course to be estimated as for non-
delivery of all the articles at this agreed time.[323]

§ 636c. Continuance of performance after repudiation.

A question of some difficulty arises where, in spite of notice
of repudiation, the plaintiff insists upon proceeding with the
performance, and attempts to charge the defendant in some
way with the cost of the complete performance. If such a
course does not enhance the damages he may clearly do so.
This is the case where the contract is for the manufacture and
delivery of goods readily salable in the market. The measure
of damages for the breach of such a contract is the difference
between the contract price and the cost of manufacture. This
difference will not be increased by the act of the manufacturer
in completing the manufacture. Indeed, it may be incumbent upon him to complete the manufacture notwithstanding

[322] United States: Cherry V. I. Works
v. Florence I. R. Co., 64 Fed. 569, 12
C. C. A. 306.
  Illinois: Delaware & H. C. Co. v.
Mitchell, 92 Ill. App. 577.
  Michigan: Goodrich v. Hubbard, 51
Mich. 62.
  Wisconsin: Hill v. Chipman, 59 Wis.
211, 18 N. W. 160.

England: Brown v. Muller, L. R. 7
Ex. 319; Ex parte Llansamlet T. P. Co.,
L. R. 16 Eq. 155; Barningham v.
Smith, 31 L. T. Rep. 540.
  [323] United States: Ralli v. Rockmore,
111 Fed. 874.
  England: Ogle v. Earl Vane, L. R. 2
Q. B. 275.

the notice of repudiation. If, for instance, the notice should reach the manufacturer of such goods at the time when his product was incomplete, it would cause a waste of his labor and material to leave the product uncompleted. If he could stop at that time and charge the defendant with the waste caused by the incompletion of his product, he would thereby not diminish, but unnecessarily increase the damages to be paid by the wrongdoer; the waste of labor and material would be unnecessary, and for this reason he could not compel the defendant to pay for it. In such a case, therefore, the manufacturer must complete the process of manufacture, and thus enable himself to obtain the market price for his goods.

If, on the other hand, any further expenditure in performance of the contract after the reception of the notice of repudiation would be a mere waste, the plaintiff cannot incur such an expense, but must cease performance upon reception of the notice of repudiation. This doctrine was first clearly established in the leading case of Clark v. Marsiglia.[324] In that case it appeared that the defendant delivered a number of paintings to the plaintiff to clean and repair, and after the plaintiff had commenced work upon the paintings the defendant desired him not to go on, as he had concluded not to have the work done. The plaintiff, notwithstanding, finished the cleaning and repairing of the pictures and claimed to recover for doing the whole work and for materials furnished; insisting that the defendant had no right to countermand the order he had given. The court said: "The defendant, by requiring the plaintiff to stop work upon the paintings, violated his contract and thereby incurred a liability to pay such damages as would include a recompense for the labor done and material used, and such further sum in damages as might, upon legal principle, be assessed for the breach of the contract; but the plaintiff had no right, by obstinately persisting in the work, to make the penalty upon the defendant greater than it would have otherwise been." And again: "In all such cases the just claims of the party employed are satisfied when he is fully recompensed for his part performance and indemnified for his loss in respect of the part left

[324] 1 Denio (N. Y.) 317.

unexecuted; and to persist in accumulating a large demand is not consistent with good faith toward the employer." This decision has been almost universally followed.[325] Occasion for the application of the principle of Clark v. Marsiglia usually occurs where the contract is for work to be done on the property of the defendant,[326] or where a specific article is to be made for the defendant which will be of use to no one else.[327] But the same rule applies even in the case of a sale of ordinary goods salable in the market, when the plaintiff insists upon shipping the goods to the place of delivery, at considerable expense for carriage, although he has received notice that the goods will not be accepted by the purchaser.[328]

Even in the case of a contract of special value to the defendant, it might be less wasteful to continue to work after notice of repudiation than to stop work, though so far as the defendant is concerned the performance of the contract would be

[325] *United States:* Rhodes v. Cleveland R. M. Co., 17 Fed. 426; Kingman v. Western Mfg. Co., 92 Fed. 486, 34 C. C. A. 489.
Maryland: Heaver v. Lanahan, 74 Md. 493, 22 Atl. 263, 20 L. R. A. 126.
Minnesota: Gibbons v. Bente, 51 Minn. 499, 53 N. W. 756, 22 L. R. A. 80.
Missouri: American P. & E. Co. v. Walker, 87 Mo. App. 503; Peck v. Kansas City M. R. & C. Co., 96 Mo. App. 212, 70 S. W. 169.
New York: Dillon v. Anderson, 43 N. Y. 231; Butler v. Butler, 77 N. Y. 472, 33 Am. Rep. 648; Mendell v. Willyoung, 42 Misc. 210, 85 N. Y. Supp. 647; Dunham v. Hastings Pavement Co., 95 App. Div. 390, 88 N. Y. Supp. 835; Sharp's Pub. Co. v. Grant, 1 N. Y. City Ct. 314.
North Carolina: Heiser v. Mears, 120 N. C. 443, 27 S. E. 117.
North Dakota: Davis v. Bronson, 2 N. Dak. 300, 50 N. W. 836, 16 L. R. A. 655.
Rhode Island: Collyer v. Moulton, 9 R. I. 90, 98 Am. Dec. 370.

Tennessee: Gardner v. Deeds, 116 Tenn. 128, 92 S. W. 518; Ault v. Dustin, 100 Tenn. 366, 45 S. W. 981.
Vermont: Danforth v. Walker, 37 Vt. 239, 40 Vt. 257.
Williston's Pollock on Contracts, p. 349.
[326] *Maryland:* Heaver v. Lanahan, 74 Md. 493, 22 Atl. 263, 20 L. R. A. 126.
Minnesota: Gibbons v. Bente, 51 Minn. 499, 53 N. W. 756, 22 L. R. A. 80.
New York: Clark v. Marsiglia, 1 Den. 317.
North Dakota: Davis v. Bronson, 2 N. Dak. 300, 50 N. W. 836, 16 L. R. A. 655.
[327] *United States:* Kingman v. Western Mfg. Co., 92 Fed. 486, 34 C. C. A. 489.
Missouri: American P. & E. Co. v. Walker, 87 Mo. App. 503; Sharp's Pub. Co. v. Grant, 1 N. Y. City Ct. 314.
[328] Sonka v. Chatham, 2 Tex. Civ. App. 312, 21 S. W. 948. But see Roebling v. Lock Stitch Fence Co., 130 Ill. 660, 22 N. E. 518.

useless to him. This happens where the work for the defendant is only part of the entire process. So where the article to be delivered to the defendant was only a by-product of manufacture the plaintiff would of course not be called upon to stop the whole manufacture.[329] This principle was involved in the interesting case of Martin v. Meles.[330] This was a contract by which the plaintiff was to bring and prosecute a test case in defence of a patent. The suit was brought for the benefit of a large number of persons interested, who severally agreed to pay a share of the cost of services and expenses. After suit had begun, one of the parties gave notice to the plaintiff to discontinue on his behalf. In spite of the notice the plaintiff continued to prosecute the suit and charged the defendant with his portion of the expenses; although if the suit had been dropped upon receipt of his notice of repudiation a large part of the expenses would have been avoided. The court held that the plaintiff was not obliged, under the circumstances, to discontinue the suit at the defendant's request. Mr. Chief Justice Holmes said that the doctrine of Clark v. Marsiglia would not apply in such a case, where there was a common interest in the performance, and where what had been done and what remained to do probably were to a large extent interdependent. So where a railway advertising company agreed to place defendant's cards in the street cars of a certain city and defendant repudiated the contract the next day, the company was held entitled to recover the entire contract price, having gone on with the performance;[331] but this was not on the ground of performance, but because it appeared that the plaintiff was unable otherwise to rent the space.[332]

The doctrine of Clark v. Marsiglia practically prevents the plaintiff from keeping the contract alive for the defendant's benefit in any case to which it applies. In Ault v. Dustin[333] the defendant agreed to manufacture special sizes of rope for

[329] Southern Cotton Oil Co. v. Hefflin, 99 Fed. 339, 39 C. C. A. 546; but see James H. Rice Co. v. Penn. P. G. Co., 81 Ill. App. 407.

[330] 179 Mass. 114, 60 N. E. 397.

[331] Railway Advertising Co. v. Standard R. C. Co., 178 N. Y. 570, 70 N. E. 1108, affirming 83 App. Div. 191, 83 N. Y. Supp. 338.

[332] *Ante,* § 633f.

[333] 100 Tenn. 366, 45 S. W. 981.

the plaintiff, and before manufacture plaintiff cancelled the contract, but defendant wrote refusing to permit cancellation. Later, the price of rope having risen greatly, plaintiff wrote ordering shipment; but defendant had not manufactured the rope, and it was then too late to do so. The court held that the defendant was forbidden, by the doctrine of Clark *v.* Marsiglia, to manufacture the rope, and he was therefore not in default for failure to deliver it in spite of his refusal to accept cancellation as a breach.

§ 636d. Anticipatory breach: damages upon breach before time for performance.

In England and most of the United States, the repudiation of a contract by one of the parties to it before the time for performance has arrived amounts to a tender of a breach of the contract; and if it is accepted as such by the other party it constitutes a so-called "anticipatory breach," and the injured party is at liberty to begin suit at once and to recover entire damages.[334] The damages are to be assessed, of course,

[334] *United States:* Roehm *v.* Horst, 178 U. S. 1, 20 Sup. Ct. 780, 44 L. ed. 953; In re Neff, 157 Fed. 57, 84 C. C. A. 561 (by bankruptcy); Golden C. M. Co. *v.* Repson C. M. Co., 188 Fed. 179.
California: Remy *v.* Olds, 88 Cal. 537, 26 Pac. 355.
Florida: Sullivan *v.* McMillan, 26 Fla. 543, 557, 8 So. 450; Thompson *v.* Kyle, 39 Fla. 582, 23 So. 12, 63 Am. St. Rep. 193; Hall *v.* Northern & Southern Co., 55 Fla. 242, 46 So. 178.
Illinois: Fox *v.* Kitton, 19 Ill. 519, 534; Follansbee *v.* Adams, 86 Ill. 13; Lake Shore & M. S. Ry. *v.* Richards, 152 Ill. 59, 38 N. E. 773, 30 L. R. A. 33.
Indiana: Adams *v.* Byerly, 123 Ind. 368, 24 N. E. 130.
Iowa: Crabtree *v.* Messersmith, 19 Iowa, 179; McCormick *v.* Basal, 46 Iowa, 235.
Maryland: Dugan *v.* Anderson, 36 Md. 567, 11 Am. Rep. 509.

Michigan: Hosmer *v.* Wilson, 7 Mich. 294, 304, 74 Am. Dec. 716; Platt *v.* Brand, 26 Mich. 173.
Minnesota: Kalkhoff *v.* Nelson, 60 Minn. 284, 62 N. W. 332.
New Jersey: O'Neil *v.* Supreme Council, 70 N. J. L. 410, 57 Atl. 463.
New York: Burtis *v.* Thompson, 42 N. Y. 246, 1 Am. Rep. 516; Howard *v.* Daly, 61 N. Y. 362, 374, 19 Am. Rep. 285; Ferris *v.* Spooner, 102 N. Y. 10, 5 N. E. 773; Windmuller *v.* Pope, 107 N. Y. 674, 14 N. E. 436; Nichols *v.* Scranton Steel Co., 137 N. Y. 471, 487, 33 N. E. 561.
Pennsylvania: Girard *v.* Taggart, 5 S. & R. 19; Hocking *v.* Hamilton, 158 Pa. 107, 27 Atl. 836, 38 Am. St. Rep. 830; Mountjoy *v.* Metzger, 9 Phila. 10.
Virginia: Burke *v.* Shaver, 92 Va. 345, 23 S. E. 749; Lee *v.* Mutual Life Ass'n, 97 Va. 160, 33 S. E. 556.
West Virginia: Davis *v.* Grand Rapids S. F. Co., 41 W. Va. 717, 24 S. E. 630.

as of the date of the breach; nevertheless, they are to be a compensation for the loss caused by depriving the plaintiff of the benefit of the contract as it was originally made. The doctrine of anticipatory breach is not a doctrine which fictitiously moves the performance ahead to the time of the repudiation, and regards the repudiation as a failure to perform the contract. The anticipatory breach takes effect as a premature destruction of the contract rather than as a failure to perform it in its terms. The damage caused by such a premature destruction is, to be sure, due to the consequent failure to secure performance; but this is a failure to secure performance according to its original terms, that is, performance at the time and place when performance was required according to the terms of the agreement. Since the injury is the destruction of the contract, regarded as an article of property, the measure of damages is the value of such property at the time of its destruction; but since the value of a contract will ordinarily be determined by the benefit which its performance would confer, the exact measure of damages upon an anticipatory breach is in the ordinary case precisely the same as it would be if the repudiation were not accepted as a breach and the injured party brought suit, after the time of performance, for the non-performance at the time set. In other words, though the plaintiff sues at once for an anticipatory breach of the contract, his damages are to be assessed according to the cost of performance, not at the time and place of the breach, but at the time and place set for performance.[335]

Wisconsin: Walsh v. Myers, 92 Wis. 397, 66 N. W. 250.

England: Hochster v. De la Tour, 2 E. & B. 678, 22 L. J. Q. B. 455.

Canada: Ontario L. Co. v. Hamilton B. M. Co., 27 Ont. App. 346.

Contra, Massachusetts: Daniels v. Newton, 114 Mass. 530, 19 Am. Rep. 384.

Nebraska: Carstens v. McDonald, 38 Neb. 858, 57 N. W. 757; King v. Waterman, 55 Neb. 324, 75 N. W. 830.

North Dakota: Stanford v. McGill,

6 N. D. 536, 72 N. W. 938, 38 L. R. A. 760.

And see 14 Harvard Law Review, 428 *et seq.*

[335] *United States:* Roehm v. Horst, 178 U. S. 1, 20 Sup. Ct. 780, 44 L. ed. 953; Missouri Furnace Co. v. Cochran, 8 Fed. 463; Cherry V. I. W. v. Florence I. R. Co., 64 Fed. 569, 12 C. C. A. 306.

Kansas: York D. M. Co. v. Lusk, 6 Kan. App. 629, 49 Pac. 788.

Michigan: Lee v. Briggs, 99 Mich. 487, 58 N. W. 477.

Thus in the leading case of Roper v. Johnson [336] it appeared that a contract by the defendant to deliver certain goods had been repudiated by him before the time for performance, and that this repudiation had been accepted as a breach by the plaintiff, who brought suit at once. The court held that the measure of damages was the difference between the contract price and the market price at the time for performance. So in the case of Roehm v. Horst,[337] where the purchaser repudiated a contract of sale before the time for delivery and the seller brought suit at once, it was held that the basis of damages in the absence of special circumstances was the cost of performance at the time fixed therefor by the contract.

§ 636e. Damages affected by fluctuations in the market.

Where the trial of the action is not had until after the time fixed by the contract for performance this rule will not result in any uncertainty as to the amount of damages; for market values at the time fixed for performance can be shown, and the amount of damages is therefore no more uncertain than it would have been if suit had been brought after the time fixed for performance. If, however, suit is brought and actually comes to trial before the time fixed for performance, there is an element of uncertainty, because the jury can tell only by conjecture what would be the actual cost of performance at the time set therefor. This, however, should be regarded as no objection to the application of the ordinary rule of damages. It is true that in such a case values at the time of breach, or rather at the time of trial, will be introduced in evidence and will probably form the basis upon which the jury will find the values at the date for performance; but such actual

---

New York: Windmuller v. Pope, 107 N. Y. 674, 14 N. E. 436; Todd v. Gamble, 148 N. Y. 382, 42 N. E. 982.

Pennsylvania: Woldert Grocery Co. v. Wilkinson, 39 Pa. Super. Ct. 100.

West Virginia: Davis v. Grand Rapids S. F. Co., 41 W. Va. 717, 24 S. E. 630.

England: Roper v. Johnson, L. R. 8 C. P. 167.

Canada: Ontario Lantern Co. v. Hamilton B. M. Co., 27 Ont. App. 346.

In case of a contract for the entire product of a manufactory, the profit made by other employment of the factory should be subtracted. Allen v. Field, 130 Fed. 641.

[336] L. R. 8 C. P. 167.

[337] 178 U. S. 1, 44 L. ed. 953, 20 Sup. Ct. 780.

values are introduced in evidence not because values at the time of breach are of any importance in themselves, but merely as evidence to prove the probable values at the time of performance. It is also true that by this means the plaintiff may in fact get a larger verdict than he would have obtained if the trial had been held after the date for performance. This will happen, for instance, when the market unexpectedly rises or falls, as the case may be, between the time of trial and time of performance. But as Mr. Chief Justice Fuller said in the case of Roehm v. Horst,[338] "Although he may receive his money earlier in this way, and may gain or lose by the estimate of his damage in advance of the time for performance, still, as we have seen, he has the right to accept the situation tendered him, and the other party cannot complain."

This is the generally accepted view; but in the important case of Masterton v. Mayor of Brooklyn[339] a different view was taken by the majority of the court. The doctrine of the decision is examined in another connection.[340] The argument in favor of the view there taken, so far as it is applied to cases of anticipatory breach, is often put in the following form. Damages are to be assessed as of the time of breach. Since the breach occurs at the moment of repudiation, damages are to be assessed as of that moment; and therefore when the assessment of damages involves an estimation of the value of commodities, that estimation should be made as of the time of the breach. This conclusion, however, is fallacious. It is true that the damage is to be assessed as of the time of the breach, but what is that damage? Suppose, for instance, we take a contract for the delivery of a thousand bushels of oats on the first of July, and suppose the contract is repudiated by the seller on the first of April; the loss thereby caused to the purchaser is not the loss at the time of so many bushels of oats. He had no right to the oats at that time by the original contract, nor did he gain a right to a thousand bushels of oats at that time by the repudiation of the original contract. His right at that time was a right to have one thou-

[338] 178 U. S. 1, 44 L. ed. 953, 20 Sup. Ct. 780.   [339] 7 Hill (N. Y.), 62.   [340] Post, § 636j.

sand bushels of oats delivered to him on the first of July; and it was the right to have the oats on the first of July, and not to oats on the first of April, that he lost by the repudiation. Now a right to a delivery of oats on the first of July is a right, the value of which, in the ordinary case, depends and can only depend upon the value of the oats to be delivered at the time for delivery. The value of oats on the first of April is utterly immaterial.

To this statement, however, there may be one apparent exception which is, however, really an illustration. The thing lost on the first of April, as has been seen, is a contract for delivery of July oats. While the value of a contract is ordinarily measured by the value of the performance of it, that is not true in every case. There are certain contracts for the future delivery of commodities which have a present market value, not directly dependent upon the ultimate value of performance. For instance, in the case just stated, if there were a produce exchange in which oats could be bought for future delivery, in other words, in which there was a market for contracts for the future delivery of oats, a contract for the delivery of oats on the first of July would, on the first of April, have a certain market value fixed by bargains on the floor of the produce exchange; and on general principles of the law of damages that market value would be taken as the value of the contract, and not the benefit ultimately to come from the performance of it. If then the defendant destroyed this contract on April first by a repudiation of it, the loss caused would be measured not by the value of the future delivery but by the market value of that contract on April first. It must be clearly noticed that this market value of the contract on April first is not the same thing as the difference between the contract price and the actual value of oats on April first. July oats may be quoted at a very different price from April oats; and the value of the contract would be the value of July oats on April first, not the value of April oats. In the case of an anticipatory breach of such a contract, therefore, the true measure of damages would seem to be the market quotation of goods of the sort for future delivery, and not the conjectural or even the actually proved profit arising from the contract in July.[341] If there is no market for July oats, the market value cannot be resorted to.

This doctrine, as will be seen, applies only in a narrow class of cases; namely, those where there is a market value for "futures." In several such cases, however, the courts, not noticing this distinction but seeing that the current quotations furnished the proper measure of damages, have attempted to work this out by some application of the rule denying recovery for avoidable consequences. It therefore will be necessary, in order to complete the consideration of this subject, to consider the applicability of the rule of avoidable consequences to breaches of contract before the time for performance.

In a recent New York case [342] the action was against a telegraph company for negligence in transmission. Plaintiff in December ordered a sale of 20,000 bales of cotton for March delivery at 12.70 per pound; as received by his agent the message read "1207." The cotton was sold at prices below 12.70, and the plaintiff replaced himself by purchases of March cotton at the best prices then obtainable. The Court of Appeals held the measure of damages to be the cost of this replacement (which was in accordance with the custom of the Cotton Exchange), and as untenable the argument that the plaintiffs might have done better in March, and were consequently bound to await the entirely uncertain and speculative developments of a future market. The judgment below was reversed, but the opinion of the Appellate Court as to the measure of damages seems conclusive. It was argued that the order was to sell cotton actually on hand, deliverable in March, but the decision appears to involve the view that the action was for recovery of damages representing losses caused by a December replacement on March contracts.

§ 636f. Avoidance of loss by making forward contracts.

It appears to be the accepted doctrine in the English courts

---

[341] The value of anything for which there is a market is the market value, even though the actual economic worth of it may be different. National Bank of Commerce v. New Bedford, 175 Mass. 257, 56 N. E. 257, 78 Am. St. Rep. 487. *Ante*, § 242.

[342] Weld v. Postal T. C. Co., 199 N. Y. 88, 92 N. E. 415. In the Appellate Division there was no opinion. 132 App. Div. 924, 116 N. Y. Supp. 1150.

that where the plaintiff has elected to consider notice of repudiation as a breach of the contract it is his business to go into the market, if such is the reasonable course to pursue, and buy or sell, as the case may be, for future delivery, as a means of avoiding the loss caused by the breach. This doctrine was certainly not established by the earlier cases; [343] but in the case of Roth v. Taysen [344] the court laid down a novel doctrine which appears to have been accepted in England. In that case the buyer of goods repudiated his contract at a time when the market was obviously falling. The court held that the seller was bound to sell the goods at once upon accepting the notice as a breach, and that he could charge the defendant with only such damages as would have accrued if he had sold within a reasonable time. The court in this case relied on the special circumstance that by a clause in the contract either party, upon breach by the other, might, after written notice, resell or repurchase on the other's account. In view of this clause it seems clear that it was the plaintiff's business, in accordance with the doctrine of Clark v. Marsiglia, to sell on the defendant's account. In the later case of Nickol v. Ashton,[345] the court expressed *obiter* its concurrence in this decision upon the general principle that it was the business of the injured party to reduce his damages.

[343] In the early case of Lee v. Paterson, 8 Taunt. 540, where the notice of repudiation was not accepted as a breach, Burrough, J., in holding that damages should be based on the market price at the time for performance, said: "The plaintiff was not bound to go into the market and buy. He never assented to *rescind* the contract." This has been thought by some courts to indicate that if he had accepted the repudiation as a breach, he might have been obliged to go into the market and buy; it is entirely clear, however, that in using the word *rescind* Mr. Justice Burrough did not have in mind the doctrine of anticipatory breach; which was not laid down by any English court until more than fifty years after his time. He had in mind the rescission of the contract in the true sense. In the later case of Brown v. Muller, L. R. 7 Ex. 319, where also notice of repudiation was not accepted as a breach, the court said distinctly that the plaintiff need not go into the market and buy other goods on the defendant's account. In Roper v. Johnson, L. R. 8 C. P. 167, where the repudiation was accepted and suit brought at once, the court clearly expressed the view, *obiter*, that the plaintiff was under no obligation to go into the market and attempt to get a new contract.

[344] 12 T. L. R. 211, 73 L. T. Rep. 628.

[345] [1900], 2 Q. B. 298.

In this country actual authorities on the point are few. In the case of Kadish v. Young,[346] where the plaintiff refused to accept notice of repudiation as a breach, the court held that the plaintiff was not bound to make a forward contract for the purchase of property. In the case of Missouri Furnace Co. v. Cochran,[347] where after receiving notice of repudiation the buyer at once brought suit and immediately made a forward contract for the purchase at the then market rate, which afterwards and before the time set for performance declined, the court held that the measure of damages was to be governed by the actual market price at the time fixed by the contract for delivery, and that he could not get damages based upon the contract for future delivery which he had made at the time of repudiation.[348]   There was no claim in this case that it was unwise for the plaintiff to make a second contract; and in fact it appears ·that a consequential loss would have followed, if other goods had not been bought.   The case seems to have been one of a proper attempt to avoid consequential loss, and the decision is therefore questionable on that ground.[349]   In Hinckley v. Pittsburgh Steel Co.,[350] where the plaintiff had contracted to manufacture and deliver steel rails and the defendant had cancelled the order before the time for delivery, the court held that the plaintiff need not reduce the damages by completing the manufacture of these particular rails and selling them to others, but that the measure of damages was the difference between the contract price and the cost of manufacture.[351]   In Roehm v. Horst [352] the court appeared to take it for granted that the damages would be reduced by any circumstances of which the plaintiff ought reasonably to have availed himself, and added, "He may show what was the value of the contract by showing for what price he could have made sub-contracts."   The contract was for the sale of hops, a commodity in which futures were

[346] 108 Ill. 170, 48 Am. Rep. 548.
[347] 8 Fed. 463.
[348] See Danforth v. Walker, 40 Vt. 257.
[349] Ante, § 226b.
[350] 121 U. S. 264, 7 Sup. Ct. 875, 30 L. ed. 967.
[351] Acc., Allen v. Field, 130 Fed. 641; and see United States v. Withers, 130 Fed. 696.
[352] 178 U. S. 1, 44 L. ed. 953, 20 Sup. Ct. 780.

bought and sold, and the buyer repudiated. The suggestion of the court therefore is that since "futures" in hops could be bought in the market the market price of the futures furnished a measure of the value of the contract. The court evidently does not mean to suggest that it was the duty of the plaintiff to mitigate the damages by entering into a future contract. Indeed, as the plaintiff was the seller he could have reduced his damages in the sense of the English decisions only by *selling* for future delivery, not by buying. The suggestion of the court was neither that he should sell nor that he should buy, but that the value of his contract was determined by subtracting from the contract price the cost at the time of breach of a similar contract for the future delivery of hops. In other words, this case is an application of the principle already explained, that where future performance of a contract has a market value at the time of the breach that value is to be the basis of recovery, and not the profit of the contract at the time fixed for delivery. It thus appears that the doctrine of Roth *v.* Taysen finds no support in the Supreme Court of the United States.

On principle it seems perfectly clear that the repudiator of a contract cannot under any circumstances call upon the other party to make forward contracts for his benefit, merely for the purpose of lessening or seeming to lessen the direct loss of profits of the contract.

If, however, the plaintiff would be entitled to consequential damages by reason of the fact that he had given notice to the other party, or that the contract itself is notice, that in case of breach consequential damages would happen, then it is quite true that if notice of repudiation is given and is accepted as a breach he should take steps to avoid such consequential damages. If, for instance, the plaintiff makes a contract for the purchase of goods for future delivery, giving notice of a profitable contract of resale, and the seller repudiates before the time for performance, the buyer, if he accepts the repudiation as a breach, must buy elsewhere, if he can, to avoid the consequential loss of the resale; if he could buy elsewhere and fails to do so he cannot charge the defendant with the loss of the resale.

IV.—PROSPECTIVE DAMAGES

§ 636g. Entire and divisible contracts.

A question of interest and importance is sometimes presented in regard to prospective damages, or damages which accrue after the suit is brought. In the case of continuing agreements, or agreements to do specified acts at certain successive periods,* it has been doubted whether the damage should be assessed as at the time of the first breach, or whether the whole period of the contract is to be gone through, and an estimate made of the damages sustained, with reference to each period fixed for performance. This, again, depends, to a certain extent, on another question, whether the contract will admit of more than one action being brought on it, or whether the first recovery is conclusive of the plaintiff's rights. It is an ancient rule of our law that one action only can be maintained for the breach of an entire contract; and a judgment obtained by the plaintiff in one suit may be pleaded in bar of any second proceeding;[353]** if a plaintiff recover compensation for part of a single cause of action, it satisfies the whole.[354] But a recovery of nominal damages for the infringement of a right will not bar a suit for actual damages sustained after the bringing of the first suit; and in the case of severable contracts, successive suits for actual damages may be brought from time to time as the damages are sustained, and in each suit the party may recover such damages as he has sustained before its commencement not barred by a previous recovery.[355]

When a continuing contract is broken, and suit is brought before the completion of the term, damages are generally recoverable only for breaches suffered up to the date of the writ;[356] but all damages, prospective as well as past, arising

[353] *Massachusetts:* Badger v. Titcomb, 15 Pick. 409, 26 Am. Dec. 611.

New York: Bendernagle v. Cocks, 19 Wend. 207, 32 Am. Dec. 448.

England: Rudder v. Price, 1 H. Bl. 547.

[354] *Connecticut:* Marlborough v. Sisson, 31 Conn. 332.

New Jersey: Baker v. Baker, 28 N.

J. L. 13; Veghte v. Hoagland, 29 N. J. L. 125.

[355] McConnel v. Kibbe, 33 Ill. 175.

[356] *Kansas:* Kansas & C. P. Ry. v. Curry, 6 Kan. App. 561, 51 Pac. 576 (to issue annual pass).

Massachusetts: Fay v. Guynon, 131 Mass. 31.

Nebraska: Wittenberg v. Mollyneaux,

from such breaches must be recovered in such an action, since no further action will lie for such breaches.[357]

If, however, there has been such a breach of the contract as to destroy the whole purpose of it, so that no future performance is possible if the object of the agreement is to be preserved, entire damages may be recovered.[358] * The difficulty is to determine in what cases the contract is entire. The question was first presented on contracts to pay debts by instalments. Debt was then the only form of action to recover a sum certain; and it was held that on a bond or other contract to pay divers sums on divers days, no action of debt would lie until all the days were past.[359] So stood the law until the reign of Elizabeth, when the decision in Slade's case introduced the action of assumpsit into general practice.[360] The rule was then modified as regards the action of assumpsit, and in cases of money payable by instalments, the plaintiff was allowed to proceed upon the first default; but it was still held that the judgment was a full satisfaction, and the plaintiff therefore recovered damages for all the prospective breaches.[361] This latter rule in regard to assumpsit was further modified by a decision made in the reign of Charles II, when, in an action on an award to pay several sums at several times, the court held that an action might be brought for each sum when due, and that the plaintiff should recover damages accordingly, and have a new action as the other sums became

59 Neb. 203, 80 N. W. 824 (not to use property sold as a hotel for two years).

New York: Wharton v. Winch, 140 N. Y. 287, 35 N. E. 589; Cummins v. Hanson, 10 Daly, 493 (to board with plaintiff for a term).

[357] *Florida:* Griffing Bros. Co. v. Winfield, 53 Fla. 589, 43 So. 687.

Illinois: Crabtree v. Hagenbaugh, 25 Ill. 233, 79 Am. Dec. 324.

[358] *Maine:* Sutherland v. Wyer, 67 Me. 64.

Massachusetts: Amos v. Oakley, 131 Mass. 413; Parker v. Russell, 133 Mass. 74; R. H. White Co. v. Jerome H. Remick & Co., 198 Mass. 41, 84 N. E. 113.

Michigan: Mott v. Penoyar, 153 Mich. 273, 116 N. W. 1110.

New Hampshire: Lamoreaux v. Rolfe, 36 N. H. 33.

New York: Howard v. Daly, 61 N. Y. 362, 19 Am. Rep. 285.

North Carolina: Wilkinson v. Dunbar, 149 N. C. 20, 62 S. E. 748.

Vermont: Royalton v. Royalton & W. T. Co., 14 Vt. 311; Remelee v. Hall, 31 Vt. 582, 76 Am. Dec. 140.

[359] Fitzh. Nat. B. 131; Taylor v. Foster, Cro. Eliz. 807; Milles v. Milles, Cro. Car. 241.

[360] 4 Co. 92b.

[361] Beckwith v. Nott, Cro. Jac. 504.

due, *toties quoties*.[362] The rule in debt, however, appears to have remained unaltered.[363] So stands the matter in regard to agreements for the payment of money at specific future periods. In New York the rule which enforces the indivisibility of entire demands has been applied to open accounts for goods sold; and it has been held that the whole of such an account must be recovered, if at all, in one suit.[364] But in Massachusetts the doctrine of this case has been denied.[365] **

In any case of continuing contract, an absolute refusal by one party to go on with the contract when the time has arrived for him to perform, or after part performance, constitutes an entire breach of the contract.[366] If there is an entire breach, all damages prospective as well as past, must be recovered in the one action; the plaintiff, failing to obtain entire damages in his first suit, cannot maintain a later action.[367]

§ 636h. Contract to repair.

* The question becomes more complicated when we approach the consideration of agreements to do specific acts at various periods. In a case in New York,[368] where the defendant had covenanted with the plaintiff to keep a certain gate in repair, and to use common care in shutting it when passing and repassing, it was held that if the gate was left unrepaired or open, the defendant would be responsible in an action on the covenant, and that the true measure of damages would be the amount of the plaintiff's loss by the breach proved; that for every second breach a fresh action would lie; that a refusal to rebuild the gate did not amount to a total and final breach of

[362] Cooke *v.* Whorwood, 2 Saund. 337.
[363] Rudder *v.* Price, 1 H. Bl. 547.
[364] Guernsey *v.* Carver, 8 Wend. (N. Y.) 492, 24 Am. Dec. 60; Bendernagle *v.* Cocks, 19 Wend. (N. Y.) 207, 32 Am. Dec. 448, n.; Clark *v.* Jones, 1 Denio (N. Y.), 516, 43 Am. Dec. 706.
[365] Badger *v.* Titcomb, 15 Pick. (Mass.) 409.
[366] *Maine:* Sutherland *v.* Wyer, 67 Me. 64.
Massachusetts: Mullaly *v.* Austin, 97 Mass. 30.

New Hampshire: Lamoreaux *v.* Rolfe, 36 N. H. 33.
Vermont: Parker *v.* McKannon, 76 Vt. 96, 56 Atl. 311.
[367] *Maine:* Fales *v.* Hemenway, 64 Me. 373.
Massachusetts: Parker *v.* Russell, 133 Mass. 74.
[368] Crain *v.* Beach, 2 Barb. 120, and s. c. on appeal, Beach *v.* Crain, 2 N. Y. 86; and see, also, Fish *v.* Folley, 6 Hill (N. Y.), 54.

the covenant, nor could the damages recovered in a suit brought for one breach be presumed to have been given as a compensation for the non-performance of the covenant through all future time, so as to bar further suits.[369] ** In Keith v. Hinkston [370] it was held that on breach of a contract to keep a "switch or spur" in good repair, and to furnish cars for transportation, the plaintiff could only recover for the damage already sustained. But it has been held that all the breaches which have actually taken place must be embraced in the first suit; and that even if they are not, a second suit will not lie for them.[371]

§ 636i. To support.

Where a contract has been made to support the plaintiff for life, or a bond given conditioned to furnish the plaintiffs their support during their natural lives, a complete failure to provide for the plaintiff according to the obligation, amounts to a total breach and full and final damages may be recovered.[372] So where the plaintiff was induced to take care of a paralytic old man till his death, by his promise to "provide for her, and give her full and plenty after he was gone," she was allowed to recover such a reasonable sum, ascertained by the annuity tables or otherwise, as would provide her with an annuity which would keep her in her condition of life, relieved from the necessity of work,[373] or in other words, "such an amount as, with its interest, will give a sufficient support for life, leaving nothing at death." [374] In analogy with contracts to provide for support, it has been held in Alabama that a refusal by a college to permit the plaintiff to enjoy the benefit of a permanent

[369] Acc., Phelps v. New Haven & N. Co., 43 Conn. 453. But contra, Erie & P. R. R. v. Johnson, 101 Pa. 555.

[370] 9 Bush (Ky.), 283.

[371] Bristowe v. Fairclough, 1 M. & G. 143; Pinney v. Barnes, 17 Conn. 420; Colvin v. Corwin, 15 Wend. (N. Y.) 557; Bendernagle v. Cocks, 19 Wend. (N. Y.) 207.

[372] Maine: Philbrook v. Burgess, 52 Me. 271, 83 Am. Dec. 509; Fales v. Hemenway, 64 Me. 373.

Massachusetts: Canada v. Canada, 6 Cush. 15; Amos v. Oakley, 131 Mass.

413; Parker v. Russell, 133 Mass. 74.

New York: Schell v. Plumb, 55 N. Y. 592; Shaffer v. Lee, 8 Barb. 413; Empie v. Empie, 35 App. Div. 51, 54 N. Y. Supp. 402.

Oregon: Tippin v. Ward, 5 Ore. 450.

But unless the defendant's conduct was such as to put an end entirely to the contract, recovery can be had only for a partial breach. Fay v. Guynon, 131 Mass. 31.

[373] Thompson v. Stevens, 71 Pa. 161.

[374] Freeman v. Fogg, 82 Me. 408.

scholarship which he had purchased, by denying him the right to appoint a pupil, is a total breach.[375]

§ 636j. Fluctuations in value during contract: Masterton v. The Mayor.

There is another class of cases, namely, where the contract covers a long space of time, and during that period the services and commodities which enter into the cost of performance have fluctuated in value. Thus in a case in New York, which we have already had occasion to notice in reference to another branch of this subject,[376] the plaintiff, in 1836, agreed to furnish and deliver marble to build a city hall, at successive periods in five successive years. In 1837 the defendants refused to receive any more. The suit was brought before, but the trial did not take place till after the period for performance had elapsed, and it was shown that the difference between the cost of the marble and the contract price, which was the measure of damages, had fluctuated considerably in the five years. On this state of facts the circuit judge charged, that "in fixing damages to be allowed the plaintiffs, the jury were to take things as they were *at the time the work was suspended*, and not allow for any increased benefit they would have received from the subsequent fall of wages or subsequent circumstances." And of this opinion was the majority of the court, on a motion for a new trial. Nelson, C. J., who delivered the leading opinion, said:

"It has been argued that, inasmuch as the furnishing of the marble would have run through a period of five years—of which about one year and a half only had expired at the time of the suspension—the benefits which the party might have realized from the execution of the contract must necessarily be speculative and conjectural; the court and jury having no certain data upon which to make the estimate. If it were necessary to make the estimate upon any such basis, the argument would be decisive of the present claim; but in my judgment no such necessity exists. Where the contract, as in this case, is broken before the arrival of the time for full performance, and the op-

---

[375] Howard College v. Turner, 71 Ala. 429, 46 Am. Rep. 326.

[376] Masterton v. Mayor of Brooklyn, 7 Hill (N. Y.), 61, 42 Am. Dec. 38.

posite party elects to consider it in that light, *the market price on the day of the breach* is to govern in the assessment of damages. *In other words, the damages are to be settled and ascertained according to the existing state of the market at the time the cause of action arose, and not at the time fixed for full performance.* The basis upon which to estimate the damages, therefore, is just as fixed and easily ascertained in cases like the present as in actions predicated upon a failure to perform at the day."

And Bronson, J., said:

"There may have been fluctuations in the prices of labor and materials between the day of the breach and the time when the contract was to have been fully performed, and this makes the question upon which my brethren are not agreed. I concur in opinion with the chief justice, that such fluctuations in prices should not be taken into the account in ascertaining the amount of damages, but that the court and jury should be governed entirely by the state of things which existed at the time the contract was broken. This is the most plain and simple rule; it will best preserve the analogies of the law, and will be as likely as any other to do substantial justice to both parties."

Beardsley, J., however, dissented on this point, saying:

"The plaintiffs were not bound to wait till the period had elapsed for the complete performance of the agreement, nor to make successive offers of performance, in order to recover all their damages. They might regard the contract as broken up so far as to absolve them from making further efforts to perform, and give them a right to recover full damages as for a total breach. I am not prepared to say that the plaintiffs might not have brought successive suits on this covenant, had they from time to time made repeated offers to perform on their part, which were refused by the defendants; but this the plaintiffs were not bound to do. There can be no serious difficulty in assessing damages according to the principles which have been stated. The contract was made in 1836, and, according to the testimony, about five years would have been a reasonable time for its execution. That time has gone by. The expense of executing the contract must necessarily depend upon the prices of labor and materials. If prices fluctuated during the period in question, that may be shown by testimony. In this respect there is no need of resorting to conjecture; for all the data necessary to form a correct estimate of the entire expense of executing the contract can now be furnished by witnesses.

"If the cause had been brought to trial before the time for completing the contract expired, it would have been impracticable to make an accurate assessment of the damages. This is no reason, however, why the injured party should not have his damages, although the difficulty in making a just assessment in such a case has been deemed a sufficient ground for decreeing specific performance. No rule which will be absolutely certain to do justice between the parties can be laid down for such a case. Some time must be taken arbitrarily, at which prices are to be ascertained and estimated, and the day of the breach of the contract, or of the commencement of the suit, should perhaps be adopted under such circumstances. But we need not, in the present case, express any opinion on that point. No conjectural estimate is required to ascertain what would have been the expense of a complete execution of this contract; but the state of the market in respect to prices is now susceptible of explicit and intelligible proof; and where that is so, it seems to me unsuitable to adopt an arbitrary period, especially as the estimate of damages must, in any event. be somewhat conjectural." [377]

So in a case in Alabama,[378] where the plaintiff had agreed to let the defendants have all the pine timber on his lands, suitable for good lumber, the defendants to saw it into lumber, sell it as soon as they could, and pay the plaintiff one-fifth of the gross proceeds of the lumber sold and collected by them, it was held that for the breach of this contract by the defendant in not sawing all the lumber, but one action lay, in which, notwithstanding the period allowed for the performance had not expired at the time of the breach, he was entitled to the damages resulting from the prospective as well as the actual failure, to be assessed on the basis of value at the time of the breach.

In Shaffer v. Lee,[379] Hand, J., said of the case of Masterton v.

[377] The rule laid down by the majority of the court was followed in New York & H. R. R. v. Story, 6 Barb. (N. Y.) 419.

[378] Fail v. McRee, 36 Ala. 61.

[379] 8 Barb. (N. Y.) 412.

The Mayor, "As I understand the opinions delivered, all the judges considered the plaintiff entitled to recover entire and final damages for the non-fulfilment." And it is to be noticed that this was the only question actually before the court for decision. That part of the charge in the trial court quoted above was favorable to the defendant, and as the plaintiff did not except to it, the question of its correctness, upon which, as we have seen, the judges differed in opinion, was not directly involved in the decision.

The dictum of the majority of the judges in Masterton v. The Mayor has been followed in a few States only,[380] and appears not to represent the present law in New York.[381]

§ 636k. Goodrich v. Hubbard.

The contract may be sued upon either after the time for its performance has expired, or while it is still running. In the case just cited the plaintiff sued at once on breach. In a Michigan case [382] a logging contract provided that the logger should haul the logs during the winter next ensuing if the weather should permit; if the weather should be unfavorable, the contract was to be continued to another winter. Owing to the weather, the logger postponed what remained undone the first winter; but the defendants prevented complete performance by removing the logs before the next winter. In the ensuing winter the logger could have delivered the logs for half the contract rate, being much less than it would have cost him the first winter. It was held that he was entitled to recover the difference between the contract price and what it would have cost him to deliver the logs during the second winter.[383] In this Michigan case the

---

[380] *Alabama:* Fail v. McRee, 36 Ala. 61, *supra.*

Florida: Sullivan v. McMillan, 26 Fla. 543, 8 So. 450.

Illinois: James H. Rice Co. v. Penn P. G. Co., 88 Ill. App. 407.

Louisiana: Seaton v. Second Municipality, 3 La. Ann. 44.

The question was left open in *Nebraska:* Nebraska Bridge S. & L. Co. v. Owen Conway & Sons, 127 Ia. 237, 103 N. W. 122.

[381] Windmuller v. Pope, 107 N. Y. 674, 14 N. E. 436; Todd v. Gamble, 148 N. Y. 382, 42 N. E. 982; St. Regis P. Co. v. Santa Clara L. Co., 173 N. Y. 149, 65 N. E. 967.

[382] Goodrich v. Hubbard, 51 Mich. 62, 16 N. W. 232.

[383] *Acc.,* Leo Austrian & Co. v. Springer, 94 Mich. 343, 54 N. W. 50, 34 Am. St. Rep. 350; Greenwood v. Davis, 106 Mich. 230, 64 N. W. 266.

point at issue was whether the plaintiff's recovery must be the contract price, less the cost of performance, during the first or the second winter, because although the time of performance was the second winter, the time when the defendants prevented performance was earlier. The Supreme Court of Michigan said: [384]

"It is objected that the profits must be ascertained on the day of the breach; that to attempt to ascertain the damages in any other way would be speculative, uncertain, and conjectural. The case of Masterton v. Mayor of Brooklyn is cited as authority, but an examination of that case shows that the court made the market price on the day of the breach of the contract to govern in assessment of damages to depend upon the opposite party having elected to consider the contract broken before the arrival of the time for full performance. The facts of this case were somewhat exceptional, there being a claim for a breach of a contract running through a period of five years, of which about one year and a half only had expired, the court and jury having no certain data upon which to estimate the profits for the remaining three years and a half.[385] That case is not applicable here, where the election of the plaintiff to consider the contract broken before arrival of the time for its full performance does not appear; and upon the facts found it does appear that there are certain data for estimating the damages found. The consideration of profits cannot be separated in this case from the circumstances under which the work was to be done, and the prevention of which constitutes the breach making the defendants liable.

"There is no element of uncertainty regarding the profits the plaintiff would have realized from the performance of the contract, and which must govern in the estimate of damages. There are no contingencies modifying or taking the case out of the rule laid down by this court in the case of Burrell v. New York & Saginaw Solar Salt Co." [386]

§ 6361. Probable future expense of performing.

In a case in Vermont a similar rule was laid down. The de-

[384] 51 Mich. 62, 70, per Sherwood, J.

[385] This seems to be a mistake. See statement of the case above.

[386] 14 Mich. 34.

fendants, a bridge company, had, in September, 1830, agreed with the plaintiffs to keep a bridge in repair for twelve years, on the plaintiffs paying twenty-five dollars every year. The plaintiffs paid the annual sum until 1838, when the defendants ceased to repair; and the judge charged at the trial, that the jury "should limit their inquiries to the time when both the parties ceased in fact to act under the contract." But on motion for a new trial the court said: "The rule of damages in this case should have been, to give the plaintiffs the difference between what they were to pay the defendants, and the probable expense of performing the contract, and thus assess the entire damages for the remaining twelve years." [387]

In Roper v. Johnson [388] the defendant agreed to deliver coal to the plaintiff for a certain price during the months of May, June, July, and August. In June, the defendants refused to deliver any more coal; suit was brought in July, and the trial took place in August, before the expiration of the time for performance. The price of coal was continually rising. A verdict was found, based on the actual price of coal to the time of trial, and a *probable further rise in price during the remainder of August.* This verdict was sustained by the Court of Common Pleas. Brett, J., said: "When you come to estimate the damages, it must be by the difference between the contract price and the market price at the day or days appointed for performance, and not at the time of breach." The defendant might, however, reduce these damages by showing that the plaintiff should have secured another contract at the time of breach.

§ 636m. General conclusions.

It will be seen from the foregoing that two extreme rules have been laid down: one, that in calculating the cost of performance, the market rates at the time of breach are to govern; the other, that the market rates down to the time of trial, and even the *probable future course of the market* (if the time of performance extends beyond the time of trial), may be con-

---

[387] Royalton v. R. & W. Turnpike Co., 14 Vt. 311. *Acc.*, McCall v. Icks, 107 Wis. 232, 83 N. W. 300.

[388] L. R. 8 C. P. 167; *acc.*, Brown v. Muller, L. R. 7 Ex. 319, 323, per Kelley, C. B.; Leigh v. Patterson, 8 Taunt. 540.

sidered. Under the first rule, the recovery would not be affected by the time selected for the trial; under the second rule, if the trial took place in advance of the time fixed for performance the measure of recovery would be dependent partly on rates existing at the time of the breach and partly upon conjecture as to the future course of the market. If the trial were postponed, for the conjectural rates would be substituted the now ascertained market rates. The case may easily be supposed of a new trial for error, in which second trial it will appear that the conjectural rates allowed in the first trial were not justified by the actual course of the market. Of course in all such cases, the *measure of damages* is always the same; but the actual recovery, as we have seen, may be more or less, according as the time of trial is earlier or later. But the allowance of conjectural rates, or the consideration of the probable future course of the market, seems to be in conflict with all the rules requiring certainty of proof. It would be almost impossible to foretell, with that degree of certainty required of a plaintiff in proving the amount of his ' damages, that the price of performance would decrease by any certain amount during the period fixed for performance; and, on the other hand, after the plaintiff had shown what the cost of performance would be, reckoned according to circumstances at the time of trial, it would be as difficult for the defendant to show that a change would take place. The principle requiring certainty of proof would lead to the rule that damages on account of all work to be done after *the date of the trial* should in the ordinary case be estimated according to the state of affairs *at the time of trial*. If, however, the period fixed for the complete performance of the contract has passed before the trial, there is no uncertainty as to the actual cost of performance, as Beardsley, J., points out in his opinion in the case of Masterton *v.* The Mayor. The contract price and the exact cost of performance can be shown, and the difference between them is the measure of damages. This is not affected by the fact that at the time of breach the amount could not be certainly known. In many cases circumstances occurring after the injury determine the amount of damages. The opinion of the majority of the court in Masterton *v.* The

Mayor in this respect seems to have been based upon the old notion, now abandoned, that no circumstances occurring after the injury can be resorted to for aid in fixing the amount of loss.[389]

Perhaps, on principle, a distinction should be made among agreements of this class. If the contract is, in its nature, capable of division, as to deliver the crops of a farm for several successive years, and if the periods have arrived before suit brought, there seems no reason why a separate action may not be brought for every refusal to perform, nor why the damages should not be estimated as at every period fixed for performance.[390]   But where the contract is intrinsically indivisible, as in the case of a building contract, for instance, one refusal may properly be considered as an absolute breach; and then we have presented the question involved in Masterton v. The Mayor. If the periods specified in the contract have not arrived before the trial of the cause, any effort to fix the rights of the parties at those various times must be mere matter of conjecture; and *probable expense* is neither a precise nor a safe direction for a jury.

§ 636n. Mutual covenants.

The question whether mutual covenants in a contract are dependent or independent also involves the entirety of the contract. In a recent case in the United States Circuit Court of Appeals [391] the question arose upon the construction of a lease by a railroad company. By this contract (renewable forever) the company leased to H. a tract of land near the

---

[389] § 85.

[390] Brown v. Muller, L. R. 7 Ex. 319.
  In England, it has been several times held in chancery, in regard to future agreements, that the difficulty of arriving at any true rule of damages is a good ground for a decree for specific performance. Buxton v. Lister, 3 Atk. 383, and Taylor v. Neville, cited therein; Ball v. Coggs, 1 Bro. Parl. Cas. 140; and Adderley v. Dixon, 1 Sim. & Stuart, 607. In this last case the vice-chancellor said: "The profit

upon the contract being to depend upon future events, cannot be correctly estimated in damages, where the calculation must proceed upon conjecture. Damages might be no complete remedy, being to be calculated merely by conjecture." This language seems to imply that, at law, the whole period of the contract would be inquired into, on the principle of the Vermont decision.

[391] Union Pacific Ry. v. Travelers' Ins. Co., 83 Fed. 676, 49 U. S. App. 752, 28 C. C. A. 1.

center of a town, H. agreeing to construct upon it a hotel and station, the company agreeing to stop all passenger trains passing at reasonable hours, a sufficient time to allow the passengers to take their meals. It also covenanted not to permit the use of its property to injure the business of the hotel. After a time the trains ceased to stop sufficiently long to comply with the contract. The value of the improvements put upon the leased premises was $40,000 and the court below held that the measure of damages caused by the breach was the value of these improvements. On appeal it was agreed that this was the proper measure on the grounds that the covenants of the lessor to stop its trains for meals, and not to permit the use of its property to injure the business of the hotel, and the covenant of the lessor to keep a first-class hotel were mutually dependent covenants, each of which went to the whole consideration; second, that the continuing breach by the lessor gave the lessee the right to recover damages as for a total breach of the entire contract; and, third, that the lessee was entitled to recover whatever it had expended in preparing to fulfil its part of the contract—which was alleged to be more than the estimated value of the hotel. But the Circuit Court of Appeals ordered a new trial, holding that the true measure of damages was the difference between what the lessee earned after breach, and what it would have earned if the contract had been fully performed by the railroad company.

In such cases the test is whether the covenants go to the whole consideration on both sides. If they do, then "they are mutual conditions," "the one precedent to the other." If not, the damages for any breach may be separately assessed.[392] In the first case, the injured party may treat the contract as broken in its entirety, and recover damages for a total breach.[393] But in the second case, the contract is still binding upon

[392] *United States:* Lawler v. Bangs, 2 Wall. 728, 736, 17 L. ed. 768.

England: Boone v. Eyric, 1 H. Bl. 273; Ritchie v. Anderson, 10 East. 295; Stavers v. Cushing, 3 Bing. N. C. 355.

[393] *Illinois:* Leopold v. Salkey, 89 Ill. 412, 31 Am. Rep. 93, *n.*

Iowa: Richmond v. The D. & S. C. R. R., 40 Ia., 264 275.

Massachusetts: Parker v. Russell, 133 Mass. 74.

Michigan: Grand R. & B. C. R. R. v. Van Dusen, 29 Mich. 431.

the injured party, and he can only recover his actual damages, the *damnum emergens*, or the *lucrum cessans*.[394] It should be observed, however, that rules for determining whether covenants are dependent or independent "are merely aids in ascertaining the intention of the minds of those who execute the instruments. Often the intention is so clear that rules are of no service."

[394] *United States:* Central A. Co. v. Buchanan, 73 Fed. 1006, 43 U. S. App. 265, 275, 20 C. C. A. 33.

Missouri: Butler v. Manny, 52 Mo. 497, 506; Turner v. Mellier, 59 Mo. 526, 536.

New York: Pepper v. Haight, 20 Barb. 429, 440.

Pennsylvania: Obermyer v. Nichols, 6 Binney, 159, 164.

England: Pordage v. Cole, 1 Saund. 320; Campbell v. Jones, 6 T. R. 570, 573; Surplice v. Farnsworth, 7 Man. & Gr. 576, 584.

CHAPTER XXVIII

BREACH OF PROMISE OF MARRIAGE

§ 637. Exceptional nature of the action.

*The action for breach of promise of marriage, as has been already said, though nominally an action founded on the breach of an agreement, presents a striking exception to the general rules which govern contracts. This action is given as an indemnity to the injured party for the loss she has sustained, and has been always held to embrace the injury to the feelings, affections, and wounded pride, as well as the loss of marriage.[1] From the nature of the case, it has been found impossible to fix the amount of compensation by any precise rule; and, as in tort, the measure of damages is a question for the sound discretion of the jury in each particular instance,[2]

[1] *Arkansas:* Collins v. Mack, 31 Ark. 684.

Maine: Tobin v. Shaw, 45 Me. 331, 71 Am. Dec. 547; Tyler v. Salley, 82 Me. 128.

Michigan: Vanderpool v. Richardson, 52 Mich. 336, 17 N. W. 936.

Missouri: Wilbur v. Johnson, 58 Mo. 600.

New York: Wells v. Padgett, 8 Barb. 323.

North Carolina: Allen v. Baker, 86 N. C. 91, 41 Am. Rep. 444.

Texas: Daggett v. Wallace, 75 Tex. 352, 13 S. W. 49, 16 Am. St. Rep. 908.

[2] *Georgia:* Parker v. Forehand, 99 Ga. 743, 28 S. E. 400.

Illinois: Fidler v. McKinley, 21 Ill. 308.

Iowa: Rine v. Rater, 108 Ia. 61, 78 N. W. 835.

Kansas: Kennedy v. Rodgers, 2 Kan. App. 764, 44 Pac. 47.

Maine: Tobin v. Shaw, 45 Me. 331.

Missouri: Green v. Spencer, 3 Mo.

1272

subject, of course, to the general restriction that a verdict influenced by prejudice, passion, or corruption, will not be allowed to stand.[3] ** "Damages in this action," said Mr. Justice E. D. Smith, in a case in the New York Court of Appeals, "have never been limited to the simple rule governing actions upon simple contracts for the payment of money."[4] The injury is accompanied by circumstances affording no definite standard by which the amount lost can be measured, and from the necessity of the case the jury must be left to

318, 26 Am. Dec. 672; Hill *v.* Maupin, 3 Mo. 323.

Nebraska: Schreckengast *v.* Ealy, 16 Neb. 510, 20 N. W. 853.

New Jersey: Coryell *v.* Colbaugh, 1 N. J. L. 77, 1 Am. Dec. 192; Stout *v.* Prall, 1 N. J. L. 79, 1 Am. Dec. 193.

New York: Southard *v.* Rexford, 6 Cow. 254.

Rhode Island: Drury *v.* Merrill, 20 R. I. 2, 36 Atl. 835.

South Carolina: Torre *v.* Summers, 2 Nott & M'C. 267, 10 Am. Dec. 597.

Wisconsin: Olson *v.* Solverson, 71 Wis. 663, 38 N. W. 329.

[3] *Connecticut:* Hattin *v.* Chapman, 46 Conn. 607 (a very strong case).

Illinois: Richmond *v.* Roberts, 98 Ill. 472.

Indiana: Eve *v.* Rodgers, 12 Ind. App. 623, 40 N. E. 25.

In the following cases the court refused to set aside a verdict: Geiger *v.* Payne, 102 Iowa, 581, 69 N. W. 554 (verdict for $16,000; circumstances of aggravation, defendant worth from $50,000 to $75,000); Salchert *v.* Reinig, 135 Wis. 194, 115 N. W. 132 (verdict for $10,000; circumstances of aggravation); McKenzie *v.* Gray, 143 Ia. 112, 120 N. W. 71 (verdict for $8,000; breach after long engagement, defendant worth $75,000); Daggett *v.* Wallace, 75 Tex. 352, 13 S. W. 49, 16 Am. St. Rep. 908 (verdict for $7,500; circumstances of aggravation); Musselman *v.* Barker, 26 Neb. 737, 42 N. W. 759

(verdict for $7,000; circumstances of aggravation); Fisher *v.* Kenyon, 56 Wash. 8, 104 Pac. 1127 (verdict for $6,000); Kerns *v.* Hagenbuchle, 60 N. Y. Super. Ct. 222, 17 N. Y. Supp. 367 (verdict for $5,000; circumstances of aggravation); Douglas *v.* Gausman, 68 Ill. 170 (verdict for $3,600; defendant worth $25,000); Brown *v.* Odill, 104 Tenn. 250, 56 S. W. 840, 78 Am. St. Rep. 914 (verdict for $2,800; defendant worth less than $10,000, no special aggravating circumstances); Mainz *v.* Lederer, 21 R. I. 370, 374, 43 Atl. 876 (verdict for $1,200; circumstances of aggravation, defendant worth $75,000).

In the following cases the court set aside a verdict: McCarty *v.* Heryford, 125 Fed. 46 (verdict for $22,500; defendant worth $50,000, circumstances of mitigation); Johnson *v.* Levy, 122 La. 118, 47 So. 422 (verdict for $20,000); Kolsch *v.* Jewell, 21 App. Div. 581, 48 N. Y. Supp. 527 (verdict for $7,500; plaintiff sewing machine teacher, defendant received salary of $30 a week; circumstances of aggravation; verdict cut down to $2,500); Kellett *v.* Robie, 99 Wis. 303, 47 N. W. 781 (verdict for $3,500; defendant worth $6,000, no circumstances of aggravation).

In Hooker *v.* Phillippe, 26 Ind. App. 501, 60 N. E. 167, a verdict for one cent damages was set aside as inadequate.

[4] Thorn *v.* Knapp, 42 N. Y. 474, 483, 1 Am. Rep. 561.

exercise a large discretion in arriving at the amount. The verdict will not be interfered with unless it is obviously and grossly excessive, although in a sufficiently flagrant case the court may set the verdict aside.[5]

§ 637a. Exemplary damages.

In jurisdictions in which exemplary damages are allowed, it is almost universally agreed that exemplary damages may be allowed in actions for breach of promise of marriage where the proper circumstances are shown to justify such damages.[6] In a few States, however, the courts appear to refuse to allow exemplary damages.[7] As has been seen, in no other action for breach of contract can such damages be allowed; and if the form of action be regarded rather than the substance, no such damages could be allowed in this case. In every case, of course, a proper foundation must be laid for the recovery of exemplary damages, or the recovery will be limited to compensatory damages.[8]

[5] *Connecticut:* Smith *v.* Hall, 69 Conn. 651, 38 Atl. 386.
Michigan: Hahiat *v.* Codde, 106 Mich. 387, 6 N. W. 194.
Minnesota: Hahn *v.* Bettingen, 84 Minn. 512, 88 N. W. 10.
Tennessee: Goodall *v.* Thurman, 1 Head, 209.
Wisconsin: Olson *v.* Solverson, 71 Wis. 663, 38 N. W. 329.
England: Gough *v.* Farr, 1 Y. & J. 477.
[6] *California:* Moore *v.* Hopkins, 83 Cal. 270, 23 Pac. 318, 17 Am. St. Rep. 248 (*semble*).
Illinois: Jacoby *v.* Stark, 205 Ill. 34, 68 N. E. 557; Churan *v.* Sebasta, 131 Ill. App. 330.
Indiana: Kurtz *v.* Frank, 76 Ind. 594, 40 Am. Rep. 275; Hughes *v.* Nolte, 7 Ind. App. 526, 34 N. E. 725.
Michigan: McPherson *v.* Ryan, 59 Mich. 33; Roberts *v.* Druillard, 123 Mich. 286, 82 N. W. 49.
Minnesota: Tamke *v.* Vangsnes, 72 Minn. 236, 75 N. W. 217.
New Jersey: Coryell *v.* Colbaugh, Coxe (1 N. J. L.), 77.

New York: Johnson *v.* Jenkins, 24 N. Y. 252; Thorn *v.* Knapp, 42 N. Y. 474, 1 Am. Rep. 561; Chellis *v.* Chapman, 125 N. Y. 214, 26 N. E. 308, 11 L. R. A. 784, 21 Am. St. Rep. 736; Wolters *v.* Schultz, 1 Misc. 196, 21 N. Y. Supp. 768; Jacobs *v.* Sire, 4 Misc. 398, 23 N. Y. Supp. 1063; Kerns *v.* Hagenbuchle, 60 N. Y. Super. Ct. 222, 17 N. Y. Supp. 367.
Ohio: Duvall *v.* Fuhrman, 3 Ohio C. Ct. 305, 2 Oh. Circ. Dec. 174.
Oregon: Kelley *v.* Highfield, 15 Ore. 277, 14 Pac. 744.
Pennsylvania: Baldy *v.* Stratton, 11 Pa. 316.
Texas: Clark *v.* Reese, 26 Tex. Civ. App. 619, 64 S. W. 783.
[7] Trammell *v.* Vaughan, 158 Mo. 214, 59 S. W. 79, 51 L. R. A. 854, 81 Am. St. Rep. 302.
In States where no exemplary damages are allowed in any case, the action for breach of promise cannot constitute an exception: Harrison *v.* Swift, 13 All. (Mass.) 144.
[8] *California:* Moore *v.* Hopkins, 83

§ 638. Loss of marriage.

In estimating compensatory damages for breach of promise of marriage the jury may allow compensation for loss of the advantages of the marriage; the reasonable expectation of sharing in the husband's wealth, the permanent home and advantageous establishment, and the social standing which might follow the marriage.[9] For the purpose of properly estimating the advantages of the proposed marriage it is admissible to show the pecuniary position of the defendant at the time of the breach of the contract.[10] This can be done by proving the de-

---

Cal. 270, 23 Pac. 318, 17 Am. St. Rep. 248.

Illinois: LaPorte *v.* Wallace, 89 Ill. App. 517.

[9] *Connecticut:* Smith *v.* Hall, 69 Conn. 651, 38 Atl. 386.

Illinois: Jacoby *v.* Stark, 205 Ill. 34, 68 N. E. 557.

Iowa: Royal *v.* Smith, 40 Ia. 615; Vierling *v.* Binder, 113 Ia. 337, 85 N. W. 621; McKenzie *v.* Gray, 143 Ia. 112, 120 N. W. 71; Lauer *v.* Banning, 131 N. W. 783.

Kansas: Kennedy *v.* Rogers, 2 Kan. App. 764, 44 Pac. 47.

Kentucky: Grubbs *v.* Pence, 24 Ky. L. Rep. 2183, 73 S. W. 785.

Maine: Lawrence *v.* Cooke, 56 Me. 187, 96 Am. Dec. 443.

Massachusetts: Coolidge *v.* Neat, 129 Mass. 146.

Michigan: Goddard *v.* Westcott, 82 Mich. 180, 46 N. W. 242; Rutter *v.* Collins, 103 Mich. 143, 62 N. W. 267; Spencer *v.* Simmons, 160 Mich. 292, 125 N. W. 9.

Minnesota: Tamke *v.* Vangsnes, 72 Minn. 236, 75 N. W. 217.

Missouri: Trammell *v.* Vaughan, 158 Mo. 214, 59 S. W. 79, 51 L. R. A. 854, 81 Am. St. Rep. 302.

Montana: Dupont *v.* McAdow, 6 Mont. 226, 9 Pac. 925.

Nebraska: Stratton *v.* Dole, 45 Neb. 472, 63 N. W. 875.

New York: Chellis *v.* Chapman, 125

N. Y. 214, 26 N. E. 308, 11 L. R. A. 784, 21 Am. St. Rep. 736.

North Carolina: Allen *v.* Baker, 86 N. C. 91, 41 Am. Rep. 444.

Rhode Island: Perkins *v.* Hersey, 1 R. I. 493.

Tennessee: Brown *v.* Odill, 104 Tenn. 250, 56 S. W. 840, 78 Am. St. Rep. 914.

England: James *v.* Biddington, 6 C. & P. 589.

[10] *Arkansas:* Collins *v.* Mack, 31 Ark. 684.

California: Reed *v.* Clark, 47 Cal. 194.

Illinois: Douglas *v.* Gausman, 68 Ill. 170; Richmond *v.* Roberts, 98 Ill. 472.

Indiana: Hunter *v.* Hatfield, 68 Ind. 416.

Iowa: Holloway *v.* Griffith, 32 Ia. 409, 7 Am. Rep. 208; McKenzie *v.* Gray, 143 Ia. 112, 120 N. W. 71.

Maine: Lawrence *v.* Cooke, 56 Me. 187.

Michigan: Miller *v.* Rosier, 31 Mich. 475; Bennett *v.* Bean, 42 Mich. 346, 4 N. W. 8, 36 Am. Rep. 442; McPherson *v.* Ryan, 59 Mich. 33, 26 N. W. 321.

Minnesota: Johnson *v.* Travis, 33 Minn. 231, 22 N. W. 624.

Missouri: Casey *v.* Gill, 154 Mo. 181, 55 S. W. 219.

New York: Kniffen *v.* McConnell, 30 N. Y. 285; Crosier *v.* Craig, 47 Hun, 83; Totten *v.* Read, 16 Daly, 282, 10 N. Y. Supp. 318, 32 N. Y. St. 46.

fendant's wealth by reputation [11] especially as this directly affects the social position which the plaintiff would have gained by the marriage.[12] In some States it is held not allowable to prove his ownership of any particular property, unless the marriage would have given the wife a legal interest in such property, as might happen in case of real estate in which she would get by the marriage an inchoate right of dower; [13] but in most States the actual value of his property may be shown.[14] No evidence of property coming to the defendant at a time subsequent to the breach is allowed to be given,[15] but evidence of facts happening after the breach which fix the value of the property accruing before the breach may be shown.[16] The social standing of the defendant may be put in evidence, to show the loss of social standing suffered by the plaintiff through the breach.[17]

North Carolina: Allen *v.* Baker, 86 N. C. 91, 41 Am. Rep. 444.

Ohio: Stribley *v.* Welz, 1 Ohio Dec. 621, 624, 8 Ohio C. Ct. 571.

Texas: Ortiz *v.* Navarro, 10 Tex. Civ. App. 195, 30 S. W. 581.

West Virginia: Dent *v.* Pickens, 34 W. Va. 240, 12 S. E. 698, 26 Am. St. Rep. 921.

Wisconsin: Olson *v.* Solveson, 71 Wis. 663, 38 N. W. 329; Salchert *v.* Reinig, 135 Wis. 194, 115 N. W. 132.

England: James *v.* Biddington, 6 C. & P. 589.

[11] *Nebraska:* Stratton *v.* Dole, 45 Neb. 472, 63 N. W. 875.

New Jersey: Smith *v.* Compton, 67 N. J. L. 548, 52 Atl. 386, 58 L. R. A. 480.

New York: Chellis *v.* Chapman, 125 N. Y. 214, 26 N. E. 308, 11 L. R. A. 784, 21 Am. St. Rep. 736.

[12] Chellis *v.* Chapman, 125 N. Y. 214, 26 N. E. 308, 11 L. R. A. 784, 21 Am. St. Rep. 736.

[13] *New Jersey:* Smith *v.* Compton, 67 N. J. L. 548, 52 Atl. 386, 58 L. R. A. 480.

New York: Kniffen *v.* McConnell,

30 N. Y. 285; Chellis *v.* Chapman, 125 N. Y. 214, 26 N. E. 308, 11 L. R. A. 784, 21 Am. St. Rep. 736.

See Kerfoot *v.* Marsden, 2 F. & F. 160.

[14] *Illinois:* Sprague *v.* Craig, 51 Ill. 288; Douglas *v.* Gausman, 68 Ill. 170.

Iowa: Rime *v.* Rater, 108 Ia. 61, 78 N. W. 835; Vierling *v.* Binder, 113 Ia. 337, 85 N. W. 621.

Vermont: Clark *v.* Hodges, 65 Vt. 273, 26 Atl. 726.

[15] In Vierling *v.* Binder, 113 Ia. 337, 85 N. W. 621, it seems to have been assumed that the plaintiff could not claim damages based on property acquired after the promise was made; and see to the same effect Dent *v.* Pickens, 34 W. Va. 240, 12 S. E. 698, 26 Am. St. Rep. 921.

[16] *Vermont:* Clark *v.* Hodges, 65 Vt. 273, 26 Atl. 726.

Washington: Fisher *v.* Kenyon, 56 Wash. 8, 104 Pac. 1127 (defendant's property at time of trial, a few months after breach, admissible to prove property at time of breach).

[17] Ortiz *v.* Navarro, 10 Tex. Civ. App. 195, 30 S. W. 581.

Evidence of the wealth of defendant's wife [18] or parent [19] cannot be shown; nor can he introduce evidence of his own poverty.[20]

§ 638a. Injury to affections.

The plaintiff is also allowed to recover damages for her wounded affections and loss of the comfort and companionship of a husband.[21] For the purpose of estimating loss of this sort evidence may be introduced of the existence of lack of feeling of affection for the defendant,[22] and of the plaintiff's grief at the termination of the engagement.[23] Compensation cannot be recovered for injury to the feelings of plaintiff's family and friends.[24]

§ 638b. Mental suffering.

The plaintiff may also recover compensation for mortification and shame caused by the termination of the engagement, distress of mind, disgrace and loss of standing in the community.[25] For the purpose of estimating this loss she may show the

[18] Crandall v. Quin, 51 N. Y. Super. Ct. 276.

[19] *Michigan:* Miller v. Rosea, 31 Mich. 475; Spencer v. Simmons, 160 Mich. 292, 125 N. W. 9.

New York: Aldis v. Stewart, 4 Misc. 389, 24 N. Y. Supp. 329, 53 N. Y. St. 518.

[20] Wilbur v. Johnson, 58 Mo. 600.

[21] *Georgia:* Parker v. Forehand, 99 Ga. 743, 28 S. E. 400.

Hawaii: Ayers v. Mahuka, 9 Haw. 377.

Iowa: Robinson v. Craver, 88 Ia. 381, 55 N. W. 492.

Kansas: Kennedy v. Rodgers, 2 Kan. App. 764, 44 Pac. 47.

Louisiana: Johnson v. Levy, 118 La. 447, 43 So. 46.

Maine: Lawrence v. Cooke, 56 Me. 187, 96 Am. Dec. 443.

Massachusetts: Coolidge v. Neat, 129 Mass. 146.

Michigan: Spencer v. Simmons, 160 Mich. 292, 125 N. W. 9.

Missouri: Trammell v. Vaughan, 158 Mo. 214, 59 S. W. 79, 51 L. R. A. 854, 81 Am. St. Rep. 302; Liese v. Meyer, 143 Mo. 547, 45 S. W. 282.

Montana: Dupont v. McAdow, 6 Mont. 226, 9 Pac. 925.

New York: Wolters v. Schultz, 1 Misc. 196, 21 N. Y. Supp. 768.

Rhode Island: Perkins v. Hersey, 1 R. I. 493.

Tennessee: Brown v. Odill, 104 Tenn. 250, 56 S. W. 840, 78 Am. St. Rep. 914.

[22] *Iowa:* Robinson v. Craver, 88 Ia. 381, 55 N. W. 492 (*semble*).

Michigan: Miller v. Rosea, 31 Mich. 475.

Montana: Dupont v. McAdow, 6 Mont. 226, 9 Pac. 925.

[23] *Michigan:* Bennett v. Beam, 42 Mich. 346, 4 N. W. 8, 36 Am. Rep. 442.

Texas: Ortiz v. Navarro, 10 Tex. Civ. App. 195, 30 S. W. 581.

[24] Bell v. Giberson, 30 N. Br. 10.

[25] *Georgia:* Parker v. Forehand, 99

length of time during which the engagement had subsisted,[26] and that knowledge of the engagement had been communicated to her friends.[27]

§ 638c. Consequential damages.

In addition to these elements of compensation the plaintiff may recover compensation for any damages suffered as a consequence of the breach of contract. For instance, the plaintiff may recover on the actual outlay in preparation for the marriage.[28] The plaintiff, if a woman, may also show that the engagement subsisted for so long a time that other suitors were discouraged from approaching her with offers of marriage and that she has therefore lost the opportunity of becoming engaged to others.[29] The fact, however, that at the defendant's solicitation she terminated an engagement with another suitor cannot be shown.[30] It has been held that injury to health caused by manual labor which, as defendant knew would be the case, plaintiff was compelled to undergo in order to support herself after the breach was chargeable to the defendant.[31]

Ga. 743, 28 S. E. 400; Graves v. Rivers, 123 Ga. 224, 51 S. E. 318.

Hawaii: Ayers v. Mahuka, 9 Haw. 377.

Iowa: Royal v. Smith, 40 Iowa, 615; Robinson v. Craver, 88 Iowa, 381, 55 N. W. 492; Rime v. Rater, 108 Iowa, 61, 78 N. W. 835.

Kansas: Kennedy v. Rodgers, 2 Kan. App. 764, 44 Pac. 47.

Kentucky: Grubbs v. Pence, 24 Ky. L. Rep. 2183, 73 S. W. 785.

Maine: Lawrence v. Cooke, 56 Me. 187, 96 Am. Dec. 443; Tyler v. Salley, 82 Me. 128, 19 Atl. 107.

Massachusetts: Coolidge v. Neat, 129 Mass. 146.

Michigan: Goddard v. Westcott, 82 Mich. 180, 46 N. W. 242; Rutter v. Collins, 103 Mich. 143, 62 N. W. 267.

Missouri: Trammell v. Vaughan, 158 Mo. 214, 59 S. W. 79, 51 L. R. A. 854, 81 Am. St. Rep. 302.

New York: Wolters v. Schultz, 1 Misc. 196, 21 N. Y. Supp. 768.

Tennessee: Brown v. Odill, 104 Tenn. 250, 56 S. W. 840, 78 Am. St. Rep. 914.

[26] Olmstead v. Hoy, 112 Ia. 349, 83 N. W. 1056.

[27] Reed v. Clark, 47 Cal. 194; Liebrandt v. Sorg, 133 Cal. 571, 65 Pac. 1098.

[28] *Illinois:* Dunlap v. Clark, 25 Ill. App. 573.

Iowa: Olmstead v. Hoy, 112 Ia. 349, 83 N. W. 1056.

Michigan: Goddard v. Westcott, 82 Mich. 180, 46 N. W. 242.

New York: Wolters v. Schultz, 1 Misc. 196, 21 N. Y. Supp. 768.

Texas: Glasscock v. Shell, 57 Tex. 215.

[29] Olmstead v. Hoy, 112 Iowa, 349, 83 N. W. 1056.

[30] Hahn v. Bettingen, 81 Minn. 91, 83 N. W. 467, 83 Am. St. Rep. 366.

[31] Duff v. Judson, 160 Mich. 386, 125 N. W. 371.

§ 639. Aggravation. Seduction under promise of marriage.

Circumstances which show that the injury was particularly serious may be shown in aggravation of damages. Thus it may be shown, in order to increase the damages, that the plaintiff was seduced by the defendant under promise of marriage [32]

[32] *Arkansas:* Collins *v.* Mack, 31 Ark. 684.
Connecticut: Hattin *v.* Chapman, 46 Conn. 607.
Georgia: Graves *v.* Rivers, 123 Ga. 224, 51 S. E. 318.
Illinois: Tubbs *v.* Van Kleek, 12 Ill. 446; Burnett *v.* Simpkins, 24 Ill. 264; Poehlmann *v.* Kertz, 105 Ill. App. 249; Churan *v.* Sebasta, 131 Ill. App. 330.
Indiana: Whalen *v.* Layman, 2 Blackf. 194, 18 Am. Dec. 157; King *v.* Kersey, 2 Ind. 402.
Indian Territory: Davis *v.* Pryor, 3 Ind. Ty. 396, 58 S. W. 660.
Iowa: Geiger *v.* Payne, 102 Ia. 581, 69 N. W. 554; Lauer *v.* Banning, 131 N. W. 783.
Louisiana: Smith *v.* Braun, 37 La. Ann. 225; Johnson *v.* Levy, 122 La. 118, 47 So. 422.
Maine: Tyler *v.* Salley, 82 Me. 128.
Maryland: Sauer *v.* Schulenberg, 33 Md. 288, 3 Am. Rep. 174.
Massachusetts: Paul *v.* Frazier, 3 Mass. 71, 3 Am. Dec. 95; Kelley *v.* Riley, 106 Mass. 339, 8 Am. Rep. 336.
Michigan: Bennett *v.* Beam, 42 Mich. 346, 4 N. W. 8, 36 Am. Rep. 442.
Minnesota: Schmidt *v.* Dunham, 46 Minn. 227, 49 N. W. 126.
Missouri: Green *v.* Spencer, 3 Mo. 318, 26 Am. Dec. 672; Hill *v.* Maupin, 3 Mo. 323, 26 Am. Dec. 672; Roper *v.* Clay, 18 Mo. 383; Wilbur *v.* Johnson, 58 Mo. 600; Bird *v.* Thompson, 96 Mo. 424; Liese *v.* Meyer, 143 Mo. 547, 45 S. W. 282; Clemons *v.* Seba, 131 Mo. App. 378, 111 S. W. 522.
Nebraska: Musselman *v.* Barker, 26 Neb. 737, 42 N. W. 759.
New Jersey: Coil *v.* Wallace, 24 N. J. L. 291.

New York: Kniffen *v.* McConnell' 30 N. Y. 285; Wells *v.* Padgett, 8 Barb· 323; Jennette *v.* Sullivan, 63 Hun, 361, 18 N. Y. Supp. 266, 43 N. Y. St. 647; Kolsch *v.* Jewell, 21 App. Div. 581, 48 N. Y. Supp. 527.
Ohio: Matthews *v.* Cribbett, 11 Oh. St. 330.
Oregon: Osmun *v.* Winters, 25 Ore. 260, 35 Pac. 250.
Tennessee: Conn *v.* Wilson, 2 Overt. 233, 5 Am. Dec. 663; Goodal *v.* Thurman, 1 Head, 209; Williams *v.* Hollingsworth, 6 Baxter, 12; Spellings *v.* Parks, 104 Tenn. 351, 58 S. W. 126.
Texas: Daggett *v.* Wallace, 75 Tex. 352, 13 S. W. 49, 16 Am. St. Rep. 908.
West Virginia: McKinsey *v.* Squires, 32 W. Va. 41, 9 S. E. 55; Dent *v.* Pickens, 34 W. Va 240, 12 S. E. 698, 26 Am. St. Rep. 921.
Wisconsin: Giese *v.* Schultz, 69 Wis. 521, 34 N. W. 913.
England: Berry *v.* DaCosta, L. R. 1 C. P. 331; Millington *v.* Loring, 6 Q. B. Div. 190.
Canada: Bell *v.* Giberson, 30 N. Br. 10.
The rule is otherwise in *Pennsylvania*, on the ground that there is a separate action for the seduction, at suit of the father. Weaver *v.* Bachert, 2 Pa. St. 80, 44 Am. Dec. 159; Baldy *v.* Stratton, 11 Pa. 316.
Burks *v.* Shain, 2 Bibb (Ky.), 341, 5 Am. Dec. 616, is often cited as a decision that seduction cannot be shown in aggravation. In that case, however, it was pointed out that several special circumstances prevented such use of the evidence; the father had obtained damages for the seduction, the seduction was not

and that she was delivered of a bastard child.[33] Such seduction must be alleged in the pleadings.[34] It is not the mere fact of seduction that aggravates the damages, but seduction which results from the promise.[35] Thus seduction before the promise of marriage cannot be shown; [36] nor can loss of time and medical attendance in giving birth to a child,[37] nor the care and maintenance of the child.[38] Nor can disease supervening on the intercourse be shown.[39]

In an action for breach of promise, it was held by the Supreme Court of Massachusetts, that although it might be true that damages for the seduction, as a distinct ground of action, could not be added to the damages to which the plaintiff was entitled for the breach of the alleged promise, and these damages must be awarded solely for the suffering which resulted from the defendant's refusal to perform his promise, yet that it would not follow that the act of seduction was not to be taken into consideration by the jury. The damages, even under this rule, could not be justly estimated without regarding the increased exposure to mortification and distress to which the

pleaded, and it had taken place before the promise was made.

In *Rhode Island* it was at first held that seduction could not be shown in aggravation. Perkins *v.* Hersey, 1 R. I. 493. This case was overruled and the general rule adopted in Mainz *v.* Lederer, 21 R. I. 370, 43 Atl. 876. But this case was in turn overruled and the doctrine that seduction cannot be shown in aggravation was restored in Wrynn *v.* Downey, 27 R. I. 454, 63 Atl. 401, 4 L. R. A. (N. S.) 615.

[33] *Indiana:* Wilds *v.* Bogan, 57 Ind. 453.

Louisiana: Johnson *v.* Levy, 122 La. 118, 47 So. 422.

Minnesota: Schmidt *v.* Durnham, 46 Minn. 227, 49 N. W. 126.

Tennessee: Conn *v.* Wilson, 2 Overt. 233, 5 Am. Dec. 663.

[34] *Indiana:* Cates *v.* McKinney, 48 Ind. 562, 17 Am. Rep. 768.

Kentucky: Burks *v.* Shain, 2 Bibb, 341, 5 Am. Dec. 616.

Maine: Tyler *v.* Salley, 82 Me. 128.

West Virginia: Dent *v.* Pickens, 34 W. Va. 240, 12 S. E. 698, 26 Am. St. Rep. 921.

Wisconsin: Leavitt *v.* Cutler, 37 Wis. 46.

[35] Salchert *v.* Reinig, 135 Wis. 194, 115 N. W. 132, and cases cited.

[36] *Alabama:* Espy *v.* Jones, 37 Ala. 379.

Kentucky: Burks *v.* Shain, 2 Bibb, 341, 5 Am. Dec. 616.

[37] Giese *v.* Schultz, 53 Wis. 462, 10 N. W. 598, 65 Wis. 487, 27 N. W. 353. See, however, Stiles *v.* Tilford, 10 Wend. (N. Y.) 338.

[38] Wilds *v.* Bogan, 57 Ind. 453.

[39] Churan *v.* Sebasta, 131 Ill. App. 330 (because the disease would equally have resulted from keeping the contract).

Contra, however, Millington *v.* Loring, 6 Q. B. Div. 190.

plaintiff had been exposed by a seduction under a promise of marriage afterwards broken.[40]

§ 639a. Circumstances of the breach.

Any circumstances attending the breach of promise which would tend to increase the plaintiff's damage may be shown in aggravation. Thus circumstances of abruptness and humiliation with which the engagement was broken may be shown to aggravate the damages,[41] and the length of time during which an engagement has subsisted is a proper circumstance for the jury to consider.[42] The jury may take into account the plaintiff's altered social position in consequence of the defendant's misconduct.[43] And for that purpose evidence of the plaintiff's poverty may be shown.[44] The fact that the defendant entered into the contract with a bad motive may be shown in aggravation.[45] Slanderous statements with regard to the plaintiff made by the defendant at or about the time of the breach may also be shown to increase the damages, according to the better view; [46] though in Illinois this is not allowed, because a separate action would lie for the slander.[47]

§ 640. Events after suit brought.

No evidence can generally be given of any fact having a tendency to aggravate the damages, which has occurred after

[40] Sherman v. Rawson, 102 Mass. 395. See, to the same purport:
Maryland: Sauer v. Schulenberg, 33 Md. 288, 3 Am. Rep. 174.
Michigan: Sheahan v. Barry, 27 Mich. 217.
New York: Getzelson v. Bernstein, 37 N. Y. Supp. 220.
Wisconsin: Salchert v. Reinig, 135 Wis. 194, 115 N. W. 132.
[41] *Michigan:* McPherson v. Ryan, 59 Mich. 33, 26 N. W. 321.
Pennsylvania: Baldy v. Stratton, 11 Pa. 316.
[42] Grant v. Willey, 101 Mass. 356.
[43] *Nebraska:* Musselman v. Barker, 26 Neb. 737, 42 N. W. 759.
England: Berry v. Da Costa, L. R.

1 C. P. 331. See Smith v. Woodfine, 1 C. B. (N. S.) 660, where the cases are reviewed.
[44] Vanderpool v. Richardson, 52 Mich. 336, 17 N. W. 936.
[45] Kaufman v. Fye, 99 Tenn. 145, 42 S. W. 25.
[46] *Maine:* Lawrence v. Cooke, 56 Me. 187, 96 Am. Dec. 443.
Missouri: Liese v. Meyer, 143 Mo. 547, 45 S. W. 282.
New Hampshire: Chesley v. Chesley, 10 N. H. 327.
Oregon: Kelley v. Highfield, 15 Ore. 290, 14 Pac. 744.
[47] Greenup v. Stoker, 7 Ill. 688; Dunlap v. Clark, 25 Ill. App. 573.

the commencement of the suit.[48]   So it has been held that in an action for breach of promise, an indecent and insulting letter written by defendant to the plaintiff after suit brought cannot be proved.[49]

But in Osmun v. Winters [50] an article published under defendant's signature, attacking plaintiff's character, and an insulting letter addressed by defendant to plaintiff, both written after the commencement of the action, were held admissible and were allowed to be considered in aggravation of damages, on the ground that it tended to show the animus of defendant in refusing to perform the marriage contract, upon like grounds as unproved allegations of unchastity in the pleadings may be considered in aggravation of damages.

§ 640a. Plea of justification interposed in bad faith.

If the defendant sets up in bad faith, or without reasonable grounds for believing that he will be able to establish the truth of it a plea of justification which constitutes an attack on the plaintiff's character, this will be allowed to aggravate the damages.[51]   This is held even though the attempt is not made in the formal pleadings, but only in the evidence produced at the trial.[52]

In a few jurisdictions this doctrine appears to be carried so far that the defendant sets up a scandalous justification at his peril; and if he fails to prove it the attempt aggravates the damage, in whatever good faith it was made.[53]   In other States, however, this is regarded as unsound, on the ground that it restricts the right of the defendant to interpose a perfectly legal

[48] Dent v. Pickens, 34 W. Va. 240, 12 S. E. 698, 26 Am. St. Rep. 921.

[49] Greenleaf v. McColley, 14 N. H. 303.

[50] 30 Ore. 177, 46 Pac. 780.

[51] *California:* Reed v. Clark, 47 Cal. 194.

Indiana: Haymond v. Saucer, 84 Ind. 3.

Missouri: Davis v. Slagle, 27 Mo. 600; Cole v. Holliday, 4 Mo. App. 94.

New York: Kniffen v. McConnell, 30 N. Y. 285.

Ohio: Duvall v. Fuhrman, 3 Ohio C. Ct. 305, 2 Oh. Cir. Dec. 174.

But see Spencer v. Simmons, 160 Mich. 292, 125 N. W. 9.

[52] Kniffen v. McConnell, 30 N. Y. 285.

[53] *Colorado:* Fleetwood v. Barnett, 11 Col. App. 77, 52 Pac. 293.

New York: Southard v. Rexford, 6 Cow. 260; Thorn v. Knapp, 42 N. Y. 474, 1 Am. Rep. 561.

Oregon: Osmun v. Winters, 30 Ore. 177, 46 Pac. 780.

Tennessee: Kaufman v. Fye, 99 Tenn. 145, 167, 42 S. W. 25.

plea; and the justification is allowed to aggravate the damages only where it was interposed in bad faith.[54] An unsuccessful attempt of the defendant to prove that while the plaintiff claimed to be waiting for the defendant to marry her she was trying to marry another man, should not aggravate the damages.[55]

§ 641. Mitigation. Bad character or conduct of plaintiff.

Any circumstance tending to diminish the damages which would otherwise be recovered by the plaintiff may be shown in mitigation of damages. Thus it may be shown that the plaintiff's character and reputation for chastity, sobriety, or otherwise is bad.[56] This evidence tends directly to diminish the damages which she claims for loss of reputation and for humiliation and wounded feelings.

* Bad conduct of the plaintiff may be shown either in bar of the action altogether or in mitigation of damages. Dissolute conduct on the part of the woman after the promise (or before if unknown) discharges the contract altogether. *Indecent* conduct *before* the promise, if unknown to the defendant, or *after* the promise, goes in mitigation of damages.[57] ** The plaintiff's

[54] *California:* Powers *v.* Wheatley, 45 Cal. 113; Reed *v.* Clark, 47 Cal. 194; *Illinois:* Fidler *v.* McKinley, 21 Ill. 308; Blackburn *v.* Mann, 85 Ill. 222. *Indiana:* Hunter *v.* Hatfield, 68 Ind. 416.

Iowa: Denslow *v.* Van Horn, 16 Ia. 476.

Ohio: White *v.* Thomas, 12 Oh. St. 312, 80 Am. Dec. 347.

Wisconsin: Leavitt *v.* Cutler, 37 Wis. 46; Albertz *v.* Albertz, 78 Wis. 72, 47 N. W. 95.

[55] Simpson *v.* Black, 27 Wis. 206.

[56] *Connecticut:* Woodward *v.* Bellamy, 2 Root, 354.

Illinois: Doubet *v.* Kirkman, 15 Ill. App. 622.

Missouri: Cole *v.* Holliday, 4 Mo. App. 94; Markham *v.* Herrick, 82 Mo. App. 327.

New York: Johnson *v.* Caulkins, 1 Johns. Cas. 116.

Tennessee: Williams *v.* Hollingsworth, 6 Baxter, 12.

Canada: McGregor *v.* McArthur, 5 U. C. C. P. 493.

In Capehart *v.* Carradine, 4 Strobh. (S. C.) 42, it is held that reports of immoral acts of the plaintiff may be proved in mitigation if they are based on good foundation.

In Gross *v.* Hochstim, 130 N. Y. Supp. 315, undesirable traits and objectionable characteristics of the (male) plaintiff were allowed to be shown in mitigation: as that he lived beyond his means, failed to pay his board bill, and pawned the engagement ring given him by defendant.

[57] *Illinois:* Butler *v.* Eschleman, 18 Ill. 44.

Indiana: Conaway *v.* Shelton, 3 Ind. 334.

Iowa: Denslow *v.* Van Horn, 16 Iowa, 476.

breach of the criminal law by profanity, is said to go in mitigation;[58] and so does his habit of getting intoxicated.[59]

The fact of a female plaintiff's having had an illegitimate child, if known to the defendant at the time of the promise, is no defense to the action, but goes in mitigation.[60] So in Illinois, the woman's connection with a man other than the defendant, before as well as after the promise, although the engagement was formed or continued by the defendant, with knowledge of the fact, goes in mitigation of the damages, on the ground that an unchaste woman cannot be injured by a breach of the marriage promise to the same extent with a virtuous one.[61] So far, however, as the damages are a pecuniary compensation for the loss of an advantageous match, the measure should not be affected by previous misconduct of the woman which had been forgiven by the defendant. Indeed, a reputable woman's pecuniary loss would perhaps not be so great as that of one whose reputation is tarnished, as it would generally be more easily made good. Perhaps, moreover, as regards other damages, the loss of the opportunity of retrieving her name, and reassuming a position of respectability, is an injury practically equivalent to the keener mortification which a virtuous woman may be thought to sustain from the breach of such a contract. In the case, however, of the continuance of the woman's wrongdoing, if such continuance be without the suitor's knowledge, she is entitled to nothing, and if with his acquiescence, to nom-

---

Massachusetts: Boynton v. Kellogg, 3 Mass. 189, 3 Am. Dec. 122.

Nebraska: Stratton v. Dole, 45 Neb. 472, 63 N. W. 875.

New Jersey: Budd v. Crea, 6 N. J. L. 370.

New York: Johnson v. Caulkins, 1 Johns. Cas. 116, 1 Am. Dec. 102; Willard v. Stone, 7 Cow. 22, 17 Am. Dec. 496; Palmer v. Andrews, 7 Wend. 142; Kniffen v. McConnell, 30 N. Y. 285.

Pennsylvania: Van Storch v. Griffen, 71 Pa. 240.

South Carolina: Capehart v. Carradine, 4 Strob. 42.

Texas: Clark v. Reese, 26 Tex. Civ. App. 619, 64 S. W. 783.

Wisconsin: Albertz v. Albertz, 78 Wis. 72, 47 N. W. 95, 10 L. R. A. 584.

England: Irving v. Greenwood, 1 C. & P. 350.

In Tompkins v. Wadley, 3 Thomps. & C. (N. Y.) 424, an unchaste act 27 years before the trial was allowed to be shown in mitigation.

[58] Berry v. Bakeman, 44 Me. 164.

[59] Button v. McCauley, 5 Abb. Pr. (N. S.) 29, 4 Transcr. App. 447, 1 Abb. Dec. 282.

[60] Denslow v. Van Horn, 16 Ia. 476.

[61] Burnett v. Simpkins, 24 Ill. 264; acc., Sheahan v. Barry, 27 Mich. 217.

inal damages only, both on the ground of her misconduct, and because the loss of a husband who has connived at his wife's shame inflicts no damage.

Incontinence between the plaintiff and the defendant before the promise should not be shown in mitigation of damages.[62] The fact that the plaintiff shot the defendant [63] or abused the defendant's relatives [64] cannot be shown in mitigation.

§ 641a. Feelings of the parties.

The feelings of the plaintiff toward the defendant during the existence of the engagement may be shown, as bearing directly on the compensation for wounded affections; but not her feelings after the breach of the engagement. Thus in Miller *v.* Hayes [65] it was held that declarations made by the plaintiff after the commencement of the suit, to the effect that she would not marry the defendant except for his money, were not admissible in mitigation of damages. But in Miller *v.* Rosier [66] similar declarations, made a few days after the engagement was broken, were admitted, as showing her feelings during the engagement. The fact that the plaintiff had been engaged to another person previous to her promise to the defendant cannot be shown in mitigation.[67]

In the case of Leeds *v.* Cook [68] the defendant, just before her projected marriage with the plaintiff, had eloped with another man. In mitigation of damages it was shown that the plaintiff had conducted himself with extreme indifference toward the defendant, had entertained no serious affection for her, and had immediately after defendant's elopement made proposals of marriage to another woman. Lord Ellenborough said that if the plaintiff appeared to be of gross manners and destitute of feeling, as he complained by this action of an injury in the loss of the society of a woman which he appeared never to have

[62] *Alabama:* Espy *v.* Jones, 37 Ala. 379.

Colorado: Fleetwood *v.* Barnett, 11 Col. App. 77, 52 Pac. 293.

See, however, an intimation to the contrary effect in Wells *v.* Padgett, 8 Barb. (N. Y.) 323.

[63] Schmidt *v.* Durnham, 46 Minn. 227, 49 N. W. 126.

[64] Albertz *v.* Albertz, 78 Wis. 72, 47 N. W. 95, 10 L. R. A. 584.

[65] 34 Ia. 496, 11 Am. Rep. 154.

[66] 31 Mich. 475.

[67] Edge *v.* Griffin (Tex. Civ. App.), 63 S. W. 148.

[68] 4 Esp. 256.

valued, and the pleasures of which society he seemed little calculated to taste, the jury should take it into their consideration in their verdict.

On the other hand, the defendant should not be allowed to prove his own feelings in order to mitigate the damages; for that would be allowing him to shelter himself behind his own wrong. Thus in Piper *v.* Kingsbury [69] it was held that the jury could not consider in mitigation of damages the possible consequences of an unhappy marriage with the defendant, rendered such by the want of that love and affection which a husband should bear his wife, the court saying: "It would virtually have been saying that the plaintiff ought not to recover the damage actually sustained, because the defendant might have inflicted a greater."

It has been held by a majority of the New York Court of Appeals that the defendant might show in mitigation of damages in this action, that the breach proceeded from no change of feeling on his part, but was in deference to the wishes of his mother, a woman in infirm health.[70] But such evidence must be taken merely as tending to reduce the standard to compensatory, and to exclude exemplary damages. The plaintiff cannot be the less entitled to compensation for the injury sustained, because of the circumstances which palliate the defendant's conduct.

§ 641b. Physical defects of the parties.

Physical defects or bad health on the part of either party may be shown in mitigation. Thus, it may be shown in mitigation, that the defendant was affected with an incurable disease at the time of his breach of the promise.[71] So bad health on the part of the plaintiff may be shown, on the ground that damages may be affected by any condition of mind or body which unfits a party to fulfil the position of wife or husband.[72] If, however, this condition was known to the defendant at the time of entering into the engagement the case is otherwise. Thus in Lohner

---

[69] 48 Vt. 480, 486.
[70] Johnson *v.* Jenkins, 24 N. Y. 252.
[71] *Illinois:* Sprague *v.* Craig, 51 Ill. 288, 2 Am. Rep. 301.

Indiana: Mabin *v.* Webster, 129 Ind. 430, 28 N. E. 863, 28 Am. St. Rep. 199.
[72] Walker *v.* Johnson, 6 Ind. App. 600, 33 N. E. 267.

v. Coldwell [73] the defendant attempted to mitigate damages by showing that there was insanity in the plaintiff's family. The court held that this could not be done in the absence of evidence that the defendant was ignorant of the fact when he entered into the engagement, and that he broke off the engagement in consequence of the insanity.

Close kinship of the parties cannot be shown in mitigation of damages.[74]

§ 641c. Offer of performance after breach.

An offer of the defendant, after breach, to marry the plaintiff may be shown as bearing on the amount of damages.[75] This is perhaps not properly mitigation of damages, but on general principles it would show that the plaintiff had an opportunity to avoid the loss of the pecuniary advantages of the marriage, and therefore should not recover compensation for the loss of such advantages.

Under certain circumstances the offer will not mitigate the damages; as where the defendant by his misconduct has made an acceptance of the offer impossible. In such a case the Supreme Court of Michigan said:[76]

"The contract of marriage is one so dependent upon affection that where this is wanting, a union would be more likely to add to than lessen the damages; instead of bringing happiness to the parties, it would be more likely to entail lifelong misery on one or both. The affection which the plaintiff may have had for the defendant, and under the influence of which she may even eagerly have accepted a matrimonial alliance with him, may by his subsequent conduct have been turned into loathing and contempt, so that a marriage which at a certain time would have been to her one of the most desirable of events, would at a subsequent period, even in thought, be repulsive.

[73] 15 Tex. Civ. App. 444, 39 S. W. 591.
[74] Albertz *v.* Albertz, 78 Wis. 72, 47 N. W. 95, 10 L. R. A. 584.
[75] *United States:* McCarty *v.* Heryford, 125 Fed. 46.
Alabama: Kelly *v.* Renfro, 9 Ala. 325, 44 Am. Dec. 441.

Indiana: Kurtz *v.* Frank, 76 Ind. 594, 40 Am. Rep. 275.
Contra, Holloway *v.* Griffith, 32 Iowa, 409, 7 Am. Rep. 208.
[76] Bennett *v.* Beam, 42 Mich. 346, 352, 4 N. W. 8, 36 Am. Rep. 442.

"A supposed virtuous man of wealth, refinement, and respectability, gains the affections of a young lady, and under a promise of marriage accomplishes her ruin, then abandons her and enters upon a life of open and notorious profligacy and debauchery, and when sued he offers to carry out his agreement—offers himself in marriage, when any woman with even a spark of virtue or sensibility would shrink from his polluted touch. To hold that the offer of such a skeleton, and refusal to accept, could be considered even in mitigation of damages, would shock the sense of justice and be simply a legal outrage. Such an offer could in no way atone for the past, or have any tendency to show that the defendant had not, and was not acting in a most heartless and outrageous manner."

But these remarks must be taken in the light of the peculiar circumstances. This is, indeed, true in every case where evidence of circumstances of mitigation or aggravation is offered. It is not to be supposed that in a proper case, as, for instance, where defendant had honestly believed the plaintiff to be of bad character, and subsequently discovered his mistake offered reparation, the court would have rejected evidence of the facts.

CHAPTER XXIX

§ 642. Damages recoverable by builder.

Where the owner cancels the contract, or refuses to permit performance by the defendant, the measure of damages is the profit of the contract, that is, the contract price less the cost of completing performance.[1] The prevailing opinion is, that if the contractor has made sub-contracts which he is

[1] *Alabama:* Tutwiler v. Burns, 160 Ala. 386, 49 So. 455.

Arkansas: Womble v. Hickson, 91 Ark. 266, 121 S. W. 401.

California: O'Connell v. Main & T. S. H. Co., 90 Cal. 515, 27 Pac. 373, 25 Am. St. Rep. 145.

Illinois: Ryan v. Miller, 153 Ill. 138, 38 N. E. 642.

Massachusetts: John Soley & Sons v. Jones (Mass.), 95 N. E. 94.

Michigan: Scheible v. Klein, 89 Mich. 376, 50 N. W. 857.

Minnesota: Swanson v. Andrews, 83 Minn. 505, 86 N. W. 465.

Nebraska: Von Dorn v. Mengedoht, 41 Neb. 525, 59 N. W. 800.

New Jersey: Wilson v. Borden, 68 N. J. L. 627, 54 Atl. 815; Sullivan v. Moffatt, 70 N. J. L. 4, 56 Atl. 304.

New York: McMaster v. State, 108 N. Y. 542, 15 N. E. 417; Miller v. Hahn, 23 App. Div. 48, 48 N. Y. Supp. 346; Schlesinger v. Ritchie, 115 N. Y. Supp. 116.

Pennsylvania: Shallenberger v. Standard S. M. Co., 223 Pa. 220, 72 Atl. 500.

South Carolina: Feaster v. Richland Cotton Mills, 51 S. C. 143, 28 S. E. 301.

Texas: Joske v. Pleasants, 15 Tex. Civ. App. 433, 39 S. E. 586.

Washington: Chase v. Smith, 35 Wash. 631, 77 Pac. 1069.

See *ante,* § 614.

If the plaintiff has already received more than his outlay and the profits he is able to prove, he can recover nothing. McElwee v. Bridgeport L. & I. Co., 54 Fed. 627, 13 U. S. App. 195, 4 C. C. A. 525.

obliged to break on account of the cancellation of the contract he is not entitled to compensation for the damage he must pay the sub-contractor; apparently on the ground that the loss is remote.[2] Any materials of the builder which are used by the owner after the breach are of course to be paid for,[3] though if they are considered in the profit the builder of course cannot a second time recover their value.[4] It has been held in New York that the plaintiff cannot prove subcontracts into which he has entered in order to show what profit he would have made on the contract;[5] but on the other hand, when after the breach the house was completed by the defendant, it has been held in Alabama that the defendant might show the cost of completion for the purpose of showing the amount of profit plaintiff would have made.[6] In Swanson v. Andrews[7] a builder was to receive an additional amount if certain changes were made in the plans. This builder was discharged, and another was employed to build the house, and the changes were in fact made. It was held nevertheless that the first builder was not entitled to compensation based on the extra work, since he was not entitled by the contract to do it.

Where upon a contract to construct, the defendant delayed the construction, the plaintiff, who was the contractor, was allowed to recover the increased cost of construction caused thereby.[8] Mitchell, J., said:

"Where a contractor in good faith enters upon the performance of a contract, and incurs expense, the employer having notice of that fact, if the employer, either by an order or by negligently failing to perform an essential part to be performed by him, suspends the execution of the contract, upon a resumption and completion of the work it will be

[2] Smith v. United States, 11 Ct. Cl. 707.
Contra, Smith v. Flanders, 129 Mass. 322.
[3] Alabama: Tutwiler v. Burns, 160 Ala. 386, 49 So. 455.
New York: Carlin v. New York, 132 App. Div. 90, 116 N. Y. Supp. 346.
[4] Smith v. Davis, 150 Ala. 106, 43 So. 729.

[5] Brodie v. Fost, 123 App. Div. 749, 108 N. Y. Supp. 414; Wetter v. Kleinert, 139 App. Div. 220, 123 N. Y. Supp. 755.
[6] Smith v. Davis, 150 Ala. 106, 43 So. 729.
[7] 83 Minn. 505, 86 N. W. 465.
[8] Louisville & N. R. R. v. Hollerbach, 105 Ind. 137, 145, 151, 5 N. E. 28.

implied that all loss, necessarily occasioned by such suspension, of which the employer is at the time notified, shall fall upon him. The contractor may not acquiesce in the suspension in silence, and upon the resumption and completion of the work claim the contract price, and damages for that which may have occurred with his acquiescence. If, however, notice be given of his readiness and willingness to prosecute the work to completion within the time agreed upon, and that its suspension will involve him in loss, we can discover no principle upon which it can be held that the loss must fall upon the contractor in case of a voluntary resumption of the contract. . . . The plaintiff may recover as damages any direct loss which he sustained by the unreasonable suspension or delay of the work by the employer. The employer must have had notice that the suspension would result in loss, and the suspension must not have been consented to by the contractor."

In this case the contractor recovered compensation for injury to tools, and interest for the period of delay upon all moneys invested upon materials furnished for the work, and labor necessary in furnishing them.[9] So where the plaintiff and defendant entered into a written contract, by which the former agreed for a certain sum to be paid him by the latter to do the carpenter's work on a school-house to be built, and furnish and use the necessary materials, and that he would "commence said work and proceed therewith without delay, and in such a manner as not to delay the contractor for the mason work," it was held that this covenant implied a correlative obligation on the part of the defendant to have his building in readiness for the plaintiff to perform the condition; and that the plaintiff, having sustained damages from the defendant's delay in having the building ready for him to do the work, could maintain an action to recover the amount of his damages, in which was included his increased expense from the delay.[10] The contractor is entitled to recover all

[9] Acc., Langford v. United States, 95 Fed. 933; Kellogg Bridge Co. v. United States, 15 Ct. Cl. 206.

[10] Allamon v. Albany, 43 Barb. (N. Y.) 33; Weeks v. Rector, etc., of Trinity Church, 36 App. Div. 195, 67 N. Y. Supp. 670.

other expenses and inconvenience caused by the delay,[11] such as wages necessarily paid while the work was delayed,[12] enhanced cost of labor after the work was resumed,[13] enhanced price of materials,[14] and deterioration of materials during the delay.[15] But he cannot recover for any interruption of his work which he should have foreseen and guarded against.[16]

§ 643. Damages for failure to build.

The measure of damages for the failure of a contractor to construct a building is the reasonable cost of having the building constructed by another contractor less the contract price.[17] Where a certain portion of the building is left undone the same rule applies; that is, the increased cost of completion is the measure of damages for failure to complete.[18] So where a builder was to build a cornice in the ceiling of a room at a certain price and failed to do so, the measure of damages

[11] *Illinois:* Cook County *v.* Sexton, 16 Ill. App. 93.

South Dakota: Hickok *v.* W. E. Adams Co., 18 S. D. 14, 99 N. W. 77.

Texas: Hood *v.* Raines, 19 Tex. 400.

[12] *United States:* Figh *v.* United States, 8 Ct. Cl. 319; Bitting *v.* United States, 25 Ct. Cl. 502.

New Hampshire: Hutt *v.* Hickey, 67 N. H. 411, 29 Atl. 456.

[13] Figh *v.* United States, 8 Ct. Cl. 319; Bitting *v.* United States, 25 Ct. Cl. 502; Langford *v.* United States, 95 Fed. 933.

[14] Figh *v.* United States, 8 Ct. Cl. 319; Kelly *v.* United States, 31 Ct. Cl. 361.

[15] Figh *v.* United States, 8 Ct. Cl. 319; Langford *v.* United States, 95 Fed. 933.

[16] Thomas W. Finucane Co. *v.* Board of Education, 190 N. Y. 76, 82 N. E. 737.

[17] *United States:* Hunt *v.* Oregon P. Ry., 36 Fed. 481; American Surety Co. *v.* Woods, 106 Fed. 263, 45 C. C. A. 282.

Massachusetts: Hebb *v.* Welch, 185 Mass. 335, 70 N. E. 440.

New York: National Contracting Co.

v. Hudson River W. P. Co., 118 App. Div. 665, 103 N. Y. Supp. 641.

Oregon: Savage *v.* Glenn, 10 Ore. 440.

So in a covenant by landlord to build a wall for the tenant, the wall not being built, the measure of damages is the cost of building the wall with compensation for loss of use of the premises during rebuilding. Fisher *v.* Goebel, 40 Mo. 475; *acc.,* Candler Inv. Co. *v.* Cox, 4 Ga. App. 763, 62 S. E. 479.

Where the contract gives the owner the right to complete the contract at the expense of the builder, and he does so in good faith, he may recover the cost of so doing without the necessity of proving the cost reasonable. Bair *v.* Sleicher, 153 Fed. 129, 82 C. C. A. 281.

[18] *New York:* McGrath *v.* Horgan, 72 App. Div. 152, 76 N. Y. Supp. 412; Deeves *v.* Richardson & Boynton Co., 59 N. Y. Super. Ct. 423, 14 N. Y. Supp. 633; Watts *v.* Board of Education, 9 App. Div. 143, 41 N. Y. Supp. 141.

Texas: Mills *v.* Paul (Tex. Civ. App.), 30 S. W. 558.

was the cost of placing the cornice in the ceiling less the contract price for doing so.[19] If the building is left incompleted it is immaterial that in its incomplete condition its value for purposes of sale is not lessened by reason of the work left undone; so where the owner of a house which the defendant had failed to complete sold it in the condition in which the defendant left it and there was no evidence that the price he received was less than he would have received if the defendant's contract had been fully performed, he nevertheless was entitled to recover the cost of completing according to the contract.[20]

§ 644. Defective construction.

Where the building is completed but the construction is in some respect defective, the principle upon which damages are to be estimated will depend on whether the defect can be remedied by the expenditure of a reasonable amount of money. If in view of the expense it is reasonable to remedy the defect, then the measure of damages is the cost of remedying it.[21] If, on the other hand, the value of the building with the defect is greater than its value without the defect less the cost of applying the remedy, then the measure of damages is the diminution in the value of the building by reason of the defect.[22]

[19] New York Metal Ceiling Co. v. City Homes Imp. Co., 88 N. Y. Supp. 233.

[20] Ekstrand v. Barth, 41 Wash. 321, 83 Pac. 305.

[21] *California:* Carpenter v. Ibbetson, 1 Cal. App. 272, 81 Pac. 1114.

Kentucky: Forbes v. Hunter, 31 Ky. L. Rep. 285, 102 S. W. 246.

Massachusetts: Goddard v. Barnard, 16 Gray, 205.

Michigan: Germain v. Union School District, 158 Mich. 214, 122 N. W. 524.

Missouri: Hirt v. Hahn, 61 Mo. 496; Wright v. Sanderson, 20 Mo. App. 534.

Ohio: Somerby v. Tappan, Wright, 229.

Pennsylvania: Morgan v. Gambol, 230 Pa. 165, 79 Atl. 410.

Tennessee: Gibson v. Carlin, 13 Lea, 440.

Virginia: Lambert v. Jenkins, 71 S. E. 718.

[22] *Colorado:* Schafer v. Gildea, 3 Colo. 15.

Kentucky: Taulbee v. Moore, 106 Ky. 749, 51 S. W. 564; Short v. Moore, 19 Ky. L. Rep. 1225, 43 S. W. 211; Hartford Mill Co. v. Hartford T. W. Co., 121 S. W. 477.

Massachusetts: White v. McLaren, 151 Mass. 553, 24 N. E. 911.

New York: Walter v. Hangen, 71 App. Div. 40, 75 N. Y. Supp. 683; Haist v. Bell, 24 App. Div. 252, 48 N. Y. Supp. 405.

Oregon: Chamberlin v. Hibbard, 26 Ore. 428, 38 Pac. 437.

But see American Surety Co. v Lyons, 44 Tex. Civ. App. 150, 97 S. W. 1080. In this case the court, in answer to the contention that the dif-

In no case can the measure of damages be reduced to the cost of a remedy for the defect which does not really give to the owner substantially what he had contracted for. So, where a flue in a building was faultily constructed, and it was claimed that the defect could be remedied by putting on a certain kind of ventilator, the court held that damages could not be confined to the cost of putting in the ventilator if the ventilator injured the appearance of the building or for other reasons was undesirable.[23]

Where the building is defectively constructed, consequential damages may be recoverable in addition to the cost of remedying the defect or the diminution in value.[24] So in case of a defective roof, the owner may recover compensation for injuries to the contents of the building by rain.[25] Loss of use of the building during the necessary repairs may also be recovered.[26]

§ 645. Delay in construction.

Where a contractor does not finish a house in the time agreed, but is afterward allowed to go on with the contract, the owner recovers the value of the use of the building during the delay, or in other words the rental value of the building.[27]

erence in value, if less than the cost of completion, was the limit of recovery said: "To adopt the measure of damages contended for would be to force appellee to forego the benefit of her bargain and accept and pay for a building different from that contracted for. She had the right to demand that the building be completed according to the contract, and, if the contractor refused to remedy the defects in the building as constructed by him, she was entitled to recover as damages the amount it would cost her over and above the contract price to have the defects remedied and the building completed in accordance with the contract."

[23] Larrimore v. Comanche County (Tex. Civ. App.), 32 S. W. 367.

[24] Wright v. Sanderson, 20 Mo. App.

534 (improper foundation; recover for injury to building by cracks in wall caused by defect in foundation).

[25] Missouri: Haysler v. Owen, 61 Mo. 270.

Tennessee: Gibson v. Carlin, 13 Lea, 440.

In Goddard v. Barnard, 16 Gray (Mass.), 205, the form of the contract was held to prevent recovery of such damage.

[26] Massachusetts: White v. McLaren, 151 Mass. 553, 24 S. E. 911.

Ohio: Somerby v. Tappan, Wright, 229.

See Lord v. Comstock, 52 N. Y. Super. Ct. 548 (cannot recover for loss of particular chance to let the building during the delay).

[27] Colorado: McIntire v. Barnes, 4 Colo. 285.

The owner cannot recover rent which could have been realized from any particular lease; that not having been contemplated by the builder; [28] and it is therefore immaterial to show that the building could have been rented. [29]

Damages for loss of a particular use cannot be recovered in the absence of evidence that notice of this use was given to the defendant. [30] So rent paid by the plaintiff for another house cannot be recovered. [31]

If, however, there is notice of the special use, damages may be recovered for consequential damages in a proper case. So where there was notice of the intended use of the house for a

Georgia: Cannon *v.* Hunt, 113 Ga. 501, 38 S. E. 983.

Illinois: Korf *v.* Lull, 70 Ill. 420; Hawley *v.* Florsheim, 44 Ill. App. 320; Galbraith *v.* Chicago A. I. Works, 50 Ill. App. 246.

Iowa: Novelty Iron Works *v.* Capitol City Oatmeal Co., 88 Ia. 524, 55 N. W. 518.

Kentucky: Simon *v.* Lanius, 9 Ky. L. Rep. 59.

Maryland: Abbott *v.* Gatch, 13 Md. 314, 71 Am. Dec. 635.

Massachusetts: C. W. Hunt Co. *v.* Boston El. Ry., 199 Mass. 220, 85 N. E. 446.

Michigan: Covode *v.* Principaal, 110 Mich. 672, 68 N. W. 987.

Missouri: McConey *v.* Wallace, 22 Mo. App. 377; Dengler *v.* Auer, 55 Mo. App. 548.

New York: Ruff *v.* Rinaldo, 55 N. Y. 664; Hexter *v.* Knox, 63 N. Y. 561; Lord *v.* Comstock, 52 N. Y. Super. Ct. 548.

Oregon: Savage *v.* Glenn, 10 Ore. 440.

Pennsylvania: Rogers *v.* Bemus, 69 Pa. 432; Finch *v.* Heermans, 5 Luz. Leg. Reg. 125.

South Carolina: Harwood *v.* Tappan, 2 Spear, 536.

Texas: J. T. Stark Grain Co. *v.* Harry Bros. Co. (Tex. Civ. App.), 122 S. W. 947.

If no rental value or value of use can be proved, the plaintiff may recover at least nominal damages. Smith *v.* Green (Tex. Civ. App.), 122 S. W. 919.

[28] *Georgia:* Cannon *v.* Hunt, 113 Ga. 501, 38 S. E. 983.

Illinois: Hawley *v.* Forsheim, 44 Ill. App. 320.

Maryland: Abbott *v.* Gatch, 13 Md. 314, 71 Am. Dec. 635.

New York: Lord *v.* Comstock, 52 N. Y. Super. Ct. 548.

In Consaul *v.* Sheldon, 35 Neb. 247, 52 N. W. 1104, the plaintiff was allowed to show an actual lease of the building, it appearing that the rent was less than the reasonable rental value. The court intimated that under these circumstances the plaintiff would be restricted to the agreed rent; but this would seem a mistake. See § 243a.

[29] *Illinois:* Galbraith *v.* Chicago A. I. Works, 50 Ill. App. 246.

Michigan: Covode *v.* Principaal, 110 Mich. 672, 68 N. W. 987.

A few decisions to the contrary must be regarded as erroneous, and overruled by the late cases: *e. g.* Wagner *v.* Corkhill, 40 Barb. (N. Y.) 175.

[30] Galbraith *v.* Chicago Architectural Iron Works, 50 Ill. App. 246.

[31] *Georgia:* Cannon *v.* Hunt, 113 Ga. 501, 38 S. E. 983.

Kentucky: Jaudes *v.* Fisher, 5 Ky. L. Rep. 768.

dwelling house for plaintiff into which his furniture must be put at a certain time, he may recover the cost of storing the furniture.[32] So where the defendant knew that the plaintiff needed the structure in order to land coal from vessels during a coal strike, he was responsible for the loss to plaintiff from failure to have it for such use; and the cost of furnishing a substitute for the purpose was recoverable.[33] And where defendant contracted to build a gas-holder to be furnished December 1, and he had notice that it would be needed during each December and January only, the owner could recover a year's rental for a two months' delay.[34] Where defendant had notice that the building which he agreed to construct was leased, he is liable for loss of rent; though not for special damages paid by plaintiff to the lessee under a special clause in the lease of which he had no notice.[35] So where the plaintiff and defendant owned adjoining buildings and the defendant wished to take down a party wall between them and contracted with plaintiff that it should be rebuilt within three weeks, and plaintiff thereupon with knowledge of the defendant made an agreement with her tenant that if the repairs lasted more than three weeks she should pay a large compensation per day, and defendant did not complete the repairs within three weeks, it was held that he was responsible for the amount of money plaintiff had to pay her tenant under the agreement.[36] In any case the specific profits anticipated from use of the building cannot be recovered; they are too uncertain.[37]

[32] Hexter v. Knox, 63 N. Y. 561.

[33] C. W. Hunt Co. v. Boston El. Ry. 199 Mass. 220, 85 N. E. 446.

[34] Wood v. Joliet Gaslight Co., 111 Fed. 463.

[35] Albany Phosphate Co. v. Hugger Bros., 4 Ga. App. 771, 62 S. E. 533.

[36] McLaren v. Fischer, 45 App. Div. 13, 61 N. Y. Supp. 808.

In Haven v. Wakefield, 39 Ill. 509, the plaintiff sued for delay in performance of a contract to build a building and lease it to the plaintiff for storing broom brush and manufacturing brooms. By reason of delay the brush had to be stored in the building before it was completed and was injured by the weather. The plaintiff was also delayed in harvesting his crop, and some of it suffered injury from frost. Such damage was held proximate, and could be recovered.

[37] *Illinois:* Haven v. Wakefield, 39 Ill. 509.

Pennsylvania: Rogers v. Bemus, 69 Pa. 432; Finch v. Heermans, 5 Luz. Leg. Reg. 125.

South Carolina: Harwood v. Tappan, 2 Spear, 536.

Texas: J. T. Stark Grain Co. v. Harry Bros. Co. (Tex. Civ. App.), 122 S. W. 947.

But while the profits expected from the use of the building cannot be recovered as themselves furnishing the measure of damages, the cost of the building, its depreciation and the depreciation of its machinery while in operation and the profits that could be made with the building, are proper to be considered in arriving at the rental value.[38]

§ 646. On contract to supply machinery or power for buildings.

For breach of a contract to supply machinery or power for a building, the direct damage is the expense of procuring the machine or power elsewhere, less the contract price.[39] Since in the case of such a contract there is knowledge of the purpose of the supply, the plaintiff may also recover compensation for loss of use of the premises, which will amount to the rental value,[40] not the expected profits.[41] Where the machinery supplied is defective, the plaintiff may recover the cost of remedying the defect.[42] If the premises were reasonably operated, and the defect caused an injury to the premises, the amount of this injury may also be recovered;[43] and so where the attempt

[38] Novelty Iron Works v. Capital City Oatmeal Co., 88 Ia. 524, 55 N. W. 518.

[39] Citizens' Elec. Light & P. Co. v. Gonzales Water Power Co. (Tex. Civ. App.), 76 S. W. 577 (failure to furnish water wheel).

[40] Illinois: Consumers' Pure Ice Co. v. Jenkins, 58 Ill. App. 519 (machine to break ice).

Michigan: McKinnon v. McEwan, 48 Mich. 106, 11 N. W. 828, 42 Am. Rep. 458 (boilers for power).

[41] Illinois: Consumers' P. I. Co. v. Jenkins, 58 Ill. App. 519.

Kansas: Paola Gas Co. v. Paola Glass Co., 56 Kan. 614, 44 Pac. 621, 54 Am. St. Rep. 598 (failure to furnish gas for fuel).

Michigan: McKinnon v. McEwan, 48 Mich. 106, 11 N. W. 828, 42 Am. Rep. 458; Doud v. Duluth Milling Co., 55 Minn. 53, 56 N. W. 463 (barrel plant for flour mill). But see Bryson

v. McCone, 121 Cal. 153, 53 Pac. 637. In that case the business was established, and the contract was for the replacing of one machine by another; it was rightly held that recovery could be had for loss of profits of an established business.

[42] New York: Davis v. Talcott, 14 Barb. 611 (machinery in mill).

Pennsylvania: Dixon-Woods Co. v. Phillips Glass Co., 169 Pa. 167, 32 Atl. 432 (furnace for making glass); Morse v. Arnfield, 15 Pa. Super. Ct. 140 (elevator).

Vermont: Clifford v. Richardson, 18 Vt. 620 (machinery in mill).

Canada: Crompton & K. L. Works v. Hoffman, 5 Ont. L. R. 554 (loom in factory). Colton v. Good, 11 Up. Can. Q. B. 153, contra, must be regarded as overruled on this point.

[43] New York: Cassidy v. Le Fevre, 45 N. Y. 562 (damage by exploding boiler).

82

to operate with the defective machine caused loss of material.[44] If the defect results in a stoppage of the plant, the rental value of the plant may also be recovered,[45] but not compensation for the expected profits, since they are ordinarily too conjectural.[46] It would seem, however, that if the defendant had notice that the premises would be stopped if the machine were defective, and the business was an established one, so that the profits could be proved with reasonable certainty, recovery might be had for loss of profits.[47] When the fitting out of a building with machinery is delayed, the owner may recover for the loss of use of the building, measured by the rental value.[48] No recovery can be had for loss of anticipated profits,[49] though in the case

Pennsylvania: Erie City Iron Works *v.* Barber, 102 Pa. 156 (damage by explosion of boiler).

Canada: Colton *v.* Good, 11 Up. Can. Q. B. 153 (damage by mill stone broken during operation).

[44] *Kansas:* Paola Gas Co. *v.* Paola Glass Co., 56 Kan. 614, 44 Pac. 621, 54 Am. St. Rep. 598.

Pennsylvania: Dixon-Woods Co. *v.* Phillips Glass Co., 169 Pa. 167, 32 Atl. 434 (loss of material in operating defective furnace).

[45] *New York:* Cassidy *v.* Le Fevre, 45 N. Y. 562.

Pennsylvania: Dixon-Woods Co. *v.* Phillips Glass Co., 169 Pa. 167, 32 Atl. 432.

[46] *New York:* Cassidy *v.* Le Fevre, 45 N. Y. 562.

Pennsylvania: Fleming *v.* Beck, 48 Pa. 309; Erie City Iron Works *v.* Barber, 102 Pa. 156; Dixon-Woods Co. *v.* Phillips Glass Co., 169 Pa. 167, 32 Atl. 432.

[47] They appear to have been allowed on this principle in the following cases:

New York: Davis *v.* Talcott, 14 Barb. 611.

Vermont: Clifford *v.* Richardson, 18 Vt. 620.

Canada: Crompton & K. Loom Works *v.* Hoffman, 5 Ont. L. R. 554.

[48] *Illinois:* Consumers' Pure Ice Co.

v. Jenkins, 58 Ill. App. 519 (ice machine).

Iowa: Novelty Iron Works *v.* Capital City Oatmeal Co., 88 Iowa, 524, 55 N. W. 518 (machinery for mill).

Michigan: John Hutchinson Mfg. Co. *v.* Pinch, 91 Mich. 156, 51 N. W. 930, 30 Am. St. Rep. 463 (machinery for mill: overruling on this point Allis *v.* McLean, 48 Mich. 428, 12 N. W. 640, 42 Am. Rep. 474, which was criticised in the previous edition of this work, § 186).

North Carolina: Boyle *v.* Reeder, 1 Ired. 607 (engine for mill).

[49] *United States:* Howard *v.* Stillwell & Bierce Manuf. Co., 139 U. S. 199, 11 Sup. Ct. 500, 35 L. ed. 147 (machinery for mill).

Illinois: Consumers' Pure Ice Co. *v.* Jenkins, 58 Ill. App. 519.

Iowa: Novelty Iron Works *v.* Capital City Oatmeal Co., 88 Ia. 524, 55 N. W. 518.

Michigan: John Hutchinson Mfg. Co. *v.* Pinch, 91 Mich. 156, 51 N. W. 930, 30 Am. St. Rep. 463.

Minnesota: Doud *v.* Duluth Milling Co., 55 Minn. 53, 56 N. W. 463 (barrel shop for mill).

Nebraska: Bridges *v.* Lanham, 14 Neb. 369, 15 N. W. 704, 45 Am. Rep. 121 (float for mill).

New York: Reilly *v.* Connors, 65

of an established business past profits may be shown to indicate the business value of the premises.[50] In one case damages were claimed for injury to stock by the delay, but they were not allowed.[51]

§ 646a. On contract to furnish materials for building.

For failure to furnish materials for building, the direct loss would be the difference between the contract and the market prices.[52]

For delay in furnishing materials for building the owner cannot usually recover compensation for loss of use of the building, on the ground that the completion of the building is thereby delayed; since such delay in completion would usually be remote, or at least unforeseen.[53] Such delay will, however, often cause a natural waste of time of workmen employed on the building; and compensation for time so lost may be recovered.[54]

When the materials supplied do not conform to the contract, and the defect is discovered at a time when it can be remedied by supplying proper materials, the measure of damages is the cost of supplying these.[55] If the materials have been used in the building, and it is too late to replace them by other materials, the measure of damages is the difference in value of the building; as when an inferior quality of lumber is supplied and used in building.[56] If because of the defect in the materials,

App. Div. 470, 72 N. Y. Supp. 834 (heating plant; cannot recover anticipated rent).

North Carolina: Boyle *v.* Reeder, 1 Ired. 607.

[50] Williams *v.* Island City M. & M. Co., 25 Ore. 573, 37 Pac. 49 (machinery for mill).

[51] Boyle *v.* Reeder, 1 Ired. (N. C.) 607 (machinery for mill).

[52] *Minnesota:* Liljengren Furniture & L. Co. *v.* Mead, 42 Minn. 420, 44 N. W. 306.

New York: Woolf *v.* Schaefer, 103 App. Div. 567, 93 N. Y. Supp. 184.

[53] *Minnesota:* Liljengren Furniture & L. Co. *v.* Mead, 42 Minn. 420, 44 N. W. 306.

New York: Woolf *v.* Schaefer, 103 App. Div. 567, 93 N. Y. Supp. 184.

Vermont: Eddy *v.* Clement, 38 Vt. 486.

[54] *Kentucky:* Clark *v.* Koerner, 61 S. W. 30.

Ohio: Block-Pollak Iron Co. *v.* Cincinnati C. I. Co., 10 Ohio Dec. 51.

[55] *Iowa:* Indianapolis Terra Cotta Co. *v.* Murphy, 99 Iowa, 633, 68 N. W. 898.

Missouri: Spink *v.* Mueller, 77 Mo. App. 85.

[56] *Indiana:* Elwood Planing Mills Co. *v.* Harting, 21 Ind. App. 408, 52 N. E. 621.

Minnesota: Wheaton *v.* Lund, 61 Minn. 94, 63 N. W. 251.

not discoverable while they were being used, the building is injured, the owner may recover compensation for such injury.[57]

§ 646b. On contract to repair.

If a contract to repair premises is not properly performed, the plaintiff may recover the cost of completing the repairs.[58] Compensation may also be recovered for loss of use of the premises until the repairs are properly completed, based on the rental value of the premises,[59] or if the premises can be used in part, the difference in rental value with and without the repairs,[60] but ordinarily not damage to business or loss of profits.[61] Consequential damage may be recovered in a proper case, where the defendant had notice; as for idleness of hands on breach of contract to make repairs in a mill,[62] or injury to tenants on defective repair of a roof.[63]

§ 647. Building and repairing roads.

Upon delay in building a road for the plaintiff, he may recover the cost of building a temporary road to use during the delay.[64]

Where the contractor for building a road is delayed by the defendant, he may recover compensation for the increased cost of labor and materials caused by the delay.[65]

[57] *Ohio:* Block-Pollak Iron Co. v. Cincinnati C. I. Co., 10 Ohio Dec. 51 (defect in iron furnished; recovery for consequent blowing off of roof).

Pennsylvania: Haines v. Young, 13 Pa. Super. Ct. 303 (defect in metal supports for marble slabs; marble slab fell and broke; recovery for loss).

[58] *Tennessee:* Fort v. Orndoff, 7 Heisk. 167.

Vermont: Clifford v. Richardson, 18 Vt. 620.

[59] *Michigan:* John Hutchinson Mfg. Co. v. Pinch, 91 Mich. 156, 51 N. W. 930.

Oregon: Williams v. Island City Milling Co., 25 Ore. 573, 37 Pac. 49.

Texas: Bounds v. Hickerson, 26 Tex. Civ. App. 608, 63 S. W. 887. If the

plaintiff had the right under the contract to make the repairs himself at the defendant's expense, he cannot charge the defendant with loss of use of the mill after he might himself have made the repairs. Fort v. Orndoff, 7 Heisk. (Tenn.) 167.

[60] Winne v. Kelley, 34 Iowa, 339.

[61] *Georgia:* Coweta Falls Mfg. Co. v. Rogers, 19 Ga. 416, 65 Am. Dec. 602.

Kansas: Walrath v. Whittekind, 26 Kan. 482.

[62] Coweta Falls Manuf. Co. v. Rogers, 19 Ga. 416, 65 Am. Dec. 602.

[63] Malony v. Brady, 18 N. Y. Supp. 757.

[64] Smith v. Smith, 45 Vt. 433.

[65] King v. Des Moines, 99 Iowa, 432, 68 N. W. 708.

For breach of a contract to keep a road in repair the plaintiff may recover the reasonable cost of making the repairs.[66] Where the road was improperly built, the diminution in value should be recoverable. In such a case it was held that the county for which the road was being built was entitled to the amount saved by the contractors by their imperfect construction,[67] and it seems clear that such an amount at least is recoverable.

§ 647a. Building or repairing a bridge.

Where a contract to build a bridge is cancelled, the builder may recover the profits of the contract.[68] If the owner delays the work, the builder may recover damages caused by the delay, including interest on the amount of money invested in the work during the time of delay.[69]

If the builder erects the bridge defectively, as where the iron used is not as heavy as was agreed, the measure of damages is the difference in value of the bridge. This is to be arrived at by finding the increased cost of the additional weight of metal, including also the profit which the evidence showed a contractor would have added, to the actual cost to him of the metal.[70] In Railroad Co. v. Smith,[71] the plaintiff was allowed to recover for the delay of trains and for extra men to work a defectively built bridge.

For delay in erecting a railroad bridge, the railroad may recover for loss of use of the road; which in case of a new road will be measured by interest on the cost of the unused portion.[72]

Where the defendant undertook to keep a bridge standing and in repair and it was carried away by a flood, the measure of damages was held to be the cost of rebuilding the bridge plus

---

[66] *Massachusetts:* Clark v. Russell, 110 Mass. 133.

New York: Mayor, etc., v. Second Ave. R. R., 102 N. Y. 572, 55 Am. Rep. 839, 7 N. E. 905.

[67] Board of Commissioners v. Wolff (Ind.), 72 N. E. 860.

[68] Insley v. Shepard, 31 Fed. 869.

[69] Louisville & N. R. R. v. Hollerbach, 105 Ind. 137, 5 N. E. 28.

[70] Modern Steel Structural Co. v. Van Buren County, 126 Iowa, 606, 102 N. W. 536.

[71] 21 Wall. 255, 22 L. ed. 513

[72] American Bridge Co. v. Camden Interstate Ry., 135 Fed. 323, 68 C. C. A. 131.

the premium that might be necessary to procure an insurance against similar loss for the remainder of the term for which covenant to keep it in repair was to remain in force.[73]

§ 647b. Constructing a railroad.

For breach by the company of a contract to construct for it the whole or a portion of the roadbed of a railroad, the measure of damages is the difference between the contract price and the cost of construction;[74] and if the company wrongfully delays the work, the contractor may recover the loss caused by delay, such as wages lost,[75] but not conjectural or remote damages.[76]

For delay by the contractor the company cannot recover compensation based on the expected profits, as they are too

---

[73] Gathwright v. Callaway County, 10 Mo. 663. This must be regarded as the case of a special contract. In the ordinary case the defendant would be discharged from his obligation by the destruction of the bridge without his fault. Livingston Co. v. Graves, 32 Mo. 479.

[74] *Alabama:* Danforth v. Tennessee & C. R. R., 93 Ala. 614, 11 So. 60. Tennessee & C. R. R. v. Danforth, 13 So. 51, 112 Ala. 80, 20 So. 502.

Missouri: Hammond v. Beeson, 112 Mo. 190, 20 S. W. 646.

Tennessee: Smith v. O'Donnell, 8 Lea, 468.

Texas: O'Connor v. Smith, 84 Tex. 232, 19 S. W. 168.

In Brucker v. Manistee & G. R. R. R. (Mich.), 130 N. W. 822, defendant refused to let plaintiff complete performance of contract to build road. The defendants after refusing to allow plaintiff to proceed, themselves completed the contract at a price greater than the contract price. It was held that plaintiff was not bound by this price, but might show that it could have been done cheaper. The defendant having by the contract the option of changing the route, the

plaintiff could recover only the profit on building the road according to the route as it was changed, although this change happened after the breach.

[75] *United States:* Phillips & C. C. Co. v. Seymour, 91 U. S. 646, 23 L. ed. 341.

Alabama: Hardaway-Wright Co. v. Bradley Bros. (Ala.), 57 So. 21.

Iowa: Graves v. Glass, 86 Ia. 261, 53 N. W. 231.

Missouri: Hammond v. Beeson, 112 Mo. 190, 20 S. W. 646.

New York: Curnan v. Delaware & O. R. R. R., 138 N. Y. 480, 34 N. E. 201.

Texas: O'Connor v. Smith, 84 Tex. 232, 19 S. W. 168.

[76] *United States:* Phillips & C. C. Co. v. Seymour, 91 U. S. 646, 23 L. ed. 341.

Indiana: Louisville & N. R. R. v. Hollerbach, 105 Ind. 137, 5 N. E. 28.

Missouri: Tucker v. Deering S. W. Ry., 133 Mo. App. 122, 113 S. W. 242.

Tennessee: Smith v. O'Donnell, 8 Lea, 468.

Texas: O'Connor v. Smith, 84 Tex. 232, 19 S. W. 168.

Virginia: Atlantic & D. Ry. v. Delaware Const. Co., 98 Va. 503, 37 S. E. 13.

conjectural.[77] The proper measure of recovery is the rental value of the road during the period of delay.[78]

If the company, rightly or wrongly, puts an end to the contract after part performance, it cannot retain any portion of payments due which by agreement were to be retained as security for performance, as such an agreement is one for a penalty.[79]

§ 647c. Other contracts of construction.

The rules for the assessment of damages are the same in the case of other contracts of construction. Where the contractor fails to perform his contract to do certain work, the measure of damages is the cost to the owner of having it done by another, less the contract price if that has not been paid.[80] The owner, since he can have the work done by another, cannot recover for any loss that accrues by reason of the work remaining undone after the lapse of a reasonable time,[81] nor can he recover compensation for loss of expected profits.[82] For delay in construction, the owner may recover damages for loss of use of the property rendered useless during the delay,[83] but not for loss of expected profits.[84] For improper construction, the

[77] *Georgia:* Florida N. R. R. v. Southern Supply Co., 112 Ga. 1, 37 S. E. 130.

Pennsylvania: Jolly v. Parral & D. R. R., 35 Pittsb. L. J. (N. S.) 37.

A fortiori the expected profits by enhancement of the value of land owned by the company cannot be recovered. Coos Bay R. & E. R. & N. Co. v. Nosler, 30 Ore. 547, 48 Pac. 361.

[78] Jolly v. Parral & D. R. R., 35 Pittsb. L. J. (N. S.) 37.

[79] *Georgia:* Florida N. R. R. v. Southern Supply Co., 112 Ga. 1, 37 S. E. 130.

New York: Curnan v. Delaware & O. R. R. R., 138 N. Y. 480, 34 N. E. 201.

[80] *Kentucky:* Hazlip v. Austill, 4 Ky. L. Rep. 982 (to dig well).

Louisiana: Hammond O. & D. Co. v. Feitel, 115 La. 132, 38 So. 941 (to dig well).

Vermont: Keyes v. Western V. S. Co., 34 Vt. 81 (to repair drain).

American Surety Co. v. Woods, 105 Fed. 741, 45 C. C. A. 282, *contra*, cannot be regarded as a sound decision.

[81] *Kentucky:* Hazlip v. Austill, 4 Ky. L. Rep. 982.

Vermont: Keyes v. Western Vermont Slate Co., 34 Vt. 81.

[82] Smith v. Curran, 138 Fed. 150 (irrigating works).

[83] *Georgia:* Water Lot Co. v. Leonard, 30 Ga. 560 (mill flume; recover value of use of mill).

Massachusetts: Willey v. Fredericks, 10 Gray, 357 (sea wall to protect land; recover value of use of land).

[84] *Nebraska:* Bridges v. Lanham, 14 Neb. 369, 45 Am. Rep. 121, 15 N. W. 704 (mill flume).

Virginia: Atlantic & D. Ry. v. Delaware Construction Co., 98 Va. 503, 37 S. E. 13 (pier).

owner may recover the cost of remedying the defect,[85] with proper compensation for loss of use of the premises during the time necessary to do so.[86] For breach of contract of construction by the owner, the ordinary measure of damages is the profits of the contract.[87] Where part of the work had been performed by the contractor, but had been rendered more costly by fault of the owner, the contractor was allowed compensation for the increased cost.[88] Where the owner delays the work the contractor may recover compensation for wages of laborers and value of the use of machinery kept idle,[89] and for the increased cost of performance caused by the delay.[90]

§ 648. Actions by or against architects.

Where an architect was to obtain a certain fee for drawing plans and superintending construction, and he was prevented by the owner from superintending the construction, he is entitled to his entire fee, subject to the right of the owner to show that he might have earned a fee elsewhere in the time saved.[91]

Where an architect employed to superintend construction negligently failed to discover a defect in construction, the measure of damages recoverable against him was the cost of remedying the defect.[92]

§ 648a. Breach of contract by sub-contractor.

Where a sub-contractor fails to carry out his contract, the measure of damages is the increased cost of procuring the work

---

[85] Fisher v. Goebel, 40 Mo. 475, or the difference between the value as constructed and the value as it should have been constructed. Culbertson v. Ashland C. & C. Co. (Ky.), 139 S. W. 792 (cement walk).

[86] Saluda Manuf. Co. v. Pennington, 2 Spear (S. C.), 735.

[87] Gaffey v. United Shoe Machinery Co., 202 Mass. 48, 88 N. E. 330 (to remove ledge).

[88] Vicksburg W. S. Co. v. Gorman, 70 Miss. 360, 11 So. 680 (to build waterworks).

[89] United States: Cotton v. United States, 38 Ct. Cl. 536.

Iowa: Graves v. Glass, 86 Iowa, 261, 53 N. W. 231.

[90] Williston v. Matthews, 55 Minn. 422, 56 N. W. 1112.

[91] Graf v. Law, 120 Wis. 177, 97 N. W. 898.

[92] Straus v. Buchman, 96 App. Div. 270, 89 N. Y. Supp. 226; Schwartz v. Kuhn, 126 N. Y. Supp. 568.

to be done by another.[93] If the sub-contractor performs the contract improperly, he is responsible for damages recovered against the contractor by the owner on account of the defect.[94] If by reason of the defect or by the sub-contractor's delay the completion of the building is delayed, so that the contractor suffers damage thereby, the sub-contractor is responsible.[95] In Meyer v. Haven [96] the defendant had contracted to build railroad shops; and the plaintiff made a sub-contract with him for the structural ironwork. The plaintiff delayed furnishing the ironwork and notice was given of the danger by reason of delay. As a result of delay the walls were blown down. In an action to enforce a mechanic's lien, the defendant sought to set off damages for this loss. It was held that defendant could set off value of the property destroyed and the cost of reconstructing the walls, and also (if the terms of the contract with the railroad were communicated to plaintiffs at the time the sub-contract was made) could set off damages resulting from the breach of that contract because of the delay. This included loss of interest and payment delayed, and increased expense of doing the work in the winter. The loss of rents is not a natural consequence of the delay.[97]

Where the sub-contractor breaks his contract with the contractor, he is responsible for all damages which the company could recover against the contractor, provided they were within his contemplation. Snell v. Cottingham [98] was an action on an agreement by Cottingham with Snell to build the road of the L. B. & M. Co. by a certain time. The company had leased its line to the T. W. & W. Co., agreeing to have the

---

[93] *Illinois:* National Surety Co. *v.* Townsend B. & C. Co., 176 Ill. 156, 52 N. E. 938.

Kansas: McCullough *v.* S. J. Hayde Contracting Co., 82 Kan. 734, 109 Pac. 176.

Kentucky: Seventh St. P. M. Co. *v.* Schaefer, 30 Ky. L. Rep. 623, 99 S. W. 341.

Maryland: Ætna Indemnity Co. *v.* George A. Fuller Co., 111 Md. 321, 73 Atl. 738.

[94] Hoppaugh *v.* McGrath, 53 N. J.

L. 81, 21 Atl. 106. In this case it was held immaterial that the judgment against the contractor had not been paid.

[95] Noyes *v.* F. A. Noullet & Co., 118 La. 888, 43 So. 539.

[96] 70 App. Div. 529, 75 N. Y. Supp. 261; and on an earlier appeal 37 App. Div. 201, 55 N. Y. Supp. 864.

[97] Friedland *v.* McNeil, 33 Mich. 40 (loss of pew rents, upon delay in completion of a church).

[98] 72 Ill. 161.

line finished by a certain day, and to pay the interest on certain bonds. Snell assumed the obligations of the L. B. & M. Co. and agreed with the T. W. & W. Co. that if the road should be completed before the time agreed between the two companies the interest on the bonds should be saved for all the time gained. The time fixed by Cottingham's contract was earlier than that of the contract between the companies. Snell had made his agreement with Cottingham with reference to his contract with the company, but this Cottingham did not know. Cottingham did not finish the road within the time agreed. It was held that Snell could only recover the value of the use of the road during the delay, and that the other contract could not be considered, as it was not in the contemplation of the parties.

If the amount of damages is agreed upon between the company and the contractor by way of compromise, the subcontractor is in no case bound by the compromise.[99]

[99] Laing v. Hanson, 36 Tex. Civ. App. 116, 36 S. W. 116.

CHAPTER XXX

I.—No Express Contract

§ 649. Quantum meruit.

* We have thus far spoken of express contracts made by the parties; we have still to speak of the agreements which, in the absence of any express stipulation, the law implies from a given state of facts. For property transferred or services rendered by one to another, the law implies a promise to pay what the thing or the property is worth. The party then recovers, to use technical language, on a *quantum meruit* or a *quantum*

1307

valebat; and the measure of damages becomes a question of evidence as to the value of the property or services. Nor can this rule be varied, except by express agreement. Thus, where a father, whose infant daughter was employed by a manufacturing company, forbade them to employ her any longer, and gave them notice that if they did so he should demand a given sum for her time and labor, it was held, in an action of assumpsit against the company, that the notice was unavailing to fix the measure of compensation, and that he could only recover what her services were reasonably worth.** ¹

§ 650. Measure of compensation on a quantum meruit.
When recovery is had on a *quantum meruit* for services rendered to or benefit conferred upon the defendant at his request, the measure of compensation is the value of the work done, or in some cases the money paid, not the benefit derived by the defendant from it; ² and the same is true where the services or benefit are accepted by the defendant, though not originally rendered at his request.³ If the plaintiff has rendered services

¹ Adams *v.* Woonsocket Co., 11 Met. (Mass.) 327.

So where through the fraud of an architect the amount to be paid upon a building contract was greater in the builder's copy than in the owner's, and neither party discovered the discrepancy until the builder in good faith completed his work, it was held that he might recover on a *quantum meruit* the fair value of the labor and materials. Vickery *v.* Ritchie, 202 Mass. 247, 88 N. E. 835, 26 L. R. A. (N. S.) 810. The amount of recovery in such a case would of course be limited to the price named in the builder's copy.

² *Delaware:* Verderame *v.* Hansen, 75 Atl. 785; White *v.* Dougherty, 76 Atl. 609.

Kansas: Turner *v.* Webster, 24 Kan. 38, 36 Am. Rep. 251.

Massachusetts: Bradley *v.* Rea, 14 All. 20; Stowe *v.* Buttrick, 125 Mass. 449; Vickery *v.* Ritchie, 202 Mass. 247, 88 N. E. 835, 26 L. R. A. (N. S.) 810.

Michigan: Mooney *v.* York Iron Co., 82 Mich. 263, 46 N. W. 376.

New York: Bluemner *v.* Garvin, 120 App. Div. 29, 104 N. Y. Supp. 1009.

Tennessee: Edington *v.* Pickle, 1 Sneed, 122.

Where there was no agreement on the price except that it should not exceed $6.00 per day, the plaintiff recovers the value of his services up to that amount. Russell *v.* Wylly, 119 N. Y. Supp. 155.

No compensation can be recovered in this action for labor performed with the expectation of making it available in the performance of a contract with the defendant, which contract the defendant terminated before any part had been performed. Curtis *v.* Smith, 48 Vt. 116.

³ Hayward *v.* Leonard, 7 Pick. (Mass.) 181, 19 Am. Dec. 268; Bee Printing Co. *v.* Hitchborn, 4 All. 63; Chase *v.* Corcoran, 106 Mass. 286.

the measure of recovery is the value of the services, not of the product of the service; [4] and if the plaintiff has leased property, it is the value of the use. [5] The amount paid by the plaintiff to his own workmen hired by him to do the work is not recoverable, but only the value of their work. [6] Thus, where an agent without his principal's authority borrows money and invests it in property, the principals, by afterwards appropriating and selling the property for their own benefit, will be held to have ratified the act; and the measure of their liability is the amount borrowed, and not that realized from the sale. [7] It has been held that if the plaintiff has once charged a certain amount, which has been paid, and a receipt taken in full, no greater amount can be recovered, because the jury should put no greater estimate on the value of his services than he himself put upon them. [8] The true bar to recovery in such a case seems to be that the acceptance of a certain amount in full is an accord and satisfaction.

§ 651. Contract void by statute of frauds.

In an action for work and labor, the rule of damages is the value of the service rendered, and not an oral agreement as to wages, ruled out under the statute of frauds. [9] Where a parol

[4] *United States:* Charleston I. M. Co. v. Joyce, 63 Fed. 916, 11 C. C. A. 496 (boring well).
Illinois: Ennis v. Pullman P. C. Co., 165 Ill. 161, 46 N. E. 439 (professional services).
Massachusetts: Snow v. Ware, 13 Met. 42 (building road).
Michigan: Turner v. Mason, 65 Mich. 662, 32 N. W. 846 (painting portrait).
It is the net value, deducting an allowance for defective workmanship: Wright v. Cumpsty, 41 Pa. 102.
[5] Adamson v. Adamson, 9 Ark. 26 (slaves).
[6] Hauptman v. Catlin, 1 E. D. Smith (N. Y.), 729.
[7] Watson v. Bigelow, 47 Mo. 413.
[8] Danziger v. Hoyt, 46 Hun (N. Y.), 270.

[9] *Illinois:* Butcher Steel Works v. Atkinson, 68 Ill. 421.
New Hampshire: Emery v. Smith, 46 N. H. 151.
New York: Day v. New York C. R. R., 51 N. Y. 583, 590; Rosepaugh v. Vredenburgh, 16 Hun, 60.
But *contra,* Fuller v. Rice, 52 Mich. 435; La Du-King M. Co. v. La Du, 36 Minn. 473.
In King v. Brown, 2 Hill (N. Y.), 485, plaintiff agreed to do forty dollars worth of work and defendant in payment agreed to convey four acres of land. The work was done. The defendant refused to convey, and the contract was void by the statute of frauds. It was held that plaintiff could recover for his labor, but the amount recovered was the actual value of the labor, and not the greater value of the

contract for the sale of land is void or unenforceable by the statute of frauds, a vendee can frequently recover the consideration, generally under one of the common counts.[10]   In Bender v. Bender [11] the rule is stated to be "Compensation for all that the plaintiff did in pursuance of the contract and in satisfaction of his part thereof, and for all permanent improvements made upon the land in reliance upon the contract with the knowledge of the defendant, deducting the value of the rents and profits during the plaintiff's occupancy." In California the measure of an intended vendee's damages is the money he has advanced, with interest, or the reasonable value of the services rendered, without reference to the express contract, and evidence of the value of the land is inadmissible.[12]   In New Hampshire it is held that the actual loss sustained and expense incurred under all the circumstances of the case, taking the agreement into consideration, furnish the measure of the damages which the jury, if they see fit, may make equal to the value of the land.[13]   In Mississippi, where the proposed vendor of land in bad faith refuses to consummate a parol agreement for the sale of land, the proposed vendee is entitled to compensation for the trouble and loss of time incurred in consequence of his confidence in the other, but not for the loss of his bargain.[14]

Statutes frequently make contracts to leave a legacy void unless they are in writing. In a jurisdiction in which such a statute is in force it is held that where services are rendered in pursuance of a mutual understanding that payment shall be made by bequest or devise, and the party dies without making the expected compensation, the one rendering the services may recover the value of the services from the estate.[15]

land. If the contract had been simply for a specified amount of work which was to be the consideration for the conveyance of the land, the value of the land could be shown as establishing the value of the work; but where the parties themselves had agreed on labor of a certain value, that alone could be recovered.

[10] Tripp v. Bishop, 56 Pa. 424; Harris v. Harris, 70 Pa. 170.

[11] 37 Pa. 419; acc., Wright v. Haskell, 45 Me. 489.

[12] Fuller v. Reed, 38 Cal. 99.

[13] Ham v. Goodrich, 37 N. H. 185.

[14] Welch v. Lawson, 32 Miss. 170.

[15] Robinson v. Raynor, 28 N. Y. 494; Collier v. Rutledge, 136 N. Y. 621, 32 N. E. 626; Ritchie v. Bennett, 35 App. Div. 68, 54 N. Y. Supp. 379; Lane v. Calby, 95 App. Div. 11, 88 N. Y. Supp.

§ 652. Failure of consideration.

The amount paid, with interest, is the measure of damages in assumpsit to recover for failure of consideration.[16] In James *v.* Hodsden [17] the plaintiff had given his notes for a patent fraudulently represented to have some value. He compromised some of the notes. In assumpsit to recover for the failure of consideration, it was held that he could recover the amount paid to compromise the notes, even assuming that he could have defended them, for he was not bound to follow them through a long course of litigation, and it would be presumed he did his best.

§ 653. Compensation for work and labor.

Where one has incurred necessary expense or sustained damages in protecting another's property which is accidentally beyond the owner's control, and it is afterwards reclaimed by the owner, the law implies a promise to pay the expense or compensate for the damage.[18] But for services rendered gratuitously without request there can be no recovery.[19]

§ 654. Waiver of tort.

Where a person who has suffered an injury to his property is allowed to waive the tort and sue in assumpsit, the measure of damages in contract, as in tort, is the value of the property taken or destroyed.[20]

§ 655. Deviation from contract by consent—Extra work.

* So, also, where work is done under a special agreement at estimated prices, and there is a deviation from the original plan, by the *consent of the parties*, the contract is made the rule of payment, as far as it can be traced, and for the extra labor the party is entitled to his *quantum meruit.*** [21] Where the

---

[16] Tyler *v.* Bailey, 71 Ill. 34.
[17] 47 Vt. 127.
[18] Sheldon *v.* Sherman, 42 Barb. 368.
[19] *Post,* § 673d.
[20] *Indiana:* Board of Commissioners *v.* Trees, 12 Ind. App. 479, 40 N. E. 535.
New Jersey: Moore *v.* Richardson, 68 N. J. L. 305, 53 Atl. 1032.

[21] *California:* De Boom *v.* Priestly, 1 Cal. 206.
Illinois: Brigham *v.* Hawley, 17 Ill. 38; McClelland *v.* Snider, 18 Ill. 58; Chicago & G. E. R. R. *v.* Vosburgh, 45 Ill. 311.
Kentucky: Wright *v.* Wright, 1 Litt. 179; Western *v.* Sharp, 14 B. Mon. 177.

performance of a special contract was prevented by the defendant, and suit brought on the common counts, the Supreme Court of New York said: [22]

"The defendant may give the contract in evidence with a view to lessen the quantum of damages. So far as the work was done under the special contract, the prices specified in it are, as a general rule, to be taken as the best evidence of the value of the work. Where it does not appear that the work was rendered more expensive to the plaintiff than was contemplated when the contract was made, or than it otherwise would have been, in consequence of the improper interference of the defendant, or of his neglect or omission to perform what by the contract he was bound to do, the contract prices should be held conclusive between the parties. But if the defendant neglect to furnish the materials which he was to find in due time, so that the plaintiff is obliged to do his work at a less favorable season, and at an additional expense, such expense ought to be taken into consideration and added to the contract price."

It is the duty of a contractor who has undertaken a piece of work, such as the erection of a house for a specified price, but without specification as to the manner or style of the work, when he proposes to do any part of it in a more costly style than would be justified by the agreed price, to inform the employer of the difference in cost. The employer has *prima facie* a right to suppose, unless apprised of the contrary, that every proposition as to different parts of the work is made under the contract for the whole, and is intended merely to present him with a choice of modes within that contract. To get rid of this inference, the contractor must show, either that he notified his employer that his proposition was a departure from the original

---

Louisiana: Jones v. Adams, 12 La. Ann. 621.

Maryland: Annapolis & B. S. L. R. R. v. Ross, 68 Md. 310.

New Hampshire: Wheeden v. Fiske, 50 N. H. 125.

New York: Hollinshead v. Mactier, 13 Wend. 276; Nason Mfg. Co. v. Stephens, 127 N. Y. 602, 28 N. E. 411.

Pennsylvania: McGrann v. North Lebanon R. R., 29 Pa. 82.

South Carolina: McCormick v. Connoly, 2 Bay, 401.

Wyoming: Hood v. Smiley, 5 Wyo. 70, 96 Pac. 856.

England: Robson v. Godfrey, 1 Holt N. P. 236.

[22] Koon v. Greenman, 7 Wend. (N. Y.) 121, 123.

design and contract, and would be attended with increased cost, or that its character necessarily gave him this information; otherwise there can be no recovery for extra work.[23] As to costly work done in his absence, and in a manner not previously approved by him, it is not enough to show that on his return he was pleased with its appearance, and did not order it to be removed. The rule sanctioning payments for alterations and additions not originally contemplated, as far as the work can be traced under the contract, must be so applied as not to violate the above principles. Nor, it seems, should extra work, either in quantity or quality, unless done under an express agreement or on a statement of the price, be charged for at a greater rate in reference to the market value of such work than the contract bears to the market value of the work contracted to be done.[24]

If, however, circumstances have occurred which made the extra work more costly than it was at the time the contract was entered into, the contract price ceases to be a guide in estimating the compensation for the extra work.[25] So in a case where the plaintiff entered into a written contract with the defendants to construct a section of a canal, to receive nine cents per cubic foot for excavation, forty cents per cubic yard for rock, and eleven cents for embankment; and the defendants had so far rescinded the contract as to enable the plaintiff to recover in the form of a *quantum meruit*, the plaintiff was held at liberty to recover for excavating *hard pan* (that not being mentioned nor included in the contract), at the rate which it was worth; and to prove the value of his labor in this respect, wholly irrespective of the contract. The contract contained a

[23] *Alabama:* Badders v. Davis, 88 Ala. 367, 6 So. 834.
England: Lovelock v. King, 1 Moo. & R. 60.
Where the contract provides that no work shall be regarded as extra work unless expressly so contracted for in writing before the work is begun, extra work done expressly as such under a parol contract must be paid for, since the parol contract is a modification of the written contract. Er-

skine v. Johnson, 23 Neb. 261, 36 N. W. 510; McLeod v. Genius, 31 Neb. 1, 47 N. W. 473.
[24] Jones v. Woodbury, 11 B. Mon. (Ky.) 167.
[25] *Indiana:* Harrison Co. v. Byrne, 67 Ind. 21.
Iowa: Slusser v. Burlington, 47 Ia. 300 (hard pan).
Michigan: Turner v. Grand Rapids, 20 Mich. 390 (bad state of weather).

provision that the judgment of the defendant's engineer should, in case of a difference between the parties, be conclusive; but this was held not to apply to the hard pan.[26] Where the deviation consisted in a cheapening of the construction, it has been held that the difference in value between the parts so constructed, and constructed as the contract required, should be deducted from the contract price.[27] If the extra work is so different from the work provided for in the contract that the price named in the contract furnishes no proper guide to the value of the extra work, or if the nature of the contract is so modified by the changes that the original prices cannot be traced in the new work, the plaintiff may recover the value of the work.[28]

II.—RESCISSION OF EXPRESS CONTRACT

§ 655a. Nature of rescission.

The term Rescission should legally be confined to cases where a contract is rightfully put an end to during the performance of it and before the performance is completed. This may be done by mutual consent of the parties or it may under certain circumstances be the act of one party to the contract alone. For instance, if a party is induced to enter into a contract by the fraud of the other party to it, he may avoid or

[26] Dubois v. Delaware & Hudson Canal Co., 4 Wend. (N. Y.) 285; s. c. 12 Wend. (N. Y.) 334; and s. c. in error, 15 Wend. (N. Y.) 87. In Alabama, see Aiken v. Bloodgood, 12 Ala. 221.

[27] Alabama: Badders v. Davis, 88 Ala. 367, 6 So. 834.

Illinois: Holmes v. Stummel, 17 Ill. 455.

Missouri: Lindemann v. Dennis, 65 Mo. App. 511.

Ohio: Goldsmith v. Hand, 26 Oh. St. 101.

Washington: Adamant P. M. Co. v. Nat. Bank of Commerce, 5 Wash. 232, 31 Pac. 634.

Therefore if a change is made at the instance of the builder and for his benefit there can be no recovery for

extra work. Spence v. Board of Commissioners, 117 Ind. 573, 18 N. E. 513.

[28] United States: Charleston Ice Manuf. Co. v. Joyce, 63 Fed. 916, 11 C. C. A. 496.

Illinois: Chicago & Gr. W. R. R. v. Vosburgh, 45 Ill. 311; Western Union R. R. v. Smith, 75 Ill. 496; Elgin v. Joslyn, 136 Ill. 525, 26 N. E. 1090.

Indiana: Street v. Swain, 21 Ind. 203.

New Hampshire: Bailey v. Woods, 17 N. H. 365; Wheeden v. Fiske, 50 N. H. 125.

New York: Hollinshead v. Mactier, 13 Wend. 276.

Utah: Rhodes v. Clute, 17 Utah, 137, 53 Pac. 990.

Wyoming: Hood v. Smiley, 5 Wyo. 70, 96 Pac. 856.

rescind the contract. Even if the contract was legally entered into, one party, according to most authorities, may elect to rescind the contract if full performance of it is prevented by the other party. Under some circumstances it has even been held that one party may rescind a contract because of a breach of it by the other party although it is still entirely possible for the former to continue and complete the performance on his side. In all these cases the rescission is legally accomplished because of a right given by law to the rescinding party.

Rescission, properly so called, is sometimes confounded with repudiation of the contract by one party. This, however, is an entirely improper use of the term.

Whenever a party to the contract is given the right to rescind because of a breach by the other party this is merely an optional right. He may, if he choose, continue to claim his right to the performance of the contract and may bring suit upon the special agreement and recover damages for the breach of it which will include loss of profits if any can be proved. On the other hand if he choose he may rescind the contract and claim the rights which arise from rescission.[29]

If a party to a contract elects to rescind it he cannot then continue to claim the benefits of the contract. He cannot go on and perform it nor can he claim compensation for loss of profits of it. His election involves an abandonment of any claim whatever to the performance of the contract and he can make no other claim than for a return of the benefit conferred by him.[30] Consequently, where the non-payment of an instalment under a contract is held to justify rescission, a party cannot sue for breach of the contract on such non-payment and recover for loss of profits of the contract. If he chooses to keep the contract alive, he must continue performance; but if he

[29] *Illinois:* Wilson v. Bauman, 80 Ill. 493.
Maryland: North v. Mallory, 94 Md. 305, 51 Atl. 89.
Nebraska: Thompson v. Gaffey, 52 Neb. 317, 72 N. W. 314.
Vermont: Derby v. Johnson, 21 Vt. 17.
[30] Therefore if the plaintiff continues

performance after his right to rescind accrues, he cannot afterward change his mind, and claim to recover on a *quantum meruit.*
New York: Meyer v. Hallock, 2 Robert. 284.
Pennsylvania: Shaw v. Turnpike, 3 P. & W. 445.

elects to regard the contract as rescinded, he has no claim to the profits.[31]

Upon the rescission of a contract both parties to it have the right to be replaced so far as that is possible in the condition in which they were before performance of the contract began. In other words, each side is entitled to a return of anything which it has given to the other on account of the contract or in performance of it. Since one of the parties is in the wrong the other party must be preferred on both sides of this return; and if a complete return of the benefits can be made without injustice to the other party, then the return must be made to the rescinding party and not to the wrongdoing party. In most cases, however, no difficulty will be found in securing a return of benefits. If the rescinding party has been overpaid in advance, the other may recover the excess of such payments over the value of the work done before abandonment.[32]

§ 655b. Rescission for default of defendant.

According to the prevailing opinion, where there is a contract for labor, and an entire sum to be paid for it, and the plaintiff has performed a part according to its terms, and has been prevented from performing the whole by the defendant, he may sue either on the contract to recover damages for the breach of it, or in general assumpsit to recover for the value of what he has done. If he sue on the contract, he must set it forth specially, and then his damages for what he has done under it must be regulated by the contract price, and he will recover such a proportion of the whole of that price as the work he has done bears to the whole work. And in such a suit he may recover whatever other damages he may have sustained by the defendant's breach; as, for instance, if the contract were a profitable one, the profit he would have made by being allowed to complete it, and the damages he may have incurred in providing labor and means to perform the residue. If he

[31] *California:* Cox v. McLaughlin, 54 Cal. 605.
Illinois: Christian County v. Oveholt, 18 Ill. 223.
Minnesota: Beatty v. Howe Lumber Co., 77 Minn. 272, 79 N. W. 1013.

New York: Wharton v. Winch, 140 N. Y. 287, 35 N. E. 589; Jones v. N. Y., 57 App. Div. 403, 68 N. Y. Supp. 228.
[32] Watson v. DeWitt County, 19 Tex. Civ. App. 150, 46 S. W. 1061.

choose to waive the contract and sue in general assumpsit for work and labor, then his measure of damages will be a reasonable compensation for the work actually performed. He is not then limited to a recovery of his *pro rata* share of the agreed price.[33] So where the plaintiff had agreed with the defendants to make a section of an aqueduct, to be paid one dollar per cubic yard for rock excavation, the defendants stopped the work when about half of it was done. The plaintiff proved that he had lost on the part of the work which he had executed (that being the most expensive), estimating it at the contract price of one dollar per yard, the sum of $46,800, and that he would have made a profit on that portion of the contract which remained to be executed when the work was suspended, equal to the amount of his loss on the work done. The New York Court of Appeals, overruling the Supreme Court, held that the plaintiff should recover the actual value of the work done, without regard to the contract price.[34] Pratt, J., said:

"When parties deviate from the terms of a special contract, the contract price will, as far as applicable, generally be the rule of damages. But when the contract is terminated by one party against the consent of the other, the latter will not be confined to the contract price, but may bring his action for a breach of the contract, and recover as damages all that he may lose by way of profits in not being allowed to fulfil the contract; or he may waive the contract and bring his action on the common counts for work and labor generally, and recover what the work done is actually worth."

The Supreme Court of Ohio, in discussing this decision, dissent from these views and declare it as a rule in all cases that "the express contract furnishes the measure of damages to the

---

[33] *Connecticut:* Valente v. Weinberg, 80 Conn. 134, 67 Atl. 369, 13 L. R. A. (N. S.) 448.

Illinois: Lincoln v. Schwartz, 70 Ill. 134.

Michigan: Kearney v. Doyle, 22 Mich. 294; Cadman v. Markle, 76 Mich. 448.

Missouri: McCullough v. Baker, 47 Mo. 401.

New York: Merrill v. Ithaca & O. R.

R., 16 Wend. 586, 30 Am. Dec. 130; Moran v. McSwegan, 33 N. Y. Super. Ct. 350.

North Carolina: Buffkin v. Baird, 73 N. C. 283.

Vermont: Chamberlin v. Scott, 33 Vt. 80.

[34] Clark v. Mayor of New York, 4 N. Y. 338, 343, 53 Am. Dec. 379, reversing 3 Barb. 288.

extent of the evidence it affords, and to the same extent as in cases where the contract continues in force, but remains neglected and unperformed by the defendant," and that this rule remains the same, notwithstanding the contract was terminated by the defendant against the plaintiff's consent.[35]

When the rescinded party to a contract has given property or has performed services either in consideration for the contract or in partial performance of it, he is entitled upon rescission, as has been seen, to a return of the property or the services. In case of property this return can often be made in specie. In case of service there can be no return in specie. Where no return can be made of the exact benefit conferred, the plaintiff is entitled to recover in an action on a *quantum meruit* or *quantum valebat*, the value of the services conferred [36] or the property given [37] in lieu of a return in specie; and since this is not a suit on the contract, but merely a recovery of the benefit conferred by performance for the purpose of replacing the parties in their original position, the contract price is immaterial,[38] and so is the value of the services to the defendant.[39] The cost to the plaintiff may be shown as evidence of

[35] Doolittle v. McCullough, 12 Oh. St. 360; acc., Preble v. Bottom, 27 Vt. 249.

[36] *Georgia:* Britt v. Hays, 21 Ga. 157. *Illinois:* Selby v. Hutchinson, 9 Ill. 319; Webster v. Enfield, 10 Ill. 298; Dobbins v. Higgins, 78 Ill. 440; Wilson v. Bauman, 80 Ill. 493. *Iowa:* Fitch v. Casey, 2 G. Greene, 300; Marquis v. Lauretson, 76 Ia. 23, 40 N. W. 73; Thompson v. Brown, 106 Ia. 367, 67 N. W. 819. *Maryland:* Black v. Woodrow, 39 Md. 194. *Michigan:* Bush v. Brooks, 70 Mich. 446, 38 N. W. 562. *New York:* Simmons v. Ocean Causeway, 21 App. Div. 30, 47 N. Y. Supp. 360; Hardiman v. Mayor, 21 App. Div. 614, 47 N. Y. Supp. 786. *Rhode Island:* Green v. Haley, 5 R. I. 260. *Vermont:* Preble v. Bottom, 27 Vt. 249.

[37] *Iowa:* Fagan v. Hook, 134 Ia. 381, 111 N. W. 981. *Minnesota:* Bennett v. Phelps, 12 Minn. 326. *New York:* Tabak v. Fettner, 139 App. Div. 248, 123 N. Y. Supp. 982. [38] *Iowa:* Fitch v. Casey, 2 G. Greene, 300. *Maryland:* Rodemer v. Hazelhurst, 9 Gill, 288; North v. Mallory, 94 Md. 305, 51 Atl. 89. *Massachusetts:* Connolly v. Sullivan, 173 Mass. 1, 53 N. E. 143. *Michigan:* Hemminger v. Western Assur. Co., 95 Mich. 355, 54 N. W. 949, 35 Am. St. Rep. 566. *Nebraska:* Thompson v. Gaffey, 52 Neb. 317, 72 N. W. 314. *New York:* Merrill v. Ithaca & O. R. R., 16 Wend. 586 (*cf.* Koon v. Greenman, 7 Wend. 121). *Vermont:* Derby v. Johnson, 21 Vt. 17. [39] San Francisco Bridge Co. v. Dum-

the value.[40] In a few States, however, the courts, overlooking the consideration that this is not a suit for breach of contract, but to recover for goods delivered or services rendered on a consideration failed, hold that the recovery must be at the contract rate,[41] or at least cannot exceed the contract price,[42] unless the circumstances are such as to show that the expense of the part performance was greater than the average expense of full performance.[43] This amounts to giving the defendant the benefit of the contract which by his default it is agreed that the plaintiff has a right to destroy.

Where the contract is divisible, so that a contract price is named for each of several acts of performance, and some of the acts have been completed before rescission, the contract price alone is recoverable for these acts; the value of the performance cannot be demanded.[44]

§ 655c. Rescission by act of God or of the law: impossibility of performance.

Where through the plaintiff's illness, or otherwise through the act of God or of the law, a contract is not completed, a recovery can be had for what is done under it to an amount measured by the value of the service, but limited by the terms of the contract.[45] So where an agent was employed to superin-

barton Land & Imp. Co., 119 Cal. 272, 51 Pac. 335 (to build a levee).

[40] Simmons v. Ocean Causeway, 21 App. Div. 30, 47 N. Y. Supp. 360.

[41] *Arkansas:* Wiegel v. Boone, 64 Ark. 228, 41 S. W. 763.

California: Reynolds v. Jourdan, 6 Cal. 108.

Illinois: Chicago Training School v. Davies, 64 Ill. App. 503; Rice v. Partello, 88 Ill. App. 52.

Indiana: Hoyle v. Stellwagen, 28 Ind. App. 681, 63 N. E. 780.

New Jersey: Kehoe v. Rutherford, 56 N. J. L. 23, 27 Atl. 912.

[42] *Illinois:* Folliott v. Hunt, 21 Ill. 654.

Missouri: Steinburg v. Gebhardt, 41 Mo. 519.

[43] Wellston Coal Co. v. Franklin Paper Co., 57 Oh. St. 182, 48 N. E.

888 (agreement to buy coal for a year at a certain rate; after coal had been received during the period of highest price, buyer repudiated; seller may recover for portion delivered at market rate).

[44] *Iowa:* Marquis v. Lauretson, 76 Ia. 23, 40 N. W. 73.

Maryland: Rodemer v. Hazlehurst, 9 Gill, 288.

See Wiegel v. Boone, 64 Ark. 228, 41 S. W. 763.

[45] *Georgia:* Doster v. Brown, 25 Ga. 24, 71 Am. Dec. 153.

Kentucky: Fuller v. Brown, 11 Met. 440.

Massachusetts: Harrington v. Fall River Iron Works, 119 Mass. 82.

Minnesota: La Du-King M. Co. v. La Du, 36 Minn. 473.

tend the construction of an engineering work under a contract by which he was to receive as compensation a third of the profits besides a salary, but died after the greater part of the work had been done, and it was afterwards finished at a large profit, it was held, in an action brought by his executors, that they were entitled to recover the *pro rata* proportion of the salary and of the profits under the contract, which last were measured by taking one-third of such a proportion of the whole profits earned and received by the defendant, as the cost of the work done at the time of the testator's death bore to that of the completed undertaking.[46]

In Louisiana, a contract made by a partnership as undertakers for the construction of a railroad will be cancelled by the death of any of the parties, and the other contracting party is only bound to pay the value of the work already done, and that of the materials already prepared, proportionably to the price agreed on.[47]

Where by a change of law during the progress of the work the completion of a contract is made impossible, the contractor may recover at the contract rate for the work already done.[48] And so when the full performance of work is prevented by an injunction, recovery may be had for the part performed before the injunction was issued at the contract rate, or at least according to the value of the services rendered.[49]

When one undertakes to do work upon the property of another, and before the completion of the work the property is destroyed by act of God the contractor is entitled to recover

Missouri: Callahan *v.* Shotwell, 60 Mo. 398.

New York: Jones *v.* Judd, 4 N. Y. 411; Wolfe *v.* Howes, 20 N. Y. 197, 75 Am. Dec. 384.

In Fahy *v.* North, 19 Barb. 341, the recovery was held not to be governed by the contract rate. In Hubbard *v.* Belden, 27 Vt. 645; Patrick *v.* Putnam, 27 Vt. 759, the amount recovered was reduced by the damages sustained by the employer from the plaintiff's absence.

For cases of service involving this point, see *post*, § 672.

[46] Clark *v.* Gilbert, 26 N. Y. 279, 84 Am. Dec. 189.

[47] McCord *v.* West Feliciana R. R., 3 La. Ann. 285.

[48] Jones *v.* Judd, 4 N. Y. 411; Heine *v.* Meyer, 61 N. Y. 171, 20 Am. Rep. 475 (construction of a building).

[49] *Mississippi:* Whitfield *v.* Zellnor, 24 Miss. 663 (recovery of what the services were worth).

New Hampshire: Theobald *v.* Burleigh, 66 N. H. 574, 23 Atl. 367 (what the services were worth).

Vermont: Doolittle *v.* Nash, 48 Vt. 441.

compensation for the work he has done.[50] So where a contractor undertakes to do work on the defendant's building, and the building is blown down before completion of the work, the contractor may recover compensation for his work.[51] And if both sides of the contract have been partly executed before the destruction, compensation may be recovered on both sides for what has been done.[52]

So where one is to make repairs on the house of another under a special contract, or is to furnish a part of the work and materials used in the erection of a house, and his contract becomes impossible of performance on account of the destruction of the house by fire, he may recover for what he has done or furnished.[53] And on the same principle recovery may be had for labor and materials where the plaintiff had undertaken to install a heating or lighting plant in a building,[54] to

[50] See on this doctrine all the cases subsequently cited in this section.

The opposite doctrine prevails in England: Appleby v. Myers, L. R. 2 C. P. 651 (contract to put machinery into defendant's building). And see Brumby v. Smith, 3 Ala. 123; Shanks v. Griffin, 14 B. Mon. 153.

If it is still possible to restore and complete the work the plaintiff must do so before he will be entitled to recover compensation; as where he undertakes to erect a building on land, and it is blown or burned down before completion, the plaintiff is not thereby discharged from his obligation to perform.

Illinois: Schwartz v. Saunders, 46 Ill. 18.

Massachusetts: Adams v. Nichols, 19 Pick. 275, 31 Am. Dec. 137.

New Jersey: School Trustees v. Bennett, 27 N. J. L. 513, 72 Am. Dec. 373.

New York: Tompkins v. Dudley, 25 N. Y. 272, 82 Am. Dec. 349.

Tennessee: Galyon v. Ketchen, 85 Tenn. 55, 1 S. W. 508.

Texas: Weis v. Devlin, 67 Tex. 507, 3 S. W. 726, 60 Am. Rep. 38.

[51] *Illinois:* Schwartz v. Saunders, 46 Ill. 18.

Iowa: Garretty v. Brazell, 34 Iowa, 100.

[52] Butterfield v. Byron, 153 Mass. 517, 27 N. E. 667, 25 Am. St. Rep. 654, 12 L. R. A. 571.

[53] *Illinois:* Rawson v. Clark, 70 Ill. 656.

Massachusetts: Cleary v. Sohier, 120 Mass. 210; Butterfield v. Byron, 153 Mass. 517, 27 N. E. 667, 25 Am. St. Rep. 654, 12 L. R. A. 571.

New York: Niblo v. Binsse, 1 Keyes, 476; Hayes v. Gross, 9 App. Div. 12, 40 N. Y. Supp. 1098.

Texas: Hollis v. Chapman, 36 Tex. 1; Weis v. Devlin, 67 Tex. 507, 3 S. W. 726, 60 Am. Rep. 38.

West Virginia: Hysell v. Sterling Coal & Manuf. Co., 46 W. Va. 158, 33 S. E. 95.

Wisconsin: Cook v. McCabe, 53 Wis. 250, 10 N. W. 507, 40 Am. Rep. 765.

[54] *Illinois:* Kenwood Bridge Co. v. Dunderdale, 50 Ill. App. 581.

New York: Niblo v. Binsse, 1 Keyes, 476.

move a building,[55] to build a house from the defendant's materials,[56] to make gloves from the defendant's materials,[57] or to repair the defendant's vessel,[58] and the building, the materials, or the vessel is destroyed by fire before complete performance. According to the weight of authority this recovery is to be had at the contract rate, so far as this can be applied to the case.[59] In some States, however, the reasonable value of the work and materials is to be recovered, and not the *pro rata* portion of the contract price.[60] Since neither party is in fault, neither has forfeited the right to rely on the contract; and the better view therefore is to allow recovery at the contract rate.

§ 655d. Cancellation according to the terms of the contract.

When the contract contains a clause permitting one party to cancel it upon notice to the other, and the contract is so cancelled after part performance, the party who has partly performed may recover compensation for the work he has done at the contract rate.[61]

§ 655e. Rescission by mutual consent or mistake.

When a contract is rescinded after part performance by the

[55] Angus v. Scully, 176 Mass. 357, 57 N. E. 674, 49 L. R. A. 562, 79 Am. St. Rep. 318.

[56] Wilson v. Knott, 3 Humph. 473, 39 Am. Dec. 165.

[57] Labowitz v. Frankfort, 4 N. Y. Misc. 275, 23 N. Y. Supp. 1038.

[58] Menetone v. Athawes, 3 Burr. 1592.

[59] *Illinois:* Schwartz v. Saunders, 46 Ill. 18; Rawson v. Clark, 70 Ill. 656; Clark v. Busse, 82 Ill. 515.

Massachusetts: Butterfield v. Byron, 153 Mass. 517, 27 N. E. 667, 25 Am. St. Rep. 654, 12 L. R. A. 571.

New York: Niblo v. Binsse, 1 Keyes, 476; Hayes v. Gross, 9 App. Div. 12, 40 N. Y. Supp. 1098; Labowitz v. Frankfort, 4 Misc. 275, 23 N. Y. Supp. 1038.

Texas: Hollis v. Chapman, 36 Tex. 1.

Virginia: Clark v. Franklin, 7 Leigh,

1.

Wisconsin: Cook v. McCabe, 53 Wis. 250, 10 N. W. 507, 40 Am. Rep. 765.

[60] Wilson v. Knott, 3 Humph. (Tenn.) 473, 39 Am. Dec. 165.

[61] *Illinois:* Chicago v. Sexton, 115 Ill. 230, 2 N. E. 263.

Massachusetts: Fitzgerald v. Allen, 128 Mass. 232.

New York: Dolan v. Rodgers, 149 N. Y. 489, 44 N. E. 167.

In Lyman v. Lincoln, 38 Neb. 794, 57 N. W. 531, however, where the city cancelled a contract to build an engine house under a power reserved to it in the contract, it was held that it could not thereafter use the contract price for the purpose of diminishing plaintiff's claim. Plaintiff is entitled to recover the amount of actual benefit which the city received independently of the terms of the contract.

mutual consent of the parties, a party who has partially performed the contract may in the ordinary case recover the value of such performance according to the contract price; the amount recoverable depending upon the ratio of the value of the labor and materials actually furnished to the total value of all the labor and materials which would have been required for the performance of the contract.[62]   So where the contract is rescinded or avoided for the mutual mistake of the parties, either party may recover the value of his performance.[63]

If, however, the circumstances of the rescission are such as to make it clear that neither party was to have compensation, this will not be allowed. So when the plaintiff, who had contracted to build a mill, built it so badly that it was entirely useless, and by agreement of the parties the mill was entirely rebuilt, the builder was allowed to recover nothing for the first building, but was restricted to compensation for the rebuilding.[64]

III.—EXPRESS CONTRACT PERFORMED

§ 655f. Full performance of express contract.

Where an express contract for labor or for the delivery of goods is completely performed on the side of the contractor, leaving nothing undone but the payment of the contract price, the contractor may sue on the common counts as for a debt; but the measure of recovery is the contract price, and the plaintiff cannot recover the value of the services or the goods beyond that price.[65]

[62] *United States:* Charleston Ice Manuf. Co. *v.* Joyce, 63 Fed. 916, 11 C. C. A. 496.
Illinois: Schillo *v.* McEwen, 90 Ill. 77.
Iowa: McAfferty *v.* Hale, 24 Ia. 355.
Massachusetts: Connolly *v.* Sullivan, 173 Mass. 1, 53 N. E. 143.
New York: Delaware & H. Canal Co. *v.* Dubois, 15 Wend. 87, affirming Dubois *v.* C. Co., 12 Wend. 334.
North Carolina: Farmer *v.* Francis, 12 Ire. 282.
[63] Vickery *v.* Ritchie, 202 Mass. 247, 88 N. E. 835, 26 L. R. A. (N. S.) 810.

[64] Simpson *v.* McDonald, 2 Ark. 370.
[65] *United States:* Chesapeake & O. Canal Co. *v.* Knapp, 9 Pet. 541, 9 L. ed. 222; Dermott *v.* Jones, 2 Wall. 1, 17 L. ed. 762.
Delaware: Massey *v.* Greenabaum, 5 Pennew. 20, 58 Atl. 804.
Kansas: Houghton *v.* Kittleman, 7 Kan. App. 207, 52 Pac. 898.
Maryland: City & Suburban Ry. *v.* Basshor, 82 Md. 397, 33 Atl. 635; Southern Building & Loan Assoc. *v.* Price, 88 Md. 155, 42 L. R. A. 206, 41 Atl. 53.

§ 656. Acceptance of work not according to the contract.

If a contracting party does work in performance of a contract, but does not fulfil the terms of the contract, the other party by accepting the work as it was done renders himself liable to pay compensation.

And where by the terms of the contract one party on abandonment of the contract uncompleted has a right to complete it at the other's expense, the election to complete the contract involves an acceptance of the work so far as it is done, and entitles the contractor to recover compensation for the work he has done,[66] making allowance for the damages (as for delay) caused by the non-performance.[67]

Where work was done on land, as by building a house or other structure, the owner by occupying the building does not accept the work, since he cannot make use of his own land without using the building and his doing so is no waiver of his right to claim that the contract has not been performed.[68] In such a case the enforced occupation of the building by the owner is not a waiver of the condition precedent, and although the owner of the land necessarily becomes the owner also of the

Massachusetts: Morse *v.* Potter, · 4 Gray, 292.

Missouri: Kick *v.* Boerste, 45 Mo. App. 134.

New York: Clark *v.* Fairchild, 22 Wend. 576; Ladue *v.* Seymour, 24 Wend. 60.

Rhode Island: McDermott *v.* St. Wilhelmina B. A. Soc., 24 R. I. 527, 54 Atl. 58.

Tennessee: Allen *v.* McNew, 8 Humph. 46.

Virginia: Baltimore & O. R. R. *v.* Polly, 14 Gratt. 447.

[66] *New York:* Van Clief *v.* Van Vechten, 130 N. Y. 571, 29 N. E. 1017; Watts *v.* Board of Education, 9 App. Div. 143, 41 N. Y. Supp. 141.

Wisconsin: Arndt *v.* Keller, 96 Wis. 274, 71 N. W. 651.

Contra, Sumpter *v.* Hedges, [1898] 1 Q. B. 673.

[67] *New York:* McGrath *v.* Horgan, 72 App. Div. 152, 76 N. Y. Supp. 412.

Wisconsin: Nichols *v.* Superior, 109 Wis. 643, 85 N. W. 428.

[68] *Alabama:* English *v.* Wilson, 34 Ala. 201.

Arkansas: Bertrand *v.* Byrd, 5 Ark. 651.

California: Zottman *v.* San Francisco, 20 Cal. 96, 81 Am. Dec. 96, *n.;* J. M. Griffith Co. *v.* Los Angeles (Cal.), 54 Pac. 383.

Illinois: Eldridge *v.* Rowe, 7 Ill. 91, 43 Am. Dec. 41.

Kentucky: Morford *v.* Mastin, 6 T. B. Mon. 609, 17 Am. Dec. 188.

Missouri: Lowe *v.* Sinklear, 27 Mo. 308, 72 Am. Dec. 266; Yeats *v.* Ballentine, 56 Mo. 530.

New Jersey: Bozarth *v.* Dudley, 44 N. J. L. 304, 43 Am. Rep. 373.

England: Munro *v.* Butt, 8 El. & Bl. 738.

structure thus attached to his freehold, and cannot be obliged to tear it down, he is nevertheless under no obligation to pay for it. The main question is whether, under the circumstances of the particular case, there has been *a voluntary acceptance by the defendant of the plaintiff's incomplete performance.* If the acceptance was involuntary, or was compelled only by the necessity of the case, or the defendant's wish to retain property of his own to which the plaintiff's work was an incident or a necessary adjunct, there is no right of recovery. The courts are, however, acute to find an acceptance even in such cases, and any act of approval is sufficient for the purpose. The measure of damages in an action on the common counts for work accepted, but not done according to the contract, should be the value of the work,[69] not exceeding the contract price,[70] with the right in the defendant to recoup damages for the non-performance.[71] The same is true when the defendant impliedly accepts the work by seeing it performed without ob-

[69] *Alabama:* Merriweather *v.* Taylor, 15 Ala. 735; Hawkins *v.* Gilbert, 19 Ala. 54; Bell *v.* Teague, 85 Ala. 211, 3 So. 861.

Arkansas: Simpson *v.* McDonald, 2 Ark. 370.

California: Lacy Mfg. Co. *v.* Los Angeles, G. & E. Co., 12 Cal. App. 37, 106 Pac. 413.

Delaware: Webster *v.* Beebe, 77 Atl. 769.

Indiana: McClure *v.* Secrist, 5 Ind. 31, 61 Am. Dec. 74.

Missouri: Williams *v.* Porter, 51 Mo. 441.

Vermont: Viles *v.* Barre & M. T. & P. Co., 79 Vt. 311, 65 Atl. 104.

West Virginia: Baltimore & O. R. R. *v.* Lafferty, 2 W. Va. 104.

Wisconsin: Taylor *v.* Williams, 6 Wis. 363.

[70] *Maryland:* Walsh *v.* Jenvey, 85 Md. 240, 36 Atl. 817.

Michigan: Eaton *v.* Gladwell, 121 Mich. 444, 80 N. W. 292.

North Carolina: Farmer *v.* Francis, 12 Ired. 282.

[71] *United States:* Dermott *v.* Jones, 23 How. 220, 16 L. ed. 442.

Alabama: Sheppard *v.* Dowling, 103 Ala. 563, 15 So. 846.

Colorado: Bush *v.* Finucane, 8 Colo. 192, 6 Pac. 514.

Delaware: Webster *v.* Beebe, 77 Atl. 769.

Illinois: Adlard *v.* Muldoon, 45 Ill. 193; Estep *v.* Fenton, 66 Ill. 467.

Indiana: Epperly *v.* Bailey, 3 Ind. 72; Barkalow *v.* Pfeiffer, 38 Ind. 214.

Maine: Jewett *v.* Weston, 11 Me. 346.

Massachusetts: Bee Printing Co. *v.* Hichborn, 4 All. 63.

Michigan: Phelps *v.* Beebe, 71 Mich. 554.

Missouri: Keith *v.* Ridge, 146 Mo. 90, 47 S. W. 904.

New Hampshire: Horn *v.* Batchelder, 41 N. H. 86.

New York: Pullman *v.* Corning, 9 N. Y. 93.

Vermont: Barker *v.* Troy & Rutland R. R., 27 Vt. 766; Viles *v.* Barre & M. T. & P. Co., 79 Vt. 311, 65 Atl. 104.

jection. Thus where the contractor is in default, so that he
cannot sue upon his contract, but the other party has stood by
and seen him prosecute the work without objection, and been
benefited by his labor and materials, the contractor is entitled
to compensation to the extent of such benefit. But the profits
which he might have made if he had complied with his engagement, cannot be included in his damages.[72] The law in such
case implies a promise on the other's part to pay what the labor
was reasonably worth, of which the special contract will furnish evidence.[73] Where work is to be done within a certain
time, the employer, by allowing it to go on after the time has
expired, waives his right to rescind on that account, and can
only claim such damages from the employee as he may have
sustained by the delay.[74] But other objections are not thereby
waived.[75] Where the work accepted was in an incomplete
state, the contract price is to be reduced by the sum required
to complete it.[76] But where it was completed, but lacking in
quality, the contract price is to be reduced by the difference in
value of the work as it should have been by the contract and
as it actually was.[77]

§ 657. Substantial performance.

Where a contractor performing his contract in good faith
substantially complies with his obligation, but makes some
comparatively slight deviation, he may recover compensation
for the work done.[78]

[72] Carland v. New Orleans, 13 La.
Ann. 43.
[73] Jewell v. Schroeppel, 4 Cow. 564.
[74] *California:* Lacy Mfg. Co. v. Los
Angeles G. & E. Co., 12 Cal. App. 37,
106 Pac. 413.
New York: Sinclair v. Tallmadge, 35
Barb. 602.
[75] Nibbe v. Brauhn, 24 Ill. 268.
[76] *Arkansas:* Walworth v. Finnegan,
33 Ark. 751.
Connecticut: Blakeslee v. Holt, 42
Conn. 226.
Indiana: Manville v. McCoy, 3 Ind.
148.
Maine: Hayden v. Madison, 7 Me. 76.

Ohio: Goldsmith v. Hand, 26 Oh. St.
101.
Wisconsin: Arndt v. Keller, 96 Wis.
274, 71 N. W. 651.
[77] *United States:* The Isaac Newton,
1 Abb. Adm. 11.
Alabama: Sheppard v. Dowling, 103
Ala. 563, 15 So. 846.
New York: Morton v. Harrison, 52
N. Y. Super. Ct. 305; Walter v. Hangen, 71 App. Div. 40, 75 N. Y. Supp.
683.
[78] Stude v. Koehler (Tex. Civ. App.),
138 S. W. 193.
He cannot, strictly speaking, recover
on the special contract, and therefore

While there is general agreement on this point among the authorities, the rule for determining the amount of recovery is very differently stated by the different courts. The rule most commonly laid down is that the contractor may recover the contract price less an allowance for the damage caused by the deviation.[79] In such a case where one who had contracted to build a house had slightly deviated from the contract the jury were told at the trial to consider what *the house was worth* to the defendant, and give that sum in damages. On a motion for a

if the original obligation was in the form of a covenant an action of covenant will not lie on substantial performance. Clayton *v.* Blake, 4 Ired. (N. C.) 497.

[79] *United States:* The Lucille Manor, 70 Fed. 233; Springfield Milling Co. *v.* Barnard & Leas Manuf. Co., 81 Fed. 261, 26 C. C. A. 389.

Indiana: Barkalow *v.* Pfeiffer, 38 Ind. 214.

Iowa: Ætna Iron & Steel Works *v.* Kossuth County, 79 Iowa, 40, 44 N. W. 215.

Massachusetts: Bassett *v.* Sanborn, 9 Cush. 58; Gleason *v.* Smith, 9 Cush. 484, 57 Am. Dec. 62; Kenworthy *v.* Stevens, 132 Mass. 123; Norwood *v.* Lathrop, 178 Mass. 208, 59 N. E. 650.

Minnesota: Leeds *v.* Little, 42 Minn. 414, 44 N. W. 309.

Missouri: Yeats *v.* Ballentine, 56 Mo. 530; Decker *v.* School District, 101 Mo. App. 115, 74 S. W. 390.

New Jersey: Bozarth *v.* Dudley, 44 N. J. L. 304, 43 Am. Rep. 373; Feeney *v.* Bardsley, 66 N. J. L. 239, 49 Atl. 443.

New York: Phillip *v.* Gallant, 62 N. Y. 256; Woodward *v.* Fuller, 80 N. Y. 312; Nolan *v.* Whitney, 88 N. Y. 648; Smith *v.* Gugerty, 4 Barb. 614; Sinclair *v.* Tallmadge, 35 Barb. 602.

Ohio: Goldsmith *v.* Hand, 26 Oh. St. 101; Johnson *v.* Slaymaker, 18 Oh. C. Ct. 104.

Pennsylvania: Chambers *v.* Jaynes, 4 Pa. 39; Danville Bridge Co. *v.* Pom-

roy, 15 Pa. 151; Truesdale *v.* Watts, 12 Pa. 73; Wade *v.* Haycock, 25 Pa. 382; Moore *v.* Carter, 146 Pa. 492, 23 Atl. 243; White *v.* Braddock Borough School Dist., 159 Pa. 201, 28 Atl. 136; Shires *v.* O'Connor, 4 Pa. Super. Ct. 465.

South Dakota: Aldrich *v.* Wilmarth, 3 S. D. 523, 54 N. W. 811.

Wisconsin: Bishop *v.* Price, 24 Wis. 480.

It is generally held that the burden of bringing in evidence of the damage caused by the deviation is on the defendant.

Iowa: Fitts *v.* Reinhart, 102 Iowa, 311, 71 N. W. 227.

Minnesota: Leeds *v.* Little, 42 Minn. 414, 44 N. W. 309.

Pennsylvania: Filbert *v.* Philadelphia, 181 Pa. 530, 37 Atl. 545, 59 Am. St. Rep. 676.

In Massachusetts in one case the burden was thought to be on the plaintiff. Gillis *v.* Cobe, 177 Mass. 584, 59 N. E. 455. But this decision seems to be qualified by later cases. Vickery *v.* Ritchie, 202 Mass. 247, 88 N. E. 835, 26 L. R. A. (N. S.) 810.

In a few cases full recovery of the contract price upon substantial performance appears to have been allowed, but the court was probably not dealing with the question of reduction. Linch *v.* Paris Lumber & Grain Elevator Co., 80 Tex. 23, 15 S. W. 208.

See Jennings *v.* Willer (Tex. Civ. App.), 32 S. W. 24.

new trial, this was held wrong, the court saying: "The house might have been worth the whole stipulated price, notwithstanding the departures from the contract. They should have been instructed to deduct so much from the contract price as the house was worth less on account of these departures." And a new trial was granted.[80] In an action for negligence in building a cellar under a house, the rule of damages is the amount in money which the value of the cellar and building falls short of what it would have been if the work had been done according to the contract. This difference includes both the cost of supplying such deficiencies as could be supplied without expense disproportioned to the value of the building, and also in the case of such as could not be so supplied, the further or independent diminution in value thereby caused.[81] In this case the action was tort, but there had been a contract, and the decision seems to be rested by the court upon the general principle in such cases.

Where work is completed, though not within the agreed time, there may be a recovery in *indebitatus assumpsit* for its value, if time is not of the essence of the contract. The special contract will furnish a rule to measure the damages. So far as performance is defective in *time*, it admits of compensation. Where there was delay in completing a steamboat within the time, the measure of damages was not what it should cost the party to hire another boat for the time, but what would be the *ordinary* hire of such a boat; and in case of defective work,

[80] Hayward v. Leonard, 7 Pick. (Mass.) 181, 19 Am. Dec. 268.

To the same effect are the following cases:

Iowa: Crookshank v. Mallory, 2 Greene, 257; Tait v. Sherman, 10 Ia. 60; Corwin v. Wallace, 17 Ia. 374.

Maine: White v. Oliver, 36 Me. 92.

Michigan: White v. Brockway, 40 Mich. 209.

Missouri: Marsh v. Richards, 29 Mo. 99.

New Hampshire: Wadleigh v. Sutton, 6 N. H. 15, 23 Am. Dec. 703; Laton v. King, 19 N. H. 280; Davis v. Barring-

ton, 30 N. H. 517; Horn v. Batchelder, 41 N. H. 86.

Ohio: Kane v. Ohio Stone Co., 39 Oh. St. 1.

Texas: Davidson v. Edgar, 5 Tex. 492; Hillyard v. Crabtree, 11 Tex. 264, 62 Am. Dec. 475.

Vermont: Merrow v. Huntoon, 25 Vt. 9; Morrison v. Cummings, 26 Vt. 486.

Wisconsin: Bishop v. Price, 24 Wis. 480.

England: Cutler v. Close, 5 C. & P. 337; Thornton v. Place, 1 Moo. & Rob. 218.

[81] Moulton v. McOwen, 103 Mass. 587.

what would be the cost of repairs and the ordinary hire of a boat during the time necessary to make them.[82] If time is of the essence of the contract, a failure to complete the performance in time should prevent recovery altogether by the plaintiff.[83]

This rule is often stated more specifically in this form— that where performance substantially conforms to the contract but varies in some particulars from the specifications, the amount to be deducted from the contract price is the reasonable cost of remedying such defects as are remediable without unreasonable expenditure,[84] and so far as the defects cannot be remedied, the diminished value of the performance, compared with complete performance.[85]

It is often held, however, that the measure of recovery is the value of the performance,[86] or the amount of benefit con-

---

[82] Brown v. Foster, 51 Pa. 165.

[83] Slater v. Emerson, 19 How. 224, 15 L. ed. 626.

[84] *Connecticut:* Pinches v. Swedish Lutheran Church, 55 Conn. 183, 10 Atl. 264, 3 Am. St. Rep. 43.

Illinois: Keeler v. Herr, 157 Ill. 57, 41 N. E. 750.

Massachusetts: Walker v. Orange, 16 Gray, 193.

Michigan: Sheldon v. Leahy, 111 Mich. 29, 69 N. W. 76.

Minnesota: Leeds v. Little, 42 Minn. 414, 44 N. W. 309.

Missouri: Haysler v. Owen, 61 Mo. 270.

New York: Crouch v. Gutmann, 134 N. Y. 45, 31 N. E. 271, 30 Am. St. Rep. 608.

Pennsylvania: Pallman v. Smith, 135 Pa. 188, 19 Atl. 188; Shires v. O'Connor, 4 Pa. Super. Ct. 465.

Wisconsin: Foeller v. Heintz, 137 Wis. 169, 118 N. W. 543, 24 L. R. A. (N. S.) 327, explaining and qualifying Ashland L. S. & C. Co. v. Shores, 105 Wis. 122, 81 N. W. 136.

England: Cutler v. Close, 5 C. & P. 337.

[85] *Alabama:* Fleming v. Lunsford, 163 Ala. 540, 50 So. 921.

Massachusetts: Cullen v. Sears, 112 Mass. 299.

Michigan: Eaton v. Gladwell, 121 Mich. 444, 449, 80 N. W. 211.

New York: Morton v. Harrison, 52 N. Y. Super. Ct. 305.

Wisconsin: Foeller v. Heintz, 137 Wis. 169, 118 N. W. 543, 24 L. R. A. (N. S.) 327, explaining and qualifying Ashland L. S. & C. Co. v. Shores, 105 Wis. 122, 81 N. W. 136.

[86] *United States:* Woodruff v. Hough, 91 U. S. 596, 23 L. ed. 332.

Connecticut: Pinches v. Swedish Lutheran Church, 55 Conn. 183, 10 Atl. 264, 3 Am. St. Rep. 43.

Kentucky: Morford v. Ambrose, 3 J. J. Marsh. 688.

Maine: Norris v. School Dist., 12 Me. 293, 28 Am. Dec. 182; Veazie v. Bangor, 51 Me. 509.

Massachusetts: Smith v. First Cong. Meeting House, 8 Pick. 178; Lord v. Wheeler, 1 Gray, 282; Atkins v. Barnstable, 97 Mass. 428; Powell v. Howard, 109 Mass. 192.

Michigan: Allen v. McKibbin, 5 Mich. 449; Wildey v. School Dist., 25 Mich. 419; Phelps v. Beebe, 71 Mich. 554, 39 N. W. 761.

Missouri: Williams v. Porter, 51

ferred on the defendant,[87] though in every case where the point
is raised it is of course held that this recovery cannot exceed
the contract price [88] to the benefit of which the defendant has a
right,[89] deducting therefrom the damages for non-performance.[90]
The true doctrine appears to be that recovery can in no case
exceed the contract price less proper allowance for the defective
performance; nor on the other hand can it exceed the benefit
conferred.[91] Since the plaintiff has not exactly performed his
contract he cannot justly claim the benefit of any profit that
would have come to him by performing it; and on the other
hand the defendant is entitled to be left in no worse position
than he would have occupied had the contract been performed,
and therefore should be held to pay no more than the contract
price less the allowance for non-performance.

IV.—EXPRESS CONTRACT UNPERFORMED

§ 658. Abandonment or substantial non-performance of contract.

Where the contract is, on its face, an entire one, and has

Mo. 441; Freeman v. Aylor, 62 Mo.
App. 613; Decker v. School Dist., 101
Mo. App. 115, 74 S. W. 390.

Ohio: Newman v. McGregor, 5
Ohio, 349, 24 Am. Dec. 293.

[87] *Arkansas:* Bertrand v. Byrd, 5 Ark.
651.

Maryland: Walsh v. Jenvey, 85 Md.
240, 36 Atl. 817.

Massachusetts: Bassett v. Sanborn, 9
Cush. 58; Cardell v. Bridge, 9 Allen,
355; Norwood v. Lathrop, 178 Mass.
208, 59 N. E. 650.

[88] *Connecticut:* Pinches v. Swedish
Lutheran Church, 55 Conn. 183, 10
Atl. 264, 3 Am. St. Rep. 43.

Kentucky: Morford v. Ambrose, 3
J. J. Marsh. 688.

Maryland: Walsh v. Jenvey, 85 Md.
240, 36 Atl. 817.

Massachusetts: Atkins v. Barnstable,
97 Mass. 428; Powell v. Howard, 109
Mass. 192.

[89] Ætna S. & I. Works v. Kossuth
County, 79 Ia. 40, 44 N. W. 215.

[90] *Kentucky:* Escott v. White, 10
Bush, 169.

Michigan: Allen v. McKibbin, 5
Mich. 449; Wildey v. School District,
25 Mich. 419; Phelps v. Beebe, 71
Mich. 554, 39 N. W. 761; Germain v.
Union School Dist., 158 Mich. 214, 122
N. W. 524.

Missouri: Freeman v. Aylor, 62 Mo.
App. 613; Decker v. School Dist., 101
Mo. App. 115, 74 S. W. 390.

[91] *Massachusetts:* Gillis v. Cobe, 177
Mass. 584, 59 N. E. 455. This, however, has been explained not to mean
that where a useless building is built
the rule would give the contractor nothing because the total value of the land
was not increased by the building; the
benefit conferred is the value of the
structure in itself, without regard to
whether it is useful where the defendant
had it placed. See Vickery v. Ritchie,
202 Mass. 247, 88 N. E. 835, 26 L. R. A.
(N. S.) 810.

Missouri: Yeats v. Ballentine, 56 Mo.
530.

been performed only in part, a substantial portion of the contract being left unperformed; or where, after substantial performance, the contractor wilfully and without excuse abandons further performance, compensation is sometimes sought for what has been actually done.[92] * Such are cases of agreements to work for a specified time for a given sum, where the party employed quits his employment without the consent of the other, and before the period fixed; agreements to deliver a certain quantity of goods, and delivery of only a part; agreements to do work, as building, for instance, according to certain specifications, where the work is done, but the specifications are departed from; whether in these cases the party failing to perform his agreement strictly has any redress whatever, and to what extent, is a very delicate and much vexed question, which perhaps more properly belongs to the subject of the right of action than that of the measure of damages. The better and sounder rule would seem to be, that unless there is a waiver of the privileged performance, or an acceptance of the partial performance, there can be no recovery. In cases of this kind, where the plaintiff is held entitled to recover anything, the agreement of the parties, not having been completely performed, cannot be conclusive as to the remuneration. Other evidence must be resorted to, and other considerations affect the result. Still, the contract to a certain extent furnishes the measure of remuneration.** As to the right to recover, the authorities are in conflict.

§ 659. Jurisdictions refusing recovery.

According to the better view, in the case of an entire executory contract, which the plaintiff without legal excuse has failed to fulfil on his part, he can recover nothing, either on the contract itself or on a *quantum meruit*. Some courts have refused in such case to modify the contract of the parties, or substitute another by sanctioning a recovery to any extent.[93] In the case

[92] Campbell v. Gates, 10 Pa. 483.

[93] *United States:* Dermott v. Jones, 2 Wall. 1, 17 L. ed. 762.

California: Hutchinson v. Wetmore, 2 Cal. 310, 56 Am. Dec. 337.

Maryland: Gill v. Vogler, 52 Md. 663.

Massachusetts: Olmstead v. Beale, 19 Pick. 528; Veazie v. Hosmer, 11 Gray, 369.

Mississippi: Wooten v. Read, 2 Sm. & M. 585.

Missouri: Posey v. Garth, 7 Mo. 94,

of Smith *v.* Brady [94] the subject is fully discussed, and the principle applied to the case of a contract by a builder to erect a building (for which he is to be paid on its completion) on another's land, according to certain specifications, between which and the building as erected there is a substantial disagreement.

§ 660. Jurisdictions allowing recovery—Britton v. Turner.

Recovery was first allowed in such cases in the leading case of Britton *v.* Turner.[95] In an action for work and labor, it ap-

37 Am. Dec. 183; Caldwell *v.* Dickson, 17 Mo. 575; Schnerr *v.* Lemp, 19 Mo. 40.

New York: Champlin *v.* Rowley, 18 Wend. 187, 31 Am. Dec. 376; Pullman *v.* Corning, 9 N. Y. 93; Lawson *v.* Hogan, 93 N. Y. 39; Neville *v.* Frost, 2 E. D. Smith, 62.

Ohio: Allen *v.* Curles, 6 Oh. St. 505; Larkin *v.* Buck, 11 Oh. St. 561.

Pennsylvania: Martin *v.* Schoenberger, 8 W. & S. 367; Bryant *v.* Stilwell, 24 Pa. 314.

Vermont: Jones *v.* Marsh, 22 Vt. 144 (followed, as to law in Vermont, in Jordan *v.* Fitz, 63 N. H. 227).

England: Cutter *v.* Powell, 6 T. R. 320; Sinclair *v.* Bowles, 9 B. & C. 92; Kingdom *v.* Cox, 5 C. B. 522.

This is the case when there is a voluntary abandonment of the contract without excuse:

United States: Hansbrough *v.* Peck, 5 Wall. 497, 18 L. ed. 520.

Alabama: Hawkins *v.* Gilbert, 19 Ala. 54.

California: Golden Gate Lumber Co. *v.* Sahrbacher, 105 Cal. 114, 38 Pac. 635.

Maryland: Denmead *v.* Coburn, 15 Md. 29.

Massachusetts: Homer *v.* Shaw, 177 Mass. 1, 58 N. E. 160.

New York: Jennings *v.* Camp, 13 Johns. 94. 7 Am. Dec. 367; Brown *v.* Weber. 38 N. Y. 187; Glacius *v.* Black, 50 N. Y. 145, 10 Am. Rep. 449; Crane

v. Knubel, 61 N. Y. 645; Cunningham *v.* Jones, 4 Abb. Pr. 433.

So where the work is completed, but fails in some substantial particular to comply with the requirements of the contract:

Minnesota: Elliott *v.* Caldwell, 43 Minn. 357, 45 N. W. 845, 9 L. R. A. 52.

New Jersey: Bozarth *v.* Dudley, 44 N. J. L. 304, 43 Am. Rep. 373; Feeney *v.* Bardsley, 66 N. J. L. 239, 49 Atl. 443.

New York: Smith *v.* Brady, 17 N. Y. 173, 72 Am. Dec. 442; Glacius *v.* Black, 50 N. Y. 145, 10 Am. Rep. 449.

Ohio: Mehurin *v.* Stone, 37 Oh. St. 49.

Pennsylvania: Shires *v.* O'Connor, 4 Pa. Super. Ct. 465.

South Dakota: Hulst *v.* Benevolent Hall Assoc., 9 S. D. 144, 68 N. W. 200.

England: Ellis *v.* Hamlen, 3 Taunt. 52; Whitaker *v.* Dunn, 3 T. L. Rep. 602.

Canada: Sherlock *v.* Powell, 26 Ont. App. 407.

It seems that if the contractor upon abandonment forfeits his right to compensation, this is an end to rights on the contract for either party. The owner cannot sue the contractor for damages for non-performance without making allowance for the work done by the contractor. Griffin *v.* Miner, 54 N. Y. Super. Ct. 46.

[94] 17 N. Y. 173, 72 Am. Dec. 442.

[95] 6 N. H. 481, 488, 26 Am. Dec. 713.

peared that the plaintiff had agreed to work for the defendant one year for a given sum, and that before the expiration of the time agreed on he had quitted his service without the defendant's consent, and on this he was held entitled to recover for the time he was employed. Parker, C. J., after commenting on the extreme disagreement and want of harmony among the cases, and calling particular attention to those where a recovery had been allowed on partial performance of agreements to build, proceeded to say:

"We hold, then, where a party undertakes to pay upon a special contract for the performance of labor or the furnishing of materials, he is not to be charged upon such special agreement until the money is earned according to the terms of it; and where the parties have made an express contract, the law will not imply and raise a contract different from that which the parties have entered into, except upon some farther transaction between the parties.

"In case of a failure to perform such special contract, by the default of the party contracting to do the service, if the money is not due by the terms of the special agreements, he is not entitled to recover for his labor, or for the materials furnished, unless the other party receives what has been done or furnished, and upon the whole case derives a benefit from it.

"But if, where a contract is made of such a character, a party actually receives labor or materials, and thereby derives a benefit and advantage over and above the damage which has resulted from the breach of the contract by the other party, the labor actually done, and the value received, furnish a new consideration, and the law thereupon raises a promise to pay to the extent of the reasonable worth of such excess. This may be considered as making a new case, one not within the original agreement, and the party is entitled to recover on his new case for the work done, not as agreed, yet accepted by the defendant.

"If, on such failure to perform the whole, the nature of the contract be such that the employer can reject what has been done, and refuse to receive any benefit from the part performance, he is entitled so to do, and in such case is not liable to be charged, unless he has before assented to and accepted of what has been done, however much the other party may have done toward the performance. He has, in such case, received nothing, and having contracted to receive nothing but the entire matter contracted for, he is not bound to pay; because his express promise was only to pay on receiving the whole, and having actually received nothing, the law cannot and ought not to raise an implied promise to pay.

"But where the party receives value, takes and uses the materials, or has advantage from the labor, he is liable to pay the reasonable worth of what he has received. And the rule is the same, whether it was received and accepted by the assent of the party prior to the breach, under a contract by which, from its nature, he was to receive labor, from time to time, until the completion of the whole contract; or whether it was received and accepted by an assent subsequent to the performance of all which was in fact done. If he received it under such circumstances as precluded him from rejecting it afterwards, that does not alter the case; it has still been received by his assent. . . . The amount, however, for which the employer ought to be charged, where the laborer abandons his contract, is only the reasonable worth, or the amount of advantage he received upon the whole transaction; and in estimating the value of the labor, the contract price for the service cannot be exceeded."

The case of Britton v. Turner has been followed, with more or less modification, in perhaps a majority of the jurisdictions in this country.[96]

---

[96] *Indiana:* McKinney v. Springer, 3 Ind. 59, 54 Am. Dec. 470, n., by which the prior cases of Swift v. Williams, 2 Ind. 365, and Hoagland v. Moore, 2 Blackf. 167, are overruled as to the point in question.

Iowa: Barr v. Van Duyn, 45 Ia. 228.

Kansas: Duncan v. Baker, 21 Kan. 99.

Michigan: Wilson v. Wagar, 26 Mich. 452; Begole v. McKenzie, 26 Mich. 470; Keystone L. & S. M. Co. v. Dole, 43 Mich. 370; Fuller v. Rice, 52 Mich. 435.

Missouri: Downey v. Burke, 23 Mo. 228; Barcus v. Hannibal R. C. & P. P.

R., 26 **Mo.** 102; Marsh v. Richards, 29 Mo. 99.

Nebraska: Parcell v. McComber, 11 Neb. 209, 38 Am. Rep. 366.

North Carolina: Gorman v. Bellamy, 82 N. C. 496.

Oregon: Steeples v. Newton, 7 Ore. 110, 83 Am. Rep. 705.

Tennessee: Jones v. Jones, 2 Swan, 605.

Texas: Carroll v. Welch, 26 Tex. 147. The cases in which this doctrine is laid down are usually cases where the work was completed, but there were serious defects in it.

Kentucky: Nance v. Patterson Building Co., 140 Ky. 564, 131 S. W. 484.

§ 661. Rule in Vermont.

In Vermont the right of recovery seems to turn, not only where the contract is substantially performed, but in all cases, not on the plaintiff's voluntary acceptance, but on the benefit supposed to be conferred by the work done. In the case of Kelly v. Bradford,[97] Aldis, J., delivering the opinion of the Supreme Court of that State, says:

"Where a contract has been substantially though not strictly performed—where the party failing to perform according to the terms of his contract has not been guilty of a voluntary abandonment or wilful departure from the contract, has acted in good faith, intending to perform the contract according to its stipulations, but has failed in a strict compliance with its provisions, and where from the nature of the contract, and of the labor performed, the parties cannot rescind and stand in *statu quo*, but one of them must derive some benefit from the labor or money of the other,—in such case the party failing to perform his contract strictly, may recover of the other as upon a *quantum meruit* for such a sum only as the contract as performed has been of real and actual benefit to the other party, estimating such benefit by reference to the contract price of the whole work."

Missouri: Heman v. Compton Hill Imp. Co., 58 Mo. App. 480; Muller v. Gillick, 66 Mo. App. 500.

New Hampshire: Danforth v. Freeman, 69 N. H. 466, 43 Atl. 621.

North Carolina: Twitty v. McGuire, 3 Murph. 501.

Tennessee: Cox v. Estell, Peck, 175; Elliott v. Wilkinson, 8 Yerg. 411; Porter v. Woods, 3 Humph. 56, 39 Am. Dec. 153; Gibson v. Carlin, 13 Lea, 440; Deberry v. Young, 1 Tenn. Cas. 51; Bush v. Jones, 2 Tenn. Cas. 224.

Texas: Gonzales College v. McHugh, 21 Tex. 256.

But in many States, the plaintiff is allowed to recover if his work has been of actual benefit to the defendant, even though he has intentionally abandoned the work before completion and without excuse.

Arkansas: Walworth v. Finnegan, 33 Ark. 751.

Maine: Jewett v. Weston, 11 Me. 346; Norris v. School District, 12 Me. 292, 28 Am. Dec. 182.

Tennessee: Porter v. Woods, 3 Humph. 56, 39 Am. Dec. 153.

Texas: Hillyard v. Crabtree, 11 Tex. 264, 62 Am. Dec. 475; Gonzales College v. McHugh, 21 Tex. 256; Carroll v. Welch, 26 Tex. 147; Watson v. DeWitt County, 19 Tex. Civ. App. 150, 46 S. W. 1061.

West Virginia: Baltimore & O. R. R. v. Lafferty, 2 W. Va. 104.

The rule is otherwise in Vermont (*infra*, § 661) and in Kentucky. Escott v. White, 10 Bush (Ky.), 169.

[97] 33 Vt. 35.

And the rule by which compensation is to be made for the partial performance of the contract, is thus declared: "The party failing to perform must first deduct from the contract price such sum as will enable the other party to get the contract completed according to its terms; or where that is impossible or unreasonable, such a sum as will fully compensate him for the imperfection in the work and insufficiency of the materials, so that he shall in this respect be made as good, pecuniarily, as if the contract had been strictly performed. 2d. Whatever additional damages his breach of the contract may have occasioned to the other."

Later decisions firmly maintain in that State the same *quasi* equitable doctrine in actions at law, holding that where the stipulations are not in the nature of conditions precedent, a party who but partly fulfils his contract may recover for what has been done under it to the extent that such partial performance has benefited the other.[98] So in the same State, where one agrees to work for another a certain time, he can maintain an action for his compensation without making up time he has reasonably lost during the period, and the time so lost will be deducted.[99]

If however the plaintiff voluntarily abandoned the contract before completing performance, he is not allowed to recover.[100]

§ 662. Measure of recovery.

But the party in default must not gain by his default, nor the other lose by it. Parties often agree to give excessive prices to have an entire contract literally performed, when a partial performance would never have been contracted for. And though the contract price, as far as practicable and equitable, furnishes the measure of damages on such a *quantum meruit*, and the defaulting party can in no case recover more, yet he can have his

[98] Dyer v. Jones, 8 Vt. 205; Gilman v. Hall, 11 Vt. 510, 34 Am. Dec. 700; Brackett v. Morse, 23 Vt. 554; Merrow v. Huntoon, 25 Vt. 9; Morrison v. Cummings, 26 Vt. 486; Hubbard v. Belden, 27 Vt. 645; Barker v. Troy & Rutland R. R., 27 Vt. 766; Kettle v. Harvey, 21 Vt. 301; Swift v. Harriman, 30 Vt. 607; Smith v. Foster, 36 Vt. 705.

[99] McDonald v. Montague, 30 Vt. 357.
[100] Kettle v. Harvey, 21 Vt. 301; Austin v. Austin, 47 Vt. 311. Unless, indeed, where the contract is divisible, he may recover for the portion of it that has been completely performed, deducting damages for non-performance of the remainder. Booth v. Tyson, 15 Vt. 515.

quantum meruit only, and is not entitled to the contract price for what is worth less.[101] The mode of ascertaining the real benefit received from the part performance of work, in such case, is to estimate the whole work at the price fixed by the contract, and to deduct from that the amount requisite to complete the part of the work left unfinished. If any loss is occasioned by the unfinished part costing more in proportion than the whole was undertaken for, the loss must be borne by the party who originally contracted to do the whole. The amount to be allowed may in some cases be less than the proportion which the work done would bear to the cost of the whole, but cannot exceed it.[102]

The rule is sometimes less perfectly stated in the form that the plaintiff may recover the benefit which he conferred on the defendant.[103] The better form of statement is that the plaintiff is entitled to recover the value of the benefit conferred on the defendant, not however exceeding the contract price, reduced by any damages occasioned by failure properly to perform.[104]

§ 663. Recovery by an infant.

An infant who serves under a contract which he has a right

[101] *Illinois:* Clement v. State Reform School, 84 Ill. 311.
Michigan: Allen v. McKibbin, 5 Mich. 449.
[102] *Arkansas:* Walworth v. Finnegan, 33 Ark. 751.
Illinois: Dobbins v. Higgins, 78 Ill. 440.
Indiana: McKinney v. Springer, 3 Ind. 59, 54 Am. Dec. 470.
Maine: Jewett v. Weston, 11 Me. 346.
Michigan: Keystone L. & S. M. Co. v. Dole, 43 Mich. 370; Fuller v. Rice, 52 Mich. 435.
Missouri: Barcus v. Hannibal R. C. & P. P. R., 26 Mo. 102; Marsh v. Richards, 29 Mo. 99.
New Hampshire: Danforth v. Freeman, 69 N. H. 466, 43 Atl. 621.
North Carolina: Twitty v. McGuire, 3 Murph. 501.

Tennessee: Porter v. Woods, 3 Humph. 56, 39 Am. Dec. 153; Gibson v. Carlin, 13 Lea, 440; Bush v. Jones, 2 Tenn. Cas. 224.
Texas: Hillyard v. Crabtree, 11 Tex. 264, 62 Am. Dec. 475; Gonzales College v. McHugh, 21 Tex. 256; Watson v. DeWitt County, 19 Tex. Civ. App. 150, 46 S. W. 1061.
[103] *Maine:* Norris v. School Dist., 12 Me. 293, 28 Am. Dec. 182.
Tennessee: Elliott v. Wilkinson, 8 Yerg. 411.
[104] *Missouri:* Heman v. Compton Hill Imp. Co., 58 Mo. App. 480; Muller v. Gillick, 66 Mo. App. 500.
New Hampshire: Danforth v. Freeman, 69 N. H. 466, 43 Atl. 621.
Tennessee: Deberry v. Young, 1 Tenn. Cas. 51.
Texas: Carroll v. Welch, 26 Tex. 147.

to repudiate may recover upon such repudiation the value of his services.[105]

In Vermont it has been held, in accordance with the rule in that State, that when an infant makes a contract with an adult to serve for a given time, and leaves before he has performed the whole of the service, he is entitled to recover what his services are reasonably worth, taking into consideration the injury to the other.[106]   But in Maine it has been held that a minor who has agreed to work for a certain time, and not to leave without giving notice a certain time beforehand, but does not complete the agreed term, and does not give the notice, is not liable to have the damages thereby occasioned deducted from the amount he would otherwise recover, the minor not being bound by his contract.[107]

[105] *Post*, § 673a.
[106] Hoxie *v*. Lincoln, 25 Vt. 206; *acc.*, Moses *v*. Stevens, 2 Pick. 332; Gaffney *v*. Hayden, 110 Mass. 137, 14 Am. Rep. 580; Hagerty *v*. Nashua Lock Co., 62 N. H. 576.
[107] Derocher *v*. Continental Mills, 58 Me. 217, 4 Am. Rep. 286.

9 7 8 1 5 8 7 9 8 0 6 3 3